# Forecasting, Time Series, and Regression

*An Applied Approach*

## Duxbury Titles of Related Interest

DUXBURY

# Forecasting, Time Series, and Regression

## An Applied Approach

FOURTH EDITION

Bruce L. Bowerman
*Miami University, Ohio*

Richard T. O'Connell
*Miami University, Ohio*

Anne B. Koehler
*Miami University, Ohio*

THOMSON
━━━★━━ ™
BROOKS/COLE

Australia • Canada • Mexico • Singapore • Spain
United Kingdom • United States

**THOMSON**

**BROOKS/COLE**

Publisher: Curt Hinrichs
Assistant Editor: Ann Day
Editorial Assistant: Katherine Brayton
Technology Project Manager: Burke Taft
Marketing Assistant: Jessica Bothwell
Advertising Project Manager:
  Nathaniel Bergson-Michelson
Project Manager, Editorial Production:
  Hal Humphrey

Print/Media Buyer: Doreen Suruki
Permission Editor: Kiely Sexton
Production Service: Hal Lockwood, Penmarin Books
Text Designer: Andrew Ogus
Copy Editor: Anita Wagner
Cover Image: Photodisc/Getty Images
Compositor: International Typesetting
  and Composition
Printer: Phoenix Color Corp

For more information about our products, contact us at:

**Thomson Learning Academic Resource Center**
**1-800-423-0563**

For permission to use material from this text or product, submit a request online at **www.thomsonrights.com.**

Any additional questions about permissions can be submitted by email to thomsonrights@thomson.com

Library of Congress Control Number: 2003115455

ISBN: 0-534-40977-6

**Thomson Brooks/Cole**
**10 Davis Drive**
**Belmont, CA 94002**
**USA**

**Asia**
Thomson Learning
5 Shenton Way #01-01
UIC Building
Singapore 068808

**Australia/New Zealand**
Thomson Learning
102 Dodds Street
Southbank, Victoria 3006
Australia

**Canada**
Nelson
1120 Birchmount Road
Toronto, Ontario M1K 5G4
Canada

**Europe/Middle East/Africa**
Thomson Learning
High Holborn House
50/51 Bedford Row
London WC1R 4LR
United Kingdom

**Latin America**
Thomson Learning
Seneca, 53
Colonia Polanco
11560 Mexico D.F.
Mexico

**Spain/Portugal**
Paraninfo
Calle Magallanes, 25
28015 Madrid, Spain

# *About the Authors*

**Bruce L. Bowerman** is a professor of decision sciences at Miami University in Oxford, Ohio. He received his Ph.D. in statistics from Iowa State University in 1974 and has more than 32 years of experience teaching basic statistics, regression analysis, time series forecasting, and design of experiments to both undergraduate and graduate students. In 1987 Professor Bowerman received an Outstanding Teaching award from the Miami University senior class, and in 1992 he received the Effective Educator award from the Richard T. Farmer School of Business Administration. Together with Richard T. O'Connell, Professor Bowerman has written ten textbooks. In addition to the earlier editions of this forecasting textbook, these textbooks include *Business Statistics in Practice* and *Linear Statistical Models: An Applied Approach*. The first edition of *Forecasting and Time Series* earned an Outstanding Academic Book award from *Choice* magazine. Professor Bowerman has also published a number of articles in applied stochastic processes, time series forecasting, and statistical education.

**Richard T. O'Connell** is an associate professor of decision sciences at Miami University in Oxford, Ohio. He has more than 27 years of experience teaching basic statistics, statistical quality control and process improvement, regression analysis, time series analysis, and design of experiments to both undergraduate and graduate business students. He also has extensive consulting experience and has taught workshops dealing with statistical quality control and process improvement for a variety of companies in the Midwest. In 2000 Professor O'Connell received an Effective Educator award from the Richard T. Farmer School of Business Administration.

Together with Bruce L. Bowerman he has written ten textbooks. In addition to the earlier editions of this forecasting textbook, these textbooks include *Business Statistics in Practice* and *Linear Statistical Models: An Applied Approach.* Professor O'Connell has published numerous articles in the area of innovative statistical education and statistical quality control. He is one of the first college instructors in the United States to integrate statistical process control and process improvement methodology into his basic business statistics course. Professor O'Connell received an M.S. degree in decision sciences from Northwestern University in 1973, and he is currently a member of both the Decision Sciences Institute and the American Statistical Association.

**Anne B. Koehler** is a professor of decision sciences and the George and Mildred Panuska Professor of Business Administration at Miami University in Oxford, Ohio. She received a Ph.D. in mathematics in 1968 from Indiana University. Her interest in forecasting began with an internship at the J. M. Smucker Company in 1980. Professor Koehler began teaching statistics in 1975 and forecasting in 1990. She teaches courses in basic statistics, regression analysis, time series forecasting, and survey sampling. She is coauthor of a paper in the *Journal of the American Statistical Society* (1997) that presented a state space model for the Holt–Winters multiplicative model and provided that method with a sound statistical basis. Professor Koehler has numerous publications, many of which are on forecasting with seasonal models and exponential smoothing methods. She is an associate editor for the *International Journal of Forecasting,* and for many years was the editor of the software reviews for that journal. She served on the Board of Directors of the International Institute of Forecasters for 10 years. She is also as associate editor for *Decision Sciences* and has twice served on the Board of Directors of the Decision Sciences Institute.

# Brief Contents

# Contents

* Optional

PART **III**

# *Time Series Regression, Decomposition Methods, and Exponential Smoothing*

PART **IV**

*The Box–Jenkins Methodology*

# 9   Nonseasonal Box–Jenkins Models and Their Tentative Identification   401

# 10   Estimation, Diagnostic Checking, and Forecasting for Nonseasonal Box–Jenkins Models   449

# 11 Box–Jenkins Seasonal Modeling   489

# 12 Advanced Box–Jenkins Modeling   539

## APPENDIXES

# A Statistical Tables   591

# B   Matrix Algebra for Regression Calculations   603

# C   Directions and Programs to Implement Regression Analysis in SAS Version 8   631

# D Directions and Programs to Implement the Box–Jenkins Methodology in SAS Version 8  649

# *Preface*

*Forecasting, Time Series, and Regression: An Applied Approach,* Fourth Edition, provides an accessible yet broad introduction to the most widely used methodologies in forecasting practice. This book is designed for use as a textbook in applied courses on forecasting, time series analysis, and regression and as a reference book for practitioners, who must make real-world forecasts. It is appropriate for advanced (junior or senior) undergraduate students and graduate students in business and economics, engineering, and the sciences (including mathematics, statistics, operations research, and computer science). The required mathematical and statistical background for this book is basic algebra and an introductory statistics course.

## OBJECTIVES AND APPROACH

We have two major objectives in this text. One is to help students develop an understanding of concepts and methodologies. The second is to help them develop the ability to apply these concepts and methodologies to real-world problems and interpret the results of those problems. We have placed a premium in this book on illustrating concepts by using many real-world data sets in the examples and exercises. We believe that students learn best when they can relate the concepts to realistic yet tractable examples.

# THE ROLE OF THE COMPUTER

Examining and understanding computer output is a fundamental part of this textbook. Although we have chosen to feature Excel, MINITAB, JMP IN, and SAS in the text, any computer software that produces output required for the analysis may be used for implementation by students and professionals. The hands-on analysis in the text provides a sound basis for the analysis of corresponding output from other computer software. Thus, if you prefer to use other software, we are confident it will work well with the presentation in this textbook. To facilitate this possibility, we have provided all the data files formatted for SPSS, Stata, S-Plus, and EViews in addition to the formats of software featured in the text. One last note on computing: the SAS programs corresponding to the SAS output in the text are provided in appendices and on the Instructor's CD.

# CHANGES TO THE FOURTH EDITION

The fourth edition includes several significant improvements.

- Regression analysis has been expanded and contains many more exercises. This expansion is designed for courses that cover primarily regression analysis or for courses that wish to cover both regression and forecasting.

- The chapter on exponential smoothing is entirely new and incorporates some of the latest research, which has provided the exponential smoothing methods with a sound statistical basis. The notation for the exponential smoothing methods has been simplified, and the use of spreadsheets has been added. The formulas for the prediction intervals in exponential smoothing are now based on statistical models. These statistical models for exponential smoothing are given in an optional section and may be used to teach exponential smoothing in a model-based approach.

- The Box–Jenkins chapters have been streamlined and reorganized into four chapters in the fourth edition.

- Many new exercises appear throughout the book. In addition, many examples and exercises featuring data sets have been updated.

- An optional appendix with matrix algebra for regression may be taught concurrently with the material in the main part of the textbook. The examples in this appendix are the same as those in the main part of the textbook, and additional exercises in regression analysis that require the use of matrix algebra are included.

- Throughout the text, computer output and graphics have been modernized and reflect the latest software releases. The book now includes a data disk containing all of the data files utilized in the examples and exercises in the text formatted for MINITAB, SAS, Excel, JMP IN, Stata, SPSS, S-Plus, and EViews.

- A new Instructor's CD containing worked-out solutions to every exercise and SAS programs is available to qualified faculty.

## ORGANIZATION AND COVERAGE

The book is organized into four parts. Some instructors may wish to teach a course that covers all four parts, although we have found that most instructors choose to cover only selected chapters. For instance, some instructors will wish to build their course around regression analysis, while others will want to build their course around the Box–Jenkins methodology. The book is designed to be flexible and easily adapted to several different course syllabi.

Part I consists of an introduction (Chapter 1) and review of basic statistical concepts (Chapter 2). Chapter 2 can easily be delayed or skipped if you prefer to review inference and estimation in the context of regression, forecasting, and time series analysis.

Part II discusses estimation and forecasting by using regression analysis. This part begins with Chapter 3, which presents simple linear regression. Chapter 4 discusses multiple regression analysis, including the advanced topics of interaction and dummy variables. Chapter 5 covers model building, residual analysis, and diagnostics for outlying and influential observations. The residual analysis is split into two sections. The first of these sections uses only simple regression models and may be taught earlier with Chapter 3. Appendix B, which covers matrix algebra for regression, may be integrated with the material in Chapter 4.

Courses that have a prerequisite of regression analysis may start with Part III. Part III opens with Chapter 6, which covers time series regression. This includes modeling trends and seasonal effects by using polynomial functions of time, dummy variables, and trigonometric functions. The chapter also introduces modeling of autocorrelated error terms. Chapter 7 discusses time series decomposition methods. Part III concludes with Chapter 8, which presents exponential smoothing. Included are discussions of simple exponential smoothing, Holt's trend corrected exponential smoothing, Holt–Winters methods, and damped trend methods. The exponential smoothing methods are presented in the classical way and implemented in spreadsheets. In addition, the error correction form of the smoothing equations is given, and this form provides a link to an optional section on state space models for exponential smoothing.

Part IV discusses forecasting with the Box–Jenkins methodology. This part is written from first principles and can be read without reading Part II or Part III. Therefore, an instructor may begin a course with Chapters 9 and 10, which discuss nonseasonal Box–Jenkins modeling. Chapter 11 presents an introduction to seasonal Box–Jenkins modeling. Time series regression models with Box–Jenkins models for the error terms are also covered in Chapter 11. It is important to note that, in order to simplify notation, we have delayed use of the backshift operator until Chapter 12. Therefore, the reader can obtain from Chapters 9, 10, and 11 a complete knowledge of nonseasonal Box–Jenkins modeling, an introduction to seasonal Box–Jenkins modeling, and an introduction to Box–Jenkins error term models in time series regression without using this operator. Chapter 12 begins by introducing the backshift operator and then discusses general Box–Jenkins modeling. The chapter continues with a discussion of intervention models and finishes with transfer function models.

## COURSE OPTIONS

Below we list some possible courses that can be based on this book. All courses are assumed to include any needed basic statistical review from Chapter 2.

1. A course on forecasting using regression analysis, time series regression, decomposition methods, and exponential smoothing would consist of Chapter 1 and Parts II and III. A more intensive course would also include the basic techniques of the Box–Jenkins methodology, as given by Chapters 9, 10, and 11 from Part IV.

2. A course on forecasting using time series regression, decomposition methods, exponential smoothing, and the basic techniques from the Box–Jenkins methodology would consist of Chapter 1, Part III, and Chapters 9, 10, and 11 from Part IV. A more intensive course would also include the advanced techniques of the Box–Jenkins methodology, as given in Chapter 12.

3. A course on forecasting using Box–Jenkins methodology would consist of Chapter 1 and Part IV.

4. A course on forecasting using regression analysis and Box–Jenkins methodology would consist of Chapter 1, Part II, Chapter 6 from Part III, and Chapters 9, 10, and 11 from Part IV. A more intensive course would also include Chapter 12.

5. A course on regression analysis that would include material on simple and multiple regression, time series regression, and matrix algebra for regression would consist of Part II, Chapter 6 from Part III, and Appendix B.

## ACKNOWLEDGMENTS

We wish to thank the people at Thomson Learning for all their work on this book. We are especially grateful to Curt Hinrichs of Duxbury for initiating the idea to do this revision and for his continual support. A special thank you goes to the production managers, Hal Lockwood and Hal Humphrey, and the copy editor, Anita Wagner. We would like to thank the reviewers for this project: Mack C. Shelley II, Iowa State University, and William Struning, Seton Hall University. We also gratefully acknowledge the reviewers for the earlier editions of this book: S. Chakraborti, University of Alabama; Terry Dielman, Texas Christian University; Benito Flores, Texas A&M University; Michael L. Hand, Willamette University; Robert McAuliffe, Babson College; Helmut Schneider, Louisiana State University; and Stanley R. Schultz, Cleveland State University. Finally, we thank our families for their love and encouragement.

Bruce L. Bowerman<br>
Richard T. O'Connell<br>
Anne B. Kochler

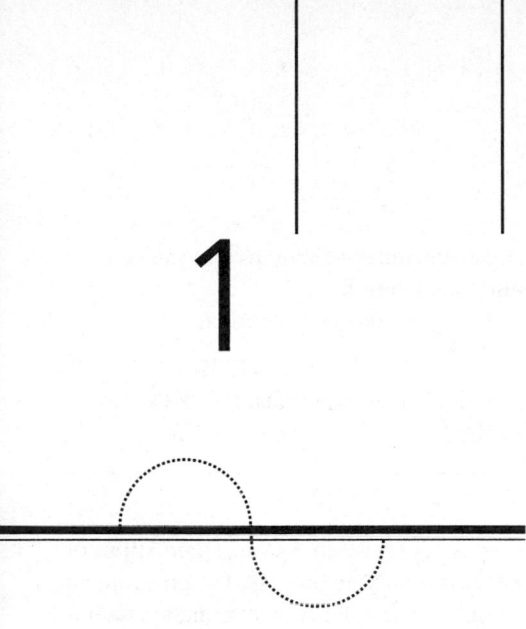

# 1

# *An Introduction to Forecasting*

This chapter introduces the topic of **forecasting.** We begin in Section 1.1 by discussing cross-sectional and time series data. Then, in Section 1.2, we explain the general natures of different kinds of forecasting methods. Both **qualitative** and **quantitative** methods are considered. Section 1.3 discusses the fact that forecasts of future time series values are not likely to be perfectly accurate and explains how to measure **forecast errors.** In Section 1.4 we present some important factors that must be considered when choosing a forecasting method. Section 1.5 presents an overview of the quantitative forecasting techniques discussed in this book.

1

# 1.1   FORECASTING AND DATA

This book is about forecasting and some of the statistical techniques that can be used to produce forecasts. We begin with the following definition.

> Predictions of future events and conditions are called **forecasts,** and the act of making such predictions is called **forecasting.**

Forecasting is very important in many types of organizations since predictions of future events must be incorporated into the decision-making process. The government of a country must be able to forecast such things as air quality, water quality, unemployment rate, inflation rate, and welfare payments in order to formulate its policies. A university must be able to forecast student enrollment in order to make decisions concerning faculty resources and housing availability. The university might also wish to forecast daily mean temperature so that it can plan its fuel purchases for the coming months. A local school board must be able to forecast the number of children of elementary school age who will be living in the school district years in the future in order to decide whether a new school should be built. Any organization must be able to make forecasts in order to make intelligent decisions.

Business firms, in particular, require forecasts of many events and conditions in all phases of their operations. The following are some examples of situations in which business forecasts are needed.

- *In marketing departments,* reliable forecasts of demand must be available so that sales strategies can be planned. For example, total demand for products must be forecasted in order to plan total promotional effort. Besides this, demand in various market regions and among various consumer groups must be predicted in order to plan effective advertising strategies.

- *In finance,* interest rates must be predicted so that new capital acquisitions can be planned and financed. Financial planners must also forecast receipts and expenditures in order to predict cash flows and maintain company liquidity.

- *In personnel management,* forecasts of the number of workers required in different job categories are required in order to plan job recruiting and training programs. In addition, personnel managers need predictions of the supply of labor in various areas and of the amount of absenteeism and the rate of labor turnover to be expected.

- *In production scheduling,* predictions of demand for each product line are needed. Such predictions are made for specific time periods, such as for specific weeks and months. These forecasts allow the firm to plan production schedules and inventory maintenance. Forecasts of demand for individual products can be translated into forecasts of raw material requirements so that purchases can be planned. The planning of resource purchases also requires predictions about resource availabilities and prices.

- *Process control* requires forecasts of the future behavior of the process. For example, an industrial process may begin to produce increasing numbers of defective items as the process operates over time. If the behavior of this process can be predicted accurately, it will be possible to determine when it should be shut down and overhauled so that the number of defective items produced can be minimized.

- *Strategic management* requires forecasts of general economic conditions, price and cost changes, technological change, market growth, and the like in order to plan the long-term future of the company. For example, such forecasts might be used to determine whether investment in new plant and equipment will be needed in the future.

In forecasting events that will occur in the future, a forecaster must rely on information concerning events that have occurred in the past. That is, in order to prepare a forecast, the forecaster must analyze past data and must base the forecast on the results of this analysis. Forecasters use past data in the following way. First, *the forecaster analyzes the data in order to identify a pattern* that can be used to describe it. Then *this pattern is extrapolated, or extended, into the future in order to prepare a forecast.* This basic strategy is employed in most forecasting techniques and *rests on the assumption that the pattern that has been identified will continue in the future.* A forecasting technique cannot be expected to give good predictions unless this assumption is valid. If the data pattern that has been identified does not persist in the future, this indicates that the forecasting technique being used is likely to produce inaccurate predictions. A forecaster should not be surprised by such a situation, but must try to anticipate when such a change in pattern will take place so that appropriate changes in the forecasting system can be made before the predictions become too inaccurate.

Although most of the data in this book are time series data, we also examine cross-sectional data.

---

**Cross-sectional data** are values observed at one point in time.

---

A few examples of cross-sectional data are listed below.

- Starting salary and GPA for graduates last spring
- Home upkeep cost in the past year and current value for homes in an area
- Labor hours, occupied bed days, and average length of stay for hospitals last month

In these examples, values of the first variable would be predicted from the values of the remaining variables for a particular graduate, home, or hospital. We discuss making predictions with this type of data in Section 1.5 and in Chapters 3, 4, and 5.

---

A **time series** is a chronological sequence of observations on a particular variable.

---

As an example, the data in Table 1.1 are a time series that gives the quarterly total value of time deposits held by the Baarth Regional Bank during 2001 and 2002. Notice that the value of time deposits was observed at equally spaced time points (quarterly). Equally spaced time points are used in most time series studies. Business time series often consist of yearly, quarterly, or monthly observations, but any other period may be used. There are many, many examples of time series data, some of which are listed below.

- Unit sales of a product over time
- Total dollar sales for a company over time
- Number of unemployed over time
- Unemployment rate over time
- Production of a product over time
- Air or water quality over time
- Inventory level for a product over time
- Population of a city over time
- Daily mean temperature over time

Time series data are often examined in hopes of discovering a historical pattern that can be exploited in the preparation of a forecast. In order to identify this

**TABLE 1.1** Time Series Data: Quarterly Values of Time Deposits

| Year | Quarter | Value of Time Deposits (in millions of dollars) |
|------|---------|-------------------------------------------------|
| 2001 | 1       | 35.3                                            |
|      | 2       | 37.6                                            |
|      | 3       | 38.1                                            |
|      | 4       | 39.5                                            |
| 2002 | 1       | 37.9                                            |
|      | 2       | 39.9                                            |
|      | 3       | 4'.1                                            |
|      | 4       | ⸱1.2                                            |

pattern, it is often convenient to think of a time series as consisting of several components.

---

The components of a time series are

1. Trend
2. Cycle
3. Seasonal variations
4. Irregular fluctuations

---

We consider each of these components in turn.

**Trend** refers to the upward or downward movement that characterizes a time series over a period of time. Thus trend reflects the long-run growth or decline in the time series.

Trend movements can represent a variety of factors. For example, long-run movements in the sales of a particular industry might be determined by one, some, or all of the following factors:

- Technological change in the industry
- Changes in consumer tastes
- Increases in per capita income
- Increases in total population
- Market growth
- Inflation or deflation (price changes)

**Cycle** refers to recurring up and down movements around trend levels. These fluctuations can have a duration of anywhere from two to ten years or even longer measured from peak to peak or trough to trough.

One of the common cyclical fluctuations found in time series data is the "business cycle." The business cycle is represented by fluctuations in the time series caused by recurrent periods of prosperity alternating with recession. Economists have identified several phases in the business cycle. A period of *expansion* in economic or business activity (boom) ends at the *peak* or upper turning point of the business cycle. This peak is followed by a period of *contraction* in economic activity (bust) during which economic activity diminishes. This contraction ends at the lower turning point or *trough* of activity and is then followed by a renewed period of expansion or increase in economic activity.

Cyclical fluctuations need not be caused by changes in economic factors, however. For example, cyclical fluctuations in agricultural yields might reflect changes in weather cycles; the cyclical fluctuations in sales of a particular item of clothing might reflect changes in clothing styles, which are determined by the whims of fashion designers who are bored with the current length of hemlines.

Because there is no single explanation for cyclical fluctuations, they vary greatly in both length and magnitude.

**Seasonal variations** are periodic patterns in a time series that complete themselves within a calendar year and are then repeated on a yearly basis. Seasonal variations are usually caused by such factors as weather and customs. For example, the average monthly temperature clearly is seasonal in nature since it directly measures changes in the weather. Similarly, the number of monthly housing starts might have a seasonal pattern due to changes in the weather. There might be a high level of housing starts in the spring and early summer because of good weather expected in future months. Housing starts might then decline through the late summer and fall, reaching a low point during the coldest months of winter, and then increase rapidly again in the early spring. Another time series that might contain a seasonal component is the monthly sales volume in a department store. Here seasonal variation might be caused by the observance of various holidays. Thus department store sales volumes might reach high points in December and April as a result of shopping for the Christmas and Easter holidays.

Ordinarily, series of monthly or quarterly data are used to examine seasonal variations. Clearly, a single yearly observation would not reveal variations that occur during the year.

**Irregular fluctuations** are erratic movements in a time series that follow no recognizable or regular pattern. Such movements represent what is "left over" in a time series after trend, cycle, and seasonal variations have been accounted for. Many irregular fluctuations in a time series are caused by "unusual" events that cannot be forecasted—earthquakes, accidents, hurricanes, wars, wildcat strikes, and the like. Irregular fluctuations can also be caused by errors on the part of the time series analyst.

Time series that exhibit trend, seasonal, and cyclical components are illustrated in Figure 1.1. In Figure 1.1(a) a time series of sales observations that has an essentially straight line or linear trend is plotted. Figure 1.1(b) portrays a time series of sales observations that contains a seasonal pattern that repeats annually. Figure 1.1(c) exhibits a time series of agricultural yields that is cyclical in nature, repeating a cycle about once every ten years.

It should be pointed out that the time series components we have discussed do not always occur alone; they can occur in any combination or all can occur together. For this reason, *no single best forecasting model exists*. A forecasting model that can be used to forecast a time series characterized by trend alone may not be appropriate in forecasting a time series characterized by a combination of trend and seasonal variations. Thus one of the most important problems to be solved in forecasting is that of *trying to match the appropriate forecasting model to the pattern of the available time series data*. Once an appropriate model has been selected, the methodology usually involves estimating the time series components (model parameters). The estimates are then used to compute a forecast. For example, if a time series is characterized by a combination of trend and seasonal components, the appropriate forecasting technique would first estimate these two components.

**FIGURE 1.1**
Time series exhibiting trend, seasonal, and cyclical components

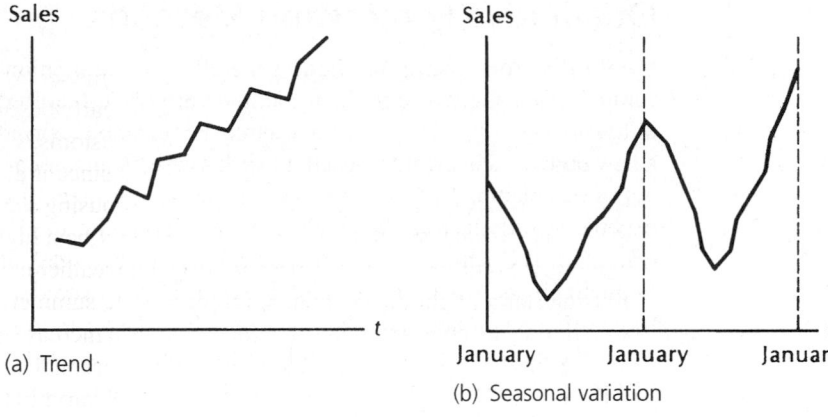

(a) Trend

(b) Seasonal variation

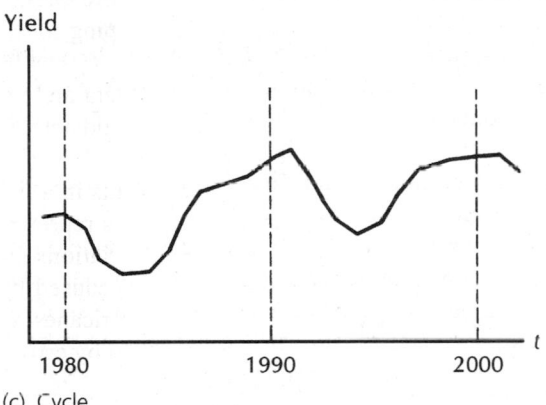

(c) Cycle

Forecasts would then be obtained by combining the estimate of the trend component with the estimate of the seasonal component. Again, however, it should be emphasized that the key to this methodology is finding a model that matches the pattern of the historical data that are available.

# 1.2   FORECASTING METHODS

In Section 1.1 we pointed out that no single best forecasting model exists. In fact, there are many forecasting methods that can be used to predict future events. These methods can be divided into two basic types—**qualitative** methods and **quantitative** methods.

## Qualitative Forecasting Methods

**Qualitative forecasting methods** generally use the opinions of experts to predict future events subjectively. Such methods are often required when historical data either are not available at all or are scarce. For example, consider a situation in which a new product is being introduced. In such a case, no historical sales data for the product are available. To forecast sales for the new product, a company must rely on expert opinion, which can be supplied by members of its sales force and market research team. Other situations in which historical data are not available might involve trying to predict if and when new technologies will be discovered and adopted. Qualitative forecasting techniques are also used to predict changes in historical data patterns. Since the use of historical data to predict future events is based on the assumption that the pattern of the historical data will persist, changes in the data pattern cannot be predicted on the basis of historical data. Thus qualitative methods are often used to predict such changes.

We will briefly describe several commonly used qualitative forecasting techniques. The first of these techniques involves **subjective curve fitting.** Consider a firm that is introducing a new product and wishes to forecast sales of this product over the next several years so that it can estimate the productive capacity needed to produce the product. In predicting sales of a new product, it is often convenient to consider what is known as the "product life cycle." This life cycle is usually thought of as consisting of several stages. During the first stage (growth), sales of the product start slowly, then increase rapidly, and then continue to increase, but at a slower rate. During the next stage (maturity), sales of the product stabilize, increasing slowly, reaching a plateau, and then decreasing slowly. During the last stage (decline), sales of the product decline at an increasing rate. This product life cycle is illustrated in Figure 1.2. In forecasting sales of the product during the growth stage, the company might use the expert opinions of its sales and marketing personnel to subjectively construct an S-curve, as illustrated in Figure 1.3. Such an

**FIGURE 1.2**
Product life cycle

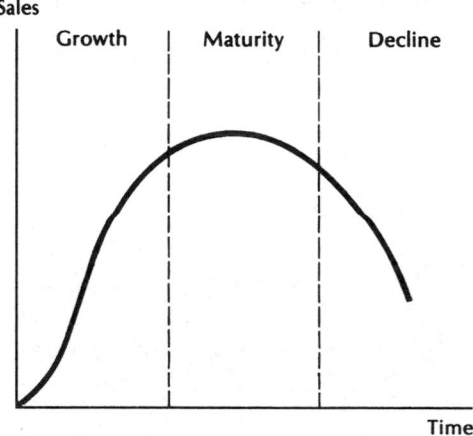

**FIGURE 1.3**
S-curve

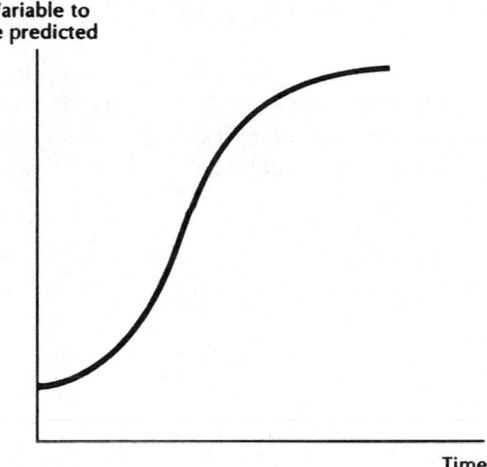

**FIGURE 1.4**
Exponential curve

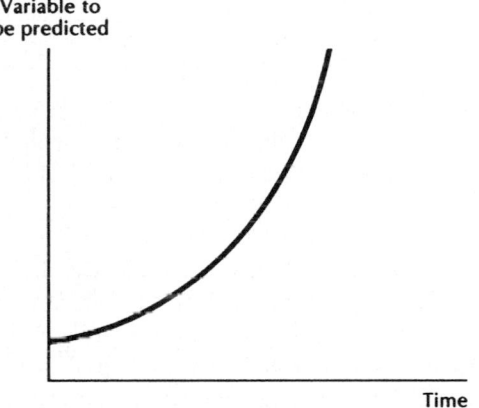

S-curve could then be used to forecast sales during this stage. In constructing this S-curve, the company must use its experience with other products and all its knowledge concerning the new product in order to predict how long it will take for the rapid increase in sales to begin, how long this rapid growth will continue, and when sales of the product will begin to stabilize. Note that the construction of this curve is done subjectively since there will be few or no sales data available for the new product. Estimating such a curve is an example of subjective curve fitting. Of course, one of the biggest problems in using this technique is deciding on the form of the curve to be used. In a product life cycle situation, the use of an S-curve may be appropriate. But many other functional forms can be used. For example, an exponential curve, as illustrated in Figure 1.4, might be appropriate in some situations. Other situations might call for the use of a logarithmic curve. Thus the forecaster first must subjectively determine the form of the curve to be used. The subjective construction of such curves is difficult and requires a great deal of expertise and judgment.

Another common qualitative forecasting method is called the **Delphi method.** In this technique, which was developed by the RAND Corporation, a panel of experts is used to produce predictions concerning a specific question, such as when a new development will occur in a particular field. The use of the Delphi method assumes that the panel members are recognized experts in the field of interest, and it also assumes that the combined knowledge of the panel members will produce predictions at least as good as those that would be produced by any one member. When a panel of experts is called upon to make predictions, a panel discussion might seem to be appropriate. But such discussions are often dominated by one individual or by a small group of individuals. Also, the decisions made in panel discussions can be influenced by various kinds of social pressure. The Delphi method attempts to avoid these problems by keeping the panel members physically separated. Each participant is asked to respond to a series of questionnaires and to return the completed questionnaires to a panel coordinator. After the first questionnaire has been completed and sent, subsequent questionnaires are accompanied by information concerning the opinions of the group as a whole. Thus the participants can review their predictions relative to the group response. It is hoped that after several rounds of questionnaires the group's responses will converge on a consensus that can be used as a forecast. It should be noted, however, that the Delphi method does not require that a consensus be reached. Instead, the method allows for justified differences of opinion rather than attempting to produce unanimity. We will not present a more detailed discussion of the Delphi method here. The interested reader is referred to Rowe and Wright (2001).

A third qualitative forecasting technique involves the use of time-independent **technological comparisons.** In this method, which is often used in predicting technological change, changes in one area are predicted by monitoring changes that take place in another area. That is, the forecaster tries to determine a pattern of change in one area, often called a **primary trend,** which he or she believes will result in new developments in some other area. A forecast of developments in the second area can then be made by monitoring developments in the first area. For example, consider the problem of trying to forecast when a new metal alloy of very high tensile strength will be used commercially. Suppose that the forecaster determines that metallurgical advances made in industry are related to metallurgical advances in the space program. Then, by following metallurgical advances in the space program, the forecaster can predict when similar advances will take place in industry. Thus the development of high-tensile-strength alloys in the space program would allow the forecaster to predict when such alloys will be available for commercial use. This type of forecasting poses two basic problems. First, the forecaster must identify a primary trend that will reliably predict events in the area of interest. Second, the forecaster must use his or her expertise to determine the precise relationship between the primary trend and the events to be forecast. Once these determinations have been made, forecasts in the area of interest can be made by monitoring the primary trend. For a further discussion of this technique, the reader is referred to Gerstenfeld (1971).

The qualitative forecasting techniques we have discussed—subjective curve fitting, the Delphi method, and time-independent technological comparisons—represent only some of the subjective forecasting methods available. These subjective methods are frequently called **judgmental forecasting methods.** The interested reader is referred to a book on principles of forecasting that is edited by J. S. Armstrong (2001). This book is a collection of papers, many of which are concerned with judgmental forecasting.

## Quantitative Forecasting Methods

The rest of this book is devoted to a discussion of **quantitative forecasting techniques.** These techniques involve the analysis of historical data in an attempt to predict future values of a variable of interest. Quantitative forecasting models can be grouped into two kinds—univariate models and causal models.

A **univariate forecasting model** predicts future values of a time series *solely on the basis of the past values of the time series.* When a univariate model is used, historical data are analyzed in an attempt to identify a data pattern. Then, on the assumption that it will continue in the future, this data pattern is extrapolated in order to produce forecasts. Univariate forecasting models are, therefore, most useful when conditions are expected to remain the same; they are not very useful in forecasting the impact of changes in management policies. For example, while a univariate model can be used to predict sales if a firm expects to continue using its present marketing strategy, such a model will not be useful in predicting the changes in sales that might result from a price increase, increased advertising expenditures, or a new advertising campaign.

The use of **causal forecasting models** involves the identification of other variables that are related to the variable to be predicted. Once these related variables have been identified, a statistical model that describes the relationship between these variables and the variable to be forecasted is developed. The statistical relationship derived is then used to forecast the variable of interest. For example, the sales of a product might be related to the price of the product, advertising expenditures to promote the product, competitors' prices for similar products, and so on. In such a case, sales would be referred to as the **dependent variable,** while the other variables would be referred to as the **independent variables.** The forecaster's job is to estimate statistically the functional relationship between sales and the independent variables. Having determined this relationship, the forecaster would use predicted future values of the independent variables (price of the product, advertising expenditures, competitors' prices, etc.) to predict the future values of sales (the dependent variable).

In the business world, causal models are advantageous because they allow management to evaluate the impact of various alternative policies. For example, management might wish to predict how various price structures and levels of advertising expenditures will affect sales. A causal model relating these variables could be used here. However, causal models have several disadvantages as well. First, they are quite difficult to develop. Also, they require historical data on all the variables included in the model. Moreover, the ability to predict the dependent variable depends on the ability of the forecaster to accurately predict future values of the independent variables. Despite these disadvantages, causal models are often used.

To summarize our discussion of forecasting methods, quantitative forecasting methods are used when historical data are available: univariate models predict future values of the variable of interest solely on the basis of the historical pattern of that variable, assuming that the historical pattern will continue; and causal models predict future values of the variable of interest based on the relationship between that variable and other variables. Qualitative forecasting techniques are used when historical data are scarce or not available at all, and they depend on the opinions of experts who subjectively predict future events. In actual practice most forecasting systems employ both quantitative and qualitative methods. For example, quantitative methods are used when the existing data pattern is expected to persist, and qualitative methods are used to predict when the existing data pattern might change. Thus forecasts generated by quantitative methods are almost always subjectively evaluated by management. This evaluation may result in a modification of the forecast based on the manager's "expert opinion."

# 1.3  ERRORS IN FORECASTING

Unfortunately, all forecasting situations involve some degree of uncertainty. We recognize this fact by including an irregular component in the description of a time series. The presence of this irregular component, which represents unexplained or unpredictable fluctuations in the data, means that some error in forecasting must be expected. If the effect of the irregular component is substantial, our ability to forecast accurately will be limited. If, however, the effect of the irregular component is small, determination of the appropriate trend, seasonal, or cyclical patterns should allow us to forecast with more accuracy.

The irregular component is not the only source of errors in forecasting, however. The accuracy with which we can predict each of the other components of a time series also influences the magnitude of error in our forecasts. Since these components cannot be perfectly predicted in a practical situation, the errors in forecasting represent the combined effects of the irregular component and the accuracy with which the forecasting technique can predict trend, seasonal, or cyclical patterns. Hence large forecasting errors may indicate that the irregular component is so large that no forecasting technique will produce accurate forecasts, or they may indicate that the forecasting technique is not capable of accurately predicting the trend, seasonal, or cyclical components and, therefore, that the technique is inappropriate.

## Types of Forecasts

The fact that forecasting techniques often produce predictions that are somewhat in error has a bearing on the form of the forecasts we require. In this book we consider two types of forecasts: (1) the **point forecast** and (2) the **prediction interval forecast.**

Whereas a point forecast is a single number that represents our best prediction (or guess) of the actual value of the variable being forecasted, a prediction interval forecast is an interval (or range) of numbers that is calculated so that we are very confident—(for instance, 95% confident) that the actual value will be contained in the interval. Suppose, for example, that the Olympia Paper Company, Inc., produces Absorbent Paper Towels and for the past 120 weeks has recorded weekly sales of those towels. In Chapter 9 we present and forecast this time series. We will find that a point forecast of sales in week 121 is 258,889 rolls, and that a 95% prediction interval forecast of sales in week 121 is [238,517 rolls, 279,261 rolls]. The prediction interval says that the Olympia Paper Company is 95% confident that the sales of Absorbent Paper Towels in week 121 will be no less than 238,517 rolls and no more than 279,261 rolls. The company might use the fact that it is quite sure that sales will be no more than 279,261 rolls to determine the level of inventory it should carry for that week. It might also use the fact that sales are not likely to be less than 238,517 rolls to help determine the minimum amount of revenue that will be generated by this product next week.

## Measuring Forecast Errors

We now consider the problem of measuring forecasting errors. We can denote the actual value of the variable of interest in time period $t$ as $y_t$, and the predicted value as $\hat{y}_t$. Then we can subtract the predicted value of $y_t$ from the actual value $y_t$ to obtain the forecast error $e_t$. That is,

---

The **forecast error** for a particular forecast $\hat{y}_t$ is

$$e_t = y_t - \hat{y}_t$$

---

In Section 1.1 we noted the importance of matching a forecasting technique to the pattern of data characterizing a time series. An examination of forecast errors over time can often indicate whether the forecasting technique does or does not match this pattern. For example, if a forecasting technique is accurately forecasting the trend, seasonal, or cyclical components that are present in a time series, the forecast errors should reflect only the irregular component. In such a case, the forecast errors should appear purely random. Figure 1.5(a) (page 14) illustrates forecast errors that indicate that the forecasting technique appropriately accounts for the trend, seasonal, or cyclical components present in the time series. Sometimes, when the forecasting technique does not match the data pattern, the forecasting errors will exhibit a pattern over time. In Figure 1.5(b) the forecast errors show an upward trend, which indicates that the forecasting methodology does not account for an upward trend in the time series. The forecast errors in Figure 1.5(c) indicate that a seasonal

**FIGURE 1.5**
Plots of forecast
errors

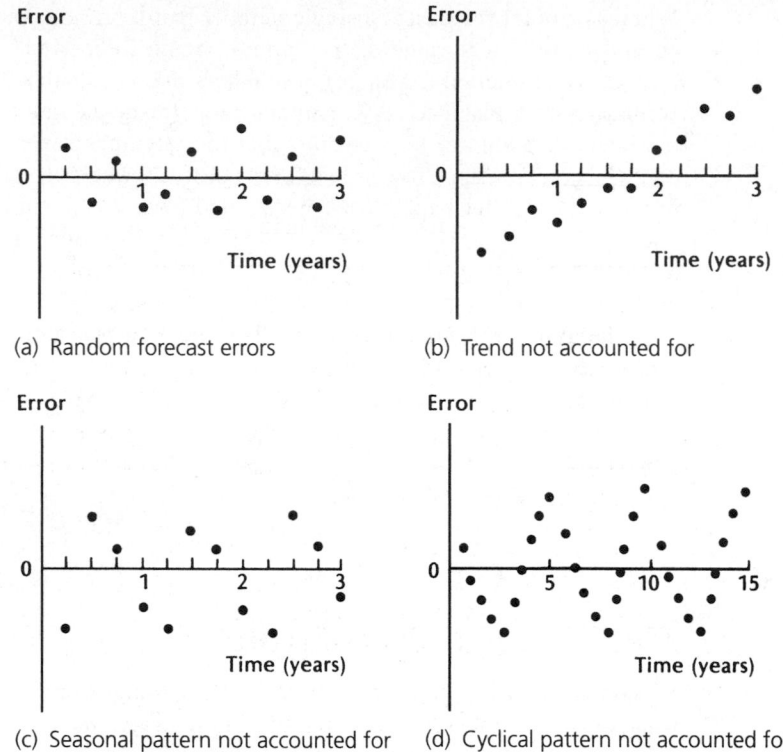

(a)  Random forecast errors

(b)  Trend not accounted for

(c)  Seasonal pattern not accounted for

(d)  Cyclical pattern not accounted for

pattern in the data is not accounted for, and the forecast errors in Figure 1.5(d) indicate that a cyclical pattern in the data is not accounted for. Patterns of forecast
errors such as those illustrated in Figure 1.5(b), (c), and (d) indicate that the forecasting technique being employed is not appropriate; that is, it does not match the
pattern of the time series data.

   If the forecasting errors over time indicate that the forecasting methodology is
appropriate (random distribution of errors), it is important to *measure the magnitude
of the errors* so that we can determine whether accurate forecasting is possible. In order
to do this, one might consider the sum of all forecast errors over time. That is, one
might calculate

$$\sum_{t=1}^{n} (y_t - \hat{y}_t)$$

which reads "the summation of the differences between the predicted $(\hat{y}_t)$ and actual
$(y_t)$ values from time period $t = 1$ through time period $t = n$, where $n$ is the total
number of observed time periods." However, this quantity is not used because if the
errors display a random pattern, some errors will be positive while other errors will
be negative, and the sum of the forecast errors will be near zero regardless of the size

of the errors. That is, the positive and negative errors, no matter how large or small, will cancel each other out.

One way to solve this problem is to consider the absolute values of the forecasting errors. These absolute values are called the **absolute deviations.**

$$\text{Absolute deviation} = |e_t| = |y_t - \hat{y}_t|$$

Given the absolute deviations, we can then define a measure known as the **mean absolute deviation (MAD).** This measure is simply the average of the absolute deviations for all forecasts. That is,

$$\text{Mean absolute deviation (MAD)} = \frac{\sum_{t=1}^{n} |e_t|}{n} = \frac{\sum_{t=1}^{n} |y_t - \hat{y}_t|}{n}$$

An example of the calculations involved in computing the MAD is given in Table 1.2. This measure can be used to determine the magnitude of the forecast errors generated by a forecasting methodology.

Another way to prevent positive and negative forecast errors from canceling each other out is to square the forecast errors. These squares are called the **squared errors:**

$$\text{Squared error} = (e_t)^2 = (y_t - \hat{y}_t)^2$$

**TABLE 1.2** Computation of Mean Absolute Deviation

| Actual Value $y_t$ | Predicted Value $\hat{y}_t$ | Error $e_t = y_t - \hat{y}_t$ | Absolute Deviation $|e_t| = |y_t - \hat{y}_t|$ |
|---|---|---|---|
| 25 | 22 | 3 | 3 |
| 28 | 30 | -2 | 2 |
| 29 | 30 | -1 | 1 |
| | | | $\sum_{t=1}^{3} |e_t| = 6$ |

$$\text{Mean absolute deviation} = \frac{\sum_{t=1}^{3} |e_t|}{3} = \frac{6}{3} = 2$$

Given the squared errors, we can define the **mean squared error (MSE).** This measure is simply the average of the squared errors for all forecasts. That is,

$$\text{Mean squared error (MSE)} = \frac{\sum_{t=1}^{n}(e_t)^2}{n} = \frac{\sum_{t=1}^{n}(y_t - \hat{y}_t)^2}{n}$$

An example of the calculations involved in computing the MSE is given in Table 1.3.

Having shown that both the MAD and the MSE can be used to measure the magnitude of forecast errors, we now describe how these two measures differ. The basic difference between these measures is that *the MSE, unlike the MAD, penalizes a forecasting technique much more for large errors than for small errors.* For example, an error of 2 produces a squared error of 4 while an error of 4 (an error twice as large) produces a squared error of 16 (a squared error four times as large). So, when using the MSE, the forecaster would prefer several smaller forecast errors to one large error. This situation is illustrated in Table 1.4, where we consider two different sets of forecasts generated by methods A and B. Forecasting method A has produced predictions yielding moderate forecast errors, while forecasting method B has produced predictions yielding two small errors along with one large error. Notice that forecasting method A has the larger MAD, while forecasting method B has the larger MSE. This is so because in the calculation of the MSE, forecasting method B is heavily penalized for its large error in forecasting the actual value 67.

Measures such as the MAD and MSE can be used in two different ways. First, they can be used to aid in the process of selecting a forecasting model. Suppose that

**TABLE 1.3 Computation of Mean Squared Error**

| Actual Value $y_t$ | Predicted Value $\hat{y}_t$ | Error $e_t = y_t - \hat{y}_t$ | Squared Error $(e_t)^2 = (y_t - \hat{y}_t)^2$ |
|---|---|---|---|
| 25 | 22 | 3 | 9 |
| 28 | 30 | -2 | 4 |
| 29 | 30 | -1 | 1 |
| | | | $\sum_{t=1}^{3}(e_t)^2 = 14$ |

$$\text{Mean squared error} = \frac{\sum_{t=1}^{3}(e_t)^2}{3} = \frac{14}{3} = 4.67$$

**TABLE 1.4** Comparisons of the Errors Produced by Two Different Forecasting Methods

|  | Actual $y_t$ | Predicted $\hat{y}_t$ | Error | Absolute Deviation | Squared Error |
|---|---|---|---|---|---|
| Forecasting method A | 60 | 57 | +3 | 3 | 9 |
|  | 64 | 61 | +3 | 3 | 9 |
|  | 67 | 70 | −3 | 3 | 9 |
|  |  |  |  | 9 | 27 |

$$\text{Mean absolute deviation} = \frac{9}{3} = 3$$

$$\text{Mean squared error} = \frac{27}{3} = 9$$

|  | Actual $y_t$ | Predicted $\hat{y}_t$ | Error | Absolute Deviation | Squared Error |
|---|---|---|---|---|---|
| Forecasting method B | 60 | 59 | +1 | 1 | 1 |
|  | 64 | 65 | −1 | 1 | 1 |
|  | 67 | 73 | −6 | 6 | 36 |
|  |  |  |  | 8 | 38 |

$$\text{Mean absolute deviation} = \frac{8}{3} = 2.67$$

$$\text{Mean squared error} = \frac{38}{3} = 12.67$$

we are trying to choose among several forecasting models in an attempt to determine which is likely to produce the most accurate predictions of future values of some variable of interest. A common strategy used in making such a selection involves the simulation of historical data. In the simulation process we pretend that we do not know the values of the historical data. Then we use each of the forecasting models to produce "predictions" of the historical data. We next compare these "predictions" with the actual values of the historical data and measure their accuracy using the MAD or MSE. Now, in order to choose the technique we will use in actual forecasting, we compare the performance of the various techniques in "forecasting" the historical data to see which of them provided the most accurate simulated "predictions."

Second, the MAD or the MSE can be used to monitor a forecasting system in order to detect when something has "gone wrong" with the system. For example, in Section 1.1, we stated that forecasts cannot be expected to be accurate unless the historical data pattern that has been identified continues in the future. Consider a situation in which a data pattern that has persisted for an extended period suddenly changes. Any forecasting method we have been using to forecast the variable of interest might now become inaccurate because of this change. In such a situation we would like to discover the change in pattern as quickly as possible before forecasts become very inaccurate. This can be done by using measures that incorporate the MAD or MSE to monitor the forecast errors and to "signal" us when these errors become "too large." We return to this problem in Chapter 8.

A way of measuring the forecasting error that allows comparison across different time series with values of different magnitude is to divide the absolute deviations by the actual value $y_t$ and then multiply by 100. Here we assume that the values of the time series are positive. These percentages are called the **absolute percentage errors.** That is,

$$\text{Absolute percentage error} = \text{APE}_t = \frac{|e_t|}{y_t}(100) = \frac{|y_t - \hat{y}_t|}{y_t}(100)$$

We can now define the **mean absolute percentage error** as the average of the absolute percentage errors. That is,

$$\text{Mean absolute percentage error (MAPE)} = \frac{\sum_{t=1}^{n} \text{APE}_t}{n}$$

An example of the calculations involved in computing the MAPE is given in Table 1.5.

**TABLE 1.5  Computation of Mean Absolute Percentage Error**

| Actual Value $y_t$ | Predicted Value $\hat{y}_t$ | Error $|e_t| = |y_t - \hat{y}_t|$ | Absolute Percentage Error $\text{APE}_t = (|e_t|/y_t)(100)$ |
|---|---|---|---|
| 25 | 22 | 3 | 12.0 |
| 28 | 30 | 2 | 7.1 |
| 29 | 30 | 1 | 3.5 |
| | | | $\sum_{t=1}^{3} \text{APE}_t = 22.6$ |

$$\text{Mean absolute percentage error} = \frac{\sum_{t=1}^{3} \text{APE}_t}{3} = \frac{22.6}{3} = 7.5$$

# 1.4 CHOOSING A FORECASTING TECHNIQUE

In choosing a forecasting technique, the forecaster must consider the following factors:

1. The time frame
2. The pattern of data
3. The cost of forecasting
4. The accuracy desired
5. The availability of data
6. The ease of operation and understanding

The first factor that can influence the choice of a forecasting method is the **time frame** of the forecasting situation. Forecasts are generated for points in time that may be a number of days, weeks, months, quarters, or years in the future. This length of time is called the time frame or time horizon. The length of the time frame is usually categorized as follows:

- Immediate—less than one month
- Short term—one to three months
- Medium—more than three months to less than two years
- Long term—two years or more

In general the length of the time frame will influence the choice of the forecasting technique. Typically, a longer time frame makes accurate forecasting more difficult, with qualitative forecasting techniques becoming more useful as the time frame lengthens.

As discussed in Section 1.1, the pattern of data must also be considered when choosing a forecasting model. The components present (trend, cycle, seasonal, or some combination of these) will help determine the model that will be used. Thus it is extremely important to identify the existing data pattern.

When choosing a forecasting technique, several costs are relevant. The cost of developing the model must be considered. We will see in later chapters that the development of a forecasting model requires that a set of procedures be followed. The complexity, and hence the cost, of these procedures varies from technique to technique. Also, the cost of the actual operation of the forecasting technique is important. Some forecasting methods are operationally simple, while others are very complex. The degree of complexity can have a definite influence on the total cost of forecasting.

Another important factor in the choice of a forecasting technique is the desired accuracy of the forecast. In some situations a forecast that is in error by as much as 20% may be acceptable; in other situations a forecast that is in error by 1% might be disastrous. The accuracy that can be obtained using any particular forecasting method is always an important consideration.

We have pointed out that historical data on the variable of interest are used when quantitative forecasting methods are employed. The availability of this information is a factor that may determine the forecasting method to be used. Since various forecasting methods require different amounts of historical data, the quantity of data available is important. Beyond this, the accuracy and the timeliness of the data that are available must be examined, since the use of inaccurate or outdated historical data will yield inaccurate predictions. If the needed historical data are not available, special data-collection procedures may be necessary.

Last, the ease with which the forecasting method is operated and understood is important. Managers are held responsible for the decisions they make, and if they are to be expected to base their decisions on predictions, they must be able to understand the techniques used to obtain these predictions. A manager simply will not have confidence in the predictions obtained from a forecasting technique he or she does not understand, and if the manager does not have confidence in these predictions, they will not be used in the decision-making process. Thus the manager's understanding of the forecasting system is crucial.

Choosing the forecasting method to be used in a particular situation involves finding a technique that balances the factors just discussed. The "best" forecasting method for a given situation is not always the "most accurate." Instead, *the forecasting method that should be used is one that meets the needs of the situation at the least cost and with the least inconvenience.*

Suppose that a company wants to predict sales one month in advance. To accomplish this task, the firm develops a complicated forecasting system and finds that the mean absolute deviation for the technique is 2000 units. The firm must then determine whether the cost and inconvenience of this forecasting system are justified. In order to make this decision, the mean absolute deviation of 2000 units must be placed in perspective. If monthly sales average 5000 units, then the mean absolute deviation of 2000 units is very large and the forecasts will be quite inaccurate. In this case, using such a complex forecasting system is probably not justified. If, however, monthly sales average 40,000 units, then the forecasts will be quite accurate (on a percentage basis). But the knowledge that the forecasting method produces accurate forecasts is not enough to tell the firm whether the method is *appropriate*. Suppose that in the past, monthly sales have differed from 40,000 units by no more than 3000 units. Then the firm could forecast sales of 40,000 units each month and predict sales nearly as well as with the complex forecasting system, and with much less cost and effort. Thus if a forecast that is accurate within 3000 units is adequate, the company should simply forecast sales of 40,000 units each month rather than use the complicated forecasting system; if greater accuracy were required, the more complicated forecasting system would be justified. Thus the low cost and the ease of using a simple forecasting method must be balanced against the greater accuracy but higher cost of a more complex forecasting technique.

# 1.5 AN OVERVIEW OF QUANTITATIVE FORECASTING TECHNIQUES

The quantitative forecasting techniques covered in this book include regression analysis, time series regression, decomposition methods, exponential smoothing, and the Box–Jenkins methodology.

## Regression Analysis

Regression analysis is a statistical methodology that is used to relate variables. Here we wish to relate a variable of interest, which is called the **dependent variable** or **response variable,** to one or more **predictor, or independent, variables.** The dependent variable is denoted by $y$, and the independent variables are denoted by $x_1, x_2, \ldots, x_k$. The objective is to build a **regression model** or **prediction equation**—an equation relating $y$ to $x_1, x_2, \ldots, x_k$. We use the model to **describe, predict,** and **control** $y$ on the basis of the independent variables.

A regression model can employ **quantitative independent variables** and/or **qualitative independent variables.** A *quantitative independent variable* assumes numerical values corresponding to points on the real line. A *qualitative independent variable* is nonnumerical. The levels of such a variable are defined by describing them. As an example, suppose that we wish to build a regression model relating the dependent variable

$$y = \text{demand for a consumer product}$$

to the independent variables

$x_1 =$ the price of the product

$x_2 =$ the average industry price of competitors' similar products

$x_3 =$ advertising expenditures made to promote the product

$x_4 =$ the type of advertising campaign (television, radio, print media, etc.) used to promote the product

Here $x_1$, $x_2$, and $x_3$ are quantitative independent variables. In contrast, $x_4$ is a qualitative independent variable, since we would define the levels of $x_4$ by describing the different advertising campaigns. After constructing an appropriate regression model relating $y$ to $x_1$, $x_2$, $x_3$, and $x_4$, we would use the model for the following purposes:

1.  To **describe** the relationships between $y$ and $x_1, x_2, x_3,$ and $x_4$. For instance, we might wish to describe the effect that increasing advertising expenditure has on the demand for the product. We might also wish to determine whether this effect depends on the price of the product.

2. To **predict** future demands for the product on the basis of future values of $x_1$, $x_2$, $x_3$, and $x_4$.

3. To **control** future demands for the product by controlling the price of the product, advertising expenditures, and the types of advertising campaigns used.

Note that we cannot control the price of competitors' products, nor can we control competitors' advertising expenditures or other factors that affect demand. Therefore, we cannot perfectly control or predict future demands.

We develop a regression model by using observed values of the dependent and independent variables. If these values are observed over time, the data are called **time series data.** On the other hand, if these values are observed at one point in time, the data are called **cross-sectional data.** For example, suppose we observe values of the demand for a product, the price of the product, and the advertising expenditures made to promote the product. If we observe these values in one sales region over thirty consecutive months, the data are time series data. If we observe these values in thirty different sales regions for a particular month of the year, the data are cross-sectional data.

The point prediction of interest in regression analysis may not be at a future time period. For example, a sales manager may be able to use a multiple regression model that predicts a representative's sales performance on the basis of variables such as time with the company and the product's market potential, advertising expenditure, market share, and recent change in the market share. Suppose a random sample of twenty-five sales representatives, each of whom is responsible for one sales territory, is selected from all the representatives that the company considers to be effective. These values would form a cross-sectional data set. A regression model based on this sample might be used to evaluate a questionable sales representative by comparing the actual sales of this representative with the prediction interval from the model.

In Part II of this book (Chapters 3, 4, and 5), we discuss using regression to analyze and forecast both time series and cross-sectional data. Specifically, Chapter 3, Sections 4.1 through 4.6 of Chapter 4, and Sections 5.2 and 5.3 of Chapter 5 discuss the basic tools of regression analysis. These are the tools that are needed in Part III. The remaining sections of Chapters 4 and 5 present various optional advanced topics in regression analysis. These topics are not needed for studying any other chapter in this book, but they would be studied by a reader interested in a more complete discussion of using regression analysis in forecasting (prediction).

## Univariate Time Series: Time Series Regression, Classical Decomposition, Exponential Smoothing

Part III (Chapters 6, 7, and 8) discusses using univariate forecasting models. The examples of regression analysis in Part II illustrate the use of causal forecasting models. For example, we illustrate predicting product demand on the basis of price and advertising expenditure, and we illustrate predicting sales performance on the

**FIGURE 1.6**
A time series
exhibiting a trend
with a slope that
remains constant

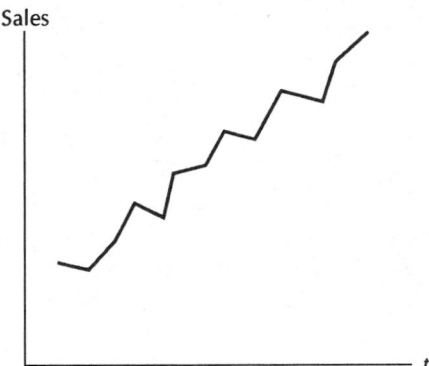

basis of time with the company, market potential, advertising expenditures, market share, and change in market share. In contrast, recall that univariate models predict future values of a time series solely on the basis of past values of the time series. Chapter 6 considers **time series regression.** This technique basically relates the dependent variable to functions of time describing trend and seasonal components. It is most profitably used when the components describing the times series to be forecasted remain constant over time. For example, if a time series exhibits a linear trend, then the slope of the trend line remains constant (see Figure 1.6). As another example, if the time series can be described by using monthly seasonal effects, then the seasonal effect for each of the twelve months remains the same from one year to the next.

In Chapter 7 we discuss **decomposition methods.** These methods decompose a time series into trend, seasonal, and irregular (error) components. Estimates of these components are used to describe and forecast the time series. As with time series regression, decomposition methods assume that the components describing the time series remain constant over time.

In ongoing forecasting systems, forecasts of a time series are made in each period for succeeding periods. Hence, the estimates of time series components need to be updated at the end of each time period to account for possible changes in the components that may be occurring over time. In addition, such changes may imply that unequal weight should be applied to the time series observations when the components are updated. **Exponential smoothing,** which is discussed in Chapter 8, is a forecasting method that weights recent observations more heavily than remote observations. For example, this technique might be appropriate for forecasting the sales time series in Figure 1.7 (page 24). Historically, the exponential smoothing methods were not based on statistical models. However, recent work (Ord, Koehler, and Snyder, 1997) has provided a solid statistical basis for the exponential smoothing methods. This work has shown that state space models with a single source of error produce the same point forecasts as the exponential smoothing methods and can also be used to find prediction interval forecasts. The traditional methods for finding point forecasts are described in Chapter 8, and the new model-based formulas for finding prediction interval forecasts are presented with each exponential smoothing method.

**FIGURE 1.7**
JMP IN plot of time series exhibiting a trend line with a slope that is changing over time

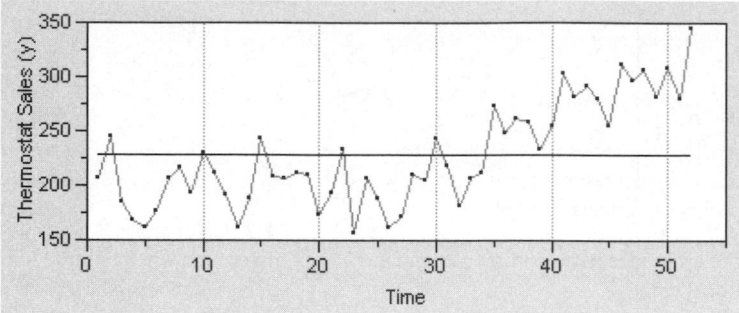

In optional Section 8.6, the state space models are introduced and related to the methods and prediction intervals in the earlier sections.

## Box–Jenkins Methods

Part IV covers the **Box–Jenkins methodology** (note that Part IV is written from first principles and can be read without reading Part II or Part III). Identification of an appropriate model from among those presented in Parts II and III requires combining the examination of data plots with a great deal of intuition, whereas the Box–Jenkins methodology provides a more extensive collection of models and a much more systematic procedure for identifying an appropriate model. Because of this identification process, the Box–Jenkins methodology frequently requires more observations of the time series than the other techniques. In theory the Box–Jenkins methodology can be used to forecast any type of time series. It is probably most appropriate when the components describing the time series are changing over time.

Chapters 9, 10, and 11 present a complete discussion of nonseasonal univariate Box–Jenkins modeling and an introduction to seasonal univariate Box–Jenkins modeling. The last section of Chapter 10 shows the relationship between exponential smoothing and the Box–Jenkins methodology in the nonseasonal case. Section 11.3 shows how to combine the time series regression of Chapter 6 with a Box–Jenkins model for error terms that are correlated. Chapter 12 discusses advanced techniques of Box–Jenkins modeling. Specifically, more details on seasonal univariate Box–Jenkins modeling are presented in the first section. Section 12.2 presents a brief explanation of **intervention models,** used to model the effects of exceptional external events (such as a strike) that affect the variable that we wish to forecast. Finally, Section 12.3 introduces **transfer function models,** which are Box–Jenkins causal models. That is, a transfer function model predicts future values of a time series on the basis of past values of the time series and on the basis of one or more related time series. For example, we might predict future sales of a product on the basis of past sales of the product and on the basis of advertising expenditures for the product.

# Exercises

**1.1** Discuss the need for forecasting.

**1.2** Discuss what a time series is, and discuss the meaning of trend effects, seasonal variations, cyclical variations, and irregular effects.

**1.3** Discuss the difference between time series data and cross-sectional data.

**1.4** Discuss the difference between point forecasts and prediction interval forecasts.

**1.5** Table 1.6 gives the forecast errors produced using three different sales forecasting models.
a. Graph these forecast errors for each model.
b. Which error patterns appear to be random?
c. Decide whether models A, B, and C adequately fit the data pattern characterizing sales. Explain your conclusions.

**1.6** Table 1.7 (page 26) presents predicted monthly sales and actual monthly sales for a company over the first six months of 2002.
a. Calculate the forecast error for each month.
b. Calculate the MAD.
c. Calculate the MSE.
d. Calculate the MAPE.

**1.7** Given the following sales forecasting models, determine whether these forecasting models are univariate models or causal models. Note that Sales($t$) denotes sales in time $t$.
a. Sales($t + 1$) = .8[Forecasted Sales($t$)] + .2[Sales($t$)]
b. Sales($t + 1$) = 500 + 2.5(Advertising Expenditure in Year $t$) + 5(Number of Customer Calls by Salespeople in Year $t$)
c. Sales($t + 1$) = $(1/t) \sum_{i=1}^{t}$ Sales($i$)

**1.8** Table 1.8 (page 26) contains the predicted and actual per capita income for a certain area of the United States.

## TABLE 1.6

| Year | Quarter | Model A Forecast Error | Model B Forecast Error | Model C Forecast Error |
|------|---------|------------------------|------------------------|------------------------|
| 1998 | 1 | +25 | +15 | −20 |
|      | 2 | +12 | +6 | +6 |
|      | 3 | +7 | −10 | +15 |
|      | 4 | +5 | −3 | −10 |
| 1999 | 1 | +3 | +12 | +8 |
|      | 2 | 0 | +4 | −5 |
|      | 3 | −4 | −7 | +7 |
|      | 4 | −11 | −1 | −8 |
| 2000 | 1 | −17 | +9 | +3 |
|      | 2 | −21 | +7 | +10 |
|      | 3 | −28 | −12 | −12 |
|      | 4 | −34 | −5 | +4 |
| 2001 | 1 | −21 | +17 | −7 |
|      | 2 | −13 | +3 | +9 |
|      | 3 | −7 | −9 | +19 |
|      | 4 | −2 | −3 | −7 |
| 2002 | 1 | +5 | +13 | +16 |
|      | 2 | +9 | +5 | −6 |
|      | 3 | +15 | −10 | −9 |
|      | 4 | +19 | −6 | +5 |

**TABLE 1.7 (for Exercise 1.6)**

|  | Actual Sales | Predicted Sales |
|---|---|---|
| January | 270 | 265 |
| February | 263 | 268 |
| March | 275 | 269 |
| April | 262 | 267 |
| May | 250 | 245 |
| June | 278 | 275 |

**TABLE 1.8 (for Exercise 1.8)**

| Year | Per Capita Income ($) | Predicted Per Capita Income ($) |
|---|---|---|
| 1979 | 3074 | 3292 |
| 1980 | 3135 | 3250 |
| 1981 | 3206 | 3230 |
| 1982 | 3267 | 3255 |
| 1983 | 3310 | 3266 |
| 1984 | 3362 | 3283 |
| 1985 | 3418 | 3300 |
| 1986 | 3500 | 3337 |

a. Calculate the forecast error for each year.
b. Plot these 0forecast errors against time.
c. Do you think the forecasting method that was used adequately fits the data pattern present? Why or why not?
d. Calculate the MAD.
e. Calculate the MSE.
f. Calculate the MAPE.

**1.9** Table 1.9 contains actual yearly sales for a company along with the predictions of yearly sales generated using two different forecasting methods.
a. Calculate the MAD for both forecasting methods.
b. Calculate the MSE for both forecasting methods.
c. Explain why these measures of accuracy yield different results in this case.

**TABLE 1.9 (for Exercise 1.9)**

| Year | Actual Sales (in millions) | Method A Predicted Sales | Method B Predicted Sales |
|---|---|---|---|
| 1998 | 8.0 | 9.0 | 9.5 |
| 1999 | 12.0 | 11.5 | 10.5 |
| 2000 | 14.0 | 14.0 | 12.0 |
| 2001 | 16.0 | 16.5 | 13.0 |
| 2002 | 10.0 | 19.0 | 15.0 |

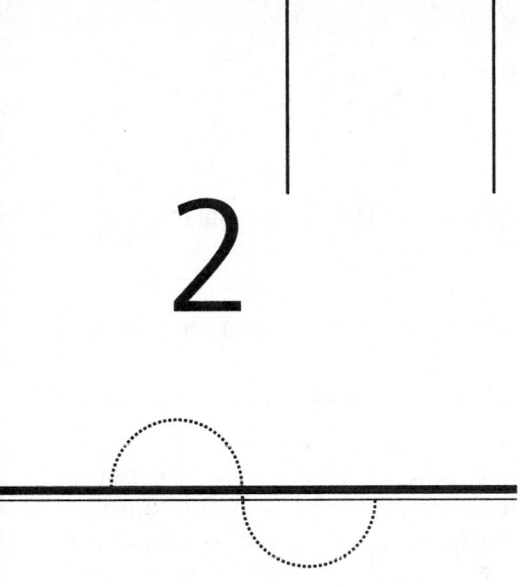

# 2

# *Basic Statistical Concepts*

In this chapter we discuss some basic statistical concepts. We begin in Section 2.1 by considering **populations.** We see that populations are described by **population parameters.** We define four such parameters—the population **mean, range, variance,** and **standard deviation.** Section 2.2 presents some elementary concepts concerning probability. In Section 2.3 we find that since the true values of population parameters are unknown, we must compute estimates of these parameters. To compute such estimates, we must randomly select a sample from the population of interest. Section 2.3 describes how this is done. We also show how sample statistics, which are descriptive measures of samples, can be used as point estimates of population parameters. To compute probabilities, we use probability distributions. We introduce **continuous probability distributions** in Section 2.4. In Sections 2.5 and 2.6 we discuss several useful continuous probability distributions—the **normal,** $t$, $F$, and **chi-square** distributions. In Section 2.7 we discuss **confidence intervals** for a population mean, and in Section 2.8 we study **hypothesis tests** about a population mean.

# 2.1   POPULATIONS

Frequently, we seek information about a collection of objects, or **elements.**

> We define a **population** to be the entire collection of elements about which information is desired.

A population may contain a finite number of elements. In this case we call the population **finite.** We denote the size of a finite population by the symbol $N$. If there is no finite limit to the number of elements that could potentially exist in a population, we say that the population is **infinite.** We are often interested in studying properties of some numerical characteristic of the population elements. Here each element in the population possesses a particular value of the numerical characteristic under study. In this book a value of a numerical characteristic is always a number on the real line.

Table 2.1 lists a numerical characteristic that might be of interest for each of the indicated finite populations.

We now consider a population of numerical values. A **parameter** is a descriptive measure of the population. We define four parameters—the population mean, range, variance, and standard deviation—in the following box.

**TABLE 2.1  Examples of Population Characteristics**

| Finite Population of Elements | Numerical Characteristic of an Element |
| --- | --- |
| The countries on the planet Earth | Number of inhabitants below poverty level in a country |
| The states in the United States | Number of family farms in a state |
| The cities with a population of at least 5000 in the state of Nebraska | Percentage of workers unemployed in a city |
| The inhabitants of Cleveland, Ohio | Yearly income (in dollars) of an inhabitant |
| The members of the United States Senate | Number of votes missed during 2004 by a senator |
| The teams in the National Football League | Number of games won last year by a team |

> ## SOME POPULATION PARAMETERS
>
> 1. The **population mean,** denoted $\mu$, is the average of the values in the population.
> 2. The **population range,** denoted RNG, is the difference between the largest value and the smallest value in the population.
> 3. The **population variance,** denoted $\sigma^2$, is the average of the squared deviations of the values in the population from the population mean $\mu$.
> 4. The **population standard deviation,** denoted $\sigma$, is the positive square root of the population variance.

**EXAMPLE 2.1**   National Motors Company, Inc., is an automobile manufacturer that produces a model called the Hawk. The company wishes to study the gasoline mileage (measured in miles per gallon, or mpg) obtained by the Hawk when it is driven 50,000 miles under normal conditions.

Consider the population of the first $N = 3$ Hawks produced by National Motors. Assume that each automobile is driven under the above conditions and that the mileages obtained are 32.4, 30.6, and 31.8. For this population,

1. The mean is

$$\mu = \frac{32.4 + 30.6 + 31.8}{3} = \frac{94.8}{3} = 31.6$$

2. The range is

$$RNG = 32.4 - 30.6 = 1.8$$

3. The variance is

$$\sigma^2 = \frac{(32.4 - 31.6)^2 + (30.6 - 31.6)^2 + (31.8 - 31.6)^2}{3}$$

$$= \frac{(.8)^2 + (-1)^2 + (.2)^2}{3} = \frac{.64 + 1 + .04}{3}$$

$$= \frac{1.68}{3} = .56$$

4. The standard deviation is

$$\sigma = \sqrt{\sigma^2} = \sqrt{.56} = .7483$$

The population mean is a measure of the central tendency of the values in the population, while the population range, variance, and standard deviation are measures of the spread, or variation, of the values. To see that the population variance is a measure of spread, first suppose that the values are spread far apart. Then many values will be far away from the mean $\mu$. This means that many of the squared deviations will be large. Thus the sum of the squared deviations will be large, and the average of the squared deviations—the population variance—will be relatively large. On the other hand, if the values are clustered close together, many values will be close to $\mu$. This means that many of the squared deviations will be small. Therefore, the average of the squared deviations—the population variance—will be small. We conclude that the greater the spread of the values, the larger the population variance. One might be tempted at this point to look for some "hidden meaning" behind (or practical interpretation of) the population variance. However, for now all that should be understood is that (1) the population variance is as defined above, and (2) the reason we are studying the population variance is that the population standard deviation will be found to be important in later sections.

In Example 2.1 we can calculate $\mu$, RNG, $\sigma^2$, and $\sigma$ because the population is small. In many situations the population is so large that the parameters cannot be computed. It would simply be too time consuming and/or expensive to do so. For instance, it would be impossible to calculate the mean $\mu$ of the population of mileages that would be obtained by the (theoretically) infinite population of all Hawks that could potentially be produced by the manufacturing process for this automobile. Suppose that, in general, the value of a population parameter is unknown. Then if information concerning the parameter is desired, our only recourse is to take a **sample,** or a subset of elements, from the population of interest. **Statistical inference** is the science of using the information contained in a sample to make a generalization about a population. One type of statistical inference is **statistical estimation.** This is the science of using the information contained in a sample (1) to find an estimate of an unknown population parameter and (2) to place a reasonable bound on how far the estimate might deviate from the unknown population parameter. That is, we wish to place a reasonable bound on how wrong the estimate might be. We continue our discussion of estimation in Section 2.3.

# 2.2   PROBABILITY

The concept of probability is employed in describing populations and in using sample information to make statistical inferences. To begin our discussion of probability, we first define an **experiment** to be any process of observation that has an uncertain outcome. An **event** is an experimental outcome that may or may not take place. The **probability** of an event is a number that measures the chance, or likelihood, that the event will occur when the experiment is performed. Let the symbol $A$ denote an event that may or may not occur when an experiment, denoted by EXP, is performed. We denote the probability that the event $A$ will occur by $P(A)$. Suppose that the experiment is performed $n_{EXP}$ times and the event $A$ occurs $n_A$ of these $n_{EXP}$ times. Then the proportion of the time event $A$ has occurred is

$$\frac{n_A}{n_{EXP}}$$

To interpret $P(A)$, consider repeating the experiment a number of times approaching infinity, and consider the sequence of numbers obtained by calculating the ratio $n_A/n_{EXP}$ after each repetition. The limit of this sequence is interpreted to be the probability of the event $A$. Stated mathematically,

$$P(A) = \lim_{n_{EXP} \to \infty} \frac{n_A}{n_{EXP}}$$

For example, the probability of a head appearing when we toss a fair coin is .5. This means that if we were to toss the coin a number of times approaching infinity, the proportion of heads obtained would approach one-half. For instance, suppose that we toss a fair coin a number of times and obtain the results in Table 2.2 (where H denotes a head and T denotes a tail). If we define the event $A$ as "a head appears," Table 2.2 shows $n_A$ (the number of repetitions on which a head has appeared), $n_{EXP}$ (the number of times the coin has been tossed), and the ratio $n_A/n_{EXP}$ for each repetition. Thus we obtain the following sequence of ratios $n_A/n_{EXP}$.

$$\frac{1}{1} \quad \frac{1}{2} \quad \frac{2}{3} \quad \frac{3}{4} \quad \frac{3}{5} \quad \frac{4}{6} \quad \frac{4}{7} \quad \frac{4}{8} \quad \frac{5}{9} \quad \frac{6}{10} \quad \cdots$$

When we say that the probability of a head is .5, we are saying that the limit of this sequence as $n_{EXP}$ approaches infinity is .5.

Of course, in practice we cannot perform an experiment a number of times approaching infinity. So from a practical standpoint, the probability of an event is

**TABLE 2.2** Calculation of the Ratio $n_A/n_{EXP}$ for Repeated Coin Tosses

| Repetition | Outcome | Number of Heads, $n_A$ | Number of Repetitions, $n_{EXP}$ | $n_A/n_{EXP}$ |
|:---:|:---:|:---:|:---:|:---:|
| 1 | H | 1 | 1 | 1/1 |
| 2 | T | 1 | 2 | 1/2 |
| 3 | H | 2 | 3 | 2/3 |
| 4 | H | 3 | 4 | 3/4 |
| 5 | T | 3 | 5 | 3/5 |
| 6 | H | 4 | 6 | 4/6 |
| 7 | T | 4 | 7 | 4/7 |
| 8 | T | 4 | 8 | 4/8 |
| 9 | H | 5 | 9 | 5/9 |
| 10 | H | 6 | 10 | 6/10 |
| ⋮ | ⋮ | ⋮ | ⋮ | ⋮ |

roughly equal to the proportion of the time the event would occur if the experiment were performed a very large number of times. Consequently, one way to estimate the probability of an event is to perform the related experiment a great many times. Then we estimate the probability as the proportion of times the event occurs during the repetitions of the experiment.

Since $P(A)$ is a long-run proportion, it follows that $P(A)$ is greater than or equal to zero and less than or equal to 1. If the event $A$ never occurs, then $P(A) = 0$. If the event $A$ is certain to occur, then $P(A) = 1$. Sometimes we wish to estimate the probability of an event when we cannot perform the related experiment a very large number of times. Then we might estimate this probability using previous experience with similar situations and intuitive judgment. For example, a company president might estimate the probability of success for a one-time business venture to be .7. Here, on the basis of his knowledge of the success of previous similar ventures, the opinions of company personnel, and other pertinent information, he believes that there is a 70% chance that the venture will be successful. If we can neither perform the related experiment a very large number of times nor use subjective judgment, many other methods are available to estimate the probability of an event. One such method—the use of continuous probability distributions—is discussed in Section 2.4.

# 2.3   RANDOM SAMPLES AND SAMPLE STATISTICS

The calculation of many population parameters—such as a mean or standard deviation—requires knowledge of all the values in the (finite or infinite) population. If we do not know all the values, we must randomly select a sample of $n$ values from the population. Then the information contained in the sample can be used to make statistical inferences concerning the population parameter. For example, the parameter can be estimated.

We can randomly select a sample of $n$ values by first randomly selecting a sample of $n$ elements from the population of elements. This is done in such a way that on any particular selection *each element remaining in this population on that selection is given the same probability, or chance, of being selected.* Here we can randomly select the sample with or without replacement. If we **sample with replacement,** we place the element selected on a particular selection back into the population. Thus we give this element a chance to be selected on any succeeding selection. In such a case all the elements in the population remain for each and every selection. If we **sample without replacement,** we do not place the element chosen on a particular selection back into the population. Thus we do not give this element a chance to be selected on any succeeding selection. In this case the elements remaining in the population for a particular selection are all the elements except for the elements that have previously been selected. *It is best* *to sample without replacement.* To see why this is so, suppose that on a particular selection we randomly select an element from the population that is unrepresentative of the population. That is, the element is considerably different from the other elements in the population. This might throw off our estimates of population parameters. Then, if we sample with replacement, we might select the unrepresentative element again. This would result in our estimates of population parameters being thrown off even more drastically. On the other hand, if we sample without replacement, the unrepresentative element cannot be selected again. We assume in this book that all sampling is done *without* replacement.

If we have randomly selected a sample of $n$ elements, the values of the numerical characteristic of interest possessed by these elements make up a randomly selected sample of $n$ numerical values. For $i = 1, 2, \ldots, n$ we let $y_i$ denote the value of the numerical characteristic under study possessed by the $i$th randomly selected element. Therefore, the set

$$\{y_1, y_2, \ldots, y_n\}$$

denotes the randomly selected sample of $n$ numerical values.

We now define a **sample statistic** to be a descriptive measure of the randomly selected sample of numerical values. We often use sample statistics as point estimates of population parameters.

---

A **point estimate** of a population parameter is a single number used as an estimate, or guess, of the population parameter.

---

Following are definitions of three sample statistics that are used as point estimates of the population mean, variance, and standard deviation.

## POINT ESTIMATES OF THE POPULATION MEAN, VARIANCE, AND STANDARD DEVIATION

Suppose that the sample

$$\{y_1, y_2, \ldots, y_n\}$$

has been randomly selected from a finite or an infinite population.

1.  The **sample mean** is defined to be

$$\bar{y} = \frac{\sum_{i=1}^{n} y_i}{n}$$

and is a point estimate of the population mean $\mu$.

2. The **sample variance** is defined to be

$$s^2 = \frac{\sum_{i=1}^{n}(y_i - \bar{y})^2}{n - 1}$$

and is a point estimate of the population variance $\sigma^2$.

3. The **sample standard deviation** is defined to be

$$s = \sqrt{s^2} = \sqrt{\frac{\sum_{i=1}^{n}(y_i - \bar{y})^2}{n - 1}}$$

and is a point estimate of the population standard deviation $\sigma$.

The rationale behind the use of these sample statistics as point estimates is that each sample statistic is exactly, or nearly, the sample counterpart of the corresponding population parameter. Here we define the *sample counterpart* of a population parameter to be the same function of the $n$ values in the sample that the population parameter is of the values in the population. For example, the sample mean

$$\bar{y} = \frac{\sum_{i=1}^{n} y_i}{n}$$

is the sample counterpart of the population mean. However, although

$$\frac{\sum_{i=1}^{n}(y_i - \bar{y})^2}{n}$$

is the sample counterpart of the population variance, we use the sample variance (with $n - 1$ as divisor) as the point estimate of $\sigma^2$. This is done because it can be shown that dividing by $n - 1$ rather than by $n$ makes $s^2$ a better estimate (in some senses) of $\sigma^2$.

**EXAMPLE 2.2**    Suppose that we wish to estimate the mean $\mu$ and standard deviation $\sigma$ of the (theoretically) infinite population of all Hawk gasoline mileages. To do this, we will randomly select a sample of $n = 5$ mileages from this population. We first randomly select a sample of five Hawks from a subpopulation of 1000 Hawks that National Motors has produced and that we assume is representative of the population of all Hawks. Then we will test drive each randomly selected automobile under the previously described conditions and record the mileage obtained.

Suppose that we obtain the following sample of mileages:

$$\{y_1, y_2, y_3, y_4, y_5\} = \{30.7, 31.8, 30.2, 32.0, 31.3\}$$

1. The sample mean is

$$\bar{y} = \frac{\sum_{i=1}^{5} y_i}{5} = \frac{30.7 + 31.8 + 30.2 + 32.0 + 31.3}{5}$$

$$= \frac{156}{5} = 31.2$$

and is the point estimate of the population mean $\mu$.

2. The sample variance is

$$s^2 = \frac{\sum_{i=1}^{5} (y_i - \bar{y})^2}{5 - 1}$$

$$= \frac{(y_1 - \bar{y})^2 + (y_2 - \bar{y})^2 + (y_3 - \bar{y})^2 + (y_4 - \bar{y})^2 + (y_5 - \bar{y})^2}{4}$$

$$= [(30.7 - 31.2)^2 + (31.8 - 31.2)^2 + (30.2 - 31.2)^2 + (32.0 - 31.2)^2$$
$$+ (31.3 - 31.2)^2] \div 4$$

$$= \frac{(-.5)^2 + (.6)^2 + (-1)^2 + (.8)^2 + (.1)^2}{4}$$

$$= \frac{2.26}{4} = .565$$

and is the point estimate of the population variance $\sigma^2$.

3. The sample standard deviation is

$$s = \sqrt{s^2} = \sqrt{.565} = .7517$$

and is the point estimate of the population standard deviation $\sigma$.

Note that $\bar{y}$, $s^2$, and $s$ have been calculated from a sample of $n = 5$ mileages. Therefore, unless we are very lucky, these estimates will not be equal to the respective population parameters $\mu$, $\sigma^2$, and $\sigma$. For example, suppose (a supernatural power knows) that $\mu$, the true mean Hawk mileage, is 31.5 mpg. Then the sample mean $\bar{y} = 31.2$ is .3 mpg smaller than $\mu$. The difference

$$\bar{y} - \mu = 31.2 - 31.5 = -.3$$

is called the **error of estimation** obtained when estimating $\mu$ by $\bar{y}$. We do not know the size of this error of estimation because we do not know the true value of $\mu$. However, we will see in Section 2.7 that we can utilize the sample standard deviation $s$ (along with other quantities) to provide a bound on the error of estimation. This bound will tell us the farthest that $\bar{y}$ might reasonably be from $\mu$.

# 2.4   CONTINUOUS PROBABILITY DISTRIBUTIONS

Before we randomly select a value $y$ from a population, $y$ potentially can be any of the values in the population. Thus we can consider calculating probabilities concerning the value $y$ might attain when the random selection is actually made. Specifically, consider the closed interval from $a$ to $b$ ($a < b$) on the real line. Denoting this interval as $[a, b]$, we often wish to find

$$P(y \text{ will be in the interval } [a, b])$$

which can be written more simply as

$$P(a \leq y \leq b)$$

This probability can be interpreted as the proportion of values in the population that are greater than or equal to $a$ and less than or equal to $b$.

We can often use a **continuous probability distribution** to calculate probabilities concerning $y$. Specifically, such distributions assign probabilities to intervals of numbers on the real line. To understand this idea, suppose that $f(v)$ is a continuous function of the numbers on the real line. Consider the continuous curve that results when $f(v)$ is graphed. A hypothetical curve $f(v)$ is illustrated in Figure 2.1.

> The curve $f(v)$ is the **continuous probability distribution** of $y$ if the probability that $y$ will be in the interval $[a, b]$ is the area under the curve $f(v)$ corresponding to the interval $[a, b]$.

**FIGURE 2.1**
A hypothetical
continuous
probability curve
$f(v)$

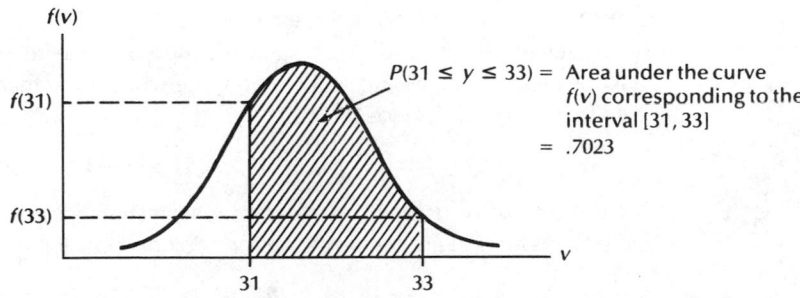

$P(31 \leq y \leq 33) =$ Area under the curve $f(v)$ corresponding to the interval $[31, 33]$
$= .7023$

As an example, suppose that the curve $f(v)$ illustrated in Figure 2.1 is the continuous probability distribution of $y$, the mileage of a randomly selected automobile. Assume that we wish to find the probability that $y$ will be between 31 mpg and 33 mpg. Then we would find the area under the curve $f(v)$ corresponding to the interval [31, 33]. If, for instance, this area were found to equal .7023, then, as shown in Figure 2.1,

$$P(31 \leq y \leq 33) = .7023$$

This says that 70.23% of all mileages are between 31 mpg and 33 mpg.

Suppose that the curve $f(v)$ is the continuous probability distribution of $y$. Then we say that the population of values from which $y$ will be randomly selected *is distributed according to the continuous probability curve $f(v)$*. Alternatively, we say that the population has the continuous probability distribution defined by $f(v)$. In Sections 2.5 and 2.6 we discuss several methods for determining the specific curve that describes a given population. We also show how to use statistical tables to find areas under probability curves.

The height of the curve $f(v)$ at a given point on the real line represents the relative probability, or chance, that $y$ will be in a small interval of numbers around the given point. For example, suppose that the continuous probability distribution of $y$ is as shown in Figure 2.1. From this figure we see that $f(31)$, the height of the curve at the point 31, is greater than $f(33)$, the height of the curve at the point 33. Thus it is more probable that $y$ will be in a small interval of numbers around 31 than in a small interval of numbers around 33. Said another way, the height of the curve at a given point represents the relative proportion of values in the population that are in a small interval of numbers around the given point.

We next consider two general properties that are satisfied by a continuous probability distribution.

1. For any number $v$, $f(v) \geq 0$. Intuitively, this property must be satisfied because the height of the probability curve $f(v)$ at the point $v$ represents a relative probability and because any probability must be greater than or equal to zero.

2. The total area under a continuous probability curve equals 1. This property holds because the total area under $f(v)$ equals the probability that $y$ will fall between $-\infty$ and $\infty$, and $y$ is sure to fall between $-\infty$ and $\infty$.

Two common shapes displayed by continuous probability curves describing actual populations are shown in Figure 2.2 (page 38). The curve illustrated in Figure 2.2(a) is symmetrical. Thus in this figure, $f(\mu + \varepsilon)$ equals $f(\mu - \varepsilon)$. The second shape, the curve depicted in Figure 2.2(b), is skewed, in this case to the right. Notice that whereas the population mean $\mu$ is not located under the highest point of the skewed curve, it is located under the highest point of the symmetrical curve. We further discuss the location of $\mu$ for probability distributions with various shapes in Section 2.6.

Again consider Figure 2.2(a). By the symmetry of the curve $f(v)$, the area under this curve to the right of $\mu$ equals the area under the curve to the left of $\mu$. Since the total area under the curve equals 1, these equal areas must each equal .5. Thus if a population is described by a symmetrical continuous probability curve, then 50% of the values are less than or equal to the population mean $\mu$ and 50% of the values are greater than or equal to $\mu$.

**FIGURE 2.2**
Some common
shapes of
continuous
probability
distributions

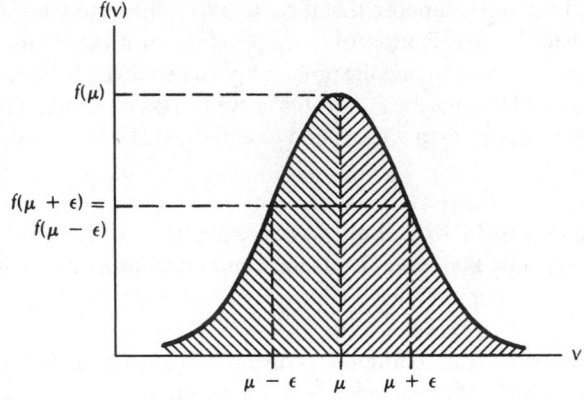

(a)  A symmetrical continuous probability distribution

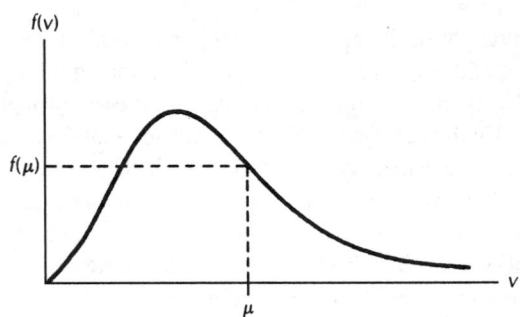

(b)  A continuous probability distribution that is skewed to the right

# 2.5  THE NORMAL PROBABILITY DISTRIBUTION

## The Normal Curve

Consider a population with mean $\mu$ and standard deviation $\sigma$. Sometimes such a population is distributed according to a **normal probability distribution.**

### THE NORMAL PROBABILITY CURVE

The **normal probability distribution** is defined by the probability curve

$$f(v) = \frac{1}{\sigma\sqrt{2\pi}} \exp\left(-\frac{(v-\mu)^2}{2\sigma^2}\right) \quad \text{for} \quad -\infty < v < \infty$$

Here $\pi = 3.14159\ldots$ is the ratio of the circumference to the diameter of a circle, and exp denotes taking $e = 2.71828\ldots$, the base of Naperian logarithms, to the power in parentheses. If a population is distributed according to a normal distribution, we say that $y$ is **normally distributed** with mean $\mu$ and standard deviation $\sigma$.

We denote the normal probability distribution by $N(\mu, \sigma)$. This means that the shape of the **normal (probability) curve** that results when $f(v)$ as defined above is graphed depends on the mean and standard deviation of the population. The normal probability curve is illustrated in Figure 2.3. It is often described as a bell-shaped curve. The following are several important properties of this curve.

1. The normal curve is centered at the population mean $\mu$.

2. The mean $\mu$ corresponds to the highest point on the normal curve.

3. The normal curve is symmetrical around the population mean.

4. Since the normal curve is a probability distribution, the total area under the curve is equal to 1.

5. Since the normal curve is symmetrical, the area under the normal curve above the mean equals the area under the curve below the mean, and each of these areas equals .5 (see Figure 2.3).

The population mean $\mu$ centers the normal curve on the real line. This is illustrated in Figure 2.4 (page 40). This figure shows two normal curves with different means $\mu_1$ and $\mu_2$ (where $\mu_1 > \mu_2$) and with the same standard deviation $\sigma$. The variance $\sigma^2$ (or the standard deviation $\sigma$) measures the spread of the normal curve. This is illustrated in Figure 2.5 (page 40), which shows two normal curves with the same mean $\mu$ but different standard deviations $\sigma_1$ and $\sigma_2$. Since $\sigma_1 > \sigma_2$, the normal curve with standard deviation $\sigma_1$ is more spread out than the normal curve with standard deviation $\sigma_2$.

If $y$ is normally distributed with mean $\mu$ and standard deviation $\sigma$, then

$$P(a \le y \le b)$$

**FIGURE 2.3**
The normal
probability curve

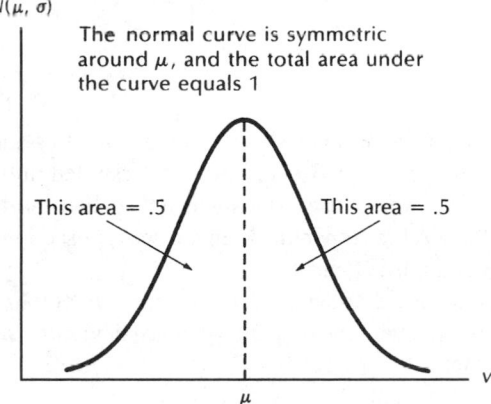

**FIGURE 2.4**
Two normal curves with different means and equal standard deviations

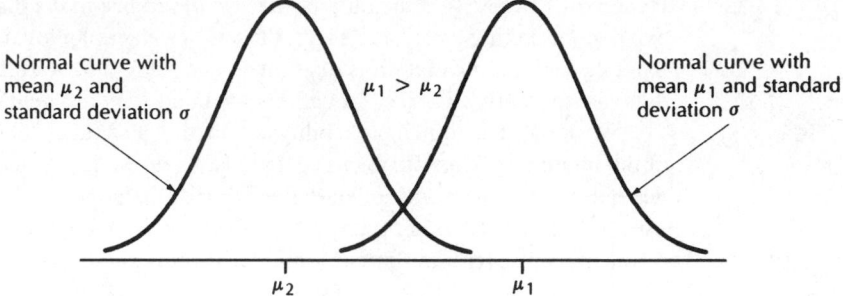

Normal curve with mean $\mu_2$ and standard deviation $\sigma$

$\mu_1 > \mu_2$

Normal curve with mean $\mu_1$ and standard deviation $\sigma$

$\mu_2$   $\mu_1$

**FIGURE 2.5**
Two normal curves with the same mean and different standard deviations

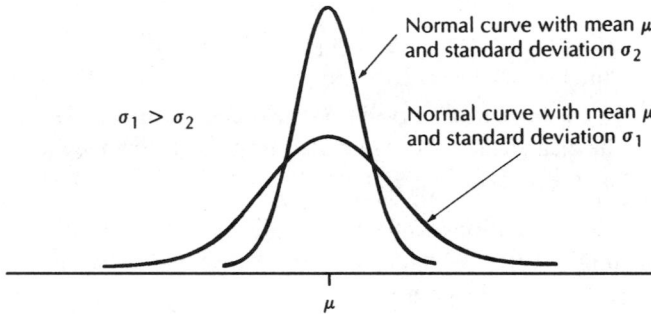

Normal curve with mean $\mu$ and standard deviation $\sigma_2$

Normal curve with mean $\mu$ and standard deviation $\sigma_1$

$\sigma_1 > \sigma_2$

$\mu$

**FIGURE 2.6**
An area under a normal curve corresponding to the interval [a, b]

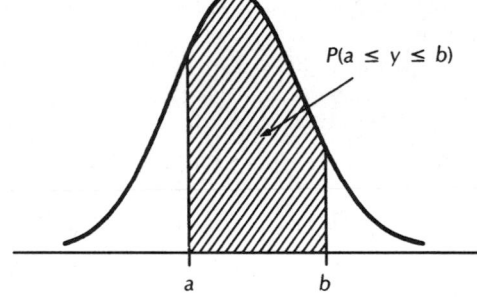

$P(a \leq y \leq b)$

$a$   $b$

equals the area under the normal curve with mean $\mu$ and standard deviation $\sigma$ corresponding to the interval [a, b]. Such an area is illustrated in Figure 2.6. To find areas under a normal curve, we can use a statistical table called a **normal table.** Such a table is presented as Table A1 in Appendix A. In the next subsection we briefly discuss how to find areas under a normal curve.

Three important areas under the normal curve are emphasized in Figure 2.7. If $y$ is normally distributed with mean $\mu$ and standard deviation $\sigma$, it can be shown (using a normal table) that

**FIGURE 2.7**
Three important
percentages
concerning a
normally
distributed
population with
mean μ and
standard
deviation σ

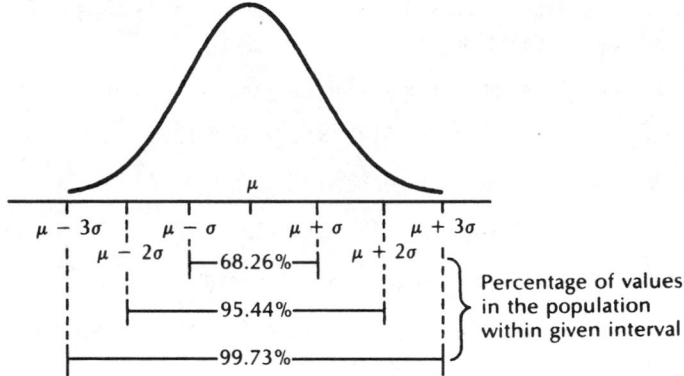

1.  $P(\mu - \sigma \leq y \leq \mu + \sigma) = .6826$

    This means that 68.26% of the values in the population are within (plus or minus) 1 standard deviation of the population mean.

2.  $P(\mu - 2\sigma \leq y \leq \mu + 2\sigma) = .9544$

    This means that 95.44% of the values in the population are within (plus or minus) 2 standard deviations of the population mean.

3.  $P(\mu - 3\sigma \leq y \leq \mu + 3\sigma) = .9973$

    This means that 99.73% of the values in the population are within (plus or minus) 3 standard deviations of the population mean.

**EXAMPLE 2.3**   In the gasoline mileage problem, suppose that the population of all mileages is normally distributed with mean $\mu = 31.5$ and standard deviation $\sigma = .8$. Then

1.  68.26% of all mileages lie in the interval

    $$[\mu - \sigma, \ \mu + \sigma] = [31.5 - .8, \ 31.5 + .8]$$
    $$- [30.7, \ 32.3]$$

2.  95.44% of all mileages lie in the interval

    $$[\mu - 2\sigma, \ \mu + 2\sigma] = [31.5 - 2(.8), \ 31.5 + 2(.8)] = [31.5 - 1.6, \ 31.5 + 1.6]$$
    $$= [29.9, \ 33.1]$$

3.  99.73% of all mileages lie in the interval

    $$[\mu - 3\sigma, \ \mu + 3\sigma] = [31.5 - 3(.8), \ 31.5 + 3(.8)] = [31.5 - 2.4, \ 31.5 + 2.4]$$
    $$= [29.1, \ 33.9]$$

Since National Motors does not know the true values of μ and σ, it cannot calculate these intervals. However, we can use the sample mean $\bar{y} = 31.2$ as the point estimate of μ and the sample standard deviation $s = .7517$ as the point estimate of $\sigma$ (see Example 2.2). Thus we can *estimate* that

1. 68.26% of the mileages in this population lie in the interval

$$[31.2 - 1(.7517),\ 31.2 + 1(.7517)] = [30.4483,\ 31.9517]$$

2. 95.44% of the mileages lie in the interval

$$[31.2 - 2(.7517),\ 31.2 + 2(.7517)] = [29.6966,\ 32.7034]$$

3. 99.73% of the mileages lie in the interval

$$[31.2 - 3(.7517),\ 31.2 + 3(.7517)] = [28.9449,\ 33.4551]$$

The results of Example 2.3 depend on the assumption that the population of mileages is normally distributed. If we wish to verify the validity of this assumption, a sample of only $n = 5$ mileages is not sufficient. We would need to select a larger sample of mileages.

Table 2.3 lists a sample of $n = 49$ randomly selected mileages. Table 2.4 groups the 49 mileages into a **frequency distribution** having six intervals. We have chosen the number of intervals by using a general rule that says that the number of intervals should be the smallest integer $K$ such that $2^K > n$. Here $n$ is the number of observations

**TABLE 2.3  A Sample of *n* = 49 Mileages**

| | | | | |
|---|---|---|---|---|
| $y_1 = 30.8$ | $y_{11} = 30.9$ | $y_{21} = 32.0$ | $y_{31} = 32.3$ | $y_{41} = 32.6$ |
| $y_2 = 31.7$ | $y_{12} = 30.4$ | $y_{22} = 31.4$ | $y_{32} = 32.7$ | $y_{42} = 31.4$ |
| $y_3 = 30.1$ | $y_{13} = 32.5$ | $y_{23} = 30.8$ | $y_{33} = 31.2$ | $y_{43} = 31.8$ |
| $y_4 = 31.6$ | $y_{14} = 30.3$ | $y_{24} = 32.8$ | $y_{34} = 30.6$ | $y_{44} = 31.9$ |
| $y_5 = 32.1$ | $y_{15} = 31.3$ | $y_{25} = 30.6$ | $y_{35} = 31.7$ | $y_{45} = 32.8$ |
| $y_6 = 33.3$ | $y_{16} = 32.1$ | $y_{26} = 31.5$ | $y_{36} = 31.4$ | $y_{46} = 31.5$ |
| $y_7 = 31.3$ | $y_{17} = 32.5$ | $y_{27} = 32.4$ | $y_{37} = 32.2$ | $y_{47} = 31.6$ |
| $y_8 = 31.0$ | $y_{18} = 31.8$ | $y_{28} = 31.0$ | $y_{38} = 31.5$ | $y_{48} = 32.2$ |
| $y_9 = 32.0$ | $y_{19} = 30.4$ | $y_{29} = 29.8$ | $y_{39} = 31.7$ | $y_{49} = 32.0$ |
| $y_{10} = 32.4$ | $y_{20} = 30.5$ | $y_{30} = 31.1$ | $y_{40} = 30.6$ | |

$$\bar{y} = \frac{\sum_{i=1}^{49} y_i}{49} = \frac{1546.1}{49} = 31.553061 \approx 31.6$$

$$s^2 = \frac{\sum_{i=1}^{49} (y_i - \bar{y})^2}{48} = \frac{30.666}{48} = .638875 \approx .64$$

$$s = \sqrt{s^2} = \sqrt{.638875} = .799 \approx .8$$

**TABLE 2.4** A Frequency Distribution of the $n$ = 49 Mileages

| Interval | Frequency |
|----------|-----------|
| [29.8, 30.3] | 3 |
| [30.4, 30.9] | 9 |
| [31.0, 31.5] | 12 |
| [31.6, 32.1] | 13 |
| [32.2, 32.7] | 9 |
| [32.8, 33.3] | 3 |

**FIGURE 2.8**
A histogram of the
$n$ = 49 mileages

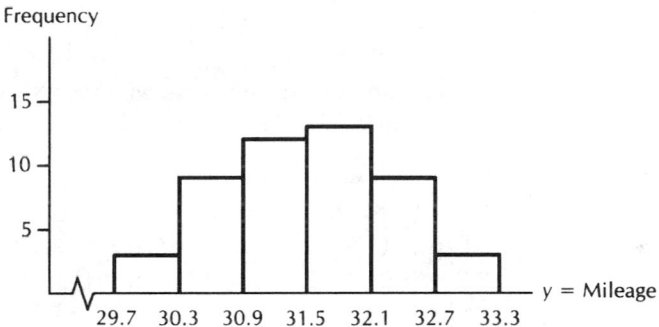

that we wish to group into a frequency distribution. Since $n$ = 49, and since $2^5$ = 32 < 49 and $2^6$ = 64 > 49, it follows that we should use $K$ = 6 intervals. The first interval, [29.8, 30.3], is then formed by adding .5 to 29.8, the smallest mileage in Table 2.3. This yields an interval containing six measurement values—29.8, 29.9, 30.0, 30.1, 30.2, and 30.3. The decision to include six measurement values in the first interval (and in the other intervals) is based on calculating

$$\frac{[\text{Largest mileage} - \text{Smallest mileage}]}{K} = \frac{33.3 - 29.8}{6} = \frac{3.5}{6} \approx .6$$

This means that to include the smallest measurement and the largest measurement in the $K$ = 6 classes, each class should contain six measurement values. The five other intervals are formed in exactly the same way. The frequency distribution of Table 2.4 is depicted graphically in the form of a histogram in Figure 2.8. We see that this histogram looks reasonably bell shaped and symmetrical. Since it is customary to look for pronounced rather than subtle departures from the normality assumption, the histogram in Figure 2.8 does not seriously contradict the assumption that the population is normally distributed.

Finally, note that an alternative to constructing a frequency distribution and histogram is to make a **stem-and-leaf diagram.** The procedure for doing this is best illustrated by an example.

Consider the $n = 49$ mileages in Table 2.3. These mileages range from 29.8 to 33.3. To construct a stem-and-leaf diagram, the first two digits of the mileages—29, 30, 31, 32, and 33—are placed in a column on the left of the diagram. The respective third digits are recorded in the appropriate row. Therefore, the first three mileages—30.8, 31.7, and 30.1—would be represented as

```
29 |
30 | 8  1
31 | 7
32 |
33 |
```

We continue this procedure, and for neatness we order the data within each row (although this is not required). We obtain the following stem-and-leaf diagram:

```
29 | 8
30 | 1 3 4 4 5 6 6 6 8 8 9
31 | 0 0 1 2 3 3 4 4 4 5 5 5 6 6 7 7 7 8 8 9
32 | 0 0 0 1 1 2 2 3 4 4 5 5 6 7 8 8
33 | 3
```

Alternatively, we can obtain more classes by placing 29, 30*, 30, 31*, 31, 32*, 32, and 33 in the column on the left side of the diagram. Here, for instance, in the row headed by 30* we place the mileages from 30.0 to 30.4, and in the row headed by 30 we place the mileages from 30.5 to 30.9. By doing this, we obtain the following stem-and-leaf diagram:

```
29  | 8
30* | 1 3 4 4
30  | 5 6 6 6 8 8 9
31* | 0 0 1 2 3 3 4 4 4
31  | 5 5 5 6 6 7 7 7 8 8 9
32* | 0 0 0 1 1 2 2 3 4 4
32  | 5 5 6 7 8 8
33  | 3
```

As we see, a stem-and-leaf diagram looks like a histogram turned sideways. The advantage of the stem-and-leaf diagram is that it not only reflects frequencies but also contains all of the observations. Note that the above stem-and-leaf display looks reasonably bell shaped and symmetrical. Therefore, it does not provide much evidence to contradict the normality assumption.

# z Values and Finding Normal Probabilities

If $y$ is randomly selected from a normally distributed population with mean $\mu$ and standard deviation $\sigma$, then we define the $z$ value corresponding to $y$ to be

$$z = \frac{y - \mu}{\sigma} = \text{the number of standard deviations that } y \text{ is from the mean } \mu$$

Clearly, there is a $z$ value corresponding to each value in the population. Therefore, there is a population of $z$ values corresponding to the population of $y$ values. Thus we can assume that $z$ is randomly selected from the population of $z$ values. Moreover, it can be proved that if $y$ is normally distributed, with mean $\mu$ and standard deviation $\sigma$, then $z$ (or the population of $z$ values) is normally distributed with mean zero and standard deviation 1. A normal distribution with mean zero and standard deviation 1 is referred to as a **standard normal distribution.**

If we subtract $\mu$ from the inequality

$$a \leq y \leq b$$

and divide by $\sigma$, we obtain the following inequalities:

$$\frac{a - \mu}{\sigma} \leq \frac{y - \mu}{\sigma} \leq \frac{b - \mu}{\sigma}$$

$$\frac{a - \mu}{\sigma} \leq z \leq \frac{b - \mu}{\sigma}$$

$$z_a \leq z \leq z_b$$

Here $z_a = (a - \mu)/\sigma$ is the $z$ value corresponding to $a$, and $z_b - (b - \mu)/\sigma$ is the $z$ value corresponding to $b$. We see that

$$P(a \leq y \leq b) = P(z_a \leq z \leq z_b)$$

Thus to find the probability

$$P(a \leq y \leq b)$$

we can calculate the $z$ values corresponding to $a$ and $b$ and then find

$$P(z_a \leq z \leq z_b)$$

This is the area under the standard normal curve corresponding to the interval $[z_a, z_b]$. We illustrate this procedure in Figure 2.9 (page 46).

**EXAMPLE 2.4**    In the gasoline mileage problem, the population of all mileages is normally distributed with mean $\mu = 31.5$ and standard deviation $\sigma = .8$. We now show that

$$P(29.9 \leq y \leq 33.1) = .9544$$

**FIGURE 2.9**   $P(a \leq y \leq b) = P(z_a \leq z \leq z_b)$

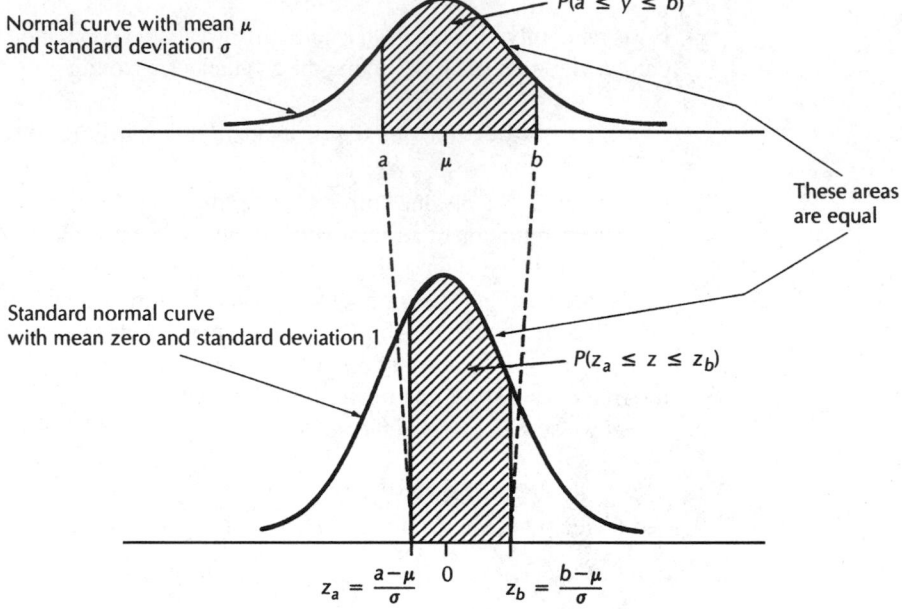

The z value corresponding to the mileage 29.9 mpg is

$$z_{29.9} = \frac{29.9 - \mu}{\sigma} = \frac{29.9 - 31.5}{.8} = \frac{-1.6}{.8} = -2$$

This says that the mileage 29.9 is 2 standard deviations below $\mu = 31.5$. The z value corresponding to the mileage 33.1 mpg is

$$z_{33.1} = \frac{33.1 - \mu}{\sigma} = \frac{33.1 - 31.5}{.8} = \frac{1.6}{.8} = 2$$

This says that the mileage 33.1 is 2 standard deviations above $\mu = 31.5$. It follows that

$$P(29.9 \leq y \leq 33.1) = P(z_{29.9} \leq z \leq z_{33.1})$$
$$= P(-2 \leq z \leq 2)$$

This probability can be found using the normal table (Table A1) in Appendix A. This table gives

$$P(0 \leq z \leq z_c)$$

for values of $z_c$ ranging from .00 to 3.09. Looking at this table, we see that

$$P(0 \leq z \leq 2) = .4772$$

**FIGURE 2.10**

$z_{[\gamma]}$ is the point on the scale of the standard normal curve such that the area under this curve to the right of this point is γ

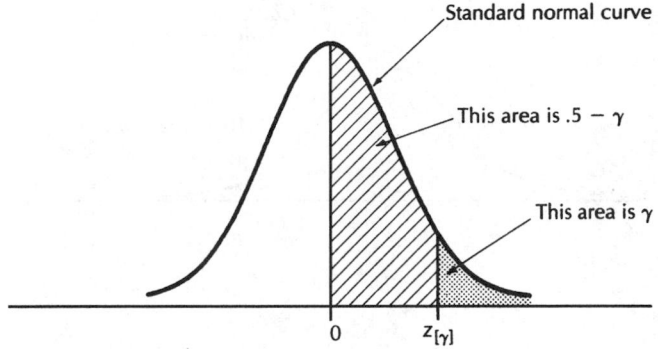

Standard normal curve

This area is .5 − γ

This area is γ

0    $z_{[\gamma]}$

Since the curve of the standard normal distribution is symmetrical about its mean, it follows that

$$P(-2 \leq z \leq 2) = P(-2 \leq z \leq 0) + P(0 \leq z \leq 2)$$
$$= .4772 + .4772 = .9544$$

Thus

$$P(29.9 \leq y \leq 33.1) = P(-2 \leq z \leq 2) = .9544$$

To perform the calculations involved in some statistical inference procedures, we need to find the $z$ value such that the area to its right under the standard normal curve is γ. We denote this $z$ value as $z_{[\gamma]}$. We refer to $z_{[\gamma]}$ as **the point on the scale of the standard normal curve such that the area under this curve to the right of this point is γ.** The point $z_{[\gamma]}$ is illustrated in Figure 2.10. This point can be easily found. For example, suppose we wish to find $z_{[.025]}$, which is the point on the scale of the standard normal curve such that the area under this curve to the right of this point is .025. Then we note that the area under the standard normal curve between zero and $z_{[.025]}$ must equal .5 − .025 = .475. Looking at Table A1, we see that the $z$ value corresponding to an area of .4750 is 1.96. Thus $z_{[.025]}$ equals 1.96. This says that we must be 1.96 standard deviations above the mean of a standard normal distribution to obtain a *right-hand tail area* of .025.

# 2.6   THE *t*-DISTRIBUTION, THE *F*-DISTRIBUTION, AND THE CHI-SQUARE DISTRIBUTION

## The *t*-Distribution

Sometimes a population has what is called a *t*-**distribution.** The probability curve of the *t*-distribution has the following properties:

**FIGURE 2.11**
$t_{[\gamma]}^{(df)}$ is the point on the scale of the $t$-distribution having $df$ degrees of freedom such that the area under this curve to the right of this point is $\gamma$

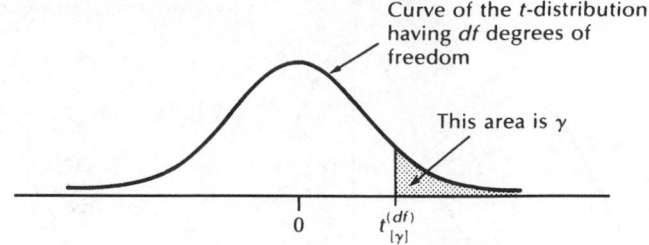

Curve of the $t$-distribution having $df$ degrees of freedom

This area is $\gamma$

0    $t_{[\gamma]}^{(df)}$

1. The curve is symmetrical and bell shaped.

2. The curve is symmetrical about zero, which is the mean of the $t$-distribution.

3. The standard deviation $\sigma$ of the $t$-distribution is always greater than 1.

4. The exact spread, or standard deviation $\sigma$, of the $t$-distribution depends on a parameter that is called **the number of degrees of freedom.**

5. As the number of degrees of freedom approaches infinity, the standard deviation $\sigma$ of the $t$-distribution approaches 1.

6. As the number of degrees of freedom approaches infinity, the curve approaches (that is, becomes shaped more and more like) the probability curve of a standard normal distribution.

To carry out the calculations in later chapters, we must find the point on the scale of the $t$-distribution having a given number of degrees of freedom such that the area under this curve to the right of this point is $\gamma$. Such a point is illustrated in Figure 2.11 and is denoted $t_{[\gamma]}^{(df)}$. Here the superscript $(df)$ refers to the number of degrees of freedom and the subscript $[\gamma]$ refers to the size of the area under the curve to the right of the point $t_{[\gamma]}^{(df)}$. In general, we refer to the point $t_{[\gamma]}^{(df)}$ as **the point on the scale of the $t$-distribution having $df$ degrees of freedom such that the area under this curve to the right of this point is $\gamma$.**

The $t$-point $t_{[\gamma]}^{(df)}$ can be found by using a **$t$-table** (see Table A2 of Appendix A). This table lists values of $t_{[\gamma]}^{(df)}$ for values of $\gamma$ ranging from .10 to .005. The values of $t_{[\gamma]}^{(df)}$ are tabulated according to the number of degrees of freedom, $df$. For example, $t_{[.025]}^{(11)}$ is 2.201. Notice that the $t$-table lists values of $t_{[\gamma]}^{(df)}$ for degrees of freedom from 1 to 29 and $\infty$. Values of $df$ greater than 29 are not listed because when the number of degrees of freedom is large, the value $t_{[\gamma]}^{(df)}$ is very close to the value $z_{[\gamma]}$. Values of $z_{[\gamma]}$ for values of $\gamma$ ranging from .10 to .005 are given in the $t$-table in the row corresponding to $\infty$. Generally, if the number of degrees of freedom is 30 or more, it is sufficient to use the value $z_{[\gamma]}$ for $t_{[\gamma]}^{(df)}$.

## The *F*-Distribution

Sometimes a population has what is called an **$F$-distribution.** The probability curve of the $F$-distribution has the following properties:

**FIGURE 2.12**

$F_{[\gamma]}^{(r_1, r_2)}$ is the point on the scale of the *F*-distribution having $r_1$ and $r_2$ degrees of freedom such that the area under this curve to the right of this point is $\gamma$.

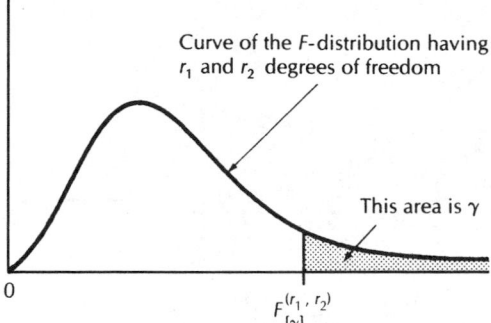

Curve of the *F*-distribution having $r_1$ and $r_2$ degrees of freedom

This area is $\gamma$

0

$F_{[\gamma]}^{(r_1, r_2)}$

1.  The curve $f(v)$ of the *F*-distribution is positive for all values of $v > 0$.

2.  The curve is skewed to the right.

3.  The exact form of the curve depends on two parameters, called the numerator degrees of freedom (denoted $r_1$) and the denominator degrees of freedom (denoted $r_2$).

To perform manipulations in later chapters, we must know how to find the **point on the scale of the *F*-distribution having $r_1$ and $r_2$ degrees of freedom such that the area under this curve to the right of this point is $\gamma$.** Such a point is illustrated in Figure 2.12 and is denoted as $F_{[\gamma]}^{(r_1, r_2)}$. This point can be found using Table A3. This table lists values of $F_{[.05]}^{(r_1, r_2)}$ tabulated according to values of the parameters $r_1$ and $r_2$. To find the point $F_{[.05]}^{(r_1, r_2)}$, we scan across the top of the *F*-table to find the column corresponding to the parameter $r_1$, and we scan down the side to find the row corresponding to the parameter $r_2$. The value in the column corresponding to $r_1$ and in the row corresponding to $r_2$ is $F_{[.05]}^{(r_1, r_2)}$. Thus, for example, $F_{[.05]}^{(8,10)}$ is 3.07. Although Table A3 tabulates values of $F_{[\gamma]}^{(r_1, r_2)}$ for the value $\gamma = .05$, tables for other values of $\gamma$ are also available. For example, see Table A4 in Appendix A, which tabulates $F_{[.01]}^{(r_1, r_2)}$.

In Chapters 3 and 4 we will need to find points on the scale of the *F*-distribution. In those chapters we will simplify the notation from $F_{[\gamma]}^{(r_1, r_2)}$ to $F_{[\gamma]}$, but the values for $r_1$ and $r_2$ will be known from the context of the problem. Since we must use the values of $r_1$ and $r_2$ to find values in the tables for the *F*-distribution, some readers might prefer to continue to use the more sophisticated notation in their own work. For example, one could continue to write $F_{[.05]}^{(8,10)} = 3.07$ instead of writing $F_{[.05]} = 3.07$ when the degrees of freedom are $r_1 = 8$ and $r_2 = 10$.

## The Chi-Square Distribution

Sometimes a population has what is called a **chi-square distribution.** The probability curve of the chi-square distribution is similar in shape to the probability curve of the *F*-distribution:

**FIGURE 2.13**
$\chi^2_{[\gamma]}(df)$ is the point on the scale of the chi-square distribution having *df* degrees of freedom such that the area under this curve to the right of this point is $\gamma$.

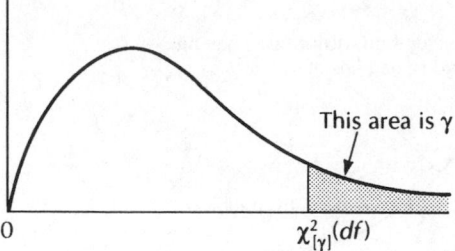

1. The curve $f(v)$ of the chi-square distribution is positive for all values of $v > 0$.
2. The curve is skewed to the right.
3. The exact form of the curve depends on a parameter that is called the number of degrees of freedom and is denoted as *df*.

We refer to the point $\chi^2_{[\gamma]}(df)$ as the **point on the scale of the chi-square distribution having *df* degrees of freedom such that the area under this curve to the right of this point is $\gamma$;** see Figure 2.13. A table of chi-square points is given in Table A7 of Appendix A. This table lists values of $\chi^2_{[\gamma]}(df)$ for values of $\gamma$ ranging from .995 to .005. For example, $\chi^2_{[.05]}(4) = 9.48773$.

# 2.7   CONFIDENCE INTERVALS FOR A POPULATION MEAN

## A Confidence Interval Based on the *t*-Distribution

Suppose that we randomly select a sample of *n* values

$$\{y_1, y_2, \ldots, y_n\}$$

from a population. Then we use the sample mean and the sample standard deviation

$$\bar{y} = \frac{\sum_{i=1}^{n} y_i}{n} \quad \text{and} \quad s = \sqrt{\frac{\sum_{i=1}^{n} (y_i - \bar{y})^2}{n-1}}$$

as the point estimates of the population mean $\mu$ and population standard deviation $\sigma$. In this section we consider using a *confidence interval* to estimate the population mean. The reason for doing this is that the point estimate $\bar{y}$ does not provide any indication of how close it is to the unknown $\mu$. A **confidence interval** for the population mean $\mu$ is an interval constructed around the sample mean $\bar{y}$ so that we are reasonably sure, or confident, that this interval contains $\mu$.

We can construct a confidence interval so that we are 99%, 95%, 90%, and so on, confident that this interval contains $\mu$. In general, we let $100(1 - \alpha)\%$ denote our **level of confidence.** For example, if $\alpha = .05$, we are $100(1 - \alpha)\% = 100(1 - .05)\% = 95\%$ confident. The following box presents the formula for a $100(1 - \alpha)\%$ confidence interval for $\mu$ based on the $t$-distribution. After illustrating the use of this interval, we discuss the logic behind deriving the interval.

---

## A CONFIDENCE INTERVAL FOR $\mu$ BASED ON THE $t$-DISTRIBUTION

Suppose that $\bar{y}$ is the mean and $s$ is the standard deviation of a sample of $n$ values that has been randomly selected from a normally distributed population having mean $\mu$ and standard deviation $\sigma$. Then a **$100(1 - \alpha)\%$ confidence interval for $\mu$** is

$$\left[ \bar{y} \pm t_{[\alpha/2]}^{(n-1)}\left(\frac{s}{\sqrt{n}}\right) \right] = \left[ \bar{y} - t_{[\alpha/2]}^{(n-1)}\left(\frac{s}{\sqrt{n}}\right), \bar{y} + t_{[\alpha/2]}^{(n-1)}\left(\frac{s}{\sqrt{n}}\right) \right]$$

Here, $t_{[\alpha/2]}^{(n-1)}$ is the point on the scale of the $t$-distribution having $n - 1$ degrees of freedom such that the area under this curve to the right of this point is $\alpha/2$.

---

The $100(1 - \alpha)\%$ confidence interval for $\mu$ says that we are $100(1 - \alpha)\%$ confident that $\mu$ is greater than or equal to the lower bound

$$\bar{y} - t_{[\alpha/2]}^{(n-1)}\left(\frac{s}{\sqrt{n}}\right)$$

and less than or equal to the upper bound

$$\bar{y} + t_{[\alpha/2]}^{(n-1)}\left(\frac{s}{\sqrt{n}}\right)$$

Since we do not know the true value of $\mu$, we are not absolutely certain (not 100% confident) that $\mu$ is contained in the $100(1 - \alpha)\%$ confidence interval. Exactly what we mean by $100(1 - \alpha)\%$ confidence is discussed later. For now, suffice it to say that if we choose a high level of confidence, we are very sure that $\mu$ is in the interval.

Before presenting an example we make three comments. First, if the number of degrees of freedom for the $t$-point $t_{[\alpha/2]}^{(n-1)}$ is 30 or more, it is sufficient to use the normal point $z_{[\alpha/2]}$. Second, it has been shown that the confidence interval formula approximately holds for many populations that are not normally distributed. In particular, the formula approximately holds for a population described by a probability curve that is mound-shaped (even if this curve is somewhat skewed to the right or left). This assumption can be checked by using sample data to construct a histogram. Third, although the formula applies to infinite populations, it also approximately applies to many finite (mound-shaped) populations. However, better formulas, which yield shorter confidence intervals, often exist for finite populations.

**EXAMPLE 2.5**

Federal gasoline mileage standards state that $\mu$, the mean gasoline mileage obtained by the fleet of all Hawks, must be at least 30 mpg. If this standard is not met, a heavy fine will be imposed. To demonstrate that this standard is being met, National Motors randomly selects a sample of $n = 5$ Hawks and tests them for gasoline mileage. The sample

$$\{y_1, y_2, y_3, y_4, y_5\} = \{30.7, 31.8, 30.2, 32.0, 31.3\}$$

is obtained. In Example 2.2 we saw that for this sample the sample mean is $\bar{y} = 31.2$ mpg and the sample standard deviation is $s = .7517$ mpg. This sample of mileages has been randomly selected from the (theoretically) infinite population of all Hawk mileages. Therefore, $\bar{y} = 31.2$ is the point estimate of $\mu$.

Suppose that we wish to calculate a 95% confidence interval for $\mu$. Since $100(1 - \alpha)\% = 95\%$ implies that $\alpha = .05$, we use $t_{[\alpha/2]}^{(n-1)} = t_{[.05/2]}^{(5-1)} = t_{[.025]}^{(4)} = 2.776$. (See Table A2 in Appendix A.) It follows that a 95% confidence interval for $\mu$ is

$$\left[ \bar{y} \pm t_{[\alpha/2]}^{(n-1)} \left( \frac{s}{\sqrt{n}} \right) \right] = \left[ 31.2 \pm 2.776 \left( \frac{.7517}{\sqrt{5}} \right) \right] = [31.2 \pm .9333]$$

$$= [30.3, \ 32.1]$$

This interval says that we can be 95% confident that $\mu$ is between 30.3 and 32.1 mpg. Therefore, since the lower bound of this interval is above 30 mpg, we can be at least 95% confident that $\mu$ is greater than 30 mpg. We conclude that we have strong evidence that the Hawk not only meets but exceeds the federal mileage standard.

Next, suppose that we wish to calculate a 99% confidence interval for $\mu$. Since $100(1 - \alpha)\% = 99\%$ implies that $\alpha = .01$, we use $t_{[\alpha/2]}^{(n-1)} = t_{[.01/2]}^{(5-1)} = t_{[.005]}^{(4)} = 4.604$ . It follows that a 99% confidence interval for $\mu$ is

$$\left[ \bar{y} \pm t_{[\alpha/2]}^{(n-1)} \left( \frac{s}{\sqrt{n}} \right) \right] = \left[ 31.2 \pm 4.604 \left( \frac{.7517}{\sqrt{5}} \right) \right] = [31.2 \pm 1.5479]$$

$$= [29.7, \ 32.7]$$

This interval is longer than the 95% confidence interval for $\mu$. Hence increasing the level of confidence from 95% to 99% (1) has the advantage of making us more confident that $\mu$ is contained in our interval for $\mu$, but (2) has the disadvantage of increasing the length of our confidence interval. This results in a less precise guess of the true value of $\mu$. Note that the lower bound of the 99% confidence interval for $\mu$ is not greater than or equal to 30. Therefore, on the basis of this confidence interval we cannot be 99% confident that $\mu$ is at least 30. However, since National Motors is at least 95% confident that $\mu$ is greater than 30, there is substantial evidence that current gasoline mileage standards are being met.

Suppose that federal mileage standards also state that three years from now, $\mu$ must be at least 33 mpg. The 95% confidence interval for $\mu$ makes us at least 95% confident that $\mu$ is less than 33 mpg. Therefore, the company is very confident that the current model of the Hawk will not meet gasoline mileage standards three years from now. The company should probably begin a research and development project to increase Hawk gasoline mileage.

To complete this example, we discuss the meaning of 95% confidence as it pertains to the 95% confidence interval we calculated above. Figure 2.14(a) (page 54) depicts three possible samples from the *population of all possible samples of five mileages* that could have been randomly selected from the infinite population of all Hawk mileages. Note that the population of all mileages is illustrated as normally distributed with mean $\mu$ and standard deviation $\sigma$ equal to 31.5 and .8, respectively. In Figure 2.14(b) we summarize and depict the sample mean $\bar{y}$, sample standard deviation $s$, and 95% confidence interval for $\mu$ — $[\bar{y} \pm 2.776(s/\sqrt{5})]$—given by each of the three possible samples. Note that two of the three 95% confidence intervals for $\mu = 31.5$ in Figure 2.14 contain $\mu$. The interpretation of 95% confidence here is that 95% of the 95% confidence intervals for $\mu$ *in the population of all such intervals* contain $\mu = 31.5$, and 5% of the confidence intervals in this population do not contain $\mu$. Thus when we compute a 95% confidence interval for $\mu$, we can be 95% confident that $\mu$ is contained in our interval. This is so because 95% of the intervals in the population of all possible 95% confidence intervals for $\mu$ contain $\mu$ and because we have obtained one of the confidence intervals in this population.

## The Derivation of the Interval

To derive the $100(1 - \alpha)\%$ confidence interval for $\mu$, we state several important results.

### PROPERTIES OF THE POPULATION OF ALL POSSIBLE SAMPLE MEANS

The **population of all possible sample means** (that is, point estimates of $\mu$)

1.  Has *mean* $\mu_{\bar{y}} = \mu$
2.  Has *variance* $\sigma_{\bar{y}}^2 = \sigma^2/n$ (if the population sampled is infinite)
3.  Has *standard deviation* $\sigma_{\bar{y}} = \sigma/\sqrt{n}$ (if the population sampled is infinite)
4.  Has a *normal distribution* (if the population sampled has a normal distribution)

Result 1,

$$\mu_{\bar{y}} = \mu$$

**FIGURE 2.14** Illustration of the meaning of a 95% confidence interval for $\mu$

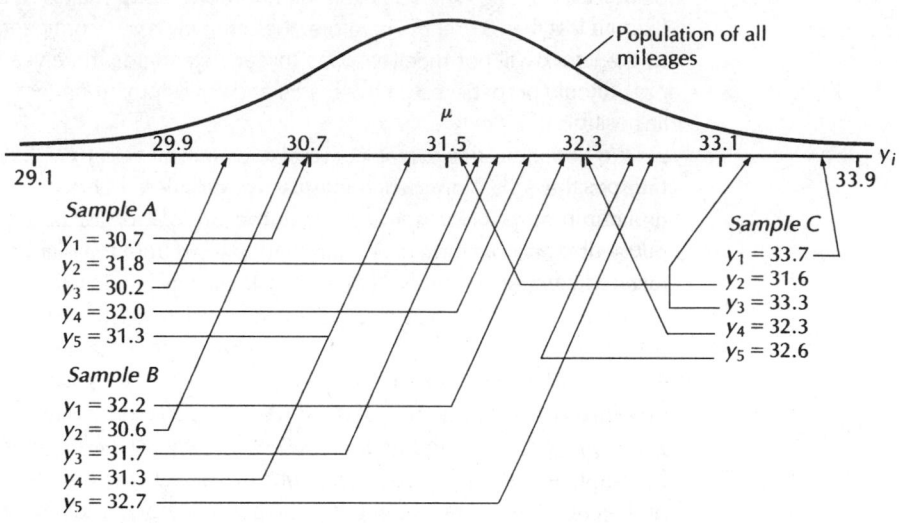

(a) Three possible samples

Sample A
$\bar{y} = 31.2$
$s = .7517$
$$\left[31.2 \pm 2.776 \frac{.7517}{\sqrt{5}}\right]$$
$= [30.3, 32.1]$

Sample B
$\bar{y} = 31.7$
$s = .8093$
$$\left[31.7 \pm 2.776 \frac{.8093}{\sqrt{5}}\right]$$
$= [30.7, 32.7]$

Sample C
$\bar{y} = 32.7$
$s = .8276$
$$\left[32.7 \pm 2.776 \frac{.8276}{\sqrt{5}}\right]$$
$= [31.7, 33.7]$

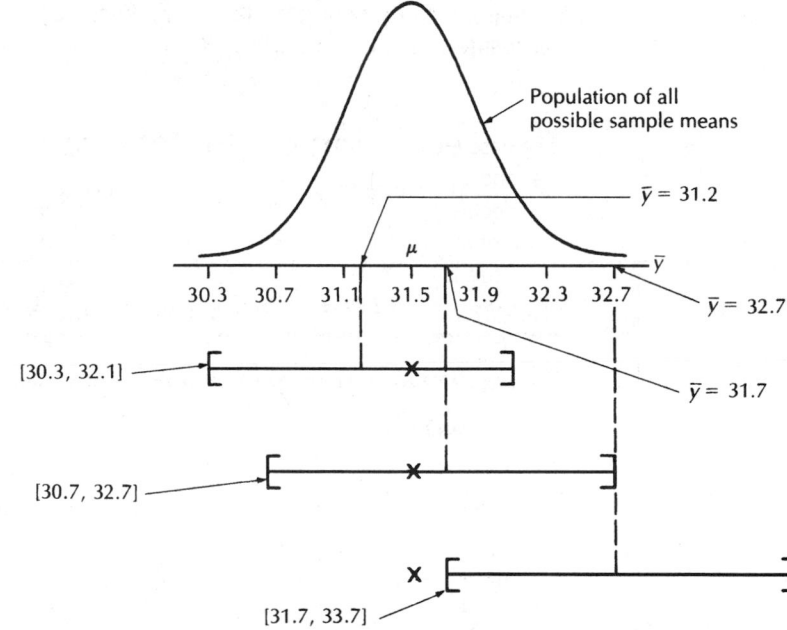

(b) The sample mean $\bar{y}$, sample standard deviation $s$, and 95% confidence interval for $\mu$, $\left[\bar{y} \pm 2.776 \dfrac{s}{\sqrt{5}}\right]$, given by each of the three possible samples says that $\mu_{\bar{y}}$, the mean of all possible sample means, equals $\mu$, the population mean. For this reason, when we use the sample mean $\bar{y}$ as the point estimate of $\mu$, we are using an **unbiased** estimation procedure. This property of unbiasedness tells us that although the sample mean $\bar{y}$ that we calculate probably does not equal $\mu$, the average of all the different sample means that we could have calculated (from all the different possible samples) *is* equal to $\mu$.

We note that $\sigma_{\bar{y}}^2$ and $\sigma_{\bar{y}}$, the variance and standard deviation of the population of all possible sample means, measure the variation, or spread, of the different possible sample means. Here a large variance $\sigma_{\bar{y}}^2$ indicates that the sample means are widely dispersed around $\mu$. A small variance $\sigma_{\bar{y}}^2$ indicates that the sample means are clustered closely around $\mu$. Now consider result 2:

$$\sigma_{\bar{y}}^2 = \frac{\sigma^2}{n}$$

Note that since each possible sample mean is an average of $n$ sample values, the sample mean "averages out" high and low sample values. Therefore, we would expect the sample means to be more closely clustered around $\mu$ than the individual population values. That is, intuitively, $\sigma_{\bar{y}}^2$ should be smaller than the population variance $\sigma^2$. Result 2 says that this is the case—that the division by $n$ makes $\sigma_{\bar{y}}^2$ smaller than $\sigma^2$. Furthermore, this result says that the larger the sample size, the smaller is $\sigma_{\bar{y}}^2$. That is, when $n$ is larger, more sample values are used to compute each possible sample mean. This results in the sample means clustering even more closely around $\mu$.

**EXAMPLE 2.6**

In the gasoline mileage problem, recall that the true values of $\mu$, $\sigma^2$, and $\sigma$ (the mean, variance, and standard deviation of the infinite population of all mileages) are 31.5, .64, and .8, respectively. Therefore, the mean, variance, and standard deviation of the infinite population of all possible sample means (that would be calculated by using all possible samples of size $n = 5$) are, respectively,

$$\mu_{\bar{y}} = \mu = 31.5$$

$$\sigma_{\bar{y}}^2 = \frac{\sigma^2}{n} = \frac{.64}{5} = .128$$

$$\sigma_{\bar{y}} = \frac{\sigma}{\sqrt{n}} = \frac{.8}{\sqrt{5}} = .358$$

Since $\sigma = .8$ and $\sigma_{\bar{y}} = .358$, we see that the sample means are more closely clustered around $\mu$ than are the individual mileages. Moreover, assume that the population of all mileages is normally distributed. Then the population of all possible sample means is also normally distributed (see Figure 2.14). Thus, as discussed in Section 2.5, 68.26%, 95.44%, and 99.73% of all possible sample means lie in, respectively, the intervals

$$[\mu_{\bar{y}} \pm \sigma_{\bar{y}}] = [31.5 \pm .358] = [31.142, 31.858]$$

$$[\mu_{\bar{y}} \pm 2\sigma_{\bar{y}}] = [31.5 \pm 2(.358)] = [31.5 \pm .716] = [30.784, 32.216]$$

$$[\mu_{\bar{y}} \pm 3\sigma_{\bar{y}}] = [31.5 \pm 3(.358)] = [31.5 \pm 1.074] = [30.426, 32.574]$$

These intervals are narrower than the intervals containing 68.26%, 95.44%, and 99.73% of the individual mileages. (See Example 2.3.)

Results 1, 2, and 3 imply that if the population that is sampled is normally distributed, then the population of all possible values of

$$\frac{\bar{y} - \mu_{\bar{y}}}{\sigma_{\bar{y}}} = \frac{\bar{y} - \mu}{\sigma/\sqrt{n}}$$

has a standard normal distribution. We estimate $\sigma_{\bar{y}} = \sigma/\sqrt{n}$ by $s_{\bar{y}} = s/\sqrt{n}$, which is called the **standard error of the estimate** $\bar{y}$. Then it can be proved that if the population that is sampled is normally distributed, the population of all possible values of

$$\frac{\bar{y} - \mu}{s_{\bar{y}}} = \frac{\bar{y} - \mu}{s/\sqrt{n}}$$

has a $t$-distribution with $n - 1$ degrees of freedom. This implies that

$$P\left(-t_{[\alpha/2]}^{(n-1)} \leq \frac{\bar{y} - \mu}{s/\sqrt{n}} \leq t_{[\alpha/2]}^{(n-1)}\right)$$

is the area under the curve of the $t$-distribution having $n - 1$ degrees of freedom between $t_{[\alpha/2]}^{(n-1)}$ and $t_{[\alpha/2]}^{(n-1)}$. As illustrated in Figure 2.15, this area equals $1 - \alpha$. Multiplying the inequality in the probability statement

$$P\left(-t_{[\alpha/2]}^{(n-1)} \leq \frac{\bar{y} - \mu}{s/\sqrt{n}} \leq t_{[\alpha/2]}^{(n-1)}\right) = 1 - \alpha$$

by $s/\sqrt{n}$ (which is positive), we obtain

$$P\left[-t_{[\alpha/2]}^{(n-1)}\left(\frac{s}{\sqrt{n}}\right) \leq \bar{y} - \mu \leq t_{[\alpha/2]}^{(n-1)}\left(\frac{s}{\sqrt{n}}\right)\right] = 1 - \alpha$$

**FIGURE 2.15**   $P\left(-t_{[\alpha/2]}^{(n-1)} \leq \dfrac{\bar{y} - \mu}{s/\sqrt{n}} \leq t_{[\alpha/2]}^{(n-1)}\right) = 1 - \alpha$

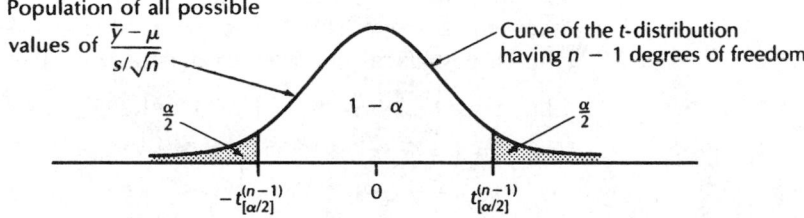

Population of all possible values of $\dfrac{\bar{y} - \mu}{s/\sqrt{n}}$

Curve of the $t$-distribution having $n - 1$ degrees of freedom

$\dfrac{\alpha}{2}$

$1 - \alpha$

$\dfrac{\alpha}{2}$

$-t_{[\alpha/2]}^{(n-1)}$       $0$       $t_{[\alpha/2]}^{(n-1)}$

This implies (subtracting $\bar{y}$ through the above inequality) that

$$P\left[-\bar{y} - t_{[\alpha/2]}^{(n-1)}\left(\frac{s}{\sqrt{n}}\right) \leq -\mu \leq -\bar{y} + t_{[\alpha/2]}^{(n-1)}\left(\frac{s}{\sqrt{n}}\right)\right] = 1 - \alpha$$

which in turn implies (multiplying the above inequality by $-1$) that

$$P\left[\bar{y} + t_{[\alpha/2]}^{(n-1)}\left(\frac{s}{\sqrt{n}}\right) \geq \mu \geq \bar{y} - t_{[\alpha/2]}^{(n-1)}\left(\frac{s}{\sqrt{n}}\right)\right] = 1 - \alpha$$

This probability statement is equivalent to

$$P\left[\bar{y} - t_{[\alpha/2]}^{(n-1)}\left(\frac{s}{\sqrt{n}}\right) \leq \mu \leq \bar{y} + t_{[\alpha/2]}^{(n-1)}\left(\frac{s}{\sqrt{n}}\right)\right] = 1 - \alpha$$

This says that the proportion of confidence intervals containing the population mean $\mu$ in the population of all possible $100(1 - \alpha)\%$ confidence intervals for $\mu$ is equal to $1 - \alpha$. That is, suppose that we compute a $100(1 - \alpha)\%$ confidence interval for $\mu$ by using the formula

$$\left[\bar{y} \pm t_{[\alpha/2]}^{(n-1)}\left(\frac{s}{\sqrt{n}}\right)\right]$$

Then $100(1 - \alpha)\%$ (for example, 95%) of the confidence intervals in the population of all possible $100(1 - \alpha)\%$ confidence intervals for $\mu$ contain $\mu$, and $100(\alpha)\%$ (for example, 5%) of the confidence intervals in this population do not contain $\mu$.

## Confidence Intervals Based on the Normal Distribution

The preceding confidence interval is based on the $t$-distribution. It assumes that the population sampled is normally distributed (or at least is mound-shaped). We now consider a confidence interval that is valid for any population.

---

**A LARGE SAMPLE CONFIDENCE INTERVAL FOR $\mu$ BASED ON THE NORMAL DISTRIBUTION**

The **central limit theorem** states that if the sample size $n$ is large (say, at least 30), then the population of all possible sample means approximately has a normal distribution (with mean $\mu_{\bar{y}} = \mu$ and standard deviation $\sigma_{\bar{y}} = \sigma/\sqrt{n}$), no matter what probability distribution describes the population sampled (see Figure 2.16, page 58). Therefore, *if n is large,* the population of all possible values of

$$\frac{\bar{y} - \mu_{\bar{y}}}{\sigma_{\bar{y}}} = \frac{\bar{y} - \mu}{\sigma/\sqrt{n}}$$

approximately has a **standard normal distribution.** This implies that

$$\left[\bar{y} \pm z_{[\alpha/2]}\left(\frac{\sigma}{\sqrt{n}}\right)\right] \quad \text{and} \quad \left[\bar{y} \pm z_{[\alpha/2]}\left(\frac{s}{\sqrt{n}}\right)\right]$$

are **approximately correct $100(1 - \alpha)\%$ confidence intervals for $\mu$,** *no matter what probability distribution describes the population sampled.* Here the second interval follows from the first by approximating $\sigma$ by $s$.

To derive the first of these intervals, consider the $z$ value $z_{[\alpha/2]}$ and Figure 2.17. The fact that the population of all possible values of

$$\frac{\bar{y} - \mu}{\sigma/\sqrt{n}}$$

approximately has a standard normal distribution implies that

$$P\left(-z_{[\alpha/2]} \leq \frac{\bar{y} - \mu}{\sigma/\sqrt{n}} \leq z_{[\alpha/2]}\right) \approx 1 - \alpha$$

This probability is the area under the curve of the standard normal distribution between $-z_{[\alpha/2]}$ and $z_{[\alpha/2]}$. Using algebraic manipulations analogous to those carried out in the preceding subsection, we find that

$$P\left[\bar{y} - z_{[\alpha/2]}\left(\frac{\sigma}{\sqrt{n}}\right) \leq \mu \leq \bar{y} + z_{[\alpha/2]}\left(\frac{\sigma}{\sqrt{n}}\right)\right] \approx 1 - \alpha$$

**FIGURE 2.16** The central limit theorem

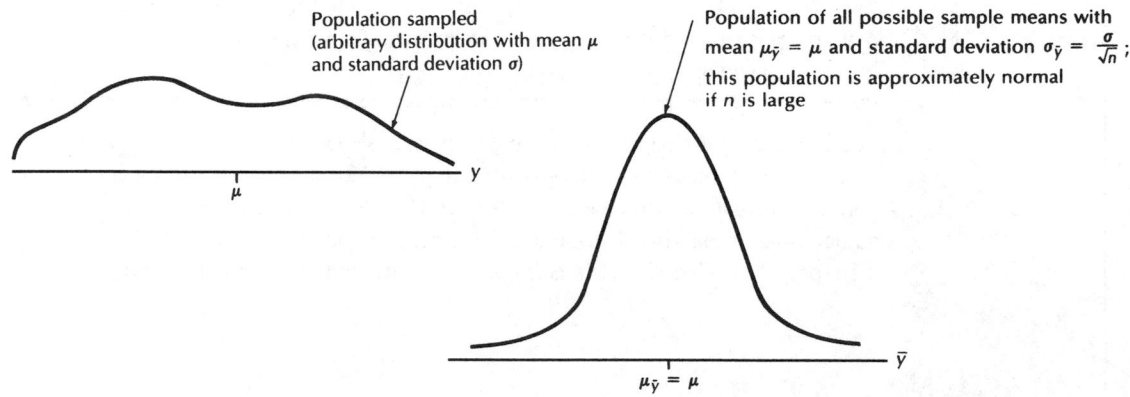

Population sampled (arbitrary distribution with mean $\mu$ and standard deviation $\sigma$)

Population of all possible sample means with mean $\mu_{\bar{y}} = \mu$ and standard deviation $\sigma_{\bar{y}} = \frac{\sigma}{\sqrt{n}}$; this population is approximately normal if $n$ is large

$\mu$

$y$

$\mu_{\bar{y}} = \mu$

$\bar{y}$

**FIGURE 2.17** $P\left(-z_{[\alpha/2]} \leq \dfrac{\bar{y} - \mu}{\sigma/\sqrt{n}} \leq z_{[\alpha/2]}\right) \approx 1 - \alpha$

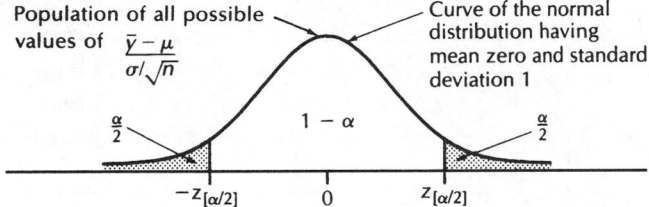

This implies that $[\bar{y} \pm z_{[\alpha/2]}(\sigma/\sqrt{n})]$ is an approximately correct $100(1 - \alpha)\%$ confidence interval for $\mu$.

A more precise statement of the central limit theorem says that the larger the sample size $n$ is, the more nearly normally distributed is the population of all possible sample means. This is illustrated in Figure 2.18 (page 60) for several sampled population shapes. This figure also illustrates that the larger $n$ is, then the smaller is $\sigma_{\bar{y}} = \sigma/\sqrt{n}$. Recall that $\sigma_{\bar{y}}$ measures the spread of the population of all possible sample means. Figure 2.18 shows that as $n$ increases, the spread of this population decreases. There are some indications that for many populations, computing sample means for samples of size $n = 10$, or possibly even $n = 5$, will produce an approximately normally distributed population of all possible sample means. In such cases

$$[\bar{y} \pm z_{[\alpha/2]}(s/\sqrt{n})]$$

is an approximately correct $100(1 - \alpha)\%$ confidence interval for $\mu$.

However, in practice we rarely know the true value of the population standard deviation $\sigma$. Moreover, practice indicates that $n$ should be at least 30 for the sample standard deviation $s$ to be an accurate point estimate of $\sigma$. Therefore, $n$ should probably be at least 30 for $[\bar{y} \pm z_{[\alpha/2]}(s/\sqrt{n})]$ to be an approximately correct $100(1 - \alpha)\%$ confidence interval for $\mu$.

To summarize, when we do not know the true value of the population standard deviation $\sigma$, we should use the $100(1 - \alpha)\%$ confidence interval for $\mu$ based on the normal distribution

$$\left[\bar{y} \pm z_{[\alpha/2]}\left(\frac{s}{\sqrt{n}}\right)\right]$$

if the sample size $n$ is large (say, at least 30). If the sample size $n$ is small and the population sampled is normally distributed (or at least mound shaped), we should use the $100(1 - \alpha)\%$ confidence interval for $\mu$ based on the $t$-distribution

$$\left[\bar{y} \pm t_{[\alpha/2]}^{(n-1)}\left(\frac{s}{\sqrt{n}}\right)\right]$$

**FIGURE 2.18**
Illustration of the
central limit
theorem

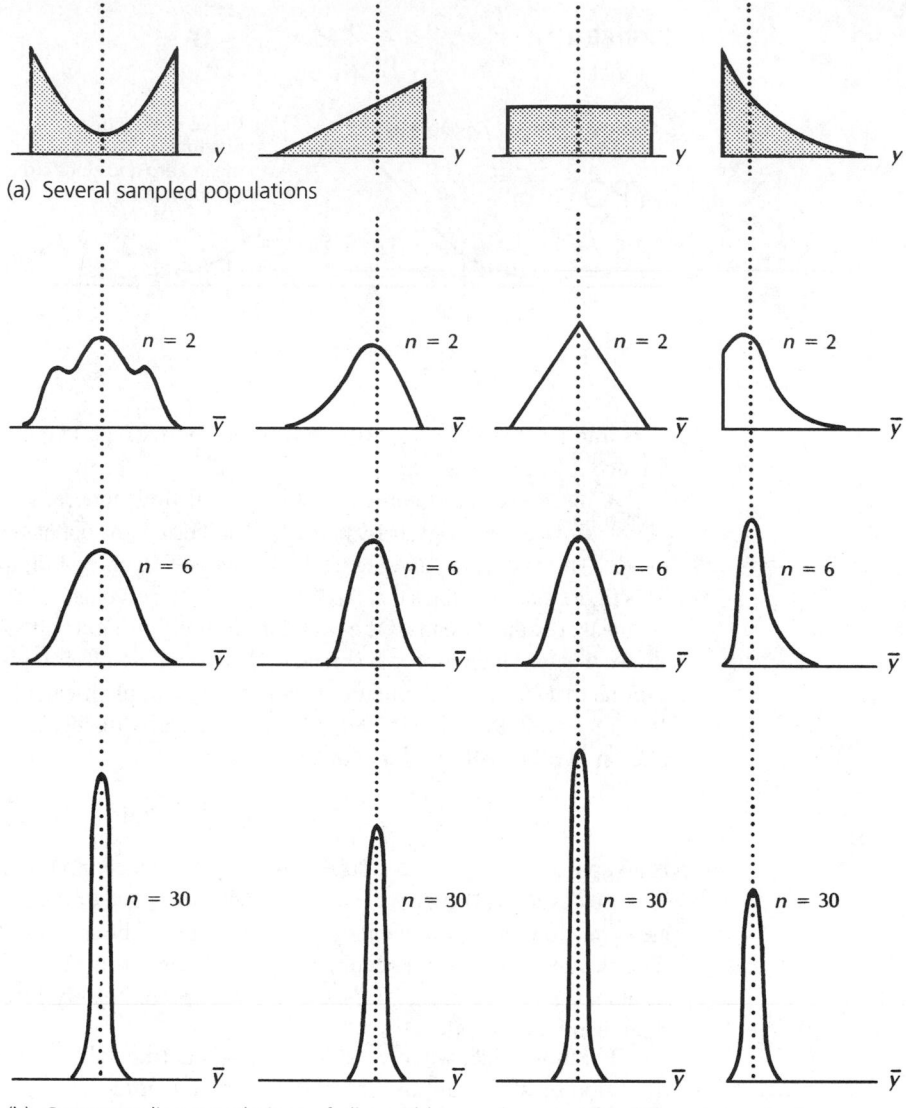

(a)  Several sampled populations

(b)  Corresponding populations of all possible sample means for different sample sizes

**EXAMPLE 2.7**    Suppose that National Motors wishes to claim that the mean of all Hawk mileages is greater than the 31 mpg average claimed by a competitor. The company randomly selects the sample of $n = 49$ mileages in Table 2.3. This sample has mean $\bar{y} = 31.5531$ and standard deviation $s = .799$. It follows that $\bar{y} = 31.5531$ is the point estimate of the population mean, $\mu$. Moreover, since $n = 49$ is large, a 95% confidence interval for $\mu$ is

$$\left[ \bar{y} \pm z_{[.025]}\left( \frac{s}{\sqrt{n}} \right) \right] = \left[ 31.5531 \pm 1.96\left( \frac{.799}{\sqrt{49}} \right) \right] = [31.5531 \pm .2237]$$

$$= [31.3, \ 31.8]$$

Here $z_{[.025]}$ is obtained from Table A1 in Appendix A. Since this 95% interval for $\mu$ has a lower bound of 31.3, we can be very confident that $\mu$ is greater than 31 mpg. This convinces the company that it can legitimately claim in a new advertising campaign that $\mu$ is greater than 31 mpg.

# 2.8 HYPOTHESIS TESTING FOR A POPULATION MEAN

## Testing $H_0$: $\mu = c$ versus $H_a$: $\mu \neq c$

**EXAMPLE 2.8**

The G & B Corporation produces a 16-ounce bottle of Gem Shampoo. The bottles are filled by an automated bottle-filling process. If a particular adjustment to the bottle-filling process results in substantial overfilling or underfilling of bottles, then the line must be shut down and readjusted. Overfilling results in lost profits for G & B, while underfilling is unfair to consumers. For a given adjustment to the bottle-filling process, we consider the infinite population of all bottles that potentially could be produced. For each bottle there is a corresponding bottle fill (measured in ounces). We let $\mu$ denote the mean of the infinite population of all the bottle fills that potentially could be produced by (the particular adjustment to) the bottle-filling process. G & B has decided that it will shut down and readjust the process if it can be very certain that it should reject the null hypothesis $H_0$: $\mu = 16$ in favor of the alternative hypothesis $H_a$: $\mu \neq 16$. Here $H_0$ says that the mean bottle fill is at the appropriate level. $H_a$ says that the mean fill is above or below the desired 16 ounces.

As illustrated in Example 2.8, we sometimes wish to test the **null hypothesis, $H_0$:** $\mu = c$ versus the **alternative hypothesis, $H_a$:** $\mu \neq c$. Here $\mu$ is a population mean, and $c$ is an arbitrary constant. The classical approach to testing these hypotheses utilizes the **test statistic:**

$$t = \frac{\bar{y} - c}{s/\sqrt{n}}$$

Here $\bar{y}$ and $s$ are the mean and standard deviation of a sample of size $n$ that has been randomly selected from the population having mean $\mu$. The test statistic $t$ measures the distance between $\bar{y}$ and $c$ (the value that makes $H_0$ true). A test statistic nearly (or exactly) equal to zero results when $\bar{y}$ is nearly (or exactly) equal to $c$. Such a test statistic provides little or no evidence to support rejecting $H_0$ in favor of $H_a$. This is so because the point estimate $\bar{y}$ indicates that $\mu$ is nearly or exactly equal to $c$. However, a positive test statistic substantially greater than zero results when $\bar{y}$ is substantially greater than $c$. This provides evidence to support rejecting $H_0$ in favor of $H_a$ because the point estimate $\bar{y}$ indicates that $\mu$ is greater than $c$. Similarly, a negative test statistic substantially less than zero results when $\bar{y}$ is substantially smaller than $c$. This also provides evidence to support rejecting $H_0$ in favor of $H_a$ because the point estimate $\bar{y}$ indicates that $\mu$ is smaller than $c$.

**TABLE 2.5** Type I and Type II errors in Gem Bottle-Filling Example

| Decisions Made in Hypothesis Test | State of Nature | |
|---|---|---|
| | **Null hypothesis $H_0$: $\mu = 16$ is true: process mean is at the correct level** | **Null hypothesis $H_0$: $\mu = 16$ is false: process mean is not correct** |
| **Reject null hypothesis $H_0$: $\mu = 16$. Readjust the process** | Type 1 error. Readjust the process when the process mean is at the correct level | Correct action: Readjust the process when the process mean is not correct |
| **Do not reject null hypothesis $H_0$: $\mu = 16$. Do not readjust the process** | Correct action: Do not readjust the process when the process mean is at the correct level | Type II error: Do not readjust the process when the process mean is not correct |

To decide how large in absolute value the test statistic must be before we reject $H_0$, we consider the errors that can be made in hypothesis testing. These errors are summarized in Table 2.5 in the context of the Gem Shampoo bottle-filling example. A **Type I error** is committed if we reject $H_0$: $\mu = 16$ when $H_0$ is true. This means that we would readjust the process when the process mean is at the correct level. A **Type II error** is committed if we do not reject $H_0$: $\mu = 16$ when $H_0$ is false. This means that we would not readjust the process when the process mean is not correct.

We obviously desire that both *the probability of a Type I error, denoted by $\alpha$, and the probability of a Type II error be small*. It is common procedure to base a hypothesis test on taking a sample of a fixed size and on setting $\alpha$ equal to a specified value. Here we sometimes choose $\alpha$ to be as high as .1, but we usually choose $\alpha$ to be between .05 and .01. The most frequent choice for $\alpha$ is .05. We usually do not set $\alpha$ lower than .01 because setting $\alpha$ extremely small often leads to a probability of a Type II error that is unacceptably large. Generally, for a fixed sample size the lower the probability of a Type I error, the higher the probability of a Type II error. We consider how to determine the precise value of $\alpha$ that should be used after discussing the procedure for testing $H_0$.

---

### TESTING $H_0$: $\mu = c$ VERSUS $H_a$: $\mu \neq c$ USING REJECTION POINTS

Define the test statistic

$$t = \frac{\bar{y} - c}{s/\sqrt{n}}$$

If the population sampled is normally distributed with mean $\mu$, we can reject $H_0$: $\mu = c$ in favor of $H_a$: $\mu \neq c$ by setting the probability of a Type I error equal to $\alpha$ if and only if

$$|t| > t_{[\alpha/2]}^{(n-1)} \quad \text{that is, if} \quad t > t_{[\alpha/2]}^{(n-1)} \quad \text{or} \quad t < -t_{[\alpha/2]}^{(n-1)}$$

In the above procedure we call the points $-t_{[\alpha/2]}^{(n-1)}$ and $t_{[\alpha/2]}^{(n-1)}$ **rejection points** because they tell us how different from zero $t$ must be for us to be able to reject $H_0$ by setting the probability of a Type I error equal to $\alpha$.

We now consider why using this rejection point procedure ensures that the probability of a Type I error equals $\alpha$. Recall that if the population sampled is normally distributed with mean $\mu$, then the population of all possible values of

$$\frac{\bar{y} - \mu}{s/\sqrt{n}}$$

has a $t$-distribution with $n - 1$ degrees of freedom. It follows that if the null hypothesis $H_0$: $\mu = c$ is true, then the population of all possible values of the test statistic

$$t = \frac{\bar{y} - c}{s/\sqrt{n}}$$

has a $t$-distribution with $n - 1$ degrees of freedom. Therefore, using the above rejection points says that if $H_0$: $\mu = c$ is true, then, as illustrated in Figure 2.19:

1. The probability that

$$-t_{[\alpha/2]}^{(n-1)} \leq t \leq t_{[\alpha/2]}^{(n-1)}$$

is $1 - \alpha$. That is, $100(1 - \alpha)\%$ (for example, $100(1 - .05)\% = 95\%$) of all possible values of $t$ are between $-t_{[\alpha/2]}^{(n-1)}$ and $t_{[\alpha/2]}^{(n-1)}$ and thus lead us to fail to reject $H_0$: $\mu = c$ (when $H_0$: $\mu = c$ is true), a correct decision.

**FIGURE 2.19**
The rejection points for testing $H_0$: $\mu = c$ versus $H_a$: $\mu \neq c$. The probability that we reject $H_0$: $\mu = c$ when $H_0$ is true is $\alpha/2 + \alpha/2 = \alpha$.

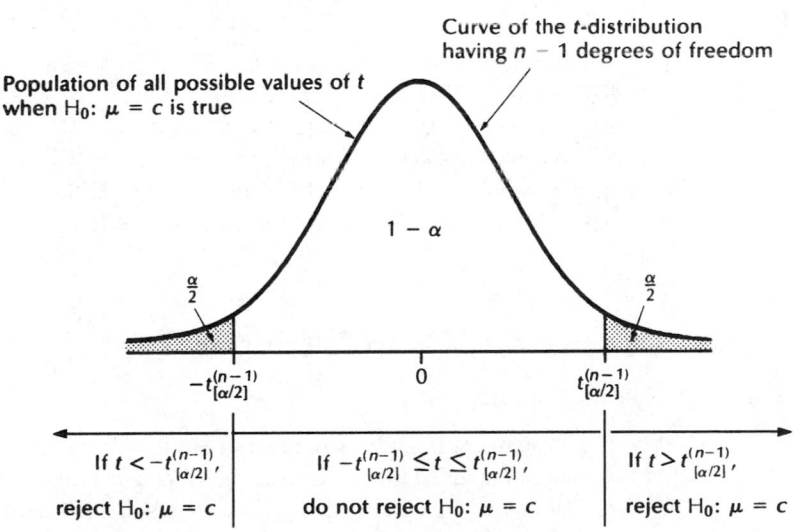

2.  The probability that

$$t < -t_{[\alpha/2]}^{(n-1)} \quad \text{or} \quad t > t_{[\alpha/2]}^{(n-1)}$$

is $\alpha$. That is, $100(\alpha)\%$ (for example, $100(.05)\% = 5\%$) of all possible values of $t$ are either less than $-t_{[\alpha/2]}^{(n-1)}$ or greater than $t_{[\alpha/2]}^{(n-1)}$ and lead us to reject $H_0$: $\mu = c$ (when $H_0$: $\mu = c$ is true), a Type I error.

Therefore, using these rejection points implies that the probability of a Type I error equals $\alpha$.

**EXAMPLE 2.9**   To test $H_0$: $\mu = 16$ versus $H_a$: $\mu \neq 16$, G & B Corporation will randomly select a sample of $n = 6$ bottle fills from the current adjustment of the Gem bottle-filling process. We assume that the population of all possible bottle fills is normally distributed or at least mound shaped. The rejection point condition tells us that we can reject $H_0$: $\mu = 16$ by setting $\alpha$, the probability of a Type I error, equal to .05 if and only if the absolute value of

$$t = \frac{\bar{y} - 16}{s/\sqrt{n}} = \frac{\bar{y} - 16}{s/\sqrt{6}}$$

is greater than $t_{[\alpha/2]}^{(n-1)} = t_{[.05/2]}^{(6-1)} = t_{[.025]}^{(5)} = 2.571$. That is, we can reject $H_0$ if $t$ is greater than $t_{[.025]}^{(5)} = 2.571$ or less than $-t_{[.025]}^{(5)} = -2.571$.

Now suppose that G & B Corporation observes the following sample of $n = 6$ bottle fills:

$$\{y_1, y_2, y_3, y_4, y_5, y_6\} = \{15.68, 16.00, 15.61, 15.93, 15.86, 15.72\}$$

It can be verified that this sample has mean $\bar{y} = 15.8$ and standard deviation $s = .1532$. It follows that

$$t = \frac{\bar{y} - 16}{s/\sqrt{n}} = \frac{15.8 - 16}{.1532/\sqrt{6}} = -3.2$$

Since $|t| = 3.2 > 2.571 = t_{[.025]}^{(5)}$, we can reject $H_0$: $\mu = 16$ by setting $\alpha$ equal to .05.

As another example, we can reject $H_0$: $\mu = 16$ in favor of $H_a$: $\mu \neq 16$ by setting $\alpha$ equal to .01 if and only if the absolute value of $t$ is greater than $t_{[\alpha/2]}^{(n-1)} = t_{[.01/2]}^{(6-1)} = t_{[.005]}^{(5)} = 4.032$. That is, we can reject $H_0$ if $t > 4.032$ or $t < -4.032$. Specifically, since $t = -3.2$ is between $-4.032$ and $4.032$, we cannot reject $H_0$: $\mu = 16$ by setting $\alpha$ equal to .01.

## Considerations in Setting $\alpha$

Note the following:

1.  If we can reject $H_0$: $\mu = c$ in favor of $H_a$: $\mu \neq c$ by setting $\alpha$ equal to .05, then we have concluded that $H_0$ is false by using a test that allows only a .05 probability of concluding that $H_0$ is false when it is true. This is usually regarded as *strong evidence* that $H_0$ is false and $H_a$ is true.

2.   If we can reject $H_0$: $\mu = c$ in favor of $H_a$: $\mu \neq c$ by setting $\alpha$ *equal to .01*, this is usually regarded as *very strong evidence* that $H_0$ is false and $H_a$ is true.

3.   The smaller the value of $\alpha$ at which $H_0$: $\mu = c$ can be rejected in favor of $H_a$: $\mu \neq c$, the stronger the evidence that $H_0$ is false and $H_a$ is true.

Usually we do not require that $H_0$ be rejected in favor of $H_a$ at a value of $\alpha$ less than .01 before deciding that $H_0$ is false and $H_a$ is true. This is so because, as previously stated, setting $\alpha$ extremely small leads to an unacceptably large probability of a Type II error (not rejecting $H_0$ when $H_0$ is false). For example, consider the Gem Shampoo bottle-filling problem. We saw in Example 2.9 that we can reject $H_0$: $\mu = 16$ in favor of $H_a$: $\mu \neq 16$ by setting $\alpha$ equal to .05 but not by setting $\alpha$ equal to .01. Therefore, we have strong evidence that $H_0$: $\mu = 16$ is false and $H_a$: $\mu \neq 16$ is true.

If we have decided to take a particular action if and only if we can reject $H_0$: $\mu = c$ in favor of $H_a$: $\mu \neq c$ by setting the probability of a Type I error equal to $\alpha$, then we must decide how to set $\alpha$. We stated previously that it is reasonable to set $\alpha$ between .05 and .01. In setting a specific value of $\alpha$ (say, between .05 and .01) we should take into account the relative costs of making Type I and Type II errors. For example, suppose that the G & B Corporation has decided that it will shut down and readjust the bottle-filling process if it can reject $H_0$: $\mu = 16$ in favor of $H_a$: $\mu \neq 16$ by setting $\alpha$ equal to .05. From Table 2.5 it is clear that setting $\alpha$ equal to .05 implies that this procedure will cause the process to be readjusted 5% of the time when the process mean is at the correct level. Here G & B has decided to set $\alpha$ at .05 rather than .01 because the company feels that making a Type II error (not readjusting when the process mean is not correct) is very serious. Setting $\alpha$ at .05 makes the probability of a Type II error smaller than would setting $\alpha$ at .01.

## Testing $H_0$: $\mu = c$ versus $H_a$: $\mu > c$

**EXAMPLE 2.10**   In the gasoline mileage problem, recall that mileage standards state that the mean mileage $\mu$ must be at least 30 mpg. Here we might be tempted to say that National Motors can "prove" that $\mu \geq 30$ if it can accept the null hypothesis $H_0$: $\mu \geq 30$ instead of the alternative hypothesis $H_a$: $\mu < 30$. However, *hypothesis testing seeks to find how confident we can be that the null hypothesis should be rejected in favor of the alternative hypothesis. It does not seek to find how confident we can be that the null hypothesis should be accepted.* Therefore, we cannot use hypothesis testing to "prove" that a null hypothesis is true. Thus we cannot make the statement that National Motors wishes to prove (that is, $\mu \geq 30$) the null hypothesis. It might, therefore, be tempting to make $\mu \geq 30$ the alternative hypothesis. But we cannot do this either because in hypothesis testing the alternative hypothesis always involves a strict inequality ($>$ or $<$ or $\neq$), and the null hypothesis involves an equality ($=$) or a nonstrict inequality ($\geq$ or $\leq$). The only way out of this predicament is to use the following procedure:

1.   State what you wish to justify in the form of a *strict inequality* ($<$, $>$, or $\neq$), and make it the **alternative hypothesis $H_a$.**

2.   State what is reasonably possible if the alternative hypothesis is false, and make this statement the **null hypothesis $H_0$.**

National Motors can use this procedure by rewriting what it wishes to prove ($\mu \geq 30$) as the inequality $\mu > 30$. This statement becomes the alternative hypothesis. We then make $\mu \leq 30$ (which is reasonably possible if $\mu > 30$ is false) the null hypothesis. We then attempt to justify that the mileage standard is being met by attempting to reject $H_0$: $\mu \leq 30$ in favor of $H_a$: $\mu > 30$ by setting $\alpha$, the probability of a Type I error, equal to .05. Here $H_a$ says that the mileage standard is in fact being exceeded.

As illustrated in Example 2.10, we sometimes need to test $H_0$: $\mu \leq c$ versus $H_a$: $\mu > c$. We note that it can be shown that testing these hypotheses is equivalent to testing $H_0$: $\mu = c$ versus $H_a$: $\mu > c$, and we consider the following result.

---

### TESTING $H_0$: $\mu = c$ VERSUS $H_a$: $\mu > c$ BY USING A REJECTION POINT

Define the test statistic

$$t = \frac{\bar{y} - c}{s/\sqrt{n}}$$

If the population sampled has a normal distribution with mean $\mu$, we can reject $H_0$: $\mu = c$ in favor of $H_a$: $\mu > c$ by setting the probability of a Type I error equal to $\alpha$ if and only if

$$t > t_{[\alpha]}^{(n-1)}$$

---

**EXAMPLE 2.11**    Consider Example 2.10 and note that testing $H_0$: $\mu \leq 30$ versus $H_a$: $\mu > 30$ is equivalent to testing $H_0$: $\mu = 30$ versus $H_a$: $\mu > 30$. Suppose that we use a sample of $n = 5$ mileages. Then we can reject $H_0$ with $\alpha = .05$ if and only if

$$t = \frac{\bar{y} - 30}{s/\sqrt{n}}$$

is greater than

$$t_{[\alpha]}^{(n-1)} = t_{[.05]}^{(5-1)} = t_{[.05]}^{(4)} = 2.132$$

This condition is intuitively reasonable because a value of $t$ substantially greater than zero results when $\bar{y}$ is substantially greater than 30. This provides substantial evidence for rejecting $H_0$: $\mu = 30$ in favor of $H_a$: $\mu > 30$. Setting $\alpha$ equal to .05 means that if $H_0$: $\mu = 30$ is true, then

1.  $100(1 - \alpha)\% = 95\%$ of all possible values of $t$ are less than or equal to the rejection point $t_{[.05]}^{(4)} = 2.132$ and thus lead us to fail to reject $H_0$: $\mu = 30$ (when $H_0$ is true), a correct decision.

2.  $100(\alpha)\% = 5\%$ of all possible values of $t$ are greater than the rejection point $t_{[.05]}^{(4)} = 2.132$ and lead us to reject $H_0$: $\mu = 30$ (when $H_0$ is true), a Type I error.

Now, from Example 2.5, $\bar{y} = 31.2$ is the mean and $s = .7517$ is the standard deviation of the sample of $n = 5$ mileages that National Motors has randomly selected from the population of all mileages. It follows that

$$t = \frac{\bar{y} - 30}{s/\sqrt{n}} = \frac{31.2 - 30}{.7517/\sqrt{5}} = 3.569$$

Since $t = 3.569 > 2.132 = t_{[.05]}^{(4)}$, we can reject $H_0$: $\mu = 30$ in favor of $H_a$: $\mu > 30$ by setting $\alpha$ equal to .05.

## Testing $H_0$: $\mu = c$ versus $H_a$: $\mu < c$

**EXAMPLE 2.12**  National Motors equips the Hawk with a newly designed disk brake system. A major competitor claims that its automobile achieves a mean stopping distance of 60 feet. Here we define the stopping distance to be the distance (in feet) required to bring an automobile to a complete stop from a speed of 35 mph under normal driving conditions. National Motors would like to conduct a new television advertising campaign claiming that the mean stopping distance achieved by the Hawk is less than the 60-foot distance claimed by its competitor.

We define $\mu$ to be the mean of the (theoretically) infinite population of all Hawk stopping distances. The television networks will allow National Motors to make its claim only if the company can justify statistically that $\mu$ is less than 60 feet. To do this, the company establishes an alternative hypothesis of $H_a$: $\mu < 60$; this is the claim we wish to make. Therefore, the null hypothesis becomes $H_0$: $\mu \geq 60$. If we can reject $H_0$ in favor of $H_a$ by setting the probability of a Type I error equal to .05, National Motors will be allowed to make the claim in the television ad campaign.

As illustrated in Example 2.12, we sometimes need to test $H_0$: $\mu \geq c$ versus $H_a$: $\mu < c$. We note that testing these hypotheses can be shown to be equivalent to testing $H_0$: $\mu = c$ versus $H_a$: $\mu < c$, and we consider the following result.

---

**TESTING $H_0$: $\mu = c$ VERSUS $H_a$: $\mu < c$ BY USING A REJECTION POINT**

Define the test statistic

$$t = \frac{\bar{y} - c}{s/\sqrt{n}}$$

If the population sampled has a normal distribution with mean $\mu$, we can reject $H_0$: $\mu = c$ in favor of $H_a$: $\mu < c$ by setting the probability of a Type I error equal to $\alpha$ if and only if

$$t < -t_{[\alpha]}^{(n-1)}$$

---

**EXAMPLE 2.13** Consider Example 2.12 and note that testing $H_0: \mu \geq 60$ versus $H_a: \mu < 60$ is equivalent to testing $H_0: \mu = 60$ versus $H_a: \mu < 60$. Suppose that we employ a sample of $n = 64$ stopping distances. Then we can reject $H_0$ in favor of $H_a$ by setting $\alpha$ equal to .05 if and only if

$$t = \frac{\bar{y} - 60}{s/\sqrt{n}}$$

is less than

$$-t_{[\alpha]}^{(n-1)} = -t_{[.05]}^{(64-1)} = -t_{[.05]}^{(63)} \approx -z_{[.05]} = -1.645$$

Here the point $-t_{[.05]}^{(63)}$ employs more than 30 degrees of freedom. Therefore, we approximate this $t$-point by using the normal point $-z_{[.05]} = -1.645$. The use of this rejection point is intuitively reasonable because a value of $t$ substantially less than zero results when $\bar{y}$ is substantially less than 60. This provides substantial evidence to support rejecting $H_0: \mu = 60$ in favor of $H_a: \mu < 60$. Setting $\alpha$ equal to .05 means that if $H_0: \mu = 60$ is true, then

1. $100(1 - \alpha)\% = 95\%$ of all possible values of $t$ are greater than or equal to the rejection point $-t_{[.05]}^{(63)} \approx -1.645$ and thus lead us to not reject $H_0: \mu = 60$ (when $H_0: \mu = 60$ is true), a correct decision.

2. $100(\alpha)\% = 5\%$ of all possible values of $t$ are less than the rejection point $-t_{[.05]}^{(63)} \approx -1.645$ and lead us to reject $H_0: \mu = 60$ (when $H_0: \mu = 60$ is true), a Type I error.

National Motors randomly selects a sample of $n = 64$ Hawks and obtains a stopping distance for each automobile. It calculates the mean and standard deviation of the sample to be $\bar{y} = 58.12$ feet and $s = 6.13$ feet. It follows that

$$t = \frac{\bar{y} - 60}{s/\sqrt{n}} = \frac{58.12 - 60}{6.13/\sqrt{64}} = -2.45$$

Since $t = -2.45 < -1.645 \approx -t_{[.05]}^{(63)}$, we can reject $H_0: \mu = 60$ in favor of $H_a: \mu < 60$ by setting $\alpha$ equal to .05. On the basis of this result, National Motors will be allowed to make the television claim that $\mu$ is less than 60.

## A Summary of Testing $H_0: \mu = c$

We now summarize our results concerning testing $H_0: \mu = c$.

### TESTING $H_0: \mu = c$ USING THE $t$-DISTRIBUTION

*Suppose that the population sampled is normally distributed* with mean $\mu$ and define the test statistic

$$t = \frac{\bar{y} - c}{s/\sqrt{n}}$$

Then we can reject $H_0$: $\mu = c$ in favor of a particular alternative hypothesis by setting the probability of a Type I error equal to $\alpha$ by using the following rejection point conditions.

| Alternative Hypothesis | Rejection Point Condition: Reject $H_0$ in Favor of $H_a$ If and Only If |
|---|---|
| $H_a$: $\mu \neq c$ | $\lvert t \rvert > t_{[\alpha/2]}^{(n-1)}$ |
| $H_a$: $\mu > c$ | $t > t_{[\alpha]}^{(n-1)}$ |
| $H_a$: $\mu < c$ | $t < -t_{[\alpha]}^{(n-1)}$ |

As demonstrated in the preceding examples, for 30 or more degrees of freedom we approximate the $t$-points $t_{[\alpha/2]}^{(n-1)}$ and $t_{[\alpha]}^{(n-1)}$ by the normal points $z_{[\alpha/2]}$ and $z_{[\alpha]}$. Furthermore, when $n$ is at least 30, the central limit theorem tells us that the population of all possible values of

$$\frac{\bar{y} - \mu}{s/\sqrt{n}}$$

approximately has a standard normal distribution, no matter what probability distribution describes the population being sampled. Therefore, we obtain the following large sample tests of $H_0$: $\mu = c$.

## TESTING $H_0$: $\mu = c$ USING THE NORMAL DISTRIBUTION

Define the test statistic

$$z = \frac{\bar{y} - c}{s/\sqrt{n}}$$

and *suppose that the sample size $n$ is large* (say, at least 30). Then we can reject $H_0$: $\mu = c$ in favor of a particular alternative hypothesis by setting the probability of a Type I error equal to $\alpha$ by using the following rejection point conditions.

| Alternative Hypothesis | Rejection Point Condition: Reject $H_0$ in Favor of $H_a$ If and Only If |
|---|---|
| $H_a$: $\mu \neq c$ | $\lvert z \rvert > z_{[\alpha/2]}$ |
| $H_a$: $\mu > c$ | $z > z_{[\alpha]}$ |
| $H_a$: $\mu < c$ | $z < -z_{[\alpha]}$ |

## Using *p*-Values

We next introduce a **probability value** (or *p*-**value**) condition for testing $H_0$: $\mu = c$ versus $H_a$: $\mu \neq c$.

---

### TESTING $H_0$: $\mu = c$ VERSUS $H_a$: $\mu \neq c$ BY USING *p*-VALUES

Define the *p-value* to be twice the area under the curve of the *t*-distribution having $n - 1$ degrees of freedom to the right of the absolute value of

$$t = \frac{\bar{y} - c}{s/\sqrt{n}}$$

Then if the population sampled is normally distributed with mean $\mu$, we can reject $H_0$: $\mu = c$ in favor of $H_a$: $\mu \neq c$ by setting the probability of a Type I error equal to $\alpha$ if and only if

$$p\text{-value} < \alpha$$

---

Although we have initially defined the *p*-value in terms of an area under a curve, we will soon show that the *p*-value is a *probability* that has an important interpretation. First, however, we note that the above *p*-value condition for rejecting $H_0$: $\mu = c$ in favor of $H_a$: $\mu \neq c$ is equivalent to the previously discussed rejection point condition. To see this, suppose that the *p*-value is less than a specified value of $\alpha$. Then

$$\begin{bmatrix} \text{The area under the curve of} \\ \text{the } t\text{-distribution having } n-1 \\ \text{degrees of freedom to the right} \\ \text{of } |t| \end{bmatrix} < \alpha/2$$

This implies (as seen in Figure 2.20) that $|t| > t_{[\alpha/2]}^{(n-1)}$. Therefore, we can reject $H_0$: $\mu = c$ in favor of $H_a$: $\mu \neq c$ by setting the probability of a Type I error equal to $\alpha$.

In comparing the rejection-point and *p*-value conditions, first note that the rejection-point condition is simpler from a computational standpoint. This is so because it requires only that we calculate the test statistic $t$ and look up the value $t_{[\alpha/2]}^{(n-1)}$ in a *t*-table. The *p*-value condition is more complicated; it requires that we calculate an area under the *t*-curve. However, this problem is not serious, since most regression computer packages (and some handheld calculators) compute areas under *t*-curves and *p*-values. Furthermore, the *p*-value condition has an advantage. Suppose that several hypothesis testers all wished to use different values of $\alpha$. Then, using the rejection-point condition, each hypothesis tester would have to look up a different rejection point $t_{[\alpha/2]}^{(n-1)}$ to decide whether to reject $H_0$. However, when the *p*-value condition is used,

**FIGURE 2.20**
The equivalence of the rejection-point and p-value conditions for rejecting $H_0: \mu = c$ in favor of $H_a: \mu \neq c$

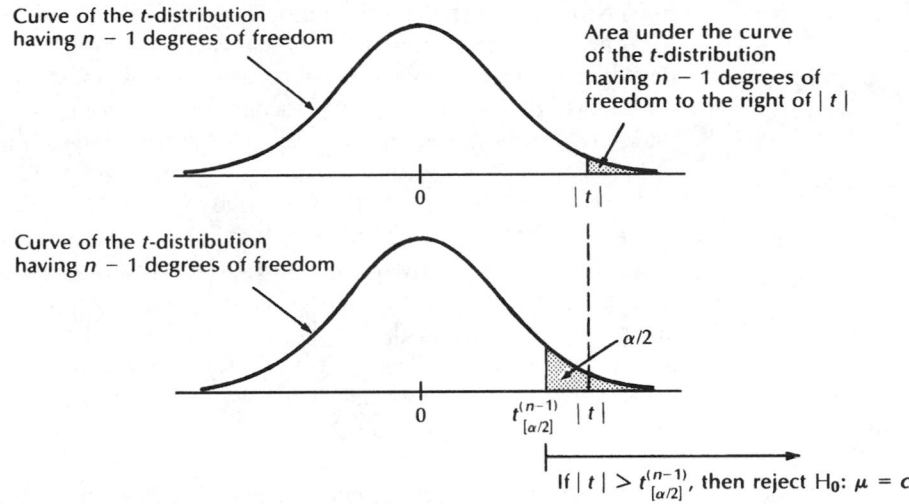

Curve of the *t*-distribution having $n - 1$ degrees of freedom

Area under the curve of the *t*-distribution having $n - 1$ degrees of freedom to the right of $|t|$

$|t|$

Curve of the *t*-distribution having $n - 1$ degrees of freedom

$\alpha/2$

$t^{(n-1)}_{[\alpha/2]}$  $|t|$

If $|t| > t^{(n-1)}_{[\alpha/2]}$, then reject $H_0: \mu = c$

only the *p*-value needs to be calculated. Then each hypothesis tester knows that if the *p*-value is less than his or her particular chosen value of $\alpha$, $H_0$ should be rejected. Another advantage of the *p*-value is that it may be interpreted as a measure of probabilistic doubt about the validity of $H_0$. This is illustrated in Example 2.14.

**EXAMPLE 2.14**   We saw in Example 2.9 that the *t*-statistic for testing $H_0: \mu = 16$ versus $H_a: \mu \neq 16$ in the Gem Shampoo bottle-filling problem was

$$t = \frac{\bar{y} - 16}{s/\sqrt{n}} = \frac{15.8 - 16}{.1532/\sqrt{6}} = -3.2$$

It follows that the *p*-value for testing these hypotheses is twice the area under the curve of the *t*-distribution having $n - 1 = 6 - 1 = 5$ degrees of freedom to the right of $|t| = |-3.2| = 3.2$. This *p*-value can be calculated by computer to be .026. We see that the *p*-value is less than .05 but, for example, not less than .02. It follows that we can reject $H_0: \mu = 16$ in favor of $H_a: \mu \neq 16$ by setting $\alpha$ equal to .05 but not by setting $\alpha$ equal to .02. We would regard this as strong evidence that $H_0: \mu = 16$ is false and $H_a: \mu \neq 16$ is true.

In addition to its use as a decision rule, the *p*-value can be interpreted as a probability. If $H_0: \mu = 16$ is true, then the population of all possible values of the test statistic

$$t = \frac{\bar{y} - 16}{s/\sqrt{n}}$$

has a *t*-distribution with $n - 1 = 5$ degrees of freedom. Furthermore, twice the area under the curve of the *t*-distribution having $n - 1$ degrees of freedom to the right of $|t|$ is (by the symmetry of the *t*-distribution) equal to the area to the right of $|t|$ plus the area to the left of $-|t|$. It follows that the *p*-value equals the sum of these latter two areas. Therefore, the *p*-value equals the proportion of all possible values of *t* that, if $H_0: \mu = 16$ is true, are at least as far away from zero as the value of *t* that we have actually observed ($t = -3.2$). Notice here that the larger (in absolute value) *t* is, the more this test statistic contradicts $H_0$. It follows that the *p*-value equals the proportion of all possible values of *t* that are at least as contradictory to $H_0$ as the value of *t* that we have actually observed. The *p*-value of .026 leads us to reach one of two possible conclusions. The first conclusion is that $H_0: \mu = 16$ is true and only .026 (that is, 26 in 1000) of all possible values of *t* contradict $H_0$ at least as much as the value of *t* that we have observed. That is, if we believe that $H_0$ is true, we must also believe that we have observed a value of *t* so rare that it can be described as a 26 in 1000 chance. The second conclusion is that $H_0: \mu = 16$ is false and $H_a: \mu \neq 16$ is true. A reasonable person would probably believe the second conclusion. That is, the fact that the *p*-value .026 is small casts strong doubt on the validity of the null hypothesis $H_0: \mu = 16$ and thus lends strong support to the validity of the alternative hypothesis $H_a: \mu \neq 16$.

We now consider testing one-sided hypotheses by using *p*-values.

### TESTING $H_0: \mu = c$ VERSUS $H_a: \mu > c$ BY USING *p*-VALUES

Define the *p*-value as the area under the curve of the *t*-distribution having $n - 1$ degrees of freedom to the right of

$$t = \frac{\bar{y} - c}{s/\sqrt{n}}$$

Then, if the population sampled is normally distributed with mean $\mu$, we can reject $H_0: \mu = c$ in favor of $H_a: \mu > c$ by setting the probability of a Type I error equal to $\alpha$ if and only if

$$p\text{-value} < \alpha$$

The *p*-value condition for rejecting $H_0: \mu = c$ in favor of $H_a: \mu > c$ is equivalent to the previously discussed rejection-point condition. To see this, suppose that for a specified value of $\alpha$,

$$p\text{-value} = \left[ \begin{array}{l} \text{The area under the curve of} \\ \text{the } t\text{-distribution having } n - 1 \\ \text{degrees of freedom to the} \\ \text{right of } t \end{array} \right] < \alpha$$

This implies (as seen in Figure 2.21) that $t > t_{[\alpha]}^{(n-1)}$. Therefore, we can reject $H_0: \mu = c$ in favor of $H_a: \mu > c$ by setting the probability of a Type I error equal to $\alpha$.

**FIGURE 2.21**
The equivalence of the rejection-point and *p*-value conditions for rejecting $H_0$: $\mu = c$ in favor of $H_a$: $\mu > c$

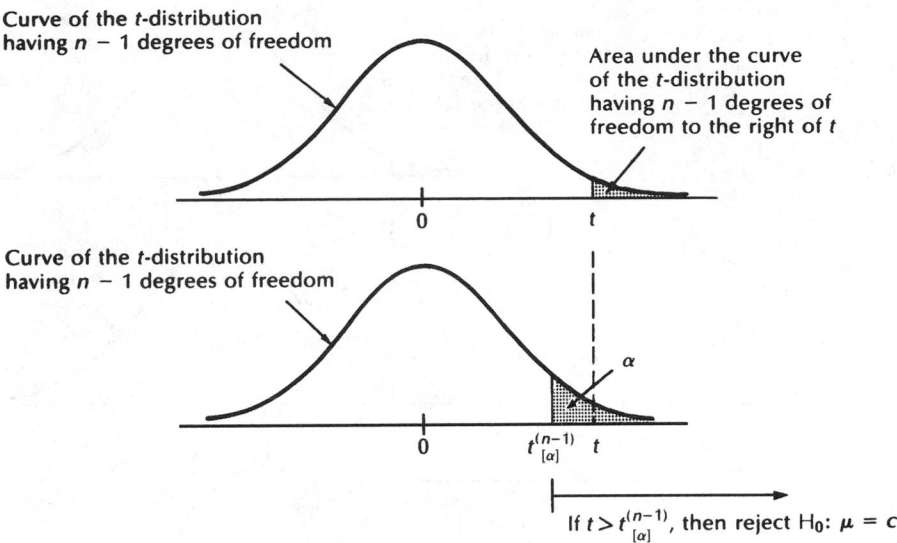

Curve of the *t*-distribution having $n - 1$ degrees of freedom

Area under the curve of the *t*-distribution having $n - 1$ degrees of freedom to the right of *t*

Curve of the *t*-distribution having $n - 1$ degrees of freedom

If $t > t_{[\alpha]}^{(n-1)}$, then reject $H_0$: $\mu = c$

**EXAMPLE 2.15**

We saw in Example 2.11 that the *t*-statistic for testing $H_0$: $\mu = 30$ versus $H_a$: $\mu > 30$ is

$$t = \frac{\bar{y} - 30}{s/\sqrt{n}} = \frac{31.2 - 30}{.7517/\sqrt{5}} = 3.569$$

The corresponding *p*-value is the area under the curve of the *t*-distribution having $n - 1 = 4$ degrees of freedom to the right of $t = 3.569$. This *p*-value can be calculated by computer to be .013. We see that the *p*-value is less than .05 but not less than .01. It follows that we can reject $H_0$: $\mu = 30$ in favor of $H_a$: $\mu > 30$ by setting $\alpha$ equal to .05 but not by setting $\alpha$ equal to .01. As a probability, the *p*-value says that if we are to believe that $H_0$: $\mu = 30$ is true, then we must believe that we have observed a value of *t* that is so rare that only .013 (that is, 13 in 1000) of all possible values of *t* are at least as contradictory to $H_0$: $\mu = 30$.

---

**TESTING $H_0$: $\mu = c$ VERSUS $H_a$: $\mu < c$ BY USING *p*-VALUES**

Define the *p*-value as the area under the curve of the *t*-distribution having $n - 1$ degrees of freedom to the left of

$$t = \frac{\bar{y} - c}{s/\sqrt{n}}$$

Then, if the population sampled is normally distributed with mean $\mu$, we can reject $H_0$: $\mu = c$ in favor of $H_a$: $\mu < c$ by setting the probability of a Type I error equal to $\alpha$ if and only if

$$p\text{-value} < \alpha$$

**FIGURE 2.22**
The equivalence of the rejection-point and p-value conditions for rejecting $H_0$: $\mu = c$ in favor of $H_a$: $\mu < c$

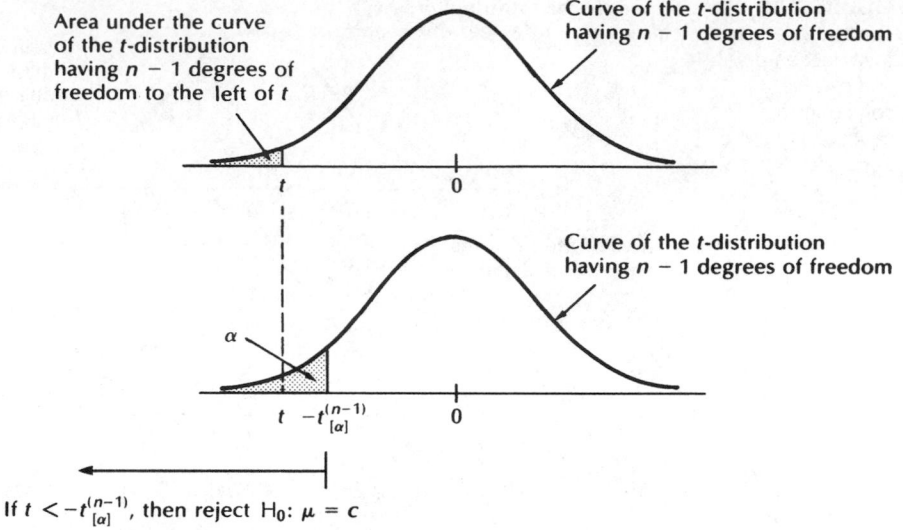

Area under the curve of the t-distribution having $n - 1$ degrees of freedom to the left of $t$

Curve of the t-distribution having $n - 1$ degrees of freedom

Curve of the t-distribution having $n - 1$ degrees of freedom

If $t < -t_{[\alpha]}^{(n-1)}$, then reject $H_0$: $\mu = c$

The p-value condition for rejecting $H_0$: $\mu = c$ in favor of $H_a$: $\mu < c$ is equivalent to the previously discussed rejection-point condition. To see this, suppose that for a specified value of $\alpha$

$$p\text{-value} = \left[ \begin{array}{c} \text{The area under the curve of} \\ \text{the } t\text{-distribution having } n - 1 \\ \text{degrees of freedom to the} \\ \text{left of } t \end{array} \right] < \alpha$$

This implies (as seen in Figure 2.22) that $t < -t_{[\alpha]}^{(n-1)}$. Therefore, we can reject $H_0$: $\mu = c$ in favor of $H_a$: $\mu < c$ by setting the probability of a Type I error equal to $\alpha$.

**EXAMPLE 2.16**    We saw in Example 2.13 that the t-statistic for testing $H_0$: $\mu = 60$ versus $H_a$: $\mu < 60$ is

$$t = \frac{\bar{y} - 60}{s/\sqrt{n}} = \frac{58.12 - 60}{6.13/\sqrt{64}} = -2.45$$

The corresponding p-value is the area under the curve of the t-distribution having $n - 1 = 63$ degrees of freedom to the left of $-2.45$. This is approximately the area under the standard normal curve to the left of $-2.45$. This area equals $(.5 - .4929) = .0071$. (See Table A1.) Since this p-value is less than .01, we can reject $H_0$: $\mu = 60$ in favor of $H_a$: $\mu < 60$ by setting $\alpha$ equal to .01. We would regard this as very strong evidence that $H_0$ is false and $H_a$ is true. As a probability, the p-value says that if we are to believe that $H_0$: $\mu = 60$ is true, then we must believe that we have observed a value of $t$ that is so rare that only .0071 (that is, 7 in 1000) of all possible values of $t$ are at least as contradictory to $H_0$: $\mu = 60$.

In general, recall that if the sample size $n$ is large (say, at least 30), we use the test statistic

$$z = \frac{\bar{y} - c}{s/\sqrt{n}}$$

In this case we redefine the $p$-values in the above results to be the corresponding areas under the standard normal curve. It follows by the central limit theorem that if $n$ is large, the previous $p$-value results approximately hold for populations that are not normally distributed.

We can summarize our discussion of the $p$-value for testing $H_0$: $\mu = c$ as follows:

1.  If the *p-value is less than .05*, we can reject $H_0$: $\mu = c$ by setting $\alpha$ equal to .05. This means that we have *strong evidence* that $H_0$: $\mu = c$ is false.

2.  If the *p-value is less than .01*, we can reject $H_0$: $\mu = c$ by setting $\alpha$ equal to .01. This means that we have *very strong evidence* that $H_0$: $\mu = c$ is false.

3.  The smaller the $p$-value is, the stronger the evidence that $H_0$: $\mu = c$ is false.

One way to report the result of a statistical test is to state whether we "reject" or "do not reject" $H_0$ on the basis of setting the probability of a Type I error equal to $\alpha$. As an alternative to this, reporting the $p$-value is becoming increasingly popular. This is so because the result of the statistical test may be used by several people to make different decisions at different times. Thus by reporting the $p$-value, the individual performing the test permits any other decision makers to reach their own conclusions.

## Exercises

**2.1** Consider the following sample of six gasoline mileages:

$$32.3 \quad 30.5 \quad 31.7 \quad 31.6 \quad 31.4 \quad 32.6$$

a.  Calculate the sample mean $\bar{y}$.
b.  Calculate the sample variance $s^2$.
c.  Calculate the sample standard deviation $s$.

**2.2** Consider the following sample of seven dollar amounts owed by customers with delinquent charge accounts:

$$\$99 \quad \$123 \quad \$75 \quad \$138 \quad \$105 \quad \$65 \quad \$116$$

a.  Calculate the sample mean $\bar{y}$.
b.  Calculate the sample variance $s^2$.
c.  Calculate the sample standard deviation $s$.

**2.3** Consider the following sample of "percent berry content" values for eight randomly selected jars of strawberry preserves:

$$65.4 \quad 64.9 \quad 65.2 \quad 65.7 \quad 65.0 \quad 65.7 \quad 65.3 \quad 64.7$$

a.  Calculate the sample mean $\bar{y}$.
b.  Calculate the sample variance $s^2$.
c.  Calculate the sample standard deviation $s$.

**2.4** An engine manufacturer tests nine engines for pollution (measured in milligrams of particulate matter per cubic yard) with the following results:

$$72 \quad 74 \quad 75 \quad 75 \quad 79 \quad 81 \quad 70 \quad 77 \quad 85$$

a.  Calculate the sample mean $\bar{y}$.
b.  Calculate the sample variance $s^2$.
c.  Calculate the sample standard deviation $s$.

**2.5** Consider the first thirty observations in Table 2.3.
a.  Calculate the sample mean $\bar{y}$.
b.  Calculate the sample variance $s^2$.
c.  Calculate the sample standard deviation $s$.
d.  Construct a histogram for the data.
e.  Construct a stem-and-leaf display of the data.

**2.6** The following is a sample of "bag weights" (in pounds) for an industrial bagging operation:

| | | | | | |
|---|---|---|---|---|---|
| 50.6 | 49.8 | 50.8 | 50.5 | 50.2 | 50.4 |
| 50.6 | 51.4 | 50.4 | 50.3 | 49.9 | 50.1 |
| 50.8 | 50.8 | 50.6 | 50.8 | 52.2 | 50.7 |
| 50.8 | 50.6 | 50.7 | 50.6 | 50.3 | 49.8 |
| 50.8 | 50.6 | 49.1 | 51.2 | 50.2 | 52.0 |
| 49.8 | 50.8 | 49.0 | 51.1 | 46.8 | 50.5 |

a. Calculate the sample mean $\bar{y}$.
b. Calculate the sample variance $s^2$.
c. Calculate the sample standard deviation $s$.
d. Construct a histogram for the data.
e. Construct a stem-and-leaf display of the data.

**2.7** Suppose that the population of all gasoline mileages for the GSX-50 is normally distributed with mean $\mu = 31.5$ mpg and standard deviation $\sigma = 0.8$ mpg. Let $y$ denote a mileage randomly selected from this population. Find the following probabilities:
a. $P(30.7 \leq y \leq 32.3)$
b. $P(29.1 \leq y \leq 33.9)$
c. $P(29.5 \leq y \leq 32.3)$
d. $P(31.0 \leq y \leq 31.3)$
e. $P(y \leq 29.5)$
f. $P(y \geq 29.5)$
g. $P(y \geq 33.4)$
h. $P(y \leq 33.4)$

**2.8** Using Table A1 in Appendix A, find
a. $z_{[.05]}$
b. $z_{[.02]}$
c. $z_{[.01]}$
d. $z_{[.005]}$

**2.9** Using Table A2 in Appendix A, find
a. $t_{[.05]}^{(7)}$
b. $t_{[.01]}^{(7)}$
c. $t_{[.005]}^{(7)}$

**2.10** Using Table A3 in Appendix A, find
a. $F_{[.05]}^{(2,5)}$
b. $F_{[.05]}^{(5,2)}$

**2.11** Using Table A7 in Appendix A, find
a. $\chi_{[.05]}^2(3)$
b. $\chi_{[.01]}^2(2)$

**2.12** The daily water consumption for an Ohio community is normally distributed with a mean consumption of 300,000 gallons and a standard deviation of 20,000 gallons.
a. Find the probability that daily water consumption will be less than 250,000 gallons.
b. Find the probability that daily water consumption will be between 260,000 gallons and 330,000 gallons.
c. The community water system will experience a noticeable drop in water pressure when daily water consumption exceeds 346,000 gallons. What is the probability of experiencing such a drop in water pressure?

**2.13** Assume that the population of all Hawk mileages is normally distributed. Use the following sample of $n = 5$ mileages:

$$\{32.3, 30.5, 31.7, 31.4, 32.6\}$$

to find 90%, 95%, 98%, and 99% confidence intervals for $\mu$, the population mean Hawk mileage.

**2.14** Consider Figure 2.14 on page 54.
a. Using the three samples in Figure 2.14, calculate three 99% confidence intervals for $\mu$.
b. What percentage of these three confidence intervals contain $\mu$ (=31.5)?
c. Explain the meaning of 99% confidence in this situation.

**2.15** Zenex Radio Corporation has developed a new way to assemble an electronic component used in the manufacture of radios. The company wishes to determine whether $\mu$, the mean assembly time of this component using the new method, is less than 20 minutes, which is known to be the mean assembly time of the component using the current method. Suppose that Zenex Radio randomly selects a sample of $n = 6$ employees. The company thoroughly trains each employee to use the new assembly method and has each employee assemble one component using the new method. The company records the assembly times and calculates the mean and standard deviation of the sample of $n = 6$ assembly times to be $\bar{y} = 14.29$ minutes and $s = 2.19$ minutes.
a. Assuming that the population of all assembly times has a normal distribution, calculate a 99% confidence interval for $\mu$.

b. Using the confidence interval that you calculated in part (a), can Zenex Radio be at least 99% confident that $\mu$ is less than 20 minutes? Justify your answer.

**2.16** National Motors has equipped the ZX-900 with a new disk brake system. We define the stopping distance for a ZX-900 to be the distance (in feet) required to bring the automobile to a complete stop from a speed of 35 mph under normal driving conditions using this new brake system. In addition, we define $\mu$ to be the mean stopping distance of all ZX-900s. One of the ZX-900's major competitors is advertised as achieving a mean stopping distance of 60 feet. National Motors would like to claim in a new advertising campaign that the ZX-900 achieves a shorter mean stopping distance.

Suppose that National Motors randomly selects a sample of $n = 81$ ZX-900s. The company records the stopping distance of each of these automobiles and calculates the mean and standard deviation of the sample of $n = 81$ stopping distances to be $\bar{y} = 57.8$ feet and $s = 6.02$ feet.
a. Calculate 90%, 95%, 98%, and 99% confidence intervals for $\mu$.
b. Using the 95% confidence interval, can National Motors be at least 95% confident that $\mu$ is less than 60 feet? Explain.
c. Using the 98% confidence interval, can National Motors be at least 98% confident that $\mu$ is less than 60 feet? Explain.

**2.17** Consider the Gem Shampoo problem. Suppose that a sample of $n = 6$ bottle fills is randomly selected from a particular adjustment to the Gem bottle-filling process. A sample mean of $\bar{y} = 15.7665$ and a sample standard deviation of $s = .1524$ are obtained.
a. Test $H_0: \mu = 16$ versus $H_a: \mu \neq 16$ by setting $\alpha = .05$. On the basis of this test, should the process be readjusted?
b. Test $H_0: \mu = 16$ versus $H_a: \mu \neq 16$ by setting $\alpha = .01$. On the basis of this test, should the process be readjusted?

**2.18** Use the sample information in Exercise 2.15 to test $H_0: \mu = 20$ versus $H_a: \mu < 20$. Set $\alpha = .05$.

**2.19** Use the sample information in Exercise 2.16 to test $H_0: \mu = 60$ versus $H_a: \mu < 60$. Set $\alpha = .05$. Also calculate the $p$-value.

**2.20** The *bad debt ratio* for a financial institution is defined to be the dollar value of loans defaulted divided by the total dollar value of all loans made. A random sample of seven Ohio banks is selected. The bad debt ratios (written as percentages) for these banks are 7, 4, 6, 7, 5, 4, and 9%.
a. The mean bad debt ratio for all federally insured banks is 3.5%. Federal banking officials claim that the mean bad debt ratio for Ohio banks is higher than the mean for all federally insured banks. Set up the null and alternative hypotheses that should be used to justify this claim statistically.
b. Assuming that bad debt ratios for Ohio banks are normally distributed, use the sample results given above to test the hypotheses you set up in part (a) with $\alpha = .01$. Interpret the outcome of the test.

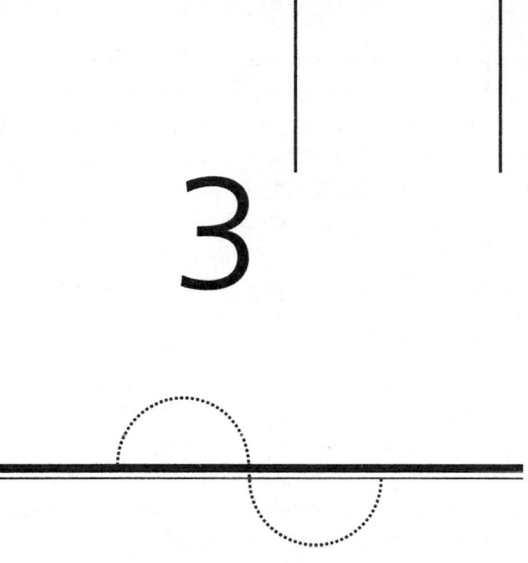

# 3

# *Simple Linear Regression*

In this chapter we begin our study of regression analysis by discussing the **simple linear regression model.** In Section 3.1 we describe this model. We will see that the model employs two parameters: the **slope** and the **y-intercept.** Sections 3.2 and 3.3 show how to compute "least squares point estimates" of these parameters and how to use these estimates to compute point predictions of the dependent variable. In Section 3.4 we explain the assumptions behind the simple linear regression model. Sections 3.5 and 3.6 discuss testing the significance of the independent variable, calculating confidence intervals for means, and calculating prediction intervals for individual values of the dependent variable. In Sections 3.7 and 3.8 we explain several measures of the utility of the simple linear regression model. These include the simple coefficient of determination and an $F$-test for the simple linear model. We conclude this chapter with optional Section 3.9, which shows some computational formulas.

## 3.1 THE SIMPLE LINEAR REGRESSION MODEL

The **simple linear regression model** assumes that the relationship between the **dependent variable, which is denoted $y$,** and the **independent variable, denoted $x$,** can be approximated by a straight line. We can tentatively decide whether there is an approximate straight-line relationship between $y$ and $x$ by making a **scatter diagram,** or **scatter plot,** of $y$ versus $x$. First, data concerning the two variables are observed in pairs. To construct the scatter plot, each value of $y$ is plotted against its corresponding value of $x$. If the $y$ values tend to increase or decrease in a straight-line fashion as the $x$ values increase, and if there is a scattering of the $(x, y)$ points around the straight line, then it is reasonable to describe the relationship between $y$ and $x$ by using the simple linear regression model. We illustrate this in the following case study, which shows how regression analysis can help a natural gas company improve its gas ordering process.

**EXAMPLE 3.1**   When the natural gas industry was deregulated in 1993, natural gas companies became responsible for acquiring the natural gas needed to heat the homes and businesses in the cities they serve. To do this, natural gas companies purchase natural gas from marketers (usually through long-term contracts) and periodically (daily, weekly, monthly, or the like) place orders for natural gas to be transmitted by pipeline transmission systems to their cities. There are hundreds of pipeline transmission systems in the United States, and many of these systems supply a large number of cities.

To place an order (called a *nomination*) for an amount of natural gas to be transmitted to its city over a period of time (day, week, month), a natural gas company makes its best prediction of the city's natural gas needs for that period. The natural gas company then instructs its marketer(s) to deliver this amount of gas to its pipeline transmission system. If most of the natural gas companies being supplied by the transmission system can predict their cities' natural gas needs with reasonable accuracy, then the overnominations of some companies will tend to cancel the undernominations of other companies. As a result, the transmission system will probably have enough natural gas to efficiently meet the needs of the cities it supplies.

In order to encourage natural gas companies to make accurate transmission nominations and to help control costs, pipeline transmission systems charge, in addition to their usual fees, transmission fines. A natural gas company is charged a transmission fine if it substantially undernominates natural gas, which can lead to an excessive number of unplanned transmissions, or if it substantially overnominates natural gas, which can lead to excessive storage of unused gas. Typically, pipeline transmission systems allow a certain percentage nomination error before they impose a fine. For example, some systems do not impose a fine unless the actual amount of natural gas used by a city differs from the nomination by more than 10%. Beyond the allowed percentage nomination error, fines are charged on a sliding scale—the larger the nomination error, the larger the transmission fine. Furthermore, some transmission systems evaluate nomination errors and assess fines more often than others. For instance, some transmission systems do this daily, while others do it weekly or monthly (this frequency depends on the number of storage fields to which the transmission system has access, the system's accounting practices, and other factors). In any case, each natural gas company needs a way to accurately predict its city's natural gas needs so it can make accurate transmission nominations.

Suppose we are analysts in a management consulting firm. The natural gas company serving a small city has hired the consulting firm to develop an accurate way to predict the amount of fuel (in millions of cubic feet—MMcf—of natural gas) that will be required to heat the city. Because the pipeline transmission system supplying the city evaluates nomination errors and assesses fines weekly, the natural gas company wants predictions of future weekly fuel consumptions. Moreover, since the pipeline transmission system allows a 10% nomination error before assessing a fine, the natural gas company would like the actual and predicted weekly fuel consumptions to differ by no more than 10%. Our experience suggests that weekly fuel consumption substantially depends on the average hourly temperature (in degrees Fahrenheit) measured in the city during the week. Therefore, we will try to predict the **dependent (response) variable** weekly fuel consumption ($y$) on the basis of the **independent (predictor) variable** average hourly temperature ($x$) during the week. To this end, we observe values of $y$ and $x$ for eight weeks. The data are given in Table 3.1. In Figure 3.1 (page 82) we give a scatter plot of $y$ versus $x$. This plot shows

1. A tendency for the fuel consumption to decrease in a straight-line fashion as the temperatures increase

2. A scattering of points around the straight line

A **regression model** describing the relationship between $y$ and $x$ must represent these two characteristics. We now develop such a model.

We begin by considering a specific average hourly temperature $x$. For example, consider the average hourly temperature 28°F, which was observed in week 1, or consider the average hourly temperature 45.9°F, which was observed in week 5 (there is nothing special about these two average hourly temperatures, but we will use them throughout this example to help explain the idea of a regression model). For the specific average hourly temperature $x$ that we consider, there are, in theory, many weeks that could have this temperature. However, although these weeks each have the same average hourly temperature, other factors that affect fuel consumption could vary from week to week. For example, these weeks might have different average hourly wind velocities, different

**TABLE 3.1 The Fuel Consumption Data**

| Week, $i$ | Average Hourly Temperature, $x_i$ (°F) | Weekly Fuel Consumption, $y_i$ (tons) |
|---|---|---|
| 1 | $x_1 = 28.0$ | $y_1 = 12.4$ |
| 2 | $x_2 = 28.0$ | $y_2 = 11.7$ |
| 3 | $x_3 = 32.5$ | $y_3 = 12.4$ |
| 4 | $x_4 = 39.0$ | $y_4 = 10.8$ |
| 5 | $x_5 = 45.9$ | $y_5 = 9.4$ |
| 6 | $x_6 = 57.8$ | $y_6 = 9.5$ |
| 7 | $x_7 = 58.1$ | $y_7 = 8.0$ |
| 8 | $x_8 = 62.5$ | $y_8 = 7.5$ |

**FIGURE 3.1**
A scatter plot relating $y$ (weekly fuel consumption) to $x$ (average hourly temperature)

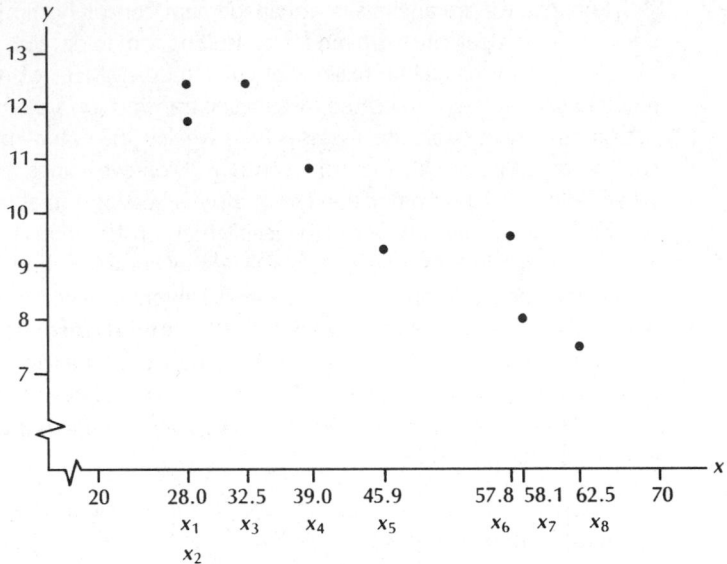

thermostat settings, and so forth. Therefore, the weeks could have different fuel consumptions. It follows that there is a population of weekly fuel consumptions that could be observed when the average hourly temperature is $x$. Furthermore, this population has a mean, which we denote as $\mu_{y|x}$ (pronounced **mu of $y$ given $x$**).

We can represent the straight-line tendency we observe in Figure 3.1 by assuming that $\mu_{y|x}$ is related to $x$ by the equation

$$\mu_{y|x} = \beta_0 + \beta_1 x$$

This is the equation of a straight line with **$y$-intercept** $\beta_0$ (pronounced **beta zero**) and **slope** $\beta_1$ (pronounced **beta one**). To better understand the straight line and the meanings of $\beta_0$ and $\beta_1$, we must first realize that the values of $\beta_0$ and $\beta_1$ determine the precise value of the mean weekly fuel consumption $\mu_{y|x}$ that corresponds to a given value of the average hourly temperature $x$. We cannot know the true values of $\beta_0$ and $\beta_1$, and in the next section we learn how to estimate these values. However, for illustrative purposes, let us suppose that the true value of $\beta_0$ is 15.77 and the true value of $\beta_1$ is $-.1281$. It would then follow, for example, that the mean of the population of all weekly fuel consumptions that could be observed when the average hourly temperature is 28°F is

$$\mu_{y|28} = \beta_0 + \beta_1(28)$$
$$= 15.77 - .1281(28)$$
$$= 12.18 \text{ MMcf of natural gas}$$

As another example, it would also follow that the mean of the population of all weekly fuel consumptions that could be observed when the average hourly temperature is

45.9°F is

$$\mu_{y|45.9} = \beta_0 + \beta_1(45.9)$$
$$= 15.77 - .1281(45.9)$$
$$= 9.89 \text{ MMcf of natural gas}$$

Note that as the average hourly temperature increases from 28°F to 45.9°F, mean weekly fuel consumption decreases from 12.18 MMcf to 9.89 MMcf of natural gas. This makes sense because we would expect to use less fuel if the average hourly temperature increases. Of course, because we do not know the true values of $\beta_0$ and $\beta_1$, we cannot actually calculate these mean weekly fuel consumptions. However, when we learn in the next section how to estimate $\beta_0$ and $\beta_1$, we will then be able to estimate the mean weekly fuel consumptions. For now, when we say that the equation $\mu_{y|x} = \beta_0 + \beta_1 x$ is the equation of a straight line, we mean that the different mean weekly fuel consumptions that correspond to different average hourly temperatures lie exactly on a straight line. For example, consider the eight mean weekly fuel consumptions that correspond to the eight average hourly temperatures in Table 3.1. In Figure 3.2(a) (page 84) we depict these mean weekly fuel consumptions as triangles that lie exactly on the straight line defined by the equation $\mu_{y|x} = \beta_0 + \beta_1 x$. Furthermore, in this figure we draw arrows pointing to the triangles that represent the previously discussed means $\mu_{y|28}$ and $\mu_{y|45.9}$. Sometimes we refer to the straight line defined by the equation $\mu_{y|x} = \beta_0 + \beta_1 x$ as the **line of means.**

In order to interpret the slope $\beta_1$ of the line of means, consider two different weeks. Suppose that for the first week the average hourly temperature is $c$. The mean weekly fuel consumption for all such weeks is

$$\beta_0 + \beta_1(c)$$

For the second week, suppose that the average hourly temperature is $(c + 1)$. The mean weekly fuel consumption for all such weeks is

$$\beta_0 + \beta_1(c + 1)$$

It is easy to see that the difference between these mean weekly fuel consumptions is $\beta_1$. Thus, as illustrated in Figure 3.2(b), the slope $\beta_1$ is the change in mean weekly fuel consumption that is associated with a one-degree increase in average hourly temperature. To interpret the meaning of the $y$-intercept $\beta_0$, consider a week having an average hourly temperature of 0°F. The mean weekly fuel consumption for all such weeks is

$$\beta_0 + \beta_1(0) = \beta_0$$

Therefore, as illustrated in Figure 3.2(c), the $y$-intercept $\beta_0$ is the mean weekly fuel consumption when the average hourly temperature is 0°F. However, because we have not observed any weeks with temperatures near 0, we have no data to tell us what the relationship between mean weekly fuel consumption and average hourly temperature looks like for temperatures near 0. Therefore, the interpretation of $\beta_0$ is of dubious practical value. More will be said about this later.

Now recall that the observed weekly fuel consumptions are not exactly on a straight line. Rather, they are scattered around a straight line. To represent this phenomenon, we

**FIGURE 3.2**
The simple linear regression model relating weekly fuel consumption ($y$) to average hourly temperature ($x$)

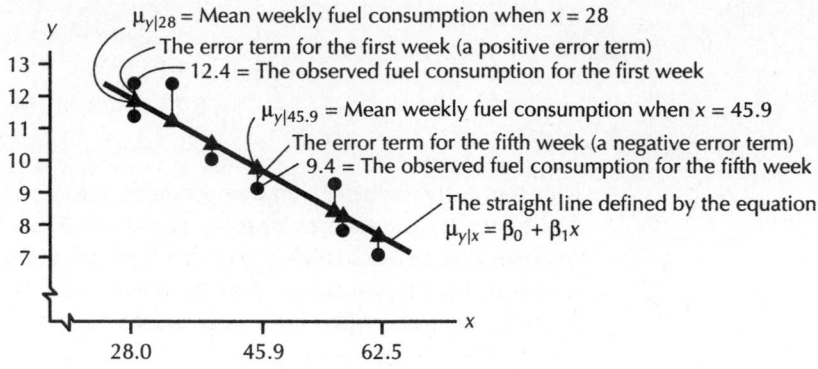

(a) The line of means and the error terms

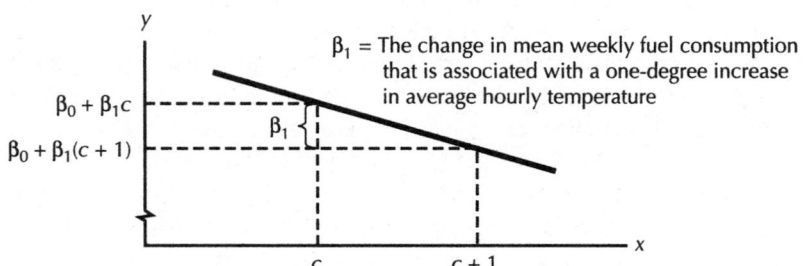

(b) The slope of the line of means

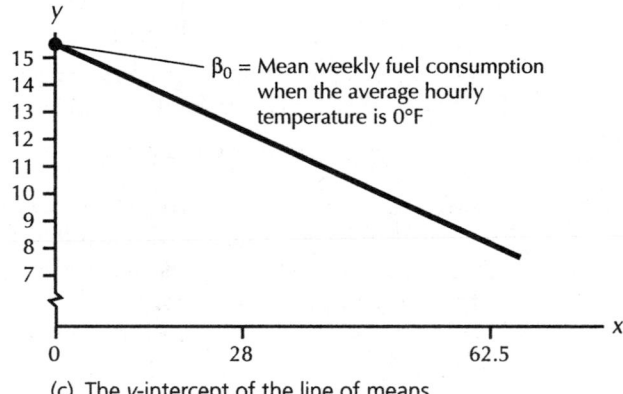

(c) The $y$-intercept of the line of means

use the **simple linear regression model**

$$y = \mu_{y|x} + \varepsilon$$
$$= \beta_0 + \beta_1 x + \varepsilon$$

This model says that the weekly fuel consumption $y$ observed when the average hourly temperature is $x$ differs from the mean weekly fuel consumption $\mu_{y|x}$ by an amount equal to $\varepsilon$ **(epsilon).** Here $\varepsilon$ is called an **error term.** The error term describes the effect on $y$ of all factors other than the average hourly temperature. Such factors would include the average hourly wind velocity and the average hourly thermostat setting in the city. For example, Figure 3.2(a) shows that the error term for the first week is positive. Therefore, the observed fuel consumption $y = 12.4$ in the first week was above the corresponding mean weekly fuel consumption for all weeks when $x = 28$. As another example, Figure 3.2(a) also shows that the error term for the fifth week was negative. Therefore, the observed fuel consumption $y = 9.4$ in the fifth week was below the corresponding mean weekly fuel consumption for all weeks when $x = 45.9$. More generally, Figure 3.2(a) illustrates that the simple linear regression model says that the eight observed fuel consumptions (the dots in the figure) deviate from the eight mean fuel consumptions (the triangles in the figure) by amounts equal to the error terms (the vertical line segments in the figure). Of course, since we do not know the true values of $\beta_0$ and $\beta_1$, the relative positions of the quantities pictured in the figure are only hypothetical.

With the fuel consumption example as background, we are ready to define the **simple linear regression model relating the dependent variable $y$ to the independent variable $x$.** We suppose that we have gathered $n$ observations—each observation consists of an observed value of $x$ and its corresponding value of $y$. Then:

---

**THE SIMPLE LINEAR REGRESSION MODEL**

The **simple linear** (or **straight-line**) **regression model** is

$$y = \mu_{y|x} + \varepsilon = \beta_0 + \beta_1 x + \varepsilon.$$

Here

1. $\mu_{y|x} = \beta_0 + \beta_1 x$ is the **mean value** of the dependent variable $y$ when the value of the independent variable is $x$.

2. $\beta_0$ is the **y-intercept.** $\beta_0$ is the mean value of $y$ when $x$ equals 0.

3. $\beta_1$ is the **slope.** $\beta_1$ is the change (amount of increase or decrease) in the mean value of $y$ associated with a one-unit increase in $x$. If $\beta_1$ is positive, the mean value of $y$ increases as $x$ increases. If $\beta_1$ is negative, the mean value of $y$ decreases as $x$ increases.

4. $\varepsilon$ is an error term that describes the effects on $y$ of all factors other than the value of the independent variable $x$.

---

This model is illustrated in Figure 3.3 (page 86) (note that $x_0$ in this figure denotes a specific value of the independent variable $x$). The $y$-intercept $\beta_0$ and the slope $\beta_1$ are called **regression parameters.** Because we do not know the true values of these parameters, we must use the sample data to estimate these values. We see how this is done in the next section. In later sections we show how to use these estimates to predict $y$.

**FIGURE 3.3**
The simple linear
regression model
(Here $\beta_1 > 0$)

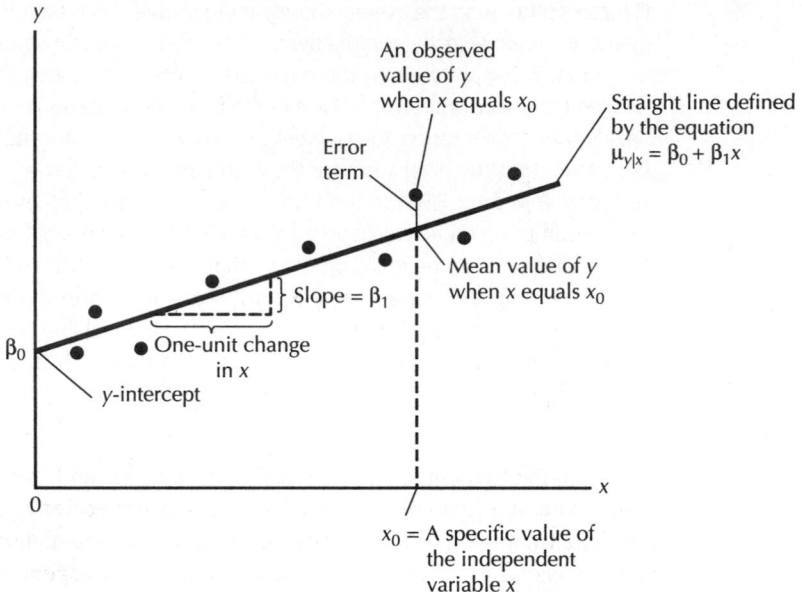

The fuel consumption data in Table 3.1 were observed sequentially over time (in eight consecutive weeks). When data are observed in time sequence, the data are called **time series data.** Many applications of regression utilize such data. Another frequently used type of data is called **cross-sectional data.** This kind of data is observed at a single point in time.

**EXAMPLE 3.2**    Quality Home Improvement Center (QHIC) operates five stores in a large metropolitan area. The marketing department at QHIC wishes to study the relationship between $x$, home value (in thousands of dollars), and $y$, yearly expenditure on home upkeep (in dollars). A random sample of 40 homeowners is taken, and they are asked to estimate their expenditures during the previous year on the types of home upkeep products and services offered by QHIC. Public records of the county auditor are used to obtain the previous year's assessed values of the homeowner's homes. The resulting $x$ and $y$ values are given in Table 3.2. Because the 40 observations are for the same year (for different homes), these data are cross-sectional.

The MINITAB output of a scatter plot of $y$ versus $x$ is given in Figure 3.4. We see that the observed values of $y$ tend to increase in a straight-line (or slightly curved) fashion as $x$ increases. Assuming that $\mu_{y|x}$ and $x$ have a straight-line relationship, it is reasonable to relate $y$ to $x$ by using the simple linear regression model having a positive slope ($\beta_1 > 0$):

$$y = \beta_0 + \beta_1 x + \varepsilon$$

The slope $\beta_1$ is the change (increase) in mean dollar yearly upkeep expenditure that is associated with each $1000 increase in home value. In later examples the marketing department at QHIC will use predictions given by this simple linear regression model to help determine which homes should be sent advertising brochures promoting QHIC's products and services.

**TABLE 3.2** The QHIC Upkeep Expenditure Data

| Home | Value of Home, x (× $1000) | Upkeep Expenditure, y($) | Home | Value of Home, x (× $1000) | Upkeep Expenditure, y($) |
|---|---|---|---|---|---|
| 1 | 237.00 | 1412.08 | 21 | 153.04 | 849.14 |
| 2 | 153.08 | 797.20 | 22 | 232.18 | 1313.84 |
| 3 | 184.86 | 872.48 | 23 | 125.44 | 602.06 |
| 4 | 222.06 | 1003.42 | 24 | 169.82 | 642.14 |
| 5 | 160.68 | 852.90 | 25 | 177.28 | 1038.80 |
| 6 | 99.68 | 288.48 | 26 | 162.82 | 697.00 |
| 7 | 229.04 | 1288.46 | 27 | 120.44 | 324.34 |
| 8 | 101.78 | 423.08 | 28 | 191.10 | 965.10 |
| 9 | 257.86 | 1351.74 | 29 | 158.78 | 920.14 |
| 10 | 96.28 | 378.04 | 30 | 178.50 | 950.90 |
| 11 | 171.00 | 918.08 | 31 | 272.20 | 1670.32 |
| 12 | 231.02 | 1627.24 | 32 | 48.90 | 125.40 |
| 13 | 228.32 | 1204.76 | 33 | 104.56 | 479.78 |
| 14 | 205.90 | 857.04 | 34 | 286.18 | 2010.64 |
| 15 | 185.72 | 775.00 | 35 | 83.72 | 368.36 |
| 16 | 168.78 | 869.26 | 36 | 86.20 | 425.60 |
| 17 | 247.06 | 1396.00 | 37 | 133.58 | 626.90 |
| 18 | 155.54 | 711.50 | 38 | 212.86 | 1316.94 |
| 19 | 224.20 | 1475.18 | 39 | 122.02 | 390.16 |
| 20 | 202.04 | 1413.32 | 40 | 198.02 | 1090.84 |

**FIGURE 3.4**
MINITAB plot of upkeep expenditure versus value of home for the QHIC data

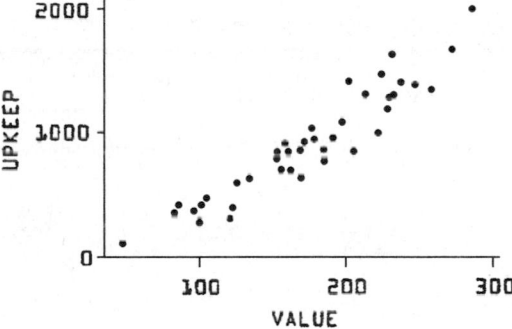

We have interpreted the slope $\beta_1$ of the simple linear regression model to be the change in the mean value of $y$ associated with a one-unit increase in $x$. We sometimes refer to this change as the effect of the independent variable $x$ on the dependent variable $y$. However, we cannot prove that *a change in an independent variable causes a change in the dependent variable*. Rather, regression can be used only to establish that the two variables move together and that the independent variable contributes information for predicting the dependent variable. For instance, regression analysis might be used to establish that as liquor sales have increased over the years, college professors' salaries have also increased. However, this does not prove that increases in liquor sales cause increases in college professors' salaries. Rather, both variables are influenced by a third variable—long-run growth in the national economy.

# 3.2 THE LEAST SQUARES POINT ESTIMATES

Although we do not know the true values of the parameters $\beta_0$ and $\beta_1$ in the simple linear regression model

$$y = \mu_{y|x} + \varepsilon$$
$$= \beta_0 + \beta_1 x + \varepsilon$$

we can use the $n$ observed values of the independent variable $x$,

$$x_1, x_2, \ldots, x_n$$

and the $n$ observed values of the dependent variable $y$,

$$y_1, y_2, \ldots, y_n$$

to calculate point estimates $b_0$ and $b_1$ of $\beta_0$ and $\beta_1$. These estimates are called the **least squares point estimates** of the parameters $\beta_0$ and $\beta_1$. We first present the formulas for computing $b_0$ and $b_1$. We then present an example in which we use these formulas and discuss the rationale for the formulas.

---

## THE LEAST SQUARES POINT ESTIMATES

For the simple linear regression model:

1.  The **least squares point estimate of the slope** $\beta_1$ is $b_1 = \dfrac{SS_{xy}}{SS_{xx}}$, where

$$SS_{xy} = \sum (x_i - \bar{x})(y_i - \bar{y}) = \sum x_i y_i - \frac{\left(\sum x_i\right)\left(\sum y_i\right)}{n}$$

and

$$SS_{xx} = \sum (x_i - \bar{x})^2 = \sum x_i^2 - \frac{\left(\sum x_i\right)^2}{n}$$

2.  The **least squares point estimate of the $y$-intercept** $\beta_0$ is $b_0 = \bar{y} - b_1\bar{x}$, where

$$\bar{y} = \frac{\sum y_i}{n} \quad \text{and} \quad \bar{x} = \frac{\sum x_i}{n}$$

Here $n$ is the number of observations (an observation is an observed value of $x$ and its corresponding value of $y$). In order to simplify notation, we will often drop the limits on summations in this and subsequent chapters. That is, instead of using the summation

$$\sum_{i=1}^{n}$$

we will simply write $\sum$.

The following example illustrates how to calculate these point estimates and how to use these point estimates to estimate mean values and predict individual values of the dependent variable. Note that the quantities $SS_{xy}$ and $SS_{xx}$ used to calculate the least squares point estimates are also used throughout this chapter to perform other important calculations.

**EXAMPLE 3.3**   In order to calculate least squares point estimates of the parameters $\beta_1$ and $\beta_0$ in the fuel consumption model,

$$y = \mu_{y|x} + \varepsilon$$
$$= \beta_0 + \beta_1 x + \varepsilon$$

we first consider the summations that are shown in Table 3.3 (page 90).
Using these summations, we calculate $SS_{xy}$ and $SS_{xx}$ as follows:

$$SS_{xy} = \sum x_i y_i - \frac{\left(\sum x_i\right)\left(\sum y_i\right)}{n}$$

$$= 3413.11 - \frac{(351.8)(81.7)}{8} = -179.6475$$

$$SS_{xx} = \sum x_i^2 - \frac{\left(\sum x_i\right)^2}{n}$$

$$= 16,874.76 - \frac{(351.8)^2}{8} = 1404.355$$

It follows that the least squares point estimate of the slope $\beta_1$ is

$$b_1 = \frac{SS_{xy}}{SS_{xx}} = \frac{-179.6475}{1404.355} = -.1279$$

Furthermore, because

$$\bar{y} = \frac{\sum y_i}{8} = \frac{81.7}{8} = 10.2125 \quad \text{and} \quad \bar{x} = \frac{\sum x_i}{8} = \frac{351.8}{8} = 43.98$$

**TABLE 3.3** The Calculation of Point Estimates $b_0$ and $b_1$ of the Parameters in the Fuel Consumption Model $y = \mu_{y|x} + \varepsilon = \beta_0 + \beta_1 x + \varepsilon$

| $y_i$ | $x_i$ | $x_i^2$ | $x_i y_i$ |
|---|---|---|---|
| 12.4 | 28.0 | $(28.0)^2 = 784$ | $(28.0)(12.4) = 347.2$ |
| 11.7 | 28.0 | $(28.0)^2 = 784$ | $(28.0)(11.7) = 327.6$ |
| 12.4 | 32.5 | $(32.5)^2 = 1{,}056.25$ | $(32.5)(12.4) = 403$ |
| 10.8 | 39.0 | $(39.0)^2 = 1{,}521$ | $(39.0)(10.8) = 421.2$ |
| 9.4 | 45.9 | $(45.9)^2 = 2{,}106.81$ | $(45.9)(9.4) = 431.46$ |
| 9.5 | 57.8 | $(57.8)^2 = 3{,}340.84$ | $(57.8)(9.5) = 549.1$ |
| 8.0 | 58.1 | $(58.1)^2 = 3{,}375.61$ | $(58.1)(8.0) = 464.8$ |
| 7.5 | 62.5 | $(62.5)^2 = 3{,}906.25$ | $(62.5)(7.5) = 468.75$ |
| $\sum y_i = 81.7$ | $\sum x_i = 351.8$ | $\sum x_i^2 = 16{,}874.76$ | $\sum x_i y_i = 3{,}413.11$ |

the least squares point estimate of the y-intercept $\beta_0$ is

$$b_0 = \bar{y} - b_1\bar{x} = 10.2125 - (-.1279)(43.98) = 15.84$$

Since $b_1 = -.1279$, we estimate that mean weekly fuel consumption decreases (since $b_1$ is negative) by .1279 MMcf of natural gas when average hourly temperature increases by one degree. Since $b_0 = 15.84$, we estimate that mean weekly fuel consumption is 15.84 MMcf of natural gas when average hourly temperature is 0°F. However, we have not observed any weeks with temperatures near 0, so making this interpretation of $b_0$ might be dangerous. We discuss this point more fully in the next section.

Now we explain the meaning of the term **least squares.** Note that for a particular observation $(x_i, y_i)$, we can use the point estimates $b_0$ and $b_1$ of the parameters $\beta_0$ and $\beta_1$ to calculate the **point prediction**

$$\hat{y}_i = b_0 + b_1 x_i$$
$$= 15.84 - .1279x_i$$

of the fuel consumption $y_i$ in the $i$th week. According to the simple linear regression model, the fuel consumption $y_i$ and the average hourly temperature $x_i$ are related by

$$y_i = \beta_0 + \beta_1 x_i + \varepsilon_i$$

Here we have predicted $\varepsilon_i$, the error term in week $i$, to be zero because of several assumptions to be discussed in Section 3.4. One implication of these assumptions is that $\varepsilon_i$ has a 50% chance of being positive and a 50% chance of being negative. For example, since the average hourly temperature in the fifth week was $x_5 = 45.9$, it follows that the point prediction of $y_5$ is

$$\hat{y}_5 = b_0 + b_1 x_5$$
$$= 15.84 - .1279(45.9)$$
$$= 9.9663$$

In general, if any particular values of $b_0$ and $b_1$ are good point estimates of $\beta_0$ and $\beta_1$, they will, for $i = 1, 2, \ldots, 8$, make $\hat{y}_i$ fairly close to $y_i$. Therefore, the **$i$th residual**

$$e_i = y_i - \hat{y}_i = y_i - (b_0 + b_1 x_i)$$

will be fairly small. We use the previously given formulas to calculate the point estimates $b_0$ and $b_1$ of the parameters $\beta_0$ and $\beta_1$ because it can be proved that these point estimates give a value of the **sum of squared residuals**

$$SSE = \sum_{i=1}^{8} e_i^2 = \sum_{i=1}^{8} (y_i - \hat{y}_i)^2$$

$$= \sum_{i=1}^{8} [y_i - (b_0 + b_i x_i)]^2$$

that is smaller than would be given by any other values of $b_0$ and $b_1$. Since these point estimates minimize SSE, we call them the **least squares point estimates.**

To illustrate the fact that the least squares point estimates minimize SSE, consider Table 3.4. In comparing the two parts of the table, we see that SSE = 2.57, the value given by the least squares point estimates $b_0 = 15.84$ and $b_1 = -.1279$, is less than SSE = 9.8877,

**TABLE 3.4** Comparison of SSE Values Given by the Least Squares Point Estimates $b_0 = 15.84$ and $b_1 = -.1279$ and by the Point Estimates $b_0 = 16.22$ and $b_1 = -.1152$

(a) Predictions Using the Least Squares Point Estimates $b_0 = 15.84$ and $b_1 = -.1279$

| Week, $i$ | Average Hourly Temperature, $x_i$ (°F) | Observed Fuel Consumption, $y_i$ (tons) | Predicted Fuel Consumption, $\hat{y}_i = b_0 + b_1 x_i$ = 15.84 − .1279$x_i$ | Residual, $e_i = y_i - \hat{y}_i$ |
|---|---|---|---|---|
| 1 | 28.0 | 12.4 | 12.2560 | .1440 |
| 2 | 28.0 | 11.7 | 12.2560 | −.5560 |
| 3 | 32.5 | 12.4 | 11.6804 | .7196 |
| 4 | 39.0 | 10.8 | 10.8489 | −.0489 |
| 5 | 45.9 | 9.4 | 9.9663 | −.5663 |
| 6 | 57.8 | 9.5 | 8.4440 | 1.0560 |
| 7 | 58.1 | 8.0 | 8.4056 | −.4056 |
| 8 | 62.5 | 7.5 | 7.8428 | −.3428 |

$$SSE = \sum_{i=1}^{8} e_i^2 = 2.57$$

(b) Predictions Using the Point Estimates $b_0 = 16.22$ and $b_1 = -.1152$

| Week, $i$ | Average Hourly Temperature, $x_i$ (°F) | Observed Fuel Consumption, $y_i$ (tons) | Predicted Fuel Consumption, $\hat{y}_i = b_0 + b_1 x_i$ = 16.22 − .1152$x_i$ | Residual, $e_i = y_i - \hat{y}_i$ |
|---|---|---|---|---|
| 1 | 28.0 | 12.4 | 12.9944 | −.5944 |
| 2 | 28.0 | 11.7 | 12.9944 | −1.2944 |
| 3 | 32.5 | 12.4 | 12.4760 | −.0760 |
| 4 | 39.0 | 10.8 | 11.7272 | −.9272 |
| 5 | 45.9 | 9.4 | 10.9323 | −1.5323 |
| 6 | 57.8 | 9.5 | 9.5614 | −.0614 |
| 7 | 58.1 | 8.0 | 9.5269 | −1.5269 |
| 8 | 62.5 | 7.5 | 9.0200 | −1.5200 |

$$SSE = \sum_{i=1}^{8} e_i^2 = 9.8877$$

**FIGURE 3.5**
The eight residuals given by the prediction equation

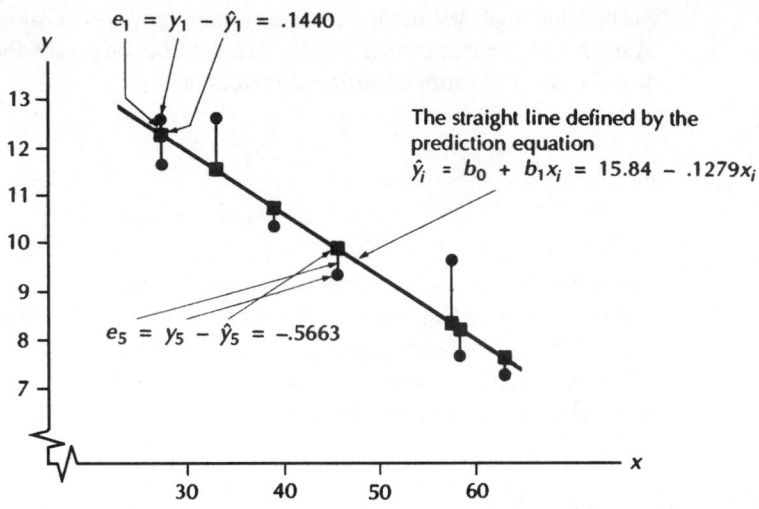

the value given by $b_0 = 16.22$ and $b_1 = -.1152$, which are not the least squares point estimates. There is nothing special about the values 16.22 and $-.1152$. The point is that if we choose any values of $b_0$ and $b_1$ that are different from the least squares values, we will obtain a larger SSE.

In Figure 3.5 we plot the eight observed fuel consumptions (the dots in the figure) and the eight predicted fuel consumptions (the squares in the figure). Note that the predicted fuel consumptions lie on the straight line defined by the prediction equation

$$\hat{y} = b_0 + b_1 x$$
$$= 15.84 - .1279x$$

Furthermore, the distances between the observed and predicted fuel consumptions are the residuals. Since the least squares point estimates minimize SSE, we can interpret them as positioning the straight-line prediction equation so as to minimize the sum of squared distances between the observed and predicted fuel consumptions. In this sense we can say that the straight line defined by the above prediction equation is the best straight line that can be fit to the eight observed fuel consumptions. This straight line is called the **least squares regression line** and the equation

$$\hat{y} = b_0 + b_1 x$$

is called the **least squares prediction equation.**

# 3.3   POINT ESTIMATES AND POINT PREDICTIONS

We now consider using the simple linear regression model to estimate and predict.

**EXAMPLE 3.4**    Consider the fuel consumption problem. We define the **experimental region** to be the range of the previously observed values of the average hourly temperature $x$. Because we have observed average hourly temperatures between 28°F and 62.5°F (see Table 3.4), the experimental region consists of the range of average hourly temperatures from 28°F to 62.5°F. The simple linear regression model relates weekly fuel consumption $y$ to average hourly temperature $x$ for values of $x$ that are in the experimental region. For such values of $x$, the least squares line is the estimate of the line of means. This implies that the point on the least squares line that corresponds to the average hourly temperature $x$

$$\hat{y} = b_0 + b_1 x$$
$$= 15.84 - .1279x$$

is the point estimate of the mean of all the weekly fuel consumptions that could be observed when the average hourly temperature is $x$:

$$\mu_{y|x} = \beta_0 + \beta_1 x$$

Note that $\hat{y}$ is an intuitively logical point estimate of $\mu_{y|x}$. This is because the expression $b_0 + b_1 x$ used to calculate $\hat{y}$ has been obtained from the expression $\beta_0 + \beta_1 x$ for $\mu_{y|x}$ by replacing the unknown values of $\beta_0$ and $\beta_1$ by their least squares point estimates $b_0$ and $b_1$.

The quantity $\hat{y}$ is also the point prediction of the individual value

$$y = \beta_0 + \beta_1 x + \varepsilon$$

which is the amount of fuel consumed in a single week when average hourly temperature equals $x$. To understand why $\hat{y}$ is the point prediction of $y$, note that $y$ is the sum of the mean $\beta_0 + \beta_1 x$ and the error term $\varepsilon$. We have already seen that $\hat{y} = b_0 + b_1 x$ is the point estimate of $\beta_0 + \beta_1 x$. In Section 3.2 we reasoned that we should predict the error term $\varepsilon$ to be 0, which implies that $\hat{y}$ is also the point prediction of $y$. To see why we should predict the error term to be 0, note that in the next section we discuss several assumptions concerning the simple linear regression model. One implication of these assumptions is that the error term has a 50% chance of being positive and a 50% chance of being negative. Therefore, it is reasonable to predict the error term to be 0 and to use $\hat{y}$ as the point prediction of a single value of $y$ when the average hourly temperature equals $x$.

Now suppose a weather forecasting service predicts that the average hourly temperature in the next week will be 40°F. Because 40°F is in the experimental region,

$$\hat{y} = 15.84 - .1279(40)$$
$$= 10.72 \text{ MMcf of natural gas}$$

is (1) the point estimate of the mean weekly fuel consumption when the average hourly temperature is 40°F and (2) the point prediction of an individual weekly fuel consumption when the average hourly temperature is 40°F. This says that (1) we estimate that the average of all possible weekly fuel consumptions that could potentially be observed when the average hourly temperature is 40°F equals 10.72 MMcf of natural gas, and (2) we predict that the fuel consumption in a single week when the average hourly temperature is 40°F will be 10.72 MMcf of natural gas.

Figure 3.6 (page 94) illustrates (1) the point estimate of mean fuel consumption when $x$ is 40°F (the square on the least squares line), (2) the true mean fuel consumption

**FIGURE 3.6**

Point estimation
and point
prediction in the
fuel consumption
problem

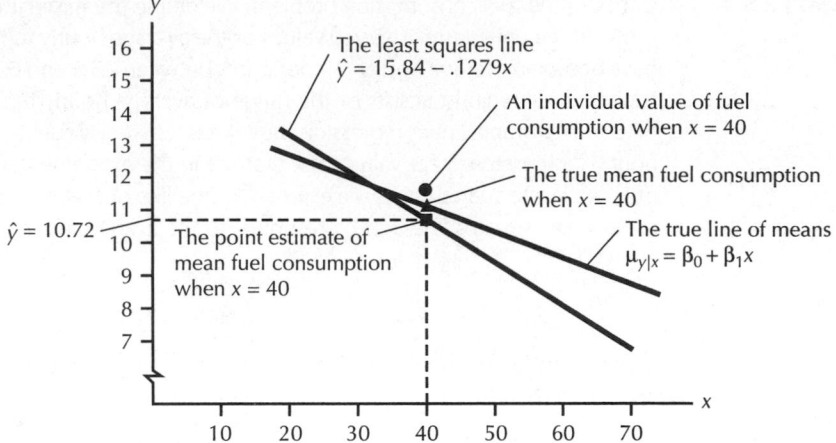

when $x$ is 40°F (the triangle on the true line of means), and (3) an individual value of fuel consumption when $x$ is 40°F (the dot in the figure). Of course this figure is only hypothetical. However, it illustrates that the point estimate of the mean value of $y$ (which is also the point prediction of the individual value of $y$) will differ from both the true mean value of $y$ and the individual value of $y$, unless we are extremely fortunate. Therefore, it is very likely that the point prediction $\hat{y} = 10.72$, which is the natural gas company's transmission nomination for next week, will differ from next week's actual fuel consumption, $y$. It follows that we might wish to predict the largest and smallest that $y$ might reasonably be. We will see how to do this in Section 3.6.

To conclude this example, note that Figure 3.7 illustrates the potential danger of using the least squares line to predict outside the experimental region. In the figure, we extrapolate the least squares line far beyond the experimental region to obtain a prediction for a temperature of −10°F. As shown in Figure 3.1, for values of $x$ in the experimental region the observed values of $y$ tend to decrease in a straight-line fashion as the values of $x$ increase. However, for temperatures lower than 28°F the relationship between $y$ and $x$ might become curved. If it does, extrapolating the straight-line prediction equation to obtain a prediction for $x = -10$ might badly underestimate mean weekly fuel consumption (see Figure 3.7).

The previous example illustrates that when we are using a least squares regression line, we should not estimate a mean value or predict an individual value unless the corresponding value of $x$ is in the **experimental region**—the range of the previously observed values of $x$. Often the value $x = 0$ is not in the experimental region. For example, consider the fuel consumption problem. Figure 3.7 illustrates that the average hourly temperature 0°F is not in the experimental region. In such a situation, it would not be appropriate to interpret the $y$-intercept $b_0$ as the estimate of the mean value of $y$ when $x$ equals 0. In the case of the fuel consumption problem, it would not be appropriate to use $b_0 = 15.84$ as the point estimate of the mean weekly

**FIGURE 3.7**
The danger of extrapolation outside the experimental region

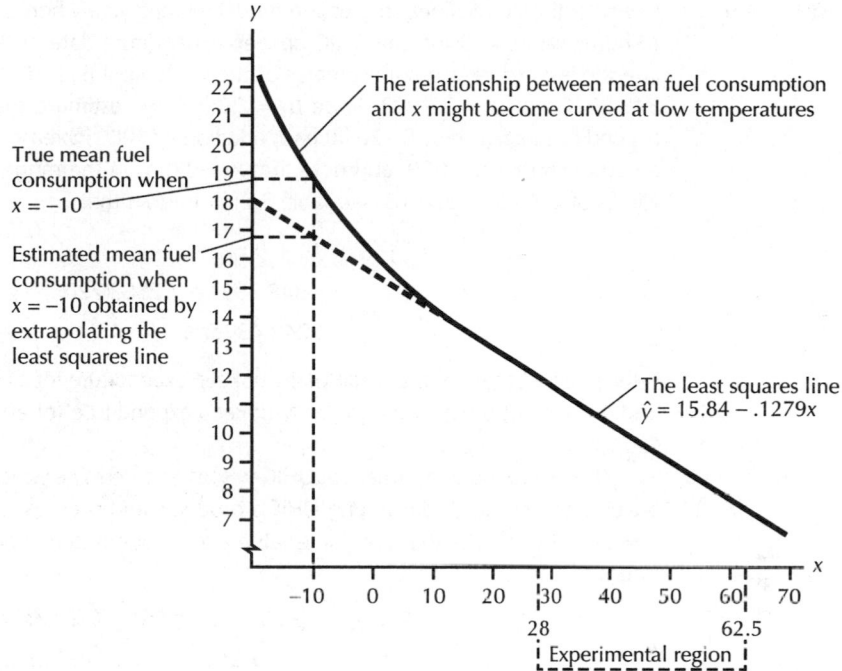

fuel consumption when average hourly temperature is 0. Therefore, because it is not meaningful to interpret the *y*-intercept in many regression situations, we often omit such interpretations.

We now present a general procedure for estimating a mean value and predicting an individual value.

---

## POINT ESTIMATION AND POINT PREDICTION IN SIMPLE LINEAR REGRESSION

Let $b_0$ and $b_1$ be the least squares point estimates of the *y*-intercept $\beta_0$ and the slope $\beta_1$ in the simple linear regression model, and suppose that $x_0$, a specified value of the independent variable *x*, is inside the experimental region. Then

$$\hat{y} = b_0 + b_1 x_0$$

is the **point estimate** of the **mean value of the dependent variable** when the value of the independent variable is $x_0$. In addition, $\hat{y}$ is the **point prediction** of an **individual value of the dependent variable** when the value of the independent variable is $x_0$. Here we predict the error term to be 0.

**EXAMPLE 3.5**    Consider the simple linear regression model relating yearly home upkeep expenditure, $y$, to home value, $x$. Using the QHIC upkeep expenditure data in Table 3.2, we can calculate the least squares point estimates of the $y$-intercept $\beta_0$ and the slope $\beta_1$ to be $b_0 = -348.3921$ and $b_1 = 7.2583$. Since $b_1 = 7.2583$, we estimate that mean yearly upkeep expenditure increases by $7.26 for each additional $1000 increase in home value. Consider a home worth $220,000, and note that $x_0 = 220$ is in the range of previously observed values of $x$: 48.9 to 286.18 (see Table 3.2). It follows that

$$\hat{y} = b_0 + b_1 x_0$$
$$= -348.3921 + 7.2583(220)$$
$$= 1248.43 \ (\text{or } \$1248.43)$$

is the point estimate of the mean yearly upkeep expenditure for all homes worth $220,000 and is the point prediction of a yearly upkeep expenditure for an individual home worth $220,000.

The marketing department at QHIC wishes to determine which homes should be sent advertising brochures promoting QHIC's products and services. The prediction equation $\hat{y} = b_0 + b_1 x$ implies that the home value $x$ corresponding to a predicted upkeep expenditure of $\hat{y}$ is

$$x = \frac{\hat{y} - b_0}{b_1} = \frac{\hat{y} - (-348.3921)}{7.2583} = \frac{\hat{y} + 348.3921}{7.2583}$$

Therefore, for example, if QHIC wishes to send an advertising brochure to any home that has a predicted upkeep expenditure of at least $500, then QHIC should send this brochure to any home that has a value of at least

$$x = \frac{\hat{y} + 348.3921}{7.2583} = \frac{500 + 348.3921}{7.2583} = 116.886 \ (\$116,886)$$

# 3.4 MODEL ASSUMPTIONS AND THE STANDARD ERROR

## Model Assumptions

In order to perform hypothesis tests and set up various types of intervals when using the simple linear regression model

$$y = \mu_{y|x} + \varepsilon$$
$$= \beta_0 + \beta_1 x + \varepsilon$$

we need to make certain assumptions about the error term $\varepsilon$. At any given value of $x$, there is a population of error term values that could potentially occur. These error term values describe the different potential effects on $y$ of all factors other than the value of $x$. Therefore, these error term values explain the variation in the $y$ values that could be observed when the independent variable is $x$. Our statement of the simple linear regression model assumes that $\mu_{y|x}$, the mean of the population of all $y$ values that could be observed when the independent variable is $x$, is $\beta_0 + \beta_1 x$. This model also implies that $\varepsilon = y - (\beta_0 + \beta_1 x)$, so this is equivalent to assuming that the mean of the corresponding population of potential error term values is 0. In total, we make four assumptions—called the **regression assumptions**—about the simple linear regression model. These assumptions can be stated in terms of potential $y$ values or, equivalently, in terms of potential error term values. Following tradition, we begin by stating these assumptions in terms of potential error term values.

## THE REGRESSION ASSUMPTIONS

1.  At any given value of $x$, the population of potential error term values has a **mean equal to** 0.

2.  **Constant variance assumption.** At any given value of $x$, the population of potential error term values has a variance that does not depend on the value of $x$. That is, the different populations of potential error term values corresponding to different values of $x$ have **equal variances.** We denote the **constant variance as** $\sigma^2$.

3.  **Normality assumption.** At any given value of $x$, the population of potential error term values has a **normal distribution.**

4.  **Independence assumption.** Any one value of the error term $\varepsilon$ is **statistically independent** of any other value of $\varepsilon$. That is, the value of the error term $\varepsilon$ corresponding to an observed value of $y$ is statistically independent of the value of the error term corresponding to any other observed value of $y$.

Taken together, the first three assumptions say that at any given value of $x$, the population of potential error term values is *normally distributed* with *mean zero* and a *variance $\sigma^2$ that does not depend on the value of $x$.* Because the potential error term values cause the variation in the potential $y$ values, these assumptions imply that the population of all $y$ values that could be observed when the independent variable is $x$

**FIGURE 3.8**
An illustration of
the model
assumptions

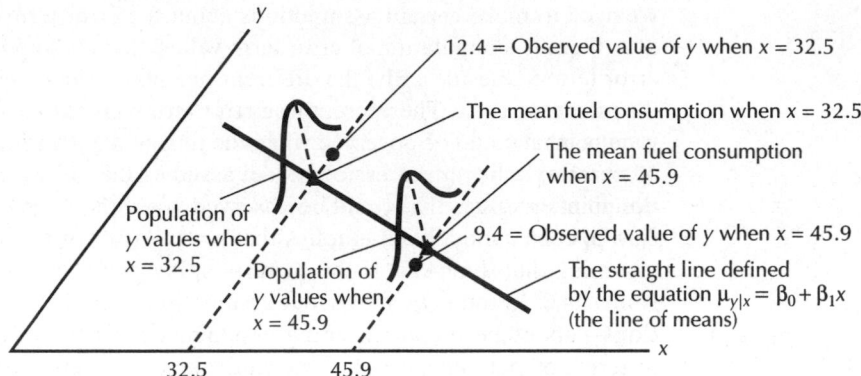

is *normally distributed* with *mean* $\beta_0 + \beta_1 x$ and *a variance* $\sigma^2$ *that does not depend on x.* These three assumptions are illustrated in Figure 3.8 in the context of the fuel consumption problem. Specifically, this figure depicts the populations of weekly fuel consumptions corresponding to two values of average hourly temperature— 32.5 and 45.9. Note that these populations are shown to be normally distributed with different means (each of which is on the line of means) and with the same variance (or spread).

The independence assumption is most likely to be violated when time series data are utilized in a regression study. Intuitively, this assumption says that there is no pattern of positive error terms being followed (in time) by other positive error terms, and there is no pattern of positive error terms being followed by negative error terms. That is, there is no pattern of higher-than-average *y* values being followed by other higher-than-average *y* values, and there is no pattern of higher-than-average *y* values being followed by lower-than-average *y* values.

It is important to point out that the regression assumptions very seldom, if ever, hold exactly in any practical regression problem. However, it has been found that regression results are not extremely sensitive to mild departures from these assumptions. In practice, only pronounced departures from these assumptions require attention. In Chapter 5 we show how to check the regression assumptions. Until then, we will suppose that the assumptions are valid in our examples.

In Sections 3.2 and 3.3 we stated that when we predict an individual value of the dependent variable, we predict the error term to be 0. To see why we do this, note that the regression assumptions state that at any given value of the independent variable, the population of all error term values that can potentially occur is normally distributed with a mean equal to 0. Since we also assume that successive error terms (observed over time) are statistically independent, each error term has a 50% chance of being positive and a 50% chance of being negative. Therefore, it is reasonable to predict any particular error term value to be 0.

## The Mean Square Error and the Standard Error

To present statistical inference formulas in later sections, we need to be able to compute point estimates of $\sigma^2$ and $\sigma$, the constant variance and standard deviation of the error term populations. The point estimate of $\sigma^2$ is called the **mean square error** and the point estimate of $\sigma$ is called the **standard error.** In the following box, we show how to compute these estimates.

---

**THE MEAN SQUARE ERROR AND THE STANDARD ERROR**

If the regression assumptions are satisfied and SSE is the sum of squared residuals, then

1. The point estimate of $\sigma^2$ is the **mean square error**

$$s^2 = \frac{\text{SSE}}{n - 2}$$

2. The point estimate of $\sigma$ is the **standard error**

$$s = \sqrt{\frac{\text{SSE}}{n - 2}}$$

Here the sum of squared residuals

$$\text{SSE} = \sum_{i=1}^{n} (y_i - \hat{y}_i)^2 \quad \text{where} \quad \hat{y}_i = b_0 + b_1 x_i$$

can be calculated by the alternative formula

$$\text{SSE} = \sum_{i=1}^{n} y_i^2 - \left[ b_0 \sum_{i=0}^{n} y_i + b_1 \sum_{i=1}^{n} x_i y_i \right]$$

---

In order to understand these point estimates, recall that $\sigma^2$ is the variance of the population of $y$ values (for a given value of $x$) around the mean value $\mu_{y|x}$. Because $\hat{y}$ is the point estimate of this mean, it seems natural to use

$$\text{SSE} = \sum_{i=1}^{n} (y_i - \hat{y}_i)^2$$

to help construct a point estimate of $\sigma^2$. We divide SSE by $n - 2$ because it can be proven that doing so makes the resulting $s^2$ an unbiased point estimate of $\sigma^2$. Here we call $n - 2$ the **number of degrees of freedom** associated with SSE.

**EXAMPLE 3.6**   Recall that $b_0 = 15.84$ and $b_1 = -.1279$ are the least squares point estimates of $\beta_0$ and $\beta_1$ in the fuel consumption regression model

$$y = \mu_{y|x} + \varepsilon$$
$$= \beta_0 + \beta_1 x + \varepsilon$$

It follows, as illustrated in Table 3.4, that

$$\hat{y}_i = b_0 + b_1 x_i = 15.84 - .1279 x_i$$

is the point prediction of $y_i$ and thus that the sum of squared residuals is

$$SSE = \sum_{i=1}^{8} (y_i - \hat{y}_i)^2$$
$$= (.1440)^2 + (-.5560)^2 + \cdots + (-.3428)^2 = 2.57$$

Also, recall from Table 3.3 that

$$\sum_{i=1}^{8} y_i = 81.7 \quad \text{and} \quad \sum_{i=1}^{8} x_i y_i = 3413.11$$

and note that

$$\sum_{i=1}^{8} y_i^2 = y_1^2 + y_2^2 + \cdots + y_8^2$$
$$= (12.4)^2 + (11.7)^2 + \cdots + (7.5)^2 = 859.91$$

It follows that SSE can be calculated in the following alternative fashion:

$$SSE = \sum_{i=1}^{8} y_i^2 - \left[ b_0 \sum_{i=1}^{8} y_i + b_1 \sum_{i=1}^{8} x_i y_i \right]$$
$$= 859.91 - [15.84(81.7) + (-.1279)(3413.11)]$$
$$= 859.91 - 857.34$$
$$= 2.57$$

Therefore, a point estimate of $\sigma^2$ is the mean square error

$$s^2 = \frac{SSE}{n - 2} = \frac{2.57}{8 - 2} = \frac{2.57}{6} = .428$$

and a point estimate of $\sigma$ is the standard error

$$s = \sqrt{s^2} = \sqrt{.428} = .6542$$

# 3.5 TESTING THE SIGNIFICANCE OF THE SLOPE AND *y*-INTERCEPT

## Testing the Significance of the Slope

A simple linear regression model is not likely to be useful unless there is a *significant relationship between y and x*. In order to judge the significance of the relationship between *y* and *x*, we test the null hypothesis

$$H_0: \beta_1 = 0$$

which says that there is no change in the mean value of *y* associated with an increase in *x*, versus the alternative hypothesis

$$H_a: \beta_1 \neq 0$$

which says that there is a (positive or negative) change in the mean value of *y* associated with an increase in *x*. It would be reasonable to conclude that *x* is significantly related to *y* if we can be quite certain that we should reject $H_0$ in favor of $H_a$.

In order to test these hypotheses, recall that we compute the least squares point estimate $b_1$ of the true slope $\beta_1$ by using a sample of *n* observed values of the dependent variable *y*. A different sample of *n* observed *y* values would yield a different least squares point estimate $b_1$. For example, consider the fuel consumption problem, and recall that we have observed eight average hourly temperatures. Corresponding to each temperature there is a (theoretically) infinite population of fuel consumptions that could potentially be observed at that temperature [see Table 3.5(a)] (page 102). Sample 1 in Table 3.5(b) is the sample of eight fuel consumptions that we have actually observed from these populations (these are the same fuel consumptions originally given in Table 3.1). Samples 2 and 3 in Table 3.5(b) are two other samples that we could have observed. In general, an infinite number of such samples could be observed. Because each sample yields its own unique values of $b_1$, $b_0$, $s^2$, and $s$ [see Table 3.5(c)–(f)], there is an infinite population of potential values of each of these estimates.

If the regression assumptions hold, then the population of all possible values of $b_1$ is normally distributed with a mean of $\beta_1$ and with a standard deviation of

$$\sigma_{b_1} = \frac{\sigma}{\sqrt{SS_{xx}}}$$

The standard error *s* is the point estimate of $\sigma$, so it follows that a point estimate of $\sigma_{b_1}$ is

$$s_{b_1} = \frac{s}{\sqrt{SS_{xx}}}$$

**TABLE 3.5** Three Samples in the Fuel Consumption Case

**(a) The Eight Populations of Fuel Consumptions**

| Week | Average Hourly Temperature $x$ | Population of Potential Weekly Fuel Consumptions |
|------|------------------------------|--------------------------------------------------|
| 1 | 28.0 | Population of fuel consumptions when $x = 28.0$ |
| 2 | 28.0 | Population of fuel consumptions when $x = 28.0$ |
| 3 | 32.5 | Population of fuel consumptions when $x = 32.5$ |
| 4 | 39.0 | Population of fuel consumptions when $x = 39.0$ |
| 5 | 45.9 | Population of fuel consumptions when $x = 45.9$ |
| 6 | 57.8 | Population of fuel consumptions when $x = 57.8$ |
| 7 | 58.1 | Population of fuel consumptions when $x = 58.1$ |
| 8 | 62.5 | Population of fuel consumptions when $x = 62.5$ |

**(b) Three Possible Samples**

| Sample 1 | Sample 2 | Sample 3 |
|----------|----------|----------|
| $y_1 = 12.4$ | $y_1 = 12.0$ | $y_1 = 10.7$ |
| $y_2 = 11.7$ | $y_2 = 11.8$ | $y_2 = 10.2$ |
| $y_3 = 12.4$ | $y_3 = 12.3$ | $y_3 = 10.5$ |
| $y_4 = 10.8$ | $y_4 = 11.5$ | $y_4 = 9.8$ |
| $y_5 = 9.4$ | $y_5 = 9.1$ | $y_5 = 9.5$ |
| $y_6 = 9.5$ | $y_6 = 9.2$ | $y_6 = 8.9$ |
| $y_7 = 8.0$ | $y_7 = 8.5$ | $y_7 = 8.5$ |
| $y_8 = 7.5$ | $y_8 = 7.2$ | $y_8 = 8.0$ |

**(c) Three Possible Values of $b_1$**

$b_1 = -.1279$    $b_1 = -.1285$    $b_1 = -.0666$

**(d) Three Possible Values of $b_0$**

$b_0 = 15.84$    $b_0 = 15.85$    $b_0 = 12.44$

**(e) Three Possible Values of $s^2$**

$s^2 = .428$    $s^2 = .47$    $s^2 = .0667$

**(f) Three Possible Values of $s$**

$s = .6542$    $s = .686$    $s = .2582$

which is called the **standard error of the estimate $b_1$.** Furthermore, if the regression assumptions hold, then the population of all values of

$$\frac{b_1 - \beta_1}{s_{b_1}}$$

has a *t*-distribution with $n - 2$ degrees of freedom. It follows that if the null hypothesis $H_0: \beta_1 = 0$ is true, then the population of all possible values of the test statistic

$$t = \frac{b_1}{s_{b_1}}$$

has a *t*-distribution with $n - 2$ degrees of freedom. Therefore, we can test the significance of the regression relationship as follows.

---

### TESTING THE SIGNIFICANCE OF THE REGRESSION RELATIONSHIP: TESTING THE SIGNIFICANCE OF THE SLOPE

Define the test statistic

$$t = \frac{b_1}{s_{b_1}} \quad \text{where} \quad s_{b_1} = \frac{s}{\sqrt{SS_{xx}}}$$

and suppose that the regression assumptions hold. Then we can reject $H_0: \beta_1 = 0$ in favor of a particular alternative hypothesis at significance level $\alpha$ (that is, by setting the probability of a Type I error equal to $\alpha$) if and only if the appropriate rejection point condition holds, or equivalently, the corresponding *p*-value is less than $\alpha$.

| Alternative Hypothesis | Rejection Point Condition: Reject $H_0$ if | *p*-Value |
|---|---|---|
| $H_a: \beta_1 \neq 0$ | $|t| > t_{[\alpha/2]}^{(n-2)}$ | Twice the area under the *t* curve to the right of $|t|$ |
| $H_a: \beta_1 > 0$ | $t > t_{[\alpha]}^{(n-2)}$ | The area under the *t* curve to the right of *t* |
| $H_a: \beta_1 < 0$ | $t < -t_{[\alpha]}^{(n-2)}$ | The area under the *t* curve to the left of *t* |

Here all the *p*-values are also based on $n - 2$ degrees of freedom.

---

We usually use the two-sided alternative $H_a: \beta_1 \neq 0$ for this test of significance. However, sometimes a one-sided alternative is appropriate. For example, in the fuel consumption problem we can say that if the slope $\beta_1$ is not 0, then it must be negative. A negative $\beta_1$ would say that mean fuel consumption decreases as temperature $x$

increases. Because of this, it would be appropriate to decide that $x$ is significantly related to $y$ if we can reject $H_0$: $\beta_1 = 0$ in favor of the one-sided alternative $H_a$: $\beta_1 < 0$. Although this test would be slightly more effective than the usual two-sided test, there is little practical difference between using the one-sided or two-sided alternative. Furthermore, computer packages (such as MINITAB, SAS, and Excel) present results for testing a two-sided alternative hypothesis. For these reasons we will emphasize the two-sided test.

It should also be noted that

1. *If we can decide that the slope is significant at the .05 significance level,* then we have concluded that $x$ is significantly related to $y$ by using a test that allows only a .05 probability of concluding that $x$ is significantly related to $y$ when it is not. *This is usually regarded as strong evidence that the regression relationship is significant.*

2. *If we can decide that the slope is significant at the .01 significance level, this is usually regarded as very strong evidence that the regression relationship is significant.*

3. The smaller the significance level $\alpha$ at which $H_0$ can be rejected, the stronger the evidence that the regression relationship is significant.

**EXAMPLE 3.7**    Again consider the fuel consumption model

$$y = \beta_0 + \beta_1 x + \varepsilon$$

For this model $SS_{xx} = 1404.355$, $b_1 = -.1279$, and $s = .6542$ (see Examples 3.3 and 3.6). Therefore

$$s_{b_1} = \frac{s}{\sqrt{SS_{xx}}} = \frac{.6542}{\sqrt{1,404.355}} = .01746$$

and

$$t = \frac{b_1}{s_{b_1}} = \frac{-.1279}{.01746} = -7.33$$

To test the significance of the slope we compare $|t|$ with $t_{[\alpha/2]}^{(n-2)}$ based on $n - 2 = 8 - 2 = 6$ degrees of freedom. Because

$$|t| = 7.33 > t_{[.025]}^{(6)} = 2.447$$

we can reject $H_0$: $\beta_1 = 0$ in favor of $H_a$: $\beta_1 \neq 0$ at level of significance .05.

The $p$-value for testing $H_0$ versus $H_a$ is twice the area to the right of $|t| = 7.33$ under the curve of the $t$ distribution having $n - 2 = 6$ degrees of freedom. Since this $p$-value can be shown to be .00033, we can reject $H_0$ in favor of $H_a$ at level of significance .05, .01, or .001. We therefore have extremely strong evidence that $x$ is significantly related to $y$ and that the regression relationship is significant.

Figure 3.9 presents the MINITAB and Excel outputs of a simple linear regression analysis of the fuel consumption data. Note that the values $b_0 = 15.84$, $b_1 = -.1279$, $s = .6542$, $s_{b_1} = .01746$, and $t = -7.33$ (each of which has been previously calculated)

**FIGURE 3.9** MINITAB and Excel output of a simple linear regression analysis of the fuel consumption data

```
The regression equation is
Fuelcons = 15.8 - 0.128 Temp
```

| Predictor | Coef | SE Coef | T | P[g] |
|---|---|---|---|---|
| Constant | 15.8379[a] | 0.8018[c] | 19.75[e] | 0.000 |
| Temp | -0.12792[b] | 0.01746[d] | -7.33[f] | 0.000 |

S = 0.654209[h]   R-Sq = 89.9%[i]   R-Sq(adj) = 88.3%

Analysis of Variance

| Source | DF | SS | MS | F | P |
|---|---|---|---|---|---|
| Regression | 1 | 22.981[j] | 22.981 | 53.69[m] | 0.000[n] |
| Residual Error | 6 | 2.568[k] | 0.428 | | |
| Total | 7 | 25.549[l] | | | |

| Fit[o] | SE Fit[p] | 95% CI[q] | 95% PI[r] |
|---|---|---|---|
| 10.721 | 0.241 | (10.130, 11.312) | (9.015, 12.427) |

[a] $b_0$ [b] $b_1$ [c] $s_{b_0}$ [d] $s_{b_1}$ [e] $t$ for testing $H_0$: $\beta_0 = 0$ [f] $t$ for testing $H_0$: $\beta_1 = 0$ [g] $p$-values for $t$-statistics [h] $s$ = standard error [i] $r^2$ [j] Explained variation [k] SSE = Unexplained variation [l] Total variation [m] $F$(model) statistic [n] $p$-value for $F$(model) [o] $\hat{y}$ when $x = 40$ [p] $s_{\hat{y}}$ [q] 95% confidence interval when $x = 40$ [r] 95% prediction interval when $x = 40$

(a) The MINITAB output

| Regression Statistics | |
|---|---|
| Multiple R | 0.948414 |
| R Square | 0.899489[h] |
| Adjusted R Square | 0.882737 |
| Standard Error | 0.654209[g] |
| Observations | 8 |

**ANOVA**

| | df | SS | MS | F[l] | Significance F |
|---|---|---|---|---|---|
| Regression | 1 | [i]22.98081629 | 22.98082 | 53.6949 | 0.000330052[m] |
| Residual | 6 | [j]2.567933713 | 0.427989 | | |
| Total | 7 | [k]25.54875 | | | |

| | Coefficients | Standard Error | t Stat[e] | P-Value[f] | Lower 95%[n] | Upper 95%[n] |
|---|---|---|---|---|---|---|
| Intercept | [a]15.83786 | [c]0.801773385 | 19.75353 | 1.1E-06 | 13.87598718 | 17.79973 |
| Temp | [b]–0.127922 | [d]0.01745733 | –7.32768 | 0.00033 | –0.17063829 | –0.085205 |

[a] $b_0$ [b] $b_1$ [c] $s_{b_1}$ [d] $s_{b_0}$ [e] $t$ statistics for testing $H_0$: $\beta_0 = 0$ and $H_0$: $\beta_1 = 0$ [f] $p$-values for $t$-statistics [g] $s$ = standard error [h] $r^2$ [i] Explained variation [j] SSE = Unexplained variation [k] Total variation [l] $F$(model) statistic [m] $p$-value for $F$(model) [n] 95% confidence intervals for $\beta_0$ and $\beta_1$

(b) The Excel output

are given on these outputs. Also note that Excel gives the $p$-value of .00033, and MINITAB has rounded this $p$-value to .000 (which means less than .001). Other quantities on the MINITAB and Excel outputs will be discussed later.

In addition to testing the significance of the slope, it is often useful to calculate a confidence interval for $\beta_1$. We show how this is done in the following box.

---

### A CONFIDENCE INTERVAL FOR THE SLOPE

If the regression assumptions hold, a **$100(1 - \alpha)\%$ confidence interval for the true slope $\beta_1$** is

$$\left[ b_1 \pm t_{[\alpha/2]}^{(n-2)} s_{b_1} \right]$$

---

**EXAMPLE 3.8**    The MINITAB and Excel outputs in Figure 3.9 for the fuel consumption data tell us that $b_1 = -.1279$ and $s_{b_1} = .01746$. Thus, for instance, a 95% confidence interval for $\beta_1$ is

$$\left[ b_1 \pm t_{[.025]}^{(8-2)} s_{b_1} \right] = [-.1279 \pm 2.447(.01746)]$$
$$= [-.1706, -.0852]$$

This interval says we are 95% confident that if average hourly temperature increases by one degree, then mean weekly fuel consumption will decrease (because both the lower bound and the upper bound of the interval are negative) by at least .0852 MMcf of natural gas and by at most .1706 MMcf of natural gas. Also, because the 95% confidence interval for $\beta_1$ does not contain 0, we can reject $H_0$: $\beta_1 = 0$ in favor of $H_a$: $\beta_1 \neq 0$ at level of significance .05. Note that the 95% confidence interval for $\beta_1$ is given on the Excel output but not on the MINITAB output.

**EXAMPLE 3.9**    Figure 3.10 presents the SAS output of a simple linear regression analysis of the QHIC data. Below we summarize some important quantities from the output (we discuss the other quantities later):

$$b_0 = -348.39206 \qquad b_1 = 7.25826 \qquad s = 146.89735$$

$$s_{b_1} = .41557 \qquad t = \frac{b_1}{s_{b_1}} = 17.47 \qquad p\text{-value for } t < .0001$$

Since the $p$-value for testing the significance of the slope is less than .001, we can reject $H_0$: $\beta_1 = 0$ in favor of $H_a$: $\beta_1 \neq 0$ at the .001 level of significance. It follows that we have extremely strong evidence that the regression relationship is significant.

**FIGURE 3.10** SAS output of a simple linear regression analysis of QHIC data

### Analysis of Variance

| Source | DF | Sum of Squares | Mean Square | F Value | Pr > F |
|---|---|---|---|---|---|
| Model | 1 | 6582760[j] | 6582760 | 305.06[m] | <.0001[n] |
| Error | 38 | 819996[k] | 21579 | | |
| Corrected Total | 39 | 7402755[l] | | | |

| Root MSE | 146.89735[h] | R-Square | 0.8892[i] |
|---|---|---|---|
| Dependent Mean | 918.09150 | Adj R-Sq | 0.8863 |
| Coeff Var | 16.00029 | | |

### Parameter Estimates

| Variable | Label | DF | Parameter Estimate | Standard Error | t Value | Pr > \|t\|[g] |
|---|---|---|---|---|---|---|
| Intercept | Intercept | 1 | -348.39206[a] | 76.14100[c] | -4.58[e] | <.0001 |
| Value | Value | 1 | 7.25826[b] | 0.41557[d] | 17.47[f] | <.0001 |

| Obs | Dep Var Upkeep | Predicted[o] Value | Std Error[p] Mean Predict | 95% CL Mean[q] | | 95% CL Predict[r] | |
|---|---|---|---|---|---|---|---|
| 41 | . | 1248 | 29.9529 | 1188 | 1309 | 944.9288 | 1552 |

[a]$b_0$  [b]$b_1$  [c]$s_{b_0}$  [d]$s_{b_1}$  [e]t for testing $H_0: \beta_0 = 0$  [f]t for testing $H_0: \beta_1 = 0$  [g]p-values for t-statistics  [h]s = standard error  [i]$r^2$
[j]Explained variation  [k]SSE = Unexplained variation  [l]Total variation  [m]F(model) statistic  [n]p-value for F(model)  [o]$\hat{y}$ when $x = 220$
[p]$s_{\hat{y}}$  [q]95% confidence interval when $x = 220$  [r]95% prediction interval when $x = 220$

Although the SAS output does not include a 95% confidence interval for $\beta_1$, it does give the values for $b_1$ and $s_{b_1}$. A complete t-table would show us that $t_{[.025]}^{(40-2)} = t_{[.025]}^{(38)} = 2.024$. Since our t-table does not include a row for 38 degrees of freedom and 38 > 30, we could replace $t_{[.025]}^{(38)}$ by the approximate value of $z_{[.025]} = 1.96$. We use the approximation to obtain

$$\left[b_1 \pm t_{[.025]}^{(40-2)} s_{b_1}\right] \approx \left[b_1 \pm z_{[.025]} s_{b_1}\right] = [7.25826 \pm 1.96(.41557)]$$
$$= [6.4437, 8.0728]$$

This interval says we are 95% confident that mean yearly upkeep expenditures increase by between $6.44 and $8.07 for each additional $1000 increase in the home value.

## Testing the Significance of the y-Intercept

We can also test the significance of the y-intercept $\beta_0$. We do this by testing the null hypothesis $H_0: \beta_0 = 0$ versus the alternative hypothesis $H_a: \beta_0 \neq 0$. To carry out this test we use the test statistic

$$t = \frac{b_0}{s_{b_0}}$$

where

$$s_{b_0} = s\sqrt{\frac{1}{n} + \frac{\bar{x}^2}{SS_{xx}}}$$

Here the rejection point and $p$-value conditions for rejecting $H_0$ are the same as those given previously for testing the significance of the slope, except that $t$ is calculated as $b_0/s_{b_0}$. For example, if we consider the fuel consumption problem and the MINITAB output in Figure 3.9, we see that $b_0 = 15.8379$, $s_{b_0} = .8018$, $t = 19.75$, and $p$-value = .000. Because $t = 19.75 > t_{[.025]}^{(8-2)} > 2.447$ and $p$-value $< .05$, we can reject $H_0: \beta_0 = 0$ in favor of $H_a: \beta_0 \neq 0$ at the .05 level of significance. In fact, since the $p$-value $< .001$, we can also reject $H_0$ at the .001 level of significance. This provides extremely strong evidence that the $y$-intercept $\beta_0$ does not equal 0 and that we should include $\beta_0$ in the fuel consumption model.

In general, if we fail to conclude that the intercept is significant at a level of significance of .05, it might be reasonable to drop the $y$-intercept from the model. However, remember that $\beta_0$ equals the mean value of $y$ when $x$ equals 0. If, logically speaking, the mean value of $y$ would not equal 0 when $x$ equals 0 (for example, in the fuel consumption problem, mean fuel consumption would not equal 0 when the average hourly temperature is 0), it is common practice to include the $y$-intercept whether or not $H_0: \beta_0 = 0$ is rejected. In fact, experience suggests that it is definitely safest, when in doubt, to include the intercept $\beta_0$.

# 3.6  CONFIDENCE AND PREDICTION INTERVALS

The point on the least squares line corresponding to a particular value $x_0$ of the independent variable $x$ is

$$\hat{y} = b_0 + b_1 x_0$$

Unless we are very lucky, $\hat{y}$ will not exactly equal either the mean value of $y$ when $x$ equals $x_0$ or a particular individual value of $y$ when $x$ equals $x_0$. Therefore, we need to place bounds on how far $\hat{y}$ might be from these values. We can do this by calculating a **confidence interval for the mean value of $y$** and a **prediction interval for an individual value of $y$.**

Both of these intervals employ a quantity called the **distance value**. For simple linear regression this quantity is calculated as follows.

## THE DISTANCE VALUE FOR SIMPLE LINEAR REGRESSION

In simple linear regression the **distance value** for a particular value $x_0$ of $x$ is

$$\text{Distance value} = \frac{1}{n} + \frac{(x_0 - \bar{x})^2}{SS_{xx}}$$

This quantity is given its name because it is a measure of the distance between the value $x_0$ of $x$ and $\bar{x}$, the average of the previously observed values of $x$. Notice from the above formula that the farther $x_0$ is from $\bar{x}$, which can be regarded as the center of the experimental region, the larger the distance value. The significance of this fact will become apparent shortly.

We now consider establishing a confidence interval for the mean value of $y$ when $x$ equals a particular value $x_0$ (for later reference, we call this mean value $\mu_{y|x_0}$. Because each possible sample of $n$ values of the dependent variable gives values of $b_0$ and $b_1$ that differ from the values given by other samples, different samples give different values of the point estimate

$$\hat{y} = b_0 + b_1 x_0$$

It can be shown that if the regression assumptions hold, then the population of all possible values of $\hat{y}$ is normally distributed with mean $\mu_{y|x_0}$ and standard deviation

$$\sigma_{\hat{y}} = \sigma\sqrt{\text{Distance value}}$$

The point estimate of $\sigma_{\hat{y}}$ is

$$s_{\hat{y}} = s\sqrt{\text{Distance value}}$$

which is called the **standard error of the estimate $\hat{y}$.** Using this standard error, we form a confidence interval as follows.

## A CONFIDENCE INTERVAL FOR A MEAN VALUE OF *y*

If the regression assumptions hold, a **$100(1 - \alpha)\%$ confidence interval for the mean value of $y$** when the independent variable is $x_0$ is

$$\left[ \hat{y} \pm t_{[\alpha/2]}^{(n-2)} s\sqrt{\text{Distance value}} \right]$$

**EXAMPLE 3.10**    In the fuel consumption problem, suppose we wish to compute a 95% confidence interval for the mean value of weekly fuel consumption when the average hourly temperature is $x_0 = 40°F$. From Example 3.4, the point estimate of this mean is

$$\hat{y} = b_0 + b_1 x_0$$
$$= 15.84 - .1279(40)$$
$$= 10.72 \text{ MMcf of natural gas}$$

Furthermore, using the information in Example 3.3, we compute

$$\text{Distance value} = \frac{1}{n} + \frac{(x_0 - \bar{x})^2}{SS_{xx}}$$
$$= \frac{1}{8} + \frac{(40 - 43.98)^2}{1404.355}$$
$$= .1362$$

Since $s = .6542$ (see Example 3.6), it follows that the desired 95% confidence interval is

$$\left[\hat{y} \pm t_{[.025]}^{(8-2)} s \sqrt{\text{Distance value}}\right] = \left[10.72 \pm 2.447(.6542)\sqrt{.1362}\right]$$
$$= [10.72 \pm .59]$$
$$= [10.13, 11.31]$$

This interval says we are 95% confident that the mean (or average) of all the weekly fuel consumptions that would be observed in all weeks having an average hourly temperature of 40°F is between 10.13 MMcf of natural gas and 11.31 MMcf of natural gas.

We develop an interval for an individual value of $y$ when $x$ equals a particular value $x_0$ by considering the **prediction error** $y - \hat{y}$. After observing each possible sample and calculating the point prediction based on that sample, we could observe any one of an infinite number of different individual values of $y$ (because of different possible error terms). Therefore, there are an infinite number of different prediction errors that could be observed. If the regression assumptions hold, it can be shown that the population of all possible prediction errors is normally distributed with mean 0 and standard deviation

$$\sigma_{(y-\hat{y})} = \sigma\sqrt{1 + \text{Distance value}}$$

The point estimate of $\sigma_{(y-\hat{y})}$ is

$$s_{(y-\hat{y})} = s\sqrt{1 + \text{Distance value}}$$

which is called the **standard error of the prediction error.** Using this quantity we obtain a **prediction interval** as follows.

### A PREDICTION INTERVAL FOR AN INDIVIDUAL VALUE OF $y$

If the regression assumptions hold, a **100(1 − α)% prediction interval for an individual value of $y$** when the independent variable is $x_0$ is

$$\left[\hat{y} \pm t_{[\alpha/2]}^{(n-2)} s \sqrt{1 + \text{Distance value}}\right]$$

**EXAMPLE 3.11**

In the fuel consumption problem, suppose we wish to compute a 95% prediction interval for an individual weekly fuel consumption when average hourly temperature equals 40°F. Recalling that $\hat{y} = 10.72$ when $x_0 = 40$, the desired interval is

$$\left[\hat{y} \pm t_{[.025]}^{(8-2)} s\sqrt{1 + \text{Distance value}}\right] = [10.72 \pm 2.447(.6542)\sqrt{1.1362}]$$

$$= [10.72 \pm 1.71]$$

$$= [9.01, 12.43]$$

This interval says we are 95% confident that the individual fuel consumption in a future single week having an average hourly temperature of 40°F will be between 9.01 MMcf of natural gas and 12.43 MMcf of natural gas. Because the weather forecasting service has predicted that the average hourly temperature in the next week will be 40°F, we can use the prediction interval to evaluate how well our regression model is likely to predict next week's fuel consumption and to evaluate whether the natural gas company will be assessed a transmission fine. First, recall that the point prediction $\hat{y} = 10.72$ given by our model is the natural gas company's transmission nomination for next week. Also, note that the half-length of the 95% prediction interval given by our model is 1.71, which is (1.71/10.72)100% = 15.91% of the transmission nomination. It follows that we are 95% confident that the actual amount of natural gas that will be used by the city next week will differ from the natural gas company's transmission nomination by no more than 15.91%. That is, we are 95% confident that the natural gas company's percentage nomination error will be less than or equal to 15.91%. Although this does not imply that the natural gas company is likely to make a terribly inaccurate nomination, we are not confident that the company's percentage nomination error will be within the 10% allowance granted by the pipeline transmission system. Therefore, the natural gas company may be assessed a transmission fine. In Chapter 4 we use a **multiple regression model** to substantially reduce the natural gas company's percentage nomination errors.

Below we repeat the bottom of the MINITAB output in Figure 3.9(a). This output gives the point estimate and prediction $\hat{y} = 10.72$, the 95% confidence interval for the mean value of $y$ when $x$ equals 40, and the 95% prediction interval for an individual value of $y$ when $x$ equals 40.

```
    Fit   SE Fit      95% CI            95% PI
 10.721    0.241  (10.130,  11.312)  (9.015,  12.427)
```

Although the MINITAB output does not directly give the distance value, it does give $s_{\hat{y}} = s\sqrt{\text{Distance value}}$ under the heading "SE Fit." A little algebra shows that this implies that the distance value equals $(s_{\hat{y}}/s)^2$. Specifically, because $s_{\hat{y}} = .241$ and $s = .6542$ [see the MINITAB output in Figure 3.9(a)], it follows that the distance value equals $(.241/.6542)^2 = .1357$. This distance value is (within rounding) equal to the distance value that we hand calculated in Example 3.10.

Figure 3.11 (page 112) illustrates and compares the 95% confidence interval for the mean value of $y$ when $x$ equals 40 and the 95% prediction interval for an individual value of $y$ when $x$ equals 40. We see that both intervals are centered at $\hat{y} = 10.72$. However, the prediction interval is longer than the confidence interval. This is because the formula for the prediction interval has an "extra 1 under the radical," which accounts for the added

**FIGURE 3.11**
Comparison of a
confidence interval
for the mean value
of y when x = 40
and a prediction
interval for an
individual value of y
when x = 40

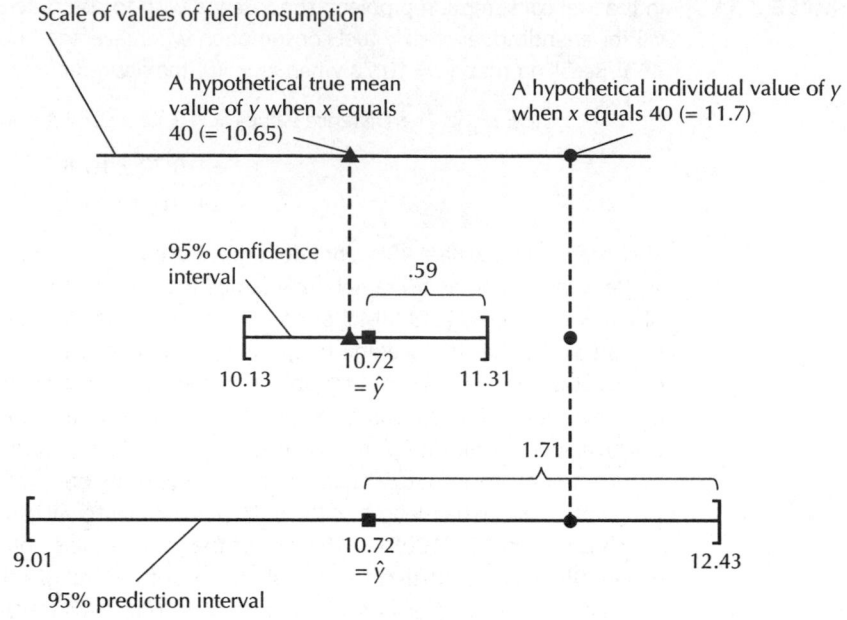

uncertainty introduced by our not knowing the value of the error term (which we nevertheless predict to be 0, though it probably will not equal 0). Figure 3.11 hypothetically supposes that the true values of $\beta_0$ and $\beta_1$ are 15.77 and –.1281, and also supposes that in a future week when x equals 40 the error term will equal 1.05—no human being would actually know these facts. Assuming these values, the mean value of y when x equals 40 would be

$$\beta_0 + \beta_1(40) = 15.77 - .1281(40) = 10.65$$

and in the future week the individual value of y when x equals 40 would be

$$\beta_0 + \beta_1(40) + \varepsilon = 10.65 + 1.05 = 11.7$$

As illustrated in Figure 3.11, the 95% confidence interval contains the mean 10.65. However, this interval is not long enough to contain the individual value 11.7; remember, it is not meant to contain this individual value of y. In contrast, the 95% prediction interval is long enough and does contain the individual value 11.7. Of course, the relative positions of the quantities shown in Figure 3.11 will vary in different situations. However, this figure emphasizes that we must be careful to include the extra 1 under the radical when computing a prediction interval for an individual value of y.

To conclude this example, note that Figure 3.12 illustrates the MINITAB output of the 95% confidence and prediction intervals corresponding to all values of x in the experimental region. Here $\bar{x}$ = 43.98 can be regarded as the center of the experimental region. Notice that the farther x is from $\bar{x}$ = 43.98, the larger is the distance value and, therefore, the

**FIGURE 3.12**
MINITAB output of
95% confidence
and prediction
intervals for the
fuel consumption
data

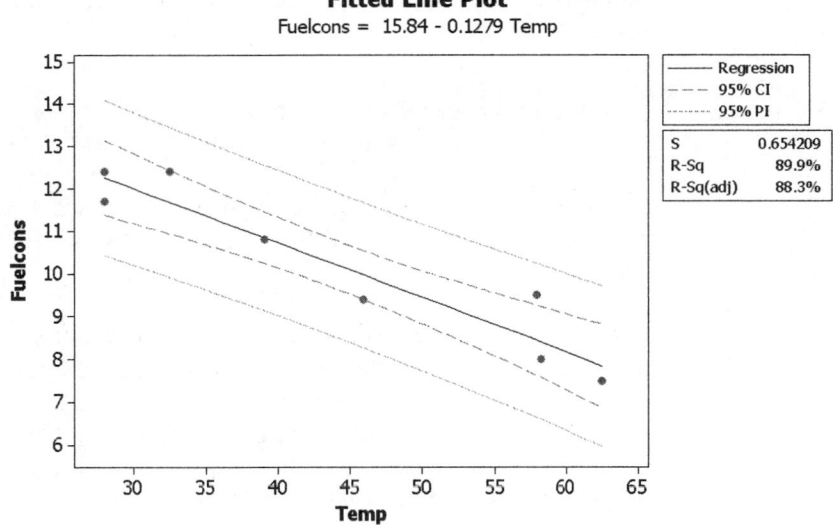

**Fitted Line Plot**
Fuelcons = 15.84 - 0.1279 Temp

| | |
|---|---|
| Regression | |
| 95% CI | |
| 95% PI | |

| S | 0.654209 |
|---|---|
| R-Sq | 89.9% |
| R-Sq(adj) | 88.3% |

longer are the 95% confidence and prediction intervals. These longer intervals are undesirable because they give us less information about mean and individual values of y.

In general, the prediction interval is useful if, as in the fuel consumption problem, it is important to predict an individual value of the dependent variable. A confidence interval is useful if it is important to estimate the mean value. Although it is not important to estimate a mean value in the fuel consumption problem, it is important to estimate a mean value in other situations. To understand this, recall that the mean value is the average of all the values of the dependent variable that could potentially be observed when the independent variable equals a particular value. Therefore, it might be important to estimate the mean value if we will observe and are affected by a very large number of values of the dependent variable when the independent variable equals a particular value. We illustrate this in the following example.

**EXAMPLE 3.12**   Consider a home worth $220,000. We have seen in Example 3.5 for the QHIC upkeep expenditure data that the predicted yearly upkeep expenditure for such a home is

$$\hat{y} = b_0 + b_1 x_0$$
$$= -348.3921 + 7.2583(220)$$
$$= 1248.43 \text{ (that is, } \$1248.43)$$

This predicted value is given at the bottom of the SAS output in Figure 3.10, which we repeat here:

```
          Dep Var Predicted     Std Error
Obs       Upkeep    Value Mean Predict      95% CL Mean        95% CL Predict
 41          .        1248      29.9529      1188     1309  944.9288      1552
```

In addition to giving $\hat{y} = 1248$, the SAS output shows the 95% prediction interval for the yearly upkeep expenditure of an individual house worth \$220,000:

$$\left[\hat{y} \pm t^{(40-2)}_{[.025]} s\sqrt{1 + \text{Distance value}}\right] = [945,\ 1552]$$

Because there are many homes worth roughly \$220,000 in the metropolitan area, QHIC is more interested in the mean upkeep expenditure for all such homes than in the individual upkeep expenditure for one such home. The SAS output tells us that a 95% confidence interval for this mean upkeep expenditure is [1188, 1309]. This interval says that QHIC is 95% confident that the mean upkeep expenditure for all homes worth \$220,000 is at least \$1188 and is no more than \$1309.

# 3.7   SIMPLE COEFFICIENTS OF DETERMINATION AND CORRELATION

## The Simple Coefficient of Determination

The **simple coefficient of determination** is a measure of the usefulness of a simple linear regression model. To introduce this quantity, which is denoted $r^2$ (pronounced **r squared**), suppose we have observed $n$ values of the dependent variable $y$. However, we choose to predict $y$ without using a predictor (independent) variable $x$. In such a case the only reasonable prediction of a specific value of $y$, say $y_i$, would be $\bar{y}$, which is simply the average of the n observed values $y_1, y_2, \ldots, y_n$. Here the error of prediction in predicting $y_i$ would be $(y_i - \bar{y})$. For example, Figure 3.13(a) illustrates the prediction errors obtained for the fuel consumption data when we do not use the information provided by the independent variable $x$, average hourly temperature.

Next, suppose we decide to employ the predictor variable $x$ and observe the values $x_1, x_2, \ldots, x_n$ corresponding to the observed values of $y$. In this case the prediction of $y_i$ is

$$\hat{y}_i = b_0 + b_1 x_i$$

and the error of prediction is $y_i - \hat{y}_i$. For example, Figure 3.13(b) illustrates the prediction errors obtained in the fuel consumption problem when we use the predictor variable $x$. Together, Figure 3.13(a) and (b) show the reduction in the prediction errors accomplished by employing the predictor variable $x$ (and the least squares line).

**FIGURE 3.13**
Reduction in
prediction errors
accomplished by
employing the
predictor variable $x$

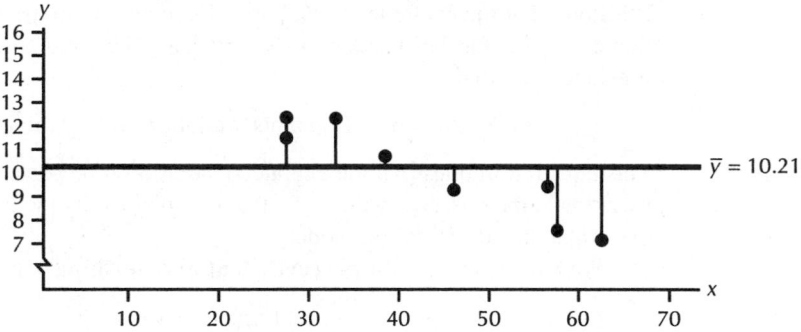

(a) Prediction errors for the fuel consumption problem when we do not use the information contributed by $x$

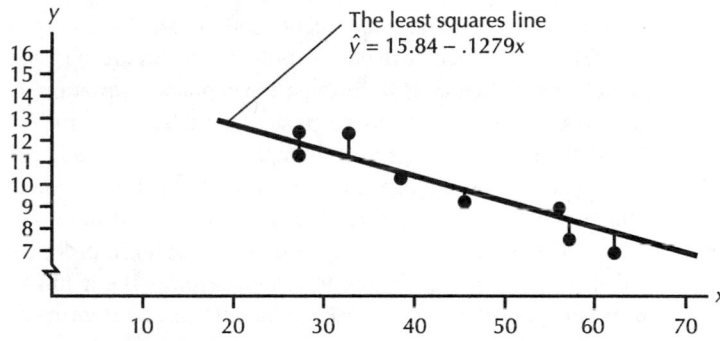

(b) Prediction errors for the fuel consumption problem when we use the information contributed by $x$ by using the least squares line

Using the predictor variable $x$ decreases the prediction error in predicting $y_i$ from $(y_i - \bar{y})$ to $(y_i - \hat{y}_i)$, or by an amount equal to

$$(y_i - \bar{y}) - (y_i - \hat{y}_i) = (\hat{y}_i - \bar{y})$$

It can be shown that in general

$$\sum (y_i - \bar{y})^2 - \sum (y_i - \hat{y}_i)^2 = \sum (\hat{y}_i - \bar{y})^2$$

The sum of squared prediction errors obtained when we do not employ the predictor variable $x$, $\sum(y_i - \bar{y})^2$, is called the **total variation.** It measures the total amount of variation exhibited by the observed values of $y$. The sum of squared prediction errors obtained when we use the predictor variable $x$, $\sum(y_i - \hat{y}_i)^2$, is called the **unexplained variation** (this is another name for SSE). It measures the amount of variation in the values of $y$ that is not explained by the predictor variable. The quantity $\sum(\hat{y}_i - \bar{y})^2$ is called the **explained variation.** Using these definitions and the above equation involving these summations, we see that

Total variation − Unexplained variation = Explained variation

It follows that the explained variation is the reduction in the sum of squared prediction errors that has been accomplished by using the predictor variable $x$ to predict $y$. It also follows that

$$\text{Total variation} = \text{Explained variation} + \text{Unexplained variation}$$

This equation implies that the explained variation represents the amount of the total variation in the observed values of $y$ that is explained by the predictor variable $x$ (and the simple linear regression model).

We now define the **simple coefficient of determination** to be

$$r^2 = \frac{\text{Explained variation}}{\text{Total variation}}$$

That is, $r^2$ is the proportion of the total variation in the $n$ observed values of $y$ that is explained by the simple linear regression model. Neither the explained variation nor the total variation can be negative (both quantities are sums of squares). Therefore, $r^2$ is greater than or equal to 0. Because the explained variation must be less than or equal to the total variation, $r^2$ cannot be greater than 1. The nearer $r^2$ is to 1, the larger is the proportion of the total variation that is explained by the model, and the greater is the utility of the model in predicting $y$. If the value of $r^2$ is not reasonably close to 1, the independent variable in the model does not provide accurate predictions of $y$. In such a case, a different predictor variable must be found in order to accurately predict $y$. It is also possible that no regression model employing a single predictor variable will accurately predict $y$. In this case the model must be improved by including more than one independent variable. We see how to do this in Chapter 4.

In the following box we summarize the results of this section.

---

**THE SIMPLE COEFFICIENT OF DETERMINATION, $r^2$**

For the simple linear regression model,

1. **Total variation** = $\sum(y_i - \bar{y})^2$
2. **Explained variation** = $\sum(\hat{y}_i - \bar{y})^2$
3. **Unexplained variation** = $\sum(y_i - \hat{y}_i)^2$
4. **Total variation = Explained variation + Unexplained variation**
5. The **simple coefficient of determination** is

$$r^2 = \frac{\text{Explained variation}}{\text{Total variation}}$$

6. $r^2$ is the proportion of the total variation in the $n$ observed values of the dependent variable that is explained by the simple linear regression model.

**EXAMPLE 3.13**   Below we present the middle portion of the MINITAB output for the fuel consumption data in Figure 3.9(a):

```
S = 0.654209    R-Sq = 89.9%    R-Sq(adj) = 88.3%


Analysis of Variance

Source           DF       SS       MS       F       P
Regression        1   22.981   22.981   53.69   0.000
Residual Error    6    2.568    0.428
Total             7   25.549
```

This output tells us that the explained variation is 22.981 (see "SS Regression"), the unexplained variation is 2.568 (see "SS Residual Error"), and the total variation is 25.549 (see "SS Total"). It follows that

$$r^2 = \frac{\text{Explained variation}}{\text{Total variation}} = \frac{22.981}{25.549} = .899$$

This value of $r^2$ says that the regression model explains 89.9% of the total variation in the eight observed fuel consumptions. Note that $r^2$ is given on the MINITAB output (see "R–Sq") and is expressed as a percentage. Also note that the quantities discussed here are given in the Excel output in Figure 3.9(b).

**EXAMPLE 3.14**   Below we present the top portion of the SAS output for the QHIC upkeep expenditure data in Figure 3.10

```
                       Analysis of Variance

                               Sum of         Mean
Source                DF      Squares        Square     F Value     Pr > F

Model                  1      6582760       6582760     305.06      <.0001
Error                 38       819996         21579
Corrected Total       39      7402755


         Root MSE            146.89735    R-Square      0.8892
         Dependent Mean      918.09150    Adj R-Sq      0.8863
         Coeff Var            16.00029
```

This output gives the explained variation, the unexplained variation, and the total variation under the respective headings "Sum of Squares/Model," "Sum of Squares/Error," and "Sum of Squares/Corrected Total." The output also tells us that $r^2$ equals .889. Therefore, the simple linear regression model that employs home value as a predictor variable explains 88.9% of the total variation in the 40 observed home upkeep expenditures.

Before continuing, note that in optional Section 3.9 we present some shortcut formulas for calculating the total, explained, and unexplained variations.

## The Simple Correlation Coefficient, $r$

People often claim that two variables are correlated. For example, a college admissions officer might feel that the academic performance of college students (measured by grade point average) is correlated with the students' scores on a standardized college entrance examination. This means that college students' grade point averages are related to their college entrance exam scores. One measure of the relationship between two variables $y$ and $x$ is the **simple correlation coefficient.** We define this quantity as follows:

---

**THE SIMPLE CORRELATION COEFFICIENT**

The **simple correlation coefficient between $y$ and $x$,** denoted by $r$, is

$$r = +\sqrt{r^2} \text{ if } b_1 \text{ is positive} \quad \text{and} \quad r = -\sqrt{r^2} \text{ if } b_1 \text{ is negative}$$

where $b_1$ is the slope of the least squares line relating $y$ to $x$. This correlation coefficient *measures the strength of the linear relationship between $y$ and $x$.*

---

Because $r^2$ is always between 0 and 1, the correlation coefficient $r$ is between $-1$ and 1. A value of $r$ near 0 implies little linear relationship between $y$ and $x$. A value of $r$ close to 1 says that $y$ and $x$ have a strong tendency to move together in a straight-line fashion with a positive slope and, therefore, that $y$ and $x$ are highly related and **positively correlated.** A value of $r$ close to $-1$ says that $y$ and $x$ have a strong tendency to move together in a straight-line fashion with a negative slope and, therefore, that $y$ and $x$ are highly related and **negatively correlated.** Figure 3.14 illustrates these relationships. Notice that when $r = 1$, $y$ and $x$ have a perfect linear relationship with a positive slope, whereas when $r = -1$, $y$ and $x$ have a perfect linear relationship with a negative slope.

**EXAMPLE 3.15**    In the fuel consumption problem we have previously found that $b_1 = -.1279$ and $r^2 = .899$. It follows that the simple correlation coefficient between $y$ (weekly fuel consumption) and $x$ (average hourly temperature) is

$$r = -\sqrt{r^2} = -\sqrt{.899} = -.948$$

This simple correlation coefficient says that $x$ and $y$ have a strong tendency to move together in a linear fashion with a negative slope. We have seen this tendency in Figure 3.1, which indicates that $y$ and $x$ are negatively correlated.

**FIGURE 3.14**
An illustration of
different values of
the simple
correlation
coefficient

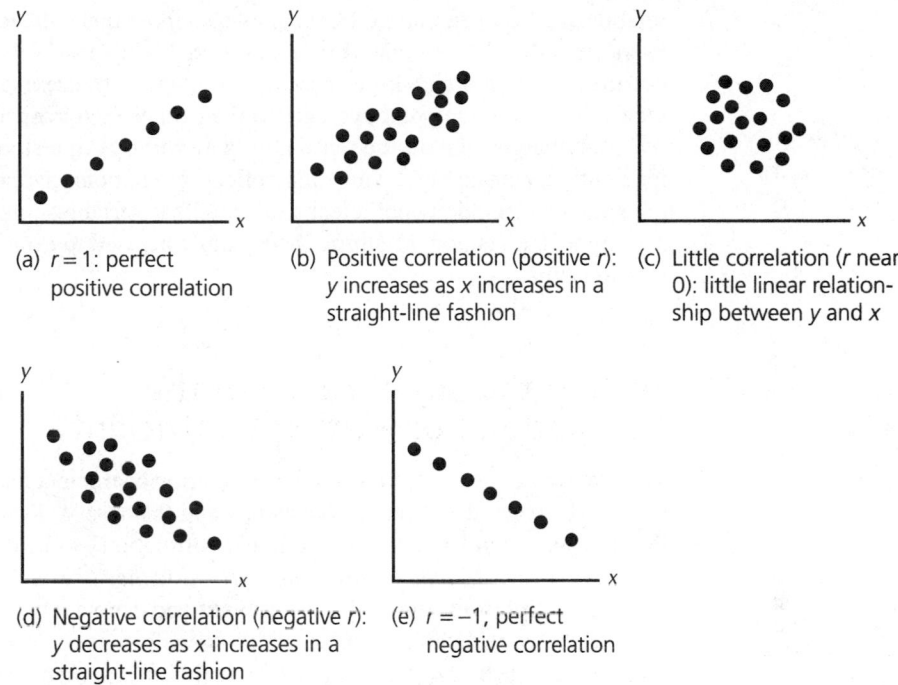

(a) $r = 1$: perfect
positive correlation

(b) Positive correlation (positive $r$):
$y$ increases as $x$ increases in a
straight-line fashion

(c) Little correlation ($r$ near
0): little linear relationship between $y$ and $x$

(d) Negative correlation (negative $r$):
$y$ decreases as $x$ increases in a
straight-line fashion

(e) $r = -1$, perfect
negative correlation

If we have computed the least squares slope $b_1$ and $r^2$, the method given in the previous box provides the easiest way to calculate $r$. The simple correlation coefficient can also be calculated using the formula

$$r = \frac{SS_{xy}}{\sqrt{SS_{xx}SS_{yy}}}$$

Here $SS_{xy}$ and $SS_{xx}$ have been defined in Section 3.2, and $SS_{yy}$ denotes the total variation, which has been defined in this section. Furthermore, this formula for $r$ automatically gives $r$ the correct (+ or −) sign. For instance, in the fuel consumption problem, $SS_{xy} = -179.6475$, $SS_{xx} = 1404.355$, and $SS_{yy} = 25.549$ (see Table 3.3 and Figure 3.9). Therefore

$$r = \frac{SS_{xy}}{\sqrt{SS_{xx}SS_{yy}}} = \frac{-179.6475}{\sqrt{(1404.355)(25.549)}} = -.948$$

It is important to make a couple of points. First, *the value of the simple correlation coefficient is not the slope of the least squares line*. If we wish to find this slope, we should use the previously given formula for $b_1$. Second, *high correlation does not imply that a cause-and-effect relationship exists*. When $r$ indicates that $y$ and $x$ are highly correlated, this says that $y$ and $x$ have a strong tendency to move together in a straight-line fashion. The correlation does not mean that changes in $x$ cause changes in $y$. Instead, some other variable (or variables) could be causing the apparent relationship between $y$ and $x$. For example, suppose that college students' grade point averages and college entrance exam scores are highly positively correlated. This does not mean that earning a high score on a college entrance exam causes students to receive a high grade point average. Rather, other factors such as intellectual ability, study habits, and attitude probably determine both a student's score on a college entrance exam and a student's college grade point average. In general, while the simple correlation coefficient can show that variables tend to move together in a straight-line fashion, scientific theory must be used to establish cause-and-effect relationships.

## Testing the Significance of the Population Correlation Coefficient

Thus far we have seen that the simple correlation coefficient measures the linear relationship between the observed values of $x$ and the observed values of $y$ that make up the sample. A similar coefficient of linear correlation can be defined for the population of *all possible combinations of observed values of x and y*. We call this coefficient the **population correlation coefficient** and denote it by the symbol $\rho$ (rho). We use $r$ as the point estimate of $\rho$. In addition, we can also carry out a hypothesis test. Here we test the *null hypothesis* $H_0$: $\rho = 0$, *which says there is no linear relationship between x and y*. We test $H_0$ against the *alternative* $H_a$: $\rho \neq 0$, *which says there is a positive or negative linear relationship between x and y*. This test can be done by using $r$ to compute the test statistic

$$t = \frac{r\sqrt{n-2}}{\sqrt{1-r^2}}$$

The test is based on the assumption that the population of all possible observed combinations of values of $x$ and $y$ has a *bivariate normal probability distribution*. See Wonnacott and Wonnacott (1981) for a discussion of this distribution. It can be shown that the preceding test statistic $t$ and the $p$-value used to test $H_0$: $\rho = 0$ versus $H_a$: $\rho \neq 0$ are equal to, respectively, the test statistic $t = b_1/s_{b_1}$ and the $p$-value used to test $H_0$: $\beta_1 = 0$ versus $H_a$: $\beta_1 \neq 0$, where $\beta_1$ is the slope in the simple linear regression model. Keep in mind, however, that although the mechanics involved in these hypothesis tests are the same, these tests are based on different assumptions (the test for significance of the slope is based on the regression assumptions). If the bivariate normal distribution assumption for the test concerning $\rho$ is badly violated, we can use a nonparametric approach to correlation—see Bowerman and O'Connell (2003).

**EXAMPLE 3.16**   Again consider testing the significance of the slope in the fuel consumption problem. Recall that in Example 3.7 we found that $t = -7.33$ and that the $p$-value related to this $t$ statistic is less than .001. We therefore (if the regression assumptions hold) can reject $H_0$: $\beta_1 = 0$

at level of significance .05, .01, or .001, and we have extremely strong evidence that $x$ is significantly related to $y$. This also implies (if the population of all possible observed combinations of $x$ and $y$ has a bivariate normal probability distribution) that we can reject $H_0$: $\rho = 0$ in favor of $H_a$: $\rho \neq 0$ at level of significance .05, .01, or .001. It follows that we have extremely strong evidence of a linear relationship, or correlation, between $x$ and $y$. Furthermore, because we have previously calculated $r$ to be $-.948$, we estimate that $x$ and $y$ are negatively correlated.

# 3.8 AN *F*-TEST FOR THE MODEL

In this section we discuss an *F*-test that can be used to test the significance of the regression relationship between $x$ and $y$. Sometimes people refer to this as testing the significance of the simple linear regression model. For simple linear regression, this test is another way to test the null hypothesis $H_0$: $\beta_1 = 0$ (the relationship between $x$ and $y$ is not significant) versus $H_a$: $\beta_1 \neq 0$ (the relationship between $x$ and $y$ is significant). If we can reject $H_0$ at level of significance $\alpha$, we often say that *the simple linear regression model is significant at level of significance $\alpha$*.

---

**AN *F*-TEST FOR THE SIMPLE LINEAR REGRESSION MODEL**

Suppose that the regression assumptions hold, and define the **overall *F*-statistic** to be

$$F(\text{model}) = \frac{\text{Explained variation}}{(\text{Unexplained variation}) / (n-2)}$$

Also define the *p*-value related to $F(\text{model})$ to be the area under the curve of the *F*-distribution (having 1 numerator and $n-2$ denominator degrees of freedom) to the right of $F(\text{model})$—*see* Figure 3.15(b).

We can reject $H_0$: $\beta_1 = 0$ in favor of $H_a$: $\beta_1 \neq 0$ at level of significance $\alpha$ if either of the following equivalent conditions hold:

1. $F(\text{model}) > F_{[\alpha]}$
2. *p*-value $< \alpha$

Here the point $F_{[\alpha]}$ is based on 1 numerator and $n-2$ denominator degrees of freedom.

The first condition in the box says we should reject $H_0$: $\beta_1 = 0$ (and conclude that the relationship between $x$ and $y$ is significant) when $F$(model) is large. This is intuitive because a large overall $F$-statistic would be obtained when the explained variation is large compared to the unexplained variation. This would occur if $x$ is significantly related to $y$, which would imply that the slope $\beta_1$ is not equal to 0. Figure 3.15(a) illustrates that we reject $H_0$ when $F$(model) is greater than $F_{[\alpha]}$. As can be seen in Figure 3.15(b), when $F$(model) is large, the related $p$-value is small. When the $p$-value is small enough [resulting from an $F$(model) statistic that is large enough], we reject $H_0$. Figure 3.15(b) illustrates that the second condition in the box ($p$-value $< \alpha$) is an equivalent way to carry out this test.

**EXAMPLE 3.17**   Consider the fuel consumption problem and the MINITAB output in Example 3.13 of the simple linear regression model relating weekly fuel consumption $y$ to average hourly

**FIGURE 3.15**
An $F$-test for the simple linear regression model

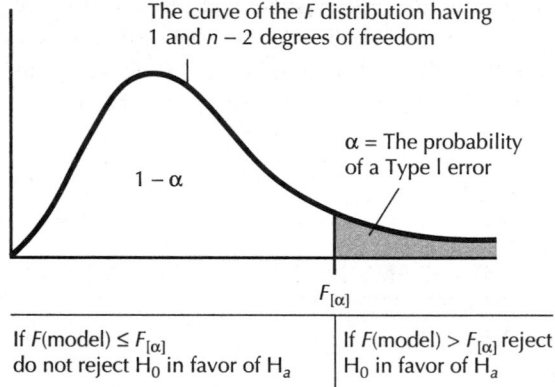

(a) The rejection point $F_{[\alpha]}$ based on setting the probability of a Type I error equal to $\alpha$

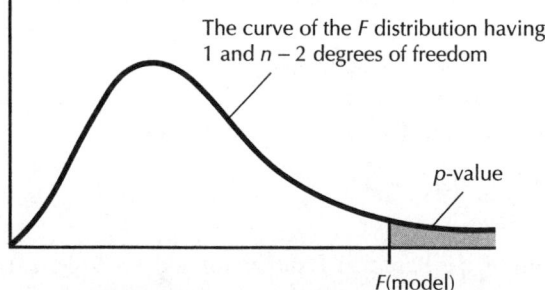

(b) If the $p$-value is smaller than $\alpha$, then $F$ (model) $> F_{[\alpha]}$ and we reject $H_0$.

temperature *x*. Looking at this output, we see that the explained variation is 22.981 and the unexplained variation is 2.568. It follows that

$$F(\text{model}) = \frac{\text{Explained variation}}{(\text{Unexplained variation})/(n-2)}$$

$$= \frac{22.981}{2.568/(8-2)} = \frac{22.981}{.428}$$

$$= 53.69$$

Note that this overall *F*-statistic is given on the MINITAB output (it is labeled "*F*"). The *p*-value related to *F*(model) is the area to the right of 53.69 under the curve of the *F*- distribution having 1 numerator and 6 denominator degrees of freedom. This *p*-value is also given on the MINITAB output (labeled "*P*"). Here MINITAB tells us that the *p*-value is .000 (which means less than .001). If we wish to test the significance of the regression relationship with level of significance $\alpha = .05$, we use the rejection point $F_{[.05]}$ based on 1 numerator and 6 denominator degrees of freedom. Using Table A3, we find that $F_{[.05]} = 5.99$. Since $F(\text{model}) = 53.69 > F_{[.05]} = 5.99$, we can reject $H_0: \beta_1 = 0$ in favor of $H_a: \beta_1 \neq 0$ at level of significance .05. Alternatively, since *p*-value = .000 is smaller than .05, .01, and .001, we can reject $H_0$ at level of significance .05, .01, or .001. Therefore, we have extremely strong evidence that $H_0: \beta_1 = 0$ should be rejected and that the regression relationship between *x* and *y* is significant. That is, we might say that we have extremely strong evidence that the simple linear model relating *y* to *x* is significant.

As another example, the SAS output in Example 3.14 tells us that for the QHIC simple linear regression model, *F*(model) is 305.06 and the related *p*-value is less than .0001. Here *F*(model) is labeled "F value." Because the *p*-value is less than .001, we have extremely strong evidence that the regression relationship is significant.

Testing the significance of the regression relationship between *y* and *x* by using the overall *F*-statistic and its related *p*-value is equivalent to doing this test by using the *t*-statistic and its related *p*-value. Specifically, it can be shown that $(t)^2 = F(\text{model})$ and that $(t_{[\alpha/2]}^{(n-2)})^2$, which is based on $n - 2$ degrees of freedom, equals $F_{[\alpha]}$ based on 1 numerator and $n - 2$ denominator degrees of freedom. It follows that the rejection point conditions

$$|t| > t_{[\alpha/2]}^{(n-2)} \quad \text{and} \quad F(\text{model}) > F_{[\alpha]}$$

are equivalent. Furthermore, the *p*-values related to *t* and *F*(model) can be shown to be equal. Because these tests are equivalent, it would be logical to ask why we have presented the *F*-test. There are two reasons. First, most standard regression computer packages include the results of the *F*-test as a part of the regression output. Second, the *F*-test has a useful generalization in multiple regression analysis (where we employ more than one predictor variable). The *F*-test in multiple regression is not equivalent to a *t*-test. This is further explained in Chapter 4.

# 3.9   SOME SHORTCUT FORMULAS

## Calculating the Sum of Squared Residuals

A shortcut formula for the sum of squared residuals is

$$SSE = SS_{yy} - \frac{SS_{xy}^2}{SS_{xx}}$$

where

$$SS_{yy} = \sum (y_i - \bar{y})^2 = \sum y_i^2 - \frac{\left(\sum y_i\right)^2}{n}$$

For example, consider the fuel consumption case. If we square each of the eight observed fuel consumptions in Table 3.1 and add up the resulting squared values, we find that $\sum y_i^2 = 859.91$. We have also found in Table 3.3 that $\sum y_i = 81.7$, $SS_{xy} = -179.6475$, and $SS_{xx} = 1404.355$. It follows that

$$SS_{yy} = \sum y_i^2 - \frac{\left(\sum y_i\right)^2}{n}$$

$$= 859.91 - \frac{(81.7)^2}{8} = 25.549$$

and

$$SSE = SS_{yy} - \frac{SS_{xy}^2}{SS_{xx}} = 25.549 - \frac{(-179.6475)^2}{1404.355}$$

$$= 25.549 - 22.981 = 2.568$$

Finally, note that $SS_{xy}^2/SS_{xx}$ equals $b_1 SS_{xy}$. However, we recommend using the first of these expressions, because doing so usually gives less round-off error.

## Calculating the Total, Explained, and Unexplained Variations

The *unexplained variation* is SSE, and thus the shortcut formula for SSE is a shortcut formula for the unexplained variation. The quantity $SS_{yy}$ is the *total variation,* and thus the shortcut formula for $SS_{yy}$ is a shortcut formula for the total variation. Lastly, it can be shown that the expression $SS_{xy}^2/SS_{xx}$ equals the *explained variation* and thus is a shortcut formula for this quantity.

# Exercises

**3.1** The chairman of the marketing department at a large state university undertakes a study to relate starting salary ($y$) after graduation for marketing majors to grade point average (GPA) in major courses. To do this, records of seven recent marketing graduates are randomly selected (Table 3.6).
a. Construct a scatter plot of $y$ versus $x$.
b. Using the scatter plot of $y$ versus $x$, explain why the simple linear regression model

$$y = \mu_{y|x} + \varepsilon$$
$$= \beta_0 + \beta_1 x + \varepsilon$$

might appropriately relate $y$ to $x$.

**3.2** Consider the simple linear regression model describing the starting salary data of Exercise 3.1.
a. Explain the meaning of $\mu_{y|x = 4.00} = \beta_0 + \beta_1(4.00)$.
b. Explain the meaning of $\mu_{y|x = 2.50} = \beta_0 + \beta_1(2.50)$.
c. Interpret the meaning of the slope parameter $\beta_1$.
d. Interpret the meaning of the $y$-intercept $\beta_0$. Why does this interpretation fail to make practical sense?
e. The error term $\varepsilon$ describes the effects of many factors on starting salary $y$. What are these factors? Give two specific examples.

**3.3** Use Figure 3.16, an output of the least squares prediction equation for the starting salary data, to do the following.
a. Identify and interpret the least squares point estimates $b_0$ and $b_1$. Does the interpretation of $b_0$ make practical sense?
b. Use the least squares line to obtain a point estimate of the mean starting salary for all marketing graduates having a grade point average of 3.25 and a point prediction of the starting salary for an individual marketing graduate having a grade point average of 3.25.
c. Verify that $b_0 = 14.8156$ and $b_1 = 5.70657$ by using the formulas in Section 3.2.

**3.4** Refer to the starting salary data of Exercise 3.1.
a. Given that SSE = 1.438, calculate $s^2$ and $s$.
b. Verify that SSE = 1.438 by using the formula in Section 3.4.

**3.5** Accu-Copiers, Inc., sells and services the Accu-500 copying machine. As part of its standard service

**TABLE 3.6** GPA and Starting Salary

| Marketing Graduate | GPA, $x$ | Starting Salary, $y$ ($\times$ \$1000) |
|---|---|---|
| 1 | 3.26 | 33.8 |
| 2 | 2.60 | 29.8 |
| 3 | 3.35 | 33.5 |
| 4 | 2.86 | 30.4 |
| 5 | 3.82 | 36.4 |
| 6 | 2.21 | 27.6 |
| 7 | 3.47 | 35.3 |

**FIGURE 3.16**

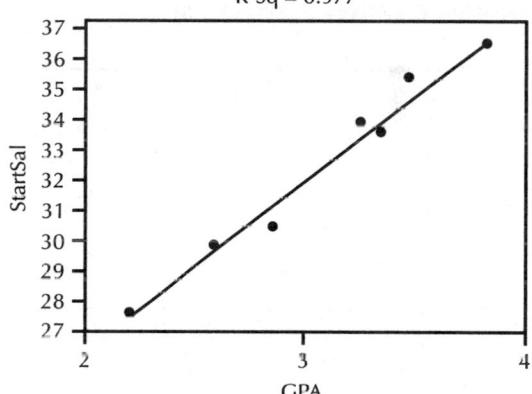

Regression Plot
Y = 14.8156 + 5.70657X
R-Sq = 0.977

contract, the company agrees to perform routine service on this copier. To obtain information about the time it takes to perform routine service, Accu-Copiers has collected data for 11 service calls. The data are shown in Table 3.7 (page 126) and plotted in Figure 3.17 (page 126).

Using the scatter plot of $y$ versus $x$, discuss why the simple linear regression model might appropriately relate $y$ to $x$.

**3.6** Consider the simple linear regression model describing the service time data in Exercise 3.5.
a. Explain the meaning of $\mu_{y|x = 4} = \beta_0 + \beta_1(4)$.
b. Explain the meaning of $\mu_{y|x = 6} = \beta_0 + \beta_1(6)$.
c. Interpret the meaning of the slope parameter $\beta_1$.
d. Interpret the meaning of the $y$-intercept $\beta_0$. Does this interpretation make practical sense?

**TABLE 3.7 (for Exercise 3.5)**
Copier Service Time

| Service Call | Number of Copiers Serviced, $x$ | Number of Minutes Required, $y$ |
|---|---|---|
| 1 | 4 | 109 |
| 2 | 2 | 58 |
| 3 | 5 | 138 |
| 4 | 7 | 189 |
| 5 | 1 | 37 |
| 6 | 3 | 82 |
| 7 | 4 | 103 |
| 8 | 5 | 134 |
| 9 | 2 | 68 |
| 10 | 4 | 112 |
| 11 | 6 | 154 |

**FIGURE 3.18**

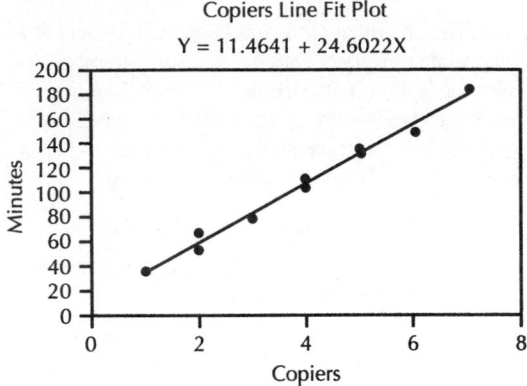

Copiers Line Fit Plot

$Y = 11.4641 + 24.6022X$

**FIGURE 3.17 (for Exercise 3.5)**

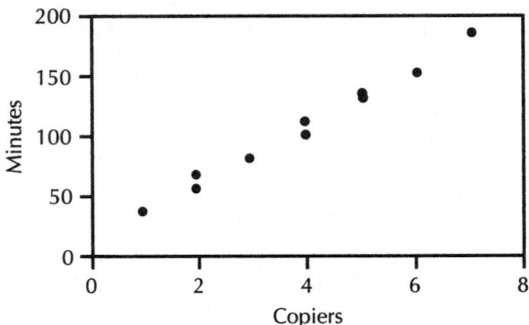

e.  The error term $\varepsilon$ describes the effects of many factors on service time. What are these factors? Give two specific examples.

**3.7** Use Figure 3.18, an output of the least squares prediction equation for the service time data, to do the following.

a.  Identify and interpret the least squares point estimates $b_0$ and $b_1$. Does the interpretation of $b_0$ make practical sense?

b.  Use the least squares line to obtain a point estimate of the mean time to service four copiers and a point prediction of the time to service four copiers on a single call.

c.  Verify that $b_0 = 11.4641$ and $b_1 = 24.6022$ by using the formulas in Section 3.2.

**3.8** Refer to the service time data in Exercise 3.5.

a.  Given that SSE = 191.70166, calculate $s^2$ and $s$.

b.  Verify that SSE = 191.70166 by using the formula in Section 3.4.

**3.9** Enterprise Industries produces Fresh, a brand of liquid laundry detergent. In order to study the relationship between price and demand for the large bottle of Fresh, the company has gathered the data in Table 3.8 concerning demand for Fresh over the last 30 sales periods (each sales period is four weeks). Here, for each sales period,

$y$ = demand for the large bottle of Fresh (in hundreds of thousands of bottles) in the sales period

$x_1$ = the price (in dollars) of Fresh as offered by Enterprise Industries in the sales period

$x_2$ = the average industry price (in dollars) of competitors' similar detergents in the sales period

$x_4 = x_2 - x_1$ = the "price difference" in the sales period

Note: We denote the "price difference" as $x_4$ (rather than, for example, $x_3$) to be consistent with other notation to be introduced in the Fresh detergent case in Example 4.12.

Using Figure 3.19, the scatter plot (from MINITAB) of $y$ versus $x_4$ shown below, discuss why the simple linear regression model might appropriately relate $y$ to $x_4$.

**3.10** Consider the simple linear regression model relating demand, $y$, to the price difference, $x_4$, and the Fresh demand data of Exercise 3.9.

a.  Explain the meaning of $\mu_{y|x_4=.10} = \beta_0 + \beta_1(.10)$.

b.  Explain the meaning of $\mu_{y|x_4=-.05} = \beta_0 + \beta_1(-.05)$.

**TABLE 3.8** Fresh Detergent Demand Data

| Sales Period | $x_1$ | $x_2$ | $x_4 = x_2 - x_1$ | $y$ | Sales Period | $x_1$ | $x_2$ | $x_4 = x_2 - x_1$ | $y$ |
|---|---|---|---|---|---|---|---|---|---|
| 1 | 3.85 | 3.80 | −.05 | 7.38 | 16 | 3.80 | 4.10 | .30 | 8.87 |
| 2 | 3.75 | 4.00 | .25 | 8.51 | 17 | 3.70 | 4.20 | .50 | 9.26 |
| 3 | 3.70 | 4.30 | .60 | 9.52 | 18 | 3.80 | 4.30 | .50 | 9.00 |
| 4 | 3.70 | 3.70 | 0 | 7.50 | 19 | 3.70 | 4.10 | .40 | 8.75 |
| 5 | 3.60 | 3.85 | .25 | 9.33 | 20 | 3.80 | 3.75 | −.05 | 7.95 |
| 6 | 3.60 | 3.80 | .20 | 8.28 | 21 | 3.80 | 3.75 | −.05 | 7.65 |
| 7 | 3.60 | 3.75 | .15 | 8.75 | 22 | 3.75 | 3.65 | −.10 | 7.27 |
| 8 | 3.80 | 3.85 | .05 | 7.87 | 23 | 3.70 | 3.90 | .20 | 8.00 |
| 9 | 3.80 | 3.65 | −.15 | 7.10 | 24 | 3.55 | 3.65 | .10 | 8.50 |
| 10 | 3.85 | 4.00 | .15 | 8.00 | 25 | 3.60 | 4.10 | .50 | 8.75 |
| 11 | 3.90 | 4.10 | .20 | 7.89 | 26 | 3.65 | 4.25 | .60 | 9.21 |
| 12 | 3.90 | 4.00 | .10 | 8.15 | 27 | 3.70 | 3.65 | −.05 | 8.27 |
| 13 | 3.70 | 4.10 | .40 | 9.10 | 28 | 3.75 | 3.75 | 0 | 7.67 |
| 14 | 3.75 | 4.20 | .45 | 8.86 | 29 | 3.80 | 3.85 | .05 | 7.93 |
| 15 | 3.75 | 4.10 | .35 | 8.90 | 30 | 3.70 | 4.25 | .55 | 9.26 |

**FIGURE 3.19**

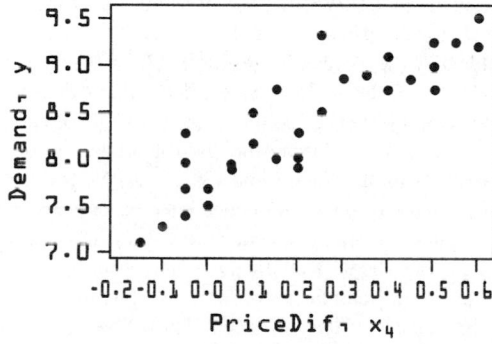

**FIGURE 3.20**

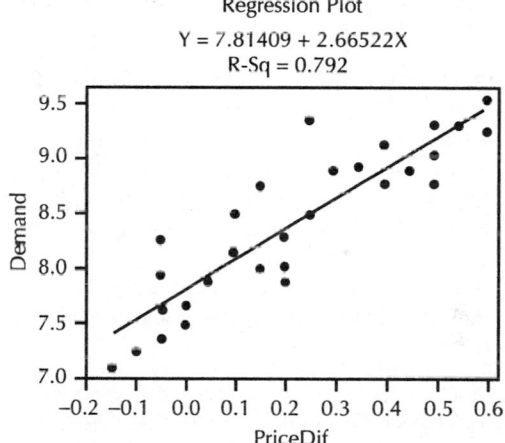

c. Explain the meaning of the slope parameter $\beta_1$.
d. Explain the meaning of the intercept $\beta_0$. Does this explanation make practical sense?
e. What factors are represented by the error term in this model? Give two specific examples.

**3.11** Use Figure 3.20, an output of the least squares prediction equation for the fresh demand data, to do the following.
a. Identify and interpret the least squares point estimates $b_0$ and $b_1$. Does the interpretation of $b_0$ make practical sense?
b. Use the least squares line to obtain a point estimate of the mean demand in all sales periods when the

price difference is .10 and a point prediction of the actual demand in an individual sales period when the price difference is .10.
c. If Enterprise Industries wishes to maintain a price difference that corresponds to a predicted demand of 850,000 bottles (that is, $\hat{y} = 8.5$), what should this price difference be?
d. Given that SSE = 2.8059, calculate $s^2$ and $s$.

**3.12** An accountant wishes to predict direct labor cost ($y$) on the basis of the batch size ($x$) of a product

**TABLE 3.9** Direct Labor Cost Data

| Direct Labor Cost, $y$ (× \$100) | Batch Size, $x$ |
|---|---|
| 71 | 5 |
| 663 | 62 |
| 381 | 35 |
| 138 | 12 |
| 861 | 83 |
| 145 | 14 |
| 493 | 46 |
| 548 | 52 |
| 251 | 23 |
| 1024 | 100 |
| 435 | 41 |
| 772 | 75 |

produced in a job shop. Data for 12 production runs are given in Table 3.9.

a. Construct a scatter plot of $y$ versus $x$.

b. Discuss whether the scatter plot suggests that a simple linear regression model might appropriately relate $y$ to $x$.

**3.13** Consider the simple linear regression model describing the direct labor cost data of Exercise 3.12.

a. Explain the meaning of $\mu_{y|x=60} = \beta_0 + \beta_1(60)$.

b. Explain the meaning of $\mu_{y|x=30} = \beta_0 + \beta_1(30)$.

c. Explain the meaning of the slope parameter $\beta_1$.

d. Explain the meaning of the intercept $\beta_0$. Does this explanation make practical sense?

e. What factors are represented by the error term in this model? Give two specific examples of these factors.

**3.14** Consider the direct labor cost data given in Table 3.9, and suppose that a simple linear regression model is appropriate.

a. Verify that $b_0 = 18.48751$ and $b_1 = 10.14626$ by using the formulas from Section 3.2.

b. Interpret the meanings of $b_0$ and $b_1$. Does the interpretation of $b_0$ make practical sense?

c. Write the least squares prediction equation.

d. Use the least squares line to obtain a point estimate of the mean direct labor cost for all batches of size 60 and a point prediction of the direct labor cost for an individual batch of size 60.

**3.15** Refer to the direct labor cost data in Table 3.9.

a. Given that SSE = 747, calculate $s^2$ and $s$.

b. Verify that SSE = 747 by using the formula in Section 3.4.

**In Exercises 3.16 through 3.19, we refer to Figures 3.21–3.24, which give MINITAB and SAS output of simple linear regression analyses of the data sets related to the four situations introduced in the previous exercises. Using the appropriate output for each data set,**

a. Identify the least squares point estimates $b_0$ and $b_1$ of $\beta_0$ and $\beta_1$.

b. Identify SSE, $s^2$, and $s$.

c. Identify $s_{b_1}$ and the $t$-statistic for testing the significance of the slope. Show how $t$ has been calculated by using $b_1$ and $s_{b_1}$.

d. Using the $t$-statistic and appropriate rejection points, test $H_0$: $\beta_1 = 0$ versus $H_a$: $\beta_1 \neq 0$ by setting $\alpha$ equal to .05. What do you conclude about the relationship between $y$ and $x$?

e. Using the $t$-statistic and appropriate rejection points, test $H_0$: $\beta_1 = 0$ versus $H_a$: $\beta_1 \neq 0$ by setting $\alpha$ equal to .01. What do you conclude about the relationship between $y$ and $x$?

f. Identify the $p$-value for testing $H_0$: $\beta_1 = 0$ versus $H_a$: $\beta_1 \neq 0$. Using the $p$-value, determine whether we can reject $H_0$ by setting $\alpha$ equal to .10, .05, .01, and .001. What do you conclude about the relationship between $y$ and $x$?

g. Calculate the 95% confidence interval for $\beta_1$. Discuss one practical application of this interval.

h. Calculate the 99% confidence interval for $\beta_1$.

i. Identify $s_{b_0}$ and the $t$-statistic for testing the significance of the $y$ intercept. Show how $t$ has been calculated using $b_0$ and $s_{b_0}$.

j. Identify the $p$-value for testing $H_0$: $\beta_0 = 0$ versus $H_a$: $\beta_0 \neq 0$. Using the $p$-value, determine whether we can reject $H_0$ by setting $\alpha$ equal to .10, .05, .01, and .001. What do you conclude?

k. Using the appropriate data set, show how $s_{b_1}$ has been calculated. Hint: Calculate $SS_{xx}$.

**3.16** The MINITAB output of a simple linear regression analysis of the starting salary data (see Table 3.6 on page 125) is given in Figure 3.21. Recall that a labeled MINITAB regression output is in Figure 3.9 of Section 3.5.

**3.17** The SAS output of a simple linear regression analysis of the service time data (see Table 3.7 on

**FIGURE 3.21 (for Exercises 3.16, 3.20, 3.24, and 3.28)** MINITAB output of a simple linear regression analysis of the starting salary data

```
The regression equation is
SALARY = 14.8 + 5.71 GPA


Predictor    Coef   SE Coef       T      P
Constant   14.816     1.235   12.00  0.000
GPA        5.7066    0.3953   14.44  0.000


S = 0.536321    R-Sq = 97.7%    R-Sq(adj) = 97.2%


Analysis of Variance

Source            DF       SS       MS       F      P
Regression         1   59.942   59.942  208.39  0.000
Residual Error     5    1.438    0.288
Total              6   61.380

     Fit   SE Fit       95% CI            95% PI
  33.362    0.213   (32.813, 33.910)   (31.878, 34.846)
```

**FIGURE 3.22 (for Exercises 3.17, 3.21, 3.25, and 3.29)** SAS output of a simple linear regression analysis of the service time data

```
                           Analysis of Variance

                                    Sum of        Mean
  Source               DF          Squares      Square    F Value    Pr > F

  Model                 1            19919       19919     935.15    <.0001
  Error                 9        191.70166    21.30018
  Corrected Total      10            20111


              Root MSE          4.61521     R-Square    0.9905
              Dependent Mean  107.63636     Adj R-Sq    0.9894
              Coeff Var         4.28778


                          Parameter Estimates

                                 Parameter    Standard
  Variable    Label     DF        Estimate       Error    t Value    Pr > |t|

  Intercept   Intercept  1        11.46409     3.43903       3.33      0.0087
  Copiers     Copiers    1        24.60221     0.80451      30.58     <.0001

         Dep Var  Predicted    Std Error
  Obs    Minutes      Value  Mean Predict     95% CL Mean       95% CL Predict
   12          .   109.8729        1.3935  106.7207  113.0252  98.9671  120.7788
   13          .   134.4751        1.6452  130.7535  138.1968  123.3913  145.5590
```

**FIGURE 3.23 (for Exercises 3.18, 3.22, 3.26, and 3.30)** MINITAB output of a simple regression analysis of the Fresh detergent demand data

```
The regression equation is
Demand = 7.81 + 2.67 PriceDif


Predictor      Coef   SE Coef       T       P
Constant    7.81409   0.07988   97.82   0.000
PriceDif     2.6652    0.2585   10.31   0.000


S = 0.316561   R-Sq = 79.2%   R-Sq(adj) = 78.4%


Analysis of Variance

Source          DF      SS      MS       F       P
Regression       1  10.653  10.653  106.30   0.000
Residual Error  28   2.806   0.100
Total           29  13.459

   Fit   SE Fit      95% CI            95% PI
8.0806   0.0648  (7.9479, 8.2133)  (7.4187, 8.7425)
8.4804   0.0586  (8.3604, 8.6004)  (7.8209, 9.1398)
```

**FIGURE 3.24 (for Exercises 3.19, 3.23, 3.27, and 3.31)** SAS output of a simple linear regression analysis of the direct labor cost data

```
                          Analysis of Variance

                                 Sum of          Mean
Source                DF        Squares        Square    F Value   Pr > F

Model                  1        1024593       1024593    13720.5   <.0001
Error                 10      746.76238      74.67624
Corrected Total       11        1025340


              Root MSE            8.64154   R-Square   0.9993
              Dependent Mean    481.83333   Adj R-Sq   0.9992
              Coeff Var           1.79347


                        Parameter Estimates

                              Parameter       Standard
Variable    Label     DF       Estimate          Error   t Value   Pr > |t|

Intercept   Intercept  1       18.48751        4.67658      3.95     0.0027
Bsize       Bsize      1       10.14626        0.08662    117.13     <.0001

        Dep Var  Predicted   Std Error
  Obs      Cost  Value Mean Predict      95% CL Mean       95% CL Predict
   13        .   627.2630      2.7865   621.0544  633.4717   607.0322  647.4939
```

page 126) is given in Figure 3.22 (page 129). Recall that a labeled SAS regression output is in Figure 3.10 of Section 3.5.

**3.18** The MINITAB output of a simple linear regression analysis of the Fresh detergent data (see Table 3.8 on page 127) is given in Figure 3.23. Recall that a labeled MINITAB regression output is in Figure 3.9 of Section 3.5.

**3.19** The SAS output of a simple linear regression analysis of the direct labor cost data (see Table 3.9 on page 128) is given in Figure 3.24. Recall that a labeled SAS regression output is in Figure 3.10 of Section 3.5.

**3.20** The information at the bottom of the MINITAB output for the starting salary data in Figure 3.21 (page 129) relates to marketing graduates having a grade point average of 3.25.
a. Report a point estimate of and a 95% confidence interval for the mean starting salary of all marketing graduates having a grade point average of 3.25.
b. Report a point prediction of and a 95% prediction interval for the starting salary of an individual marketing graduate having a grade point average of 3.25.
c. Verify the results in (a) and (b) (within rounding) by hand calculation.

**3.21** The information at the bottom of the SAS output for the service time data in Figure 3.22 (page 129) corresponds to future service calls in which the number of copiers will be 4 and 5, respectively.
a. Report a point estimate of and a 95% confidence interval for the mean time to service four copiers.
b. Report a point prediction of and a 95% prediction interval for the time to service four copiers on a single call.
c. If we examine the service time data, we see that there was at least one call on which Accu-Copiers serviced each of 1, 2, 3, 4, 5, 6, and 7 copiers. The 95% confidence intervals for the mean service times on these calls might be used to schedule future service calls. To understand this, note that a person making service calls will (in, say, a year or more) make a very large number of service calls. Some of the person's individual service times will be below, and some will be above, the corresponding mean service times. However, since the very large number of individual service times will average out to the mean service times, it seems fair to both the efficiency of the company and to the person

making service calls to schedule service calls by using estimates of the mean service times. Therefore, suppose we wish to schedule a call to service five copiers. Examining the SAS output, we see that a 95% confidence interval for the mean time to service five copiers is [130.7535, 138.1968]. Since the mean time might be 138.1968 minutes, it would seem fair to allow 138 minutes to make the service call. Now suppose we wish to schedule a call to service four copiers. Determine how many minutes to allow for the service call.

**3.22** The information at the bottom of the MINITAB output for the Fresh demand data in Figure 3.23 corresponds to future sales periods in which the price difference will be .10 and .25, respectively.
a. Report a point estimate of and a 95% confidence interval for the mean demand for Fresh in all sales periods when the price difference is .10.
b. Report a point prediction of and a 95% prediction interval for the actual demand for Fresh in an individual sales period when the price difference is .10.
c. Locate the confidence interval and prediction interval you found in parts (a) and (b) on the MINITAB output in Figure 3.25 below.
d. Find 99% confidence and prediction intervals for the mean and actual demands referred to in parts (a) and (b). Hint: Solve for the distance value—see Example 3.11.
e. Repeat parts (a), (b), (c), and (d) for sales periods in which the price difference is .25.

**FIGURE 3.25**

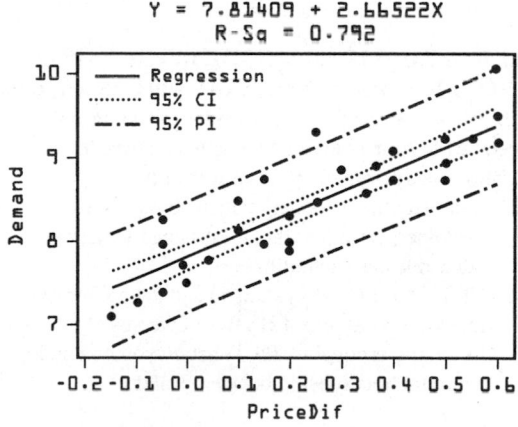

$$Y = 7.81409 + 2.66522X$$
$$R\text{-}Sq = 0.792$$

**3.23** The information on the bottom of the SAS output for the direct labor cost data in Figure 3.24 (page 130) relates to a batch of size 60.

a. Report a point estimate of and a 95% confidence interval for the mean direct labor cost of all batches of size 60.

b. Report a point estimate of and a 95% prediction interval for the actual direct labor cost of an individual batch of size 60.

c. Find 99% confidence and prediction intervals for the mean and actual direct labor costs referred to in parts (a) and (b). Hint: Solve for the distance value—see Example 3.11.

**In Exercises 3.24 through 3.27, we refer to Figures 3.21–3.24, which give MINITAB and SAS output of simple linear regression analyses of the data sets related to four previously discussed situations.**

a. Find the total variation, the unexplained variation, the explained variation, the simple coefficient of determination ($r^2$), and the simple correlation coefficient ($r$). Interpret $r^2$.

b. Using a $t$-statistic involving $r$ and appropriate rejection points, test $H_0: \rho = 0$ versus $H_a: \rho \neq 0$ by setting $\alpha$ equal to .05 and by setting $\alpha$ equal to .01. What do you conclude?

**3.24** Use the MINITAB output in Figure 3.21 (page 129) for the starting salary data.

**3.25** Use the SAS output in Figure 3.22 (page 129) for the service time data.

**3.26** Use the MINITAB output in Figure 3.23 (page 130) for the Fresh demand data.

**3.27** Use the SAS output in Figure 3.24 (page 130) for the direct labor cost data.

**In Exercises 3.28 through 3.31, we refer to Figures 3.21–3.24, which give MINITAB and SAS output of simple linear regression analyses of the data sets related to four previously discussed situations. Using the appropriate computer output,**

a. Calculate the $F$(model) statistic by using the explained variation, the unexplained variation, and other relevant quantities.

b. Utilize the $F$(model) statistic and the appropriate rejection point to test $H_0: \beta_1 = 0$ versus $H_a: \beta_1 \neq 0$ by setting $\alpha$ equal to .05. What do you conclude about the relationship between $y$ and $x$?

c. Utilize the $F$(model) statistic and the appropriate rejection point to test $H_0: \beta_1 = 0$ versus $H_a: \beta_1 \neq 0$ by setting $\alpha$ equal to .01. What do you conclude about the relationship between $y$ and $x$?

d. Find the $p$-value related to $F$(model). Using the $p$-value, determine whether we can reject $H_0: \beta_1 = 0$ in favor of $H_a: \beta_1 \neq 0$ by setting $\alpha$ equal to .10, .05, .01, and .001. What do you conclude?

e. Show that the $F$(model) statistic is the square of the $t$-statistic for testing $H_0: \beta_1 = 0$ versus $H_a: \beta_1 \neq 0$. Also, show that the $F_{[.05]}$ rejection point is the square of the $t_{[.025]}^{(n-2)}$ rejection point.

**3.28** Use the MINITAB output in Figure 3.21 (page 129) for the starting salary data.

**3.29** Use the SAS output in Figure 3.22 (page 129) for the service time data.

**3.30** Use the MINITAB output in Figure 3.23 (page 130) for the Fresh demand data.

**3.31** Use the SAS output in Figure 3.24 (page 130) for the direct labor cost data.

**3.32** On January 28, 1986, the space shuttle *Challenger* exploded soon after takeoff, killing all eight astronauts aboard. The temperature at the Kennedy Space Center at liftoff was 31°F. Before the launch, several scientists argued that the launch should be delayed because the shuttle's O-rings might harden in the cold and leak. Other scientists used the data plot in Figure 3.26 to argue that there was no relationship between temperature and O-ring failure. On the basis of this figure and other considerations, *Challenger* was launched to its disastrous last flight.

Scientists using the data plot in Figure 3.26 made a horrible mistake. They relied on a data plot that was

**FIGURE 3.26** A data plot based on seven launches

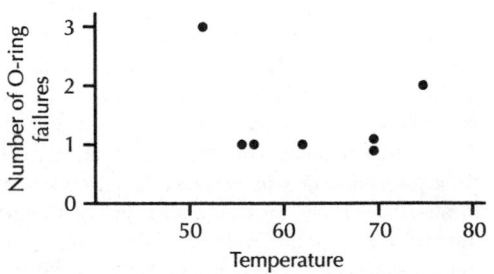

**FIGURE 3.27** A data plot based on all 24 launches

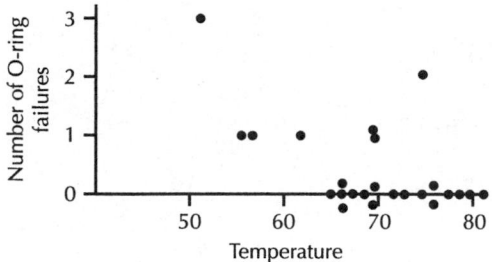

**TABLE 3.10** The Smoking and Lung Cancer Death Data

| Occupational Group | Smoking Index | Lung Cancer Death Index |
|---|---|---|
| Farmers, foresters, and fishermen | 77 | 84 |
| Miners and quarrymen | 137 | 116 |
| Gas, coke, and chemical makers | 117 | 123 |
| Glass and ceramics makers | 94 | 128 |
| Furnace, forge, foundry, and rolling mill workers | 116 | 155 |
| Electrical and electronics workers | 102 | 101 |
| Engineering and allied trades | 111 | 118 |
| Woodworkers | 93 | 113 |
| Leather workers | 88 | 104 |
| Textile workers | 102 | 88 |
| Clothing workers | 91 | 104 |
| Food, drink, and tobacco workers | 104 | 129 |
| Paper and printing workers | 107 | 86 |
| Makers of other products | 112 | 96 |
| Construction workers | 113 | 144 |
| Painters and decorators | 110 | 139 |
| Drivers of stationary engines, cranes, etc. | 125 | 113 |
| Laborers not included elsewhere | 133 | 146 |
| Transport and communications workers | 115 | 128 |
| Warehousemen, storekeepers, packers, and bottlers | 105 | 115 |
| Clerical workers | 87 | 79 |
| Sales workers | 91 | 85 |
| Service, sport, and recreation workers | 100 | 120 |
| Administrators and managers | 76 | 60 |
| Professionals, technical workers, and artists | 66 | 51 |

created by using only the seven previous launches where there was at least one O-ring failure. A plot based on all 24 previous launches—17 of which had no O-ring failures—is given in Figure 3.27.

a. Intuitively, do you think that Figure 3.27 indicates that there is a relationship between temperature and O-ring failure? Use simple linear regression to justify your answer.

b. Even though the figure using only seven launches is incomplete, what about it should have cautioned the scientists not to make the launch?

**3.33** The data in Table 3.10 concerning the relationship between smoking and lung cancer death were presented in a course of The Open University, *Statistics in Society,* Unit C4, The Open University Press, Milton Keynes, England, 1983. The original source of the data is *Occupational Mortality: The Registrar General's Decennial Supplement for England and Wales, 1970–1972,* Her Majesty's Stationery Office, London, 1978. In the table, a smoking index value greater (less) than 100 indicates that men in the occupational group smoke more (less) than average when compared to all men of the same age. Similarly for lung cancer deaths, an index value greater (less) than 100 indicates that men in the occupational group have a greater (less) than average lung cancer death rate when compared to all men of the same age. In Figure 3.28 (page 134) we present a portion of a MINITAB output of a simple linear regression analysis relating the lung cancer death index to the smoking index. In Figure 3.29 (page 134) we present a plot of the lung cancer death index versus the smoking index.

a. Although the data do not prove that smoking increases your chance of getting lung cancer, can you think of a third factor that would cause the two indexes to move together?

**FIGURE 3.28 (for Exercise 3.33)** MINITAB output of a simple linear regression analysis of the data in Table 3.10

```
The regression equation is
DeathIdx = -2.9 + 1.09 SmokeIdx

Predictor          Coef        SE Coef              T            P
Constant          -2.89          23.03          -0.13        0.901
SmokeIdx          1.0875        0.2209           4.92        0.000

S = 18.62         R-Sq = 51.3%          R-Sq(adj) = 49.2%
```

**FIGURE 3.29 (for Exercise 3.33)** A plot of the lung cancer death index versus the smoking index

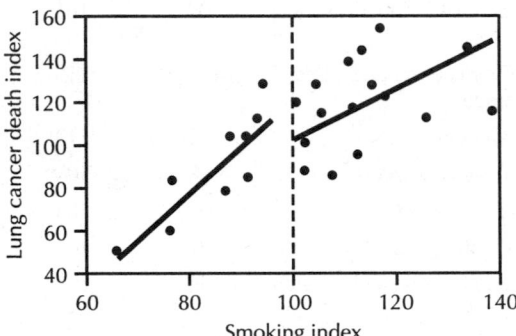

b. Does the slope of the hypothetical line relating the two indexes when the smoking index is less than 100 seem to equal the slope of the hypothetical line relating the two indexes when the smoking index is greater than 100? If you wish, use simple linear regression to make a more precise determination. What practical conclusion might you make?

**3.34** In New Jersey, banks have been charged with withdrawing from counties having a high percentage of minorities. To substantiate this charge, P. D'Ambrosio and S. Chambers (1995) present the data in Table 3.11 concerning the percentage, $x$, of minority population and the number of county residents, $y$, per bank branch in each of New Jersey's 21 counties. If we use Excel to perform a simple linear regression analysis of this data, we obtain the output given in Figure 3.30.
a. Determine if there is a significant relationship between $x$ and $y$.
b. Describe the exact nature of any relationship that exists between $x$ and $y$. (Hint: Estimate $\beta_1$ by a point estimate and a confidence interval.)

**TABLE 3.11 The New Jersey Bank Data**

| County | Percentage of Minority Population, $x$ | Number of Residents Per Bank Branch, $y$ |
|---|---|---|
| Atlantic | 23.3 | 3,073 |
| Bergen | 13.0 | 2,095 |
| Burlington | 17.8 | 2,905 |
| Camden | 23.4 | 3,330 |
| Cape May | 7.3 | 1,321 |
| Cumberland | 26.5 | 2,557 |
| Essex | 48.8 | 3,474 |
| Gloucester | 10.7 | 3,068 |
| Hudson | 33.2 | 3,683 |
| Hunterdon | 3.7 | 1,998 |
| Mercer | 24.9 | 2,607 |
| Middlesex | 18.1 | 3,154 |
| Monmouth | 12.6 | 2,609 |
| Morris | 8.2 | 2,253 |
| Ocean | 4.7 | 2,317 |
| Passaic | 28.1 | 3,307 |
| Salem | 16.7 | 2,511 |
| Somerset | 12.0 | 2,333 |
| Sussex | 2.4 | 2,568 |
| Union | 25.6 | 3,048 |
| Warren | 2.8 | 2,349 |

*Source*: P. D'Ambrosio and S. Chambers, "No Checks and Balances," *Asbury Park Press*, September 10, 1995. Copyright ©1995 Asbury Park Press.

**3.35** The State Department of Taxation wishes to investigate the effect of experience, $x$, on the amount of time, $y$, required to fill out Form ST 1040AVG, the state income-averaging form. In order to do this, nine people whose financial status makes income averaging advantageous are chosen at random. Each is asked to fill out Form ST 1040AVG and to report (1) the time $y$ (in hours) required to complete the form and (2) the number of times $x$ (including this one) that he or she has filled out this form. The following data are obtained:

**FIGURE 3.30** Excel output of a simple linear regression analysis of the New Jersey bank data

### Regression Statistics

| | |
|---|---|
| Multiple R | 0.72562918 |
| R Square | 0.52653771 |
| Adjusted R Square | 0.50161864 |
| Standard Error | 400.254553 |
| Observations | 21 |

### ANOVA

| | df | SS | MS | F | Significance F |
|---|---|---|---|---|---|
| Regression | 1 | 3385090.234 | 3385090 | 21.129912 | 0.000196916 |
| Residual | 19 | 3043870.432 | 160203.7 | | |
| Total | 20 | 6428960.667 | | | |

| | Coefficients | Standard Error | t Stat | P-Value | Lower 95% | Upper 95% |
|---|---|---|---|---|---|---|
| Intercept | 2082.01531 | 159.1069986 | 13.08563 | 5.921E-11 | 1749.000427 | 2415.03018 |
| PCT | 35.2877366 | 7.676706896 | 4.596728 | 0.0001969 | 19.22019946 | 51.3552738 |

**FIGURE 3.31** Plot of y versus x in Exercise 3.35

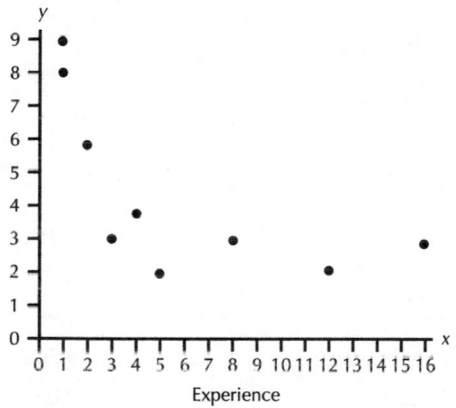

Experience

**FIGURE 3.32** Plot of y versus 1/x in Exercise 3.35

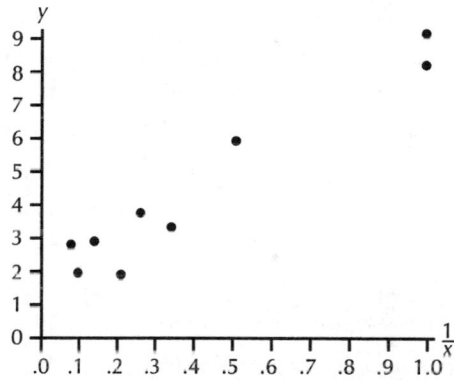

| Completion time, y (in Hours) | 8.0 | 4.7 | 3.7 | 2.8 | 8.9 |
|---|---|---|---|---|---|
| Experience, x | 1 | 8 | 4 | 16 | 1 |
| | 5.8 | 2.0 | 1.9 | 3.3 | |
| | 2 | 12 | 5 | 3 | |

A plot of these data is given in Figure 3.31 and indicates that the model

$$y = \mu_{y|x} + \varepsilon = \beta_0 + \beta_1\left(\frac{1}{x}\right) + \varepsilon$$

might appropriately relate y to x. To understand this model, note that as x increases, 1/x decreases and thus

$\mu_{y|x}$ decreases. This seems to be what the data plot indicates is happening. To further understand this model, note that a plot of the values of y versus the values of 1/x in Figure 3.32 has a straight-line appearance. This indicates that a simple linear regression model having y as the dependent variable and 1/x as the independent variable—that is, the model we are considering—might be appropriate. Using the formulas of simple linear regression analysis, the least squares point estimates of $\beta_0$ and $\beta_1$ can be calculated to be $b_0 = 2.0572$ and $b_1 = 6.3545$. Furthermore, consider the completion time of an individual filling out the form for the fifth time (that

**TABLE 3.12 (for Exercise 3.36) Accounting Rates on Stocks and Market Returns for 54 Companies**

| Company | Market Rate | Accounting Rate | Company | Market Rate | Accounting Rate |
|---|---|---|---|---|---|
| McDonnell Douglas | 17.73 | 17.96 | Caterpillar Tractor | 13.38 | 17.66 |
| NCR | 4.54 | 8.11 | Georgia Pacific | 13.43 | 14.59 |
| Honeywell | 3.96 | 12.46 | Minnesota Mining & Manufacturing | 10.00 | 20.94 |
| TRW | 8.12 | 14.70 | Standard Oil (Ohio) | 16.66 | 9.62 |
| Raytheon | 6.78 | 11.90 | American Brands | 9.40 | 16.32 |
| W. R. Grace | 9.69 | 9.67 | Aluminum Company of America | .24 | 8.19 |
| Ford Motors | 12.37 | 13.35 | General Electric | 4.37 | 15.74 |
| Textron | 15.88 | 16.11 | General Tire | 3.11 | 12.02 |
| Lockheed Aircraft | −1.34 | 6.78 | Borden | 6.63 | 11.44 |
| Getty Oil | 18.09 | 9.41 | American Home Products | 14.73 | 32.58 |
| Atlantic Richfield | 17.17 | 8.96 | Standard Oil (California) | 6.15 | 11.89 |
| Radio Corporation of America | 6.78 | 14.17 | International Paper | 5.96 | 10.06 |
| Westinghouse Electric | 4.74 | 9.12 | National Steel | 6.30 | 9.60 |
| Johnson & Johnson | 23.02 | 14.23 | Republic Steel | .68 | 7.41 |
| Champion International | 7.68 | 10.43 | Warner Lambert | 12.22 | 19.88 |
| R. J. Reynolds | 14.32 | 19.74 | U.S. Steel | .90 | 6.97 |
| General Dynamics | −1.63 | 6.42 | Bethlehem Steel | 2.35 | 7.90 |
| Colgate-Palmolive | 16.51 | 12.16 | Armco Steel | 5.03 | 9.34 |
| Coca-Cola | 17.53 | 23.19 | Texaco | 6.13 | 15.40 |
| International Business Machines | 12.69 | 19.20 | Shell Oil | 6.58 | 11.95 |
| Allied Chemical | 4.66 | 10.76 | Standard Oil (Indiana) | 14.26 | 9.56 |
| Uniroyal | 3.67 | 8.49 | Owens Illinois | 2.60 | 10.05 |
| Greyhound | 10.49 | 17.70 | Gulf Oil | 4.97 | 12.11 |
| Cities Service | 10.00 | 9.10 | Tenneco | 6.65 | 11.53 |
| Philip Morris | 21.90 | 17.47 | Inland Steel | 4.25 | 9.92 |
| General Motors | 5.86 | 18.45 | Kraft | 7.30 | 12.27 |
| Philips Petroleum | 10.81 | 10.06 | | | |
| FMC | 5.71 | 13.30 | | | |

*Source:* Data from Benzion Barlev and Haim Levy, "On the Variability of Accounting Income Numbers," *Journal of Accounting Research* (Autumn 1979), pp. 305–315.

is, $x = 5$). Then, it can be verified that a point prediction of and a 95% prediction interval for this completion time are, respectively, 3.3281 and [.7225, 5.9337]. Show how the point prediction has been calculated.

**3.36** In an article in the *Journal of Accounting Research,* Benzion Barlev and Haim Levy consider relating accounting rates on stocks and market returns. Fifty-four companies were selected. For each company the authors recorded values of $x$, the mean yearly accounting rate for the period 1959 to 1974, and $y$, the mean yearly market return rate for the

period 1959 to 1974. The data in Table 3.12 (page 136) were obtained. Here the accounting rate can be interpreted to represent input into investment and therefore is a logical predictor of market return. Use the simple linear regression model and a computer to do the following.

a. Find a point estimate of and a 95% confidence interval for the mean market return rate of all stocks having an accounting rate of 15.00.

b. Find a point prediction of and a 95% prediction interval for the market return rate of an individual stock having an accounting rate of 15.00.

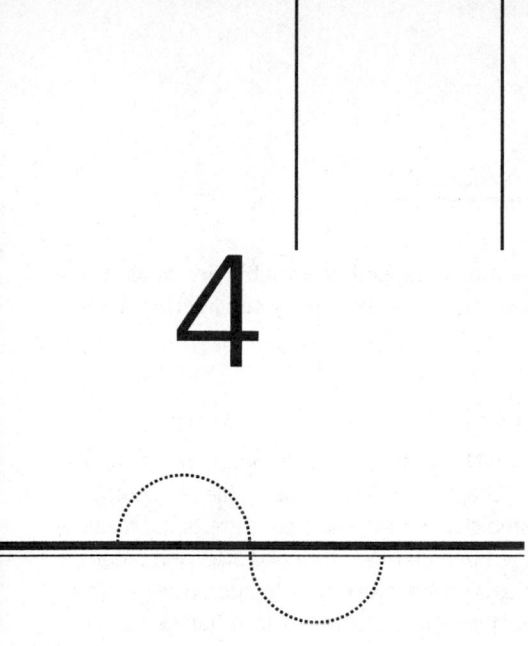

# 4

# *Multiple Linear Regression*

In this chapter we extend our discusssion of regression analysis by studying regression models that employ more than one independent variable. Sometimes these models are called **multiple regression models.** Sections 4.1 through 4.6 cover the basic concepts in multiple regression. We begin in Section 4.1 by introducing the (multiple) linear regression model along with the regression assumptions: model appropriateness, constant variance, independence, and normality. In Section 4.2 we show how to find the least squares estimates of the model parameters, and we use the model to compute point estimates and point predictions. In Section 4.3 we examine the mean square error and the standard error. Section 4.4 considers some ways to judge overall model utility. Included are the overall $F$-test, $R^2$, and adjusted $R^2$. In Section 4.5 we study statistical inference for a single regression parameter $\beta_j$ (including the test of $H_0$: $\beta_j = 0$ versus $H_a$: $\beta_j \neq 0$), and in Section 4.6 we study how to find confidence intervals for means and prediction intervals for individual values.

Sections 4.7 through 4.10 introduce more advanced models. In Section 4.7 we examine the quadratic regression model, and in Section 4.8 we discuss the use of what we call interaction terms in regression models. Section 4.9 illustrates using dummy variables to model the effects of the different levels of a qualitative (that is, nonnumeric) independent variable. Finally, in Section 4.10 we present the partial $F$-test, which is a test of significance for a portion of the regression model.

# 4.1   THE LINEAR REGRESSION MODEL

Regression models that employ more than one independent variable are called **multiple regression models.** We begin our study of these models by considering the following example.

**EXAMPLE 4.1**   **Part 1: The Data and a Regression Model**

Consider the fuel consumption problem in which the natural gas company wishes to predict weekly fuel consumption for its city. In Chapter 3 we used the single predictor variable $x$, average hourly temperature, to predict $y$, weekly fuel consumption. We now consider predicting $y$ on the basis of average hourly temperature and a second predictor variable—the chill index. The chill index for a given average hourly temperature expresses the combined effects of all other major weather-related factors that influence fuel consumption, such as wind velocity, cloud cover, and the passage of weather fronts. The chill index is expressed as a whole number between 0 and 30. A weekly chill index near 0 indicates that, given the average hourly temperature during the week, all other major weather-related factors will only slightly increase weekly fuel consumption. A weekly chill index near 30 indicates that, given the average hourly temperature during the week, other weather-related factors will greatly increase weekly fuel consumption.

The company has collected data concerning weekly fuel consumption ($y$), average hourly temperature ($x_1$), and the chill index ($x_2$) for the last eight weeks. These data are given in Table 4.1. Figure 4.1 presents a scatter plot of $y$ versus $x_1$. This plot shows that $y$ tends to decrease in a straight-line fashion as $x_1$ increases. This suggests that if we wish to predict $y$ on the basis of $x_1$ only, the simple linear regression model (having a negative slope)

$$y = \beta_0 + \beta_1 x_1 + \varepsilon$$

relates $y$ to $x_1$. Figure 4.2 presents a scatter plot of $y$ versus $x_2$. This plot shows that $y$ tends to increase in a straight-line fashion as $x_2$ increases. This suggests that if we wish to predict

**TABLE 4.1  Fuel Consumption Data**

| Week | Average Hourly Temperature, $x_1$ (°F) | Chill Index, $x_2$ | Fuel Consumption, $y$ (MMcf) |
|------|------|------|------|
| 1 | 28.0 | 18 | 12.4 |
| 2 | 28.0 | 14 | 11.7 |
| 3 | 32.5 | 24 | 12.4 |
| 4 | 39.0 | 22 | 10.8 |
| 5 | 45.9 | 8 | 9.4 |
| 6 | 57.8 | 16 | 9.5 |
| 7 | 58.1 | 1 | 8.0 |
| 8 | 62.5 | 0 | 7.5 |

**FIGURE 4.1**

Plot of y (weekly fuel consumption) versus $x_1$ (average hourly temperature)

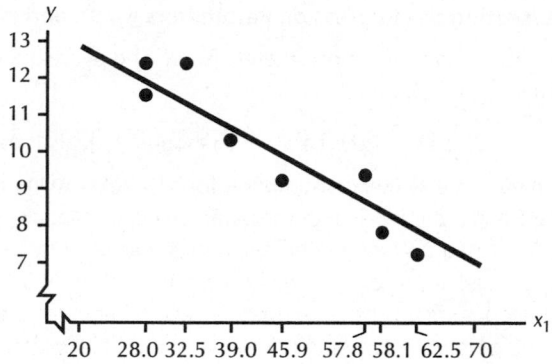

**FIGURE 4.2**

Plot of y (weekly fuel consumption) versus $x_2$ (the chill index)

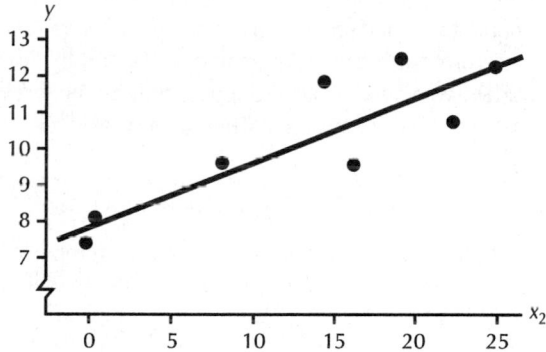

y on the basis of $x_2$ only, the simple linear regression model (having a positive slope)

$$y = \beta_0 + \beta_1 x_2 + \varepsilon$$

relates y to $x_2$. Since we wish to predict y on the basis of both $x_1$ and $x_2$, it seems reasonable to combine these models to form the model

$$y = \beta_0 + \beta_1 x_1 + \beta_2 x_2 + \varepsilon$$

to relate y to $x_1$ and $x_2$. Here we have arbitrarily placed the $\beta_1 x_1$ term first and the $\beta_2 x_2$ term second, and we have renumbered $\beta_1$ and $\beta_2$ to be consistent with the subscripts on $x_1$ and $x_2$. This regression model says that

1. $\beta_0 + \beta_1 x_1 + \beta_2 x_2$ is the mean value of y when the average hourly temperature is $x_1$ and the chill index is $x_2$. For instance,

$$\beta_0 + \beta_1(45.9) + \beta_2(8)$$

   is the average fuel consumption for all weeks having an average hourly temperature equal to 45.9 and a chill index equal to 8.

2. $\beta_0$, $\beta_1$, and $\beta_2$ are regression parameters relating the mean value of y to $x_1$ and $x_2$.

3. $\varepsilon$ is an error term that describes the effects on y of all factors other than $x_1$ and $x_2$.

### Part 2: Interpreting the Regression Parameters $\beta_0$, $\beta_1$, and $\beta_2$

The exact interpretations of the parameters $\beta_0$, $\beta_1$, and $\beta_2$ are quite simple. First, suppose that $x_1 = 0$ and $x_2 = 0$. Then

$$\beta_0 + \beta_1 x_1 + \beta_2 x_2 = \beta_0 + \beta_1(0) + \beta_2(0) = \beta_0$$

So $\beta_0$ is the mean weekly fuel consumption for all weeks having an average hourly temperature of 0°F and a chill index of 0. The parameter $\beta_0$ is called the **intercept** in the regression model. One might wonder whether $\beta_0$ has any practical interpretation, since it is unlikely that a week having an average hourly temperature of 0°F would also have a chill index of 0. Indeed, sometimes the parameter $\beta_0$ and other parameters in a regression analysis do not have practical interpretations because the situations related to the interpretations would not be likely to occur in practice. In fact, sometimes each parameter does not, by itself, have much practical importance. Rather, the parameters relate the mean of the dependent variable to the independent variables in an overall sense.

We next interpret the individual meanings of $\beta_1$ and $\beta_2$. To examine the interpretation of $\beta_1$, consider two different weeks. Suppose that for the first week the average hourly temperature is $c$ and the chill index is $d$. The mean weekly fuel consumption for all such weeks is

$$\beta_0 + \beta_1(c) + \beta_2(d)$$

For the second week, suppose that the average hourly temperature is $c + 1$ and the chill index is $d$. The mean weekly fuel consumption for all such weeks is

$$\beta_0 + \beta_1(c + 1) + \beta_2(d)$$

It is easy to see that the difference between these mean fuel consumptions is $\beta_1$. Since weeks 1 and 2 differ only in that the average hourly temperature during week 2 is one degree higher than the average hourly temperature during week 1, we can interpret the parameter $\beta_1$ as the change in mean weekly fuel consumption that is associated with a one-degree increase in average hourly temperature when the chill index does not change.

The interpretation of $\beta_2$ can be established similarly. We can interpret $\beta_2$ as the change in mean weekly fuel consumption that is associated with a one-unit increase in the chill index when the average hourly temperature does not change.

### Part 3: A Geometric Interpretation of the Regression Model

We now interpret our fuel consumption model geometrically. We begin by defining the **experimental region** to be the range of the combinations of the observed values of $x_1$ and $x_2$. From the data in Table 4.1, it is reasonable to depict the experimental region as the shaded region in Figure 4.3. Here the combinations of $x_1$ and $x_2$ values are the ordered pairs in the figure.

We next write the mean value of $y$ when average hourly temperature is $x_1$ and the chill index is $x_2$ as $\mu_{y|x_1,x_2}$ (pronounced *mu of y given $x_1$ and $x_2$*) and consider the equation

$$\mu_{y|x_1,x_2} = \beta_0 + \beta_1 x_1 + \beta_2 x_2$$

which relates mean fuel consumption to $x_1$ and $x_2$. Since this is a linear equation in two variables, geometry tells us that this equation is the equation of a plane in three-dimensional

**FIGURE 4.3**
The experimental
region

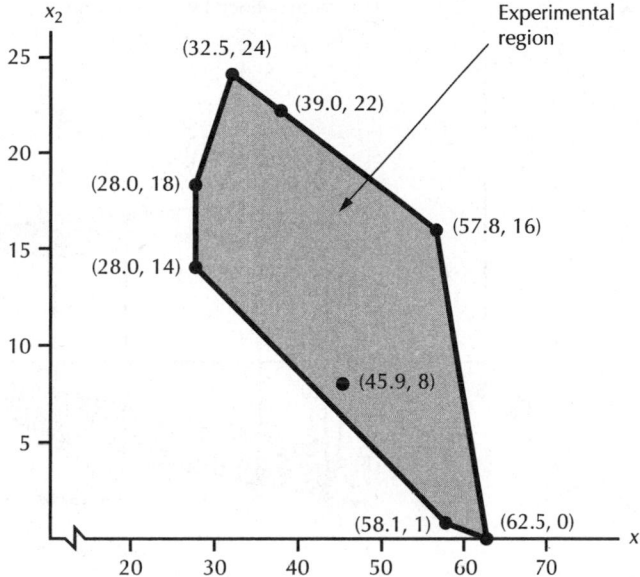

space. We sometimes refer to this plane as the **plane of means,** and we illustrate the portion of this plane corresponding to the $(x_1, x_2)$ combinations in the experimental region in Figure 4.4 (page 144). As illustrated in this figure, the model

$$y = \mu_{y|x_1,x_2} + \varepsilon$$
$$= \beta_0 + \beta_1 x_1 + \beta_2 x_2 + \varepsilon$$

says that the eight error terms cause the eight observed fuel consumptions (the dots in the upper portion of the figure) to deviate from the eight mean fuel consumptions (the triangles in the figure), which exactly lie on the plane of means

$$\mu_{y|x_1,x_2} = \beta_0 + \beta_1 x_1 + \beta_2 x_2$$

For example, consider the data for week 1 in Table 4.1 ($y = 12.4$, $x_1 = 28.0$, $x_2 = 18$). Figure 4.4 shows that the error term for this week is positive, causing $y$ to be higher than $\mu_{y|28.0,18}$ (mean fuel consumption when $x_1 = 28$ and $x_2 = 18$). Here factors other than $x_1$ and $x_2$ (for instance, thermostat settings that are higher than usual) have resulted in a positive error term. As another example, the error term for week 5 in Table 4.1 ($y = 9.4$, $x_1 = 45.9$, $x_2 = 8$) is negative. This causes $y$ for week 5 to be lower than $\mu_{y|45.9,8}$ (mean fuel consumption when $x_1 = 45.9$ and $x_2 = 8$). Here factors other than $x_1$ and $x_2$ (for instance, lower-than-usual thermostat settings) have resulted in a negative error term.

The fuel consumption model expresses the dependent variable as a function of two independent variables. In general, we can use a multiple regression model to express a dependent variable as a function of any number of independent variables. For example, the Cincinnati Gas and Electric Company predicts daily natural gas consumption as a function of four independent variables—average temperature,

**FIGURE 4.4**
A geometrical
interpretation of
the regression
model relating $y$ to
$x_1$ and $x_2$

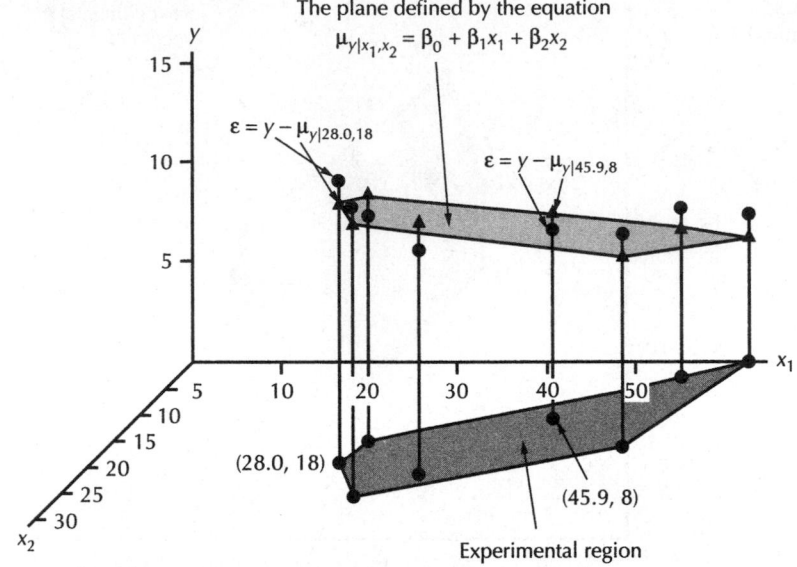

When looking at this figure, it is best to pretend that you are sitting high in a football
stadium and are looking down at the playing field, which is the $(x_1, x_2)$ plane.

average wind velocity, average sunlight, and change in average temperature from the previous day. The general form of a multiple regression model expresses the dependent variable $y$ as a function of $k$ independent variables $x_1, x_2, \ldots, x_k$. We call this general form the (multiple) **linear regression model** and express it as shown in the following box.

## THE LINEAR REGRESSION MODEL

The **linear regression model relating $y$ to $x_1, x_2, \ldots, x_k$** is

$$y = \mu_{y|x_1,x_2,\ldots,x_k} + \varepsilon = \beta_0 + \beta_1 x_1 + \beta_2 x_2 + \cdots + \beta_k x_k + \varepsilon$$

Here

1.  $\mu_{y|x_1,x_2,\ldots,x_k} = \beta_0 + \beta_1 x_1 + \beta_2 x_2 + \cdots + \beta_k x_k$ is the mean value of the dependent variable $y$ when the values of the independent variables are $x_1$, $x_2, \ldots, x_k$.

2.  $\beta_0, \beta_1, \beta_2, \ldots, \beta_k$ are (unknown) **regression parameters** relating the mean value of $y$ to $x_1, x_2, \ldots, x_k$.

3.  $\varepsilon$ is an **error term** that describes the effects on $y$ of all factors other than the values of the independent variables $x_1, x_2, \ldots, x_k$.

Here we assume that we have obtained $n$ observations, with each observation consisting of an observed value of $y$ and corresponding observed values of $x_1, x_2, \ldots, x_k$.

We call this model a *linear regression model* because the expression

$$\beta_0 + \beta_1 x_1 + \beta_2 x_2 + \cdots + \beta_k x_k$$

*expresses the mean value of $y$ as a linear function of the parameters $\beta_0, \beta_1, \beta_2, \ldots, \beta_k$.* We will talk more about this later. The concept of linearity is important because the techniques of regression are easiest to use and best developed when we employ a linear model.

In addition to employing a linear regression model, we make several assumptions about the populations of error terms. These assumptions are stated in the following box.

---

### ASSUMPTIONS FOR THE LINEAR REGRESSION MODEL

1. At any given combination of values of $x_1, x_2, \ldots, x_k$, the population of potential error term values has a mean equal to 0.

2. **Constant variance assumption:** At any given combination of values of $x_1, x_2, \ldots, x_k$, the population of potential error term values has a variance that does not depend on the combination of values of $x_1, x_2, \ldots, x_k$. That is, the different populations of potential error term values corresponding to different combinations of values of $x_1, x_2, \ldots, x_k$ have equal variances. We denote the constant variance as $\sigma^2$.

3. **Normality assumption:** At any given combination of values of $x_1, x_2, \ldots, x_k$, the population of potential error term values has a *normal distribution.*

4. **Independence assumption:** Any one value of the error term $\varepsilon$ is *statistically independent* of any other value of $\varepsilon$. That is, the value of the error term $\varepsilon$ corresponding to an observed value of $y$ is statistically independent of the error term corresponding to any other observed value of $y$.

---

Taken together, the first three assumptions say that at any given combination of values of $x_1, x_2, \ldots, x_k$, the population of potential error term values is normally distributed with mean 0 and a variance $\sigma^2$ that does not depend on the combination of values of $x_1, x_2, \ldots, x_k$. The model

$$y = \beta_0 + \beta_1 x_1 + \beta_2 x_2 + \cdots + \beta_k x_k + \varepsilon$$

implies that at any given combination of values of $x_1, x_2, \ldots, x_k$, the variation in the $y$ values is caused by and thus is the same as the variation in the $\varepsilon$ values. Therefore, the first three assumptions imply that at any given combination of values of $x_1, x_2, \ldots, x_k$, the population of $y$ values that could be observed is normally distributed with mean

$\beta_0 + \beta_1 x_1 + \beta_2 x_2 + \cdots + \beta_k x_k$ and a variance $\sigma^2$ that does not depend on the combination of values of $x_1, x_2, \ldots, x_k$. Furthermore, the independence assumption says that when time series data are utilized in a regression study, there are no patterns in the error term values. In Sections 5.3 and 5.4 we show how to check the validity of the regression assumptions. Those sections can be read at any time after Section 4.6. As in simple linear regression, only pronounced departures from the assumptions must be remedied.

We next consider another example of the linear regression model.

**EXAMPLE 4.2**   Suppose the sales manager of a company wishes to evaluate the performance of the company's sales representatives. Each sales representative is solely responsible for one sales territory, and the manager decides that it is reasonable to measure the performance, $y$, of a sales representative by using the yearly sales of the company's product in the representative's sales territory. The manager feels that sales performance $y$ substantially depends on five independent variables:

$x_1$ = number of months the representative has been employed by the company

$x_2$ = sales of the company's product and competing products in the sales
     territory

$x_3$ = dollar advertising expenditure in the territory

$x_4$ = weighted average of the company's market share in the territory for the
     previous four years

$x_5$ = change in the company's market share in the territory over the previous
     four years

In Table 4.2 we present values of $y$ and $x_1$ through $x_5$ for 25 randomly selected sales representatives. To understand the values of $y$ and $x_2$ in the table, note that sales of the company's product or any competing product are measured in hundreds of units of the product sold. Therefore, for example, the first sales figure of 3669.88 in Table 4.2 means that the first randomly selected sales representative sold 366,988 units of the company's product during the year.

Plots of $y$ versus $x_1$ through $x_5$ are given next to Table 4.2. Since each plot has an approximate straight-line appearance, it is reasonable to relate $y$ to $x_1$ through $x_5$ by using the regression model

$$y = \beta_0 + \beta_1 x_1 + \beta_2 x_2 + \beta_3 x_3 + \beta_4 x_4 + \beta_5 x_5 + \varepsilon$$

Here, $\mu_{y|x_1, x_2, \ldots, x_5} = \beta_0 + \beta_1 x_1 + \beta_2 x_2 + \beta_3 x_3 + \beta_4 x_4 + \beta_5 x_5$ is, intuitively, the mean sales in all sales territories where the values of the previously described five independent variables are $x_1, x_2, x_3, x_4,$ and $x_5$. Furthermore, for example, the parameter $\beta_3$ equals the increase in mean sales that is associated with a \$1 increase in advertising expenditure ($x_3$) when the other four independent variables do not change. The main objective of the regression analysis is to help the sales manager evaluate sales performance by comparing actual performance to predicted performance. The manager has randomly selected the 25 representatives

**TABLE 4.2 Sales Territory Performance Data**

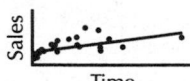

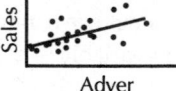

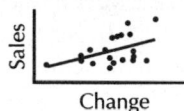

| Sales, $y$ | Time with Company, $x_1$ | Market Potential, $x_2$ | Advertising, $x_3$ | Market Share, $x_4$ | Market Share Change, $x_5$ |
|---|---|---|---|---|---|
| 3669.88 | 43.10 | 74,065.11 | 4,582.88 | 2.51 | 0.34 |
| 3473.95 | 108.13 | 58,117.30 | 5,539.78 | 5.51 | 0.15 |
| 2295.10 | 13.82 | 21,118.49 | 2,950.38 | 10.91 | −0.72 |
| 4675.56 | 186.18 | 68,521.27 | 2,243.07 | 8.27 | 0.17 |
| 6125.96 | 161.79 | 57,805.11 | 7,747.08 | 9.15 | 0.50 |
| 2134.94 | 8.94 | 37,806.94 | 402.44 | 5.51 | 0.15 |
| 5031.66 | 365.04 | 50,935.26 | 3,140.62 | 8.54 | 0.55 |
| 3367.45 | 220.32 | 35,602.08 | 2,086.16 | 7.07 | −0.49 |
| 6519.45 | 127.64 | 46,176.77 | 8,846.25 | 12.54 | 1.24 |
| 4876.37 | 105.69 | 42,053.24 | 5,673.11 | 8.85 | 0.31 |
| 2468.27 | 57.72 | 36,829.71 | 2,761.76 | 5.38 | 0.37 |
| 2533.31 | 23.58 | 33,612.67 | 1,991.85 | 5.43 | −0.65 |
| 2408.11 | 13.82 | 21,412.79 | 1,971.52 | 8.48 | 0.64 |
| 2337.38 | 13.82 | 20,416.87 | 1,737.38 | 7.80 | 1.01 |
| 4586.95 | 86.99 | 36,272.00 | 10,694.20 | 10.34 | 0.11 |
| 2729.24 | 165.85 | 23,093.26 | 8,618.61 | 5.15 | 0.04 |
| 3289.40 | 116.26 | 26,878.59 | 7,747.89 | 6.64 | 0.68 |
| 2800.78 | 42.28 | 39,571.96 | 4,565.81 | 5.45 | 0.66 |
| 3264.20 | 52.84 | 51,866.15 | 6,022.70 | 6.31 | −0.10 |
| 3453.62 | 165.04 | 58,749.82 | 3,721.10 | 6.35 | −0.03 |
| 1741.45 | 10.57 | 23,990.82 | 860.97 | 7.37 | −1.63 |
| 2035.75 | 13.82 | 25,694.86 | 3,571.51 | 8.39 | −0.43 |
| 1578.00 | 8.13 | 23,736.35 | 2,845.50 | 5.15 | 0.04 |
| 4167.44 | 58.54 | 34,314.29 | 5,060.11 | 12.88 | 0.22 |
| 2799.97 | 21.14 | 22,809.53 | 3,552.00 | 9.14 | −0.74 |

*Source:* This data set is from a research study published in "An Analytical Approach for Evaluation of Sales Territory Performance," *Journal of Marketing*, January 1972, 31–37 (authors are David W. Cravens, Robert B. Woodruff, and Joseph C. Stamper). We have updated the situation in our case study to be more modern.

from all the representatives the company considers to be effective and wishes to use a regression model based on effective representatives to evaluate questionable representatives. Questionable representatives whose performance is substantially lower than performance predictions will get special training aimed at improving their sales techniques.

# 4.2 THE LEAST SQUARES ESTIMATES, AND POINT ESTIMATION AND PREDICTION

The regression parameters $\beta_0, \beta_1, \beta_2, \ldots, \beta_k$ in the linear regression model are unknown. Therefore, they must be estimated from data (observations of $y, x_1, x_2, \ldots, x_k$). To see how we might do this, let $b_0, b_1, b_2, \ldots, b_k$ denote point estimates of the unknown parameters. Then, a point prediction of an observed value of the dependent variable

$$y = \beta_0 + \beta_1 x_1 + \beta_2 x_2 + \cdots + \beta_k x_k + \varepsilon$$

is

$$\hat{y} = b_0 + b_1 x_1 + b_2 x_2 + \cdots + b_k x_k$$

Here, since the regression assumptions imply that the error term $\varepsilon$ has a 50% chance of being positive and a 50% chance of being negative, we predict $\varepsilon$ to be 0. Next, let $y_i$ and $\hat{y}_i$ denote the observed and predicted values of the dependent variable for the $i$th observation, and define the **residual** for the $i$th observation to be $e_i = y_i - \hat{y}_i$. We then consider the **sum of squared residuals**

$$\text{SSE} = \sum_{i=1}^{n} (y_i - \hat{y}_i)^2$$

Intuitively, if any particular values of $b_0, b_1, b_2, \ldots, b_k$ are good point estimates, they will make (for $i = 1, 2, \ldots, n$) the predicted value $\hat{y}_i$ fairly close to the observed value $y_i$ and thus will make SSE fairly small. We define the **least squares point estimates** to be the values of $b_0, b_1, b_2, \ldots, b_k$ that minimize SSE.

It can be shown that a formula exists for computing the least squares point estimates of the parameters in the linear regression model. This formula is written using a branch of mathematics called *matrix algebra* and is presented in Appendix B. In practice, the least squares point estimates can be easily computed using many standard statistical computer packages. In our discussion of multiple regression, we rely on MINITAB, Excel, and SAS to compute the needed estimates.

**EXAMPLE 4.3**    **Part 1: The Least Squares Point Estimates**

Consider the fuel consumption model of Example 4.1:

$$y = \beta_0 + \beta_1 x_1 + \beta_2 x_2 + \varepsilon$$

The MINITAB and Excel output in Figure 4.5 tells us that if we use the data in Table 4.1 to calculate the least squares point estimates of the parameters $\beta_0$, $\beta_1$, and $\beta_2$, we obtain $b_0 = 13.1087$, $b_1 = -0.09001$, and $b_2 = 0.08249$.

The point estimate $b_1 = -.09001$ of $\beta_1$ says we estimate that mean weekly fuel consumption decreases (since $b_1$ is negative) by .09001 MMcf of natural gas when average hourly temperature increases by one degree and the chill index does not change. The point

**FIGURE 4.5** MINITAB and Excel output of a regression analysis of the fuel consumption data in Table 4.1 using the model $y = \beta_0 + \beta_1 x_1 + \beta_2 x_2 + \varepsilon$

```
The regression equation is
FUELCONS = 13.1 - 0.0900 TEMP + 0.0825 CHILL
```

| Predictor | Coef | SE Coef[d] | T[e] | P[f] |
|-----------|------|-----------|------|------|
| Constant | 13.1087[a] | 0.8557 | 15.32 | 0.000 |
| TEMP | -0.09001[b] | 0.01408 | -6.39 | 0.001 |
| CHILL | 0.08249[c] | 0.02200 | 3.75 | 0.013 |

$S = 0.367078$[g]   R-Sq = 97.4%[h]   R-Sq(adj) = 96.3%

Analysis of Variance

| Source | DF | SS | MS | F | P |
|--------|----|----|----|----|----|
| Regression | 2 | 24.875[i] | 12.438 | 92.30[l] | 0.000[m] |
| Residual Error | 5 | 0.674[j] | 0.135 | | |
| Total | 7 | 25.549[k] | | | |

| Fit[n] | SE Fit[o] | 95% CI[p] | 95% PI[q] |
|--------|-----------|-----------|-----------|
| 10.333 | 0.170 | (9.895, 10.771) | (9.293, 11.374) |

(a) The MINITAB output

**Regression Statistics**

| | |
|---|---|
| Multiple R | 0.986726685 |
| R Square | 0.97362955[h] |
| Adjusted R Square | 0.963081371 |
| Standard Error | 0.3670782[g] |
| Observations | 8 |

ANOVA

| | df | SS | MS | F | Significance F |
|---|----|----|----|----|----------------|
| Regression | 2 | 24.87501798[i] | 12.43751 | 92.30309[l] | 0.000112926[m] |
| Residual | 5 | 0.673732024[j] | 0.134746 | | |
| Total | 7 | 25.54875[k] | | | |

| | Coefficients | Standard Error[d] | t Stat[e] | P-Value[f] | Lower 95%[r] | Upper 95%[r] |
|---|--------------|-------------------|-----------|------------|--------------|--------------|
| Intercept | 13.10873722[a] | 0.855698052 | 15.31935 | 2.15E-05 | 10.90909894 | 15.30037549 |
| TEMP | -0.090013872[b] | 0.014077361 | -6.39423 | 0.001386 | -0.12620082 | -0.053826924 |
| CHILL | 0.082494974[c] | 0.022002548 | 3.749337 | 0.013303 | 0.025935717 | 0.139054231 |

(b) The Excel output

---

[a]$b_0$   [b]$b_1$   [c]$b_2$   [d]$s_{b_j}$   [e]t-statistics   [f]p-values for t-statistics   [g]$s$ = standard error   [h]$R^2$   [i]Explained variation   [j]SSE = unexplained variation   [k]Total variation   [l]F (model) statistic   [m]p-value for F(model)   [n]$\hat{y}$   [o]$s_{\hat{y}}$   [p]95% confidence interval when $x_1 = 40$ and $x_2 = 10$   [q]95% prediction interval when $x_1 = 40$ and $x_2 = 10$   [r]95% confidence interval for $\beta_j$

estimate $b_2 = .08249$ of $\beta_2$ says we estimate that mean weekly fuel consumption increases (since $b_2$ is positive) by .08249 MMcf of natural gas when there is a one-unit increase in the chill index and average hourly temperature does not change.

The equation

$$\hat{y} = b_0 + b_1 x_1 + b_2 x_2$$
$$= 13.1087 - 0.09001 x_1 + 0.08249 x_2$$

is called the **least squares prediction equation.** It is obtained by replacing $\beta_0$, $\beta_1$, and $\beta_2$, by their estimates $b_0$, $b_1$, and $b_2$ and by predicting the error term to be 0. This equation is given on the MINITAB output (labeled as the "regression equation"—note that $b_0$, $b_1$, and $b_2$ have been rounded to 13.1, −0.0900, and 0.0825). We can use this equation to compute a prediction for any observed value of $y$. For instance, a point prediction of $y_1 = 12.4$ (when $x_1 = 28.0$ and $x_2 = 18$) is

$$\hat{y}_1 = 13.1087 - 0.09001(28.0) + 0.08249(18)$$
$$= 12.0733$$

This results in a residual equal to

$$e_1 = y_1 - \hat{y}_1 = 12.4 - 12.0733 = .3267$$

Table 4.3 gives the point prediction obtained using the least squares prediction equation and the residual for each of the eight observed fuel consumption values. In addition, this table tells us that the sum of squared residuals (SSE) equals .674.

The least squares prediction equation is the equation of a plane, which we sometimes call the **least squares plane.** Figure 4.6 illustrates a portion of this plane—the portion that corresponds to the $(x_1, x_2)$ combinations in the experimental region. Figure 4.6 also shows the residuals for the eight weeks. These residuals are depicted as line segments drawn between the observed fuel consumptions (the dots scattered around the least

**TABLE 4.3** The Point Predictions and Residuals Using the Least Squares Point Estimates, $b_0 = 13.1$, $b_1 = -.0900$, and $b_2 = .0825$

| Week | Average Hourly Temperature, $x_1$(°F) | Chill Index, $x_2$ | Observed Fuel Consumption, $y$ (MMcf) | Predicted Fuel Consumption, $\hat{y} = b_0 + b_1 x_1 + b_2 x_2$ $= 13.1 - .0900 x_1 + .0825 x_2$ | Residual, $e = y - \hat{y}$ |
|------|------|------|------|------|------|
| 1 | 28.0 | 18 | 12.4 | 12.0733 | .3267 |
| 2 | 28.0 | 14 | 11.7 | 11.7433 | −.0433 |
| 3 | 32.5 | 24 | 12.4 | 12.1632 | .2368 |
| 4 | 39.0 | 22 | 10.8 | 11.4131 | −.6131 |
| 5 | 45.9 | 8 | 9.4 | 9.6371 | −.2371 |
| 6 | 57.8 | 16 | 9.5 | 9.2259 | .2741 |
| 7 | 58.1 | 1 | 8.0 | 7.9614 | .0386 |
| 8 | 62.5 | 0 | 7.5 | 7.4829 | .0171 |

$$\text{SSE} = (.3267)^2 + (-.0433)^2 + \cdots + (.0171)^2 = .674$$

**FIGURE 4.6**

A geometrical interpretation of the prediction equation relating $\hat{y}$ to $x_1$ and $x_2$

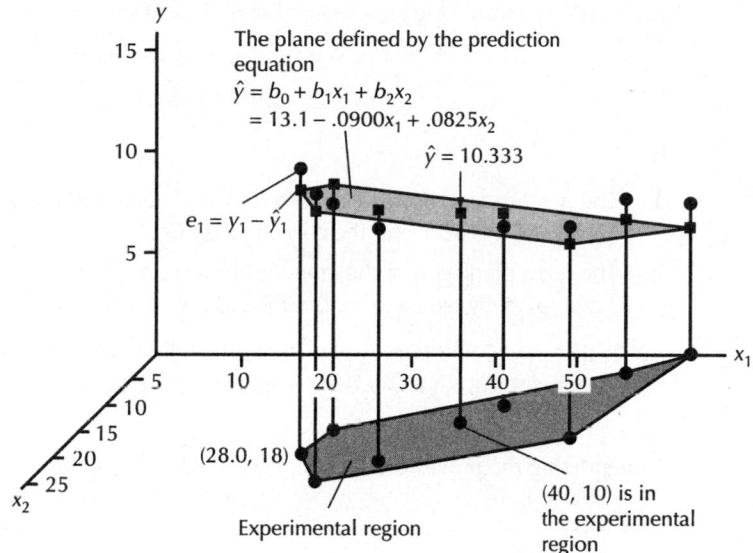

squares plane) and the predicted fuel consumptions (the squares on the least squares plane). Since the least squares point estimates minimize the sum of squared residuals, we can interpret them as positioning the planar prediction equation in three-dimensional space so as to minimize the sum of squared distances between the observed and predicted fuel consumptions. In this sense we can say that the plane defined by the least squares point estimates is the best plane that can be positioned between the observed fuel consumptions.

### Part 2: Estimating Means and Predicting Individual Values

For combinations of values of $x_1$ and $x_2$ that are in the experimental region, the **least squares plane** (see Figure 4.6) is the estimate of the **plane of means** (see Figure 4.4). This implies that the point on the least squares plane corresponding to the average hourly temperature $x_1$ and the chill index $x_2$

$$\hat{y} = b_0 + b_1x_1 + b_2x_2$$
$$= 13.1087 - .09001x_1 + .08249x_2$$

is the point estimate of $\mu_{y|x_1,x_2}$, the mean of all the weekly fuel consumptions that could be observed when the average hourly temperature is $x_1$ and the chill index is $x_2$. In addition, since we predict the error term to be 0, $\hat{y}$ is also the point prediction of $y = \mu_{y|x_1,x_2} + \varepsilon$, which is the amount of fuel consumed in a single week when the average hourly temperature is $x_1$ and the chill index is $x_2$.

For example, suppose a weather forecasting service predicts that in the next week the average hourly temperature will be 40°F and the chill index will be 10. Since this combination is inside the experimental region (see Figure 4.6), we see that

$$\hat{y} = 13.1087 - .09001(40) + .08249(10)$$
$$= 10.333 \text{ MMcf of natural gas}$$

is

1.  The point estimate of the mean weekly fuel consumption when the average hourly temperature is 40°F and the chill index is 10

2.  The point prediction of the amount of fuel consumed in a single week when the average hourly temperature is 40°F and the chill index is 10

Notice that $\hat{y} = 10.333$ is given at the bottom of the MINITAB output in Figure 4.5. In addition, Figure 4.6 illustrates this point estimate and prediction.

Generalizing the previous example, we obtain the following.

---

### POINT ESTIMATION AND POINT PREDICTION IN MULTIPLE REGRESSION

Let $b_0, b_1, b_2, \ldots, b_k$ be the least squares point estimates of the parameters $\beta_0$, $\beta_1, \beta_2, \ldots, \beta_k$ in the linear regression model, and suppose that $x_{01}, x_{02}, \ldots, x_{0k}$ are specified values of the independent variables $x_1, x_2, \ldots, x_k$. If the combination of specified values is inside the experimental region, then

$$\hat{y} = b_0 + b_1 x_{01} + b_2 x_{02} + \cdots + b_k x_{0k}$$

is the **point estimate** of the **mean value of the dependent variable** when the values of the independent variables are $x_{01}, x_{02}, \ldots, x_{0k}$. In addition, $\hat{y}$ is the **point prediction** of an **individual value of the dependent variable** when the values of the independent variables are $x_{01}, x_{02}, \ldots, x_{0k}$. Here we predict the error term to be 0.

---

**EXAMPLE 4.4**    Figure 4.7 presents the SAS output of a regression analysis of the sales territory performance data in Table 4.2 using the model

$$y = \beta_0 + \beta_1 x_1 + \beta_2 x_2 + \beta_3 x_3 + \beta_4 x_4 + \beta_5 x_5 + \varepsilon$$

On this output $x_1, x_2, x_3, x_4$, and $x_5$ are denoted as Time, MktPoten, Adver, MktShare, and Change, respectively. The SAS output tells us that the least squares point estimates of the model parameters are $b_0 = -1113.7879$, $b_1 = 3.6121$, $b_2 = .0421$, $b_3 = .1289$, $b_4 = 256.9555$, and $b_5 = 324.5335$. These estimates give the least squares prediction equation

$$\hat{y} = -1113.7879 + 3.6121 x_1 + .0421 x_2 + .1289 x_3 + 256.9555 x_4 + 324.5335 x_5$$

**FIGURE 4.7** SAS output of a regression analysis of the sales territory performance data using the model $y = \beta_0 + \beta_1 x_1 + \beta_2 x_2 + \beta_3 x_3 + \beta_4 x_4 + \beta_5 x_5 + \varepsilon$

Analysis of Variance

| Source | DF | Sum of Squares | Mean Square | F Value | Pr > F |
|---|---|---|---|---|---|
| Model | 5 | 37862659[a] | 7572532 | 40.91[d] | <.0001[e] |
| Error | 19 | 3516890[b] | 185099 | | |
| Corrected Total | 24 | 41379549[c] | | | |

| | | | | |
|---|---|---|---|---|
| Root MSE | 430.23189[k] | R-Square | 0.9150[f] | |
| Dependent Mean | 3374.56760 | Adj R-Sq | 0.8926 | |
| Coeff Var | 12.74924 | | | |

Parameter Estimates

| Variable | Label | DF | Parameter[g] Estimate | Standard[h] Error | t Value[i] | Pr > \|t\|[j] |
|---|---|---|---|---|---|---|
| Intercept | Intercept | 1 | -1113.78788 | 419.88690 | -2.65 | 0.0157 |
| Time | Time | 1 | 3.61210 | 1.18170 | 3.06 | 0.0065 |
| MktPoten | MktPoten | 1 | 0.04209 | 0.00673 | 6.25 | <.0001 |
| Adver | Adver | 1 | 0.12886 | 0.03704 | 3.48 | 0.0025 |
| MktShare | MktShare | 1 | 256.95554 | 39.13607 | 6.57 | <.0001 |
| Change | Change | 1 | 324.53345 | 157.28308 | 2.06 | 0.0530 |

| Obs | Dep Var Sales | Predicted[l] Value | Std Error[o] Mean Predict | 95% CL Mean[m] | | 95% CL Predict[n] | |
|---|---|---|---|---|---|---|---|
| 26 | . | 4182 | 141.8220 | 3885 | 4479 | 3234 | 5130 |

[a]Explained variation  [b]SSE = unexplained variation  [c]Total variation  [d]F (model)  [e]p-value for F (model)  [f]$R^2$  [g]$b_j$  [h]$s_{b_j}$  [i]t-statistic  [j]p-value for t-statistic  [k]s = standard error  [l]$\hat{y}$  [m]95% confidence interval for mean  [n]95% prediction interval  [o]$s_{\hat{y}}$

Recalling that the sales values in Table 4.2 are measured in hundreds of units of the product sold, the point estimate $b_3 = .1289$ says we estimate that mean sales increase by .1289 hundreds of units—that is, by 12.89 units—for each dollar increase in advertising expenditure when the other four independent variables do not change. If the company sells each unit for $1.10, this implies that we estimate that mean sales revenue increases by ($1.10)(12.89) = $14.18 for each dollar increase in advertising expenditure when the other four independent variables do not change. The other $\beta$ values in the model can be interpreted similarly.

Consider a questionable sales representative for whom Time = 85.42, MktPoten = 35,182.73, Adver = 7281.65, MktShare = 9.64, and Change = .28. The point prediction of the sales corresponding to this combination of values of the independent variables is

$$\hat{y} = -1113.7879 + 3.6121(85.42) + .0421(35,182.73)$$

$$+ .1289(7281.65) + 256.9555(9.64) + 324.5335(.28)$$

$$= 4182 \text{ (that is, } 418,200 \text{ units)}$$

which is given on the SAS output. The actual sales for the questionable sales representative were 3088. This sales figure is 1094 less than the point prediction $\hat{y} = 4182$. However, we will have to wait until we study prediction intervals in multiple regression (see Section 4.6) to determine whether there is strong evidence that this sales figure is unusually low.

# 4.3 THE MEAN SQUARE ERROR AND THE STANDARD ERROR

In order to compute intervals and test hypotheses when using the linear regression model, we must calculate point estimates of $\sigma^2$ and $\sigma$ (the constant variance and standard deviation of the different error term populations). We show how to do this in the following box.

---

**THE MEAN SQUARE ERROR AND THE STANDARD ERROR**

Suppose that the linear regression model

$$y = \beta_0 + \beta_1 x_1 + \beta_2 x_2 + \cdots + \beta_k x_k + \varepsilon$$

utilizes $k$ independent variables and thus has $(k + 1)$ parameters $\beta_0, \beta_1, \beta_2, \ldots, \beta_k$. Then, if the regression assumptions are satisfied, and if SSE denotes the sum of squared residuals for the model:

1.  A point estimate of $\sigma^2$ is the **mean square error**

$$s^2 = \frac{\text{SSE}}{n - (k + 1)}$$

2.  A point estimate of $\sigma$ is the **standard error**

$$s = \sqrt{\frac{\text{SSE}}{n - (k + 1)}}$$

---

In order to explain these point estimates, recall that $\sigma^2$ is the variance of the population of $y$ values (for given values of $x_1, x_2, \ldots, x_k$) around the mean value $\mu_{y|x_1, x_2, \ldots, x_k}$. Since $\hat{y}$ is the point estimate of this mean, it seems natural to use SSE $= \Sigma(y_i - \hat{y}_i)^2$ to help construct a point estimate of $\sigma^2$. We divide SSE by $n - (k + 1)$ because it can be proven that doing so makes the resulting $s^2$ an unbiased point estimate of $\sigma^2$. We call $n - (k + 1)$ the **number of degrees of freedom** associated with SSE.

We will see in Section 4.6 that if a particular regression model gives a small standard error, then the model will give short prediction intervals and thus accurate predictions of individual $y$ values. For example, Table 4.3 shows that SSE for the fuel consumption model

$$y = \beta_0 + \beta_1 x_1 + \beta_2 x_2 + \varepsilon$$

is .674. Since this model utilizes $k = 2$ independent variables and thus has $k + 1 = 3$ parameters ($\beta_0$, $\beta_1$, and $\beta_2$), a point estimate of $\sigma^2$ is the mean square error

$$s^2 = \frac{\text{SSE}}{n - (k + 1)} = \frac{.674}{8 - 3} = \frac{.674}{5} = .1348$$

and a point estimate of $\sigma$ is the standard error $s = \sqrt{.1348} = .3671$. Note that SSE = .674, $s^2 = .1348 \approx .135$, and $s = .3671$ are given on the MINITAB and Excel outputs in Figure 4.5. Also note that the $s$ of .3671 for the model with two independent variables is less than the $s$ of .6542 for the simple linear regression model that uses only the average hourly temperature to predict weekly fuel consumption (see Example 3.6).

As another example, the SSE for the sales territory performance model

$$y = \beta_0 + \beta_1 x_1 + \beta_2 x_2 + \beta_3 x_3 + \beta_4 x_4 + \beta_5 x_5 + \varepsilon$$

is 3,516,890. Since this model utilizes $k = 5$ independent variables and thus has $k + 1 = 6$ parameters, a point estimate of $\sigma^2$ is the mean square error

$$s^2 = \frac{\text{SSE}}{n - (k + 1)} = \frac{3,516,890}{25 - 6} = 185,099$$

and a point estimate of $\sigma$ is the standard error $s = \sqrt{185,099} = 430.23$. Note that these values of SSE, $s^2$, and $s$ are given on the SAS output in Figure 4.7.

# 4.4  MODEL UTILITY: $R^2$, ADJUSTED $R^2$, AND THE OVERALL $F$-TEST

We indicated in the previous section that if a regression model gives a small $s$, then the model will accurately predict individual $y$ values. For this reason, $s$ is one measure of the usefulness, or utility, of a regression model. In this section we discuss three other ways to assess the utility of a regression model.

## The Multiple Coefficient of Determination, $R^2$

We first discuss a quantity called the **multiple coefficient of determination,** which is denoted $R^2$. The formulas for $R^2$ and several other related quantities are given in the following box.

## THE MULTIPLE COEFFICIENT OF DETERMINATION, $R^2$

For the linear regression model:

1.  **Total variation** = $\Sigma(y_i - \bar{y})^2$
2.  **Explained variation** = $\Sigma(\hat{y}_i - \bar{y})^2$
3.  **Unexplained variation** = $\Sigma(y_i - \hat{y}_i)^2$
4.  **Total variation = Explained variation + Unexplained variation**
5.  The **multiple coefficient of determination** is

$$R^2 = \frac{\text{Explained variation}}{\text{Total variation}}$$

6.  $R^2$ is the proportion of the total variation in the $n$ observed values of the dependent variable that is explained by the overall regression model.
7.  **Multiple correlation coefficient** = $R = \sqrt{R^2}$

As an example, consider the fuel consumption model

$$y = \beta_0 + \beta_1 x_1 + \beta_2 x_2 + \varepsilon$$

The MINITAB and Excel output in Figure 4.5 tells us that the total, explained, and unexplained variations for this model are, respectively, 25.549, 24.875, and .674. This output also tells us that the multiple coefficient of determination is

$$R^2 = \frac{\text{Explained variation}}{\text{Total variation}} = \frac{24.875}{25.549} = .974$$

which implies that the multiple correlation coefficient is $R = \sqrt{.974} = .9869$. The value of $R^2 = .974$ says that the fuel consumption model with two independent variables explains 97.4% of the total variation in the eight observed fuel consumptions. Furthermore, this $R^2$ value is larger than the $r^2$ of .899 for the simple linear regression model that uses only the average hourly temperature to predict weekly fuel consumption (see Figure 3.9).

As another example, consider the sales territory performance model

$$y = \beta_0 + \beta_1 x_1 + \beta_2 x_2 + \beta_3 x_3 + \beta_4 x_4 + \beta_5 x_5 + \varepsilon$$

The SAS output in Figure 4.7 tells us that the total, explained, and unexplained variations for this model are, respectively, 41,379,549, 37,862,659, and 3,516,890. The SAS output also tells us that $R^2$ equals .915.

# Adjusted $R^2$

Even if the independent variables in a regression model are unrelated to the dependent variable, they will make $R^2$ somewhat greater than 0. To avoid overestimating the importance of the independent variables, many analysts recommend calculating an *adjusted* multiple coefficient of determination.

---

### ADJUSTED $R^2$

The **adjusted multiple coefficient of determination (adjusted $R^2$)** is

$$\overline{R}^2 = \left( R^2 - \frac{k}{n-1} \right)\left( \frac{n-1}{n-(k+1)} \right)$$

where $R^2$ is the multiple coefficient of determination, $n$ is the number of observations, and $k$ is the number of independent variables in the model under consideration.

---

To briefly explain this formula, note that it can be shown that subtracting $k/(n-1)$ from $R^2$ helps avoid overestimating the importance of the $k$ independent variables. Furthermore, multiplying

$$\left( R^2 - \frac{k}{n-1} \right)$$

by $(n-1)/[n-(k+1)]$ makes $\overline{R}^2$ equal to 1 when $R^2$ equals 1.

As an example, consider the fuel consumption model

$$y = \beta_0 + \beta_1 x_1 + \beta_2 x_2 + \varepsilon$$

Since we have seen that $R^2 = .974$, it follows that

$$\overline{R}^2 = \left( R^2 - \frac{k}{n-1} \right)\left( \frac{n-1}{n-(k+1)} \right)$$

$$= \left( .974 - \frac{2}{8-1} \right)\left( \frac{8-1}{8-(2+1)} \right)$$

$$= .963$$

which is given on the MINITAB and Excel output in Figure 4.5. Similarly, in addition to telling us that $R^2 = .915$ for the five independent variable sales territory performance model, the SAS output in Figure 4.7 tells us that $\overline{R}^2 = .893$ for this model.

If $R^2$ is less than $k/(n - 1)$ (which can happen), then $\bar{R}^2$ will be negative. In this case, statistical software systems set $\bar{R}^2$ equal to 0. Historically, $R^2$ and $\bar{R}^2$ have been popular measures of model utility—possibly because they are unitless and between 0 and 1. In general, we desire $R^2$ and $\bar{R}^2$ to be near 1. However, sometimes even if a regression model has an $R^2$ and an $\bar{R}^2$ that are near 1, the standard error $s$ is still too large for the model to predict accurately. The best that can be said for an $R^2$ and an $\bar{R}^2$ near 1 is that they give us hope that the model will predict accurately. Of course, the only way to know is to see if $s$ is small enough. In other words, since we usually are judging a model's ability to predict, $s$ is a better measure of model utility than are $R^2$ and $\bar{R}^2$. We will say more later about using $s$, $R^2$, and $\bar{R}^2$ to help choose a regression model.

## The Overall *F*-Test

Another way to assess the utility of a regression model is to test the significance of the regression relationship between $y$ and $x_1, x_2, \ldots, x_k$. For the linear regression model, we test the null hypothesis

$$H_0: \beta_1 = \beta_2 = \cdots = \beta_k = 0$$

which says that *none of the independent variables $x_1, x_2, \ldots, x_k$ is significantly related to $y$* **(the regression relationship is not significant),** versus the alternative hypothesis

$$H_a: \text{At least one of } \beta_1, \beta_2, \ldots, \beta_k \text{ does not equal } 0$$

which says that *at least one of the independent variables is significantly related to $y$* **(the regression relationship is significant)**. If we can reject $H_0$ at level of significance $\alpha$, we say that **the linear regression model is significant at level of significance $\alpha$.** We carry out the test as follows.

---

### AN *F*-TEST FOR THE LINEAR REGRESSION MODEL

Suppose that the regression assumptions hold and that the linear regression model has $(k + 1)$ parameters, and consider testing

$$H_0: \beta_1 = \beta_2 = \cdots = \beta_k = 0$$

versus

$$H_a: \text{At least one of } \beta_1, \beta_2, \ldots, \beta_k \text{ does not equal } 0$$

We define the **overall *F*-statistic** to be

$$F(\text{model}) = \frac{(\text{Explained variation}) / k}{(\text{Unexplained variation}) / [n - (k + 1)]}$$

Also define the $p$-value related to $F$(model) to be the area under the curve of the $F$-distribution (having $k$ and $[n - (k + 1)]$ degrees of freedom) to the right of $F$(model). Then, we can reject $H_0$ in favor of $H_a$ at level of significance $\alpha$ if either of the following equivalent conditions holds:

1. $F(\text{model}) > F_{[\alpha]}$

2. $p$-value $< \alpha$

Here the point $F_{[\alpha]}$ is based on $k$ numerator and $n - (k + 1)$ denominator degrees of freedom.

Condition 1 is intuitively reasonable because a large value of $F$(model) would be caused by an explained variation that is large relative to the unexplained variation. This would occur if at least one independent variable in the regression model significantly affects $y$, which would imply that $H_0$ is false and $H_a$ is true.

**EXAMPLE 4.5**    Consider the fuel consumption model

$$y = \beta_0 + \beta_1 x_1 + \beta_2 x_2 + \varepsilon$$

The MINITAB and Excel output in Figure 4.5 tells us that the explained and unexplained variations for this model are, respectively, 24.875 and .674. It follows, since there are $k = 2$ independent variables, that

$$F(\text{model}) = \frac{(\text{Explained variation}) / k}{(\text{Unexplained variation}) / [n - (k + 1)]}$$

$$= \frac{24.875 / 2}{.674 / [8 - (2 + 1)]} = \frac{12.438}{.135}$$

$$= 92.30$$

Note that this overall $F$-statistic is given on the MINITAB and Excel output. The $p$-value related to $F$(model) is the area to the right of 92.30 under the curve of the $F$-distribution having $k = 2$ numerator and $n - (k + 1) = 8 - 3 = 5$ denominator degrees of freedom. Both the MINITAB and Excel output in Figure 4.5 say this $p$-value is less than .001.

If we wish to test the significance of the regression model at level of significance $\alpha = .05$, we use the rejection point $F_{[.05]}$ based on 2 numerator and 5 denominator degrees of freedom. Using Table A3, we find that $F_{[.05]} = 5.79$. Since $F(\text{model}) = 92.30 > F_{[.05]} = 5.79$, we can reject $H_0$ in favor of $H_a$ at level of significance .05. Alternatively, since the $p$-value is smaller than .05, .01, and .001, we can reject $H_0$ at level of significance .05, .01, and .001. Therefore, we have extremely strong evidence that the fuel consumption model is significant. That is, we have extremely strong evidence that at least one of the independent variables $x_1$ and $x_2$ in the model is significantly related to $y$.

Similarly, the SAS output in Figure 4.7 tells us that $F(\text{model}) = 40.91$ for the sales territory performance model with five independent variables. Furthermore, since the SAS output also tells us that the *p*-value related to *F*(model) is less than .001, we have extremely strong evidence that at least one of the five independent variables in this model is significantly related to sales territory performance.

If the overall *F*-test tells us that at least one independent variable in a regression model is significant, we next attempt to decide which independent variables are significant. In the next section we discuss one way to do this.

# 4.5 TESTING THE SIGNIFICANCE OF AN INDEPENDENT VARIABLE

Consider the linear regression model

$$y = \beta_0 + \beta_1 x_1 + \beta_2 x_2 + \cdots + \beta_k x_k + \varepsilon$$

In order to gain information about which independent variables significantly affect *y*, we can test the significance of a single independent variable. We arbitrarily refer to this variable as $x_j$ and assume that it is multiplied by the parameter $\beta_j$. For example, if $j = 1$, we are testing the significance of $x_1$, which is multiplied by $\beta_1$; if $j = 2$, we are testing the significance of $x_2$, which is multiplied by $\beta_2$. To test the significance of $x_j$, we test the null hypothesis

$$H_0: \beta_j = 0$$

We usually test $H_0$ versus the alternative hypothesis

$$H_a: \beta_j \neq 0$$

It is reasonable to conclude that $x_j$ is significantly related to *y* in the regression model under consideration if $H_0$ can be rejected in favor of $H_a$ at a small level of significance. Here the phrase *in the regression model under consideration* is very important. This is because it can be shown that whether $x_j$ is significantly related to *y* in a particular regression model can depend on what other independent variables are included in the model. This issue is discussed in detail in Chapter 5.

Testing the significance of $x_j$ in a multiple regression model is similar to testing the significance of the slope in the simple linear regression model (recall that we test $H_0: \beta_1 = 0$ in simple regression). It can be proved that if the regression assumptions hold, the population of all possible values of the least squares point estimate $b_j$ is normally distributed with mean $\beta_j$ and standard deviation $\sigma_{b_j}$. The point estimate of $\sigma_{b_j}$ is called the **standard error of the estimate $b_j$** and is denoted $s_{b_j}$. The formula for $s_{b_j}$ involves matrix algebra and is discussed in Appendix B. In our discussion here, we rely on MINITAB, SAS, and Excel to compute $s_{b_j}$. It can be shown that if the regression assumptions hold, then the population of all possible values of

$$\frac{b_j - \beta_j}{s_{b_j}}$$

has a $t$-distribution with $n - (k + 1)$ degrees of freedom. It follows that if the null hypothesis $H_0$: $\beta_j = 0$ is true, then the population of all possible values of the test statistic

$$t = \frac{b_j}{s_{b_j}}$$

has a $t$-distribution with $n - (k + 1)$ degrees of freedom. Therefore, we can test the significance of $x_j$ as follows.

---

### TESTING THE SIGNIFICANCE OF THE INDEPENDENT VARIABLE $x_j$

Define the test statistic

$$t = \frac{b_j}{s_{b_j}}$$

and suppose that the regression assumptions hold. Then we can reject $H_0$: $\beta_j = 0$ in favor of a particular alternative hypothesis at significance level $\alpha$ if and only if the appropriate rejection point condition holds, or equivalently, the corresponding $p$-value is less than $\alpha$.

| Alternative Hypothesis | Rejection Point Condition: Reject $H_0$ if | $p$-Value |
|---|---|---|
| $H_a$: $\beta_j \neq 0$ | $|t| > t_{[\alpha/2]}^{(n-(k+1))}$ | Twice the area under the $t$ curve to the right of $|t|$ |
| $H_a$: $\beta_j > 0$ | $t > t_{[\alpha]}^{(n-(k+1))}$ | The area under the $t$ curve to the right of $t$ |
| $H_a$: $\beta_j < 0$ | $t < -t_{[\alpha]}^{(n-(k+1))}$ | The area under the $t$ curve to the left of $t$ |

Here all the $p$-values are also based on $n - (k + 1)$ degrees of freedom.

---

As in testing $H_0$: $\beta_1 = 0$ in simple linear regression, we usually use the two-sided alternative hypothesis $H_a$: $\beta_j \neq 0$ unless we have theoretical reasons to believe that $\beta_j$ has a particular (plus or minus) sign. Moreover, MINITAB, SAS, and Excel present the results for the two-sided test.

It is customary to test the significance of each and every independent variable in a regression model. Generally speaking,

1. If we can reject $H_0$: $\beta_j = 0$ at the .05 level of significance, we have strong evidence that the independent variable $x_j$ is significantly related to $y$ in the regression model.

2. If we can reject $H_0$: $\beta_j = 0$ at the .01 level of significance, we have very strong evidence that $x_j$ is significantly related to $y$ in the regression model.

3. The smaller the significance level $\alpha$ at which $H_0$ can be rejected, the stronger the evidence that $x_j$ is significantly related to $y$ in the regression model.

**TABLE 4.4** *t*-Statistics and *p*-Values for Testing the Significance of the Intercept, $x_1$, and $x_2$ in the Fuel Consumption Model $y = \beta_0 + \beta_1 x_1 + \beta_2 x_2 + \varepsilon$

| Independent Variable | Null Hypothesis | $b_j$ | $s_{b_j}$ | $t = \dfrac{b_j}{s_{b_j}}$ | *p*-Value |
|---|---|---|---|---|---|
| Intercept | $H_0: \beta_0 = 0$ | $b_0 = 13.1087$ | $s_{b_0} = .8557$ | $t = \dfrac{b_0}{s_{b_0}} = \dfrac{13.1087}{.8557} = 15.32$ | .000 |
| $x_1$ | $H_0: \beta_1 = 0$ | $b_1 = -0.09001$ | $s_{b_1} = .01408$ | $t = \dfrac{b_1}{s_{b_1}} = \dfrac{-.09001}{.01408} = -6.39$ | .001 |
| $x_2$ | $H_0: \beta_2 = 0$ | $b_2 = 0.08249$ | $s_{b_2} = .02200$ | $t = \dfrac{b_2}{s_{b_2}} = \dfrac{.08249}{.02200} = 3.75$ | .013 |

**EXAMPLE 4.6**   Again consider the fuel consumption model

$$y = \beta_0 + \beta_1 x_1 + \beta_2 x_2 + \varepsilon$$

Table 4.4 summarizes the calculation of the *t*-statistics and related *p*-values for testing the significance of the intercept and each of the independent variables $x_1$ and $x_2$. Here the values of $b_j$, $s_{b_j}$, $t$, and the *p*-value have been obtained from the MINITAB and Excel output of Figure 4.5. If we wish to carry out tests at the .05 level of significance, we use the rejection point.

$$t_{[\alpha/2]}^{(n-(k+1))} = t_{[.05/2]}^{(8-3)} = t_{[.025]}^{(5)} = 2.571$$

Looking at Table 4.4, we see that

1.   For the intercept, $|t| = 15.32 > 2.571$.
2.   For $x_1$, $|t| = 6.39 > 2.571$.
3.   For $x_2$, $|t| = 3.75 > 2.571$.

Since in each case $|t| > t_{[.025]}^{(5)}$, we reject each of the null hypotheses in Table 4.4 at the .05 level of significance. Furthermore, since the *p*-values related to the intercept and $x_1$ are each less than .01, we can reject $H_0: \beta_0 = 0$ and $H_0: \beta_1 = 0$ at the .01 level of significance. Since the *p*-value related to $x_2$ is less than .05 but not less than .01, we can reject $H_0: \beta_2 = 0$ at the .05 level of significance, but not at the .01 level of significance. On the basis of these results, we have very strong evidence that in the above model the intercept $\beta_0$ is significant and $x_1$ (average hourly temperature) is significantly related to $y$. We also have strong evidence that in this model $x_2$ (the chill index) is significantly related to $y$.

**EXAMPLE 4.7**   Consider the sales territory performance model

$$y = \beta_0 + \beta_1 x_1 + \beta_2 x_2 + \beta_3 x_3 + \beta_4 x_4 + \beta_5 x_5 + \varepsilon$$

Since the SAS output in Figure 4.7 tells us that the *p*-values associated with Time, MktPoten, Adver, and MktShare are all less than .01, we have very strong evidence that these variables are important in this model. Since the *p*-value associated with Change is .0530, we have close to strong evidence that this variable is important.

We next consider how to calculate a confidence interval for a regression parameter.

### A CONFIDENCE INTERVAL FOR THE REGRESSION PARAMETER $\beta_j$

If the regression assumptions hold, a **$100(1 - \alpha)\%$ confidence interval for the regression parameter $\beta_j$** is

$$\left[ b_j \pm t_{[\alpha/2]}^{(n-(k+1))} s_{b_j} \right]$$

**EXAMPLE 4.8**

Consider the fuel consumption model

$$y = \beta_0 + \beta_1 x_1 + \beta_2 x_2 + \varepsilon$$

The MINITAB and Excel output in Figure 4.5 tells us that $b_1 = -.09001$ and $s_{b_1} = .01408$. It follows, since

$$t_{[\alpha/2]}^{(n-(k+1))} = t_{[.05/2]}^{(8-3)} = t_{[.025]}^{(5)} = 2.571$$

that a 95% confidence interval for $\beta_1$ is (see the Excel output)

$$\left[ b_1 \pm t_{[.025]}^{(8-3)} s_{b_1} \right] = [-.09001 \pm 2.571(.01408)]$$
$$= [-.1262, -.0538]$$

This interval says we are 95% confident that if average hourly temperature increases by one degree and the chill index does not change, then mean weekly fuel consumption will decrease by at least .0538 MMcf of natural gas and by at most .1262 MMcf of natural gas. Furthermore, since this 95% confidence interval does not contain 0, we can reject $H_0$: $\beta_1 = 0$ in favor of $H_a$: $\beta_1 \neq 0$ at the .05 level of significance.

## 4.6 CONFIDENCE AND PREDICTION INTERVALS

In this section we show how to use the linear regression model to find a **confidence interval for a mean value of $y$** and a **prediction interval for an individual value of $y$.** We first present two examples of these intervals, and we then discuss the logic behind and the formulas used to compute the intervals.

**EXAMPLE 4.9**

In the fuel consumption problem, recall that the weather forecasting service has predicted that in the next week the average hourly temperature will be $x_{01} = 40°F$ and the chill index will be $x_{02} = 10$. Also, recall from Example 4.3 that

$$\hat{y} = 13.1087 - .09001x_{01} + .08249x_{02}$$
$$= 13.1087 - .09001(40) + .08249(10)$$
$$= 10.333 \text{ MMcf of natural gas}$$

is the point estimate of mean weekly fuel consumption when $x_1$ equals 40 and $x_2$ equals 10, and is the point prediction of fuel consumption in a single week when $x_1$ equals 40 and $x_2$ equals 10. This point estimate and prediction are given at the bottom of the MINITAB output in Figure 4.5, which we repeat here:

```
   Fit  SE Fit       95% CI            95% PI
10.333   0.170   (9.895, 10.771)   (9.293, 11.374)
```

In addition to giving $\hat{y} = 10.333$, the MINITAB output tells us that a 95% confidence interval for mean weekly fuel consumption when $x_1$ equals 40 and $x_2$ equals 10 is [9.895, 10.771]. This interval says we are 95% confident that mean weekly fuel consumption for all weeks having an average hourly temperature of 40°F and a chill index of 10 is between 9.895 MMcf of natural gas and 10.771 MMcf of natural gas. The MINITAB output also tells us that a 95% prediction interval for fuel consumption in a single week when $x_1$ equals 40 and $x_2$ equals 10 is [9.293, 11.374]. This interval says we are 95% confident that the amount of fuel consumed next week will be between 9.293 MMcf of natural gas and 11.374 MMcf of natural gas.

Recall from Example 3.11 that the simple linear regression model, which predicts next week's fuel consumption on the basis of the average hourly temperature being 40°F, makes us 95% confident that the natural gas company's percentage nomination error will be no more than 15.91%. We now wish to determine if our new model, which predicts next week's fuel consumption on the basis of the average hourly temperature being 40°F and the chill index being 10, is likely to produce a percentage nomination error that is within the 10% allowance granted by the pipeline transmission system. First, recall that the point prediction $\hat{y} = 10.333$ given by our new model would be the natural gas company's transmission nomination for next week. Also note that $\hat{y} = 10.333$ is the midpoint of the 95% prediction interval, [9.293, 11.374], for next week's fuel consumption. The half-length of this interval is $(11.374 - 9.293)/2 = 1.041$, which implies that the interval can be expressed as [10.333 ± 1.041]. Therefore, since 1.041 is $(1.041/10.333)100\% = 10.07\%$ of the transmission nomination of 10.333, the model makes us 95% confident that the actual amount of natural gas that will be used by the city next week will differ from the natural gas company's transmission nomination by no more than 10.07%. That is, we are 95% confident that the natural gas company's percentage nomination error will be less than or equal to 10.07%. Therefore, this error will probably be within the 10% allowance granted by the pipeline transmission system, and it is unlikely that the natural gas company will be required to pay a transmission fine.

**EXAMPLE 4.10**    In the sales territory performance problem, consider a questionable sales representative for whom Time = 85.42, MktPoten = 35,182.73, Adver = 7281.65, MktShare = 9.64, and Change = .28. We have seen in Example 4.4 that the point prediction of the sales corresponding to this combination of values of the independent variables is

$$\hat{y} = -1113.7879 + 3.6121(85.42) + .0421(35,182.73)$$
$$+ .1289(7281.65) + 256.9555(9.64) + 324.5335(.28)$$
$$= 4182 \text{ (that is, } 418,200 \text{ units)}$$

This point prediction is given at the bottom of the SAS output in Figure 4.7, which we repeat here:

| Obs | Dep Var Sales | Predicted Value | Std Error Mean Predict | 95% CL Mean | | 95% CL Predict | |
|-----|-----|-----|-----|-----|-----|-----|-----|
| 26 | . | 4182 | 141.8220 | 3885 | 4479 | 3234 | 5130 |

In addition to giving $\hat{y} = 4182$, the SAS output tells us that a 95% prediction interval for $y$ is [3234, 5130]. Furthermore, the actual sales $y$ for the questionable representative were 3082. This actual sales figure is less than the point prediction $\hat{y} = 4182$ and is less than the lower bound of the 95% prediction interval for $y$, [3234, 5130]. Therefore, we conclude that there is strong evidence that the actual performance of the questionable representative is less than the predicted performance. We should investigate the reason for this. Perhaps the questionable representative needs special training.

In general

$$\hat{y} = b_0 + b_1 x_{01} + \cdots + b_k x_{0k}$$

is the point estimate of the mean value of $y$ when the values of the independent variables are $x_{01}, x_{02}, \ldots, x_{0k}$. Calling this mean value $\mu_{y|x_{01}, x_{02}, \ldots, x_{0k}}$, it can be proved that if the regression assumptions hold, then the population of all possible values of $\hat{y}$ is normally distributed with mean $\mu_{y|x_{01}, x_{02}, \ldots, x_{0k}}$ and standard deviation

$$\sigma_{\hat{y}} = \sigma \sqrt{\text{Distance value}}$$

The formula for the distance value involves matrix algebra and is given in Appendix B. We will soon see how to use MINITAB or SAS output to find the distance value. It can be shown that the farther the values $x_{01}, x_{02}, \ldots, x_{0k}$ are from the center of the experimental region, the larger is the distance value. We regard the center of the experimental region to be the point $(\bar{x}_1, \bar{x}_2, \ldots, \bar{x}_k)$, where $\bar{x}_1$ is the average of the observed $x_1$ values, $\bar{x}_2$ is the average of the observed $x_2$ values, and so forth. Since $s$ is the point estimate of $\sigma$, the point estimate of $\sigma_{\hat{y}}$ is

$$s_{\hat{y}} = s \sqrt{\text{Distance value}}$$

which is called the **standard error of the estimate** $\hat{y}$. Using this standard error, we can form a confidence interval.

## A CONFIDENCE INTERVAL FOR A MEAN VALUE OF $y$

If the regression assumptions hold, a $100(1 - \alpha)\%$ **confidence interval for the mean value of** $y$ when the values of the independent variables are $x_{01}, x_{02}, \ldots, x_{0k}$ is

$$\left[ \hat{y} \pm t_{[\alpha/2]}^{(n-(k+1))} s \sqrt{\text{Distance value}} \right]$$

To develop an interval for an individual value of $y$, we consider the prediction error $y - \hat{y}$. It can be proved that if the regression assumptions hold, then the population of all possible prediction errors is normally distributed with mean 0 and standard deviation

$$\sigma_{(y-\hat{y})} = \sigma\sqrt{1 + \text{Distance value}}$$

The point estimate of $\sigma_{(y-\hat{y})}$ is

$$s_{(y-\hat{y})} = s\sqrt{1 + \text{Distance value}}$$

which is called the **standard error of the prediction error.** Using this standard error, we can form a prediction interval.

---

## A PREDICTION INTERVAL FOR AN INDIVIDUAL VALUE OF $y$

If the regression assumptions hold, a **$100(1 - \alpha)\%$ prediction interval for an individual value of $y$** when the values of the independent variables are $x_{01}, x_{02}, \ldots, x_{0k}$ is

$$\left[\hat{y} \pm t_{[\alpha/2]}^{(n-(k+1))}s\sqrt{1 + \text{Distance value}}\right]$$

---

Recall that the farther the values $x_{01}, x_{02}, \ldots, x_{0k}$ are from the center of the experimental region, the larger is the distance value. It follows that the farther the values $x_{01}, x_{02}, \ldots, x_{0k}$ are from the center of the experimental region, the longer (less precise) are the confidence intervals and prediction intervals provided by a regression model.

MINITAB gives $s_{\hat{y}} = s\sqrt{\text{Distance value}}$ under the heading "SE Fit." Since the MINITAB output also gives $s$, the distance value can be found by calculating $(s_{\hat{y}}/s)^2$. For example, the MINITAB output in Example 4.9 tells us that $\hat{y} = 10.333$ (see "Fit") and $s_{\hat{y}} = .170$ (see "SE Fit"). Therefore, since $s$ for the fuel consumption model with two variables equals .3671, the distance value equals $(.170/.3671)^2 = .2144515$. It follows that the 95% confidence and prediction intervals given on the MINITAB output of Example 4.9 have been calculated as follows.

$$\left[\hat{y} \pm t_{[.025]}^{(8-3)}s\sqrt{\text{Distance value}}\right] = \left[10.333 \pm 2.571(.3671)\sqrt{.2144515}\right]$$
$$= [10.333 \pm .438]$$
$$= [9.895, \ 10.771]$$

$$\left[\hat{y} \pm t_{[.025]}^{(8-3)}s\sqrt{1 + \text{Distance value}}\right] = \left[10.333 \pm 2.571(.3671)\sqrt{1 + .2144515}\right]$$
$$= [10.333 \pm 1.041]$$
$$= [9.293, \ 11.374]$$

As another example, the SAS output in Example 4.10 tells us that $\hat{y} = 4182$ (see "Predicted Value") and $s_{\hat{y}} = 141.8220$ (see "Std Error Mean Predict"). Therefore, since *s* for the sales territory performance model equals 430.23188, the distance value equals $(s_{\hat{y}}/s)^2 = (141.8220/430.23188)^2 = .109$. It follows that the 95% prediction interval given on the SAS output of Example 4.10 has been calculated as follows:

$$\left[\hat{y} \pm t^{(25-6)}_{[.025]}s\sqrt{1 + \text{Distance value}}\right] = \left[4182 \pm 2.093(430.232)\sqrt{1 + .109}\right]$$
$$= [3234, 5130]$$

# 4.7 THE QUADRATIC REGRESSION MODEL

One useful form of the linear regression model is what we call the *quadratic regression model*. Assuming that we have obtained *n* observations—each consisting of an observed value of *y* and a corresponding value of *x*—the model is as follows.

---

## THE QUADRATIC REGRESSION MODEL

The **quadratic regression model** relating *y* to *x* is

$$y = \beta_0 + \beta_1 x + \beta_2 x^2 + \varepsilon$$

where

1. $\beta_0 + \beta_1 x + \beta_2 x^2$ is $\mu_{y|x}$, the mean value of the dependent variable *y* when the value of the independent variable is *x*.

2. $\beta_0$, $\beta_1$, and $\beta_2$ are (unknown) *regression parameters* relating the mean value of *y* to *x*.

3. $\varepsilon$ is an error term that describes the effects on *y* of all factors other than *x* and $x^2$.

---

The quadratic equation $\mu_{y|x} = \beta_0 + \beta_1 x + \beta_2 x^2$ that relates $\mu_{y|x}$ to *x* is the equation of a **parabola.** Two parabolas are shown in Figure 4.8(a) and (b) (page 168) and help to explain the meanings of the parameters $\beta_0$, $\beta_1$, and $\beta_2$. Here $\beta_0$ is the **y-intercept** of the parabola (the value of $\mu_{y|x}$ when *x* = 0). Furthermore, $\beta_1$ is the **shift parameter** of the parabola: the value of $\beta_1$ shifts the parabola to the left or right. Specifically, increasing the value of $\beta_1$ shifts the parabola to the left. Lastly, $\beta_2$ is the **rate of curvature** of the parabola. If $\beta_2$ is greater than 0, the parabola opens upward [see Figure 4.8(a)]. If $\beta_2$ is less than 0, the parabola opens downward [see Figure 4.8(b)].

**FIGURE 4.8** The mean value of the dependent variable changing in a quadratic fashion as $x$ increases ($\mu_{y|x} = \beta_0 + \beta_1 x + \beta_2 x^2$)

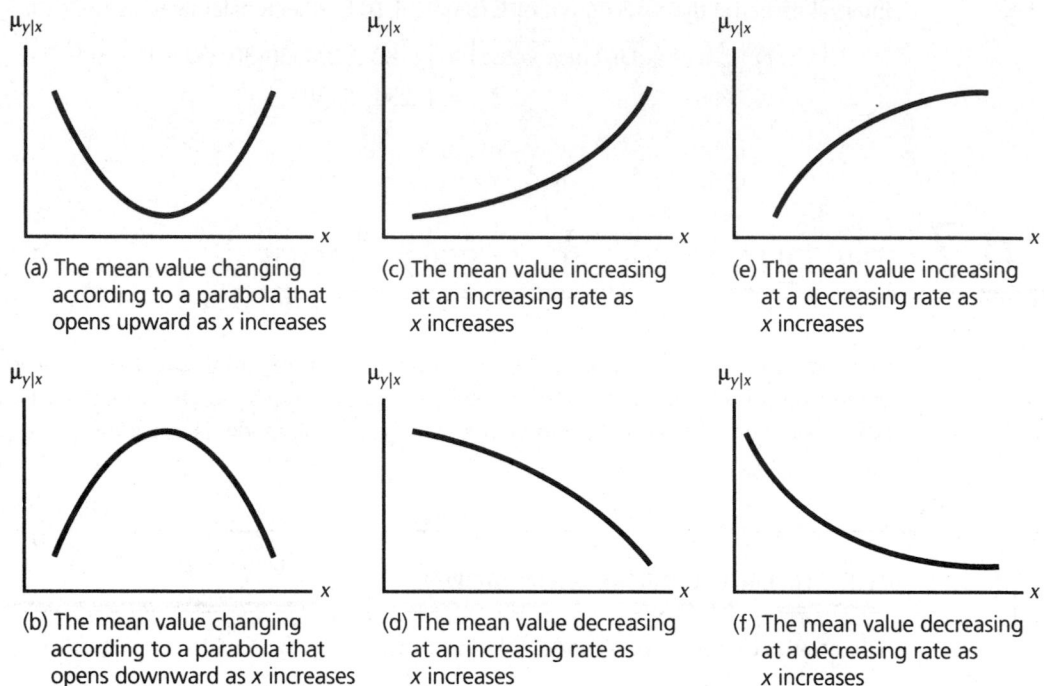

(a) The mean value changing according to a parabola that opens upward as $x$ increases

(c) The mean value increasing at an increasing rate as $x$ increases

(e) The mean value increasing at a decreasing rate as $x$ increases

(b) The mean value changing according to a parabola that opens downward as $x$ increases

(d) The mean value decreasing at an increasing rate as $x$ increases

(f) The mean value decreasing at a decreasing rate as $x$ increases

If a scatter plot of $y$ versus $x$ shows points scattered around a parabola, or a part of a parabola [some typical parts are shown in Figure 4.8(c), (d), (e), and (f)], then the quadratic regression model might appropriately relate $y$ to $x$.

It is important to note that although the quadratic model employs the squared term $x^2$ and therefore assumes a curved relationship between the mean value of $y$ and $x$, this model is a **linear regression model.** This is because the expression $\beta_0 + \beta_1 x + \beta_2 x^2$ expresses the mean value of $y$ as a **linear function of the parameters** $\beta_0$, $\beta_1$, and $\beta_2$. In general, as long as the mean value of $y$ is a *linear function of the regression parameters,* we are using a linear regression model.

**EXAMPLE 4.11**    An oil company wishes to improve the gasoline mileage obtained by cars that use its premium unleaded gasoline. Company chemists suggest that an additive, ST-3000, be blended with the gasoline. In order to study the effects of this additive, mileage tests are carried out in a laboratory using test equipment that simulates driving under prescribed conditions. The amount of additive ST-3000 blended with the gasoline is varied, and the gasoline mileage for each test run is recorded. Table 4.5 gives the results of the test runs.

**TABLE 4.5** The Gasoline Mileage Data

| Number of Units, $x$, of Additive ST-3000 | Gasoline Mileage, $y$ (mpg) |
|:---:|:---:|
| 0 | 25.8 |
| 0 | 26.1 |
| 0 | 25.4 |
| 1 | 29.6 |
| 1 | 29.2 |
| 1 | 29.8 |
| 2 | 32.0 |
| 2 | 31.4 |
| 2 | 31.7 |
| 3 | 31.7 |
| 3 | 31.5 |
| 3 | 31.2 |
| 4 | 29.4 |
| 4 | 29.0 |
| 4 | 29.5 |

**FIGURE 4.9**
Scatter plot of gasoline mileage ($y$) versus number of units ($x$) of additive ST-3000

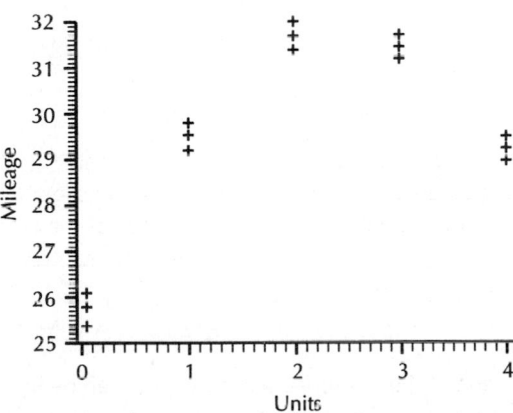

Here the dependent variable $y$ is gasoline mileage (in miles per gallon, mpg) and the independent variable $x$ is the amount of additive ST-3000 used (measured as the number of units of additive added to each gallon of gasoline). One of the study's goals is to determine the number of units of additive that should be blended with the gasoline to maximize gasoline mileage. The company would also like to predict the maximum mileage that can be achieved using additive ST-3000.

Figure 4.9 gives a scatter plot of $y$ versus $x$. Since the scatter plot has the appearance of a quadratic curve (that is, part of a parabola), it seems reasonable to relate $y$ to $x$ by using the quadratic model

$$y = \beta_0 + \beta_1 x + \beta_2 x^2 + \varepsilon$$

**FIGURE 4.10**
MINITAB output of a regression analysis of the gasoline mileage data using the quadratic model

```
The regression equation is
Mileage = 25.7 + 4.98 Units - 1.02 UnitsSq


Predictor        Coef   SE Coef        T      P
Constant      25.7152    0.1554   165.43  0.000
Units          4.9762    0.1841    27.02  0.000
UnitsSq      -1.01905   0.04414   -23.09  0.000


S = 0.286079    R-Sq = 98.6%    R-Sq(adj) = 98.3%


Analysis of Variance

Source          DF       SS       MS       F      P
Regression       2   67.915   33.958  414.92  0.000
Residual Error  12    0.982    0.082
Total           14   68.897

    Fit   SE Fit          95% CI                95% PI
31.7901   0.1111  (31.5481, 32.0322)  (31.1215, 32.4588)
```

Figure 4.10 gives the MINITAB output of a regression analysis of the data using this quadratic model. Here the squared term $x^2$ is denoted as UnitsSq on the output. The MINITAB output tells us that the least squares point estimates of the model parameters are $b_0 = 25.7152$, $b_1 = 4.9762$, and $b_2 = -1.01905$. These estimates give us the least squares prediction equation

$$\hat{y} = 25.7152 + 4.9762x - 1.01905x^2$$

This is the equation of the best quadratic curve that can be fitted to the data plotted in Figure 4.9. The MINITAB output also tells us that the p-values related to $x$ and $x^2$ are less than .001. This implies that we have very strong evidence that each of these model components is significant. The fact that $x^2$ seems significant confirms the graphical evidence that there is a quadratic relationship between $y$ and $x$. Once we have such confirmation, we usually retain the linear term $x$ in the model no matter what the size of its p-value. The reason is that geometrical considerations indicate that it is best to use both $x$ and $x^2$ to model a quadratic relationship.

The oil company wishes to find the value of $x$ that results in the highest predicted mileage. Using calculus, it can be shown that the value $x = 2.44$ maximizes predicted gas mileage. Therefore, the oil company can maximize predicted mileage by blending 2.44 units of additive ST-3000 with each gallon of gasoline. This will result in a predicted gas mileage equal to

$$\hat{y} = 25.7152 + 4.9762(2.44) - 1.01905(2.44)^2$$
$$= 31.7901 \text{ miles per gallon}$$

This predicted mileage is the point estimate of the mean mileage that would be obtained by all gallons of the gasoline (when blended as just described) and is the point prediction of the mileage that would be obtained by an individual gallon of the gasoline. Note that $\hat{y} = 31.7901$ is given at the bottom of the MINITAB output in Figure 4.10. In addition, the MINITAB output tells us that a 95% confidence interval for the mean mileage that would be obtained by all gallons of the gasoline is [31.5481, 32.0322]. If the test equipment simulates driving conditions in a particular automobile, this confidence interval implies that an owner of the automobile can be 95% confident that he or she will average between 31.5481 mpg and 32.0322 mpg when using a very large number of gallons of the gasoline. The MINITAB output also tells us that a 95% prediction interval for the mileage that would be obtained by an individual gallon of the gasoline is [31.1215, 32.4588].

We now consider a model that employs both a linear and a quadratic term for one independent variable and also employs another linear term for a second independent variable.

**EXAMPLE 4.12**

Enterprise Industries produces Fresh, a brand of liquid laundry detergent. In order to more effectively manage its inventory and make revenue projections, the company would like to better predict demand for Fresh. To develop a prediction model, the company has gathered data concerning demand for Fresh over the last 30 sales periods (each sales period is defined to be a four-week period). The demand data are presented in Table 4.6 (page 172). Here, for each sales period,

> $y$ = the demand for the large size bottle of Fresh (in hundreds of thousands of bottles) in the sales period
>
> $x_1$ = the price (in dollars) of Fresh as offered by Enterprise Industries in the sales period
>
> $x_2$ = the average industry price (in dollars) of competitors' similar detergents in the sales period
>
> $x_3$ = Enterprise Industries' advertising expenditure (in hundreds of thousands of dollars) to promote Fresh in the sales period
>
> $x_4 = x_2 - x_1$ = the "price difference" in the sales period

To begin our analysis, suppose that Enterprise Industries believes on theoretical grounds that the single independent variable $x_4$ adequately describes the effects of $x_1$ and $x_2$ on $y$. That is, perhaps demand for Fresh depends more on how the price for Fresh compares to competitors' prices than it does on the absolute levels of the prices for Fresh and other competing detergents. This makes sense since most consumers must buy a certain amount of detergent no matter what the price might be.

Figures 4.11 and 4.12 (page 173) present scatter plots of $y$ versus $x_4$ and $y$ versus $x_3$. The plot in Figure 4.11 indicates that $y$ tends to increase in a straight-line fashion as $x_4$ increases. This suggests that the simple linear model

$$y = \beta_0 + \beta_1 x_4 + \varepsilon$$

**TABLE 4.6** Historical Data, Including Price Differences, Concerning Demand for Fresh Detergent

| Sales Period | Price for Fresh, $x_1$ ($) | Average Industry Price, $x_2$ ($) | Price Difference, $x_4 = x_2 - x_1$ ($) | Advertising Expenditure for Fresh, $x_3$ (× $100,000) | Demand for Fresh, $y$ (× 100,000 Bottles) |
|---|---|---|---|---|---|
| 1 | 3.85 | 3.80 | −.05 | 5.50 | 7.38 |
| 2 | 3.75 | 4.00 | .25 | 6.75 | 8.51 |
| 3 | 3.70 | 4.30 | .60 | 7.25 | 9.52 |
| 4 | 3.70 | 3.70 | 0 | 5.50 | 7.50 |
| 5 | 3.60 | 3.85 | .25 | 7.00 | 9.33 |
| 6 | 3.60 | 3.80 | .20 | 6.50 | 8.28 |
| 7 | 3.60 | 3.75 | .15 | 6.75 | 8.75 |
| 8 | 3.80 | 3.85 | .05 | 5.25 | 7.87 |
| 9 | 3.80 | 3.65 | −.15 | 5.25 | 7.10 |
| 10 | 3.85 | 4.00 | .15 | 6.00 | 8.00 |
| 11 | 3.90 | 4.10 | .20 | 6.50 | 7.89 |
| 12 | 3.90 | 4.00 | .10 | 6.25 | 8.15 |
| 13 | 3.70 | 4.10 | .40 | 7.00 | 9.10 |
| 14 | 3.75 | 4.20 | .45 | 6.90 | 8.86 |
| 15 | 3.75 | 4.10 | .35 | 6.80 | 8.90 |
| 16 | 3.80 | 4.10 | .30 | 6.80 | 8.87 |
| 17 | 3.70 | 4.20 | .50 | 7.10 | 9.26 |
| 18 | 3.80 | 4.30 | .50 | 7.00 | 9.00 |
| 19 | 3.70 | 4.10 | .40 | 6.80 | 8.75 |
| 20 | 3.80 | 3.75 | −.05 | 6.50 | 7.95 |
| 21 | 3.80 | 3.75 | −.05 | 6.25 | 7.65 |
| 22 | 3.75 | 3.65 | −.10 | 6.00 | 7.27 |
| 23 | 3.70 | 3.90 | .20 | 6.50 | 8.00 |
| 24 | 3.55 | 3.65 | .10 | 7.00 | 8.50 |
| 25 | 3.60 | 4.10 | .50 | 6.80 | 8.75 |
| 26 | 3.65 | 4.25 | .60 | 6.80 | 9.21 |
| 27 | 3.70 | 3.65 | −.05 | 6.50 | 8.27 |
| 28 | 3.75 | 3.75 | 0 | 5.75 | 7.67 |
| 29 | 3.80 | 3.85 | .05 | 5.80 | 7.93 |
| 30 | 3.70 | 4.25 | .55 | 6.80 | 9.26 |

might appropriately relate $y$ to $x_4$. The plot in Figure 4.12 indicates that $y$ tends to increase in a curved fashion as $x_3$ increases. Since this curve appears to have the shape of Figure 4.8(c), this suggests that the quadratic model

$$y = \beta_0 + \beta_1 x_3 + \beta_2 x_3^2 + \varepsilon$$

might appropriately relate $y$ to $x_3$.

To construct a prediction model based on both $x_3$ and $x_4$, it seems reasonable to combine these two models to form the regression model

$$y = \beta_0 + \beta_1 x_4 + \beta_2 x_3 + \beta_3 x_3^2 + \varepsilon$$

**FIGURE 4.11**

Plot of $y$ (demand for Fresh detergent) versus $x_4$ (price difference)

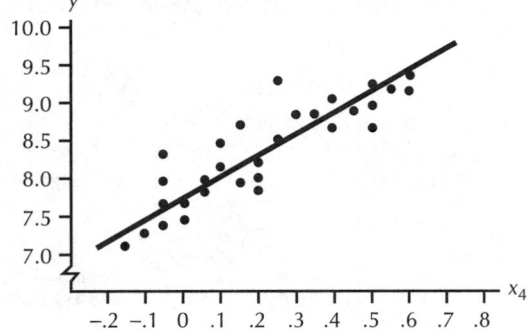

**FIGURE 4.12**

Plot of $y$ (demand for Fresh detergent) versus $x_3$ (advertising expenditure for Fresh)

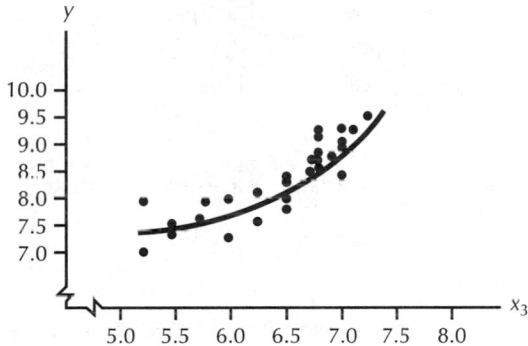

Here we have arbitrarily ordered the $x_4$, $x_3$, and $x_3^2$ terms in the combined model, and we have renumbered the subscripts on the $\beta$s appropriately. In the combined model

$$\beta_0 + \beta_1 x_4 + \beta_2 x_3 + \beta_3 x_3^2$$

is the mean demand for Fresh when the price difference is $x_4$ and the advertising expenditure is $x_3$. The error term describes the effects on demand of all factors other than $x_4$ and $x_3$.

Figure 4.13 (page 174) presents the SAS output of a regression analysis of the Fresh demand data using the combined model. The output tells us that the least squares point estimates of the model parameters are $b_0 = 17.32437$, $b_1 = 1.30699$, $b_2 = -3.69559$, and $b_3 = .34861$. The output also tells us that the $p$-values related to $x_4$, $x_3$, and $x_3^2$ are .0002, .0564, and .0293. Therefore, we have strong evidence that each of the model components $x_4$ and $x_3^2$ is significant. Furthermore, although the $p$-value related to $x_3$ is slightly greater than .05, we will (as discussed in Example 4.11) retain $x_3$ in the model because $x_3^2$ is significant.

In order to predict demand in a future sales period, Enterprise Industries must determine future values of $x_3$ and $x_4 = x_2 - x_1$. Of course, the company can set $x_1$ (its price for Fresh) and $x_3$ (its advertising expenditure). Also, it feels that by examining the prices of competitors'

**FIGURE 4.13** SAS output of a regression analysis of the Fresh demand data in Table 4.6 using the model $y = \beta_0 + \beta_1 x_4 + \beta_2 x_3 + \beta_3 x_3^2 + \varepsilon$

Analysis of Variance

| Source | DF | Sum of Squares | Mean Square | F Value | Pr > F |
|---|---|---|---|---|---|
| Model | 3 | 12.18532 | 4.06177 | 82.94 | <.0001 |
| Error | 26 | 1.27327 | 0.04897 | | |
| Corrected Total | 29 | 13.45859 | | | |

| | | | | |
|---|---|---|---|---|
| Root MSE | 0.22130 | R-Square | 0.9054 | |
| Dependent Mean | 8.38267 | Adj R-Sq | 0.8945 | |
| Coeff Var | 2.63992 | | | |

Parameter Estimates

| Variable | Label | DF | Parameter Estimate | Standard Error | t Value | Pr > \|t\| |
|---|---|---|---|---|---|---|
| Intercept | Intercept | 1 | 17.32437 | 5.64146 | 3.07 | 0.0050 |
| X4 | PriceDif | 1 | 1.30699 | 0.30361 | 4.30 | 0.0002 |
| X3 | AdvExp | 1 | -3.69559 | 1.85027 | -2.00 | 0.0564 |
| X3SQ | X3 ** 2 | 1 | 0.34861 | 0.15118 | 2.31 | 0.0293 |

| Obs | Dep Var Demand | Predicted Value | Std Error Mean Predict | 95% CL Mean | | 95% CL Predict | |
|---|---|---|---|---|---|---|---|
| 31 | . | 8.2933 | 0.0581 | 8.1738 | 8.4128 | 7.8230 | 8.7636 |

similar products immediately prior to a future period, it can very accurately predict $x_2$ (the average industry price for competitors' similar detergents). Furthermore, the company can react to any change in competitors' price to maintain any desired price difference $x_4 = x_2 - x_1$. This is an advantage of predicting on the basis of $x_4$ rather than on the basis of $x_1$ and $x_2$ (which the company cannot control). Therefore, suppose that the company will maintain a price difference of $.20 ($x_{04}$ = .20) and will spend $650,000 on advertising ($x_{03}$ = 6.50) in a future sales period. Since this combination of price difference and advertising expenditure is in the experimental region defined by the data in Table 4.6, a point prediction of demand in the future sales period is

$$\hat{y} = 17.32437 + 1.30699 x_{04} - 3.69559 x_{03} + .34861 x_{03}^2$$

$$= 17.32437 + 1.30699(.20) - 3.69559(6.50) + .34861(6.50)^2$$

$$= 8.2933 \text{ (that is, } 829,330 \text{ bottles)}$$

This quantity, in addition to being the point prediction of demand in a single sales period when the price difference is $.20 and the advertising expenditure is $650,000, is also the point estimate of the mean of all possible demands when $x_4 = .20$ and $x_3 = 6.5$. Note that $\hat{y} = 8.2933$ is given on the SAS output of Figure 4.13. The output also gives a 95% confidence interval for mean demand when $x_4$ equals .20 and $x_3$ equals 6.50, which is [8.1738, 8.4128], and a 95% prediction interval for an individual demand when $x_4$ equals .20 and $x_3$ equals 6.50, which is [7.8230, 8.7636]. This latter interval says we are 95%

confident that the actual demand in the future sales period will be between 782,300 bottles and 876,360 bottles. The upper limit of this interval can be used for inventory control. It says that if Enterprise Industries plans to have 876,360 bottles on hand to meet demand in the future sales period, then the company can be very confident that it will have enough bottles. The lower limit of the interval can be used to better understand Enterprise Industries' cash flow situation. It says the company can be very confident that it will sell at least 782,300 bottles in the future sales period. Therefore, for example, if the average competitors' price is $3.90 and thus Enterprise Industries' price is $3.70, the company can be very confident that its minimum revenue from the large size bottle of Fresh in the future period will be at least 782,300 × $3.70 = $2,894,510.

# 4.8 INTERACTION

Multiple regression models often contain **interaction variables.** We form an interaction variable by multiplying two independent variables together. For instance, if a regression model includes the independent variables $x_1$ and $x_2$, then we can form the interaction variable $x_1x_2$. It is appropriate to employ an interaction variable if the relationship between the mean value of the dependent variable $y$ and one of the independent variables is dependent on (that is, is different depending on) the value of the other independent variable. We explain the concept of interaction in the following example.

**EXAMPLE 4.13**    **Part 1: The Data and Data Plots**

Bonner Frozen Foods, Inc., has designed an experiment to study the effects of two types of advertising expenditures on sales of one of its lines of frozen foods. Twenty-five sales regions of equal sales potential were selected. Different combinations of $x_1$ = radio and television expenditures (measured in units of $1000) and $x_2$ = print expenditures (measured in units of $1000) were specified and randomly assigned to the sales regions. Table 4.7 (page 176) shows the expenditure combinations along with the associated values of sales volume, measured in units of $10,000 and denoted $y$, for the sales regions during August of last year.

To help decide whether interaction exists between $x_1$ and $x_2$, we can plot the data in Table 4.7. To do this, we first plot $y$ versus $x_1$. In constructing this plot, we make the plot character for each point the corresponding value of $x_2$ ($x_2$ = 1, 2, 3, 4, 5). The resulting plot (shown in Figure 4.14) (page 176) is called a **plot of $y$ versus $x_1$ for the different "levels" of $x_2$.** Looking at this plot, we see that the straight line relating $y$ to $x_1$ when $x_2$ equals 5 appears to have a smaller slope than does the line relating $y$ to $x_1$ when $x_2$ equals 1. That is, the rate of increase of the line corresponding to $x_2$ = 5 is less steep than the rate of increase

**TABLE 4.7** Bonner Frozen Foods, Inc., Sales Volume Data

| Sales Region | Radio and Television Spending, $x_1$ | Print Spending, $x_2$ | Sales Volume, y | Sales Region | Radio and Television Spending, $x_1$ | Print Spending, $x_2$ | Sales Volume, y |
|---|---|---|---|---|---|---|---|
| 1 | 1 | 1 | 3.27 | 14 | 3 | 4 | 17.99 |
| 2 | 1 | 2 | 8.38 | 15 | 3 | 5 | 19.85 |
| 3 | 1 | 3 | 11.28 | 16 | 4 | 1 | 9.46 |
| 4 | 1 | 4 | 14.50 | 17 | 4 | 2 | 12.61 |
| 5 | 1 | 5 | 19.63 | 18 | 4 | 3 | 15.50 |
| 6 | 2 | 1 | 5.84 | 19 | 4 | 4 | 17.68 |
| 7 | 2 | 2 | 10.01 | 20 | 4 | 5 | 21.02 |
| 8 | 2 | 3 | 12.46 | 21 | 5 | 1 | 12.23 |
| 9 | 2 | 4 | 16.67 | 22 | 5 | 2 | 13.58 |
| 10 | 2 | 5 | 19.83 | 23 | 5 | 3 | 16.77 |
| 11 | 3 | 1 | 8.51 | 24 | 5 | 4 | 20.56 |
| 12 | 3 | 2 | 10.14 | 25 | 5 | 5 | 21.05 |
| 13 | 3 | 3 | 14.75 | | | | |

**FIGURE 4.14**
Plot of y versus $x_1$ (plot character is the corresponding value of $x_2$): the larger $x_2$ is, the smaller is the slope of the straight line relating y to $x_1$

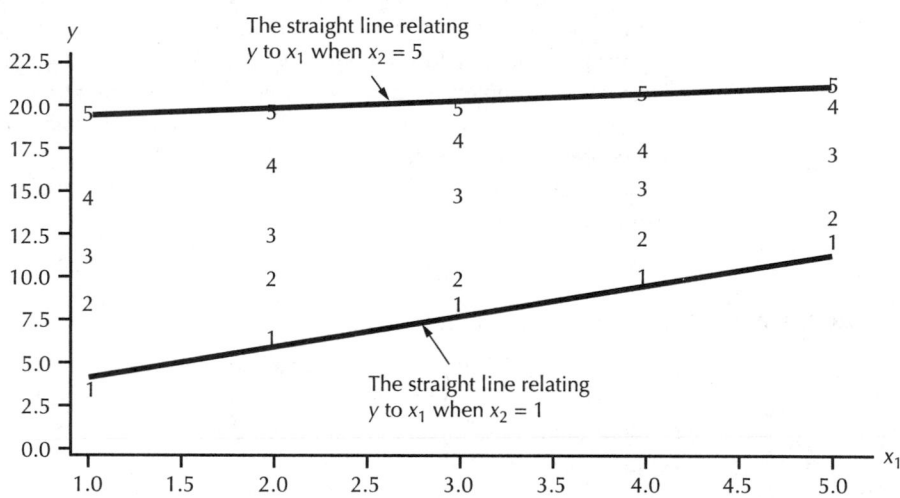

of the line corresponding to $x_2 = 1$. Examining the entire data plot, Figure 4.14 might suggest that the larger $x_2$ is, the smaller is the slope of the straight line relating y to $x_1$.

In Figure 4.15 we plot y versus $x_2$ for the different levels of $x_1$ ($x_1 = 1, 2, 3, 4, 5$). Here the plot character for each point is the corresponding value of $x_1$. We see that the straight line relating y to $x_2$ when $x_1$ equals 5 appears to have a smaller slope than does the straight line relating y to $x_2$ when $x_1$ equals 1. Looking at the entire data plot, Figure 4.15 might suggest that the larger $x_1$ is, the smaller is the slope of the straight line relating y to $x_2$.

In summary, Figures 4.14 and 4.15 seem to imply that the more money spent on one type of advertising, the smaller is the slope of the straight line relating sales volume to

**FIGURE 4.15**

Plot of $y$ versus $x_2$ (plot character is the corresponding value of $x_1$): the larger $x_1$ is, the smaller is the slope of the straight line relating $y$ to $x_2$

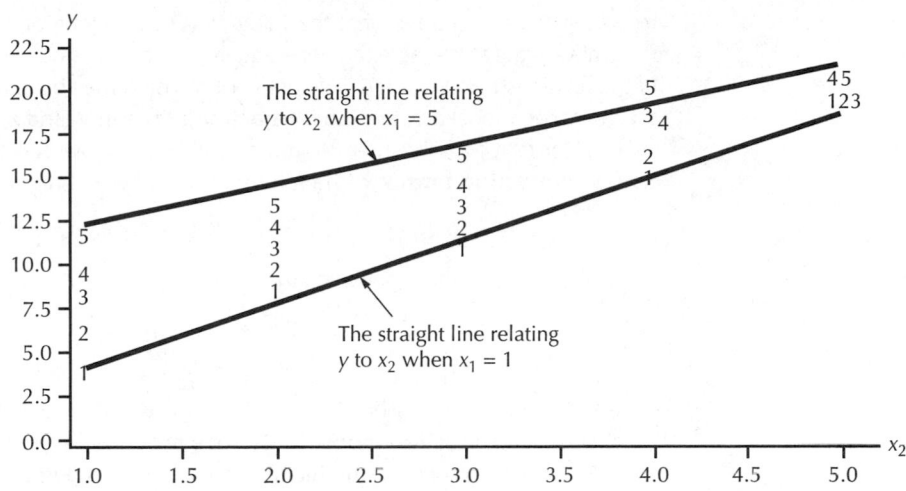

the amount spent on the other type of advertising. This says that there is **interaction** between $x_1$ and $x_2$ because

1.  The relationship between $y$ and $x_1$ (the slope of the line relating $y$ to $x_1$) is different for different values of $x_2$.

2.  The relationship between $y$ and $x_2$ (the slope of the line relating $y$ to $x_2$) is different for different values of $x_1$.

Intuitively, interaction between $x_1$ and $x_2$ makes sense because as Bonner Frozen Foods spends more money on one type of advertising, increases in spending on the other type of advertising might become less effective.

### Part 2: Modeling the Interaction between $x_1$ and $x_2$

The regression model

$$y = \beta_0 + \beta_1 x_1 + \beta_2 x_2 + \varepsilon$$

cannot describe the interaction between $x_1$ and $x_2$ because this model says that mean sales volume equals

$$\beta_0 + \beta_1 x_1 + \beta_2 x_2 = (\beta_0 + \beta_1 x_1) + \beta_2 x_2$$

This implies that for any particular value of $x_1$, the slope of the straight line relating the mean value of $y$ to $x_2$ will always be $\beta_2$. That is, no matter what the value of $x_1$ is, the slope of the line relating mean $y$ to $x_2$ is always the same. This rules out the possibility of describing the relationships illustrated in Figure 4.15 by using the above model. The model also says that mean sales volume equals

$$\beta_0 + \beta_1 x_1 + \beta_2 x_2 = (\beta_0 + \beta_2 x_2) + \beta_1 x_1$$

This implies that no matter what the value of $x_2$ is, the slope of the line relating mean $y$ to $x_1$ is always the same (here the slope equals $\beta_1$). This rules out the possibility of describing the relationships illustrated in Figure 4.14 by using the above model. In short, we say that the above model assumes **no interaction** between $x_1$ and $x_2$.

In order to model the interaction between $x_1$ and $x_2$ we can use the **cross-product term** or **interaction term** $x_1x_2$. Therefore, we consider the model

$$y = \beta_0 + \beta_1x_1 + \beta_2x_2 + \beta_3x_1x_2 + \varepsilon$$

This model says that mean sales volume equals

$$\beta_0 + \beta_1x_1 + \beta_2x_2 + \beta_3x_1x_2$$

which can be rewritten as $(\beta_0 + \beta_1x_1) + (\beta_2 + \beta_3x_1)x_2$. This implies that the slope of the line relating mean $y$ to $x_2$, which is $(\beta_2 + \beta_3x_1)$, will be different for different values of $x_1$. This allows the **interaction model** to describe relationships such as those illustrated in Figure 4.15. Furthermore, for this model the mean sales volume

$$\beta_0 + \beta_1x_1 + \beta_2x_2 + \beta_3x_1x_2$$

can also be rewritten as $(\beta_0 + \beta_2x_2) + (\beta_1 + \beta_3x_2)x_1$. This implies that the slope of the line relating mean $y$ to $x_1$, which is $(\beta_1 + \beta_3x_2)$, will be different for different values of $x_2$. This allows the interaction model to describe relationships such as those illustrated in Figure 4.14. In short, we say that the model employing the term $x_1x_2$ assumes that **interaction exists** between $x_1$ and $x_2$.

### Part 3: Statistical Inference

Figure 4.16 gives the MINITAB output of a regression analysis of the data in Table 4.7 by using the model

$$y = \beta_0 + \beta_1x_1 + \beta_2x_2 + \beta_3x_1x_2 + \varepsilon$$

Note that $x_1x_2$ is denoted as Interact on the output. Since all of the $p$-values related to the intercept and the independent variables are less than .01, we have very strong evidence that each of $\beta_0$, $x_1$, $x_2$, and $x_1x_2$ is significant in the above model. In particular, the very small $p$-value related to $x_1x_2$ confirms that interaction exists between $x_1$ and $x_2$ as was originally suggested by the plots in Figures 4.14 and 4.15 (if there were little or no interaction between $x_1$ and $x_2$, the term $x_1x_2$ would be insignificant since it would not help us to model the data).

Next, suppose that Bonner Frozen Foods will spend \$2000 on radio and television advertising ($x_1 = 2$) and will spend \$5000 on print advertising ($x_2 = 5$) in a future month in a particular sales region. If there are no trend, seasonal, or other time-related influences affecting monthly sales volume, then it is reasonable to believe that the regression relationship between $y$ and $x_1$ and $x_2$ that we have developed probably applies to the future month and particular sales region. It follows that

$$\hat{y} = -2.3497 + 2.3611(2) + 4.1831(5) - 0.3489(2)(5)$$
$$= 19.799 \text{ (that is, } \$197,990)$$

**FIGURE 4.16** MINITAB output of a regression analysis of the Bonner sales volume data in Table 4.7 using the model $y = \beta_0 + \beta_1 x_1 + \beta_2 x_2 + \beta_3 x_1 x_2 + \varepsilon$

```
The regression equation is
Volume = - 2.35 + 2.36 RadioTV + 4.18 Print - 0.349 Interact


Predictor         Coef   SE Coef        T       P
Constant       -2.3497    0.6883    -3.41   0.003
RadioTV         2.3611    0.2075    11.38   0.000
Print           4.1831    0.2075    20.16   0.000
Interact       -0.34890   0.06257   -5.58   0.000


S = 0.625710     R-Sq = 98.6%    R-Sq(adj) = 98.4%


Analysis of Variance

Source           DF       SS       MS       F       P
Regression        3    590.41   196.80   502.67   0.000
Residual Error   21      8.22     0.39
Total            24    598.63

    Fit   SE Fit       95% CI            95% PI
 19.799    0.265   (19.247, 20.351)   (18.385, 21.213)
```

is a point estimate of mean sales volume when $2000 is spent on radio and television advertising and $5000 is spent on print advertising. In addition, $\hat{y}$ is a point prediction of the individual sales volume that will be observed in the future month in the particular sales region. Besides giving $\hat{y} = 19.799$, the MINITAB output in Figure 4.16 tells us that the 95% confidence interval for mean sales volume is [19.247, 20.351] and that the 95% prediction interval for an individual sales volume is [18.385, 21.213]. This prediction interval says we are 95% confident that the individual sales volume in the future month in the particular sales region will be between $183,850 and $212,130.

It is easy to construct data plots to check for interaction in the Bonner Frozen Foods example because the company has carried out a designed experiment. In many regression problems, however, we do not carry out a designed experiment, and the data are "unstructured." In such a case, it may not be possible to construct the data plots needed to detect interaction between independent variables. For example, if we consider the Fresh demand data in Table 4.6, we might suspect that there is interaction between $x_3$ (advertising expenditure) and $x_4$ (the price difference). That is, we might suspect that the relationship between mean demand for Fresh and advertising expenditure is different for different levels of the price difference. For instance, increases in advertising expenditures might be more effective at some price differences than at others. To detect such interaction, we would like to construct plots of demand versus $x_3$ for different levels of $x_4$. However, examination of the Fresh demand data reveals that there are only a few observations at any one level of the price difference, and therefore the needed data plots cannot easily be made. In such a case we can use $t$-statistics and $p$-values related to potential interaction terms to try to assess the importance of inter-action. We illustrate this in the following example.

**EXAMPLE 4.14**    **Part 1: An Interaction Model and Statistical Inference**

In Example 4.12 we considered the Fresh demand model

$$y = \beta_0 + \beta_1 x_4 + \beta_2 x_3 + \beta_3 x_3^2 + \varepsilon$$

Since we might logically suspect that there is interaction between $x_4$ and $x_3$, we add the interaction term $x_4 x_3$ to this model and form the model

$$y = \beta_0 + \beta_1 x_4 + \beta_2 x_3 + \beta_3 x_3^2 + \beta_4 x_4 x_3 + \varepsilon$$

Figure 4.17 presents the SAS output obtained by using this model to perform a regression analysis of the Fresh demand data. This output shows that each of the $p$-values for testing the significance of the intercept and the independent variables is less than .05. Therefore, we have strong evidence that the intercept and each of $x_4$, $x_3$, $x_3^2$, and $x_4 x_3$ are significant. In particular, since the $p$-value related to $x_4 x_3$ is .0361, we have strong evidence that the interaction variable $x_4 x_3$ is important. This confirms that the interaction between $x_4$ and $x_3$ that we suspected really does exist.

**FIGURE 4.17** SAS output of a regression analysis of the Fresh demand data using the interaction model
$y = \beta_0 + \beta_1 x_4 + \beta_2 x_3 + \beta_3 x_3^2 + \beta_4 x_4 x_3 + \varepsilon$

### Analysis of Variance

| Source | DF | Sum of Squares | Mean Square | F Value | Pr > F |
|---|---|---|---|---|---|
| Model | 4 | 12.39419 | 3.09855 | 72.78 | <.0001 |
| Error | 25 | 1.06440 | 0.04258 | | |
| Corrected Total | 29 | 13.45859 | | | |

| | | | | |
|---|---|---|---|---|
| Root MSE | 0.20634 | R-Square | 0.9209 | |
| Dependent Mean | 8.38267 | Adj R-Sq | 0.9083 | |
| Coeff Var | 2.46150 | | | |

### Parameter Estimates

| Variable | Label | DF | Parameter Estimate | Standard Error | t Value | Pr > \|t\| |
|---|---|---|---|---|---|---|
| Intercept | Intercept | 1 | 29.11329 | 7.48321 | 3.89 | 0.0007 |
| X4 | PriceDif | 1 | 11.13423 | 4.44585 | 2.50 | 0.0192 |
| X3 | AdvExp | 1 | -7.60801 | 2.46911 | -3.08 | 0.0050 |
| X3SQ | X3 ** 2 | 1 | 0.67125 | 0.20270 | 3.31 | 0.0028 |
| X4X3 | X4 * X3 | 1 | -1.47772 | 0.66716 | -2.21 | 0.0361 |

| Obs | Dep Var Demand | Predicted Value | Std Error Mean Predict | 95% CL Mean | | 95% CL Predict | |
|---|---|---|---|---|---|---|---|
| 31 | . | 8.3272 | 0.0563 | 8.2112 | 8.4433 | 7.8867 | 8.7678 |

Suppose again that Enterprise Industries wishes to predict demand for Fresh in a future sales period when the price difference will be \$.20 ($x_4 = .20$) and when the advertising expenditure for Fresh will be \$650,000 ($x_3 = 6.50$). Using the least squares point estimates in Figure 4.17, the needed point prediction is

$$\hat{y} = 29.11329 + 11.13423(.20) - 7.60801(6.50) + .67125(6.50)^2 - 1.47772(.20)(6.50)$$
$$= 8.3272 \ (832{,}720 \text{ bottles})$$

This point prediction is given on the SAS output of Figure 4.17, which also tells us that the 95% confidence interval for mean demand when $x_4$ equals .20 and $x_3$ equals 6.50 is [8.2112, 8.4433] and that the 95% prediction interval for an individual demand when $x_4$ equals .20 and $x_3$ equals 6.50 is [7.8867, 8.7678]. Notice that this prediction interval is shorter than the 95% interval—[7.8230, 8.7636]—obtained using the model that omits the interaction term $x_4x_3$ and predicts $y$ on the basis of $x_4$, $x_3$, and $x_3^2$. This is another indication that it is useful to include the interaction variable $x_4x_3$ in the model.

### Part 2: The Nature of Interaction between $x_3$ and $x_4$

To understand the exact nature of the interaction between $x_3$ and $x_4$, consider the prediction equation

$$\hat{y} = 29.1133 + 11.1342x_4 - 7.6080x_3 + .6712x_3^2 - 1.4777x_4x_3$$

obtained by using the Fresh demand interaction model. If we set $x_4$ equal to .10 and place this value of $x_4$ into the prediction equation, we obtain

$$\hat{y} = 29.1133 + 11.1342x_4 - 7.6080x_3 + .6712x_3^2 - 1.4777x_4x_3$$
$$= 29.1133 + 11.1342(.10) - 7.6080x_3 + .6712x_3^2 - 1.4777(.10)x_3$$
$$= 30.2267 - 7.7558x_3 + .6712x_3^2$$

This quadratic equation shows us how predicted demand changes as advertising expenditure $x_3$ increases when the price difference is .10. Next we set $x_4$ equal to .30. If we place this value of $x_4$ into the Fresh prediction equation, we obtain

$$\hat{y} = 29.1133 + 11.1342x_4 - 7.6080x_3 + .6712x_3^2 - 1.4777x_4x_3$$
$$= 29.1133 + 11.1342(.30) - 7.6080x_3 + .6712x_3^2 - 1.4777(.30)x_3$$
$$= 32.4535 - 8.0513x_3 + .6712x_3^2$$

This quadratic equation shows us how predicted demand changes as advertising expenditure $x_3$ increases when the price difference is .30.

In Figure 4.18(a) and (b) (page 182) we calculate three points (predicted demands) on each of these quadratic curves. Figure 4.18(c) shows graphs of the two quadratic curves with the predicted demands plotted on these graphs. Comparing these graphs, we see that predicted demand is higher when $x_4$ equals .30 than when $x_4$ equals .10. This makes sense—predicted demand should be higher when Enterprise Industries has a larger price

**FIGURE 4.18** Interaction between $x_4$ and $x_3$ in the Fresh detergent case

(a) Calculating values of predicted demand when $x_4$ equals .10

$x_3$ $\quad \hat{y} = 30.2267 - 7.7558x_3 + .6712x_3^2$
6.0 $\quad \hat{y} = 30.2267 - 7.7558(6.0) + .6712(6.0)^2 = 7.86$
6.4 $\quad \hat{y} = 30.2267 - 7.7558(6.4) + .6712(6.4)^2 = 8.08$
6.8 $\quad \hat{y} = 30.2267 - 7.7558(6.8) + .6712(6.8)^2 = 8.52$

(b) Calculating values of predicted demand when $x_4$ equals .30

$x_3$ $\quad \hat{y} = 32.4535 - 8.0513x_3 + .6712x_3^2$
6.0 $\quad \hat{y} = 32.4535 - 8.0513(6.0) + .6712(6.0)^2 = 8.31$
6.4 $\quad \hat{y} = 32.4535 - 8.0513(6.4) + .6712(6.4)^2 = 8.42$
6.8 $\quad \hat{y} = 32.4535 - 8.0513(6.8) + .6712(6.8)^2 = 8.74$

(c) Illustrating the interaction

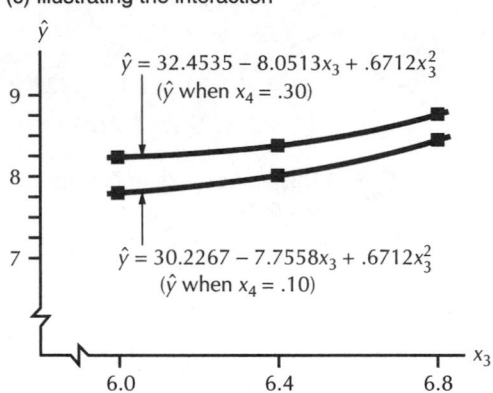

advantage. Furthermore, for each curve we see that predicted demand increases at an increasing rate as $x_3$ increases. However, the rate of increase in predicted demand is slower when $x_4$ equals .30 than when $x_4$ equals .10—this is the effect of the interaction between $x_3$ and $x_4$.

This type of interaction is logical because when the price difference is large (the price for Fresh is low relative to the average industry price), the mean demand for Fresh will be high (assuming the quality of Fresh is comparable to competing brands). Thus with mean demand already high because many consumers are buying Fresh on the basis of price, there may be little opportunity for increased advertising expenditure to increase mean demand. However, when the price difference is smaller, there may be more potential consumers who are not buying Fresh who can be convinced to do so by increased advertising. Thus when the price difference is smaller, increased advertising expenditure is more effective than it is when the price difference is larger.

It should be noted that this type of interaction between $x_4$ and $x_3$ was estimated from the observed Fresh demand data in Table 4.6. This is because we obtained the least squares point estimates using these data. We are not hypothesizing the existence of the interaction; the importance of the $x_4 x_3$ term and the least squares point estimates tell us that this type of interaction exists. However, we can only hypothesize the reasons behind the interaction. We should also point out that this type of interaction can be assumed to exist only for values of $x_4$ and $x_3$ inside the experimental region. Examination of the Fresh demand data shows that Fresh was being sold at either a price advantage (when the price of Fresh is lower than the average industry price) or at a slight price disadvantage (when the price of Fresh is slightly higher than the average industry price). However, if Fresh were sometimes sold at a large price disadvantage, the type of interaction that exists between $x_4$ and $x_3$ might be different. In such a case, increases in advertising expenditure might be very ineffective because most consumers will not wish to buy a product with a much higher price.

As another example, if we perform a regression analysis of the fuel consumption data by using the model

$$y = \beta_0 + \beta_1 x_1 + \beta_2 x_2 + \beta_3 x_1 x_2 + \varepsilon$$

we find that the $p$-value for testing $H_0$: $\beta_3 = 0$ is .787. Therefore, we conclude that the interaction term $x_1 x_2$ is not needed and that there is little or no interaction between the average hourly temperature and the chill index.

A final comment is in order. If a $p$-value indicates that an interaction term (say, $x_1 x_2$) is important, then it is usual practice to retain the corresponding linear terms ($x_1$ and $x_2$) in the model no matter what the size of their $p$-values. The reason is that doing so can be shown to give a model that will better describe the interaction between $x_1$ and $x_2$.

# 4.9 USING DUMMY VARIABLES TO MODEL QUALITATIVE INDEPENDENT VARIABLES

The levels (or values) of a quantitative independent variable are numerical, whereas the levels of a **qualitative** independent variable are defined by describing them. For instance, the type of sales technique used by a door-to-door salesperson is a qualitative independent variable. Here we might define three different levels—high pressure, medium pressure, and low pressure.

We can model the effects of the different levels of a qualitative independent variable by using what we call **dummy variables** (also called **indicator variables**). Such variables are usually defined so that they take on two values—either 0 or 1. To see how we use dummy variables, we begin with an example.

**EXAMPLE 4.15**   **Part 1: The Data and Data Plots**

Suppose that Electronics World, a chain of stores that sells audio and video equipment, has gathered the data in Table 4.8 (page 184). These data concern store sales volume in July of last year ($y$, measured in thousands of dollars), the number of households in the store's area ($x$, measured in thousands), and the location of the store (on a suburban street or in a suburban shopping mall—a qualitative independent variable). Figure 4.19 (page 184) gives a data plot of $y$ versus $x$. Stores having a street location are plotted as solid dots, while stores having a mall location are plotted as asterisks. Notice that the line relating $y$ to $x$ for mall locations has a higher $y$-intercept than does the line relating $y$ to $x$ for street locations.

**Part 2: A Dummy Variable Model**

In order to model the effects of the street and shopping mall locations, we define a dummy variable denoted $D_M$ as follows:

$$D_M = \begin{cases} 1 & \text{if a store is in a mall location} \\ 0 & \text{otherwise} \end{cases}$$

**TABLE 4.8** The Electronics World Sales Volume Data

| Store | Number of Households, $x$ (× 1000) | Location | Sales Volume, $y$ (× 1000) |
|-------|------------------------------------|----------|----------------------------|
| 1 | 161 | Street | 157.27 |
| 2 | 99 | Street | 93.28 |
| 3 | 135 | Street | 136.81 |
| 4 | 120 | Street | 123.79 |
| 5 | 164 | Street | 153.51 |
| 6 | 221 | Mall | 241.74 |
| 7 | 179 | Mall | 201.54 |
| 8 | 204 | Mall | 206.71 |
| 9 | 214 | Mall | 229.78 |
| 10 | 101 | Mall | 135.22 |

**FIGURE 4.19** Plot of the sales volume data and a geometrical interpretation of the model $y = \beta_0 + \beta_1 x + \beta_2 D_M + \varepsilon$

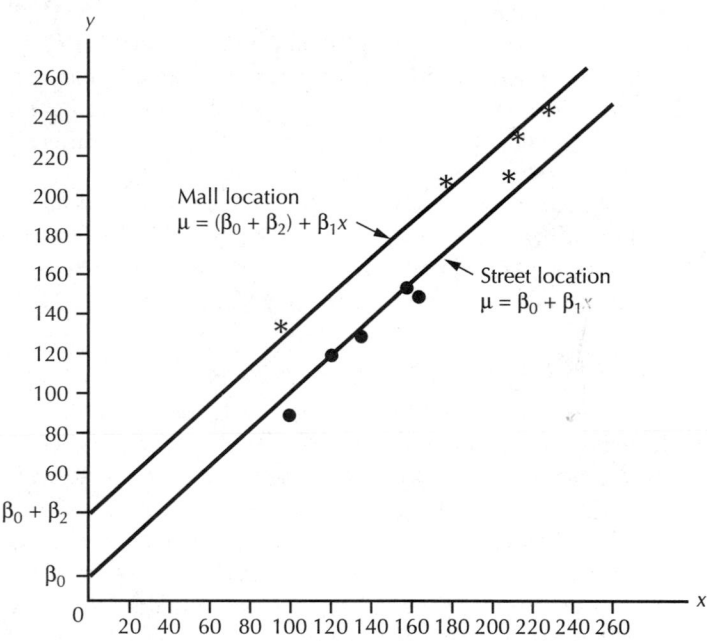

**FIGURE 4.20** Excel output of a regression analysis of the sales volume data using the model $y = \beta_0 + \beta_1 x + \beta_2 D_M + \varepsilon$

**Regression Statistics**

| Multiple R | 0.991334181 |
|---|---|
| R Square | 0.982743458 |
| Adjusted R Square | 0.977813018 |
| Standard Error | 7.328824987 |
| Observations | 10 |

**ANOVA**

| | df | SS | MS | F | Significance F |
|---|---|---|---|---|---|
| Regression | 2 | 21411.79772 | 10705.89886 | 199.3216321 | 6.75054E-07 |
| Residual | 7 | 375.9817298 | 53.71167568 | | |
| Total | 9 | 21787.77945 | | | |

| | Coefficients | Standard Error | t Stat | P-value | Lower 95% | Upper 95% |
|---|---|---|---|---|---|---|
| Intercept | 17.35982415 | 9.447024979 | 1.837596935 | 0.10872748 | −4.97882424 | 39.69847254 |
| X | 0.85104695 | 0.06524481 | 13.04390258 | 3.62598E-06 | 0.6967676 | 1.005326301 |
| DM | 29.21574639 | 5.593973003 | 5.222718517 | 0.001222158 | 15.98811162 | 42.44338115 |

Using this dummy variable, we consider the regression model

$$y = \beta_0 + \beta_1 x + \beta_2 D_M + \varepsilon$$

This model and the definition of $D_M$ imply that

1. For a street location, mean sales volume equals

$$\beta_0 + \beta_1 x + \beta_2 D_M = \beta_0 + \beta_1 x + \beta_2(0)$$
$$= \beta_0 + \beta_1 x$$

2. For a mall location, mean sales volume equals

$$\beta_0 + \beta_1 x + \beta_2 D_M = \beta_0 + \beta_1 x + \beta_2(1)$$
$$= (\beta_0 + \beta_2) + \beta_1 x$$

Thus the dummy variable allows us to model the situation illustrated in Figure 4.19. Here, the lines relating mean sales volume to $x$ for street and mall locations have different $y$ intercepts—$\beta_0$ and $(\beta_0 + \beta_2)$—and the same slope $\beta_1$. It follows that this dummy variable model assumes no interaction between $x$ and store location—note the **parallel** data patterns for the street and mall locations in Figure 4.19. Also, note that $\beta_2$ is the difference between the mean monthly sales volume for stores in mall locations and the mean monthly sales volume for stores in street locations, when all these stores have the same number of households in their areas. The Excel output in Figure 4.20 tells us that the least squares point estimate of $\beta_2$ is $b_2 = 29.216$. This says that for any given number of households in a store's area, we estimate that the mean monthly sales volume in a mall location is $29,216 greater than the mean monthly sales volume in a street location.

### Part 3: A Dummy Variable Model for Comparing Three Locations

In addition to the data concerning street and mall locations in Table 4.8, Electronics World has also collected data concerning downtown locations. The complete data set is given in Table 4.9 and plotted in Figure 4.21. Here stores having a downtown location are plotted as open circles. A model describing these data is

$$y = \beta_0 + \beta_1 x + \beta_2 D_M + \beta_3 D_D + \varepsilon$$

Here the dummy variable $D_M$ is as previously defined and the dummy variable $D_D$ is defined as follows:

$$D_D = \begin{cases} 1 & \text{if a store is in a downtown location} \\ 0 & \text{otherwise} \end{cases}$$

It follows that

1.   For a street location, mean sales volume equals

$$\begin{aligned} \beta_0 + \beta_1 x + \beta_2 D_M + \beta_3 D_D &= \beta_0 + \beta_1 x + \beta_2(0) + \beta_3(0) \\ &= \beta_0 + \beta_1 x \end{aligned}$$

2.   For a mall location, mean sales volume equals

$$\begin{aligned} \beta_0 + \beta_1 x + \beta_2 D_M + \beta_3 D_D &= \beta_0 + \beta_1 x + \beta_2(1) + \beta_3(0) \\ &= (\beta_0 + \beta_2) + \beta_1 x \end{aligned}$$

3.   For a downtown location, mean sales volume equals

$$\begin{aligned} \beta_0 + \beta_1 x + \beta_2 D_M + \beta_3 D_D &= \beta_0 + \beta_1 x + \beta_2(0) + \beta_3(1) \\ &= (\beta_0 + \beta_3) + \beta_1 x \end{aligned}$$

Thus the dummy variables allow us to model the situation illustrated in Figure 4.21. Here the lines relating mean sales volume to $x$ for street, mall, and downtown locations have different $y$-intercepts—$\beta_0$, $(\beta_0 + \beta_2)$, and $(\beta_0 + \beta_3)$—and the same slope $\beta_1$. It follows that this dummy variable model assumes no interaction between $x$ and store location.

### Part 4: Comparing the Locations

To compare the effects of the street, shopping mall, and downtown locations, consider comparing three means, which we denote as $\mu_{h,S}$, $\mu_{h,M}$, and $\mu_{h,D}$. These means represent the mean sales volumes at stores having $h$ households in the area and located on streets, in shopping malls, and downtown, respectively. If we set $x = h$, it follows that

$$\begin{aligned} \mu_{h,S} &= \beta_0 + \beta_1 h + \beta_2(0) + \beta_3(0) \\ &= \beta_0 + \beta_1 h \\ \mu_{h,M} &= \beta_0 + \beta_1 h + \beta_2(1) + \beta_3(0) \\ &= \beta_0 + \beta_1 h + \beta_2 \end{aligned}$$

**TABLE 4.9** The Complete Electronics World Sales Volume Data

| Store | Number of Households, $x$ ($\times$ 1000) | Location | Sales Volume, $y$ ($\times$ 1000) |
|---|---|---|---|
| 1 | 161 | Street | 157.27 |
| 2 | 99 | Street | 93.28 |
| 3 | 135 | Street | 136.81 |
| 4 | 120 | Street | 123.79 |
| 5 | 164 | Street | 153.51 |
| 6 | 221 | Mall | 241.74 |
| 7 | 179 | Mall | 201.54 |
| 8 | 204 | Mall | 206.71 |
| 9 | 214 | Mall | 229.78 |
| 10 | 101 | Mall | 135.22 |
| 11 | 231 | Downtown | 224.71 |
| 12 | 206 | Downtown | 195.29 |
| 13 | 248 | Downtown | 242.16 |
| 14 | 107 | Downtown | 115.21 |
| 15 | 205 | Downtown | 197.82 |

**FIGURE 4.21** Plot of the complete Electronics World sales volume data and a geometrical interpretation of the model $y = \beta_0 + \beta_1 x + \beta_2 D_M + \beta_3 D_D + \varepsilon$

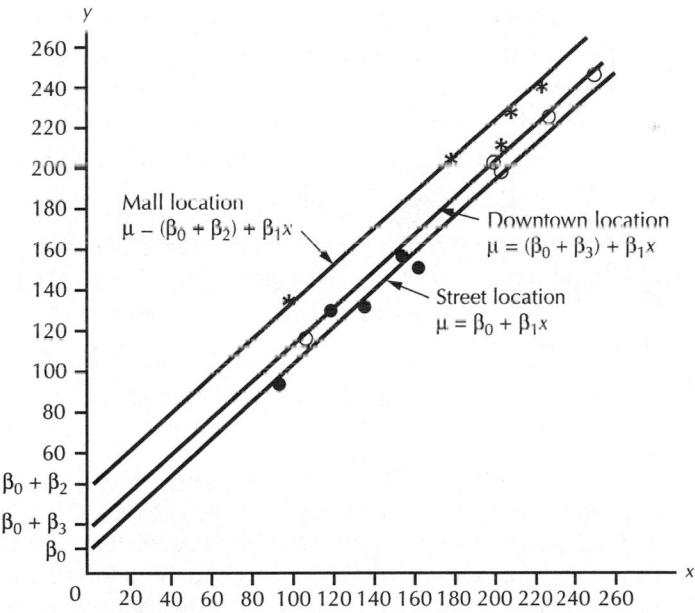

and

$$\mu_{h,D} = \beta_0 + \beta_1 h + \beta_2(0) + \beta_3(1)$$
$$= \beta_0 + \beta_1 h + \beta_3$$

In order to compare street and mall locations, we look at

$$\mu_{h,M} - \mu_{h,S} = (\beta_0 + \beta_1 h + \beta_2) - (\beta_0 + \beta_1 h) = \beta_2$$

which is the difference between the mean sales volume for stores in mall locations having $h$ households in the area and the mean sales volume for stores in street locations having $h$ households in the area. Figure 4.22 gives the MINITAB and Excel output of a regression analysis of the data in Table 4.9 by using the dummy variable model. The output tells us that the least squares point estimate of $\beta_2$ is $b_2 = 28.374$. This says that for any given number of households in a store's area, we estimate that the mean monthly sales volume in a mall location is $28,374 greater than the mean monthly sales volume in a street location. Furthermore, since the output tells us that $s_{b_2} = 4.461$, it follows that a 95% confidence interval for $\beta_2$ is

$$[b_2 \pm t_{[.025]}^{(15-4)} s_{b_2}] = [28.374 \pm 2.201(4.461)]$$
$$= [18.554, \ 38.193]$$

This interval says we are 95% confident that for any given number of households in a store's area, the mean monthly sales volume in a mall location is between $18,554 and $38,193 greater than the mean monthly sales volume in a street location. The MINITAB and Excel output also shows that the $t$-statistic for testing $H_0: \beta_2 = 0$ versus $H_a: \beta_2 \neq 0$ equals 6.36 and that the related $p$-value is less than .001. Therefore, we have very strong evidence that there is a difference between the mean monthly sales volumes in mall and street locations.

In order to compare downtown and street locations, we look at

$$\mu_{h,D} - \mu_{h,S} = (\beta_0 + \beta_1 h + \beta_3) - (\beta_0 + \beta_1 h) = \beta_3$$

Since the MINITAB and Excel output in Figure 4.22 tells us that $b_3 = 6.864$, we estimate that for any given number of households in a store's area, the mean monthly sales volume in a downtown location is $6864 greater than the mean monthly sales volume in a street location. Furthermore, since the output tells us that $s_{b_3} = 4.770$, it follows that a 95% confidence interval for $\beta_3$ is

$$\left[ b_3 \pm t_{[.025]}^{(11)} s_{b_3} \right] = [6.864 \pm 2.201(4.770)]$$
$$= [-3.636, \ 17.363]$$

This says we are 95% confident that for any given number of households in a store's area, the mean monthly sales volume in a downtown location is between $3636 less than and $17,363 greater than the mean monthly sales volume in a street location. The MINITAB and Excel output also show that the $t$-statistic and $p$-value for testing $H_0: \beta_3 = 0$ versus $H_a: \beta_3 \neq 0$ are $t = 1.44$ and $p$-value $= .178$. Therefore, we do not have strong evidence

**FIGURE 4.22** MINITAB and Excel output of a regression analysis of the sales volume data using the model $y = \beta_0 + \beta_1 x + \beta_2 D_M + \beta_3 D_D + \varepsilon$

```
The regression equation is
y = 15.0 + 0.869 x + 28.4 DM + 6.86 DD


Predictor      Coef   SE Coef       T       P
Constant     14.978     6.188    2.42   0.034
x           0.86859   0.04049   21.45   0.000
DM           28.374     4.461    6.36   0.000
DD            6.864     4.770    1.44   0.178


S = 6.34941    R-Sq = 98.7%    R-Sq(adj) = 98.3%


Analysis of Variance

Source           DF      SS      MS       F       P
Regression        3   33269   11090  275.07   0.000
Residual Error   11     443      40
Total            14   33712

   Fit    SE Fit        95% CI              95% PI
217.07      2.91  (210.65, 223.48)   (201.69, 232.45)
```
(a) The MINITAB output

### Regression Statistics

| | |
|---|---|
| Multiple R | 0.993401001 |
| R Square | 0.986845548 |
| Adjusted R Square | 0.98325797 |
| Standard Error | 6.349409429 |
| Observations | 15 |

### ANOVA

| | df | SS | MS | F | Significance F |
|---|---|---|---|---|---|
| Regression | 3 | 33268.69529 | 11089.5651 | 275.0729275 | 1.26776E-10 |
| Residual | 11 | 443.4650011 | 40.3150001 | | |
| Total | 14 | 33712.16029 | | | |

| | Coefficients | Standard Error | t Stat | P-Value | Lower 95% | Upper 95% |
|---|---|---|---|---|---|---|
| Intercept | 14.97769322 | 6.188445404 | 2.420267489 | 0.033990776 | 1.357009832 | 28.59837661 |
| X | 0.868588415 | 0.040489928 | 21.45196249 | 2.51663E-10 | 0.77947064 | 0.957706191 |
| DM | 28.37375607 | 4.4613066 | 6.359965502 | 5.37015E-05 | 18.55448148 | 38.19303066 |
| DD | 6.863776795 | 4.770476502 | 1.438803187 | 0.178046589 | −3.635976504 | 17.36353009 |

(b) The Excel output

that there is a difference between the mean monthly sales volumes in downtown and street locations.

In order to compare mall and downtown locations, we look at

$$\mu_{h,M} - \mu_{h,D} = (\beta_0 + \beta_1 h + \beta_2) - (\beta_0 + \beta_1 h + \beta_3) = \beta_2 - \beta_3$$

The least squares point estimate of this difference is

$$b_2 - b_3 = 28.374 - 6.864 = 21.51$$

This says that for any given number of households in a store's area we estimate that the mean monthly sales volume in a mall location is $21,510 greater than the mean monthly sales volume in a downtown location. Near the end of this section we will show how to calculate a confidence interval for and test a hypothesis about $\mu_{h,M} - \mu_{h,D}$. We will see that there is very strong evidence that the mean monthly sales volume in a mall location is greater than the mean monthly sales volume in a downtown location. In summary, the mall location seems to give a greater mean monthly sales volume than either the street or downtown location.

### Part 5: Predicting a Future Sales Volume

Suppose that Electronics World wishes to predict the sales volume in a future month for an individual store that has 200,000 households in its area and is located in a shopping mall. The needed point prediction is (since $D_M = 1$ and $D_D = 0$ when a store is in a shopping mall)

$$\hat{y} = b_0 + b_1(200) + b_2(1) + b_3(0)$$
$$= 14.978 + .8686(200) + 28.374(1)$$
$$= 217.07$$

This point prediction is given at the bottom of the MINITAB output in Figure 4.22(a). The corresponding 95% prediction interval, which is [201.69, 232.45], says we are 95% confident that the sales volume in a future sales period for an individual mall store that has 200,000 households in its area will be between $201,690 and $232,450.

### Part 6: An Interaction Model

In modeling the sales volume data we might consider using the model

$$y = \beta_0 + \beta_1 x + \beta_2 D_M + \beta_3 D_D + \beta_4 x D_M + \beta_5 x D_D + \varepsilon$$

This model implies that

1. For a street location, mean sales volume equals (since $D_M = 0$ and $D_D = 0$)

$$\beta_0 + \beta_1 x + \beta_2(0) + \beta_3(0) + \beta_4 x(0) + \beta_5 x(0)$$
$$= \beta_0 + \beta_1 x$$

2. For a mall location, mean sales volume equals (since $D_M = 1$ and $D_D = 0$)

$$\beta_0 + \beta_1 x + \beta_2(1) + \beta_3(0) + \beta_4 x(1) + \beta_5 x(0)$$
$$= (\beta_0 + \beta_2) + (\beta_1 + \beta_4)x$$

3. For a downtown location, mean sales volume equals (since $D_M = 0$ and $D_D = 1$)

$$\beta_0 + \beta_1 x + \beta_2(0) + \beta_3(1) + \beta_4 x(0) + \beta_5 x(1)$$
$$= (\beta_0 + \beta_3) + (\beta_1 + \beta_5)x$$

As illustrated in Figure 4.23(a) (page 192), if we use this model, then the straight lines relating mean sales volume to $x$ for the street, mall, and downtown locations have different $y$-intercepts and different slopes. Therefore, this model assumes **interaction** between $x$ and store location. Figure 4.23(b) gives the SAS output of a regression analysis of the sales volume data using the above interaction model. Here $D_M$, $D_D$, $xD_M$, and $xD_D$ are labeled as DM, DD, xDM, and xDD, respectively, on the output. The SAS output tells us that the $p$-values related to the significance of $xD_M$ and $xD_D$ are large—.5334 and .8132, respectively. Therefore, these interaction terms are not important. It follows that the no-interaction model seems best.

In the sales volume situation of the preceding example, when we use the model

$$y = \beta_0 + \beta_1 x + \beta_2 D_M + \beta_3 D_D + \varepsilon$$

we are able to compare the effects of three store locations by using two dummy variables. Furthermore, the parameters $\beta_2$ and $\beta_3$ multiplied by $D_M$ and $D_D$ express the effects of the mall and downtown locations with respect to the effect of a street location. That is, $\beta_2 = \mu_{h,M} - \mu_{h,S}$ and $\beta_3 = \mu_{h,D} - \mu_{h,S}$. However, this model also implies that $\mu_{h,M} - \mu_{h,D} = \beta_2 - \beta_3$, and we cannot use our MINITAB, Excel, or SAS output to calculate a confidence interval or test a hypothesis about a difference in regression parameters. To make statistical inferences about $\mu_{h,M} - \mu_{h,D}$, we need to express $\mu_{h,M} - \mu_{h,D}$ as a single regression parameter. To do this, we must realize that we can write a dummy variable regression model describing sales volume by using *any two* of the three dummy variables $D_M$, $D_D$, and $D_S$. Here $D_S$ equals 1 if a store has a street location and $D_S = 0$ otherwise. If, instead of using $D_M$ and $D_D$, we use $D_S$ and $D_D$, the parameters $\beta_2$ and $\beta_3$ express the effects of the street and downtown locations with respect to the effect of the mall location. If we use $D_S$ and $D_M$, the parameters $\beta_2$ and $\beta_3$ express the effects of the street and mall locations with respect to the effect of the downtown location. Specifically, consider the model that uses $D_S$ and $D_M$,

$$y = \beta_0 + \beta_1 x + \beta_2 D_S + \beta_3 D_M + \varepsilon$$

The Excel output of the least squares point estimates of the parameters of this model is shown at the top of page 193.

**FIGURE 4.23** Regression analysis of the sales volume data using the model
$y = \beta_0 + \beta_1 x + \beta_2 D_M + \beta_3 D_D + \beta_4 x D_M + \beta_5 x D_D + \varepsilon$

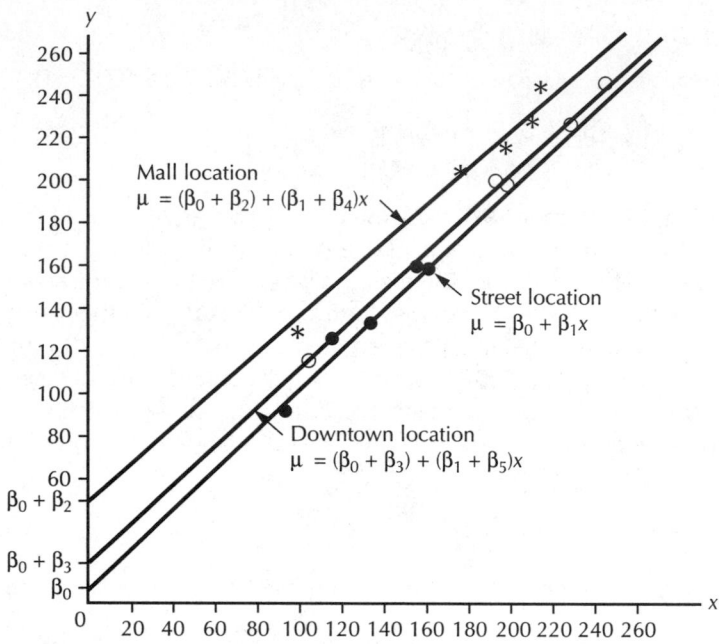

(a) Geometrical interpretation of the model

```
                         Analysis of Variance

                                  Sum of        Mean
  Source              DF         Squares       Square    F Value    Pr > F

  Model                5           33296    6659.21152     144.03    <.0001
  Error                9       416.10268      46.23363
  Corrected Total     14           33712


              Root MSE              6.79953    R-Square    0.9877
              Dependent Mean      176.98933    Adj R-Sq    0.9808
              Coeff Var             3.84177


                        Parameter Estimates

                              Parameter    Standard
  Variable    Label      DF    Estimate       Error    t Value    Pr > |t|

  Intercept   Intercept   1     7.90042    17.03513       0.46      0.6538
  x           x           1     0.92070     0.12343       7.46      <.0001
  DM          DM          1    42.72974    21.50420       1.99      0.0782
  DD          DD          1    10.25503    21.28319       0.48      0.6414
  xDM         x * DM      1    -0.09172     0.14163      -0.65      0.5334
  xDD         x * DD      1    -0.03363     0.13819      -0.24      0.8132
```

(b) SAS output using the model

|           | Coefficients  | Standard Error | t Stat        | P-value      | Lower 95%     | Upper 95%   |
|-----------|---------------|----------------|---------------|--------------|---------------|-------------|
| Intercept | 21.84147001   | 8.55847513     | 2.552028216   | 0.026897774  | 3.004383732   | 40.67855629 |
| X         | 0.868588415   | 0.040489928    | 21.45196249   | 2.51663E-10  | 0.77947064    | 0.957706191 |
| DS        | −6.863776795  | 4.770476502    | −1.438803187  | 0.178046589  | −17.36353009  | 3.635976504 |
| DM        | 21.50997928   | 4.065091975    | 5.291388094   | 0.00025577   | 12.56276764   | 30.45719091 |

Since $\beta_3$ expresses the effect of the mall location with respect to the effect of the downtown location, $\beta_3$ equals $\mu_{h,M} - \mu_{h,D}$. The Excel output tells us that the least squares point estimate of $\beta_3$ is 21.51 and that the standard error of this estimate is 4.0651. It follows that a 95% confidence interval for $\mu_{h,M} - \mu_{h,D}$ is

$$[21.51 \pm 2.201(4.0651)] = [12.563, 30.457]$$

This says we are 95% confident that for any given number of households in a store's area, the mean monthly sales volume in a mall location is between \$12,563 and \$30,457 greater than the mean monthly sales volume in a downtown location. The Excel output also shows that the *t*-statistic and *p*-value for testing the significance of $\mu_{h,M} - \mu_{h,D}$ are, respectively, 5.29 and 0.000256. Therefore, we have very strong evidence that there is a difference between the mean monthly sales volumes in mall and downtown locations.

In general, if we wish to model the effect of a qualitative independent variable having $a$ levels, we use $a - 1$ dummy variables. The parameter multiplied by a particular dummy variable expresses the effect of the level represented by that dummy variable with respect to the effect of the level that is not represented by a dummy variable. For example, if we wish to compare the effects on sales, $y$, of four different types of advertising campaigns—television $(T)$, radio $(R)$, magazine $(M)$, and mailed coupons $(C)$—we might use the model

$$y - \beta_0 + \beta_1 D_I + \beta_2 D_R + \beta_3 D_M + \varepsilon$$

The parameter $\beta_1$ is the difference between mean sales when a television advertising campaign is used and mean sales when a mailed coupon advertising campaign is used. The interpretations of $\beta_2$ and $\beta_3$ follow similarly. In the exercises we consider in more detail an example of this type.

# 4.10   THE PARTIAL *F*-TEST: TESTING THE SIGNIFICANCE OF A PORTION OF A REGRESSION MODEL

We now present a **partial *F*-test** that allows us to test the significance of a set of independent variables in a regression model. That is, we can use this *F*-test to test the significance of a *portion* of a regression model. For example, in the Electronics World situation, we employed the dummy variable model

$$y = \beta_0 + \beta_1 x + \beta_2 D_M + \beta_3 D_D + \varepsilon$$

It might be useful to test the significance of the dummy variables $D_M$ and $D_D$. We can do this by testing the null hypothesis

$$H_0: \beta_2 = \beta_3 = 0$$

which says that neither dummy variable significantly affects $y$, versus the alternative hypothesis

$$H_a: \text{At least one of } \beta_2 \text{ and } \beta_3 \text{ does not equal } 0$$

which says at least one of the dummy variables significantly affects $y$. Intuitively, since $D_M$ and $D_D$ represent the effects of the mall and downtown locations with respect to the street location, the null hypothesis says that the effects of the mall, downtown, and street locations on mean sales volume do not differ (insignificant dummy variables). The alternative hypothesis says that at least two locations have different effects on mean sales volume (at least one significant dummy variable). These intuitive interpretations will be more fully justified in the next example.

In general, consider the regression model

$$y = \beta_0 + \beta_1 x_1 + \cdots + \beta_g x_g + \beta_{g+1} x_{g+1} + \cdots + \beta_k x_k + \varepsilon$$

Suppose we wish to test the null hypothesis

$$H_0: \beta_{g+1} = \beta_{g+2} = \cdots = \beta_k = 0$$

which says that **none of the independent variables $x_{g+1}, x_{g+2}, \ldots, x_k$ affects $y$,** versus the alternative hypothesis

$$H_a: \text{At least one of } \beta_{g+1}, \beta_{g+2}, \ldots, \beta_k \text{ does not equal } 0$$

which says that **at least one of the independent variables $x_{g+1}, x_{g+2}, \ldots, x_k$ affects $y$.** If we can reject $H_0$ in favor of $H_a$ by specifying a *small* probability of a Type I error, then it is reasonable to conclude that at least one of $x_{g+1}, x_{g+2}, \ldots, x_k$ **significantly** affects $y$. In this case we should use $t$-statistics and other techniques to determine which of $x_{g+1}, x_{g+2}, \ldots, x_k$ significantly affect $y$. To test $H_0$ versus $H_a$, consider the following two models:

**Complete model:** $y = \beta_0 + \beta_1 x_1 + \cdots + \beta_g x_g + \beta_{g+1} x_{g+1} + \cdots + \beta_k x_k + \varepsilon$

**Reduced model:** $y = \beta_0 + \beta_1 x_1 + \cdots + \beta_g x_g + \varepsilon$

Here the complete model is assumed to have $k$ independent variables, the reduced model is the complete model under the assumption that $H_0$ is true, and $(k - g)$ denotes the number of regression parameters we have set equal to 0 in the statement of $H_0$.

To carry out this test, we calculate $\text{SSE}_C$, **the unexplained variation for the complete model,** and $\text{SSE}_R$, **the unexplained variation for the reduced model.** The appropriate test statistic is based on the difference

$$\text{SSE}_R - \text{SSE}_C$$

which is called *the drop in the unexplained variation attributable to the independent variables $x_{g+1}, x_{g+2}, \ldots, x_k$.* In the following box we give the formula for the test statistic and show how to carry out the test.

---

## THE PARTIAL *F*-TEST: AN *F*-TEST FOR A PORTION OF A REGRESSION MODEL

Suppose that the regression assumptions hold and consider testing

$$H_0: \beta_{g+1} = \beta_{g+2} = \cdots = \beta_k = 0$$

versus

$$H_a: \text{At least one of } \beta_{g+1}, \beta_{g+2}, \ldots, \beta_k \text{ does not equal } 0$$

We define the **partial *F*-statistic** to be

$$F = \frac{(\text{SSE}_R - \text{SSE}_C)/(k - g)}{\text{SSE}_C/[n - (k + 1)]}$$

Also define the *p*-value related to $F$ to be the area under the curve of the $F$ distribution [having $k - g$ and $n - (k + 1)$ degrees of freedom] to the right of $F$. Then, we can reject $H_0$ in favor of $H_a$ at level of significance $\alpha$ if either of the following equivalent conditions holds:

1. $F > F_{[\alpha]}$
2. *p*-value $< \alpha$

Here the point $F_{[\alpha]}$ is based on $k - g$ numerator and $n - (k + 1)$ denominator degrees of freedom.

---

It can be shown that the "extra" independent variables $x_{g+1}, x_{g+2}, \ldots, x_k$ will always explain some of the variation in the observed $y$ values and, therefore, will always make $\text{SSE}_C$ somewhat smaller than $\text{SSE}_R$. Condition 1 says that we should reject $H_0$ if

$$F = \frac{(\text{SSE}_R - \text{SSE}_C)/(k - g)}{\text{SSE}_C/[n - (k + 1)]}$$

is large. This is reasonable because a large value of $F$ would result from a large value of $(SSE_R - SSE_C)$, which would be obtained if at least one of the independent variables $x_{g+1}, x_{g+2}, \ldots, x_k$ makes $SSE_C$ substantially smaller than $SSE_R$. This would suggest that $H_0$ is false and that $H_a$ is true.

Before looking at an example, we should point out that testing the significance of a single independent variable by using a partial $F$-test is equivalent to carrying out this test by using the previously discussed $t$-test (see Section 4.5). It can be shown that when we test $H_0: \beta_j = 0$ versus $H_a: \beta_j \neq 0$ using a partial $F$-test

$$F = t^2 \quad \text{and} \quad F_{[\alpha]} = \left( t_{[\alpha/2]}^{(n-(k+1))} \right)^2$$

Here $F_{[\alpha]}$ is based on 1 numerator and $n - (k + 1)$ degrees of freedom. Hence, the rejection conditions

$$|t| > t_{[\alpha/2]}^{(n-(k+1))} \quad \text{and} \quad F > F_{[\alpha]}$$

are equivalent. It can also be shown that in this case the $p$-value related to $t$ equals the $p$-value related to $F$.

**EXAMPLE 4.16**   In Example 4.15 we used the dummy variable model

$$y = \beta_0 + \beta_1 x + \beta_2 D_M + \beta_3 D_D + \varepsilon$$

to make pairwise comparisons of the street, mall, and downtown store locations by carrying out a $t$-test for each of the parameters $\beta_2$, $\beta_3$, and $\beta_2 - \beta_3$. There is a theoretical problem with this because, although we can set the probability of a Type I error equal to .05 for each individual test, it is possible to show that the probability of falsely rejecting $H_0$ in *at least one* of these tests is greater than .05. Because of this problem, some people feel that before making pairwise comparisons we should test for differences between the effects of the locations by testing the single hypothesis

$$H_0: \mu_{h,S} = \mu_{h,M} = \mu_{h,D}$$

which says that the street, mall, and downtown locations have the same effects on mean sales volume (no differences between locations).

To carry out this test we consider the following:

**Complete model:** $y = \beta_0 + \beta_1 x + \beta_2 D_M + \beta_3 D_D + \varepsilon$

In Example 4.15 we saw that for this model

$$\beta_2 = \mu_{h,M} - \mu_{h,S} \quad \text{and} \quad \beta_3 = \mu_{h,D} - \mu_{h,S}$$

It follows that the null hypothesis $H_0: \mu_{h,S} = \mu_{h,M} = \mu_{h,D}$ is equivalent to $H_0: \beta_2 = \beta_3 = 0$ and that the alternative hypothesis

$$H_a: \text{At least two of } \mu_{h,S}, \mu_{h,M}, \text{ and } \mu_{h,D} \text{ differ}$$

which says that at least two locations have different effects on mean sales volume, is equivalent to

$$H_a: \text{At least one of } \beta_2 \text{ and } \beta_3 \text{ does not equal } 0$$

Because of these equivalencies, we can test $H_0$ versus $H_a$ by using a partial $F$-test. For the previously given complete model (which has $k = 3$ independent variables), we obtain an unexplained variation equal to $SSE_C = 443.4650$. The reduced model is the complete model when $H_0$ is true. Therefore, we obtain

$$\text{Reduced model: } y = \beta_0 + \beta_1 x + \varepsilon$$

For this model the unexplained variation is $SSE_R = 2467.8067$. Noting that two parameters ($\beta_2$ and $\beta_3$) are set equal to 0 in the statement of $H_0$, we have $k - g = 2$. Therefore, the needed partial $F$-statistic is

$$F = \frac{(SSE_R - SSE_C)/(k - g)}{SSE_C/[n - (k + 1)]}$$

$$= \frac{(2467.8067 - 443.4650)/2}{443.4650/[15 - 4]}$$

$$= 25.1066$$

We compare $F$ with $F_{[.01]} = 7.21$, which is based on $k - g = 2$ numerator and $n - (k + 1) = 15 - 4 = 11$ denominator degrees of freedom. Since

$$F = 25.1066 > 7.21$$

we can reject $H_0$ at the .01 level of significance, and we have very strong statistical evidence that at least two locations have different effects on mean sales volume. Having reached this conclusion, it makes sense to compare the effects of specific pairs of locations. We have already done this in Example 4.15. It should also be noted that even if $H_0$ were not rejected, some practitioners feel that pairwise comparisons should still be made. This is because there is always a possibility that we have erroneously decided to not reject $H_0$.

## Exercises

**4.1** A real estate agency collects the data in Table 4.10 concerning

$y$ = sales price of a house (in thousands of dollars)
$x_1$ = home size (in hundreds of square feet)
$x_2$ = rating (an overall "niceness rating" for the house expressed on a scale from 1 [worst] to 10 [best], and provided by the real estate agency)

The agency wishes to develop a regression model that can be used to predict the sales prices of future houses it will list. Consider relating $y$ to $x_1$ and $x_2$ by using the model

$$y = \mu_{y|x_1, x_2} + \varepsilon$$

$$= \beta_0 + \beta_1 x_1 + \beta_2 x_2 + \varepsilon$$

**TABLE 4.10** Real Estate Sales Price Data

| Sales Price, $y$ ($\times$ \$1000) | Home Size, $x_1$ ($\times$ 100 ft$^2$) | Rating, $x_2$ |
|---|---|---|
| 180 | 23 | 5 |
| 98.1 | 11 | 2 |
| 173.1 | 20 | 9 |
| 136.5 | 17 | 3 |
| 141 | 15 | 8 |
| 165.9 | 21 | 4 |
| 193.5 | 24 | 7 |
| 127.8 | 13 | 6 |
| 163.5 | 19 | 7 |
| 172.5 | 25 | 2 |

*Source:* Data from R. L. Andrews and J. T. Ferguson, "Integrating Judgement with a Regression Appraisal," *The Real Estate Appraiser and Analyst* 52, no. 2 (1986).

**FIGURE 4.24** Real estate sales price plots

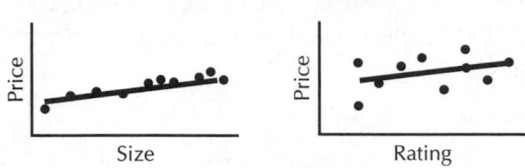

a. Discuss why the data plots in Figure 4.24 indicate that this model might be reasonable.
b. Explain the meaning of

$$\mu_{y|x_1=20,x_2=9} = \beta_0 + \beta_1(20) + \beta_2(9)$$

c. Explain the meanings of $\beta_0$, $\beta_1$, and $\beta_2$.
d. What factors are represented by the error term in this model? Give a specific example of these factors.

**4.2** Table 4.11 presents data concerning the need for labor in 17 U.S. Navy hospitals. Here

$y$ = monthly labor hours required
$x_1$ = monthly X-ray exposures
$x_2$ = monthly occupied bed days (a hospital has one occupied bed day if one bed is occupied for an entire day)
$x_3$ = average length of patients' stay (in days)

The main objective of the regression analysis is to help the navy evaluate the performance of its hospitals in terms of how many labor hours are used relative to how many labor hours are needed. The navy selected hospitals 1 through 17 from hospitals that it thought were efficiently run and wishes to use a regression model based on efficiently run hospitals to evaluate the efficiency of questionable hospitals. Consider relating $y$ to $x_1$, $x_2$, and $x_3$ by using the model

$$y = \beta_0 + \beta_1 x_1 + \beta_2 x_2 + \beta_3 x_3 + \varepsilon$$

**TABLE 4.11 (for Exercises 4.2 and 4.4)  Hospital Labor Needs Data**

| Hospital | Monthly X-Ray Exposures, $x_1$ | Monthly Occupied Bed Days, $x_2$ | Average Length of Stay, $x_3$ | Monthly Labor Hours Required, $y$ |
|---|---|---|---|---|
| 1 | 2,463 | 472.92 | 4.45 | 566.52 |
| 2 | 2,048 | 1,339.75 | 6.92 | 696.82 |
| 3 | 3,940 | 620.25 | 4.28 | 1,033.15 |
| 4 | 6,505 | 568.33 | 3.90 | 1,603.62 |
| 5 | 5,723 | 1,497.60 | 5.50 | 1,611.37 |
| 6 | 11,520 | 1,365.83 | 4.60 | 1,613.27 |
| 7 | 5,779 | 1,687.00 | 5.62 | 1,854.17 |
| 8 | 5,969 | 1,639.92 | 5.15 | 2,160.55 |
| 9 | 8,461 | 2,872.33 | 6.18 | 2,305.58 |
| 10 | 20,106 | 3,655.08 | 6.15 | 3,503.93 |
| 11 | 13,313 | 2,912.00 | 5.88 | 3,571.89 |
| 12 | 10,771 | 3,921.00 | 4.88 | 3,741.40 |
| 13 | 15,543 | 3,865.67 | 5.50 | 4,026.52 |
| 14 | 36,194 | 7,684.10 | 7.00 | 10,343.81 |
| 15 | 34,703 | 12,446.33 | 10.78 | 11,732.17 |
| 16 | 39,204 | 14,098.40 | 7.05 | 15,414.94 |
| 17 | 86,533 | 15,524.00 | 6.35 | 18,854.45 |

*Source: Procedures and Analysis for Staffing Standards Development Regression Analysis Handbook* (San Diego, CA: Navy Manpower and Material Analysis Center, 1979).

**FIGURE 4.25** Hospital labor needs plots

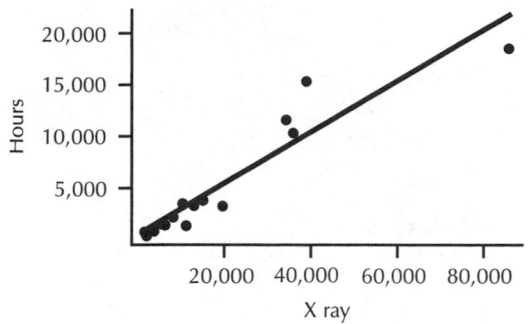

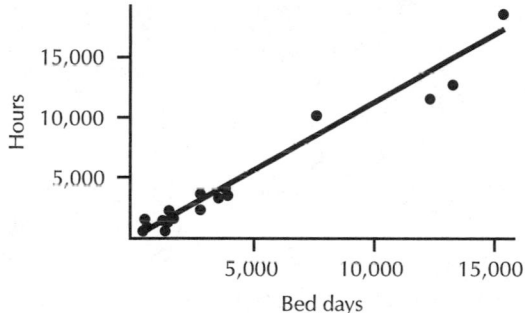

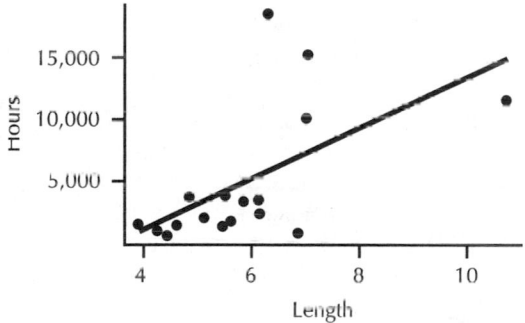

Discuss why the data plots in Figure 4.25 indicate that this model might be reasonable. Explain the meanings of $\beta_0$, $\beta_1$, $\beta_2$, $\beta_3$, and $\varepsilon$ in this model.

**4.3** Figures 4.26 and 4.27 (page 200) give the MINITAB and Excel output of a regression analysis of the real estate sales price data in Table 4.10 using the model

$$y = \beta_0 + \beta_1 x_1 + \beta_2 x_2 + \varepsilon$$

a. Using the MINITAB or Excel output, identify and interpret $b_0$, $b_1$, and $b_2$, the least squares point estimates of $\beta_0$, $\beta_1$, and $\beta_2$.
b. Calculate a point estimate of the mean sales price of all houses having 2000 square feet and a rating of 8, and a point prediction of the sales price of an individual house having 2000 square feet and a rating of 8. Identify the point estimate (prediction), which is given at the bottom of the MINITAB output.

**4.4** Figure 4.28 (page 201) gives the SAS output of a regression analysis of the hospital labor needs data in Table 4.11 using the model

$$y = \beta_0 + \beta_1 x_1 + \beta_2 x_2 + \beta_3 x_3 + \varepsilon$$

Note that the variables $x_1$, $x_2$, and $x_3$ are denoted as Xray, BedDays, and Length on the output.
a. Identify and interpret $b_0$, $b_1$, $b_2$, and $b_3$, the least squares point estimates of $\beta_0$, $\beta_1$, $\beta_2$, and $\beta_3$.
b. Consider a questionable hospital for which Xray = 56,194, BedDays = 14,077.88, and Length = 6.89. A point prediction of the labor hours corresponding to this combination of values of the independent variables is given on the SAS output. Identify this point prediction and show how it has been calculated.
c. If the actual number of labor hours used by the questionable hospital was $y = 17,207.31$, how does this $y$ value compare with the point prediction?

**In Exercises 4.5 and 4.6 we refer to MINITAB, SAS, and Excel output of regression analyses of the data sets related to the situations introduced in Exercises 4.1 and 4.2. Using the appropriate output,**
a. Identify SSE, $s^2$, and $s$. Show how $s^2$ has been calculated from SSE and other numbers.
b. Find the total variation, the unexplained variation, and the explained variation.
c. Find and interpret $R^2$ and $\bar{R}^2$. Show how $\bar{R}^2$ has been calculated from $R^2$ and other numbers.
d. Calculate the $F(\text{model})$ statistic by using the explained variation, the unexplained variation, and other relevant quantities as given on the computer output.
e. Use the $F(\text{model})$ statistic and the appropriate rejection point to test the significance of the linear regression model under consideration by setting $\alpha$ equal to .05.
f. Use the $F(\text{model})$ statistic and the appropriate rejection point to test the significance of the linear

**FIGURE 4.26 (for Exercises 4.3, 4.5, 4.7, and 4.9)** MINITAB output of a regression analysis of the real estate sales price data using the model $y = \beta_0 + \beta_1 x_1 + \beta_2 x_2 + \varepsilon$

```
The regression equation is
Y = 29.3 + 5.61 X1 + 3.83 X2


Predictor    Coef   SE Coef       T      P
Constant    29.347    4.891    6.00  0.001
X1          5.6128   0.2285   24.56  0.000
X2          3.8344   0.4332    8.85  0.000


S = 3.24164   R-Sq = 99.0%   R-Sq(adj) = 98.7%


Analysis of Variance

Source           DF      SS       MS        F      P
Regression        2  7374.0   3687.0   350.87  0.000
Residual Error    7    73.6     10.5
Total             9  7447.5

   Fit   SE Fit       95% CI            95% PI
172.28     1.57  (168.56, 175.99)  (163.76, 180.80)
```

**FIGURE 4.27 (for Exercises 4.3, 4.5, and 4.7)** Excel output of a regression analysis of the real estate sales price data using the model $y = \beta_0 + \beta_1 x_1 + \beta_2 x_2 + \varepsilon$

**Regression Statistics**

| | |
|---|---|
| Multiple R | 0.99504936 |
| R Square | 0.99012322 |
| Adjusted R Square | 0.98730128 |
| Standard Error | 3.24163564 |
| Observations | 10 |

**ANOVA**

| | df | SS | MS | F | Significance F |
|---|---|---|---|---|---|
| Regression | 2 | 7373.951588 | 3686.975794 | 350.86649 | 9.57533E-08 |
| Residual | 7 | 73.55741155 | 10.50820165 | | |
| Total | 9 | 7447.509 | | | |

| | Coefficients | Standard Error | t Stat | P-Value | Lower 95% | Upper 95% |
|---|---|---|---|---|---|---|
| Intercept | 29.3468118 | 4.891442017 | 5.999623777 | 0.0005425 | 17.78039768 | 40.91322597 |
| X Variable 1 | 5.61280584 | 0.228520722 | 24.5614743 | 4.725E-08 | 5.072440585 | 6.153171094 |
| X Variable 2 | 3.83442234 | 0.43320097 | 8.851370612 | 4.753E-05 | 2.81006555 | 4.858779125 |

regression model under consideration by setting $\alpha$ equal to .01.

g. Find the *p*-value related to *F*(model). Using the *p*-value, test the significance of the linear regression model by setting $\alpha = .10, .05, .01$, and .001. What do you conclude?

**4.5** Use the MINITAB and Excel output in Figures 4.26 and 4.27 for the real estate sales price data.

**4.6** Use the SAS output in Figure 4.28 for the hospital labor needs data.

**FIGURE 4.28 (for Exercises 4.4, 4.6, 4.8, and 4.10)** SAS output of a regression analysis of the hospital labor needs data using the model $y = \beta_0 + \beta_1 x_1 + \beta_2 x_2 + \beta_3 x_3 + \varepsilon$

Analysis of Variance

| Source | DF | Sum of Squares | Mean Square | F Value | Pr > F |
|--------|-----|----------------|-------------|---------|--------|
| Model | 3 | 489799142 | 163266381 | 431.97 | <.0001 |
| Error | 13 | 4913399 | 377954 | | |
| Corrected Total | 16 | 494712540 | | | |

| | | | | |
|--|--|--|--|--|
| Root MSE | 614.77942 | R-Square | 0.9901 | |
| Dependent Mean | 4978.48000 | Adj R-Sq | 0.9878 | |
| Coeff Var | 12.34874 | | | |

Parameter Estimates

| Variable | Label | DF | Parameter Estimate | Standard Error | t Value | Pr > \|t\| |
|----------|-------|-----|--------------------|-----------------|---------|------------|
| Intercept | Intercept | 1 | 1523.38924 | 786.89772 | 1.94 | 0.0749 |
| Xray | Xray | 1 | 0.05299 | 0.02009 | 2.64 | 0.0205 |
| BedDays | BedDays | 1 | 0.97848 | 0.10515 | 9.31 | <.0001 |
| Length | Length | 1 | -320.95083 | 153.19222 | -2.10 | 0.0563 |

| Obs | Dep Var Hours | Predicted Value | Std Error Mean Predict | 95% CL Mean | | 95% CL Predict | |
|-----|---------------|------------------|-------------------------|-------------|--|----------------|--|
| 18 | . | 16065 | 373.0980 | 15259 | 16871 | 14511 | 17618 |

In Exercises 4.7 and 4.8 we refer to MINITAB, SAS, and Excel output of regression analyses of the data sets related to the situations introduced in Exercises 4.1 and 4.2. Using the appropriate output, do the following for *each parameter* $\beta_j$ in the model under consideration:

a. Identify $b_j$, $s_{b_j}$, and the *t*-statistic for testing $H_0$: $\beta_j = 0$. Show how $t$ has been calculated by using $b_j$ and $s_{b_j}$

b. Using the *t*-statistic and appropriate rejection points, test $H_0$: $\beta_j = 0$ versus $H_a$: $\beta_j \neq 0$ by setting $\alpha$ equal to .05. Which independent variables are significantly related to $y$ in the model with $\alpha = .05$?

c. Using the *t*-statistic and appropriate rejection points, test $H_0$: $\beta_j = 0$ versus $H_a$: $\beta_j \neq 0$ by setting $\alpha$ equal to .01. Which independent variables are significantly related to $y$ in the model with $\alpha = .01$?

d. Identify the *p*-value for testing $H_0$: $\beta_j = 0$ versus $H_a$: $\beta_j \neq 0$. Using the *p*-value, determine whether we can reject $H_0$ by setting $\alpha$ equal to .10, .05, .01, and .001. What do you conclude about the significance of the independent variables in the model?

e. Calculate the 95% confidence interval for $\beta_j$.

f. Calculate the 99% confidence interval for $\beta_j$. Discuss one practical application of this interval.

**4.7** Use the MINITAB and Excel output in Figures 4.26 and 4.27 for the real estate sales price data. Do (a) through (f) for each of $\beta_0$, $\beta_1$, and $\beta_2$

**4.8** Use the SAS output in Figure 4.28 for the hospital labor needs data . Do (a) through (f) for each of $\beta_0$, $\beta_1$, $\beta_2$, and $\beta_3$.

**4.9** Consider the MINITAB output in Figure 4.26 for the real estate price data. The information at the bottom of the MINITAB output relates to a house having 2000 square feet and a rating of 8.

a. Report a point estimate of and a 95% confidence interval for the mean sales price of all houses having 2000 square feet and a rating of 8.

b. Report a point prediction of and a 95% prediction interval for the actual sales price of an individual house having 2000 square feet and a rating of 8.

c. Find 99% confidence and prediction intervals for the mean and actual sales prices referred to in parts (a) and (b). Hint: Solve for the distance value.

**4.10** In the hospital labor needs problem, consider a questionable hospital for which Xray = 56,194, BedDays = 14,077.88, and Length = 6.89. A 95% prediction interval for the labor hours corresponding to this combination of values of the independent variables is given on the SAS output in Figure 4.28. Identify the prediction interval. Then, use this interval to determine if the actual number of labor hours used by the questionable hospital ($y$ = 17,207.31) is unusually low or high.

**4.11** In a September 1982 article in *Business Economics,* C. I. Allmon related $y$ = Crest toothpaste sales in a given year (in thousands of dollars) to $x_1$ = Crest advertising budget in the year (in thousands of dollars), $x_2$ = ratio of Crest's advertising budget to Colgate's advertising budget in the year, and $x_3$ = U.S. personal disposable income in the year (in billions of dollars). The data analyzed are given in Table 4.12 and plotted in Figure 4.29. When we perform a regression analysis of these data using the model

$$y = \beta_0 + \beta_1 x_1 + \beta_2 x_2 + \beta_3 x_3 + \varepsilon$$

we find that the least squares point estimates of the model parameters and their associated $p$-values (given

**TABLE 4.12 (for Exercise 4.11)  Crest Toothpaste Sales Data**

| Year | Crest Sales, $y$ | Crest Budget, $x_1$ | Ratio, $x_2$ | U.S. Personal Disposable Income, $x_3$ |
|---|---|---|---|---|
| 1967 | 105,000 | 16,300 | 1.25 | 547.9 |
| 1968 | 105,000 | 15,800 | 1.34 | 593.4 |
| 1969 | 121,600 | 16,000 | 1.22 | 638.9 |
| 1970 | 113,750 | 14,200 | 1.00 | 695.3 |
| 1971 | 113,750 | 15,000 | 1.15 | 751.8 |
| 1972 | 128,925 | 14,000 | 1.13 | 810.3 |
| 1973 | 142,500 | 15,400 | 1.05 | 914.5 |
| 1974 | 126,000 | 18,250 | 1.27 | 998.3 |
| 1975 | 162,000 | 17,300 | 1.07 | 1096.1 |
| 1976 | 191,625 | 23,000 | 1.17 | 1194.4 |
| 1977 | 189,000 | 19,300 | 1.07 | 1311.5 |
| 1978 | 210,000 | 23,056 | 1.54 | 1462.9 |
| 1979 | 224,250 | 26,000 | 1.59 | 1641.7 |

*Source:* C. I. Allmon, "Advertising and Sales Relationships for Toothpaste: Another Look," *Business Economics* (September 1982), pp. 17, 58. Reprinted by permission. Copyright © 1982 National Association for Business Economics.

**FIGURE 4.29 (for Exercise 4.11)** Plots of toothpaste sales

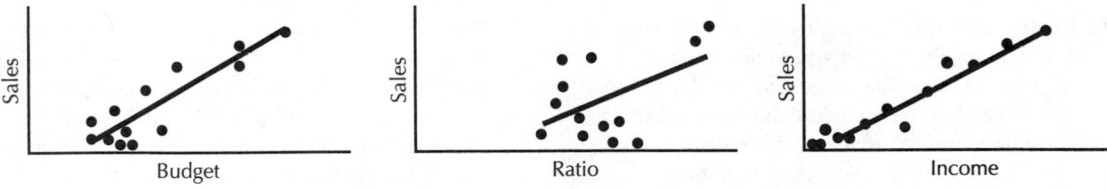

in parentheses) are $b_0 = 30,626(.156)$, $b_1 = 3.893(.094)$, $b_2 = -29,607(.245)$, and $b_3 = 86.52(<.001)$. Suppose it was estimated at the end of 1979 that in 1980 the advertising budget for Crest would be 28,000; the ratio of Crest's advertising budget to Colgate's advertising budget would be 1.56; and the U.S. personal disposable income would be 1,821.7. Using the model, a point prediction of and a 95% prediction interval for Crest sales in 1980 are 251,059 and [221.988,    280,130]. Show how the point prediction has been calculated.

**4.12** The trend in home building in recent years has been to emphasize open spaces and great rooms, rather than smaller living rooms and family rooms. A builder of speculative homes in the college community of Oxford, Ohio, had been building such homes, but his homes had been taking many months to sell and selling for substantially less than the asking price. In order to determine what types of homes would attract residents of the community, the builder contacted a statistician at a local college. The statistician went to a local real estate agency and obtained the data in Table 4.13 (page 204). This table presents the sales price $y$, square footage $x_1$, number of rooms $x_2$, number of bedrooms $x_3$, and age $x_4$ for each of 63 single-family residences recently sold in the community. When we perform a regression analysis of these data using the model

$$y = \beta_0 + \beta_1 x_1 + \beta_2 x_2 + \beta_3 x_3 + \beta_4 x_4 + \varepsilon$$

we find that the least squares point estimates of the model parameters and their associated $p$-values (given in parentheses) are $b_0 = 10.3676(.3710)$, $b_1 = .0500(<.001)$, $b_2 = 6.3218(.0152)$, $b_3 = -11.1032(.0635)$, and $b_4 = -.4319(.0002)$. Discuss why the estimates $b_2 = 6.3218$ and $b_3 = -11.1032$ suggest that it might be more profitable when building a house of a specified square footage (1) to include both a (smaller) living room and family room rather than a (larger) great room and (2) to not increase the number of bedrooms (at the cost of another type of room) that would normally be included in a house of the specified square footage.

Note: Based on the statistical results, the builder realized that there are many families with children in a college town and that the parents in such families would rather have one living area for the children (the family room) and a separate living area for themselves (the living room). The builder started modifying his open-space homes accordingly and greatly increased his profits.

**4.13** Figure 4.30 (page 205) presents the MINITAB output of a regression analysis of the real estate sales price data (see Exercise 4.1) using the model

$$y = \beta_0 + \beta_1 x_1 + \beta_2 x_2 + \beta_3 x_2^2 + \varepsilon$$

a. Discuss why the plots of $y$ versus $x_1$ and $y$ versus $x_2$ in Figure 4.24 indicate that this model might appropriately relate $y$ to $x_1$ and $x_2$.

b. Do the $p$-values for the independent variables in this model indicate that these independent variables are significant? Explain your answer.

c. Report and interpret a point prediction of and a 95% prediction interval for the sales price of an individual house having 2000 square feet and a rating of 8 (see the bottom of the MINITAB output in Figure 4.30).

**4.14** United Oil Company is attempting to develop a reasonably priced unleaded gasoline that will deliver higher gasoline mileages than can be achieved by its current unleaded gasolines. As part of its development process, United Oil wishes to study the effect of two independent variables—$x_1$, amount of gasoline additive RST (0, 1, or 2 units), and $x_2$, amount of gasoline additive XST (0, 1, 2, or 3 units), on gasoline mileage $y$. Mileage tests are carried out using equipment that simulates driving under prescribed conditions. The combinations of $x_1$ and $x_2$ used in the experiment, along with the corresponding values of $y$, are given in Table 4.14 (page 206).

a. Discuss why the data plots given in Figure 4.31 (page 206) indicate that the model

$$y = \beta_0 + \beta_1 x_1 + \beta_2 x_1^2 + \beta_3 x_2 + \beta_4 x_2^2 + \varepsilon$$

might appropriately relate $y$ to $x_1$ and $x_2$.

b. If we use SAS to analyze the data in Table 4.14 by using the model in part (a), we obtain the output in Figure 4.32 (page 206). Noting from Table 4.14 that the combination of one unit of gasoline additive RST and two units of gasoline additive XST seems to maximize gasoline mileage, assume that United Oil Company will use this combination to make its unleaded gasoline. The estimation and prediction results at the bottom of the SAS output are for the combination $x_1 = 1$ and $x_2 = 2$.

**TABLE 4.13 (for Exercise 4.12) Measurements Taken on 63 Single-Family Residences**

| Home | Sales Price, y (× $1000) | Square Feet, $x_1$ | Rooms, $x_2$ | Bedrooms, $x_3$ | Age, $x_4$ |
|---|---|---|---|---|---|
| 1 | 53.5 | 1008 | 5 | 2 | 35 |
| 2 | 49.0 | 1290 | 6 | 3 | 36 |
| 3 | 50.5 | 860 | 8 | 2 | 36 |
| 4 | 49.9 | 912 | 5 | 3 | 41 |
| 5 | 52.0 | 1204 | 6 | 3 | 40 |
| 6 | 55.0 | 1204 | 5 | 3 | 10 |
| 7 | 80.5 | 1764 | 8 | 4 | 64 |
| 8 | 86.0 | 1600 | 7 | 3 | 19 |
| 9 | 69.0 | 1255 | 5 | 3 | 16 |
| 10 | 149.0 | 3600 | 10 | 5 | 17 |
| 11 | 46.0 | 864 | 5 | 3 | 37 |
| 12 | 38.0 | 720 | 4 | 2 | 41 |
| 13 | 49.5 | 1008 | 6 | 3 | 35 |
| 14 | 105.0 | 1950 | 8 | 3 | 52 |
| 15 | 152.5 | 2086 | 7 | 3 | 12 |
| 16 | 85.0 | 2011 | 9 | 4 | 76 |
| 17 | 60.0 | 1465 | 6 | 3 | 102 |
| 18 | 58.5 | 1232 | 5 | 2 | 69 |
| 19 | 101.0 | 1736 | 7 | 3 | 67 |
| 20 | 79.4 | 1296 | 6 | 3 | 11 |
| 21 | 125.0 | 1996 | 7 | 3 | 9 |
| 22 | 87.9 | 1874 | 5 | 2 | 14 |
| 23 | 80.0 | 1580 | 5 | 3 | 11 |
| 24 | 94.0 | 1920 | 5 | 3 | 14 |
| 25 | 74.0 | 1430 | 9 | 3 | 16 |
| 26 | 69.0 | 1486 | 6 | 3 | 27 |
| 27 | 63.0 | 1008 | 5 | 2 | 35 |
| 28 | 67.5 | 1282 | 5 | 3 | 20 |
| 29 | 35.0 | 1134 | 5 | 2 | 74 |
| 30 | 142.5 | 2400 | 9 | 4 | 15 |
| 31 | 92.2 | 1701 | 5 | 3 | 15 |
| 32 | 56.0 | 1020 | 6 | 3 | 16 |
| 33 | 63.0 | 1053 | 5 | 2 | 24 |
| 34 | 60.0 | 1728 | 6 | 3 | 26 |
| 35 | 34.0 | 416 | 3 | 1 | 42 |
| 36 | 52.0 | 1040 | 5 | 2 | 9 |
| 37 | 75.0 | 1496 | 6 | 3 | 30 |
| 38 | 93.0 | 1936 | 8 | 4 | 39 |
| 39 | 60.0 | 1904 | 7 | 4 | 32 |
| 40 | 73.0 | 1080 | 5 | 2 | 24 |
| 41 | 71.0 | 1768 | 8 | 4 | 74 |
| 42 | 83.0 | 1503 | 6 | 3 | 14 |
| 43 | 90.0 | 1736 | 7 | 3 | 16 |
| 44 | 83.0 | 1695 | 6 | 3 | 12 |
| 45 | 115.0 | 2186 | 8 | 4 | 12 |
| 46 | 50.0 | 888 | 5 | 2 | 34 |
| 47 | 55.2 | 1120 | 6 | 3 | 29 |
| 48 | 61.0 | 1400 | 5 | 3 | 33 |
| 49 | 147.0 | 2165 | 7 | 3 | 2 |
| 50 | 210.0 | 2353 | 8 | 4 | 15 |
| 51 | 60.0 | 1536 | 6 | 3 | 36 |
| 52 | 100.0 | 1972 | 8 | 3 | 37 |
| 53 | 44.5 | 1120 | 5 | 3 | 27 |
| 54 | 55.0 | 1664 | 7 | 3 | 79 |
| 55 | 53.4 | 925 | 5 | 3 | 20 |
| 56 | 65.0 | 1288 | 5 | 3 | 2 |
| 57 | 73.0 | 1400 | 5 | 3 | 2 |
| 58 | 40.0 | 1376 | 6 | 3 | 103 |
| 59 | 141.0 | 2038 | 12 | 4 | 62 |
| 60 | 68.0 | 1572 | 6 | 3 | 29 |
| 61 | 139.0 | 1545 | 6 | 3 | 9 |
| 62 | 140.0 | 1993 | 6 | 3 | 4 |
| 63 | 55.0 | 1130 | 5 | 2 | 21 |

*Source:* RE/MAX Alpha Real Estate, Oxford, Ohio.

**FIGURE 4.30 (for Exercise 4.13)** MINITAB output of a regression analysis of the real estate sales price data using the model $y = \beta_0 + \beta_1 x_1 + \beta_2 x_2 + \beta_3 x_2^2 + \varepsilon$

```
The regression equation is
Y = 19.1 + 5.56 X1 + 9.22 X2 - 0.513 X2SQ


Predictor      Coef    SE Coef      T       P
Constant     19.074      3.632    5.25   0.002
X1           5.5596     0.1255   44.29   0.000
X2            9.223      1.312    7.03   0.000
X2SQ        -0.5129     0.1228   -4.18   0.006


S = 1.77128    R-Sq = 99.7%    R-Sq(adj) = 99.6%


Analysis of Variance

Source           DF      SS       MS       F       P
Regression        3   7428.7   2476.2   789.25   0.000
Residual Error    6     18.8      3.1
Total             9   7447.5

   Fit   SE Fit        95% CI                95% PI
171.222   0.895   (169.033, 173.411)   (166.367, 176.078)
```

1. Find a point estimate of and a 95% confidence interval for the mean mileage obtained by all gallons of the gasoline when it is made using one unit of RST and two units of XST.
2. Find a point prediction of and a 95% prediction interval for the mileage that would be obtained by an individual gallon of the gasoline when it is made using one unit of RST and two units of XST.

**4.15** We concluded in Exercise 4.13 that the real estate sales price model

$$y = \beta_0 + \beta_1 x_1 + \beta_2 x_2 + \beta_3 x_2^2 + \varepsilon$$

might appropriately relate $y$ to $x_1$ and $x_2$. To investigate whether interaction exists between $x_1$ and $x_2$, we consider the model

$$y = \beta_0 + \beta_1 x_1 + \beta_2 x_2 + \beta_3 x_2^2 + \beta_4 x_1 x_2 + \varepsilon$$

Figure 4.33 (page 207) presents the MINITAB output of a regression analysis of the real estate sales price data using this model.

a. Does the $p$-value for $x_1 x_2$ indicate that this interaction variable is important? Do the $p$-values for the other independent variables in the model indicate that these variables are important? Explain your answer.
b. Report and interpret a point prediction of and a 95% prediction interval for the sales price of an individual house having 2000 square feet and a rating of 8 (see the bottom of the MINITAB output in Figure 4.33). Is the 95% prediction interval given by the model

$$y = \beta_0 + \beta_1 x_1 + \beta_2 x_2 + \beta_3 x_2^2 + \beta_4 x_1 x_2 + \varepsilon$$

shorter than the 95% prediction interval given by the model

$$y = \beta_0 + \beta_1 x_1 + \beta_2 x_2 + \beta_3 x_2^2 + \varepsilon$$

(see the MINITAB output in Figure 4.30)? If so, what does this mean?

**4.16** In this exercise we study the nature of the interaction between $x_1$, square footage, and $x_2$, rating, for the real estate sales price data.

**TABLE 4.14 (for Exercise 4.14)** United Oil Company Unleaded Gasoline Mileage Data

| Gasoline Mileage, $y$ (mpg) | Amount of Gasoline Additive RST, $x_1$ | Amount of Gasoline Additive XST, $x_2$ |
|---|---|---|
| 27.4 | 0 | 0 |
| 28.0 | 0 | 0 |
| 28.6 | 0 | 0 |
| 29.6 | 1 | 0 |
| 30.6 | 1 | 0 |
| 28.6 | 2 | 0 |
| 29.8 | 2 | 0 |
| 32.0 | 0 | 1 |
| 33.0 | 0 | 1 |
| 33.3 | 1 | 1 |
| 34.5 | 1 | 1 |
| 32.3 | 0 | 2 |
| 33.5 | 0 | 2 |
| 34.4 | 1 | 2 |
| 35.0 | 1 | 2 |
| 35.6 | 1 | 2 |
| 33.3 | 2 | 2 |
| 34.0 | 2 | 2 |
| 34.7 | 2 | 2 |
| 33.4 | 1 | 3 |
| 32.0 | 2 | 3 |
| 33.0 | 2 | 3 |

**FIGURE 4.31 (for Exercise 4.14)** Scatter plots for the United Oil Mileage data

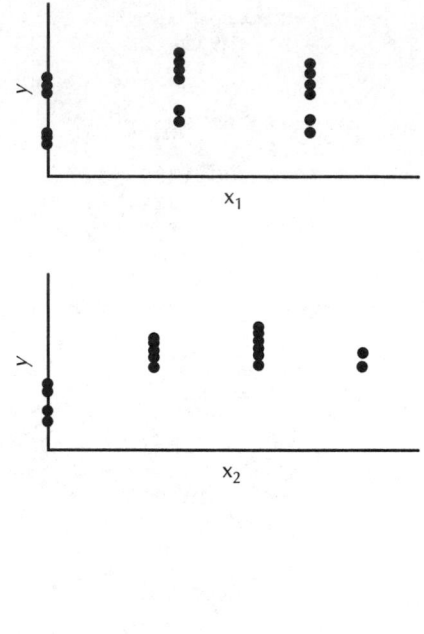

**FIGURE 4.32 (for Exercise 4.14)** SAS output of a regression analysis of the United Oil Company data using the model $y = \beta_0 + \beta_1 x_1 + \beta_2 x_1^2 + \beta_3 x_2 + \beta_4 x_2^2 + \varepsilon$

Analysis of Variance

| Source | DF | Sum of Squares | Mean Square | F Value | Pr > F |
|---|---|---|---|---|---|
| Model | 4 | 120.71374 | 30.17844 | 75.90 | <.0001 |
| Error | 17 | 6.75898 | 0.39759 | | |
| Corrected Total | 21 | 127.47273 | | | |

| | | |
|---|---|---|
| Root MSE | 0.63055 | R-Square 0.9470 |
| Dependent Mean | 32.11818 | Adj R-Sq 0.9345 |
| Coeff Var | 1.96320 | |

Parameter Estimates

| Variable | Label | DF | Parameter Estimate | Standard Error | t Value | Pr > \|t\| |
|---|---|---|---|---|---|---|
| Intercept | Intercept | 1 | 28.15892 | 0.29018 | 97.04 | <.0001 |
| X1 | X1 | 1 | 3.31331 | 0.58963 | 5.62 | <.0001 |
| X2 | X2 | 1 | 5.27521 | 0.41289 | 12.78 | <.0001 |
| X1SQ | X1 ** 2 | 1 | -1.41108 | 0.28156 | -5.01 | 0.0001 |
| X2SQ | X2 ** 2 | 1 | -1.39637 | 0.15085 | -9.26 | <.0001 |

| Obs | Dep Var Y | Predicted Value | Std Error Mean Predict | 95% CL Mean | | 95% CL Predict | |
|---|---|---|---|---|---|---|---|
| 23 | . | 35.0261 | 0.2495 | 34.4997 | 35.5525 | 33.5954 | 36.4568 |

**FIGURE 4.33 (for Exercises 4.15 and 4.16)** MINITAB output of a regression analysis of the real estate sales price data using the model $y = \beta_0 + \beta_1 x_1 + \beta_2 x_2 + \beta_3 x_2^2 + \beta_4 x_1 x_2 + \varepsilon$

```
The regression equation is
Y = 27.4 + 5.08 X1 + 7.29 X2 - 0.531 X2SQ + 0.115 X1X2


Predictor      Coef   SE Coef       T       P
Constant     27.438     3.059    8.97   0.000
X1           5.0813    0.1476   34.42   0.000
X2           7.2899    0.9089    8.02   0.000
X2SQ        -0.53110   0.06978   -7.61   0.001
X1X2         0.11473   0.03103    3.70   0.014


S = 1.00404    R-Sq = 99.9%    R-Sq(adj) = 99.9%


Analysis of Variance

Source          DF      SS       MS        F       P
Regression       4  7442.5   1860.6  1845.66   0.000
Residual Error   5     5.0      1.0
Total            9  7447.5

    Fit   SE Fit         95% CI              95% PI
171.751    0.527  (170.396, 173.105)  (168.836, 174.665)
```

a. Consider all houses with a rating of 2. In this case, predicted sales price is (using the least squares point estimates in Figure 4.33)

$$\hat{y} = b_0 + b_1 x_1 + b_2 x_2 + b_3 x_2^2 + b_4 x_1 x_2$$
$$= 27.438 + 5.0813 x_1 + 7.2899(2)$$
$$- .5311(2)^2 + .11473 x_1 (2)$$

Calculate $\hat{y}$ when $x_1 = 13$ and 22. Plot $\hat{y}$ versus $x_1$, for $x_1 = 13$ and 22.

b. Consider all houses with a rating of 8. In this case, predicted sales price is (using the least squares point estimates in Figure 4.33)

$$\hat{y} = b_0 + b_1 x_1 + b_2 x_2 + b_3 x_2^2 + b_4 x_1 x_2$$
$$= 27.438 + 5.0813 x_1 + 7.2899(8)$$
$$- .5311(8)^2 + .11473 x_1 (8)$$

Calculate $\hat{y}$ when $x_1 = 13$ and 22. Plot $\hat{y}$ versus $x_1$, for $x_1 = 13$ and 22.

c. By comparing the plots you made in (a) and (b), discuss the nature of the interaction between $x_1$ and $x_2$.

**4.17** A study examined the profit $y$ per sales dollar earned by a construction company and its relationship to the size $x_1$ of the construction contract (in hundreds of thousands of dollars) and the number $x_2$ of years of experience of the construction supervisor. Data were obtained from a sample of $n = 18$ construction projects undertaken by the construction company over the past two years. These data are presented in Table 4.15 (page 208), where $y$, $x_1$, and $x_2$ denote the profit, contract size, and supervisor experience associated with a particular construction project. To investigate whether interaction exists between $x_1$ and $x_2$, we consider Figure 4.34 (page 208), which gives plots of $y$ versus $x_1$ for different values of $x_2$. Plot (a) in Figure 4.34 shows that when $x_2$ (supervisor experience) equals 2, $y$ (profit) decreases as $x_1$ (contract size) increases. This says that less experienced supervisors handle large contracts less effectively than smaller contracts. Plot (b) shows that when $x_2$ equals 4, $y$ also decreases as $x_1$ increases. Plot (c) shows that when $x_2$ equals 6, $y$ increases as $x_1$ increases. This says that more experienced supervisors handle larger contracts more effectively than smaller contracts. These plots suggest that the relationship between mean profit and

**FIGURE 4.34 (for Exercises 4.17 and 4.18)** Plots of $y$ versus $x_1$ for different values of $x_2$ for the construction profit data

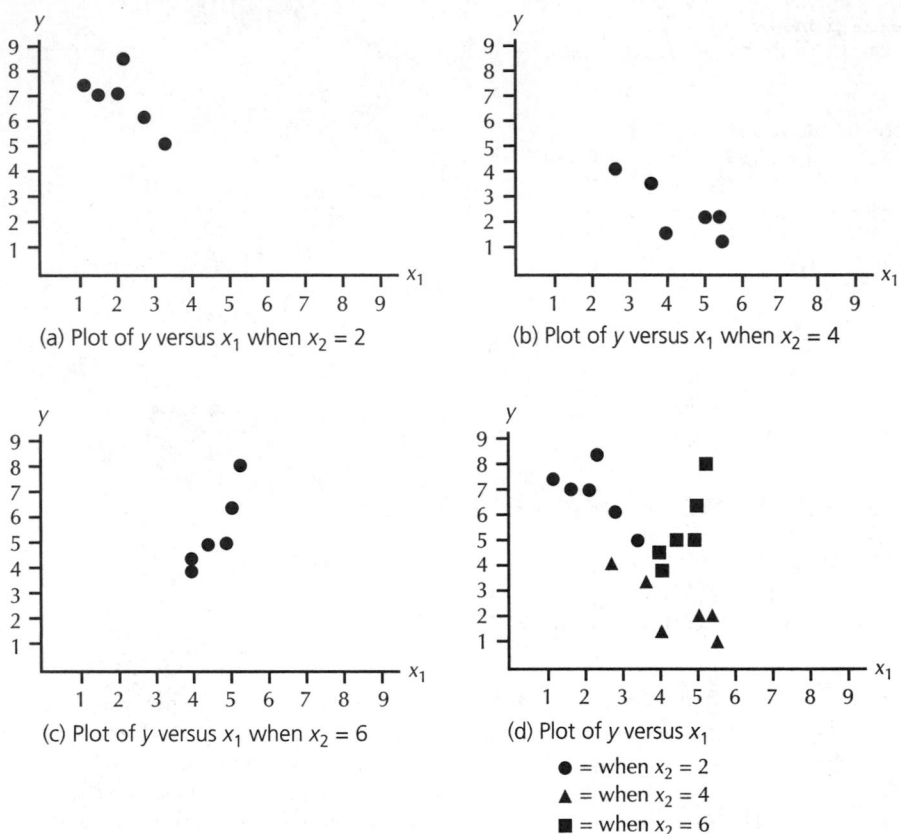

(a) Plot of $y$ versus $x_1$ when $x_2 = 2$

(b) Plot of $y$ versus $x_1$ when $x_2 = 4$

(c) Plot of $y$ versus $x_1$ when $x_2 = 6$

(d) Plot of $y$ versus $x_1$

● = when $x_2 = 2$
▲ = when $x_2 = 4$
■ = when $x_2 = 6$

**TABLE 4.15 (for Exercises 4.17 and 4.18) The Construction Profit Data**

| Construction Project | Contract Size, $x_1$ (× $100,000) | Supervisor Experience, $x_2$ (years) | Profit, $y$ (%) | Construction Project | Contract Size, $x_1$ (× $100,000) | Supervisor Experience, $x_2$ (years) | Profit, $y$ (%) |
|---|---|---|---|---|---|---|---|
| 1 | 5.1 | 4 | 2.0 | 10 | 4.3 | 6 | 5.0 |
| 2 | 3.5 | 4 | 3.5 | 11 | 2.9 | 2 | 6.0 |
| 3 | 2.4 | 2 | 8.5 | 12 | 1.1 | 2 | 7.5 |
| 4 | 4.0 | 6 | 4.5 | 13 | 2.6 | 4 | 4.0 |
| 5 | 1.7 | 2 | 7.0 | 14 | 4.0 | 6 | 4.0 |
| 6 | 2.0 | 2 | 7.0 | 15 | 5.3 | 4 | 1.0 |
| 7 | 5.0 | 4 | 2.0 | 16 | 4.9 | 6 | 5.0 |
| 8 | 3.2 | 2 | 5.0 | 17 | 5.0 | 6 | 6.5 |
| 9 | 5.2 | 6 | 8.0 | 18 | 3.9 | 4 | 1.5 |

*Source:* © 1982. Reprinted with permission of Brooks/Cole, an imprint of the Wadsworth Group, a division of Thomson Learning. Fax 800-730-2215.

**FIGURE 4.35 (for Exercises 4.17 and 4.18)** SAS output of a regression analysis of the construction profit data using the model $y = \beta_0 + \beta_1 x_1 + \beta_2 x_2 + \beta_3 x_1^2 + \beta_4 x_1 x_2 + \varepsilon$

```
                          Analysis of Variance

                                  Sum of         Mean
      Source            DF        Squares        Square     F Value    Pr > F

      Model              4       77.02982       19.25745     20.44    <.0001
      Error             13       12.24796        0.94215
      Corrected Total   17       89.27778


                 Root MSE              0.97064    R-Square     0.8628
                 Dependent Mean        4.88889    Adj R-Sq     0.8206
                 Coeff Var            19.85409


                          Parameter Estimates

                                  Parameter     Standard
      Variable    Label     DF    Estimate      Error      t Value    Pr > |t|

      Intercept   Intercept  1    19.30496      2.05206      9.41     <.0001
      CSIZE       CSIZE      1     -1.48660      1.17773     -1.26      0.2290
      SUPEXP      SUPEXP     1     -6.37145      1.04231     -6.11     <.0001
      CSIZESQ     CSIZE ** 2 1     -0.75225      0.22524     -3.34      0.0053
      INTER       CSIZE * SUPEXP 1  1.71705      0.25378      6.77     <.0001

              Dep Var  Predicted    Std Error
      Obs     Profit   Value Mean Predict     95% CL Mean        95% CL Predict
      19        .       6.0599    0.4397     5.1099   7.0098     3.7578    8.3620
```

contract size ($x_1$) depends on supervisor experience ($x_2$). This says that interaction exists between $x_1$ and $x_2$ as these variables affect $y$. Figure 4.35 presents the SAS output of a regression analysis of the construction profit data using the model

$$y = \beta_0 + \beta_1 x_1 + \beta_2 x_2 + \beta_3 x_1^2 + \beta_4 x_1 x_2 + \varepsilon$$

Report and interpret a point prediction of and a 95% prediction interval for the actual profit associated with a future construction project for which the contract size will be $480,000 and the supervisor will have six years of experience (see the predicted values given at the bottom of the SAS Output).

**4.18** We next use the nature of the interaction between $x_1$ and $x_2$ in the construction profit data to decide how supervisors should be assigned to different contract sizes.

a. Consider all contracts for which the supervisor has two years of experience. In this case, predicted profit is (using the least squares point estimates in Figure 4.35)

$$\hat{y} = b_0 + b_1 x_1 + b_2 x_2 + b_3 x_1^2 + b_4 x_1 x_2$$
$$= 19.3050 - 1.4866 x_1 - 6.3715(2)$$
$$- .7522 x_1^2 + 1.7171 x_1(2)$$

Calculate $\hat{y}$ when $x_1 = 3$, 4, and 5. Plot $\hat{y}$ versus $x_1$, for $x_1 = 3$, 4, and 5.

b. Consider all contracts for which the supervisor has four years of experience. In this case, predicted profit is (using the least squares point estimates in Figure 4.35 )

$$\hat{y} = b_0 + b_1 x_1 + b_2 x_2 + b_3 x_1^2 + b_4 x_1 x_2$$
$$= 19.3050 - 1.4866 x_1 - 6.3715(4)$$
$$- .7522 x_1^2 + 1.7171 x_1(4)$$

Calculate $\hat{y}$ when $x_1 = 3$, 4, and 5. Plot $\hat{y}$ versus $x_1$, for $x_1 = 3$, 4, and 5. Plot on the same set of axes that you used in part (a).

c. Consider all contracts for which the supervisor has six years of experience. In this case, predicted profit is (using the least squares point estimates in Figure 4.35 )

$$\hat{y} = b_0 + b_1 x_1 + b_2 x_2 + b_3 x_1^2 + b_4 x_1 x_2$$
$$= 19.3050 - 1.4866 x_1 - 6.3715(6)$$
$$- .7522 x_1^2 + 1.7171 x_1(6)$$

Calculate $\hat{y}$ when $x_1 = 3, 4,$ and $5$. Plot $\hat{y}$ versus $x_1$, for $x_1 = 3, 4,$ and $5$. Use the same set of axes that you did in parts (a) and (b).

d. The curves of the equations for $\hat{y}$ as a function of $x_1$ when $x_2 = 2$, $\hat{y}$ as a function of $x_1$ when $x_2 = 4$, and $\hat{y}$ as a function of $x_1$ when $x_2 = 6$ all intersect at one point, which we denote as $(x_1^*, y^*)$. To find $x_1^*$, we can set the equation for $\hat{y}$ as a function of $x_1$ when $x_2 = 2$ equal to the equation for $\hat{y}$ as a function of $x_1$ when $x_2 = 4$ as follows:

$$19.3050 - 1.4866 x_1 - 6.3715(2)$$
$$- .7522 x_1^2 + 1.7171 x_1(2)$$
$$= 19.3050 - 1.4866 x_1 - 6.3715(4)$$
$$- .7522 x_1^2 + 1.7171 x_1(4)$$

Solve this equation for $x_1$, which is $x_1^*$. By looking at the plots you made, determine

1. Which of the three plotted curves gives higher predicted profits $\hat{y}$ when $x_1$ is less than $x_1^*$. Decide what level of supervisory experience should be assigned to contract sizes less than $x_1^*$.
2. Which of the three plotted curves gives higher predicted profits $\hat{y}$ when $x_1$ is greater than $x_1^*$. Decide what level of supervisory experience should be assigned to contract sizes greater than $x_1^*$.
3. Which contract sizes should be assigned to supervisors with the level of experience that you did not choose in (1) and (2). Note that although predicted profit will not be optimal for these supervisors, the company must make this decision because it has supervisors with this level of experience.

**4.19** In the article "The Effect of Promotion Timing on Major League Baseball Attendance" (*Sport Marketing Quarterly,* December 1999), T. C. Boyd and T. C. Krehbiel use data from six major league baseball teams having outdoor stadiums to study the effect of promotion timing on major league baseball attendance. One of their regression models describes game attendance in 1996 as follows (*p*-values less than .10 are shown in parentheses under the appropriate independent variables):

Attendance
$$= 2521 + 106.5\ Temperature + 12.33\ Winning\ \%$$
$$\qquad\qquad (<.001) \qquad\qquad\qquad (<.001)$$
$$+ .2248\ OpWin\ \% - 424.2\ DayGame$$
$$\qquad (<.001)$$
$$+ 4845\ Weekend + 1192\ Rival$$
$$\qquad (<.001) \qquad\qquad (<.10)$$
$$+ 4745\ Promotion + 5059\ Promo*DayGame$$
$$\qquad (<.001) \qquad\qquad\qquad (<.001)$$
$$- 4690\ Promo*Weekend$$
$$\qquad (<.001)$$
$$+ 696.5\ Promo*Rival$$

In this model, *Temperature* is the high temperature recorded in the city on game day; *Winning %* is the home team's winning percentage at the start of the game; *OpWin %* is a dummy variable that equals 1 if the opponent's winning percentage was .500 or higher and 0 otherwise; *DayGame* is a dummy variable that equals 1 if the game was a day game and 0 otherwise; *Weekend* is a dummy variable that equals 1 if the game was on a Friday, Saturday, or Sunday and 0 otherwise; *Rival* is a dummy variable that equals 1 if the opponent was a rival and 0 otherwise; *Promotion* is a dummy variable that equals 1 if the home team ran a promotion during the game and 0 otherwise. Using the model, which is based on 475 games and has an $R^2$ of .6221, Boyd and Krehbiel conclude that "promotions run during day games and on weekdays are likely to result in greater attendance increases." Explain these conclusions by using the least squares point estimates 5059 and −4690, which are multiplied by the interaction terms *Promo*DayGame* and *Promo*Weekend*. Given that major league baseball teams tend to run promotions during night games and on weekends, what are the practical consequences of the authors' conclusions?

**4.20** Neter, Kutner, Nachtsheim, and Wasserman (1996) relate the speed, $y$, with which a particular insurance innovation is adopted to the size of the insurance firm, $x$, and the type of firm. The dependent variable $y$ is measured by the number of months elapsed between the time the first firm adopted the innovation and the time the firm being considered adopted the innovation. The size of the firm, $x$, is measured by the total assets of the firm, and the type of the firm—a qualitative independent variable—is

**TABLE 4.16 (for Exercise 4.20)** Insurance Innovation Data

| Firm | Number of Months Elapsed, $y$ | Size of Firm, ($\times$ \$1 million), $x$ | Type of Firm | Firm | Number of Months Elapsed, $y$ | Size of Firm, ($\times$ \$1 million), $x$ | Type of Firm |
|---|---|---|---|---|---|---|---|
| 1 | 17 | 151 | Mutual | 11 | 28 | 164 | Stock |
| 2 | 26 | 92 | Mutual | 12 | 15 | 272 | Stock |
| 3 | 21 | 175 | Mutual | 13 | 11 | 295 | Stock |
| 4 | 30 | 31 | Mutual | 14 | 38 | 68 | Stock |
| 5 | 22 | 104 | Mutual | 15 | 31 | 85 | Stock |
| 6 | 0 | 277 | Mutual | 16 | 21 | 224 | Stock |
| 7 | 12 | 210 | Mutual | 17 | 20 | 166 | Stock |
| 8 | 19 | 120 | Mutual | 18 | 13 | 305 | Stock |
| 9 | 4 | 290 | Mutual | 19 | 30 | 124 | Stock |
| 10 | 16 | 238 | Mutual | 20 | 14 | 246 | Stock |

**FIGURE 4.36 (for Exercise 4.20)** Plot of the insurance innovation data

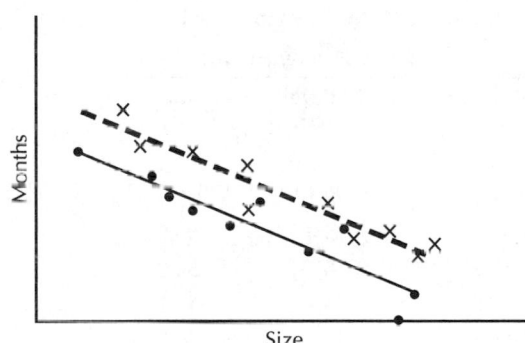

Size

- ● Mutual
- ✕ Stock
- ——— Linear (Mutual)
- – – – Linear (Stock)

either a mutual company or a stock company. The data in Table 4.16 are observed.

a. Discuss why the data plot in Figure 4.36 indicates that the model

$$y = \beta_0 + \beta_1 x + \beta_2 D_S + \varepsilon$$

might appropriately describe the observed data. Here $D_S$ equals 1 if the firm is a stock company and 0 if the firm is a mutual company.

b. Let $\mu_{a,M}$ denote the mean adoption time of the insurance innovation by mutual companies having an asset size of $a$, and let $\mu_{a,S}$ denote the mean adoption time of the insurance innovation by stock companies having an asset size of $a$. The model in part (a) implies that

$$\mu_{a,M} = \beta_0 + \beta_1 a + \beta_2(0) = \beta_0 + \beta_1 a$$

and

$$\mu_{a,S} = \beta_0 + \beta_1 a + \beta_2(1) = \beta_0 + \beta_1 a + \beta_2$$

This implies that $\mu_{a,S} - \mu_{a,M} = \beta_2$. In your own words, interpret $\beta_2$.

c. Figure 4.37 (page 212) presents the Excel output of a regression analysis of the insurance innovation data using the model of part (a). Test $H_0: \beta_2 = 0$ versus $H_a: \beta_2 \neq 0$ by setting $\alpha = .05$ and .01. Also, identify and interpret a 95% confidence interval for $\beta_2$. What do you conclude about the importance of firm type when we are predicting adoption speed?

d. If we add the interaction term $xD_S$ to the model of part (a), we find that the $p$-value related to this term is .9821. What does this imply?

**FIGURE 4.37 (for Exercise 4.20)** Excel output of a regression analysis of the insurance innovation data using the model $y = \beta_0 + \beta_1 x + \beta_2 D_S + \varepsilon$

**Regression Statistics**

| | |
|---|---|
| Multiple R | 0.946075002 |
| R Square | 0.89505791 |
| Adjusted R Square | 0.882711781 |
| Standard Error | 3.221131199 |
| Observations | 20 |

**ANOVA**

| | df | SS | MS | F | Significance F |
|---|---|---|---|---|---|
| Regression | 2 | 1504.413335 | 752.2066673 | 72.49705253 | 4.76511E-09 |
| Residual | 17 | 176.3866654 | 10.3756862 | | |
| Total | 19 | 1680.8 | | | |

| | Coefficients | Standard Error | t Stat | P-value | Lower 95% | Upper 95% |
|---|---|---|---|---|---|---|
| Intercept | 33.87406904 | 1.813858297 | 18.67514628 | 9.14527E-13 | 30.0471572 | 37.70098087 |
| x | −0.101742115 | 0.008891218 | −11.4429901 | 2.07469E-09 | −0.120500971 | −0.08298326 |
| Ds | 8.055469205 | 1.4591057 | 5.520826355 | 3.74187E-05 | 4.97702097 | 11.13391744 |

**4.21** The Tastee Bakery Company supplies a bakery product to many supermarkets in a metropolitan area. The company wishes to study the effect of the height of the shelf display employed by the supermarkets on monthly sales, $y$ (measured in cases of 10 units each), for this product. Shelf display height has three levels—bottom ($B$), middle ($M$), and top ($T$). For each shelf display height, six supermarkets of equal sales potential will be randomly selected, and each supermarket will display the product using its assigned shelf height for a month. At the end of the month, sales of the bakery product at the 18 participating stores will be recorded. When the experiment is carried out, the data in Table 4.17 are obtained. Here we assume that the set of sales amounts for each display height is a sample that has been randomly selected from the population of all sales amounts that could be obtained (at supermarkets of the given sales potential) when using that display height. To compare the population mean sales amounts $\mu_B$, $\mu_M$, and $\mu_T$ that would be obtained by using the bottom, middle, and top display heights, we use the following dummy variable regression model:

$$y = \beta_B + \beta_M D_M + \beta_T D_T + \varepsilon$$

**TABLE 4.17 (for Exercise 4.21)  Bakery Sales Study Data (Sales in Cases)**

| Shelf Display Height | | |
|---|---|---|
| Bottom (B) | Middle (M) | Top (T) |
| 58.2 | 73.0 | 52.4 |
| 53.7 | 78.1 | 49.7 |
| 55.8 | 75.4 | 50.9 |
| 55.7 | 76.2 | 54.0 |
| 52.5 | 78.4 | 52.1 |
| 58.9 | 82.1 | 49.9 |

Here $D_M$ equals 1 if a middle display height is used and 0 otherwise; $D_T$ equals 1 if a top display height is used and 0 otherwise. Figure 4.38 presents the MINITAB output of a regression analysis of the bakery sales study data using this model.

a.  By using the definitions of the dummy variables, show that

$$\mu_B = \beta_B \qquad \mu_M = \beta_B + \beta_M \qquad \mu_T = \beta_B + \beta_T$$

**FIGURE 4.38 (for Exercise 4.21)** MINITAB output of a dummy variable regression analysis of the bakery sales data in Table 4.17

```
The regression equation is
Y = 55.8 + 21.4 DM - 4.30 DT


Predictor    Coef   SE Coef      T      P
Constant   55.800    1.013   55.07  0.000
DM         21.400    1.433   14.93  0.000
DT         -4.300    1.433   -3.00  0.009


S = 2.48193    R-Sq = 96.1%    R-Sq(adj) = 95.6%


Analysis of Variance

Source          DF      SS      MS       F      P
Regression       2  2273.9  1136.9  184.57  0.000
Residual Error  15    92.4     6.2
Total           17  2366.3

   Fit   SE Fit       95% CI            95% PI
77.200    1.013  (75.040, 79.360)  (71.486, 82.914)
```

**FIGURE 4.39 (for Exercise 4.21)** MINITAB output for the model $y = \beta_T + \beta_B D_B + \beta_M D_M + \varepsilon$

```
Predictor    Coef       SE Coef        T          P

Constant   51.500        1.013      50.83      0.000
DB          4.300        1.433       3.00      0.009
DM         25.700        1.433      17.94      0.000
```

b. Use the overall $F$-statistic to test $H_0: \beta_M = \beta_T = 0$, or, equivalently, $H_0: \mu_B = \mu_M = \mu_T$.

c. Show that your results in part (a) imply that

$$\mu_M - \mu_B = \beta_M \qquad \mu_T - \mu_B = \beta_T$$

$$\mu_M - \mu_T = \beta_M - \beta_T$$

Then use the least squares point estimates of the model parameters to find a point estimate of each of the three differences in means. Also, find a 95% confidence interval for and test the significance of each of the first two differences in means.

d. Find a point estimate of mean sales when using a middle display height, a 95% confidence interval for mean sales when using a middle display height,

and a 95% prediction interval for sales at an individual supermarket that employs a middle display height (see the bottom of the MINITAB output in Figure 4.38).

e. Consider the following alternative model

$$y = \beta_T + \beta_B D_B + \beta_M D_M + \varepsilon$$

Here $D_B$ equals 1 if a bottom display height is used and 0 otherwise. The MINITAB output of the least squares point estimates of the parameters of this model is shown in Figure 4.39. Since $\beta_M$ expresses the effect of the middle display height with respect to the effect of the top display height, $\beta_M$ equals $\mu_M - \mu_T$. Calculate a 95% confidence interval for and test the significance of $\mu_M - \mu_T$.

**4.22** Recall from Example 4.12 that Enterprise Industries has observed the historical data in Table 4.6 concerning $y$ (demand for Fresh liquid laundry detergent), $x_4$ (the price difference), and $x_3$ (Enterprise Industries' advertising expenditure for Fresh). To ultimately increase the demand for Fresh, Enterprise Industries' marketing department is comparing the effectiveness of three different advertising campaigns. These campaigns are denoted as compaigns $A$, $B$, and $C$. Campaign $A$ consists entirely of television commercials, campaign $B$ consists of a balanced mixture of television and radio commercials, and campaign $C$ consists of a balanced mixture of television, radio, newspaper, and magazine ads. To conduct the study, Enterprise Industries has randomly selected one advertising campaign to be used in each of the 30 sales periods in Table 4.6. Although logic would indicate that each of campaigns $A$, $B$, and $C$ should be used in 10 of the 30 sales periods, Enterprise Industries has made previous commitments to the advertising media involved in the study. As a result, campaigns $A$, $B$, and $C$ were randomly assigned to, respectively, 9, 11, and 10 sales periods. Furthermore, advertising was done in only the first three weeks of each sales period, so that the carryover effect of the campaign used in a sales period to the next sales period would be minimized. Table 4.18 lists the campaigns used in the sales periods.

To compare the effectiveness of advertising campaigns $A$, $B$, and $C$, we define two dummy variables. Specifically, we define the dummy variable $D_B$ to equal 1 if campaign $B$ is used in a sales period and 0 otherwise. Furthermore, we define the dummy variable $D_C$ to equal 1 if campaign $C$ is used in a sales period and 0 otherwise. Figure 4.40 presents the SAS output of a regression analysis of the Fresh demand data by using the model

$$y = \beta_0 + \beta_1 x_4 + \beta_2 x_3 + \beta_3 x_3^2 + \beta_4 x_4 x_3$$
$$+ \beta_5 D_B + \beta_6 D_C + \varepsilon$$

The $p$-value for each independent variable in the model is less than .05. The importance of $x_3^2$ in the model implies that there is a *quadratic* relationship between $y$ and $x_3$. This quadratic relationship is suggested by the *curvature* in the plot of $y$ versus $x_3$ in Figure 4.12. The importance of $x_4 x_3$ in the model implies that there is

**TABLE 4.18 (for Exercise 4.22)**
**Advertising Campaigns**

| Sales Period | Advertising Campaign |
|---|---|
| 1 | B |
| 2 | B |
| 3 | B |
| 4 | A |
| 5 | C |
| 6 | A |
| 7 | C |
| 8 | C |
| 9 | B |
| 10 | C |
| 11 | A |
| 12 | C |
| 13 | C |
| 14 | A |
| 15 | B |
| 16 | B |
| 17 | B |
| 18 | A |
| 19 | B |
| 20 | B |
| 21 | C |
| 22 | A |
| 23 | A |
| 24 | A |
| 25 | A |
| 26 | B |
| 27 | C |
| 28 | B |
| 29 | C |
| 30 | C |

*interaction* between $x_4$ and $x_3$. To compare the advertising campaigns, consider comparing three means, denoted $\mu_{[d,a,A]}$, $\mu_{[d,a,B]}$, and $\mu_{[d,a,C]}$. These means represent the mean demands for Fresh when the price difference is $d$, the advertising expenditure is $a$, and we use advertising campaigns $A$, $B$, and $C$, respectively. If we set $x_4 = d$ and $x_3 = a$ in the expression

$$\beta_0 + \beta_1 x_4 + \beta_2 x_3 + \beta_3 x_3^2 + \beta_4 x_4 x_3 + \beta_5 D_B + \beta_6 D_C$$

**FIGURE 4.40 (for Exercise 4.22)** SAS output of a dummy variable regression model analysis of the Fresh demand data

```
                      Analysis of Variance

                            Sum of        Mean
Source              DF      Squares       Square     F Value    Pr > F

Model                6     13.06502      2.17750     127.25    <.0001
Error               23      0.39357      0.01711
Corrected Total     29     13.45859


           Root MSE              0.13081   R-Square    0.9708
           Dependent Mean        8.38267   Adj R-Sq    0.9631
           Coeff Var             1.56050


                      Parameter Estimates

                            Parameter    Standard
Variable   Label      DF    Estimate     Error       t Value    Pr > |t|

Intercept  Intercept   1    25.61270     4.79378      5.34     <.0001
X4         X4          1     9.05868     3.03170      2.99      0.0066
X3         X3          1    -6.53767     1.58137     -4.13      0.0004
X3SQ       X3 ** 2     1     0.58444     0.12987      4.50      0.0002
X4X3       X3 * X4     1    -1.15648     0.45574     -2.54      0.0184
DB         DB          1     0.21369     0.06215      3.44      0.0022
DC         DC          1     0.38178     0.06125      6.23     <.0001


         Dep Var  Predicted    Std Error
  Obs       Y     Value  Mean Predict    95% CL Mean      95% CL Predict
   31       .     8.5007      0.0469    8.4037   8.5977   8.2132   8.7881
```

it follows that

$$\mu_{[d,a,A]} = \beta_0 + \beta_1 d + \beta_2 a + \beta_3 a^2 + \beta_4 da$$
$$+ \beta_5(0) + \beta_6(0)$$
$$= \beta_0 + \beta_1 d + \beta_2 a + \beta_3 a^2 + \beta_4 da$$

$$\mu_{[d,a,B]} = \beta_0 + \beta_1 d + \beta_2 a + \beta_3 a^2 + \beta_4 da$$
$$+ \beta_5(1) + \beta_6(0)$$
$$= \beta_0 + \beta_1 d + \beta_2 a + \beta_3 a^2 + \beta_4 da + \beta_5$$

and

$$\mu_{[d,a,C]} = \beta_0 + \beta_1 d + \beta_2 a + \beta_3 a^2 + \beta_4 da + \beta_5(0) + \beta_6(1)$$
$$= \beta_0 + \beta_1 d + \beta_2 a + \beta_3 a^2 + \beta_4 da + \beta_6$$

These equations imply that

$$\mu_{[d,a,B]} - \mu_{[d,a,A]} = \beta_5 \qquad \mu_{[d,a,C]} - \mu_{[d,a,A]} = \beta_6$$

and

$$\mu_{[d,a,C]} - \mu_{[d,a,B]} = \beta_6 - \beta_5$$

a. Use the least squares point estimates of the model parameters to find a point estimate of each of the three differences in means. Also, find a 95% confidence interval for and test the significance of each of the first two differences in means.

b. The prediction results at the bottom of the SAS output correspond to a future period when the price difference will be $x_4 = .20$, the advertising expenditure will be $x_3 = 6.50$, and campaign $C$ will be used. Show how $\hat{y} = 8.5007$ is calculated. Identify

**FIGURE 4.41 (for Exercise 4.22)** SAS output for the Fresh demand model
$y = \beta_0 + \beta_1 x_4 + \beta_2 x_3 + \beta_3 x_3^2 + \beta_4 x_4 x_3 + \beta_5 D_A + \beta_6 D_C + \varepsilon$

```
                              Parameter Estimates

                              Parameter     Standard
Variable     Label      DF    Estimate      Error      t Value    Pr > |t|
Intercept    Intercept   1     25.82638     4.79456      5.39     <.0001
X3           X3          1     -6.53767     1.58137     -4.13      0.0004
X4           X4          1      9.05868     3.03170      2.99      0.0066
X3SQ         X3 ** 2     1      0.58444     0.12987      4.50      0.0002
X4X3         X3 * X4     1     -1.15648     0.45574     -2.54      0.0184
DA           DA          1     -0.21369     0.06215     -3.44      0.0022
DC           DC          1      0.16809     0.06371      2.64      0.0147
```

and interpret a 95% confidence interval for the mean demand and a 95% prediction interval for an individual demand when $x_4 = .20$, $x_3 = 6.50$, and campaign $C$ is used.

c. Consider the alternative model

$$y = \beta_0 + \beta_1 x_4 + \beta_2 x_3 + \beta_3 x_3^2 + \beta_4 x_4 x_3$$
$$+ \beta_5 D_A + \beta_6 D_C + \varepsilon$$

Here $D_A$ equals 1 if advertising campaign $A$ is used and 0 otherwise. The SAS output of the least squares point estimates of the parameters of this model is shown in Figure 4.41. Since $\beta_6$ compares the effect of advertising campaign $C$ with respect to the effect of advertising campaign $B$, $\beta_6$ equals $\mu_{[d,a,C]} - \mu_{[d,a,B]}$. Find a 95% confidence interval for and test the significance of $\mu_{[d,a,C]} - \mu_{[d,a,B]}$.

**4.23** Figure 4.42 presents the SAS output of a regression analysis of the Fresh demand data using the model

$$y = \beta_0 + \beta_1 x_4 + \beta_2 x_3 + \beta_3 x_3^2 + \beta_4 x_4 x_3 + \beta_5 D_B$$
$$+ \beta_6 D_C + \beta_7 x_3 D_B + \beta_8 x_3 D_C + \varepsilon$$

a. When there are many independent variables in a model, we might not be able to trust the $p$-values to tell us what is important. This is because of a condition called **multicollinearity,** which is discussed in Chapter 5. Note, however, that the $p$-value for $x_3 D_C$ is the smallest of the $p$-values for the independent variables $D_B$, $D_C$, $x_3 D_B$, and $x_3 D_C$. This might be regarded as "some evidence" that "some interaction" exists between advertising

expenditure and advertising campaign. To further investigate this interaction, note that the model utilizing $x_3 D_B$ and $x_3 D_C$ implies that

$$\mu_{[d,a,A]} = \beta_0 + \beta_1 d + \beta_2 a + \beta_3 a^2 + \beta_4 da + \beta_5(0)$$
$$+ \beta_6(0) + \beta_7 a(0) + \beta_8 a(0)$$
$$\mu_{[d,a,B]} = \beta_0 + \beta_1 d + \beta_2 a + \beta_3 a^2 + \beta_4 da + \beta_5(1)$$
$$+ \beta_6(0) + \beta_7 a(1) + \beta_8 a(0)$$
$$\mu_{[d,a,C]} = \beta_0 + \beta_1 d + \beta_2 a + \beta_3 a^2 + \beta_4 da + \beta_5(0)$$
$$+ \beta_6(1) + \beta_7 a(0) + \beta_8 a(1)$$

Using these equations, verify that $\mu_{[d,a,C]} - \mu_{[d,a,A]}$ equals $\beta_6 + \beta_8 a$. Then, using the least squares point estimates, show that a point estimate of $\mu_{[d,a,C]} - \mu_{[d,a,A]}$ equals .3266 when $a = 6.2$ and equals .4080 when $a = 6.6$. Also, verify that $\mu_{[d,a,C]} - \mu_{[d,a,B]}$ equals $\beta_6 - \beta_5 + \beta_8 a - \beta_7 a$. Using the least squares point estimates, show that a point estimate of $\mu_{[d,a,C]} - \mu_{[d,a,B]}$ equals .14266 when $a = 6.2$ and equals .18118 when $a = 6.6$. Discuss why these results imply that the larger the advertising expenditure $a$ is, the larger is the improvement in mean sales that is obtained by using advertising campaign $C$ rather than advertising campaign $A$ or $B$.

b. Identify a point prediction of and a 95% prediction interval for Fresh demand in a future period when the price difference will be $x_4 = .20$, the advertising expenditure will be $x_3 = 6.50$, and campaign $C$ will be used (see the bottom of the SAS output in Figure 4.42). Is the 95% prediction interval shorter or longer than the 95% prediction interval given by the first model of Exercise 4.22?

**FIGURE 4.42 (for Exercise 4.23)** SAS output of a regression analysis of the Fresh demand data using the model
$y = \beta_0 + \beta_1 x_4 + \beta_2 x_3 + \beta_3 x_3^2 + \beta_4 x_4 x_3 + \beta_5 D_B + \beta_6 D_C + \beta_7 x_3 D_B + \beta_8 x_3 D_C + \varepsilon$

Parameter Estimates

| Variable | Label | DF | Parameter Estimate | Standard Error | t Value | Pr > \|t\| |
|----------|-------|----|--------------------|-----------------|---------|-----------|
| Intercept | Intercept | 1 | 28.68734 | 5.12847 | 5.59 | <.0001 |
| X3 | X3 | 1 | -7.41146 | 1.66169 | -4.46 | 0.0002 |
| X4 | X4 | 1 | 10.82532 | 3.29880 | 3.28 | 0.0036 |
| X3SQ | X3 ** 2 | 1 | 0.64584 | 0.13460 | 4.80 | <.0001 |
| X4X3 | X3 * X4 | 1 | -1.41562 | 0.49287 | -2.87 | 0.0091 |
| DB | DB | 1 | -0.48068 | 0.73089 | -0.66 | 0.5179 |
| DC | DC | 1 | -0.93507 | 0.83572 | -1.12 | 0.2758 |
| X3DB | X3 * DB | 1 | 0.10722 | 0.11169 | 0.96 | 0.3480 |
| X3DC | X3 * DC | 1 | 0.20349 | 0.12882 | 1.58 | 0.1291 |

| Obs | Dep Var Y | Predicted Value | Std Error Mean Predict | 95% CL Mean | | 95% CL Predict | |
|-----|-----------|-----------------|------------------------|-------------|--|----------------|--|
| 31 | . | 8.5118 | 0.0479 | 8.4123 | 8.6114 | 8.2249 | 8.7988 |

In Exercises 4.24 through 4.26, you will perform partial $F$-tests by using the following three Fresh detergent models:

**Model 1:** $y = \beta_0 + \beta_1 x_4 + \beta_2 x_3 + \beta_3 x_3^2 + \beta_4 x_4 x_3 + \varepsilon$

**Model 2:** $y = \beta_0 + \beta_1 x_4 + \beta_2 x_3 + \beta_3 x_3^2 + \beta_4 x_4 x_3$
$\qquad + \beta_5 D_B + \beta_6 D_C + \varepsilon$

**Model 3:** $y = \beta_0 + \beta_1 x_4 + \beta_2 x_3 + \beta_3 x_3^2 + \beta_4 x_4 x_3$
$\qquad + \beta_5 D_B + \beta_6 D_C + \beta_7 x_3 D_B + \beta_8 x_3 D_C + \varepsilon$

The values of SSE for models 1, 2, and 3 are, respectively, 1.0644, .3936, and .3518.

**4.24** In Model 2, test $H_0: \beta_5 = \beta_6 = 0$ by setting $\alpha$ equal to .05 and .01. Reason that testing $H_0: \beta_5 = \beta_6 = 0$ is equivalent to testing $H_0: \mu_{[d,a,A]} = \mu_{[d,a,B]} = \mu_{[d,a,C]}$. Interpret what this says.

**4.25** In Model 3, test $H_0: \beta_5 = \beta_6 = \beta_7 - \beta_8 - 0$ by setting $\alpha$ equal to .05 and .01. Interpret.

**4.26** In Model 3, test $H_0: \beta_7 = \beta_8 = 0$ by setting $\alpha$ equal to .05 and .01. Interpret your results.

**4.27** In a study of the effectiveness of offering a price reduction on a given product, 300 households having similar incomes were selected. A coupon offering a price reduction, $x$, on the product, as well as advertising material for the product, was sent to each household. The coupons offered different price reductions (10, 20, 30, 40, 50, and 60 dollars), and 50

**TABLE 4.19 (for Exercise 4.27)**
**Coupon Redemption Data**

| Coupon Value, $x$ ($\times \$10$) | Households Redeeming Coupon | |
|------------------------------------|------------------|------------------|
| | Number, $y$ | Proportion, $\hat{p}$ |
| 1 | 4 | .08 |
| 2 | 7 | .14 |
| 3 | 20 | .40 |
| 4 | 35 | .70 |
| 5 | 44 | .88 |
| 6 | 46 | .92 |

homes were assigned at random to each price reduction. Table 4.19 summarizes the number, $y$, and proportion, $\hat{p}$, of households redeeming coupons for each price reduction. In Figure 4.43 (page 218) we plot the $\hat{p}$ values versus the $x$ values and draw a hypothetical curve through the plotted points. A theoretical curve having the shape of the curve in Figure 4.43 is the **logistic curve**

$$p(x) = \frac{e^{(\beta_0 + \beta_1 x)}}{1 + e^{(\beta_0 + \beta_1 x)}}$$

where $p(x)$ denotes the probability that a household receiving a coupon having a price reduction of $x$ will redeem the coupon. The MINITAB output in Figure 4.43 tells us that the least squares point estimates of $\beta_0$ and $\beta_1$ are $b_0 = -3.7456$ and $b_1 = 1.1109$. Using these estimates, it follows that, for example

**FIGURE 4.43 (for Exercise 4.27)** MINITAB output of a logistic regression of the product name data

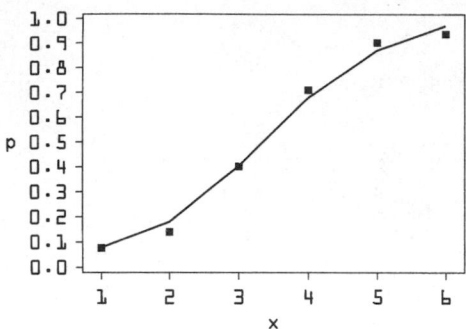

```
Logistic Regression Table

Predictor       Coef    SE Coef       Z      P
Constant    -3.74558   0.434355   -8.62  0.000
x            1.11095   0.119364    9.31  0.000


     x      p̂(x)        x      p̂(x)

     1   0.066943      4   0.667791
     2   0.178920      5   0.859260
     3   0.398256      6   0.948831
```

$$\hat{p}(5) = \frac{e^{(-3.7456+1.1109(5))}}{1 + e^{(-3.7456+1.1109(5))}} = \frac{6.1037}{1 + 6.1037} = .8593$$

That is, $\hat{p}(5) = .8593$ is the point estimate of the probability that a household receiving a coupon having a price reduction of \$50 will redeem the coupon. The MINITAB output in Figure 4.43 gives the values of $\hat{p}(x)$ for $x = 1, 2, 3, 4, 5,$ and 6. Find a point estimate of $p(4.5)$, the probability that a household receiving a coupon having a price reduction of \$45 will redeem the coupon.

**4.28** The personnel director of a firm has developed two tests to help determine whether potential employees would perform successfully in a particular position. To help estimate the usefulness of the tests, the director gives both tests to 43 current employees that currently hold the position. Table 4.20 gives the scores of each employee on both tests and indicates whether the employee is currently performing successfully or unsuccessfully in the position. If the employee is performing successfully, we say that the employee is in group 1; if the employee is performing unsuccessfully, we say that the employee is in group 0. Let $x_1$ and $x_2$ denote the scores of a potential employee on tests 1 and 2, and let $p(x_1, x_2)$ denote the probability that a potential employee having the scores $x_1$ and $x_2$ will perform successfully in the position. We can estimate the relationship between $p(x_1, x_2)$ and $x_1$ and $x_2$ by using the **multiple logistic function**

$$p(x_1, x_2) = \frac{e^{(\beta_0+\beta_1x_1+\beta_2x_2)}}{1 + e^{(\beta_0+\beta_1x_1+\beta_2x_2)}}$$

The output in Figure 4.44(a) tells us that the least squares point estimates of $\beta_0$, $\beta_1$, and $\beta_2$ are $b_0 = -56.17$, $b_1 = .4833$, and $b_2 = .1652$.

a. Consider, for example, a potential employee who scores a 93 on test 1 and an 84 on test 2. It follows that a point estimate of the probability that the potential employee will perform successfully in the position is

$$\hat{p}(93, 84) = \frac{e^{(-56.17+.4833(93)+.1652(84))}}{1 + e^{(-56.17+.4833(93)+.1652(84))}}$$

$$= \frac{14.206506}{15.206506} = .9342$$

If we *classify* a potential employee into group 1 ("will perform successfully") if and only if $\hat{p}(x_1, x_2)$ is greater than .5, this potential employee is classified into group 1. Next, consider a potential employee who scores an 85 on test 1 and an 82 on test 2. Calculate $\hat{p}(85, 82)$, and classify this employee into group 0 or group 1.

b. Another way to classify a potential employee into group 0 or group 1 is to use **discriminant analysis.** For example, Figure 4.44(b) and (c) present the MINITAB output of a discriminant analysis of the data in Table 4.20. Figure 4.44(b) gives a *discriminant equation for group 0* and a *discriminant equation for group 1*. Denoting these equations as $\hat{y}_{(0)}$ and $\hat{y}_{(1)}$, the MINITAB output tells us that

$$\hat{y}_{(0)} = -298.27 + 5.20x_1 + 1.97x_2$$

**FIGURE 4.44 (for Exercise 4.28)** MINITAB output of a logistic regression and a discriminant analysis of the performance data

```
Predictor        Coef      SE Coef         Z        P
Constant       -56.17        17.45     -3.22    0.001
Test 1         0.4833       0.1578      3.06    0.002
Test 2         0.1652       0.1021      1.62    0.106
```

(a) The logistic regression

```
Linear Discriminant Function for Group
                     0            1
Constant       -298.27      -351.65
test1             5.20         5.68
test2             1.97         2.10
```

(b) The discriminant equations

```
Summary of Classification
put into        ....True Group....
Group              0            1
0                 16            5
1                  4           18
Total N           20           23
N Correct         16           18
Proport.       0.800        0.783
N = 43         N Correct =    34
Prop. Correct = 0.791
```

(c) The summary of classification table

and

$$\hat{y}_{(1)} = -351.65 + 5.68x_1 + 2.10x_2$$

A prospective employee is classified into group 1 if and only if $\hat{y}_{(1)}$ is greater than $\hat{y}_{(0)}$. For example, consider a prospective employee who scores a 93 on test 1 and an 84 on test 2. For this prospective employee, $\hat{y}_{(0)} = 350.81$ and $\hat{y}_{(1)} = 352.99$. Since $\hat{y}_{(1)}$ is greater than $\hat{y}_{(0)}$, the prospective employee is classified into group 1. Calculate $\hat{y}_{(0)}$ and $\hat{y}_{(1)}$ for a prospective employee who scores an 85 on test 1 and an 82 on test 2. Then, classify this employee into group 0 or group 1. Also, interpret the *summary of classification table* in Figure 4.44(c). This table gives the results of classifying the 43 employees that were used to develop the discriminant equations into group 0 or 1.

**TABLE 4.20 (for Exercise 4.28)** Performance Data

| Group | Test 1 | Test 2 | Group | Test 1 | Test 2 |
|-------|--------|--------|-------|--------|--------|
| 1 | 96 | 85 | 0 | 93 | 74 |
| 1 | 96 | 88 | 0 | 90 | 84 |
| 1 | 91 | 81 | 0 | 91 | 81 |
| 1 | 95 | 78 | 0 | 91 | 78 |
| 1 | 92 | 85 | 0 | 88 | 78 |
| 1 | 93 | 87 | 0 | 86 | 86 |
| 1 | 98 | 84 | 0 | 79 | 81 |
| 1 | 92 | 82 | 0 | 83 | 84 |
| 1 | 97 | 89 | 0 | 79 | 77 |
| 1 | 95 | 96 | 0 | 88 | 75 |
| 1 | 99 | 93 | 0 | 81 | 85 |
| 1 | 89 | 90 | 0 | 85 | 83 |
| 1 | 94 | 90 | 0 | 82 | 72 |
| 1 | 92 | 94 | 0 | 82 | 81 |
| 1 | 94 | 84 | 0 | 81 | 77 |
| 1 | 90 | 92 | 0 | 86 | 76 |
| 1 | 91 | 70 | 0 | 81 | 84 |
| 1 | 90 | 81 | 0 | 85 | 78 |
| 1 | 86 | 81 | 0 | 83 | 77 |
| 1 | 90 | 76 | 0 | 81 | 71 |
| 1 | 91 | 79 | | | |
| 1 | 88 | 83 | | | |
| 1 | 87 | 82 | | | |

*Source:* T. Dielman, *Applied Regression Analysis for Business and Economics,* second edition. © 1996. Reprinted with permission of Brooks/Cole, an imprint of the Wadsworth Group, a division of Thomson Learning. Fax 800-730-2215.

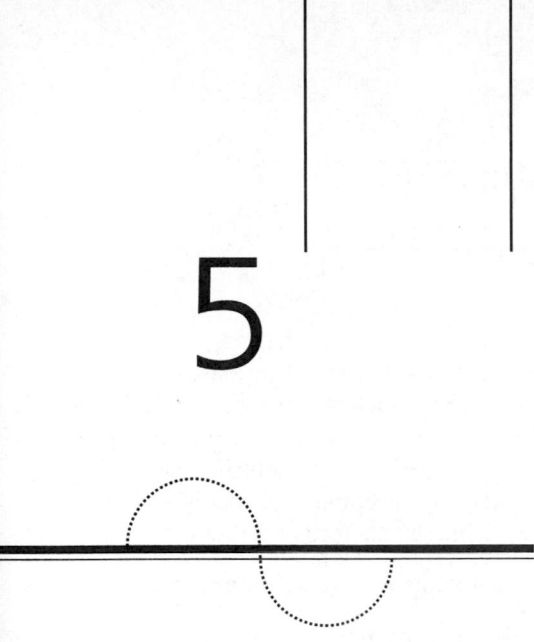

# 5

# *Model Building and Residual Analysis*

In this chapter we continue our discussion of regression analysis. In Section 5.1 we examine procedures for building an appropriate regression model. We begin the section with a discussion of multicollinearity. Then we examine advanced methods of model comparison. We also present several computerized screening procedures (stepwise regression, backward elimination, maximum adjusted $R^2$ improvement) that can be used to identify a set or sets of independent variables that might be important when there are a large number of potentially important independent variables. Section 5.2 considers residual analysis to check the validity of the regression assumptions and includes remedying a violation of the constant variance assumption. All the examples in Section 5.2 are for simple regression models. In Section 5.3, we extend the residual analysis to multiple regression models. Finally, in Section 5.4 we discuss outlying and influential observations.

# 5.1 MODEL BUILDING, AND THE EFFECTS OF MULTICOLLINEARITY

## Multicollinearity

Recall the sales territory performance data in Table 4.2. These data consist of values of the dependent variable $y$ (SALES) and of the independent variables $x_1$ (TIME), $x_2$ (MKTPOTEN), $x_3$ (ADVER), $x_4$ (MKTSHARE), and $x_5$ (CHANGE). The complete sales territory performance data analyzed by Cravens, Woodruff, and Stomper (1972) consist of the data presented in Table 4.2 and data concerning three additional independent variables. These three additional variables are defined as follows:

$x_6$ = number of accounts handled by the representative (we will sometimes denote this variable as ACCTS)

$x_7$ = average workload per account, measured by using a weighting based on the sizes of the orders by the accounts and other workload-related criteria (we will sometimes denote this variable as WKLOAD)

$x_8$ = an aggregate rating on eight dimensions of the representative's performance, made by a sales manager and expressed on a 1–7 scale (we will sometimes denote this variable as RATING)

Table 5.1 gives the observed values of $x_6$, $x_7$, and $x_8$, and Figure 5.1 presents the MINITAB output of a **correlation matrix** for the sales territory performance data. Examining the first column of this matrix, we see that the simple correlation coefficient between SALES and WKLOAD is −.117 and that the $p$-value for testing the significance of the relationship between SALES and WKLOAD is .577. This indicates that there is little or no relationship between SALES and WKLOAD. However, the simple correlation coefficients between SALES and the other seven independent variables range from .402 to .754, with associated $p$-values ranging from .046 to .000.

**TABLE 5.1** Values of ACCTS, WKLOAD, and RATING

| Accounts, $x_6$ | Workload, $x_7$ | Rating, $x_8$ | Accounts, $x_6$ | Workload, $x_7$ | Rating, $x_8$ | Accounts, $x_6$ | Workload, $x_7$ | Rating, $x_8$ |
|---|---|---|---|---|---|---|---|---|
| 74.86 | 15.05 | 4.9 | 119.51 | 21.41 | 2.8 | 78.86 | 16.00 | 4.2 |
| 107.32 | 19.97 | 5.1 | 116.26 | 16.32 | 3.1 | 136.58 | 17.44 | 3.6 |
| 96.75 | 17.34 | 2.9 | 142.28 | 14.51 | 4.2 | 138.21 | 17.98 | 3.1 |
| 195.12 | 13.40 | 3.4 | 89.43 | 19.35 | 4.3 | 75.61 | 20.99 | 1.6 |
| 180.44 | 17.64 | 4.6 | 84.55 | 20.02 | 4.2 | 102.44 | 21.66 | 3.4 |
| 104.88 | 16.22 | 4.5 | 119.51 | 15.26 | 5.5 | 76.42 | 21.46 | 2.7 |
| 256.10 | 18.80 | 4.6 | 80.49 | 15.87 | 3.6 | 136.58 | 24.78 | 2.8 |
| 126.83 | 19.86 | 2.3 | 136.58 | 7.81 | 3.4 | 88.62 | 24.96 | 3.9 |
| 203.25 | 17.42 | 4.9 | | | | | | |

**FIGURE 5.1** MINITAB output of a correlation matrix for the sales territory performance data

|          | Sales   | Time    | MktPoten | Adver   | MktShare | Change  | Accts   | WkLoad  |
|----------|---------|---------|----------|---------|----------|---------|---------|---------|
| Time     | 0.623   |         |          |         |          |         |         |         |
|          | 0.001   |         |          |         |          |         |         |         |
| MktPoten | 0.598   | 0.454   |          |         |          |         |         |         |
|          | 0.002   | 0.023   |          |         |          |         |         |         |
| Adver    | 0.596   | 0.249   | 0.174    |         |          |         |         |         |
|          | 0.002   | 0.230   | 0.405    |         |          |         |         |         |
| MktShare | 0.484   | 0.106   | -0.211   | 0.264   |          |         |         |         |
|          | 0.014   | 0.613   | 0.312    | 0.201   |          |         |         |         |
| Change   | 0.489   | 0.251   | 0.268    | 0.377   | 0.085    |         |         |         |
|          | 0.013   | 0.225   | 0.195    | 0.064   | 0.685    |         |         |         |
| Accts    | 0.754   | 0.758   | 0.479    | 0.200   | 0.403    | 0.327   |         |         |
|          | 0.000   | 0.000   | 0.016    | 0.338   | 0.046    | 0.110   |         |         |
| WkLoad   | -0.117  | -0.179  | -0.259   | -0.272  | 0.349    | -0.288  | -0.199  |         |
|          | 0.577   | 0.391   | 0.212    | 0.188   | 0.087    | 0.163   | 0.341   |         |
| Rating   | 0.402   | 0.101   | 0.359    | 0.411   | -0.024   | 0.549   | 0.229   | -0.277  |
|          | 0.046   | 0.631   | 0.078    | 0.041   | 0.911    | 0.004   | 0.272   | 0.180   |

Cell Contents: Pearson correlation
P-Value

This indicates the existence of potentially useful relationships between SALES and these seven independent variables.

Although simple correlation coefficients (and scatter plots) give us a preliminary understanding of the data, they cannot be relied upon alone to tell us which independent variables are significantly related to the dependent variable. One reason for this is a condition called multicollinearity. **Multicollinearity** is said to exist among the independent variables in a regression situation if these independent variables are related to or dependent upon each other. One way to investigate multicollinearity is to examine the correlation matrix. To understand this, note that all of the simple correlation coefficients not located in the first column of this matrix measure the *simple correlations between the independent variables*. For example, the simple correlation coefficient between ACCTS and TIME is .758, which says that the ACCTS values increase as the TIME values increase. Such a relationship makes sense because it is logical that the longer a sales representative has been with the company, the more accounts he or she handles. Statisticians often regard multicollinearity in a data set to be severe if at least one simple correlation coefficient between the independent variables is at least .9. Since the largest such simple correlation coefficient in Figure 5.1 is .758, this is not true for the sales territory performance data. Note, however, that even moderate multicollinearity can be a potential problem. This will be demonstrated later using the sales territory performance data.

**FIGURE 5.2** SAS output of the $t$-statistics, $p$-values, and variance inflation factors for the sales territory performance model $y = \beta_0 + \beta_1 x_1 + \beta_2 x_2 + \beta_3 x_3 + \beta_4 x_4 + \beta_5 x_5 + \beta_6 x_6 + \beta_7 x_7 + \beta_8 x_8 + \varepsilon$

| Variable | Label | DF | Parameter Estimate | Standard Error | t Value | Pr > \|t\| | Variance Inflation |
|---|---|---|---|---|---|---|---|
| Intercept | Intercept | 1 | -1507.81373 | 778.63494 | -1.94 | 0.0707 | 0 |
| Time | Time | 1 | 2.00957 | 1.93065 | 1.04 | 0.3134 | 3.34262 |
| MktPoten | MktPoten | 1 | 0.03720 | 0.00820 | 4.54 | 0.0003 | 1.97762 |
| Adver | Adver | 1 | 0.15099 | 0.04711 | 3.21 | 0.0055 | 1.91021 |
| MktShare | MktShare | 1 | 199.02354 | 67.02792 | 2.97 | 0.0090 | 3.23576 |
| Change | Change | 1 | 290.85513 | 186.78200 | 1.56 | 0.1390 | 1.60173 |
| Accts | Accts | 1 | 5.55096 | 4.77555 | 1.16 | 0.2621 | 5.63932 |
| WkLoad | WkLoad | 1 | 19.79389 | 33.67669 | 0.59 | 0.5649 | 1.81835 |
| Rating | Rating | 1 | 8.18928 | 128.50561 | 0.06 | 0.9500 | 1.80856 |

Another way to measure multicollinearity is to use **variance inflation factors.** Consider a regression model relating a dependent variable $y$ to a set of independent variables $x_1, \ldots, x_{j-1}, x_j, x_{j+1}, \ldots, x_k$. The **variance inflation factor VIF$_j$** for the independent variable $x_j$ in this set is denoted VIF$_j$ and is defined by the equation

$$\text{VIF}_j = \frac{1}{1 - R_j^2}$$

where $R_j^2$ is the multiple coefficient of determination for the regression model that relates $x_j$ to all the other independent variables $x_1, \ldots, x_{j-1}, x_{j+1}, \ldots, x_k$ in the set. For example, Figure 5.2 gives the SAS output of the $t$-statistics, $p$-values, and variance inflation factors for the sales territory performance model that relates $y$ to all eight independent variables. The largest variance inflation factor is VIF$_6 = 5.639$. To calculate VIF$_6$, SAS first calculates the multiple coefficient of determination for the regression model that relates $x_6$ to $x_1, x_2, x_3, x_4, x_5, x_7$, and $x_8$ to be $R_6^2 = .822673$. It then follows that

$$\text{VIF}_6 = \frac{1}{1 - R_6^2} = \frac{1}{1 - .822673} = 5.639$$

In general, if $R_j^2 = 0$, which says that $x_j$ is not related to the other independent variables, then the variance inflation factor VIF$_j$ equals 1. On the other hand, if $R_j^2 > 0$, which says that $x_j$ is related to the other independent variables, then $(1 - R_j^2)$ is less than 1, making VIF$_j$ greater than 1. Both the largest variance inflation factor among the independent variables and the mean $\overline{\text{VIF}}$ of the variance inflation factors for the independent variables indicate the severity of multicollinearity. Generally, the multicollinearity between independent variables is considered severe if

1.  The largest variance inflation factor is greater than 10 (which means that the largest $R_j^2$ is greater than .9).

2.  The mean $\overline{\text{VIF}}$ of the variance inflation factors is substantially greater than 1.

The largest variance inflation factor in Figure 5.2 is not greater than 10, and the average of the variance inflation factors, which is 2.667, would probably not be considered substantially greater than 1. Therefore, we would probably not consider the multicollinearity among the eight independent variables to be severe.

**FIGURE 5.3**
The picket fence
display

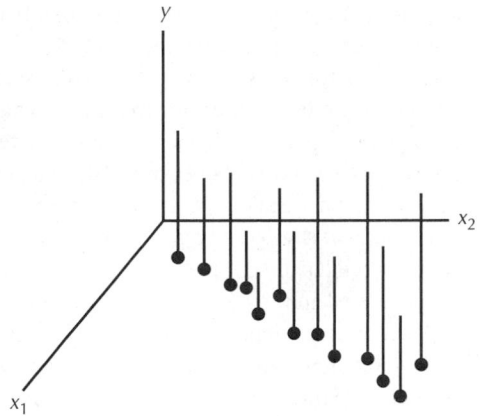

VIF$_j$ is called the variance inflation factor because it can be shown that when VIF$_j$ is greater than 1, then the standard deviation $\sigma_{b_j}$ of the population of all possible values of the least squares point estimate $b_j$ is likely to be inflated beyond its value when $R_j^2 = 0$. If $\sigma_{b_j}$ is greatly inflated, two slightly different samples of values of the dependent variable can yield two substantially different values of $b_j$. To intuitively understand why strong multicollinearity can significantly affect the least squares point estimates, consider the so-called "picket fence" display in Figure 5.3. This figure depicts two independent variables ($x_1$ and $x_2$) exhibiting strong multicollinearity (note that as $x_1$ increases, $x_2$ increases). The heights of the pickets on the fence represent the $y$ observations. If we assume that the model

$$y = \beta_0 + \beta_1 x_1 + \beta_2 x_2 + \varepsilon$$

adequately describes this data, then calculating the least squares point estimates is like fitting a plane to the points on the top of the picket fence. Clearly, this plane would be quite unstable. That is, a slightly different height of one of the pickets (a slightly different $y$ value) could cause the slant of the fitted plane (and the least squares point estimates that determine this slant) to radically change. It follows that when strong multicollinearity exists, sampling variation can result in least squares point estimates that differ substantially from the true values of the regression parameters. In fact, some of the least squares point estimates may have a sign (positive or negative) that differs from the sign of the true value of the parameter (we will see an example of this in the exercises). Therefore, when strong multicollinearity exists, it is dangerous to individually interpret the least squares point estimates.

The most important problem caused by multicollinearity is that even when multicollinearity is not severe, it can hinder our ability to use the $t$-statistics and related $p$-values to assess the importance of the independent variables. Recall that we can reject H$_0$: $\beta_j = 0$ in favor of H$_a$: $\beta_j \neq 0$ at level of significance $\alpha$ if and only if the absolute value of the corresponding $t$-statistic is greater than $t_{[\alpha/2]}^{(n-(k+1))}$, or equivalently, if and only if the related $p$-value is less than $\alpha$. Thus the larger (in absolute value) the $t$-statistic is and the smaller the $p$-value is, the stronger is the evidence that we should reject

$H_0$: $\beta_j = 0$ and the stronger is the evidence that the independent variable $x_j$ is significant. When multicollinearity exists, the sizes of the $t$-statistic and of the related $p$-value **measure the additional importance of the independent variable $x_j$ over the combined importance of the other independent variables in the regression model.** Since two or more correlated independent variables contribute redundant information, multicollinearity often causes the $t$-statistics obtained by relating a dependent variable to a set of correlated independent variables to be smaller (in absolute value) than the $t$-statistics that would be obtained if separate regression analyses were run, where each separate regression analysis relates the dependent variable to a smaller set (for example, only one) of the correlated independent variables. Thus multicollinearity can cause some of the correlated independent variables to appear less important—in terms of having small absolute $t$-statistics and large $p$-values—than they really are. Another way to understand this is to note that since multicollinearity inflates $\sigma_{b_j}$, it inflates the point estimate $s_{b_j}$ of $\sigma_{b_j}$. Since $t = b_j / s_{b_j}$, an inflated value of $s_{b_j}$ can (depending on the size of $b_j$) cause $t$ to be small (and the related $p$-value to be large). This would suggest that $x_j$ is not significant even though $x_j$ may really be important.

For example, Figure 5.2 tells us that when we perform a regression analysis of the sales territory performance data using a model that relates $y$ to all eight independent variables, the $p$-values related to TIME, MKTPOTEN, ADVER, MKTSHARE, CHANGE, ACCTS, WKLOAD, and RATING are, respectively, .3134, .0003, .0055, .0090, .1390, .2621, .5649, and .9500. By contrast, recall from Figure 4.7 that when we perform a regression analysis of the sales territory performance data using a model that relates $y$ to the first five independent variables, the $p$-values related to TIME, MKTPOTEN, ADVER, MKTSHARE, and CHANGE are, respectively, .0065, .0001, .0025, .0001, and .0530. Note that TIME ($p$-value = .0065) seems *highly significant* and CHANGE ($p$-value = .0530) seems *somewhat significant* in the five-independent-variable model. However, when we consider the model that uses all eight independent variables, TIME ($p$-value = .3134) seems *insignificant* and CHANGE ($p$-value = .1390) seems *somewhat insignificant.* The reason that TIME and CHANGE seem more significant in the model with five independent variables is that since this model uses fewer variables, TIME and CHANGE contribute less overlapping information and thus have additional importance in this model.

## Comparing Regression Models on the Basis of $R^2$, $s$, Adjusted $R^2$, Prediction Interval Length, and the C Statistic

We have seen that when multicollinearity exists in a model, the $p$-value associated with an independent variable in the model measures the additional importance of the variable over the combined importance of the variables in the model. Therefore, it can be difficult to use the $p$-values to determine which variables to retain in and which variables to remove from a model. The implication is that we need to evaluate more than the *additional importance* of each independent variable in a regression model.

We also need to evaluate how well the independent variables *work together* to accurately describe, predict, and control the dependent variable. One way to do this is to determine if the *overall* model gives a high $R^2$ and $\overline{R}^2$, a small $s$, and short prediction intervals.

It can be proved that **adding any independent variable to a regression model, even an unimportant independent variable, will decrease the unexplained variation and will increase the explained variation.** Therefore, since the total variation $\sum(y_i - \overline{y})^2$ depends only on the observed $y$ values and thus remains unchanged when we add an independent variable to a regression model, it follows that **adding any independent variable to a regression model will increase the multiple coefficient of determination**

$$R^2 = \frac{\text{Explained variation}}{\text{Total variation}}$$

This implies that $R^2$ cannot tell us (by decreasing) that adding an independent variable is undesirable. That is, although we wish to obtain a model with a large $R^2$, there are better criteria than $R^2$ that can be used to compare regression models.

One better criterion is the standard error

$$s = \sqrt{\frac{\text{SSE}}{n - (k + 1)}}$$

When we add an independent variable to a regression model, the number of model parameters $(k + 1)$ increases by one, and thus the number of degrees of freedom $n - (k + 1)$ decreases by one. If the decrease in $n - (k + 1)$, which is used in the denominator to calculate $s$, is proportionally more than the decrease in SSE (the unexplained variation) that is caused by adding the independent variable to the model, then $s$ will increase. **If $s$ increases, this tells us that we should not add the independent variable to the model.** To see one reason why, consider the formula for the prediction interval for $y$

$$[\hat{y} \pm t_{[\alpha/2]}^{(n-(k+1))} s\sqrt{1 + \text{Distance value}}]$$

Since adding an independent variable to a model decreases the number of degrees of freedom, adding the variable will increase the $t_{[\alpha/2]}^{(n-(k+1))}$ point used to calculate the prediction interval. To understand this, look at any column of the $t$-table in Table A2 and scan from the bottom of the column to the top — you can see that the $t$ points increase as the degrees of freedom decrease. It can also be shown that adding any independent variable to a regression model will not decrease (and usually increases) the distance value. Therefore, since adding an independent variable increases $t_{[\alpha/2]}^{(n-(k+1))}$ and does not decrease the distance value, **if $s$ increases, the length of the prediction interval for $y$ will increase.** This means the model will predict less accurately and thus we should not add the independent variable.

On the other hand, if adding an independent variable to a regression model decreases $s$, the length of a prediction interval for $y$ will decrease if and only if the decrease in $s$ is enough to offset the increase in $t_{[\alpha/2]}^{(n-(k+1))}$ and the (possible) increase in the distance value. Therefore, **an independent variable should not be included in a**

**final regression model unless it reduces $s$ enough to reduce the length of the desired prediction interval for $y$.** However, we must balance the length of the prediction interval, or in general, the "goodness" of any criterion, against the difficulty and expense of using the model. For instance, predicting $y$ requires knowing the corresponding values of the independent variables. So we must decide whether including an independent variable reduces $s$ and prediction interval lengths enough to offset the potential errors caused by possible inaccurate determination of values of the independent variables, or the possible expense of determining these values. If adding an independent variable provides prediction intervals that are only slightly shorter while making the model more difficult and/or more expensive to use, we might decide that including the variable is not desirable.

Since a key factor is the length of the prediction intervals provided by the model, one might wonder why we do not simply make direct comparisons of prediction interval lengths (without looking at $s$). It is useful to compare interval lengths, but these lengths depend on the distance value, which depends on how far the values of the independent variables we wish to predict for are from the center of the experimental region. We often wish to compute prediction intervals for several different combinations of values of the independent variables (and thus for several different values of the distance value). Thus we would compute prediction intervals having slightly different lengths. However, the standard error $s$ is a constant factor with respect to the length of prediction intervals (as long as we are considering the same regression model). Thus it is common practice to compare regression models on the basis of $s$ (and $s^2$). Finally, note that it can be shown that **the standard error $s$ decreases if and only if $\bar{R}^2$ (adjusted $R^2$) increases.** It follows that if we are comparing regression models, **the model that gives the smallest $s$ gives the largest $\bar{R}^2$.**

**EXAMPLE 5.1**    Figure 5.4 gives MINITAB and SAS output resulting from calculating $R^2$, $\bar{R}^2$, and $s$ for **all possible regression models** based on all possible combinations of the eight independent variables in the sales territory performance situation (the values of $C_p$ on the output will be explained after we complete this example). The MINITAB output gives the two best models of each size in terms of $s$ and $\bar{R}^2$—the two best one-variable models, the two best two-variable models, and so on. The first SAS output gives the eight best models of any size, and the second SAS output gives the output for the best model on this list. Examining Figures 5.4(a) and (b), we see that the three models having the smallest values of $s$ and the largest values of $\bar{R}^2$ are

1.    The six-variable model that contains

TIME, MKTPOTEN, ADVER, MKTSHARE, CHANGE, ACCTS

and has $s = 428.00$ and $\bar{R}^2 = 89.4$; we refer to this model as Model 1.

2.    The five-variable model that contains

TIME, MKTPOTEN, ADVER, MKTSHARE, CHANGE

and has $s = 430.23$ and $\bar{R}^2 = 89.3$; we refer to this model as Model 2.

**FIGURE 5.4** MINITAB and SAS output of some of the best sales territory performance regression models

| Vars | R-Sq | R-Sq(adj) | Mallows C-p | s | MktPoten | Adv | MktShare | Change | Accts | WkLoad | Rating |
|------|------|-----------|-------------|--------|------|---|------|------|---|------|---|
| 1 | 56.8 | 55.0 | 67.6 | 881.09 | | | | | X | | |
| 1 | 38.8 | 36.1 | 104.6 | 1049.3 | X | | | | | | |
| 2 | 77.5 | 75.5 | 27.2 | 650.39 | | X | | X | | | |
| 2 | 74.6 | 72.3 | 33.1 | 691.11 | X | X | | | | | |
| 3 | 84.9 | 82.7 | 14.0 | 545.51 | X | X | X | | | | |
| 3 | 82.8 | 80.3 | 18.4 | 582.64 | X | X | | X | | | |
| 4 | 90.0 | 88.1 | 5.4 | 453.84 | X | X | X | X | | | |
| 4 | 89.6 | 87.5 | 6.4 | 463.95 | X | X | X | X | | | |
| 5 | 91.5 | 89.3 | 4.4 | 430.23 | X | X | X | X | | | |
| 5 | 91.2 | 88.9 | 5.0 | 436.75 | X | X | X | X | | | |
| 6 | 92.0 | 89.4 | 5.4 | 428.00 | X | X | X | X | X | | |
| 6 | 91.6 | 88.9 | 6.1 | 438.20 | X | X | X | X | X | X | |
| 7 | 92.2 | 89.0 | 7.0 | 435.67 | X | X | X | X | X | X | |
| 7 | 92.0 | 88.8 | 7.3 | 440.30 | X | X | X | X | X | X | X |
| 8 | 92.2 | 88.3 | 9.0 | 449.03 | X | X | X | X | X | X | X |

(a) The MINITAB output of the two best models of each size

Adjusted R-Square Selection Method

| Number in Model | Adjusted R-Square | R-Square | C(p) | Root MSE | Variables in Model |
|-----------------|-------------------|----------|--------|----------|--------------------|
| 6 | 0.8938 | 0.9203 | 5.3540 | 428.00388 | Time MktPoten Adver MktShare Change Accts |
| 5 | 0.8926 | 0.9150 | 4.4428 | 430.23189 | Time MktPoten Adver MktShare Change |
| 7 | 0.8899 | 0.9220 | 7.0041 | 435.67416 | Time MktPoten Adver MktShare Change Accts WkLoad |
| 5 | 0.8894 | 0.9124 | 4.9750 | 436.74618 | MktPoten Adver MktShare Change Accts |
| 6 | 0.8886 | 0.9165 | 6.1423 | 438.19670 | MktPoten Adver MktShare Change Accts WkLoad |
| 7 | 0.8876 | 0.9204 | 7.3455 | 440.29880 | Time MktPoten Adver MktShare Change Accts Rating |
| 6 | 0.8872 | 0.9154 | 6.3573 | 440.93586 | Time MktPoten Adver MktShare Change Rating |
| 6 | 0.8867 | 0.9150 | 6.4385 | 441.96639 | Time MktPoten Adver MktShare Change WkLoad |

(b) The SAS output of the best eight models in terms of s (Root MSE) and $\bar{R}^2$ (adjusted R-Square)

| Variable | Label | DF | Parameter Estimate | Standard Error | t Value | Pr > \|t\| |
|----------|-------|----|--------------------|----------------|---------|-----------|
| Intercept | Intercept | 1 | -1165.47855 | 420.37272 | -2.77 | 0.0126 |
| Time | Time | 1 | 2.26935 | 1.69898 | 1.34 | 0.1983 |
| MktPoten | MktPoten | 1 | 0.03828 | 0.00755 | 5.07 | <.0001 |
| Adver | Adver | 1 | 0.14067 | 0.03839 | 3.66 | 0.0018 |
| MktShare | MktShare | 1 | 221.60469 | 50.58309 | 4.38 | 0.0004 |
| Change | Change | 1 | 285.10928 | 160.55966 | 1.78 | 0.0927 |
| Accts | Accts | 1 | 4.37770 | 3.99904 | 1.09 | 0.2881 |

| Obs | Dep Var Sales | Predicted Value | Std Error Mean Predict | 95% CL Mean | | 95% CL Predict | |
|-----|---------------|-----------------|------------------------|-------------|------|----------------|------|
| 26 | . | 4144 | 145.3483 | 3838 | 4449 | 3194 | 5093 |

(c) The SAS output of Model 1 $y = \beta_0 + \beta_1 x_1 + \beta_2 x_2 + \beta_3 x_3 + \beta_4 x_4 + \beta_5 x_5 + \beta_6 x_6 + \varepsilon$

**3.** The seven-variable model that contains

TIME, MKTPOTEN, ADVER, MKTSHARE, CHANGE, ACCTS, WKLOAD

and has $s = 435.67$ and $\bar{R}^2 = 89.0$; we refer to this model as Model 3.

To see that $s$ can increase when we add an independent variable to a regression model, note that $s$ increases from 428.00 to 435.67 when we add WKLOAD to Model 1 to form Model 3. In this case, although it can be verified that adding WKLOAD decreases the unexplained variation from 3,297,279.3342 to 3,226,756.2751, this decrease has not been enough to offset the change in the denominator of

$$s^2 = \frac{SSE}{n - (k + 1)}$$

which decreases from $25 - 7 = 18$ to $25 - 8 = 17$. To see that prediction interval lengths might increase even though $s$ decreases, consider adding ACCTS to Model 2 to form Model 1. This decreases $s$ from 430.23 to 428.00. However, consider a questionable sales representative for whom TIME = 85.42, MKTPOTEN = 35,182.73, ADVER = 7281.65, MKTSHARE = 9.64, CHANGE = .28, and ACCTS = 120.61. The 95% prediction interval given by Model 2 for sales corresponding to this combination of values of the independent variables is [3234, 5130] (see Figure 4.7) and has length $5130 - 3234 = 1896$. The 95% prediction interval given by Model 1 for such values is [3194, 5093] [see Figure 5.4(c)] and has length $5093 - 3194 = 1899$. In other words, the slight decrease in $s$ accomplished by adding ACCTS to Model 2 to form Model 1 is not enough to offset the increases in $t_{[\alpha/2]}^{(n-(k+1))}$ and the distance value (which can be shown to increase from .109 to .115), and thus the length of the prediction interval given by Model 1 increases. In addition, the extra independent variable ACCTS in Model 1 has a $p$-value of .2881. Therefore, we conclude that Model 2 is better than Model 1 and is, in fact, the "best" sales territory performance model (using only linear terms).

Another quantity that can be used for comparing regression models is called the **$C$-statistic** (also often called the **$C_p$-statistic**). To show how to calculate the $C$-statistic, suppose that we wish to choose an appropriate set of independent variables from $p$ potential independent variables. We first calculate the mean square error, which we denote as $s_p^2$, for the model using all $p$ potential independent variables. Then, if SSE denotes the unexplained variation for another particular model that has $k$ independent variables, it follows that the $C$-statistic for this model is

$$C = \frac{SSE}{s_p^2} - [n - 2(k + 1)]$$

For example, consider the sales territory performance case. It can be verified that the mean square error for the model using all $p = 8$ independent variables is 201,621.21 and that the SSE for the model using the first $k = 5$ independent variables (Model 2 in the previous example) is 3,516,812.7933. It follows that the $C$-statistic for this latter model is

$$C = \frac{3,516,812.7933}{201,621.21} - [25 - 2(5 + 1)] = 4.4$$

Since the $C$-statistic for a given model is a function of the model's SSE, and since we want SSE to be small, **we want $C$ to be small.** Although adding an unimportant independent variable to a regression model will decrease SSE, adding such a variable can increase $C$. This can happen when the decrease in SSE caused by the addition of the extra independent variable is not enough to offset the decrease in $n - 2(k + 1)$ caused by the addition of the extra independent variable (which increases $k$ by 1). It should be noted that although adding an unimportant independent variable to a regression model can increase both $s^2$ and $C$, there is no exact relationship between $s^2$ and $C$.

Although we want $C$ to be small, it can be shown from the theory behind the $C$-statistic that **we also wish to find a model for which the $C$-statistic roughly equals $k + 1$,** the number of parameters in the model. **If a model has a $C$-statistic substantially greater than $k + 1$, it can be shown that this model has substantial bias and is undesirable.** Thus, although we want to find a model for which $C$ is as small as possible, if $C$ for such a model is substantially greater than $k + 1$, we may prefer to choose a different model for which $C$ is slightly larger and more nearly equal to the number of parameters in that (different) model. **If a particular model has a small value of $C$ and $C$ for this model is less than $k + 1$, then the model should be considered desirable.** Finally, it should be noted that for the model that includes all $p$ potential independent variables (and thus utilizes $p + 1$ parameters), it can be shown that $C = p + 1$.

If we examine Figure 5.4, we see that Model 2 of the previous example has the smallest $C$-statistic. The $C$-statistic for this model equals 4.4. Since $C = 4.4$ is less than $k + 1 = 6$, the model is not biased. Therefore, this model should be considered best with respect to the $C$ statistic.

Thus far we have considered how to find the best model using linear independent variables. In Exercise 5.3 we illustrate, using the sales territory performance case, a systematic procedure for deciding which squared and interaction terms (see Sections 4.7 and 4.8) to include in a regression model. We have found that this systematic procedure often identifies important squared and interaction terms that are not identified by simply using scatter and residual plots. After finding one or more potential final regression models, we use the techniques of Sections 5.2 and 5.3 to check the regression assumptions and the techniques of Section 5.4 to identify outlying and influential observations. Based on this analysis, we make needed improvements and eventually find one or more final regression models that can be used to describe, predict, and control the dependent variable.

# Stepwise Regression and Backward Elimination

In some situations it is useful to employ an **iterative model selection procedure,** where at each step a single independent variable is added to or deleted from a regression model, and a new regression model is evaluated. We discuss here two such procedures—**stepwise regression and backward elimination.**

## Stepwise Regression

There are slight variations in the way different computer packages carry out **stepwise regression.** Assuming that $y$ is the dependent variable and $x_1, x_2, \ldots, x_p$ are the $p$ potential independent variables (where $p$ is generally large), we explain how most of the computer packages perform stepwise regression. Stepwise regression uses $t$-statistics (and related $p$-values) to determine the significance of the independent variables in various regression models. In this context we say that *the t-statistic indicates that the independent variable $x_j$ is significant at the $\alpha$ level if and only if the related p-value is less than $\alpha$.* Then stepwise regression is carried out as follows.

*Choice of $\alpha_{entry}$ and $\alpha_{stay}$*   Before beginning the stepwise procedure we choose a value of $\alpha_{entry}$, which we call **the probability of a Type I error related to entering an independent variable into the regression model.** We also choose a value of $\alpha_{stay}$, which we call **the probability of a Type I error related to retaining an independent variable that was previously entered into the model.** Although there are many considerations in choosing these values, it is common practice to set both $\alpha_{entry}$ and $\alpha_{stay}$ equal to .05 or .10.

*Step 1*   The stepwise procedure considers the $p$ possible one-independent-variable regression models of the form

$$y = \beta_0 + \beta_1 x_j + \varepsilon$$

Each different model includes a different potential independent variable. For each model the $t$-statistic (and $p$-value) related to testing $H_a\colon \beta_1 = 0$ versus $H_a\colon \beta_1 \neq 0$ is calculated. Denoting the independent variable giving the largest absolute value of the $t$-statistic (and the smallest $p$-value) by the symbol $x_{[1]}$, we consider the model

$$y = \beta_0 + \beta_1 x_{[1]} + \varepsilon$$

If the $t$-statistic does not indicate that $x_{[1]}$ is significant at the $\alpha_{entry}$ level, then the stepwise procedure terminates by concluding that none of the independent variables are significant at the $\alpha_{entry}$ level. If the $t$-statistic indicates that the independent variable $x_{[1]}$ is significant at the $\alpha_{entry}$ level, then $x_{[1]}$ is retained for use in step 2.

*Step 2*   The stepwise procedure considers the $p - 1$ possible two-independent-variable regression models of the form

$$y = \beta_0 + \beta_1 x_{[1]} + \beta_2 x_j + \varepsilon$$

Each different model includes $x_{[1]}$, the independent variable chosen in step 1, and a different potential independent variable chosen from the remaining $p - 1$ independent variables that were not chosen in step 1. For each model the $t$-statistic (and $p$-value) related to testing $H_0\colon \beta_2 = 0$ versus $H_a\colon \beta_2 \neq 0$ is calculated. Denoting the independent variable giving the largest absolute value of the $t$-statistic (and the smallest $p$-value) by the symbol $x_{[2]}$, we consider the model

$$y = \beta_0 + \beta_1 x_{[1]} + \beta_2 x_{[2]} + \varepsilon$$

If the $t$-statistic indicates that $x_{[2]}$ is significant at the $\alpha_{entry}$ level, then $x_{[2]}$ is retained in this model, and the stepwise procedure checks to see whether $x_{[1]}$ should be allowed to stay in the model. This check should be made because multicollinearity will probably cause the $t$-statistic related to the importance of $x_{[1]}$ to change when $x_{[2]}$ is added to the model. If the $t$-statistic does not indicate that $x_{[1]}$ is significant at the $\alpha_{stay}$ level, then the stepwise procedure returns to the beginning of step 2. Starting with a new one-independent-variable model that uses the new significant independent variable $x_{[2]}$, the stepwise procedure attempts to find a new two-independent-variable model

$$y = \beta_0 + \beta_1 x_{[2]} + \beta_2 x_j + \varepsilon$$

If the $t$-statistic indicates that $x_{[1]}$ is significant at the $\alpha_{stay}$ level in the model

$$y = \beta_0 + \beta_1 x_{[1]} + \beta_2 x_{[2]} + \varepsilon$$

then both the independent variables $x_{[1]}$ and $x_{[2]}$ are retained for use in further steps.

*Further steps*   The stepwise procedure continues by adding independent variables one at a time to the model. At each step an independent variable is added to the model if it has the largest (in absolute value) $t$-statistic of the independent variables not in the model and if its $t$-statistic indicates that it is significant at the $\alpha_{entry}$ level. After adding an independent variable, the stepwise procedure checks all the independent variables already included in the model and removes an independent variable if it has the smallest (in absolute value) $t$-statistic of the independent variables already included in the model and if its $t$-statistic indicates that it is not significant at the $\alpha_{stay}$ level. This removal procedure is sequentially continued, and only after the necessary removals are made does the stepwise procedure attempt to add another independent variable to the model. The stepwise procedure terminates when all the independent variables not in the model are insignificant at the $\alpha_{entry}$ level or when the variable to be added to the model is the one just removed from it.

   For example, again consider the sales territory performance data. We let $x_1, x_2, x_3, x_4, x_5, x_6, x_7,$ and $x_8$ be the eight potential independent variables employed in the stepwise procedure. Figure 5.5(a) (page 234) gives the MINITAB output of the stepwise regression employing these independent variables where both $\alpha_{entry}$ and $\alpha_{stay}$ have been set equal to .10. The stepwise procedure

1.   Adds ACCTS $(x_6)$ on the first step.
2.   Adds ADVER $(x_3)$ and retains ACCTS on the second step.
3.   Adds MKTPOTEN $(x_2)$ and retains ACCTS and ADVER on the third step.
4.   Adds MKTSHARE $(x_4)$ and retains ACCTS, ADVER, and MKTPOTEN on the fourth step.

The procedure terminates after step 4 when no more independent variables can be added. Therefore, the stepwise procedure arrives at the model that utilizes $x_2, x_3, x_4,$ and $x_6$.

**FIGURE 5.5** The MINITAB output of stepwise regression and backward elimination for the sales territory performance problem

| Step | 1 | 2 | 3 | 4 |
|---|---|---|---|---|
| Constant | 709.32 | 50.30 | -327.23 | -1441.93 |
| Accts | 21.7 | 19.0 | 15.6 | 9.2 |
| T-Value | 5.50 | 6.41 | 5.19 | 3.22 |
| P-Value | 0.000 | 0.000 | 0.000 | 0.004 |
| Adver | | 0.227 | 0.216 | 0.175 |
| T-Value | | 4.50 | 4.77 | 4.74 |
| P-Value | | 0.000 | 0.000 | 0.000 |
| MktPoten | | | 0.0219 | 0.0382 |
| T-Value | | | 2.53 | 4.79 |
| P-Value | | | 0.019 | 0.000 |
| MktShare | | | | 190 |
| T-Value | | | | 3.82 |
| P-Value | | | | 0.001 |
| S | 881 | 650 | 583 | 454 |
| R-Sq | 56.85 | 77.51 | 82.77 | 90.04 |
| R-Sq(adj) | 54.97 | 75.47 | 80.31 | 88.05 |
| Mallows C-p | 67.6 | 27.2 | 18.4 | 5.4 |

(a) Stepwise regression ($\alpha_{entry} = \alpha_{stay} = .10$)

| Step | 1 | 2 | 3 | 4 | 5 |
|---|---|---|---|---|---|
| Constant | -1508 | -1486 | -1165 | -1114 | -1312 |
| Time | 2.0 | 2.0 | 2.3 | 3.6 | 3.8 |
| T-Value | 1.04 | 1.10 | 1.34 | 3.06 | 3.01 |
| P-Value | 0.313 | 0.287 | 0.198 | 0.006 | 0.007 |
| MktPoten | 0.0372 | 0.0373 | 0.0383 | 0.0421 | 0.0444 |
| T-Value | 4.54 | 4.75 | 5.07 | 6.25 | 6.20 |
| P-Value | 0.000 | 0.000 | 0.000 | 0.000 | 0.000 |
| Adver | 0.151 | 0.152 | 0.141 | 0.129 | 0.152 |
| T-Value | 3.21 | 3.51 | 3.66 | 3.48 | 4.01 |
| P-Value | 0.006 | 0.003 | 0.002 | 0.003 | 0.001 |
| MktShare | 199 | 198 | 222 | 257 | 259 |
| T-Value | 2.97 | 3.09 | 4.38 | 6.57 | 6.15 |
| P-Value | 0.009 | 0.007 | 0.000 | 0.000 | 0.000 |
| Change | 291 | 296 | 285 | 325 | |
| T-Value | 1.56 | 1.80 | 1.78 | 2.06 | |
| P-Value | 0.139 | 0.090 | 0.093 | 0.053 | |
| Accts | 5.6 | 5.6 | 4.4 | | |
| T-Value | 1.16 | 1.23 | 1.09 | | |
| P-Value | 0.262 | 0.234 | 0.288 | | |
| WkLoad | 20 | 20 | | | |
| T-Value | 0.59 | 0.61 | | | |
| P-Value | 0.565 | 0.550 | | | |
| Rating | 8 | | | | |
| T-Value | 0.06 | | | | |
| P-Value | 0.950 | | | | |
| S | 449 | 436 | 428 | 430 | 464 |
| R-Sq | 92.20 | 92.20 | 92.03 | 91.50 | 89.60 |
| R-Sq(adj) | 88.31 | 88.99 | 89.38 | 89.26 | 87.52 |
| Mallows C-p | 9.0 | 7.0 | 5.4 | 4.4 | 6.4 |

(b) Backward elimination ($\alpha_{stay} = .05$)

## Backward Elimination

To carry out **backward elimination,** we perform a regression analysis by using a regression model containing all the $p$ potential independent variables. Then the independent variable having the smallest (in absolute value) $t$-statistic is chosen. If the $t$-statistic indicates that this independent variable is significant at the $\alpha_{stay}$ level ($\alpha_{stay}$ is chosen prior to the beginning of the procedure), then the procedure terminates by choosing the regression model containing all $p$ independent variables. If this independent variable is not significant at the $\alpha_{stay}$ level, then it is removed from the model, and a regression analysis is performed by using a regression model containing all the remaining independent variables. The procedure continues by removing independent variables one at a time from the model. At each step an independent variable is removed from the model if it has the smallest (in absolute value) $t$-statistic of the independent variables remaining in the model and if it is not significant at the $\alpha_{stay}$ level. The procedure terminates when no independent variable remaining in the model can be removed. Backward elimination is generally considered a reasonable procedure, especially for analysts who like to start with all possible independent variables in the model so that they will not "miss any important variables."

To illustrate backward elimination, we first note that choosing the independent variable that has the smallest (in absolute value) $t$-statistic in a model is equivalent to choosing the independent variable that has the largest $p$-value in the model. With this in mind, Figure 5.5(b) gives the MINITAB output of a backward elimination of the sales territory performance data. Here the backward elimination uses $\alpha_{stay} = .05$, begins with the model using all eight independent variables, and removes (in order) RATING ($x_8$), then WKLOAD ($x_7$), then ACCTS ($x_6$), and finally CHANGE ($x_5$). The procedure terminates when no independent variable remaining can be removed—that is, when no independent variable has a related $p$-value greater than $\alpha_{stay} = .05$—and arrives at a model that uses TIME ($x_1$), MKTPOTEN ($x_2$), ADVER ($x_3$), and MKTSHARE ($x_4$). This model has an $s$ of 464 and an $\overline{R}^2$ of .8752 and is inferior to the model arrived at by stepwise regression, which has an $s$ of 454 and an $\overline{R}^2$ of .8805 [see Figure 5.5(a)]. However, the backward elimination process allows us to find a model that is better than either of these. If we look at the model considered by backward elimination after RATING ($x_8$), WKLOAD ($x_7$), and ACCTS ($x_6$) have been removed, we have the model using $x_1$, $x_2$, $x_3$, $x_4$, and $x_5$. This model has an $s$ of 430 and an $\overline{R}^2$ of .8926, and in Example 5.1 we reasoned that this model is perhaps the best sales territory performance model. Interestingly, this is the model that backward elimination would arrive at if we were to set $\alpha_{stay}$ equal to .10 rather than .05—note that this model has no $p$-values greater than .10.

The sales territory performance example brings home two important points. First, the models obtained by backward elimination and stepwise regression depend on the choices of $\alpha_{entry}$ and $\alpha_{stay}$ (whichever is appropriate). Second, it is best not to think of these methods as "automatic model-building procedures." Rather, they should be regarded as processes that allow us to find and evaluate a variety of model choices.

# 5.2 RESIDUAL ANALYSIS IN SIMPLE REGRESSION

In this section we explain how to check the validity of the regression assumptions. The required checks are carried out by analyzing the **regression residuals.** The residuals are defined as follows.

---

For any particular observed value of $y$, the corresponding **residual** is

$$e = y - \hat{y} = (\text{observed value of } y - \text{predicted value of } y)$$

where the predicted value of $y$ is calculated using the **least squares prediction equation**

$$\hat{y} = b_0 + b_1 x$$

---

The linear regression model $y = \beta_0 + \beta_1 x + \varepsilon$ implies that the error term $\varepsilon$ is given by the equation $\varepsilon = y - (\beta_0 + \beta_1 x)$. Since $\hat{y}$ in the box is clearly the point estimate of $\beta_0 + \beta_1 x$, we see that the residual $e = y - \hat{y}$ is the point estimate of the error term $\varepsilon$. If the regression assumptions are valid, then for any given value of the independent variable, the population of potential error term values is normally distributed with mean 0 and variance $\sigma^2$ (see the regression assumptions in Section 3.4). Furthermore, the different error terms are statistically independent. Because the residuals provide point estimates of the error terms, it follows that

---

If the regression assumptions hold, the residuals should look like they have been randomly and independently selected from normally distributed populations having mean 0 and variance $\sigma^2$.

---

In any real regression problem, the regression assumptions will not hold exactly. In fact, it is important to point out that mild departures from the regression assumptions do not seriously hinder our ability to use a regression model to make statistical inferences. Therefore, we are looking for pronounced, rather than subtle, departures from the regression assumptions. Because of this, we will require that the residuals only approximately fit the description just given.

## Residual Plots

One useful way to analyze residuals is to plot them versus various criteria. The resulting plots are called **residual plots.** To construct a residual plot, we compute the residual for each observed $y$ value. The calculated residuals are then plotted versus some criterion. To validate the regression assumptions, we make residual plots against (1) values of the independent variable $x$; (2) values of $\hat{y}$, the predicted value of the dependent variable; and (3) the time order in which the data have been observed (if the regression data are time series data).

We next look at an example of constructing residual plots. Then we explain how to use these plots to check the regression assumptions.

**EXAMPLE 5.2**   Table 5.2 presents the predicted home upkeep expenditures and residuals that are given by the simple linear regression model describing the QHIC data. Here each residual is computed as

$$e = y - \hat{y} = y - (b_0 + b_1x) = y - (-348.3921 + 7.2583x)$$

For instance, for the first observation (home) when $y = 1412.08$ and $x = 237.00$ (see Table 3.2), the residual is

$$e = 1412.08 - [-348.3921 + 7.2583(237)]$$
$$= 1412.08 - 1371.816 = 40.264$$

The MINITAB output in Figure 5.6(a) and (b) (page 238) gives plots of the residuals for the QHIC simple linear regression model against values of $x$ and $\hat{y}$. To understand how these plots are constructed, recall that for the first observation (home) $y = 1412.08$, $x = 237.00$, $\hat{y} = 1371.816$, and the residual is 40.264. It follows that the point plotted in Figure 5.6(a) corresponding to the first observation has a horizontal axis coordinate of the $x$ value

**TABLE 5.2 Residuals for the QHIC Simple Linear Regression Model**

| Observation | Upkeep | Predicted | Residual | Observation | Upkeep | Predicted | Residual |
|---|---|---|---|---|---|---|---|
| 1 | 1412.080 | 1371.816 | 40.264 | 21 | 849.140 | 762.413 | 86.727 |
| 2 | 797.200 | 762.703 | 34.497 | 22 | 1313.840 | 1336.832 | −22.992 |
| 3 | 872.480 | 993.371 | −120.891 | 23 | 602.060 | 562.085 | 39.975 |
| 4 | 1003.420 | 1263.378 | −259.958 | 24 | 642.140 | 884.206 | −242.066 |
| 5 | 852.900 | 817.866 | 35.034 | 25 | 1038.800 | 938.353 | 100.447 |
| 6 | 288.480 | 375.112 | −86.632 | 26 | 697.000 | 833.398 | −136.398 |
| 7 | 1288.460 | 1314.041 | −25.581 | 27 | 324.340 | 525.793 | −201.453 |
| 8 | 423.080 | 390.354 | 32.726 | 28 | 965.100 | 1038.662 | −73.562 |
| 9 | 1351.740 | 1523.224 | −171.484 | 29 | 920.140 | 804.075 | 116.065 |
| 10 | 378.040 | 350.434 | 27.606 | 30 | 950.900 | 947.208 | 3.692 |
| 11 | 918.080 | 892.771 | 25.309 | 31 | 1670.320 | 1627.307 | 43.013 |
| 12 | 1627.240 | 1328.412 | 298.828 | 32 | 125.400 | 6.537 | 118.863 |
| 13 | 1204.760 | 1308.815 | −104.055 | 33 | 479.780 | 410.532 | 69.248 |
| 14 | 857.040 | 1146.084 | −289.044 | 34 | 2010.640 | 1728.778 | 281.862 |
| 15 | 775.000 | 999.613 | −224.613 | 35 | 368.360 | 259.270 | 109.090 |
| 16 | 869.260 | 876.658 | −7.398 | 36 | 425.600 | 277.270 | 148.330 |
| 17 | 1396.000 | 1444.835 | −48.835 | 37 | 626.900 | 621.167 | 5.733 |
| 18 | 711.500 | 780.558 | −69.058 | 38 | 1316.940 | 1196.602 | 120.338 |
| 19 | 1475.180 | 1278.911 | 196.269 | 39 | 390.160 | 537.261 | −147.101 |
| 20 | 1413.320 | 1118.068 | 295.252 | 40 | 1090.840 | 1088.889 | 1.951 |

**FIGURE 5.6** MINITAB output of residual plots for the QHIC simple linear regression model

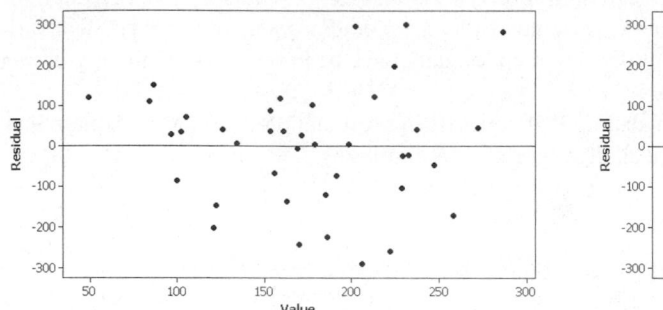

(a) MINITAB output of residual plot versus $x$

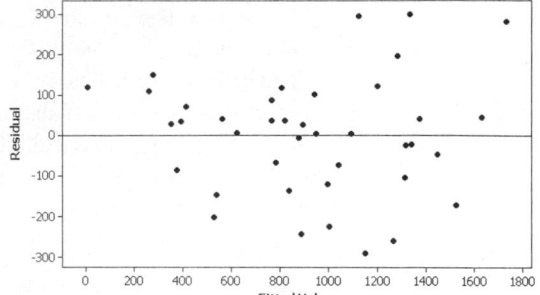

(b) MINITAB output of residual plot versus $\hat{y}$

**FIGURE 5.7**
Residual plots and
the constant
variance
assumption

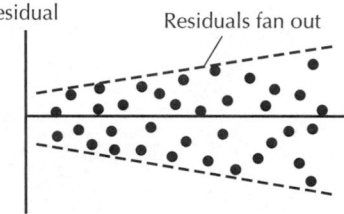

(a) Increasing error variance

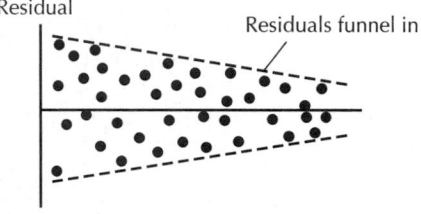

(b) Decreasing error variance

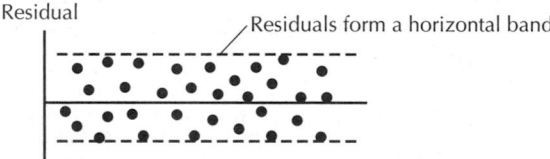

(c) Constant error variance

237.00 and a vertical axis coordinate of the residual 40.264. It also follows that the point plotted in Figure 5.6(b) corresponding to the first observation has a horizontal axis coordinate of the $\hat{y}$ value 1371.816, and a vertical axis coordinate of the residual 40.264. Finally, note that the QHIC data are cross-sectional data, not time series data. Therefore, we cannot make a residual plot versus time.

## The Constant Variance Assumption

To check the validity of the constant variance assumption, we examine plots of the residuals against values of $x, \hat{y}$, and time (if the regression data are time series data). When we look at these plots, the pattern of the residuals' fluctuation around 0 tells us about the validity of the constant variance assumption. A residual plot that "fans out" [as in Figure 5.7(a)] suggests that the error terms are becoming more spread out as the horizontal plot value increases and that the constant variance assumption is violated. Here we would say that an **increasing error variance** exists. A residual plot that "funnels in" [as in Figure 5.7(b)] suggests that the spread of the error terms is decreasing as the horizontal plot value increases and that again the constant variance assumption is violated. In this case we would say that a **decreasing error variance** exists. A residual plot with a horizontal band appearance [as in Figure 5.7(c)] suggests that the spread of the error terms around 0 is not changing much as the horizontal plot value increases. Such a plot tells us that the constant variance assumption (approximately) holds.

As an example, consider the QHIC case and the residual plot in Figure 5.6(a). This plot appears to fan out as $x$ increases, indicating that the spread of the error terms is increasing as $x$ increases. That is, an increasing error variance exists. This is equivalent to saying that the variance of the population of potential yearly upkeep expenditures for houses worth $x$ (thousand dollars) appears to increase as $x$ increases. The reason is that the model $y = \beta_0 + \beta_1 x + \varepsilon$ says that the variation of $y$ is the same as the variation of $\varepsilon$. For example, the variance of the population of potential yearly upkeep expenditures for houses worth \$200,000 would be larger than the variance of the population of potential yearly upkeep expenditures for houses worth \$100,000. Increasing variance makes some intuitive sense because people with more expensive homes generally have more discretionary income. These people can choose to spend either a substantial amount or a much smaller amount on home upkeep, thus causing a relatively large variation in upkeep expenditures.

Another residual plot showing the increasing error variance in the QHIC case is Figure 5.6(b). This plot tells us that the residuals appear to fan out as $\hat{y}$ (predicted $y$) increases, which is logical because $\hat{y}$ is an increasing function of $x$. Also, note that the original scatter plot of $y$ versus $x$ in Figure 3.4 shows the increasing error variance—the $y$ values appear to fan out as $x$ increases. In fact, one might ask why we need to consider residual plots when we can simply look at scatter plots. One answer is that, in general, because of possible differences in scaling between residual plots and scatter plots, one of these types of plots might be more informative in a particular situation. Therefore, we should always consider both types of plots.

When the constant variance assumption is violated, we cannot use the regression formulas presented in this book to make statistical inferences. Later in this section we discuss how we can make statistical inferences when a nonconstant error variance exists.

## The Assumption of Correct Functional Form

If the functional form of a regression model is incorrect, the residual plots constructed by using the model often display a pattern suggesting the form of a more appropriate model. For instance, if we use a simple linear regression model when the true relationship between $y$ and $x$ is curved, the residual plot will have a curved appearance. For example, the scatter plot of upkeep expenditure, $y$, versus home value, $x$, in Figure 3.4 has either a straight-line or slightly curved appearance. We used a simple linear regression model to describe the relationship between $y$ and $x$, but note that there is a "dip," or slightly curved appearance, in the upper left portion of each residual plot in Figure 5.6. Therefore, both the scatter plot and residual plots indicate that there might be a slightly curved relationship between $y$ and $x$. Later in this section we discuss one way to model curved relationships.

## The Normality Assumption

If the normality assumption holds, a histogram and/or stem-and-leaf display of the residuals should look reasonably bell shaped and reasonably symmetric about 0. Figure 5.8(a) gives the MINITAB output of a stem-and-leaf display of the residuals from the simple linear regression model describing the QHIC data. The stem-and-leaf display looks fairly bell shaped and symmetric about 0. However, the tails of the display look somewhat long and "heavy" or "thick," indicating a possible violation of the normality assumption.

Another way to check the normality assumption is to construct a **normal plot** of the residuals. To make a normal plot, we first arrange the residuals in order from smallest to largest. Letting the ordered residuals be denoted as $e_{(1)}, e_{(2)}, \ldots, e_{(n)}$ we denote the $i$th residual in the ordered listing as $e_{(i)}$. In the traditional normal plot we plot $e_{(i)}$ on the horizontal axis against a point called $z_{(i)}$ on the vertical axis. Here $z_{(i)}$ is defined to be the point on the horizontal axis under the standard normal curve so that the area under the curve to the left of the $z_{(i)}$ is $(3i - 1)/(3n + 1)$. For example, recall that in the QHIC case there are $n = 40$ residuals given in Table 5.2. When $i = 1$, it follows that

$$\frac{3i - 1}{3n + 1} = \frac{3(1) - 1}{3(40) + 1} = \frac{2}{121} = .0165$$

Therefore, $z_{(1)}$ is the normal point having an area of .0165 under the standard normal curve to its left. This implies that the area under the normal curve between $z_{(1)}$ and 0 is $.5 - .0165 = .4835$. Thus, as illustrated in Figure 5.8(b), $z_{(1)}$ equals $-2.13$. Because the smallest residual in Table 5.2 is $-289.044$, the first point plotted in the normal plot is $e_{(1)} = -289.044$ on the horizontal scale versus $z_{(1)} = -2.13$ on the vertical scale. When $i = 2$, it follows that $(3i - 1)/(3n + 1)$ equals .0413 and thus that $z_{(2)} = -1.74$. Therefore, because the second smallest residual in Table 5.2 is $-259.958$, the second point plotted is $e_{(2)} = -259.958$ on the horizontal scale versus $z_{(2)} = -1.74$ on the vertical scale. This process is continued until the entire normal plot is constructed. The MINITAB 13 output of this plot is given in Figure 5.8(c).

An equivalent plot is shown in Figure 5.8(d), which is a MINITAB 14 output. In Figure 5.8(d), we plot the percentage $p_{(i)}$ of the area under the standard normal curve to the left of $z_{(i)}$ on the vertical axis. Thus, the first point plotted in this normal plot is $e_{(1)} = -289.044$ on the horizontal scale versus $p_{(1)} = (.0165)(100) = 1.65$, and the second point plotted is $e_{(2)} = -259.958$ on the horizontal scale versus $p_{(2)} =$

**FIGURE 5.8** Stem-and-leaf display and normal plot of the residuals from the simple linear regression model describing the QHIC data

```
Stem-and-leaf of RESI1    N  = 40
Leaf Unit = 10

 2      -2   85
 5      -2   420
 6      -1   7
10      -1   4320
13      -0   876
17      -0   4220
(11)     0   00022333344
12       0   68
10       1   001124
 4       1   9
 3       2
 3       2   899
```

(a) MINITAB output of the stem-and-leaf display

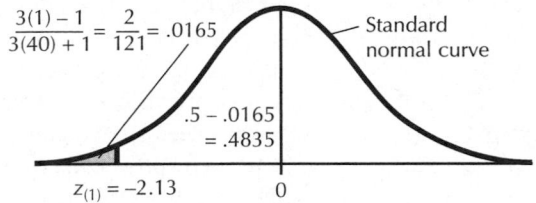

$$\frac{3(1)-1}{3(40)+1} = \frac{2}{121} = .0165$$

Standard normal curve

$.5 - .0165 = .4835$

$z_{(1)} = -2.13$      0

(b) Calculating $z_{(1)}$ for a normal plot

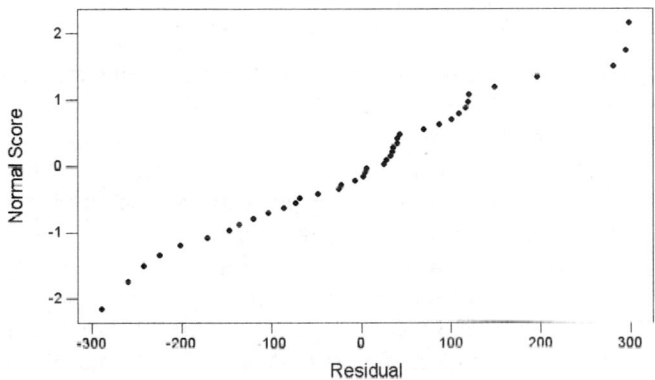

(c) MINITAB 13 output of the normal plot

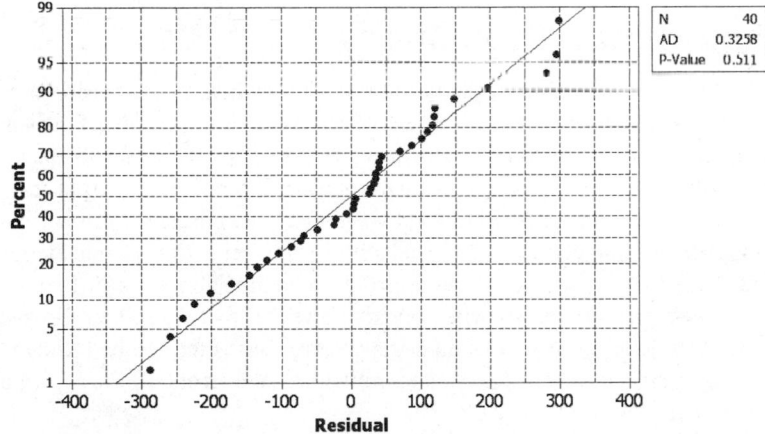

| N | 40 |
|---|---|
| AD | 0.3258 |
| P-Value | 0.511 |

(d) MINITAB 14 output of the normal plot

$(.0413)(100) = 4.13$ on the vertical scale. It is important to note that the scale on the vertical axis does not have the usual spacing between the percentages. The spacing reflects the distance between the $z$-scores that correspond to the percentages in the standard normal distribution. Hence, if we wished to create the plot in Figure 5.8(d) by hand, we would need special graphing paper with this vertical scale.

It can be proven that if the normality assumption holds, then the expected value of the $i$th ordered residual $e_{(i)}$ is proportional to $z_{(i)}$. Therefore, a plot of the $e_{(i)}$ values on the horizontal scale versus the $z_{(i)}$ values on the vertical scale (or equivalently, the $e_{(i)}$ values on the horizontal scale versus the $p_{(i)}$ values on the vertical scale) should have a straight-line appearance. That is, if the normality assumption holds, then the normal plot should have a straight-line appearance. A normal plot that does not look like a straight line (admittedly a subjective decision) indicates that the normality assumption is violated. Since the normal plot in Figure 5.8(c) and the equivalent normal plot in Figure 5.8(d) have some curvature (particularly in the upper right portion), there may be a violation of the normality assumption. However, the Anderson–Darling statistic, as shown in Figure 5.8(d), is .3258. This statistic is used to test

$H_0$: The residuals have a normal distribution

$H_a$: The residuals do not have a normal distribution

Since the $p$-value for this statistic is .511, we do not have sufficient evidence to reject $H_0$ even at $\alpha = .10$. Thus, we do not have statistical evidence by this test to say that the normality assumption is violated.

It is important to realize that violations of the constant variance and correct functional form assumptions can often cause a histogram and/or stem-and-leaf display of the residuals to look nonnormal and can cause the normal plot to have a curved appearance. Because of this, it is usually a good idea to use residual plots to check for nonconstant variance and incorrect functional form before making any final conclusions about the normality assumption. Later in this section we discuss a procedure that sometimes remedies simultaneous violations of the constant variance, correct functional form, and normality assumptions.

## The Independence Assumption

The independence assumption is most likely to be violated when the regression data are **time series data**—that is, data that have been collected in a time sequence. For such data the time-ordered error terms can be **autocorrelated.** Intuitively, we say that error terms occurring over time have **positive autocorrelation** if a positive error term in time period $i$ tends to produce, or be followed by, another positive error term in time period $i + k$ (some later time period) and if a negative error term in time period $i$ tends to produce, or be followed by, another negative error term in time period $i + k$. In other words, positive autocorrelation exists when positive error terms tend to be followed over time by positive error terms and when negative error terms tend to be followed over time by negative error terms. Positive autocorrelation in the error terms is depicted

**FIGURE 5.9**
Positive
autocorrelation in
the error terms:
cyclical pattern

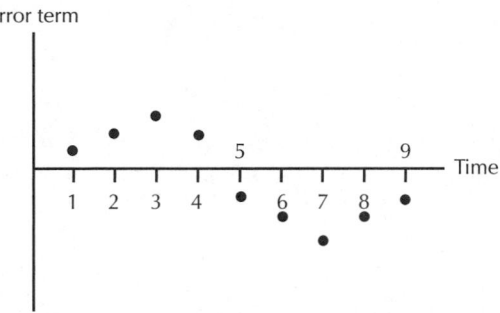

in Figure 5.9, which illustrates that **positive autocorrelation can produce a cyclical error term pattern over time.** The simple linear regression model implies that a positive error term produces a greater-than-average value of $y$ and a negative error term produces a smaller-than-average value of $y$. It follows that positive autocorrelation in the error terms means that greater-than-average values of $y$ tend to be followed by greater-than-average values of $y$, and smaller-than-average values of $y$ tend to be followed by smaller-than-average values of $y$. An example of positive autocorrelation could hypothetically be provided by a simple linear regression model relating demand for a product to advertising expenditure. Here we assume that the data are time series data observed over a number of consecutive sales periods. One of the factors included in the error term of the simple linear regression model is competitors' advertising expenditure for their similar products. If, for the moment, we assume that competitors' advertising expenditure significantly affects the demand for the product, then a higher-than-average competitors' advertising expenditure probably causes demand for the product to be lower than average and hence probably causes a negative error term. On the other hand, a lower-than-average competitors' advertising expenditure probably causes the demand for the product to be higher than average and hence probably causes a positive error term. So if competitors tend to spend money on advertising in a cyclical fashion—spending large amounts for several consecutive sales periods (during an advertising campaign) and then spending lesser amounts for several consecutive sales periods—a negative error term in one sales period will tend to be followed by a negative error term in the next sales period, and a positive error term in one sales period will tend to be followed by a positive error term in the next sales period. In this case the error terms would display positive autocorrelation, and thus these error terms would not be statistically independent.

Intuitively, error terms occurring over time have **negative autocorrelation** if a positive error term in time period $i$ tends to produce, or be followed by, a negative error term in time period $i + k$ and if a negative error term in time period $i$ tends to produce, or be followed by, a positive error term in time period $i + k$. In other words, negative autocorrelation exists when positive error terms tend to be followed over time by negative error terms and negative error terms tend to be followed over time by positive error terms. An example of negative autocorrelation in the error terms is depicted

**FIGURE 5.10**
Negative
autocorrelation in
the error terms:
alternating pattern

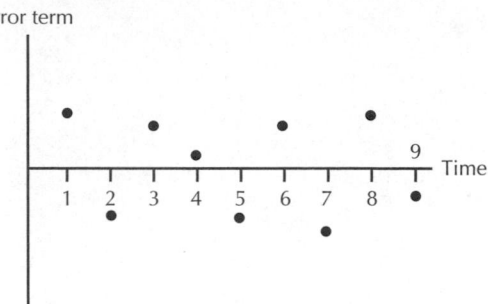

in Figure 5.10, which illustrates that **negative autocorrelation in the error terms can produce an alternating pattern over time.** It follows that negative autocorrelation in the error terms means that greater-than-average values of $y$ tend to be followed by smaller-than-average values of $y$ and smaller-than-average values of $y$ tend to be followed by greater-than-average values of $y$. An example of negative autocorrelation might be provided by a retailer's weekly stock orders. Here a larger-than-average stock order one week might result in an oversupply and hence a smaller-than-average order the next week.

The **independence assumption** basically says that the time-ordered error terms display no positive or negative autocorrelation. This says that **the error terms occur in a random pattern over time.** Such a random pattern would imply that the error terms (and their corresponding $y$ values) are statistically independent.

Because the residuals are point estimates of the error terms, a residual plot versus time is used to check the independence assumption. If a residual plot versus the data's time sequence has a cyclical appearance, the error terms are positively autocorrelated, and the independence assumption is violated. If a plot of the time-ordered residuals has an alternating pattern, the error terms are negatively autocorrelated, and again the independence assumption is violated. However, if a plot of the time-ordered residuals displays a random pattern, the error terms have little or no autocorrelation. In such a case, it is reasonable to conclude that the independence assumption holds.

**EXAMPLE 5.3**    Table 5.3 presents data concerning weekly sales at Pages' Bookstore (Sales), Pages' weekly advertising expenditure (Adver), and the weekly advertising expenditure of Pages' main competitor (Compadv). Here the sales values are expressed in thousands of dollars, and the advertising expenditure values are expressed in hundreds of dollars. Table 5.3 also gives the residuals that are obtained from a simple linear regression analysis relating Pages' sales to Pages' advertising expenditure. These residuals are plotted versus time in Figure 5.11. We see that the residual plot has a cyclical pattern. This tells us that the error terms for the model are positively autocorrelated and the independence assumption is violated. Furthermore, there tend to be positive residuals when the competitor's advertising expenditure is lower (in weeks 1 through 8 and weeks 14, 15, and 16) and negative residuals

**TABLE 5.3** Pages' Bookstore Sales Data, and Residuals from a Simple Linear Regression Relating Sales to Advertising Expenditure

| Observation | Adver | Compadv | Sales | Predicted | Residual |
|---|---|---|---|---|---|
| 1 | 18 | 10 | 22 | 18.7 | 3.3 |
| 2 | 20 | 10 | 27 | 23.0 | 4.0 |
| 3 | 20 | 15 | 23 | 23.0 | −0.0 |
| 4 | 25 | 15 | 31 | 33.9 | −2.9 |
| 5 | 28 | 15 | 45 | 40.4 | 4.6 |
| 6 | 29 | 20 | 47 | 42.6 | 4.4 |
| 7 | 29 | 20 | 45 | 42.6 | 2.4 |
| 8 | 28 | 25 | 42 | 40.4 | 1.6 |
| 9 | 30 | 35 | 37 | 44.7 | −7.7 |
| 10 | 31 | 35 | 39 | 46.9 | −7.9 |
| 11 | 34 | 35 | 45 | 53.4 | −8.4 |
| 12 | 35 | 30 | 52 | 55.6 | −3.6 |
| 13 | 36 | 30 | 57 | 57.8 | −0.8 |
| 14 | 38 | 25 | 62 | 62.1 | −0.1 |
| 15 | 41 | 20 | 73 | 68.6 | 4.4 |
| 16 | 45 | 20 | 84 | 77.3 | 6.7 |

**FIGURE 5.11**
A plot of the residuals in Table 5.3 versus time

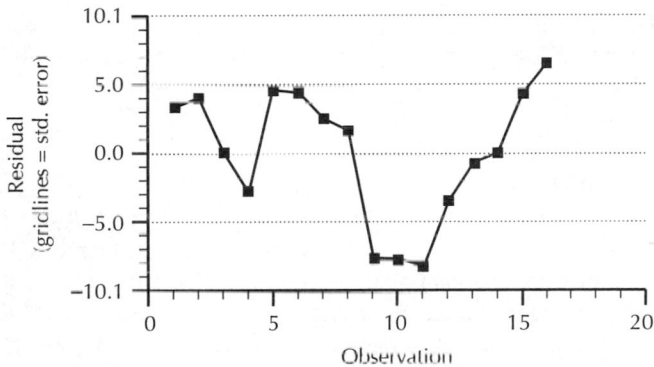

when the competitor's advertising expenditure is higher (in weeks 9 through 13). Therefore, the competitor's advertising expenditure seems to be causing the positive autocorrelation.

When the independence assumption is violated, various remedies can be employed. One approach is to identify which independent variable left in the error term (for example, competitors' advertising expenditure) is causing the error terms to be autocorrelated. We can then remove this independent variable from the error term and insert it directly into the regression model to form a *multiple regression model*—see Chapter 4. We further discuss how to detect and remedy violations of the independence assumption in Chapter 6 and in Chapters 9 through 12.

# Transforming the Dependent Variable: A Possible Remedy for Violations of the Constant Variance, Correct Functional Form, and Normality Assumptions

In general, if a data or residual plot indicates that the error variance of a regression model increases as an independent variable or the predicted value of the dependent variable increases, then we can sometimes remedy the situation by transforming the dependent variable. One transformation that works well is to take each $y$ value to a fractional power. As an example, we might use a transformation in which we take the square root (or one-half power) of each $y$ value. Letting $y^*$ denote the value obtained when the transformation is applied to $y$, we would write the **square root transformation** as

$$y^* = \sqrt{y} = y^{.5}$$

Another commonly used transformation is the **quartic root transformation.** Here we take each $y$ value to the one-fourth power. That is,

$$y^* = y^{.25}$$

If we consider a transformation that takes each $y$ value to a fractional power (such as .5, .25, or the like), as the power approaches 0, the transformed value $y^*$ approaches the natural logarithm of $y$ (commonly written ln $y$). In fact, we sometimes use the **logarithmic transformation**

$$y^* = \ln y$$

which takes the natural logarithm of each $y$ value. In general, when we take a fractional power (including the natural logarithm) of the dependent variable, the transformation not only tends to equalize the error variance but also tends to "straighten out" certain types of nonlinear data plots. Specifically, if a data plot indicates that the dependent variable is increasing at an increasing rate (as in Figure 3.4), then a fractional power transformation tends to straighten out the data plot. A fractional power transformation can also help to remedy a violation of the normality assumption. Because we cannot know which fractional power to use before we actually take the transformation, we recommend taking all of the square root, quartic root, and natural logarithm transformations and seeing which one best equalizes the error variance and (possibly) straightens out a nonlinear data plot.

**EXAMPLE 5.4**    Consider the QHIC upkeep expenditures. In Figures 5.12, 5.13, and 5.14 we show the plots that result when we take the square root, quartic root, and natural logarithmic transformations of the upkeep expenditures and plot the transformed values versus the home values. The square root transformation seems to best equalize the error variance and straighten out the curved data plot in Figure 3.4. Note that the natural logarithmic transformation seems to "overtransform" the data—the error variance tends to decrease

**FIGURE 5.12**
MINITAB plot of
the square roots
of the upkeep
expenditures versus
the home values

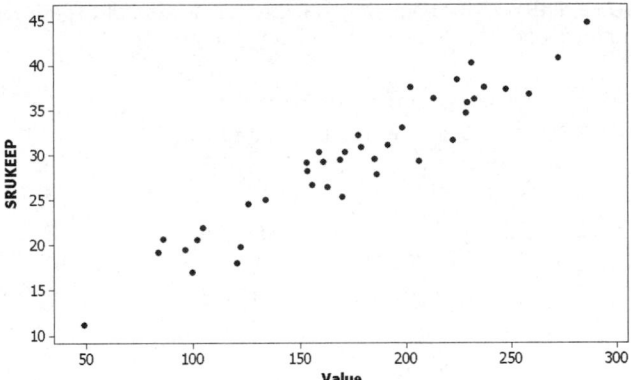

**FIGURE 5.13**
MINITAB plot of
the quartic roots
of the upkeep
expenditures versus
the home values

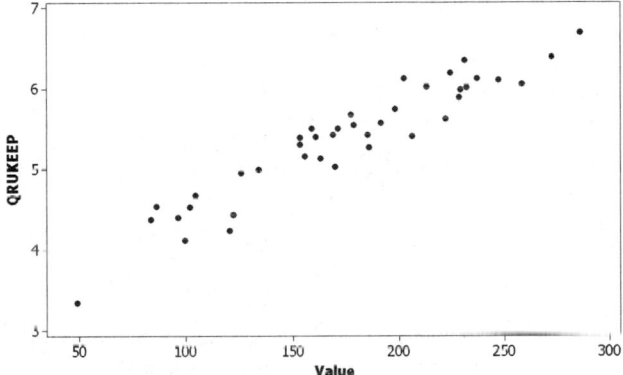

**FIGURE 5.14**
MINITAB plot of the
natural logarithms
of the upkeep
expenditures versus
home values

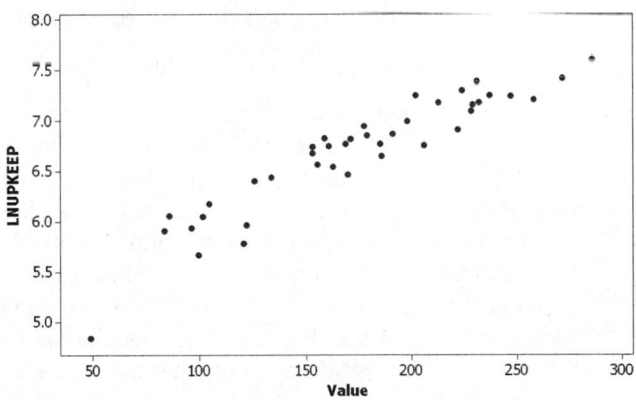

**FIGURE 5.15** MINITAB output of a regression analysis of the upkeep expenditure data using the model $y^* = \beta_0 + \beta_1 x + \varepsilon$ where $y^* = y^{.5}$

```
The regression equation is
SRUKEEP = 7.20 + 0.127 Value


Predictor        Coef    SE Coef        T       P
Constant        7.201      1.205     5.98   0.000
Value        0.127047   0.006577    19.32   0.000


S = 2.32479    R-Sq = 90.8%    R-Sq(adj) = 90.5%


Analysis of Variance

Source            DF        SS        MS         F       P
Regression         1    2016.8    2016.8    373.17   0.000
Residual Error    38     205.4       5.4
Total             39    2222.2

    Fit    SE Fit         95% CI              95% PI
 35.151     0.474   (34.191, 36.111)    (30.348, 39.954)
```

as the home value increases and the data plot seems to "bend down." The plot of the quartic roots indicates that the quartic root transformation also seems to overtransform the data (but not by as much as the logarithmic transformation). In general, as the fractional power gets smaller, the transformation gets stronger. Different fractional powers are best in different situations.

Since the plot in Figure 5.12 of the square roots of the upkeep expenditures versus the home values has a straight-line appearance, we consider the model

$$y^* = \beta_0 + \beta_1 x + \varepsilon \quad \text{where} \quad y^* = y^{.5}$$

The MINITAB output of a regression analysis using this transformed model is given in Figure 5.15, and the MINITAB output of an analysis of the model's residuals is given in Figure 5.16. Note that the residual plot versus $x$ for the transformed model in Figure 5.16(a) has a horizontal band appearance. It can also be verified that the transformed model's residual plot versus $\hat{y}$, which we do not give here, has a similar horizontal band appearance. Therefore, we conclude that the constant variance and the correct functional form assumptions approximately hold for the transformed model. Next, note that the stem-and-leaf display of the transformed model's residuals in Figure 5.16(b) looks reasonably bell shaped and symmetric, and note that the normal plot of these residuals in

**FIGURE 5.16** MINITAB output of residual analysis for the upkeep expenditure model
$y^* = \beta_0 + \beta_1 x + \varepsilon$ where $y^* = y^{.5}$

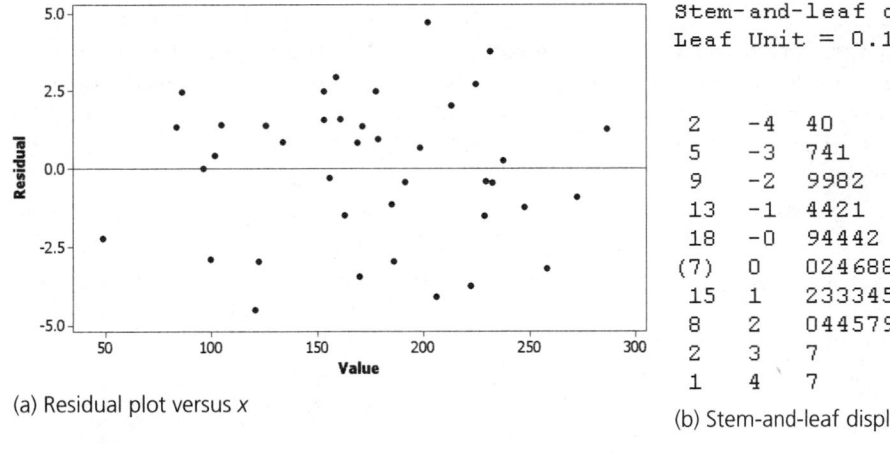

(a) Residual plot versus $x$

```
Stem-and-leaf of RESI2   N   = 40
Leaf Unit = 0.10

  2     -4   40
  5     -3   741
  9     -2   9982
 13     -1   4421
 18     -0   94442
 (7)     0   0246889
 15      1   2333455
  8      2   044579
  2      3   7
  1      4   7
```

(b) Stem-and-leaf display of the residuals

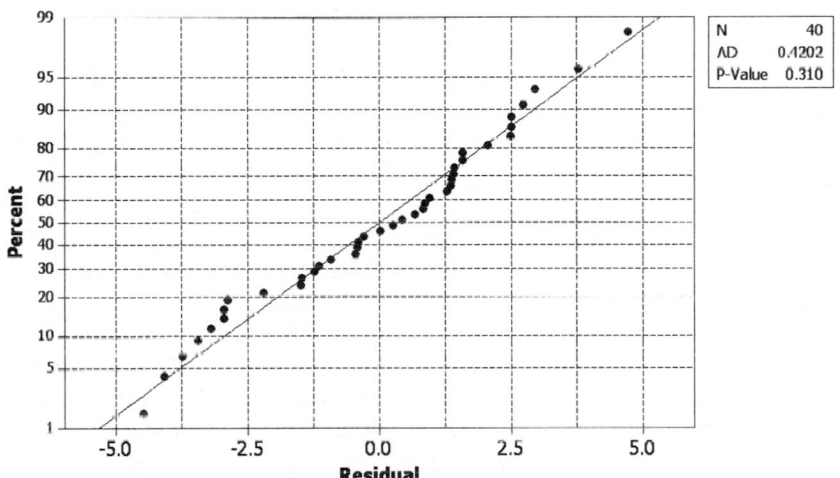

|     |       |
| --- | ----- |
| N   | 40    |
| AD  | 0.4202 |
| P-Value | 0.310 |

(c) Normal plot of the residuals

Figure 5.16(c) looks straighter than the normal plot for the untransformed model (see Figure 5.8). In addition, we cannot reject the null hypothesis that the residuals have a normal distribution because the $p$-value for the Anderson–Darling statistic is .310, which is well above $\alpha = .05$. Therefore, we also conclude that the normality assumption approximately holds for the transformed model.

Because the regression assumptions approximately hold for the transformed regression model, we can use this model to make statistical inferences. Consider a home worth $220,000. Using the least squares point estimates on the MINITAB output in Figure 5.15, it follows that a point prediction of $y*$ for such a home is

$$\hat{y}* = 7.201 + .127047(220)$$

$$= 35.151$$

This point prediction is given at the bottom of the MINITAB output, as is the 95% prediction interval for $y*$, which is [30.348, 39.954]. It follows that a point prediction of the upkeep expenditure for a home worth $220,000 is $(35.151)^2 = \$1235.59$ and that a 95% prediction interval for this upkeep expenditure is $[(30.348)^2, (39.954)^2] = [\$921.00, \$1596.32]$.

Suppose that QHIC wishes to send an advertising brochure to any home that has a predicted upkeep expenditure of at least $500. Solving the prediction equation $\hat{y}* = b_0 + b_1 x$ for $x$, and noting that a predicted upkeep expenditure of $500 corresponds to a $\hat{y}*$ of $\sqrt{500} = 22.36068$, it follows that QHIC should send the advertising brochure to any home that has a value of at least

$$x = \frac{\hat{y}* - b_0}{b_1} = \frac{22.36068 - 7.201}{.127047} = 119.3234 \text{ (or } \$119,323)$$

Recall that because there are many homes of a particular value in the metropolitan area, QHIC is interested in estimating the mean upkeep expenditure corresponding to this value. Consider all homes worth, for example, $220,000. The MINITAB output in Figure 5.15 tells us that a point estimate of the mean of the square roots of the upkeep expenditures for all such homes is 35.151 and that a 95% confidence interval for this mean is [34.191, 36.111]. Unfortunately, because it can be shown that the mean of the square root is not the square root of the mean, we cannot transform the results for the mean of the square roots back into a result for the mean of the original upkeep expenditures. This is a major drawback to transforming the dependent variable and one reason why many statisticians avoid transforming the dependent variable unless the regression assumptions are badly violated. In Chapter 4 and Section 5.3 we discuss other remedies for violations of the regression assumptions that do not have some of the drawbacks of transforming the dependent variable. Some of these remedies involve transforming the independent variable—a procedure introduced in Exercise 5.11. Furthermore, if we reconsider the residual analysis of the original, untransformed QHIC model in Figures 5.6 and 5.8, we might conclude that the regression assumptions are not badly violated for the untransformed model. Also, note that the point prediction, 95% prediction interval, and value of $x$ obtained here using the transformed model are not very different from the results obtained in Examples 3.5 and 3.12 using the untransformed model. This implies that it might be reasonable to rely on the results obtained using the untransformed model, or to at least rely on the results for the mean upkeep expenditures obtained using the untransformed model.

In this section we have concentrated on analyzing the residuals for the QHIC simple linear regression model. If we analyze the residuals in Table 3.4 for the fuel consumption simple linear regression model (recall that the fuel consumption data are time series data), we conclude that the regression assumptions approximately hold for this model.

# 5.3 RESIDUAL ANALYSIS IN MULTIPLE REGRESSION

In Section 5.2 we showed how to use residual analysis to check the regression assumptions for a simple linear regression model. In multiple regression we proceed similarly. Specifically, for a multiple regression model we plot the residuals given by the model against (1) values of each independent variable, (2) values of the predicted value of the dependent variable, and (3) the time order in which the data have been observed (if the regression data are time series data). A fanning-out pattern on a residual plot indicates an increasing error variance; a funneling-in pattern indicates a decreasing error variance. Both violate the constant variance assumption. A curved pattern on a residual plot indicates that the functional form of the regression model is incorrect. If the regression data are time series data, a cyclical pattern on the residual plot versus time suggests positive autocorrelation, and an alternating pattern suggests negative autocorrelation. Both violate the independence assumption. On the other hand, if all residual plots have (at least approximately) a horizontal band appearance, then it is reasonable to believe that the constant variance, correct functional form, and independence assumptions approximately hold. To check the normality assumption, we can construct a histogram, stem-and-leaf display, and normal plot of the residuals. The histogram and stem-and-leaf display should look bell shaped and symmetric about 0; the normal plot should have a straight-line appearance.

To illustrate these ideas, consider the sales territory performance data in Table 4.2. Figure 4.7 gives the SAS output of a regression analysis of these data using the model

$$y = \beta_0 + \beta_1 x_1 + \beta_2 x_2 + \beta_3 x_3 + \beta_4 x_4 + \beta_5 x_5 + \varepsilon$$

The least squares point estimates on the output give the prediction equation

$$\hat{y} = -1113.7879 + 3.6121 x_1 + .0421 x_2 + .1289 x_3 + 256.9555 x_4 + 324.5335 x_5$$

Using this prediction equation, we can calculate the predicted sales values and residuals given in Table 5.4 (page 252). For example, observation 10 in this data set corresponds to a sales representative for whom $x_1 = 105.69$, $x_2 = 42{,}053.24$, $x_3 = 5673.11$, $x_4 = 8.85$, and $x_5 = .31$. If we insert these values into the prediction equation, we obtain a predicted sales value of $\hat{y}_{10} = 4143.597$. Since the actual sales for the sales representative are $y_{10} = 4876.370$, the residual $e_{10}$ equals the difference between $y_{10} = 4876.370$ and $\hat{y}_{10} = 4143.597$, which is 732.773. The normal plot of the residuals in Figure 5.17(a) (page 252) has a straight-line appearance. Observe that in Figure 5.17(a) the normal plot has the residuals $e_{(i)}$ on the vertical axis versus the normal score $z_{(i)}$ on the horizontal axis, in contrast to the MINITAB output in Figure 5.8(c) which has the residuals on the horizontal axis and the percentage $p_{(i)}$ on the vertical axis. In either form of the normal plot, we look for a straight-line appearance. In addition, the plot of the residuals versus predicted sales in Figure 5.17(b) has a horizontal band appearance, as do the plots of the residuals versus the independent variables [the plot versus $x_3$, advertising, is

**TABLE 5.4** Residuals for the Sales Territory Performance Model $y = \beta_0 + \beta_1 x_1 + \beta_2 x_2 + \beta_3 x_3 + \beta_4 x_4 + \beta_5 x_5 + \varepsilon$

| Observation | Sales | Predicted | Residual | Observation | Sales | Predicted | Residual |
|---|---|---|---|---|---|---|---|
| 1 | 3669.880 | 3504.990 | 164.890 | 14 | 2337.380 | 2351.344 | −13.964 |
| 2 | 3473.950 | 3901.180 | −427.230 | 15 | 4586.950 | 4797.688 | −210.738 |
| 3 | 2295.100 | 2774.866 | −479.766 | 16 | 2729.240 | 2904.099 | −174.859 |
| 4 | 4675.560 | 4911.872 | −236.312 | 17 | 3289.400 | 3362.660 | −73.260 |
| 5 | 6125.960 | 5415.196 | 710.764 | 18 | 2800.780 | 2907.376 | −106.596 |
| 6 | 2134.940 | 2026.090 | 108.850 | 19 | 3264.200 | 3625.026 | −360.826 |
| 7 | 5031.660 | 5126.127 | −94.467 | 20 | 3453.620 | 4056.443 | −602.823 |
| 8 | 3367.450 | 3106.925 | 260.525 | 21 | 1741.450 | 1409.835 | 331.615 |
| 9 | 6519.450 | 6055.297 | 464.153 | 22 | 2035.750 | 2494.101 | −458.351 |
| 10 | 4876.370 | 4143.597 | 732.773 | 23 | 1578.000 | 1617.561 | −39.561 |
| 11 | 2468.270 | 2503.165 | −34.895 | 24 | 4167.440 | 4574.903 | −407.463 |
| 12 | 2533.310 | 1827.065 | 706.245 | 25 | 2799.970 | 2488.700 | 311.270 |
| 13 | 2408.110 | 2478.083 | −69.973 | | | | |

**FIGURE 5.17** Residual plots for the sales territory performance model in Table 5.4

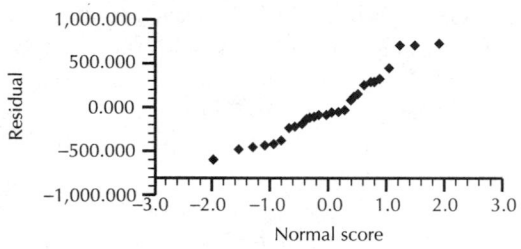

(a) Normal plot of the residuals

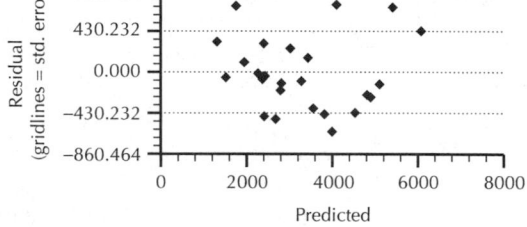

(b) Plot of the residuals versus predicted sales

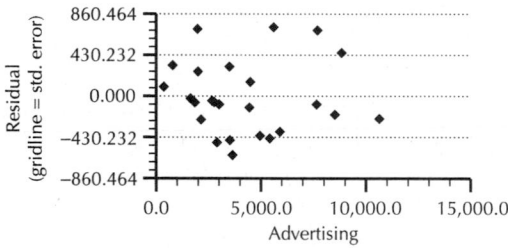

(c) Plot of the residuals versus advertising

shown in Figure 5.17(c)]. We conclude that the regression assumptions approximately hold for the sales territory performance model (note that since the data are cross-sectional, a residual plot versus time is not appropriate).

We next consider the QHIC data in Table 3.2. When we performed a regression analysis of these data by using the simple linear regression model, plots of the model's residuals versus $x$ (home value) and $\hat{y}$ (predicted upkeep expenditure) both fanned out

**FIGURE 5.18**

MINITAB plot of the quadratic QHIC model residuals versus $x$

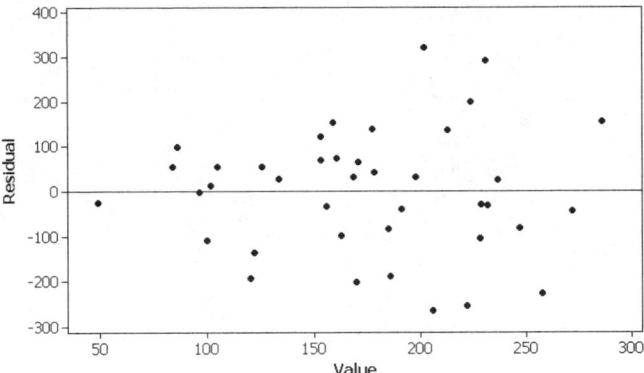

and had a "dip," or slightly curved appearance (see Figure 5.6). In order to remedy the indicated violations of the assumptions of constant variance and correct functional form, we transformed the dependent variable by taking the square roots of the upkeep expenditures. An alternative approach consists of two steps. First, the slightly curved appearance of the residual plots implies that it is reasonable to add the squared term $x^2$ to the simple linear regression model. This gives the *quadratic regression model*

$$y = \beta_0 + \beta_1 x + \beta_2 x^2 + \varepsilon$$

The MINITAB output in Figure 5.18 shows that the plot of this model's residuals versus $x$ fans out, indicating a violation of the constant variance assumption. The second step of the alternative approach remedies this violation by *dividing through the model by $x$*. How this is done is discussed in Exercise 5.11. We will see that the final model obtained will allow us to do what the square root transformation of Section 5.2 would not allow us to do—make statistical inferences about *mean* upkeep expenditures.

# 5.4 DIAGNOSTICS FOR DETECTING OUTLYING AND INFLUENTIAL OBSERVATIONS

An observation that is well separated from the rest of the data is called an **outlier.** An observation that would cause some important aspect of the regression analysis (for example, the least squares point estimates or the standard error $s$) to substantially change if it were removed from the data set is called **influential.** An observation may be an outlier with respect to its $y$ value and/or its $x$ values, but an outlier may or may not be

**FIGURE 5.19**
Data plot
illustrating outlying
and influential
observations

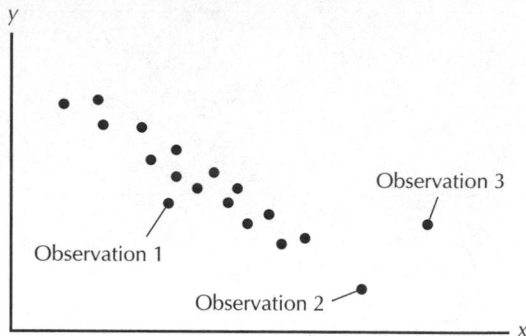

influential. We illustrate these ideas by considering Figure 5.19, which is a hypothetical plot of the values of a dependent variable $y$ against an independent variable $x$. Observation 1 in this figure is outlying with respect to its $y$ value. However, it is not outlying with respect to its $x$ value, since its $x$ value is near the middle of the other $x$ values. Moreover, observation 1 may not be influential because there are several observations with similar $x$ values and nonoutlying $y$ values, which will keep the least squares point estimates from being excessively influenced by observation 1. Observation 2 in Figure 5.19 is outlying with respect to its $x$ value, but since its $y$ value is consistent with the regression relationship displayed by the nonoutlying observations, it is probably not influential. Observation 3, however, is probably influential, because it is outlying with respect to its $x$ value and because its $y$ value is not consistent with the regression relationship displayed by the other observations.

In addition to using data plots (such as Figure 5.19), we can use more sophisticated procedures to detect outlying and influential observations. These procedures are particularly important when we are performing a multiple regression analysis and thus simple data plots are unlikely to tell us what we need to know. To illustrate, we consider the data in Table 5.5, which concerns the need for labor in 17 U.S. Navy hospitals. Specifically, this table gives values of the dependent variable Hours ($y$, monthly labor hours required) and of the independent variables Xray ($x_1$, monthly X-ray exposures), BedDays ($x_2$, monthly occupied bed days—a hospital has one occupied bed day if one bed is occupied for an entire day), and Length ($x_3$, average length of patients' stay, in days). When we perform a regression analysis of these data using the model

$$y = \beta_0 + \beta_1 x_1 + \beta_2 x_2 + \beta_3 x_3 + \varepsilon$$

we find that the least squares point estimates of the model parameters and their associated $p$-values (given in parentheses) are $b_0 = 1523.3892(.0749)$, $b_1 = .0530(.0205)$, $b_2 = .9785(<.0001)$ and $b_3 = -320.9508(.0563)$. In addition, Figure 5.20 (page 256) gives the SAS and MINITAB output of outlying and influential observation diagnostics for the model. The main objective of the regression analysis is to help the navy evaluate the performance of its hospitals in terms of how many labor hours are used relative

**TABLE 5.5 Hospital Labor Needs Data**

| Hospital | Hours $y$ | Xray $x_1$ | BedDays $x_2$ | Length $x_3$ |
|----------|-----------|------------|---------------|--------------|
| 1 | 566.52 | 2,463 | 472.92 | 4.45 |
| 2 | 696.82 | 2,048 | 1,339.75 | 6.92 |
| 3 | 1,033.15 | 3,940 | 620.25 | 4.28 |
| 4 | 1,603.62 | 6,505 | 568.33 | 3.90 |
| 5 | 1,611.37 | 5,723 | 1,497.60 | 5.50 |
| 6 | 1,613.27 | 11,520 | 1,365.83 | 4.60 |
| 7 | 1,854.17 | 5,779 | 1,687.00 | 5.62 |
| 8 | 2,160.55 | 5,969 | 1,639.92 | 5.15 |
| 9 | 2,305.58 | 8,461 | 2,872.33 | 6.18 |
| 10 | 3,503.93 | 20,106 | 3,655.08 | 6.15 |
| 11 | 3,571.89 | 13,313 | 2,912.00 | 5.88 |
| 12 | 3,741.40 | 10,771 | 3,921.00 | 4.88 |
| 13 | 4,026.52 | 15,543 | 3,865.67 | 5.50 |
| 14 | 10,343.81 | 36,194 | 7,684.10 | 7.00 |
| 15 | 11,732.17 | 34,703 | 12,446.33 | 10.78 |
| 16 | 15,414.94 | 39,204 | 14,098.40 | 7.05 |
| 17 | 18,854.45 | 86,533 | 15,524.00 | 6.35 |

*Source: Procedures and Analysis for Staffing Standards Development: Regression Analysis Handbook* (San Diego, CA: Navy Manpower and Material Analysis Center, 1979).

to how many labor hours are needed. The navy selected hospitals 1 through 17 from hospitals that it thought were efficiently run and wishes to use a regression model based on efficiently run hospitals to evaluate the efficiency of questionable hospitals.

## Leverage Values

To interpret the diagnostics in Figure 5.20, we first identify outliers with respect to their $x$ values. One way to do this is to employ leverage values. The **leverage value** for an observation is the **distance value,** discussed in Section 4.6, and is used to calculate a prediction interval for the $y$ value of the observation. This value is a measure of the distance between the observation's $x$ values and the center of the experimental region. The leverage value is labeled as "Hat Diag H" on the SAS output and as "HI1" on the MINITAB output. **If the leverage value for an observation is large, the observation is outlying with respect to its $x$ values.** A *leverage value* is considered to be *large if it is greater than twice the average of all of the leverage values.* Note that twice this average can be shown to be equal to $2(k + 1)/n$. For example, since there are $n = 17$ observations in Table 5.5 and since the model

$$y = \beta_0 + \beta_1 x_1 + \beta_2 x_2 + \beta_3 x_3 + \varepsilon$$

utilizes $k = 3$ independent variables, twice the average leverage value is $2(k + 1)/n = 2(3 + 1)/17 = .4706$. Looking at Figure 5.20(a) and (b), we see that the leverage values for hospitals 15, 16, and 17 are, respectively, .682, .785, and .863. Since these leverage

**FIGURE 5.20** MINITAB and SAS output of the outlying and influential observation diagnostics for the model $y = \beta_0 + \beta_1 x_1 + \beta_2 x_2 + \beta_3 x_3 + \varepsilon$

|    | Xray | BedDays | Length | Hours | FITS1 | RESI1 | SRES1 | TRES1 | HI1 | COOK1 |
|----|------|---------|--------|-------|-------|-------|-------|-------|-----|-------|
| 1  | 2463  | 472.9   | 4.45  | 566.5   | 688.4   | -121.89 | -0.21144 | -0.20350 | 0.120749 | 0.00153 |
| 2  | 2048  | 1339.8  | 6.92  | 696.8   | 721.8   | -25.03  | -0.04628 | -0.04447 | 0.226128 | 0.00016 |
| 3  | 3940  | 620.3   | 4.28  | 1033.2  | 965.4   | 67.76   | 0.11814  | 0.11356  | 0.129664 | 0.00052 |
| 4  | 6505  | 568.3   | 3.90  | 1603.6  | 1172.5  | 431.16  | 0.76464  | 0.75174  | 0.158762 | 0.02759 |
| 5  | 5723  | 1497.6  | 5.50  | 1611.4  | 1526.8  | 84.59   | 0.14384  | 0.13830  | 0.084914 | 0.00048 |
| 6  | 11520 | 1365.8  | 4.60  | 1613.3  | 1993.9  | -380.60 | -0.65697 | -0.64194 | 0.112011 | 0.01361 |
| 7  | 5779  | 1687.0  | 5.62  | 1854.2  | 1676.6  | 177.61  | 0.30187  | 0.29105  | 0.084078 | 0.00209 |
| 8  | 5969  | 1639.9  | 5.15  | 2160.6  | 1791.4  | 369.14  | 0.62704  | 0.61176  | 0.083005 | 0.00890 |
| 9  | 8461  | 2872.3  | 6.18  | 2305.6  | 2798.8  | -493.18 | -0.83846 | -0.82827 | 0.084596 | 0.01624 |
| 10 | 20106 | 3655.1  | 6.15  | 3503.9  | 4191.3  | -687.40 | -1.19211 | -1.21359 | 0.120262 | 0.04857 |
| 11 | 13313 | 2912.0  | 5.88  | 3571.9  | 3191.0  | 380.93  | 0.64507  | 0.62993  | 0.077335 | 0.00872 |
| 12 | 10771 | 3921.0  | 4.88  | 3741.4  | 4364.5  | -623.10 | -1.11726 | -1.12900 | 0.177058 | 0.06714 |
| 13 | 15543 | 3865.7  | 5.50  | 4026.5  | 4364.2  | -337.71 | -0.56794 | -0.55255 | 0.064498 | 0.00556 |
| 14 | 36194 | 7684.1  | 7.00  | 10343.8 | 8713.3  | 1630.50 | 2.87070  | 4.55845  | 0.146451 | 0.35349 |
| 15 | 34703 | 12446.3 | 10.78 | 11732.2 | 12080.9 | -348.69 | -1.00542 | -1.00588 | 0.681763 | 0.54140 |
| 16 | 39204 | 14098.4 | 7.05  | 15414.9 | 15133.0 | 281.91  | 0.99006  | 0.98925  | 0.785480 | 0.89729 |
| 17 | 86533 | 15524.0 | 6.35  | 18854.5 | 19260.5 | -406.00 | -1.78584 | -1.97506 | 0.863247 | 5.03294 |

(a) MINITAB output

```
                Std Error    Student                          Cook's               Hat Diag
Obs   Residual  Residual    Residual   -2-1  0  1  2            D   RStudent        H
  1  -121.8894   576.5      -0.211    |         |           |   0.002   -0.2035    0.1207
  2   -25.0283   540.8      -0.0463   |         |           |   0.000   -0.0445    0.2261
  3    67.7570   573.5       0.118    |         |           |   0.001    0.1136    0.1297
  4   431.1560   563.9       0.765    |         | *         |   0.028    0.7517    0.1588
  5    84.5898   588.1       0.144    |         |           |   0.000    0.1383    0.0849
  6  -380.5990   579.3      -0.657    |       * |           |   0.014   -0.6419    0.1120
  7   177.6121   588.4       0.302    |         |           |   0.002    0.2911    0.0841
  8   369.1446   588.7       0.627    |         | *         |   0.009    0.6118    0.0830
  9  -493.1810   588.2      -0.838    |       * |           |   0.016   -0.8283    0.0846
 10  -687.4035   576.6      -1.192    |      ** |           |   0.049   -1.2136    0.1203
 11   380.9328   590.5       0.645    |         | *         |   0.009    0.6299    0.0773
 12  -623.1021   557.7      -1.117    |      ** |           |   0.067   -1.1290    0.1771
 13  -337.7088   594.6      -0.568    |       * |           |   0.006   -0.5526    0.0645
 14      1631    568.0       2.871    |         | ***** |   0.353    4.5584    0.1465
 15  -348.6937   346.8      -1.005    |      ** |           |   0.541   -1.0059    0.6818
 16   281.9136   284.7       0.990    |         | *         |   0.897    0.9892    0.7855
 17  -406.0026   227.3      -1.786    |     *** |           |   5.033   -1.9751    0.8632
```

(b) SAS output

values are greater than .4706, we conclude that *hospitals 15, 16, and 17 are outliers with respect to their x values.* This is because, as Table 5.5 shows, $x_1$ (monthly X-ray exposures) and $x_2$ (monthly occupied bed days) are substantially larger for hospitals 15, 16, and 17 than for hospitals 1 through 14. In other words, hospitals 15, 16, and 17 are substantially larger hospitals than hospitals 1 through 14.

## Residuals and Studentized Residuals

To identify outliers with respect to their $y$ values, we can use residuals. Any residual that is substantially different from the others is suspect. For example, note from Table 5.5 that hospital 14's values of Xray, BedDays, and Length are 36,194, 7684.1, and 7. Using the least squares point estimates for our model, it follows that the point prediction of labor hours for hospital 14 is

$$\hat{y}_{14} = 1523.3892 + .0530(36,194) + .9785(7684.1) - 320.9508(7)$$
$$= 8713.31$$

Since the actual number of labor hours for hospital 14 is $y_{14} = 10,343.81$, the residual $e_{14}$ for hospital 14 is the difference between $y_{14} = 10,343.81$ and $\hat{y}_{14} = 8713.31$, which is 1630.50. Figure 5.20 shows the residuals for all 17 hospitals. Since $e_{14} = 1630.50$ is much larger than the other residuals, it seems that hospital 14 used a number of labor hours that is much larger than predicted by the regression model. To obtain a somewhat more precise idea about whether an observation is an outlier with respect to its $y$ value, we can calculate the studentized residual for the observation. The **studentized residual** for an observation is the observation's residual divided by the residual's standard error. As a very rough rule of thumb, if the studentized residual for an observation is greater than 2 in absolute value, we have some evidence that the observation is an outlier with respect to its $y$ value. For example, since Figure 5.20 tells us that the studentized residual (see "Student Residual" on the SAS output and "SRES1" on the MINITAB output) for hospital 14 is 2.871, we have some evidence that hospital 14 is an outlier with respect to its $y$ value. (The formula for the residual's standard error, as well as the formulas for the other outlying and influential observation diagnostics discussed in this section, are given in an optional technical note at the end of this section.)

## Deleted Residuals and Studentized Deleted Residuals

Many statisticians feel that an excellent way to identify an outlier with respect to its $y$ value is to use the **PRESS, or deleted, residual.** To calculate the deleted residual for observation $i$, we subtract from $y_i$ the point prediction $\hat{y}_{(i)}$ computed using least squares point estimates based on all $n$ observations except for observation $i$. We do this because if observation $i$ is an outlier with respect to its $y$ value, using this observation to compute the usual least squares point estimates might "draw" the usual point prediction $\hat{y}_i$ toward $y_i$ and thus cause the resulting usual residual to be small. This would falsely imply that observation $i$ is not an outlier with respect to its $y$ value. For example, consider using observation 3 in Figure 5.19 to determine the least squares line. Doing this might draw the least squares line toward observation 3, causing the point prediction $\hat{y}_3$ given by the line to be near $y_3$ and thus the usual residual $y_3 - \hat{y}_3$ to be small. This would falsely imply that observation 3 is not an outlier with respect to its $y$ value. To illustrate more precisely the concept of the deleted residual, recall that hospital 14's values of Xray, BedDays, and Length are 36,194, 7684.1, and 7.

Furthermore, let $b_0^{(14)}, b_1^{(14)}, b_2^{(14)},$ and $b_3^{(14)}$ denote the least squares point estimates of $\beta_0, \beta_1, \beta_2$ and $\beta_3$ that are calculated by using all 17 observations in Table 5.5 except for observation 14. Then, it can be shown that the point prediction of $y_{14}$ using these least squares point estimates

$$\hat{y}_{(14)} = b_0^{(14)} + b_1^{(14)}(36,194) + b_2^{(14)}(7684.1) + b_3^{(14)}(7)$$

equals 8433.43. It follows that the deleted residual for hospital 14 is the difference between $y_{14} = 10,343.81$ and $\hat{y}_{(14)} = 8433.43$, which is 1910.38. Standard statistical software packages calculate the deleted residual for each observation and divide this residual by its standard error to form the **studentized deleted residual.** The studentized deleted residual is labeled as "RStudent" on the SAS output and as "TRES1" on the MINITAB output. Examining Figure 5.20, we see that the studentized deleted residual for hospital 14 is 4.558.

To evaluate the studentized deleted residual for an observation, we compare this quantity with two $t$-distribution points—$t_{[.025]}^{(n-(k+2))}$ and $t_{[.005]}^{(n-(k+2))}$. Specifically, if the studentized deleted residual is greater in absolute value than $t_{[.025]}^{(n-(k+2))}$, then there is *some evidence* that the observation is an outlier with respect to its $y$ value. If the studentized deleted residual is greater in absolute value than $t_{[.005]}^{(n-(k+2))}$, then there is *strong evidence* that the observation is an outlier with respect to its $y$ value. The data analysis experience of the authors leads us to suggest that one should not be overly concerned that an observation is an outlier with respect to its $y$ value unless the studentized deleted residual is greater in absolute value than $t_{[.005]}^{(n-(k+2))}$. For the hospital labor needs model, $n - (k + 2) = 17 - 3 - 2 = 12$, and therefore $t_{[.025]}^{(12)} = 2.179$ and $t_{[.005]}^{(12)} = 3.055$. The studentized deleted residual for hospital 14, which equals 4.558, is greater in absolute value than both $t_{[.025]}^{(12)} = 2.179$ and $t_{[.005]}^{(12)} = 3.055$. Therefore, we should be very concerned that *hospital 14 is an outlier with respect to its y value.*

## Cook's Distance Measure

One way to determine if an observation is influential is to calculate **Cook's distance measure,** which we sometimes refer to as **Cook's D,** or simply $D$. Cook's $D$ is labeled as "Cook's D" on the SAS output and as "Cook 1" on the MINITAB output in Figure 5.20. It can be shown that if Cook's $D$ for observation $i$ is large, then the least squares point estimates calculated by using all $n$ observations differ substantially (*as a group*) from the least squares point estimates calculated by using all $n$ observations except for observation $i$. This would say that observation $i$ is influential. To determine whether $D$ is large, we compare $D$ with two $F$-distribution points—$F_{[.80]}$, the 20th percentile of the $F$-distribution, and $F_{[.50]}$, the 50th percentile of the $F$-distribution—based on $(k + 1)$ numerator and $[n - (k + 1)]$ denominator degrees of freedom. If $D$ is less than $F_{[.80]}$, the observation should not be considered influential. If $D$ is greater than $F_{[.50]}$, the observation should be considered influential. If $D$ is between $F_{[.80]}$ and $F_{[.50]}$, then the nearer $D$ is to $F_{[.50]}$, the greater the influence of the observation. Examining Figure 5.20, we see that for observation 17 Cook's $D$ is 5.033 and is the largest value of Cook's $D$ on the output. This value of Cook's $D$ is greater than $F_{[.05]} = 3.18$, which is based on $k + 1 = 4$ numerator and $n - (k + 1) = 17 - 4 = 13$ denominator degrees of freedom. Since $F_{[.05]}$ is itself greater than $F_{[.50]}$, Cook's $D$ for observation 17 is greater than $F_{[.50]}$, which says that *removing hospital 17 from the data set would substantially change (as a group) the least squares point estimates* of the parameters $\beta_0, \beta_1, \beta_2,$ and $\beta_3$. Therefore, hospital 17 is *influential*.

In general, if we decide (by using Cook's $D$) that removing observation $i$ from the data set would substantially change (as a group) the least squares point estimates, we might wish to determine whether the point estimate of a particular parameter $\beta_j$ would change substantially. We might also wish to determine if the point prediction of $y_i$ would change substantially. In Exercises 5.17 and 5.18 we discuss how to make such determinations.

## What to Do about Outlying and Influential Observations

To illustrate how we deal with outlying and influential observations, we summarize what we have learned in the hospital labor needs case:

1.   Hospitals 15, 16, and 17, outliers with respect to their $x$ values, are larger than the other hospitals. Hospital 17 is influential in that removing it from the data set would substantially change (as a group) the least squares point estimates of the parameters $\beta_0, \beta_1, \beta_2,$ and $\beta_3$.

2.   Hospital 14 is an outlier with respect to its $y$ value. Furthermore, hospital 14 is influential in that, since its residual ($e_{14} = 1630.5$) is large, the sum of squared residuals and thus the standard error $s$ (which equals 614.779) are larger than they would be if hospital 14 were removed from the data set.

We recommend first dealing with outliers with respect to their $y$ values, because they affect the overall fit of the model. Often when we decide what to do with such outliers, other problems become much less important or disappear. In general, we should first check to see if the $y$ value in question was recorded correctly. If it was recorded incorrectly, it should be corrected and the regression should be rerun. If it cannot be corrected, the corresponding observation should be discarded and the regression should be rerun. We will assume that the labor hours for hospital 14 ($y_{14} = 10,343.8$) were recorded correctly.

If the $y$ value has been recorded correctly, we must search for a reason for it. The $y$ value could have resulted from a situation that we do not wish the regression model to describe. For example, the fact that $y_{14} = 10,343.8$ is substantially greater than the point prediction $\hat{y}_{14} = 8713.3$ might have resulted from a one-time disaster at the naval base—such as a fire on a ship—that we are not building a model to describe. We will assume there was no such disaster at the naval base. In this case—and in the absence of any other reason—we might conclude that $y_{14} = 10,343.8$ resulted from the fact that hospital 14 was run significantly more inefficiently than any other hospital. We should then talk to the administrative staff at hospital 14 and try to correct the problem. From the point of view of using the regression model to predict and evaluate labor needs for other hospitals, we would remove hospital 14 from the data set. This is because we do not wish the model to be based on a hospital that is run inefficiently. In the exercises we will consider the output of a regression analysis when we remove hospital 14 from the data set.

Before deciding, however, that hospital 14 has been run inefficiently, we should consider the possibility that our regression model does not contain an independent variable that would explain the seemingly large $y$ value. For example, we have seen that hospitals 15, 16, and 17 are "large" hospitals, and we note from Table 5.5 that hospital 14 is "fairly large." It is possible that there is an *inherent inefficiency* due to large hospitals. This would suggest using a *dummy variable* to model this inefficiency. Therefore, we might consider the model

$$y = \beta_0 + \beta_1 x_1 + \beta_2 x_2 + \beta_3 x_3 + \beta_4 D_L + \varepsilon$$

In this model the dummy variable $D_L$ equals 1 if we are considering a "large hospital" (hospitals 14, 15, 16, and 17) and equals 0 otherwise (hospitals 1 through 13). It follows that $\beta_4$ is an extra expected number of labor hours that is associated with the inefficiency of large hospitals. In the exercises we will consider the output of a regression analysis using this model. If we conclude that there is an important effect due to the inefficiency of large hospitals and that, given this effect, hospital 14 is no longer an outlier with respect to its $y$ value, then we would conclude that hospital 14 has not been run inefficiently and should remain in the data set.

## A Technical Note (Optional)

Suppose we perform a regression analysis of $n$ observations by using a regression model that utilizes $k$ independent variables. Let SSE and $s$ denote the unexplained variation and the standard error for the regression model. Also, let $h_i$ and $e_i = y_i - \hat{y}_i$ denote the leverage value and the usual residual for observation $i$. Then, the standard error of the residual $e_i$ can be proven to equal $s\sqrt{1 - h_i}$. This implies that the *studentized residual* for observation $i$ equals $e_i/(s\sqrt{1 - h_i})$. Furthermore, let $d_i = y_i - \hat{y}_{(i)}$ denote the **deleted residual** for observation $i$, and let $s_{d_i}$ denote the standard error of $d_i$. Then, it can be shown that the **deleted residual** $d_i$ and the **studentized deleted residual** $d_i/s_{d_i}$ can be calculated by using the equations

$$d_i = \frac{e_i}{1 - h_i} \quad \text{and} \quad \frac{d_i}{s_{d_i}} = e_i\left[\frac{n - k - 2}{\text{SSE}(1 - h_i) - e_i^2}\right]^{1/2}$$

Finally, if $D_i$ denotes the value of the Cook's $D$ statistic for observation $i$, it can be proven that

$$D_i = \frac{e_i^2}{(k + 1)s^2}\left[\frac{h_i}{(1 - h_i)^2}\right]$$

# Exercises

**5.1** Table 5.5 presents data concerning the need for labor in 17 U.S. Navy hospitals. This table gives values of the dependent variable Hours (monthly labor hours) and of the independent variables Xray (monthly X-ray exposures), BedDays (monthly occupied bed days—a hospital has one occupied bed day if one bed is occupied for an entire day), and Length (average length of patients' stay, in days). The data in Table 5.5 are part of a larger data set analyzed by the navy. The complete data set consists of two additional independent variables—Load (average daily patient load) and Pop (eligible population in the area, in thousands)—values of which are given in Table 5.6. Figure 5.21 (page 262) gives MINITAB and SAS output of multicollinearity analysis and model building for the complete hospital labor needs data set.

a. Find the three largest simple correlation coefficients between the independent variables in Figure 5.21(a). Also, find the three largest variance inflation factors in Figure 5.21(b).

b. Based on your answers to part (a), which independent variables are most strongly involved in multicollinearity?

c. Do any least squares point estimates have a sign (positive or negative) that is different from what we would intuitively expect—another indication of multicollinearity?

d. The p-value associated with $F$(model) for the model in Figure 5.21(b) is less than .0001. In general, if the p-value associated with $F$(model) is much smaller than all of the p-values associated with the independent variables, this is another indication of multicollinearity. Is this true in this situation?

e. Figure 5.21(c) and (d) indicate that the two best hospital labor needs models are the model using Xray, BedDays, Pop, and Length, which we will call Model 2, and the model using Xray, BedDays, and Length, which we will call Model 1. Which model gives the smallest value of $s$ and the largest

**TABLE 5.6** Values of Load and Pop

| Hospital | Load ($x_4$) | Pop ($x_5$) |
|---|---|---|
| 1 | 15.57 | 18.0 |
| 2 | 44.02 | 9.5 |
| 3 | 20.42 | 12.8 |
| 4 | 18.74 | 36.7 |
| 5 | 49.20 | 35.7 |
| 6 | 44.92 | 24.0 |
| 7 | 55.48 | 43.3 |
| 8 | 59.28 | 46.7 |
| 9 | 94.39 | 78.7 |
| 10 | 128.02 | 180.5 |
| 11 | 96.00 | 60.9 |
| 12 | 131.42 | 103.7 |
| 13 | 127.21 | 126.8 |
| 14 | 252.90 | 157.7 |
| 15 | 409.20 | 169.4 |
| 16 | 463.70 | 331.4 |
| 17 | 510.22 | 371.6 |

value of $\bar{R}^2$? Which model gives the smallest value of $C$? Consider a questionable hospital for which Xray = 56,194, BedDays = 14,077.88, Pop = 329.7, and Length = 6.89. The 95% prediction intervals given by Models 1 and 2 for labor hours corresponding to this combination of values of the independent variables are, respectively, [14,511, 17,618], and [14,460, 17,601]. Which model gives the shortest prediction interval? Consider Figure 5.22 (page 263). Which model is chosen by both stepwise regression and backward elimination? Overall, which model seems best?

**FIGURE 5.21 (for Exercise 5.1)** MINITAB and SAS output of multicollinearity analysis and model building for the hospital labor needs data for 17 hospitals

```
              Xray   BedDays   Length     Load      Pop
BedDays      0.907
             0.000
                            Cell Contents:  Pearson correlation
                                               P-Value
Length       0.447    0.671
             0.072    0.003

Load         0.907    1.000    0.671
             0.000    0.000    0.003

Pop          0.910    0.933    0.463    0.936
             0.000    0.000    0.061    0.000

Hours        0.945    0.986    0.579    0.986    0.940
             0.000    0.000    0.015    0.000    0.000
```
(a) The MINITAB output of a correlation matrix

```
Predictor      Coef    SE Coef       T       P      VIF
Constant       1963       1071    1.83   0.094
Xray        0.05593    0.02126    2.63   0.023      7.9
BedDays       1.590      3.092    0.51   0.617   8933.1
Length       -394.3      209.6   -1.88   0.087      4.3
Load         -15.85      97.65   -0.16   0.874   9597.6
Pop          -4.219      7.177   -0.59   0.569     23.3
```
(b) The MINITAB output of the variance inflation factors

```
                          R-Square Selection Method

Number in            Adjusted                        Root
  Model    R-Square   R-Square       C(p)             MSE   Variables in Model

    1       0.9722     0.9703     20.3812       957.85555   BedDays
   ----------------------------------------------------------------------------
    2       0.9867     0.9848      4.9416       685.16852   Xray BedDays
   ----------------------------------------------------------------------------
    3       0.9901     0.9878      2.9177       614.77942   Xray BedDays Length
   ----------------------------------------------------------------------------
    4       0.9908     0.9877      4.0263       615.48868   Xray BedDays Length Pop
   ----------------------------------------------------------------------------
    5       0.9908     0.9867      6.0000       642.08838   Xray BedDays Length Load Pop
```
(c) The SAS output of the best single model of each size

```
                       Adjusted R-Square Selection Method

Number in   Adjusted                               Root
  Model     R-Square   R-Square       C(p)          MSE    Variables in Model

    3        0.9878     0.9901      2.9177     614.77942   Xray BedDays Length
    4        0.9877     0.9908      4.0263     615.48868   Xray BedDays Length Pop
    4        0.9875     0.9906      4.2643     622.09422   Xray Length Load Pop
    4        0.9874     0.9905      4.3456     624.33413   Xray BedDays Length Load
    3        0.9870     0.9894      3.7142     634.99196   Xray Length Load
```
(d) The SAS output of the best five models

**FIGURE 5.22 (for Exercise 5.1)** MINITAB output of a stepwise regression and a backward elimination of the hospital labor needs data

| Step | 1 | 2 | 3 |
|---|---|---|---|
| Constant | -28.13 | -68.31 | 1523.39 |
| | | | |
| BedDays | 1.117 | 0.823 | 0.978 |
| T-Value | 22.90 | 9.92 | 9.31 |
| P-Value | 0.000 | 0.000 | 0.000 |
| | | | |
| Xray | | 0.075 | 0.053 |
| T-Value | | 3.91 | 2.64 |
| P-Value | | 0.002 | 0.021 |
| | | | |
| Length | | | -321 |
| T-Value | | | -2.10 |
| P-Value | | | 0.056 |
| | | | |
| S | 958 | 685 | 615 |
| R-Sq | 97.22 | 98.67 | 99.01 |
| R-Sq(adj) | 97.03 | 98.48 | 98.78 |
| Mallows C-p | 20.4 | 4.9 | 2.9 |

(a) Stepwise regression ($\alpha_{entry} - \alpha_{stay} - .10$)

| Step | 1 | 2 | 3 |
|---|---|---|---|
| Constant | 1963 | 2032 | 1523 |
| | | | |
| Xray | 0.056 | 0.056 | 0.053 |
| T-Value | 2.63 | 2.75 | 2.64 |
| P-Value | 0.023 | 0.017 | 0.021 |
| | | | |
| BedDays | 1.59 | 1.09 | 0.98 |
| T-Value | 0.51 | 7.10 | 9.31 |
| P-Value | 0.617 | 0.000 | 0.000 |
| | | | |
| Length | -394 | -410 | -321 |
| T-Value | -1.88 | -2.30 | -2.10 |
| P-Value | 0.087 | 0.040 | 0.056 |
| | | | |
| Load | -16 | | |
| T-Value | -0.16 | | |
| P-Value | 0.874 | | |
| | | | |
| Pop | -4.2 | -5.0 | |
| T-Value | -0.59 | -0.98 | |
| P-Value | 0.569 | 0.344 | |
| | | | |
| S | 642 | 615 | 615 |
| R-Sq | 99.08 | 99.08 | 99.01 |
| R-Sq(adj) | 98.67 | 98.77 | 98.78 |
| Mallows C-p | 6.0 | 4.0 | 2.9 |

(b) Backward elimination ($\alpha_{stay} = .10$)

**5.2** Market Planning, Inc., a marketing research firm, has obtained the prescription sales data in Table 5.7 (page 264) for $n = 20$ independent pharmacies.* In this table $y$ is the average weekly prescription sales over the past year (in units of $1000), $x_1$ is the floor space (in square feet), $x_2$ is the percentage of floor space allocated to the prescription department, $x_3$ is

the number of parking spaces available to the store, $x_4$ is the weekly per capita income for the surrounding community (in units of $100), and $x_5$ is a *dummy variable* that equals 1 if the pharmacy is located in a shopping center and 0 otherwise. Use the SAS and MINITAB output in Figure 5.23 (page 265) to discuss why the model using FloorSp and PresPct might be the best model describing prescription sales. The least squares point estimates of the parameters of this model can be calculated to be $b_0 = 48.2909$, $b_1 = -.003842$, and $b_2 = -.5819$.

Discuss what $b_1$ and $b_2$ say about obtaining high prescription sales.

* This problem is taken from an example in L. Ott, *An Introduction to Statistical Methods and Data Analysis*, 2nd ed. (Boston: PWS-KENT Publishing Company, 1987). Used with permission.

**TABLE 5.7 (for Exercise 5.2)** Prescription Sales Data

| Pharmacy | Sales, $y$ | Floor Space, $x_1$ | Prescription Percentage, $x_2$ | Parking, $x_3$ | Income, $x_4$ | Shopping Center, $x_5$ |
|----------|------------|---------------------|-------------------------------|----------------|---------------|------------------------|
| 1  | 22 | 4900 | 9  | 40 | 18 | 1 |
| 2  | 19 | 5800 | 10 | 50 | 20 | 1 |
| 3  | 24 | 5000 | 11 | 55 | 17 | 1 |
| 4  | 28 | 4400 | 12 | 30 | 19 | 0 |
| 5  | 18 | 3850 | 13 | 42 | 10 | 0 |
| 6  | 21 | 5300 | 15 | 20 | 22 | 1 |
| 7  | 29 | 4100 | 20 | 25 | 8  | 0 |
| 8  | 15 | 4700 | 22 | 60 | 15 | 1 |
| 9  | 12 | 5600 | 24 | 45 | 16 | 1 |
| 10 | 14 | 4900 | 27 | 82 | 14 | 1 |
| 11 | 18 | 3700 | 28 | 56 | 12 | 0 |
| 12 | 19 | 3800 | 31 | 38 | 8  | 0 |
| 13 | 15 | 2400 | 36 | 35 | 6  | 0 |
| 14 | 22 | 1800 | 37 | 28 | 4  | 0 |
| 15 | 13 | 3100 | 40 | 43 | 6  | 0 |
| 16 | 16 | 2300 | 41 | 20 | 5  | 0 |
| 17 | 8  | 4400 | 42 | 46 | 7  | 1 |
| 18 | 6  | 3300 | 42 | 15 | 4  | 0 |
| 19 | 7  | 2900 | 45 | 30 | 9  | 1 |
| 20 | 17 | 2400 | 46 | 16 | 3  | 0 |

*Source: From Introduction to Statistical Methods and Data Analysis, Second Edition,* by L. Ott. © 1984.
Reprinted with permission of Brooks/Cole, an imprint of the Wadsworth Group, a division of Thomson
Learning. Fax 800-730-2215.

**5.3** Recall from Example 5.1 that we have concluded that perhaps the best sales territory performance model using only linear terms is the model using TIME, MKTPOTEN, ADVER, MKTSHARE, and CHANGE. For this model, $s = 430.23$ and $\overline{R}^2 = .893$. To decide which squared and pairwise interaction terms should be added to this model, we consider all possible squares and pairwise interactions of the five linear independent variables in this model. Figure 5.24 (page 266) gives the MINITAB notation for these squares and pairwise interactions so that we can better understand the next figure.

Consider having MINITAB evaluate all possible models involving these squared and pairwise interaction terms, where the five linear terms TIME, MKTPOTEN, ADVER, MKTSHARE, and CHANGE are included in each possible model. If we have MINITAB do this and find the best single model of each size, we obtain the output in Figure 5.25 (page 266). The model using 12 squared and pairwise interaction terms has the smallest $s$. However, if we desire a somewhat simpler model, note that $s$ does not increase substantially until we move from a model having seven squared and pairwise interaction terms to a model having six such

(Continues on page 266)

**FIGURE 5.23 (for Exercise 5.2)** SAS and MINITAB output for the prescription sales data

R-Square Selection Method

| Number in Model | R-Square | Adjusted R-Square | C(p) | Root MSE | Variables in Model |
|---|---|---|---|---|---|
| 1 | 0.4393 | 0.4082 | 10.1709 | 4.83511 | PresPct |
| 2 | 0.6657 | 0.6263 | 1.6062 | 3.84200 | FloorSp PresPct |
| 3 | 0.6907 | 0.6327 | 2.4364 | 3.80893 | FloorSp PresPct ShopCtr |
| 4 | 0.6987 | 0.6184 | 4.0623 | 3.88253 | FloorSp PresPct Parking ShopCtr |
| 5 | 0.7001 | 0.5930 | 6.0000 | 4.00990 | FloorSp PresPct Parking Income ShopCtr |

(a) The SAS output of the single best model of each size

| Predictor | Coef | SE Coef | T | P |
|---|---|---|---|---|
| Constant | 48.291 | 6.890 | 7.01 | 0.000 |
| Floor3p | -0.003842 | 0.001133 | -3.39 | 0.003 |
| PresPct | -0.5819 | 0.1026 | -5.67 | 0.000 |

(b) The MINITAB output of the model
$y = \beta_0 + \beta_1 x_1 + \beta_2 x_2 + \varepsilon$

| Predictor | Coef | SE Coef | T | P |
|---|---|---|---|---|
| Constant | 42.827 | 8.348 | 5.13 | 0.000 |
| Floor3p | -0.002473 | 0.001645 | -1.50 | 0.152 |
| PresPct | -0.5294 | 0.1117 | -4.74 | 0.000 |
| ShopCtr | -3.038 | 2.668 | -1.14 | 0.272 |

(c) The MINITAB output of the model
$y = \beta_0 + \beta_1 x_1 + \beta_2 x_2 + \beta_3 x_5 + \varepsilon$

**FIGURE 5.24 (for Exercise 5.3)** Squared terms and pairwise interaction terms for the sales territory performance problem

```
SQT   = TIME*TIME              TC    = TIME*CHANGE
SQMP  = MKTPOTEN*MKTPOTEN      MPA   = MKTPOTEN*ADVER
SQA   = ADVER*ADVER            MPMS  = MKTPOTEN*MKTSHARE
SQMS  = MKTSHARE*MKTSHARE      MPC   = MKTPOTEN*CHANGE
SQC   = CHANGE*CHANGE          AMS   = ADVER*MKTSHARE
TMP   = TIME*MKTPOTEN          AC    = ADVER*CHANGE
TA    = TIME*ADVER             MSC   = MKTSHARE*CHANGE
TMS   = TIME*MKTSHARE
```

**FIGURE 5.25 (for Exercise 5.3)** MINITAB output of sales territory performance models with squared and interaction terms

The following variables are included in all models: TIME MKTPOTEN ADVER MKTSHARE CHANGE

```
                                       S     S                    M
                                    S  Q  S  Q  S  T     T        M  P  M  A        M
                                    Q  M  Q  M  Q  M  T  M  T  P  M  P  M  A        S
  Vars  R-Sq  R-Sq(adj)   C-p    S     T  P  A  S  C  P  A  S  C  A  S  C  S  C  C
    1   94.2    92.2     43.2  365.87                       X
    2   95.8    94.1     29.7  318.19  X                    X
    3   96.5    94.7     25.8  301.61  X                    X     X
    4   97.0    95.3     22.5  285.53  X              X  X        X
    5   97.5    95.7     20.3  272.05  X              X  X        X     X
    6   98.1    96.5     16.4  244.00  X        X     X  X        X           X
    7   98.7    97.4     13.0  210.70  X  X           X  X        X     X  X
    8   99.0    97.8     12.3  193.95  X  X        X  X  X        X     X  X
    9   99.2    98.0     12.7  185.44  X  X     X     X  X        X     X  X  X
   10   99.3    98.2     13.3  175.70  X  X     X     X  X        X  X  X  X  X
   11   99.4    98.2     14.6  177.09  X  X     X     X  X  X  X  X  X  X  X
   12   99.5    98.2     15.8  174.60  X  X     X  X  X  X  X     X  X  X  X
   13   99.5    98.1     17.5  183.22  X  X  X     X  X  X  X  X  X  X  X  X
   14   99.6    97.9     19.1  189.77  X  X     X  X  X  X  X  X  X  X  X  X  X
   15   99.6    97.4     21.0  210.78  X  X  X  X  X  X  X  X  X  X  X  X  X  X  X
```

terms. It can also be verified that the model having seven squared and pairwise interaction terms is the largest model for which all of the independent variables have *p*-values less than .05. Therefore, we might consider this model to have an optimal mix of a small *s* and simplicity. Identify *s* and $\overline{R}^2$ for this model. How do the *s* and $\overline{R}^2$ values you have identified compare with those for the model using only the linear terms TIME, MKTPOTEN, ADVER, MKTSHARE, and CHANGE (Figure 4.7 on page 153)?

**5.4** Recall that Table 3.4 gives the residuals from the simple linear regression model relating weekly fuel consumption to average hourly temperature. Figure 5.26 gives the Excel output of a plot of these residuals versus average hourly temperature. Describe the appearance of this plot. Does the plot indicate any violations of the regression assumptions?

**FIGURE 5.26 (for Exercise 5.4)** Excel residual plot

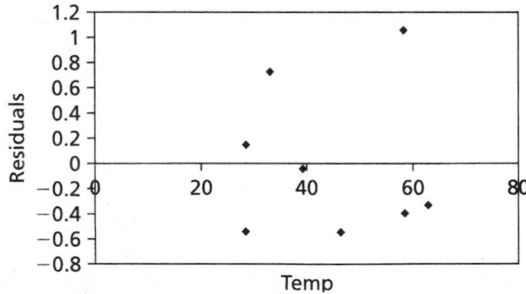

**5.5** Figure 5.27 (page 267) gives the MINITAB output of residual diagnostics that are obtained when the simple linear regression model is fit to the Fresh detergent demand data in Exercise 3.9. Interpret the

**FIGURE 5.27 (for Exercise 5.5)** MINITAB residual diagnostics for the Fresh detergent demand data

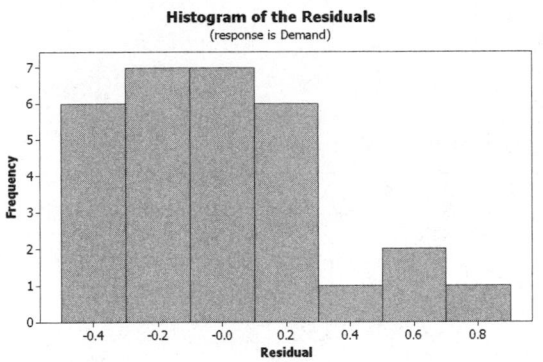

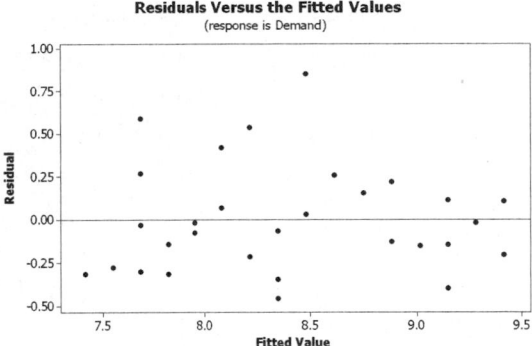

## Normal Probability Plot of the Residuals
(response is Demand)

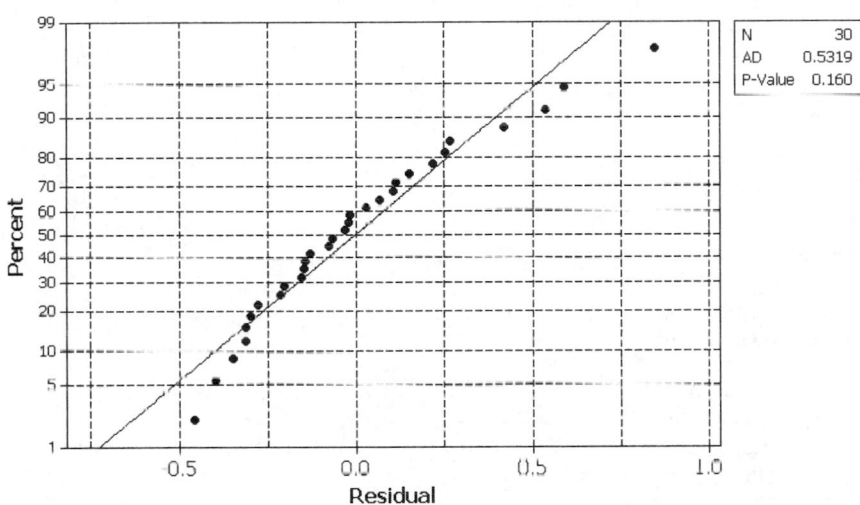

diagnostics and determine if they indicate any violations of the regression assumptions.

**5.6** Recall that Figure 3.17 gives the SAS output of a simple linear regression analysis of the service time data in Exercise 3.5. The residuals given by this model are shown in Table 5.8 (page 268), and MINITAB output of residual plots versus $x$ and $\hat{y}$ is given in Figure 5.28 (page 268). Do the plots indicate any violations of the regression assumptions?

**5.7** Table 5.8 (page 268) gives the residuals from the simple linear regression model describing the service time data in Exercise 3.5.

a. In this exercise we construct a normal plot of the residuals from the simple linear regression model. To construct this plot, we must first arrange the residuals in order from smallest to largest. These ordered residuals are given in Table 5.9 (page 269). Denoting the $i$th ordered residual as $e_{(i)}(i = 1, 2, \ldots, 11)$, we next compute for each value of $i$ the point $p_{(i)}$. These computations are summarized in Table 5.9. Show how $p_{(4)} = 32.35$ and $p_{(10)} = 85.29$ have been obtained.

b. The ordered residuals (the $e_{(i)}$ values) are plotted against the $p_{(i)}$ values on the MINITAB output of

**TABLE 5.8 (for Exercises 5.6 and 5.7)**
**Residuals for the Service Time Model**

| Observation | Minutes | Predicted | Residual |
|---|---|---|---|
| 1 | 109.0 | 109.9 | −0.9 |
| 2 | 58.0 | 60.7 | −2.7 |
| 3 | 138.0 | 134.5 | 3.5 |
| 4 | 189.0 | 183.7 | 5.3 |
| 5 | 37.0 | 36.1 | 0.9 |
| 6 | 82.0 | 85.3 | −3.3 |
| 7 | 103.0 | 109.9 | −6.9 |
| 8 | 134.0 | 134.5 | −0.5 |
| 9 | 68.0 | 60.7 | 7.3 |
| 10 | 112.0 | 109.9 | 2.1 |
| 11 | 154.0 | 159.1 | −5.1 |

Figure 5.28(c). Does this figure indicate a violation of the normality assumption?

**5.8** A simple linear regression model is employed to analyze the 24 monthly observations of sales and advertising given in Table 5.10 (page 269). Residuals are computed and are plotted versus time. The resulting residual plot is shown in Figure 5.29 (page 269). Discuss why the residual plot suggests the existence of positive autocorrelation.

**5.9** Table 5.11 (page 270) presents data concerning the time, $y$, required to perform service and the number of desktop computers serviced, $x$, for 15 service calls. Figure 5.30(a) (page 270) gives a plot of $y$ versus $x$, and Figure 5.31 (page 270) gives the Excel output of a simple linear regression relating $y$ to $x$. Furthermore, Figure 5.30(b) gives the Excel output of a plot of the residuals versus $x$ for the simple linear regression model. Using Figures 5.30(a) and (b), discuss why the constant variance assumption seems to be violated.

**5.10** It can be verified that if we take the square root, quartic root, and natural logarithmic transformations of the service times and plot the transformed values versus the numbers of desktop computers serviced, the natural logarithmic transformation seems to best equalize the error variance. Figure 5.32(a) (page 271) gives a plot of the natural logarithms of the service times versus the numbers of desktop computers

**FIGURE 5.28 (for Exercises 5.6 and 5.7)**
MINITAB residual plots for the service time model

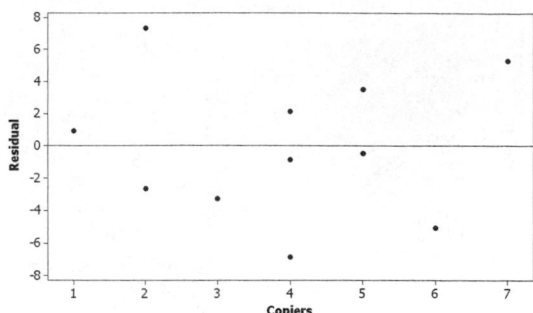

(a) Plot of the residuals versus number of copiers serviced

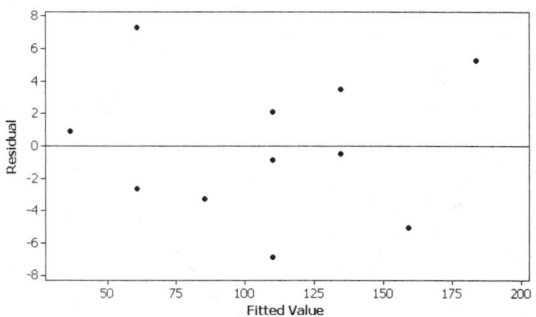

(b) Plot of the residuals versus predicted service time (in minutes)

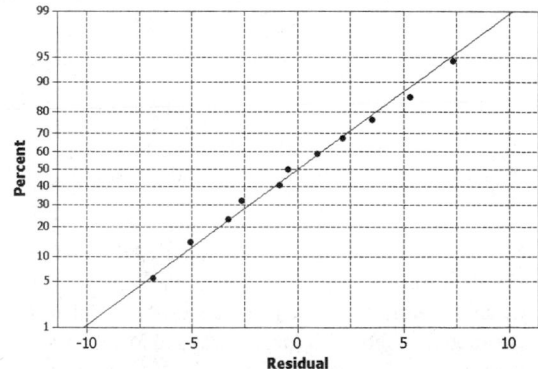

(c) Normal plot of the residuals

serviced, and Figure 5.33 (page 272) gives the SAS output of a regression analysis of the service time data by using the model $y^* = \beta_0 + \beta_1 x + \varepsilon$ where $y^* = \ln y$.

(Continues on page 270)

**TABLE 5.9 (for Exercise 5.7)** Ordered
Residuals and Normal Plot Calculations

| $i$ | Ordered Residual, $e_{(i)}$ | $\dfrac{3i-1}{3n+1}$ | $p_{(i)}$ |
|---|---|---|---|
| 1 | −6.9 | .0588 | 5.88 |
| 2 | −5.1 | .1470 | 14.20 |
| 3 | −3.3 | .2353 | 23.53 |
| 4 | −2.7 | .3235 | 32.35 |
| 5 | −0.9 | .4118 | 41.18 |
| 6 | −0.5 | .5000 | 50.00 |
| 7 | 0.9 | .5882 | 58.82 |
| 8 | 2.1 | .6765 | 67.65 |
| 9 | 3.5 | .7647 | 76.47 |
| 10 | 5.3 | .8529 | 85.29 |
| 11 | 7.3 | .9412 | 94.12 |

**FIGURE 5.29 (for Exercise 5.8)** Residual plot

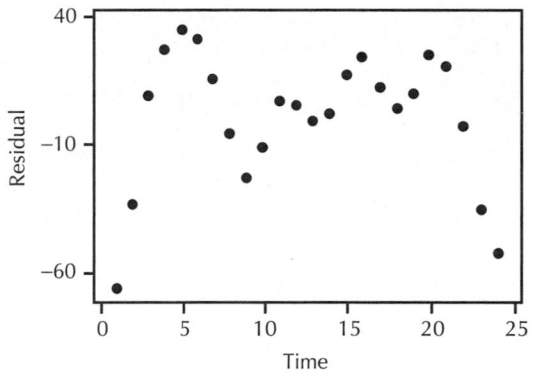

**TABLE 5.10 (for Exercise 5.8)** Sales and Advertising Data

| Month | Monthly Total Sales, $y$ | Advertising Expenditures, $x$ | Month | Monthly Total Sales, $y$ | Advertising Expenditures, $x$ |
|---|---|---|---|---|---|
| 1 | 202.66 | 116.44 | 13 | 260.51 | 129.85 |
| 2 | 232.91 | 119.58 | 14 | 266.34 | 122.65 |
| 3 | 272.07 | 125.74 | 15 | 281.24 | 121.64 |
| 4 | 290.97 | 124.55 | 16 | 286.19 | 127.24 |
| 5 | 299.09 | 122.35 | 17 | 271.97 | 132.35 |
| 6 | 296.95 | 120.44 | 18 | 265.01 | 130.86 |
| 7 | 279.49 | 123.24 | 19 | 274.44 | 122.90 |
| 8 | 255.75 | 127.55 | 20 | 291.81 | 117.15 |
| 9 | 242.78 | 121.19 | 21 | 290.91 | 109.47 |
| 10 | 255.34 | 118.00 | 22 | 264.95 | 114.34 |
| 11 | 271.58 | 121.81 | 23 | 228.40 | 123.72 |
| 12 | 268.27 | 126.54 | 24 | 209.33 | 130.33 |

*Source: Forecasting Methods and Applications*, "Sales and Advertising Data," by S. Makridakis, S. C. Wheelwright, and V. E. McGee, *Forecasting: Methods and Applications* (Copyright © 1983 John Wiley & Sons, Inc.). Reprinted by permission of John Wiley & Sons, Inc.

**TABLE 5.11 (for Exercises 5.9, 5.10, and 5.11)**
**Service Time Data for 15 Service Calls**

| Service Time, $y$ (Minutes) | Number of Desktop Computers Serviced, $x$ |
|---|---|
| 92 | 3 |
| 63 | 2 |
| 126 | 6 |
| 247 | 8 |
| 49 | 2 |
| 90 | 4 |
| 119 | 5 |
| 114 | 6 |
| 67 | 2 |
| 115 | 4 |
| 188 | 6 |
| 298 | 11 |
| 77 | 3 |
| 151 | 10 |
| 27 | 1 |

**FIGURE 5.30 (for Exercises 5.9 and 5.10)** The data plot and residual plot for the service time data

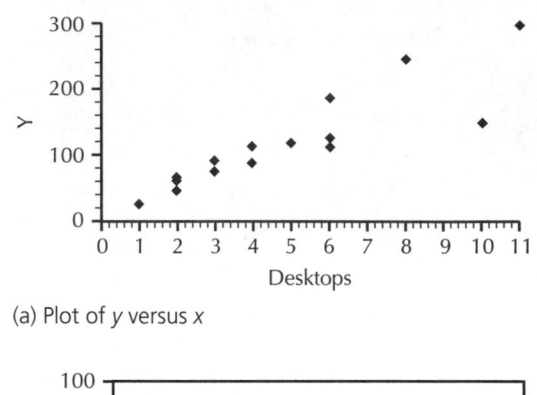

(a) Plot of $y$ versus $x$

(b) The Excel residual plot

**FIGURE 5.31 (for Exercise 5.9)** Excel output of a simple linear regression analysis of the service time data in Table 5.11

**Regression Statistics**

| | |
|---|---|
| Multiple R | 0.890796713 |
| R Square | 0.793518784 |
| Adjusted R Square | 0.777635614 |
| Standard Error | 34.91277748 |
| Observations | 15 |

**ANOVA**

| | df | SS | MS | F | Significance F |
|---|---|---|---|---|---|
| Regression | 1 | 60896.00693 | 60896.00693 | 49.95972225 | 8.43917E-06 |
| Residual | 13 | 15845.72641 | 1218.902031 | | |
| Total | 14 | 76741.73333 | | | |

| | Coefficients | Standard Error | t Stat | P-value | Lower 95% | Upper 95% |
|---|---|---|---|---|---|---|
| Intercept | 14.43054083 | 17.63137142 | 0.818458218 | 0.427844007 | −23.65971402 | 52.52079567 |
| Desktops | 22.00742312 | 3.113573955 | 7.068219171 | 8.43917E-06 | 15.28095683 | 28.7338894 |

a. The bottom of the SAS output in Figure 5.33 on page 272 corresponds to a future service call on which seven desktop computers will be serviced. Find a point prediction of and a 95% prediction interval for (1) $y^*$ for the service call and (2) the actual service time for the service call.

b. A plot of the model's residuals versus $x$ is given in Figure 5.32(b) on page 271. What problem is indicated by the residual plot?

**5.11** Consider the simple linear regression model describing the service time data in Table 5.11.

**FIGURE 5.32 (for Exercises 5.10 and 5.11)** The data plot and residual plots

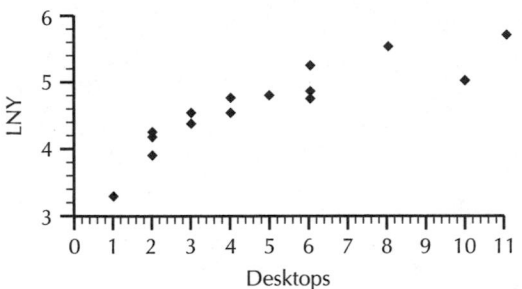

(a) Plot of natural logarithm of *y* versus *x*

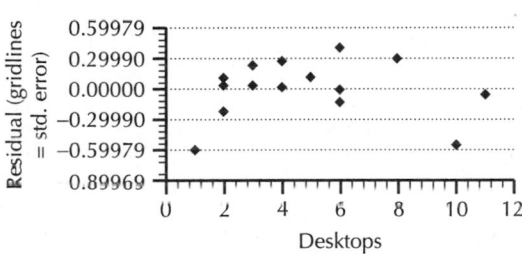

(b) The residual plot for Exercise 5.10

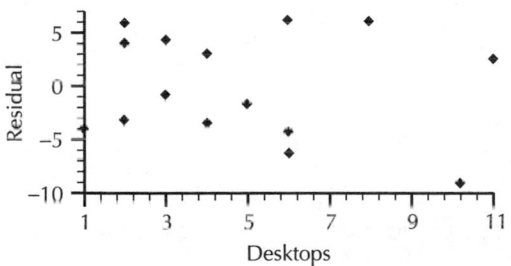

(c) The residual plot for Exercise 5.11

Figure 5.30(b) (page 270) shows that the residual plot versus $x$ for this model fans out, indicating that the error term $\varepsilon$ tends to become larger in magnitude as $x$ increases. To remedy this violation of the constant variance assumption, we divide all terms in the simple linear regression model by $x$. This gives the transformed model

$$\frac{y}{x} = \beta_0\left(\frac{1}{x}\right) + \beta_1 + \frac{\varepsilon}{x}$$

or equivalently

$$\frac{y}{x} = \beta_0 + \beta_1\left(\frac{1}{x}\right) + \frac{\varepsilon}{x}$$

Figure 5.34 (page 272) and Figure 5.32(c) (on this page) give a regression output and a residual plot versus $x$ for this model.

a. Does the residual plot indicate that the constant variance assumption holds for the transformed model?

b. Consider a future service call on which seven desktop computers will be serviced. Let $\mu_0$ represent the mean service time for all service calls on which seven desktop computers will be serviced, and let $y_0$ represent the actual service time for an individual service call on which seven desktop computers will be serviced. The bottom of the SAS output in Figure 5.34 tells us that

$$\frac{\hat{y}}{7} = 24.0406 + 6.7642\left(\frac{1}{7}\right) = 25.0069$$

is a point estimate of $\mu_0/7$ and a point prediction of $y_0/7$. Multiply this result by 7 to obtain $\hat{y}$. Multiply the ends of the confidence interval and prediction interval shown on the SAS output by 7. This will give a 95% confidence interval for $\mu_0$ and a 95% prediction interval for $y_0$. If the number of minutes we will allow for the future service call is the upper limit of the 95% confidence interval for $\mu_0$, how many minutes will we allow?

**5.12** Recall that Table 4.6 gives values for $n = 30$ sales periods of demand for Fresh liquid laundry detergent ($y$), price difference ($x_4$), and advertising expenditure ($x_3$).

a. Figure 5.35(a) (page 273) gives the residual plot versus $x_3$ that is obtained when the regression model relating $y$ to $x_4$ and $x_3$ is used to analyze the Fresh detergent data. Discuss why the residual plot indicates that we should add $x_3^2$ to the model.

b. Figure 5.35(b) gives the residual plot versus $x_3$ when the regression model relating to $y$ to $x_4$, $x_3$, and $x_3^2$ is used to analyze the Fresh detergent data. Discuss why the residual plot indicates that we now have the correct functional form.

**5.13** Consider the quadratic regression model describing the QHIC data. Figure 5.18 (page 253) shows that the residual plot versus $x$ for this model

(Continues on page 273)

**FIGURE 5.33 (for Exercise 5.10)** SAS output of a regression analysis of the service time data in Table 5.11 using the model $y^* = \beta_0 + \beta_1 x + \varepsilon$ where $y^* = \ln y$

Analysis of Variance

| Source | DF | Sum of Squares | Mean Square | F Value | Pr > F |
|---|---|---|---|---|---|
| Model | 1 | 4.20324 | 4.20324 | 46.73 | <.0001 |
| Error | 13 | 1.16920 | 0.08994 | | |
| Corrected Total | 14 | 5.37243 | | | |

| | | |
|---|---|---|
| Root MSE | 0.29990 | R-Square 0.7824 |
| Dependent Mean | 4.63051 | Adj R-Sq 0.7656 |
| Coeff Var | 6.47655 | |

Parameter Estimates

| Variable | Label | DF | Parameter Estimate | Standard Error | t Value | Pr > \|t\| |
|---|---|---|---|---|---|---|
| Intercept | Intercept | 1 | 3.74070 | 0.15145 | 24.70 | <.0001 |
| Desktops | Desktops | 1 | 0.18284 | 0.02675 | 6.84 | <.0001 |

| Obs | Dep Var LNY | Predicted Value | Std Error Mean Predict | 95% CL Mean | | 95% CL Predict | |
|---|---|---|---|---|---|---|---|
| 16 | . | 5.0206 | 0.0962 | 4.8128 | 5.2284 | 4.3402 | 5.7010 |

**FIGURE 5.34 (for Exercise 5.11)** SAS output of a regression analysis of the service time data in Table 5.11 using the model $y/x = \beta_0 + \beta_1(1/x) + \varepsilon/x$

Analysis of Variance

| Source | DF | Sum of Squares | Mean Square | F Value | Pr > F |
|---|---|---|---|---|---|
| Model | 1 | 36.26846 | 36.26846 | 1.36 | 0.2640 |
| Error | 13 | 345.88574 | 26.60660 | | |
| Corrected Total | 14 | 382.15420 | | | |

| | | |
|---|---|---|
| Root MSE | 5.15816 | R-Square 0.0949 |
| Dependent Mean | 26.15217 | Adj R-Sq 0.0253 |
| Coeff Var | 19.72363 | |

Parameter Estimates

| Variable | Label | DF | Parameter Estimate | Standard Error | t Value | Pr > \|t\| |
|---|---|---|---|---|---|---|
| Intercept | Intercept | 1 | 24.04058 | 2.24606 | 10.70 | <.0001 |
| InvDesktop | 1 / Desktops | 1 | 6.76420 | 5.79357 | 1.17 | 0.2640 |

| Obs | Dep Var TRANSY | Predicted Value | Std Error Mean Predict | 95% CL Mean | | 95% CL Predict | |
|---|---|---|---|---|---|---|---|
| 16 | . | 25.0069 | 1.6541 | 21.4335 | 28.5803 | 13.3044 | 36.7094 |

**FIGURE 5.35 (for Exercise 5.12)** MINITAB residual plots

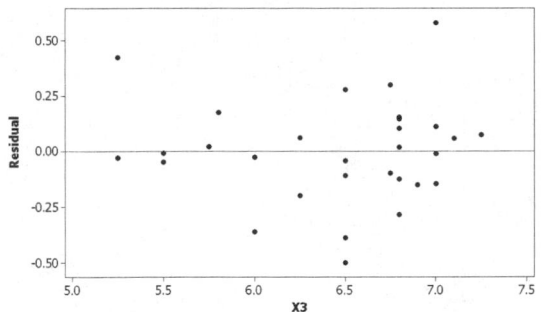

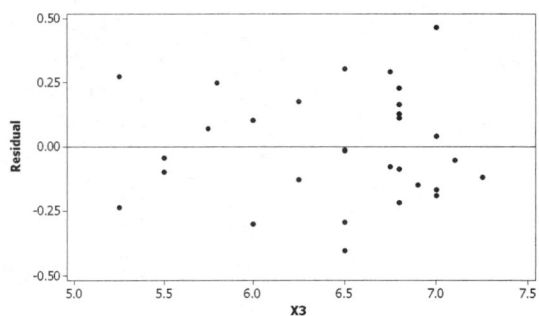

(a) Plot of the residuals versus $x_3$ for the model
$y = \beta_0 + \beta_1 x_4 + \beta_2 x_3 + \varepsilon$

(b) Plot of the residuals versus $x_3$ for the model
$y = \beta_0 + \beta_1 x_4 + \beta_2 x_3 + \beta_3 x_3^2 + \varepsilon$

fans out, indicating that the error term $\varepsilon$ tends to become larger as $x$ increases. To remedy this violation of the constant variance assumption, we divide all terms in the quadratic model by $x$. This gives the transformed model

$$\frac{y}{x} = \beta_0\left(\frac{1}{x}\right) + \beta_1 + \beta_2 x + \frac{\varepsilon}{x}$$

Figure 5.36 (page 274) gives a regression output and a residual plot versus $x$ for this model.

a. Does the residual plot indicate that the constant variance assumption holds for the transformed model?

b. Consider a home worth \$220,000. We let $\mu_0$ represent the mean yearly upkeep expenditure for all homes worth \$220,000, and we let $y_0$ represent the yearly upkeep expenditure for an individual home worth \$220,000. The bottom of the MINITAB output in Figure 5.36(a) tells us that $\hat{y}/220 = 5.635$ is a point estimate of $\mu_0/220$ and a point prediction of $y_0/220$. Multiply this result by 220 to obtain $\hat{y}$. Multiply the ends of the confidence interval and prediction interval shown on the MINITAB output by 220. This will give a 95% confidence interval for $\mu_0$ and a 95% prediction interval for $y_0$.

**5.14** Consider the hospital labor needs data in Table 5.5 (page 255). Figure 5.37 (page 275) gives residual plots that are obtained when we perform a regression

analysis of these data by using the model

$$y = \beta_0 + \beta_1 x_1 + \beta_2 x_2 + \beta_3 x_3 + \varepsilon$$

a. Interpret the normal plot of the residuals.

b. Interpret the residual plots versus predicted labor hours, BedDays ($x_2$), and Length ($x_3$). Note: the first two of these plots, as well as the unshown plot versus Xray ($x_1$), indicate that there are 4 hospitals that are substantially larger than the other 13 hospitals. We discuss the potential *influence* of these 4 large hospitals in Section 5.4.

**5.15** Consider having SAS perform a regression analysis of the hospital labor needs data with hospital 14 removed ($n = 16$) and the model

$$y = \beta_0 + \beta_1 x_1 + \beta_2 x_2 + \beta_3 x_3 + \varepsilon$$

If we do this analysis, we find that the least squares point estimates of the model parameters and their associated $p$ values (given in parentheses) are $b_0 = 1946.8020(.0023)$, $b_1 = .0386(.0120)$, $b_2 = 1.0394$ (<.0001), and $b_3 = -413.7578(.0012)$. Also, the standard error $s$ is 387.160. In addition, Figure 5.38 (page 275) gives the SAS output of the outlying and influential observation diagnostics for this model.

a. Do all of the residuals on the output seem to be of the same magnitude?

b. The studentized deleted residual (see "RStudent") having the largest absolute value is the studentized deleted residual for hospital 12, which equals $-2.2241$. Compare this studentized deleted residual

**FIGURE 5.36 (for Exercise 5.13)** MINITAB regression analysis
and residual plots

```
Predictor          Coef    SE Coef       T       P
Noconstant
1/V              -53.50      83.20   -0.64   0.524
One               3.409      1.321    2.58   0.014
Value          0.011224   0.004627    2.43   0.020

    Fit   SE Fit      95% CI             95% PI
  5.635    0.162   (5.306, 5.964)   (3.994, 7.276)
```

$$\frac{\hat{y}}{220} = \frac{-53.50}{220} + 3.409 + .011224(220) = 5.635$$

(a) Regression estimates and prediction interval

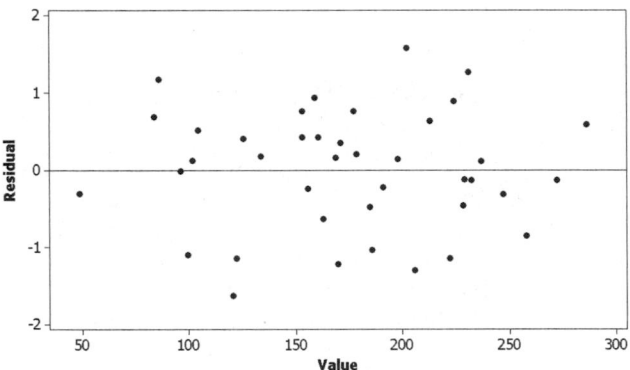

(b) The plot of the residuals versus Value

with $t_{[.025]}$ and $t_{[.005]}$ based on the appropriate
number of degrees of freedom. Based on this
comparison, should we be very concerned that
there are any outliers with respect to their $y$ values?

c. The leverage values (see "Hat Diag H") for
hospitals 14, 15, and 16 (which are the original
hospitals 15, 16, and 17) are, respectively, .7144,
.7868, and .9334. Are these hospitals outliers with
respect to their $x$ values?

d. Cook's distance measure (see "Cook's $D$") for
hospital 16 (the original hospital 17) is 1.317. Has
removing hospital 14 from the data set made the
original hospital 17 seem less influential? Explain
your answer. Hint: See Figure 5.20 in Section 5.4.

e. Hospital 15 (the original hospital 16) has the
largest Cook's $D$ ( = 1.384) on the output. Does
hospital 15 seem less influential than the original
hospital 17 did when we used all 17 hospitals
(including hospital 14) to perform the regression

analysis? Explain your answer. Hint: See Figure
5.20 in Section 5.4.

**5.16** Consider having SAS perform a regression
analysis of the hospital labor needs data using all 17
hospitals and the model

$$y = \beta_0 + \beta_1 x_1 + \beta_2 x_2 + \beta_3 x_3 + \beta_4 D_L + \varepsilon$$

where $D_L$ is a dummy variable for large hospitals 14,
15, 16, and 17. If we do this, we find that the least
squares point estimates of the model parameters and
their associated $p$-values (given in parentheses) are
$b_0 = 2462.2164(.0004)$, $b_1 = .0482(.0016)$, $b_2 =
.7843(<.0001)$, $b_3 = -432.4095(.0006)$, and $b_4 =
2871.7828(.0003)$. In addition, Figure 5.39 (page 276)
gives the SAS output of outlying and influential
observation diagnostics for this model.

a. By interpreting $b_4 = 2871.7828$ and its associated
$p$-value of .0003, discuss why there seems to be an

(Continues on page 276)

**FIGURE 5.37 (for Exercise 5.14)** SAS residual analysis for the hospital labor needs model
$y = \beta_0 + \beta_1 x_1 + \beta_2 x_2 + \beta_3 x_3 + \varepsilon$

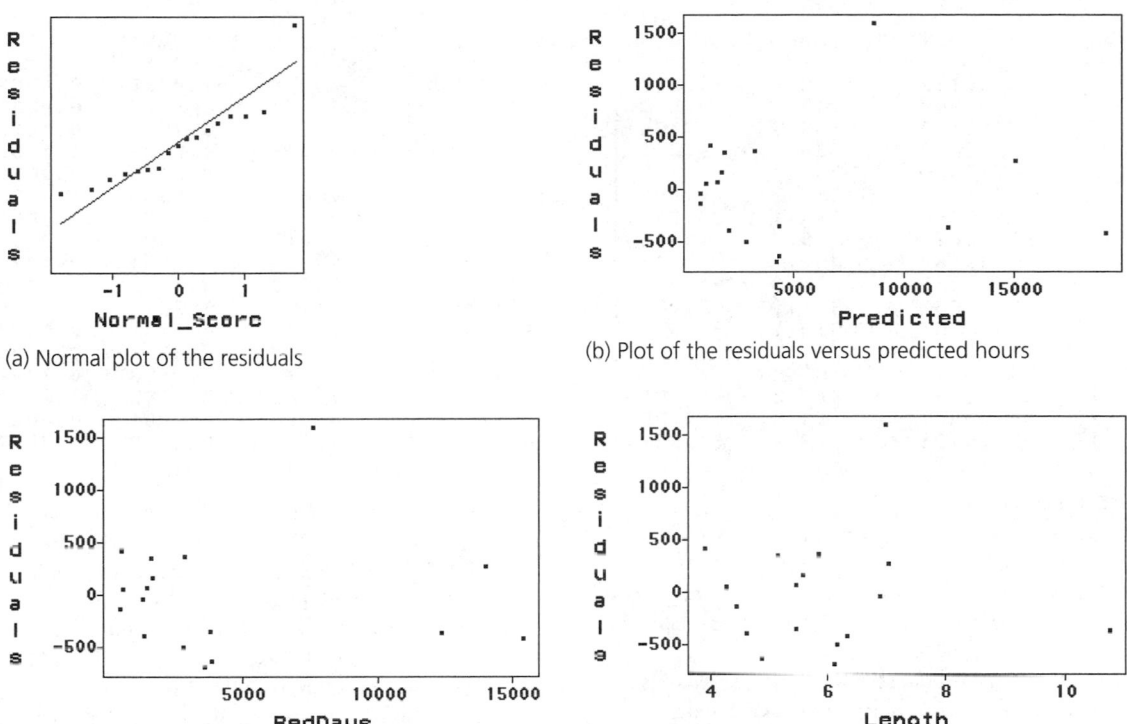

(a) Normal plot of the residuals

(b) Plot of the residuals versus predicted hours

(c) Plot of the residuals versus BedDays

(d) Plot of the residuals versus Length

**FIGURE 5.38 (for Exercise 5.15)** SAS output of outlying and influential observation diagnostics for the hospital labor needs model $y - \beta_0 + \beta_1 x_1 + \beta_2 x_2 + \beta_3 x_3 + \varepsilon$ with hospital 14 removed

| Obs | Residual | Std Error Residual | Student Residual | -2-1 0 1 2 | Cook's D | RStudent | Hat Diag H |
|---|---|---|---|---|---|---|---|
| 1 | -125.6245 | 363.0 | -0.346 | \| | 0.004 | -0.3330 | 0.1208 |
| 2 | 141.6906 | 338.6 | 0.418 | \| | 0.013 | 0.4036 | 0.2351 |
| 3 | 60.5547 | 361.2 | 0.168 | \| | 0.001 | 0.1607 | 0.1297 |
| 4 | 428.8118 | 355.1 | 1.208 | \|** | 0.069 | 1.2336 | 0.1588 |
| 5 | 162.8657 | 370.0 | 0.440 | \| | 0.005 | 0.4249 | 0.0869 |
| 6 | -294.2870 | 364.3 | -0.808 | *\| | 0.021 | -0.7953 | 0.1144 |
| 7 | 256.2955 | 370.1 | 0.692 | \|* | 0.011 | 0.6766 | 0.0861 |
| 8 | 409.8143 | 370.6 | 1.106 | \|** | 0.028 | 1.1171 | 0.0835 |
| 9 | -396.0764 | 369.8 | -1.071 | **\| | 0.028 | -1.0783 | 0.0876 |
| 10 | -472.9534 | 360.1 | -1.313 | **\| | 0.067 | -1.3591 | 0.1350 |
| 11 | 517.6976 | 370.7 | 1.397 | \|** | 0.044 | 1.4612 | 0.0833 |
| 12 | -677.2337 | 351.0 | -1.929 | ***\| | 0.202 | -2.2241 | 0.1780 |
| 13 | -262.1642 | 374.1 | -0.701 | *\| | 0.009 | -0.6851 | 0.0663 |
| 14 | -29.6792 | 206.9 | -0.143 | \| | 0.013 | -0.1375 | 0.7144 |
| 15 | 218.9904 | 178.8 | 1.225 | \|** | 1.384 | 1.2537 | 0.7868 |
| 16 | 61.2977 | 99.947 | 0.613 | \|* | 1.317 | 0.5966 | 0.9334 |

**FIGURE 5.39 (for Exercise 5.16)** SAS output of outlying and influential observation diagnostics for the hospital labor needs model $y = \beta_0 + \beta_1 x_1 + \beta_2 x_2 + \beta_3 x_3 + \beta_4 D_L + \varepsilon$

| Obs | Residual | Std Error Residual | Student Residual | -2-1 0 1 2 | Cook's D | RStudent | Hat Diag H |
|---|---|---|---|---|---|---|---|
| 1 | -461.0116 | 334.4 | -1.379 | \*\*\| | 0.070 | -1.4388 | 0.1553 |
| 2 | 77.4562 | 319.4 | 0.242 | \| | 0.003 | 0.2327 | 0.2293 |
| 3 | -254.5770 | 333.3 | -0.764 | \*\| | 0.022 | -0.7498 | 0.1609 |
| 4 | 68.7689 | 325.8 | 0.211 | \| | 0.002 | 0.2025 | 0.1983 |
| 5 | 77.1924 | 348.1 | 0.222 | \| | 0.001 | 0.2128 | 0.0849 |
| 6 | -485.9099 | 342.2 | -1.420 | \*\*\| | 0.053 | -1.4903 | 0.1153 |
| 7 | 220.6348 | 348.1 | 0.634 | \|\* | 0.007 | 0.6172 | 0.0846 |
| 8 | 351.5576 | 348.4 | 1.009 | \|\*\* | 0.018 | 1.0099 | 0.0831 |
| 9 | -144.6460 | 341.1 | -0.424 | \| | 0.005 | -0.4091 | 0.1211 |
| 10 | -134.0155 | 322.9 | -0.415 | \| | 0.009 | -0.4002 | 0.2124 |
| 11 | 727.1552 | 342.6 | 2.122 | \|\*\*\*\* | 0.115 | 2.5712 | 0.1134 |
| 12 | -204.6980 | 319.3 | -0.641 | \*\| | 0.025 | -0.6245 | 0.2297 |
| 13 | 162.0928 | 337.5 | 0.480 | \| | 0.007 | 0.4643 | 0.1396 |
| 14 | 266.8015 | 197.4 | 1.352 | \|\*\* | 0.877 | 1.4058 | 0.7058 |
| 15 | -373.6246 | 205.2 | -1.821 | \*\*\*\| | 1.422 | -2.0492 | 0.6819 |
| 16 | 183.7427 | 167.4 | 1.098 | \|\*\* | 0.898 | 1.1081 | 0.7884 |
| 17 | -76.9195 | 117.4 | -0.655 | \*\| | 0.738 | -0.6386 | 0.8958 |

(Exercise 5.16 Continued)

important effect due to the inefficiency of large hospitals.

b. Given the large-hospital inefficiency, is hospital 14 an outlier with respect to its $y$ value? Explain your answer.

c. Identify the hospital having the largest Cook's $D$. Does this hospital seem less influential than hospital 17 did when we used all 17 observations (including hospital 14) and no dummy variable to perform the regression analysis? See the output in Figure 5.20 (page 256). Explain your answer.

d. Although the remedial actions taken in Exercise 5.15 (remove hospital 14) and in this exercise (use a dummy variable) have lessened the influence of the larger hospitals (hospitals 14, 15, 16, and 17), these larger hospitals generally seem more influential than the small to medium-sized hospitals. This probably implies that we need more data concerning large hospitals to develop a better regression model for evaluating hospitals whose efficiency the navy questions. Since we do not now have such data, we will use the data we have to choose a model for evaluating questionable hospitals. To do this, first note that the $s$ for the dummy variable model of this exercise is 363.8542 and the $s$ for the model of Exercise 5.15 is 387.1598. Also, note that both of these values of $s$ are substantially smaller than the $s$ of 614.7794 for the model using all 17 hospitals and no dummy variable.

Next, consider a questionable large hospital ($D_L = 1$) for which Xray = 56,194, BedDays = 14,077.88, and Length = 6.89. Such a hospital has the following 95% prediction intervals for labor needs; [15,175, 17,030] if using the dummy variable model in this exercise, [14,906, 16,886] if using the model in Exercise 5.15, and [14,511, 17,618] if using the model of Exercise 4.4 (page 199), which does not employ a dummy variable and uses all 17 hospitals. Which of the three models gives the shortest prediction interval?

e. Figure 5.40(a) presents the plots of the residuals versus the predicted values for the model in Exercise 5.15 when hospital 14 is omitted. Figure 5.40(b) presents the same graph for the dummy variable model in this exercise when using all 17 hospitals. Which residual plot has the most "horizontal band" appearance (or constant variance)?

f. Combining all the available information in Exercises 4.4, 5.14, 5.15, and 5.16, and in Figure 5.20, which of the three models seems best for evaluating the efficiency of questionable hospitals?

**5.17** Consider the difference between the least squares point estimate $b_j$ of $\beta_j$, computed using all $n$ observations, and the least squares point estimate $b_j^{(i)}$ of $\beta_j$, computed using all $n$ observations except for observation $i$. SAS calculates this difference for each observation and divides the difference by its standard error to form the **difference in estimate of $\beta_j$ statistic.**

**FIGURE 5.40 (for Exercise 5.16)** SAS plots of residuals versus predicted values

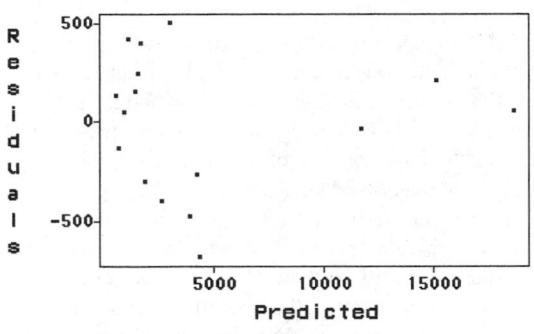

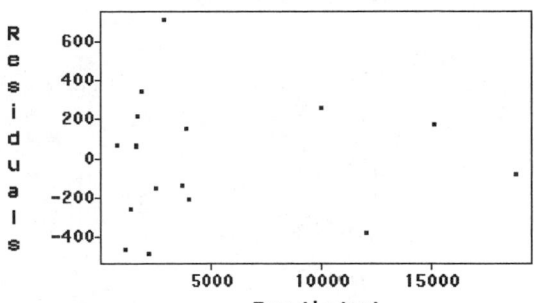

(a) Model in Exercise 5.15 with hospital 14 removed      (b) Dummy variable model for 17 hospitals

**FIGURE 5.41 (for Exercise 5.17)** SAS output of the difference in estimate of $\beta_j$ statistics

| Obs | INTERCEP Dfbetas | X1 Dfbetas | X2 Dfbetas | X3 Dfbetas |
|---|---|---|---|---|
| 1 | -0.0477 | 0.0157 | -0.0083 | 0.0309 |
| 2 | 0.0138 | -0.0050 | 0.0119 | -0.0183 |
| 3 | 0.0307 | -0.0084 | 0.0060 | -0.0216 |
| 4 | 0.2416 | -0.0217 | 0.0251 | -0.1821 |
| 5 | 0.0035 | 0.0014 | -0.0099 | 0.0074 |
| 6 | -0.0881 | -0.0703 | 0.0724 | 0.0401 |
| 7 | 0.0045 | -0.0008 | -0.0180 | 0.0179 |
| 8 | 0.0764 | -0.0319 | 0.0063 | -0.0314 |
| 9 | 0.0309 | 0.0243 | 0.0304 | -0.0873 |
| 10 | 0.1787 | -0.2924 | 0.3163 | -0.2544 |
| 11 | -0.0265 | 0.0560 | -0.0792 | 0.0680 |
| 12 | -0.4387 | 0.3549 | -0.3782 | 0.3864 |
| 13 | -0.0671 | 0.0230 | -0.0243 | 0.0390 |
| 14 | -0.8544 | 1.1389 | -0.4148 | 0.9620 |
| 15 | 0.9616 | 0.1324 | -0.0133 | -0.9561 |
| 16 | 0.9880 | -1.4284 | 1.7339 | -1.1027 |
| 17 | 0.0294 | -3.0114 | 1.2688 | 0.3155 |

If the absolute value of this statistic is greater than 2 (a sometimes-used critical value for this statistic), then removing observation *i* from the data set would substantially change the least squares point estimate of $\beta_j$. For example, consider the hospital labor needs model of Section 5.4 that uses all 17 observations to relate *y* to $x_1$, $x_2$, and $x_3$. Also consider the columns labeled "Dfbetas" in Figure 5.41. Notice that there are four such columns—one for each model parameter—which are labeled INTERCEP, X1, X2, and X3. Each of these columns contains the *difference in estimate of*

$\beta_j$ *statistic* related to the column's parameter label for each observation. We see that for observation 17 "INTERCEP Dftbetas" (= .0294), "X2 Dfbetas" (= 1.2688), and "X3 Dfbetas" (= .3155) are all less than 2 in absolute value. This says that the least squares point estimates of $\beta_0$, $\beta_2$, and $\beta_3$ probably would not change substantially if hospital 17 were removed from the data set. However, for observation 17 "X1 Dfbetas" (= −3.0114) is greater than 2 in absolute value. What does this say?

(Continues on page 278)

**FIGURE 5.42 (for Exercise 5.18)**
SAS output of the difference in fits
statistics

| Obs | Dffits |
|-----|---------|
| 1 | -0.0754 |
| 2 | -0.0240 |
| 3 | 0.0438 |
| 4 | 0.3266 |
| 5 | 0.0421 |
| 6 | -0.2280 |
| 7 | 0.0882 |
| 8 | 0.1841 |
| 9 | -0.2518 |
| 10 | -0.4487 |
| 11 | 0.1824 |
| 12 | -0.5237 |
| 13 | -0.1451 |
| 14 | 1.8882 |
| 15 | -1.4723 |
| 16 | 1.8930 |
| 17 | -4.9623 |

Note: If we remove hospital 14 from the data set or use a dummy variable to model the inefficiency of large hospitals (see Exercises 5.15 and 5.16), then hospital 17 becomes much less influential with respect to the difference in estimate of $\beta_j$ statistic.

Note: The formula for the difference in estimate of $\beta_j$ statistic involves a fairly complicated matrix algebra expression and will not be given in this book. The interested reader is referred to Bowerman and O'Connell (1990). MINITAB does not give this statistic.

**5.18** Consider the difference between the point prediction $\hat{y}_i$ of $y_i$ computed using least squares point estimates based on all $n$ observations and the point prediction $\hat{y}_{(i)}$ of $y_i$ computed using least squares point estimates based on all $n$ observations except for observation $i$. Standard statistical software packages calculate this difference for each observation and divide the difference by its standard error to form the **difference in fits statistic.** If the absolute value of this statistic is greater than 2 (a sometimes-used critical value for this statistic), then removing observation $i$ from the data set would substantially change the point prediction of $y_i$. For example, consider the hospital labor needs model of Section 5.4 that uses all 17 observations to relate $y$ to $x_1$, $x_2$, and $x_3$. Also consider the column labeled "Dffits" in Figure 5.42. This column contains the **difference in fits statistic** for each observation. The value of this statistic for observation 17 is −4.9623. What does this say?

Note: If we remove hospital 14 from the data set or use a dummy variable to model the inefficiency of large hospitals (see Exercises 5.15 and 5.16), then hospital 17 becomes much less influential with respect to the difference in fits statistic.

Note: The formula for the difference in fits statistic for observation $i$ is found by multiplying the formula for the studentized deleted residual for observation $i$ by $[h_i/(1 - h_i)]^{1/2}$. Here $h_i$ is the leverage value for observation $i$. MINITAB gives this statistic.

# 6

# *Time Series Regression*

In this chapter we discuss **time series regression models.** Such models relate the dependent variable $y_t$ to functions of time. These models are most profitably used when the parameters describing the time series to be forecast remain constant over time. For example, if a time series exhibits a linear trend, then the slope of the trend line remains constant. As another example, if the time series can be described by using monthly seasonal parameters, then the seasonal parameters for each of the twelve months remain the same from one year to the next. To begin this chapter, Section 6.1 shows how to model **trend** by using **polynomial functions** of time. In particular, we consider **no trend, linear trend,** and **quadratic trend** models. In Section 6.2 we see that the error terms for a time series regression can be **autocorrelated.** In this section we define **positive and negative autocorrelation,** and we discuss detecting autocorrelation by using **residual plots** and the **Durbin–Watson statistic** (which is used to test for **first-order autocorrelation**). In Section 6.3 we begin to analyze **seasonal data.** We consider two types of seasonal variation—**constant seasonal variation** and **increasing seasonal variation**—and we show how data **transformations** can be employed to obtain a transformed series that displays constant seasonal variation. Section 6.4 discusses modeling seasonal variation by using **dummy variables** and **trigonometric functions.** Section 6.5 shows how to employ **growth curve models.**

The error terms for time series regression models are often autocorrelated. Therefore, Section 6.6 deals with handling autocorrelated errors. We discuss modeling the error terms for a time series regression by using the **first-order autoregressive process.**

# 6.1   MODELING TREND BY USING POLYNOMIAL FUNCTIONS

We sometimes can describe a time series $y_t$ by using a **trend model.** Such a model is defined as follows.

---

The **trend model** is

$$y_t = TR_t + \varepsilon_t$$

where

$$y_t = \text{the value of the time series in period } t$$
$$TR_t = \text{the \textbf{trend} in time period } t$$
$$\varepsilon_t = \text{the \textbf{error term} in time period } t$$

---

This model says that the time series $y_t$ can be represented by an average level (denoted $\mu_t$) that changes over time according to the equation $\mu_t = TR_t$ and by the error term $\varepsilon_t$. This error term represents random fluctuations that cause the $y_t$ values to deviate from the average level $\mu_t$.

Some useful trends are given in the following box.

---

## NO TREND, LINEAR TREND, AND QUADRATIC TREND

1.   **No trend,** which is modeled as $TR_t = \beta_0$, implies that there is **no long-run growth or decline** in the time series over time; see Figure 6.1(a).

2.   **Linear trend,** which is modeled as $TR_t = \beta_0 + \beta_1 t$, implies that there is a **straight-line long-run growth** (if the slope $\beta_1$ is greater than zero) **or decline** (if $\beta_1$ is less than zero) over time; see Figure 6.1(b) and (c).

3.   **Quadratic trend,** which is modeled as $TR_t = \beta_0 + \beta_1 t + \beta_2 t^2$, implies that there is a **quadratic (or curvilinear) long-run change** over time. This quadratic change can either be *growth at an increasing or decreasing rate*—see Figure 6.1(d) and (e)—or *decline at an increasing or decreasing rate;* see Figure 6.1(f) and (g).

---

These trends are the most commonly used. However, other, more complicated trends also exist. For example, we can model trend by using the *p***th-order polynomial function.**

**FIGURE 6.1** Different types of trend

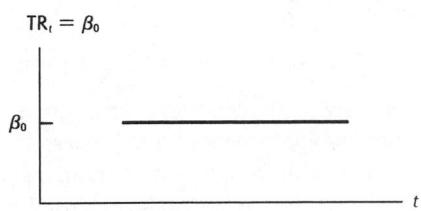

$TR_t = \beta_0$

$\beta_0$

(a) No long-run growth or decline

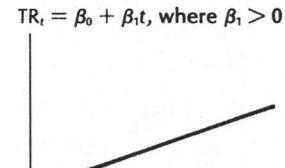

$TR_t = \beta_0 + \beta_1 t$, where $\beta_1 > 0$

(b) Straight-line growth

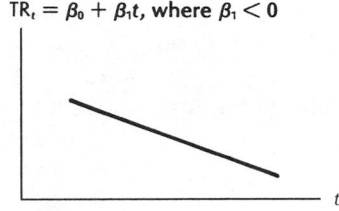

$TR_t = \beta_0 + \beta_1 t$, where $\beta_1 < 0$

(c) Straight-line decline

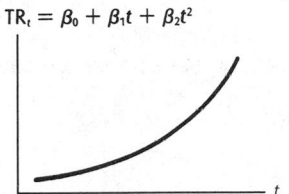

$TR_t = \beta_0 + \beta_1 t + \beta_2 t^2$

(d) Growth at an increasing rate

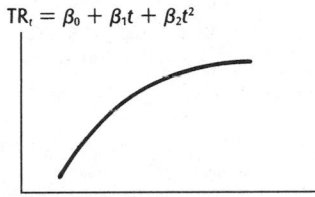

$TR_t = \beta_0 + \beta_1 t + \beta_2 t^2$

(e) Growth at a decreasing rate

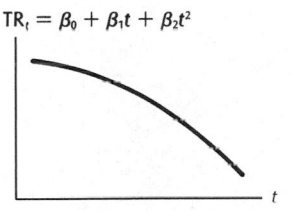

$TR_t = \beta_0 + \beta_1 t + \beta_2 t^2$

(f) Decline at an increasing rate

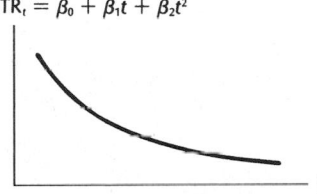

$TR_t = \beta_0 + \beta_1 t + \beta_2 t^2$

(g) Decline at a decreasing rate

---

**The $p$th-order polynomial trend model** is

$$y_t = TR_t + \varepsilon_t$$
$$= \beta_0 + \beta_1 t + \beta_2 t^2 + \cdots + \beta_p t^p + \varepsilon_t$$

---

Third-order ($p = 3$) and higher-order ($p > 3$) polynomials model trends with one or more reversals in curvature. For instance, a third-order polynomial trend

$$TR_t = \beta_0 + \beta_1 t + \beta_2 t^2 + \beta_3 t^3$$

describes a trend with one reversal of curvature.

Least squares point estimates of the parameters in these trend models may be obtained by using regression techniques. Here we assume that the error term $\varepsilon_t$ satisfies the constant variance, independence, and normality assumptions. Violations of the constant variance assumption would be suggested by a fanning-out or funneling-in residual plot versus time. The normality assumption can be checked by constructing histograms, stem-and-leaf diagrams, and normal plots of the residuals. We discuss checking the independence assumption in Section 6.2.

**EXAMPLE 6.1**    The Bay City Seafood Company owns a fleet of fishing trawlers and operates a fish processing plant. In order to forecast its minimum and maximum possible revenues from cod sales and to plan the operations of its fish processing plant, the company desires to make both point forecasts and prediction interval forecasts of its monthly cod catch (measured in tons). The company has recorded the monthly cod catch for the previous two years (years 1 and 2). The cod catch history is given in Table 6.1. When these data are plotted, they appear to fluctuate randomly around a constant average level (see the JMP IN plot in Figure 6.2). Since the company subjectively believes that this data pattern will continue in the future, it seems reasonable to use the regression model

$$y_t = TR_t + \varepsilon_t = \beta_0 + \varepsilon_t$$

to forecast the cod catch in future months.

**TABLE 6.1  Cod Catch (In Tons)**

| Month | Year 1 | Year 2 |
|---|---|---|
| January | 362 | 276 |
| February | 381 | 334 |
| March | 317 | 394 |
| April | 297 | 334 |
| May | 399 | 384 |
| June | 402 | 314 |
| July | 375 | 344 |
| August | 349 | 337 |
| September | 386 | 345 |
| October | 328 | 362 |
| November | 389 | 314 |
| December | 343 | 365 |

**FIGURE 6.2**
JMP IN plot of cod catch (tons) versus time (months)

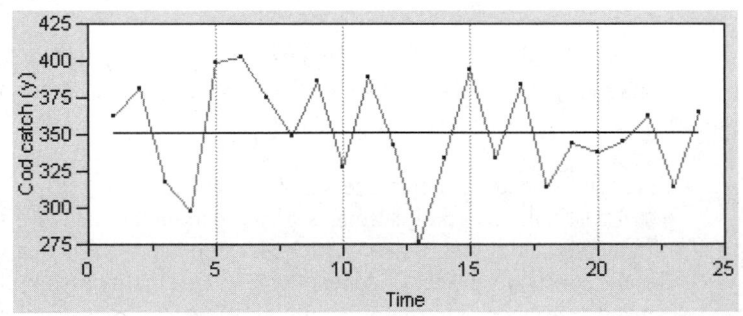

**FIGURE 6.3** MINITAB output of a regression analysis of the cod catch data using the model $y_t = \beta_0 + \varepsilon_t$

```
Predictor         Coef        SE Coef           T           P
Noconstant
Intercep        351.292        6.904          50.88       0.000

S = 33.82        Durbin-Watson statistic = 2.12

Predicted Values for New Observations

New Obs      Fit      SE Fit        95.0% CI               95.0% PI
1          351.29      6.90     ( 337.01,  365.57)    ( 279.88,  422.71)
```

The MINITAB output of a regression analysis of the cod catch data using this model is given in Figure 6.3. Note that the least squares point estimate of $\beta_0$ can be shown to be equal to

$$\bar{y} = \frac{y_1 + y_2 + \cdots + y_{24}}{24} = \frac{362 + 381 + \cdots + 365}{24} = 351.29$$

which is the mean of the $n = 24$ observed cod catches. Thus

$$\hat{y}_t = \bar{y} = 351.29$$

is the point prediction of the cod catch ($y_t$) in any future month. Moreover, a $100(1 - \alpha)\%$ prediction interval for $y_t$ is

$$\left[ \bar{y} \pm t_{[\alpha/2]}^{(n-1)} s \sqrt{1 + \left(\frac{1}{n}\right)} \right]$$

where

$$s = \sqrt{\frac{\sum_{t=1}^{n} (y_t - \bar{y})^2}{n - 1}} = \sqrt{\frac{(362 - 351.29)^2 + \cdots + (365 - 351.29)^2}{24 - 1}}$$

$$= 33.82$$

If we wish to compute a 95% prediction interval, we use

$$t_{[\alpha/2]}^{(n-1)} = t_{[.05/2]}^{(24-1)} = t_{[.025]}^{(23)} = 2.069$$

and we compute the interval to be

$$\left[ \bar{y} \pm t_{[.025]}^{(23)} s \sqrt{1 + (1/n)} \right] = \left[ 351.29 \pm 2.069(33.82)\sqrt{1 + (1/24)} \right]$$

$$= [351.29 \pm 71.42]$$

$$= [279.88, 422.71]$$

This interval, which is also given on the MINITAB output of Figure 6.3, says that Bay City Seafood is 95% confident that the cod catch $y_t$ in any future month will be between 279.88 tons and 422.71 tons.

**EXAMPLE 6.2**

For the past two years, Smith's Department Stores, Inc., has carried a new type of electronic calculator called the Bismark X-12. Sales of this calculator have generally been increasing over these two years. Smith's uses an inventory policy that attempts to ensure that its stores will have enough Bismark X-12 calculators to meet practically all of the demand for the Bismark X-12, while ensuring that Smith's does not needlessly tie up its money by ordering many more calculators than it can reasonably expect to sell. In order to implement this inventory policy in future months, Smith's requires both point predictions and prediction intervals for total monthly Bismark X-12 demand.

The monthly calculator demand data for the past two years are given in Table 6.2. A JMP IN plot of the demand data versus time is shown in Figure 6.4. The demands appear

**TABLE 6.2 Calculator Sales Data**

| Month | Year 1 | Year 2 |
|---|---|---|
| January | 197 | 296 |
| February | 211 | 276 |
| March | 203 | 305 |
| April | 247 | 308 |
| May | 239 | 356 |
| June | 269 | 393 |
| July | 308 | 363 |
| August | 262 | 386 |
| September | 258 | 443 |
| October | 256 | 308 |
| November | 261 | 358 |
| December | 288 | 384 |

**FIGURE 6.4**
JMP IN plot of calculator sales versus time (months)

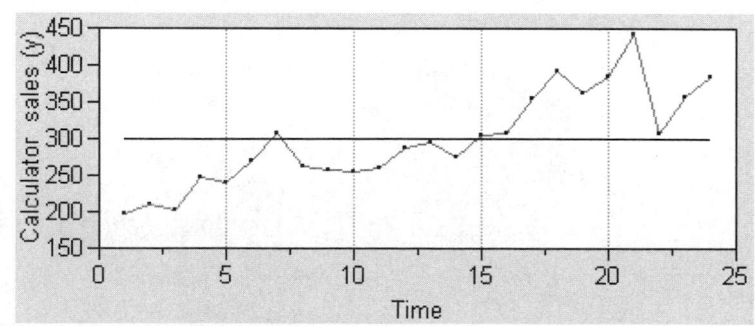

to fluctuate randomly around an average level that increases over time in a linear fashion. Furthermore, Smith's believes that this trend will continue for at least the next two years. Thus it is reasonable to use the regression model

$$y_t = \text{TR}_t + \varepsilon_t = \beta_0 + \beta_1 t + \varepsilon_t$$

to forecast calculator sales in future months. The least squares point estimates of $\beta_1$ and $\beta_0$ are, respectively,

$$b_1 = \frac{SS_{ty}}{SS_{tt}} = \frac{\sum\limits_{t=1}^{24} ty_t - \dfrac{\left(\sum\limits_{t=1}^{24} t\right)\left(\sum\limits_{t=1}^{24} y_t\right)}{24}}{\sum\limits_{t=1}^{24} t^2 - \dfrac{\left(\sum\limits_{t=1}^{24} t\right)^2}{24}} = 8.07435$$

and

$$b_0 = \bar{y} - b_1\bar{t} = \frac{\sum\limits_{t=1}^{24} y_t}{24} - b_1 \frac{\sum\limits_{t=1}^{24} t}{24} = 198.02899$$

The SAS output of a regression analysis of the demand data using the linear trend model is given in Figure 6.5. For this model both the intercept and the variable $t$ are significant— each has a $p$-value less than .0001. Furthermore, $R^2 = .7726$ and $s = 31.67061$.

Using this model, the point forecast of a future demand $y_t$ is

$$\hat{y}_t = b_0 + b_1 t = 198.02899 + 8.07435t$$

Therefore, point forecasts of Bismark X-12 demand in January and February of year 3 are, respectively,

$$\ddot{y}_{25} = 198.02899 + 8.07435(25) = 399.9$$

and

$$\hat{y}_{26} = 198.02899 + 8.07435(26) = 408.0$$

Moreover, a 95% prediction interval for $y_{25}$ is

$$\left[\hat{y}_{25} \pm t_{[.025]}^{(24-2)} s \sqrt{1 + \frac{1}{24} + \frac{(25 - \bar{t})^2}{\sum\limits_{t=1}^{24} (t - \bar{t})^2}}\right] = [399.9 \pm 71.3] = [328.6, 471.2]$$

Note that these point predictions and the prediction interval are given on the SAS output of Figure 6.5. This figure also shows that a 95% prediction interval for $y_{26}$ is [336.0, 479.9]. The prediction intervals can be used to help implement Smith's inventory policy. For instance, if Smith's stocks 471 Bismark X-12 calculators in January of year 3, we can be very sure that monthly demand will be met.

**FIGURE 6.5** SAS output of a regression analysis of the calculator sales data using the model $y_t = \beta_0 + \beta_1 t + \varepsilon_t$

Analysis of Variance

| Source | DF | Sum of Squares | Mean Square | F Value | Pr > F |
|---|---|---|---|---|---|
| Model | 1 | 74974 | 74974 | 74.75 | <.0001 |
| Error | 22 | 22067 | 1003.02735 | | |
| Corrected Total | 23 | 97041 | | | |

| | | | | |
|---|---|---|---|---|
| Root MSE | 31.67061 | R-Square | 0.7726 | |
| Dependent Mean | 298.95833 | Adj R-Sq | 0.7623 | |
| Coeff Var | 10.59365 | | | |

Parameter Estimates

| Variable | Label | DF | Parameter Estimate | Standard Error | t Value | Pr > \|t\| |
|---|---|---|---|---|---|---|
| Intercept | Intercept | 1 | 198.02899 | 13.34443 | 14.84 | <.0001 |
| T | | 1 | 8.07435 | 0.93392 | 8.65 | <.0001 |

| Obs | Dep Var y | Predicted Value | Std Error Mean Predict | 95% CL Mean | | 95% CL Predict | |
|---|---|---|---|---|---|---|---|
| 25 | . | 399.8877 | 13.3444 | 372.2130 | 427.5623 | 328.6146 | 471.1608 |
| 26 | . | 407.9620 | 14.1687 | 378.5780 | 437.3460 | 336.0080 | 479.9161 |
| 27 | . | 416.0364 | 15.0057 | 384.9164 | 447.1564 | 343.3561 | 488.7167 |
| 28 | . | 424.1107 | 15.8537 | 391.2323 | 456.9892 | 350.6603 | 497.5611 |

Durbin-Watson D    1.682

**TABLE 6.3 Loan Requests (in $1000s)**

| Month | Year 1 | Year 2 |
|---|---|---|
| January | 297 | 808 |
| February | 249 | 809 |
| March | 340 | 867 |
| April | 406 | 855 |
| May | 464 | 965 |
| June | 481 | 921 |
| July | 549 | 956 |
| August | 553 | 990 |
| September | 556 | 1019 |
| October | 642 | 1021 |
| November | 670 | 1033 |
| December | 712 | 1127 |

**EXAMPLE 6.3**   The State University Credit Union, a savings institution open to the faculty and staff of State University, handles savings accounts and makes loans to members. In order to plan its investment strategies, the credit union requires both point predictions and prediction intervals of monthly loan requests (in thousands of dollars) to be made by the faculty and staff in future months.

The credit union has recorded monthly loan requests for its past two years of operation (see Table 6.3). A JMP IN plot of the loan request data versus time is given in Figure 6.6. This plot suggests that loan requests tend to fluctuate around an average level that

**FIGURE 6.6**

JMP IN plot of loan requests ($\times$ \$1000) versus time (months)

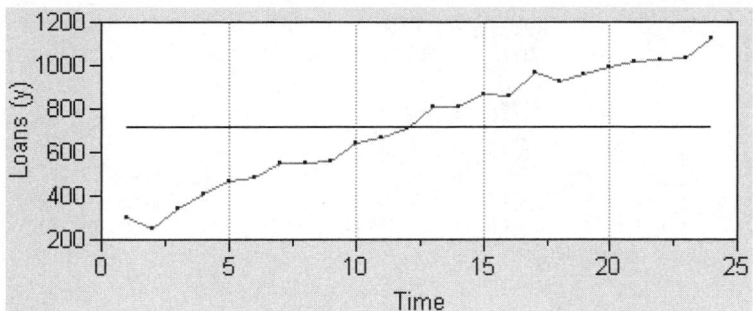

**FIGURE 6.7** MINITAB output of a regression analysis of the loan request data using the model $y_t = \beta_0 + \beta_1 t + \beta_2 t^2 + \varepsilon_t$

```
The regression equation is
y = 200 + 50.9 Time - 0.568 TimeSQ

Predictor        Coef      SE Coef           T           P
Constant       199.62        20.85        9.58       0.000
Time           50.937         3.842       13.26       0.000
TimeSQ        -0.5677         0.1492        3.00       0.001

S = 31.25        R-Sq = 98.7%      R-Sq(adj) = 98.6%

Analysis of Variance

Source            DF           SS          MS           F           P
Regression         2      1566730      783365      802.33       0.000
Residual Error    21        20504         976
Total             23      1587234

        Durbin-Watson statistic = 2.10

Predicted Values for New Observations
    Fit      SE Fit          95.0% CI              95.0% PI
1118.21       20.85   ( 1074.85, 1161.56)   ( 1040.09, 1196.32)
1140.19       24.44   ( 1089.37, 1191.01)   ( 1057.70, 1222.68)
```

increases at a decreasing rate over time. The quadratic trend of loan requests is consistent with the credit union's historical membership pattern, and the credit union expects this trend to continue in future months. Thus it seems reasonable to forecast loan requests by using the quadratic regression model

$$y_t = TR_t + \varepsilon_t = \beta_0 + \beta_1 t + \beta_2 t^2 + \varepsilon_t$$

The MINITAB output of a regression analysis of the loan request data using this model is shown in Figure 6.7. This figure shows that the least squares point estimates of $\beta_0$, $\beta_1$, and $\beta_2$ are $b_0 = 199.62$, $b_1 = 50.937$, and $b_2 = -0.5677$. Furthermore, each of the terms in this model—the intercept, the linear term $t$, and the quadratic term $t^2$—is significant (both $\beta_0$ and $t$ have a $p$-value of .000, and $t^2$ has a $p$-value of .001). In addition, we find that $R^2 = .987$ and $s = 31.25$. Using this model, the point forecast of a future value of loan requests $y_t$ is

$$\hat{y}_t = b_0 + b_1 t + b_2 t^2$$
$$= 199.62 + 50.937t - .5677t^2$$

For example, point forecasts of loan requests in January and February of year 3 are, respectively,

$$\hat{y}_{25} = 199.62 + 50.937(25) - .5677(25)^2$$
$$= 1118.21$$
$$\hat{y}_{26} = 199.62 + 50.937(26) - .5677(26)^2$$
$$= 1140.19$$

These point predictions are given in the output of Figure 6.7. This figure also shows that 95% prediction intervals for $y_{25}$ and $y_{26}$ are, respectively, [1040.09, 1196.32] and [1057.70, 1222.68]. For example, the first interval says that the credit union can be very sure that loan requests in January of year 3 will be no higher than $1,196,320.

# 6.2  DETECTING AUTOCORRELATION

The validity of the regression methods illustrated in Section 6.1 requires that the independence assumption be satisfied. However, when time series data are being analyzed, this assumption is often violated. It is quite common for the time-ordered error terms to be autocorrelated. We say that error terms occurring over time have **positive autocorrelation** if a positive error term in time period $t$ tends to produce, or be followed by, another positive error term in time period $t + k$ (a later time period) and if a negative error term in time period $t$ tends to produce, or be followed by, another negative error term in time period $t + k$. In other words, positive autocorrelation exists when positive error terms tend to be followed over time by positive error terms and negative error terms tend to be followed over time by negative error terms. An example of positive autocorrelation in the error terms is depicted in Figure 6.8(a). This figure illustrates that positive autocorrelation in the error terms can produce a cyclical pattern over time. Thus positive autocorrelation in the error terms means that greater than average values of $y_t$ tend to be followed by greater than average values of $y_t$, and smaller than average values of $y_t$ tend to be followed by smaller than average values of $y_t$.

Error terms occurring over time have **negative autocorrelation** if a positive error term in time period $t$ tends to produce, or be followed by, a negative error term in time period $t + k$ and if a negative error term in time period $t$ tends to produce, or be followed by, a positive error term in time period $t + k$. In other words, negative autocorrelation exists when positive error terms tend to be followed over time by negative error terms and negative error terms tend to be followed over time by positive error terms. An example of negative autocorrelation in the error terms is depicted in Figure 6.8(b).

**FIGURE 6.8**
Positive and negative autocorrelation

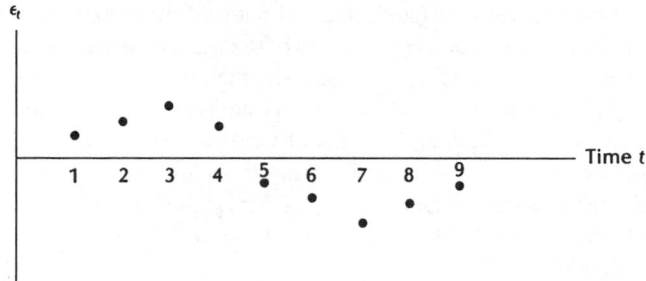

(a)  Positive autocorrelation in the error terms: Cyclical pattern

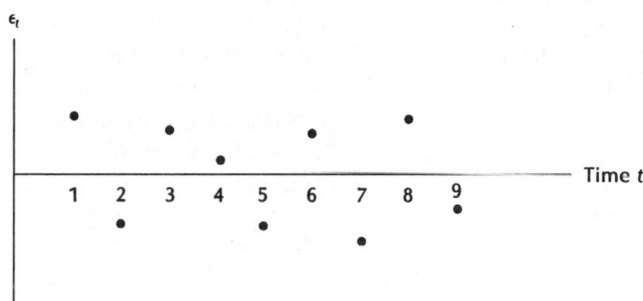

(b)  Negative autocorrelation in the error terms: Alternating pattern

**FIGURE 6.9**
Little or no autocorrelation in the error terms: random pattern

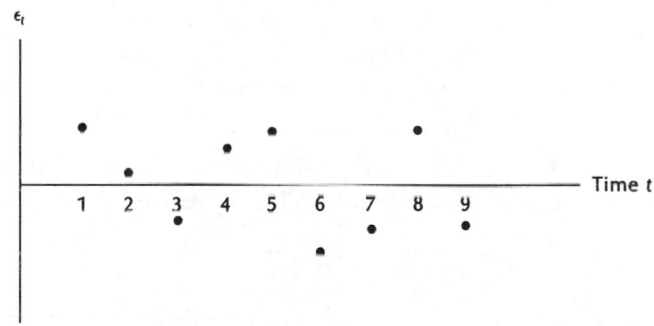

This figure illustrates that negative autocorrelation in the error terms can produce an alternating pattern over time. It follows that negative autocorrelation in the error terms means that greater than average values of $y_t$ tend to be followed by smaller than average values of $y_t$ and smaller than average values of $y_t$ tend to be followed by greater than average values of $y_t$. An example of negative autocorrelation might be provided by a retailer's weekly stock orders. Here a larger than average stock order one week might result in an oversupply and hence a smaller than average order the next week.

The independence assumption says that the time-ordered error terms display no positive or negative autocorrelation. This says that the error terms occur in a random pattern over time, as illustrated in Figure 6.9. Such a pattern would imply that these error terms are statistically independent, which would in turn imply that the time-ordered values of $y_t$ are statistically independent.

Since the residuals are point estimates of the error terms, a residual plot against time can be used to detect violations of the independence assumption. If a residual plot against time has a cyclical appearance, the error terms are positively autocorrelated, and the independence assumption does not hold. Another way to detect positive auto-correlation is to look at the signs of the time-ordered residuals. Letting $+$ denote a positive residual and $-$ denote a negative residual, we call a sequence of residuals with the same sign (for instance, $+\,+\,+$) a **run.** If positive autocorrelation exists, the signs of the residuals should display relatively few runs of fairly long duration. For instance, the pattern $+\,+\,+\,+\,-\,-\,-\,+\,+\,+\,-\,-\,-\,-\,+\,+\,+\,+\,-\,-\,-$ in the time-ordered resid-uals would indicate that positive autocorrelation exists.

If a plot of the time-ordered residuals has an alternating pattern, the error terms are negatively autocorrelated. If we look at the signs of the time-ordered residuals, negative autocorrelation is characterized by many runs of relatively short duration. For example, the pattern $+\,-\,+\,-\,+\,+\,-\,+\,-\,+\,-\,-\,+\,-$ in the time-ordered residuals would indicate that negative autocorrelation exists and that the independence assumption is violated.

However, if a plot of the time-ordered residuals displays a random pattern, the error terms have little or no autocorrelation. This suggests that these error terms are independent.

**EXAMPLE 6.4**   Figures 6.10, 6.11 (page 292), and 6.12 (page 292) give plots of the time-ordered residuals for the no trend cod catch model of Example 6.1, the linear trend calculator sales model of Example 6.2, and the quadratic trend loan requests model of Example 6.3. None of these plots exhibit a well-defined cyclical pattern or a well-defined alternating pattern. That is, each residual plot probably displays a random pattern. For each model we conclude that little or no autocorrelation exists and that the independence assumption holds.

One type of positive or negative autocorrelation is called **first-order autocorre-lation.** It says that $\varepsilon_t$, the error term in time period $t$, is related to $\varepsilon_{t-1}$, the error term

**FIGURE 6.10**
MINITAB plot of residuals versus time for the cod catch model

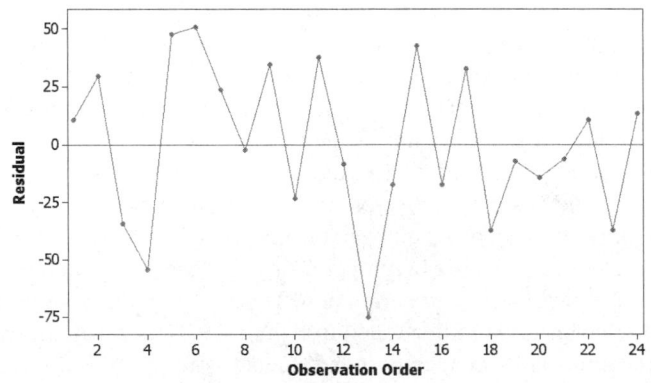

in time period $t - 1$, by the equation

$$\varepsilon_t = \phi_1 \varepsilon_{t-1} + a_t$$

Here we assume that $\phi_1^{\dagger}$ is the correlation coefficient between error terms separated by one time period and $a_1, a_2, \ldots$ are values randomly and independently selected from a normal distribution having mean zero and a variance independent of time. We now present the **Durbin–Watson test,** which is a formal test for first-order (positive or negative) autocorrelation.

---

## DURBIN–WATSON TEST: (FIRST-ORDER) POSITIVE AUTOCORRELATION

The **Durbin–Watson statistic** is

$$d = \frac{\sum\limits_{t=2}^{n} (e_t - e_{t-1})^2}{\sum\limits_{t=1}^{n} e_t^2}$$

where $e_1, e_2, \ldots, e_n$ are the time-ordered residuals.

Consider testing the null hypothesis

$H_0$: The error terms are not autocorrelated

versus the alternative hypothesis

$H_a$: The error terms are positively autocorrelated

Durbin and Watson have shown that there are points (denoted $d_{L,\alpha}$ and $d_{U,\alpha}$) such that if $\alpha$ is the probability of a Type I error, then

1. If $d < d_{L,\alpha}$, we reject $H_0$.
2. If $d > d_{U,\alpha}$, we do not reject $H_0$.
3. If $d_{L,\alpha} \leq d \leq d_{U,\alpha}$, the test is inconclusive.

---

Here small values of $d$ lead to the conclusion of positive autocorrelation, because if $d$ is small, the differences $(e_t - e_{t-1})$ are small. This indicates that the adjacent residuals $e_t$ and $e_{t-1}$ are of the same magnitude, which in turn says that the adjacent error terms $\varepsilon_t$ and $\varepsilon_{t-1}$ are positively correlated.

---

[†]In this and subsequent chapters we use the subscripted symbol $\phi$ (rather than the sometimes used $\rho$) to denote the parameter(s) in an autoregressive process. We do so because this notation is consistent with that used when writing autoregressive terms in the Box–Jenkins methodology.

**FIGURE 6.11**
SAS plot of residuals versus time for the calculator sales model

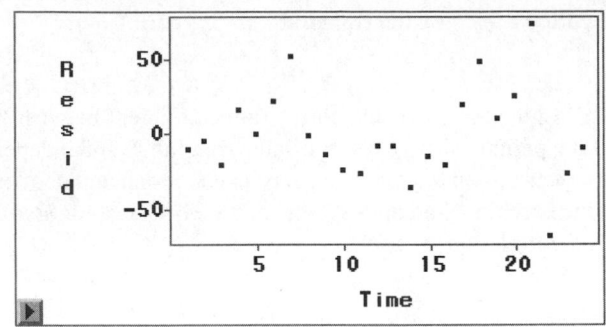

**FIGURE 6.12**
MINITAB plot of residuals versus time for the loan request model

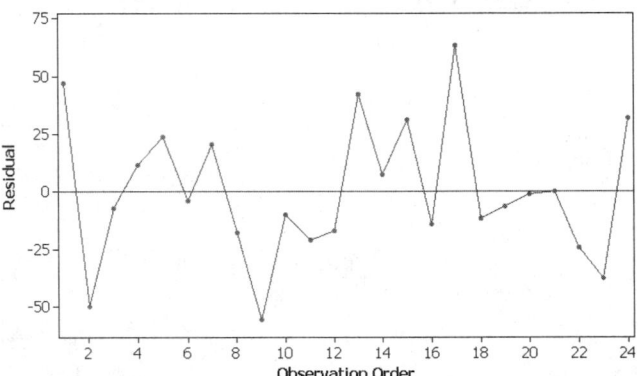

So that the Durbin–Watson test may be easily done, tables containing the points $d_{L,\alpha}$ and $d_{U,\alpha}$ have been constructed. These tables give the appropriate $d_{L,\alpha}$ and $d_{U,\alpha}$ points for various values of $\alpha$; $k$, the number of independent variables; and $n$, the number of observations. Tables A5 and A6 in Appendix A give values for $\alpha = .05$ and $\alpha = .01$. Note that, for instance, $k$ equals 1 for the simple linear trend model.

**EXAMPLE 6.5**

Consider the calculator sales analysis of Example 6.2. The linear trend model of this example yields the prediction equation

$$\hat{y}_t = 198.02899 + 8.07435\,t$$

The residuals obtained by using the linear trend model are computed using the equation

$$e_t = y_t - \hat{y}_t = y_t - (198.02899 + 8.07435\,t)$$

For example, the first three residuals are:

$$e_1 = y_1 - \hat{y}_1 = 197 - (198.02899 + 8.07435(1)) = -9.1033$$
$$e_2 = y_2 - \hat{y}_2 = 211 - (198.02899 + 8.07435(2)) = -3.1777$$
$$e_3 = y_3 - \hat{y}_3 = 203 - (198.02899 + 8.07435(3)) = -19.2520$$

If we wish to test

$$H_0: \text{The error terms are not autocorrelated}$$

versus the alternative

$$H_a: \text{The error terms are positively autocorrelated}$$

we compute the Durbin–Watson statistic to be

$$d = \frac{\sum_{t=2}^{24} (e_t - e_{t-1})^2}{\sum_{t=1}^{24} e_t^2}$$

$$= \frac{(-3.1777-(-9.1033))^2 + (-19.2520-(-3.1777))^2 + \cdots + (-7.8133-(-25.7390))^2}{(-9.1033)^2 + (-3.1777)^2 + \cdots + (-7.8133)^2}$$

$$= 1.682$$

Notice that the Durbin–Watson statistic is given on the SAS output of Figure 6.5. To test for positive autocorrelation at $\alpha = .05$, we use (see Table A5) $d_{L,.05} = 1.27$ and $d_{U,.05} = 1.45$. Since $d = 1.682 > d_{U,.05} = 1.45$, we do not reject $H_0$. That is, there is no evidence of positive (first-order) autocorrelation.

As a second example, the MINITAB output of Figure 6.7 shows that the Durbin–Watson statistic for the loan requests quadratic trend model is 2.10. Since $d = 2.10 > d_{U,.05} = 1.55$ (note that $k = 2$ for the quadratic trend model), we do not reject $H_0$. Again we conclude that there is no evidence of positive (first-order) autocorrelation.

The Durbin–Watson test can also be used to test for negative autocorrelation.

---

## DURBIN–WATSON TEST: (FIRST-ORDER) NEGATIVE AUTOCORRELATION

Consider testing the null hypothesis

$$H_0: \text{The error terms are not autocorrelated}$$

versus the alternative hypothesis

$$H_a: \text{The error terms are negatively autocorrelated}$$

Durbin and Watson have shown that based on setting the probability of a Type I error equal to $\alpha$, the points $d_{L,\alpha}$ and $d_{U,\alpha}$ are such that

1.  If $(4 - d) < d_{L,\alpha}$, we reject $H_0$.
2.  If $(4 - d) > d_{U,\alpha}$, we do not reject $H_0$.
3.  If $d_{L,\alpha} \leq (4 - d) \leq d_{U,\alpha}$, the test is inconclusive.

Here large values of $d$ (and hence small values of $4 - d$) lead to the conclusion of negative autocorrelation because if $d$ is large, this indicates that the differences $(e_t - e_{t-1})$ are large. This says that the adjacent error terms $\varepsilon_t$ and $\varepsilon_{t-1}$ are negatively autocorrelated. As an example, for the data and model in Example 6.2 we see that

$$(4 - d) = (4 - 1.682) = 2.318 > d_{U,.05} = 1.45$$

Therefore, on the basis of setting $\alpha$ equal to .05, we fail to reject the null hypothesis of no negative autocorrelation. That is, there is no evidence of negative (first-order) autocorrelation.

Finally, we can also use the Durbin–Watson statistic to test for positive or negative autocorrelation.

---

### DURBIN–WATSON TEST: (FIRST-ORDER) POSITIVE OR NEGATIVE AUTOCORRELATION

Consider testing the null hypothesis

$H_0$: The error terms are not autocorrelated

versus the alternative hypothesis

$H_a$: The error terms are positively or negatively autocorrelated

Durbin and Watson have shown that, based on setting the probability of a Type I error equal to $\alpha$,

1. If $d < d_{L,\alpha/2}$ or if $(4 - d) < d_{L,\alpha/2}$, we reject $H_0$.
2. If $d > d_{U,\alpha/2}$ and if $(4 - d) > d_{U,\alpha/2}$, we do not reject $H_0$.
3. If $d_{L,\alpha/2} \leq d \leq d_{U,\alpha/2}$ or $d_{L,\alpha/2} \leq (4 - d) \leq d_{U,\alpha/2}$, the test is inconclusive.

---

Before we conclude our presentation of the Durbin–Watson test, several comments are relevant. First, the validity of the Durbin–Watson test depends on the assumption that the population of all possible residuals at any time $t$ has a normal distribution. Second, positive autocorrelation is found in practice more commonly than negative autocorrelation. Therefore, the first test we presented (the test for positive autocorrelation) is used more often than the others. Third, most regression computer packages print the Durbin–Watson $d$-statistic. Fourth, first-order autocorrelation is not the only type of autocorrelation. Time series data can exhibit more complicated autocorrelated error structures. In such cases autocorrelation is detected by using what is called the **sample autocorrelation function.** We discuss this function in subsequent chapters.

When the error terms for a time series are autocorrelated, we must model the autocorrelation. We begin to explain how this is done in Section 6.6.

# 6.3 TYPES OF SEASONAL VARIATION

We now consider time series that display **seasonal variation.** We define two types of seasonal variation. If the magnitude of the seasonal swing does not depend on the level of the time series, we say that the time series exhibits **constant seasonal variation.** A time series with constant seasonal variation is illustrated in Figure 6.13. This time series appears to possess an increasing linear trend. Note that the size of the seasonal swing remains the same as the level of the time series increases. If the magnitude of the seasonal swing depends on the level of the time series, we say that the time series exhibits **increasing seasonal variation.** Figure 6.14 illustrates a time series that exhibits increasing seasonal variation. Notice that the magnitude of the seasonal swing (the size of the peaks and troughs) becomes larger as the level of the time series increases.

When a time series displays increasing seasonal variation, it is common practice to apply a transformation to the data in order to produce a transformed series that displays constant seasonal variation. A transformation of the form

$$y_t^* = y_t^\lambda \quad \text{where} \quad 0 < \lambda < 1$$

**FIGURE 6.13**
A time series exhibiting constant seasonal variation

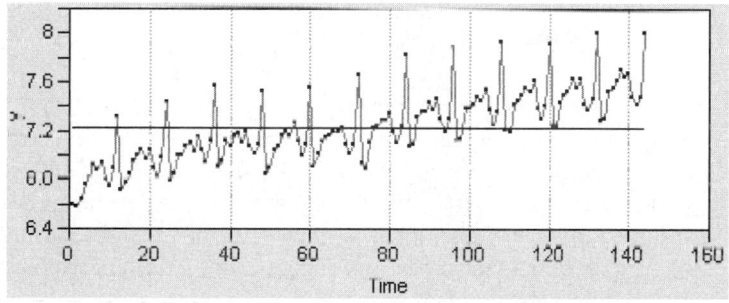

**FIGURE 6.14**
A time series exhibiting increasing seasonal variation

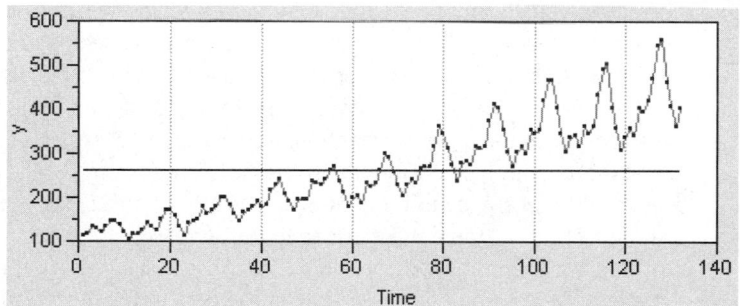

is often used. For instance, we might employ the square root transformation

$$y_t^* = y_t^{.5}$$

or the quartic root transformation

$$y_t^* = y_t^{.25}$$

It can be shown that as the power $\lambda$ approaches zero, the transformed value $y_t^\lambda$ approaches ln $y_t$, the natural logarithm of $y_t$. In fact, it is common practice to employ the transformation

$$y_t^* = \ln y_t$$

in order to obtain a transformed series that displays constant seasonal variation.

**EXAMPLE 6.6**   Traveler's Rest, Inc., operates four hotels in a midwestern city. The analysts in the operating division of the corporation were asked to develop a model that could be used to obtain short-term forecasts (up to one year) of the number of occupied rooms in the hotels. These forecasts were needed by various personnel to assist in decision making with regard to hiring additional help during the summer months, ordering materials that have long delivery lead times, budgeting of local advertising expenditures, and so forth.

The available historical data consisted of the number of occupied rooms during each day for the previous 15 years, starting on the first day of January. Because it was desired to obtain monthly forecasts, these data were reduced to monthly averages by dividing each monthly total by the number of days in the month. The monthly room averages for the first 14 of the 15 years, denoted by $y_1, y_2, \ldots, y_{168}$, are given in Table 6.4 and plotted in Figure 6.15.

At the outset it was decided to perform all analysis with the data from the first 14 of the previous 15 years so that forecasts for the 15th year could be used as a check on the validity of the model. Figure 6.15 shows that the monthly room averages follow a strong trend and that they have a seasonal pattern with one major and several minor peaks during the year. It also appears that the amount of seasonal variation is increasing with the level of the time series. This suggests that a transformation should be used in order to obtain a transformed series that displays constant seasonal variation.

Figure 6.16 gives a JMP IN plot of the square roots ($y_t^* = y_t^{.5}$) of the room averages. This plot suggests that the square root transformation is not strong enough to equalize the seasonal variation. Figure 6.17 shows a plot of the quartic roots ($y_t^* = y_t^{.25}$) of the room averages. The quartic root transformation seems to produce a transformed series with constant seasonal variation. Figure 6.18 gives a plot of the natural logarithms ($y_t^* = \ln y_t$) of the room averages. It might be concluded that this transformation has also equalized the seasonal variation. However, careful examination of the plot suggests that the logarithmic transformation may be overtransforming the data (note a slight funneling in appearance in the plot after $t = 120$ or so). Since both the logarithmic and the quartic root transformations seem to be reasonably effective, and since the logarithmic transformation is commonly used, we will try using the logarithmic transformation. We continue our analysis of these data in the next section.

**TABLE 6.4 Monthly Hotel Room Averages for 14 Years**

| $t$ | $y_t$ | $t$ | $y_t$ | $t$ | $y_t$ | $t$ | $y_t$ | $t$ | $y_t$ | $t$ | $y_t$ | $t$ | $y_t$ |
|---|---|---|---|---|---|---|---|---|---|---|---|---|---|
| 1 | 501 | 25 | 555 | 49 | 585 | 73 | 645 | 97 | 665 | 121 | 723 | 145 | 748 |
| 2 | 488 | 26 | 523 | 50 | 553 | 74 | 593 | 98 | 626 | 122 | 655 | 146 | 731 |
| 3 | 504 | 27 | 532 | 51 | 576 | 75 | 617 | 99 | 649 | 123 | 658 | 147 | 748 |
| 4 | 578 | 28 | 623 | 52 | 665 | 76 | 686 | 100 | 740 | 124 | 761 | 148 | 827 |
| 5 | 545 | 29 | 598 | 53 | 656 | 77 | 679 | 101 | 729 | 125 | 768 | 149 | 788 |
| 6 | 632 | 30 | 683 | 54 | 720 | 78 | 773 | 102 | 824 | 126 | 885 | 150 | 937 |
| 7 | 728 | 31 | 774 | 55 | 826 | 79 | 906 | 103 | 937 | 127 | 1067 | 151 | 1076 |
| 8 | 725 | 32 | 780 | 56 | 838 | 80 | 934 | 104 | 994 | 128 | 1038 | 152 | 1125 |
| 9 | 585 | 33 | 609 | 57 | 652 | 81 | 713 | 105 | 781 | 129 | 812 | 153 | 840 |
| 10 | 542 | 34 | 604 | 58 | 661 | 82 | 710 | 106 | 759 | 130 | 790 | 154 | 864 |
| 11 | 480 | 35 | 531 | 59 | 584 | 83 | 600 | 107 | 643 | 131 | 692 | 155 | 717 |
| 12 | 530 | 36 | 592 | 60 | 644 | 84 | 676 | 108 | 728 | 132 | 782 | 156 | 813 |
| 13 | 518 | 37 | 578 | 61 | 623 | 85 | 645 | 109 | 691 | 133 | 758 | 157 | 811 |
| 14 | 489 | 38 | 543 | 62 | 553 | 86 | 602 | 110 | 649 | 134 | 709 | 158 | 732 |
| 15 | 528 | 39 | 565 | 63 | 599 | 87 | 601 | 111 | 656 | 135 | 715 | 159 | 745 |
| 16 | 599 | 40 | 648 | 64 | 657 | 88 | 709 | 112 | 735 | 136 | 788 | 160 | 844 |
| 17 | 572 | 41 | 615 | 65 | 680 | 89 | 706 | 113 | 748 | 137 | 794 | 161 | 833 |
| 18 | 659 | 42 | 697 | 66 | 759 | 90 | 817 | 114 | 837 | 138 | 893 | 162 | 935 |
| 19 | 739 | 43 | 785 | 67 | 878 | 91 | 930 | 115 | 995 | 139 | 1046 | 163 | 1110 |
| 20 | 758 | 44 | 830 | 68 | 881 | 92 | 983 | 116 | 1040 | 140 | 1075 | 164 | 1124 |
| 21 | 602 | 45 | 645 | 69 | 705 | 93 | 745 | 117 | 809 | 141 | 812 | 165 | 868 |
| 22 | 587 | 46 | 643 | 70 | 684 | 94 | 735 | 118 | 793 | 142 | 822 | 166 | 860 |
| 23 | 497 | 47 | 551 | 71 | 577 | 95 | 620 | 119 | 692 | 143 | 714 | 167 | 762 |
| 24 | 558 | 48 | 606 | 72 | 656 | 96 | 698 | 120 | 763 | 144 | 802 | 168 | 877 |

**FIGURE 6.15**
JMP IN plot of monthly hotel room averages for 14 years

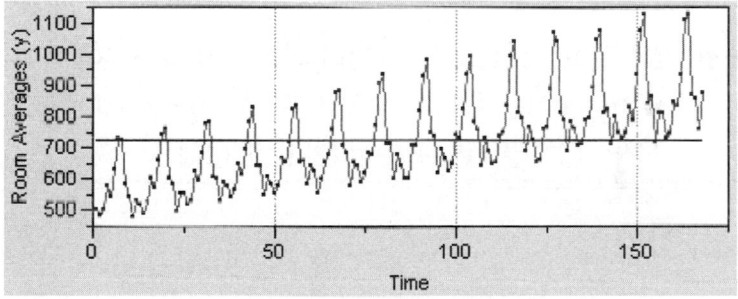

**FIGURE 6.16**
JMP IN plot of square roots of room averages

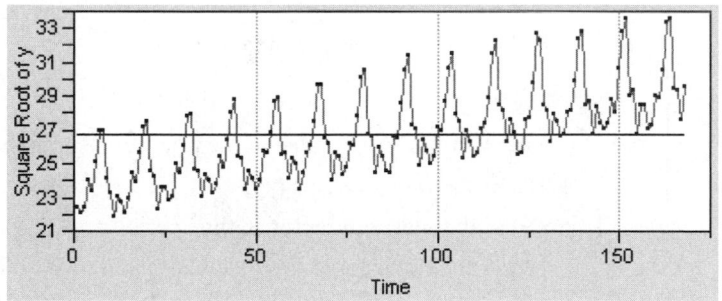

**FIGURE 6.17**
JMP IN plot of
quartic roots of
room averages

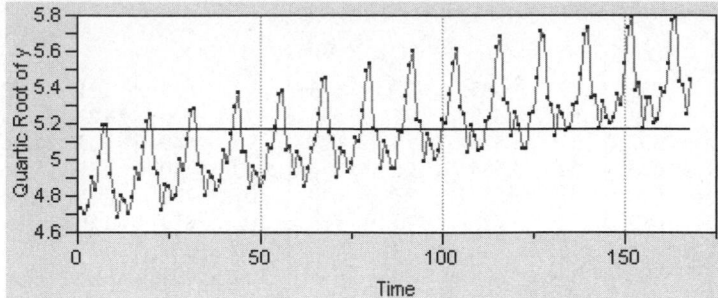

**FIGURE 6.18**
JMP IN plot of
natural logarithms
of room averages

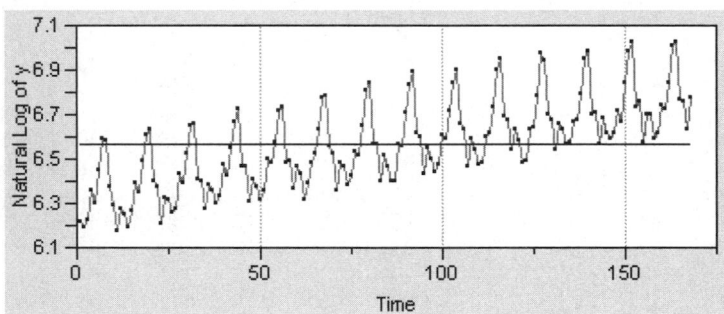

# 6.4   MODELING SEASONAL VARIATION BY USING DUMMY VARIABLES AND TRIGONOMETRIC FUNCTIONS

When analyzing a time series that exhibits constant seasonal variation, we often use a model of the following form.

$$y_t = TR_t + SN_t + \varepsilon_t$$

where

$y_t$ = the observed value of the time series in time period $t$

$TR_t$ = the **trend** in time period $t$

$SN_t$ = the **seasonal factor** in time period $t$

$\varepsilon_t$ = the **error term** (irregular factor) in time period $t$

This model says that the time series $y_t$ can be represented by an average level (denoted $\mu_t$) that changes over time according to the equation

$$\mu_t = TR_t + SN_t$$

combined with random fluctuations (represented by the error term $\varepsilon_t$) that cause the observations to deviate from the average level. We assume that the error term $\varepsilon_t$ satisfies the usual regression assumptions—constant variance, independence, and normality. Notice that this model implies that the magnitude of the seasonal swing is independent of the trend (constant seasonal variation). Furthermore, if $tr_t$ and $sn_t$ denote estimates of $TR_t$ and $SN_t$, respectively, then this model gives an estimate of $y_t$ that is equal to

$$\hat{y}_t = tr_t + sn_t$$

One way to model seasonal patterns is to employ **dummy variables.** Assuming that there are $L$ seasons (months, quarters, etc.) per year, we express the seasonal factor $SN_t$ as follows:

The **seasonal factor** expressed using *dummy variables* is

$$SN_t = \beta_{s1}x_{s1,t} + \beta_{s2}x_{s2,t} + \cdots + \beta_{s(L-1)}x_{s(L-1),t}$$

where $x_{s1,t}, x_{s2,t}, \ldots, x_{s(L-1),t}$ are **dummy variables** that are defined as follows:

$$x_{s1,t} = \begin{cases} 1 & \text{if time period } t \text{ is season 1} \\ 0 & \text{otherwise} \end{cases}$$

$$x_{s2,t} = \begin{cases} 1 & \text{if time period } t \text{ is season 2} \\ 0 & \text{otherwise} \end{cases}$$

$$\vdots$$

$$x_{s(L-1),t} = \begin{cases} 1 & \text{if time period } t \text{ is season } L-1 \\ 0 & \text{otherwise} \end{cases}$$

When $L = 12$, we have monthly data, and we will simplify the notation for the dummy variables by using $M_1$ for $x_{s1,t}$, $M_2$ for $x_{s2,t}, \ldots$, and $M_{11}$ for $x_{s11,t}$. When $L = 4$, we have quarterly data, and we will simplify the notation for the dummy variables by using $Q_1$ for $x_{s1,t}$, $Q_2$ for $x_{s2,t}$, and $Q_3$ for $x_{s3,t}$. For example, if $L = 12$ and the trend is linear, we have

$$y_t = TR_t + SN_t + \varepsilon_t$$
$$= \beta_0 + \beta_1 t + \beta_2 M_1 + \beta_3 M_2 + \cdots + \beta_{12} M_{11} + \varepsilon_t$$

If $L = 12$, the trend is linear, and the time period $t$ is season 2 (February), we have

$$y_t = \beta_0 + \beta_1 t + \beta_2(0) + \beta_3(1) + \cdots + \beta_{12}(0) + \varepsilon_t$$
$$= \beta_0 + \beta_1 t + \beta_3 + \varepsilon_t$$

The use of the dummy variables ensures that a seasonal parameter for season 2 (February) is added to the linear trend in each appropriate time period (periods that correspond to February). This seasonal parameter $\beta_3$ accounts for the seasonality of the time series in February. In general, the purpose of the dummy variable is to ensure that an appropriate seasonal parameter is included in the regression model in each time period.

We have, quite arbitrarily, set the seasonal parameter for season 12 (the last month, December) equal to zero. Thus the other 11 seasonal parameters ($\beta_2, \beta_3, \ldots, \beta_{12}$ for $L = 12$ and linear trend) are defined with respect to December. For example, $\beta_3$ is the difference, excluding the trend, between the level of the time series in February and the level of the time series in December. A positive $\beta_3$ implies that, excluding trend, the level of the time series in February can be expected to be greater than the level in December. A negative $\beta_3$ implies that, excluding trend, the level of the time series in February can be expected to be less than the level in December.

We do not have to set the seasonal parameter for season $L$ equal to zero. We must, however, set the seasonal parameter of one of the seasons equal to zero (and thus define the other seasonal parameters with respect to that season). If we do not, it can be shown that the least squares estimates of the model parameters cannot be calculated in the usual fashion. Also note that the dummy variable model assumes that the time series displays **constant** (sometimes called **additive**) **seasonal variation.** When a time series exhibits increasing seasonal variation, we generally apply a transformation to equalize the seasonal variation before fitting the dummy variable model.

**EXAMPLE 6.7**

We now consider using dummy variable regression to forecast the monthly hotel room averages in Table 6.4. The plot of Figure 6.15 suggests that the room averages are described by a linear trend and increasing seasonal variation. The plot of Figure 6.18 says that taking natural logarithms of the room averages may equalize the seasonal variation reasonably well. Thus we consider the regression model

$$y_t^* = TR_t + SN_t + \varepsilon_t$$
$$= \beta_0 + \beta_1 t + \beta_2 M_1 + \beta_3 M_2 + \cdots + \beta_{12} M_{11} + \varepsilon_t$$

where $y_t^* = \ln y_t$ and $M_1, M_2, \ldots, M_{11}$ are seasonal dummy variables. For example,

$$M_1 = \begin{cases} 1 & \text{if period } t \text{ is January} \\ 0 & \text{otherwise} \end{cases}$$

Note that we have not defined a dummy variable for December. Assuming that the constant variance, independence, and normality assumptions are satisfied, Figure 6.19 gives relevant portions of the SAS output of a regression analysis of the room average data using the above dummy variable model. The output shows that the model is significant ($F = 1126.61$ and $p$-value $< .0001$) and that the linear trend and each of the seasonal

**FIGURE 6.19** SAS output of an analysis of the logged room averages using dummy variable regression

```
                          Analysis of Variance

                              Sum of          Mean
Source              DF        Squares        Square      F Value    Pr > F

Model               12        6.06828       0.50569      1126.61    <.0001
Error              155        0.06957       0.00044886
Corrected Total    167        6.13785

          Root MSE            0.02119    R-Square      0.9887
          Dependent Mean      6.56389    Adj R-Sq      0.9878
          Coeff Var           0.32277

                         Parameter Estimates

                      Parameter      Standard
        Variable   DF  Estimate        Error      t Value    Pr > |t|

        Intercept   1   6.28756       0.00643      978.26     <.0001
        Time        1   0.00273       0.00003379    80.65     <.0001
        M1          1  -0.04161       0.00802       -5.19     <.0001
        M2          1  -0.11208       0.00801      -13.98     <.0001
        M3          1  -0.08446       0.00801      -10.54     <.0001
        M4          1   0.03983       0.00801        4.97     <.0001
        M5          1   0.02040       0.00801        2.55      0.0119
        M6          1   0.14691       0.00801       18.34     <.0001
        M7          1   0.28902       0.00801       36.09     <.0001
        M8          1   0.31119       0.00801       38.86     <.0001
        M9          1   0.05599       0.00801        6.99     <.0001
        M10         1   0.03954       0.00801        4.94     <.0001
        M11         1  -0.11222       0.00801      -14.01     <.0001

          Durbin-Watson D                   1.190

      Dep Var  Predicted    Std Error
Obs     Lny    Value  Mean Predict     95% CL Mean         95% CL Predict
169      .     6.7065    0.006427    6.6938   6.7192    6.6628    6.7503
170      .     6.6388    0.006427    6.6261   6.6515    6.5950    6.6825
171      .     6.6691    0.006427    6.6564   6.6818    6.6254    6.7129
172      .     6.7961    0.006427    6.7834   6.8088    6.7524    6.8399
173      .     6.7794    0.006427    6.7667   6.7921    6.7357    6.8232
174      .     6.9087    0.006427    6.8960   6.9214    6.8649    6.9524
175      .     7.0535    0.006427    7.0408   7.0662    7.0098    7.0972
176      .     7.0784    0.006427    7.0657   7.0911    7.0347    7.1221
177      .     6.8259    0.006427    6.8132   6.8386    6.7822    6.8697
178      .     6.8122    0.006427    6.7995   6.8249    6.7685    6.8559
179      .     6.6632    0.006427    6.6505   6.6759    6.6194    6.7069
180      .     6.7781    0.006427    6.7654   6.7908    6.7344    6.8218
```

dummy variables are significant (every $t$-statistic has a related $p$-value that is less than .05). In addition, $R^2 = .9887$ and $s = 0.02119$.

Using the least squares estimates given on the SAS output, we compute a point forecast of $y^*_{169} = \ln y_{169}$ to be

$$\hat{y}^*_{169} = b_0 + b_1(169) + b_2(1)$$

$$= 6.28756 + .00273(169) + (-.04161)(1)$$

$$= 6.7065$$

Note that this point forecast is given on the SAS output of Figure 6.19. Therefore, a point prediction of $y_{169}$ is

$$\hat{y}_{169} = e^{6.7065} = 817.70$$

Similarly, a point forecast of $y^*_{170} = \ln y_{170}$ is

$$\hat{y}^*_{170} = b_0 + b_1(170) + b_3(1)$$
$$= 6.28756 + .00273(170) + (-.11208)$$
$$= 6.6388$$

and a point forecast of $y_{170}$ is

$$\hat{y}_{170} = e^{6.6388} = 764.18$$

Furthermore, the SAS output shows that a 95% prediction interval for $y^*_{169} = \ln y_{169}$ is [6.6628, 6.7503]. It follows that a 95% prediction interval for $y_{169}$ is

$$[e^{6.6628}, e^{6.7503}] = [782.74, 854.32]$$

This interval says that Traveler's Rest, Inc., can be 95% confident that the monthly hotel room average occupancy in period 169 will be no less than 782.74 rooms per day and no more than 854.32 rooms per day.

The Durbin–Watson statistic for the above model (1.190 for the logged data model) is small. Although Tables A5 and A6 do not provide critical values for $n = 168$ and $k = 12$, this value of the Durbin–Watson statistic suggests that the independence assumption is violated. In Section 6.6 we demonstrate how to find an improved model.

Sometimes regression models involving **trigonometric terms** can be used to forecast time series exhibiting either constant or increasing seasonal variation. Two such models that can be useful when modeling constant seasonal variation are as follows (here $L$ is the number of seasons in a year).

---

**TRIGONOMETRIC MODELS FOR CONSTANT SEASONAL VARIATION**

1. $y_t = \beta_0 + \beta_1 t + \beta_2 \sin\left(\dfrac{2\pi t}{L}\right) + \beta_3 \cos\left(\dfrac{2\pi t}{L}\right) + \varepsilon_t$

and

2. $y_t = \beta_0 + \beta_1 t + \beta_2 \sin\left(\dfrac{2\pi t}{L}\right) + \beta_3 \cos\left(\dfrac{2\pi t}{L}\right) + \beta_4 \sin\left(\dfrac{4\pi t}{L}\right)$

   $+ \beta_5 \cos\left(\dfrac{4\pi t}{L}\right) + \varepsilon_t$

These models assume a linear trend, but they can be altered to handle other trends. The first of these models is useful in modeling a very regular seasonal time series that exhibits constant seasonal variation. The second model possesses terms that allow the modeling of a time series displaying constant seasonal variation and having a more complicated seasonal pattern.

**EXAMPLE 6.8**   Again consider forecasting the monthly hotel room averages given in Table 6.4. Since this time series seems to have a linear trend and increasing seasonal variation, we consider the trigonometric regression model

$$y_t^* = \beta_0 + \beta_1 t + \beta_2 \sin\left(\frac{2\pi t}{12}\right) + \beta_3 \cos\left(\frac{2\pi t}{12}\right) + \beta_4 \sin\left(\frac{4\pi t}{12}\right) + \beta_5 \cos\left(\frac{4\pi t}{12}\right) + \varepsilon_t$$

where $y_t^* = \ln y_t$.

Figure 6.20 gives relevant portions of the SAS output that is obtained when this model is fit to the monthly room averages. We find that the model is significant ($F = 358.75$ and p-value $<.0001$) and that the linear trend and each of the sine and cosine terms are significant (every t-statistic has a related p-value that is less than .05). In addition, $R^2 = .9172$ and $s = .05602$.

Using the least squares estimates given on the SAS output, we compute a point forecast of $y_{169}^* = \ln y_{169}$ to be

$$\hat{y}_{169}^* = 6.33275 + .00274t - .10092 \sin\left(\frac{2\pi(169)}{12}\right) - .12665\left(\frac{2\pi(169)}{12}\right)$$

$$+ .06626\left(\frac{4\pi(169)}{12}\right) + .01898\left(\frac{4\pi(169)}{12}\right)$$

$$- 6.7018$$

Note that this point forecast is given on the SAS output of Figure 6.20. Therefore, a point prediction of $y_{169}$ is

$$\hat{y}_{169} - e^{6.7018} = 813.87$$

Furthermore, the SAS output shows that a 95% prediction interval for $y_{169}^* = \ln y_{169}$ is $[6.5885, 6.8150]$. It follows that a 95% prediction interval for $y_{169}$ is

$$[e^{6.5885}, e^{6.8150}] = [726.69, 911.42]$$

Note that this interval is much less precise (length $911.42 - 726.69 = 184.73$) than the 95% prediction interval obtained by fitting the dummy variable model of Example 6.7 (length $854.32 - 782.74 = 71.58$).

Trigonometric time series models sometimes give useful predictions. However, the authors generally consider dummy variable regression (and other methods presented later) to be superior to trigonometric models for modeling seasonal variation. This is because dummy variable models (and other techniques) use a different parameter to model the effect of each different season in a year.

**FIGURE 6.20** SAS output of an analysis of monthly room averages using a trigonometric model

Analysis of Variance

| Source | DF | Sum of Squares | Mean Square | F Value | Pr > F |
|---|---|---|---|---|---|
| Model | 5 | 5.62944 | 1.12589 | 358.75 | <.0001 |
| Error | 162 | 0.50842 | 0.00314 | | |
| Corrected Total | 167 | 6.13785 | | | |

| | | | |
|---|---|---|---|
| Root MSE | 0.05602 | R-Square | 0.9172 |
| Dependent Mean | 6.56389 | Adj R-Sq | 0.9146 |
| Coeff Var | 0.85348 | | |

Parameter Estimates

| Variable | Label | DF | Parameter Estimate | Standard Error | t Value | Pr > \|t\| |
|---|---|---|---|---|---|---|
| Intercept | Intercept | 1 | 6.33275 | 0.00870 | 728.22 | <.0001 |
| Time | Time | 1 | 0.00274 | 0.00008930 | 30.63 | <.0001 |
| sintwo | | 1 | -0.10092 | 0.00612 | -16.49 | <.0001 |
| costwo | | 1 | -0.12665 | 0.00611 | -20.72 | <.0001 |
| sinfour | | 1 | 0.06626 | 0.00611 | 10.84 | <.0001 |
| cosfour | | 1 | 0.01898 | 0.00611 | 3.10 | 0.0022 |

Durbin-Watson D                 2.630

| Obs | Dep Var Lny | Predicted Value | Std Error Mean Predict | 95% CL Mean | | 95% CL Predict | |
|---|---|---|---|---|---|---|---|
| 169 | . | 6.7018 | 0.0124 | 6.6773 | 6.7262 | 6.5885 | 6.8150 |
| 170 | . | 6.6949 | 0.0126 | 6.6701 | 6.7198 | 6.5815 | 6.8083 |
| 171 | . | 6.6806 | 0.0126 | 6.6556 | 6.7056 | 6.5672 | 6.7940 |
| 172 | . | 6.7123 | 0.0126 | 6.6874 | 6.7371 | 6.5989 | 6.8257 |
| 173 | . | 6.8173 | 0.0125 | 6.7926 | 6.8420 | 6.7039 | 6.9307 |
| 174 | . | 6.9543 | 0.0125 | 6.9296 | 6.9791 | 6.8410 | 7.0677 |
| 175 | . | 7.0385 | 0.0126 | 7.0136 | 7.0633 | 6.9251 | 7.1519 |
| 176 | . | 7.0128 | 0.0126 | 6.9879 | 7.0377 | 6.8994 | 7.1262 |
| 177 | . | 6.8989 | 0.0126 | 6.8741 | 6.9236 | 6.7855 | 7.0122 |
| 178 | . | 6.7768 | 0.0125 | 6.7522 | 6.8015 | 6.6635 | 6.8902 |
| 179 | . | 6.7153 | 0.0126 | 6.6905 | 6.7401 | 6.6019 | 6.8286 |
| 180 | . | 6.7174 | 0.0128 | 6.6922 | 6.7427 | 6.6040 | 6.8309 |

# 6.5  GROWTH CURVE MODELS

All of the models presented so far in this chapter describe trend and seasonal effects by using deterministic functions of time that are *linear in the parameters*. For example, the model

$$y_t = \text{TR}_t + \text{SN}_t + \varepsilon_t$$
$$= \beta_0 + \beta_1 t + \beta_2 t^2 + \beta_3 Q_1 + \beta_4 Q_2 + \beta_5 Q_3 + \varepsilon_t$$

is linear in the parameters $\beta_0$, $\beta_1$, $\beta_2$, $\beta_3$, $\beta_4$, and $\beta_5$. That is, each term in the model is the product of a model parameter and a numeric value determined by the observed data.

Sometimes, however, useful models are not linear in the parameters. For instance, consider what we call the **growth curve model.**

---

The **growth curve model** is

$$y_t = \beta_0 \left( \beta_1^t \right) \varepsilon_t$$

---

This model is not linear in the parameters since the independent variable $t$ enters as an exponent and $\beta_0$ is multiplied by $\beta_1^t$. The model further departs from the usual linear model since the error term $\varepsilon_t$ is multiplicative rather than additive [that is, multiplied by—rather than added to—$\beta_0(\beta_1^t)$]. To apply the techniques of estimation and prediction we presented in previous discussions, we must transform such a nonlinear model to one that is linear in the parameters. The model

$$y_t = \beta_0 \left( \beta_1^t \right) \varepsilon_t$$

can be transformed to a linear model by taking logarithms on both sides. Either base 10 logarithms (denoted log) or natural (base $e$) logarithms (denoted ln) can be used. Both base 10 and natural logarithms can easily be obtained on many modern pocket calculators or by using computer routines. Two important properties of logarithms are given by

$$\log(AB) = \log(A) + \log(B)$$

and

$$\log(A^r) = r \log(A)$$

where $A$ and $B$ are positive numbers. These properties allow us to transform some nonlinear models to achieve models that are linear in the parameters.

If $\beta_0 > 0$ and $\beta_1 > 0$, applying a logarithmic transformation to the model $y_t = \beta_0(\beta_1^t)$ yields

$$\log(y_t) = \log(\beta_0) + \log(\beta_1)t + \log(\varepsilon_t)$$

If we let $\alpha_0 = \log(\beta_0)$, $\alpha_1 = \log(\beta_1)$, and $u_t = \log(\varepsilon_t)$, the transformed version of the model becomes

$$\log(y_t) = \alpha_0 + \alpha_1 t + u_t$$

Thus the model with the dependent variable $\log(y_t)$ is linear in the parameters $\alpha_0$ and $\alpha_1$.

Cases in which a model

$$y_t = \beta_0 \left( \beta_1^t \right) \varepsilon_t$$

may be appropriate can be identified by data plots of $y_t$ versus $t$. Plots of the expression $\beta_0(\beta_1^t)$ for several combinations of $\beta_0$ and $\beta_1$ are shown in Figure 6.21. Plots of

**FIGURE 6.21**
Exponential curves
of the form
$y_t = \beta_0(\beta_1^t)$

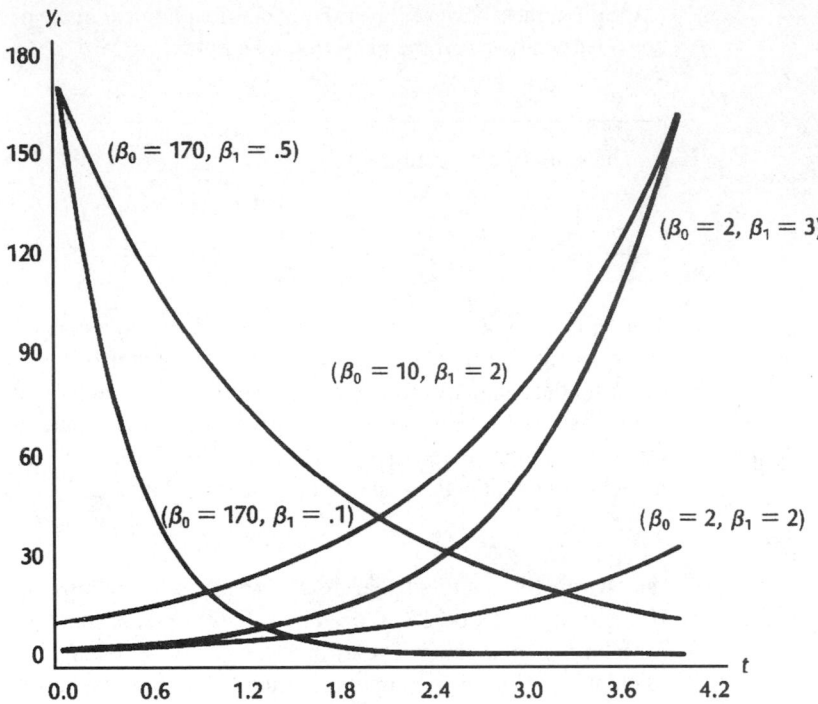

observed data would have points "scattered about" such a function. The multiplicative error term would cause more variation around the high parts of the curve and less variation around the low parts, since the variation in $y_t$ is dependent on the level of $\beta_0(\beta_1^t)$—that is, given the same error term $\varepsilon_t$, the larger $\beta_0(\beta_1^t)$ is, the larger is the variation in $y_t$.

Figure 6.21 shows that the curves described by

$$y_t = \beta_0(\beta_1^t)$$

may be increasing ($\beta_1 > 1$) or decreasing ($0 < \beta_1 < 1$) functions of $t$. We can see that $\beta_0$ is the intercept and that $\beta_1$ determines the amount of curvature in the plot. The curvature gets more pronounced as $\beta_1$ moves away from 1 in either direction. We now present an example.

**EXAMPLE 6.9**   Western Steakhouses, a fast-food chain, opened 15 years ago. Each year since then the number of steakhouses in operation, $y_t$, was recorded. An analyst for the firm wishes to use these data to predict the number of steakhouses that will be in operation next year.

The steakhouse data ($y_t$) are plotted against time ($t$) in Figure 6.22. This plot shows an exponential increase reminiscent of the plots in Figure 6.21 where $\beta_1$ is greater than 1.

**TABLE 6.5** Western Steakhouse Openings over the Last 15 Years

| Year ($t$) | $y_t$ | ln $y_t$ | Year ($t$) | $y_t$ | ln $y_t$ |
|---|---|---|---|---|---|
| 1 | 11 | 2.398 | 9 | 82 | 4.407 |
| 2 | 14 | 2.639 | 10 | 99 | 4.595 |
| 3 | 16 | 2.773 | 11 | 119 | 4.779 |
| 4 | 22 | 3.091 | 12 | 156 | 5.050 |
| 5 | 28 | 3.332 | 13 | 257 | 5.549 |
| 6 | 36 | 3.584 | 14 | 284 | 5.649 |
| 7 | 46 | 3.829 | 15 | 403 | 5.999 |
| 8 | 67 | 4.205 | | | |

**FIGURE 6.22**
JMP IN plot of Western Steakhouse openings versus time (years)

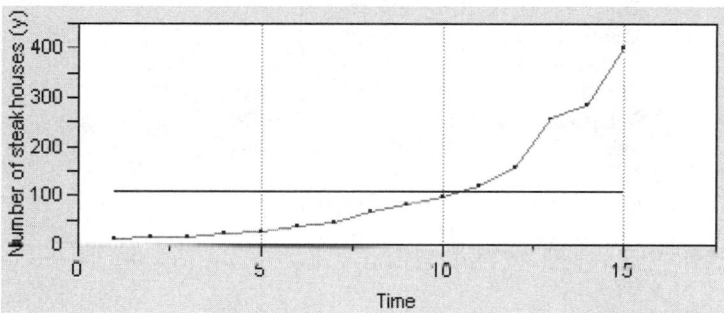

This suggests that the model

$$y_t = \beta_0\left(\beta_1^t\right)\varepsilon_t$$

may be appropriate. The natural logarithms of the steakhouse data (ln $y_t$) are given in Table 6.5 and are plotted in Figure 6.23. This plot suggests that the relationship between ln $y_t$ and $t$ is linear. Applying the logarithmic transformation to the model

$$y_t = \beta_0\left(\beta_1^t\right)\varepsilon_t$$

we obtain

$$\ln y_t = \ln(\beta_0) + t\ln(\beta_1) + \ln\varepsilon_t$$

Defining $\alpha_0 = \ln(\beta_0)$, $\alpha_1 = \ln(\beta_1)$, and $u_t = \ln\varepsilon_t$, we have

$$\ln y_t = \alpha_0 + \alpha_1 t + u_t$$

When this model is fitted to the steakhouse data, we obtain the MINITAB output given in Figure 6.24. Using this MINITAB output, we can see that

1. The least squares point estimates of $\alpha_0$ and $\alpha_1$ are

$$\hat{\alpha}_0 = 2.07012 \quad \text{and} \quad \hat{\alpha}_1 = .25688$$

**FIGURE 6.23**
JMP IN plot of the natural logarithms of Western Steakhouse openings

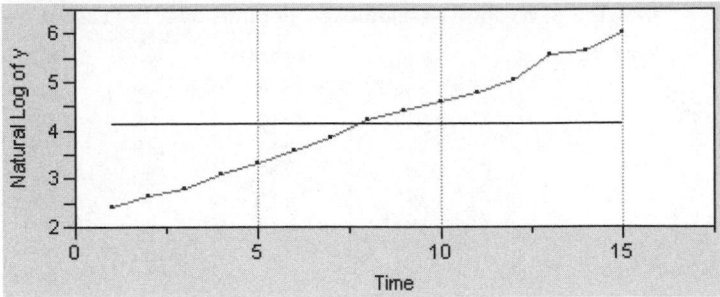

**FIGURE 6.24**
MINITAB output of a regression analysis of the steakhouse data using a growth curve model

```
The regression equation is
Lny = 2.07 + 0.257 Year

Predictor         Coef      SE Coef          T         P
Constant       2.07012      0.04103      50.45     0.000
Year          0.256880     0.004513      56.92     0.000

S = 0.07552     R-Sq = 99.6%     R-Sq(adj) = 99.6%

Analysis of Variance

Source           DF          SS          MS          F         P
Regression        1      18.477      18.477    3239.97     0.000
Residual Error   13       0.074       0.006
Total            14      18.551

         Durbin-Watson statistic = 1.88

Predicted Values for New Observations

New Obs     Fit     SE Fit        95.0% CI              95.0% PI
1        6.1802     0.0410   ( 6.0916, 6.2689)   ( 5.9945, 6.3659)
```

Since $\alpha_1 = \ln(\beta_1)$, it follows that

$$\beta_1 = e^{\alpha_1}$$

Thus a point estimate of $\beta_1$ is

$$\hat{\beta}_1 = e^{\hat{\alpha}_1} = e^{.25688} = 1.293$$

The model

$$y_t = \beta_0\left(\beta_1^t\right)\varepsilon_t = \left[\beta_0\left(\beta_1^{t-1}\right)\right]\beta_1\varepsilon_t \approx (y_{t-1})\beta_1\varepsilon_t$$

implies that we expect $y_t$ to be approximately $\beta_1$ times $y_{t-1}$. Therefore, since the point estimate of $\beta_1$ is 1.293, we estimate $y_t$ to be approximately 1.293 times $y_{t-1}$, and thus we estimate $y_t$ to be

$$100(\hat{\beta}_1 - 1)\% = 100(1.293 - 1)\% = 29.3\%$$

greater than $y_{t-1}$. Here, $100(\hat{\beta}_1 - 1)\% = 29.3\%$ is the point estimate of the **growth rate** $100(\beta_1 - 1)\%$.

2.  The point prediction of $\ln y_{16}$, where $y_{16}$ is the number of steakhouses that will be in operation in period 16, is

$$\widehat{\ln y_{16}} = \hat{\alpha}_0 + \hat{\alpha}_1 t = 2.07012 + .25688(16) = 6.1802$$

Thus a point prediction of $y_{16}$ is

$$\hat{y}_{16} = e^{6.1802} = 483.09$$

3.  The 95% prediction interval for $\ln y_{16}$ is

$$[5.9945, 6.3659]$$

and thus a 95% prediction interval for $y_{16}$ is

$$[e^{5.9945}, e^{6.3659}] = [401.22, 581.67]$$

Finally, note that if we consider testing

$$H_0: \text{The error terms are not autocorrelated}$$

the Durbin–Watson statistic is $d = 1.88$. Since $d = 1.88 > d_{U,.05} = 1.36$, we do not reject $H_0$. Thus there is no evidence to suggest that the error terms for this model display first-order autocorrelation.

# 6.6 HANDLING FIRST-ORDER AUTOCORRELATION

We have seen that the error terms for time series regression models are often auto-correlated. We have also seen that the Durbin–Watson statistic can be used to detect first-order autocorrelation. In this section we consider how to model a time series that possesses a first-order autocorrelated error structure.

When the error terms for a time series regression model are autocorrelated, the model is inadequate. In such a case we should remedy the problem by modeling the autocorrelation. If we ignore autocorrelated error terms, we will pay a penalty in terms of wider prediction intervals. By taking autocorrelation into account, we can obtain more precise prediction intervals.

One autocorrelated error structure that is frequently encountered is the **first-order autoregressive process**. This model relates $\varepsilon_t$, the error term in time period $t$, to $\varepsilon_{t-1}$, the error term in time period $t - 1$, as follows.

---

The **first-order autoregressive process** is defined by

$$\varepsilon_t = \phi_1 \varepsilon_{t-1} + a_t$$

---

Here $a_t$ is assumed to be an error term (often called a **random shock**) with mean zero that satisfies the constant variance, independence, and normality assumptions. We define $\phi_1$ to be the **correlation coefficient** between $\varepsilon_t$ and $\varepsilon_{t-1}$. That is, $\phi_1$ is defined to be the correlation coefficient between error terms separated by one time period. If $\phi_1 > 0$, this indicates that the error terms are positively autocorrelated. It is easy to see that if $\phi_1 > 0$, then a positive error term $\varepsilon_{t-1}$ tends to produce another positive error term $\varepsilon_t$. Likewise, a negative error term $\varepsilon_{t-1}$ tends to produce another negative error term $\varepsilon_t$. On the other hand, if $\phi_1 < 0$, the error terms are negatively autocorrelated. Therefore, if $\phi_1 < 0$, then a positive error term $\varepsilon_{t-1}$ tends to produce a negative error term $\varepsilon_t$. However, a negative error term $\varepsilon_{t-1}$ tends to produce a positive error term $\varepsilon_t$.

Now, letting $x_{t1}, x_{t2}, \ldots, x_{tk}$ denote the values of the independent variables $x_1$, $x_2, \ldots, x_k$ that have been or will be observed in the time period $t$, consider the time series regression model

$$y_t = \beta_0 + \beta_1 x_{t1} + \beta_2 x_{t2} + \cdots + \beta_k x_{tk} + \varepsilon_t$$

where $\varepsilon_t$ is described by a first-order autoregressive process. That is,

$$\varepsilon_t = \phi_1 \varepsilon_{t-1} + a_t$$

We can employ SAS PROC ARIMA to obtain point estimates $b_0, b_1, b_2, \ldots, b_k$, and $\hat{\phi}_1$ of the model parameters $\beta_0, \beta_1, \beta_2, \ldots, \beta_k$, and $\phi_1$. Using these estimates, we can obtain point predictions as follows (here we denote predictions of $y_t$ and $\varepsilon_t$ as $\hat{y}_t$ and $\hat{\varepsilon}_t$).

---

A *point prediction* made at time $T$ for the future value $y_{T+\tau}$ is

$$\hat{y}_{T+\tau} = b_0 + b_1 x_{T+\tau,1} + b_2 x_{T+\tau,2} + \cdots + b_k x_{T+\tau,k} + \hat{\phi}_1 \hat{e}_{T+\tau-1}$$

Here, if $\tau = 1$ (the prediction is for one time period ahead), then

$$\hat{\varepsilon}_{T+\tau-1} = \hat{\varepsilon}_T$$
$$= y_T - [b_0 + b_1 x_{T1} + b_2 x_{T2} + \cdots + b_k x_{Tk}]$$

since $y_T$ has been observed. If $\tau > 1$ (the prediction is for more than one time period ahead), then $y_{T+\tau-1}$ has not been observed. Therefore, if $\tau > 1$

$$\hat{\varepsilon}_{T+\tau-1} = \hat{y}_{T+\tau-1} - [b_0 + b_1 x_{T+\tau-1,1} + b_2 x_{T+\tau-1,2} + \cdots + b_k x_{T+\tau-1,k}]$$

---

Furthermore, approximate $100(1 - \alpha)\%$ prediction intervals are obtained as follows.

---

1. If $\tau = 1$, then an **approximate $100(1 - \alpha)\%$ prediction interval for $y_{T+1}$ is**

$$[\hat{y}_{T+1} \pm z_{[\alpha/2]}s]$$

2. If $\tau = 2$, then an **approximate $100(1 - \alpha)\%$ prediction interval for $y_{T+2}$ is**

$$\left[\hat{y}_{T+2} \pm z_{[\alpha/2]}s\sqrt{1 + (\hat{\phi}_1)^2}\right]$$

3. If $\tau \geq 3$, then an **approximate $100(1 - \alpha)\%$ prediction interval for $y_{T+\tau}$ is**

$$\left[\hat{y}_{T+\tau} \pm z_{[\alpha/2]}s\sqrt{1 + (\hat{\phi}_1)^2 + \cdots + (\hat{\phi}_1)^{2(\tau-1)}}\right]$$

---

In these formulas, $z_{[\alpha/2]}$ is defined as usual, $s$ is the standard error, and $\hat{\phi}_1$ is the estimate of $\phi_1$.

**EXAMPLE 6.10**    In Example 6.7 we considered analyzing the monthly hotel room averages given in Table 6.4 by using the dummy variable regression model

$$y_t^* = \beta_0 + \beta_1 t + \beta_2 M_1 + \beta_3 M_2 + \cdots + \beta_{12} M_{11} + \varepsilon_t$$

where

$$y_t^* = \ln y_t$$

Recall that the Durbin–Watson statistic (see Figure 6.19) for this model suggests that the error terms may be autocorrelated. Therefore, consider the model

$$y_t^* = \beta_0 + \beta_1 t + \beta_2 M_1 + \beta_3 M_2 + \cdots + \beta_{12} M_{11} + \varepsilon_t$$

where

$$\varepsilon_t = \phi_1 \varepsilon_{t-1} + a_t$$

Here $a_t$ is a random shock with mean zero that satisfies the constant variance, independence, and normality assumptions. That is, we suppose that $\varepsilon_t$ is described by a first-order autoregressive process. Figure 6.25 gives relevant portions of the SAS output that

**FIGURE 6.25** PROC ARIMA analysis of logged hotel room averages using the model
$y_t^* = \beta_0 + \beta_1 t + \beta_2 M_1 + \beta_3 M_2 + \cdots + \beta_{12} M_{11} + \varepsilon_t$ where $\varepsilon_t = \phi_1 \varepsilon_{t-1} + a_t$

```
                      Conditional Least Squares Estimation

                              Standard                Approx
Parameter       Estimate        Error     t Value   Pr > |t|    Lag   Variable

MU               6.28537      0.0072031     872.59    <.0001      0    Lny
AR1,1            0.39838      0.07462         5.34    <.0001      1    Lny
NUM1             0.0027377    0.00005105     53.63    <.0001      0    Time
NUM2            -0.03994      0.0063323      -6.31    <.0001      0    M1
NUM3            -0.11070      0.0074140     -14.93    <.0001      0    M2
NUM4            -0.08321      0.0077914     -10.68    <.0001      0    M3
NUM5             0.04103      0.0079329       5.17    <.0001      0    M4
NUM6             0.02156      0.0079842       2.70    0.0077      0    M5
NUM7             0.14805      0.0079958      18.52    <.0001      0    M6
NUM8             0.29014      0.0079796      36.36    <.0001      0    M7
NUM9             0.31229      0.0079215      39.42    <.0001      0    M8
NUM10            0.05703      0.0077673       7.34    <.0001      0    M9
NUM11            0.04047      0.0073634       5.50    <.0001      0    M10
NUM12           -0.11156      0.0062314     -17.90    <.0001      0    M11

                Constant Estimate      3.781419
                Variance Estimate      0.000382
                Std Error Estimate     0.019533
                AIC                   -832.233
                SBC                   -788.497
                Number of Residuals     168
        * AIC and SBC do not include log determinant.
```

(a) Estimation of model parameters

```
                    Forecasts for variable Lny

Obs      Forecast      Std Error      95% Confidence Limits

169       6.7205        0.0195         6.6822        6.7588
170       6.6450        0.0210         6.6038        6.6862
171       6.6723        0.0213         6.6306        6.7139
172       6.7981        0.0213         6.7563        6.8398
173       6.7809        0.0213         6.7391        6.8226
174       6.9099        0.0213         6.8682        6.9516
175       7.0547        0.0213         7.0129        7.0964
176       7.0795        0.0213         7.0378        7.1212
177       6.8270        0.0213         6.7852        6.8687
178       6.8131        0.0213         6.7714        6.8549
179       6.6639        0.0213         6.6221        6.7056
180       6.7782        0.0213         6.7364        6.8199
```

(b) Forecasts of $y_t^* = \ln y_t$ for $t = 169, \ldots, 180$

```
Obs    Forecasty     L95CI     U95CI
169     829.26      798.11    861.62
170     768.95      737.91    801.30
171     790.20      757.96    823.81
172     896.11      859.49    934.30
173     880.83      844.82    918.37
174    1002.15      961.18   1044.87
175    1158.24     1110.89   1207.61
176    1187.39     1138.85   1238.00
177     922.40      884.69    961.71
178     909.73      872.54    948.51
179     783.57      751.54    816.97
180     878.45      842.54    915.89
```

(c) Forecasts of $y_{169}$ through $y_{180}$

is obtained when we use PROC ARIMA to analyze the logged hotel room averages using this model. Note that the SAS output includes least squares estimates $b_0, b_1, b_2, b_3, \ldots, b_{12}$, and $\hat{\phi}_1$ of the parameters $\beta_0, \beta_1, \beta_2, \beta_3, \ldots, \beta_{12}$, and $\phi_1$. Using these estimates, a point prediction made in time period 168 for $y_{169}^*$ is

$$
\begin{aligned}
\hat{y}_{169}^* &= 6.28537 + .0027377(169) - .03994M_1 - .1107M_2 \\
&\quad + \cdots + .04047M_{10} - .11156M_{11} + .39838\hat{\varepsilon}_{T+\tau-1} \\
&= 6.28537 + .0027377(169) - .03994(1) - .1107(0) + \cdots + .04047(0) \\
&\quad - .11156(0) + .39838\hat{\varepsilon}_{168} \\
&= 6.28537 + .0027377(169) - .03994 + .39838\hat{\varepsilon}_{168} \\
&= 6.7081 + .39838\hat{\varepsilon}_{168}
\end{aligned}
$$

Since $y_{168}$ is 877, it follows that

$$
\begin{aligned}
\hat{\varepsilon}_{168} &= \ln 877 - [6.28537 + .0027377(168)] \\
&= 6.7765 - 6.7453 \\
&= .0312
\end{aligned}
$$

Thus

$$
\hat{y}_{169}^* = 6.7081 + .39838(.0312) - 6.7205
$$

Note that this point prediction is given in the SAS output of Figure 6.25(b). Furthermore, an approximate 95% prediction interval for $y_{169}^*$ (also given in the SAS output) is

$$
\begin{aligned}
[\hat{y}_{169}^* \pm z_{[\alpha/2]}s] &= [6.7205 \pm z_{[.025]}(.019533)] \\
&= [6.7205 \pm 1.96(.019533)] = [6.7205 \pm .0383] \\
&= [6.6822, 6.7588]
\end{aligned}
$$

As another example, a point prediction made in time period 168 for $y_{170}^*$ is

$$
\begin{aligned}
\hat{y}_{170}^* &= 6.28537 + .0027377(170) - .1107(1) + .39838\hat{\varepsilon}_{169} \\
&= 6.6401 + .39838\hat{\varepsilon}_{169}
\end{aligned}
$$

where

$$
\begin{aligned}
\hat{\varepsilon}_{169} &= \hat{y}_{169}^* - [6.28537 + .0027377(169) - .03994] \\
&= 6.7205 - 6.7081 = .0124
\end{aligned}
$$

Thus

$$
\begin{aligned}
\hat{y}_{170}^* &= 6.6401 + .39838(.0124) \\
&= 6.6450
\end{aligned}
$$

Moreover, an approximate 95% prediction interval for $y_{170}^*$ is

$$\left[\hat{y}_{170}^* \pm z_{[\alpha/2]} s \sqrt{1 + (\hat{\phi}_1)^2}\right] = \left[6.6450 \pm 1.96(.019533)\sqrt{1 + (.39838)^2}\right]$$

$$= [6.6450 \pm .0412]$$

$$= [6.6038, 6.6862]$$

Both the point prediction of $y_{170}^*$ and this approximate 95% prediction interval are also given in the SAS output of Figure 6.25(b). Similarly, we find that a point prediction made in time period 168 for $y_{171}^*$ is $\hat{y}_{171}^* = 6.6723$ and that an approximate 95% prediction interval for $y_{171}^*$ is

$$\left[\hat{y}_{171}^* \pm z_{[\alpha/2]} s \sqrt{1 + (\hat{\phi}_1)^2 + (\hat{\phi}_1)^4}\right] = \left[6.6723 \pm 1.96(.019533)\sqrt{1 + (.39838)^2 + (.39838)^4}\right]$$

$$= [6.6723 \pm .0416]$$

$$= [6.6306, 6.7139]$$

Having computed point predictions and prediction intervals for $y_{169}^*$, $y_{170}^*$, and $y_{171}^*$, it follows that, for instance, the point prediction of $y_{169}$ is

$$\hat{y}_{169} = e^{6.7205} = 829.26$$

and a 95% prediction interval for $y_{169}$ is

$$[e^{6.6822}, e^{6.7588}] = [798.11, 861.62]$$

Note that this interval is also given in the SAS output.

Finally, note that the SAS output of Figure 6.25(a) shows that the autoregressive term $\phi_1 \varepsilon_{t-1}$ (denoted AR1,1 on the output) is significant ($t = 5.34$). This says that the first-order autoregressive term helps us to model the autocorrelated error structure of the time series.

In addition to the first-order autoregressive process, other autocorrelated error structures exist. For instance, consider the following.

> The **autoregressive process of order $p$** is defined as
>
> $$\varepsilon_t = \phi_1 \varepsilon_{t-1} + \phi_2 \varepsilon_{t-2} + \cdots + \phi_p \varepsilon_{t-p} + a_t$$

This process relates $\varepsilon_t$, the error term in time period $t$, to the previous error terms $\varepsilon_{t-1}$, $\varepsilon_{t-2}, \ldots, \varepsilon_{t-p}$. Here $\phi_1, \phi_2, \ldots, \phi_p$ are unknown parameters and $a_t$ is an error term (random shock) with mean zero that satisfies the constant variance, independence, and normality assumptions. In later chapters we consider using an autoregressive process of order $p$ to find an improved model for the autocorrelated error structure exhibited by the monthly room averages.

# Exercises

**6.1** In this problem we consider annual U.S. lumber production over 30 years. The data were obtained from the U.S. Department of Commerce *Survey of Current Business* and are presented in Table 6.6. (This exercise was suggested by an example in Abraham and Ledolter, 1983). Figure 6.26 gives a plot of the lumber production versus time. Figure 6.27 presents the

**TABLE 6.6** Annual Total U.S. Lumber Production (Millions of Board Feet)

| | | | | |
|---|---|---|---|---|
| 35,404 | 36,762 | 32,901 | 38,902 | 37,515 |
| 37,462 | 36,742 | 36,356 | 37,858 | 38,629 |
| 32,901 | 33,385 | 37,166 | 32,926 | 32,019 |
| 33,178 | 34,171 | 35,733 | 35,697 | 35,710 |
| 34,449 | 36,124 | 35,791 | 34,548 | 36,693 |
| 38,044 | 38,658 | 34,592 | 32,087 | 37,153 |

*Note:* Table reads from left to right.

**FIGURE 6.26** JMP IN plot of total U.S. lumber production versus time

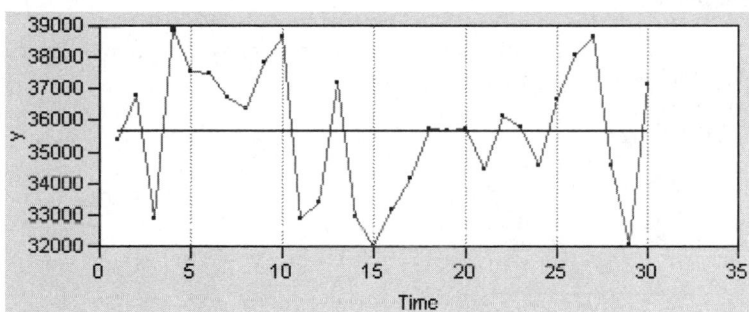

**FIGURE 6.27** MINITAB regression analysis of the lumber production data using the model $y_t = \beta_0 + \varepsilon_t$

```
The regression equation is
y = 35652 Intercept

Predictor      Coef     SE Coef         T        P
Noconstant
Intercep     35651.9     372.0      95.85    0.000

S = 2037

Analysis of Variance

Source         DF          SS         MS        F        P
Regression      1 38131667905 38131667905  9186.50    0.000
Residual Error 29   120374229    4150835
Total          30 38252042134
        Durbin-Watson statistic = 1.58
Predicted Values for New Observations

New Obs     Fit    SE Fit        95.0% CI            95.0% PI
1         35652       372  (   34891,   36413)  (   31416,   39888)
```

MINITAB output of a regression analysis of these data using the model

$$y_t = \beta_0 + \varepsilon_t$$

Figure 6.28 presents the MINITAB output of a plot of the residuals from the model against time.

a. Discuss why the plot in Figure 6.26 indicates that the above model is reasonable.

b. Identify, on the output, a point forecast and 95% prediction interval for total U.S. lumber production in any future time period. Show how these quantities are calculated.

c. Does the plot of the time-ordered residuals in Figure 6.28 exhibit either positive autocorrelation or negative correlation?

**6.2** The past twenty monthly sales figures for a new type of watch sold at Lambert's Discount Stores are given in Table 6.7. Figure 6.29 gives the JMP IN plot

**TABLE 6.7  Watch Sales**

| Month | Sales | Month | Sales |
|-------|-------|-------|-------|
| 1 | 298 | 11 | 356 |
| 2 | 302 | 12 | 371 |
| 3 | 301 | 13 | 399 |
| 4 | 351 | 14 | 392 |
| 5 | 336 | 15 | 425 |
| 6 | 361 | 16 | 411 |
| 7 | 407 | 17 | 455 |
| 8 | 351 | 18 | 457 |
| 9 | 357 | 19 | 465 |
| 10 | 346 | 20 | 481 |

of these data versus time. Figure 6.30 presents the MINITAB output of a regression analysis of these data using the model

$$y_t = \beta_0 + \beta_1 t + \varepsilon_t$$

**FIGURE 6.28**  MINITAB residual plot versus time for the lumber production model

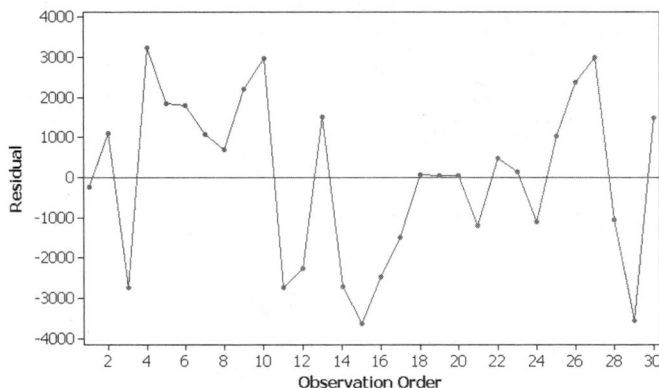

**FIGURE 6.29**  JMP IN plot of monthly watch sales

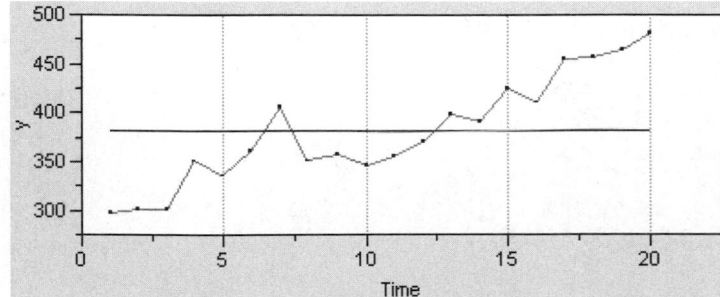

**FIGURE 6.30** MINITAB regression analysis of the watch sales data using the model $y_t = \beta_0 + \beta_1 t + \varepsilon_t$

```
y = 290 + 8.67 Time

Predictor        Coef      SE Coef           T         P
Constant        290.09       10.15       28.59     0.000
Time            8.6677      0.8469       10.23     0.000

S = 21.84      R-Sq = 85.3%     R-Sq(adj) = 84.5%

Analysis of Variance

Source           DF          SS          MS         F        P
Regression        1       49960       49960    104.75    0.000
Residual Error   18        8585         477
Total            19       58546
            Durbin-Watson statistic = 1.37

Predicted Values for New Observations
    Fit      SE Fit         95.0% CI                95.0% PI
 472.11       10.15   ( 450.80,   493.42)   ( 421.52,   522.70)
 480.78       10.90   ( 457.89,   503.67)   ( 429.50,   532.05)
 489.45       11.66   ( 464.95,   513.94)   ( 437.43,   541.46)
```

**FIGURE 6.31** MINITAB plot of the residuals from the watch sales model versus time

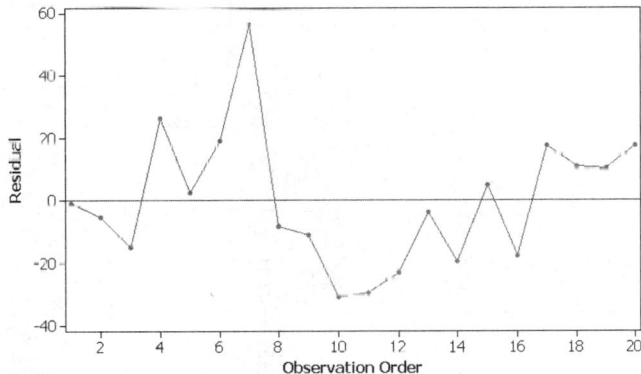

Figure 6.31 presents the MINITAB plot of the residuals from this model versus time.

a. Discuss why the plot in Figure 6.29 indicates that the above model is reasonable.

b. Using the computer output in Figure 6.30, determine whether there is statistical support for a linear trend model.

c. The predicted values at the bottom of the output in Figure 6.30 are for watch sales in months 21, 22, and 23. Identify the point forecasts and 95% prediction intervals for watch sales in months 21, 22, and 23.

d. Write the prediction equation for the model, and use it to show how the point forecasts in part (c) are calculated.

e.  Test for positive autocorrelation by using the Durbin–Watson statistic with $\alpha = .05$. Does the residual plot in Figure 6.31 seem consistent with the outcome of the test?

**6.3**  The quarterly sales of the TRK-50 mountain bike for the previous four years by a bicycle shop in Switzerland is presented in Table 6.8. Figure 6.32 gives the plot of these sales versus time. Figure 6.33 presents the MINITAB output of a regression analysis of the bike sales by using the model

$$y_t = \beta_0 + \beta_1 t + \beta_2 Q_2 + \beta_3 Q_3 + \beta_4 Q_4 + \varepsilon_t$$

where $Q_2$, $Q_3$, and $Q_4$ are the appropriately defined dummy variables for quarters 2, 3, and 4.
a.  From Figure 6.32, what kind of trend appears to exist?
b.  From Figure 6.32, what type of seasonal variation appears to exist? Is a transformation needed to obtain a series that displays constant variation?
c.  From the computer output in Figure 6.33, do all the independent variables seem to be important? Justify your answer statistically.
d.  Write out the definitions of the dummy variables $Q_2$, $Q_3$, and $Q_4$.
e.  The predicted values at the bottom of the MINITAB output in Figure 6.33 are for the bike sales in year 5. Find and identify $\hat{y}_{17}$, $\hat{y}_{18}$, $\hat{y}_{19}$, and $\hat{y}_{20}$, the point predictions of $y_{17}$, $y_{18}$, $y_{19}$, and $y_{20}$.
f.  Write the prediction equation for the model, and use it to calculate $\hat{y}_{17}$ and $\hat{y}_{18}$.

g.  Find and identify the 95% prediction intervals for $y_{17}$, $y_{18}$, $y_{19}$, and $y_{20}$. Interpret these intervals.
h.  Test for positive autocorrelation by using the Durbin-Watson statistic with $\alpha = .05$.

**6.4**  Table 6.9 presents the quarterly energy bills for a school system. The energy bills are the combined gas, oil, and electric bills for the school system and are expressed in units of $100. A plot of the energy bills versus time is displayed in Figure 6.34.
a.  From the plot in Figure 6.34, what kind of trend appears to exist?

**TABLE 6.8  Quarterly Sales of the TRK-50 Mountain Bike**

| Year | Quarter | $t$ | $y_t$ |
|------|---------|-----|-------|
| 1    | 1       | 1   | 10    |
|      | 2       | 2   | 31    |
|      | 3       | 3   | 43    |
|      | 4       | 4   | 16    |
| 2    | 1       | 5   | 11    |
|      | 2       | 6   | 33    |
|      | 3       | 7   | 45    |
|      | 4       | 8   | 17    |
| 3    | 1       | 9   | 13    |
|      | 2       | 10  | 34    |
|      | 3       | 11  | 48    |
|      | 4       | 12  | 19    |
| 4    | 1       | 13  | 15    |
|      | 2       | 14  | 37    |
|      | 3       | 15  | 51    |
|      | 4       | 16  | 21    |

**FIGURE 6.32**  JMP IN plot of quarterly bike sales

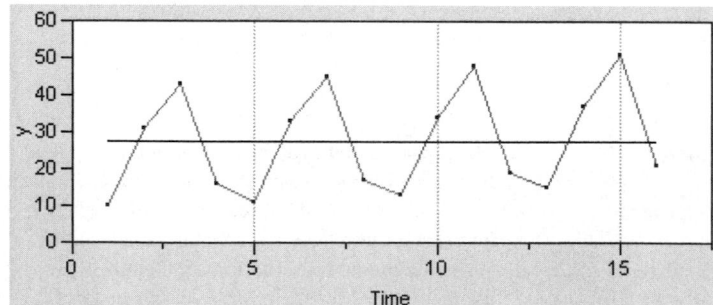

**FIGURE 6.33** MINITAB regression analysis of the bike sales data using the model $y_t = \beta_0 + \beta_1 t + \beta_2 Q_2 + \beta_3 Q_3 + \beta_4 Q_4 + \varepsilon_t$

```
The regression equation is
y = 8.75 + 0.500 Time + 21.0 Q2 + 33.5 Q3 + 4.50 Q4

Predictor         Coef     SE Coef          T        P
Constant        8.7500      0.4281      20.44    0.000
Time           0.50000     0.03769      13.27    0.000
Q2             21.0000      0.4782      43.91    0.000
Q3             33.5000      0.4827      69.41    0.000
Q4              4.5000      0.4900       9.18    0.000

S = 0.6742      R-Sq = 99.8%      R-Sq(adj) = 99.8%
Predicted Values for New Observations
   Fit     SE Fit          95.0% CI               95.0% PI
17.250      0.506   ( 16.137,  18.363)   ( 15.395,  19.105)
38.750      0.506   ( 37.637,  39.863)   ( 36.895,  40.605)
51.750      0.506   ( 50.637,  52.863)   ( 49.895,  53.605)
23.250      0.506   ( 22.137,  24.363)   ( 21.395,  25.105)

        Durbin-Watson statistic = 2.20
```

**TABLE 6.9 Quarterly Energy Bills for the School System (× $100)**

| Year | Quarter 1 | Quarter 2 | Quarter 3 | Quarter 4 |
|------|-----------|-----------|-----------|-----------|
| 1  | 344.39 (= $y_1$) | 246.63 (= $y_2$) | 131.53 (= $y_3$) | 288.87 (= $y_4$) |
| 2  | 313.45 (= $y_5$) | 189.76 (= $y_6$) | 179.10 (= $y_7$) | 221.10 (= $y_8$) |
| 3  | 246.84 | 209.00 | 51.21 | 133.89 |
| 4  | 277.01 | 197.98 | 50.68 | 218.08 |
| 5  | 365.10 | 207.51 | 54.63 | 214.09 |
| 6  | 267.00 | 230.28 | 230.32 | 426.41 |
| 7  | 467.06 | 306.03 | 253.23 | 279.46 |
| 8  | 336.56 | 196.67 | 152.15 | 319.67 |
| 9  | 440.00 | 315.04 | 216.42 | 339.78 |
| 10 | 434.66 (= $y_{37}$) | 399.66 (= $y_{38}$) | 330.80 (= $y_{39}$) | 539.78 (= $y_{40}$) |

**FIGURE 6.34** Quarterly energy bills for the school system

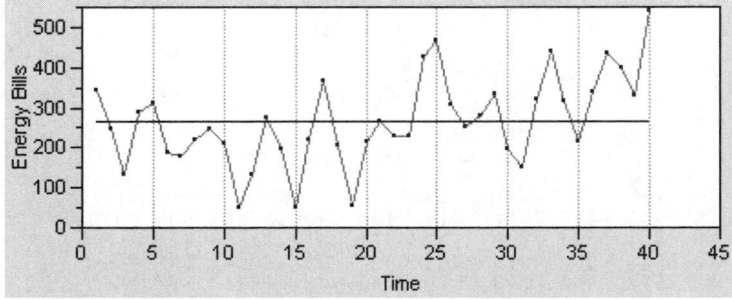

b. From the plot in Figure 6.34, what type of seasonal variation appears to exist? Is a transformation needed to obtain a series that displays constant variation?

c. Figure 6.35 presents the SAS output of a regression analysis of the above data using the model

$$y_t = \beta_0 + \beta_1 t + \beta_2 t^2 + \beta_3 Q_1 + \beta_4 Q_2 + \beta_5 Q_3 + \varepsilon_t$$

1. Write out the definitions of the dummy variables $Q_1$, $Q_2$, and $Q_3$.
2. Do all the independent variables in the model seem important? Justify your answer statistically.
3. Write the prediction equation for the model, and use it to calculate $\hat{y}_{41}$ and $\hat{y}_{42}$.
4. Find and report point forecasts and 95% prediction intervals for the energy bills in periods 41, 42, 43, and 44.

5. Test for positive autocorrelation by using the Durbin–Watson statistic and setting $\alpha = .05$.

d. Figure 6.36 presents the SAS PROC ARIMA output of an analysis of the energy bill data using the model

$$y_t = \beta_0 + \beta_1 t + \beta_2 t^2 + \beta_3 Q_1 + \beta_4 Q_2 + \beta_5 Q_3 + \varepsilon_t$$

where

$$\varepsilon_t = \phi_1 \varepsilon_{t-1} + a_t$$

1. Identify the value for $\hat{\phi}_1$. Is it statistically different from 0?
2. Do the other independent variables in the model seem important? Justify your answer statistically.
3. Find and report the point forecasts and 95% prediction intervals for the energy bills in periods 41, 42, 43, and 44.

**FIGURE 6.35** SAS regression analysis of the energy bill data using the model
$y_t = \beta_0 + \beta_1 t + \beta_2 t^2 + \beta_3 Q_1 + \beta_4 Q_2 + \beta_5 Q_3 + \varepsilon_t$

### Analysis of Variance

| Source | DF | Sum of Squares | Mean Square | F Value | Pr > F |
|--------|----|----------------|-------------|---------|--------|
| Model | 5 | 361967 | 72393 | 19.80 | <.0001 |
| Error | 34 | 124336 | 3656.93152 | | |
| Corrected Total | 39 | 486303 | | | |

| | | | |
|--|--|--|--|
| Root MSE | 60.47257 | R-Square | 0.7443 |
| Dependent Mean | 265.54575 | Adj R-Sq | 0.7067 |
| Coeff Var | 22.77294 | | |

### Parameter Estimates

| Variable | Label | DF | Parameter Estimate | Standard Error | t Value | Pr > \|t\| |
|----------|-------|----|--------------------|----------------|---------|-----------|
| Intercept | Intercept | 1 | 276.63631 | 35.04850 | 7.89 | <.0001 |
| Time | | 1 | -7.45825 | 3.39603 | -2.20 | 0.0350 |
| Timesq | | 1 | 0.30123 | 0.08030 | 3.75 | 0.0007 |
| Q1 | | 1 | 65.77065 | 27.15916 | 2.42 | 0.0209 |
| Q2 | | 1 | -37.87011 | 27.09580 | -1.40 | 0.1713 |
| Q3 | | 1 | -127.61132 | 27.05743 | -4.72 | <.0001 |

Durbin-Watson D       0.840

| Obs | Dep Var y | Predicted Value | Std Error Mean Predict | 95% CL Mean | | 95% CL Predict | |
|-----|-----------|-----------------|------------------------|-------------|--|----------------|--|
| 41 | . | 542.9878 | 35.0485 | 471.7607 | 614.2149 | 400.9438 | 685.0318 |
| 42 | . | 456.8910 | 37.4591 | 380.7649 | 533.0171 | 312.3283 | 601.4537 |
| 43 | . | 385.2961 | 40.0368 | 303.9316 | 466.6607 | 237.9076 | 532.6847 |
| 44 | . | 531.6563 | 42.7513 | 444.7753 | 618.5373 | 381.1521 | 682.1605 |

**FIGURE 6.36** SAS PROC ARIMA analysis of the energy bill data using the model
$y_t = \beta_0 + \beta_1 t + \beta_2 t^2 + \beta_3 Q_1 + \beta_4 Q_2 + \beta_5 Q_3 + \varepsilon_t$ where $\varepsilon_t = \phi_1 \varepsilon_{t-1} + a_t$

Conditional Least Squares Estimation

| Parameter | Estimate | Standard Error | t Value | Approx Pr > \|t\| | Lag | Variable |
|-----------|----------|----------------|---------|-------------------|-----|----------|
| MU      | 283.94906  | 47.55019 | 5.97  | <.0001 | 0 | y      |
| AR1,1   | 0.59408    | 0.14701  | 4.04  | 0.0003 | 1 | y      |
| NUM1    | -9.21968   | 5.46550  | -1.69 | 0.1011 | 0 | Time   |
| NUM2    | 0.35348    | 0.13315  | 2.65  | 0.0121 | 0 | Timesq |
| NUM3    | 70.10688   | 17.42697 | 4.02  | 0.0003 | 0 | Q1     |
| NUM4    | -35.42856  | 19.52221 | -1.81 | 0.0787 | 0 | Q2     |
| NUM5    | -126.52509 | 16.95695 | -7.46 | <.0001 | 0 | Q3     |

|  |  |
|---|---|
| Constant Estimate | 115.2595 |
| Variance Estimate | 2525.195 |
| Std Error Estimate | 50.25132 |

| Obs | Forecast | Std Error | 95% Confidence Limits | |
|-----|----------|-----------|-----------|-----------|
| 41 | 605.3285 | 50.2513 | 506.8378 | 703.8193 |
| 42 | 505.6717 | 58.4502 | 391.1114 | 620.2320 |
| 43 | 426.9411 | 61.0817 | 307.2232 | 546.6591 |
| 44 | 569.9732 | 61.9838 | 448.4872 | 691.4592 |

4. Write the prediction equation for this model.
5. Show how the quantities in part (3) are calculated.

**6.5** In Example 6.6, we noted that the quartic roots $(y_t^* = y_t^{.25})$ of the hotel room averages seemed to produce a transformed series with constant variation. Figure 6.37 (page 322) presents the SAS output of an analysis of the quartic roots using the model

$$y_t^* = \beta_0 + \beta_1 t + \beta_2 M_1 + \beta_3 M_2 + \cdots + \beta_{12} M_{11} + \varepsilon_t$$

where

$$y_t^* = y_t^{.25}$$

a. Do all the variables seem important in the model? Justify your answer statistically.
b. Find and report $\hat{y}_{169}^*$ and $\hat{y}_{170}^*$, the point estimates of $y_{169}^*$ and $y_{170}^*$.
c. Using the least squares estimates in Figure 6.37, write the prediction equation for the model and compute $\hat{y}_{169}^*$ and $\hat{y}_{170}^*$.

d. Compute the point forecast $\hat{y}_{169} = (\hat{y}_{169}^{.25})^4$ and 95% prediction interval $[(5.2913)^4, (5.4065)^4]$ for $y_{169}$, the hotel room average in January of next year.
e. Compute the point forecast $\hat{y}_{170}$ and 95% prediction interval for $y_{170}$, the hotel room average in February of next year.
f. Test for positive autocorrelation by using the Durbin–Watson statistic with $\alpha = .05$.

**6.6** The data in Table 6.10 (page 322) give the number of reported cases $y_t$ of a newly discovered disease over the last 11 months. A plot of this data versus time is shown in Figure 6.38 (page 323). Figure 6.39 (page 323) presents a plot of the natural logarithms of the number of reported cases versus time.
a. Does the use of a growth curve model for forecasting future $y_t$ values seem appropriate? Explain your answer.
b. Has the logarithmic transformation in Figure 6.39 (page 323) linearized the data?
c. Using natural logarithms, define a transformed growth curve model that will be linear in its parameters.

Continued on page 324

**FIGURE 6.37 (for Exercise 6.5)** SAS dummy variable regression of the quartic roots of the hotel room averages

Parameter Estimates

| Variable | DF | Parameter Estimate | Standard Error | t Value | Pr > \|t\| |
|---|---|---|---|---|---|
| Intercept | 1 | 4.80732 | 0.00846 | 568.07 | <.0001 |
| Time | 1 | 0.00352 | 0.00004449 | 79.01 | <.0001 |
| M1 | 1 | -0.05247 | 0.01055 | -4.97 | <.0001 |
| M2 | 1 | -0.14079 | 0.01055 | -13.34 | <.0001 |
| M3 | 1 | -0.10710 | 0.01055 | -10.15 | <.0001 |
| M4 | 1 | 0.04988 | 0.01055 | 4.73 | <.0001 |
| M5 | 1 | 0.02542 | 0.01055 | 2.41 | 0.0171 |
| M6 | 1 | 0.19017 | 0.01055 | 18.03 | <.0001 |
| M7 | 1 | 0.38245 | 0.01055 | 36.27 | <.0001 |
| M8 | 1 | 0.41337 | 0.01054 | 39.20 | <.0001 |
| M9 | 1 | 0.07142 | 0.01054 | 6.77 | <.0001 |
| M10 | 1 | 0.05064 | 0.01054 | 4.80 | <.0001 |
| M11 | 1 | -0.14194 | 0.01054 | -13.46 | <.0001 |

Durbin-Watson D        1.262

| Obs | Dep Var QtRooty | Predicted Value | Std Error Mean Predict | 95% CL Mean | | 95% CL Predict | |
|---|---|---|---|---|---|---|---|
| 169 | . | 5.3489 | 0.008463 | 5.3322 | 5.3656 | 5.2913 | 5.4065 |
| 170 | . | 5.2641 | 0.008463 | 5.2474 | 5.2808 | 5.2065 | 5.3217 |
| 171 | . | 5.3013 | 0.008463 | 5.2846 | 5.3180 | 5.2437 | 5.3589 |
| 172 | . | 5.4618 | 0.008463 | 5.4451 | 5.4785 | 5.4042 | 5.5194 |
| 173 | . | 5.4409 | 0.008463 | 5.4241 | 5.4576 | 5.3833 | 5.4984 |
| 174 | . | 5.6091 | 0.008463 | 5.5924 | 5.6258 | 5.5515 | 5.6667 |
| 175 | . | 5.8049 | 0.008463 | 5.7882 | 5.8216 | 5.7473 | 5.8625 |
| 176 | . | 5.8394 | 0.008463 | 5.8226 | 5.8561 | 5.7818 | 5.8969 |
| 177 | . | 5.5009 | 0.008463 | 5.4842 | 5.5176 | 5.4433 | 5.5585 |
| 178 | . | 5.4837 | 0.008463 | 5.4669 | 5.5004 | 5.4261 | 5.5412 |
| 179 | . | 5.2946 | 0.008463 | 5.2779 | 5.3113 | 5.2370 | 5.3522 |
| 180 | . | 5.4400 | 0.008463 | 5.4233 | 5.4568 | 5.3825 | 5.4976 |

**TABLE 6.10 (for Exercise 6.6)** Number of Reported Cases of a New Disease over the Last 11 Months

| Month ($t$) | Number of Reported Cases ($y_t$) |
|---|---|
| 1 | 1 |
| 2 | 1 |
| 3 | 2 |
| 4 | 3 |
| 5 | 4 |
| 6 | 6 |
| 7 | 8 |
| 8 | 13 |
| 9 | 21 |
| 10 | 27 |
| 11 | 45 |

**FIGURE 6.38 (for Exercise 6.6)** JMP IN plot of the monthly number of reported cases of a new disease

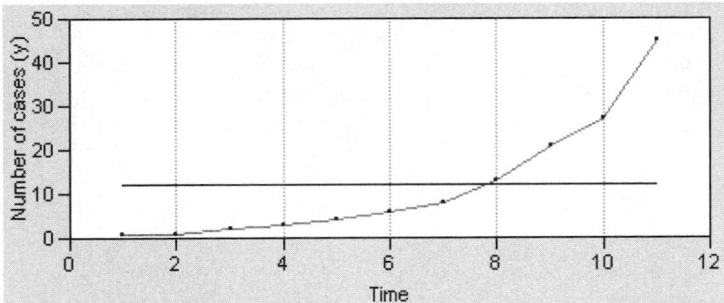

**FIGURE 6.39 (for Exercise 6.6)** JMP IN plot of monthly logged values of the disease data

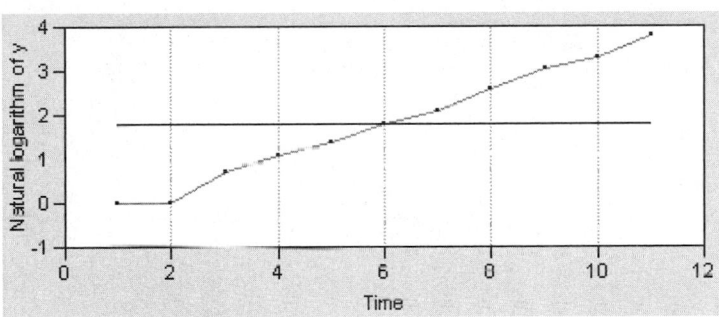

**FIGURE 6.40 (for Exercise 6.6)** MINITAB regression of the logged disease data using a growth model

```
The regression equation is
Lny = - 0.543 + 0.390 Time

Predictor        Coef     SE Coef          T        P
Constant     -0.54334     0.07344      -7.40    0.000
Time          0.38997     0.01083      36.01    0.000

S = 0.1136      R-Sq = 99.3%      R-Sq(adj) = 99.2%

Analysis of Variance

Source            DF          SS          MS          F        P
Regression         1      16.728      16.728    1296.87    0.000
Residual Error     9       0.116       0.013
Total             10      16.844

Durbin-Watson statistic = 2.73
Predicted Values for New Observations
    Fit     SE Fit           95.0% CI                 95.0% PI
 4.1363     0.0734    ( 3.9701,  4.3024)    ( 3.8303,  4.4423)
```

d. Figure 6.40 (page 323) presents a MINITAB output of the transformed growth curve model of part (c).
   1. Identify the values for $\hat{\alpha}_0$ and $\hat{\alpha}_1$ for the transformed growth model of part (c), and write the prediction equation for that model.
   2. Estimate the growth rate for this disease.
   3. Calculate a point forecast for $y_{12}$, the number of reported cases in month 12.
   4. Using the values for the transformed growth curve model at the bottom of Figure 6.40, calculate a 95% prediction interval for $y_{12}$. Interpret this interval.

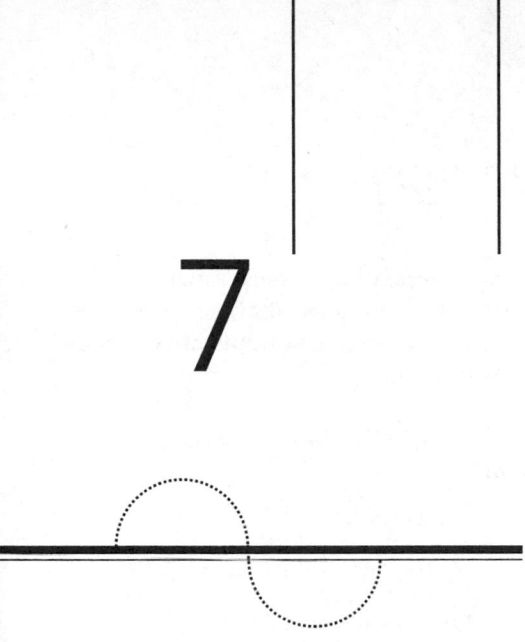

# *Decomposition Methods*

In this chapter we show how to use **decomposition models** to forecast time series that exhibit trend and seasonal effects. These models have no theoretical basis—they are strictly an intuitive approach. However, decomposition models have been found useful when the parameters describing a time series are not changing over time. The basic idea behind these models is to decompose the time series into several **factors: trend, seasonal, cyclical,** and **irregular (error).** Estimates of these factors are used to describe the time series. In addition, if the time series parameters are not changing, the estimates can be used to compute point forecasts.

Section 7.1 presents the **multiplicative decomposition model.** This model has been found useful when modeling time series that display **increasing or decreasing seasonal variation.** Section 7.2 briefly describes the **additive decomposition model,** which can be employed when modeling time series that exhibit **constant seasonal variation.** Section 7.3 gives a brief description of X-12-ARIMA, a decomposition method used by the Bureau of the Census of the U.S. Department of Commerce.

# 7.1   MULTIPLICATIVE DECOMPOSITION

Consider a time series that exhibits increasing or decreasing seasonal variation. When the parameters describing the series are not changing over time, the time series sometimes can be modeled adequately by using what is called the **multiplicative decomposition model.** This model can be stated as follows.

---

The **multiplicative decomposition model** is

$$y_t = TR_t \times SN_t \times CL_t \times IR_t$$

where

$$y_t \; = \; \text{the observed value of the time series in time period } t$$
$$TR_t \; = \; \text{the \textbf{trend component} (or factor) in time period } t$$
$$SN_t \; = \; \text{the \textbf{seasonal component} (or factor) in time period } t$$
$$CL_t \; = \; \text{the \textbf{cyclical component} (or factor) in time period } t$$
$$IR_t \; = \; \text{the \textbf{irregular component} (or factor) in time period } t$$

---

We previously discussed the nature of trend effects, seasonal variations, and irregular fluctuations. The cyclical component, $CL_t$, refers to recurring up and down movements around trend levels as caused, for example, by the business cycle. These fluctuations can last anywhere from two to longer than ten years as measured from peak to peak or trough to trough. In business, a peak would mark the end of an expansion in business activity, and a trough would mark the end of a contraction.

Notice that this decomposition model employs a **multiplicative seasonal factor.** That is, the seasonal factor is multiplied by the trend (rather than, for example, added to the trend as in dummy variable regression; see Section 6.4). To see how the multiplicative seasonal factor can model increasing seasonal variation, suppose, for instance, that sales of outboard motors by the Power Drive Corporation are seasonal. Also suppose that sales are lowest in the first quarter, highest in the second quarter, moderately high in the third quarter, and moderately low in the fourth quarter. Furthermore, assume that sales exhibit a linear trend given by

$$TR_t = 500 + 50t$$

where $t = 0$ is considered to be the fourth quarter of 2002. If trend alone is considered, outboard motor sales in the four quarters of 2003 are expected to be

$$TR_1 = 500 + 50(1) = 550 \quad (\text{quarter 1})$$
$$TR_2 = 500 + 50(2) = 600 \quad (\text{quarter 2})$$
$$TR_3 = 500 + 50(3) = 650 \quad (\text{quarter 3})$$
$$TR_4 = 500 + 50(4) = 700 \quad (\text{quarter 4})$$

However, sales are seasonal. Therefore, we can model the seasonal behavior of sales by defining seasonal factors. Suppose that the seasonal factors for quarters 1, 2, 3, and 4 are $SN_{Q1} = .4$, $SN_{Q2} = 1.6$, $SN_{Q3} = 1.2$, and $SN_{Q4} = .8$. If we assume that these seasonal factors are multiplicative, then when we consider both trend and seasonal effects, sales in the four quarters of 2003 are expected to be

$$TR_1 \times SN_{Q1} = [500 + 50(1)](.4) = 220$$
$$TR_2 \times SN_{Q2} = [500 + 50(2)](1.6) = 960$$
$$TR_3 \times SN_{Q3} = [500 + 50(3)](1.2) = 780$$
$$TR_4 \times SN_{Q4} = [500 + 50(4)](.8) = 560$$

Multiplying the trend $TR_t$ by the appropriate seasonal factors models the seasonal pattern of sales. This is illustrated in Figure 7.1.

If multiplicative seasonal factors remain constant over time, they allow us to model increasing seasonal variation. For example, in the outboard motor sales situation, when we consider both trend and seasonal effects, sales in the four quarters of 2004 are expected to be

$$TR_5 \times SN_{Q1} = [500 + 50(5)](.4) = 300$$
$$TR_6 \times SN_{Q2} = [500 + 50(6)](1.6) = 1280$$
$$TR_7 \times SN_{Q3} = [500 + 50(7)](1.2) - 1020$$
$$TR_8 \times SN_{Q4} = [500 + 50(8)](.8) = 720$$

Multiplication of the trend by the seasonal factors implies that the size of the seasonal swing is proportional to the trend. Therefore, since the trend

$$TR_t = 500 + 50t$$

is increasing, the size of the seasonal swing is increasing (increasing seasonal variation). Note again that here we are assuming that the seasonal factors remain constant over time. Sometimes the seasonal factors instead change over time; then the methods in Chapters 8 to 12 should be considered.

**FIGURE 7.1**
An illustration in Excel of multiplicative seasonal factors
$SN_{Q1} = .4$
$SN_{Q2} = 1.6$
$SN_{Q3} = 1.2$
and
$SN_{Q4} = .8$

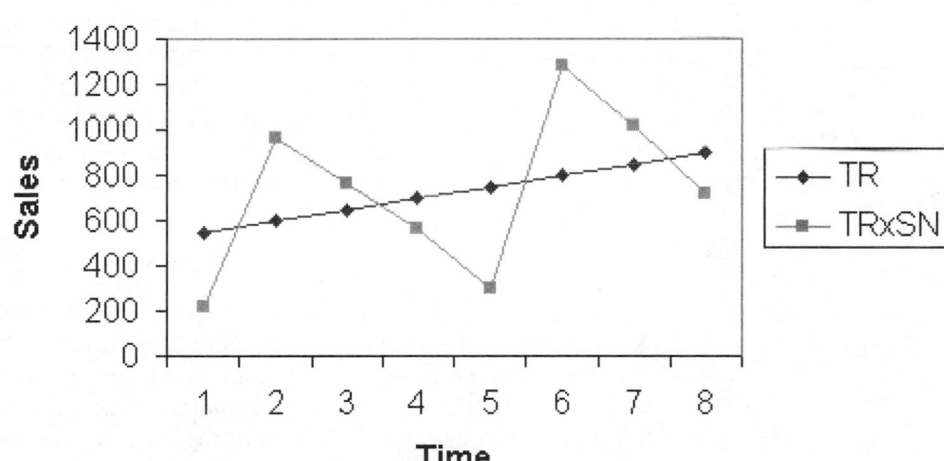

The seasonal factor $SN_t$ models cyclical patterns in a time series that are completed within one calendar year. If a time series displays a cycle that has a longer duration, a cyclical factor $CL_t$ can be defined. For instance, in the outboard motor sales situation, suppose that all four quarters of 2003 are included in a "boom period" of the business cycle. Assume that the cyclical factors describing the increased economic activity in the four quarters of 2003 are $CL_1 = 1.08$, $CL_2 = 1.09$, $CL_3 = 1.09$, and $CL_4 = 1.10$. If trend, seasonal, and cyclical effects are considered, sales in the four quarters of 2003 are expected to be

$$TR_1 \times SN_{Q1} \times CL_1 = 220(1.08) = 238$$
$$TR_2 \times SN_{Q2} \times CL_2 = 960(1.09) = 1046$$
$$TR_3 \times SN_{Q3} \times CL_3 = 780(1.09) = 850$$
$$TR_4 \times SN_{Q4} \times CL_4 = 560(1.10) = 616$$

Thus the cyclical factors increase expected sales above levels that would be expected if only trend and seasonal effects were considered. This reflects the boom in economic activity.

The **multiplicative decomposition method** can be used to obtain point estimates—denoted $tr_t$, $sn_t$, $cl_t$, and $ir_t$—of the factors $TR_t$, $SN_t$, $CL_t$, and $IR_t$. The following example illustrates the procedure.

**EXAMPLE 7.1**

The Discount Soda Shop, Inc., owns and operates ten drive-in soft drink stores. Discount Soda has been selling Tasty Cola, a soft drink that was introduced on the market just three years ago and has been gaining in popularity. Periodically, Discount Soda orders a supply of Tasty Cola from the regional distributor. The company uses an inventory policy that attempts to meet practically all of the demand for Tasty Cola, while at the same time ensuring that the company does not tie up its money needlessly by ordering much more Tasty Cola than it can reasonably expect to sell. In order to implement its inventory policy, Discount Soda needs to forecast monthly Tasty Cola sales (in hundreds of cases). At the end of each month, Discount Soda desires point forecasts and prediction interval forecasts of Tasty Cola sales in future months.

Discount Soda has recorded monthly Tasty Cola sales for the previous three years, which we will call year 1, year 2, and year 3. This time series is given in Table 7.1 and is plotted in Figure 7.2. Notice that in addition to having a linear trend, the Tasty Cola sales time series possesses seasonal variation, with sales of the soft drink being greatest in the summer and early fall months and lowest in the winter months. We show later in this example that it is reasonable to conclude that $y_t$, the sales of Tasty Cola in period $t$, is adequately described by the model

$$y_t = TR_t \times SN_t \times CL_t \times IR_t$$

Therefore, we summarize in Table 7.2 the calculations needed to find estimates—denoted $tr_t$, $sn_t$, $cl_t$, and $ir_t$—of the components $TR_t$, $SN_t$, $CL_t$, and $IR_t$ of this model.

To begin our consideration of the calculations, we will explain the calculation of **moving averages** and **centered moving averages** (the centered moving averages are denoted $CMA_t$). The purpose behind computing these averages is to eliminate seasonal

**TABLE 7.1** Monthly Sales of Tasty Cola (In Hundreds of Cases)

| Year | Month | $t$ | Sales $y_t$ | Year | Month | $t$ | Sales $y_t$ |
|------|-------|-----|-------------|------|-------|-----|-------------|
| 1 | 1 (Jan.) | 1 | 189 | 2 | 7 | 19 | 831 |
| | 2 (Feb.) | 2 | 229 | | 8 | 20 | 960 |
| | 3 (Mar.) | 3 | 249 | | 9 | 21 | 1152 |
| | 4 (Apr.) | 4 | 289 | | 10 | 22 | 759 |
| | 5 (May) | 5 | 260 | | 11 | 23 | 607 |
| | 6 (June) | 6 | 431 | | 12 | 24 | 371 |
| | 7 (July) | 7 | 660 | | | | | |
| | 8 (Aug.) | 8 | 777 | 3 | 1 | 25 | 298 |
| | 9 (Sept.) | 9 | 915 | | 2 | 26 | 378 |
| | 10 (Oct.) | 10 | 613 | | 3 | 27 | 373 |
| | 11 (Nov.) | 11 | 485 | | 4 | 28 | 443 |
| | 12 (Dec.) | 12 | 277 | | 5 | 29 | 374 |
| | | | | | 6 | 30 | 660 |
| 2 | 1 | 13 | 244 | | 7 | 31 | 1004 |
| | 2 | 14 | 296 | | 8 | 32 | 1153 |
| | 3 | 15 | 319 | | 9 | 33 | 1388 |
| | 4 | 16 | 370 | | 10 | 34 | 904 |
| | 5 | 17 | 313 | | 11 | 35 | 715 |
| | 6 | 18 | 556 | | 12 | 36 | 441 |

**FIGURE 7.2**
JMP IN plot of monthly sales of Tasty Cola (in hundreds of cases)

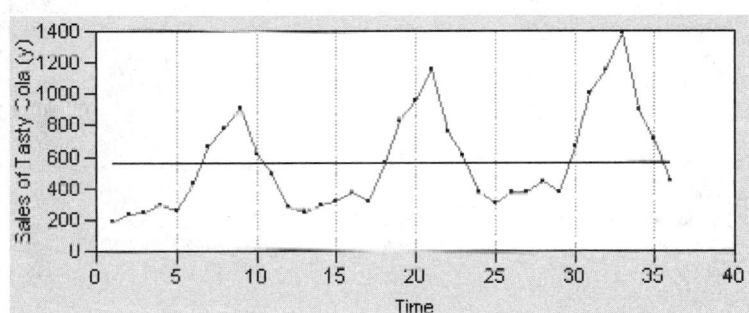

variations and irregular fluctuations from the data. The first moving average is the average of the first 12 Tasty Cola sales values

$$\frac{189 + 229 + 249 + 289 + 260 + 431 + 660 + 777 + 915 + 613 + 485 + 277}{12}$$

$$= 447.833$$

Here we use a "12-period moving average" because the Tasty Cola time series data are monthly ($L = 12$ time periods or "seasons" per year). If the data were quarterly, we would compute a "four-period moving average." The second moving average is obtained by dropping the first sales value ($y_1$) from the average and by including the next sales value ($y_{13}$)

**TABLE 7.2** Analysis of the Historical Tasty Cola Sales Time Series Using Multiplicative Decomposition

**(a) The Values of $sn_t$, $d_t$, and $tr_t$**

| $t$ | $y_t$ | 12-Period Moving Average | $CMA_t =$ $tr_t \times cl_t$ | $sn_t \times ir_t$ $= y_t/(tr_t \times cl_t)$ | $sn_t$ | $d_t = \dfrac{y_t}{sn_t}$ | $tr_t = 380.163$ $+ 9.489t$ | $\hat{y}_t = tr_t \times sn_t$ |
|---|---|---|---|---|---|---|---|---|
| 1 | 189 | | | | .493 | 383.37 | 389.652 | 192.10 |
| 2 | 229 | | | | .596 | 384.23 | 399.141 | 237.89 |
| 3 | 249 | | | | .595 | 418.49 | 408.630 | 243.13 |
| 4 | 289 | | | | .680 | 425 | 418.119 | 284.32 |
| 5 | 260 | | | | .564 | 460.99 | 427.608 | 241.17 |
| 6 | 431 | | | | .986 | 437.12 | 437.097 | 430.98 |
| 7 | 660 | 447.833 | 450.1 | 1.466 | 1.467 | 449.9 | 446.586 | 655.14 |
| 8 | 777 | 452.417 | 455.2 | 1.707 | 1.693 | 458.95 | 456.075 | 772.13 |
| 9 | 915 | 458 | 460.9 | 1.985 | 1.990 | 459.79 | 465.564 | 926.47 |
| 10 | 613 | 463.833 | 467.2 | 1.312 | 1.307 | 469.01 | 475.053 | 620.89 |
| 11 | 485 | 470.583 | 472.8 | 1.026 | 1.029 | 471.33 | 489.542 | 498.59 |
| 12 | 277 | 475 | 480.2 | .577 | .600 | 461.67 | 494.031 | 296.42 |
| 13 | 244 | 485.417 | 492.5 | .495 | .493 | 494.97 | 503.520 | 248.24 |
| 14 | 296 | 499.667 | 507.3 | .583 | .596 | 496.64 | 513.009 | 305.75 |
| 15 | 319 | 514.917 | 524.8 | .608 | .595 | 536.13 | 522.498 | 310.89 |
| 16 | 370 | 534.667 | 540.7 | .684 | .680 | 544.12 | 531.987 | 361.75 |
| 17 | 313 | 546.833 | 551.9 | .567 | .564 | 554.97 | 541.476 | 305.39 |
| 18 | 556 | 557 | 560.9 | .991 | .986 | 563.89 | 550.965 | 543.25 |
| 19 | 831 | 564.833 | 567.1 | 1.465 | 1.467 | 566.46 | 560.454 | 822.19 |
| 20 | 960 | 569.333 | 572.7 | 1.676 | 1.693 | 567.04 | 569.943 | 964.91 |
| 21 | 1152 | 576.167 | 578.4 | 1.992 | 1.990 | 578.89 | 579.432 | 1153.07 |
| 22 | 759 | 580.667 | 583.7 | 1.300 | 1.307 | 580.72 | 588.921 | 769.72 |
| 23 | 607 | 586.75 | 589.3 | 1.030 | 1.029 | 589.89 | 598.410 | 615.76 |
| 24 | 371 | 591.833 | 596.2 | .622 | .600 | 618.33 | 607.899 | 364.74 |
| 25 | 298 | 600.5 | 607.7 | .490 | .493 | 604.46 | 617.388 | 304.37 |
| 26 | 378 | 614.917 | 623.0 | .607 | .596 | 634.23 | 626.877 | 373.62 |
| 27 | 373 | 631 | 640.8 | .582 | .595 | 626.89 | 636.366 | 378.64 |
| 28 | 443 | 650.667 | 656.7 | .675 | .680 | 651.47 | 645.855 | 439.18 |
| 29 | 374 | 662.75 | 667.3 | .561 | .564 | 663.12 | 655.344 | 369.61 |
| 30 | 660 | 671.75 | 674.7 | .978 | .986 | 669.37 | 664.833 | 655.53 |
| 31 | 1004 | 677.583 | | | 1.467 | 684.39 | 674.322 | 989.23 |
| 32 | 1153 | | | | 1.693 | 681.04 | 683.811 | 1157.69 |
| 33 | 1388 | | | | 1.990 | 697.49 | 693.300 | 1379.67 |
| 34 | 904 | | | | 1.307 | 691.66 | 702.789 | 918.55 |
| 35 | 715 | | | | 1.029 | 694.85 | 712.278 | 732.93 |
| 36 | 441 | | | | .600 | 735 | 721.707 | 433.06 |

in the average. Thus we obtain

$$\frac{229 + 249 + 289 + 260 + 431 + 660 + 777 + 915 + 613 + 485 + 277 + 244}{12}$$

$$= 452.417$$

**TABLE 7.2 (Continued)**

**(b) The Values of $cl_t$ and $ir_t$**

| $t$ | $y_t$ | $tr_t \times sn_t$ | $cl_t \times ir_t = \dfrac{y_t}{tr_t \times sn_t}$ | $cl_t = \dfrac{cl_{t-1}ir_{t-1} + cl_t ir_t + cl_{t+1}ir_{t+1}}{3}$ | $ir_t = \dfrac{cl_t \times ir_t}{cl_t}$ |
|---|---|---|---|---|---|
| 1 | 189 | 192.10 | .9839 | | |
| 2 | 229 | 237.89 | .9626 | .9902 | .9721 |
| 3 | 249 | 243.13 | 1.0241 | 1.0010 | 1.0231 |
| 4 | 289 | 284.32 | 1.0165 | 1.0396 | .9778 |
| 5 | 260 | 241.17 | 1.0781 | 1.0315 | 1.0452 |
| 6 | 431 | 430.98 | 1.0000 | 1.0285 | .9723 |
| 7 | 660 | 655.14 | 1.0074 | 1.0046 | 1.0028 |
| 8 | 777 | 772.13 | 1.0063 | 1.0004 | 1.0059 |
| 9 | 915 | 926.47 | .9876 | .9937 | .9939 |
| 10 | 613 | 620.89 | .9873 | .9825 | 1.0063 |
| 11 | 485 | 498.59 | .9727 | .9648 | 1.0082 |
| 12 | 277 | 296.42 | .9345 | .9634 | .9700 |
| 13 | 244 | 248.24 | .9829 | .9618 | 1.0219 |
| 14 | 296 | 305.75 | .9681 | .9924 | .9755 |
| 15 | 319 | 310.89 | 1.0261 | 1.0567 | .9710 |
| 16 | 370 | 361.75 | 1.0228 | 1.0246 | .9982 |
| 17 | 313 | 305.39 | 1.0249 | 1.0237 | 1.0012 |
| 18 | 556 | 543.25 | 1.0235 | 1.0197 | 1.0037 |
| 19 | 831 | 822.19 | 1.0107 | 1.0097 | 1.0010 |
| 20 | 960 | 964.91 | .9949 | 1.0016 | .9933 |
| 21 | 1152 | 1153.07 | .9991 | .9934 | 1.0057 |
| 22 | 759 | 769.72 | .9861 | .9903 | .9958 |
| 23 | 607 | 615.76 | .9858 | .9964 | .9894 |
| 24 | 371 | 364.74 | 1.0172 | .9940 | 1.0233 |
| 25 | 298 | 304.37 | .9791 | 1.0027 | .9765 |
| 26 | 378 | 373.62 | 1.0117 | .9920 | 1.0199 |
| 27 | 373 | 378.64 | .9851 | 1.0018 | .9833 |
| 28 | 443 | 439.18 | 1.0087 | 1.0030 | 1.0057 |
| 29 | 374 | 369.61 | 1.0119 | 1.0091 | 1.0028 |
| 30 | 660 | 655.53 | 1.0068 | 1.0112 | .9956 |
| 31 | 1004 | 989.23 | 1.0149 | 1.0059 | 1.0089 |
| 32 | 1153 | 1157.69 | .9959 | 1.0053 | .9906 |
| 33 | 1388 | 1379.67 | 1.0060 | .9954 | 1.0106 |
| 34 | 904 | 918.55 | .9842 | .9886 | .9955 |
| 35 | 715 | 732.93 | .9755 | .9927 | .9827 |
| 36 | 441 | 433.06 | 1.0183 | | |

The third moving average is obtained by dropping $y_2$ from the average and by including $y_{14}$ in the average. We obtain

$$\frac{249 + 289 + 260 + 431 + 660 + 777 + 915 + 613 + 485 + 277 + 244 + 296}{12}$$

$$= 458$$

Successive moving averages are computed similarly until we include $y_{36}$ in the last moving average. Note that we use the term "moving average" here because as we calculate these averages, we move along by dropping the most remote observation in the previous average and by including the "next" observation in the new average.

The first moving average corresponds to a time that is midway between periods 6 and 7, the second moving average corresponds to a time that is midway between periods 7 and 8, and so forth. In order to obtain averages corresponding to time periods in the original Tasty Cola time series, we calculate **centered moving averages.** The centered moving averages are two-period moving averages of the previously computed 12-period moving averages. Thus the first centered moving average is

$$\frac{447.833 + 452.417}{2} = 450.1$$

The second centered moving average is

$$\frac{452.417 + 458}{2} = 455.2$$

Successive centered moving averages are calculated in a similar fashion. The 12-period moving averages and centered moving averages for the Tasty Cola sales time series are given in Table 7.2(a).

If the original moving averages had been computed using an odd number of time series values, the centering procedure would not have been necessary. For example, if we had three seasons per year, we would compute three-period moving averages. Then the first moving average would correspond to period 2, the second moving average would correspond to period 3, and so on. However, most seasonal time series are quarterly, monthly, or weekly, and the centering procedure is necessary.

The centered moving average in time period $t$, $CMA_t$, is considered to be equal to $tr_t \times cl_t$, the estimate of $TR_t \times CL_t$. This is because the averaging procedure is assumed to have removed (1) seasonal variations (note that each moving average is computed using exactly one observation from each season) and (2) short-term irregular fluctuations. The (longer-term) trend effects and cyclical effects, that is, $tr_t \times cl_t$, remain.

Since the model

$$y_t = TR_t \times SN_t \times CL_t \times IR_t$$

implies that

$$SN_t \times IR_t = \frac{y_t}{TR_t \times CL_t}$$

it follows that the estimate $sn_t \times ir_t$ of $SN_t \times IR_t$ is

$$sn_t \times ir_t = \frac{y_t}{tr_t \times cl_t} = \frac{y_t}{CMA_t}$$

Noting that the values of $sn_t \times ir_t$ are calculated in Table 7.2(a), we can find $sn_t$ by grouping the values of $sn_t \times ir_t$ by months and calculating an average, $\overline{sn}_t$ for each month.

**TABLE 7.3** Estimates of the Seasonal Factors of the Tasty Cola Sales Time Series

$$sn_t \times ir_t = y_t/(tr_t \times cl_t)$$

| | | Year 1 | Year 2 | $\overline{sn}_t$ | $sn_t = 1.0008758\ (\overline{sn}_t)$ |
|---|---|---|---|---|---|
| 1 | Jan. | .495 | .490 | .4925 | .493 |
| 2 | Feb. | .583 | .607 | .595 | .596 |
| 3 | Mar. | .608 | .582 | .595 | .595 |
| 4 | Apr. | .684 | .675 | .6795 | .680 |
| 5 | May | .567 | .561 | .564 | .564 |
| 6 | June | .991 | .978 | .9845 | .986 |
| 7 | July | 1.466 | 1.465 | 1.4655 | 1.467 |
| 8 | Aug. | 1.707 | 1.676 | 1.6915 | 1.693 |
| 9 | Sept. | 1.985 | 1.992 | 1.9885 | 1.990 |
| 10 | Oct. | 1.312 | 1.300 | 1.306 | 1.307 |
| 11 | Nov. | 1.026 | 1.030 | 1.028 | 1.029 |
| 12 | Dec. | .577 | .622 | .5995 | .600 |

These seasonal factors are then normalized so that they add to $L = 12$, the number of periods in a year. This normalization is accomplished by multiplying each value of $\overline{sn}_t$ by the quantity

$$\frac{L}{\displaystyle\sum_{t=1}^{L} \overline{sn}_t} = \frac{12}{11.9895} = 1.0008758$$

This normalization process results in the estimate $sn_t = 1.0008758\ (\overline{sn}_t)$, which is the estimate of $SN_t$. These calculations are summarized in Table 7.3.

Having calculated the values of $sn_t$ and placed them in Table 7.2(a), we next define the deseasonalized observation in time period $t$ to be

$$d_t = \frac{y_t}{sn_t}$$

Deseasonalized observations are computed in order to better estimate the trend component $TR_t$. Dividing $y_t$ by the estimated seasonal factor removes the seasonality from the data and allows us to better understand the nature of the trend. The deseasonalized observations are calculated in Table 7.2(a) and are plotted in Figure 7.3. Since the deseasonalized observations have a straight-line appearance, it seems reasonable to assume a linear trend

$$TR_t = \beta_0 + \beta_1 t$$

We estimate $TR_t$ by fitting a straight line to the deseasonalized data. That is, we compute the least squares point estimates of the parameters in the simple linear regression model relating the dependent variable $d_t$ to the independent variable $t$:

$$d_t = \beta_0 + \beta_1 t + \varepsilon_t$$

**FIGURE 7.3**
Excel plot of
deseasonalized
Tasty Cola sales $d_t$

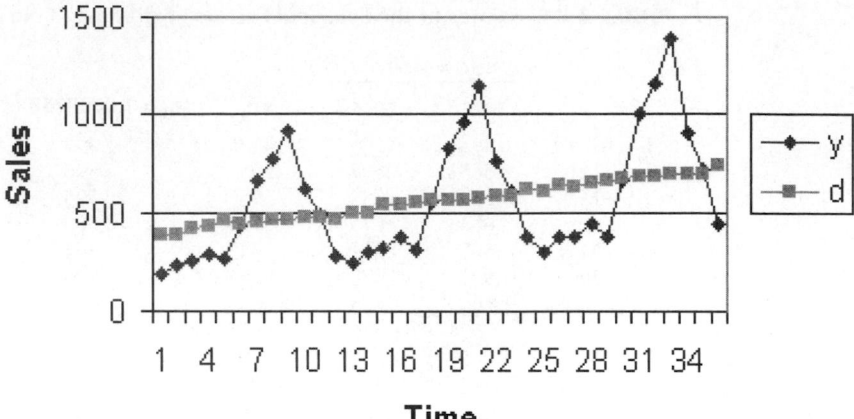

Thus, we obtain $tr_t$, the estimate of $TR_t$, by computing

$$b_1 = \frac{SS_{td}}{SS_{tt}} = \frac{\sum_{t=1}^{36} td_t - \dfrac{\left(\sum_{t=1}^{36} t\right)\left(\sum_{t=1}^{36} d_t\right)}{36}}{\sum_{t=1}^{36} t^2 - \dfrac{\left(\sum_{t=1}^{36} t\right)^2}{36}} = 9.489$$

and

$$b_0 = \bar{d} - b_1 \bar{t} = \frac{\sum_{t=1}^{36} d_t}{36} - b_1 \frac{\sum_{t=1}^{36} t}{36} = 380.163$$

Therefore,

$$tr_t = b_0 + b_1 t = 380.163 + 9.489t$$

The values of $tr_t$ are calculated in Table 7.2(a). Note that, for example, although $y_{22} = 759$ (Tasty Cola sales in period 22) is larger than $tr_{22} = 588.921$ (the estimated trend in period 22), $d_{22} = 580.72$ is smaller than $tr_{22} = 588.921$. This implies that on a deseasonalized basis, Tasty Cola sales were slightly down in October of year 2. This might have been caused by a slightly colder October than usual.

Thus far we have found estimates $sn_t$ and $tr_t$ of $SN_t$ and $TR_t$. Since the model

$$y_t = TR_t \times SN_t \times CL_t \times IR_t$$

implies that

$$CL_t \times IR_t = \frac{y_t}{TR_t \times SN_t}$$

it follows that the estimate of $CL_t \times IR_t$ is

$$cl_t \times ir_t = \frac{y_t}{tr_t \times sn_t}$$

Moreover, experience has shown that when considering either monthly or quarterly data, we can average out $ir_t$ and thus calculate the estimate $cl_t$ of $CL_t$ by using

$$cl_t = \frac{cl_{t-1}ir_{t-1} + cl_t ir_t + cl_{t+1}ir_{t+1}}{3}$$

That is, $cl_t$ is a three-period moving average of the $cl_t \times ir_t$ values.

Finally, we calculate the estimate $ir_t$ or $IR_t$ by using the equation

$$ir_t = \frac{cl_t \times ir_t}{cl_t}$$

The calculations of the values of $cl_t$ and $ir_t$ for the Tasty Cola data are summarized in Table 7.2(b). Since there are only three years of data, and since most of the values of $cl_t$ are near 1, we cannot discern a well-defined cycle. Furthermore, in examining the values of $ir_t$, we cannot detect a pattern in the estimates of the irregular factors.

Traditionally, the estimates $tr_t$, $sn_t$, $cl_t$, and $ir_t$ obtained by using the multiplicative decomposition method are used to describe the time series. However, we can also use these estimates to forecast future values of the time series. If there is no pattern in the irregular component, we predict that $IR_t$ will equal one. Therefore, the point forecast of $y_t$ is

$$\hat{y}_t = tr_t \times sn_t \times cl_t$$

if a well-defined cycle exists and can be predicted. The point forecast is

$$\hat{y}_t = tr_t \times sn_t$$

if a well-defined cycle does not exist or if $CL_t$ cannot be predicted. For our Tasty Cola example, where

$$tr_t = b_0 + b_1 t = 380.163 + 9.489t$$

the point forecasts of the $n = 36$ historical Tasty Cola sales are given in Table 7.2(a). The point forecasts of future Tasty Cola sales in the 12 months of year 4 are as given in Table 7.4. For example, the point forecast of sales in period 44 is

$$\hat{y}_{44} = tr_{44} \times sn_{44}$$
$$= [380.163 + 9.489(44)](1.693) = 797.699(1.693)$$
$$= 1350.50$$

Although there is no theoretically correct prediction interval for $y_t$, the authors have found that a fairly accurate (approximate) $100(1 - \alpha)\%$ prediction interval for $y_t$ is

$$[\hat{y}_t \pm B_t[100(1 - \alpha)]]$$

**TABLE 7.4** Forecasts of Future Values of Tasty Cola Sales Calculated Using Multiplicative Decomposition

| $t$ | $sn_t$ | $tr_t = 380.163 + 9.489t$ | $\hat{y}_t = tr_t \times sn_t$ | $B_t(95)$ | $[\hat{y}_t - B_t(95), \hat{y}_t + B_t(95)]$ | $y_t$ |
|---|---|---|---|---|---|---|
| 37 | .493 | 731.273 | 360.52 | 26.80 | [333.72, 387.32] | 352 |
| 38 | .596 | 740.762 | 441.48 | 26.92 | [414.56, 468.40] | 445 |
| 39 | .595 | 750.252 | 446.40 | 27.04 | [419.36, 473.44] | 453 |
| 40 | .680 | 759.741 | 516.62 | 27.17 | [489.45, 543.79] | 541 |
| 41 | .564 | 769.231 | 433.85 | 27.30 | [406.55, 461.15] | 457 |
| 42 | .986 | 778.720 | 767.82 | 27.44 | [740.38, 795.26] | 762 |
| 43 | 1.467 | 788.209 | 1156.30 | 27.59 | [1128.71, 1183.89] | 1194 |
| 44 | 1.693 | 797.699 | 1350.50 | 27.74 | [1322.76, 1378.24] | 1361 |
| 45 | 1.990 | 807.188 | 1606.30 | 27.89 | [1578.41, 1634.19] | 1615 |
| 46 | 1.307 | 816.678 | 1067.40 | 28.05 | [1039.35, 1095.45] | 1059 |
| 47 | 1.029 | 826.167 | 850.12 | 28.22 | [821.90, 878.34] | 824 |
| 48 | .600 | 835.657 | 501.39 | 28.39 | [473, 529.78] | 495 |

where $B_t[100(1 - \alpha)]$ is the error bound in a $100(1 - \alpha)\%$ prediction interval

$$[tr_t \pm B_t[100(1 - \alpha)]]$$

for the deseasonalized observation

$$d_t = TR_t + \varepsilon_t$$
$$= \beta_0 + \beta_1 t + \varepsilon_t$$

For example, using SAS to predict $d_t$ on the basis of $t$ by using the above trend line, we find that a 95% prediction interval for $d_{44}$ is

$$[769.959, 825.439]$$

This implies that

$$B_{44}[95] = \frac{825.439 - 769.959}{2}$$

$$= 27.74$$

It follows that an approximate 95% prediction interval for $y_{44}$ is

$$[1350.50 - 27.74, 1350.50 + 27.74] = [1322.76, 1378.24]$$

In Table 7.4 we present 95% prediction intervals (calculated by the above method) for Tasty Cola sales in the 12 months of year 4.

Suppose that we actually observe Tasty Cola sales in year 4 and that these sales are as given in Table 7.4. In Figure 7.4 we plot the observed and forecasted sales for all 48 sales periods. In practice the comparison of the observed and forecasted sales in years 1 through 3 would be used by the analyst to determine whether the forecasting equation adequately fits the historical data. An adequate fit (as indicated by Figure 7.4, for example) might prompt an analyst to use this equation to calculate forecasts for future time periods.

**FIGURE 7.4**
Forecasts of historical and future values of Tasty Cola sales calculated using multiplicative decomposition

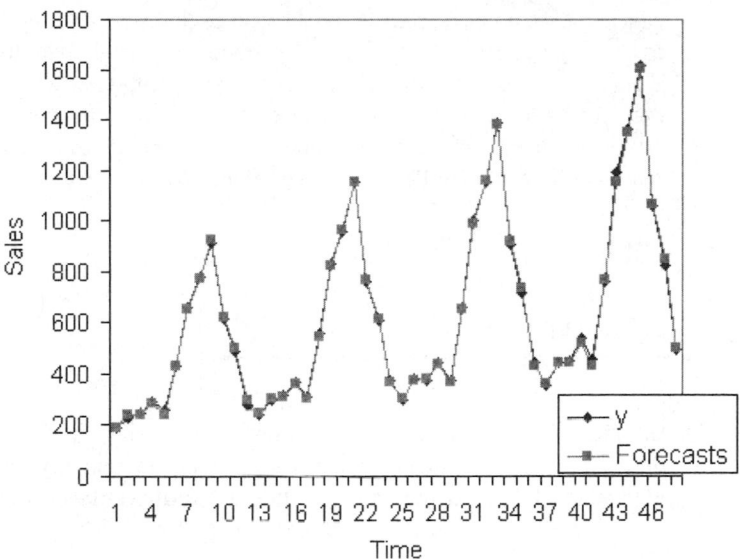

One reason that the Tasty Cola forecasting equation

$$\hat{y}_t = tr_t \times sn_t$$
$$= (380.163 + 9.489t)sn_t$$

provides reasonable forecasts is that this equation *multiplies* $sn_t$ by $tr_t$. Therefore, as the average level of the time series (determined by the trend) increases, the seasonal swing of the time series increases, which is consistent with the data plots in Figures 7.2 and 7.4. For example, note from Table 7.3 that the estimated seasonal factor for August is 1.693. The forecasting equation yields a prediction of Tasty Cola sales in August of year 1 equal to

$$\hat{y}_8 = [380.163 + 9.489(8)](1.693)$$
$$= (456.075)(1.693)$$
$$= 772.13$$

This implies a seasonal swing of $772.13 - 456.075 = 316.055$ (hundreds of cases) above 456.075, the estimated trend. The forecasting equation yields a prediction of Tasty Cola sales in August of year 2 equal to

$$\hat{y}_{20} = [380.163 + 9.489(20)](1.693)$$
$$= (569.943)(1.693)$$
$$= 964.91$$

which implies an *increased* seasonal swing of $964.91 - 569.943 = 394.967$ (hundreds of cases) above 569.943, the estimated trend. In general, then, the forecasting equation is appropriate for forecasting a time series with a seasonal swing that is proportional to the average level of the time series as determined by the trend—that is, a time series exhibiting increasing seasonal variation. In fact, sometimes increasing seasonal variation is referred to as **multiplicative seasonal variation.**

# 7.2 ADDITIVE DECOMPOSITION

Consider a time series that exhibits constant seasonal variation. When the parameters describing the series are not changing over time, the time series can sometimes be modeled adequately by using what is called the **additive decomposition model.**

---

The **additive decomposition model** is

$$y_t = TR_t + SN_t + CL_t + IR_t$$

---

Here $TR_t$, $SN_t$, $CL_t$, and $IR_t$ are again defined to be, respectively, trend, seasonal, cyclical, and irregular factors. However, in this case these factors are additive rather than multiplicative.

The **additive decomposition method** can be used to obtain point estimates $tr_t$, $sn_t$, $cl_t$, and $ir_t$ of the above factors. The procedure begins with the calculation of centered moving averages, $CMA_t$. The centered moving average is regarded as an estimate of $TR_t + CL_t$. Since the model

$$y_t = TR_t + SN_t + CL_t + IR_t$$

implies that

$$SN_t + IR_t = y_t - (TR_t + CL_t)$$

it follows that the estimate $sn_t + ir_t$ of $SN_t + IR_t$ is

$$sn_t + ir_t = y_t - (tr_t + cl_t) = y_t - CMA_t$$

In order to obtain $sn_t$, we group the values of $sn_t + ir_t$ by like seasons (months, quarters, etc., as appropriate). For each season we compute the average $\overline{sn}_t$ of the $sn_t + ir_t$ values for that season. We obtain seasonal factors by normalizing the $\overline{sn}_t$ values so that the normalized values sum to zero. The normalization is accomplished by subtracting the quantity $\sum_{t=1}^{L} \overline{sn}_t / L$ from each of the $\overline{sn}_t$ values. That is, the estimate of $SN_t$ is

$$sn_t = \overline{sn}_t - \left( \sum_{t=1}^{L} \overline{sn}_t / L \right)$$

We next calculate the deseasonalized observation in time period $t$ to be

$$d_t = y_t - \text{sn}_t$$

Subtracting $\text{sn}_t$ from the observation $y_t$ removes the seasonality from the data and allows us to estimate the trend better. We obtain the estimate $\text{tr}_t$ of the trend $\text{TR}_t$ by fitting a regression equation to the deseasonalized data. For example, a linear trend

$$\text{TR}_t = \beta_0 + \beta_1 t$$

or a quadratic trend

$$\text{TR}_t = \beta_0 + \beta_1 t + \beta_2 t^2$$

might be fitted to the deseasonalized observations.

Since the model

$$y_t = \text{TR}_t + \text{SN}_t + \text{CL}_t + \text{IR}_t$$

implies that

$$\text{CL}_t + \text{IR}_t = y_t - \text{TR}_t - \text{SN}_t$$

it follows that we compute the estimate of $\text{CL}_t + \text{IR}_t$ to be

$$\text{cl}_t + \text{ir}_t = y_t \quad \text{tr}_t - \text{sn}_t$$

In order to average out $\text{ir}_t$, we compute a three-period moving average of the $\text{cl}_t + \text{ir}_t$ values. That is, the estimate of $\text{CL}_t$ is

$$\text{cl}_t = \frac{(\text{cl}_{t-1} + \text{ir}_{t-1}) + (\text{cl}_t + \text{ir}_t) + (\text{cl}_{t+1} + \text{ir}_{t+1})}{3}$$

Finally, we calculate the estimate of $\text{IR}_t$ to be

$$\text{ir}_t = (\text{cl}_t + \text{ir}_t) - \text{cl}_t$$

The estimates $\text{tr}_t$, $\text{sn}_t$, $\text{cl}_t$, and $\text{ir}_t$ are generally used to describe the time series. We can also use these estimates to compute predictions. If there is no pattern in the irregular component, we predict $\text{IR}_t$ to equal zero. It follows that the point forecast of $y_t$ is

$$\hat{y}_t = \text{tr}_t + \text{sn}_t + \text{cl}_t$$

if a well-defined cycle exists and can be predicted. The point forecast is

$$\hat{y}_t = \text{tr}_t + \text{sn}_t$$

if no well-defined cycle exists or if $\text{CL}_t$ cannot be predicted. Although there is no theoretically correct prediction interval for $y_t$, an approximate $100(1 - \alpha)\%$ prediction interval for $y_t$ is

$$[\hat{y}_t \pm B_t[100(1 - \alpha)]]$$

where $B_t[100(1 - \alpha)]$ is the error bound in a $100(1 - \alpha)\%$ prediction interval

$$[\text{tr}_t \pm B_t[100(1 - \alpha)]]$$

for the deseasonalized observation $d_t = y_t - \text{sn}_t$.

# 7.3 THE X-12-ARIMA SEASONAL ADJUSTMENT METHOD

Seasonal adjustment, that is, removing the seasonal components or effects from the data, is a major occupation for the U.S. Census Bureau. The bureau provides both seasonally unadjusted and seasonally adjusted time series for all aspects of economics and business. Examples include time series on housing starts, retail sales, and foreign trade. In addition, it supplies other organizations, including foreign governments, with computer programs to perform seasonal adjustment. Thus, identifying the seasonal components for a time series is an important task. The latest computer program is the X-12-ARIMA Seasonal Adjustment Program (Findley et al., 1998). This program is an extension of Statistics Canada's X-11-ARIMA (Dagum, 1980) seasonal adjustment program, which in turn was an extension of the U.S. Census Bureau's X-11 (Shiskin, Young, and Musgrave, 1967). The methods in these computer programs are far more sophisticated than the multiplicative and additive decomposition methods of the previous two sections. For example, the original data are adjusted for "trading day variations." That is, the data are adjusted to account for the fact that, for example, different months or quarters consist of different numbers of business days or "trading days." There are automatic methods for detecting outliers (unusual observations). ARIMA models may be used to extend the time series by forecasting future values. As we saw in Table 7.2(a), time periods are lost at both the beginning and end of the time series when the moving averages are computed. More accurate estimates for the seasonal components are obtained by using the extended data. ARIMA (autoregressive integrated moving average) models are called Box–Jenkins models in this text and are studied in Chapters 9 to 12.

Although the latest seasonal adjustment programs are very sophisticated, one of the building blocks is the "ratio-to-moving-average" method that we employed in Example 7.1 by computing

$$\frac{y_t}{\text{CMA}_t} = \frac{y_t}{\text{tr}_t \times \text{cl}_t} = \text{sn}_t \times \text{ir}_t$$

We then averaged these values by month. We are assuming that the seasonal components do not change over time. In contrast, the X-12-ARIMA procedure performs a weighted moving average procedure on the values that correspond to the same month. This moving average procedure removes the irregular component but allows for the seasonal components that correspond to the same month of the year to change over time. For example, one choice in X-12-ARIMA is a weighted seasonal moving average that is computed as follows:

$$\overline{\text{sn}}_t = \frac{1}{9}\,\text{sn}_{t-24}^{(1)} + \frac{2}{9}\,\text{sn}_{t-12}^{(1)} + \frac{3}{9}\,\text{sn}_t^{(1)} + \frac{2}{9}\,\text{sn}_{t+12}^{(1)} + \frac{1}{9}\,\text{sn}_{t+24}^{(1)}$$

where

$$sn_t^{(1)} = \frac{y_t}{CMA_t} = \frac{y_t}{tr_t \times cl_t} = sn_t \times ir_t$$

Clearly, we need many years of data for this seasonal moving average. As was done in the classical decomposition method, these averages must be normalized. The interested reader is referred to Findley et al. (1998) for more details on the procedures in X-12-ARIMA.

Understanding the decomposition methods of Sections 7.1 and 7.2 should provide you with important knowledge to learn more about decomposition methods. Options to seasonally adjust or deseasonalize a time series are provided in many forecasting software programs. It is important in each case to understand how the seasonal component $sn_t$ is found before an observation $y_t$ is deseasonalized by computing $y_t/sn_t$. Obvious questions to ask include whether "trading days" are considered and how outliers are detected and removed.

## Exercises

**7.1** International Machinery, Inc., produces a tractor and wishes to use quarterly tractor sales data observed during the last four years to predict tractor sales for the next year. Figure 7.5 (page 342) presents an Excel output of the multiplicative decomposition analysis of these data.

a. Find and report the four seasonal factors for quarters 1, 2, 3, and 4.

b. What is the equation of the estimated trend that has been calculated using the deseasonalized data?

c. Compute (using estimated trend and seasonal factors) $\hat{y}_{17}, \hat{y}_{18}, \hat{y}_{19},$ and $\hat{y}_{20}$

d. Compute a point forecast of the total tractor sales for the next year (year 5).

e. Do the cyclical factors determine a well-defined cycle for these data? Explain your answer.

f. In Figure 7.5, find and report point forecasts of the tractor sales (based on trend and seasonal factors) for each of the quarters of next year (year 5). Do the values agree with your answers to part (c)?

g. Starting with the 16 values for the tractor sales, construct the Excel spreadsheet in Figure 7.5 to perform the steps in the multiplicative decomposition method.

h. Figure 7.6 (page 342) presents the MINITAB output of the 95% prediction interval forecasts of the deseasonalized tractor sales for each of the four quarters of the next year (year 5). Use the results in this output to compute approximate 95% prediction interval forecasts of tractor sales for each of the quarters of the next year.

**7.2** The data in Table 7.5 (page 343) give quarterly sales of the popular game Oligopoly at the J-Mart variety store.

Consider using the multiplicative decomposition method to forecast Oligopoly sales for year 4. Use of a spreadsheet is recommended for all parts except (h) and (n).

a. Compute appropriate four-period moving averages for these data.

b. Compute centered moving averages for these data.

c. Calculate $sn_t \times ir_t$ values for these data.

d. Calculate estimates of the seasonal factors for quarterly Oligopoly sales (that is, compute $sn_t$ values for these data)

e. Compute the deseasonalized observations for these data.

f. Plot the deseasonalized observations versus time. From your data plot, what kind of trend appears to exist?

g. Assuming that a linear trend

$$TR_t = \beta_0 + \beta_1 t$$

describes the deseasonalized observations, compute least squares point estimates of $\beta_0$ and $\beta_1$.

**FIGURE 7.5 (for Exercise 7.1)** Excel output of centered moving averages, seasonal factors, deseasonalized data, trend, cyclical factors, and forecasts for tractor sales

| | A | B | C | D | E | F | G | H | I | J |
|---|---|---|---|---|---|---|---|---|---|---|
| 1 | t | Data | CMA | y/CMA | sn | d | tr | yhat | cl x ir | cl |
| 2 | 1 | 293 | | | 1.191 | 245.9 | 240.5 | 286.5 | 1.023 | |
| 3 | 2 | 392 | | | 1.521 | 257.7 | 260.4 | 396.2 | 0.989 | 0.998 |
| 4 | 3 | 221 | 275.13 | 0.803 | 0.804 | 275.0 | 280.4 | 225.3 | 0.981 | 0.994 |
| 5 | 4 | 147 | 302.00 | 0.487 | 0.484 | 303.9 | 300.3 | 145.3 | 1.012 | 1.003 |
| 6 | 5 | 388 | 325.25 | 1.193 | 1.191 | 325.7 | 320.3 | 381.6 | 1.017 | 1.006 |
| 7 | 6 | 512 | 338.13 | 1.514 | 1.521 | 336.6 | 340.2 | 517.6 | 0.989 | 0.999 |
| 8 | 7 | 287 | 354.13 | 0.810 | 0.804 | 357.1 | 360.2 | 289.4 | 0.992 | 0.994 |
| 9 | 8 | 184 | 381.50 | 0.482 | 0.484 | 380.4 | 380.1 | 183.9 | 1.001 | 0.999 |
| 10 | 9 | 479 | 405.00 | 1.183 | 1.191 | 402.0 | 400.1 | 476.7 | 1.005 | 1.002 |
| 11 | 10 | 640 | 417.38 | 1.533 | 1.521 | 420.7 | 420.0 | 639.0 | 1.002 | 0.996 |
| 12 | 11 | 347 | 435.00 | 0.798 | 0.804 | 431.8 | 440.0 | 353.6 | 0.981 | 0.995 |
| 13 | 12 | 223 | 462.13 | 0.483 | 0.484 | 461.0 | 459.9 | 222.5 | 1.002 | 1.000 |
| 14 | 13 | 581 | 484.38 | 1.199 | 1.191 | 487.7 | 479.9 | 571.7 | 1.016 | 1.004 |
| 15 | 14 | 755 | 497.63 | 1.517 | 1.521 | 496.3 | 499.8 | 760.4 | 0.993 | 0.997 |
| 16 | 15 | 410 | | | | 0.804 | 510.2 | 519.8 | 417.7 | 0.982 | 0.998 |
| 17 | 16 | 266 | | | | 0.484 | 549.9 | 539.7 | 261.1 | 1.019 | |
| 18 | | Forecasts | | | | | | | | |
| 19 | 17 | 667 | | | | | Coefficients | Standard Error | t Stat | P-value |
| 20 | 18 | 882 | | | | Intercept | 220.53893 | 3.038532915 | 72.58072888 | 1.93E-19 |
| 21 | 19 | 482 | | | | X Variable | 19.949897 | 0.314237593 | 63.4866664 | 1.25E-18 |
| 22 | 20 | 300 | | | | | | | | |

**FIGURE 7.6 (for Exercise 7.1)** MINITAB output of 95% prediction interval forecasts of quarterly deseasonalized tractor sales in year 5

```
The regression equation is
y = 221 + 20.0 Time

Predictor       Coef     SE Coef         T       P
Constant     220.538       3.044     72.46   0.000
Time         19.9507       0.3148    63.38   0.000


S = 5.804      R-Sq = 99.7%     R-Sq(adj) = 99.6%

Predicted Values for New Observations

   Fit     SE Fit       95.0% CI              95.0% PI
559.70       3.04  ( 553.17,  566.23)  ( 545.64,  573.76)
579.65       3.32  ( 572.52,  586.78)  ( 565.31,  594.00)
599.60       3.61  ( 591.86,  607.34)  ( 584.94,  614.26)
619.55       3.90  ( 611.19,  627.92)  ( 604.55,  634.55)
```

**TABLE 7.5 (for Exercise 7.2)**
**Quarterly Oligopoly Sales**

| Year | Quarter | Oligopoly Sales |
|---|---|---|
| 1 | 1 | 20 |
|   | 2 | 25 |
|   | 3 | 35 |
|   | 4 | 44 |
| 2 | 1 | 28 |
|   | 2 | 29 |
|   | 3 | 43 |
|   | 4 | 48 |
| 3 | 1 | 24 |
|   | 2 | 37 |
|   | 3 | 39 |
|   | 4 | 56 |

h.  Using statistical software, such as SAS or MINITAB, do the following:
   1.  Compute least squares point estimates of $\beta_0$ and $\beta_1$, the parameters of the trend line

$$TR_t = \beta_0 + \beta_1 t$$

   describing the deseasonalized observations.
   2.  Compute point forecasts of deseasonalized Oligopoly sales for the four quarters of year 4.
   3.  Compute 95% prediction interval forecasts of deseasonalized Oligopoly sales for the four quarters of year 4.
i.  Compute $cl_t \times ir_t$ values for the Oligopoly data.
j.  Compute estimates of the cyclical factors for the Oligopoly data (that is, compute $cl_t$ values for these data).

k.  Compute estimates of the irregular factors for the Oligopoly data (that is, compute $ir_t$ values for these data).
l.  Do the $cl_t$ values determine any well-defined cycle? Explain your answer.
m.  Using estimated trend and seasonal factors, compute point forecasts of Oligopoly sales for each quarter of year 4.
n.  Using estimated trend and seasonal factors, compute approximate 95% prediction interval forecasts of Oligopoly sales for each quarter of year 4.

**7.3** Analyze the data of Exercise 7.1 by using the additive decomposition method. Does this method seem more appropriate for these data than the multiplicative decomposition method?

**7.4** Analyze the data of Exercise 7.2 by using the additive decomposition method. Does this method seem more appropriate for these data than the multiplicative decomposition method?

**7.5** Consider the hotel occupancy data in Table 6.4 of Chapter 6.
a.  Analyze this data using the multiplicative decomposition method in an Excel spreadsheet.
b.  Use statistical software, such as SAS or MINITAB, to produce point forecasts and 95% prediction intervals for the deseasonalized hotel room averages in each month of the 15th year.
c.  Using the values from part (b), compute point and 95% prediction interval forecasts of the hotel room averages in each month of the 15th year.

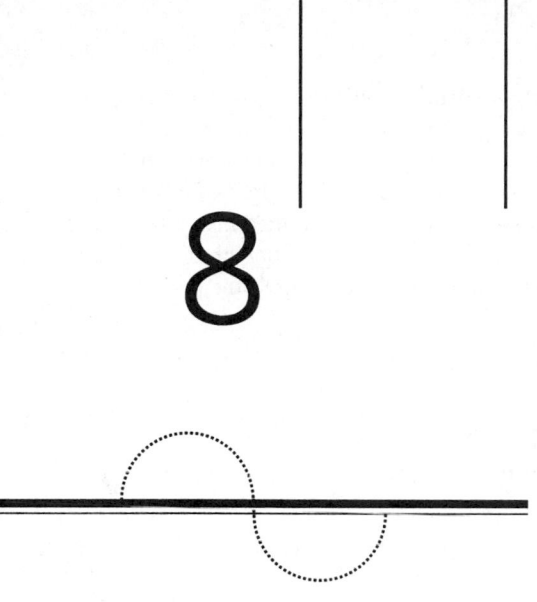

# 8

# *Exponential Smoothing*

**Exponential smoothing** provides a forecasting method that is most effective when the components (trend and seasonal factors) of the time series may be changing over time. It is a method that weights the observed time series values unequally. More recent observations are weighted more heavily than more remote observations. The unequal weighting is accomplished by using one or more **smoothing constants,** which determine how much weight is given to each observation. Historically, the exponential smoothing methods were intuitive methods not based on any formal statistical models. However, work on state space models with a single source of error (Ord, Koehler, and Snyder, 1997, and Hyndman et al., 2002) has now provided a statistical framework for the exponential smoothing methods. The formulas for the prediction intervals in this chapter are based on these models, and the models themselves are presented in the last section of the chapter.

We begin this chapter by explaining **simple exponential smoothing** in Section 8.1. This method assumes that the time series has no trend, but the level (or mean) of the time series may change over time. Section 8.2 discusses **tracking signals,** which can be used to tell us when a forecasting system is not predicting accurately. In Section 8.3 we present **Holt's trend corrected exponential smoothing,** which is a method for forecasting a time series that has a linear trend locally but a growth rate (or slope) that is changing over time. Section 8.4 discusses Holt–Winters methods, which are exponential smoothing procedures for seasonal data. Both the **additive Holt–Winters method** (which is appropriate for constant seasonal variation) and the **multiplicative Holt–Winters method** (which is appropriate for increasing seasonal variation) are presented.

345

Section 8.5 introduces **damped trend exponential smoothing,** alone and combined with additive and multiplicative seasonal components. A multiplicative seasonal model with no trend is also examined. We conclude this chapter with optional Section 8.6. In this last section we present state space models with a single source of error; these models correspond to the exponential smoothing methods examined in the preceding sections. We provide examples of how the models may be used to find prediction intervals by analytical derivation and by simulation of values for future time periods.

# 8.1   SIMPLE EXPONENTIAL SMOOTHING

If the mean (or the level) of a time series remains constant, then the no trend model (see Section 6.1)

$$y_t = \beta_0 + \varepsilon_t \quad \text{(or equivalently, } y_t = \mu + \varepsilon_t)$$

may be used to describe the data. In such a case the least squares point estimate of the mean $\beta_0$ is

$$b_0 = \bar{y} = \frac{1}{n} \sum_{t=1}^{n} y_t = \sum_{t=1}^{n} \frac{1}{n} y_t$$

When we compute the point estimate $b_0$, we are giving equal weight to each of the observed values of the time series values $y_1, y_2, \ldots, y_n$.

When the mean (or level) of the time series is changing slowly over time, the equal weighting scheme may not be appropriate. Instead, it may be desirable to weight recent observations more heavily than remote observations. The **simple exponential smoothing method** is used for forecasting a time series when there is no trend or seasonal pattern, but the mean (or level) of the time series $y_t$ is slowly changing over time. In this case, we need a different model to describe the data (see optional Section 8.6), and we need estimates for the mean (or level) that may change from one time period to the next. Instead of giving equal weights to each observation, the simple exponential smoothing method will give the most recent observation the most weight. Older observations are given successively smaller weights. The procedure allows the forecaster to update the estimate of the level of the time series so that changes in the level can be detected and incorporated into the forecasting system. We illustrate simple exponential smoothing in the following example.

**EXAMPLE 8.1**    Consider the cod catch data of Example 6.1, which are given in Table 6.1. The plot of these data (in Figure 6.2) suggests that there is no trend or seasonal pattern. It is also possible that the level (or mean) may be changing slowly over time.

We begin the simple exponential smoothing procedure by calculating an initial estimate $\ell_0$ of the level (or mean) of the series at time period $t = 0$. We compute this estimate $\ell_0$ by averaging the first twelve series values (or half the data). We obtain

$$\ell_0 = \frac{\sum_{t=1}^{12} y_t}{12} = \frac{362 + 381 + \cdots + 343}{12} = 360.6667$$

Next, assume that at the end of time period $T - 1$ we have an estimate $\ell_{T-1}$ for the level (or mean) of the time series. Then assuming in time period $T$ we obtain a new observation $y_T$, we can update $\ell_{T-1}$ to $\ell_T$, which is the new estimate of the level (or mean) in time period $T$. We compute the updated estimate by using the **smoothing equation**

$$\ell_T = \alpha y_T + (1 - \alpha)\ell_{T-1}$$

Here $\alpha$ is a **smoothing constant** between 0 and 1 ($\alpha$ is discussed in more detail later). The smoothing equation says that $\ell_T$, the estimate of the level made in time period $T$, equals a fraction $\alpha$ (for example, .1) of the newly observed time series observation $y_T$ plus a fraction $(1 - \alpha)$ (for example, .9) of $\ell_{T-1}$, the estimate of the level made in time period $T - 1$. The more the level of the process is changing, the more a newly observed time series value should influence our estimate, and thus the larger the smoothing constant $\alpha$ should be set. We will soon see how to use historical data to determine an appropriate value of $\alpha$.

We begin with the initial estimate $\ell_0 = 360.6667$ and update this initial estimate by applying the smoothing equation to the 24 observed cod catches. To do this, we arbitrarily set $\alpha$ equal to .1, and to judge the appropriateness of this choice of $\alpha$ we calculate "one-period-ahead" forecasts of the historical cod catches as we carry out the smoothing procedure. A one-period-ahead forecast of $y_T$ is the estimate $\ell_{T-1}$ of the level (or mean) made in time period $T - 1$. Thus, since the initial estimate of the level is $\ell_0 = 360.6667$, it follows that 360.6667 is the forecast of $y_1$ made at time 0. Since we see from Figure 8.1 that $y_1 = 362$, we have a forecast error of $362 - 360.6667 = 1.3333$. Using $y_1 = 362$, we can update $\ell_0$ to $\ell_1$, an estimate made in period 1 of the level (or mean) of the time series, by using

$$\ell_1 = \alpha y_1 + (1 - \alpha)\ell_0$$
$$= .1(362) + .9(360.6667)$$
$$= 360.8000$$

Since $\ell_1 = 360.8000$ is the forecast made in period 1 for $y_2$, and since we see from Figure 8.1 that $y_2 = 381$, we have a forecast error of $381 - 360.8000 = 20.2000$. Using $y_2 = 381$, we can update $\ell_1$ to $\ell_2$, an estimate of the level (or mean) made in time period 2, by using the equation

$$\ell_2 = \alpha y_2 + (1 - \alpha)\ell_1$$
$$= .1(381) + .9(360.8000)$$
$$= 362.8200$$

**FIGURE 8.1**
Excel spreadsheet of simple exponential smoothing for the cod catch data with $\alpha = .10$

| | A | B | C | D | E | F |
|---|---|---|---|---|---|---|
| **1** | n | alpha | SSE | ssquare | s | |
| **2** | 24 | 0.1 | 28735.11 | 1249.35 | 35.35 | |
| **3** | | | | | | |
| **4** | | Actual | Smoothed | Forecast | | Squared |
| **5** | Time | Cod Catch | Estimate | Made Last | Forecast | Forecast |
| **6** | Period | y | for Level | Period | Error | Error |
| **7** | 0 | | 360.6667 | | | |
| **8** | 1 | 362 | 360.8000 | 360.6667 | 1.3333 | 1.7778 |
| **9** | 2 | 381 | 362.8200 | 360.8000 | 20.2000 | 408.0400 |
| **10** | 3 | 317 | 358.2380 | 362.8200 | -45.8200 | 2099.4724 |
| **11** | 4 | 297 | 352.1142 | 358.2380 | -61.2380 | 3750.0926 |
| **12** | 5 | 399 | 356.8028 | 352.1142 | 46.8858 | 2198.2782 |
| **13** | 6 | 402 | 361.3225 | 356.8028 | 45.1972 | 2042.7887 |
| **14** | 7 | 375 | 362.6903 | 361.3225 | 13.6775 | 187.0740 |
| **15** | 8 | 349 | 361.3212 | 362.6903 | -13.6903 | 187.4230 |
| **16** | 9 | 386 | 363.7891 | 361.3212 | 24.6788 | 609.0419 |
| **17** | 10 | 328 | 360.2102 | 363.7891 | -35.7891 | 1280.8600 |
| **18** | 11 | 389 | 363.0892 | 360.2102 | 28.7898 | 828.8530 |
| **19** | 12 | 343 | 361.0803 | 363.0892 | -20.0892 | 403.5749 |
| **20** | 13 | 276 | 352.5722 | 361.0803 | -85.0803 | 7238.6501 |
| **21** | 14 | 334 | 350.7150 | 352.5722 | -18.5722 | 344.9278 |
| **22** | 15 | 394 | 355.0435 | 350.7150 | 43.2850 | 1873.5905 |
| **23** | 16 | 334 | 352.9392 | 355.0435 | -21.0435 | 442.8292 |
| **24** | 17 | 384 | 356.0452 | 352.9392 | 31.0608 | 964.7760 |
| **25** | 18 | 314 | 351.8407 | 356.0452 | -42.0452 | 1767.8023 |
| **26** | 19 | 344 | 351.0566 | 351.8407 | -7.8407 | 61.4768 |
| **27** | 20 | 337 | 349.6510 | 351.0566 | -14.0566 | 197.5893 |
| **28** | 21 | 345 | 349.1859 | 349.6510 | -4.6510 | 21.6316 |
| **29** | 22 | 362 | 350.4673 | 349.1859 | 12.8141 | 164.2016 |
| **30** | 23 | 314 | 346.8206 | 350.4673 | -36.4673 | 1329.8636 |
| **31** | 24 | 365 | 348.6385 | 346.8206 | 18.1794 | 330.4919 |

Since this implies that 362.8200 is the forecast made in period 2 for $y_3$, and since from Figure 8.1 we can see that $y_3 = 317$, we have a forecast error of $317 - 362.8200 = -45.8200$.

This procedure is continued through the entire 24 periods of historical data. Figure 8.1 presents the results for all 24 periods of the cod catch data in an Excel spreadsheet. Since the same computations are performed for each of the 24 time periods, the simple exponential smoothing is easily set up in a spreadsheet by copying the formulas for time period 1 to the other 23 time periods. Using the results in Figure 8.1, we find that for $\alpha = .1$, the sum of the squared forecast errors is 28,735.11. To find a "good" value of $\alpha$, we use Solver in Excel to find a value of $\alpha$ that provides a minimum value for the sum of squared forecast errors (SSE) when possible values of $\alpha$ range from 0 to 1. Figure 8.2(a) presents the setup of the Solver dialog box in Excel for finding a value of $\alpha$ that minimizes the SSE. Figure 8.2(b) presents an Excel spreadsheet with the solution found by Solver. We can see that when the SSE is at its minimum value of 28,089.14, the value of the smoothing

**FIGURE 8.2**
Finding the α value that minimizes SSE in simple exponential smoothing for the cod catch data

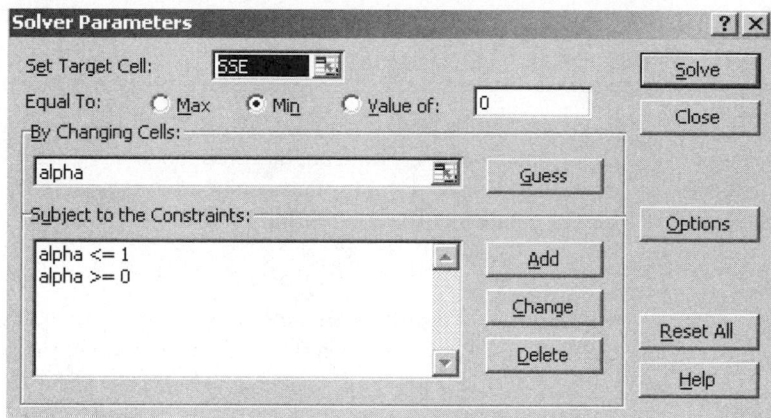

(a) Solver in Excel for finding alpha that minimizes the SSE

| | A | B | C | D | E | F |
|---|---|---|---|---|---|---|
| 1 | n | alpha | SSE | ssquare | s | |
| 2 | 24 | 0.034 | 28089.14 | 1221.27 | 34.95 | |
| 3 | | | | | | |
| 4 | | Actual | Smoothed | Forecast | | Squared |
| 5 | Time | Cod Catch | Estimate | Made Last | Forecast | Forecast |
| 6 | Period | y | for Level | Period | Error | Error |
| 7 | 0 | | 360.6667 | | | |
| 8 | 1 | 362 | 360.7125 | 360.6667 | 1.3333 | 1.7778 |
| 9 | 2 | 381 | 361.4094 | 360.7125 | 20.2875 | 411.5838 |
| 10 | 3 | 317 | 359.8838 | 361.4094 | 44.4094 | 1972.1959 |
| 28 | 21 | 345 | 355.3733 | 355.7424 | -10.7424 | 115.3987 |
| 29 | 22 | 362 | 355.6010 | 355.3733 | 6.6267 | 43.9126 |
| 30 | 23 | 314 | 354.1719 | 355.6010 | -41.6010 | 1730.6423 |
| 31 | 24 | 365 | 354.5438 | 354.1719 | 10.8281 | 117.2486 |

(b) Excel spreadsheet with values for $\alpha$, $s$, and $\ell_{24}$ when SSE has a minimum value

constant is $\alpha = .034$, and the final estimate for the level (or mean) is $\ell_{24} = 354.5438$. This small value of $\alpha$ indicates that the level (or mean) of the time series is not changing much over time.

In the simple exponential smoothing method, a point forecast at time $T$ of any future value $y_{T+\tau}$ of a time series is the last estimate $\ell_T$ for the mean of the time series because there is no trend or seasonal pattern to exploit. However, we do expect to be less accurate when we forecast further into the future. Hence, the prediction intervals will get longer. The point forecasts and prediction intervals are shown in the next box. In general, simple exponential smoothing is carried out as follows.

## SIMPLE EXPONENTIAL SMOOTHING

1. Suppose that the time series $y_1, y_2, \ldots, y_n$ has a level (or mean) that may be slowly changing over time but has no trend or seasonal pattern. Then the estimate $\ell_T$ for the level (or mean) of the time series in time period $T$ is given by the **smoothing equation**

$$\ell_T = \alpha y_T + (1 - \alpha)\ell_{T-1}$$

where $\alpha$ is a **smoothing constant** between 0 and 1, and $\ell_{T-1}$ is the estimate of the level (or mean) of the time series in time period $T - 1$.

2. A **point forecast made in time period $T$ for $y_{T+\tau}$** is

$$\hat{y}_{T+\tau}(T) = \ell_T \qquad (\tau = 1, 2, 3, \ldots)$$

3. If $\tau = 1$, then a 95% prediction interval computed in time period $T$ for $y_{T+1}$ is

$$[\ell_T \pm z_{[.025]}s]$$

If $\tau = 2$, then a 95% prediction interval computed in time period $T$ for $y_{T+2}$ is

$$\left[\ell_T \pm z_{[.025]}s\sqrt{1 + \alpha^2}\right]$$

In general for any $\tau$, **a 95% prediction interval computed in time period $T$ for $y_{T+\tau}$** is

$$\left[\ell_T \pm z_{[.025]}s\sqrt{1 + (\tau - 1)\alpha^2}\right]$$

where the standard error $s$ at time $T$ is

$$s = \sqrt{\frac{\text{SSE}}{T - 1}} = \sqrt{\frac{\sum_{t=1}^{T}[y_t - \hat{y}_t(t - 1)]^2}{T - 1}} = \sqrt{\frac{\sum_{t=1}^{T}[y_t - \ell_{t-1}]^2}{T - 1}}$$

Note: There is not general agreement on dividing the SSE by ($T$ – number of smoothing constants). However, we use this divisor because it agrees with the computation of $s$ in the equivalent Box–Jenkins models in Chapters 9 to 12.

**EXAMPLE 8.2**    In Example 8.1 we saw that $\alpha = .034$ is a "good" value of the smoothing constant when forecasting the 24 observed cod catches in Table 6.1. Therefore, we will use simple exponential smoothing with $\alpha = .034$ to forecast future monthly cod catches. From Figure 8.2(b) we see that $\ell_{24} = 354.5438$ is the estimate made in month 24 of the level (or mean) for the cod catch data. It follows that the point forecast made in month 24 for the cod catch in month 25 and for any other future monthly cod catch is

$$\hat{y}_{24+\tau}(24) = \ell_{24} = 354.5438$$

For the next step, we first need to determine the standard error:

$$s = \sqrt{\frac{\sum_{t=1}^{24}[y_t - \ell_{t-1}]^2}{24 - 1}}$$

$$= \sqrt{\frac{(y_1 - \ell_0)^2 + (y_2 - \ell_1)^2 + \cdots + (y_{24} - \ell_{23})^2}{23}}$$

$$= \sqrt{\frac{(362 - 360.6667)^2 + (381 - 360.7125)^2 + \cdots + (365 - 354.1719)^2}{23}}$$

$$= \sqrt{\frac{28,089.14}{23}}$$

$$= 34.95$$

Now, we can compute prediction intervals as follows:

- A 95% prediction interval made in month 24 for $y_{25}$ is

$$[354.5438 \pm z_{[.025]}s] = [354.5438 \pm 1.96\,(34.95)]$$
$$= [286.04, \ 423.05]$$

- A 95% prediction interval made in month 24 for $y_{26}$ is

$$\left[354.5438 \pm z_{[.025]}s\sqrt{1 + \alpha^2}\right] = \left[354.5438 \pm 1.96\,(34.95)\sqrt{1 + (.034)^2}\right]$$
$$= [286.00, \ 423.09]$$

- A 95% prediction interval made in month 24 for $y_{27}$ is

$$\left[354.5438 \pm z_{[.025]}s\sqrt{1 + 2\alpha^2}\right] = \left[354.5438 \pm 1.96\,(34.95)\sqrt{1 + 2(.034)^2}\right]$$
$$= [285.96, \ 423.12]$$

Notice that since the smoothing constant $\alpha$ is small, the increase in the length of the prediction interval is very small.

Now assume that we observe a cod catch in January of year 3 of $y_{25} - 384$. Computers have become so fast with quick access to such a large storage capacity that one could develop a forecasting system, even for thousands of items, that would repeat the process in Example 8.1 to find a new $\alpha$ and $s$ when a new observation is obtained. However, one of the traditional advantages of exponential smoothing is that we need only our last estimate to find new point forecasts. For the cod catch data, we can update $\ell_{24}$ to $\ell_{25}$ by using the smoothing equation

$$\ell_{25} = \alpha y_{25} + (1 - \alpha)\ell_{24}$$
$$= .034(384) + .966(354.5438)$$
$$= 355.5453$$

This implies that the point forecast made in month 25 of the cod catch in month 26 and of any other future month is

$$\hat{y}_{25+\tau}(25) = \ell_{25} = 355.5453$$

Furthermore, it follows that a 95% prediction interval made in month 25 for $y_{26}$ is

$$[355.5453 \pm z_{[.025]}s] = [355.5453 \pm 1.96(34.95)]$$
$$= [287.04, 424.05]$$

and a 95% prediction interval made in month 25 for $y_{27}$ is

$$\left[355.5453 \pm z_{[.025]}s\sqrt{1 + \alpha^2}\right] = \left[355.5453 \pm 1.96(34.95)\sqrt{1 + (.034)^2}\right]$$
$$= [287.00, 424.09]$$

In general, note that the smoothing equation

$$\ell_T = \alpha y_T + (1 - \alpha)\ell_{T-1}$$

implies

$$\ell_{T-1} = \alpha y_{T-1} + (1 - \alpha)\ell_{T-2}$$

Substitution, therefore, gives us

$$\ell_T = \alpha y_T + (1 - \alpha)[\alpha y_{T-1} + (1 - \alpha)\ell_{T-2}]$$
$$= \alpha y_T + (1 - \alpha)\alpha y_{T-1} + (1 - \alpha)^2 \ell_{T-2}$$

Substituting recursively for $\ell_{T-2}, \ell_{T-3}, \ldots, \ell_1$, and $\ell_0$, we obtain

$$\ell_T = \alpha y_T + (1 - \alpha)\alpha y_{T-1} + (1 - \alpha)^2 \alpha y_{T-2} + \cdots + (1 - \alpha)^{T-1}\alpha y_1 + (1 - \alpha)^T \ell_0$$

The coefficients measuring the contribution of the observations $y_T, y_{T-1}, y_{T-2}, \ldots, y_1$ are $\alpha, (1 - \alpha)\alpha, (1 - \alpha)^2\alpha, \ldots, (1 - \alpha)^{T-1}\alpha$, respectively, and are decreasing exponentially with age. For this reason we refer to this procedure as simple exponential smoothing.

Since the coefficients are decreasing exponentially, the most recent observation $y_T$ makes the largest contribution to the current estimate for the level (or mean). Older observations make smaller and smaller contributions to this estimate. Thus, remote observations are "dampened out" of the current estimate of the level (or mean) as time advances. The rate at which remote observations are dampened out depends on the smoothing constant $\alpha$. For example, if $\alpha = .9$ we obtain coefficients .9, .09, .009, .0009, .... For values of $\alpha$ near 0, remote observations are dampened out more slowly. The choice of a smoothing constant $\alpha$ is usually made by simulated forecasting of a historical data set as illustrated in Example 8.1.

The smoothing equation may be written in what is called the "error correction form" as follows.

## ERROR CORRECTION FORM

The **error correction form** for the smoothing equation in **simple exponential smoothing**:

$$\ell_T = \ell_{T-1} + \alpha(y_T - \ell_{T-1})$$

This form of the smoothing equation says that $\ell_T$, the estimate of the level at time period $T$, is the sum of $\ell_{T-1}$, the estimate of the level at time period $T - 1$, and a fraction $\alpha$ of $(y_T - \ell_{T-1})$, which is the one-period-ahead forecast error. Thus, at each time period $T$, we use the new observation $y_T$ to adjust the estimate $\ell_{T-1}$ upward or downward depending on the size and sign of our forecast error $(y_T - \ell_{T-1})$. We can easily see that the error correction form of the smoothing equation produces the same estimate $\ell_T$ as the original form of the smoothing equation because

$$\ell_T = \ell_{T-1} + \alpha(y_T - \ell_{T-1})$$
$$= \ell_{T-1} + \alpha y_T - \alpha \ell_{T-1}$$
$$= \alpha y_T + (1 - \alpha)\ell_{T-1}$$

The error correction form of the smoothing equation is better suited for understanding the state space model for the simple exponential smoothing method that is introduced in optional Section 8.6.

Many computer software packages for forecasting include exponential smoothing as a choice. These packages choose the initial value(s) and the smoothing constant(s) in different ways and also compute approximate prediction intervals in different ways. The user should carefully investigate how the computer software package implements exponential smoothing.

Figure 8.3 gives the MINITAB output of using simple exponential smoothing to forecast in month 24 the cod catches in the next three months. Figure 8.4

**FIGURE 8.3**
MINITAB output of optimization results for cod catch data

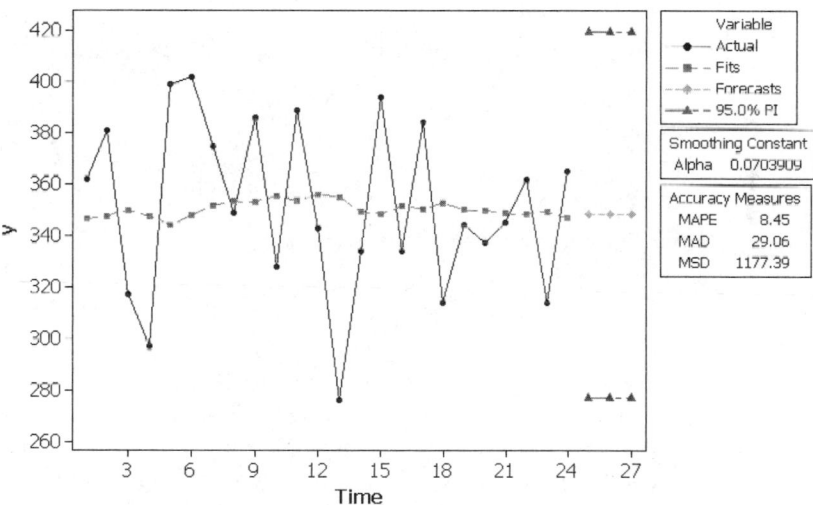

(a) Smoothing constant and graph of forecasts

| 25 | 348.168 | 276.976 | 419.360 |
| 26 | 348.168 | 276.976 | 419.360 |
| 27 | 348.168 | 276.976 | 419.360 |

(b) Point forecasts and prediction intervals

**FIGURE 8.4**
SAS output of optimization results for cod catch data

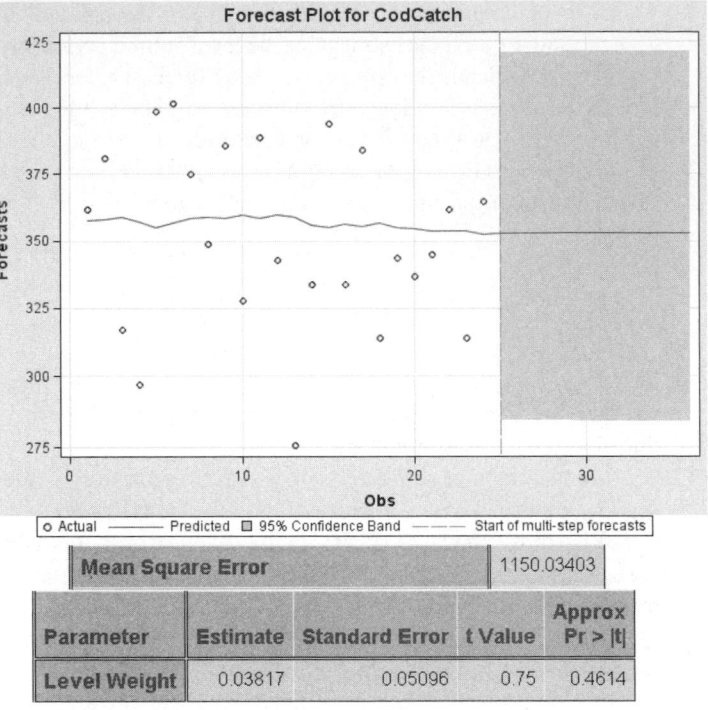

(a) Smoothing constant and graph of forecasts

| Obs | Forecasts | Standard Error | 95% Confidence Limits | |
|---|---|---|---|---|
| 25 | 352.8360 | 34.6415 | 284.9399 | 420.7322 |
| 26 | 352.8360 | 34.6668 | 284.8904 | 420.7816 |
| 27 | 352.8360 | 34.6920 | 284.8410 | 420.8310 |

(b) Point forecasts and prediction intervals

gives corresponding output from SAS Time Series Forecasting. Both MINITAB and SAS Time Series Forecasting use **backcasting** to find the initial estimate for the level. Backcasting is a procedure in which one begins at the end of the data and forecasts backward to forecast a beginning or initial level. We used the average of half the data (12 observations) as our initial estimate $\ell_0$ for the level. It can be shown that in simple exponential smoothing, using six observations is reasonable. Generally, one would expect larger smoothing constants to be selected if less data is used to find the initial estimate. The prediction intervals in the SAS Time Series Forecasting output are computed by the same formulas that we used in Example 8.2.

The smoothing constants of .070 from MINITAB and .038 from SAS Time Series Forecasting are both different from our value of .034. However, all three approaches indicate that the level of the cod catch data is not changing much. The point forecasts of 348.2 from MINITAB and 352.8 from SAS Time Series Forecasting also differ from our point forecast of 354.5. Given that there is quite a bit of variation in the data and that the level (or mean) is not changing much, these forecasts are not very different.

# 8.2 TRACKING SIGNALS

It is sometimes necessary to change the smoothing constant(s) being employed in exponential smoothing. For example, when simple exponential smoothing is being used, the rate at which the level is changing over time could change. It is possible that a different smoothing constant $\alpha$ would produce improved forecasts. A **tracking signal** might help us decide when something is wrong with a forecasting system (for instance, when we are using an inappropriate smoothing constant). Although we know that a forecasting system will never produce perfect forecasts, a tracking signal can tell us when our forecast errors are larger than an "accurate" forecasting system might reasonably be expected to produce.

The first tracking signal was the **simple cusum tracking signal,** which was suggested by R. G. Brown (1959). It is a ratio that compares the cumulative sum of errors to the smoothed mean absolute deviation. To begin with, suppose that we have a history of $T$ single-period-ahead forecast errors, $e_1(\alpha), e_2(\alpha), \ldots, e_T(\alpha)$. Here $(\alpha)$ denotes the particular value of $\alpha$ employed to obtain the single-period-ahead forecast errors. We next define the sum $(Y)$ of these forecast errors:

$$Y(\alpha, T) = \sum_{t=1}^{T} e_t(\alpha)$$

It is obvious that

$$Y(\alpha, T) - Y(\alpha, T - 1) + e_T(\alpha)$$

and we define the following smoothed mean absolute deviation (MAD):

$$MAD(\alpha, T) = \alpha|e_t(\alpha)| + (1 - \alpha)MAD(\alpha, T - 1)$$

Then:

The **simple cusum tracking signal** $C(\alpha, T)$ is defined as

$$C(\alpha, T) = \left| \frac{Y(\alpha, T)}{MAD(\alpha, T)} \right|$$

If $C(\alpha, T)$ is "large" this means that $Y(\alpha, T)$ is large relative to the mean absolute deviation MAD$(\alpha, T)$. This in turn says that the forecasting system is producing errors that are either consistently positive or consistently negative. That is, a large value of $C(\alpha, T)$ implies that the forecasting system is producing forecasts that are either consistently smaller or consistently larger than the time series values being forecasted. Since an "accurate" forecasting system should be producing roughly one-half positive errors and one-half negative errors, a large value of $C(\alpha, T)$ indicates that the forecasting system is not performing accurately. In practice, if $C(\alpha, T)$ exceeds a control limit, denoted by $K$, for two or more consecutive periods, this is taken as a strong indication that the forecast errors have been larger than an accurate forecasting system can reasonably be expected to produce.

Initial values must be assigned to $Y(\alpha, T)$ and MAD$(\alpha, T)$ when starting the forecasting procedure. Since it is reasonable to assume that the original model is correct, $Y(\alpha, 0) = 0$ is the starting value for $Y(\alpha, T)$. Since there is some random variation in the process, however, it is not reasonable to use MAD$(\alpha, 0) = 0$ as the starting value for MAD$(\alpha, T)$. One possible initial value for MAD$(\alpha, 0)$ is the average of the absolute values of the one-step-ahead forecast errors found in the forecasting of the historical data when the optimal smoothing constant $\alpha$ is used.

Values that have been recommended for the control limit $K$ apply to low values of $\alpha$ (no larger than .30). Gardner (1983) used simulations to provide a table of control limits when $\alpha = .1, .2,$ or $.3$. For control limits that have only a 5% chance of incorrectly indicating a large $C(\alpha, T)$, the values of the control limit $K$ are

| $\alpha$ | .1 | .2 | .3 |
|---|---|---|---|
| $K$ | 5.6 | 4.1 | 3.5 |

For control limits that have only a 1% chance of incorrectly indicating a large $C(\alpha, T)$, the values of the control limit $K$ are

| $\alpha$ | .1 | .2 | .3 |
|---|---|---|---|
| $K$ | 7.5 | 5.6 | 4.9 |

Another tracking signal that has had extensive use in practice is the **smoothed error tracking signal,** which was developed by Trigg (1964). It is the ratio of the smoothed one-period-ahead forecasting error to the smoothed mean absolute deviation. We define the smoothed error ($E$) of the one-period-ahead forecast errors as

$$E(\alpha, T) = e_t(\alpha) + \alpha E(\alpha, T - 1)$$

Then:

---

The **smoothed error tracking signal** is defined as

$$S(\alpha, T) = \left| \frac{E(\alpha, T)}{\text{MAD}(\alpha, T)} \right|$$

---

More information on the pros and cons of these and other tracking signals that have had successful use in practice can be found in Gardner (1983).

Tracking signals no longer play the extensive role they once did in forecasting. With the great speed and storage capacity of today's computers, the smoothing constant(s) in exponential smoothing can be reestimated frequently. It is no longer advantageous, when there is trend in the time series data, to use double exponential smoothing with one parameter instead of Holt's two-parameter smoothing (see Section 8.3). The tracking signals for time series with trend were based on smoothing methods with one parameter. Furthermore, there are new procedures based on new models for the exponential smoothing methods to aid in better identification of the correct smoothing method (see Hyndman et al., 2002).

# 8.3 HOLT'S TREND CORRECTED EXPONENTIAL SMOOTHING

Suppose that a time series displays a linear trend. If the time series is increasing or decreasing at approximately a fixed rate, then the time series may be described by the linear trend model (see Section 6.1)

$$y_t = \beta_0 + \beta_1 t + \varepsilon_t$$

The **level** (or mean) at time $T$ is $\beta_0 + \beta_1 T$, and the level (or mean) at time $T - 1$ is $\beta_0 + \beta_1(T - 1)$. Thus, the increase or decrease in the level of the time series from time period $T - 1$ to time period $T$ is

$$[\beta_0 + \beta_1 T] - [\beta_0 + \beta_1(T - 1)] = \beta_1$$

This fixed rate of increase or decrease $\beta_1$ is called the **growth rate.**

Holt's trend corrected exponential smoothing is appropriate when both the level and the growth rate are changing. A model different from the linear trend model is needed to describe the changing level and growth rate (see optional Section 8.6). To implement Holt's trend corrected exponential smoothing, we let $\ell_{T-1}$ denote the estimate of the level of the time series in time period $T - 1$, and we let $b_{T-1}$ denote the estimate of the growth rate of the time series in time $T - 1$. Then, if we observe a new time series value $y_T$ in time period $T$, we use two smoothing equations to update the estimates $\ell_{T-1}$ and $b_{T-1}$. The estimate of the level in time period $T$ uses the *smoothing constant $\alpha$* and is

$$\ell_T = \alpha y_T + (1 - \alpha)[\ell_{T-1} + b_{T-1}]$$

This equation says that $\ell_T$ equals a fraction $\alpha$ of the newly observed time series value $y_T$ plus a fraction $(1 - \alpha)$ of $[\ell_{T-1} + b_{T-1}]$, which is the estimate of the level of the time series in time period $T$, as calculated using estimates $\ell_{T-1}$ and $b_{T-1}$ computed in time period $T - 1$. The estimate of the growth rate of the time series in time period $T$ uses the *smoothing constant $\gamma$* and is

$$b_T = \gamma[\ell_T - \ell_{T-1}] + (1 - \gamma)b_{T-1}$$

This equation says that $b_T$ equals a fraction $\gamma$ of $[\ell_T - \ell_{T-1}]$, which is an estimate of the difference between the levels in periods $T$ and $T - 1$, plus a fraction $(1 - \gamma)$ of $b_{T-1}$, the estimate of the growth rate made in time period $T - 1$.

We summarize the procedure in the following box.

---

## HOLT'S TREND CORRECTED EXPONENTIAL SMOOTHING

1. Suppose that the time series $y_1, y_2, \ldots, y_n$ exhibits a linear trend for which the level and growth rate may be changing with no seasonal pattern. Then **the estimate $\ell_T$ for the level of the time series** and **the estimate $b_T$ for the growth rate of the time series** in time period $T$ are given by the smoothing equations

$$\ell_T = \alpha y_T + (1 - \alpha)[\ell_{T-1} + b_{T-1}]$$
$$b_T = \gamma[\ell_T - \ell_{T-1}] + (1 - \gamma)b_{T-1}$$

   where $\alpha$ and $\gamma$ are smoothing constants between 0 and 1, and $\ell_{T-1}$ and $b_{T-1}$ are estimates at time $T - 1$ for the level and growth rate, respectively.

2. **A point forecast made in time period $T$ for $y_{T+\tau}$ is**

$$\hat{y}_{T+\tau}(T) = \ell_T + \tau b_T \qquad (\tau = 1, 2, \ldots)$$

3. If $\tau = 1$, then **a 95% prediction interval computed in time period $T$ for $y_{T+1}$ is**

$$[(\ell_T + b_T) \pm z_{[.025]}s]$$

   If $\tau = 2$, then a 95% prediction interval computed in time period $T$ for $y_{T+2}$ is

$$\left[(\ell_T + 2b_T) \pm z_{[.025]}s\sqrt{1 + \alpha^2(1 + \gamma)^2}\right]$$

   If $\tau = 3$, then a 95% prediction interval computed in time period $T$ for $y_{T+3}$ is

$$\left[(\ell_T + 3b_T) \pm z_{[.025]}s\sqrt{1 + \alpha^2(1 + \gamma)^2 + \alpha^2(1 + 2\gamma)^2}\right]$$

   In general for $\tau \geq 2$, **a 95% prediction interval computed in time period $T$ for $y_{T+\tau}$ is**

$$\left[(\ell_T + \tau b_T) \pm z_{[.025]}s\sqrt{1 + \sum_{j=1}^{\tau-1} \alpha^2(1 + j\gamma)^2}\right]$$

   where the standard error $s$ computed in time period $T$ is

$$s = \sqrt{\frac{SSE}{T - 2}} = \sqrt{\frac{\sum_{t=1}^{T}[y_t - \hat{y}_t(t - 1)]^2}{T - 2}} = \sqrt{\frac{\sum_{t=1}^{T}[y_t - (\ell_{t-1} + b_{t-1})]^2}{T - 2}}$$

**EXAMPLE 8.3**   In this example, we use Holt's trend corrected exponential smoothing to forecast the weekly thermostat sales time series given in Table 8.1. A plot of the sales data versus time is shown in Figure 8.5. Although the plot of the sales data indicates an upward trend for the sales in the latter weeks, the growth rate of sales has clearly been changing over the 52-week period. Moreover, there is no seasonal pattern. Thus, Holt's trend corrected exponential smoothing is an appropriate forecasting procedure to apply to this time series.

To start the procedure for using the two smoothing equations, we first obtain an initial estimate $\ell_0$ for the level and an initial estimate $b_0$ for the growth rate in time period 0. One way to do this is to fit a least squares trend line to part (say half) of the historical data and let the $y$-intercept be $\ell_0$ and the slope be $b_0$. For example, consider

**TABLE 8.1  Weekly Thermostat Sales**

| 206 | 189 | 172 | 255 |
|-----|-----|-----|-----|
| 245 | 244 | 210 | 303 |
| 185 | 209 | 205 | 282 |
| 169 | 207 | 244 | 291 |
| 162 | 211 | 218 | 280 |
| 177 | 210 | 182 | 255 |
| 207 | 173 | 206 | 312 |
| 216 | 194 | 211 | 296 |
| 193 | 234 | 273 | 307 |
| 230 | 156 | 248 | 281 |
| 212 | 206 | 262 | 308 |
| 192 | 188 | 258 | 280 |
| 162 | 162 | 233 | 345 |

*Note:* Read downward left to right.

*Source:* Reprinted from R. G. Brown (1962), *Smoothing, Forecasting, and Prediction of Discrete Time Series*, p. 431, by permission of Prentice-Hall, Inc. Suggested by an example in Abraham and Ledolter (1983).

**FIGURE 8.5**
JMP IN plot of weekly thermostat sales

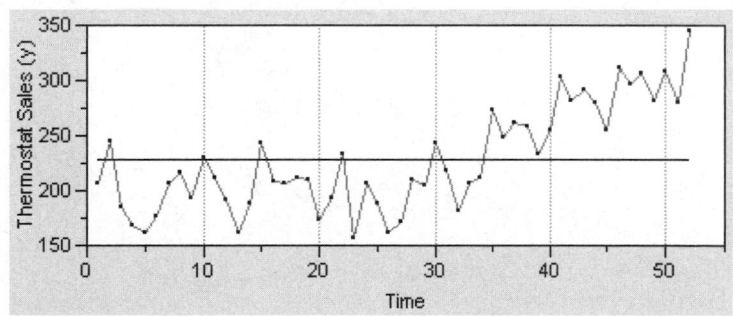

the 52 observations of the thermostat sales values in Table 8.1. If we fit a least squares trend line to the first 26 of these values, we obtain

$$\hat{y}_t = 202.6246 - .3682t$$

This would imply that $\ell_0 = 202.6246$ and $b_0 = -.3682$. We have found these two values by performing a simple linear regression analysis in Excel. Figure 8.6 presents an Excel spreadsheet with the results of the regression in the two rightmost columns. We have copied the values from the "Coefficients" column to the first cells in the columns "Level" and "Growth Rate," in the row "Time Period 0."

**FIGURE 8.6** Excel spreadsheet of Holt's trend corrected exponential smoothing for thermostat sales, $\alpha = .20$, $\gamma = .10$

| | A | B | C | D | E | F | G | H | I |
|---|---|---|---|---|---|---|---|---|---|
| 1 | n | alpha | gamma | SSE | | ssquare | s | | |
| 2 | 52 | 0.2 | 0.1 | 39182 | | 783.65 | 27.99 | | |
| 3 | | | | | | | | | |
| 4 | | Actual | | | Forecast | | Squared | | |
| 5 | Time | Themostat | | Growth | Made Last | Forecast | Forecast | | |
| 6 | Period | Sales (y) | Level | Rate | Period | Error | Error | | |
| 7 | 0 | | 202.6246 | -0.3682 | | | | SUMMARY OUTPUT | |
| 8 | 1 | 206 | 203.0051 | -0.2933 | 202.2564 | 3.7436 | 14.0145 | | |
| 9 | 2 | 245 | 211.1694 | 0.5524 | 202.7118 | 42.2882 | 1788.2923 | Regression Statistics | |
| 10 | 3 | 185 | 206.3775 | 0.0180 | 211.7219 | -26.7219 | 714.0582 | Multiple R | 0.1117696 |
| 11 | 4 | 169 | 198.9164 | -0.7299 | 206.3955 | -37.3955 | 1398.4224 | R Square | 0.0124924 |
| 12 | 5 | 162 | 190.9492 | -1.4536 | 198.1865 | -36.1865 | 1309.4608 | Adjusted R S | -0.028654 |
| 13 | 6 | 177 | 186.9964 | -1.7036 | 189.4955 | -12.4955 | 156.1383 | Standard Err | 25.555174 |
| 14 | 7 | 207 | 189.6343 | -1.2694 | 185.2929 | 21.7071 | 471.1995 | Observations | 26 |
| 15 | 8 | 216 | 193.8919 | -0.7167 | 188.3649 | 27.6351 | 763.6997 | | |
| 16 | 9 | 193 | 193.1402 | -0.7202 | 193.1752 | -0.1752 | 0.0307 | ANOVA | |
| 17 | 10 | 230 | 199.9360 | 0.0314 | 192.4199 | 37.5801 | 1412.2609 | | df |
| 18 | 11 | 212 | 202.3739 | 0.2720 | 199.9673 | 12.0327 | 144.7850 | Regression | 1 |
| 19 | 12 | 192 | 200.5167 | 0.0591 | 202.6459 | -10.6459 | 113.3354 | Residual | 24 |
| 20 | 13 | 162 | 192.8607 | -0.7124 | 200.5758 | -38.5758 | 1488.0961 | Total | 25 |
| 21 | 14 | 189 | 191.5186 | -0.7754 | 192.1483 | -3.1483 | 9.9117 | | |
| 22 | 15 | 244 | 201.3946 | 0.2898 | 190.7433 | 53.2567 | 2836.2799 | | Coefficients |
| 23 | 16 | 209 | 203.1475 | 0.4361 | 201.6844 | 7.3156 | 53.5182 | Intercept | 202.62462 |
| 24 | 17 | 207 | 204.2669 | 0.5044 | 203.5836 | 3.4164 | 11.6718 | X Variable 1 | -0.368205 |
| 25 | 18 | 211 | 206.0170 | 0.6290 | 204.7713 | 6.2287 | 38.7969 | | |
| ⋮ | ⋮ | | ⋮ | | | | | ⋮ | |
| 53 | 46 | 312 | 290.7142 | 4.9749 | 285.3928 | 26.6072 | 707.9453 | | |
| 54 | 47 | 296 | 295.7513 | 4.9811 | 295.6891 | 0.3109 | 0.0966 | | |
| 55 | 48 | 307 | 301.9860 | 5.1065 | 300.7324 | 6.2676 | 39.2823 | | |
| 56 | 49 | 281 | 301.8740 | 4.5846 | 307.0924 | -26.0924 | 680.8155 | | |
| 57 | 50 | 308 | 306.7669 | 4.6155 | 306.4586 | 1.5414 | 2.3759 | | |
| 58 | 51 | 280 | 305.1059 | 3.9878 | 311.3823 | -31.3823 | 984.8515 | | |
| 59 | 52 | 345 | 316.2750 | 4.7059 | 309.0937 | 35.9063 | 1289.2627 | | |

Starting with $\ell_0$ and $b_0$, we calculate a point forecast of $y_1$ from time origin 0 to be

$$\hat{y}_1(0) = \ell_0 + b_0 = 202.6246 + (-.3682) = 202.2564$$

This point forecast is shown in the Excel spreadsheet of Figure 8.6 in the column headed "Forecast Made Last Period." Also shown in the spreadsheet are the actual thermostat sales value $y_1 = 206$ and the forecast error, which is

$$y_1 - \hat{y}_1(0) = 206 - 202.2564 = 3.7436$$

We next choose values of the smoothing constants $\alpha$ and $\gamma$. A reasonable choice is $\alpha = .2$ and $\gamma = .1$. Then, using $y_1 = 206$ and the equation for $\ell_T$, it follows that the estimate of the level of the time series in time period 1 is

$$\ell_1 = \alpha y_1 + (1 - \alpha)[\ell_0 + b_0]$$
$$= .2(206) + .8[202.6246 + (-.3682)]$$
$$= 203.0051$$

Furthermore, using the equation for $b_T$, the estimate for the growth rate of the time series in time period 1 is

$$b_1 = \gamma[\ell_1 - \ell_0] + (1 - \gamma)b_0$$
$$= .1[203.0051 - 202.6246] + .9(-.3682)$$
$$= -.2933$$

It follows that a point forecast made in time period 1 of $y_2$ is

$$\hat{y}_2(1) = \ell_1 + b_1 - 203.0051 + (-.2933) - 202.7118$$

Since the actual thermostat sales value in period 2 is $y_2 = 245$, the forecast error is

$$y_2 - \hat{y}_2(1) = 245 - 202.7118 = 42.2882$$

The Excel spreadsheet in Figure 8.6 shows the entire process of using the two smoothing equations in Holt's trend corrected exponential smoothing to find new period-by-period estimates of the level and growth rate of the entire time series. The spreadsheet also shows the one-period-ahead forecasts, forecast errors, and squared forecast errors. Since the formulas for entries in each time period are the same, we can easily copy the formulas from time period 1 to the other 51 time periods to produce the spreadsheet in Figure 8.6. The spreadsheet also shows that the sum of the squared forecast errors (SSE) is 39,182 when $\alpha = .2$ and $\gamma = .1$.

To find "good" values for $\alpha$ and $\gamma$, we can use Solver in Excel to find the values for $\alpha$ and $\gamma$ that produce a minimum value for the SSE. Figure 8.7(a) presents the setup in the Solver dialog box for finding the values of $\alpha$ and $\gamma$ that minimize the SSE when possible values of $\alpha$ and $\gamma$ range from 0 to 1. Figure 8.7(b) gives the Excel spreadsheet of all the values when the SSE is at its minimum value of 38,884. When the SSE is minimized, $\alpha = .247$, $\gamma = .095$, $s = 27.89$, $\ell_{52} = 315.9460$, and $b_{52} = 4.5040$. We can now use these values to find forecasts and 95% prediction intervals for future thermostat sales. One note of caution is that sometimes the SSE has not reached a minimum value because it is stuck at a local minimum value. It is advisable to enter different values for the smoothing constants

**FIGURE 8.7**
Finding the values of α and γ that minimize SSE in Holt's trend corrected exponential smoothing for thermostat sales

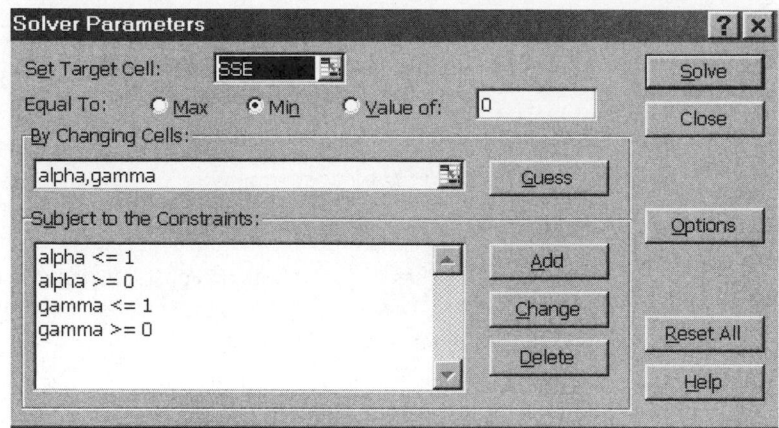

(a) Solver in Excel for finding α (alpha) and γ (gamma) that minimize the SSE

|  | A | B | C | D | E | F | G |
|---|---|---|---|---|---|---|---|
| **1** | n | alpha | gamma | SSE |  | ssquare | s |
| **2** | 52 | 0.247 | 0.095 | 38884 |  | 777.68 | 27.89 |
| **3** |  |  |  |  |  |  |  |
| **4** |  | Actual |  |  | Forecast |  | Squared |
| **5** | Time | Themostat |  | Growth | Made Last | Forecast | Forecast |
| **6** | Period | Sales (y) | Level | Rate | Period | Error | Error |
| **7** | 0 |  | 202.6246 | -0.3682 |  |  |  |
| **8** | 1 | 206 | 203.1805 | -0.2804 | 202.2564 | 3.7436 | 14.0145 |
| **9** | 2 | 245 | 213.2921 | 0.7074 | 202.9001 | 42.0999 | 1772.4001 |
| **10** | 3 | 185 | 206.8413 | 0.0270 | 213.9996 | -28.9996 | 840.9751 |
| **56** | 49 | 281 | 301.0910 | 4.2475 | 307.6757 | -26.6757 | 711.5940 |
| **57** | 50 | 308 | 305.9955 | 4.3100 | 305.3386 | 2.6614 | 7.0833 |
| **58** | 51 | 280 | 302.8248 | 3.5989 | 310.3055 | -30.3055 | 918.4226 |
| **59** | 52 | 345 | 315.9460 | 4.5040 | 306.4237 | 38.5763 | 1488.1288 |

(b) Excel spreadsheet with the values for α, γ, s, $\ell_{52}$, and $b_{52}$ when SSE is minimized

in Figure 8.6 and reoptimize (that is, run Solver with different values) to see if a minimum SSE has been found in Figure 8.7.

To illustrate the forecasting of thermostat sales, we use $\ell_{52} = 315.9460$ and $b_{52} = 4.5040$ to find the point forecasts for $y_{53}$, $y_{54}$, and $y_{55}$ as follows:

$$\hat{y}_{53}(52) = \ell_{52} + b_{52} = 315.9460 + 4.5040 = 320.45$$

$$\hat{y}_{54}(52) = \ell_{52} + 2b_{52} = 315.9460 + 2(4.5040) = 324.954$$

$$\hat{y}_{55}(52) = \ell_{52} + 3b_{52} = 315.9460 + 3(4.5040) = 329.458$$

In order to compute the 95% prediction intervals, we use the forecast errors in Figure 8.7(b) to compute the standard error s. This figure gives the one-period-ahead forecast errors when we use α = .0247 and γ = .095, the smoothing constants that minimize the SSE.

We obtain

$$s = \sqrt{\frac{\sum_{t=1}^{T} [y_t - \hat{y}_t(t-1)]^2}{T-2}}$$

$$= \sqrt{\frac{(3.7436)^2 + (42.0999)^2 + \cdots + (38.5763)^2}{50}}$$

$$= \sqrt{\frac{38,884}{50}}$$

$$= 27.89$$

Then, a 95% prediction interval for $y_{53}$ is

$$[\hat{y}_{53}(52) \pm z_{[.025]}s] = [(\ell_{52} + b_{52}) \pm z_{[.025]}s]$$
$$= [320.45 \pm 1.96(27.89)]$$
$$= [320.45 \pm 54.66]$$
$$= [265.79, \ 375.11]$$

a 95% prediction interval for $y_{54}$ is

$$\left[\hat{y}_{54}(52) \pm z_{[.025]}s\sqrt{1 + \alpha^2(1+\gamma)^2}\right]$$
$$= \left[(\ell_{52} + 2b_{52}) \pm z_{[.025]}s\sqrt{1 + \alpha^2(1+\gamma)^2}\right]$$
$$= \left[324.954 \pm 1.96(27.89)\sqrt{1 + (.247)^2(1+.095)^2}\right]$$
$$= [324.954 \pm 56.63]$$
$$= [268.32, \ 381.58]$$

and a 95% prediction interval for $y_{55}$ is

$$\left[\hat{y}_{55}(52) \pm z_{[.025]}s\sqrt{1 + \alpha^2(1+\gamma)^2 + \alpha^2(1+2\gamma)^2}\right]$$
$$- \left[(\ell_{52} + 3b_{52}) \pm z_{[.025]}s\sqrt{1 + \alpha^2(1+\gamma)^2 + \alpha^2(1+2\gamma)^2}\right]$$
$$= \left[329.458 \pm 1.96(27.89)\sqrt{1 + (.247)^2(1+.095)^2 + (.247)^2(1+2(.095))^2}\right]$$
$$= [329.458 \pm 58.86]$$
$$- [270.60, \ 388.32]$$

Furthermore, if we observe $y_{53} = 330$, we can either find a new optimal $\alpha$ and $\gamma$ that minimize the SSE for 53 time periods and compute a new $s$, or we can simply revise the estimate for the level and growth rate and our forecasts as follows:

$$\ell_{53} = \alpha y_{53} + (1-\alpha)[\ell_{52} + b_{52}]$$
$$= .247(330) + .753[315.946 + 4.5040]$$
$$= 322.8089$$
$$b_{53} = \gamma[\ell_{53} - \ell_{52}] + (1-\gamma)b_{52}$$
$$= .095[322.8089 - 315.9460] + .905(4.5040)$$
$$= 4.7281$$

Then the revised point forecasts for $y_{54}$ and $y_{55}$ are

$$\hat{y}_{54}(53) = \ell_{53} + b_{53} = 322.8089 + 4.7281 = 327.537$$

$$\hat{y}_{55}(53) = \ell_{53} + 2b_{53} = 322.8089 + 2(4.7281) = 332.2651$$

and the 95% prediction intervals for $y_{54}$ and $y_{55}$ are

$$[\hat{y}_{54}(53) \pm z_{[.025]}s] = [327.537 \pm 1.96(27.89)]$$

$$= [327.537 \pm 54.66]$$

$$= [272.88,\ 382.20]$$

$$\left[\hat{y}_{55}(53) \pm z_{[.025]}s\sqrt{1 + \alpha^2(1 + \gamma)^2}\right] = \left[332.2651 \pm 1.96(27.89)\sqrt{1 + (.247)^2(1 + .095)^2}\right]$$

$$= [332.2651 \pm 56.63]$$

$$= [275.64,\ 388.90]$$

The smoothing equations for Holt's trend corrected exponential smoothing can also be put in the error correction form. As in simple exponential smoothing, the error correction form is easier to relate to the models in optional Section 8.6.

---

## ERROR CORRECTION FORM

The error correction form for the smoothing equations in **Holt's trend corrected exponential smoothing:**

$$\ell_T = \ell_{T-1} + b_{T-1} + \alpha[y_T - (\ell_{T-1} + b_{T-1})]$$

$$b_T = b_{T-1} + \alpha\gamma[y_T - (\ell_{T-1} + b_{t-1})]$$

---

In this form of the smoothing equations, we can see that both the estimate $\ell_{T-1}$ of the level and the estimate $b_{T-1}$ of the growth rate are revised upward or downward depending on the sign of $[y_T - (\ell_{T-1} + b_{T-1})]$, which is the one-period-ahead forecast error.

Another type of exponential smoothing that has been applied to time series that exhibit a trend is Brown's double exponential smoothing. This smoothing method uses one smoothing constant to adjust both the level and the growth rate. We have chosen to examine the exponential smoothing methods that have corresponding state space models (see optional Section 8.6). The models can be used to justify the prediction intervals.

Software that provides simple exponential smoothing will most likely include Holt's trend corrected exponential smoothing. Since the software packages use different procedures for picking the initial values, finding the optimal smoothing constants, and computing prediction intervals, it is important to ask how these things are done. Figure 8.8 presents output from two such software packages. In the SAS Time Series Forecasting output of Figure 8.8(a) we see that $\gamma = .001$. This is the smallest value allowed in SAS Time Series Forecasting and indicates that the growth rate is not changing. It actually is quite common for a time series to have a level that changes without the growth rate changing. Thus, a time series can appear to have a changing trend when only the level is changing. In the MINITAB output of Figure 8.8(b) we can

**FIGURE 8.8**
Holt's trend corrected exponential smoothing for thermostat sales

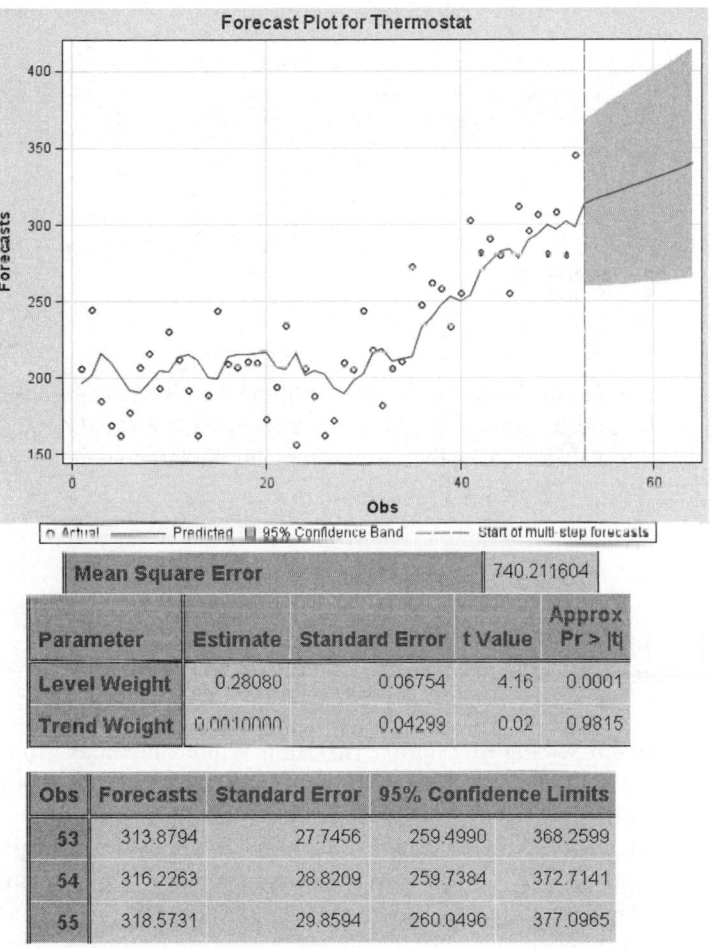

| Mean Square Error | 740.211604 |
|---|---|

| Parameter | Estimate | Standard Error | t Value | Approx Pr > \|t\| |
|---|---|---|---|---|
| Level Weight | 0.28080 | 0.06754 | 4.16 | 0.0001 |
| Trend Weight | 0.0010000 | 0.04299 | 0.02 | 0.9815 |

| Obs | Forecasts | Standard Error | 95% Confidence Limits | |
|---|---|---|---|---|
| 53 | 313.8794 | 27.7456 | 259.4990 | 368.2599 |
| 54 | 316.2263 | 28.8209 | 259.7384 | 372.7141 |
| 55 | 318.5731 | 29.8594 | 260.0496 | 377.0965 |

(a) Time Series Forecasting in SAS

**FIGURE 8.8**
(Continued)

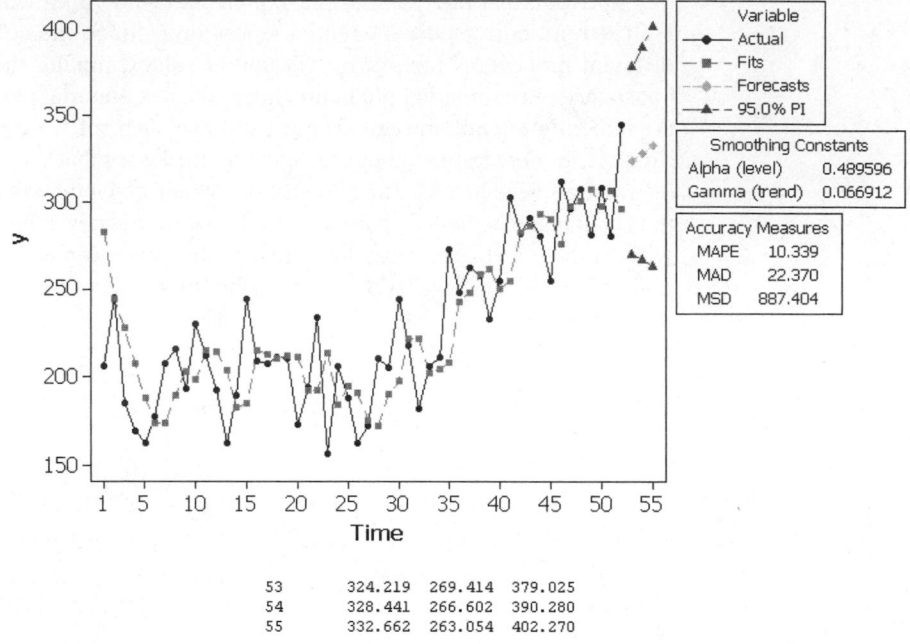

| | | | |
|---|---|---|---|
| 53 | 324.219 | 269.414 | 379.025 |
| 54 | 328.441 | 266.602 | 390.280 |
| 55 | 332.662 | 263.054 | 402.270 |

(b) MINITAB output

see that the initial values do not fit the data well. This causes a large $\alpha$ (=.4896) to be selected with a large SSE (= 887.404(52) = 46,145). As a result, the prediction intervals are wider than necessary, and the large value for $y_{52}$ may have caused the forecasts to be too high.

# 8.4  HOLT–WINTERS METHODS

In this section we examine two Holt–Winters methods. Both methods are designed for time series that exhibit linear trend at least locally, if not over the range of the entire time series. The **additive Holt–Winters method** is used for time series with constant (additive) seasonal variation, whereas the **multiplicative Holt–Winters method** is used for time series with increasing (multiplicative) seasonal variation. These two types of seasonal variation are illustrated in Section 6.3. Unlike the approach in Chapter 6 for increasing seasonal variation, the multiplicative Holt–Winters method does not require a transformation of the time series but instead models the increasing seasonal variation directly. The multiplicative Holt–Winters method is the better known of the two methods and seems to be preferred if only one of the methods is employed. We look at the additive Holt–Winters method first because it is a linear method (all the components are added), and hence it is the simpler of the two methods. However, a reader can skip the additive Holt–Winters method and study the multiplicative Holt–Winters method first without any loss of information.

## Additive Holt–Winters Method

If a time series has a linear trend with a fixed growth rate, $\beta_1$, and a fixed seasonal pattern, $SN_t$, with constant (additive) variation, then the time series may be described by the model

$$y_t = (\beta_0 + \beta_1 t) + SN_t + \varepsilon_t$$

In time series regression models, we use dummy variables to model $SN_t$ (see Chapter 6). For this model, the level of the time series at time $T - 1$ is $\beta_0 + \beta_1(T - 1)$ and at time $T$ is $\beta_0 + \beta_1 T$. Hence, the growth rate in the level from one time period to the next is $\beta_1$.

The additive Holt–Winters method is appropriate when a time series has a linear trend with an additive seasonal pattern for which the level, the growth rate, and the seasonal pattern *may be changing.* A model for these changing components of the time series can be found in optional Section 8.6. To implement the additive Holt–Winters method, we let $\ell_{T-1}$ denote the estimate of the **level** in time $T - 1$, and $b_{T-1}$ will denote the **growth rate** in time $T - 1$. Then, suppose that we observe a new time series value $y_T$ in time period $T$, and let $sn_{T-L}$ denote the "most recent" estimate of the **seasonal factor** for the season corresponding to time period $T$. Here $L$ denotes the number of seasons in a year ($L = 12$ for monthly data, and $L = 4$ for quarterly data), and thus $T - L$ denotes the time period occurring one year prior to time period $T$. Furthermore, the subscript $T - L$ of $sn_{T-L}$ denotes the fact that the time series value in time period $T - L$ is the most recent time series value observed in the season being analyzed and thus is the most recent time series value used to help find $sn_{T-L}$. Then, the estimate of the level of the time series in time period $T$ uses the smoothing constant $\alpha$ and is

$$\ell_T = \alpha(y_T - sn_{T-L}) + (1 - \alpha)(\ell_{T-1} + b_{T-1})$$

where $(y_T - sn_{T-L})$ is the deseasonalized observation in time period $T$. The estimate of the growth rate in time period $T$ uses the smoothing constant $\gamma$ and is

$$b_T = \gamma(\ell_T - \ell_{T-1}) + (1 - \gamma)b_{T-1}$$

The new estimate for the seasonal factor $SN_T$ in time period $T$ uses the smoothing constant $\delta$ and is

$$sn_T = \delta(y_T - \ell_T) + (1 - \delta)sn_{T-L}$$

where $(y_T - \ell_T)$ is an estimate of the newly observed seasonal variation.

We summarize the additive Holt–Winters method in the following box.

## ADDITIVE HOLT–WINTERS METHOD

1. Suppose that the time series $y_1, y_2, \ldots, y_n$ exhibits linear trend locally and has a seasonal pattern with constant (additive) seasonal variation and that the level, growth rate, and seasonal pattern may be changing. Then **the estimate $\ell_T$ for the level, the estimate $b_T$ for the growth rate, and the estimate $\text{sn}_T$ for the seasonal factor of the time series in time period $T$** are given by the smoothing equations

$$\ell_T = \alpha(y_T - \text{sn}_{T-L}) + (1 - \alpha)(\ell_{T-1} + b_{T-1})$$

$$b_T = \gamma(\ell_T - \ell_{T-1}) + (1 - \gamma)b_{T-1}$$

$$\text{sn}_T = \delta(y_T - \ell_T) + (1 - \delta)\text{sn}_{T-L}$$

where $\alpha$, $\gamma$, and $\delta$ are smoothing constants between 0 and 1, $\ell_{T-1}$ and $b_{T-1}$ are estimates in time period $T - 1$ for the level and growth rate, and $\text{sn}_{T-L}$ is the estimate in time period $T - L$ for the seasonal factor.

2. **A point forecast made in time period $T$ for $y_{T+\tau}$** is

$$\hat{y}_{T+\tau}(T) = \ell_T + \tau b_T + \text{sn}_{T+\tau-L} \qquad (\tau = 1, 2, \ldots)$$

where $\text{sn}_{T+\tau-L}$ is the "most recent" estimate of the seasonal factor for the season corresponding to time period $T + \tau$.

3. **A 95% prediction interval computed in time period $T$ for $y_{T+\tau}$** is

$$\left[\hat{y}_{T+\tau}(T) \pm z_{[.025]}s\sqrt{c_\tau}\right]$$

If $\tau = 1$ then $c_1 = 1$

If $2 \leq \tau \leq L$ then $c_\tau = \left[1 + \sum_{j=1}^{\tau-1} \alpha^2(1 + j\gamma)^2\right]$

If $L \leq \tau$ then $c_\tau = 1 + \sum_{j=1}^{\tau-1}[\alpha(1 + j\gamma) + d_{j,L}(1 - \alpha)\delta]^2$

where $d_{j,L} = 1$ if $j$ is an integer multiple of $L$ and 0 otherwise

The standard error $s$ computed in time period $T$ is

$$s = \sqrt{\frac{SSE}{T-3}} = \sqrt{\frac{\sum_{t=1}^{T}[y_t - \hat{y}_t(t-1)]^2}{T-3}} = \sqrt{\frac{\sum_{t=1}^{T}[y_t - (\ell_{t-1} + b_{t-1} + \text{sn}_{t-L})]^2}{T-3}}$$

The three smoothing equations of the additive Holt–Winters method can be put in the error correction form. Either form of the smoothing equations may be used to implement exponential smoothing (for example, when setting up a spreadsheet in Excel). Using the error correction form of the smoothing equations does not alter the choice of the smoothing parameters that minimize the SSE. Moreover, the formulas for the point forecasts and the 95% prediction intervals remain the same. It is, however, easier to relate the error correction form of the equations to the state space models of optional Section 8.6. The error correction form of the smoothing equations for the additive Holt–Winters method is given in the following box.

---

### ERROR CORRECTION FORM

The error correction form for the smoothing equations in the **additive Holt–Winters method:**

$$\ell_T = \ell_{T-1} + b_{T-1} + \alpha[y_T - (\ell_{T-1} + b_{T-1} + sn_{T-L})]$$
$$b_T = b_{T-1} + \alpha\gamma[y_T - (\ell_{T-1} + b_{T-1} + sn_{T-L})]$$
$$sn_T = sn_{T-L} + (1 - \alpha)\delta[y_T - (\ell_{T-1} + b_{T-1} + sn_{T-L})]$$

---

**EXAMPLE 8.4**    Consider the quarterly sales of the TRK-50 mountain bike presented in Exercise 6.3 of Chapter 6. Table 6.8 presents four years of quarterly sales of the TRK-50 mountain bike for the previous four years at a bicycle shop in Switzerland. The mountain bike sales are plotted in Figure 6.32. This plot suggests that the mountain bike sales display a linear demand and constant (additive) seasonal variation. Thus, we apply the additive Holt–Winters method to these data in order to find forecasts of future mountain bike sales.

We begin by finding estimates for the initial level, trend, and four seasonal factors. For seasonal data we need to use at least four or five years of data to find estimates for the seasonal factors. Hence, we first fit a least squares regression line to all four years of the available data rather than just half the data. As in Holt's trend corrected exponential smoothing, we let the y-intercept be $\ell_0$ and the slope of the regression line be $b_0$. For example, the Excel regression output in Figure 8.9 gives the following least squares regression equation:

$$\hat{y}_t = 20.85 + .980882t$$

Thus, we choose $\ell_0 = 20.85$ and $b_0 = .9809$. These values have been copied to the cells that correspond to the level and growth rate at time 0 in the Excel spreadsheet of Figure 8.9.

The seasonal factors are found by the following three-step procedure:

1. We use the least squares regression equation to compute $\hat{y}_t$ for each time period that is used in finding the least squares regression equation. In our case, we compute $\hat{y}_t$ for the four years of data, $t = 1, 2, \ldots, 16$.

**FIGURE 8.9** Excel spreadsheet of the additive Holt–Winters method for quarterly mountain bike sales, $\alpha = .20$, $\gamma = .10$, $\delta = .10$

| | A | B | C | D | E | F | G | H | I | J | K | L | M |
|---|---|---|---|---|---|---|---|---|---|---|---|---|---|
| 1 | n | alpha | gamma | delta | | SSE | ssquare | s | | | | | |
| 2 | 16 | 0.2 | 0.1 | 0.1 | | 25.2166 | 1.9397 | 1.3927 | | | | | |
| 3 | | | | | | | | | | | | | |
| 4 | | Actual | | | | Forecast | | Squared | | | | | |
| 5 | | Bike | | Growth | Seasonal | Made Last | Forecast | Forecast | | | | | SUMMARY OUTPUT |
| 6 | Time | Sales | Level | Rate | Factor | Period | Error | Error | | | | | |
| 7 | -3 | | | | -14.2162 | | | | | | | | |
| 8 | -2 | | | | 6.5529 | | | | | | | Regression Statistics | |
| 9 | -1 | | | | 18.5721 | | | Regression | | | Multiple R | 0.320509 | |
| 10 | 0 | | 20.8500 | 0.9809 | -10.9088 | | | | Estimates | Detrended | Average | R Square | 0.102726 |
| 11 | 1 | 10 | 22.3079 | 1.0036 | -14.0254 | 7.6147 | 2.3853 | 5.6896 | 21.8309 | -11.8309 | -14.2162 | Adjusted R | 0.038635 |
| 12 | 2 | 31 | 23.5586 | 1.0108 | 6.6418 | 29.8895 | 1.1105 | 1.2333 | 22.8118 | 8.1882 | 6.5529 | Standard E | 14.28614 |
| 13 | 3 | 43 | 24.5731 | 1.0472 | 18.5575 | 43.1815 | -0.1815 | 0.0329 | 23.7926 | 19.2074 | 18.5721 | Observatio | 16 |
| 14 | 4 | 16 | 25.8780 | 1.0729 | -10.8057 | 14.7115 | 1.2885 | 1.6603 | 24.7735 | -8.7735 | -10.9088 | | |
| 15 | 5 | 11 | 26.5658 | 1.0344 | -14.1794 | 12.9256 | -1.9256 | 3.7079 | 25.7544 | -14.7544 | 0.0000 | ANOVA | |
| 16 | 6 | 33 | 27.3518 | 1.0096 | 6.5424 | 34.2420 | -1.2420 | 1.5427 | 26.7353 | 6.2647 | | | df |
| 17 | 7 | 45 | 27.9776 | 0.9712 | 18.4040 | 46.9190 | -1.9190 | 3.6825 | 27.7162 | 17.2838 | | Regression | 1 |
| 18 | 8 | 17 | 28.7202 | 0.9483 | -10.8972 | 18.1431 | -1.1431 | 1.3067 | 28.6971 | -11.6971 | | Residual | 14 |
| 19 | 9 | 14 | 29.3707 | 0.9186 | -14.2985 | 15.4892 | -1.4892 | 2.2176 | 29.6779 | -15.6779 | | Total | 15 |
| 20 | 10 | 36 | 30.1230 | 0.9019 | 6.4759 | 36.8317 | -0.8317 | 0.6918 | 30.6588 | 5.3412 | | | |
| 21 | 11 | 50 | 31.1391 | 0.9133 | 18.4497 | 49.4289 | 0.5711 | 0.3262 | 31.6397 | 18.3603 | | | Coefficients |
| 22 | 12 | 21 | 32.0214 | 0.9102 | -10.9096 | 21.1553 | -0.1553 | 0.0241 | 32.6206 | -11.6206 | | Intercept | 20.85 |
| 23 | 13 | 19 | 33.0050 | 0.9176 | -14.2692 | 18.6331 | 0.3669 | 0.1346 | 33.6015 | -14.6015 | | X Variable | 0.980882 |
| 24 | 14 | 41 | 34.0429 | 0.9296 | 6.5240 | 40.3985 | 0.6015 | 0.3618 | 34.5824 | 6.4176 | | | |
| 25 | 15 | 55 | 35.2881 | 0.9612 | 18.5759 | 53.4222 | 1.5778 | 2.4894 | 35.5632 | 19.4368 | | | |
| 26 | 16 | 25 | 36.1813 | 0.9544 | -10.9368 | 25.3396 | -0.3396 | 0.1153 | 36.5441 | -11.5441 | | | |

These values are shown in the column of "regression estimates." For example,

$$\hat{y}_1 = 20.85 + .980882(1) = 21.8309$$

and

$$\hat{y}_5 = 20.85 + .980882(5) = 25.7544$$

2. Next we detrend the data by computing $y_t - \hat{y}_t$ for each time period that is used to estimate the least squares regression line. For the mountain bike data, we compute $y_t - \hat{y}_t$ for the four years of data, $t = 1, 2, \ldots, 16$.

These values are shown in the column of Figure 8.9 called "Detrended." For example,

$$y_1 - \hat{y}_1 = 10 - 21.8309 = -11.8309$$

and

$$y_5 - \hat{y}_5 = 11 - 25.7544 = -14.7544$$

3. Finally, the initial seasonal factor in each of the $L$ seasons, $sn_{1-L}$, $sn_{2-L}$, $\ldots$, $sn_{-1}$, $sn_0$, is found by computing the average of the detrended values for the

corresponding season. For the mountain bike data we must find $L = 4$ seasonal factors, $sn_{-3}, sn_{-2}, sn_{-1}, sn_0$. These values are computed under "Average" in Figure 8.9 and have been copied to the cells for $t = -3, -2, -1,$ and 0 under "Seasonal Factor."

For quarter 1, there are four first quarters of detrended data. Hence,

$$sn_{-3} = \frac{(y_1 - \hat{y}_1) + (y_5 - \hat{y}_5) + (y_9 - \hat{y}_9) + (y_{13} - \hat{y}_{13})}{4}$$

$$= \frac{-11.8309 + (-14.7544) + (-15.6779) + (-14.6015)}{4}$$

$$= -14.2162$$

Similarly, we find (by copying the Excel formula) that

$sn_{-2} = 6.5529$ is the seasonal factor for quarter 2

$sn_{-1} = 18.5721$ is the seasonal factor for quarter 3

$sn_0 = -10.9088$ is the seasonal factor for quarter 4

We want the average of the $L$ seasonal factors to be 0. Notice that our four initial seasonal factors for the mountain bike sales do have an average of 0, and the sum is always 0 when using these three steps.

After finding the initial values for the level, trend, and four seasonal factors, we are ready to use the smoothing equations. In this example, we use the error correction form of the smoothing equations. Either form of the smoothing equations will produce the same numbers as in Figure 8.9. Starting with the initial values, we calculate a point forecast of $y_1$ from time origin 0 to be

$$\hat{y}_1(0) = \ell_0 + b_0 + sn_{1-4} = \ell_0 + b_0 + sn_{-3}$$

$$20.85 + .9089 + (-14.2162)$$

$$= 7.6147$$

This point forecast is shown in Figure 8.9 under "Forecast Made Last Period." Also shown in the spreadsheet is the actual mountain bike sales value $y_1 = 10$ and the forecast error, which is

$$y_1 - \hat{y}_1(0) = 10 - 7.6147 = 2.3853$$

The spreadsheet in Figure 8.9 is set up using $\alpha = .2, \gamma = .1,$ and $\delta = .1$. Using $y_1 = 10$ and the error correction equation for $\ell_T$, the estimate of the level of the time series in time period 1 is

$$\ell_1 = \ell_0 + b_0 + \alpha[y_1 - (\ell_0 + b_0 + sn_{1-4})]$$

$$= \ell_0 + b_0 + \alpha[y_1 - \hat{y}_1(0)]$$

$$= 20.85 + .9809 + .2(2.3853)$$

$$= 22.3079$$

Using the error correction equation for $b_T$, the estimate for the growth rate in time period 1 is

$$b_1 = b_0 + \alpha\gamma[y_1 - (\ell_0 + b_0 + sn_{1-4})]$$
$$= b_0 + \alpha\gamma[y_1 - \hat{y}_1(0)]$$
$$= .9809 + (.2)(.1)(2.3853)$$
$$= 1.0286$$

Using the error correction equation for $sn_T$, the estimate for the seasonal factor in time period 1 is

$$sn_1 = sn_{1-4} + (1 - \alpha)\delta[y_1 - (\ell_0 + b_0 + sn_{1-4})]$$
$$= sn_{-3} + (.8)(.1)[y_1 - \hat{y}_1(0)]$$
$$= -14.2162 + (.08)(2.3853)$$
$$= -14.0254$$

It follows that a point forecast of $y_2$ in time period 1 is

$$\hat{y}_2(1) = \ell_1 + b_1 + sn_{2-4} = \ell_1 + b_1 + sn_{-2}$$
$$= 22.3079 + 1.0286 + 6.5529$$
$$= 29.8895$$

Since the actual mountain bike sales in time period 2 is $y_2 = 31$, the forecast error is

$$y_2 - \hat{y}_2(1) = 31 - 29.8895 = 1.1105$$

We continue this process for all 16 time periods. We also compute the squared forecast errors and the sum of the squared forecast errors (SSE). The results of this process are displayed in Figure 8.9, where we can see that SSE = 25.2166.

To find "good" values to use for $\alpha$, $\gamma$, and $\delta$, we select the values that minimize the sum of the squared forecast errors (SSE). Figure 8.10 shows the results of using Solver to find the minimum SSE. We see that the minimum SSE = 18.7975 is obtained using $\alpha = .561$, $\gamma = 0$, and $\delta = 0$, and that $s = 1.2025$. We also see that the final estimates for the level, growth rate, and seasonal factors are $\ell_{16} = 36.3426$, $b_{16} = .9809$, $sn_{13} = -14.2162$, $sn_{14} = 6.5529$, $sn_{15} = 18.5721$, and $sn_{16} = -10.9088$. Since the smoothing constants for the growth rate and the seasonal factors are both 0, these estimates have not changed from the initial estimates.

We now look at the process of computing point forecasts and 95% prediction intervals. We use the estimates from Figure 8.10 that produced the minimum SSE. The point forecasts of $y_{17}$, $y_{18}$, and $y_{19}$ are

$$\hat{y}_{17}(16) = \ell_{16} + b_{16} + sn_{17-4}$$
$$= \ell_{16} + b_{16} + sn_{13} = 36.3426 + .9809 - 14.2162 = 23.1073$$

$$\hat{y}_{18}(16) = \ell_{16} + 2b_{16} + sn_{14} = 36.3426 + 2(.9809) + 6.5529 = 44.8573$$

$$\hat{y}_{19}(16) = \ell_{16} + 3b_{16} + sn_{15} = 36.3426 + 3(.9809) + 18.5721 = 57.8574$$

**FIGURE 8.10** Excel spreadsheet giving the minimum SSE with the values of $\alpha$, $\gamma$, $\delta$, $s$, $\ell_{16}$, $b_{16}$, and $sn_{16}$

| | A | B | C | D | E | F | G | H | I | J | K | L | M |
|---|---|---|---|---|---|---|---|---|---|---|---|---|---|
| 1 | n | alpha | gamma | delta | | SSE | ssquare | s | | | | | |
| 2 | 16 | 0.561 | 0 | 0 | | 18.7975 | 1.4460 | 1.2025 | | | | | |
| 3 | | | | | | | | | | | | | |
| 4 | | Actual | | | | Forecast | | Squared | | | | | |
| 5 | | Bike | | Growth | Seasonal | Made Last | Forecast | Forecast | | | | | |
| 6 | Time | Sales | Level | Rate | Factor | Period | Error | Error | | | | SUMMARY OUTPUT | |
| 7 | -3 | | | | -14.2162 | | | | | | | | |
| 8 | -2 | | | | 6.5529 | | | | | | | *Regression Statistics* | |
| 9 | -1 | | | | 18.5721 | | | | Regression | | | Multiple R | 0.320509 |
| 10 | 0 | | 20.8500 | 0.9809 | -10.9088 | | | | Estimates | Detrended | Average | R Square | 0.102726 |
| 11 | 1 | 10 | 23.1682 | 0.9809 | -14.2162 | 7.6147 | 2.3853 | 5.6896 | 21.8309 | -11.8309 | -14.2162 | Adjusted R | 0.038635 |
| 12 | 2 | 31 | 24.3161 | 0.9809 | 6.5529 | 30.7020 | 0.2980 | 0.0888 | 22.8118 | 8.1882 | 6.5529 | Standard E | 14.28614 |
| 13 | 3 | 43 | 24.8098 | 0.9809 | 18.5721 | 43.8691 | -0.8691 | 0.7553 | 23.7926 | 19.2074 | 18.5721 | Observatio | 16 |
| 14 | 4 | 16 | 26.4176 | 0.9809 | -10.9088 | 14.8818 | 1.1182 | 1.2503 | 24.7735 | -8.7735 | -10.9088 | | |
| 15 | 5 | 11 | 26.1750 | 0.9809 | -14.2162 | 13.1823 | -2.1823 | 4.7622 | 25.7544 | -14.7544 | 0.0000 | ANOVA | |
| 16 | 6 | 33 | 26.7585 | 0.9809 | 6.5529 | 33.7088 | -0.7088 | 0.5024 | 26.7353 | 6.2647 | | | *df* |
| 17 | 7 | 45 | 27.0041 | 0.9809 | 18.5721 | 46.3114 | -1.3114 | 1.7198 | 27.7162 | 17.2838 | | Regression | 1 |
| 18 | 8 | 17 | 27.9423 | 0.9809 | -10.9088 | 17.0762 | -0.0762 | 0.0058 | 28.6971 | -11.6971 | | Residual | 14 |
| 19 | 9 | 14 | 28.5268 | 0.9809 | -14.2162 | 14.7070 | -0.7070 | 0.4998 | 29.6779 | -15.6779 | | Total | 15 |
| 20 | 10 | 36 | 29.4737 | 0.9809 | 6.5529 | 36.0606 | -0.0606 | 0.0037 | 30.6588 | 5.3412 | | | |
| 21 | 11 | 50 | 31.0003 | 0.9809 | 18.5721 | 49.0266 | 0.9734 | 0.9474 | 31.6397 | 18.3603 | | | *Coefficients* |
| 22 | 12 | 21 | 31.9406 | 0.9809 | -10.9088 | 21.0723 | -0.0723 | 0.0052 | 32.6206 | -11.6206 | | Intercept | 20.85 |
| 23 | 13 | 19 | 33.0867 | 0.9009 | -14.2162 | 10.7053 | 0.2947 | 0.0868 | 33.6015 | -14.6015 | | X Variable | 0.980882 |
| 24 | 14 | 41 | 34.2803 | 0.9809 | 6.5529 | 40.6205 | 0.3795 | 0.1440 | 34.5824 | 6.4176 | | | |
| 25 | 15 | 55 | 35.9153 | 0.9809 | 18.5721 | 53.8333 | 1.1667 | 1.3612 | 35.5632 | 19.4368 | | | |
| 26 | 16 | 25 | 36.3426 | 0.9809 | -10.9088 | 25.9874 | -0.9874 | 0.9749 | 36.5441 | -11.5441 | | | |

Then, a **95%** prediction interval for $y_{17}$ is

$$\left[\hat{y}_{17}(16) \pm z_{[.025]}s\sqrt{c_1}\right] = \left[23.1073 \pm 1.96(1.2025)\sqrt{1}\right]$$

$$= [23.1073 \pm 2.3569]$$

$$= [20.7504,\ 25.4642]$$

a prediction interval for $y_{18}$ is

$$\left[\hat{y}_{18}(16) \pm z_{[.025]}s\sqrt{c_2}\right] = \left[44.8573 \pm 1.96(1.2025)\sqrt{1+\alpha^2(1+\gamma)^2}\right]$$

$$= \left[44.8573 + 1.96(1.2025)\sqrt{1+(.561)^2(1+0)^2}\right]$$

$$= [44.8573 \pm 2.7025]$$

$$= [42.1548,\ 47.5598]$$

and a prediction interval for $y_{19}$ is

$$\left[\hat{y}_{19}(16) \pm z_{[.025]}s\sqrt{c_3}\right] = \left[57.8574 \pm 1.96(1.2025)\sqrt{1+\alpha^2(1+\gamma)^2+\alpha^2(1+2\gamma)^2}\right]$$

$$= \left[57.8574 \pm 1.96(1.2025)\sqrt{1+(.561)^2(1+0)^2+(.561)^2(1+2(0))^2}\right]$$

$$= [57.8574 \pm 3.0086]$$

$$= [54.8488,\ 60.8660]$$

As in the case of simple exponential smoothing and Holt's trend corrected smoothing, the point forecasts and prediction intervals can be revised by using the smoothing equations to revise the level, growth rate, and seasonal factor. Alternatively, with the power of today's computers, one can easily repeat the entire process with the new observation added.

Observe that the formulas for the 95% prediction intervals for the Holt's trend corrected exponential smoothing and for the additive Holt–Winters method are the same for the first year, except that the point forecast $\hat{y}_{t+\tau}(T)$ differs by the seasonal factor. For quarterly data, the 95% prediction intervals for both types of exponential smoothing in the first year are as follows:

$$\text{Quarter 1: } \hat{y}_{T+1}(T) \pm z_{[.025]}s$$

$$\text{Quarter 2: } \hat{y}_{T+2}(T) \pm z_{[.025]}s\sqrt{1 + \alpha^2(1 + \gamma)^2}$$

$$\text{Quarter 3: } \hat{y}_{T+3}(T) \pm z_{[.025]}s\sqrt{1 + \alpha^2(1 + \gamma)^2 + \alpha^2(1 + 2\gamma)^2}$$

$$\text{Quarter 4: } \hat{y}_{T+4}(T) \pm z_{[.025]}s\sqrt{1 + \sum_{j=1}^{3}[\alpha^2(1 + j\gamma)^2]}$$

In the second year, the 95% prediction intervals for the two exponential smoothing methods differ starting with the term that corresponds to the first quarter of the second year under the square root sign. The term for the additive Holt–Winters method is

$$[\alpha(1 + 4\gamma) + (1 - \alpha)\delta]^2$$

and the term for Holt's trend corrected exponential smoothing would be

$$\alpha^2(1 + 4\gamma)^2$$

Specifically, the intervals given by Holt–Winters method for the first and second quarters of the second year are

$$\text{Quarter 1: } \hat{y}_{T+5}(T) \pm z_{[.025]}s\sqrt{1 + \sum_{j=1}^{3}[\alpha^2(1 + j\gamma)^2] + [\alpha(1 + 4\gamma) + (1 - \alpha)\delta]^2}$$

$$\text{Quarter 2: } \hat{y}_{T+6}(T) \pm z_{[.025]}s\sqrt{1 + \sum_{j=1}^{3}[\alpha^2(1 + j\gamma)^2] + [\alpha(1 + 4\gamma) + (1 - \alpha)\delta]^2 + \alpha^2(1 + 5\gamma)^2}$$

For monthly data the difference would appear in the first month of the second year.

## Multiplicative Holt–Winters Method

If a time series has a linear trend with a fixed growth rate, $\beta_1$, and a fixed seasonal pattern, $SN_t$, with increasing (multiplicative) variation, the time series may be described by the multiplicative model

$$y_t = (\beta_0 + \beta_1 t) \times SN_t \times IR_t$$

Here $IR_t$ is an irregular component, as discussed in Chapter 1. In the classical multiplicative decomposition method, we estimated the fixed seasonal factors, $SN_t$, by using a procedure involving centered moving averages (see Chapter 7). For this model the level at time $T - 1$ is $\beta_0 + \beta_1 (T - 1)$, and the level at time $T$ is $\beta_0 + \beta_1 T$, showing that the growth rate for the level is $\beta_1$.

The **multiplicative Holt–Winters method** is appropriate when a time series has a linear trend with a multiplicative seasonal pattern for which the level, growth rate, and the seasonal pattern *may be changing rather than being fixed*. In optional Section 8.6, we discuss a model for this method. To implement the multiplicative Holt–Winters method, we let $\ell_{T-1}$ denote the estimate of the **level** in time $T-1$, and we let $b_{T-1}$ denote the estimate of the **growth rate** in time $T-1$. Then, suppose that we observe a new time series value $y_T$ in time period $T$, and let $sn_{T-L}$ denote the "most recent" estimate of the **seasonal factor** for the season corresponding to time period $T$. Here $L$ denotes the number of seasons in a year ($L = 12$ for monthly data, and $L = 4$ for quarterly data), and thus $T - L$ denotes the time period occurring one year prior to time period $T$. Furthermore, the subscript $T - L$ of $sn_{T-L}$ denotes the fact that the time series value in time period $T - L$ was the most recent time series value observed in the season being analyzed and thus was the most recent time series value used to help find $sn_{T-L}$. Then, the estimate of the level of the time series in time period $T$ uses the smoothing constant $\alpha$ and is

$$\ell_T = \alpha(y_T/sn_{T-L}) + (1 - \alpha)(\ell_{T-1} + b_{T-1})$$

where $(y_T/sn_{T-L})$ is the deseasonalized observation in time period $T$. The estimate of the growth rate in time period $T$ uses the smoothing constant $\gamma$ and is

$$b_T = \gamma(\ell_t - \ell_{T-1}) + (1 - \gamma)b_{T-1}$$

The new estimate for the seasonal factor $SN_T$ in time period $T$ uses the smoothing constant $\delta$ and is

$$sn_T = \delta(y_T/\ell_T) + (1 - \delta)sn_{T-L}$$

where $(y_T/\ell_T)$ is an estimate of the newly observed seasonal variation.

We summarize the multiplicative Holt–Winters method in the following box.

---

## MULTIPLICATIVE HOLT–WINTERS METHOD

1. Suppose that the time series $y_1, y_2, \ldots, y_n$ exhibits linear trend locally and has a seasonal pattern with increasing (multiplicative) seasonal variation and that the level, growth rate, and seasonal pattern may be changing. Then **the estimate $\ell_T$ for the level, the estimate $b_T$ for the growth rate, and the estimate $sn_T$ for the seasonal factor of the time series in time period $T$** are given by the smoothing equations

$$\ell_T = \alpha(y_T/sn_{T-L}) + (1 - \alpha)(\ell_{T-1} + b_{T-1})$$
$$b_T = \gamma(\ell_T - \ell_{T-1}) + (1 - \gamma)b_{T-1}$$
$$sn_T = \delta(y_T/\ell_T) + (1 - \delta)sn_{T-L}$$

where $\alpha$, $\gamma$, and $\delta$ are smoothing constants between 0 and 1, $\ell_{T-1}$ and $b_{T-1}$ are estimates in time period $T - 1$ for the level and growth rate, and $sn_{T-L}$ is the estimate in time period $T - L$ for the seasonal factor.

2. **A point forecast made in time period $T$ for $y_{T+\tau}$ is**

$$\hat{y}_{T+\tau}(T) = (\ell_T + \tau b_T)\operatorname{sn}_{T+\tau-L} \quad (\tau = 1, 2, \ldots)$$

where $\operatorname{sn}_{T+\tau-L}$ is the "most recent" estimate of the seasonal factor for the season corresponding to time period $T + \tau$.

3. **An approximate 95% prediction interval computed in time period $T$ for $y_{T+\tau}$ is**

$$\left[ \hat{y}_{T+\tau}(T) \pm z_{[.025]} s_r \left( \sqrt{c_\tau} \right) (\operatorname{sn}_{T+\tau-L}) \right]$$

if $\tau = 1$ then $c_1 = (\ell_T + b_T)^2$

if $\tau = 2$ then $c_2 = \alpha^2(1 + \gamma)^2(\ell_T + b_T)^2 + (\ell_T + 2b_T)^2$

if $\tau = 3$ then $c_3 = \alpha^2(1 + 2\gamma)^2(\ell_T + b_T)^2$
$$\qquad\qquad\qquad + \alpha^2(1 + \gamma)^2(\ell_T + 2b_T)^2 + (\ell_T + 3b_T)^2$$

if $2 \leq \tau \leq L$ then

$$c_\tau = \sum_{j=1}^{\tau-1} \alpha^2(1 + [\tau - j]\gamma)^2(\ell_T + jb_T)^2 + (\ell_T + \tau b_T)^2$$
$$= \alpha^2(1 + [\tau - 1]\gamma)^2(\ell_T + b_T)^2 + \cdots$$
$$+ \alpha^2(1 + \gamma)^2(\ell_T + [\tau - 1]b_T)^2 + (\ell_T + \tau b_T)^2$$

The relative standard error $s_r$ computed in time period $T$ is

$$s_r = \sqrt{\frac{\displaystyle\sum_{t=1}^{T}\left[\frac{y_t - \hat{y}_t(t-1)}{\hat{y}_t(t-1)}\right]^2}{T - 3}} = \sqrt{\frac{\displaystyle\sum_{t=1}^{T}\left[\frac{y_t - (\ell_{t-1} + b_{t-1})\operatorname{sn}_{t-L}}{(\ell_{t-1} + b_{t-1})\operatorname{sn}_{t-L}}\right]^2}{T - 3}}$$

(For a better approximation and an exact formula, see Hyndman et al., 2001.)

The three smoothing equations of the multiplicative Holt–Winters method can be put in the error correction form. Either form of the smoothing equations may be used to implement exponential smoothing (for example, when setting up a spreadsheet in Excel). Using the error correction form of the smoothing equations does not alter the choice of the smoothing parameters that minimize the SSE. Moreover, the formulas for the point forecasts and the 95% prediction intervals remain the same. It is, however, easier to relate the error correction form of the equations to the state space models of optional Section 8.6. The error correction form of the smoothing equations for the multiplicative Holt–Winters method is given in the following box.

## ERROR CORRECTION FORM

The error correction form for the smoothing equations in the **multiplicative Holt–Winters method:**

$$\ell_T = \ell_{T-1} + b_{T-1} + \alpha \frac{[y_T - (\ell_{T-1} + b_{T-1})\text{sn}_{T-L}]}{\text{sn}_{T-L}}$$

$$b_T = b_{T-1} + \alpha\gamma \frac{[y_T - (\ell_{T-1} + b_{T-1})\text{sn}_{T-L}]}{\text{sn}_{T-L}}$$

$$\text{sn}_T = \text{sn}_{T-L} + (1 - \alpha)\delta \frac{[y_T - (\ell_{T-1} + b_{T-1})\text{sn}_{T-L}]}{\ell_T}$$

**EXAMPLE 8.5**   The quarterly sales of Tiger Sports Drink for the last eight years are given in Table 8.2 and a plot of the sales is shown in Figure 8.11. The plot indicates that there is a linear increase in sales over the eight-year period and that the seasonal pattern is increasing as the level of the time series increases. This pattern suggests that multiplicative Holt–Winters might be employed to forecast future sales.

We will use the smoothing equations to construct the spreadsheet in Figure 8.12. However, we must first find initial values for the level $\ell_0$, the growth rate $b_0$, and the seasonal factors, $\text{sn}_{-3}$, $\text{sn}_{-2}$, $\text{sn}_{-1}$, and $\text{sn}_0$. We need data for at least four or five years to find

**TABLE 8.2  Quarterly Sales of Tiger Sports Drink (1000s of Cases)**

| Quarter | Year 1 | 2 | 3 | 4 | 5 | 6 | 7 | 8 |
|---|---|---|---|---|---|---|---|---|
| 1 | 72 | 77 | 81 | 87 | 94 | 102 | 106 | 115 |
| 2 | 116 | 123 | 131 | 140 | 147 | 162 | 170 | 177 |
| 3 | 136 | 146 | 158 | 167 | 177 | 191 | 200 | 218 |
| 4 | 96 | 101 | 109 | 120 | 128 | 134 | 142 | 149 |

**FIGURE 8.11**
JMP IN plot of quarterly Tiger Sports Drink sales (1000s of cases)

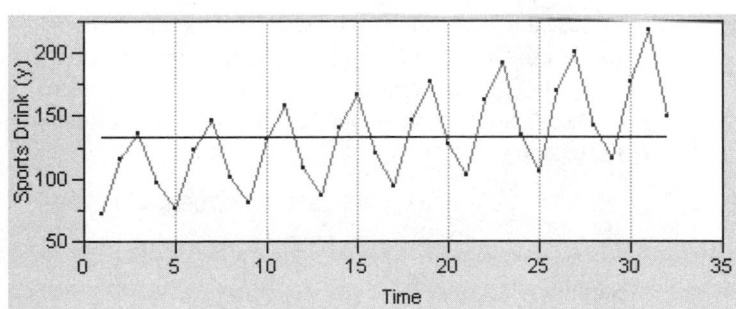

**FIGURE 8.12**

Excel spreadsheet of the multiplicative Holt–Winters method for quarterly sales of Tiger Sports Drink, $\alpha = .2$, $\gamma = .1$, $\delta = .1$

| | A | B | C | D | E | F | G | H | I |
|---|---|---|---|---|---|---|---|---|---|
| 1 | n | alpha | gamma | delta | SSE | ssquare | s | SSRE | sr |
| 2 | 32 | 0.2 | 0.1 | 0.1 | 177.3233 | 6.1146 | 2.4728 | 0.0119 | 0.0202 |
| 3 | | | | | | | | | |
| 4 | | | | | | Forecast | | Squared | Squared |
| 5 | | Actual | | | Growth | Seasonal | Made Last | Forecast | Forecast | Relative |
| 6 | Time | Demand | Level | Rate | Factor | Period | Error | Error | Error |
| 7 | -3 | | | | 0.7062 | | | | |
| 8 | -2 | | | | 1.1114 | | | | |
| 9 | -1 | | | | 1.2937 | | | | |
| 10 | 0 | | 95.2500 | 2.4706 | 0.8886 | | | | |
| 11 | 1 | 72 | 98.5673 | 2.5553 | 0.7086 | 69.0103 | 2.9897 | 8.9384 | 0.001877 |
| 12 | 2 | 116 | 101.7726 | 2.6203 | 1.1142 | 112.3876 | 3.6124 | 13.0492 | 0.001033 |
| 13 | 3 | 136 | 104.5393 | 2.6349 | 1.2944 | 135.0531 | 0.9469 | 0.8966 | 0.000049 |
| 14 | 4 | 96 | 107.3464 | 2.6521 | 0.8892 | 95.2350 | 0.7650 | 0.5852 | 0.000065 |
| 15 | 5 | 77 | 109.7310 | 2.6254 | 0.7079 | 77.9479 | -0.9479 | 0.8985 | 0.000148 |
| 16 | 6 | 123 | 111.9629 | 2.5860 | 1.1127 | 125.1919 | -2.1919 | 4.8045 | 0.000307 |
| 17 | 7 | 146 | 114.1975 | 2.5509 | 1.2928 | 148.2750 | -2.2750 | 5.1757 | 0.000235 |
| 18 | 8 | 101 | 116.1165 | 2.4877 | 0.8872 | 103.8091 | -2.8091 | 7.8913 | 0.000732 |
| | ⋮ | | | | ⋮ | | | | ⋮ |
| 39 | 29 | 115 | 161.2804 | 2.2519 | 0.7047 | 113.1314 | 1.8686 | 3.4918 | 0.000273 |
| 40 | 30 | 177 | 162.8178 | 2.1804 | 1.1046 | 180.9529 | -3.9529 | 15.6253 | 0.000477 |
| 41 | 31 | 218 | 165.7889 | 2.2595 | 1.2928 | 212.8988 | 5.1012 | 26.0220 | 0.000574 |
| 42 | 32 | 149 | 167.8900 | 2.2437 | 0.8905 | 149.7057 | -0.7057 | 0.4981 | 0.000022 |

values for the initial seasonal factors. Hence, in this example we use half of the data, 16 values, to find the initial values. As in Holt's trend corrected exponential smoothing, we use regression to fit a trend line to the first 16 sales values. In Figure 8.13, a regression output in Excel gives the following least squares regression equation:

$$\hat{y}_t = 95.2500 + 2.4706$$

Thus, for the initial values of the level and growth rate, we use $\ell_0 = 95.2500$ and $b_0 = 2.4706$. These values have been copied into the cells that correspond to the level and growth rate at time 0 in Figure 8.12.

The initial seasonal factors are found by the following four-step process:

1.  We use the least squares regression equation to compute $\hat{y}_t$ for each time period that is used in finding the least squares regression equation. In our case, we compute $\hat{y}_t$ for the four years of data, $t = 1, 2, \ldots, 16$.

    These values are shown in the column of "regression estimates" in Figure 8.13. For example,

    $$\hat{y}_1 = 95.2500 + 2.4706(1) = 97.7206$$
    $$\hat{y}_2 = 95.2500 + 2.4706(2) = 100.1912$$

    and

    $$\hat{y}_5 = 95.2500 + 2.4706(5) = 107.6029$$

**FIGURE 8.13** Using Excel to find initial estimates of the level $\ell_0$, the growth rate $b_0$, and the seasonal factors $sn_{-3}, sn_{-2}, sn_{-1}, sn_0$

| | A | B | C | D | E | F | G | H | I |
|---|---|---|---|---|---|---|---|---|---|
| **1** | Actual | | Regression | | | | | | |
| **2** | Demand | Quarter | Estimates | Detrended | Quarter 1 | Quarter 2 | Quarter 3 | Quarter 4 | Index |
| **3** | 72 | 1 | 97.7206 | 0.7368 | 0.7368 | 1.1578 | 1.3247 | 0.9131 | 0.7062 |
| **4** | 116 | 2 | 100.1912 | 1.1578 | 0.7156 | 1.1174 | 1.2973 | 0.8781 | 1.1114 |
| **5** | 136 | 3 | 102.6618 | 1.3247 | 0.6894 | 1.0921 | 1.2906 | 0.8727 | 1.2937 |
| **6** | 96 | 4 | 105.1324 | 0.9131 | 0.6831 | 1.0783 | 1.2622 | 0.8903 | 0.8886 |
| **7** | 77 | 1 | 107.6029 | 0.7156 | | | | | |
| **8** | 123 | 2 | 110.0735 | 1.1174 | | Averages by Quarter | | | Sum |
| **9** | 146 | 3 | 112.5441 | 1.2973 | 0.7062 | 1.1114 | 1.2937 | 0.8886 | 3.9999 |
| **10** | 101 | 4 | 115.0147 | 0.8781 | | | | | |
| **11** | 81 | 1 | 117.4853 | 0.6894 | | df | SS | MS | F |
| **12** | 131 | 2 | 119.9559 | 1.0921 | Regression | 1 | 2075.294 | 2075.294 | 2.727649 |
| **13** | 158 | 3 | 122.4265 | 1.2906 | Residual | 14 | 10651.71 | 760.8361 | |
| **14** | 109 | 4 | 124.8971 | 0.8727 | Total | 15 | 12727 | | |
| **15** | 87 | 1 | 127.3676 | 0.6831 | | | | | |
| **16** | 140 | 2 | 129.8382 | 1.0783 | | Coefficients | andard Err | t Stat | P-value |
| **17** | 167 | 3 | 132.3088 | 1.2622 | Intercept | 95.25 | 14.46478 | 6.584959 | 1.22E-05 |
| **18** | 120 | 4 | 134.7794 | 0.8903 | X Variable | 2.470588 | 1.495912 | 1.65156 | 0.120868 |

2. Next we detrend the data by computing $S_t = y_t/\hat{y}_t$ for each time period that is used to estimate the least squares regression line. For the sports drink data, we compute $S_t = y_t/\hat{y}_t$ for the four years of data, $t = 1, 2, \ldots, 16$.

These values are shown in the column called "Detrended" in Figure 8.13. For example,

$$S_1 = y_1/\hat{y}_1 = 72/97.7206 = .7368$$
$$S_2 = y_2/\hat{y}_2 = 116/100.1912 = 1.1578$$

and

$$S_5 = y_5/\hat{y}_5 = 77/107.6029 = .7156$$

3. Then, the average seasonal values are computed for each of the $L$ seasons. These $L$ averages, $\bar{S}_{[1]}, \bar{S}_{[2]}, \ldots, \bar{S}_{[L]}$, are found by computing the average of the detrended values for the corresponding season. For the sports drink data we must find $L = 4$ seasonal factors, $\bar{S}_{[1]}, \bar{S}_{[2]}, \bar{S}_{[3]}, \bar{S}_{[4]}$. For quarter 1, there are four first quarters of detrended data. Hence,

$$\bar{S}_{[1]} = \frac{(y_1/\hat{y}_1) + (y_5/\hat{y}_5) + (y_9/\hat{y}_9) + (y_{13}/\hat{y}_{13})}{4}$$

$$= \frac{S_1 + S_5 + S_9 + S_{13}}{4}$$

$$= \frac{.7368 + .7156 + .6894 + .6831}{4}$$

$$= .7062$$

Similarly, we find (by copying the Excel formula) that

$$\bar{S}_{[2]} = 1.1114 \text{ is the seasonal average for quarter 2}$$

$$\bar{S}_{[3]} = 1.2937 \text{ is the seasonal average for quarter 3}$$

$$\bar{S}_{[4]} = .8886 \text{ is the seasonal average for quarter 4}$$

4.  Finally, we want the average of the seasonal factors to be 1. We do this by multiplying the average seasonal values by the correction factor

$$CF = \frac{L}{\sum_{i=1}^{L} \bar{S}_{[i]}}$$

Note that if $\sum_{i=1}^{L} \bar{S}_{[i]} = L$, there is no correction to be made because $CF = 1$. In order to use the smoothing equations in the spreadsheet in Figure 8.12, the initial seasonal factors have time subscripts for which the first season is in time period $1 - L$, the second season is in time period $2 - L$, and the last season is in time period $L - L = 0$. Thus the initial seasonal factors are

$$sn_{i-L} = \bar{S}_{[i]}(CF) \qquad (i = 1, 2, \ldots, L)$$

For the quarterly sports drinks data, we find four initial seasonal factors. In this case, $CF = 4/3.9999 = 1.0000$ and

$$sn_{-3} = sn_{1-4} = \bar{S}_{[1]}(CF) = .7062(1) = .7062$$

$$sn_{-2} = sn_{2-4} = \bar{S}_{[2]}(CF) = 1.1114(1) = 1.1114$$

$$sn_{-1} = sn_{3-4} = \bar{S}_{[3]}(CF) = 1.2937(1) = 1.2937$$

$$sn_{0} = sn_{4-4} = \bar{S}_{[4]}(CF) = .8886(1) = .8886$$

These values are listed under "Index" in Figure 8.13 and copied to the cells for time periods −3, −2, −1, and 0 under "Seasonal Factor" in Figure 8.12.

After finding the initial values for the level, trend, and four seasonal factors, we are ready to use the smoothing equations. Starting with the initial values, we calculate a point forecast of $y_1$ from time origin 0 to be

$$\hat{y}_1(0) = (\ell_0 + b_0)sn_{1-4} = (\ell_0 + b_0)sn_{-3}$$
$$= (95.2500 + 2.4706)(.7062)$$
$$= 69.0103$$

This point forecast is shown in Figure 8.12 under "Forecast Made Last Period." Also shown in the spreadsheet is the actual sales value $y_1 = 72$ and the forecast error, which is

$$y_1 - \hat{y}_1(0) = 72 - 69.0103 = 2.9897$$

The spreadsheet in Figure 8.12 is set up using $\alpha = .2$, $\gamma = .1$, and $\delta = .1$. In this example, we use the original form of the smoothing equations. Either the original or the error correction form of the smoothing equations will produce the same numbers as in Figure 8.12. Using $y_1 = 72$ and the smoothing equation for $\ell_T$, the estimate of the level of the time series in time period 1 is

$$\ell_1 = \alpha(y_1/sn_{1-4}) + (1 - \alpha)(\ell_0 + b_0)$$
$$= \alpha(y_1/sn_{-3}) + (1 - \alpha)(\ell_0 + b_0)$$
$$= .2(72/7062) + .8(95.2500 + 2.4706)$$
$$= 98.5673$$

Using the smoothing equation for $b_T$, the estimate for the growth rate in time period 1 is

$$b_1 = \gamma(\ell_1 - \ell_0) + (1 - \gamma)b_0$$
$$= .1(98.5673 - 95.2500) + .9(2.4706)$$
$$= 2.5553$$

Using the smoothing equation for $sn_T$, the estimate for the seasonal factor in time period 1 is

$$sn_1 = \delta(y_1/\ell_1) + (1 - \delta)sn_{1-4}$$
$$= \delta(y_1/\ell_1) + (1 - \delta)sn_{-3}$$
$$= .1(72/98.5673) + .9(.7062)$$
$$= .7086$$

It follows that a point forecast of $y_2$ in time period 1 is

$$\hat{y}_2(1) = (\ell_1 + b_1)sn_{2-4} = (\ell_1 + b_1)sn_{-2}$$
$$= (98.5673 + 2.5553)(1.1114)$$
$$= 112.3876$$

Since the actual sales value in time period 2 is $y_2 = 116$, the forecast error is

$$y_2 - \hat{y}_2(1) = 116 - 112.3876 = 3.6124$$

Using the estimates that we just obtained, we can now compute the updated estimates $\ell_2$, $b_2$, and $sn_2$ as follows:

$$\ell_2 = \alpha(y_2/sn_{2-4}) + (1 - \alpha)(\ell_1 + b_1)$$
$$= \alpha(y_2/sn_{-2}) + (1 - \alpha)(\ell_1 + b_1)$$
$$= .2(116/1.1114) + .8(98.5673 + 2.5553)$$
$$= 101.7726$$

$$b_2 = \gamma(\ell_2 - \ell_1) + (1 - \gamma)b_1$$
$$= .1(101.7726 - 98.5673) + .9(2.5553)$$
$$= 2.6203$$

$$sn_2 = \delta(y_2/\ell_2) + (1 - \delta)sn_{2-4}$$
$$= \delta(y_2/\ell_2) + (1 - \delta)sn_{-2}$$
$$= .1(116/101.7726) + .9(1.1114)$$
$$= 1.1142$$

We continue this process for all 32 time periods. Note that the formulas for time period 1 in the spreadsheet can be copied for the remaining 31 time periods. We also compute the squared forecast errors and the sum of the squared forecast errors (SSE). The results of this process are displayed in Figure 8.12, where we can see that SSE = 177.3233.

To find "good" values to use for $\alpha$, $\gamma$, and $\delta$, we select the values that minimize the sum of the squared forecast errors (SSE). Figure 8.14 shows the results of using Solver to find the minimum SSE. We see that we obtain the minimum SSE = 168.4753 when $\alpha = .336$,

**FIGURE 8.14**
Finding $\alpha$, $\gamma$, and $\delta$ values that minimize SSE using the multiplicative Holt–Winters method for sports drink sales

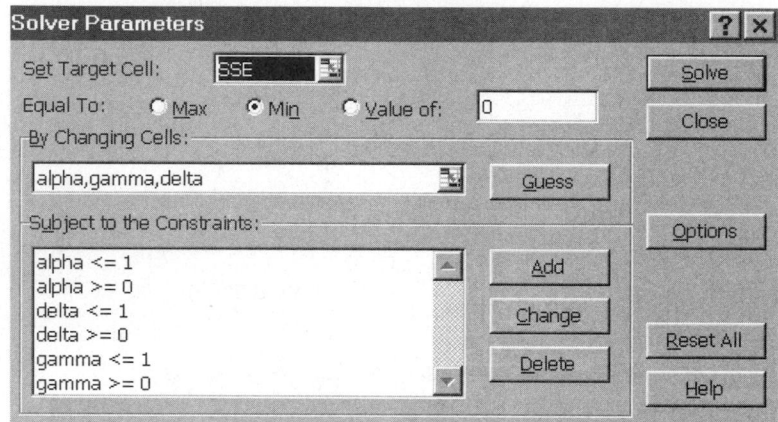

(a) Using Excel Solver for finding $\alpha$ (alpha), $\gamma$ (gamma), and $\delta$ (delta) that minimize SSE

| | A | B | C | D | E | F | G | H | I |
|---|---|---|---|---|---|---|---|---|---|
| 1 | n | alpha | gamma | delta | SSE | ssquare | s | SSRE | sr |
| 2 | 32 | 0.336 | 0.046 | 0.134 | 168.4753 | 5.8095 | 2.4103 | 0.0108 | 0.0193 |
| 3 | | | | | | | | | |
| 4 | | | | | | Forecast | | Squared | Squared |
| 5 | | Actual | | | Growth | Seasonal | Made Last | Forecast | Relative |
| 6 | Time | Demand | Level | Rate | Factor | Period | Error | Error | Error |
| 7 | -3 | | | | | 0.7062 | | | |
| 8 | -2 | | | | | 1.1114 | | | |
| 9 | -1 | | | | | 1.2937 | | | |
| 10 | 0 | | 95.2500 | 2.4706 | 0.8886 | | | | |
| 11 | 1 | 72 | 99.1415 | 2.5353 | 0.7089 | 69.0103 | 2.9897 | 8.9384 | 0.001877 |
| 12 | 2 | 116 | 102.5816 | 2.5765 | 1.1140 | 113.0036 | 2.9964 | 8.9786 | 0.000703 |
| 13 | 3 | 136 | 105.1470 | 2.5760 | 1.2937 | 136.0431 | -0.0431 | 0.0019 | 0.000000 |
| 14 | 4 | 96 | 107.8277 | 2.5808 | 0.8888 | 95.7227 | 0.2773 | 0.0769 | 0.000008 |
| ⋮ | ⋮ | | | | | ⋮ | | | ⋮ |
| 39 | 29 | 115 | 161.7496 | 2.3277 | 0.7044 | 113.1539 | 1.8461 | 3.4079 | 0.000266 |
| 40 | 30 | 177 | 162.7095 | 2.2655 | 1.1038 | 181.5084 | -4.5084 | 20.3261 | 0.000617 |
| 41 | 31 | 218 | 166.2958 | 2.3256 | 1.2934 | 212.9210 | 5.0790 | 25.7960 | 0.000569 |
| 42 | 32 | 149 | 168.1213 | 2.3028 | 0.8908 | 150.3283 | -1.3283 | 1.7643 | 0.000078 |

(b) Excel spreadsheet giving the minimum SSE with the values for $\alpha$, $\gamma$, $\delta$, $\ell_{32}$, $b_{32}$, $sn_{29}$, $sn_{30}$, $sn_{31}$, and $sn_{32}$

$\gamma = .046$, and $\delta = .134$. We also see that the final estimates for the level, growth rate, and seasonal factors are $\ell_{32} = 168.1213$, $b_{32} = 2.3028$, $sn_{29} = .7044$, $sn_{30} = 1.1038$, $sn_{31} = 1.2934$, and $sn_{32} = .8908$.

We now look at the process for computing the point forecasts and 95% prediction intervals for the next year. Using the estimates from Figure 8.14(b) that minimize the SSE, the point forecasts of $y_{33}$, $y_{34}$, $y_{35}$, and $y_{36}$ are

$$\hat{y}_{33}(32) = (\ell_{32} + b_{32})sn_{33-4}$$
$$= (\ell_{32} + b_{32})sn_{29} = (168.1213 + 2.3028)(.7044) = 120.0467$$
$$\hat{y}_{34}(32) = (\ell_{32} + 2b_{32})sn_{30} = [168.1213 + 2(2.3028)](1.1038) = 190.6560$$
$$\hat{y}_{35}(32) = (\ell_{32} + 3b_{32})sn_{31} = 226.3834$$
$$\hat{y}_{36}(32) = (\ell_{32} + 4b_{32})sn_{32} = 157.9678$$

Before we compute the 95% prediction intervals, note that the formulas in the box for these 95% prediction intervals use the relative standard error $s_r$ at time $T$ rather than the standard error $s$ at time $T$. The reason for this change is the result of using a multiplicative model where the trend is multiplied by both the seasonal factor and the irregular factor. To find $s_r$ we find the sum of the squares of the relative errors $[y_t - \hat{y}_t(t-1)]/\hat{y}_t(t-1)$, $t = 1, 2, \ldots, T$, rather than the sum of the squares of the errors, $[y_t \quad \hat{y}_t(t-1)]$, as follows:

$$s_r = \sqrt{\frac{\sum\limits_{t-1}^{32}\left[\dfrac{y_t - \hat{y}_t(t \quad 1)}{\hat{y}_t(t-1)}\right]^2}{32-3}}$$

$$= \sqrt{\frac{\left[\dfrac{72-69.0103}{69.0103}\right]^2 + \left[\dfrac{116-113.0036}{113.0036}\right]^2 + \cdots + \left[\dfrac{149-150.3283}{150.3283}\right]^2}{29}}$$

$$= \sqrt{\frac{\text{SSRE}}{29}} = \sqrt{\frac{.0108}{29}} = .0193 \qquad \text{(see Figure 8.14b)}$$

Then a 95% prediction interval for $y_{33}$ is

$$\left[\hat{y}_{33}(32) \pm z_{[.025]}s_r\left(\sqrt{c_1}\right)(sn_{33-4})\right] = \left[120.0467 \pm 1.96(.0193)\left(\sqrt{(\ell_{32}+b_{32})^2}\right)(.7044)\right]$$

$$= [120.0467 \pm 1.96(.0193)(168.1213 + 2.3028)(.7044)]$$

$$= [120.0467 \pm 4.5411]$$

$$= [115.5056, 124.5858]$$

To compute the 95% prediction interval for $y_{34}$ we first compute

$$c_2 = \alpha^2(1+\gamma)^2(\ell_{32}+b_{32})^2 + (\ell_{32}+2b_{32})^2$$
$$= (.336)^2(1+.046)^2(168.1213 + 2.3028)^2 + (168.1213 + 2(2.3028))^2$$
$$= 33,422.1814$$

Then,

$$\left[\hat{y}_{34}(32) \pm z_{[.025]}s_r\left(\sqrt{c_2}\right)(sn_{34-4})\right]$$

$$= \left[190.6560 \pm 1.96(.0193)\left(\sqrt{33,422.1814}\right)(1.1038)\right]$$

$$= [190.6560 \pm 7.6335]$$

$$= [183.0225, 198.2895]$$

Similarly, we find the 95% prediction interval for $y_{35}$ is

$$\left[\hat{y}_{35}(32) \pm z_{[.025]}s_r\left(\sqrt{c_3}\right)(sn_{35-4})\right]$$

$$= \left[226.3834 \pm 1.96(.0193)\left(\sqrt{38,230.6847}\right)(1.2934)\right]$$

$$= [226.3834 \pm 9.5665]$$

$$= [216.8169, 235.9499]$$

and the 95% prediction interval for $y_{36}$ is

$$\left[\hat{y}_{36}(32) \pm z_{[.025]}s_r\left(\sqrt{c_4}\right)(sn_{36-4})\right] = [150.9402, 164.9954]$$

If new quarterly values for the sales of Tiger Sports Drink become available, we can revise our forecasts and 95% prediction intervals by using the smoothing equations to update our estimates for the level, growth rate, and seasonal factor without reestimating the smoothing parameters. Historically, the ability to make such revisions was an advantage of exponential smoothing methods because only the most recent estimates are needed for the revision. However, with the speed and capacity of today's computers, the values of new observations can be added to the data and new estimates for the smoothing parameters can be found even when we need to forecast thousands of items.

Both the additive and multiplicative versions of the Holt–Winters methods are normally available in exponential smoothing software. If only one version is available, it will most likely be the multiplicative version. As with the other exponential smoothing methods, one should ask how such things as initial values and prediction intervals are found. Figure 8.15 presents two examples of computer output from applying the multiplicative Holt–Winters method to the monthly sales of Tasty Cola (see Table 7.1 and Figure 7.2). Since the graph in Figure 7.2 shows that the sales of Tasty Cola exhibit a linear trend with increasing seasonal variation, the multiplicative Holt–Winters method is an appropriate method for this time series. Figure 8.15(a) presents the output from the default procedure in Time Series Forecasting in SAS, which uses an automatic optimization to find the smoothing constants. Figure 8.15(b) presents a MINITAB output where the default values for the smoothing constants ($\alpha = \gamma = \delta = .2$) were used. Holt–Winters methods in MINITAB do not have the option of an automatic search for optimal smoothing constants. Notice the dramatic difference in the values of the SSE. The mean square error in Figure 8.15(a) is 88.02, and the comparable MSD in Figure 8.15(b) is 6812.61; both of the values are equal to SSE/36. A large SSE is always reflected in the length of the prediction intervals, and hence the intervals are much wider in Figure 8.15(b) than in Figure 8.15(a). It is suggested in an exercise to search for better smoothing constants in MINITAB. However, by looking at the beginning of the time series, we can see that the difference between the predicted values and the actual values is much greater in Figure 8.15(b) than in Figure 8.15(a). Hence, it is evident that the initial estimates of

**FIGURE 8.15**
Multiplicative Holt–Winters method for monthly sales of Tasty Cola

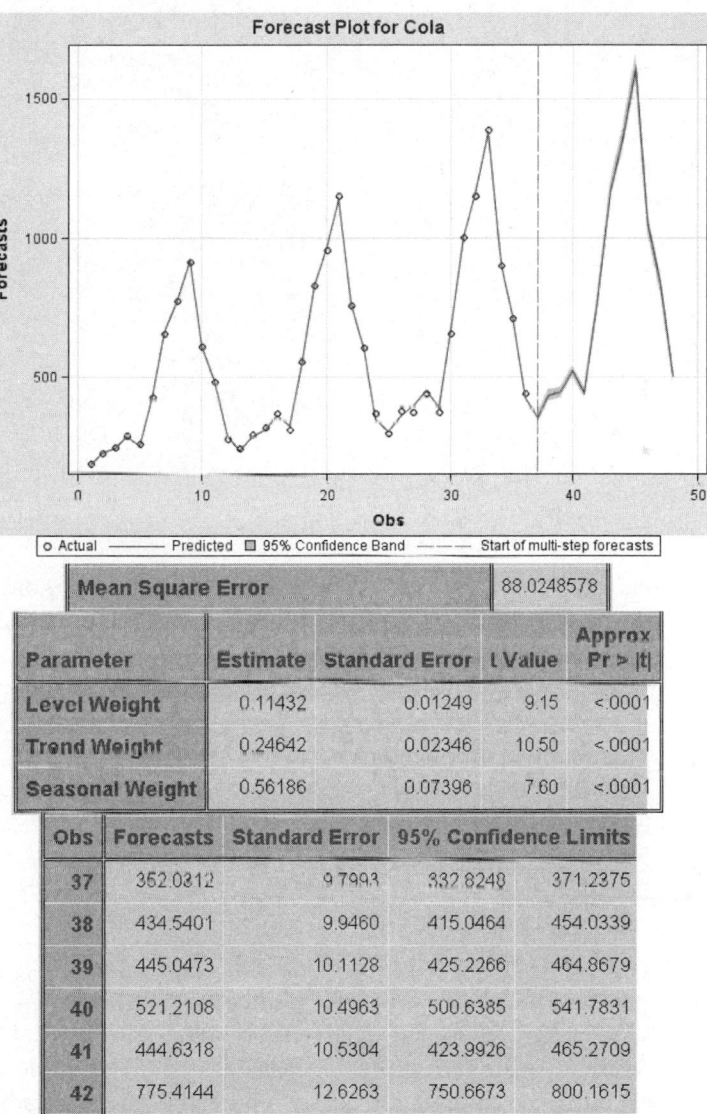

Mean Square Error: 88.0248578

| Parameter | Estimate | Standard Error | t Value | Approx Pr > |t| |
|---|---|---|---|---|
| Level Weight | 0.11432 | 0.01249 | 9.15 | <.0001 |
| Trend Weight | 0.24642 | 0.02346 | 10.50 | <.0001 |
| Seasonal Weight | 0.56186 | 0.07396 | 7.60 | <.0001 |

| Obs | Forecasts | Standard Error | 95% Confidence Limits | |
|---|---|---|---|---|
| 37 | 352.0312 | 9.7993 | 332.8249 | 371.2375 |
| 38 | 434.5401 | 9.9460 | 415.0464 | 454.0339 |
| 39 | 445.0473 | 10.1128 | 425.2266 | 464.8679 |
| 40 | 521.2108 | 10.4963 | 500.6385 | 541.7831 |
| 41 | 444.6318 | 10.5304 | 423.9926 | 465.2709 |
| 42 | 775.4144 | 12.6263 | 750.6673 | 800.1615 |

(a) Time Series Forecasting in SAS

**FIGURE 8.15**
Continued

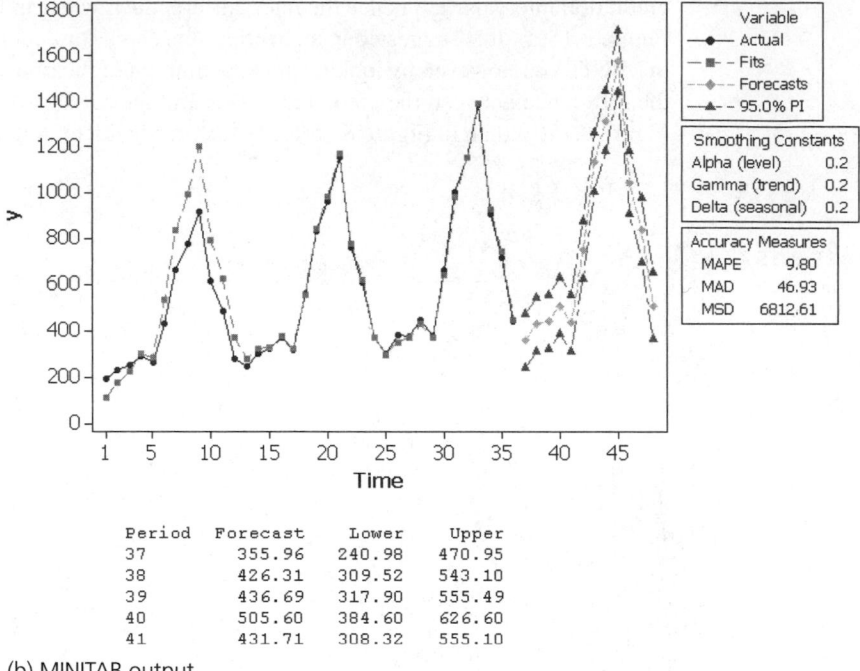

| Period | Forecast | Lower | Upper |
|--------|----------|--------|--------|
| 37 | 355.96 | 240.98 | 470.95 |
| 38 | 426.31 | 309.52 | 543.10 |
| 39 | 436.69 | 317.90 | 555.49 |
| 40 | 505.60 | 384.60 | 626.60 |
| 41 | 431.71 | 308.32 | 555.10 |

(b) MINITAB output

the level, growth rate, and seasonal factors were found by different procedures. For a short time series, the poor fit at the beginning of the time series will not be negligible and will result in wide prediction intervals.

# 8.5 DAMPED TREND AND OTHER EXPONENTIAL SMOOTHING METHODS

The methods presented so far include the most commonly used exponential methods: simple exponential smoothing, Holt's trend corrected exponential smoothing, the additive Holt–Winters method, and the multiplicative Holt–Winters method. Another common exponential smoothing method is Gardner and McKenzie's **damped trend exponential smoothing.** The damped trend method is appropriate for forecasting a time series which has a growth rate that will not be sustained into the future and whose effects should be dampened. Dampening the growth rate means to reduce it in size so that the rate of increase or decrease for the forecasts is slowing down. We first consider a method for damped trend when there is no seasonal pattern.

## DAMPED TREND METHOD

1.   Suppose that the time series $y_1, y_2, \ldots, y_n$ exhibits a linear trend for which the level and growth rate are changing somewhat with no seasonal pattern. Furthermore, suppose that we question whether the growth rate at the end of the time series will continue into the future.  Then the estimate $\ell_T$ for the **level** and the estimate $b_T$ for the **growth rate** are given by the smoothing equations

$$\ell_T = \alpha y_T + (1 - \alpha)(\ell_{T-1} + \phi b_{T-1})$$
$$b_T = \gamma(\ell_T - \ell_{T-1}) + (1 - \gamma)\phi b_{T-1}$$

where $\alpha$ and $\gamma$ are **smoothing constants** between 0 and 1, and $\phi$ is a **damping factor** between 0 and 1.

2.   A **point forecast made in time period $T$ for $y_{T+\tau}$** is

$$\hat{y}_{T+\tau}(T) = \ell_T + (\phi b_T + \phi^2 b_T + \cdots + \phi^\tau b_T)$$

3.   If $\tau = 1$, then a **95% prediction interval computed in time period $T$ for $y_{T+1}$** is

$$[\hat{y}_{T+1}(T) \pm z_{[.025]}s]$$

If $\tau = 2$, then a **95% prediction interval computed in time period $T$ for $y_{T+2}$** is

$$\left[ \hat{y}_{T+2} \pm z_{[.025]}s\sqrt{1 + \alpha^2(1 + \phi\gamma)^2} \right]$$

If $\tau = 3$, then a **95% prediction interval computed in time period $T$ for $y_{T+3}$** is

$$\left[ \hat{y}_{T+3}(T) \pm z_{[.025]}s\sqrt{1 + \alpha^2(1 + \phi\gamma)^2 + \alpha^2(1 + \phi\gamma + \phi^2\gamma)^2} \right]$$

If $\tau \geq 4$, then a **95% prediction interval computed in time period $T$ for $y_{T+\tau}$** is

$$\left[ \hat{y}_{T+\tau}(T) \pm z_{[.025]}s\sqrt{1 + \sum_{j=1}^{\tau-1} \alpha^2(1 + \phi_j\gamma)^2} \right]$$

where $\phi_j = \phi + \phi^2 + \cdots + \phi^j$.

We can see that the effect of the growth rate $b_T$ in the point forecast is reduced further for each additional time period in the future, provided $\phi$ is less than 1.  For example, if $\phi = .7$, then

$$\hat{y}_{T+1} = \ell_T + .7b_T$$
$$\hat{y}_{T+2} = \ell_T + .7b_T + (.7)^2 b_T = \ell_T + .7b_T + .49b_T$$
$$\hat{y}_{T+3} = \ell_T + .7b_T + (.7)^2 b_T + (.7)^3 b_T = \ell_T + .7b_T + .49b_T + .343b_T$$

As with the other exponential smoothing methods, the smoothing equations can be put in the error correction form.

---

## ERROR CORRECTION FORM

The error correction form for the smoothing equations in **damped trend exponential smoothing:**

$$\ell_T = \ell_{T-1} + \phi b_{T-1} + \alpha[y_T - (\ell_{T-1} + \phi b_{T-1})]$$
$$b_T = \phi b_{T-1} + \alpha\gamma[y_T - (\ell_{T-1} + \phi b_{T-1})]$$

---

For seasonal data we can use damped trend with either the additive Holt–Winters method or the multiplicative Holt–Winters method.

---

## ADDITIVE HOLT–WINTERS WITH DAMPED TREND

1.  The estimate $\ell_T$ for the **level,** the estimate $b_T$ for the **growth rate,** and the estimate $sn_T$ for the **seasonal factor** of the time series in time period $T$ are given by the smoothing equations

$$\ell_T = \alpha(y_T - sn_{T-L}) + (1 - \alpha)(\ell_{T-1} + \phi b_{T-1})$$
$$b_T = \gamma(\ell_T - \ell_{T-1}) + (1 - \gamma)\phi b_{T-1}$$
$$sn_T = \delta(y_T - \ell_T) + (1 - \delta)sn_{T-L}$$

where $\alpha$, $\gamma$, and $\delta$ are **smoothing constants** between 0 and 1, and $\phi$ is a **damping factor** between 0 and 1. The error correction form of the smoothing equations is

$$\ell_T = \ell_{T-1} + \phi b_{T-1} + \alpha[y_T - (\ell_{T-1} + \phi b_{T-1} + sn_{T-L})]$$
$$b_T = \phi b_{T-1} + \alpha\gamma[y_T - (\ell_{T-1} + \phi b_{T-1} + sn_{T-L})]$$
$$sn_T = sn_{T-L} + (1 - \alpha)\delta[y_T - (\ell_{T-1} + \phi b_{T-1} + sn_{T-L})]$$

2.  A **point forecast made in time period $T$ for $y_{T+\tau}$** is

$$\hat{y}_{T+\tau}(T) = \ell_T + (\phi b_T + \phi^2 b_T + \cdots + \phi^\tau b_T) + sn_{T+\tau-L}$$

where $sn_{T+\tau-L}$ is the "most recent" estimate of the seasonal factor for the season corresponding to time period $T + \tau$.

3.  A **95% prediction interval computed in time period** $T$ **for** $y_{T+\tau}$ **is**

$$\left[\hat{y}_{T+\tau}(T) \pm z_{[.025]}s\sqrt{c_\tau}\right]$$

If   $\tau = 1$   then   $c_1 = 1$

If   $\tau \geq 2$   then   $c_\tau = 1 + \sum_{j=1}^{\tau-1}[\alpha(1 + \phi_j\gamma) + d_{j,L}(1 - \alpha)\delta]^2$

where   $d_{j,L} = 1$   if $j$ is an integer multiple of $L$ and 0 otherwise and
$\phi_j = \phi + \phi^2 + \cdots + \phi^j$

---

## MULTIPLICATIVE HOLT–WINTERS METHOD WITH DAMPED TREND

1.  The estimate $\ell_T$ for the **level,** the estimate $b_T$ for the **growth rate,** and the estimate $sn_T$ for the **seasonal factor** of the time series in time period $T$ are given by the smoothing equations

$$\ell_T = \alpha(y_T/sn_{T-L}) + (1 - \alpha)(\ell_{T-1} + \phi b_{T-1})$$
$$b_T = \gamma(\ell_T - \ell_{T-1}) + (1 - \gamma)\phi b_{T-1}$$
$$sn_T = \delta(y_T/\ell_T) + (1 - \delta)sn_{T-L}$$

where $\alpha$, $\gamma$, and $\delta$ are **smoothing constants** between 0 and 1, and $\phi$ is a **damping factor** between 0 and 1. The error correction form of the smoothing equations is

$$\ell_T = \ell_{T-1} + \phi b_{T-1} + \alpha\frac{[y_T - (\ell_{T-1} + \phi b_{T-1})sn_{T-L}]}{sn_{T-L}}$$

$$b_T = \phi b_{T-1} + \alpha\gamma\frac{[y_T - (\ell_{T-1} + \phi b_{T-1})sn_{T-L}]}{sn_{T-L}}$$

$$sn_T = sn_{T-L} + (1 - \alpha)\delta\frac{[y_T - (\ell_{T-1} + \phi b_{T-1})sn_{T-L}]}{\ell_T}$$

2.  A **point forecast made in time period** $T$ **for** $y_{T+\tau}$ **is**

$$\hat{y}_{T+\tau}(T) = (\ell_T + \phi b_T + \phi^2 b_T + \cdots + \phi^\tau b_T)sn_{T+\tau-L}$$

where $sn_{T+\tau-L}$ is the "most recent" estimate of the seasonal factor for the season corresponding to time period $T + \tau$.

3.   An **approximate 95% prediction interval computed in time period $T$ for $y_{T+\tau}$** is

$$\left[ \hat{y}_{T+\tau}(T) \pm z_{[.025]} s_r \left( \sqrt{c_\tau} \right) (\mathrm{sn}_{T+\tau-L}) \right]$$

If   $\tau = 1$   then   $c_1 = (\ell_T + \phi b_T)^2$

If   $2 \leq \tau \leq L$   then

$$c_\tau = \sum_{j=1}^{\tau-1} \alpha^2 (1 + [\tau - j]\gamma)^2 (\ell_T + \phi_j b_T)^2 + (\ell_T + \phi_\tau b_T)^2$$

$$= \alpha^2 (1 + [\tau - 1]\gamma)^2 (\ell_T + \phi b_T)^2 + \cdots +$$

$$\alpha^2 (1 + \gamma)^2 (\ell_T + \phi_{\tau-1} b_T)^2 + (\ell_t + \phi_\tau b_T)^2$$

where   $\phi_j = \phi + \phi^2 + \cdots + \phi^j$

(For a better approximation and an exact formula, see Hyndman et al., 2001.)

When using damped trend methods, initial estimates can be obtained by utilizing the procedures presented for the Holt's trend corrected exponential smoothing, additive Holt–Winters method, or the multiplicative Holt–Winters method. The choice of smoothing constants and the damping factor is made by choosing the values that minimize the sum of the squared one-period-ahead forecast errors (SSE).

We have introduced methods for cases with no trend, linear trend, or damped trend. We have also provided methods to deal with no seasonal pattern, an additive seasonal pattern, and a multiplicative seasonal pattern. There is an exponential smoothing method that allows for exponential trend by multiplying the level by the growth rate instead of adding them. It is possible to have any combination of the four types of trend and three types of seasonality. In the next box, we show one more combination: no trend and a multiplicative seasonal pattern.

## NO TREND MULTIPLICATIVE HOLT–WINTERS METHOD

1.   The estimate $\ell_T$ for the **level,** the estimate $b_T$ for the **growth rate,** and the estimate $\mathrm{sn}_T$ for the **seasonal factor** of the time series in time period $T$ are given by the smoothing equations

$$\ell_T = \alpha(y_T/\mathrm{sn}_{T-L}) + (1 - \alpha)(\ell_{T-1})$$

$$\mathrm{sn}_T = \delta(y_T/\ell_T) + (1 - \delta)\mathrm{sn}_{T-L}$$

where $\alpha$ and $\delta$ are **smoothing constants** between 0 and 1.

2. A **point forecast made in time period $T$ for $y_{T+\tau}$** is

$$\hat{y}_{T+\tau}(T) = (\ell_T)\text{sn}_{T+\tau-L}$$

where $\text{sn}_{T+\tau-L}$ is the "most recent" estimate of the seasonal factor for the season corresponding to time period $T + \tau$.

3. An **approximate 95% prediction interval computed in time period $T$ for $y_{T+\tau}$** when $1 \le \tau \le L$ is

$$\left[\hat{y}_{T+\tau}(T) \pm z_{[.025]}s_r\left(\sqrt{1 + (\tau - 1)\alpha^2}\right)(\ell_T\text{sn}_{T+\tau-L})\right]$$

(For a better approximation and an exact formula, see Hyndman et al., 2001.)

# *8.6   MODELS FOR EXPONENTIAL SMOOTHING AND PREDICTION INTERVALS

Every exponential smoothing method has a corresponding statistical model. Statistical models are necessary for deriving formulas for prediction intervals. We will use **state space models** with a single source of error for the exponential smoothing models. The formulas for the prediction intervals in the preceding five sections were derived by using the models of this section. Before presenting the state space models, we need to introduce some new notation to distinguish the true values in the exponential smoothing models from the estimates that are found in the exponential smoothing methods. The components of exponential smoothing are called "**states**" in state space models. The notation for the components (states) is

| Component (state) | Model | Estimate |
|---|---|---|
| **Level** in time period $t$ | $L_t$ | $\ell_t$ |
| **Growth rate** in time period $t$ | $B_t$ | $b_t$ |
| **Seasonal factor** in time period $t$ | $\text{SN}_t$ | $\text{sn}_t$ |

The smoothing constants in the previous sections are estimates. To keep the notation relatively simple we change notation slightly and require that all the estimates in the previous sections for smoothing constants and the damping factor have hats (For example, $\hat{\alpha}$ is the estimate of the true value $\alpha$). The new notation is

---

* This section is optional.

| | Parameter | Estimate |
|---|---|---|
| Smoothing constant for the level | $\alpha$ | $\hat{\alpha}$ |
| Smoothing constant for the growth rate | $\gamma$ | $\hat{\gamma}$ |
| Smoothing constant for the season | $\delta$ | $\hat{\delta}$ |
| Damping factor | $\phi$ | $\hat{\phi}$ |

Each state space equation has an observation equation and one or more state equations. The **observation equation** is an equation for the value $y_t$, which can be observed. The **state equations** show how the unobserved components (states), which are the level, growth rate, and seasonal factor, change from one time period to the next. The models have a random source of error $\varepsilon_t$. The error term $\varepsilon_t$ has a value from a normal distribution that has mean zero [that is, $E(\varepsilon_t) = 0$] and a standard deviation $\sigma$ [that is, $\text{Var}(\varepsilon_t) = \sigma^2$] that is the same for each and every time period. Moreover, the error terms $\varepsilon_1, \varepsilon_2, \varepsilon_3, \ldots$ in different time periods are assumed to be statistically independent of each other.

The **state space models** for the single source of error models that we have studied in the previous sections of this chapter are presented in Table 8.3.

In order to see the relationship between the state space models and the exponential smoothing methods, one should relate the models to the error correction form of the smoothing equations. For example, looking at the model for simple exponential smoothing, we see from the observation equation that $\varepsilon_t = y_t - L_{t-1}$ and hence, the state equation is $L_t = L_{t-1} + \alpha(y_t - L_{t-1})$. Since $\ell_t$ is an estimate for the level $L_t$ and $\hat{\alpha}$ is an estimate of $\alpha$, we see that the smoothing equation, $\ell_t = \ell_{t-1} + \hat{\alpha}(y_t - \ell_{t-1})$, follows from the model.

**TABLE 8.3** State Space Models for the Exponential Smoothing Methods

| | Model | |
|---|---|---|
| **Method** | **Observation Equation** | **State Equations** |
| Simple exponential smoothing | $y_t = L_{t-1} + \varepsilon_t$ | $L_t = L_{t-1} + \alpha\varepsilon_t$ |
| Holt's trend corrected exponential smoothing | $y_t = L_{t-1} + B_{t-1} + \varepsilon_t$ | $L_t = L_{t-1} + B_{t-1} + \alpha\varepsilon_t$ <br> $B_t = B_{t-1} + \alpha\gamma\varepsilon_t$ |
| Additive Holt–Winters method | $y_t = L_{t-1} + B_{t-1} + SN_{t-L} + \varepsilon_t$ | $L_t = L_{t-1} + B_{t-1} + \alpha\varepsilon_t$ <br> $B_t = B_{t-1} + \alpha\gamma\varepsilon_t$ <br> $SN_t = SN_{t-L} + (1 - \alpha)\delta\varepsilon_t$ |
| Multiplicative Holt–Winters method | $y_t = (L_{t-1} + B_{t-1})\, SN_{t-L}\,(1 + \varepsilon_t)$ | $L_t = L_{t-1} + B_{t-1} + \alpha\,(L_{t-1} + B_{t-1})\varepsilon_t$ <br> $B_t = B_{t-1} + \alpha\gamma(L_{t-1} + B_{t-1})\varepsilon_t$ <br> $SN_t = SN_{t-L} + (1 - \alpha)\delta(SN_{t-L})\varepsilon_t$ |
| Damped trend method | $y_t = L_{t-1} + \phi B_{t-1} + \varepsilon_t$ | $L_t = L_{t-1} + \phi B_{t-1} + \alpha\varepsilon_t$ <br> $B_t = \phi B_{t-1} + \alpha\gamma\varepsilon_t$ |
| Additive Holt–Winters method with damped trend | $y_t = L_{t-1} + \phi B_{t-1} + SN_{t-L} + \varepsilon_t$ | $L_t = L_{t-1} + \phi B_{t-1} + \alpha\varepsilon$ <br> $B_t = \phi B_{t-1} + \alpha\gamma\varepsilon_t$ <br> $SN_t = SN_{t-L} + (1 - \alpha)\delta\varepsilon_t$ |
| Multiplicative Holt–Winters method with damped trend | $y_t = (L_{t-1} + \phi B_{t-1})SN_{t-L}\,(1 + \varepsilon_t)$ | $L_t = L_{t-1} + \phi B_{t-1} + \alpha(L_{t-1} + \phi B_{t-1})\varepsilon_t$ <br> $B_t = \phi B_{t-1} + \alpha\gamma\,(L_t + \phi B_{t-1})\varepsilon_t$ <br> $SN_t = SN_{t-L} + (1 - \alpha)\delta SN_{t-L}\varepsilon_t$ |
| No trend multiplicative Holt–Winters method | $y_t = L_{t-1}SN_{t-L}(1 + \varepsilon_t)$ | $L_t = L_{t-1} + \alpha L_{t-1}\varepsilon_t$ <br> $SN_t = SN_{t-L} + (1 - \alpha)\delta SN_{t-L}\varepsilon_t$ |

The relationship between the state space model and the exponential smoothing method is not so obvious for the multiplicative Holt–Winters method, where the trend, $TR_t = L_{t-1} + B_{t-1}$, the seasonal factor, $SN_{t-L}$, and the irregular factor, $IR_t = 1 - \varepsilon_t$, are multiplied together. However, the procedure to see the relationship is the same. We can rewrite the observation equation as

$$y_t = (L_{t-1} + B_{t-1})SN_{t-L}(1 + \varepsilon_t) = (L_{t-1} + B_{t-1})SN_{t-L} + (L_{t-1} + B_{t-1})SN_{t-L}\varepsilon_t$$

Then if we solve this equation for $\varepsilon_t$, we find

$$\varepsilon_t = \frac{y_t - (L_{t-1} + B_{t-1})SN_{t-L}}{(L_{t-1} + B_{t-1})SN_{t-L}}$$

If we substitute the right side of this equation for $\varepsilon_t$ in the three state equations for the multiplicative Holt–Winters method, we obtain

$$L_t = L_{t-1} + B_{t-1} + \alpha\,\frac{[y_t - (L_{t-1} + B_{t-1})SN_{t-L}]}{SN_{t-L}}$$

$$B_t = B_{t-1} + \alpha\gamma\,\frac{[y_t - (L_{t-1} + B_{t-1})SN_{t-L}]}{SN_{t-L}}$$

$$SN_t = SN_{t-L} + (1 - \alpha)\delta\,\frac{[y_t - (L_{t-1} + B_{t-1})SN_{t-L}]}{l_{t-1} + B_{t-1}}$$

With one minor change we can see that the form of these equations is the same as the error correction form if the estimates replace the true values. The minor change is in the smoothing equation for the seasonal factor, where the state space model requires that the revised values must depend on past time periods. Hence, we see a divisor of $L_{t-1} + B_{t-1}$ instead of $L_t$.

As stated at the beginning of the section, the models are needed to derive formulas for the prediction intervals. One can also check that the models give us the point forecasts for the corresponding exponential smoothing methods. In the following example we see how the point forecasts and the prediction intervals for simple exponential smoothing are based on the model.

**EXAMPLE 8.6**   Assume that we have observed the values $y_1, y_2, \ldots, y_T$ for the first $T$ time periods. If we have perfect information so that we know the values of $L_0$ and $\alpha$, then by using the observation equation and state equation repeatedly, we would know the value of $L_T$. Now the mean or expected value of $y_{T+\tau}$, which is $\tau$ periods in the future, is found as follows:

$$\text{If } \tau = 1 \quad E(y_{T+1}) = E(L_T + \varepsilon_{T+1}) = E(L_T) + E(\varepsilon_{T+1}) = L_T + 0 = L_T$$

$$\text{If } \tau = 2 \quad E(y_{T+2}) = E(L_{T+1} + \varepsilon_{T+2}) = E(L_T + \alpha\varepsilon_{T+1} + \varepsilon_{T+2})$$

$$= E(L_T) + \alpha E(\varepsilon_{T+1}) + E(\varepsilon_{T+2}) = L_T$$

$$\text{If } \tau = 3 \quad E(y_{T+3}) = E(L_{T+2} + \varepsilon_{T+3}) = E(L_{T+1} + \alpha\varepsilon_{T+2} + \varepsilon_{T+3})$$

$$= E(L_T + \alpha\varepsilon_{T+1} + \alpha\varepsilon_{T+2} + \varepsilon_{T+3}) = L_T$$

and in general,

$$E(y_{T+\tau}) = E(L_T + \alpha\varepsilon_{T+1} + \alpha\varepsilon_{T+2} + \cdots + \alpha\varepsilon_{T+\tau-1} + \varepsilon_{T+\tau}) = L_T$$

Our best forecast for $y_{T+\tau}$ is its expected or mean value. Since we do not have perfect information, we use the estimate $\ell_t$ for $L_t$. Hence, the point forecast for $y_{T+\tau}$ is

$$\hat{y}_{T+\tau}(T) = \ell_T$$

A 95% prediction interval for $y_{T+\tau}$ is

$$\hat{y}_{T+\tau}(T) \pm z_{[.025]}\sqrt{\text{Var}(y_{T+\tau} - \hat{y}_{T+\tau}(T))}$$

Again assuming that we have perfect information and thus know the value of $L_T$, we can find a formula for $\text{Var}(y_{T+\tau} - \hat{y}_{T+\tau}(T)) = \text{Var}(y_{T+\tau} - L_T)$ as follows:

$$
\begin{aligned}
\text{If } \tau = 1 \quad \text{Var}(y_{T+1} - L_T) &= \text{Var}(L_T + \varepsilon_{T+1} - L_T) = \text{Var}(\varepsilon_T) = \sigma^2 \\
\text{If } \tau = 2 \quad \text{Var}(y_{T+2} - L_T) &= \text{Var}(L_{T+1} + \varepsilon_{T+2} - L_T) \\
&= \text{Var}(L_T + \alpha\varepsilon_{T+1} + \varepsilon_{T+2} - L_T) \\
&= \text{Var}(\alpha\varepsilon_{T+1} + \varepsilon_{T+2}) \\
&= \alpha^2\text{Var}(\varepsilon_{T+1}) + \text{Var}(\varepsilon_{T+2}) \\
&= \alpha^2\sigma^2 + \sigma^2 = \sigma^2(\alpha^2 + 1)
\end{aligned}
$$

$$
\begin{aligned}
\text{If } \tau = 3 \quad \text{Var}(y_{T+3} - L_T) &= \text{Var}(L_{T+2} + \varepsilon_{T+3} - L_T) \\
&= \text{Var}(L_{T+1} + \alpha\varepsilon_{T+2} + \varepsilon_{T+3} - L_T) \\
&= \text{Var}(L_T + \alpha\varepsilon_{T+1} + \alpha\varepsilon_{T+2} + \varepsilon_{T+3} - L_T) \\
&= \text{Var}(\alpha\varepsilon_{T+1} + \alpha\varepsilon_{T+2} + \varepsilon_{T+3}) \\
&= \alpha^2\text{Var}(\varepsilon_{T+1}) + \alpha^2\text{Var}(\varepsilon_{T+2}) + \text{Var}(\varepsilon_{T+3}) \\
&= \alpha^2\sigma^2 + \alpha^2\sigma^2 + \sigma^2 = \sigma^2(2\alpha^2 + 1)
\end{aligned}
$$

and in general,

$$
\begin{aligned}
\text{Var}(y_{T+\tau} - L_T) &= \text{Var}(L_T + \alpha\varepsilon_{T+1} + \alpha\varepsilon_{T+2} + \cdots + \alpha\varepsilon_{T+\tau-1} + \varepsilon_{T+\tau} - L_T) \\
&= \alpha^2\text{Var}(\varepsilon_{T+1}) + \alpha^2\text{Var}(\varepsilon_{T+2}) + \cdots + \alpha^2\text{Var}(\varepsilon_{T+\tau-1}) + \text{Var}(\varepsilon_{T+\tau}) \\
&= (\tau - 1)\alpha^2\sigma^2 + \sigma^2 = \sigma^2[(\tau - 1)\alpha^2 + 1]
\end{aligned}
$$

Since the standard error $s$ is an estimate of $\sigma$, a 95% prediction interval for $y_{T+\tau}$ is

$$\ell_T \pm z_{[.025]}\sqrt{s^2[(\tau - 1)\hat{\alpha}^2 + 1]}$$

or

$$\ell_T \pm z_{[.025]}s\sqrt{(\tau - 1)\hat{\alpha}^2 + 1}$$

This is the formula for the 95% prediction interval that was given in Section 8.1.

In a manner similar to Example 8.6, all the point forecasts and prediction intervals for the exponential smoothing methods can be derived from the state space models of Table 8.3. These formulas are analytical formulas. We can also find the prediction intervals by using the model to simulate future values of the time series. We use the cod catch data of Examples 8.1 and 8.2 to illustrate how to simulate the lower and upper limits of a 95% prediction interval.

**EXAMPLE 8.7**

In order to find the 95% prediction interval for the cod catch data by using simulation, we begin by simulating the future values of the cod catch data. To simulate the future values of the cod catch data at time periods 25, 26, and 27, we use the state space model for simple exponential smoothing as follows:

1. We assume that the final estimates in Figure 8.2(b) are the true values for the model. We assume that $L_{24} = 354.5438$, $\sigma = 34.95$, and $\alpha = .034$.

2. We must randomly select values for the error terms $\varepsilon_{25}$, $\varepsilon_{26}$, and $\varepsilon_{27}$ from a normal distribution with mean 0 and standard deviation $\sigma = 34.95$.

3. A value for a future cod catch in time period 25 would be found with the observation equation

$$y_{25} = L_{24} + \varepsilon_{25} = 354.5438 + \varepsilon_{25}$$

4. A value for a future cod catch in time period 26 would be found by using the state equation

$$L_{25} = L_{24} + \alpha\varepsilon_{25} = 354.5438 + (.034)\varepsilon_{25}$$

and then the observation equation

$$y_{26} = L_{25} + \varepsilon_{26}$$

5. A value for a future cod catch in time period 27 would be found by using the state equation

$$L_{26} = l_{25} + \alpha\varepsilon_{26} = L_{25} + (.034)\varepsilon_{26}$$

and then the observation equation

$$y_{27} = L_{26} + \varepsilon_{27}$$

Note: If one is given values for $\varepsilon_{25}$, $\varepsilon_{26}$, and $\varepsilon_{27}$, the equations in steps 3, 4, and 5 can readily be used to compute $y_{25}$, $y_{26}$, and $y_{27}$ (see Exercise 8.23).

If we generate many values for $\varepsilon_{25}$, $\varepsilon_{26}$, and $\varepsilon_{27}$, say 10,000 of each, we would have many values for $y_{25}$, $y_{26}$, and $y_{27}$ (10,000 values of each). Then we choose

$$LL95_{25} = 2.5\text{th percentile of the 10,000 values for } y_{25}$$
$$UL95_{25} = 97.5\text{th percentile of the 10,000 values for } y_{25}$$

The 95% prediction interval for $y_{25}$ is

$$[LL95_{25}, UL95_{25}]$$

Similarly, the 95% prediction intervals for $y_{26}$ and $y_{27}$ are

$$[LL95_{26}, UL95_{26}] \quad \text{and} \quad [LL95_{27}, UL95_{27}]$$

We demonstrate this process with Crystal Ball, a simulation add-in for Excel. Table 8.4 shows where the formulas would be entered into the Excel spreadsheet of Figure 8.2(b) for the simulation of $y_{25}$, $y_{26}$, and $y_{27}$. The results of the simulation are shown in Figure 8.16. The medians should be close to the means in a simulated normal distribution, and hence the medians (50.0th percentiles) should be close to the point forecasts of 354.5438 (or 355) in Example 8.2. The medians for time periods 25, 26, and 27 are 354.8518, 353.94, and 354.33 (or 355, 354, and 354), respectively.

From Figure 8.16, we see that the 95% prediction intervals are

$$[285.7176, 422.6914] \quad \text{or} \quad [286, 423] \quad \text{for } y_{25}$$
$$[284.37, 424.47] \quad \text{or} \quad [284, 424] \quad \text{for } y_{26}$$

and

$$[284.54, 422.26] \quad \text{or} \quad [285, 422] \quad \text{for } y_{27}$$

These intervals should be compared with the analytical intervals in Example 8.2. Although the 95% prediction intervals that were derived analytically are more precise statistically, the simulated intervals are very close. Simulating intervals has some advantages. We can find intervals for which we do not have analytical formulas. For example, we can readily simulate 95% intervals for the cumulative cod catch for all three months of the cod catch data and for time series when the multiplicative Holt–Winters method is appropriate. In addition, the distribution for future values of a time series for which the multiplicative Holt–Winters method is appropriate may not have a normal distribution even if the $\varepsilon_t$ values are normally distributed. Thus simulated prediction intervals may be the most reasonable intervals.

**TABLE 8.4** Entries for Simulation of $y_{25}$, $y_{26}$, and $y_{27}$ for Cod Catch

| n | alpha | SSE | ssquare | s |
|---|---|---|---|---|
| 24 | 0.0343532 | 28089 | 1221.27 | 34.95 |

| Time Period | Actual Cod Catch y | Smoothed Estimate for Level | Forecast Made Last Period | Forecast Error | Squared Forecast Error |
|---|---|---|---|---|---|
| 0 | | 360.6667 | | | |
| 1 | 362 | 360.7125 | 360.6667 | 1.3333 | 1.7778 |
| 2 | 381 | 361.4094 | 360.7125 | 20.2875 | 411.5838 |
| 3 | 317 | 359.8838 | 361.4094 | −44.4094 | 1972.1959 |
| . | | . | | | . |
| . | | . | | | . |
| . | | . | | | . |
| 21 | 345 | 355.3733 | 355.7424 | −10.7424 | 115.3987 |
| 22 | 362 | 355.6010 | 355.3733 | 6.6267 | 43.9126 |
| 23 | 314 | 354.1719 | 355.6010 | −41.6010 | 1730.6423 |
| 24 | 365 | 354.5438 | 354.1719 | 10.8281 | 117.2486 |
| **Simulation** | | | | | |
| 25 | $y_{25} = L_{24} + \varepsilon_{25}$ | $L_{25} = L_{24} + \alpha\varepsilon_{25}$ | | $\varepsilon_{25}$ | |
| 26 | $y_{26} = L_{25} + \varepsilon_{26}$ | $L_{26} = L_{25} + \alpha\varepsilon_{26}$ | | $\varepsilon_{26}$ | |
| 27 | $y_{27} = L_{26} + \varepsilon_{27}$ | | | $\varepsilon_{27}$ | |

**FIGURE 8.16** Crystal Ball results when forecasting $y_{25}$, $y_{26}$, and $y_{27}$ for the cod catch

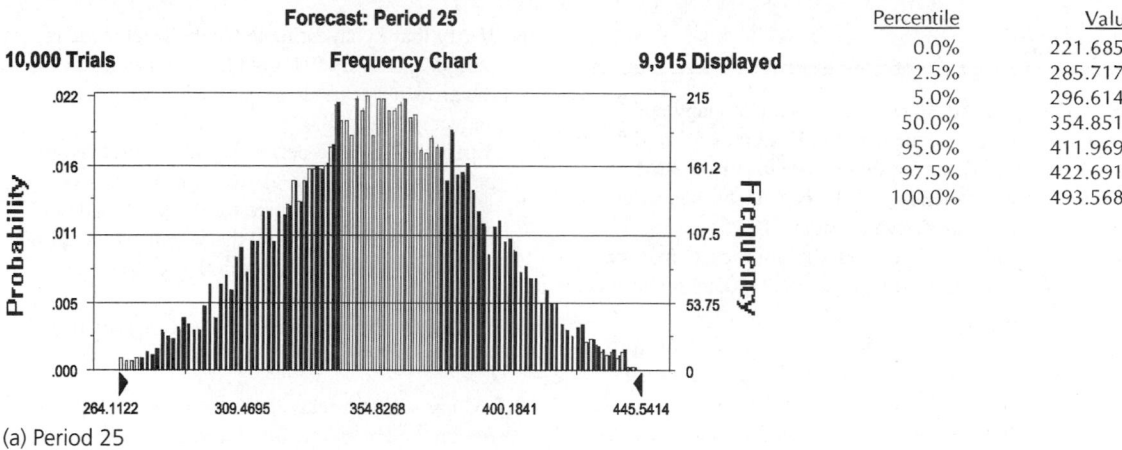

**Forecast: Period 25**

10,000 Trials     Frequency Chart     9,915 Displayed

| Percentile | Value |
|---|---|
| 0.0% | 221.6851 |
| 2.5% | 285.7176 |
| 5.0% | 296.6148 |
| 50.0% | 354.8518 |
| 95.0% | 411.9697 |
| 97.5% | 422.6914 |
| 100.0% | 493.5687 |

(a) Period 25

**Forecast: Period 26**

10,000 Trials     Frequency Chart     9,914 Displayed

| Percentile | Value |
|---|---|
| 0.0% | 209.21 |
| 2.5% | 284.37 |
| 5.0% | 295.25 |
| 50.0% | 353.94 |
| 95.0% | 413.04 |
| 97.5% | 424.47 |
| 100.0% | 482.73 |

(b) Period 26

**Forecast: Period 27**

10,000 Trials     Frequency Chart     9,911 Displayed

| Percentile | Value |
|---|---|
| 0.0% | 200.47 |
| 2.5% | 284.54 |
| 5.0% | 296.28 |
| 50.0% | 354.33 |
| 95.0% | 411.96 |
| 97.5% | 422.26 |
| 100.0% | 518.21 |

(c) Period 27

# Exercises

**8.1** Consider the Bay City Seafood Company cod catch data that were analyzed in Examples 8.1 and 8.2.
a. Verify that $\ell_3$, an estimate made in period 3 (March of year 1) of the level of the cod catch time series is 358.2380, as shown in Figure 8.1.
b. Verify that the one-period-ahead forecast error for period 4 (April of year 1) is −61.2380, as shown in Figure 8.1.
c. Verify that $\ell_4$, an estimate made in period 4 (April of year 1) of the level of the cod catch time series, is 352.1142, as shown in Figure 8.1.
d. Verify that the one-period-ahead forecast error for period 5 (May of year 1) is 46.8858, as shown in Figure 8.1.

**8.2** Consider the Bay City Seafood Company cod catch data in Figure 8.1.
a. Set up the Excel spreadsheet in Figure 8.1.
b. Use the Excel spreadsheet to find the SSE when $\alpha = .4$.
c. Use trial and error to try to find the value of $\alpha$ that minimizes the SSE.
d. Use Solver in Excel to find the value of $\alpha$ that produces the minimum value for the SSE. Your resulting spreadsheet should agree with Figure 8.2.

**8.3** Consider the Bay City Seafood Company cod catch data in Figure 8.2.
a. Using the observed values of the first two years (that is, use $T = 24$), find the point forecast and 95% prediction interval for the cod catch in month 28 (April of year 3).
b. Using the observed values of the first two years, find the point forecast and 95% prediction interval for the cod catch in month 29 (May of year 3).

**8.4** Consider the Bay City Seafood Company cod catch data in Figure 8.2.
a. If we observe a cod catch in February of year 3 to be $y_{26} = 375$, update the estimate for the level from $\ell_{25}$ to $\ell_{26}$. Recall that we already updated the level to $\ell_{25}$ in Example 8.2.
b. Find the point forecasts and 95% prediction intervals made in time period 26 for the next three months (March, April, and May).

**8.5** Consider the weekly thermostat sales in Example 8.3.

a. Verify that $\ell_2$, an estimate for the level made in period 2, is 211.1694 and that $b_2$, an estimate for the growth rate made in period 2, is .5524, as shown in Figure 8.6.
b. Verify that the one-period-ahead forecast error in period 3 is −26.7219, as shown in Figure 8.6.
c. Verify that $\ell_3$, an estimate for the level made in period 3, is 206.3775 and that $b_3$, an estimate for the growth rate made in period 3, is .0180, as shown in Figure 8.6.
d. Verify that the one-period-ahead forecast error in period 4 is −37.3955, as shown in Figure 8.6.

**8.6** Consider the weekly thermostat sales in Figure 8.6.
a. Set up the Excel spreadsheet in Figure 8.6 with $\ell_0 = 202.6246$ and $b_0 = -.3682$.
b. Use this spreadsheet to find the SSE when $\alpha = .1$ and $\gamma = .1$.
c. Use trial and error to try to find the $\alpha$ and $\gamma$ values that minimize the SSE.
d. Use Solver, starting with $\alpha = .2$ and $\gamma = .1$, to find the values of $\alpha$ and $\gamma$ that produce a minimum value for SSE. The results should agree with Figure 8.7.
e. Set up the Excel spreadsheet in Figure 8.6 using the error correction form of the smoothing equations.

**8.7** Use Excel to produce the regression output for the thermostat sales as shown in Figure 8.6.

**8.8** Consider the weekly thermostat sales in Figure 8.7(b).
a. Using the first 52 weeks of sales (that is, use $T = 52$), find the point forecast and 95% prediction interval for sales in week 56.
b. Using the first 52 weeks of sales, find the point forecast and 95% prediction interval for sales in week 57.

**8.9** Consider the weekly thermostat sales in Figure 8.7(b).
a. In Example 8.3, after observing $y_{53} = 330$ we revised the point forecasts and 95% prediction intervals for the sales in weeks 54 and 55. Continue this revision by finding revised point forecasts and 95% prediction intervals for weeks 56 and 57.
b. Suppose we now observe $y_{54} = 320$. Use this new information to revise the estimates for the level from $\ell_{53}$ to $\ell_{54}$ and the growth rate from $b_{53}$ to $b_{54}$.

c. Using the new estimates from part (b), revise the point forecasts and 95% prediction intervals for the sales in weeks 55, 56, and 57.

**8.10** Consider the calculator sales in Table 6.2 and Figure 6.4 of Chapter 6.
a. Find the initial values $\ell_0$ and $b_0$ by using Excel or some other statistical package to fit a straight line to the first half of the data.
b. Set up an Excel spreadsheet to perform Holt's trend corrected exponential smoothing.
c. Use Solver to find the values of $\alpha$ and $\gamma$ that minimize the SSE.
d. Find point forecasts and 95% prediction intervals for January, February, and March of year 3.

**8.11** Consider the sales of the TRK-50 mountain bike in Example 8.4.
a. Verify the following estimates for the level, growth rate, and seasonal factor: $\ell_2 = 23.5586$, $b_2 = 1.0508$, and $sn_2 = 6.6418$, as shown in Figure 8.9.
b. Verify that the one-period-ahead forecast error in period 3 is $-.1815$.
c. Verify the following estimates for the level, growth rate, and seasonal factor: $\ell_3 = 24.5731$, $b_3 = 1.0472$, and $sn_3 = 18.5575$.
d. Verify that the one-period-ahead forecast error in period 4 is 1.2885.

**8.12** Consider the sales of the TRK-50 mountain bike in Figure 8.9.
a. Set up the Excel spreadsheet in Figure 8.9 using $\ell_0 = 20.8500$, $b_0 = .9809$, $sn_{-3} = -14.2162$, $sn_{-2} = 6.5529$, $sn_{-1} = 18.5721$, and $sn_0 = -10.9088$.
b. Use Solver in your Excel spreadsheet from part (a) to verify that $\alpha = .561$, $\gamma = 0$, and $\delta = 0$ minimize the SSE, as shown in Figure 8.10.

**8.13** Use Excel to produce the regression output for the TRK-50 mountain bike sales as shown in Figure 8.9.

**8.14** Consider the sales of the TRK-50 mountain bike in Figure 8.10.
a. Find a point forecast and 95% prediction interval for sales of the mountain bike in the fourth quarter of year 5.
b. Find a point forecast and 95% prediction interval for sales of the mountain bike in the first quarter of year 6.

**8.15** Consider the sales of Tiger Sports Drink in Example 8.5.
a. Using the regression estimates in Figure 8.13, compute $S_2$, $S_6$, $S_{10}$, and $S_{14}$.
b. Compute $\bar{S}_{[2]}$.
c. Verify that the initial estimate of the seasonal factor for quarter 2 is $sn_{-2} = 1.1114$, as shown in Figures 8.12 and 8.13.
d. Repeat the process in parts (a) through (c) to verify that the initial estimate of the seasonal factor for quarter 3 is $sn_{-1} = 1.2937$, as shown in Figure 8.12.

**8.16** Consider the sales of the Tiger Sports Drink in Example 8.5.
a. Verify the following estimates for the level, growth rate, and seasonal factor: $\ell_3 = 104.5393$, $b_3 = 2.6349$, $sn_3 = 1.2944$, as shown in Figure 8.12.
b. Verify that the one-period-ahead forecast error in period 4 is .7650.
c. Verify the following estimates for the level, growth rate, and seasonal factor: $\ell_4 = 107.3464$, $b_4 = 2.6521$, $sn_4 = .8892$, as shown in Figure 8.12.
d. Verify that the one-period-ahead forecast error in period 5 is $-.9479$.

**8.17** Consider the sales of the Tiger Sports Drink in Figure 8.12.
a. Set up the Excel spreadsheet in Figure 8.12 using $\ell_0 = 95.2500$, $b_0 = 2.4706$, $sn_{-3} = .7062$, $sn_{-2} = 1.1114$, $sn_{-1} = 1.2937$, and $sn_0 = .8886$.
b. Use Solver, starting with $\alpha = .2$, $\gamma = .1$, and $\delta = .1$ in the Excel spreadsheet from part (a), to verify the values $\alpha = .336$, $\gamma = .046$, and $\delta = .134$ minimize the SSE, as shown in Figure 8.14(b).

**8.18** Use Excel to produce the regression output for the Tiger Sports Drink as shown in Figure 8.13.

**8.19** Consider the sales of Tiger Sports Drink in Figure 8.14.
a. Verify the point forecasts of the sales of Tiger Sports Drink for quarter 3 (time period 35) and quarter 4 (time period 36) as given in Example 8.5.
b. Verify the 95% prediction intervals for the sales of Tiger Sports Drink for quarter 3 (time period 35) and quarter 4 (time period 36) as given in Example 8.5.

**8.20** Consider the sales of Tiger Sports Drink in Figure 8.14. Suppose in the first quarter of year 9, we observe $y_{33} = 124$.

a. Without finding new values for the smoothing constants, find the estimates $\ell_{33}$, $b_{33}$, and $sn_{33}$ for the level, growth rate, and seasonal factor in time period 33.

b. Use the estimates from part (a) to revise the point forecasts and 95% prediction intervals for the sales of the sports drink in time periods 34, 35, and 36.

**8.21** Consider the Tasty Cola data of Table 7.1 and Figure 8.15. Use MINITAB to find smoothing constants that produce a smaller SSE than in Figure 8.15, where the SSE = (6812.61)(36) = 245,253.96.

**8.22** Consider the Tasty Cola data of Table 7.1.

a. Set up an Excel spreadsheet to find smoothing constants that minimize the SSE.

b. Use regression to fit a straight line to the Tasty Cola data and find initial estimates for the level and growth rate.

c. Use the procedures of Section 8.4 to find initial values for the 12 seasonal factors.

d. Use Solver in Excel to find smoothing constants that minimize the SSE.

e. Compute point forecasts and prediction intervals for the first four months of the fourth year.

**8.23** Consider the cod catch data in Example 8.7.

a. If the values for $\varepsilon_{25}$, $\varepsilon_{26}$, and $\varepsilon_{27}$ are 20, −15, and −5, respectively, simulate by hand the values for $y_{25}$, $y_{26}$, and $y_{27}$.

b. If the values of $\varepsilon_{25}$, $\varepsilon_{26}$, and $\varepsilon_{27}$ are −30, 4, and 22, respectively, simulate by hand the values for $y_{25}$, $y_{26}$, and $y_{27}$.

**8.24** Use Crystal Ball or some other simulation add-in for Excel to simulate the 95% prediction intervals for the future values of $y_{53}$, $y_{54}$, $y_{55}$, $y_{56}$, and $y_{57}$ for the weekly thermostat sales data and compare the results with the analytical prediction intervals in Example 8.3 and Exercise 8.8.

# 9

*Nonseasonal
Box–Jenkins Models
and Their Tentative
Identification*

The **Box–Jenkins methodology** consists of a four-step iterative procedure.

**Step 1:** **Tentative identification:** historical data are used to tentatively identify an appropriate Box–Jenkins model.

**Step 2:** **Estimation:** historical data are used to estimate the parameters of the tentatively identified model.

**Step 3:** **Diagnostic checking:** various diagnostics are used to check the adequacy of the tentatively identified model and, if need be, to suggest an improved model, which is then regarded as a new tentatively identified model.

**Step 4:** **Forecasting:** once a final model is obtained, it is used to forecast future time series values.

In this chapter we discuss the nature of nonseasonal Box–Jenkins models and the tentative identification of an appropriate model. We also discuss elementary concepts pertaining to estimating model parameters and then using the estimated model to forecast future time series values. A complete discussion of estimation, diagnostic checking, and forecasting is given in Chapter 10.

Classical Box–Jenkins forecasting models describe what we refer to as *stationary* time series. We begin this chapter by defining (in Section 9.1) **stationary** and **nonstationary time series** and by discussing how **differencing** can often be used to transform a nonstationary time series into a stationary time series. In Section 9.2 we introduce the **sample autocorrelation function** (the **SAC**) and the **sample partial autocorrelation function** (the **SPAC**). We will see how to characterize the *behavior* of these functions, and we discuss how to use the behavior of the SAC in order to decide whether a time series is nonstationary or stationary. Section 9.3 introduces **nonseasonal Box–Jenkins models,** using the SAC and SPAC to tentatively identify an appropriate model and forecasting future time series values by using an estimated  model. In Section 9.4 we give a general presentation of the various types—**autoregressive, moving average,** and **mixed**—of nonseasonal **Box–Jenkins models.** We also consider how to tentatively identify such models.

# 9.1   STATIONARY AND NONSTATIONARY TIME SERIES

Classical Box–Jenkins models describe *stationary* time series. Thus, in order to tentatively identify a Box–Jenkins model, we must first determine whether the time series we wish to forecast is stationary. If it is not, we must transform the time series into a series of stationary time series values. Intuitively, a time series is **stationary** if the statistical properties (for example, the mean and the variance) of the time series are essentially constant through time. If we have observed $n$ values $y_1, y_2, \ldots, y_n$ of a time series, we can use a plot of these values (against time) to help us determine whether the time series is stationary. If the $n$ values seem to fluctuate with constant variation around a constant mean $\mu$, then it is reasonable to believe that the time series is stationary (in Section 9.2 we utilize more sophisticated methods to help us determine whether a time series is stationary). If the $n$ values do not fluctuate around a constant mean or do not fluctuate with constant variation, then it is reasonable to believe that the time series is **nonstationary.** As we illustrate in the following example, if a plot of $n$ time series values $y_1, y_2, \ldots, y_n$ indicates that these values are nonstationary, we can sometimes transform the nonstationary time series values into stationary time series values by taking the **first differences** of the nonstationary time series values.

The **first differences** of the time series values $y_1, y_2, \ldots, y_n$ are

$$z_t = y_t - y_{t-1} \quad \text{where} \quad t = 2, \ldots, n$$

**EXAMPLE 9.1**   The Olympia Paper Company, Inc., makes Absorbent Paper Towels. The company would like to develop a prediction model that can be used to give point forecasts and prediction interval forecasts of weekly sales over 100,000 rolls, in units of 10,000 rolls, of Absorbent Paper Towels. With a reliable model, Olympia Paper can more effectively plan its production schedule, plan its budget, and estimate requirements for producing and storing this product. For the past 120 weeks the company has recorded weekly sales of Absorbent Paper Towels. The 120 sales figures, $y_1, y_2, \ldots, y_{120}$, are given in Table 9.1 and are plotted in Figure 9.1(a). It should be noticed from Figure 9.1(a) that the original values of the time series do not seem to fluctuate around a constant mean, and hence it would seem that these values are nonstationary.

The first differences $z_2, z_3, \ldots, z_{120}$ of the original values $y_1, y_2, \ldots, y_{120}$ are given in Table 9.2 and are calculated as follows:

$$z_2 = y_2 - y_1 = 14.4064 - 15.0000 = -.5936$$

$$z_3 = y_3 - y_2 = 14.9383 - 14.4064 = .5319$$

$$\vdots$$

$$z_{120} = y_{120} - y_{119} = 15.6453 - 15.3410 = .3043$$

**TABLE 9.1** Weekly Sales over 100,000 Rolls of Absorbent Paper Towels (In Units of 10,000 Rolls)

| $t$ | $y_t$ | $t$ | $y_t$ | $t$ | $y_t$ | $t$ | $y_t$ |
|---|---|---|---|---|---|---|---|
| 1 | 15.0000 | 31 | 10.7752 | 61 | −1.3173 | 91 | 10.5502 |
| 2 | 14.4064 | 32 | 10.1129 | 62 | −0.6021 | 92 | 11.4741 |
| 3 | 14.9383 | 33 | 9.9330 | 63 | 0.1400 | 93 | 11.5568 |
| 4 | 16.0374 | 34 | 11.7435 | 64 | 1.4030 | 94 | 11.7986 |
| 5 | 15.6320 | 35 | 12.2590 | 65 | 1.9280 | 95 | 11.8867 |
| 6 | 14.3975 | 36 | 12.5009 | 66 | 3.5626 | 96 | 11.2951 |
| 7 | 13.8959 | 37 | 11.5378 | 67 | 1.9615 | 97 | 12.7847 |
| 8 | 14.0765 | 38 | 9.6649 | 68 | 4.8463 | 98 | 13.9435 |
| 9 | 16.3750 | 39 | 10.1043 | 69 | 6.5454 | 99 | 13.6859 |
| 10 | 16.5342 | 40 | 10.3452 | 70 | 8.0141 | 100 | 14.1136 |
| 11 | 16.3839 | 41 | 9.2835 | 71 | 7.9746 | 101 | 13.8949 |
| 12 | 17.1006 | 42 | 7.7219 | 72 | 8.4959 | 102 | 14.2853 |
| 13 | 17.7876 | 43 | 6.8300 | 73 | 8.4539 | 103 | 16.3867 |
| 14 | 17.7354 | 44 | 8.2046 | 74 | 8.7114 | 104 | 17.0884 |
| 15 | 17.0010 | 45 | 8.5289 | 75 | 7.3780 | 105 | 15.8861 |
| 16 | 17.7485 | 46 | 8.8733 | 76 | 8.1905 | 106 | 14.8227 |
| 17 | 18.1888 | 47 | 8.7948 | 77 | 9.9720 | 107 | 15.9479 |
| 18 | 18.5997 | 48 | 8.1577 | 78 | 9.6930 | 108 | 15.0982 |
| 19 | 17.5859 | 49 | 7.9128 | 79 | 9.4506 | 109 | 13.8770 |
| 20 | 15.7389 | 50 | 8.7978 | 80 | 11.2088 | 110 | 14.2746 |
| 21 | 13.6971 | 51 | 9.0775 | 81 | 11.4986 | 111 | 15.1682 |
| 22 | 15.0059 | 52 | 9.3234 | 82 | 13.2778 | 112 | 15.3818 |
| 23 | 16.2574 | 53 | 10.4739 | 83 | 13.5910 | 113 | 14.1863 |
| 24 | 14.3506 | 54 | 10.6943 | 84 | 13.4297 | 114 | 13.9996 |
| 25 | 11.9515 | 55 | 9.8367 | 85 | 13.3125 | 115 | 15.2463 |
| 26 | 12.0328 | 56 | 8.1803 | 86 | 12.7445 | 116 | 17.0179 |
| 27 | 11.2142 | 57 | 7.2509 | 87 | 11.7979 | 117 | 17.2929 |
| 28 | 11.7023 | 58 | 5.0814 | 88 | 11.7319 | 118 | 16.6366 |
| 29 | 12.5905 | 59 | 1.8313 | 89 | 11.6523 | 119 | 15.3410 |
| 30 | 12.1991 | 60 | −0.9127 | 90 | 11.3718 | 120 | 15.6453 |

**FIGURE 9.1**
Original values of
and first differences
of weekly
Absorbent Paper
Towel sales

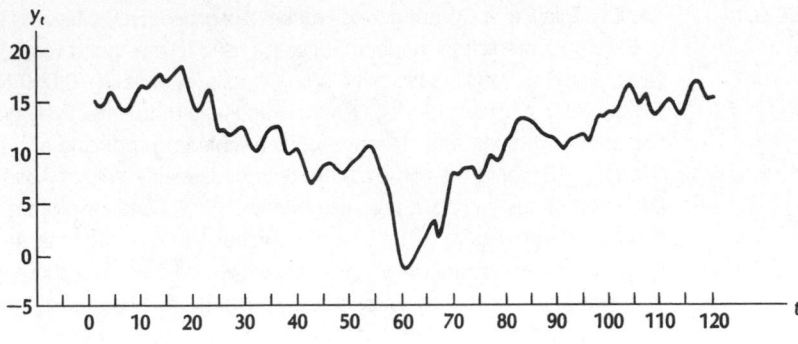

(a) Original values

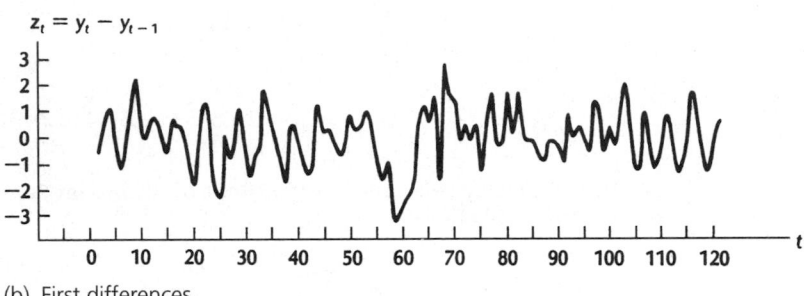

(b) First differences

These first differences are plotted in Figure 9.1(b). Since Figure 9.1(b) indicates that the first differences fluctuate with constant variation around a constant mean, it would seem that these first differences are stationary.

Although taking first differences sometimes transforms nonstationary time series values into stationary time series values, we sometimes need to use other forms of differencing to produce stationary time series values. For example, if the original time series values $y_1, y_2, \ldots, y_n$ are nonstationary, and the first differences of the original time series values $z_2 = y_2 - y_1, z_3 = y_3 - y_2, \ldots, z_n = y_n - y_{n-1}$ are nonstationary, then we can sometimes produce stationary time series values by taking the **second differences** (the first differences of the first differences) of the original time series values.

The **second differences** of the time series values $y_1, y_2, \ldots, y_n$ are

$$z_t = (y_t - y_{t-1}) - (y_{t-1} - y_{t-2})$$
$$= y_t - 2y_{t-1} + y_{t-2} \quad \text{for} \quad t = 3, 4, \ldots, n$$

**TABLE 9.2** First Differences of the Observations in Table 9.1

| $t$ | $z_t = y_t - y_{t-1}$ | $t$ | $z_t = y_t - y_{t-1}$ | $t$ | $z_t = y_t - y_{t-1}$ | $t$ | $z_t = y_t - y_{t-1}$ |
|---|---|---|---|---|---|---|---|
| 2 | −.5936 | 32 | −.6623 | 62 | .7152 | 92 | .9238 |
| 3 | .5319 | 33 | −.1798 | 63 | .7421 | 93 | .08268 |
| 4 | 1.099 | 34 | 1.810 | 64 | 1.263 | 94 | .2418 |
| 5 | −.4054 | 35 | .5154 | 65 | .5249 | 95 | .08809 |
| 6 | −1.235 | 36 | .2419 | 66 | 1.635 | 96 | −.5916 |
| 7 | −.5015 | 37 | −.9631 | 67 | −1.601 | 97 | 1.490 |
| 8 | .1805 | 38 | −1.873 | 68 | 2.885 | 98 | 1.159 |
| 9 | 2.298 | 39 | .4395 | 69 | 1.699 | 99 | −.2576 |
| 10 | .1593 | 40 | .2409 | 70 | 1.469 | 100 | .4277 |
| 11 | −.1503 | 41 | −1.062 | 71 | −.03953 | 101 | −.2186 |
| 12 | .7167 | 42 | −1.562 | 72 | .5213 | 102 | .3903 |
| 13 | .6871 | 43 | −.8918 | 73 | −.04202 | 103 | 2.101 |
| 14 | −.05226 | 44 | 1.375 | 74 | .2575 | 104 | .7016 |
| 15 | −.7344 | 45 | .3243 | 75 | −1.333 | 105 | −1.202 |
| 16 | .7475 | 46 | .3444 | 76 | .8124 | 106 | −1.063 |
| 17 | .4403 | 47 | −.07841 | 77 | 1.782 | 107 | 1.125 |
| 18 | .4109 | 48 | −.6371 | 78 | −.2790 | 108 | −.8497 |
| 19 | −1.014 | 49 | −.2449 | 79 | −.2424 | 109 | −1.221 |
| 20 | −1.847 | 50 | .8850 | 80 | 1.758 | 110 | .3976 |
| 21 | −2.042 | 51 | .2797 | 81 | .2898 | 111 | .8936 |
| 22 | 1.309 | 52 | .2459 | 82 | 1.779 | 112 | .2136 |
| 23 | 1.251 | 53 | 1.150 | 83 | .3132 | 113 | −1.195 |
| 24 | −1.907 | 54 | .2204 | 84 | −.1613 | 114 | −.1867 |
| 25 | −2.399 | 55 | −.8575 | 85 | −.1173 | 115 | 1.247 |
| 26 | .08132 | 56 | −1.656 | 86 | −.5680 | 116 | 1.772 |
| 27 | −.8186 | 57 | −.9294 | 87 | −.9465 | 117 | .2750 |
| 28 | .4881 | 58 | −2.170 | 88 | −.06604 | 118 | −.6564 |
| 29 | .8882 | 59 | −3.250 | 89 | −.07964 | 119 | −1.296 |
| 30 | −.3194 | 60 | −2.744 | 90 | −.2804 | 120 | .3043 |
| 31 | −1.424 | 61 | −.4046 | 91 | −.8216 | | |

That is, the second differences of the original time series values $y_1, y_2, \ldots, y_n$ are

$$z_3 = y_3 - 2y_2 + y_1$$
$$z_4 = y_4 - 2y_3 + y_2$$
$$\vdots$$
$$z_n - y_n - 2y_{n-1} + y_{n-2}$$

Henceforth we denote the values of the time series we are currently working with by the symbols $z_b, z_{b+1}, \ldots, z_n$. We refer to the values $z_b, z_{b+1}, \ldots, z_n$ as the "**working series.**" Note that we do not write the first value of the working series as $z_1$, because the values $z_b, z_{b+1}, \ldots, z_n$ might be obtained by differencing the nonstationary time series values $y_1, y_2, \ldots, y_n$. For example, if the values $z_b, z_{b+1}, \ldots, z_n$ are obtained by using the transformation $z_t = y_t - y_{t-1}$, then as illustrated previously, $z_b = z_2 = y_2 - y_1$, in which case $b = 2$. As another example, if the values $z_b, z_{b+1}, \ldots, z_n$ are obtained by using the transformation $z_t = y_t - 2y_{t-1} + y_{t-2}$, then $z_b = z_3 = y_3 - 2y_2 + y_1$, in which case $b = 3$.

Experience indicates that if the original time series values $y_1, y_2, \ldots, y_n$ are *nonstationary* and *nonseasonal*, then using the first differencing transformation

$$z_t = y_t - y_{t-1}$$

or the second differencing transformation

$$z_t = (y_t - y_{t-1}) - (y_{t-1} - y_{t-2})$$
$$= y_t - 2y_{t-1} + y_{t-2}$$

will usually produce stationary time series values. If the original time series values $y_1, y_2, \ldots, y_n$ are *nonstationary* and *seasonal*, then more complex transformations may be needed to provide stationary time series values. In Chapter 11 we discuss additional stationarity transformations.

# 9.2 THE SAMPLE AUTOCORRELATION AND PARTIAL AUTOCORRELATION FUNCTIONS: THE SAC AND SPAC

Box–Jenkins forecasting models are tentatively identified by examining the behavior of the **sample autocorrelation function (SAC)** and the **sample partial autocorrelation function (SPAC)** for the values of a **stationary time series** $z_b, z_{b+1}, \ldots, z_n$. Here $z_b, z_{b+1}, \ldots, z_n$ may be original time series values or transformed time series values. We first consider the SAC.

## The Sample Autocorrelation Function (SAC)

Consider the working series of time series values $z_b, z_{b+1}, \ldots, z_n$. The **sample autocorrelation at lag $k$,** denoted by $r_k$, is

$$r_k = \frac{\displaystyle\sum_{t=b}^{n-k} (z_t - \bar{z})(z_{t+k} - \bar{z})}{\displaystyle\sum_{t=b}^{n} (z_t - \bar{z})^2}$$

where

$$\bar{z} = \frac{\displaystyle\sum_{t=b}^{n} z_t}{(n - b + 1)}$$

This quantity measures the linear relationship between time series observations separated by a lag of $k$ time units. It can be proved that $r_k$ will always be between −1 and 1. A value of $r_k$ close to 1 indicates that observations separated by a lag of $k$ time units have a strong tendency to move together in a linear fashion with a positive slope, whereas a value of $r_k$ close to −1 indicates that observations separated by a lag of $k$ time units have a strong tendency to move together in a linear fashion with a negative slope.

**EXAMPLE 9.2**

In this example we consider the original values of Absorbent Paper Towel sales $y_1, y_2, \ldots, y_{120}$ given in Table 9.1. To illustrate the formula for $r_3$, the sample autocorrelation at lag 3, consider the pairs of observations for sales of Absorbent Paper Towels from Table 9.1 that are three time periods apart. These pairs $(y_t, y_{t+3})$ are displayed in Table 9.3 and a plot of $y_{t+3}$ versus $y_t$ is shown in Figure 9.2, where we can see a pattern which indicates that $r_3$ is positive.

**TABLE 9.3  Pairs of Absorbent Paper Towel Sales Three Periods Apart**

| $t$ | $y_t$ | $y_{t+3}$ |
|---|---|---|
| 1 | 15.0000 | 16.0374 |
| 2 | 14.4064 | 15.6320 |
| 3 | 14.9383 | 14.3975 |
| 4 | 16.0374 | 13.8959 |
| 5 | 15.6320 | 14.0765 |
| 6 | 14.3975 | 16.3750 |
| ⋮ | ⋮ | ⋮ |
| 116 | 17.0179 | 15.3410 |
| 117 | 17.2929 | 15.6453 |

**FIGURE 9.2**
Plot of $y_{t+3}$ versus $y_t$ for Absorbent Paper Towel sales that shows $r_3$ is positive

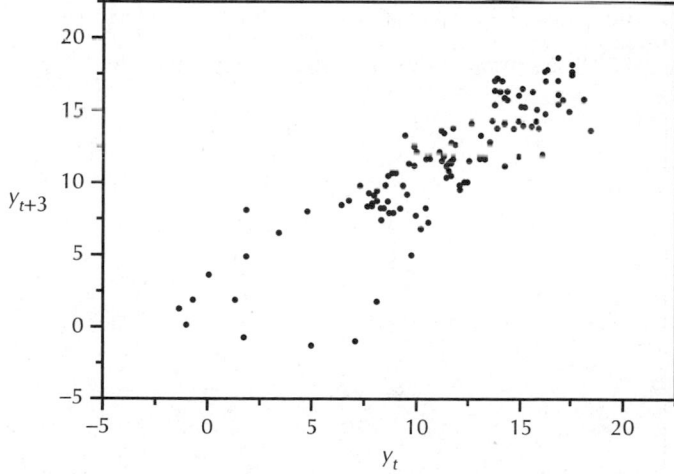

As an example of the calculations involved in computing $r_3$, note that the mean of the 120 original time series values is

$$\bar{y} = \frac{\sum_{t=1}^{120} y_t}{120} = \frac{15.0000 + 14.4064 + \cdots + 15.6453}{120} = 11.58$$

and note that $r_3$ is calculated as follows, where $z_b = y_1$, $z_{b+1} = y_2, \ldots, z_n = y_{120}$ and $\bar{z} = \bar{y}$.

$$
\begin{aligned}
r_3 &= \frac{\sum_{t=b}^{n-k} (z_t - \bar{z})(z_{t+k} - \bar{z})}{\sum_{t=b}^{n} (z_t - \bar{z})^2} = \frac{\sum_{t=1}^{120-3} (z_t - \bar{z})(z_{t+3} - \bar{z})}{\sum_{t=1}^{120} (z_t - \bar{z})^2} \\[2mm]
&= \frac{(z_1 - \bar{z})(z_4 - \bar{z}) + (z_2 - \bar{z})(z_5 - \bar{z}) + \cdots + (z_{117} - \bar{z})(z_{120} - \bar{z})}{(z_1 - \bar{z})^2 + (z_2 - \bar{z})^2 + \cdots + (z_{120} - \bar{z})^2} \\[2mm]
&= [(15.0000 - 11.58)(16.0374 - 11.58) + (14.4064 - 11.58)(15.6320 - 11.58) \\
&\quad + \cdots + (17.2929 - 11.58)(15.6453 - 11.58)] \\
&\quad \div [(15.0000 - 11.58)^2 + (14.4064 - 11.58)^2 + \cdots + (15.6453 - 11.58)^2] \\[2mm]
&= .85323
\end{aligned}
$$

In the following box we repeat the formula for $r_k$ and present (for future reference) formulas for the **standard error of $r_k$**, $s_{r_k}$, and the $t_{r_k}$-*statistic* related to $r_k$. In Sections 9.3 and 9.4 we will see how to use $s_{r_k}$ and $t_{r_k}$ to help us to tentatively identify a Box–Jenkins model. In this box we also define the **sample autocorrelation function (SAC).**

---

For the working series $z_b, z_{b+1}, \ldots, z_n$:

1. The **sample autocorrelation at lag $k$** is

$$r_k = \frac{\sum_{t=b}^{n-k} (z_t - \bar{z})(z_{t+k} - \bar{z})}{\sum_{t=b}^{n} (z_t - \bar{z})^2}$$

where

$$\bar{z} = \frac{\sum_{t=b}^{n} z_t}{n - b + 1}$$

---

2.  The **standard error of $r_k$** is

$$
s_{r_k} = \begin{cases} \dfrac{1}{(n-b+1)^{1/2}} & \text{if} \quad k = 1 \\[2em] \dfrac{\left(1 + 2\displaystyle\sum_{j=1}^{k-1} r_j^2\right)^{1/2}}{(n-b+1)^{1/2}} & \text{if} \quad k = 2, 3, \ldots \end{cases}
$$

3.  The $t_{r_k}$-statistic is

$$
t_{r_k} = \frac{r_k}{s_{r_k}}
$$

4.  The **sample autocorrelation function (SAC)** is a listing, or graph, of the sample autocorrelations at lags $k = 1, 2, \ldots$

Noting that we henceforth refer to the sample autocorrelation function as the SAC, we now present an example.

**EXAMPLE 9.3**   In Figure 9.3 we present SAS output of the SAC for the original values of the Absorbent Paper Towel sales $y_1, y_2, \ldots, y_{120}$. Here the $r_k$ values are listed under the heading "Correlation"

**FIGURE 9.3** SAS output of the SAC for the original values of paper towel sales

```
                          Name of Variable = y

                    Mean of Working Series    11.58391
                    Standard Deviation        4.377476
                    Number of Observations         120


                               Autocorrelations

Lag   Covariance   Correlation   -1 9 8 7 6 5 4 3 2 1 0 1 2 3 4 5 6 7 8 9 1    Std Error
 0    19.162294    1.00000       |                    |********************|         0
 1    18.445808    0.96260       |                    |*******************         0.091287
 2    17.388503    0.90743       |                  . |******************         0.154197
 3    16.349929    0.85323       |                  . |*****************          0.193651
 4    15.343692    0.80072       |                .   |****************           0.222787
 5    14.232902    0.74276       |                .   |***************            0.245601
 6    13.116331    0.68449       |               .    |**************             0.263656
 7    12.028851    0.62774       |              .     |************               0.278071
 8    11.088860    0.57868       |             .      |***********                0.289639
 9    10.185709    0.53155       |            .       |**********.                0.299119
10     9.493686    0.49544       |            .       |*********  .               0.306890
11     8.977998    0.46852       |           .        |*********  .               0.313484
12     8.517382    0.44449       |          .         |********     .             0.319266
13     7.970955    0.41597       |          .         |*******      .             0.324382
14     7.347767    0.38345       |         .          |*******      .             0.328797

             "." marks two standard errors
```

**FIGURE 9.4** MINITAB output of the SAC for the original values of paper towel sales

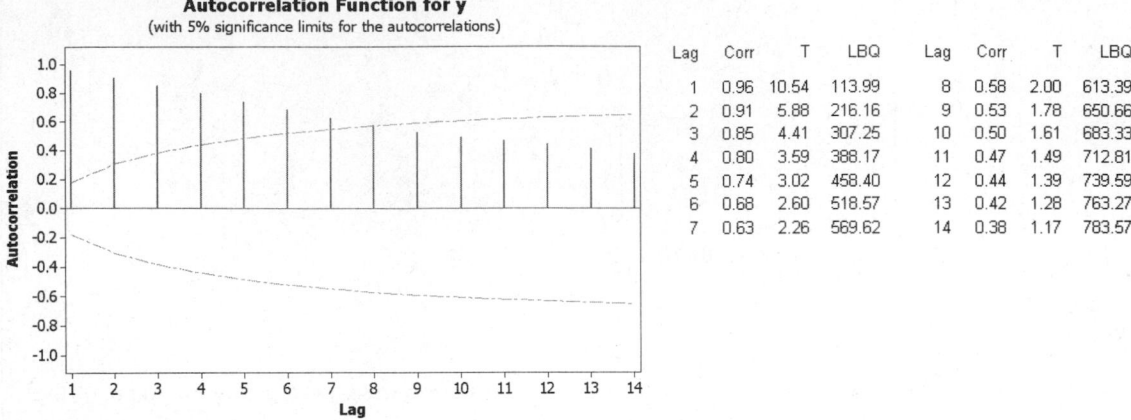

**Autocorrelation Function for y**
(with 5% significance limits for the autocorrelations)

| Lag | Corr | T | LBQ | Lag | Corr | T | LBQ |
|-----|------|------|--------|-----|------|------|--------|
| 1 | 0.96 | 10.54 | 113.99 | 8 | 0.58 | 2.00 | 613.39 |
| 2 | 0.91 | 5.88 | 216.16 | 9 | 0.53 | 1.78 | 650.66 |
| 3 | 0.85 | 4.41 | 307.25 | 10 | 0.50 | 1.61 | 683.33 |
| 4 | 0.80 | 3.59 | 388.17 | 11 | 0.47 | 1.49 | 712.81 |
| 5 | 0.74 | 3.02 | 458.40 | 12 | 0.44 | 1.39 | 739.59 |
| 6 | 0.68 | 2.60 | 518.57 | 13 | 0.42 | 1.28 | 763.27 |
| 7 | 0.63 | 2.26 | 569.62 | 14 | 0.38 | 1.17 | 783.57 |

and are plotted for lags $k = 1, 2, \ldots, 24$. Specifically, each $r_k$ value is represented by a row of asterisks. In Figure 9.4 we present the MINITAB output of the SAC for the original values of the Absorbent Paper Towel sales values, where the $r_k$ values are plotted as vertical lines.

The SAS output of the SAC also gives the standard errors of the sample autocorrelations (that is, the $s_{r_k}$ values), whereas the MINITAB output gives the $t_{r_k}$ statistics. To demonstrate how the standard errors and the associated $t_{r_k}$ values are calculated, we calculate $s_{r_3}$ and $t_{r_3}$.

$$
\begin{aligned}
s_{r_3} &= \left(1 + 2\sum_{j=1}^{k-1} r_j^2\right)^{1/2} \Big/ (n - b + 1)^{1/2} \\
&= \left(1 + 2\sum_{j=1}^{3-1} r_j^2\right)^{1/2} \Big/ (120 - 1 + 1)^{1/2} \\
&= \left(1 + 2\left[r_1^2 + r_2^2\right]\right)^{1/2} \Big/ (120)^{1/2} \\
&= (1 + 2[(.96260)^2 + (.90743)^2])^{1/2} / (120)^{1/2} \\
&= .193651
\end{aligned}
$$

$$
t_{r_3} = \frac{r_3}{s_{r_3}} = \frac{.85323}{.193651} = 4.406
$$

Although SAS does not give the $t_{r_k}$ values, it presents related "two-standard-deviation dotted bands." To understand these bands, consider Figure 9.3, and note that the "centerline" on the plot of the $r_k$ values is positioned at 0. For any lag $k$ the dot to the left of the centerline is $2(s_{r_k})$ less than 0 and the dot to the right of the centerline is $2(s_{r_k})$ greater than 0. Therefore, the dotted bands are symmetrical around the centerline. This implies in Figure 9.3 that the dots to the right of the centerline corresponding to lags 1–8, which cannot be seen because they are covered by the asterisks representing the

$r_k$ values, "bend in" toward 0 in the same manner as the dots to the left of the centerline. In general, if the last asterisk representing $r_k$ coincides with the corresponding two-standard-deviation dot (this is true for lag 8), then the absolute value of $r_k$ is roughly equal to $2(s_{r_k})$. This implies that the absolute value of

$$t_{r_k} = \frac{r_k}{s_{r_k}}$$

is roughly equal to 2. For example,

$$t_{r_8} = \frac{r_8}{s_{r_8}} = \frac{.57868}{.289639} = 1.998$$

If the last asterisk is beyond the corresponding dot (this is true for lags 1–7), then $|t_{r_k}|$ exceeds 2. If the last asterisk does not reach the corresponding dot (this is true for lags 9–24), then $|t_{r_k}|$ is less than 2. The MINITAB output also shows bands at $2(s_{r_k})$ above and $2(s_{r_k})$ below the centerline at 0. We now begin to discuss the practical implications of the $t_{r_k}$ values and of the two-standard-deviation bands.

In order to employ the Box–Jenkins methodology, we must examine and attempt to classify what we refer to as **the behavior of the SAC**. The SAC for a nonseasonal time series can display a variety of different behaviors.

First, the SAC for a nonseasonal time series can **cut off.** To see what we mean by this, we say that a **spike at lag $k$** exists in the SAC if $r_k$, the sample autocorrelation at lag $k$, is statistically large. Concluding that $r_k$ is statistically large is basically equivalent to rejecting the null hypothesis that the **theoretical autocorrelation at lag $k$** equals zero. This *theoretical* autocorrelation is denoted by the symbol $\rho_k$ and is a measure of the linear relationship between *all possible* time series values separated by a lag of $k$ time units. We can judge whether a spike at lag $k$ exists in the SAC by looking at the $t$-statistic related to $r_k$.

For nonseasonal time series, a spike is considered to exist in the SAC if the absolute value of

$$t_{r_k} = \frac{r_k}{s_{r_k}}$$

*is greater than* 2. Next we say that the SAC **cuts off after lag $k$** if there are no spikes at lags greater than $k$ in the SAC. For example, if

$$|t_{r_1}| = 3.671$$
$$|t_{r_2}| = 2.873$$
$$|t_{r_3}| = 0.517$$

and

$$|t_{r_k}| < 2$$

**FIGURE 9.5**
Examples of
behavior for
the SAC

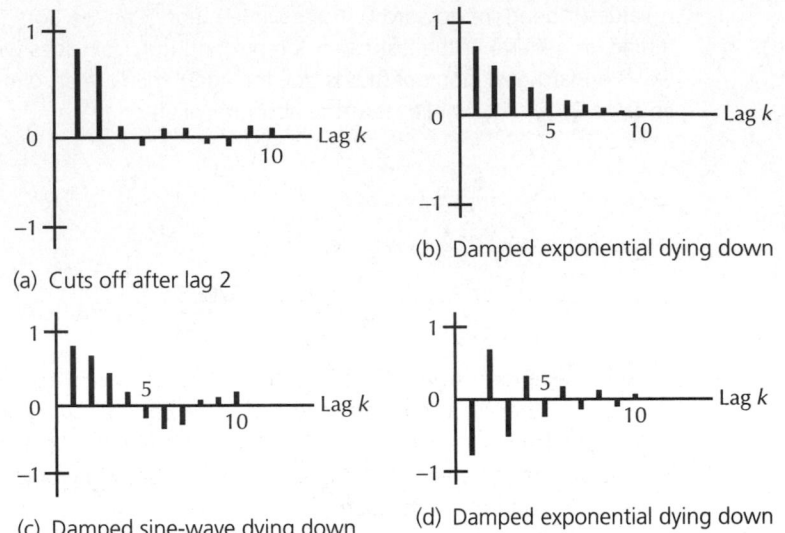

(a) Cuts off after lag 2

(b) Damped exponential dying down

(c) Damped sine-wave dying down

(d) Damped exponential dying down
with oscillation

for all lags $k > 3$, then the SAC would cut off after lag 2. A SAC that cuts off is illustrated in Figure 9.5(a). When using a SAS output, we conclude that a spike exists at lag $k$ if the last asterisk representing $r_k$ is beyond the corresponding two-standard-deviation dot. When $r_k$ appears to be near the bands at $+2(s_{r_k})$ or $-2(s_{r_k})$ in a graph, it is also helpful to examine the value of $t_{r_k}$ (calculated by hand for SAS output).

Second, we say that the SAC **dies down** if this function does not cut off but rather decreases in a "steady fashion." As illustrated in Figure 9.5, the SAC can die down in one of three ways:

1.  A damped exponential fashion (with no oscillation or with oscillation)
2.  A damped sine-wave fashion
3.  A fashion dominated by either one of or a combination of both (1) and (2)

Furthermore, the SAC can die down *fairly quickly* (as shown in Figure 9.6(a)) or can die down *extremely slowly* (as shown in Figure 9.6(b)).

## Using the SAC to Find a Stationary Time Series

The SAC can be used to help us find a working series of stationary time series values $z_b, z_{b+1}, \ldots, z_n$. This can be done because we can relate the behavior of the SAC to stationarity.

**FIGURE 9.6**
Dying down fairly
quickly versus
extremely slowly

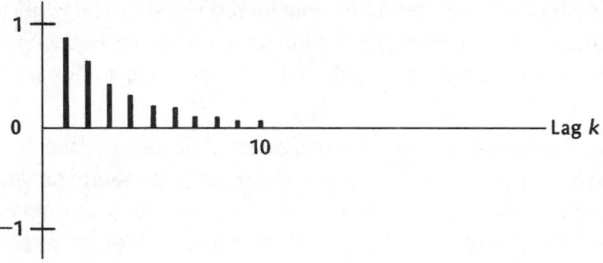

(a) Dying down fairly quickly

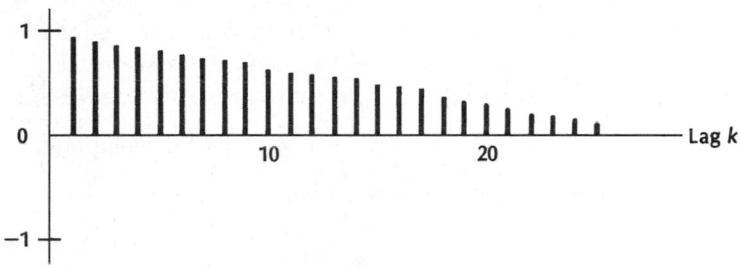

(b) Dying down extremely slowly

---

In general, it can be shown that for *nonseasonal data,*

1.   If the SAC of the time series values $z_b, z_{b+1}, \ldots, z_n$ either **cuts off fairly quickly** or **dies down fairly quickly,** then the time series values should be considered **stationary.**

2.   If the SAC of the time series values $z_b, z_{b+1}, \ldots, z_n$ **dies down extremely slowly,** then the time series values should be considered **nonstationary.**

---

The precise meanings of the terms "fairly quickly" and "extremely slowly" are somewhat arbitrary and can best be determined through experience. Moreover, experience shows that for nonseasonal data, if the SAC cuts off fairly quickly, it will often do so after a lag $k$ that is less than or equal to 2.

We can now use the following strategy to find a stationary time series. We first compute the SAC for the original time series values $y_1, y_2, \ldots, y_n$. If the SAC either cuts off fairly quickly or dies down fairly quickly, then the original time series values should be considered stationary. If the SAC dies down extremely slowly, the original time series values should be considered nonstationary. In such a case, data transformation is necessary (we would generally begin by trying first differencing). We then compute the SAC for the transformed data. If the SAC for the transformed data either cuts off fairly quickly or dies down fairly quickly, the transformed data should be considered stationary. If the SAC for the transformed data dies down extremely slowly, the transformed data should be considered nonstationary. In such a case, further data transformation (for example, second differencing) is necessary. For nonseasonal data, first or second differencing will generally produce stationary time series values.

**EXAMPLE 9.4**   Again consider the SAC of the original values of Absorbent Paper Towel sales (shown in Figure 9.3). We can use the SAC for this working series to determine whether the original values of Absorbent Paper Towel sales are stationary. To do this we note that the SAC in Figure 9.3 can (through experience with Box–Jenkins modeling) be interpreted as dying down extremely slowly (notice the very slow, reasonably steady decrease in the $r_k$ values). Since the SAC for these original values dies down extremely slowly, and since the plot of the original values of Absorbent Paper Towel sales in Figure 9.1(a) indicates that these original values do not seem to fluctuate around a constant mean, we conclude that these original values are nonstationary.

This conclusion says that we must use data transformation in order to obtain stationary time series values $z_b, z_{b+1}, \ldots, z_n$. We attempt to determine whether using the transformation

$$z_t = y_t - y_{t-1} \quad \text{(first differencing)}$$

produces stationary time series values:

$$z_b = z_2 = y_2 - y_1 = 14.4064 - 15.0000 = -.5936$$
$$z_{b+1} = z_3 = y_3 - y_2 = 14.9383 - 14.4064 = .5319$$
$$\vdots$$
$$z_n = z_{120} = y_{120} - y_{119} = 15.6453 - 15.3410 = .3043$$

Recalling that all of these first differences are given in Table 9.2, the SAC for this working series is obtained by calculating the sample autocorrelation at lag $k$ for lags $k = 1, 2, 3, \ldots$. As an example of the calculations involved, note that the mean of the 119 first differences is

$$\bar{z} = \frac{\sum\limits_{t=b}^{n} z_t}{n - b + 1} = \frac{\sum\limits_{t=2}^{120} z_t}{120 - 2 + 1} = \frac{-.5936 + .5319 + \cdots + .3043}{119}$$
$$= .005423$$

and note that $r_3$ is calculated as follows, where $z_b = z_2, z_{b+1} = z_3, \ldots, z_n = z_{120}$:

$$r_3 = \frac{\sum\limits_{t=b}^{n-k} (z_t - \bar{z})(z_{t+k} - \bar{z})}{\sum\limits_{t=b}^{n} (z_t - \bar{z})^2} = \frac{\sum\limits_{t=2}^{120-3} (z_t - \bar{z})(z_{t+3} - \bar{z})}{\sum\limits_{t=2}^{120} (z_t - \bar{z})^2}$$

$$= \frac{(z_2 - \bar{z})(z_5 - \bar{z}) + \cdots + (z_{117} - \bar{z})(z_{120} - \bar{z})}{(z_2 - \bar{z})^2 + \cdots + (z_{120} - \bar{z})^2}$$

$$= [(-.5936 - .005423)(-.4054 - .005423)$$
$$\quad + \cdots + (.2750 - .005423)(.3043 - .005423)]$$
$$\quad \div [(-.5936 - .005423)^2 + \cdots + (.3043 - .005423)^2]$$

$$= -.07166$$

In Figure 9.7 we present the SAS output of the SAC for the first differences of the Absorbent Paper Towel sales $z_2, z_3, \ldots, z_{120}$. In Figure 9.8 we present the MINITAB output of the SAC for these first differences. The SAS output also gives the values of the standard error of $r_k$. As an example, we calculate

$$
s_{r_3} = \left(1 + 2\sum_{j=1}^{k-1} r_j^2\right)^{1/2} \Big/ (n - b + 1)^{1/2}
$$

$$
= \left(1 + 2\sum_{j=1}^{3-1} r_j^2\right)^{1/2} \Big/ (120 - 2 + 1)^{1/2}
$$

$$
= \left(1 + 2[r_1^2 + r_2^2]\right)^{1/2} \Big/ (119)^{1/2}
$$

$$
= (1 + 2[(.30665)^2 + (-.06474)^2])^{1/2} / (119)^{1/2} = .100271
$$

Looking at the SAC for these first differences, we see that the SAC has a spike at lag 1 (since the last asterisk corresponding to $r_1$ is beyond the corresponding two-standard-deviation dot). Furthermore, since there are no spikes in the SAC after lag 1, we conclude that the SAC cuts off after lag 1. Therefore, since the SAC cuts off quickly, and since the plot of the first differences in Figure 9.1(b) indicates that these first differences do seem to fluctuate around a constant mean, we will assume that these first differences (that is, the time series values produced by using the transformation $z_t = y_t - y_{t-1}$) are stationary.

**FIGURE 9.7** SAS output of the SAC for the first differences of paper towel sales

Name of Variable = y

| Period(s) of Differencing | 1 |
|---|---|
| Mean of Working Series | 0.005423 |
| Standard Deviation | 1.099416 |
| Number of Observations | 119 |
| Observation(s) eliminated by differencing | 1 |

Autocorrelations

| Lag | Covariance | Correlation | -1 9 8 7 6 5 4 3 2 1 0 1 2 3 4 5 6 7 8 9 1 | Std Error |
|---|---|---|---|---|
| 0 | 1.200715 | 1.00000 | &#124;********************&#124; | 0 |
| 1 | 0.370658 | 0.30665 | &#124;****** | 0.091670 |
| 2 | -0.078249 | -.06474 | *&#124; | 0.099919 |
| 3 | -0.086619 | -.07166 | *&#124; | 0.100271 |
| 4 | 0.126391 | 0.10457 | &#124;** | 0.100700 |
| 5 | 0.101691 | 0.08413 | &#124;** | 0.101609 |
| 6 | 0.027608 | 0.02284 | &#124; | 0.102192 |
| 7 | -0.160292 | -.13261 | ***&#124; | 0.102235 |
| 8 | -0.143891 | -.11904 | **&#124; | 0.103671 |
| 9 | -0.210121 | -.17384 | ***&#124; | 0.104813 |
| 10 | -0.142910 | -.11823 | **&#124; | 0.107209 |
| 11 | -0.062396 | -.05162 | *&#124; | 0.108299 |
| 12 | 0.025252 | 0.02089 | &#124; | 0.108505 |
| 13 | 0.049984 | 0.04135 | &#124;* | 0.108539 |
| 14 | 0.023417 | 0.01937 | &#124; | 0.108672 |

"." marks two standard errors

**FIGURE 9.8** MINITAB output of the SAC for the first differences of paper towel sales

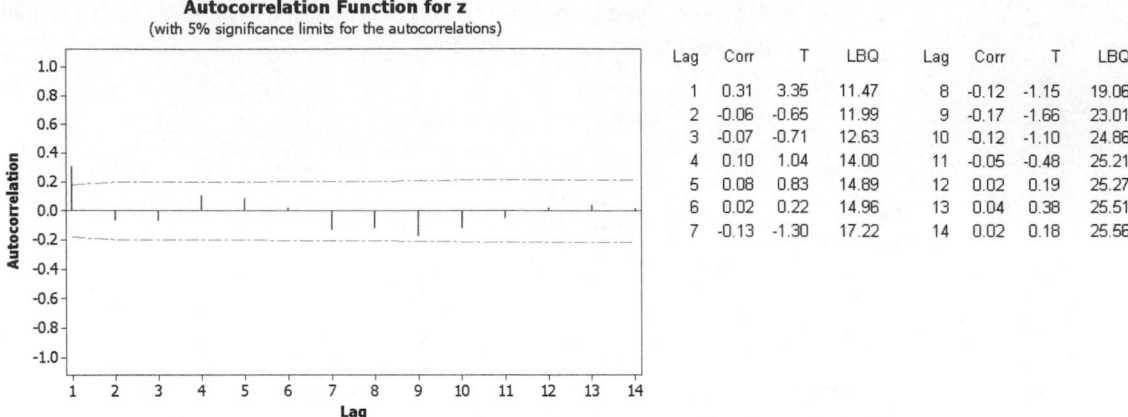

| Lag | Corr | T | LBQ | Lag | Corr | T | LBQ |
|---|---|---|---|---|---|---|---|
| 1 | 0.31 | 3.35 | 11.47 | 8 | -0.12 | -1.15 | 19.06 |
| 2 | -0.06 | -0.65 | 11.99 | 9 | -0.17 | -1.66 | 23.01 |
| 3 | -0.07 | -0.71 | 12.63 | 10 | -0.12 | -1.10 | 24.86 |
| 4 | 0.10 | 1.04 | 14.00 | 11 | -0.05 | -0.48 | 25.21 |
| 5 | 0.08 | 0.83 | 14.89 | 12 | 0.02 | 0.19 | 25.27 |
| 6 | 0.02 | 0.22 | 14.96 | 13 | 0.04 | 0.38 | 25.51 |
| 7 | -0.13 | -1.30 | 17.22 | 14 | 0.02 | 0.18 | 25.56 |

# The Sample Partial Autocorrelation Function (SPAC)

We now present formulas for the **sample partial autocorrelation at lag $k$, $r_{kk}$,** the standard error of $r_{kk}$, and the related $t$-statistic [see (3) below], and we define the **sample partial autocorrelation function** (which we henceforth refer to as the **SPAC**).

1. The **sample partial autocorrelation at lag $k$** is

$$r_{kk} = \begin{cases} r_1 & \text{if } k = 1 \\[2ex] \dfrac{r_k - \sum_{j=1}^{k-1} r_{k-1,j} r_{k-j}}{1 - \sum_{j=1}^{k-1} r_{k-1,j} r_j} & \text{if } k = 2, 3, \ldots \end{cases}$$

   where

$$r_{kj} = r_{k-1,j} - r_{kk} r_{k-1,k-j} \quad \text{for} \quad j = 1, 2, \ldots, k-1$$

2. The **standard error of $r_{kk}$** is

$$s_{r_{kk}} = 1/(n - b + 1)^{1/2}$$

3. The **$t_{r_{kk}}$-statistic** is

$$t_{r_{kk}} = \frac{r_{kk}}{s_{r_{kk}}}$$

4. The **sample partial autocorrelation function (SPAC)** is a listing, or graph, of the sample partial autocorrelations at lags $k = 1, 2, \ldots$.

It is beyond the scope of this text to give a precise interpretation of the sample partial autocorrelation at lag $k$. However, this quantity may intuitively be thought of as the sample autocorrelation of time series observations separated by a lag of $k$ time units *with the effects of the intervening observations eliminated.*

Again, in order to employ the Box–Jenkins methodology, we must examine and attempt to classify the behavior of the SPAC. The SPAC, like the SAC, can display a variety of different behaviors. First, the SPAC for a nonseasonal time series can **cut off.** To see what we mean by this, we say that a **spike at lag $k$** exists in the SPAC if $r_{kk}$, the sample partial autocorrelation at lag $k$, is statistically large. Concluding that $r_{kk}$ is statistically large is basically equivalent to rejecting the null hypothesis that the **theoretical partial autocorrelation at lag $k$,** which we denote as $\rho_{kk}$, equals zero. We can judge whether a spike at lag $k$ exists in the SPAC by looking at the $t$-statistic related to $r_{kk}$. Here we consider a spike at lag $k$ to exist in the SPAC if the absolute value of

$$ t_{r_{kk}} = \frac{r_{kk}}{s_{r_{kk}}} $$

is *greater than 2.* Moreover, we say that the SPAC **cuts off after lag $k$** if there are no spikes at lags greater than $k$ in the SPAC. For nonseasonal data, experience shows that if the SPAC cuts off, it generally does so after a lag that is less than or equal to 2. Second, we say that the SPAC **dies down** if this function does not cut off but rather decreases in a "steady fashion." As illustrated in Figure 9.5, the SPAC can die down in (1) a damped exponential fashion (with no oscillation or with oscillation), (2) a damped sine-wave fashion, or (3) a fashion dominated by either one of or a combination of (1) and (2). In later sections of this book, we will see how the behavior of the SPAC (as well as the behavior of the SAC) helps us to identify Box–Jenkins models.

**EXAMPLE 9.5**   Again consider the first differences of the Absorbent Paper Towel sales given in Table 9.2. The SPAC for these first differences is obtained by calculating the sample partial autocorrelation at lag $k$ for lags $k = 1, 2, 3, \ldots$. The sample partial autocorrelations $r_{11}$, $r_{22}$, $r_{33}$, and $r_{44}$ are computed as follows. Recall that

$$ r_{kk} = \begin{cases} r_1 & \text{if } k = 1 \\[2mm] \dfrac{r_k - \displaystyle\sum_{j=1}^{k-1} r_{k-1,j} r_{k-j}}{1 - \displaystyle\sum_{j=1}^{k-1} r_{k-1,j} r_j} & \text{if } k = 2, 3, \ldots \end{cases} $$

where

$$ r_{kj} = r_{k-1,j} - r_{kk} r_{k-1,k-j} \quad \text{for} \quad j = 1, 2, \ldots, k-1 $$

It follows that

$$r_{11} = r_1 = .307 \approx .31$$

$$r_{22} = \frac{r_2 - \sum_{j=1}^{2-1} r_{2-1,j} r_{2-j}}{1 - \sum_{j=1}^{2-1} r_{2-1,j} r_j} = \frac{r_2 - r_{11} r_1}{1 - r_1 r_1} = \frac{-.06 - (.31)(.31)}{1 - (.31)(.31)}$$

$$= -.18$$

$$r_{21} = r_{11} - r_{22} r_{11} = .31 - (-.18)(.31)$$

$$= .37$$

$$r_{33} = \frac{r_3 - \sum_{j=1}^{3-1} r_{3-1,j} r_{3-j}}{1 - \sum_{j=1}^{3-1} r_{3-1,j} r_j} = \frac{r_3 - (r_{21} r_2 + r_{22} r_1)}{1 - (r_{21} r_1 + r_{22} r_2)}$$

$$= \frac{-.07 - [(.37)(-.06) + (-.18)(.31)]}{1 - [(.37)(.31) + (-.18)(-.06)]}$$

$$= .01$$

$$r_{31} = r_{21} - r_{33} r_{22} = .37 - (.01)(-.18)$$

$$= .37$$

$$r_{32} = r_{22} - r_{33} r_{21} = -.18 - (.01)(.37)$$

$$= -.18$$

$$r_{44} = \frac{r_4 - \sum_{j=1}^{4-1} r_{4-1,j} r_{4-j}}{1 - \sum_{j=1}^{4-1} r_{4-1,j} r_j} = \frac{r_4 - (r_{31} r_3 + r_{32} r_2 + r_{33} r_1)}{1 - (r_{31} r_1 + r_{32} r_2 + r_{33} r_3)}$$

$$= \frac{.10 - [(.37)(-.07) + (-.18)(-.06) + (.01)(.31)]}{1 - [(.37)(.31) + (-.18)(-.06) + (.01)(-.07)]} = .13$$

In Figure 9.9 we present the SAS output of the SPAC for the first differences of the Absorbent Paper Towel sales. In Figure 9.10 we present the MINITAB output of the SPAC for these first differences. Although neither output gives $s_{r_{kk}}$, we can calculate this standard deviation as follows:

$$s_{r_{kk}} = \frac{1}{(n - b + 1)^{1/2}} = \frac{1}{(120 - 2 + 1)^{1/2}} = .09167 \quad \text{for} \quad k = 1, 2, \ldots$$

For any lag $k$, the dot on the SAS output to the left of the centerline is $2(s_{r_{kk}})$ less than 0, and the dot to the right of the centerline is $2(s_{r_{kk}})$ greater than 0. When analyzing the SPAC, the two-standard-deviation dotted bands are interpreted in the same way that they are when analyzing the SAC. Therefore, the SPAC in Figure 9.9 has a spike at lag 1 because

**FIGURE 9.9**

SAS output of the SPAC for the first differences of paper towel sales

**FIGURE 9.10** MINITAB output of the SPAC for the first differences of paper towel sales

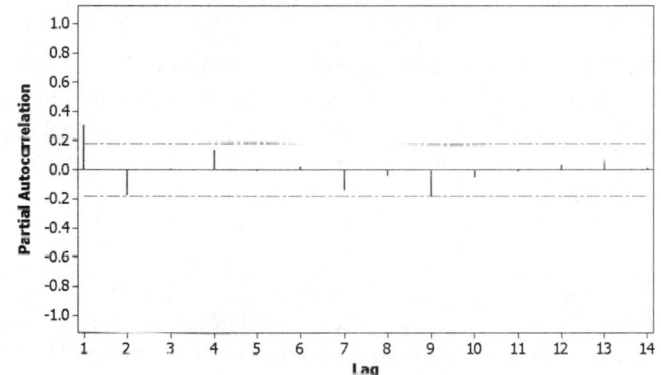

the last asterisk corresponding to $r_{11}$ is beyond the two-standard-deviation dot, which implies that $|t_{r_{11}}|$ exceeds 2. To verify this, note that

$$t_{r_{11}} = \frac{r_{11}}{s_{r_{11}}} = \frac{.30665}{.09167}$$

$$= 3.345$$

The last asterisk corresponding to $r_{22}$ coincides with the two-standard-deviation dot. However, since

$$|t_{r_{22}}| = \left| \frac{r_{22}}{s_{r_{22}}} \right| = \left| \frac{-.17525}{.09167} \right|$$

$$= 1.912$$

is slightly less than 2, and since there are no spikes in the SPAC at lags greater than 2, we might conclude that the SPAC has a spike at lag 1 and cuts off after lag 1. However, since the partial autocorrelations at lags 2 and 4 are fairly large, the cutoff is not very abrupt. Specifically, comparing the SAC of Figure 9.7 with the SPAC of Figure 9.9, we can say that (particularly at low lags) the SAC seems to cut off more abruptly than the SPAC. Since the cutoff in this SPAC is not very definite, we might also conclude that (particularly at low lags) this SPAC dies down in a fashion "dominated" by damped exponential decay (with oscillation). In the next section we see how to use the behaviors of the SAC of Figure 9.7 and the SPAC of Figure 9.9 to tentatively identify a model describing the first differences of the Absorbent Paper Towel sales.

# 9.3 AN INTRODUCTION TO NONSEASONAL MODELING AND FORECASTING

Once we have transformed the original time series $y_1, y_2, \ldots, y_n$ into stationary time series values $z_b, z_{b+1}, \ldots, z_n$, we use the SAC and SPAC to identify a Box–Jenkins model describing the stationary time series values. Two useful types of Box–Jenkins models are **autoregressive models** and **moving average models.** To introduce autoregressive models, we consider the **nonseasonal autoregressive model of order 1**

$$z_t = \phi_1 z_{t-1} + a_t$$

This model says that $z_t$ is a constant multiple of $z_{t-1}$, the time series value in the previous period, plus a **random shock**[†] $a_t$ that describes the effect of all factors other than $z_{t-1}$ on $z_t$. The constant $\phi_1$ relating $z_t$ to $z_{t-1}$ is an unknown parameter that must be estimated from sample data. The random shock $a_t$ is a value that is assumed to have been randomly selected from a *normal distribution* that has *mean zero* and a *variance* that is the *same* for each and every time period $t$. Moreover, the random shocks $a_1, a_2, a_3, \ldots$ in different time periods are assumed to be *statistically independent* of each other. We determine how to check the validity of these assumptions as we proceed through this book.

A less intuitive but equally useful model is the **nonseasonal moving average model of order 1**

$$z_t = a_t - \theta_1 a_{t-1}$$

This model says that $z_t$ equals $a_t$, a random shock corresponding to time period $t$, minus a constant multiple of $a_{t-1}$, a random shock corresponding to time period $t - 1$. The constant $\theta_1$ relating $z_t$ to $a_{t-1}$ is an unknown parameter that must be estimated from sample data. Furthermore, the random shocks are assumed to have the same properties that they have in the autoregressive model of order 1. To better understand the moving average model of order 1, suppose (for example) that the stationary time

---

[†]This text employs two fonts—one for the text discussions and exercises, and another for the examples and figures. In the text discussions and exercises a random shock is denoted as $a_t$ (as on this page). In the examples and figures a random shock is denoted as $a_t$ (as in Figure 9.11).

series values

$$z_2 = -.5936$$
$$z_3 = .5319$$
$$\vdots$$
$$z_{120} = .3043$$

in Table 9.2 are described by this model. This implies that

$$z_2 = a_2 - \theta_1 a_1$$
$$z_3 = a_3 - \theta_1 a_2$$
$$\vdots$$
$$z_{120} = a_{120} - \theta_1 a_{119}$$

We now consider how the random shocks $a_1$, $a_2$, and $a_3$ corresponding to time periods 1, 2, and 3 determine the time series values $z_2$ and $z_3$. Although we have observed the time series values $z_2 = -.5936$ and $z_3 = .5319$, we cannot know the true values of the random shocks $a_1$, $a_2$, and $a_3$. However, for the purposes of illustration, assume (a supernatural power knows) that the true value of the parameter $\theta_1$ is $-.3489$ and the true values of the random shocks $a_1$, $a_2$, and $a_3$—which are assumed to have been randomly and independently selected from three normal distributions having mean zero and a constant variance—are (see Figure 9.11)

$$a_1 - .0533 \qquad a_2 = -.6122 \quad \text{and} \quad a_3 = .7455$$

It follows that these random shocks have determined the values $z_2 = -.5936$ and $z_3 = .5319$ through the equations

$$z_2 = a_2 - \theta_1 a_1 = -.6122 - (-.3489)(.0533) = -.5936$$

and

$$z_3 = a_3 - \theta_1 a_2 = .7455 - (-.3489)(-.6122) = .5319$$

It is not intuitively obvious why the nonseasonal moving average model of order 1

$$z_t = a_t - \theta_1 a_{t-1}$$

would adequately represent a stationary time series. However, this and other Box–Jenkins models provide effective representations of many real-world time series.

**FIGURE 9.11**
The random shocks
$a_1$, $a_2$, and $a_3$

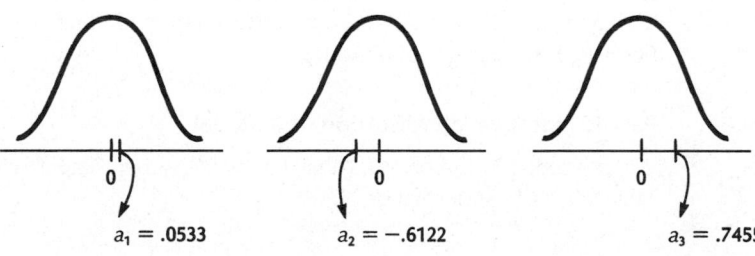

$a_1 = .0533$ $\qquad$ $a_2 = -.6122$ $\qquad$ $a_3 = .7455$

Although there are many Box–Jenkins models, each such model is characterized by its **theoretical autocorrelation function (TAC)** and its **theoretical partial autocorrelation function (TPAC).**

---

1. The **theoretical autocorrelation function (TAC)** of a model is a listing of the theoretical autocorrelations $\rho_1, \rho_2, \dots$ of time series observations described by the model.

2. The **theoretical partial autocorrelation function (TPAC)** of a model is a listing of the theoretical partial autocorrelations $\rho_{11}, \rho_{22}, \dots$ of time series observations described by the model.

---

As an example, for the nonseasonal moving average model of order 1

$$z_t = a_t - \theta_1 a_{t-1}$$

the following can be proved:

1. The TAC has a nonzero autocorrelation at lag 1 and has zero autocorrelations at all lags after lag 1 (that is, *cuts off after lag 1*). Specifically,

$$\rho_1 = \frac{-\theta_1}{1 + \theta_1^2}$$
$$\rho_k = 0 \quad \text{for} \quad k > 1$$

2. The TPAC *dies down* (that is, the values $\rho_{11}, \rho_{22}, \dots$ decrease) in a fashion dominated by damped exponential decay.

It can also be proved that for the nonseasonal autoregressive model of order 1,

1. The TAC dies down in a damped exponential fashion. Specifically,

$$\rho_k = (\phi_1)^k \quad \text{for} \quad k \geq 1$$

2. The TPAC has a nonzero partial autocorrelation at lag 1 and zero partial autocorrelations at all lags after lag 1 (that is, cuts off after lag 1).

Noting that $r_k$ and $r_{kk}$, *the sample autocorrelation* and *sample partial autocorrelation of the time series values* $z_b, z_{b+1}, \dots, z_n$ *at lag k, are the point estimates of* $\rho_k$ *and* $\rho_{kk}$, it follows that **the SAC and SPAC are the estimates of the TAC and TPAC.** Therefore, if the behavior of the SAC and SPAC of the time series values $z_b, z_{b+1}, \dots, z_n$ is consistent with (that is, similar to) the behavior of the TAC and TPAC of a particular model, then we should tentatively conclude that the time series values are described by the particular model.

**EXAMPLE 9.6**     **Part 1: Tentative Identification of a Model**

We concluded in Example 9.4 that for the Absorbent Paper Towel sales time series in Table 9.1, the transformation

$$z_t = y_t - y_{t-1}$$

produces stationary time series values. Recall that the SAC and SPAC of these stationary first differences are given in Figures 9.7 and 9.9. Also recall that we previously concluded that the SAC has a spike at lag 1 and cuts off after lag 1, and that the SPAC either (1) has a spike at lag 1 and cuts off after lag 1 or (2) dies down fairly quickly in a fashion dominated by damped exponential decay. In general, for nonseasonal data a SAC and SPAC can both die down fairly quickly or can both (appear to) cut off fairly quickly. However, in most situations, if one of these functions cuts off fairly quickly, the other will die down fairly quickly. Therefore, if both of these functions can be interpreted as cutting off, it is useful to decide which of these functions cuts off more abruptly (this usually means that the other function is dying down).

In Example 9.5 we noted that the SAC of Figure 9.7 seems to cut off more abruptly (especially at low lags) than the SPAC of Figure 9.9. It follows that it is reasonable to conclude that the SAC of Figure 9.7 has a spike at lag 1 and cuts off after lag 1. Since both the SAC and SPAC seldom cut off simultaneously, it is also reasonable to conclude that the SPAC dies down fairly quickly in a fashion dominated by damped exponential decay. Since this behavior of the SAC and SPAC is similar to the behavior of the TAC and TPAC of the nonseasonal moving average model of order 1

$$z_t = a_t - \theta_1 a_{t-1}$$

it follows that this model is a reasonable tentative model describing $z_t = y_t - y_{t-1}$. Therefore, a reasonable tentative model describing $y_t$ is

$$y_t - y_{t-1} = a_t - \theta_1 a_{t-1} \quad \text{or} \quad y_t = y_{t-1} + a_t - \theta_1 a_{t-1}$$

### Part 2: The Least Squares Point Estimate of the Model Parameter $\theta_1$

Having tentatively identified a model describing the Absorbent Paper Towel sales time series, we must now estimate the value of the model parameter $\theta_1$. Using the data of Table 9.1 and SAS, the **least squares point estimate** of $\theta_1$ in the above model can be calculated to be $\hat{\theta}_1 = -.3534$. To explain what we mean by the term "least squares," suppose that we have observed the time series values $y_1, y_2, \ldots, y_{t-1}$. In addition, suppose that we have used these $t - 1$ values, $y_1, y_2, \ldots, y_{t-1}$, to find $\hat{y}_t$, the point prediction of the future time series value $y_t$. After we observe $y_t$, we can find the point prediction of the random shock $a_t$ by computing

$$\hat{a}_t = y_t - \hat{y}_t$$

This is called the $t$th residual and is the difference between the actual value $y_t$ and its point prediction $\hat{y}_t$. The point prediction of

$$y_t = y_{t-1} + a_t - \theta_1 a_{t-1}$$

is

$$\hat{y}_t = y_{t-1} + \hat{a}_t - \hat{\theta}_1 \hat{a}_{t-1}$$

Here

1.  The point prediction $\hat{a}_t$ of the future random shock $a_t$ is zero.
2.  The point prediction $\hat{a}_{t-1}$ of the past random shock $a_{t-1}$ is the $(t - 1)$st residual $(y_{t-1} - \hat{y}_{t-1})$ if we can calculate $\hat{y}_{t-1}$ and is zero if we cannot calculate $\hat{y}_{t-1}$.

Using $\hat{\theta}_1 = -.3534$, we now calculate (when possible) the first three residuals for the Absorbent Paper Towel sales time series of Table 9.1. We start at the beginning of the historical data and attempt to predict $y_1$, the sales value in time period 1, from time origin 0. We do this by setting $t$ equal to 1 in the equation for $\hat{y}_t$. This gives us the equation

$$\hat{y}_1 = y_0 + \hat{a}_1 - (-.3534)\hat{a}_0$$

Since we have not observed $y_0$ (that is, since there is no sales value for week 0), we cannot calculate $\hat{y}_1$, and thus cannot calculate $(y_1 - \hat{y}_1)$, the first residual. We next attempt to predict $y_2$ from time origin 1. Setting $t$ equal to 2 in the equation for $\hat{y}_t$, we obtain the equation

$$\hat{y}_2 = y_1 + \hat{a}_2 - (-.3534)\hat{a}_1$$
$$= 15 + 0 + .3534(0) = 15$$

Here we have used the sales value $y_1 = 15$ in Table 9.1, and we have set $\hat{a}_1$ equal to 0 because we were not able to calculate the first residual in the previous step. Using the sales value $y_2 = 14.4064$ in Table 9.1, we are able to calculate

$$\hat{a}_2 = y_2 - \hat{y}_2 = 14.4064 - 15 = -.5936$$

Furthermore, using this second residual we can predict $y_3$ from time origin 2 as follows:

$$\hat{y}_3 = y_2 + \hat{a}_3 + .3534\hat{a}_2$$
$$= 14.4064 + .3534(-.5936) = 14.1966$$

and find

$$\hat{a}_3 = y_3 - \hat{y}_3 = 14.9383 - 14.1966 = .7417$$

If we continue this process of making one-period-ahead predictions, we eventually find that the point prediction of $y_{120}$ from time origin 119 is $\hat{y}_{120} = 14.956$. Thus the residual for time period 120 is

$$\hat{a}_{120} = y_{120} - \hat{y}_{120} = 15.6453 - 14.956 = .6893$$

When we say that $\hat{\theta}_1 = -.3534$ is the **least squares estimate** of $\theta_1$, we mean that $\hat{\theta}_1 = -.3534$ minimizes the quantity

$$\text{SSE} = \sum_{t=2}^{120} \hat{a}_t^2 = \sum_{t=2}^{120} (y_t - \hat{y}_t)^2$$

That is, $\hat{\theta}_1 = -.3534$ makes the sum of squared differences between the observed time series values and the predictions (given by the prediction equation $\hat{y}_t = y_{t-1} + \hat{a}_t + .3534\hat{a}_{t-1}$) of these time series values smaller than the value of SSE that would be obtained by using any other value of $\hat{\theta}_1$.

### Part 3: Using the Model to Forecast Future Time Series Values

Having estimated the parameter $\theta_1$, the next step is to use various diagnostics to check the adequacy of the tentative model

$$y_t = y_{t-1} + a_t - \theta_1 a_{t-1}$$

We do this in Chapter 10 and find that this is a reasonable final model, which implies that we should use this model to forecast future time series values.

In order to compute forecasts of future Absorbent Paper Towel sales, we recall that the point prediction of

$$y_t = y_{t-1} + a_t - \theta_1 a_{t-1}$$

is

$$\hat{y}_t = y_{t-1} + \hat{a}_t - \hat{\theta}_1 \hat{a}_{t-1}$$

Here

1. The point prediction $\hat{a}_t$ of the future random shock $a_t$ is zero.
2. The point prediction $\hat{a}_{t-1}$ of the past random shock $a_{t-1}$ is the $(t - 1)$st residual $(y_{t-1} - \hat{y}_{t-1})$ if we can calculate $\hat{y}_{t-1}$, and is zero if we cannot calculate $\hat{y}_{t-1}$.

Since we have observed 120 values of the Absorbent Paper Towel sales time series, we say that we are at "time origin 120." Since the equation

$$y_t = y_{t-1} + a_t - \theta_1 a_{t-1}$$

implies that

$$y_{121} = y_{120} + a_{121} - \theta_1 a_{120}$$

it follows that a point forecast of $y_{121}$ made at time origin 120 is

$$\begin{aligned}
\hat{y}_{121}(120) &= y_{120} + \hat{a}_{121} - \hat{\theta}_1 \hat{a}_{120} \\
&= y_{120} + 0 - (-.3534)(y_{120} - \hat{y}_{120}) = 15.6453 + .3534(.6893) \\
&= 15.8889
\end{aligned}$$

Furthermore, using SAS it can be shown that a 95% prediction interval forecast of $y_{121}$ is

$$[15.8889 - 2.0372, 15.8889 + 2.0372] \quad \text{or} \quad [13.8517, 17.9261]$$

To explain the meaning of "95% confidence," note that if the actual observation at time 121 is $y_{121} = 16.1099$, then this future observation is contained in the 95% prediction interval [13.8517, 17.9261], which is based on the first 120 time series observations. For this reason we say that the prediction interval–future value combination

$$\{[13.8517, 17.9261]; \quad y_{121} = 16.1099\}$$

is *successful*. Another realization of the Absorbent Paper Towel sales time series (that is, another time series generated by the model $y_t = y_{t-1} + a_t - \theta_1 a_{t-1}$ and a different sequence of random shocks) would yield a different 95% prediction interval based on the first 120 time series observations and a different future observation ($y_{121}$). If another realization yielded the 95% prediction interval [12.7654, 16.8211] and the future observation $y_{121} = 16.9712$, then the combination

$$\{[12.7654, 16.8211]; \quad y_{121} = 16.9712\}$$

would be *unsuccessful*, because the future observation $y_{121} = 16.9712$ is not contained in the 95% prediction interval [12.7654, 16.8211]. Since there are an infinite number of possible realizations of the Absorbent Paper Towel sales time series, there is an infinite population of possible prediction interval–future value combinations (where the prediction intervals are based on 95% confidence). The interpretation of "95% confidence" here is that 95% of the prediction interval–future value combinations in this population are successful, while 5% of the prediction interval–future value combinations in this population are unsuccessful. Therefore, before we calculate the 95% prediction interval based on the first 120 observations and before we subsequently observe $y_{121}$, we can be 95% confident that we will be successful (that is, obtain a 95% prediction interval such that $y_{121}$ is contained in our interval). This is because 95% of the prediction interval–future value combinations in the population of all such combinations are successful, and because we know that we will obtain one prediction interval–future value combination in this population.

Continuing, since

$$y_{122} = y_{121} + a_{122} - \theta_1 a_{121}$$

it follows that a point forecast of $y_{122}$ made at time origin 120 is

$$\begin{aligned}
\hat{y}_{122}(120) &= \hat{y}_{121}(120) + \hat{a}_{122} - \hat{\theta}_1 \hat{a}_{121} \\
&= 15.8889 + 0 - (-.3534)(0) \\
&= 15.8889
\end{aligned}$$

Note that in making the above point forecast, we used the previously calculated point forecast $\hat{y}_{121}(120) = 15.8889$ because we have not observed $y_{121}$. We have also set the point prediction $\hat{a}_{121}$ of $a_{121}$ equal to zero because, not having observed $y_{121}$, we cannot calculate the residual $y_{121} - \hat{y}_{121}(120)$. Furthermore, it can be shown that a 95% prediction interval forecast of $y_{122}$ is

$$[15.8889 - 3.4281, 15.8889 + 3.4281] = [12.4608, 19.3170]$$

In general, since

$$y_{120+\tau} = y_{120+\tau-1} + a_{120+\tau} - \theta_1 a_{120+\tau-1}$$

it follows that a point forecast of $y_{120+\tau}$ made at time origin 120 is, for $\tau \geq 2$,

$$\begin{aligned}
\hat{y}_{120+\tau}(120) &= \hat{y}_{120+\tau-1}(120) + \hat{a}_{120+\tau} - \hat{\theta}_1 \hat{a}_{120+\tau-1} \\
&= 15.8889 + 0 - (-.3534)(0) \\
&= 15.8889
\end{aligned}$$

Furthermore, the larger $\tau$ is, the wider is the 95% prediction interval forecast of $y_{120+\tau}$.

Assume now that the actual observation at time 121 is $y_{121} = 16.1099$. Then, although the only way to update the point estimate of $\theta_1$ is to refit the entire model, we can obtain a new point forecast of $y_{122}$ by using the current point estimate of $\theta_1$. Since the one-period-ahead forecast error (or residual) is

$$y_{121} - \hat{y}_{121}(120) = 16.1099 - 15.8889 = .221$$

and since

$$y_{122} = y_{121} + a_{122} - \theta_1 a_{121}$$

the point forecast of $y_{122}$ made at time origin 121 is

$$\hat{y}_{122}(121) = y_{121} + \hat{a}_{122} - \hat{\theta}_1 \hat{a}_{121}$$
$$= y_{121} + 0 - (-.3534)(y_{121} - \hat{y}_{121}(120)) = 16.1099 + .3534(.221)$$
$$= 16.1880$$

Moreover, since

$$y_{123} = y_{122} + a_{123} - \theta_1 a_{122}$$

a point forecast of $y_{123}$ made at time origin 121 is

$$\hat{y}_{123}(121) = \hat{y}_{122}(121) + \hat{a}_{123} - \hat{\theta}_1 \hat{a}_{122}$$
$$= 16.1880 + 0 - (-.3534)(0)$$
$$= 16.1880$$

It is sometimes appropriate to include a **constant term $\delta$** in a Box–Jenkins model. If we include a constant term in the *nonseasonal moving average model of order 1*, we obtain the model

$$z_t = \delta + a_t - \theta_1 a_{t-1}$$

In this case it can be proved that $\delta = \mu$, where $\mu$ is the true mean (of all possible realizations) of the stationary time series under consideration. If we include a constant term in the *nonseasonal autoregressive model of order 1*, we obtain the model

$$z_t = \delta + \phi_1 z_{t-1} + a_t$$

In this case it can be proved that $\delta = \mu(1 - \phi_1)$. In general, the constant term $\delta$ in any Box–Jenkins model is a function of the mean $\mu$ of (all possible realizations of) the stationary time series under consideration. Therefore, since the sample mean of the stationary time series values $z_b, z_{b+1}, \ldots, z_n$

$$\bar{z} = \frac{\displaystyle\sum_{t=b}^{n} z_t}{n - b + 1}$$

is one possible point estimate of $\mu$, it follows that if $\bar{z}$ is statistically different from zero, then it is reasonable to assume that $\mu$ does not equal zero and, therefore, to assume that $\delta$ does not equal zero. Thus in such a case it is reasonable to include the constant term $\delta$ in the model. On the other hand, if $\bar{z}$ is not statistically different from zero, it is reasonable to assume that $\mu$ is equal to (or nearly equal to) zero. In such a case we can, therefore, assume that $\delta$ is equal to (or nearly equal to) zero, and we do not include the constant term $\delta$ in the model. One rough rule of thumb is to decide that $\bar{z}$ is statistically different from zero if the absolute value of

$$\frac{\bar{z}}{s_z / \sqrt{n - b + 1}} \quad \text{where} \quad s_z = \left[ \frac{\displaystyle\sum_{t=b}^{n} (z_t - \bar{z})^2}{(n - b + 1) - 1} \right]^{1/2}$$

is greater than 2 (this would lead us to include the constant term $\delta$ in the model). Here the use of this rough rule of thumb yields only "approximately correct" results because the denominator $s_z/\sqrt{n-b+1}$ is only very approximate [see pp. 212–214 of Box, Jenkins, and Reinsel (1994) for a discussion of the theoretically correct denominator]. We discuss a better way to decide whether to include the constant term $\delta$ in a Box–Jenkins model in Chapter 10.

If the stationary time series values $z_b, z_{b+1}, \ldots, z_n$ are the *original time series values* $y_1, y_2, \ldots, y_n$, then the assumption that $\mu$ equals zero implies that these original time series values are fluctuating around a zero mean, whereas the assumption that $\mu$ does not equal zero implies that these original values are fluctuating around a nonzero mean. If the stationary time series values $z_b, z_{b+1}, \ldots, z_n$ are **differences** of the original time series values $y_1, y_2, \ldots, y_n$, then assuming that $\mu$ equals zero is equivalent to assuming that there is no **deterministic trend** (or drift) in the original time series values, whereas assuming that $\mu$ does not equal zero is equivalent to assuming that there is a deterministic trend in those original values. Here the term *deterministic trend* refers to a tendency for the original time series values to *move persistently in a particular direction*. If the constant term $\delta$ is positive, then the deterministic trend is upward, whereas if $\delta$ is negative, then the deterministic trend is downward. If a time series does not exhibit a deterministic trend, then any trend (that is, failure of the time series to exhibit an affinity for a central value) is **stochastic.**

**EXAMPLE 9.7**    We previously concluded that for the Absorbent Paper Towel sales time series in Table 9.1, the nonseasonal moving average model of order 1 is a reasonable tentative model describing the stationary first differences produced by the transformation

$$z_t = y_t - y_{t-1}$$

If we insert a constant term $\delta$ to form the model

$$z_t = \delta + a_t - \theta_1 a_{t-1}$$

then this model implies that

$$y_t - y_{t-1} = \delta + a_t - \theta_1 a_{t-1}$$

or, equivalently, that

$$y_t = \delta + y_{t-1} + a_t - \theta_1 a_{t-1}$$

This last equation says that $y_t$ will move persistently upward by an amount $\delta$ per time period if $\delta$ is greater than 0, or $y_t$ will move persistently downward by an amount $\delta$ per time period if $\delta$ is less than 0. Since $\delta$ is a constant, the trend defined by $\delta$ is called deterministic.

To determine whether $\delta$ should indeed be included in the model, we calculate the mean and standard deviation of the stationary time series values $z_2 = y_2 - y_1$, $z_3 = y_3 - y_2, \ldots, z_{120} = y_{120} - y_{119}$ in Table 9.2 to be

$$\bar{z} = \frac{\displaystyle\sum_{t=b}^{n} z_t}{n-b+1} = \frac{\displaystyle\sum_{t=2}^{120} z_t}{120-2+1}$$

$$= .005423$$

and

$$
s_z = \left[ \frac{\sum_{t=b}^{n} (z_t - \bar{z})^2}{(n - b + 1) - 1} \right]^{1/2} = \left[ \frac{\sum_{t=2}^{120} (z_t - \bar{z})^2}{(120 - 2 + 1) - 1} \right]^{1/2}
$$

$$
= 1.099416
$$

Since the absolute value of

$$
\frac{\bar{z}}{s_z / \sqrt{n - b + 1}} = \frac{.005423}{1.099416 / \sqrt{120 - 2 + 1}}
$$

$$
= .0538
$$

is less than 2, we conclude that $\bar{z}$ is not statistically different from zero, which implies that we should not include $\delta(= \mu)$ in the model.

The fact that we have decided to not include $\delta$ in the model

$$
z_t = a_t - \theta_1 a_{t-1}
$$

implies that this model assumes that the original time series values, which are plotted in Figure 9.1(a), do not exhibit a deterministic trend. Therefore, since Figure 9.1(a) shows that the original time series values do not exhibit an affinity for a central value, it follows that the trend exhibited by these nonstationary time series values is stochastic. Moreover, since examination of Figure 9.1(a) and (b) indicates that using the transformation

$$
z_t = y_t - y_{t-1}
$$

has reduced the nonstationary time series values $y_1, y_2, \ldots, y_{120}$ to stationary time series values $z_2 = y_2 - y_1, z_3 = y_3 - y_2, \ldots, z_{120} = y_{120} - y_{119}$, we can say that using this transformation has modeled the stochastic trend.

# 9.4 TENTATIVE IDENTIFICATION OF NONSEASONAL BOX–JENKINS MODELS

The nonseasonal moving average model of order 1 and the nonseasonal autoregressive model of order 1 are only two of many nonseasonal Box–Jenkins models. In this section we present a general discussion of nonseasonal **moving average models, autoregressive models,** and **mixed models.** We also consider how to tentatively identify such models. In expressing these models we will arbitrarily include a constant term $\delta$. However, we will see that for any nonseasonal model, $\delta$ is a function of $\mu$, the true mean of all possible values of the stationary time series described by the model. Therefore, as discussed in the previous section, we should tentatively include $\delta$ in the model only if $\bar{z}$ is statistically different from zero.

# Nonseasonal Moving Average Models

The model

$$z_t = \delta + a_t - \theta_1 a_{t-1} - \theta_2 a_{t-2} - \cdots - \theta_q a_{t-q}$$

is called the **nonseasonal moving average model of order $q$.** The term "moving average" refers to the fact that this model, in addition to using the current random shock $a_t$ (which is used by all Box–Jenkins models), uses the past random shocks $a_{t-1}, a_{t-2}, \ldots,$ $a_{t-q}$. Here $\theta_1, \theta_2, \ldots, \theta_q$ are unknown parameters relating $z_t$ to $a_{t-1}, a_{t-2}, \ldots, a_{t-q}$. Each random shock $a_t$ is a value that is assumed to have been randomly selected from a *normal distribution* that has *mean zero* and a *variance* that is the *same* for each and every time period $t$. Furthermore, the random shocks $a_1, a_2, a_3, \ldots$ are assumed to be *statistically independent*. These random shock assumptions are assumed to hold for all Box–Jenkins models in this book.

It can be proved that for the nonseasonal moving average model of order $q$, $\delta = \mu$. It can also be shown that for this model

1. The **TAC** has nonzero autocorrelations at lags $1, 2, \ldots, q$ and has zero autocorrelations at all lags after $q$ (that is, **cuts off after lag $q$**). Said equivalently,

$$\rho_k \neq 0 \quad \text{for} \quad k = 1, 2, \ldots, q$$

$$\rho_k = 0 \quad \text{for} \quad k > q$$

2. The **TPAC dies down** (that is, the values $\rho_{11}, \rho_{22}, \ldots$ decrease in a steady fashion).

Therefore, if for the time series values $z_b, z_{b+1}, \ldots, z_n$

i. the SAC has spikes at lags $1, 2, \ldots, q$ and *cuts off* after lag $q$, and

ii. the SPAC *dies down*, then

we should tentatively conclude that the time series values are described by the nonseasonal moving average model of order $q$.

For example, it can be proved that for the nonseasonal moving average model of order 1

$$z_t = \delta + a_t - \theta_1 a_{t-1}$$

1. The TAC has a nonzero autocorrelation at lag 1 and has zero autocorrelations at all lags after lag 1 (that is, *cuts off* after lag 1). Specifically,

$$\rho_1 = \frac{-\theta_1}{1 + \theta_1^2} \quad \text{and} \quad \rho_k = 0 \quad \text{for} \quad k > 1$$

2. The TPAC *dies down* (that is, the values $\rho_{11}, \rho_{22}, \ldots$ decrease) in a fashion dominated by damped exponential decay.

Therefore, if the SAC has a spike at lag 1 and cuts off after lag 1 and the SPAC dies down (as was the case for the first differences of Absorbent Paper Towel sales), then we should tentatively conclude that the time series values under consideration are described by the nonseasonal moving average model of order 1.

As another example, it can be proved that for the nonseasonal moving average model of order 2

$$z_t = \delta + a_t - \theta_1 a_{t-1} - \theta_2 a_{t-2}$$

1. The TAC has nonzero autocorrelations at lags 1 and 2 and has zero auto-correlations at all lags after lag 2 (that is, *cuts off* after lag 2). Specifically,

$$\rho_1 = \frac{-\theta_1(1 - \theta_1)}{1 + \theta_1^2 + \theta_2^2}$$

$$\rho_2 = \frac{-\theta_2}{1 + \theta_1^2 + \theta_2^2}$$

$$\rho_k = 0 \quad \text{for} \quad k > 2$$

2. The TPAC *dies down* (that is, the values $\rho_{11}, \rho_{22}, \ldots$ decrease) according to a mixture of damped exponentials and/or damped sine waves.

Therefore, if the SAC has spikes at lags 1 and 2 and cuts off after lag 2 and the SPAC dies down, then we should tentatively conclude that the time series values under consideration are described by the nonseasonal moving average model of order 2.

## Nonseasonal Autoregressive Models

The model

$$z_t = \delta + \phi_1 z_{t-1} + \phi_2 z_{t-2} + \cdots + \phi_p z_{t-p} + a_t$$

is called the **nonseasonal autoregressive model of order $p$.** The term "autoregressive" refers to the fact that this model expresses the current time series value $z_t$ as a function of past time series values $z_{t-1}, z_{t-2}, \ldots, z_{t-p}$. Here $\phi_1, \phi_2, \ldots, \phi_p$ are unknown parameters relating $z_t$ to $z_{t-1}, z_{t-2}, \ldots, z_{t-p}$. It can be proved that for the nonseasonal autoregressive model of order $p$

$$\delta = \mu(1 - \phi_1 - \phi_2 - \cdots - \phi_p)$$

It can also be shown that for this model

1. The **TAC dies down** (that is, the values $\rho_1, \rho_2, \ldots$ decrease in a steady fashion).

2. The **TPAC** has nonzero partial autocorrelations at lags $1, 2, \ldots, p$ and has zero partial autocorrelations at all lags after lag $p$ (that is, **cuts off after lag $p$**). Said equivalently,

$$\rho_{kk} \neq 0 \quad \text{for} \quad k = 1, 2, \ldots, p$$

$$\rho_{kk} = 0 \quad \text{for} \quad k > p$$

Therefore, if for the time series values $z_b, z_{b+1}, \ldots, z_n$

**i.**   the SAC *dies down,* and

**ii.**   the SPAC has spikes at lags $1, 2, \ldots, p$ and *cuts off* after lag $p$, then

we should tentatively conclude that the time series values are described by the non-seasonal autoregressive model of order $p$.

For example, it can be proved that for the nonseasonal autoregressive model of order 1

$$z_t = \delta + \phi_1 z_{t-1} + a_t$$

**1.**   The TAC *dies down* in a damped exponential fashion. Specifically,

$$\rho_k = (\phi_1)^k \quad \text{for} \quad k \geq 1$$

where $\phi_1$ is less than 1.

**2.**   The TPAC has a nonzero partial autocorrelation at lag 1 and zero partial autocorrelations at all lags after lag 1 (that is, *cuts off* after lag 1).

Therefore, if the SAC dies down and the SPAC has a spike at lag 1 and cuts off after lag 1, then we should tentatively conclude that the time series values under consideration are described by the nonseasonal autoregressive model of order 1.

As another example, it can be proved that for the nonseasonal autoregressive model of order 2

$$z_t = \delta + \phi_1 z_{t-1} + \phi_2 z_{t-2} + a_t$$

**1.**   The TAC *dies down* according to a mixture of damped exponentials and/or damped sine waves. Specifically,

$$\rho_1 = \frac{\phi_1}{1 - \phi_2}$$

$$\rho_2 = \frac{\phi_1^2}{1 - \phi_2} + \phi_2$$

$$\rho_k = \phi_1 \rho_{k-1} + \phi_2 \rho_{k-2} \quad \text{for} \quad k \geq 3$$

**2.**   The TPAC has nonzero partial autocorrelations at lags 1 and 2 and zero partial autocorrelations at all lags after lag 2 (that is, *cuts off* after lag 2).

Therefore, if the SAC dies down and the SPAC has spikes at lags 1 and 2 and cuts off after lag 2, then we should tentatively conclude that the time series values under consideration are described by the nonseasonal autoregressive model of order 2.

**EXAMPLE 9.8**   A chemical company produces Chemical Product XB-77-5, a product that must have a rather precisely controlled viscosity. In order to develop a control scheme for its production process, the company needs to develop a forecasting model that will give point forecasts and prediction interval forecasts of the daily viscosity readings of this product.

For the past 95 days the company has recorded daily readings of viscosity. The 95 daily readings, $y_1, y_2, \ldots, y_{95}$, are given in Table 9.4 and are plotted in Figure 9.12. It should be noticed from Figure 9.12 that the original values of the time series seem to fluctuate around a constant mean, and, therefore, seem to be stationary. To determine more precisely whether the original time series values are stationary or nonstationary, consider Figure 9.13, which presents the SAC and SPAC for these original time series values.

**TABLE 9.4  Daily Readings of the Viscosity of Chemical Product XB-77-5**

| t | $y_t$ | t | $y_t$ | t | $y_t$ | t | $y_t$ | t | $y_t$ |
|---|---|---|---|---|---|---|---|---|---|
| 1 | 25.0000 | 20 | 38.2418 | 39 | 33.4246 | 58 | 33.2061 | 77 | 35.9774 |
| 2 | 27.0000 | 21 | 36.8926 | 40 | 33.5719 | 59 | 34.4261 | 78 | 38.0977 |
| 3 | 33.5142 | 22 | 33.8942 | 41 | 35.9222 | 60 | 37.4511 | 79 | 33.4598 |
| 4 | 35.4962 | 23 | 34.1710 | 42 | 33.2125 | 61 | 37.3335 | 80 | 32.9278 |
| 5 | 36.9029 | 24 | 35.4268 | 43 | 37.1668 | 62 | 38.4679 | 81 | 36.5121 |
| 6 | 37.8359 | 25 | 38.5831 | 44 | 35.8138 | 63 | 33.0976 | 82 | 37.4243 |
| 7 | 34.2654 | 26 | 34.6184 | 45 | 33.6847 | 64 | 32.9285 | 83 | 35.1550 |
| 8 | 31.8978 | 27 | 33.9741 | 46 | 33.2761 | 65 | 32.2754 | 84 | 34.4797 |
| 9 | 33.7567 | 28 | 30.2072 | 47 | 38.8163 | 66 | 33.2214 | 85 | 33.2898 |
| 10 | 36.6298 | 29 | 30.5429 | 48 | 42.0838 | 67 | 34.5786 | 86 | 33.9252 |
| 11 | 36.3518 | 30 | 34.8686 | 49 | 40.0069 | 68 | 32.3448 | 87 | 36.1036 |
| 12 | 40.0762 | 31 | 35.8892 | 50 | 33.4514 | 69 | 31.5316 | 88 | 36.7351 |
| 13 | 38.0928 | 32 | 35.2035 | 51 | 30.8413 | 70 | 37.8044 | 89 | 35.4576 |
| 14 | 34.5412 | 33 | 34.4337 | 52 | 30.0655 | 71 | 36.0536 | 90 | 37.5924 |
| 15 | 34.8567 | 34 | 35.4844 | 53 | 37.0544 | 72 | 35.7297 | 91 | 34.4895 |
| 16 | 34.5316 | 35 | 33.2381 | 54 | 39.0982 | 73 | 36.7991 | 92 | 39.1692 |
| 17 | 32.3851 | 36 | 36.1684 | 55 | 37.9075 | 74 | 34.9502 | 93 | 35.8242 |
| 18 | 32.6058 | 37 | 34.4116 | 56 | 36.2393 | 75 | 33.5246 | 94 | 32.3875 |
| 19 | 34.8913 | 38 | 33.7668 | 57 | 34.9535 | 76 | 35.1012 | 95 | 31.2846 |

$$\bar{y} = 34.93$$

**FIGURE 9.12**
Daily readings of the viscosity of Chemical Product XB-77-5

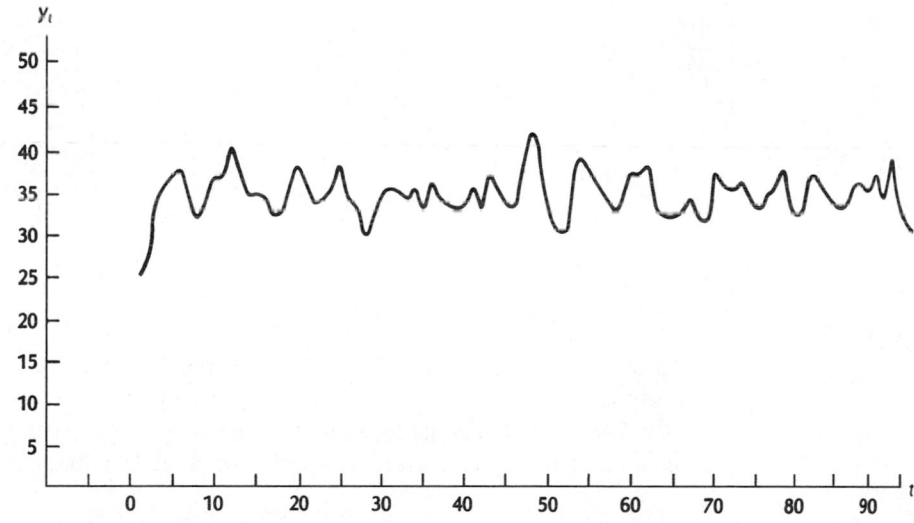

**FIGURE 9.13** SAS output of the SAC and SPAC for the original chemical viscosities

```
                    Name of Variable = y

        Mean of Working Series      34.93007
        Standard Deviation          2.647895
        Number of Observations            95


                    Autocorrelations

 Lag   Covariance   Correlation   -1 9 8 7 6 5 4 3 2 1 0 1 2 3 4 5 6 7 8 9 1      Std Error
  0    7.011350      1.00000      |                    |********************|           0
  1    3.071712      0.43811      |                 .  |*********           |    0.102598
  2   -0.786268      -.11214      |                 . **|                   .    0.120694
  3   -2.403301      -.34277      |              *******|                   .    0.121786
  4   -1.686991      -.24061      |                *****|                   .    0.131550
  5    0.020122      0.00287      |                 .   |   .               |    0.136104
  6    1.367718      0.19507      |                 .   |****.              |    0.136104
  7    0.809195      0.11541      |                 .   |**                 |    0.139016
  8   -0.332100      -.04737      |                 .  *|   .               |    0.140021
  9   -0.954314      -.13611      |                 . ***|   .              |    0.140190
 10   -0.770861      -.10994      |                 .  **|   .              |    0.141574
 11   -0.221972      -.03166      |                 .   *|   .              |    0.142470
 12    0.143892      0.02052      |                 .   |   .               |    0.142544
 13    0.273653      0.03903      |                 .   |*  .               |    0.142575
 14    0.186187      0.02656      |                 .   |*  .               |    0.142687

              "." marks two standard errors
```

(a) The SAC

```
                Partial Autocorrelations

 Lag   Correlation   -1 9 8 7 6 5 4 3 2 1 0 1 2 3 4 5 6 7 8 9 1
  1     0.43811      |                    |*********           |
  2    -0.37631      |              ********|                  |
  3    -0.15901      |                 .***|                   |
  4    -0.02400      |                 .   |   .               |
  5     0.04195      |                 .   |*  .               |
  6     0.08360      |                 .   |** .               |
  7    -0.09399      |                 . **|   .               |
  8    -0.02698      |                 .  *|   .               |
  9    -0.02374      |                 .   |   .               |
 10    -0.02836      |                 .  *|   .               |
 11    -0.03481      |                 .  *|   .               |
 12    -0.04512      |                 .  *|   .               |
 13     0.01107      |                 .   |   .               |
 14     0.00410      |                 .   |   .               |
```

(b) The SPAC

Since the SAC dies down fairly quickly in a damped sine-wave fashion, we conclude that the original time series values are stationary. Noting that the SPAC has spikes at lags 1 and 2 and cuts off after lag 2, we tentatively conclude that the original viscosity readings are described by the nonseasonal autoregressive model of order 2

$$y_t = \delta + \phi_1 y_{t-1} + \phi_2 y_{t-2} + a_t$$

Here we have included $\delta = \mu(1 - \phi_1 - \phi_2)$ in the model because

$$\bar{z} = \bar{y} = \frac{\sum\limits_{t=1}^{95} y_t}{95} = \frac{25.0000 + 27.0000 + \cdots + 31.2846}{95} = 34.93007$$

is (obviously) statistically different from zero. Since diagnostic checks (to be presented in Chapter 10) indicate that the above tentative model is a reasonable final model, we should use this model to forecast future daily chemical viscosities.

The least squares point estimates of the parameters $\delta$, $\phi_1$, and $\phi_2$ in the viscosity model

$$y_t = \delta + \phi_1 y_{t-1} + \phi_2 y_{t-2} + a_t$$

can be computer-calculated to be $\hat{\delta} = 26.8577$, $\hat{\phi}_1 = .61356$, and $\hat{\phi}_2 = -.38304$. Therefore, since we have observed 95 values of the chemical viscosity time series, it follows that point forecasts of

$$y_{96} = \delta + \phi_1 y_{95} + \phi_2 y_{94} + a_{96}$$
$$y_{97} = \delta + \phi_1 y_{96} + \phi_2 y_{95} + a_{97}$$
$$y_{98} = \delta + \phi_1 y_{97} + \phi_2 y_{96} + a_{98}$$

made at time origin 95 are

$$\hat{y}_{96}(95) = 26.8577 + .61356 y_{95} - .38304 y_{94} + \hat{a}_{96}$$
$$= 26.8577 + .61356(31.2846) - .38304(32.3875) + 0$$
$$= 33.6470$$
$$\hat{y}_{97}(95) = 26.8577 + .61356 \hat{y}_{96}(95) - .38304 y_{95} + \hat{a}_{97}$$
$$= 26.8577 + .61356(33.6470) - .38304(31.2846) + 0$$
$$= 35.5189$$
$$\hat{y}_{98}(95) = 26.8577 + .61356 \hat{y}_{97}(95) - .38304 \hat{y}_{96}(95) + \hat{a}_{98}$$
$$= 26.8577 + .61356(35.5189) - .38304(33.6470) + 0$$
$$= 35.7625$$

Moreover, it can be shown that 95% prediction intervals for $y_{96}$, $y_{97}$, and $y_{98}$ are as follows:

For $y_{96}$:  $[33.6470 \pm 4.3754] = [29.2715, 38.0224]$

For $y_{97}$:  $[35.5189 \pm 5.1333] = [30.3855, 40.6522]$

For $y_{98}$:  $[35.7625 \pm 5.1335] = [30.6291, 40.8960]$

# Nonseasonal Mixed Autoregressive–Moving Average Models

The model

$$z_t = \delta + \phi_1 z_{t-1} + \phi_2 z_{t-2} + \cdots + \phi_p z_{t-p} + a_t - \theta_1 a_{t-1} - \theta_2 a_{t-2} - \cdots - \theta_q a_{t-q}$$

is called the **nonseasonal mixed autoregressive–moving average model of order** $(p, q)$. It can be proved that for this model

$$\delta = \mu(1 - \phi_1 - \phi_2 - \cdots - \phi_p)$$

and both the TAC and TPAC die down. Therefore, if for the time series values $z_b$, $z_{b+1}, \ldots, z_n$, both the SAC and SPAC die down, we should tentatively conclude that these values are described by the mixed model. Usually, a simple form of the mixed model is appropriate. For example, it can be proved that for the nonseasonal mixed autoregressive–moving average model of order $(1, 1)$

$$z_t = \delta + \phi_1 z_{t-1} + a_t - \theta_1 a_{t-1}$$

1. The TAC dies down in a damped exponential fashion. Specifically,

$$\rho_1 = \frac{(1 - \phi_1\theta_1)(\phi_1 - \theta_1)}{1 + \theta_1^2 - 2\theta_1\phi_1}$$

$$\rho_k = \phi_1\rho_{k-1} \quad \text{for} \quad k \geq 2$$

2. The TPAC dies down in a fashion dominated by damped exponential decay.

Therefore, if for the stationary time series values $z_b, z_{b+1}, \ldots, z_n$

 i. the SAC dies down in a damped exponential fashion and

 ii. the SPAC dies down in a fashion dominated by damped exponential decay,

then we should tentatively conclude that these values are described by the mixed model of order $(1, 1)$.

## Summary of Nonseasonal Box–Jenkins Models

In Table 9.5 we summarize the TAC and TPAC for each of the general nonseasonal models we discussed in this section. In Table 9.6 we summarize the TAC and TPAC for each of the specific nonseasonal models we have discussed.

**TABLE 9.5  General Nonseasonal Models**

| Model | TAC | TPAC |
|---|---|---|
| Moving average of order $q$<br>$z_t = \delta + a_t - \theta_1 a_{t-1} - \theta_2 a_{t-2} - \ldots - \theta_q a_{t-q}$ | Cuts off after lag $q$ | Dies down |
| Autoregressive of order $p$<br>$z_t = \delta + \phi_1 z_{t-1} + \phi_2 z_{t-2} + \ldots + \phi_p z_{t-p} + a_t$ | Dies down | Cuts off after lag $p$ |
| Mixed autoregressive–moving average of order $(p, q)$<br>$z_t = \delta + \phi_1 z_{t-1} + \phi_2 z_{t-2} + \cdots + \phi_p z_{t-p}$<br>$\quad + a_t - \theta_1 a_{t-1} - \theta_2 a_{t-2} - \cdots - \theta_q a_{t-q}$ | Dies down | Dies down |

**TABLE 9.6 Specific Nonseasonal Models**

| Model | TAC | TPAC |
|---|---|---|
| First-order moving average $z_t = \delta + a_t - \theta_1 a_{t-1}$ | Cuts off after lag 1; specifically: $$\rho_1 = \frac{-\theta_1}{1 + \theta_1^2}$$ $\rho_k = 0 \quad \text{for} \quad k > 1$ | Dies down in a fashion dominated by damped exponential decay |
| Second-order moving average $z_t = \delta + a_t - \theta_1 a_{t-1} - \theta_2 a_{t-2}$ | Cuts off after lag 2; specifically: $$\rho_1 = \frac{-\theta_1(1 - \theta_1)}{1 + \theta_1^2 + \theta_2^2}$$ $$\rho_2 = \frac{-\theta_2}{1 + \theta_1^2 + \theta_2^2}$$ $\rho_k = 0 \quad \text{for} \quad k > 2$ | Dies down according to a mixture of damped exponentials and/or damped sine waves |
| First-order autoregressive $z_t = \delta + \phi_1 z_{t-1} + a_t$ | Dies down in a damped exponential fashion; specifically: $\rho_k = (\phi_1)^k \quad \text{for} \quad k \geq 1$ | Cuts off after lag 1 |
| Second-order autoregressive $z_t = \delta + \phi_1 z_{t-1} + \phi_2 z_{t-2} + a_t$ | Dies down according to a mixture of damped exponentials and/or damped sine waves; specifically: $$\rho_1 = \frac{\phi_1}{1 - \phi_2}$$ $$\rho_2 = \frac{\phi_1^2}{1 - \phi_2} + \phi_2$$ $\rho_k = \phi_1 \rho_{k-1} + \phi_2 \rho_{k-2} \quad \text{for} \quad k \geq 3$ | Cuts off after lag 2 |
| Mixed autoregressive–moving average of order $(1, 1)$ $z_t = \delta + \phi_1 z_{t-1} + a_t - \theta_1 a_{t-1}$ | Dies down in a damped exponential fashion; specifically: $$\rho_1 = \frac{(1 - \phi_1\theta_1)(\phi_1 - \theta_1)}{1 + \theta_1^2 - 2\theta_1\phi_1}$$ $\rho_k = \phi_1 \rho_{k-1} \quad \text{for} \quad k \geq 2$ | Dies down in a fashion dominated by damped exponential decay |

There is no theoretical Box–Jenkins model for which

1. The TAC has nonzero autocorrelations at lags $1, 2, \ldots, q$ and has zero autocorrelations at all lags after $q$ (that is, *cuts off* after lag $q$).

2. The TPAC has nonzero partial autocorrelations at lags $1, 2, \ldots, p$ and has zero partial autocorrelations at all lags after $p$ (that is, *cuts off* after lag $p$).

However (in practice), sometimes for the time series values $z_b, z_{b+1}, \ldots, z_n$

1. The SAC has spikes at lags $1, 2, \ldots, q$ and *cuts off* after lag $q$.

2. The SPAC has spikes at lags $1, 2, \ldots, p$ and *cuts off* after lag $p$.

If this occurs, experience indicates that (as stated in Example 9.5) we should attempt to determine which of the SAC or SPAC is cutting off more abruptly. If the SAC is cutting off more abruptly, then we should tentatively identify the nonseasonal moving average model of order $q$. If the SPAC is cutting off more abruptly, then we should tentatively identify the nonseasonal autoregressive model of order $p$. If the SAC and SPAC appear to cut off equally abruptly, then we should consider both of the models and use the techniques of Chapter 10 to select the "best" model. Some practitioners feel that any time the SAC has spikes at lags $1, 2, \ldots, q$ and cuts off after lag $q$, a moving average model is appropriate. That is, these practitioners feel that if the SAC cuts off, the behavior of the SPAC is irrelevant. However, the authors have found that although the nonseasonal moving average model of order $q$ is often the best model to use when both the SAC and SPAC cut off equally abruptly, occasionally the nonseasonal autoregressive model of order $p$ is a superior model. Therefore, we suggest that both models be considered.

Finally, note that it can be proved that for the model

$$z_t = \delta + a_t \quad \text{where} \quad \delta = \mu$$

the TAC *has zero autocorrelations* at all lags and the TPAC *has zero partial autocorrelations* at all lags. Therefore, if the SAC has no spikes at all lags and the SPAC has no spikes at all lags, we should tentatively identify this model.

## Exercises

**9.1** Consider Table 9.7, which gives 90 values $y_1$, $y_2, \ldots, y_{90}$ of weekly sales, in units of 1000 tubes, of Ultra Shine toothpaste. The JMP IN plot of these values is given in Figure 9.14. Next consider Table 9.8 (page 440), which gives the 89 first differences produced by the transformation

$$z_t = y_t - y_{t-1}$$

a. Does the plot in Figure 9.14 indicate that the weekly sales values are stationary? Explain.
b. Show how $z_2$ and $z_3$ in Table 9.8 have been calculated.
c. Plot the first 20 values in Table 9.8. Do the first differences appear to be stationary? Explain.

**9.2** Using the first 10 observations in Table 9.7, calculate $r_2$.

**9.3** Figure 9.15 (page 440) presents the SAS output of the SAC for the original toothpaste sales values in

Table 9.7. Figure 9.16 (page 441) presents the SAS output of the SAC and SPAC for the first differences of the sales values in Table 9.8. Figures 9.17 and 9.18 on page 442 present the MINITAB outputs corresponding to the SAS outputs in Figures 9.15 and 9.16.
a. Does Figure 9.15 indicate that the original values are stationary? Explain.
b. Using the values of $r_k$ in Figure 9.16(a), hand-calculate $s_{r_3}$ and $t_{r_3}$.
c. Consider Figure 9.16(b). Hand-calculate $r_{11}, r_{22}$, and $r_{33}$ by using the $r_k$ values in Figure 9.16(a). Also, hand-calculate $s_{r_{22}}$ and $t_{r_{22}}$.
d. Does Figure 9.16 indicate that the first differences are stationary? Explain.
e. Draw conclusions concerning the behaviors of the SAC and SPAC in Figure 9.16.

**9.4** Again consider the Ultra Shine toothpaste situation.
a. Using the information in Figures 9.15 and 9.16, rationalize the tentative model

$$z_t = \delta + \phi_1 z_{t-1} + a_t \quad \text{where} \quad z_t = y_t - y_{t-1}$$

b. Algebraically expand this model and express $y_t$ as a function of past times series values, $\delta$, and $a_t$.

**TABLE 9.7 (for Exercises 9.1, 9.2, and 9.3)** Weekly Sales of Ultra Shine
Toothpaste (In Units of 1000 Tubes)

| $t$ | $y_t$ | $t$ | $y_t$ | $t$ | $y_t$ | $t$ | $y_t$ | $t$ | $y_t$ |
|---|---|---|---|---|---|---|---|---|---|
| 1 | 235.000 | 19 | 434.960 | 37 | 607.028 | 55 | 791.070 | 73 | 930.786 |
| 2 | 239.000 | 20 | 445.853 | 38 | 617.541 | 56 | 805.844 | 74 | 941.306 |
| 3 | 244.090 | 21 | 455.929 | 39 | 622.941 | 57 | 815.122 | 75 | 950.305 |
| 4 | 252.731 | 22 | 465.584 | 40 | 633.436 | 58 | 822.905 | 76 | 952.373 |
| 5 | 264.377 | 23 | 477.894 | 41 | 647.371 | 59 | 830.663 | 77 | 960.042 |
| 6 | 277.934 | 24 | 491.408 | 42 | 658.230 | 60 | 839.600 | 78 | 968.100 |
| 7 | 286.687 | 25 | 507.712 | 43 | 670.777 | 61 | 846.962 | 79 | 972.477 |
| 8 | 295.629 | 26 | 517.237 | 44 | 685.457 | 62 | 853.830 | 80 | 977.408 |
| 9 | 310.444 | 27 | 524.349 | 45 | 690.992 | 63 | 860.840 | 81 | 977.602 |
| 10 | 325.112 | 28 | 532.104 | 46 | 693.557 | 64 | 871.075 | 82 | 979.505 |
| 11 | 336.291 | 29 | 538.097 | 47 | 700.675 | 65 | 877.792 | 83 | 982.934 |
| 12 | 344.459 | 30 | 544.948 | 48 | 712.710 | 66 | 881.143 | 84 | 985.833 |
| 13 | 355.399 | 31 | 551.925 | 49 | 726.513 | 67 | 884.226 | 85 | 991.350 |
| 14 | 367.691 | 32 | 557.929 | 50 | 736.429 | 68 | 890.208 | 86 | 996.291 |
| 15 | 384.003 | 33 | 564.285 | 51 | 743.203 | 69 | 894.966 | 87 | 1003.100 |
| 16 | 398.042 | 34 | 572.164 | 52 | 751.227 | 70 | 901.288 | 88 | 1010.320 |
| 17 | 412.969 | 35 | 582.926 | 53 | 764.265 | 71 | 913.138 | 89 | 1018.420 |
| 18 | 422.901 | 36 | 595.295 | 54 | 777.852 | 72 | 922.511 | 90 | 1029.480 |

**FIGURE 9.14 (for Exercise 9.1)** JMP IN plot of Ultra Shine toothpaste
weekly sales

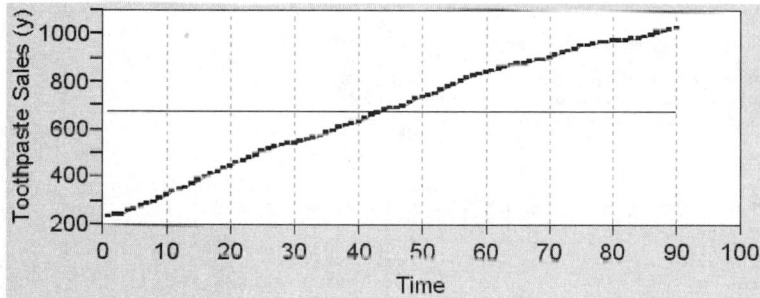

c. Explain the meaning of the constant term $\delta$.
d. The least squares point estimates of the parameters
   $\delta$ and $\phi_1$ in the model specified in (a) can be
   calculated to be $\hat{\delta} = 3.06464$ and $\hat{\phi}_1 = .64774$.
   1. Calculate the residual $y_3 - \hat{y}_3$.
   2. Calculate $\hat{y}_{91}(90)$, $\hat{y}_{92}(90)$, and $\hat{y}_{93}(90)$, which
      are point forecasts of $y_{91}$, $y_{92}$, and $y_{93}$ made at
      time origin 90.
   3. 95% prediction interval forecasts of $y_{91}$, $y_{92}$, and
      $y_{93}$ made at time origin 90 can be shown to be

of the form

$$[\text{\textemdash} \pm 5.4831]$$
$$[\text{\textemdash} \pm 10.5683]$$
$$[\text{\textemdash} \pm 15.4975]$$

Calculate these prediction interval forecasts.

**TABLE 9.8 (for Exercise 9.1)  First Differences of the Observations in Table 9.7**

| t | $z_t = y_t - y_{t-1}$ | t | $z_t = y_t - y_{t-1}$ | t | $z_t = y_t - y_{t-1}$ | t | $z_t = y_t - y_{t-1}$ | t | $z_t = y_t - y_{t-1}$ |
|---|---|---|---|---|---|---|---|---|---|
| 1 |  | 19 | 12.059 | 37 | 11.733 | 55 | 13.218 | 73 | 8.275 |
| 2 | 4.000 | 20 | 10.893 | 38 | 10.513 | 56 | 14.774 | 74 | 10.520 |
| 3 | 5.090 | 21 | 10.076 | 39 | 5.400 | 57 | 9.278 | 75 | 8.999 |
| 4 | 8.641 | 22 | 9.655 | 40 | 10.495 | 58 | 7.783 | 76 | 2.068 |
| 5 | 11.646 | 23 | 12.310 | 41 | 13.935 | 59 | 7.758 | 77 | 7.669 |
| 6 | 13.557 | 24 | 13.514 | 42 | 10.859 | 60 | 8.937 | 78 | 8.058 |
| 7 | 8.753 | 25 | 16.304 | 43 | 12.547 | 61 | 7.362 | 79 | 4.377 |
| 8 | 8.942 | 26 | 9.525 | 44 | 14.680 | 62 | 6.868 | 80 | 4.931 |
| 9 | 14.815 | 27 | 7.112 | 45 | 5.535 | 63 | 7.010 | 81 | 0.194 |
| 10 | 14.668 | 28 | 7.755 | 46 | 2.565 | 64 | 10.235 | 82 | 1.903 |
| 11 | 11.179 | 29 | 5.993 | 47 | 7.118 | 65 | 6.717 | 83 | 3.429 |
| 12 | 8.168 | 30 | 6.851 | 48 | 12.035 | 66 | 3.351 | 84 | 2.899 |
| 13 | 10.940 | 31 | 6.977 | 49 | 13.803 | 67 | 3.083 | 85 | 5.517 |
| 14 | 12.292 | 32 | 6.004 | 50 | 9.916 | 68 | 5.982 | 86 | 4.941 |
| 15 | 16.312 | 33 | 6.356 | 51 | 6.774 | 69 | 4.758 | 87 | 6.809 |
| 16 | 14.039 | 34 | 7.879 | 52 | 8.024 | 70 | 6.322 | 88 | 7.220 |
| 17 | 14.927 | 35 | 10.762 | 53 | 13.038 | 71 | 11.850 | 89 | 8.100 |
| 18 | 9.932 | 36 | 12.369 | 54 | 13.587 | 72 | 9.373 | 90 | 11.060 |

**FIGURE 9.15 (for Exercises 9.3 and 9.4)**  SAS output of the SAC of the original toothpaste sales values

```
                        Name of Variable = y

                Mean of Working Series     674.2709
                Standard Deviation         240.1522
                Number of Observations           90

                            Autocorrelations

Lag    Covariance    Correlation   -1 9 8 7 6 5 4 3 2 1 0 1 2 3 4 5 6 7 8 9 1     Std Error
 0     57673.094       1.00000      |                    |********************|            0
 1     55854.266       0.96846      |                  . |******************* |     0.105409
 2     54012.103       0.93652      |                  . |******************* |     0.178756
 3     52144.826       0.90414      |                 .  |******************  |     0.226813
 4     50267.959       0.87160      |                .   |*****************   |     0.263838
 5     48395.597       0.83914      |                .   |*****************   |     0.294096
 6     46530.410       0.80680      |               .    |***************     |     0.319594
 7     44651.675       0.77422      |              .     |**************      |     0.341475
 8     42751.481       0.74127      |              .     |**************      |     0.360452
 9     40862.523       0.70852      |             .      |*************.      |     0.377010
10     38979.443       0.67587      |            .       |*************  .    |     0.391525
11     37078.701       0.64291      |            .       |************   .    |     0.404281
12     35164.675       0.60972      |           .        |***********    .    |     0.415485
13     33249.042       0.57651      |           .        |***********    .    |     0.425311
14     31354.282       0.54366      |          .         |**********     .    |     0.433907

                    "." marks two standard errors
```

**FIGURE 9.16 (for Exercises 9.3 and 9.4)** SAS output of the SAC and SPAC for the toothpaste sales values obtained with the transformation $z_t = y_t - y_{t-1}$

```
                           Name of Variable = y

                  Period(s) of Differencing                    1
                  Mean of Working Series            8.926742
                  Standard Deviation                3.617174
                  Number of Observations                   89
                  Observation(s) eliminated by differencing   1


                              Autocorrelations

Lag    Covariance    Correlation   -1 9 8 7 6 5 4 3 2 1 0 1 2 3 4 5 6 7 8 9 1    Std Error

 0    13.083947       1.00000      |                    |********************|         0
 1     8.410177       0.64279      |                  . |************        |   0.106000
 2     4.203040       0.32124      |                  . |******              |   0.143251
 3     3.213208       0.24558      |                  . |*****.              |   0.151128
 4     3.107515       0.23751      |                  . |*****.              |   0.155547
 5     3.343641       0.25555      |                  . |*****.              |   0.159570
 6     3.424413       0.26173      |                  . |*****  .            |   0.164104
 7     2.200578       0.16819      |                  . |***    .            |   0.168729
 8     1.174906       0.08980      |                  . |**     .            |   0.170603
 9     0.542223       0.04144      |                  . |*      .            |   0.171133
10     0.553447       0.04230      |                  . |*      .            |   0.171246
11     0.587395       0.04489      |                  . |*      .            |   0.171363
12     0.891959       0.06817      |                  . |*      .            |   0.171495
13     0.668983       0.05113      |                  . |*      .            |   0.171799
14     0.489475       0.03741      |                  . |*      .            |   0.171970

                       "." marks two standard errors
```

(a) The SAC

```
                       Partial Autocorrelations

Lag    Correlation    -1 9 8 7 6 5 4 3 2 1 0 1 2 3 4 5 6 7 8 9 1

 1      0.64279      |                  . |************        |
 2     -0.15667      |                  .***|   .              |
 3      0.18771      |                  . |****              |
 4      0.04019      |                  . |*   .             |
 5      0.12233      |                  . |**  .             |
 6      0.05707      |                  . |*   .             |
 7     -0.08918      |                  . **|   .             |
 8      0.00585      |                  . |   .              |
 9     -0.06552      |                  . *|   .             |
10      0.03286      |                  . |*   .             |
11     -0.02003      |                  . *|   .             |
12      0.06615      |                  . |*   .             |
13     -0.03135      |                  . *|   .             |
14      0.03979      |                  . |*   .             |
```

(b) The SPAC

**FIGURE 9.17 (for Exercises 9.3 and 9.4)** MINITAB output of the SAC of the original toothpaste sales values

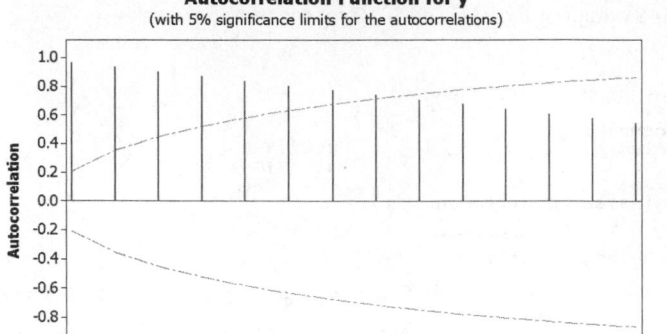

| Lag | Corr | T | LBQ | Lag | Corr | T | LBQ |
|-----|------|------|--------|-----|------|------|--------|
| 1 | 0.97 | 9.19 | 87.26 | 8 | 0.74 | 2.06 | 568.76 |
| 2 | 0.94 | 5.24 | 169.78 | 9 | 0.71 | 1.88 | 620.08 |
| 3 | 0.90 | 3.99 | 247.58 | 10 | 0.68 | 1.73 | 667.36 |
| 4 | 0.87 | 3.30 | 320.73 | 11 | 0.64 | 1.59 | 710.68 |
| 5 | 0.84 | 2.85 | 389.32 | 12 | 0.61 | 1.47 | 750.14 |
| 6 | 0.81 | 2.52 | 453.48 | 13 | 0.58 | 1.36 | 785.88 |
| 7 | 0.77 | 2.27 | 513.28 | 14 | 0.54 | 1.25 | 818.08 |

**FIGURE 9.18 (for Exercises 9.3 and 9.4)** MINITAB output of the SAC and SPAC for the toothpaste sales values obtained with the transformation $z_t = y_t - y_{t-1}$

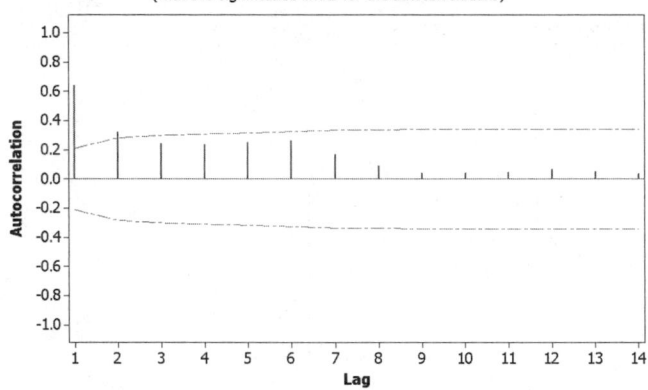

| Lag | Corr | T | LBQ | Lag | Corr | T | LBQ |
|-----|------|------|--------|-----|------|------|--------|
| 1 | 0.64 | 6.06 | 38.03 | 8 | 0.09 | 0.53 | 75.27 |
| 2 | 0.32 | 2.24 | 47.63 | 9 | 0.04 | 0.24 | 75.44 |
| 3 | 0.25 | 1.63 | 53.31 | 10 | 0.04 | 0.25 | 75.63 |
| 4 | 0.24 | 1.53 | 58.69 | 11 | 0.04 | 0.26 | 75.83 |
| 5 | 0.26 | 1.60 | 64.98 | 12 | 0.07 | 0.40 | 76.32 |
| 6 | 0.26 | 1.59 | 71.67 | 13 | 0.05 | 0.30 | 76.60 |
| 7 | 0.17 | 1.00 | 74.46 | 14 | 0.04 | 0.22 | 76.75 |

(a) The SAC

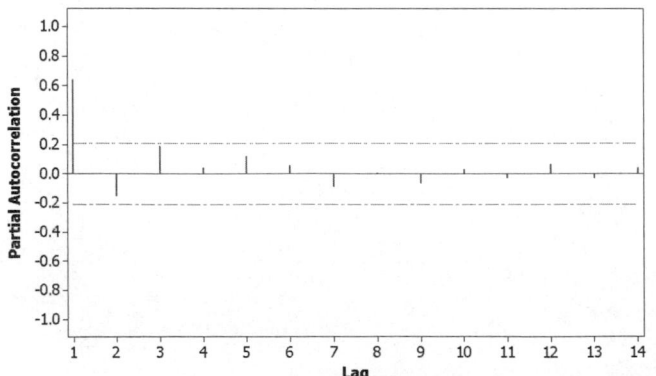

| Lag | PAC | T | Lag | PAC | T |
|-----|-------|-------|-----|-------|-------|
| 1 | 0.64 | 6.06 | 8 | 0.01 | 0.05 |
| 2 | -0.16 | -1.48 | 9 | -0.07 | -0.62 |
| 3 | 0.19 | 1.77 | 10 | 0.03 | 0.31 |
| 4 | 0.04 | 0.38 | 11 | -0.03 | -0.28 |
| 5 | 0.12 | 1.15 | 12 | 0.07 | 0.62 |
| 6 | 0.06 | 0.54 | 13 | -0.03 | -0.30 |
| 7 | -0.09 | -0.84 | 14 | 0.04 | 0.38 |

(b) The SPAC

**TABLE 9.9 (for Exercise 9.6)  Daily Viscosity Readings for Chemical Product XR-22**

| t | $y_t$ | t | $y_t$ | t | $y_t$ | t | $y_t$ | t | $y_t$ | t | $y_t$ |
|---|---|---|---|---|---|---|---|---|---|---|---|
| 1 | 39.9 | 26 | 32.5 | 51 | 36.3 | 76 | 38.0 | 101 | 33.8 | 126 | 31.7 |
| 2 | 31.9 | 27 | 37.5 | 52 | 32.1 | 77 | 36.5 | 102 | 40.2 | 127 | 37.0 |
| 3 | 37.5 | 28 | 36.2 | 53 | 34.0 | 78 | 37.2 | 103 | 35.3 | 128 | 28.7 |
| 4 | 31.7 | 29 | 36.1 | 54 | 34.5 | 79 | 36.4 | 104 | 38.8 | 129 | 38.0 |
| 5 | 37.7 | 30 | 35.5 | 55 | 34.4 | 80 | 37.2 | 105 | 39.0 | 130 | 32.2 |
| 6 | 30.3 | 31 | 37.9 | 56 | 36.2 | 81 | 34.2 | 106 | 32.2 | 131 | 33.5 |
| 7 | 38.7 | 32 | 32.3 | 57 | 39.1 | 82 | 37.0 | 107 | 38.8 | 132 | 36.3 |
| 8 | 35.3 | 33 | 36.0 | 58 | 32.6 | 83 | 35.4 | 108 | 34.3 | 133 | 37.1 |
| 9 | 34.9 | 34 | 34.5 | 59 | 38.6 | 84 | 34.4 | 109 | 30.8 | 134 | 30.5 |
| 10 | 36.4 | 35 | 32.1 | 60 | 38.5 | 85 | 35.2 | 110 | 35.9 | 135 | 36.8 |
| 11 | 35.6 | 36 | 29.2 | 61 | 30.5 | 86 | 37.1 | 111 | 31.4 | 136 | 37.7 |
| 12 | 30.5 | 37 | 39.2 | 62 | 40.1 | 87 | 32.3 | 112 | 33.0 | 137 | 33.2 |
| 13 | 34.7 | 38 | 32.6 | 63 | 32.9 | 88 | 36.9 | 113 | 34.6 | 138 | 35.2 |
| 14 | 28.4 | 39 | 35.4 | 64 | 36.2 | 89 | 34.8 | 114 | 36.4 | 139 | 35.7 |
| 15 | 34.1 | 40 | 38.4 | 65 | 32.3 | 90 | 35.8 | 115 | 33.1 | 140 | 36.0 |
| 16 | 31.9 | 41 | 31.4 | 66 | 37.1 | 91 | 36.1 | 116 | 39.4 | 141 | 34.0 |
| 17 | 35.6 | 42 | 39.3 | 67 | 30.1 | 92 | 36.7 | 117 | 35.4 | 142 | 40.3 |
| 18 | 35.2 | 43 | 32.4 | 68 | 40.3 | 93 | 36.6 | 118 | 34.4 | 143 | 37.0 |
| 19 | 31.3 | 44 | 35.1 | 69 | 36.5 | 94 | 35.1 | 119 | 36.9 | 144 | 40.2 |
| 20 | 38.3 | 45 | 33.3 | 70 | 32.9 | 95 | 37.8 | 120 | 32.8 | 145 | 34.4 |
| 21 | 30.0 | 46 | 37.3 | 71 | 35.1 | 96 | 33.9 | 121 | 35.2 | 146 | 38.5 |
| 22 | 36.5 | 47 | 34.4 | 72 | 41.1 | 97 | 37.2 | 122 | 34.6 | 147 | 35.2 |
| 23 | 32.3 | 48 | 30.4 | 73 | 25.9 | 98 | 34.3 | 123 | 36.4 | 148 | 35.6 |
| 24 | 38.4 | 49 | 38.2 | 74 | 41.3 | 99 | 38.3 | 124 | 35.8 | 149 | 31.9 |
| 25 | 41.3 | 50 | 28.7 | 75 | 32.8 | 100 | 33.9 | 125 | 35.8 | 150 | 35.2 |

**9.5** Consider Example 9.6. Assume that the actual observation at time 122 is $y_{122} = 15.9265$. Calculate $\hat{y}_{123}(122)$ and $\hat{y}_{124}(122)$, which are point forecasts of $y_{123}$ and $y_{124}$ made at time origin 122.

**9.6** Table 9.9 presents 150 daily viscosity readings for Chemical Product XR-22. The JMP IN plot of these values is given in Figure 9.19 (page 444) and the MINITAB output of the SAC and SPAC of these values is given in Figure 9.20 (page 444). Tentatively identify a model describing this time series.

**FIGURE 9.19 (for Exercise 9.6)** JMP IN plot of daily viscosity readings for Chemical Product XR-22

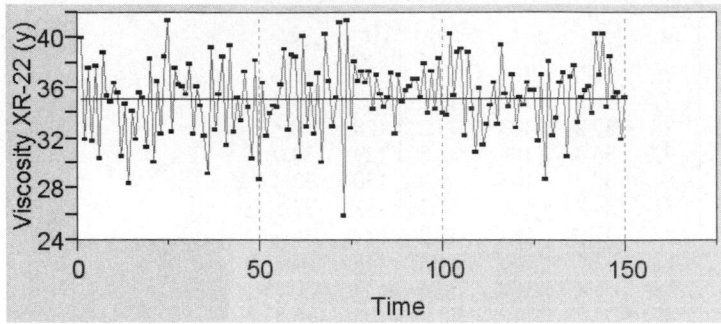

**FIGURE 9.20 (for Exercise 9.6)** MINITAB output of the SAC and SPAC for the daily viscosity readings of Chemical Product XR-22

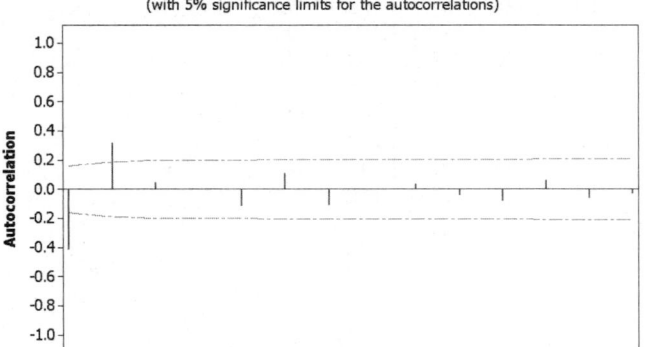

**Autocorrelation Function for y**
(with 5% significance limits for the autocorrelations)

| Lag | Corr | T | LBQ | Lag | Corr | T | LBQ |
|-----|------|------|------|-----|------|------|------|
| 1 | -0.42 | -5.08 | 26.37 | 8 | 0.00 | 0.00 | 48.24 |
| 2 | 0.32 | 3.37 | 42.02 | 9 | 0.04 | 0.35 | 48.46 |
| 3 | 0.05 | 0.48 | 42.39 | 10 | -0.04 | -0.41 | 48.75 |
| 4 | 0.00 | 0.04 | 42.39 | 11 | -0.08 | -0.80 | 49.88 |
| 5 | -0.11 | -1.12 | 44.44 | 12 | 0.06 | 0.56 | 50.46 |
| 6 | 0.11 | 1.06 | 46.31 | 13 | -0.06 | -0.60 | 51.11 |
| 7 | -0.11 | -1.07 | 48.24 | 14 | -0.03 | -0.32 | 51.30 |

(a) The SAC

**FIGURE 9.20 (Continued)**

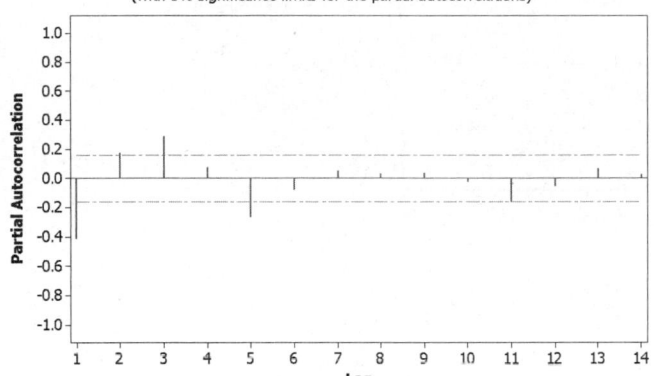

**Partial Autocorrelation Function for y**
(with 5% significance limits for the partial autocorrelations)

| Lag | PAC | T | | Lag | PAC | T |
|-----|-----|---|---|-----|-----|---|
| 1 | -0.42 | -5.08 | | 8 | 0.03 | 0.37 |
| 2 | 0.18 | 2.17 | | 9 | 0.03 | 0.42 |
| 3 | 0.29 | 3.53 | | 10 | -0.03 | -0.32 |
| 4 | 0.07 | 0.92 | | 11 | -0.16 | -2.01 |
| 5 | -0.27 | -3.27 | | 12 | -0.05 | -0.67 |
| 6 | -0.08 | -1.01 | | 13 | 0.07 | 0.83 |
| 7 | 0.05 | 0.61 | | 14 | 0.03 | 0.33 |

(b) The SPAC

**TABLE 9.10 (for Exercise 9.7)** Weekly Sales
of Shimmer Shampoo (Bottles)

| Week | Sales | Week | Sales | Week | Sales |
|------|-------|------|-------|------|-------|
| 1 | 339 | 11 | 396 | 21 | 450 |
| 2 | 319 | 12 | 396 | 22 | 444 |
| 3 | 352 | 13 | 412 | 23 | 456 |
| 4 | 330 | 14 | 387 | 24 | 449 |
| 5 | 378 | 15 | 382 | 25 | 428 |
| 6 | 392 | 16 | 423 | 26 | 444 |
| 7 | 390 | 17 | 386 | 27 | 389 |
| 8 | 395 | 18 | 420 | 28 | 447 |
| 9 | 386 | 19 | 417 | 29 | 395 |
| 10 | 383 | 20 | 474 | 30 | 417 |

**9.7** Table 9.10 provides the number of bottles of
Shimmer Shampoo sold at a grocery store over the
previous 30 weeks. The JMP IN plot appears in
Figure 9.21 (page 446). Figure 9.22 (page 446) gives
the JMP IN plot of the first differences of the Shimmer
Shampoo sales values. The SAS output for the SAC
and SPAC of the original values $y_t$ appears in Figure
9.23 (page 447), and the SAS output for the SAC and
SPAC of the first differences of the sales values $z_t$
appears in Figure 9.24 (page 448).

a. Using Figures 9.21, 9.22, 9.23(a), and 9.24(a), give
your opinion on whether to choose the original

Shimmer Shampoo sales values $y_t$ or the first
differences $z_t$ for the stationary times series.

b. Assuming that the original time series $y_t$ is
stationary, identify a tentative model for the time
series $y_t$, including the decision about whether to
include a constant term.

c. Assuming that the original data, Shimmer
Shampoo sales $y_t$, are not stationary and the first
differences $z_t$ are stationary, identify a tentative
model for the first differences $z_t$, including the
decision about whether to include a constant term.

**FIGURE 9.21 (for Exercise 9.7)** JMP IN plot of Shimmer Shampoo sales values $y_t$

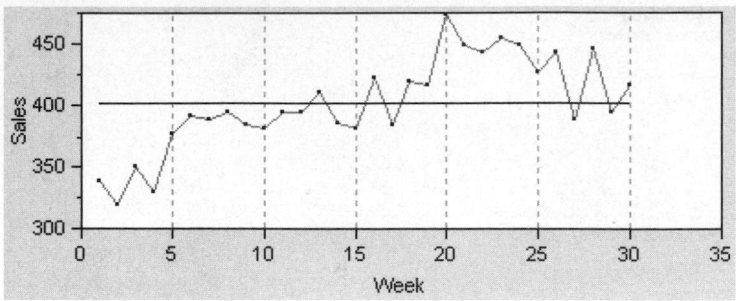

**FIGURE 9.22 (for Exercise 9.7)** JMP IN plot for first differences of
Shimmer Shampoo sales, $z_t = y_t - y_{t-1}$

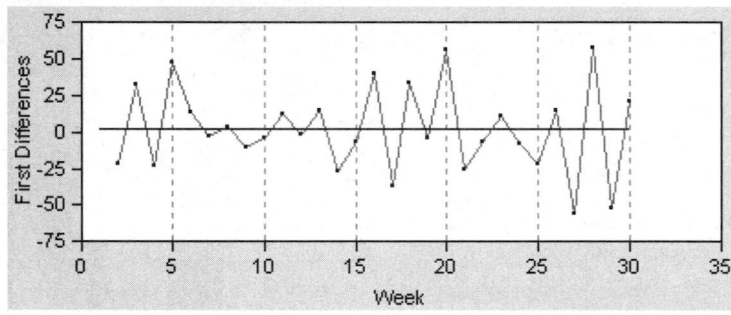

**FIGURE 9.23 (for Exercise 9.7)** SAS output of the SAC and SPAC for the original shampoo sales values

```
                        Name of Variable = y

                Mean of Working Series    402.5333
                Standard Deviation        37.12477
                Number of Observations          30


                        Autocorrelations

Lag   Covariance   Correlation   -1 9 8 7 6 5 4 3 2 1 0 1 2 3 4 5 6 7 8 9 1   Std Error

 0    1378.249     1.00000      |                    |********************|        0
 1     903.986     0.65589      |                .   |************        |     0.182574
 2     904.377     0.65618      |              .     |************        |     0.249024
 3     628.045     0.45568      |            .       |*********    .      |     0.301194
 4     465.291     0.33760      |          .         |*******     .      |     0.323359
 5     349.168     0.25334      |          .         |*****       .      |     0.334902
 6     249.010     0.18067      |        .           |****        .      |     0.341230
 7     185.656     0.13470      |        .           |***         .      |     0.344404

              "." marks two standard errors
```

(a) The SAC

```
                   Partial Autocorrelations

Lag   Correlation    -1 9 8 7 6 5 4 3 2 1 0 1 2 3 4 5 6 7 8 9 1

 1     0.65509      |                 .  |*************       |
 2     0.39659      |                 .  |********           |
 3    -0.13357      |                .***|           .       |
 4    -0.15734      |                .***|           .       |
 5     0.03571      |                .   |*          .       |
 6     0.04685      |                .   |*          .       |
 7    -0.00540      |                .   |           .       |
```

(b) The SPAC

**FIGURE 9.24  (for Exercise 9.7)** SAS output of the SAC and SPAC for the first differences of toothpaste sales, $z_t = y_t - y_{t-1}$

Name of Variable = y

```
Period(s) of Differencing                          1
Mean of Working Series                      2.689655
Standard Deviation                          28.76792
Number of Observations                            29
Observation(s) eliminated by differencing          1
```

Autocorrelations

| Lag | Covariance | Correlation | -1 9 8 7 6 5 4 3 2 1 0 1 2 3 4 5 6 7 8 9 1 | Std Error |
|-----|------------|-------------|---------------------------------------------|-----------|
| 0 | 827.593 | 1.00000 | \|                   \|\*\*\*\*\*\*\*\*\*\*\*\*\*\*\*\*\*\*\*\*\| | 0 |
| 1 | -531.160 | -.64181 | \|       \*\*\*\*\*\*\*\*\*\*\*\*\*\|      .           \| | 0.185695 |
| 2 | 323.311 | 0.39066 | \|            .      \|\*\*\*\*\*\*\* .        \| | 0.250781 |
| 3 | -142.979 | -.17276 | \|            .    \*\*\*\|          .        \| | 0.270955 |
| 4 | 22.363648 | 0.02702 | \|            .      \|\*         .        \| | 0.274727 |
| 5 | 17.551765 | 0.02121 | \|            .      \|\*         .        \| | 0.274819 |
| 6 | -59.899832 | -.07238 | \|            .     \*\|          .        \| | 0.274876 |
| 7 | -82.989954 | -.10028 | \|            .    \*\*\|          .        \| | 0.275532 |

"." marks two standard errors

(a) The SAC

Partial Autocorrelations

| Lag | Correlation | -1 9 8 7 6 5 4 3 2 1 0 1 2 3 4 5 6 7 8 9 1 |
|-----|-------------|---------------------------------------------|
| 1 | -0.64181 | \|        \*\*\*\*\*\*\*\*\*\*\*\*\*\|          .           \| |
| 2 | -0.03615 | \|              .      \*\|          .           \| |
| 3 | 0.10868 | \|              .      \|\*\*        .           \| |
| 4 | -0.05436 | \|              .     \*\|          .           \| |
| 5 | -0.03079 | \|              .      \*\|          .           \| |
| 6 | -0.06471 | \|              .     \*\|          .           \| |
| 7 | -0.30602 | \|              .\*\*\*\*\*\*\|          .           \| |

(b) The SPAC

# 10

## Estimation, Diagnostic Checking, and Forecasting for Nonseasonal Box–Jenkins Models

This chapter discusses estimation, diagnostic checking, and forecasting for nonseasonal Box–Jenkins models. We begin with Section 10.1, which presents advanced concepts pertaining to the **estimation** of model parameters. Included are discussions of **stationarity and invertibility conditions, preliminary and final point estimates,** and the use of *t*-**values** and *p*-**values** to judge the importance of model parameters. Section 10.2 covers **diagnostic checking**—checking to see whether a tentatively identified model is adequate. We discuss the **Box–Pierce** and **Ljung–Box statistics** in this section. Section 10.3 presents advanced concepts pertaining to **forecasting.** In Section 10.4 we discuss a case study, in which we use estimation, diagnostic checking, and forecasting to choose between two tentatively identified models. We end the chapter by showing how to implement two of the exponential smoothing methods in Chapter 8 by using Box–Jenkins models.

# 10.1 ESTIMATION

## Stationarity and Invertibility Conditions

The Box–Jenkins methodology requires that the model used in describing and forecasting a time series be both **stationary** and **invertible.** We previously discussed the meaning of stationarity. Although we will not formally discuss the meaning of invertibility, we will discuss it intuitively. Any Box–Jenkins model can be used to express $z_t$ as a function of past $z$ observations (that is, $z_{t-1}, z_{t-2}, \ldots$). This is obvious for the nonseasonal autoregressive model of order $p$

$$z_t = \delta + \phi_1 z_{t-1} + \phi_2 z_{t-2} + \cdots + \phi_p z_{t-p} + a_t$$

It is not obvious for the nonseasonal moving average model of order $q$

$$z_t = \delta + a_t - \theta_1 a_{t-1} - \theta_2 a_{t-2} - \cdots - \theta_q a_{t-q}$$

However, algebraic manipulation (which we omit) shows that this model can be used to express $z_t$ as an *infinite* series of past $z$-observations. A Box–Jenkins model is *not invertible* if the weights placed on the past $z$-observations when expressing $z_t$ as a function of these observations do not decline as we move further into the past. However, an **invertible** Box–Jenkins model implies that these weights do decline—a condition that intuition indicates should hold (since it seems that a recent observation should count more heavily than an observation from the more distant past). Each of the conditions of stationarity and invertibility implies that the parameters used in the model under consideration satisfy certain conditions. In Table 10.1 we present these conditions

**TABLE 10.1** Stationarity and Invertibility Conditions for Some Specific Nonseasonal Models

| Model | Stationarity Conditions | Invertibility Conditions |
|---|---|---|
| First-order moving average $z_t = \delta + a_t - \theta_1 a_{t-1}$ | None | $|\theta_1| < 1$ |
| Second-order moving average $z_t = \delta + a_t - \theta_1 a_{t-1} - \theta_2 a_{t-2}$ | None | $\theta_1 + \theta_2 < 1$ $\theta_2 - \theta_1 < 1$ $|\theta_2| < 1$ |
| First-order autoregressive $z_t = \delta + \phi_1 z_{t-1} + a_t$ | $|\phi_1| < 1$ | None |
| Second-order autoregressive $z_t = \delta + \phi_1 z_{t-1} + \phi_2 z_{t-2} + a_t$ | $\phi_1 + \phi_2 < 1$ $\phi_2 - \phi_1 < 1$ $|\phi_2| < 1$ | None |
| Mixed autoregressive–moving average of order (1, 1) $z_t = \delta + \phi_1 z_{t-1} + a_t - \theta_1 a_{t-1}$ | $|\phi_1| < 1$ | $|\theta_1| < 1$ |

for the specific nonseasonal models discussed in Chapter 9. The stationarity and invertibility conditions on the parameters of the general models discussed in Chapter 9 are complicated and are not given here. However, we will say that if a model utilizes **autoregressive** parameters, a necessary (but not sufficient) **stationarity condition** is that the sum of the values of the autoregressive parameters is less than 1. If a model utilizes **moving average** parameters, a necessary (but not sufficient) **invertibility condition** is that the sum of the values of the moving average parameters is less than 1. Furthermore, a model using only autoregressive parameters has no invertibility conditions, and a model using only moving average parameters has no stationarity conditions.

## Preliminary and Final Point Estimates

We discuss stationarity and invertibility conditions for two practical reasons. To understand these reasons, note that Box–Jenkins computer packages start with **preliminary point estimates** of the parameters to be estimated and then apply an iterative search technique to a sum of squares function to obtain final least squares point estimates of the parameters. Computer packages (for example, MINITAB and SAS) automatically supply default preliminary point estimates. However, on occasion we may wish to specify the preliminary estimates to check the stability of the final point estimates. The first reason, then, for discussing the stationarity and invertibility conditions is that the preliminary point estimates should satisfy these conditions. Moreover, it can be shown that we can obtain preliminary point estimates that do satisfy these conditions if we set the preliminary point estimate of any autoregressive or moving average parameter equal to .1. The second reason for discussing the stationarity and invertibility conditions is that when we obtain the final least squares point estimates of the parameters in our model, we should verify that these point estimates satisfy the stationarity and invertibility conditions. If they do not, this suggests that the model may not be adequate.

Although the easiest way to obtain a preliminary estimate of any autoregressive or moving average parameter is to set the preliminary estimate equal to .1, we can sometimes obtain a better preliminary point estimate (that is, a preliminary point estimate that is likely to be nearer the final point estimate that will be obtained). To see this, recall that in Table 9.6 we expressed the theoretical autocorrelations of each model in the table in terms of the parameters of that model. One application of such relationships is in obtaining better preliminary point estimates. For example, consider the first-order autoregressive model

$$z_t = \delta + \phi_1 z_{t-1} + a_t$$

Table 9.6 tells us that for this model

$$\rho_k = (\phi_1)^k \quad \text{for} \quad k \geq 1$$

This implies that

$$\rho_1 = \phi_1$$

It follows that an initial point estimate of $\phi_1$ is

$$\hat{\phi}_1 = r_1$$

where $r_1$, the point estimate of $\rho_1$, is the sample autocorrelation of the time series values $z_b, z_{b+1}, \ldots, z_n$ at lag 1. There are other methods for obtaining better preliminary estimates. For certain "simpler" Box–Jenkins models, SAS obtains better preliminary estimates by using a procedure that is beyond the scope of the discussion of this book. For more complex models, SAS uses .1 as the preliminary point estimate of any autoregressive or moving average parameter. Better preliminary point estimates are advantageous because they lead to fewer steps in the iterative search procedure to obtain a final point estimate. MINITAB uses .1 as the preliminary point estimate of any autoregressive or moving average parameter in any model.

If a nonseasonal moving average model uses a constant term $\delta = \mu$, we set the preliminary point estimate of $\delta$ equal to $\bar{z}$, the mean of the stationary time series values $z_b, z_{b+1}, \ldots, z_n$. If a nonseasonal autoregressive or mixed model uses a constant term

$$\delta = \mu(1 - \phi_1 - \phi_2 - \cdots - \phi_p)$$

we set the preliminary point estimate of $\delta$ equal to

$$\bar{z}(1 - \hat{\phi}_1 - \hat{\phi}_2 - \cdots - \hat{\phi}_p)$$

Here $\hat{\phi}_1, \hat{\phi}_2, \ldots, \hat{\phi}_p$ denote the preliminary point estimates of $\phi_1, \phi_2, \ldots, \phi_p$.

**EXAMPLE 10.1**    We said in Example 9.6 that the model

$$z_t = a_t - \theta_1 a_{t-1} \quad \text{where} \quad z_t = y_t - y_{t-1}$$

describes the original values of Absorbent Paper Towels sales. By examining Table 10.1, we see that the invertibility condition on the parameter $\theta_1$ in the nonseasonal moving average model of order 1 is $|\theta_1| < 1$. Note that the preliminary point estimate $\hat{\theta}_1 = .1$ satisfies this condition. Also note from Figure 10.1(a) that the preliminary point estimate used by SAS, $\hat{\theta}_1 = -.30665$, satisfies this condition. Figure 10.1(a) and (b) shows that SAS obtains the final point estimate $\hat{\theta}_1 = -.35343$ after four iterations. Figure 10.2 shows that MINITAB, which begins with the preliminary point estimate $\hat{\theta}_1 = .1$, obtains the final point estimate $\hat{\theta}_1 = -.3544$ after six iterations. Note that the final point estimates obtained by SAS and MINITAB satisfy the invertibility condition.

**EXAMPLE 10.2**    We said in Example 9.8 that the model

$$y_t = \delta + \phi_1 y_{t-1} + \phi_2 y_{t-2} + a_t$$

describes the viscosity readings in Table 9.4. By examining Table 10.1 we see that the stationarity conditions on the parameters $\phi_1$ and $\phi_2$ of the nonseasonal autoregressive model of order 2 are

$$\phi_1 + \phi_2 < 1 \qquad \phi_2 - \phi_1 < 1 \qquad |\phi_2| < 1$$

**FIGURE 10.1** SAS least squares estimation of $\theta_1$ in the model
$z_t = a_t - \theta_1 a_{t-1}$ where $z_t = y_t - y_{t-1}$

```
         Conditional Least Squares Estimation

Iteration        SSE       MA1,1      Lambda      R Crit

        0      127.83    -0.30665    0.00001           1
        1      127.49    -0.36024       1E-6    0.055095
        2      127.48    -0.35240       1E-7    0.008393
        3      127.48    -0.35362       1E-8    0.001299
        4      127.48    -0.35343       1E-9    0.000202
```

(a) The iterative search

```
         Conditional Least Squares Estimation

                           Standard              Approx
Parameter     Estimate        Error    t Value   Pr > |t|     Lag

MA1,1         -0.35343      0.08650      -1.09    <.0001        1


                Variance Estimate      1.080329
                Std Error Estimate     1.039389
                AIC                    347.8977
                SBC                    350.6769
                Number of Residuals         119
          * AIC and SBC do not include log determinant.
```

(b) The final point estimate and its associated *t*-value

**FIGURE 10.2** MINITAB least squares estimation of $\theta_1$ in the model
$z_t = a_t - \theta_1 a_{t-1}$ where $z_t = y_t - y_{t-1}$

```
Estimates at each iteration
Iteration        SSE      Parameters
        0    153.997       0.100
        1    130.734      -0.050
        2    130.863      -0.200
        3    127.423      -0.350
        4    127.419      -0.355
        5    127.419      -0.354
        6    127.419      -0.354
Relative change in each estimate less than  0.0010


Final Estimates of Parameters
Type          Coef     SE Coef        T        P
MA   1     -0.3544      0.0864    -4.10    0.000


Differencing: 1 regular difference
Number of observations:  Original series 120, after differencing 119
Residuals:    SS =  127.367  (backforecasts excluded)
              MS =    1.079  DF = 118
```

**FIGURE 10.3** SAS least squares estimation of the parameters in the model $y_t = \delta + \phi_1 y_{t-1} + \phi_2 y_{t-2} + a_t$

The ARIMA Procedure

Conditional Least Squares Estimation

| Iteration | SSE | MU | AR1,1 | AR1,2 | Constant | Lambda | R Crit |
|---|---|---|---|---|---|---|---|
| 0 | 458.59 | 34.93007 | 0.60297 | -0.37631 | 27.01276 | 0.00001 | 1 |
| 1 | 458.50 | 34.90449 | 0.61326 | -0.38347 | 26.88386 | 1E-6 | 0.014473 |
| 2 | 458.50 | 34.90387 | 0.61355 | -0.38305 | 26.85843 | 1E-7 | 0.000748 |
| 3 | 458.50 | 34.90370 | 0.61356 | -0.38304 | 26.85761 | 1E-8 | 0.000062 |

(a) The iterative search

Conditional Least Squares Estimation

| Parameter | Estimate | Standard Error | t Value | Approx Pr > \|t\| | Lag |
|---|---|---|---|---|---|
| MU | 34.90370 | 0.29808 | 117.10 | <.0001 | 0 |
| AR1,1 | 0.61356 | 0.09710 | 6.32 | <.0001 | 1 |
| AR1,2 | -0.38304 | 0.09754 | -3.93 | 0.0002 | 2 |

| | | | Correlations of Parameter Estimates | | |
|---|---|---|---|---|---|
| Constant Estimate | 26.85761 | | | | |
| Variance Estimate | 4.983654 | | | | |
| Std Error Estimate | 2.23241 | | Parameter | MU | AR1,1 | AR1,2 |
| AIC | 425.1355 | | | | |
| SBC | 432.7971 | | MU | 1.000 | -0.032 | -0.017 |
| Number of Residuals | 95 | | AR1,1 | -0.032 | 1.000 | -0.435 |
| * AIC and SBC do not include log determinant. | | | AR1,2 | -0.017 | -0.435 | 1.000 |

(b) The final point estimates and their associated *t*-values

Note that the preliminary point estimates $\hat{\phi}_1 = .1$ and $\hat{\phi}_2 = .1$ satisfy these conditions. Also note from Figure 10.3(a) that the preliminary point estimates used by SAS, $\hat{\phi}_1 = .60297$ and $\hat{\phi}_2 = -.37631$, satisfy these conditions. The SAS output shows that the preliminary point estimate of $\mu$ is $\bar{z} = \bar{y} = 34.93007$, the mean of the viscosity readings in Table 9.4. This implies that the preliminary point estimate of the constant term

$$\delta = \mu(1 - \phi_1 - \phi_2)$$

is

$$\hat{\delta} = \bar{z}(1 - \hat{\phi}_1 - \hat{\phi}_2)$$
$$= \bar{y}(1 - \hat{\phi}_1 - \hat{\phi}_2) = 34.93007[1 - .60297 - (-.37631)]$$
$$= 27.01276$$

Figure 10.3(a) and (b) shows that SAS uses three iterations to find the final point estimates

$$\hat{\mu} = 34.90370 \qquad \hat{\phi}_1 = .61356 \qquad \hat{\phi}_2 = -.38304$$
$$\hat{\delta} = \hat{\mu}(1 - \hat{\phi}_1 - \hat{\phi}_2)$$
$$= 34.90370(1 - .61356 - (-.38304))$$
$$= 26.85761$$

Note that $\hat{\phi}_1 = .61356$ and $\hat{\phi}_2 = -.38304$ satisfy the stationarity conditions.

To conclude this example, consider the **correlation matrix** in Figure 10.3(b). We see that, for example, the estimated correlation between $\hat{\phi}_1$ and $\hat{\phi}_2$ is $-.435$. Although the point estimates of the parameters in a Box–Jenkins model will always be correlated, very high correlations suggest that the point estimates may be of poor quality, in the sense that a slightly different realization of the time series would have yielded considerably different point estimates. As a practical rule, we should consider two point estimates to be highly correlated if the absolute estimated correlation between these point estimates is greater than .9. If this occurs, we should consider using the SAC and SPAC to find an alternative model with less correlated point estimates. Since the highest absolute estimated correlation between the point estimates in Figure 10.3(b) is .435, we conclude that the point estimates in the viscosity model are not highly correlated.

We have thus far discussed the least squares approach to obtaining point estimates. Although Box, Jenkins, and Reinsel (1994) favor the **maximum likelihood** approach to calculating point estimates, this approach can be somewhat difficult and costly to implement and so they suggest using the least squares approach. SAS (by default) and MINITAB calculate least squares point estimates. SAS has an option that allows us to calculate maximum likelihood point estimates. It can be shown that if the random shocks are normally distributed (as we assume they are) then least squares point estimates are either exactly or very nearly maximum likelihood point estimates.

## *t*-Values and *p*-Values

Associated with the **point estimate** of each parameter in a Box–Jenkins model is its **standard error** and *t*-value. Let $\theta$ denote any particular parameter in a Box–Jenkins model, let $\hat{\theta}$ denote the point estimate of $\theta$, and let $s_{\hat{\theta}}$ denote the standard error of the point estimate $\hat{\theta}$. Then the *t*-value associated with $\hat{\theta}$ is calculated by the equation

$$t = \frac{\hat{\theta}}{s_{\hat{\theta}}}$$

If the absolute value of $t$ is "large," then $\hat{\theta}$ is "large." This implies that $\theta$ does not equal zero, and thus that we should reject $H_0: \theta = 0$, which implies that we should include the parameter $\theta$ in the Box–Jenkins model. We present the following procedure for testing $H_0: \theta = 0$ versus $H_a: \theta \neq 0$.

---

### TESTING $H_0: \theta = 0$ VERSUS $H_a: \theta \neq 0$

Assume that the Box–Jenkins model under consideration utilizes $n_p$ parameters, and define

$$t = \frac{\hat{\theta}}{s_{\hat{\theta}}}$$

Also define the $p$-value to be twice the area under the curve of the $t$-distribution having $(n - n_p)$ degrees of freedom to the right of $|t|$. Then we can reject the null hypothesis $H_0: \theta = 0$ in favor of the alternative hypothesis $H_a: \theta \neq 0$ by setting the probability of a Type I error equal to $\alpha$ if and only if either of the following equivalent conditions holds.

1.  $|t| > t_{[\alpha/2]}^{(n-n_p)}$    that is,    $t > t_{[\alpha/2]}^{(n-n_p)}$    or    $t < -t_{[\alpha/2]}^{(n-n_p)}$

2.  $p$-value $< \alpha$

Note the following:

1.  If we can reject $H_0: \theta = 0$ in favor of $H_a: \theta \neq 0$ by setting $\alpha$ equal to .05, then we have concluded that $\theta$ is important in the model by using a test that allows only a .05 probability of concluding that $\theta$ is important when it is not. This is usually regarded as *strong evidence* that $\theta$ is important.

2.  If we can reject $H_0: \theta = 0$ in favor of $H_a: \theta \neq 0$ by setting $\alpha$ equal to .01, this is usually regarded as *very strong evidence* that $\theta$ is important.

3.  The smaller the value of $\alpha$ at which $H_0: \theta = 0$ can be rejected in favor of $H_a: \theta \neq 0$, the stronger the evidence that $\theta$ is important.

**EXAMPLE 10.3**    We concluded in Example 9.6 that the model

$$z_t = a_t - \theta_1 a_{t-1} \quad \text{where} \quad z_t = y_t - y_{t-1}$$

is a reasonable tentative model describing the $n = 120$ original values of Absorbent Paper Towel sales in Table 9.1. The SAS output in Figure 10.1(b) gives

1.  The least squares point estimate of $\theta_1$, which is

$$\hat{\theta}_1 = -.35343$$

2.  The standard error of the point estimate $\hat{\theta}_1$, which is

$$s_{\hat{\theta}_1} = .08650$$

3.  The $t$-value associated with $\hat{\theta}_1$, which is

$$t = \frac{\hat{\theta}_1}{s_{\hat{\theta}_1}} = \frac{-.35343}{.08650} = -4.09$$

4.  The approximate $p$-value associated with $t = -4.09$, which is twice the area under the $t$-distribution curve having $n - n_p = 120 - 1 = 119$ degrees of freedom to the right of $|t| = |-4.09| = 4.09$ and can be shown to be less than .0001.

(This value is approximate because $t$-values for estimates of parameters in Box–Jenkins models have only approximate $t$-distributions.)

Noting that the above model uses $n_p = 1$ parameters, it follows that if we wish to test $H_0$: $\theta_1 = 0$ versus $H_a$: $\theta_1 \neq 0$ by setting $\alpha$ equal to .05, we would use the rejection point

$$t_{[\alpha/2]}^{(n-n_p)} = t_{[.05/2]}^{(120-1)} = t_{[.025]}^{(119)}$$

Since $n - n_p = 119$ is at least 30, this point can be approximated by

$$z_{[\alpha/2]} = z_{[.05/2]} = z_{[.025]} = 1.96$$

Since the absolute value of $t = -4.09$ is greater than $z_{[.025]} = 1.96$, we can reject $H_0$: $\theta_1 = 0$ in favor of $H_a$: $\theta_1 \neq 0$ by setting $\alpha$ equal to .05.

Equivalently, we can reject $H_0$: $\theta_1 = 0$ in favor of $H_a$: $\theta_1 \neq 0$ because the (approximate) $p$-value is <.0001, which in turn is <.05. Hence, we have strong evidence that $\theta_1$ is important to our model for the Absorbent Paper Towel sales.

In most Box–Jenkins models $(n - n_p)$ is at least 30, and we saw in Example 10.3 that the rejection point for testing $H_0$: $\theta = 0$ versus $H_a$: $\theta \neq 0$, when $(n - n_p) \geq 30$ and $\alpha$ is set equal to .05, is $z_{[.025]} = 1.96$, which is nearly equal to 2. Therefore, as a practical rule, it is reasonable to include in a model any parameter $\theta$ whose absolute $t$-statistic is greater than 2. If the absolute $t$-value of a parameter is not greater than 2, we should seriously consider excluding the parameter from the model, because including it would be likely to produce a model that is not **parsimonious.** Here a parsimonious model is one that adequately fits the historical data without using any unnecessary parameters. Box, Jenkins, and Reinsel (1994) emphasize the importance of obtaining parsimonious models because such models usually produce more accurate forecasts.

As another example of using $t$-values, note that Figure 10.3 shows that the absolute $t$-values associated with the parameters in the model

$$y_t = \delta + \phi_1 y_{t-1} + \phi_2 y_{t-2} + a_t$$

are all greater than 2 (and the $p$-values are <.05). Thus, it seems reasonable to retain these parameters in the model.

## Multicollinearity and the Standard Error

Before leaving our discussion of using the $t$-statistic and related $p$-value to test $H_0$: $\theta = 0$ versus $H_a$: $\theta \neq 0$, we should make one final comment. Consider the viscosity model

$$y_t = \delta + \phi_1 y_{t-1} + \phi_2 y_{t-2} + a_t$$

Using the language of *regression analysis*, we call $y_t$ the *dependent variable* and $y_{t-1}$ and $y_{t-2}$ the *independent variables*. It can be proved that for any parameter $\theta$ in a time series model, the $t$-statistic and related $p$-value measure the *additional importance* of the independent variable multiplied by $\theta$ over and above the combined importance of the other independent variables in the time series model. For example, in the above model the $t$-statistic associated with $\hat{\phi}_2$ measures the additional importance of $y_{t-2}$ over and above the importance of $y_{t-1}$. For this reason **multicollinearity** (which exists when the independent variables are related to each other and thus to some extent contribute redundant information for the description and prediction of the dependent variable) can cause the $t$-statistics to make individual independent variables look unimportant when they really are important. This did not happen in our previous examples (because the absolute $t$-statistics are all greater than 2), but it can happen with other time series models. Because of multicollinearity, it is useful to have measures of the "overall fit" of a time series model. One such measure is the **standard error.**

---

The **standard error** is

$$
s = \sqrt{\frac{\text{SSE}}{n - n_p}} = \sqrt{\frac{\displaystyle\sum_{t=1}^{n} (y_t - \hat{y}_t)^2}{n - n_p}}
$$

---

Here $n$ is the number of observations in the original time series, $n_p$ is the number of parameters in the model, and the $t$th residual $(y_t - \hat{y}_t)$ is the difference between the observed time series value $y_t$ and the prediction $\hat{y}_t$ given by the model. The smaller the standard error, the better the overall fit of the model. In particular, a model with a smaller standard error often yields shorter (that is, more accurate) prediction intervals. We will use the standard error in future examples. Note that Figure 10.1 shows that $s$ for the Absorbent Paper Towels sales model is 1.039389 ($s$ is listed on the output as Std Error Estimate). Figure 10.3 shows that $s$ for the viscosity model is 2.23241.

# 10.2   DIAGNOSTIC CHECKING

A good way to check the adequacy of an *overall* Box–Jenkins model is to analyze the residuals obtained from the model in the following manner. Just as we can calculate the sample autocorrelation and partial autocorrelation functions of the time series values $z_b$, $z_{b+1}, \ldots, z_n$, we can calculate such functions for the residuals. We let RSAC denote the sample autocorrelation function of the residuals and RSPAC denote the sample partial autocorrelation function of the residuals. One way to use the residuals to check the adequacy of the overall model is to examine a statistic that determines whether the first $K$ sample autocorrelations of the residuals, considered together, indicate adequacy of the model. Two such statistics have been suggested. These statistics are summarized in the following box (the choice of $K$ is somewhat arbitrary and will be further discussed).

1. The **Box–Pierce statistic** is

$$Q = n' \sum_{l=1}^{K} r_l^2(\hat{a})$$

2. The **Ljung–Box statistic** is

$$Q^* = n'(n' + 2) \sum_{l=1}^{K} (n' - l)^{-1} r_l^2(\hat{a})$$

Here, $n' = n - d$, where $n$ is the number of observations in the original time series, and $d$ is the degree of nonseasonal differencing used to transform the original time series values into stationary time series values (note: some computer programs calculate $Q$ and $Q^*$ by using $n$ instead of $n'$). Furthermore, $r_l^2(\hat{a})$ is the square of $r_l(\hat{a})$, the sample autocorrelation of the residuals at lag $l$—that is, the sample autocorrelation of residuals separated by a lag of $l$ time units.

We can use both of these statistics to test the adequacy of the overall model in exactly the same way. However, since theory indicates that $Q^*$ is the better of the two statistics, we will discuss how to test model adequacy by using $Q^*$. The modeling process is supposed to account for the relationship between the time series observations. If it does account for these relationships, the residuals should be unrelated, and hence the autocorrelations of the residuals should be small. Thus $Q^*$ should be small. The larger $Q^*$ is, the larger are the autocorrelations of the residuals and the more related are the residuals. Hence a large value of $Q^*$ indicates that the model is inadequate. We can reject the adequacy of the model under consideration by setting the probability of a Type I error equal to $\alpha$ if and only if either of the following equivalent conditions holds.

1. $Q^*$ is greater than $\chi^2_{[\alpha]}(K - n_c)$, the point on the scale of chi-square distribution having $K - n_c$ degrees of freedom such that there is an area of $\alpha$ under the curve of this distribution above this point [see Figure 10.4(a)]. Here $n_c$ is the number of parameters other than $\delta$ that must be estimated in the model under consideration. Table A7 (in Appendix A) is a table of chi-square points.

2. $p$-value is less than $\alpha$, where the $p$-value is the area under the curve of the chi-square distribution having $K - n_c$ degrees of freedom to the right of $Q^*$ [see Figure 10.4(b)].

Frequently, $\alpha$ is chosen to equal .05, but this choice is not sacred. Usually, however, we set $\alpha$ somewhere between .01 and .05. If the $p$-value is less than .01, this is very strong evidence that the model is inadequate. If the $p$-value is greater than .01 but less than .05, this is fairly strong evidence that the model is inadequate. If

**FIGURE 10.4**
Using $Q^*$ to test model adequacy

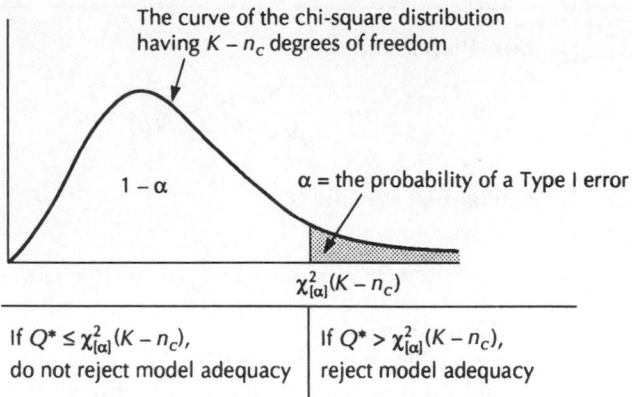

The curve of the chi-square distribution having $K - n_c$ degrees of freedom

$1 - \alpha$

$\alpha$ = the probability of a Type I error

$\chi^2_{[\alpha]}(K - n_c)$

| If $Q^* \leq \chi^2_{[\alpha]}(K - n_c)$, do not reject model adequacy | If $Q^* > \chi^2_{[\alpha]}(K - n_c)$, reject model adequacy |
|---|---|

(a) The rejection point $\chi^2_{[\alpha]}(K - n_c)$ based on setting the probability of a Type I error equal to $\alpha$

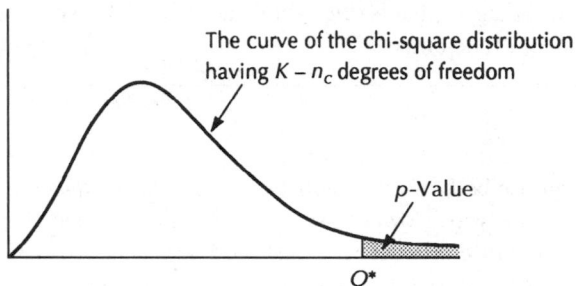

The curve of the chi-square distribution having $K - n_c$ degrees of freedom

$p$-Value

$Q^*$

(b) If the $p$-value is smaller than $\alpha$, then $Q^* > \chi^2_{[\alpha]}(K - n_c)$. Reject model adequacy.

the $p$-value is greater than .05 [or equivalently, if $Q^*$ is less than $\chi^2_{[.05]}(K - n_c)$], then it is reasonable to conclude that the model is adequate. Moreover, the greater the $p$-value is (and thus the smaller $Q^*$ is), the more we believe in the adequacy of the model.

The adequacy of the model can be further investigated by examining the individual sample autocorrelations and individual sample partial autocorrelations of the residuals. If the $Q^*$ indicates that the adequacy of the overall model should be rejected, then we might use the RSAC and RSPAC to identify spikes (that is, the sample autocorrelations or partial autocorrelations of the residuals exceeding plus or minus two standard errors) that can be used to identify an adequate model. Even if the $Q^*$ does not indicate that the adequacy of the overall model should be rejected, we might be able to improve the model by identifying spikes in the RSAC and RSPAC.

As illustrated in the following example, SAS calculates the Ljung–Box statistic $Q^*$ and its associated $p$-value for values of $K$ equal to 6, 12, 18, and 24.

**FIGURE 10.5** SAS output of the RSAC and RSPAC for the model $z_t = a_t - \theta_1 a_{t-1}$ where $z_t = y_t - y_{t-1}$

Autocorrelation Check of Residuals

| To Lag | Chi-Square | DF | Pr > ChiSq | --------------------Autocorrelations-------------------- | | | | | |
|---|---|---|---|---|---|---|---|---|---|
| 6 | 4.10 | 5 | 0.5345 | 0.006 | -0.037 | -0.102 | 0.129 | 0.028 | 0.061 |
| 12 | 10.40 | 11 | 0.4944 | -0.143 | -0.031 | -0.146 | -0.058 | -0.041 | 0.025 |
| 18 | 17.57 | 17 | 0.4165 | 0.020 | 0.038 | -0.074 | -0.003 | 0.068 | 0.196 |
| 24 | 18.67 | 23 | 0.7199 | 0.004 | -0.028 | -0.061 | 0.000 | -0.054 | 0.012 |

Autocorrelation Plot of Residuals

| Lag | Covariance | Correlation | -1 9 8 7 6 5 4 3 2 1 0 1 2 3 4 5 6 7 8 9 1 | Std Error |
|---|---|---|---|---|
| 0 | 1.080329 | 1.00000 | \|********************\| | 0 |
| 1 | 0.0059655 | 0.00552 | \| . \|* . \| | 0.091670 |
| 2 | -0.039778 | -.03682 | \| . *\| . \| | 0.091673 |
| 3 | -0.109978 | -.10180 | \| . **\| . \| | 0.091797 |
| 4 | 0.138997 | 0.12866 | \| . \|***. \| | 0.092741 |
| 5 | 0.030006 | 0.02770 | \| . \|* . \| | 0.094229 |
| 6 | 0.066126 | 0.06121 | \| . \|* . \| | 0.094297 |
| 7 | -0.154399 | -.14292 | \| .***\| . \| | 0.094631 |
| 8 | -0.033148 | -.03068 | \| . *\| . \| | 0.096428 |
| 9 | -0.157783 | -.14605 | \| .***\| . \| | 0.096510 |
| 10 | -0.063136 | -.05844 | \| . *\| . \| | 0.098349 |
| 11 | -0.044091 | -.04081 | \| . *\| . \| | 0.098641 |
| 12 | 0.027341 | 0.02531 | \| . \|* . \| | 0.098783 |
| 13 | 0.021645 | 0.02004 | \| . \|* . \| | 0.098837 |
| 14 | 0.041203 | 0.03814 | \| . \|* . \| | 0.098871 |

"." marks two standard errors

(a) The RSAC

Partial Autocorrelations

| Lag | Correlation | -1 9 8 7 6 5 4 3 2 1 0 1 2 3 4 5 6 7 8 9 1 |
|---|---|---|
| 1 | 0.00552 | \| . \|* . \| |
| 2 | -0.03685 | \| . *\| . \| |
| 3 | -0.10153 | \| . **\| . \| |
| 4 | 0.12960 | \| . \|***. \| |
| 5 | 0.01868 | \| . \|* . \| |
| 6 | 0.06077 | \| . \|* . \| |
| 7 | -0.12057 | \| . **\| . \| |
| 8 | -0.03638 | \| . *\| . \| |
| 9 | -0.15573 | \| .***\| . \| |
| 10 | -0.10387 | \| . **\| . \| |
| 11 | -0.03157 | \| . *\| . \| |
| 12 | 0.00388 | \| . \| . \| |
| 13 | 0.06414 | \| . \|* . \| |
| 14 | 0.05522 | \| . \|* . \| |

(b) The RSPAC

**EXAMPLE 10.4**   Figure 10.5 presents the SAS output of the RSAC, the RSPAC, and the $Q^*$ values and their $p$-values when the model

$$z_t = a_t - \theta_1 a_{t-1} \quad \text{where} \quad z_t = y_t - y_{t-1}$$

is fitted to the $n = 120$ original values of Absorbent Paper Towel sales in Table 9.1. Since $d = 1$ is the degree of differencing used to transform the original time series values into stationary time series values, the $n'$ used to calculate $Q^*$ is $n' = n - d = 120 - 1 = 119$. Therefore, if we let $K = 6$,

$$Q^* = n'(n' + 2) \sum_{l=1}^{6} (n' - l)^{-1} r_l^2(\hat{a})$$

$$= (119)(119 + 2) \left[ \frac{1}{(119 - 1)} (.00552)^2 + \frac{1}{(119 - 2)} (-.03682)^2 \right.$$

$$+ \frac{1}{(119 - 3)} (-.10180)^2 + \frac{1}{(119 - 4)} (.12866)^2 + \frac{1}{(119 - 5)} (.02778)^2$$

$$\left. + \frac{1}{(119 - 6)} (.06121)^2 \right]$$

$$= 4.10$$

Table A7 tells us that if we set $\alpha$, the probability of a Type I error, equal to .05, then we use the rejection point

$$\chi^2_{[\alpha]}(K - n_c) = \chi^2_{[.05]}(6 - 1 = 5) = 11.0705$$

Since $Q^* = 4.10 < 11.0705 = \chi^2_{[.05]}(5)$, we cannot reject the adequacy of the model by setting $\alpha$ equal to .05. The $p$-value is the area under the curve of the chi-square distribution having $K - n_c = 5$ degrees of freedom to the right of $Q^* = 4.10$. Figure 10.5 shows that this $p$-value is .5345. Since $p$-value $= .5345 > .05 = \alpha$, we cannot reject the adequacy of the model by setting $\alpha = .05$. This demonstrates that comparing the $p$-value with $\alpha$ yields the same conclusion as comparing $Q^*$ with $\chi^2_{[\alpha]}(K - n_c)$. Since Figure 10.5 shows that the $p$-values associated with $Q^*$ for $K = 6, 12, 18$, and 24 are all greater than .05, and since there are no spikes in the RSAC or RSPAC, we conclude that the model is adequate. Finally, note that the MINITAB output of diagnostic checking in Figure 10.6 also leads us to conclude that this model is adequate.

**EXAMPLE 10.5**   Figure 10.7 (see page 464) presents the SAS output of the RSAC, the RSPAC, and the $Q^*$ values and their $p$-values when the model

$$y_t = \delta + \phi_1 y_{t-1} + \phi_2 y_{t-2} + a_t$$

is fitted to the $n = 95$ viscosity readings in Table 9.4. Since Figure 10.7 shows that the $p$-values associated with $Q^*$ for $K = 6, 12, 18$, and 24 are greater than .05, and since there are no spikes in the RSAC or RSPAC, we conclude that this model is adequate.

# 10.3 FORECASTING

Since we have observed $n$ time series values, we say that we are at time origin $n$. We let $\hat{y}_{n+\tau}(n)$ denote a point forecast made at time origin $n$ of the time series value in time period $n + \tau$ (where $\tau \geq 1$). In Chapter 9 we discussed how to make point forecasts

**FIGURE 10.6** MINITAB output of the RSAC and RSPAC for the model $z_t = a_t - \theta_1 a_{t-1}$ where $z_t = y_t - y_{t-1}$

```
Modified Box-Pierce (Ljung-Box) Chi-Square statistic
Lag                12        24        36        48
Chi-Square       10.3      18.6      27.5      41.2
DF                 11        23        35        47
P-Value         0.500     0.725     0.815     0.710
```

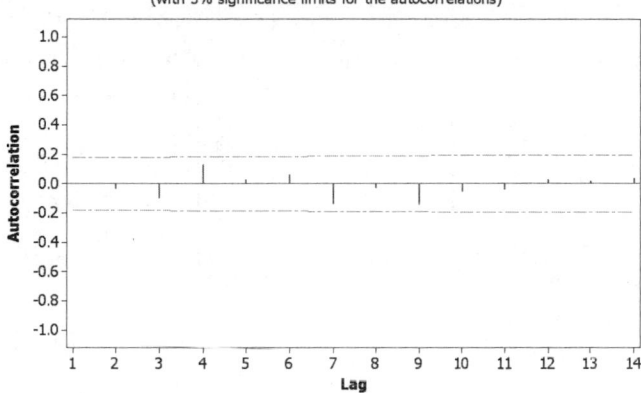

(a) The RSAC

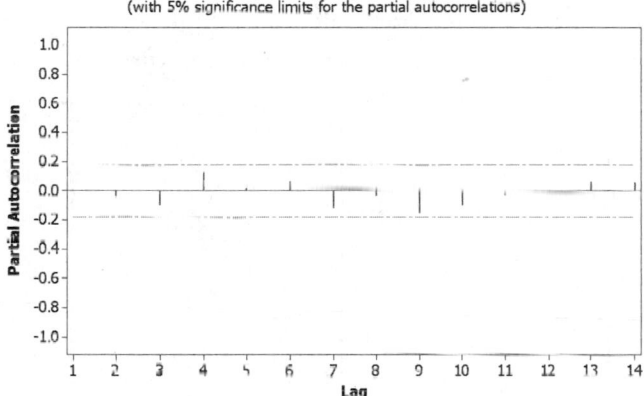

(b) The RSPAC

using Box–Jenkins models. It can also be shown that a **$100(1 - \alpha)\%$ prediction interval** calculated at time origin $n$ for the time series value in time period $n + \tau$ is

$$\left[ \hat{y}_{n+\tau}(n) \pm t_{[\alpha/2]}^{(n-n_p)} SE_{n+\tau}(n) \right]$$

Here $SE_{n+\tau}(n)$ is called the **standard error of the forecast error.** Although the formula for $SE_{n+\tau}(n)$ is beyond the scope of this book [see Box, Jenkins, and Reinsel (1994)],

**FIGURE 10.7** SAS output of the RSAC and RSPAC for the model $y_t = \delta + \phi_1 y_{t-1} + \phi_2 y_{t-2} + a_t$

### Autocorrelation Check of Residuals

| To Lag | Chi-Square | DF | Pr > ChiSq | | | Autocorrelations | | | |
|---|---|---|---|---|---|---|---|---|---|
| 6 | 3.54 | 4 | 0.4719 | -0.063 | 0.056 | -0.077 | -0.088 | -0.041 | 0.112 |
| 12 | 4.34 | 10 | 0.9305 | 0.009 | -0.034 | -0.061 | -0.047 | -0.010 | -0.015 |
| 18 | 5.93 | 16 | 0.9888 | 0.005 | 0.045 | -0.062 | 0.015 | 0.014 | -0.085 |
| 24 | 7.71 | 22 | 0.9979 | -0.085 | -0.068 | -0.050 | -0.001 | 0.009 | -0.007 |

### Autocorrelation Plot of Residuals

| Lag | Covariance | Correlation | -1 9 8 7 6 5 4 3 2 1 0 1 2 3 4 5 6 7 8 9 1 | Std Error |
|---|---|---|---|---|
| 0 | 4.983654 | 1.00000 | &#124;********************&#124; | 0 |
| 1 | -0.311869 | -.06258 | . *&#124; . | 0.102598 |
| 2 | 0.281180 | 0.05642 | . &#124;* . | 0.102999 |
| 3 | -0.382408 | -.07673 | . **&#124; . | 0.103324 |
| 4 | -0.436244 | -.08753 | . **&#124; . | 0.103922 |
| 5 | -0.205609 | -.04126 | . *&#124; . | 0.104695 |
| 6 | 0.558430 | 0.11205 | . &#124;** . | 0.104866 |
| 7 | 0.046280 | 0.00929 | . &#124; . | 0.106119 |
| 8 | -0.167766 | -.03366 | . *&#124; . | 0.106127 |
| 9 | -0.304800 | -.06116 | . *&#124; . | 0.106240 |
| 10 | -0.234292 | -.04701 | . *&#124; . | 0.106610 |
| 11 | -0.051023 | -.01024 | . &#124; . | 0.106828 |
| 12 | -0.073015 | -.01465 | . &#124; . | 0.106838 |
| 13 | 0.022551 | 0.00452 | . &#124; . | 0.106859 |
| 14 | 0.222769 | 0.04470 | . &#124;* . | 0.106861 |

"." marks two standard errors

(a) The RSAC

### Partial Autocorrelations

| Lag | Correlation | -1 9 8 7 6 5 4 3 2 1 0 1 2 3 4 5 6 7 8 9 1 |
|---|---|---|
| 1 | -0.06258 | . *&#124; . |
| 2 | 0.05271 | . &#124;* . |
| 3 | -0.07056 | . *&#124; . |
| 4 | -0.10012 | . **&#124; . |
| 5 | -0.04559 | . *&#124; . |
| 6 | 0.11363 | . &#124;** . |
| 7 | 0.01450 | . &#124; . |
| 8 | -0.06292 | . *&#124; . |
| 9 | -0.06295 | . *&#124; . |
| 10 | -0.02735 | . *&#124; . |
| 11 | -0.00180 | . &#124; . |
| 12 | -0.04208 | . *&#124; . |
| 13 | -0.02394 | . &#124; . |
| 14 | 0.04606 | . &#124;* . |

(b) The RSPAC

MINITAB and SAS calculate this quantity. It can be shown that $SE_{n+\tau}(n)$ depends on the standard error

$$s = \sqrt{\frac{SSE}{n - n_p}}$$

**FIGURE 10.8** SAS output of the point forecasts and 95% prediction intervals given by the model $z_t = a_t - \theta_1 a_{t-1}$ where $z_t = y_t - y_{t-1}$

```
            Forecasts for variable y

Obs      Forecast    Std Error      95% Confidence Limits
121      15.8889     1.0394        13.8518      17.9261
122      15.8889     1.7491        12.4608      19.3170
123      15.8889     2.2446        11.4896      20.2882
124      15.8889     2.6490        10.6970      21.0808
125      15.8889     2.9993        10.0103      21.7675
126      15.8889     3.3128         9.3959      22.3820
127      15.8889     3.5991         8.8347      22.9431
128      15.8889     3.8643         8.3151      23.4628
129      15.8889     4.1124         7.8288      23.9490
130      15.8889     4.3463         7.3703      24.4076
```

A model with a smaller standard error $s$ usually (but not always) yields smaller values of $SE_{n+\tau}(n)$ and thus shorter prediction intervals.

**EXAMPLE 10.6**  Figure 10.8 presents the SAS output of the point forecasts, values of $SE_{n+\tau}(n)$, and 95% prediction intervals when forecasting at time origin 120 the sales of Absorbent Paper Towels in weeks 121 through 130. The model used is

$$z_t = a_t - \theta_1 a_{t-1} \quad \text{where} \quad z_t = y_t - y_{t-1}$$

which we have concluded adequately describes the sales values in Table 9.1. In Example 9.6 we showed that the point forecast made at time origin 120 of sales in week $120 + \tau$ (where $\tau \geq 1$) is

$$\hat{y}_{120+\tau}(120) = 15.8889$$

This point forecast is shown on the SAS output, which also indicates that (for example)

$$SE_{121}(120) = 1.0394 \quad \text{and} \quad SE_{122}(120) = 1.7491$$

Since

$$t_{[.025]}^{(n-n_p)} = t_{[.025]}^{(120-1)} \approx z_{[.025]} = 1.96$$

the 95% prediction intervals for $y_{121}$ and $y_{122}$ are, respectively,

$$[15.8889 \pm 1.96(1.0394)] = [15.8889 \pm 2.0372] = [13.8517, 17.9261]$$

and

$$[15.8889 \pm 1.96(1.7491)] = [15.8889 \pm 3.4281] = [12.4608, 19.3170]$$

These intervals are shown (within rounding) on the SAS output. Furthermore, since

$$t_{[.005]}^{(n-n_p)} = t_{[.005]}^{(120-1)} \approx z_{[.005]} = 2.576$$

the 99% prediction intervals for $y_{121}$ and $y_{122}$ are

$$[15.8889 \pm 2.576(1.0394)] = [15.8889 \pm 2.6775] = [13.2114, 18.5664]$$

**FIGURE 10.9** MINITAB output of the point forecasts and 95% prediction intervals given by the model $z_t = a_t - \theta_1 a_{t-1}$ where $z_t = y_t - y_{t-1}$

```
Forecasts from period 120
                              95 Percent Limits
Period    Forecast      Lower         Upper
  121     15.8899      13.8532       17.9267
  122     15.8899      12.4609       19.3189
  123     15.8899      11.4891       20.2908
  124     15.8899      10.6960       21.0839
  125     15.8899      10.0088       21.7710
  126     15.8899       9.3940       22.3859
  127     15.8899       8.8326       22.9473
  128     15.8899       8.3126       23.4673
  129     15.8899       7.8261       23.9538
  130     15.8899       7.3673       24.4126
```

**FIGURE 10.10** SAS output of the point forecasts and 95% prediction intervals given by the model $y_t = \delta + \phi_1 y_{t-1} + \phi_2 y_{t-2} + a_t$

```
            Forecasts for variable y

Obs     Forecast    Std Error      95% Confidence Limits

 96      33.6470     2.2324       29.2715      38.0224
 97      35.5189     2.6191       30.3855      40.6522
 98      35.7625     2.6192       30.6291      40.8960
 99      35.1950     2.6730       29.9561      40.4339
100      34.7535     2.6923       29.4767      40.0302
101      34.6999     2.6923       29.4232      39.9767
102      34.8362     2.6953       29.5535      40.1189
103      34.9403     2.6964       29.6556      40.2251
104      34.9520     2.6964       29.6672      40.2368
105      34.9193     2.6965       29.6342      40.2044
```

and

$$[15.8889 \pm 2.576(1.7491)] = [15.8889 \pm 4.5057] = [11.3832, 20.3946]$$

Finally, note that Figure 10.9 presents the MINITAB output of the point forecasts and 95% prediction intervals when using the paper towels model to forecast at time origin 120 the sales of Absorbent Paper Towels in weeks 121 through 130.

**EXAMPLE 10.7**    Figure 10.10 presents the SAS output of the point forecasts, values of $SE_{n+\tau}(n)$, and 95% prediction intervals when forecasting at time origin 95 the viscosity readings for Chemical Product XB-77-5 in days 96 through 105. The model used is

$$y_t = \delta + \phi_1 y_{t-1} + \phi_2 y_{t-2} + a_t$$

which we have concluded adequately describes the viscosity readings in Table 9.4. In Example 9.8 we demonstrated using this model to calculate point forecasts.

**TABLE 10.2**  Weekly Sales of Super Tech DVDs (In Units of 1000 DVDs)

| t | $y_t$ | t | $y_t$ | t | $y_t$ | t | $y_t$ | t | $y_t$ | t | $y_t$ | t | $y_t$ |
|---|---|---|---|---|---|---|---|---|---|---|---|---|---|
| 1 | 45.9 | 24 | 29.0 | 47 | 52.0 | 70 | 65.5 | 93 | 73.5 | 116 | 85.7 | 139 | 76.0 |
| 2 | 45.4 | 25 | 34.8 | 48 | 53.5 | 71 | 70.6 | 94 | 70.3 | 117 | 81.3 | 140 | 74.6 |
| 3 | 42.8 | 26 | 36.8 | 49 | 53.5 | 72 | 76.0 | 95 | 68.3 | 118 | 75.9 | 141 | 70.6 |
| 4 | 34.4 | 27 | 37.2 | 50 | 52.9 | 73 | 80.1 | 96 | 64.1 | 119 | 75.0 | 142 | 67.5 |
| 5 | 31.9 | 28 | 41.7 | 51 | 53.4 | 74 | 78.6 | 97 | 62.5 | 120 | 72.5 | 143 | 67.9 |
| 6 | 36.6 | 29 | 41.2 | 52 | 52.8 | 75 | 78.3 | 98 | 62.6 | 121 | 69.6 | 144 | 68.9 |
| 7 | 39.2 | 30 | 40.7 | 53 | 51.4 | 76 | 78.1 | 99 | 60.4 | 122 | 67.3 | 145 | 67.8 |
| 8 | 41.4 | 31 | 39.5 | 54 | 52.5 | 77 | 73.6 | 100 | 61.1 | 123 | 69.8 | 146 | 65.1 |
| 9 | 40.3 | 32 | 40.4 | 55 | 52.4 | 78 | 68.8 | 101 | 64.7 | 124 | 72.2 | 147 | 65.0 |
| 10 | 43.1 | 33 | 38.0 | 56 | 51.5 | 79 | 64.4 | 102 | 65.1 | 125 | 75.2 | 148 | 67.6 |
| 11 | 43.2 | 34 | 35.6 | 57 | 51.7 | 80 | 62.4 | 103 | 61.5 | 126 | 77.2 | 149 | 67.9 |
| 12 | 41.2 | 35 | 33.9 | 58 | 53.3 | 81 | 61.1 | 104 | 64.2 | 127 | 76.8 | 150 | 66.5 |
| 13 | 38.4 | 36 | 35.2 | 59 | 55.4 | 82 | 63.1 | 105 | 67.8 | 128 | 72.4 | 151 | 68.2 |
| 14 | 38.3 | 37 | 41.8 | 60 | 56.9 | 83 | 65.3 | 106 | 66.8 | 129 | 69.4 | 152 | 71.7 |
| 15 | 41.9 | 38 | 42.4 | 61 | 60.0 | 84 | 68.3 | 107 | 64.1 | 130 | 68.7 | 153 | 71.3 |
| 16 | 37.1 | 39 | 38.9 | 62 | 60.8 | 85 | 72.5 | 108 | 66.4 | 131 | 65.1 | 154 | 68.9 |
| 17 | 34.5 | 40 | 42.1 | 63 | 62.3 | 86 | 73.2 | 109 | 68.0 | 132 | 64.4 | 155 | 70.0 |
| 18 | 31.3 | 41 | 41.7 | 64 | 62.6 | 87 | 72.9 | 110 | 71.0 | 133 | 64.2 | 156 | 73.1 |
| 19 | 30.2 | 42 | 39.2 | 65 | 63.1 | 88 | 70.5 | 111 | 76.9 | 134 | 63.2 | 157 | 69.1 |
| 20 | 28.3 | 43 | 38.5 | 66 | 62.8 | 89 | 69.4 | 112 | 84.1 | 135 | 62.1 | 158 | 67.3 |
| 21 | 25.9 | 44 | 42.5 | 67 | 64.7 | 90 | 68.2 | 113 | 85.9 | 136 | 65.8 | 159 | 72.9 |
| 22 | 26.6 | 45 | 47.9 | 68 | 66.3 | 91 | 69.3 | 114 | 85.2 | 137 | 73.7 | 160 | 78.6 |
| 23 | 26.2 | 46 | 48.6 | 69 | 63.0 | 92 | 72.3 | 115 | 86.2 | 138 | 77.1 | 161 | 82.3 |

**FIGURE 10.11**
JMP IN plot of weekly sales of Super Tech digital video disc (DVD)

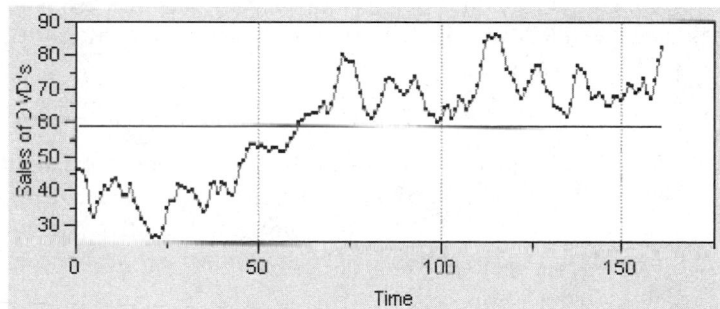

# 10.4 A CASE STUDY

A manufacturer produces and sells the Super Tech digital video disc (DVD). Sales of this DVD (in units of 1000 DVDs) over the past 161 weeks are presented in Table 10.2 and are plotted in Figure 10.11. Since Figure 10.12 shows that the SAC of the original sales values dies down very slowly, we conclude that these original values are

**FIGURE 10.12** SAS output of the SAC for the original values of DVD sales

```
                          Name of Variable = y

                    Mean of Working Series      59.29876
                    Standard Deviation          15.32488
                    Number of Observations           161


                          Autocorrelations

Lag   Covariance   Correlation  -1 9 8 7 6 5 4 3 2 1 0 1 2 3 4 5 6 7 8 9 1    Std Error

 0    234.852      1.00000      |                    |********************|         0
 1    228.692      0.97377      |                   .|******************* |    0.078811
 2    219.550      0.93485      |                  . |******************  |    0.134128
 3    211.028      0.89856      |                 .  |*****************   |    0.169843
 4    202.545      0.86244      |                .   |****************    |    0.197172
 5    193.677      0.82468      |               .    |***************     |    0.219355
 6    186.454      0.79392      |              .     |***************     |    0.237834
 7    182.484      0.77702      |             .      |***************     |    0.253761
 8    179.699      0.76516      |            .       |**************      |    0.268132
 9    176.953      0.75347      |            .       |**************      |    0.281368
10    174.970      0.74502      |           .        |**************      |    0.293633
11    173.603      0.73920      |          .         |**************      |    0.305148
12    171.550      0.73046      |          .         |**************      |    0.316074
13    167.844      0.71468      |         .          |*************       |    0.326391
14    163.182      0.69483      |         .          |*************       |    0.335971
```

nonstationary. The SAC and SPAC of the first differences of the sales values are given in Figure 10.13. One interpretation of the SAC and SPAC is that the SAC dies down and the SPAC has spikes at lags 1 and 2 and cuts off after lag 2 (we ignore the spike at lag 5). This implies that

$$\text{Model 1:} \quad z_t = \phi_1 z_{t-1} + \phi_2 z_{t-2} + a_t$$

describes the first differences of the sales values. We do not use a constant term because Figure 10.13(a) shows us that $\bar{z} = .2275$ and $s_z = 2.8136$, which implies that $\bar{z}$ is not statistically different from zero. Another interpretation of Figure 10.13 is that the SAC has spikes at lags 1 and 6 and cuts off after lag 6, and the SPAC dies down. This implies that

$$\text{Model 2:} \quad z_t = a_t - \theta_1 a_{t-1} - \theta_6 a_{t-6}$$

describes the first differences of the sales values.

Figure 10.14(b) indicates that Model 1 is inadequate, and Figure 10.15(b) indicates that Model 2 is adequate. Since the RSAC in Figure 10.14(b) has a spike at lag 6, we might modify Model 1 and consider

$$\text{Model 3:} \quad z_t = \phi_1 z_{t-1} + \phi_2 z_{t-2} + a_t - \theta_6 a_{t-6}$$

Figure 10.16(b) indicates that this model is adequate. However, in comparing Figure 10.15(a), (b), and (d) with Figure 10.16(a), (b), and (d), Model 2 might be considered

**FIGURE 10.13** SAS output of the SAC and SPAC for the first differences of DVD sales

```
                        Name of Variable = y

              Period(s) of Differencing               1
              Mean of Working Series            0.2275
              Standard Deviation             2.813604
              Number of Observations              160
              Observation(s) eliminated by differencing  1


                          Autocorrelations

Lag   Covariance    Correlation   -1 9 8 7 6 5 4 3 2 1 0 1 2 3 4 5 6 7 8 9 1    Std Error

 0    7.916369       1.00000      |                    |********************|           0
 1    3.442783       0.43489      |                 .  |*********           |    0.079057
 2   -0.065133       -.00823      |                    |.                   |    0.092813
 3    0.015437       0.00195      |                 .  |.                   |    0.092817
 4   -0.136313       -.01722      |                 .  |.                   |    0.092817
 5   -1.889516       -.23868      |              *****|                    |    0.092837
 6   -2.656235       -.33554      |            *******|                    |    0.096597
 7   -0.890803       -.11253      |                 **|.                   |    0.103625
 8   -0.523478       -.06613      |                 . *|.                  |    0.104386
 9   -0.633764       -.08006      |                 . **|.                 |    0.104648
10   -0.147157       -.01859      |                 .  |.                  |    0.105030
11    0.726406       0.09176      |                 .  |**  .              |    0.105050
12    1.183485       0.14950      |                 .  |***. |             |    0.105550
13    0.949884       0.11999      |                 .  |**  .              |    0.106865
14    0.488376       0.06169      |                 .  |*   .              |    0.107704

                  "." marks two standard errors
```

(a) The SAC

```
                      Partial Autocorrelations

Lag    Correlation   -1 9 8 7 6 5 4 3 2 1 0 1 2 3 4 5 6 7 8 9 1

 1     0.43489       |                 .  |*********           |
 2    -0.24339       |              *****|.                    |
 3     0.14715       |                 .  |***                 |
 4    -0.11389       |                 .**|.                   |
 5    -0.23959       |              *****|.                    |
 6    -0.14628       |                ***|.                    |
 7     0.08505       |                 .  |**.                 |
 8    -0.15793       |                ***|.                    |
 9     0.03666       |                 .  |*.                  |
10    -0.05646       |                 . *|.                   |
11     0.01943       |                 .  |.                   |
12     0.06090       |                 .  |*.                  |
13     0.04104       |                 .  |*.                  |
14    -0.05812       |                 . *|.                   |
```

(b) The SPAC

better than Model 3. This is because Model 2 has a smaller standard error and larger $p$-values associated with $Q^*$, and because it provides slightly shorter prediction intervals for $y_{162}$ through $y_{164}$. However, Model 3 provides shorter prediction intervals for $y_{165}$ through $y_{171}$.

**FIGURE 10.14** SAS output of estimation, diagnostic checking, and forecasting for the model $z_t = \phi_1 z_{t-1} + \phi_2 z_{t-2} + a_t$ where $z_t = y_t - y_{t-1}$

```
                    Conditional Least Squares Estimation

                                 Standard              Approx
Parameter        Estimate          Error    t Value   Pr > |t|    Lag

AR1,1            0.54567         0.07732       7.06     <.0001      1
AR1,2           -0.24146         0.07834      -3.08     0.0024      2


                   Variance Estimate         6.135022
                   Std Error Estimate        2.476898
                   AIC                       746.2899
                   SBC                       752.4403
                   Number of Residuals            160
           * AIC and SBC do not include log determinant.


                         Correlations of Parameter
                                 Estimates

                  Parameter      AR1,1      AR1,2

                  AR1,1          1.000     -0.432
                  AR1,2         -0.432      1.000
```

(a) Estimation

```
                         Autocorrelation Check of Residuals

  To      Chi-            Pr >
  Lag    Square    DF    ChiSq    ----------------------Autocorrelations--------------------

   6      22.47     4   0.0002    0.036  -0.088   0.093   0.071  -0.146  -0.300
  12      26.60    10   0.0030    0.058  -0.057  -0.070  -0.011   0.062   0.092
  18      30.15    16   0.0173    0.060   0.019   0.059  -0.107  -0.014  -0.026
  24      37.27    22   0.0221    0.040  -0.075  -0.053   0.145   0.039  -0.073
  30      41.82    28   0.0451    0.111   0.096  -0.039   0.003  -0.025  -0.002

                         Autocorrelation Plot of Residuals

  Lag   Covariance   Correlation   -1 9 8 7 6 5 4 3 2 1 0 1 2 3 4 5 6 7 8 9 1   Std Error

   0     6.135022     1.00000      |                    |********************|          0
   1     0.222138     0.03621      |                  . |*   .               |   0.079057
   2    -0.541203    -.08822       |                  .**|   .               |   0.079161
   3     0.572847     0.09337      |                  . |**.                 |   0.079773
   4     0.432599     0.07051      |                  . |*   .               |   0.080453
   5    -0.894811    -.14585       |                  ***|   .               |   0.080838
   6    -1.840764    -.30004       |               ******|   .               |   0.082466
   7     0.356735     0.05815      |                  .  |*   .              |   0.089028
   8    -0.350518    -.05713       |                  . *|   .               |   0.089265
   9    -0.429604    -.07002       |                  . *|   .               |   0.089494
  10    -0.065560    -.01069       |                  .  |   .               |   0.089835
  11     0.379688     0.06189      |                  .  |*   .              |   0.089843
  12     0.563507     0.09185      |                  .  |**  .              |   0.090109
  13     0.369160     0.06017      |                  .  |*   .              |   0.090693
  14     0.118349     0.01929      |                  .  |   .               |   0.090942

                        "." marks two standard errors
```

(b) The RSAC

**FIGURE 10.14** (Continued)

Partial Autocorrelations

| Lag | Correlation | -1 9 8 7 6 5 4 3 2 1 0 1 2 3 4 5 6 7 8 9 1 |
|-----|-------------|---------------------------------------------|
| 1 | 0.03621 | .\|\* . |
| 2 | -0.08964 | .\*\*\| . |
| 3 | 0.10104 | .\|\*\*. |
| 4 | 0.05514 | .\|\* . |
| 5 | -0.13701 | \*\*\*\| . |
| 6 | -0.29722 | \*\*\*\*\*\*\| . |
| 7 | 0.04721 | .\|\* . |
| 8 | -0.08823 | .\*\*\| . |
| 9 | 0.01702 | . \| . |
| 10 | -0.01792 | . \| . |
| 11 | -0.01183 | . \| . |
| 12 | 0.02898 | . \|\* . |
| 13 | 0.09084 | .\|\*\*. |
| 14 | -0.03730 | . \*\| . |

(c) The RSPAC

Forecasts for variable y

| Obs | Forecast | Std Error | 95% Confidence Limits | |
|-----|----------|-----------|------------|------------|
| 162 | 82.9426 | 2.4769 | 78.0880 | 87.7973 |
| 163 | 82.3999 | 4.5598 | 73.4628 | 91.3370 |
| 164 | 81.9486 | 6.0445 | 70.1015 | 93.7956 |
| 165 | 81.8333 | 7.0963 | 67.9249 | 95.7418 |
| 166 | 81.8794 | 7.9335 | 66.3300 | 97.4289 |
| 167 | 81.9324 | 8.6773 | 64.9252 | 98.9396 |
| 168 | 81.9502 | 9.3710 | 63.5834 | 100.3170 |
| 169 | 81.9471 | 10.0240 | 62.3004 | 101.5938 |
| 170 | 81.9411 | 10.6389 | 61.0892 | 102.7931 |
| 171 | 81.9386 | 11.2196 | 59.9486 | 103.9286 |

(d) Forecasts of $y_{162}$ through $y_{171}$

**FIGURE 10.15** SAS output of estimation, diagnostic checking, and forecasting for the model $z_t = a_t - \theta_1 a_{t-1} - \theta_6 a_{t-6}$ where $z_t = y_t - y_{t-1}$

Conditional Least Squares Estimation

| Parameter | Estimate | Standard Error | t Value | Approx Pr > \|t\| | Lag |
|-----------|----------|----------------|---------|-----------------|-----|
| MA1,1 | -0.61177 | 0.05499 | -11.13 | <.0001 | 1 |
| MA1,2 | 0.32354 | 0.05476 | 5.91 | <.0001 | 6 |

| | |
|---|---|
| Variance Estimate | 5.197127 |
| Std Error Estimate | 2.279721 |
| AIC | 719.7447 |
| SBC | 725.895 |
| Number of Residuals | 160 |

\* AIC and SBC do not include log determinant.

Correlations of Parameter Estimates

| Parameter | MA1,1 | MA1,2 |
|-----------|-------|-------|
| MA1,1 | 1.000 | 0.682 |
| MA1,2 | 0.682 | 1.000 |

(a) Estimation

**FIGURE 10.15** (Continued)

Autocorrelation Check of Residuals

| To Lag | Chi-Square | DF | Pr > ChiSq | | | Autocorrelations | | | |
|--------|-----------|----|-----------|--------|--------|--------|--------|-------|--------|
| 6 | 2.24 | 4 | 0.6912 | 0.011 | -0.004 | -0.001 | 0.015 | -0.107 | -0.039 |
| 12 | 5.87 | 10 | 0.8263 | -0.069 | 0.006 | -0.058 | -0.044 | 0.051 | 0.091 |
| 18 | 9.52 | 16 | 0.8905 | 0.067 | 0.034 | 0.004 | -0.107 | 0.033 | -0.045 |
| 24 | 14.69 | 22 | 0.8751 | 0.057 | -0.026 | -0.070 | 0.108 | 0.046 | -0.070 |
| 30 | 20.07 | 28 | 0.8618 | 0.115 | 0.081 | -0.053 | 0.033 | -0.063 | -0.011 |

Autocorrelation Plot of Residuals

| Lag | Covariance | Correlation | -1 9 8 7 6 5 4 3 2 1 0 1 2 3 4 5 6 7 8 9 1 | Std Error |
|-----|-----------|-------------|---------------------------------------------|-----------|
| 0 | 5.197127 | 1.00000 | \|********************\| | 0 |
| 1 | 0.058815 | 0.01132 | . \| . | 0.079057 |
| 2 | -0.021728 | -.00418 | . \| . | 0.079067 |
| 3 | -0.0068033 | -.00131 | . \| . | 0.079068 |
| 4 | 0.077402 | 0.01489 | . \| . | 0.079069 |
| 5 | -0.557956 | -.10736 | .**\| . | 0.079086 |
| 6 | -0.202080 | -.03888 | . *\| . | 0.079992 |
| 7 | -0.359223 | -.06912 | . *\| . | 0.080110 |
| 8 | 0.030045 | 0.00578 | . \| . | 0.080482 |
| 9 | -0.301465 | -.05801 | . *\| . | 0.080484 |
| 10 | -0.226584 | -.04360 | . *\| . | 0.080745 |
| 11 | 0.265393 | 0.05107 | . \|* . | 0.080892 |
| 12 | 0.472827 | 0.09098 | . \|** . | 0.081093 |
| 13 | 0.350407 | 0.06742 | . \|* . | 0.081729 |
| 14 | 0.175068 | 0.03369 | . \|* . | 0.082076 |

"." marks two standard errors

(b) The RSAC

Partial Autocorrelations

| Lag | Correlation | -1 9 8 7 6 5 4 3 2 1 0 1 2 3 4 5 6 7 8 9 1 |
|-----|-------------|---------------------------------------------|
| 1 | 0.01132 | . \| . |
| 2 | -0.00431 | . \| . |
| 3 | -0.00121 | . \| . |
| 4 | 0.01491 | . \| . |
| 5 | -0.10775 | .**\| . |
| 6 | -0.03658 | . *\| . |
| 7 | -0.07009 | . *\| . |
| 8 | 0.00608 | . \| . |
| 9 | -0.05697 | . *\| . |
| 10 | -0.05436 | . *\| . |
| 11 | 0.04533 | . \|* . |
| 12 | 0.07425 | . \|* . |
| 13 | 0.06705 | . \|* . |
| 14 | 0.02073 | . \| . |

(c) The RSPAC

Forecasts for variable y

| Obs | Forecast | Std Error | 95% Confidence Limits | |
|-----|----------|-----------|-----------------------|----------|
| 162 | 83.1502 | 2.2797 | 78.6820 | 87.6184 |
| 163 | 84.6215 | 4.3242 | 76.1463 | 93.0967 |
| 164 | 84.1300 | 5.6745 | 73.0083 | 95.2517 |
| 165 | 82.7623 | 6.7602 | 69.5125 | 96.0121 |
| 166 | 81.8336 | 7.6943 | 66.7531 | 96.9141 |
| 167 | 81.0599 | 8.5266 | 64.3481 | 97.7718 |
| 168 | 81.0599 | 9.0182 | 63.3846 | 98.7353 |
| 169 | 81.0599 | 9.4843 | 62.4710 | 99.6489 |
| 170 | 81.0599 | 9.9286 | 61.6002 | 100.5197 |
| 171 | 81.0599 | 10.3539 | 60.7667 | 101.3532 |

(d) Forecasts of $y_{162}$ through $y_{171}$

**FIGURE 10.16** SAS output of estimation, diagnostic checking, and forecasting for the model
$z_t = \phi_1 z_{t-1} + \phi_2 z_{t-2} + a_t - \theta_6 a_{t-6}$ where $z_t = y_t - y_{t-1}$

Conditional Least Squares Estimation

| Parameter | Estimate | Standard Error | t Value | Approx Pr > \|t\| | Lag |
|-----------|----------|----------------|---------|-------------------|-----|
| MA1,1 | 0.30792 | 0.07910 | 3.89 | 0.0001 | 6 |
| AR1,1 | 0.53749 | 0.07786 | 6.90 | <.0001 | 1 |
| AR1,2 | -0.25526 | 0.07845 | -3.25 | 0.0014 | 2 |

| | |
|---|---|
| Variance Estimate | 5.614383 |
| Std Error Estimate | 2.369469 |
| AIC | 733.0849 |
| SBC | 742.3104 |
| Number of Residuals | 160 |

\* AIC and SBC do not include log determinant.

Correlations of Parameter Estimates

| Parameter | MA1,1 | AR1,1 | AR1,2 |
|-----------|-------|-------|-------|
| MA1,1 | 1.000 | -0.109 | 0.060 |
| AR1,1 | -0.109 | 1.000 | -0.421 |
| AR1,2 | 0.060 | -0.421 | 1.000 |

(a) Estimation

Autocorrelation Check of Residuals

| To Lag | Chi-Square | DF | Pr > ChiSq | | | Autocorrelations | | | |
|--------|-----------|-----|-----------|---|---|---|---|---|---|
| 6 | 7.09 | 3 | 0.0691 | 0.034 | -0.082 | 0.123 | 0.036 | -0.134 | -0.020 |
| 12 | 11.39 | 9 | 0.2502 | 0.090 | -0.088 | -0.028 | -0.024 | 0.027 | 0.084 |
| 18 | 15.30 | 15 | 0.4301 | 0.114 | -0.024 | 0.037 | -0.077 | -0.000 | -0.032 |
| 24 | 22.80 | 21 | 0.3548 | 0.105 | -0.050 | -0.059 | 0.122 | 0.037 | -0.083 |
| 30 | 28.42 | 27 | 0.3897 | 0.117 | 0.089 | -0.070 | 0.015 | -0.030 | -0.035 |

Autocorrelation Plot of Residuals

| Lag | Covariance | Correlation | -1 9 8 7 6 5 4 3 2 1 0 1 2 3 4 5 6 7 8 9 1 | Std Error |
|-----|-----------|-------------|---------------------------------------------|-----------|
| 0 | 5.814383 | 1.00000 | \|********************\| | 0 |
| 1 | 0.192083 | 0.03421 | \|* . | 0.079057 |
| 2 | -0.462391 | -.08236 | .**\| . | 0.079149 |
| 3 | 0.691509 | 0.12318 | . \|** . | 0.079683 |
| 4 | 0.203489 | 0.03624 | . \|* . | 0.080885 |
| 5 | -0.751407 | -.13304 | .***\| . | 0.080966 |
| 6 | -0.112273 | -.02000 | . \| . | 0.082337 |
| 7 | 0.507512 | 0.09039 | . \|** . | 0.082368 |
| 8 | -0.493352 | -.08787 | .**\| . | 0.082985 |
| 9 | -0.157509 | -.02805 | . *\| . | 0.083565 |
| 10 | -0.134747 | -.02400 | . \| . | 0.083624 |
| 11 | 0.152878 | 0.02723 | . \|* . | 0.083667 |
| 12 | 0.470771 | 0.08385 | . \|** . | 0.083722 |
| 13 | 0.642782 | 0.11449 | . \|** . | 0.084245 |
| 14 | -0.136366 | -.02429 | . \| . | 0.085212 |

"." marks two standard errors

(b) The RSAC

**FIGURE 10.16** (Continued)

Partial Autocorrelations

```
Lag    Correlation    -1 9 8 7 6 5 4 3 2 1 0 1 2 3 4 5 6 7 8 9 1
 1      0.03421        |                    .  |* .            |
 2     -0.08363        |                    .**|  .            |
 3      0.13016        |                    .  |***            |
 4      0.01907        |                    .  |  .            |
 5     -0.11779        |                    .**|  .            |
 6     -0.02043        |                    .  |  .            |
 7      0.06832        |                    .  |* .            |
 8     -0.07145        |                    . *|  .            |
 9      0.00233        |                    .  |  .            |
10     -0.06905        |                    . *|  .            |
11      0.04120        |                    .  |* .            |
12      0.10534        |                    .  |**.            |
13      0.11232        |                    .  |**.            |
14     -0.04382        |                    . *|  .            |
```

(c) The RSPAC

Forecasts for variable y

| Obs | Forecast | Std Error | 95% Confidence Limits | |
|-----|----------|-----------|------------------------|--------|
| 162 | 82.3313 | 2.3695 | 77.6873 | 86.9754 |
| 163 | 82.8782 | 4.3458 | 74.3606 | 91.3959 |
| 164 | 82.6615 | 5.7223 | 71.4459 | 93.8770 |
| 165 | 80.8749 | 6.6770 | 67.7882 | 93.9615 |
| 166 | 79.3489 | 7.4340 | 64.7785 | 93.9194 |
| 167 | 78.1423 | 8.1126 | 62.2419 | 94.0428 |
| 168 | 77.8833 | 8.5044 | 61.2151 | 94.5515 |
| 169 | 78.0521 | 8.7798 | 60.8439 | 95.2602 |
| 170 | 78.2089 | 9.0420 | 60.4869 | 95.9309 |
| 171 | 78.2501 | 9.3164 | 59.9902 | 96.5100 |

(d) Forecasts of $y_{162}$ through $y_{171}$

# 10.5 BOX–JENKINS IMPLEMENTATION OF EXPONENTIAL SMOOTHING

Exponential smoothing methods for forecasting a time series were introduced in Chapter 8. In this section we show how to implement two of the exponential smoothing methods (simple exponential smoothing and Holt's trend corrected exponential smoothing) by using the Box–Jenkins methodology. All of the exponential smoothing methods of Chapter 8, except the multiplicative Holt–Winters method, have a corresponding Box–Jenkins model. These Box–Jenkins models are equivalent to the state space models of Section 8.6. The multiplicative Holt–Winters method is more complex because of the multiplicative or increasing seasonal pattern.

The next example illustrates the following fact.

## A BOX–JENKINS MODEL FOR SIMPLE EXPONENTIAL SMOOTHING

It can be shown that forecasting with simple exponential smoothing is equivalent to forecasting with the Box–Jenkins model

$$z_t = a_t - \theta_1 a_{t-1} \quad \text{(moving average model of order 1)}$$

where

$$z_t = y_t - y_{t-1} \quad \text{(first differences)}$$

In this case the moving average parameter $\theta_1$ in the Box–Jenkins model and the smoothing parameter $\alpha$ in the state space model are related by

$$\theta_1 = 1 - \alpha$$

It follows that we can implement simple exponential smoothing by using SAS or other forecasting software to implement the Box–Jenkins model.

**EXAMPLE 10.8**   Figure 10.17 presents the SAS output of the SAC and SPAC of the cod catch values (see Table 6.1) obtained by using the transformation to find first differences, $z_t = y_t - y_{t-1}$. For these first differences, the SAC has a spike at lag 1 and cuts off after lag 1, and the SPAC dies down. From Table 9.6, we see that this SAC and SPAC match the TAC and TPAC for the first-order moving average model

$$z_t = a_t - \theta_1 a_{t-1}$$

We omit the constant $\delta$ from the model because the absolute value of

$$\frac{\bar{z}}{s/\sqrt{n-b+1}} = \frac{0.130435}{49.30147/\sqrt{23}} = .00127$$

is less than 2.

This is the Box–Jenkins model that is equivalent to simple exponential smoothing. Figure 10.18 presents the SAS output of estimation, diagnostic checking, and forecasting for this model. Note that the point and 95% prediction interval forecasts of $y_{25}$ given by the Box–Jenkins model are (see Figure 10.18d).

$$\hat{y}_{25} = 353.4390 \quad \text{and} \quad [283.0712, 423.8069]$$

whereas the point and 95% interval forecasts of $y_{25}$ given by the simple exponential smoothing procedure carried out in Examples 8.1 and 8.2 are

$$\hat{y}_{25} = 354.5438 \quad \text{and} \quad [286.04, 423.05]$$

**FIGURE 10.17** SAS output of the SAC and SPAC of the cod catch values obtained with the transformation $z_t = y_t - y_{t-1}$

```
                        Name of Variable = y

             Period(s) of Differencing                    1
             Mean of Working Series            0.130435
             Standard Deviation                49.30147
             Number of Observations                  23
             Observation(s) eliminated by differencing    1

                           Autocorrelations

Lag   Covariance   Correlation  -1 9 8 7 6 5 4 3 2 1 0 1 2 3 4 5 6 7 8 9 1   Std Error

 0    2430.635      1.00000      |                    |********************|        0
 1   -1017.838      -.41875      |           ********|                    .        0.208514
 2    -384.039      -.15800      |              .   ***|           .              0.242336
 3     171.508      0.07056      |              .      |*          .              0.246774
 4    -75.564395    -.03109      |              .     *|           .              0.247649
 5     71.542615    0.02943      |              .      |*          .              0.247819
```

(a) The SAC

```
                     Partial Autocorrelations

Lag    Correlation   -1 9 8 7 6 5 4 3 2 1 0 1 2 3 4 5 6 7 8 9 1

 1      -0.41875     |         ********|           .              |
 2      -0.40424     |         ********|           .              |
 3      -0.27776     |          . ******|          .              |
 4      -0.29476     |          . ******|          .              |
 5      -0.24592     |          . *****|           .              |
```

(b) The SPAC

**FIGURE 10.18** SAS output of estimation, diagnostic checking, and forecasting for the model $z_t = a_t - \theta_1 a_{t-1}$ where $z_t = y_t - y_{t-1}$

```
                 Conditional Least Squares Estimation

                          Standard              Approx
Parameter    Estimate       Error    t Value   Pr > |t|    Lag

MA1,1        0.95364       0.09822     9.71     <.0001       1


                 Variance Estimate        1288.999
                 Std Error Estimate        35.90263
                 AIC                      230.9661
                 SBC                      232.1016
                 Number of Residuals            23
               * AIC and SBC do not include log determinant.
```

(a) Estimation

**FIGURE 10.18** (Continued)

Autocorrelation Check of Residuals

| To Lag | Chi-Square | DF | Pr > ChiSq | | | | Autocorrelations | | | |
|---|---|---|---|---|---|---|---|---|---|---|
| 6 | 1.56 | 5 | 0.9060 | -0.035 | -0.182 | -0.024 | -0.005 | 0.083 | 0.107 |
| 12 | 11.51 | 11 | 0.4018 | -0.142 | -0.118 | 0.233 | 0.341 | -0.119 | -0.112 |
| 18 | 12.97 | 17 | 0.7379 | -0.015 | -0.064 | 0.109 | 0.004 | 0.000 | -0.055 |

Autocorrelation Plot of Residuals

| Lag | Covariance | Correlation | -1 9 8 7 6 5 4 3 2 1 0 1 2 3 4 5 6 7 8 9 1 | Std Error |
|---|---|---|---|---|
| 0 | 1288.999 | 1.00000 | &#124;                    &#124;********************&#124; | 0 |
| 1 | -45.075516 | -.03497 | &#124;                 .        *&#124;          . &#124; | 0.208514 |
| 2 | -234.893 | -.18223 | &#124;                 .    ****&#124;          . &#124; | 0.208769 |
| 3 | -30.956127 | -.02402 | &#124;                 .        *&#124;          . &#124; | 0.215574 |
| 4 | -6.043470 | -.00469 | &#124;                 .         &#124;          . &#124; | 0.215690 |
| 5 | 106.486 | 0.08261 | &#124;                 .         &#124;**        . &#124; | 0.215695 |

(b) The RSAC

Partial Autocorrelations

| Lag | Correlation | -1 9 8 7 6 5 4 3 2 1 0 1 2 3 4 5 6 7 8 9 1 |
|---|---|---|
| 1 | -0.03497 | &#124;              .       *&#124;     . &#124; |
| 2 | -0.18368 | &#124;              .   ****&#124;     . &#124; |
| 3 | -0.03936 | &#124;              .       *&#124;     . &#124; |
| 4 | -0.04255 | &#124;              .       *&#124;     . &#124; |
| 5 | 0.07142 | &#124;              .        &#124;*    . &#124; |

(c) The RSPAC

Forecasts for variable y

| Obs | Forecast | Std Error | 95% Confidence Limits | |
|---|---|---|---|---|
| 25 | 353.4390 | 35.9026 | 283.0712 | 423.8069 |
| 26 | 353.4390 | 35.9412 | 282.9956 | 423.8825 |
| 27 | 353.4390 | 35.9797 | 282.9201 | 423.9580 |

(d) Forecasts for $y_{25}$, $y_{26}$, and $y_{27}$

The next example illustrates the following fact.

## A BOX–JENKINS MODEL FOR HOLT'S TREND CORRECTED EXPONENTIAL SMOOTHING

It can be shown that forecasting with Holt's trend corrected exponential smoothing is equivalent to forecasting with the Box–Jenkins model

$$z_t = a_t - \theta_1 a_{t-1} - \theta_2 a_{t-2} \quad \text{(moving average model of order 2)}$$

where

$$z_t = y_t - 2y_{t-1} + y_{t-2} \quad \text{(second differences)}$$

In this case the moving average parameters $\theta_1$ and $\theta_2$ in the Box–Jenkins model are related to the smoothing parameters $\alpha$ and $\gamma$ in the state space model by

$$\theta_1 = 2 - \alpha - \gamma \quad \text{and} \quad \theta_2 = \alpha - 1$$

It follows that we can implement Holt's trend corrected exponential smoothing by using SAS to implement the Box–Jenkins model.

**EXAMPLE 10.9**   In Example 8.3 we analyzed 52 values for weekly thermostat sales by using Holt's trend corrected exponential smoothing. We now analyze the thermostat sales by using the equivalent Box–Jenkins model

$$z_t = a_t - \theta_1 a_{t-1} - \theta_2 a_{t-2}$$

where

$$z_t = y_t - 2y_{t-1} + y_{t-2}$$

Figure 10.19 presents the SAS output of the estimation, diagnostic checking, and forecasting for this model. Note that the point and 95% interval forecasts of $y_{53}$ given by the Box–Jenkins model are

$$\hat{y}_{53} = 334.7299 \quad \text{and} \quad [264.7034, 404.7564]$$

whereas the point and 95% interval forecasts of $y_{53}$ given by Holt's trend corrected exponential smoothing in Example 8.3 are

$$\hat{y}_{53} = 320.45 \quad \text{and} \quad [265.79, \ 375.11]$$

In support of the Box–Jenkins methodology, advocates argue that it will identify a model equivalent to exponential smoothing if exponential smoothing is the best method and also allows one to find more appropriate models. Proponents of exponential smoothing argue that it is easier to explain the simple components of level, growth rate, and seasonal factors to users of the forecasts and that even for nonseasonal time series one should have at least 50 observations for the identification process in the Box–Jenkins method. In addition, they say that the exponential smoothing methods are easier to implement when thousands or tens of thousands of time series must be forecasted.

**FIGURE 10.19** SAS output of estimation, diagnostic checking, and forecasting for the model $z_t = a_t - \theta_1 a_{t-1} - \theta_2 a_{t-2}$ where $z_t = y_t - 2y_{t-1} + y_{t-2}$

```
                Conditional Least Squares Estimation

                             Standard              Approx
Parameter       Estimate       Error     t Value   Pr > |t|    Lag

MA1,1           1.18073       0.14016      8.42     <.0001       1
MA1,2          -0.31415       0.14049     -2.24     0.0300       2


                Variance Estimate        1276.523
                Std Error Estimate        35.72846
                AIC                      501.4475
                SBC                      505.2716
                Number of Residuals         50
          * AIC and SBC do not include log determinant.
```

(a) Estimation

```
              Autocorrelation Check of Residuals

  To     Chi-            Pr >
 Lag    Square    DF    ChiSq  --------------------Autocorrelations--------------------

   6     4.42      4    0.3521   0.033   -0.040   -0.079   -0.107    0.002    0.236
  12     7.14     10    0.7126   0.134    0.025    0.022   -0.132    0.027   -0.074
  18     9.84     16    0.8750   0.180    0.010   -0.031   -0.005   -0.013   -0.063
  24    14.85     22    0.8685   0.074    0.134   -0.124    0.085   -0.069   -0.069
```

```
              Autocorrelation Plot of Residuals

Lag   Covariance   Correlation  -1 9 8 7 6 5 4 3 2 1 0 1 2 3 4 5 6 7 8 9 1   Std Error

 0    1276.523      1.00000      |                    |********************|       0
 1      41.497825   0.03251      |                    |*       .           |   0.141421
 2     -50.593003  -.03963       |                .  *|        .           |   0.141571
 3    -101.309     -.07936       |                . **|        .           |   0.141792
 4    -136.822     -.10718       |                . **|        .           |   0.142678
 5       2.877767   0.00225      |                .   |        .           |   0.144279
 6     300.783      0.23563      |                    |*****.              |   0.144280
```

(b) The RSAC

```
                Partial Autocorrelations

Lag   Correlation  -1 9 8 7 6 5 4 3 2 1 0 1 2 3 4 5 6 7 8 9 1

 1     0.03251     |                .   |*       .           |
 2    -0.04073     |                .  *|        .           |
 3    -0.07691     |                . **|        .           |
 4    -0.10466     |                . **|        .           |
 5     0.00186     |                .   |        .           |
 6     0.22511     |                .   |*****.              |
```

(c) The RSPAC

```
                Forecasts for variable y

Obs     Forecast   Std Error    95% Confidence Limits

53     334.7299     35.7285     264.7034     404.7564
54     342.2780     46.1880     251.7512     432.8048
55     349.8261     57.3755     237.3723     462.2799
```

(d) Forecasts of $y_{53}$, $y_{54}$, and $y_{55}$

## Exercises

Figure 10.20 presents the SAS output of estimation, diagnostic checking, and forecasting when the model

$$z_t = \delta + \phi_1 z_{t-1} + a_t$$

where

$$z_t = y_t - y_{t-1}$$

is used to analyze the Ultra Shine toothpaste sales data in Table 9.7. Figure 10.21 (page 482) presents the corresponding MINITAB output. **Exercises 10.1 through 10.6 are based on these outputs.**

**10.1** Using the MINITAB output, identify the final point estimate of $\phi_1$ and verify that it satisfies the stationarity condition. Note that MINITAB finds the final point estimate of $\delta$ to be 3.0231.

**10.2** Using the SAS output, identify the final point estimate of $\phi_1$ and verify that it satisfies the stationarity condition. Note that SAS finds the final point estimate

of $\mu$ to be 8.69994 and the final point estimate of $\delta = \mu(1 - \phi_1)$ to be $8.69994(1 - .64774) = 3.06467$.

**10.3** Using the SAS and/or MINITAB output, determine whether the appropriate $t$-statistics indicate that $\delta$ and $\phi_1$ should be retained in the Ultra Shine model. Set $\alpha = .05$.

**10.4** Using the first $K = 6$ autocorrelations in Figure 10.20(b), verify that $Q^* = 8.02$. Test the adequacy of the Ultra Shine model by comparing this value of $Q^*$ with a rejection point based on setting $\alpha = .05$. What do the $p$-values say about model adequacy?

**10.5** Using the first $K = 12$ autocorrelations in Figure 10.21(b) on page 483, verify that $Q^* = 8.9$. Test the adequacy of the Ultra Shine model by comparing this value of $Q^*$ with a rejection point based on setting $\alpha = .05$.

**10.6** Using the SAS and/or MINITAB output, calculate a 99% prediction interval for $y_{91}$.

**FIGURE 10.20 (for Exercises 10.1–10.6)** SAS output of estimation, diagnostic checking, and forecasting of toothpaste sales using the model $z_t = \delta + \phi_1 z_{t-1} + a_t$ where $z_t = y_t - y_{t-1}$

The ARIMA Procedure

Conditional Least Squares Estimation

| Iteration | SSE | MU | AR1,1 | Constant | Lambda | R Crit |
|---|---|---|---|---|---|---|
| 0 | 681.46 | 8.92674 | 0.64279 | 3.188758 | 0.00001 | 1 |
| 1 | 680.86 | 8.70798 | 0.64516 | 3.089906 | 1E-6 | 0.029489 |
| 2 | 680.85 | 8.70279 | 0.64766 | 3.066321 | 1E-7 | 0.003303 |
| 3 | 680.85 | 8.69994 | 0.64774 | 3.064672 | 1E-8 | 0.000384 |

Conditional Least Squares Estimation

| Parameter | Estimate | Standard Error | t Value | Approx Pr > \|t\| | Lag |
|---|---|---|---|---|---|
| MU | 8.69994 | 0.81123 | 10.72 | <.0001 | 0 |
| AR1,1 | 0.64774 | 0.08213 | 7.89 | <.0001 | 1 |

| | | Correlations of Parameter Estimates | | |
|---|---|---|---|---|
| Constant Estimate | 3.064672 | | | |
| Variance Estimate | 7.825839 | Parameter | MU | AR1,1 |
| Std Error Estimate | 2.79747 | | | |
| AIC | 437.6596 | MU | 1.000 | -0.053 |
| SBC | 442.6369 | AR1,1 | -0.053 | 1.000 |
| Number of Residuals | 89 | | | |

\* AIC and SBC do not include log determinant.

(a) Estimation

**FIGURE 10.20** (Continued)

Autocorrelation Check of Residuals

| To Lag | Chi-Square | DF | Pr > ChiSq | ------Autocorrelations------ | | | | | |
|--------|-----------|-----|-----------|-------|--------|--------|--------|--------|-------|
| 6 | 8.02 | 5 | 0.1550 | 0.104 | -0.202 | -0.022 | 0.024 | 0.064 | 0.168 |
| 12 | 8.63 | 11 | 0.6562 | 0.016 | -0.015 | -0.048 | -0.004 | -0.013 | 0.054 |
| 18 | 13.29 | 17 | 0.7164 | 0.010 | -0.095 | 0.092 | 0.106 | -0.101 | 0.056 |
| 24 | 21.64 | 23 | 0.5418 | 0.193 | 0.008 | -0.013 | -0.116 | -0.099 | 0.097 |

Autocorrelation Plot of Residuals

| Lag | Covariance | Correlation | -1 9 8 7 6 5 4 3 2 1 0 1 2 3 4 5 6 7 8 9 1 | Std Error |
|-----|-----------|-------------|---------------------------------------------|-----------|
| 0 | 7.825839 | 1.00000 | \|                   \|********************\| | 0 |
| 1 | 0.810903 | 0.10362 | \|                   . \|** .              \| | 0.106000 |
| 2 | -1.578721 | -.20173 | \|                 ****\| .              \| | 0.107132 |
| 3 | -0.168697 | -.02156 | \|                   . \| .              \| | 0.111318 |
| 4 | 0.186704 | 0.02386 | \|                   . \| .              \| | 0.111365 |
| 5 | 0.499246 | 0.06379 | \|                   . \|* .              \| | 0.111423 |
| 6 | 1.315067 | 0.16804 | \|                   . \|*** .              \| | 0.111832 |
| 7 | 0.128687 | 0.01644 | \|                   . \| .              \| | 0.114634 |
| 8 | -0.117768 | -.01505 | \|                   . \| .              \| | 0.114661 |
| 9 | -0.377320 | -.04821 | \|                   . *\| .              \| | 0.114683 |
| 10 | -0.034512 | -.00441 | \|                   . \| .              \| | 0.114910 |
| 11 | -0.102626 | -.01311 | \|                   . \| .              \| | 0.114912 |
| 12 | 0.418786 | 0.05351 | \|                   . \|* .              \| | 0.114929 |
| 13 | 0.077975 | 0.00996 | \|                   . \| .              \| | 0.115209 |
| 14 | -0.742256 | -.09485 | \|                   . **\| .              \| | 0.115218 |

"." marks two standard errors

(b) The RSAC

Partial Autocorrelations

| Lag | Correlation | -1 9 8 7 6 5 4 3 2 1 0 1 2 3 4 5 6 7 8 9 1 |
|-----|-------------|---------------------------------------------|
| 1 | 0.10362 | \|               . \|** .              \| |
| 2 | -0.21477 | \|             ****\| .              \| |
| 3 | 0.02765 | \|               . \|* .              \| |
| 4 | -0.02142 | \|               . \| .              \| |
| 5 | 0.06812 | \|               . \|* .              \| |
| 6 | 0.16273 | \|               . \|*** .              \| |
| 7 | 0.00170 | \|               . \| .              \| |
| 8 | 0.05580 | \|               . \|* .              \| |
| 9 | -0.05029 | \|               . *\| .              \| |
| 10 | 0.00803 | \|               . \| .              \| |
| 11 | -0.05818 | \|               . *\| .              \| |
| 12 | 0.03618 | \|               . \|* .              \| |
| 13 | -0.01836 | \|               . \| .              \| |
| 14 | -0.08454 | \|               . **\| .              \| |

(c) The RSPAC

**FIGURE 10.20** (Continued)

Forecasts for variable y

| Obs | Forecast | Std Error | 95% Confidence Limits | |
|-----|----------|-----------|-----------------------|-----------|
| 91  | 1039.7086 | 2.7975  | 1034.2257 | 1045.1916 |
| 92  | 1049.3988 | 5.3920  | 1038.8307 | 1059.9668 |
| 93  | 1058.7401 | 7.9069  | 1043.2429 | 1074.2373 |
| 94  | 1067.8555 | 10.2633 | 1047.7397 | 1087.9712 |
| 95  | 1076.8245 | 12.4435 | 1052.4358 | 1101.2132 |
| 96  | 1085.6988 | 14.4545 | 1057.3684 | 1114.0292 |
| 97  | 1094.5116 | 16.3129 | 1062.5389 | 1126.4843 |
| 98  | 1103.2847 | 18.0369 | 1067.9331 | 1138.6363 |
| 99  | 1112.0320 | 19.6440 | 1073.5304 | 1150.5336 |
| 100 | 1120.7626 | 21.1501 | 1079.3093 | 1162.2159 |

(d) Forecasts of $y_{91}$ through $y_{100}$

**FIGURE 10.21 (for Exercises 10.1–10.6)**  MINITAB output of estimation, diagnostic checking, and forecasting of toothpaste sales using the model $z_t = \delta + \phi_1 z_{t-1} + a_t$ where $z_t = y_t - y_{t-1}$

Estimates at each iteration

| Iteration | SSE | Parameters | |
|-----------|---------|-------|-------|
| 0 | 1026.90 | 0.100 | 8.124 |
| 1 | 861.72  | 0.250 | 6.764 |
| 2 | 747.68  | 0.400 | 5.404 |
| 3 | 684.77  | 0.550 | 4.041 |
| 4 | 671.28  | 0.647 | 3.147 |
| 5 | 671.10  | 0.658 | 3.040 |
| 6 | 671.09  | 0.659 | 3.025 |
| 7 | 671.09  | 0.659 | 3.023 |

Relative change in each estimate less than  0.0010

Final Estimates of Parameters

| Type | Coef | SE Coef | T | P |
|------|--------|---------|-------|-------|
| AR  1   | 0.6591 | 0.0808 | 8.15  | 0.000 |
| Constant | 3.0231 | 0.2931 | 10.31 | 0.000 |

Differencing: 1 regular difference
Number of observations:  Original series 90, after differencing 89
Residuals:   SS =  665.270  (backforecasts excluded)
             MS =   7.647  DF = 87

(a) Estimation

**FIGURE 10.21** (Continued)

```
Modified Box-Pierce (Ljung-Box) Chi-Square statistic
Lag              12       24       36       48
Chi-Square      8.9     21.6     32.5     42.5
DF               10       22       34       46
P-Value       0.539    0.484    0.543    0.621
```

Autocorrelation Function for RESI1

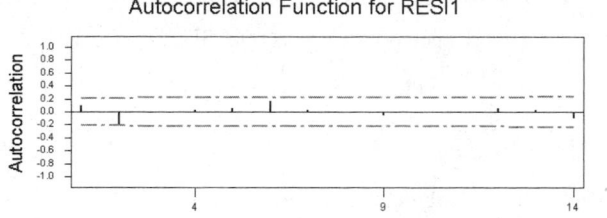

| Lag | Corr | T | LBQ | Lag | Corr | T | LBQ |
|-----|------|------|------|-----|------|------|------|
| 1 | 0.09 | 0.88 | 0.80 | 8 | -0.01 | -0.11 | 8.23 |
| 2 | -0.21 | -1.97 | 4.94 | 9 | -0.06 | -0.49 | 8.55 |
| 3 | -0.02 | -0.17 | 4.97 | 10 | -0.01 | -0.12 | 8.57 |
| 4 | 0.03 | 0.26 | 5.05 | 11 | -0.01 | -0.08 | 8.58 |
| 5 | 0.05 | 0.46 | 5.31 | 12 | 0.06 | 0.50 | 8.93 |
| 6 | 0.17 | 1.52 | 8.12 | 13 | 0.02 | 0.20 | 8.98 |
| 7 | 0.03 | 0.27 | 8.22 | 14 | -0.10 | -0.86 | 10.05 |

(b) The RSAC

Partial Autocorrelation Function for RESI1

| Lag | PAC | T | Lag | PAC | T |
|-----|------|------|-----|------|------|
| 1 | 0.09 | 0.88 | 8 | 0.06 | 0.58 |
| 2 | -0.22 | -2.09 | 9 | -0.06 | -0.57 |
| 3 | 0.03 | 0.25 | 10 | -0.00 | -0.01 |
| 4 | -0.02 | -0.19 | 11 | -0.05 | -0.50 |
| 5 | 0.00 | 0.52 | 12 | 0.03 | 0.29 |
| 6 | 0.17 | 1.61 | 13 | -0.01 | -0.05 |
| 7 | 0.02 | 0.14 | 14 | -0.09 | -0.89 |

(c) The RSPAC

```
Forecasts from period 90
                      95 Percent Limits
Period    Forecast       Lower      Upper
  91       1039.79      1034.37    1045.21
  92       1049.61      1039.11    1060.12
  93       1059.11      1043.65    1074.57
  94       1068.39      1048.25    1088.53
  95       1077.53      1053.05    1102.02
  96       1086.58      1058.08    1115.09
  97       1095.57      1063.34    1127.80
  98       1104.52      1068.82    1140.21
  99       1110.44      1074.51    1152.36
 100       1122.34      1080.38    1164.30
```

(d) Forecasts of $y_{91}$ through $y_{100}$

Figure 10.22 presents the MINITAB output of estimation, diagnostic checking, and forecasting when the model

$$y_t = \delta + a_t - \theta_1 a_{t-1} - \theta_2 a_{t-2}$$

is used to analyze the daily viscosity readings for Chemical Product XR-22 in Table 9.9. **Exercises 10.7 through 10.10 are based on this output.**

**10.7** Identify the final point estimates of $\theta_1$ and $\theta_2$ and verify that they satisfy the invertibility conditions. Identify the final point estimate of $\delta$.

**10.8** Use the appropriate $t$-statistics to determine whether $\delta$, $\theta_1$, and $\theta_2$ should be retained in the chemical product model. Set $\alpha = .05$.

**10.9** Use the $p$-values associated with $Q^*$ to determine whether the chemical product model is adequate.

**10.10** Calculate a 99% prediction interval for $y_{151}$.

*Hint:* Upper $-$ Lower $= 2(1.96)\, SE_{n+\tau}(n)$

**FIGURE 10.22  (for Exercises 10.7–10.10)** MINITAB output of estimation, diagnostic checking, and forecasting of daily viscosities using the model $y_t = \delta + a_t - \theta_1 a_{t-1} - \theta_2 a_{t-2}$

```
Final Estimates of Parameters
Type          Coef      SE Coef         T        P
MA   1       0.5237     0.0631        8.29    0.000
MA   2      -0.6569     0.0630      -10.42    0.000
Constant    35.1822     0.2223      158.23    0.000
Mean        35.1822     0.2223

Number of observations:  150
Residuals:    SS =   845.702   (backforecasts excluded)
              MS =     5.753   DF = 147
```

(a) Estimation

```
Modified Box-Pierce (Ljung-Box) Chi-Square statistic
Lag              12        24        36        48
Chi-Square     10.4      22.5      27.3      38.0
DF                9        21        33        45
P-Value       0.318     0.369     0.745     0.760
```

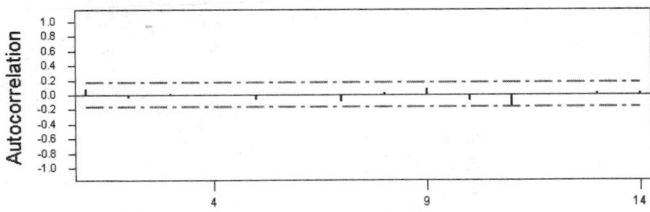

Autocorrelation Function for RESI1

(b) The RSAC

**FIGURE 10.22** (Continued)

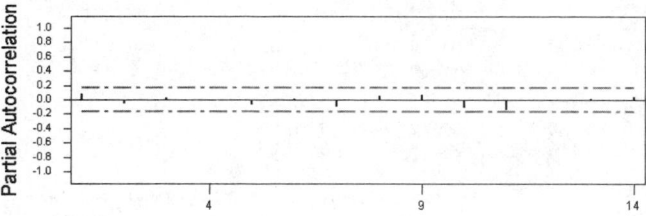

(c) The RSPAC

```
Forecasts from period 150
                            95 Percent Limits
Period     Forecast      Lower        Upper
  151      34.1996      29.4975      38.9017
  152      33.6812      28.3733      38.9891
  153      35.1822      29.0411      41.3234
  154      35.1822      29.0411      41.3234
  155      35.1822      29.0411      41.3234
  156      35.1822      29.0411      41.3234
  157      35.1822      29.0411      41.3234
  158      35.1822      29.0411      41.3234
  159      35.1822      29.0411      41.3234
  160      35.1822      29.0411      41.3234
```

(d) Forecasts of $y_{151}$ through $y_{160}$

Two possible tentative models for the Shimmer Shampoo sales values from Exercise 9.7 are

Model 1:    $y_t = \delta + \phi_1 y_{t-1} + \phi_2 y_{t-2} + a_t$

Model 2:    $z_t = \phi_1 z_{t-1} + a_t$

where    $z_t = y_t - y_{t-1}$

The SAS outputs for the estimation, diagnostic checking, and forecasting for Model 1 and Model 2 are given in Figure 10.23 (page 486) and Figure 10.24 (page 487), respectively. **Exercises 10.11 and 10.12 are based on these outputs.**

**10.11** Missing from the output for Model 1 in Figure 10.23 are the iteration steps for the estimation process that stop, in this case, after iteration 14 with a warning that "the model defined by the new estimates is unstable, and the estimates may not have converged." Using the information that is available in Figure 10.23 (page 486), identify two serious problems for Model 1.

**10.12** Using the SAS output in Figure 10.24 (page 487), check that all the conditions for a model to be suitable for forecasting are met.

Note: The difficulty in deciding whether the original sales values for Shimmer Shampoo are stationary is an example of a problem that is frequently encountered. In addition to examining the graph of the time series values, examining the SAC, and checking the stationarity conditions for the autoregressive

(Continues on page 488)

**FIGURE 10.23 (for Exercises 10.11 and 10.12)** SAS output of estimation, diagnostic checking, and forecasting of shampoo sales using Model 1, $y_t = \delta + \phi_1 y_{t-1} + \phi_2 y_{t-2} + a_t$

Conditional Least Squares Estimation

| Parameter | Estimate | Standard Error | t Value | Approx Pr > \|t\| | Lag |
|---|---|---|---|---|---|
| MU | 332.61159 | 19.42959 | 17.12 | <.0001 | 0 |
| AR1,1 | 0.35879 | 0.15150 | 2.37 | 0.0253 | 1 |
| AR1,2 | 0.64121 | 0.15316 | 4.19 | 0.0003 | 2 |

| | |
|---|---|
| Constant Estimate | 4.293E-6 |
| Variance Estimate | 532.4506 |
| Std Error Estimate | 23.07489 |
| AIC | 276.3002 |
| SBC | 280.5038 |
| Number of Residuals | 30 |

* AIC and SBC do not include log determinant.

Correlations of Parameter Estimates

| Parameter | MU | AR1,1 | AR1,2 |
|---|---|---|---|
| MU | 1.000 | -0.023 | 0.021 |
| AR1,1 | -0.023 | 1.000 | -0.934 |
| AR1,2 | 0.021 | -0.934 | 1.000 |

(a) Estimation

Autocorrelation Check of Residuals

| To Lag | Chi-Square | DF | Pr > ChiSq | --------------------Autocorrelations-------------------- | | | | | |
|---|---|---|---|---|---|---|---|---|---|
| 6 | 2.20 | 4 | 0.6990 | 0.029 | 0.116 | 0.066 | 0.007 | 0.052 | -0.191 |
| 12 | 7.72 | 10 | 0.6561 | 0.012 | 0.137 | -0.227 | 0.080 | -0.146 | 0.134 |
| 18 | 13.72 | 16 | 0.6194 | 0.158 | 0.047 | 0.251 | -0.043 | 0.052 | -0.038 |
| 24 | 21.40 | 22 | 0.4964 | -0.117 | -0.015 | -0.138 | -0.078 | 0.037 | -0.148 |

Autocorrelation Plot of Residuals

| Lag | Covariance | Correlation | -1 9 8 7 6 5 4 3 2 1 0 1 2 3 4 5 6 7 8 9 1 | Std Error |
|---|---|---|---|---|
| 0 | 532.451 | 1.00000 | \|********************\| | 0 |
| 1 | 15.248899 | 0.02864 | . \|* . | 0.182574 |
| 2 | 61.555429 | 0.11561 | . \|** . | 0.182724 |
| 3 | 35.167542 | 0.06605 | . \|* . | 0.185146 |
| 4 | 3.934699 | 0.00739 | . \| . | 0.185930 |
| 5 | 27.734240 | 0.05209 | . \|* . | 0.185939 |
| 6 | -101.505 | -.19064 | . ****\| . | 0.186425 |
| 7 | 6.333419 | 0.01189 | . \| . | 0.192814 |

(b) The RSAC

Partial Autocorrelations

| Lag | Correlation | -1 9 8 7 6 5 4 3 2 1 0 1 2 3 4 5 6 7 8 9 1 |
|---|---|---|
| 1 | 0.02864 | . \|* . |
| 2 | 0.11488 | . \|** . |
| 3 | 0.06068 | . \|* . |
| 4 | -0.00882 | . \| . |
| 5 | 0.03829 | . \|* . |
| 6 | -0.20002 | . ****\| . |

(c) The RSPAC

Forecasts for variable y

| Obs | Forecast | Std Error | 95% Confidence Limits | |
|---|---|---|---|---|
| 31 | 402.8933 | 23.0749 | 357.6674 | 448.1193 |
| 32 | 411.9387 | 24.5151 | 363.8899 | 459.9875 |
| 33 | 406.1387 | 30.2760 | 346.7989 | 465.4785 |
| 34 | 409.8577 | 32.4519 | 346.2532 | 473.4622 |

(d) Forecasts for $y_{31}$ through $y_{34}$

**FIGURE 10.24 (for Exercises 10.11 and 10.12)** SAS output of estimation, diagnostic checking, and forecasting of shampoo sales using Model 2, $z_t = \phi_1 z_{t-1} + a_t$ where $z_t = y_t - y_{t-1}$

Conditional Least Squares Estimation

| Iteration | SSE | AR1,1 | Lambda | R Crit |
|---|---|---|---|---|
| 0 | 14482 | -0.64181 | 0.00001 | 1 |
| 1 | 14482 | -0.64031 | 1E-6 | 0.001924 |
| 2 | 14482 | -0.64031 | 1E-7 | 1.941E-8 |

ARIMA Estimation Optimization Summary

| | |
|---|---|
| Estimation Method | Conditional Least Squares |
| Parameters Estimated | 1 |
| Termination Criteria | Maximum Relative Change in Estimates |
| Iteration Stopping Value | 0.001 |
| Criteria Value | 2.347E-8 |
| Alternate Criteria | Relative Change in Objective Function |
| Alternate Criteria Value | 3.77E-16 |
| Maximum Absolute Value of Gradient | 0.000357 |
| R-Square Change from Last Iteration | 1.941E-8 |
| Objective Function | Sum of Squared Residuals |
| Objective Function Value | 14482.41 |
| Marquardt's Lambda Coefficient | 1E-7 |
| Numerical Derivative Perturbation Delta | 0.001 |
| Iterations | 2 |

Conditional Least Squares Estimation

| Parameter | Estimate | Standard Error | t Value | Approx Pr > \|t\| | Lag |
|---|---|---|---|---|---|
| AR1,1 | -0.64031 | 0.14765 | -4.34 | 0.0002 | 1 |

| | |
|---|---|
| Variance Estimate | 517.2288 |
| Std Error Estimate | 22.74267 |
| AIC | 264.4869 |
| SBC | 265.8542 |
| Number of Residuals | 29 |

\* AIC and SBC do not include log determinant.

(a) Estimation

Autocorrelation Check of Residuals

| To Lag | Chi-Square | DF | Pr > ChiSq | --------------------Autocorrelations-------------------- | | | | | |
|---|---|---|---|---|---|---|---|---|---|
| 6 | 2.02 | 5 | 0.8464 | 0.029 | 0.107 | 0.056 | -0.020 | 0.030 | -0.193 |
| 12 | 7.47 | 11 | 0.7600 | 0.012 | 0.141 | -0.225 | 0.072 | -0.154 | 0.130 |
| 18 | 13.30 | 17 | 0.7156 | 0.169 | 0.045 | 0.236 | -0.041 | 0.042 | -0.061 |
| 24 | 21.56 | 23 | 0.5468 | -0.144 | -0.014 | -0.129 | -0.001 | 0.043 | -0.137 |

Autocorrelation Plot of Residuals

| Lag | Covariance | Correlation | -1 9 8 7 6 5 4 3 2 1 0 1 2 3 4 5 6 7 8 9 1 | Std Error |
|---|---|---|---|---|
| 0 | 517.229 | 1.00000 | \|********************\| | 0 |
| 1 | 14.885433 | 0.02878 | . \|* . \| | 0.185695 |
| 2 | 55.111720 | 0.10655 | . \|** . \| | 0.185849 |
| 3 | 28.961053 | 0.05599 | . \|* . \| | 0.187944 |
| 4 | -10.442400 | -.02019 | . \| . \| | 0.188518 |
| 5 | 15.494169 | 0.02996 | . \|* . \| | 0.188593 |
| 6 | -99.923700 | -.19319 | . ****\| . \| | 0.188757 |
| 7 | 6.038524 | 0.01167 | . \| . \| | 0.195456 |

(b) The RSAC

**FIGURE 10.24** (Continued)

```
                      Partial Autocorrelations

 Lag    Correlation    -1 9 8 7 6 5 4 3 2 1 0 1 2 3 4 5 6 7 8 9 1
  1        0.02878     I                .      I*   .              I
  2        0.10581     I                .      I**  .              I
  3        0.05082     I                .      I*   .              I
  4       -0.03443     I                .     *I    .              I
  5        0.02017     I                .      I    .              I
  6       -0.19448     I                .  ****I    .              I
```

(c) The RSPAC

```
                   Forecasts for variable y

 Obs       Forecast      Std Error        95% Confidence Limits
  31       402.9132       22.7427        358.3384      447.4880
  32       411.9331       24.1691        364.5625      459.3037
  33       406.1576       29.8423        347.6678      464.6474
  34       409.8557       31.9937        347.1491      472.5623
```

(d) Forecasts for $y_{31}$ through $y_{34}$

parameters, one might also employ statistical tests called unit root tests. The topic of unit root testing is beyond the scope of this book, but an interested reader might start by looking at a paper by Dickey, Bell, and Miller (1986) after mastering the notation in Chapter 12 of this text. Taking differences when it is not necessary to do so is called **overdifferencing.** This can happen when it is difficult to tell whether an original (or previously differenced) time series is stationary. However, some researchers believe that overdifferencing is not a serious problem when the analyst's goal is forecasting rather than testing an economic theory.

**10.13** Consider the thermostat sales data in Example 8.3 and Example 10.9.

a. Using a computer package, find the degree of differencing needed to make the thermostat sales time series stationary. Then use the computer package to identify a Box–Jenkins model for forecasting thermostat sales. Perform appropriate diagnostic tests.

b. Recall that in Example 8.3 we used the Box–Jenkins model that is equivalent to Holt's trend-corrected exponential smoothing to forecast the thermostat sales. Discuss the pros and cons of using the model you found in part (a) versus the Box–Jenkins equivalent Holt's trend corrected exponential smoothing model for forecasting the thermostat sales.

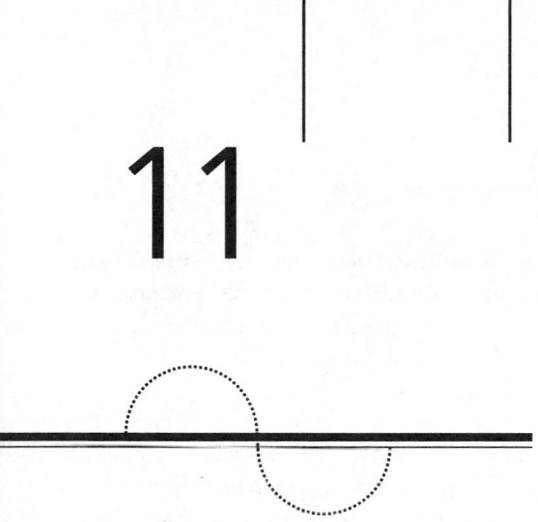

# 11

# *Box–Jenkins Seasonal Modeling*

In this chapter we begin our presentation of **seasonal Box–Jenkins models.** In Section 11.1 we discuss how to transform a seasonal time series into a stationary time series. In Section 11.2 we present three examples of tentative identification, estimation, diagnostic checking, and forecasting for seasonal Box–Jenkins models.

When we employ a time series regression model, we often find that the error terms are **autocorrelated.** That is, the error terms are not independent and, therefore, violate the usual regression assumptions. In such a case we can use the Box–Jenkins methodology to improve the model by modeling the error structure. In Section 11.3 we show how to improve time series regression models by building **Box–Jenkins error term models.**

# 11.1   TRANSFORMING A SEASONAL TIME SERIES INTO A STATIONARY TIME SERIES

We begin this section by illustrating in the following example that if the variability of a time series increases as time advances (which implies that the time series is nonstationary with respect to its variance), then we can sometimes stabilize the variance of the time series by using a "**pre-differencing transformation.**"

**EXAMPLE 11.1**   Traveler's Rest, Inc., operates four hotels in a midwestern city. The analysts in the operating division of the corporation were asked to develop a model that could be used to obtain short-term forecasts (up to one year) of the number of occupied rooms in the hotels. These forecasts were needed by various personnel to assist in decision making with regard to hiring additional help during the summer months, ordering materials that have long delivery lead times, budgeting local advertising expenditures, and so on.

The available historical data consisted of the number of occupied rooms during each day for the previous 15 years, starting on the first day of January. Because monthly forecasts were desired, these data were reduced to monthly averages by dividing each monthly total by the number of days in the month. The monthly room averages for the first 14 of the 15 years, denoted by $y_1, y_2, \ldots, y_{168}$, are given in Table 11.1 and plotted in Figure 11.1.

At the outset it was decided to perform all analyses with the data from the first 14 of the previous 15 years so that forecasts for the 15th year could be used as a check on the validity of the model. Figure 11.1 shows that the monthly room averages follow a strong trend, and that they have a seasonal pattern with one major peak and several minor peaks during the year. It also appears that the amount of seasonal variation is increasing with the level of the time series. This suggests that a predifferencing transformation should be used in order to obtain a transformed series that displays constant seasonal variation.

Figure 11.2 gives a plot of the square roots of the room averages. This plot suggests that the square root transformation is not strong enough to equalize the seasonal variation.

**FIGURE 11.1**
JMP IN plot of monthly hotel room averages for 14 years

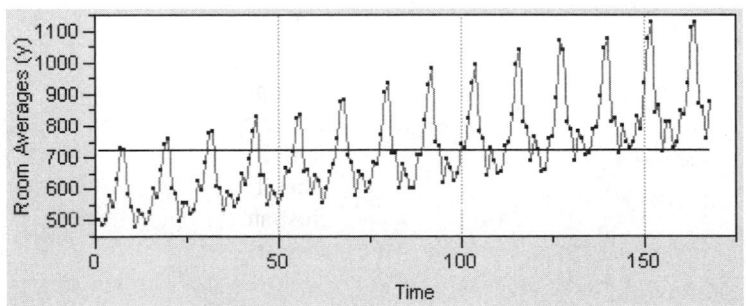

**TABLE 11.1**   Monthly Hotel Room Averages for 14 Years

| t | $y_t$ | t | $y_t$ | t | $y_t$ | t | $y_t$ | t | $y_t$ | t | $y_t$ | t | $y_t$ |
|---|---|---|---|---|---|---|---|---|---|---|---|---|---|
| 1 | 501 | 25 | 555 | 49 | 585 | 73 | 645 | 97 | 665 | 121 | 723 | 145 | 748 |
| 2 | 488 | 26 | 523 | 50 | 553 | 74 | 593 | 98 | 626 | 122 | 655 | 146 | 731 |
| 3 | 504 | 27 | 532 | 51 | 576 | 75 | 617 | 99 | 649 | 123 | 658 | 147 | 748 |
| 4 | 578 | 28 | 623 | 52 | 665 | 76 | 686 | 100 | 740 | 124 | 761 | 148 | 827 |
| 5 | 545 | 29 | 598 | 53 | 656 | 77 | 679 | 101 | 729 | 125 | 768 | 149 | 788 |
| 6 | 632 | 30 | 683 | 54 | 720 | 78 | 773 | 102 | 824 | 126 | 885 | 150 | 937 |
| 7 | 728 | 31 | 774 | 55 | 826 | 79 | 906 | 103 | 937 | 127 | 1067 | 151 | 1076 |
| 8 | 725 | 32 | 780 | 56 | 838 | 80 | 934 | 104 | 994 | 128 | 1038 | 152 | 1125 |
| 9 | 585 | 33 | 609 | 57 | 652 | 81 | 713 | 105 | 781 | 129 | 812 | 153 | 840 |
| 10 | 542 | 34 | 604 | 58 | 661 | 82 | 710 | 106 | 759 | 130 | 790 | 154 | 864 |
| 11 | 480 | 35 | 531 | 59 | 584 | 83 | 600 | 107 | 643 | 131 | 692 | 155 | 717 |
| 12 | 530 | 36 | 592 | 60 | 644 | 84 | 676 | 108 | 728 | 132 | 782 | 156 | 813 |
| 13 | 518 | 37 | 578 | 61 | 623 | 85 | 645 | 109 | 691 | 133 | 758 | 157 | 811 |
| 14 | 489 | 38 | 543 | 62 | 553 | 86 | 602 | 110 | 649 | 134 | 709 | 158 | 732 |
| 15 | 528 | 39 | 565 | 63 | 599 | 87 | 601 | 111 | 656 | 135 | 715 | 159 | 745 |
| 16 | 599 | 40 | 648 | 64 | 657 | 88 | 709 | 112 | 735 | 136 | 788 | 160 | 844 |
| 17 | 572 | 41 | 615 | 65 | 680 | 89 | 706 | 113 | 748 | 137 | 794 | 161 | 833 |
| 18 | 659 | 42 | 697 | 66 | 759 | 90 | 817 | 114 | 837 | 138 | 893 | 162 | 935 |
| 19 | 739 | 43 | 785 | 67 | 878 | 91 | 930 | 115 | 995 | 139 | 1046 | 163 | 1110 |
| 20 | 758 | 44 | 830 | 68 | 881 | 92 | 983 | 116 | 1040 | 140 | 1075 | 164 | 1124 |
| 21 | 602 | 45 | 645 | 69 | 705 | 93 | 745 | 117 | 809 | 141 | 812 | 165 | 868 |
| 22 | 587 | 46 | 643 | 70 | 684 | 94 | 735 | 118 | 793 | 142 | 822 | 166 | 860 |
| 23 | 497 | 47 | 551 | 71 | 577 | 95 | 620 | 119 | 692 | 143 | 714 | 167 | 762 |
| 24 | 558 | 48 | 606 | 72 | 656 | 96 | 698 | 120 | 763 | 144 | 802 | 168 | 877 |

Figure 11.3 shows a plot of the quartic roots of the room averages. The quartic root transformation seems to produce a transformed series with constant seasonal variation. Figure 11.4 gives a plot of the natural logarithms of the room averages. It might be concluded that this transformation has also equalized the seasonal variation. However, careful examination of the plot suggests that the logarithmic transformation may be overtransforming the data (note a slight funneling in appearance in the plot after $t = 125$ or so). Therefore, we conclude that the quartic root transformation best equalizes the amount of seasonal variation over the range of the data. Since, however, Figure 11.3 indicates that the quartic roots do not fluctuate around a constant mean (since they exhibit a strong trend and seasonal variation), the quartic roots are nonstationary. We now discuss how to use differencing to transform seasonal nonstationary time series values into stationary time series values.

In general, let $y_t^*$ represent an appropriate predifferencing transformation. For example, $y_t^* = y_t^{.25}$ if we need to take the quartic roots of the original time series values, and $y_t^* = y_t$ if we do not need a predifferencing transformation. Experience with Box–Jenkins modeling indicates that if we are analyzing a seasonal time series, then one of the four transformations illustrated in Table 11.2 will usually produce stationary time series values. The transformation

$$z_t = y_t^*$$

**FIGURE 11.2**
JMP IN plot of square roots of the room averages

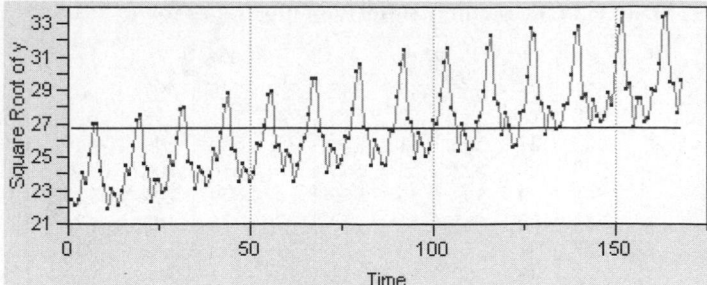

**FIGURE 11.3**
JMP IN plot of quartic roots of the room averages

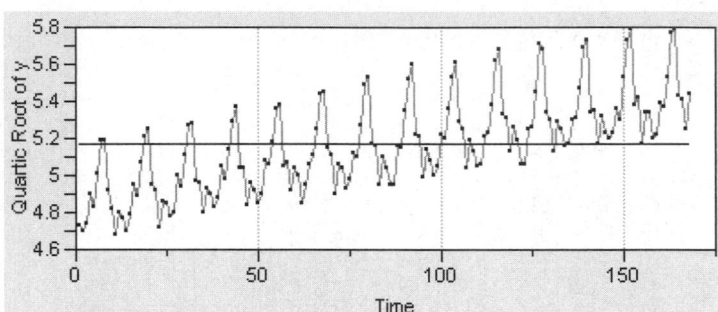

**FIGURE 11.4**
JMP IN plot of natural logarithms of the room averages

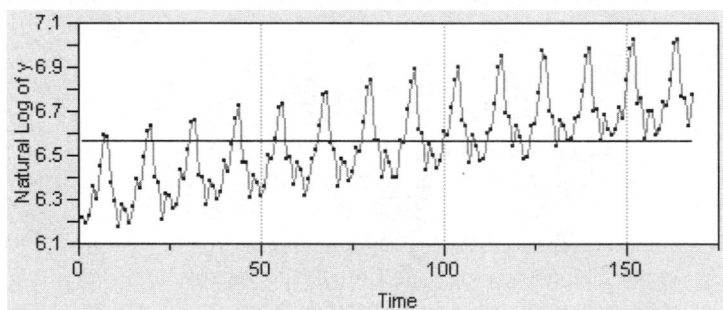

utilizes no differencing and produces the original predifferenced values $y_1^*, y_2^*, \ldots, y_n^*$ illustrated in the first column of Table 11.2. The transformation

$$z_t = y_t^* - y_{t-1}^*$$

produces the "**first regular differenced**" values illustrated in the second column of Table 11.2. The reason we use the word "regular" to describe these first differences is to distinguish them from the values obtained by using what is called "first seasonal differencing." To explain this type of differencing, we let $L$ denote the number of seasons in a year ($L = 4$ for quarterly data and $L = 12$ for monthly data). Then the transformation

$$z_t = y_t^* - y_{t-L}^*$$

**TABLE 11.2** Four Stationarity Transformations

**(1)** $z_t = y_t^*$   **(2)** $z_t = y_t^* - y_{t-1}^*$   **(3)** $z_t = y_t^* - y_{t-L}^*$   **(4)** $z_t = y_t^* - y_{t-1}^* - y_{t-L}^* + y_{t-L-1}^*$

$z_1 = y_1^*$
$z_2 = y_2^*$     $z_2 = y_2^* - y_1^*$
              $z_3 = y_3^* - y_2^*$

                              $z_{L+1} = y_{L+1}^* - y_1^*$
                              $z_{L+2} = y_{L+2}^* - y_2^*$     $z_{L+2} = y_{L+2}^* - y_{L+1}^* - y_2^* + y_1^*$
                                                $z_{L+3} = y_{L+3}^* - y_{L+2}^* - y_3^* + y_2^*$

$z_n = y_n^*$     $z_n = y_n^* - y_{n-1}^*$     $z_n = y_n^* - y_{n-L}^*$     $z_n = y_n^* - y_{n-1}^* - y_{n-L}^* + y_{n-L-1}^*$

produces the "**first seasonal differenced**" values illustrated in the third column of Table 11.2. Finally, the transformation

$$z_t = (y_t^* - y_{t-1}^*) - (y_{t-L}^* \quad y_{t-L-1}^*)$$
$$= y_t^* - y_{t-1}^* - y_{t-L}^* + y_{t-L-1}^*$$

produces the "**first regular differenced and first seasonal differenced**" values illustrated in the fourth column of Table 11.2. Whereas one of the nonseasonal differencing transformations illustrated in columns 1 and 2 sometimes transforms seasonal time series values into stationary time series values, one of the seasonal differencing transformations illustrated in columns 3 and 4 is frequently needed to produce stationary time series values.

To determine whether a particular transformation is appropriate, we examine the behavior of the SAC of the values $z_b, z_{b+1}, \ldots, z_n$ produced by the transformation at the **nonseasonal level** and at the **seasonal level.** We (somewhat arbitrarily) define the behavior of the SAC (or SPAC) at the nonseasonal level to be the behavior of this function at lags 1 through $(L - 3)$. For monthly data ($L = 12$), this is the behavior at lags 1 through 9. For quarterly data ($L = 4$), this is the behavior at lag 1. However, for quarterly data we sometimes consider lag 2 and possibly lag 3 to be part of the nonseasonal level. The behaviors displayed by the SAC and SPAC at the nonseasonal level are similar to those described in Chapter 9. Specifically, we say that a spike exists at a nonseasonal lag $k$ (1, 2, $\ldots$, $L - 3$) in the SAC if $|t_{r_k}| > 2$ (or equivalently, $|r_k| > 2s_{r_k}$) and in the SPAC if $|t_{r_{kk}}| > 2$ (or equivalently, $|r_{kk}| > 2s_{r_{kk}}$). Since it makes more sense to use recent time periods in forecasting the future, we might want to look at lags 1, 2, and possibly 3 in the SAC more closely and consider a spike to exist in the SAC at these lags if $|t_{r_k}| > 1.6$.

Next we define the behavior of the SAC and SPAC at the seasonal level to be the behavior of this function at lags equal to (or nearly equal to) $L$, $2L$, $3L$, and $4L$.

Furthermore, we define

1. The lags $L$, $2L$, $3L$, and $4L$ to be **exact seasonal lags**
2. The lags $L - 2$, $L - 1$, $L + 1$, $L + 2$, $2L - 2$, $2L - 1$, $2L + 1$, $2L + 2$, $3L - 2$, $3L - 1$, $3L + 1$, $3L + 2$, $4L - 2$, $4L - 1$, $4L + 1$, and $4L + 2$ to be **near seasonal lags**

Thus the exact seasonal lags for monthly data ($L = 12$) would be 12, 24, 36, and 48, and the near seasonal lags would be 10, 11, 13, 14, 22, 23, 25, 26, and so on. For any exact or near seasonal lag $k$, we say a **spike** exists in the SAC if $|t_{r_k}| > 2$ and in the SPAC if $|t_{r_{kk}}| > 2$. Since using the same month or quarter one year to forecast the next year seems reasonable, we might want to look at exact seasonal lags more closely. Hence, for $k = L$, $2L$, $3L$, and $4L$, we might consider a spike to exist in the SAC if $|t_{r_k}| > 1.6$.

We say that the SAC (or SPAC) **cuts off after lag $k$ at the seasonal level** if there are no spikes at exact seasonal lags or near seasonal lags greater than lag $k$ in this function. Furthermore, we say that the SAC (or SPAC) **dies down at the seasonal level** if this function does not cut off but rather decreases in a steady fashion at the seasonal level.

In general, it can be shown that if the SAC of the time series values $z_b, z_{b+1}, \ldots, z_n$ does *both* of the following:

1. Cuts off fairly quickly or dies down fairly quickly at the **nonseasonal level**
2. Cuts off fairly quickly or dies down fairly quickly at the **seasonal level**

then these values should be considered **stationary.** Otherwise, these values should be considered nonstationary. Here, if the SAC (or SPAC) cuts off fairly quickly at the non-seasonal level, it will often do so after a lag $k$ that is less than or equal to 2. Moreover, if the SAC (or SPAC) cuts off fairly quickly at the seasonal level, it will often do so after a lag that is less than or equal to $L$, the first seasonal lag.

**EXAMPLE 11.2**    Reconsider Example 11.1 and recall that the original monnthly hotel room averages are given in Table 11.1. Also recall that since the plot in Figure 11.1 indicates that the amount of seasonal variation is increasing with the level of this time series, it is appropriate to use the predifferencing transformation

$$y_t^* = y_t^{.25}$$

The SAS output of the SAC obtained by using the transformation

1. $y_t^* = y_t^{.25}$ is presented in Figure 11.5.
2. $z_t = y_t^* - y_{t-1}^*$ is presented in Figure 11.6.
3. $z_t = y_t^* - y_{t-12}^*$ is presented in Figure 11.7.
4. $z_t = y_t^* - y_{t-1}^* - y_{t-12}^* + y_{t-13}^*$ is presented in Figure 11.8.

**FIGURE 11.5** SAS output of the SAC of hotel room occupancy values given by the transformation $y_t^* = y_t^{.25}$

Name of Variable = QtRooty

| | | |
|---|---|---|
| Mean of Working Series | 5.166101 |
| Standard Deviation | 0.248479 |
| Number of Observations | 168 |

Autocorrelations

| Lag | Covariance | Correlation | -1 9 8 7 6 5 4 3 2 1 0 1 2 3 4 5 6 7 8 9 1 | Std Error |
|---|---|---|---|---|
| 0 | 0.061742 | 1.00000 | \|********************\| | 0 |
| 1 | 0.048996 | 0.79356 | \|****************\| | 0.077152 |
| 2 | 0.036500 | 0.59118 | \|************\| | 0.115971 |
| 3 | 0.023432 | 0.37952 | \|********\| | 0.132702 |
| 4 | 0.016210 | 0.26254 | \|*****.\| | 0.139013 |
| 5 | 0.0081180 | 0.13148 | \|***  .\| | 0.141934 |
| 6 | 0.0076632 | 0.12412 | \|**  .\| | 0.142657 |
| 7 | 0.0077999 | 0.12633 | \|***  .\| | 0.143298 |
| 8 | 0.014963 | 0.24235 | \|*****.\| | 0.143959 |
| 9 | 0.021188 | 0.34318 | \|*******\| | 0.146368 |
| 10 | 0.032241 | 0.52219 | \|**********\| | 0.151081 |
| 11 | 0.042517 | 0.68862 | \|*************\| | 0.161467 |
| 12 | 0.052832 | 0.85570 | \|*****************\| | 0.178092 |
| 13 | 0.041438 | 0.67114 | \|*************\| | 0.201081 |
| 14 | 0.029927 | 0.48472 | \|**********\| | 0.214000 |
| 15 | 0.017760 | 0.28765 | \|******  \| | 0.220438 |
| 16 | 0.011111 | 0.17996 | \|****  .\| | 0.222661 |
| 17 | 0.0033477 | 0.05422 | \|*  .\| | 0.223526 |
| 18 | 0.0026021 | 0.04215 | \|*  .\| | 0.223604 |
| 19 | 0.0025072 | 0.04158 | \|*  .\| | 0.223651 |
| 20 | 0.0091412 | 0.14805 | \|***  .\| | 0.223697 |
| 21 | 0.014875 | 0.24092 | \|*****.\| | 0.224280 |
| 22 | 0.025105 | 0.40661 | \|********.\| | 0.225815 |
| 23 | 0.034674 | 0.56160 | \|***********\| | 0.230132 |
| 24 | 0.044292 | 0.71737 | \|**************\| | 0.238150 |

"." marks two standard errors

In examining Figures 11.5 and 11.6, we see that

1. Since the SAC in Figure 11.5 dies down extremely slowly both at the nonseasonal level and at the seasonal level (that is, at lags equal to, or nearly equal to, $L = 12$, and $2L = 24$), it follows that the values obtained by using the transformation $y_t^* = y_t^{.25}$ should be considered nonstationary.

2. Since the SAC in Figure 11.6 dies down slowly at the nonseasonal level and extremely slowly at the seasonal level, the values obtained by using the transformation $z_t = y_t^* - y_{t-1}^*$ should also be considered nonstationary.

We next examine Figure 11.7, which presents the SAC and SPAC of the values obtained by using the transformation $z_t = y_t^* - y_{t-12}^*$. At the nonseasonal level the SAC has spikes at lags 1, 3, and 5, and the SPAC also has spikes at lags, 1, 3, and 5. Although it is some-what difficult to classify one of these functions as cutting off and one of these functions as dying down at the nonseasonal level, the spikes at lags 1, 3, and 5 in the SAC might

**FIGURE 11.6** SAS output of the SAC of hotel room occupancy values given by the transformation $z_t = y_t^* - y_{t-1}^*$

```
                    Name of Variable = QtRooty

            Period(s) of Differencing                    1
            Mean of Working Series              0.004256
            Standard Deviation                  0.155042
            Number of Observations                  167
            Observation(s) eliminated by differencing    1


                              Autocorrelations

Lag    Covariance    Correlation   -1 9 8 7 6 5 4 3 2 1 0 1 2 3 4 5 6 7 8 9 1   Std Error

 0      0.024038      1.00000       I                   I*******************I           0
 1     -0.0000366     -.00152       I                   I.                  I     0.077382
 2      0.00039127     0.01628      I                   I.                  I     0.077383
 3     -0.0054852     -.22819       I              *****I.                  I     0.077403
 4      0.00006531     0.00272      I                   I.                  I     0.081332
 5     -0.0071981     -.29945       I             ******I.                  I     0.081332
 6      0.00026608     0.01107      I                   I.                  I     0.087686
 7     -0.0068281     -.28405       I             ******I.                  I     0.087694
 8      0.00019560     0.00814      I                   I.                  I     0.093041
 9     -0.0048363     -.20120       I               ****I.                  I     0.093045
10      0.00042934     0.01786      I                   I.                  I     0.095615
11      0.00002743     0.00114      I                   I.                  I     0.095635
12      0.021748       0.90473      I                   I*****************  I     0.095635
13      0.00019786     0.00823      I                   I.                  I     0.137655
14      0.00047281     0.01967      I                   I.                  I     0.137658
15     -0.0051013     -.21222       I              . ****I.                 I     0.137675
16      0.00027543     0.01146      I                   I.                  I     0.139620
17     -0.0065139     -.27099       I             .*****I.                  I     0.139626
18     -0.0000199     -.00083       I                   I.                  I     0.142740
19     -0.0061783     -.25702       I             .*****I.                  I     0.142740
20     -0.0000390     -.00162       I                   I.                  I     0.145485
21     -0.0043944     -.18281       I              . ****I.                 I     0.145485
22      0.00017654     0.00734      I                   I.                  I     0.146854
23      0.00025176     0.01047      I                   I.                  I     0.146856
24      0.019838       0.82530      I                   I*****************  I     0.146861
```

be part of a sinusoidal dying-down pattern [see Figure 11.7(a)], while the spikes at lags 1, 3, and 5 in the SPAC appear to be more isolated [see Figure 11.7(b)]. Therefore, we conclude that *at the* **nonseasonal level** the SPAC has spikes at lags 1, 3, and 5 and cuts off after lag 5 and the SAC dies down fairly quickly (in a fashion dominated by sine-wave decay). Next, in examining the SAC and SPAC in Figure 11.7 at the **seasonal level** (that is, at lags equal to, or nearly equal to, $L = 12$ and $2L = 24$), we conclude that the SAC has a spike at lag 12 and cuts off after lag 12 (since there is no spike at a lag equal to, or nearly equal to, 24) and the SPAC dies down fairly quickly, since the spikes in this function at lags 12 and 24 are of decreasing size. In the next example we use the above conclusions to help us identify the time series model that describes the values obtained by using the transformation $z_t = y_t^* - y_{t-12}^*$. For now, it suffices to say that since the SAC in Figure 11.7(a) dies down fairly quickly at the nonseasonal level and cuts off fairly quickly (after lag 12) at the seasonal level, the values obtained by using the transformation

$$z_t = y_t^* - y_{t-12}^*$$

should be considered stationary.

**FIGURE 11.7** SAS output of the SAC and SPAC of hotel room occupancy values given by the transformation $z_t = y_t^* - y_{t-12}^*$

```
                    Name of Variable = QtRooty

        Period(s) of Differencing                    12
        Mean of Working Series                 0.042515
        Standard Deviation                     0.029756
        Number of Observations                      156
        Observation(s) eliminated by differencing    12
                    Autocorrelations
```

| Lag | Covariance | Correlation | -1 9 8 7 6 5 4 3 2 1 0 1 2 3 4 5 6 7 8 9 1 | Std Error |
|-----|-----------|-------------|---------------------------------------------|-----------|
| 0 | 0.00088540 | 1.00000 | \|                    \|********************\| | 0 |
| 1 | 0.00015434 | 0.17432 | \|                    . \|***                \| | 0.080064 |
| 2 | 0.00001267 | 0.01431 | \|                    . \| .                 \| | 0.082461 |
| 3 | -0.0002300 | -.25979 | \|                 *****\| .                 \| | 0.082477 |
| 4 | -0.0001493 | -.16860 | \|                  .***\| .                 \| | 0.087566 |
| 5 | -0.0002042 | -.23059 | \|                 *****\| .                 \| | 0.089622 |
| 6 | 0.00007130 | 0.08052 | \|                    . \|**  .              \| | 0.093348 |
| 7 | 0.00000630 | 0.09747 | \|                    . \|**                 \| | 0.093792 |
| 8 | 0.00010727 | 0.12116 | \|                    . \|**  .              \| | 0.094439 |
| 9 | 0.00003828 | 0.04323 | \|                    . \|*   .              \| | 0.095430 |
| 10 | 0.00006288 | 0.07102 | \|                   . \|*   .               \| | 0.095556 |
| 11 | -0.0000704 | -.07954 | \|                  **\| .                   \| | 0.095894 |
| 12 | -0.0003077 | -.34756 | \|              *******\| .                   \| | 0.096316 |
| 13 | -0.0000261 | -.02951 | \|                  . *\| .                   \| | 0.104045 |
| 14 | 0.00008021 | 0.09059 | \|                  . \|**                    \| | 0.104099 |
| 15 | 0.00011667 | 0.13177 | \|                  . \|***.                  \| | 0.104603 |
| 16 | 0.00008407 | 0.09495 | \|                  . \|**  .                 \| | 0.105662 |
| 17 | 0.00008387 | 0.00173 | \|                  . \|**  .                 \| | 0.106207 |
| 18 | -0.0001322 | -.14930 | \|                 .***\| .                   \| | 0.106717 |
| 19 | 0.00004830 | 0.05455 | \|                  . \|*   .                 \| | 0.108078 |
| 20 | 0.00002335 | 0.02637 | \|                  . \|*   .                 \| | 0.108254 |
| 21 | 0.00007287 | 0.08230 | \|                  . \|**  .                 \| | 0.108295 |
| 22 | -0.0000663 | -.07492 | \|                  . *\| .                   \| | 0.108695 |
| 23 | -2.0682E-6 | -.00234 | \|                  . \| .                    \| | 0.109026 |
| 24 | -0.0000561 | -.06340 | \|                  . *\| .                   \| | 0.109026 |

(a) The SAC

```
            Partial Autocorrelations
```

| Lag | Correlation | -1 9 8 7 6 5 4 3 2 1 0 1 2 3 4 5 6 7 8 9 1 |
|-----|-------------|---------------------------------------------|
| 1 | 0.17432 | \|                    . \|***                \| |
| 2 | -0.01658 | \|                    . \| .                 \| |
| 3 | -0.26764 | \|                *****\| .                 \| |
| 4 | -0.08612 | \|                  .**\| .                 \| |
| 5 | -0.19929 | \|                 ****\| .                 \| |
| 6 | 0.09310 | \|                    . \|**.                \| |
| 7 | 0.02067 | \|                    . \| .                 \| |
| 8 | -0.01442 | \|                    . \| .                 \| |
| 9 | 0.02526 | \|                    . \|*   .              \| |
| 10 | 0.07053 | \|                   . \|*   .               \| |
| 11 | -0.03408 | \|                  . *\| .                   \| |
| 12 | -0.34913 | \|              *******\| .                   \| |
| 13 | 0.14852 | \|                  . \|***                  \| |
| 14 | 0.10216 | \|                  . \|**.                  \| |
| 15 | -0.04960 | \|                  . *\| .                   \| |
| 16 | 0.00126 | \|                  . \| .                    \| |
| 17 | 0.00355 | \|                  . \| .                    \| |
| 18 | -0.06029 | \|                  . *\| .                   \| |
| 19 | 0.21451 | \|                  . \|****                 \| |
| 20 | 0.04457 | \|                  . \|*   .                 \| |
| 21 | 0.00196 | \|                  . \| .                    \| |
| 22 | 0.00585 | \|                  . \| .                    \| |
| 23 | -0.02580 | \|                  . *\| .                   \| |
| 24 | -0.12727 | \|                 ***\| .                   \| |

(b) The SPAC

**FIGURE 11.8** SAS output of the SAC of hotel room occupancy values given by the transformation $z_t = y_t^* - y_{t-1}^* - y_{t-12}^* + y_{t-13}^*$

<pre>
                    Name of Variable = QtRooty

        Period(s) of Differencing                    1,12
        Mean of Working Series                    0.000403
        Standard Deviation                        0.038058
        Number of Observations                         155
        Observation(s) eliminated by differencing       13


                            Autocorrelations

 Lag   Covariance    Correlation   -1 9 8 7 6 5 4 3 2 1 0 1 2 3 4 5 6 7 8 9 1      Std Error

  0    0.0014484      1.00000      |                    |********************|          0
  1   -0.0005853      -.40411      |           ********|  .                  |    0.080322
  2    0.00013574     0.09372      |                .   |**  .               |    0.092514
  3   -0.0003452      -.23832      |             *****  |  .                 |    0.093124
  4    0.00015446     0.10664      |                .   |**  .               |    0.096979
  5   -0.0003503      -.24182      |             *****  |  .                 |    0.097733
  6    0.00027990     0.19325      |                .   |****                |    0.101520
  7   -0.0000350      -.02414      |                .   |  .                 |    0.103866
  8    0.00010810     0.07464      |                .   |*   .               |    0.103902
  9   -0.0000803      -.05541      |                .  *|  .                 |    0.104248
 10    0.00015527     0.10720      |                .   |**  .               |    0.104438
 11    0.00006456     0.04457      |                .   |*   .               |    0.105145
 12   -0.0004876      -.33666      |           *******|    .                 |    0.105267
 13    0.00018142     0.12526      |                .   |***.                |    0.111998
 14    0.00004511     0.03114      |                .   |*   .               |    0.112898
 15    0.00007858     0.05425      |                .   |*   .               |    0.112954
 16   -0.0000402      -.02778      |                .  *|  .                 |    0.113122
 17    0.00022674     0.15654      |                .   |***  .              |    0.113166
 18   -0.0004088      -.28223      |            ******|    .                 |    0.114554
 19    0.00023575     0.16276      |                .   |***  .              |    0.118956
 20   -0.0001042      -.07192      |                .  *|  .                 |    0.120384
 21    0.00019244     0.13286      |                .   |***  .              |    0.120661
 22   -0.0001966      -.13570      |                . ***|  .                |    0.121601
 23    0.00014109     0.09741      |                .   |**  .               |    0.122574
 24   -0.0001901      -.13128      |                . ***|  .                |    0.123072
</pre>

The values of the fourth differencing transformation may be obtained by performing a first regular difference on the seasonal differences $(y_t^* - y_{t-12}^*)$, as follows:

$$z_t = (y_t^* - y_{t-12}^*) - (y_{t-1}^* - y_{t-13}^*) = y_t^* - y_{t-1}^* - y_{t-12}^* + y_{t-13}^*$$

These are the values used for the SAC in Figure 11.8. Thus, since we decided that the SAC for the seasonal differences in Figure 11.7 indicates that the seasonal differences are stationary, there is no need to do a regular difference on the stationary seasonal differences. In other words, there is no need to examine the SAC in Figure 11.8. On the other hand, if we are unsure of the decision that the seasonal differences are stationary, it is helpful to combine a first regular difference and seasonal difference to obtain the SAC in Figure 11.8.

In examining Figure 11.8, we see that this SAC might be interpreted as dying down fairly quickly at the nonseasonal level and cutting off fairly quickly at the seasonal level. However, this dying-down behavior at the nonseasonal level and cutting-off behavior at the seasonal level do not appear to be as "quick" as the dying-down behavior at the nonseasonal level and the cutting-off behavior at the seasonal level illustrated in Figure 11.7.

This implies that the values obtained by using the transformation

$$z_t = y_t^* - y_{t-1}^* - y_{t-12}^* + y_{t-13}^*$$

should probably be considered "less stationary" than the values obtained by using the transformation

$$z_t = y_t^* - y_{t-12}^*$$

# 11.2 THREE EXAMPLES OF SEASONAL MODELING AND FORECASTING

The model

$$z_t = \delta + a_t - \theta_{1,L}a_{t-L} - \theta_{2,L}a_{t-2L} - \cdots - \theta_{Q,L}a_{t-QL}$$

is called the **seasonal moving average model of order $Q$.** It can be shown that for this model the TAC has nonzero autocorrelations at lags $L, 2L, \ldots, QL$ and zero autocorrelations elsewhere and that the TPAC dies down at the seasonal lags $L, 2L, 3L, \ldots$. Therefore, if for the time series values $z_b, z_{b+1}, \ldots, z_n$, the SAC has spikes at lags $L, 2L, \ldots, QL$ and cuts off after lag $QL$ and the SPAC dies down at the seasonal level, then we might tentatively conclude that these values are described by the seasonal moving average model of order $Q$. For example, if the SAC has a spike at lag $L$ and cuts off after lag $L$ and the SPAC dies down at the seasonal level, then we might tentatively conclude that the time series values are described by the seasonal moving average model of order 1

$$z_t = \delta + a_t - \theta_{1,L}a_{t-L}$$

However, these tentative conclusions, and similar tentative conclusions discussed in the next paragraph, would be valid only if both the SAC and SPAC have no spikes at nonseasonal lags. Although this sometimes occurs for seasonal time series, often for such series the SAC and/or the SPAC do have spikes at some nonseasonal lags. We will discuss how to deal with this situation after discussing "seasonal autoregressive models."

The model

$$z_t = \delta + \phi_{1,L}z_{t-L} + \phi_{2,L}z_{t-2L} + \cdots + \phi_{P,L}z_{t-PL} + a_t$$

is called the **seasonal autoregressive model of order $P$.** It can be shown that for this model the TPAC has nonzero partial autocorrelations at lags $L, 2L, \ldots, PL$ and zero partial autocorrelations elsewhere, and the TAC dies down at the seasonal lags $L, 2L, 3L, \ldots$. Therefore, if for the time series values $z_b, z_{b+1}, \ldots, z_n$, the SPAC has spikes at lags $L, 2L, \ldots, PL$ and cuts off after lag $PL$ and the SAC dies down at the seasonal level, then we might tentatively conclude that these values are described by the seasonal autoregressive model of order $P$. For example, if the SPAC has a spike at lag $L$ and cuts off after lag $L$ and the SAC dies down at the seasonal level, then we might tentatively conclude that the time series values are described by the seasonal autoregressive model of order 1

$$z_t = \delta + \phi_{1,L}z_{t-L} + a_t$$

Since the SAC and SPAC of stationary seasonal time series values $z_b, z_{b+1}, \ldots, z_n$ often exhibit behavior at both the nonseasonal level and the seasonal level, we suggest the following three-step procedure for tentatively identifying a model describing these values.

**Step 1:** Use the behavior of the SAC and SPAC at the nonseasonal level to tentatively identify a nonseasonal model describing the time series values.

**Step 2:** Use the behavior of the SAC and SPAC at the seasonal level to tentatively identify a seasonal model describing the time series values.

**Step 3:** Combine the models obtained in steps 1 and 2 to arrive at an overall tentatively identified model. This combination is accomplished by using a method illustrated in the next three examples and in the discussion following these examples.

Estimation, diagnostic checking, and forecasting are done as discussed in Chapter 10. Note, however, that in computing the Ljung–Box statistic, we calculate $n'$ by the formula $n' = n - (d + LD)$. Here $d$ is the degree of nonseasonal differencing and $D$ is the degree of seasonal differencing used to obtain stationary time series values. Therefore, $d$ will usually be 0 or 1 and $D$ will usually be 0 or 1.

**EXAMPLE 11.3**    We concluded in Example 11.2 that for the monthly hotel room averages in Table 11.1, the transformation

$$z_t = y_t^* - y_{t-12}^* \quad \text{where} \quad y_t^* = y_t^{.25}$$

produces stationary time series values. As previously discussed, the SAC and SPAC of these stationary time series values are presented in Figure 11.7.

**Step 1:** At the nonseasonal level the SPAC has spikes at lags 1, 3, and 5 and cuts off after lag 5 and the SAC dies down. Therefore, we tentatively identify the following nonseasonal autoregressive model

$$z_t = \delta + \phi_1 z_{t-1} + \phi_3 z_{t-3} + \phi_5 z_{t-5} + a_t$$

**Step 2:** At the seasonal level the SAC has a spike at lag 12 and cuts off after lag 12 and the SPAC dies down. Therefore, we tentatively identify the seasonal moving average model of order 1

$$z_t = \delta + a_t - \theta_{1,12}a_{t-12}$$

**Step 3:** Combining these models, we obtain the overall tentatively identified model

$$z_t = \delta + \phi_1 z_{t-1} + \phi_3 z_{t-3} + \phi_5 z_{t-5} - \theta_{1,12}a_{t-12} + a_t$$

To determine whether $\delta$ should be tentatively included in the combined model, note from Figure 11.7 that $\bar{z} = .042515$ and $s_z = .029756$. Also note that since the first value of $z_t$ that can be calculated is $z_{13} = y_{13}^* - y_1^*$, then $b = 13$. Since

$$\frac{\bar{z}}{s_z/\sqrt{n - b + 1}} = \frac{.042515}{.029756/\sqrt{168 - 13 + 1}} = 17.85$$

is greater than 2, we conclude that $\bar{z}$ is statistically different from zero and that we should tentatively include $\delta$ in the model.

Figure 11.9 presents the SAS output of estimation, diagnostic checking, and forecasting for the model

$$z_t = \delta + \phi_1 z_{t-1} + \phi_3 z_{t-3} + \phi_5 z_{t-5} - \theta_{1,12} a_{t-12} + a_t$$

The $t$-statistics in Figure 11.9(a) associated with $\delta$, $\phi_1$, $\phi_3$, and $\theta_{1,12}$ are greater in absolute value than 2 and, therefore, indicate that these parameters should be retained in the model.

**FIGURE 11.9** SAS output of estimation, diagnostic checking, and forecasting for the model
$z_t = \delta + \phi_1 z_{t-1} + \phi_3 z_{t-3} + \phi_5 z_{t-5} - \theta_{1,12} a_{t-12} + a_t$

Conditional Least Squares Estimation

| Iteration | SSE | MU | MA1,1 | AR1,1 | AR1,2 | AR1,3 | Constant | Lambda | R Crit |
|---|---|---|---|---|---|---|---|---|---|
| 0 | 0.1410 | 0.04252 | 0.10000 | 0.10000 | 0.10000 | 0.10000 | 0.029761 | 0.00001 | 1 |
| 1 | 0.1000 | 0.04258 | 0.39724 | 0.14312 | -0.23635 | -0.18047 | 0.054232 | 1E-6 | 0.533821 |
| 2 | 0.09892 | 0.04264 | 0.46083 | 0.21549 | -0.22956 | -0.16215 | 0.050149 | 1E-7 | 0.095939 |
| 3 | 0.09887 | 0.04260 | 0.47239 | 0.22910 | -0.22431 | -0.15460 | 0.048981 | 1E-8 | 0.020223 |
| 4 | 0.09887 | 0.04259 | 0.47563 | 0.23162 | -0.22331 | -0.15309 | 0.048758 | 1E-9 | 0.004503 |
| 5 | 0.09887 | 0.04259 | 0.47617 | 0.23230 | -0.22306 | -0.15271 | 0.048699 | 1E-10 | 0.001007 |
| 6 | 0.09887 | 0.04259 | 0.47634 | 0.23242 | -0.22301 | -0.15263 | 0.048689 | 1E-11 | 0.000226 |

Conditional Least Squares Estimation

| Parameter | Estimate | Standard Error | t Value | Approx Pr > \|t\| | Lag |
|---|---|---|---|---|---|
| MU | 0.04259 | 0.0010110 | 42.12 | <.0001 | 0 |
| MA1,1 | 0.47634 | 0.07690 | 6.19 | <.0001 | 12 |
| AR1,1 | 0.23242 | 0.07859 | 2.96 | 0.0036 | 1 |
| AR1,2 | -0.22301 | 0.07808 | -2.82 | 0.0055 | 3 |
| AR1,3 | -0.15263 | 0.07984 | -1.91 | 0.0578 | 5 |

| | |
|---|---|
| Constant Estimate | 0.048689 |
| Variance Estimate | 0.000655 |
| Std Error Estimate | 0.025500 |
| AIC | -696.052 |
| SBC | -680.803 |
| Number of Residuals | 156 |

* AIC and SBC do not include log determinant.

Correlations of Parameter Estimates

| Parameter | MU | MA1,1 | AR1,1 | AR1,2 | AR1,3 |
|---|---|---|---|---|---|
| MU | 1.000 | 0.119 | 0.022 | 0.011 | 0.006 |
| MA1,1 | 0.119 | 1.000 | 0.092 | 0.071 | 0.117 |
| AR1,1 | 0.022 | 0.092 | 1.000 | -0.142 | 0.151 |
| AR1,2 | 0.011 | 0.071 | -0.142 | 1.000 | -0.132 |
| AR1,3 | 0.006 | 0.117 | 0.151 | -0.132 | 1.000 |

(a) Estimation

**FIGURE 11.9** (Continued)

Autocorrelation Check of Residuals

| To Lag | Chi-Square | DF | Pr > ChiSq | | | Autocorrelations | | | |
|---|---|---|---|---|---|---|---|---|---|
| 6 | 2.40 | 2 | 0.3005 | -0.012 | 0.100 | 0.016 | -0.004 | -0.009 | 0.066 |
| 12 | 6.54 | 8 | 0.5867 | 0.060 | 0.012 | -0.019 | 0.132 | 0.053 | -0.009 |
| 18 | 19.78 | 14 | 0.1372 | 0.109 | 0.159 | 0.048 | 0.051 | 0.096 | -0.155 |
| 24 | 25.52 | 20 | 0.1823 | 0.139 | 0.019 | 0.102 | -0.003 | 0.037 | -0.012 |
| 30 | 30.52 | 26 | 0.2468 | 0.115 | 0.004 | 0.105 | -0.043 | -0.008 | 0.014 |

Autocorrelation Plot of Residuals

| Lag | Covariance | Correlation | -1 9 8 7 6 5 4 3 2 1 0 1 2 3 4 5 6 7 8 9 1 | Std Error |
|---|---|---|---|---|
| 0 | 0.00065474 | 1.00000 | \|********************\| | 0 |
| 1 | -7.9819E-6 | -.01219 | \|                       \| | 0.080064 |
| 2 | 0.00006544 | 0.09995 | \|**.                    \| | 0.080076 |
| 3 | 0.00001041 | 0.01590 | \| .                     \| | 0.080872 |
| 4 | -2.4949E-6 | -.00381 | \| .                     \| | 0.080892 |
| 5 | -5.8334E-6 | -.00891 | \| .                     \| | 0.080893 |
| 6 | 0.00004353 | 0.06649 | \|*                      \| | 0.080899 |
| 7 | 0.00003950 | 0.06033 | \|*                      \| | 0.081249 |
| 8 | 8.02592E-6 | 0.01226 | \| .                     \| | 0.081535 |
| 9 | -0.0000127 | -.01945 | \| .                     \| | 0.081547 |
| 10 | 0.00008666 | 0.13236 | \|***                    \| | 0.081577 |
| 11 | 0.00003466 | 0.05294 | \|*                      \| | 0.082942 |
| 12 | -5.5993E-6 | -.00855 | \| .                     \| | 0.083159 |
| 13 | 0.00007106 | 0.10854 | \|**.                    \| | 0.083164 |
| 14 | 0.00010419 | 0.15913 | \|***                    \| | 0.084067 |
| 15 | 0.00003131 | 0.04781 | \|*                      \| | 0.085976 |
| 16 | 0.00003362 | 0.05135 | \|*                      \| | 0.086147 |
| 17 | 0.00006306 | 0.09631 | \|**.                    \| | 0.086343 |
| 18 | -0.0001016 | -.15523 | \|***                    \| | 0.087029 |
| 19 | 0.00009133 | 0.13950 | \|***.                   \| | 0.088786 |
| 20 | 0.00001238 | 0.01891 | \| .                     \| | 0.090180 |
| 21 | 0.00006650 | 0.10157 | \|**.                    \| | 0.090205 |
| 22 | -1.745E-6 | -.00267 | \| .                     \| | 0.090935 |
| 23 | 0.00002453 | 0.03746 | \|*                      \| | 0.090936 |
| 24 | -7.8704E-6 | -.01202 | \| .                     \| | 0.091035 |

(b) The RSAC

Since the absolute value of the $t$-statistic associated with $\phi_5$ ($t = -1.91$) is almost equal to 2, and since multicollinearity might be affecting the $t$-statistics, we will also retain $\phi_5$ in the model. The $p$-values associated with $Q^*$ in Figure 11.9(b) indicate that the model is adequate. It can be verified that if we remove $\phi_5$ from the model, the $p$-values associated with $Q^*$ indicate that the reduced model is inadequate.

In order to forecast the hotel room occupancies in the 15th year (months 169 through 180), we note that since $z_t = y_t^* - y_{t-12}^*$ where $y_t^* = y_t^{.25}$, we can express the model as

$$y_t^* = \delta + y_{t-12}^* + \phi_1(y_{t-1}^* - y_{t-13}^*) + \phi_3(y_{t-3}^* - y_{t-15}^*) + \phi_5(y_{t-5}^* - y_{t-17}^*) - \theta_{1,12}a_{t-12} + a_t$$

Using the least squares point estimates, it follows that a point forecast of $y_{169}^*$ made at time origin 168 is

$$\hat{y}_{169}^*(168) = .048689 + y_{157}^* + .23242(y_{168}^* - y_{156}^*) - .22301(y_{166}^* - y_{154}^*)$$
$$- .15263(y_{164}^* - y_{152}^*) - .47634(y_{157}^* - \hat{y}_{157}^*)$$

**FIGURE 11.9** (Continued)

```
                        Partial Autocorrelations

  Lag     Correlation     -1 9 8 7 6 5 4 3 2 1 0 1 2 3 4 5 6 7 8 9 1

    1      -0.01219       |                      .  |** .              |
    2       0.09981       |                      .  |** .              |
    3       0.01840       |                      .  |   .              |
    4      -0.01352       |                      .  |   .              |
    5      -0.01269       |                      .  |   .              |
    6       0.06840       |                      .  |*  .              |
    7       0.06546       |                      .  |*  .              |
    8       0.00066       |                      .  |   .              |
    9      -0.03537       |                      . *|   .              |
   10       0.13223       |                      .  |***                |
   11       0.06805       |                      .  |*  .              |
   12      -0.03748       |                      . *|   .              |
   13       0.08526       |                      .  |** .              |
   14       0.17489       |                      .  |***                |
   15       0.04898       |                      .  |*  .              |
   16       0.00351       |                      .  |   .              |
   17       0.07541       |                      .  |** .              |
   18      -0.15669       |                    ***|   .              |
   19       0.13289       |                      .  |***                |
   20       0.01470       |                      .  |   .              |
   21       0.04573       |                      .  |*  .              |
   22      -0.00729       |                      .  |   .              |
   23       0.00409       |                      .  |   .              |
   24      -0.05161       |                      . *|   .              |
```

(c) The RSPAC

```
              Forecasts for variable QtRooty

  Obs      Forecast     Std Error      95% Confidence Limits

  169       5.3841       0.0256        5.3339       5.4342
  170       5.2630       0.0263        5.2115       5.3145
  171       5.2784       0.0263        5.2268       5.3299
  172       5.4267       0.0269        5.3740       5.4793
  173       5.4025       0.0270        5.3497       5.4554
  174       5.5857       0.0274        5.5320       5.6394
  175       5.8184       0.0274        5.7647       5.8722
  176       5.8523       0.0271        5.7986       5.9060
  177       5.4783       0.0275        5.4245       5.5322
  178       5.4788       0.0275        5.4249       5.5327
  179       5.2894       0.0275        5.2355       5.3433
  180       5.4620       0.0275        5.4001       5.5160
```

(d) Forecasts of $y_{169}^*$ through $y_{180}^*$

```
  Obs      Forecasty    L95CI        U95CI
  169       840.33      809.46       872.08
  170       767.23      737.65       797.70
  171       776.24      746.35       807.01
  172       867.22      834.07       901.36
  173       851.90      819.04       885.74
  174       973.42      936.52      1011.40
  175      1146.11     1104.36      1189.04
  176      1173.02     1130.53      1216.69
  177       900.72      865.82       936.67
  178       901.01      866.07       937.00
  179       782.76      751.32       815.18
  180       890.05      855.41       925.73
```

(e) Forecasts of $y_{169}$ through $y_{180}$

**FIGURE 11.10**
95% prediction interval forecasts of actual hotel room averages for year 15

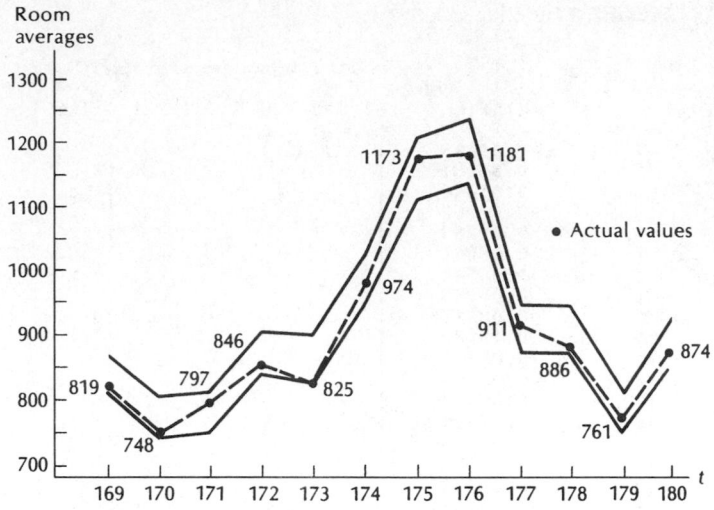

In this equation $y^*_{157}$, $y^*_{168}$, $y^*_{156}$, $y^*_{166}$, $y^*_{154}$, $y^*_{164}$, $y^*_{152}$, and $y^*_{157}$ are the quartic roots of $y_{157}$, $y_{168}$, $y_{156}$, $y_{166}$, $y_{154}$, $y_{164}$, $y_{152}$, and $y_{157}$, and $(y^*_{157} - \hat{y}^*_{157})$ is the 157th residual. The SAS output in Figure 11.9(d) tells us that when these quantities are inserted into the forecasting equation, we find that $\hat{y}^*_{169}(168) = 5.3841$. This implies that a point forecast of $y_{169}$ is $(5.3841)^4 = 840.33$, as shown in Figure 11.9(e). Figure 11.9(d) also shows that a 95% prediction interval for $y^*_{169}$ is [5.3339, 5.4342]. This implies that a 95% prediction interval for $y_{169}$ is $[(5.3339)^4, (5.4342)^4] = [809.46, 872.08]$, as shown in Figure 11.9(e). The point forecasts of and 95% prediction intervals for $y_{169}$ through $y_{180}$ are presented in Figure 11.9(e). These intervals, along with the actual monthly hotel room averages observed in the 15th year, are graphed in Figure 11.10. Since all 12 prediction intervals contain the actual hotel room averages, and since the management of Traveler's Rest thought that the prediction intervals were short enough to be useful for planning purposes, Traveler's Rest decided to consider using the model to predict monthly hotel room averages for months 181 through 192 (next year). To do this, Traveler's Rest should use the data from all 15 years to verify that the same model is still adequate (or to identify a new model, if necessary) and to estimate the parameters of an appropriate model.

It is important to make a final comment. The inclusion of the constant term $\delta$ in the model implies that we estimate that there is a deterministic, positive trend of $\hat{\delta} = .048689$ in the quartic roots of the hotel room occupancies from a specific month of a given year to the same month of the next year. If Traveler's Rest is to use this constant term for forecasting purposes, it must be convinced that this deterministic trend will persist into the future.

**EXAMPLE 11.4**

We now consider monthly passenger totals (measured in thousands of passengers) in international air travel for an 11-year period. This time series is presented in Table 11.3 and plotted in Figure 11.11. Since the plot shows the existence of increasing seasonal variation, we

**TABLE 11.3** Monthly Total International Airline Passengers (Thousands of Passengers)

| Year | Jan. | Feb. | Mar. | Apr. | May | June | July | Aug. | Sept. | Oct. | Nov. | Dec. |
|------|------|------|------|------|-----|------|------|------|-------|------|------|------|
| 1  | 112 | 118 | 132 | 129 | 121 | 135 | 148 | 148 | 136 | 119 | 104 | 118 |
| 2  | 115 | 126 | 141 | 135 | 125 | 149 | 170 | 170 | 158 | 133 | 114 | 140 |
| 3  | 145 | 150 | 178 | 163 | 172 | 178 | 199 | 199 | 184 | 162 | 146 | 166 |
| 4  | 171 | 180 | 193 | 181 | 183 | 218 | 230 | 242 | 209 | 191 | 172 | 194 |
| 5  | 196 | 196 | 236 | 235 | 229 | 243 | 264 | 272 | 237 | 211 | 180 | 201 |
| 6  | 204 | 188 | 235 | 227 | 234 | 264 | 302 | 293 | 259 | 229 | 203 | 229 |
| 7  | 242 | 233 | 267 | 269 | 270 | 315 | 364 | 347 | 312 | 274 | 237 | 278 |
| 8  | 284 | 277 | 317 | 313 | 318 | 374 | 413 | 405 | 355 | 306 | 271 | 306 |
| 9  | 315 | 301 | 356 | 348 | 355 | 422 | 465 | 467 | 404 | 347 | 305 | 336 |
| 10 | 340 | 318 | 362 | 348 | 363 | 435 | 491 | 505 | 404 | 359 | 310 | 337 |
| 11 | 360 | 342 | 406 | 396 | 420 | 472 | 548 | 559 | 463 | 407 | 362 | 405 |

*Source: FAA Statistical Handbook of Civil Aviation* (several annual issues). These data were originally presented by Box and Jenkins (see Box, Jenkins, and Reinsel, 1994).

**FIGURE 11.11**
JMP IN plot of monthly passenger totals versus time

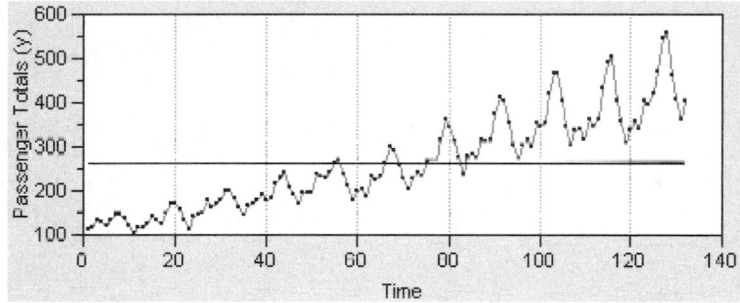

**FIGURE 11.12**
JMP IN plot of natural logarithms of monthly passenger totals versus time

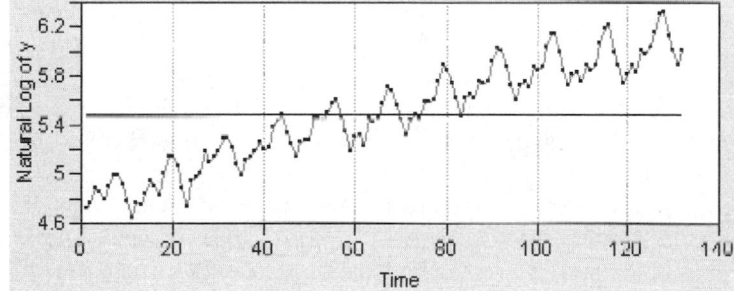

need to use a predifferencing transformation. A plot of the natural logarithms of the monthly passenger totals in Figure 11.12 indicates that the natural logarithm transformation has equalized the seasonal variation. Since the MINITAB output in Figure 11.13 shows that the SAC of the natural logarithms dies down very slowly at the nonseasonal and seasonal levels, we conclude that these values are nonstationary. Since the MINITAB output in Figure 11.14 shows that the SAC of the first regular differences of the natural logarithms dies down very

**FIGURE 11.13**
MINITAB output of
the SAC of monthly
passenger total
values given by the
transformation
$y_t^* = \ln y_t$

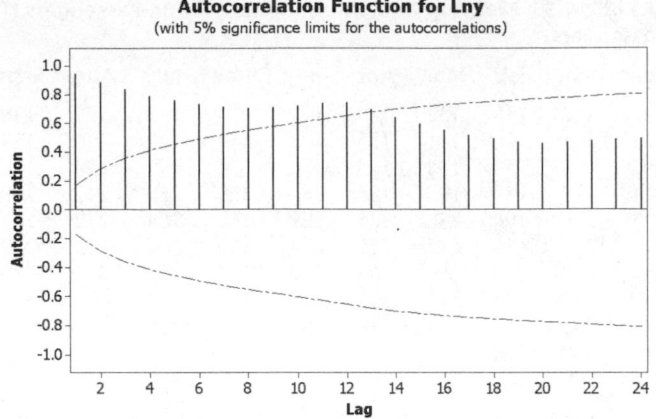

**Autocorrelation Function for Lny**
(with 5% significance limits for the autocorrelations)

**FIGURE 11.14**
MINITAB output of
the SAC of monthly
passenger total
values given by the
transformation
$z_t = y_t^* - y_{t-1}^*$

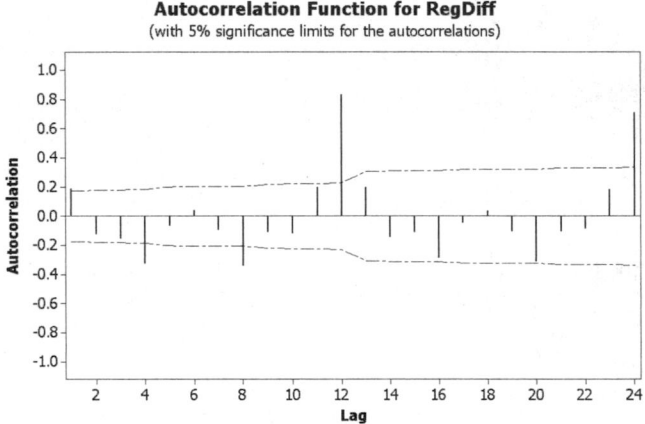

**Autocorrelation Function for RegDiff**
(with 5% significance limits for the autocorrelations)

slowly at the seasonal level, we conclude that these values are nonstationary. Since the MINITAB output in Figure 11.15 shows that the SAC of the first seasonal differences of the natural logarithms dies down very slowly at the nonseasonal level, we conclude that these values are nonstationary. Since the MINITAB output in Figure 11.16(a) shows that the SAC of the first regular differences and first seasonal differences of the natural logarithms cuts off quickly at both the nonseasonal and seasonal levels, we conclude that these values are stationary. Therefore, we now use the precise behaviors of the SAC and SPAC of these values to tentatively identify a model describing the monthly passenger totals.

**Step 1:** At the nonseasonal level the SAC in Figure 11.16(a) has a spike at lag 1 and (with the exception of a spike at lag 3) cuts off after lag 1, and the SPAC in Figure 11.16(b) dies down. Therefore, we tentatively identify the nonseasonal moving average model of order 1

$$z_t = \delta + a_t - \theta_1 a_{t-1}$$

**FIGURE 11.15**
MINITAB output of the SAC of monthly passenger total values given by the transformation
$z_t = y_t^* - y_{t-12}^*$

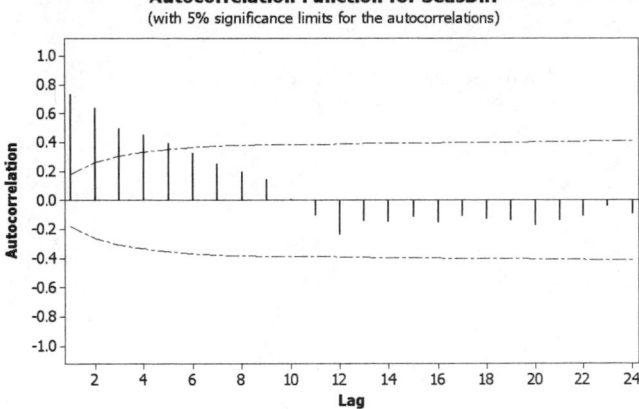

**Autocorrelation Function for SeasDiff**
(with 5% significance limits for the autocorrelations)

**Step 2:** At the seasonal level both the SAC in Figure 11.16(a) and the SPAC in Figure 11.16(b) appear to cut off after lag 12. However, since the autocorrelation at lag 24 in the SAC is smaller than the partial autocorrelation at lag 24 in the SPAC, we conclude that at the seasonal level the SAC has a spike at lag 12 and cuts off after lag 12, and the SPAC dies down. Therefore, we tentatively identify the seasonal moving average model of order 1

$$z_t = \delta + a_t - \theta_{1,12} a_{t-12}$$

**Step 3:** It might seem obvious that we would combine these models and form the model

$$z_t = \delta + a_t - \theta_1 a_{t-1} - \theta_{1,12} a_{t-12}$$

In the present situation the terms $-\theta_1 a_{t-1}$ and $-\theta_{1,12} a_{t-12}$ would be used to form the multiplicative term

$$(-\theta_1)(-\theta_{1,12}) a_{t-13} = \theta_1 \theta_{1,12} a_{t-13}$$

Here we have multiplied $-\theta_1$ by $-\theta_{1,12}$ and added the negative numbers ($-1$ and $-12$) after the $t$ in the random shock subscripts. This gives the overall tentatively identified model

$$z_t = a_t - \theta_1 a_{t-1} - \theta_{1,12} a_{t-12} + \theta_1 \theta_{1,12} a_{t-13}$$

Note that we have omitted $\delta$ in this overall model because $\bar{z}$ is not statistically different from zero ($\bar{z} = .0013$ and $s_{\bar{z}} = .045$). When using software (such as MINITAB) where $\bar{z}$ and $s_{\bar{z}}$ are not displayed, we may add $\delta$ to the tentative model and test $H_0$: $\delta = 0$ as part of the diagnostic checking.

Figure 11.17 presents the MINITAB output of estimation, diagnostic checking, and forecasting for the tentatively identified model. This output indicates that this model is adequate. Since $z_t = y_t^* - y_{t-1}^* - y_{t-12}^* + y_{t-13}^*$ where $y_t^* = n y_t$, we can forecast the

**FIGURE 11.16** MINITAB output of the SAC and SPAC of monthly passenger total values given by the transformation $z_t = y_t^* - y_{t-1}^* - y_{t-12}^* + y_{t-13}^*$

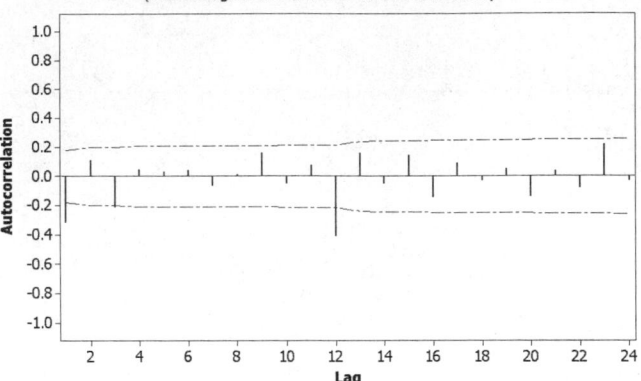

(a) The SAC

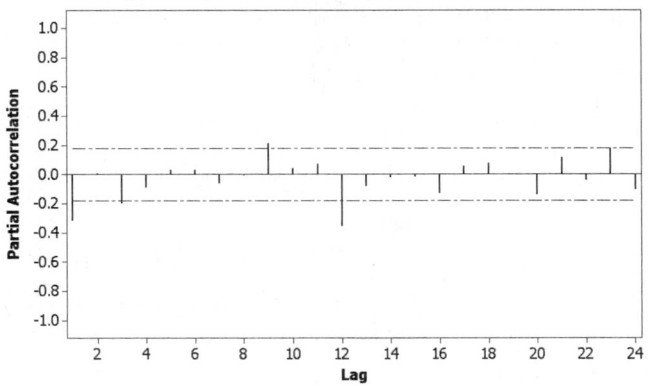

(b) The SPAC

monthly passenger totals in the next year (months 133 through 144) by expressing the model as

$$y_t^* = y_{t-1}^* + y_{t-12}^* - y_{t-13}^* + a_t - \theta_1 a_{t-1} - \theta_{1,12} a_{t-12} + \theta_1 \theta_{1,12} a_{t-13}$$

For example, Figure 11.17(d) tells us that a point forecast and 95% prediction interval for the natural logarithm of the monthly passenger totals in month 133 are, respectively, 6.03771 and [5.96718, 6.10823]. This implies that a point forecast and 95% prediction interval for the actual monthly passenger totals in month 133 are, respectively, $e^{6.03771}$ = 418.931 and $[e^{5.96718}, e^{6.10823}]$ = [390.403, 449.542]. These forecasts are shown in Figure 11.17(e). In Exercise 11.14 the reader will analyze the monthly passenger totals by using models that do not ignore the spike at lag 3 of the SAC in Figure 11.16(a).

**FIGURE 11.17** MINITAB output of estimation, diagnostic checking, and forecasting
for the model $z_t = a_t - \theta_1 a_{t-1} - \theta_{1,12} a_{t-12} + \theta_1 \theta_{1,12} a_{t-13}$

```
Estimates at each iteration
Iteration        SSE      Parameters
    0         0.209981    0.100    0.100
    1         0.184009    0.183    0.250
    2         0.167365    0.249    0.400
    3         0.158799    0.310    0.550
    4         0.155339    0.350    0.621
    5         0.155316    0.344    0.627
    6         0.155313    0.342    0.629
    7         0.155313    0.341    0.630
    8         0.155313    0.341    0.630
Relative change in each estimate less than  0.0010

Final Estimates of Parameters
Type        Coef     SE Coef       T        P
MA    1     0.3407    0.0868      3.93    0.000
SMA  12     0.6299    0.0766      8.23    0.000

Differencing: 1 regular, 1 seasonal of order 12
Number of observations:  Original series 132, after differencing 119
Residuals:      SS = 0.151421  (backforecasts excluded)
                MS = 0.001294  DF = 117
```

(a) Estimation

```
Modified Box-Pierce (Ljung-Box) Chi-Square statistic
Lag                  12        24        36        48
Chi-Square          7.5      19.6      30.5      38.7
DF                   10        22        34        46
P-Value           0.679     0.607     0.638     0.770
```

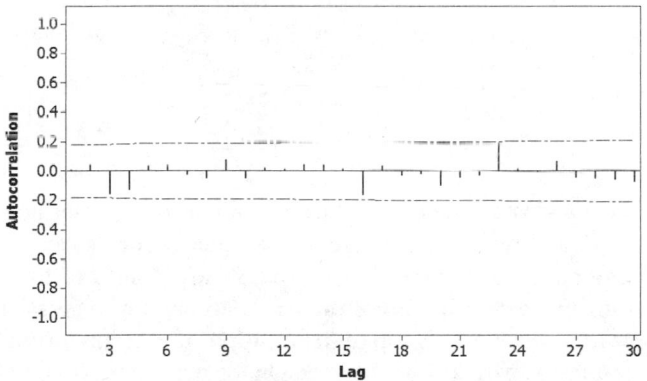

**ACF of Residuals for Lny**
(with 5% significance limits for the autocorrelations)

(b) The RSAC

**FIGURE 11.17** (Continued)

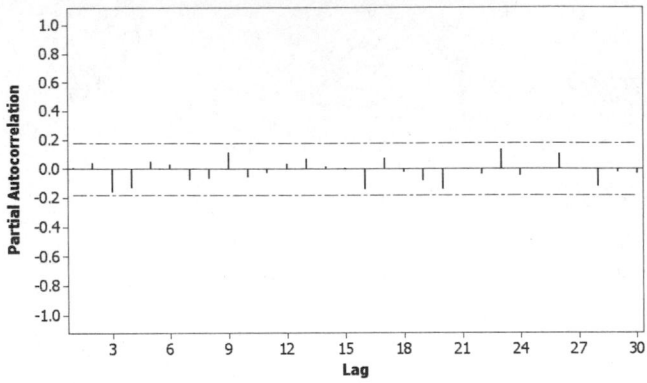

(c) The RSPAC

```
Forecasts from period 132
                        95 Percent Limits
Period      Forecast        Lower       Upper
 133        6.03771        5.96718      6.10823
 134        5.99099        5.90652      6.07546
 135        6.14666        6.05023      6.24308
 136        6.12046        6.01341      6.22751
 137        6.15698        6.04026      6.27369
 138        6.30256        6.17692      6.42819
 139        6.42828        6.29432      6.56224
 140        6.43857        6.29677      6.58037
 141        6.26527        6.11604      6.41450
 142        6.13438        5.97807      6.29069
 143        6.00539        5.84231      6.16846
 144        6.11358        5.94401      6.28316
```

(d) Forecasts of $y^*_{133}$ through $y^*_{144}$

| Period | Forecast | Lower95 | Upper95 |
|--------|----------|---------|---------|
| 133 | 418.931 | 390.403 | 449.542 |
| 134 | 399.811 | 367.424 | 435.052 |
| 135 | 467.154 | 424.212 | 514.443 |
| 136 | 455.076 | 408.876 | 506.495 |
| 137 | 471.999 | 420.004 | 530.430 |
| 138 | 545.965 | 481.508 | 619.052 |
| 139 | 619.108 | 541.486 | 707.857 |
| 140 | 625.511 | 542.814 | 720.807 |
| 141 | 525.983 | 453.066 | 610.636 |
| 142 | 461.452 | 394.678 | 539.523 |
| 143 | 405.609 | 344.575 | 477.453 |
| 144 | 451.956 | 381.461 | 535.478 |

(e) Forecasts of $y_{133}$ through $y_{144}$

In general, consider the **nonseasonal model** tentatively identified by using the non-seasonal behaviors of the SAC and SPAC, and consider the **seasonal model** tentatively identified by using the seasonal behaviors of the SAC and SPAC. **If both of these models are moving average models, or if both of these models are autoregressive models, when we combine the models, we should utilize multiplicative terms formed by combining nonseasonal terms with seasonal terms.** On the other hand, **if one of these models is a moving average model and the other is an autoregressive model, then we should not utilize multiplicative terms.** Example 11.3 is a case where the nonseasonal model was autoregressive and the seasonal model was moving average. In Example 11.4 both the nonseasonal and seasonal models are moving average. We will now consider a case where both the nonseasonal and seasonal models are autoregressive, and hence, the combined model will require multiplicative terms. In order to rationalize the exact nature of a multiplicative term (especially the sign of the term), we would need to use what is called "operator notation." **Autoregressive and moving average operators** are introduced in Chapter 12 along with the basic **backshift operator.**

**EXAMPLE 11.5**   To illustrate the situation in which a model's nonseasonal and seasonal terms are both autoregressive, consider a time series of $z_t$ values that has the SAC and SPAC given in Figure 11.18. The time series $z_t$ appears to be stationary because the SAC dies down fairly quickly at both the nonseasonal and seasonal levels. We now use the SAC and SPAC together to identify a model.

**Step 1:**   At the nonseasonal level the SPAC has spikes at lags 1 and 3 and cuts off after lag 3, and the SAC dies down. Therefore, we tentatively identify the nonseasonal autoregressive model

$$z_t = \delta + \phi_1 z_{t-1} + \phi_3 z_{t-3} + a_t$$

**Step 2:**   At the seasonal level the SPAC has a spike at lag 12 and cuts off after lag 12, and the SAC dies down. Therefore, we tentatively identify the seasonal autoregressive model of order 1

$$z_t = \delta + \phi_{1,12} z_{t-12} + a_t$$

**Step 3:**   Combining these two models and including multiplicative terms that multiply each of $\phi_1 z_{t-1}$ and $\phi_3 z_{t-3}$ by $\phi_{1,12} z_{t-12}$, we tentatively identify the overall model

$$z_t = \phi_1 z_{t-1} + \phi_3 z_{t-3} + \phi_{1,12} z_{t-12} - \phi_1 \phi_{1,12} z_{t-13} - \phi_3 \phi_{1,12} z_{t-15} + a_t$$

**A negative sign for a multiplicative term should always be used when it is derived from two autoregressive terms** (see use of operators in Chapter 12 for the rationalization). In the present situation we have omitted $\delta$ because it can be verified that $\bar{z}$ is less than twice its estimated standard error.

If we fit this model to the observed values of $z_t$, we obtain the RSAC, RSPAC, and values for the Ljung–Box statistic in Figure 11.19. The $p$ value for the Ljung–Box chi-square statistic when $K = 6$ (testing the first six lags) is .0768. Although this $p$-value is not less than .05, it is fairly small, and there is a spike at lag 5 in each of the RSAC and RSPAC. This suggests that we add the nonseasonal autoregressive term $z_{t-5}$ to our model and, therefore, tentatively identify the new model

$$z_t = \phi_1 z_{t-1} + \phi_3 z_{t-3} + \phi_5 z_{t-5} + \phi_{1,12} z_{t-12} - \phi_1 \phi_{1,12} z_{t-13} - \phi_3 \phi_{1,12} z_{t-15} - \phi_5 \phi_{1,12} z_{t-17} + a_t$$

The time series of $z_t$ values in this example is actually composed of the residuals from a time series regression model that was fitted to the monthly hotel room averages of Table 11.1. We investigate this time series regression model in the next section.

**FIGURE 11.18** SAS output for the SAC and SPAC of a time series of $z_t$ values

```
                                    Autocorrelation Plot
Lag    Covariance    Correlation    -1 9 8 7 6 5 4 3 2 1 0 1 2 3 4 5 6 7 8 9 1    Std Error

 0    0.00077814      1.00000       I                   |*******************I            0
 1    0.00027852      0.35793       I                .  |*******             I     0.077152
 2    0.00013680      0.17581       I                .  |****                I     0.086473
 3   -0.0001305      -.16766        I              .***|  .                  I     0.088575
 4   -0.0001354      -.17404        I              .***|  .                  I     0.090444
 5   -0.0001662      -.21362        I             ****|  .                   I     0.092416
 6   -0.0000774      -.09948        I              . **|  .                  I     0.095310
 7   -0.0000581      -.07466        I              .  *|  .                  I     0.095926
 8   -0.0000863      -.11086        I              . **|  .                  I     0.096272
 9   -0.0000483      -.06209        I              .  *|  .                  I     0.097029
10    0.00007297      0.09377       I                . |**  .                I     0.097265
11    0.00016465      0.21159       I                . |****                 I     0.097801
12    0.00025310      0.32526       I                . |*******              I     0.100489
13    0.00020256      0.26031       I                . |*****                I     0.106572
14    0.00012430      0.15974       I                . |***.                 I     0.110291
15   -0.0000225      -.02891        I              .   *|  .                 I     0.111660
16   -0.0000815      -.10473        I              . **|  .                  I     0.111705
17   -0.0000813      -.10442        I              . **|  .                  I     0.112288
18   -0.0001532      -.19694        I             .****|  .                  I     0.112864
19   -0.0000346      -.04449        I              .  *|  .                  I     0.114891
20   -0.0000690      -.08872        I              . **|  .                  I     0.114994
21   -3.3666E-6      -.00433        I              .    |  .                 I     0.115401
22   -0.0000132      -.01694        I              .    |  .                 I     0.115402
23    0.00011007      0.14145       I                . |*** .               I     0.115416
24    0.00014165      0.18203       I                . |****.               I     0.116444
```

(a) The SAC

```
                                 Partial Autocorrelations
Lag    Correlation    -1 9 8 7 6 5 4 3 2 1 0 1 2 3 4 5 6 7 8 9 1

 1      0.35793       I                .  |*******              I
 2      0.05470       I                .  |*  .                 I
 3     -0.28383       I              ******|  .                 I
 4     -0.04957       I                . *|  .                  I
 5     -0.07951       I                .**|  .                  I
 6     -0.01766       I                .  |  .                  I
 7     -0.05209       I                . *|  .                  I
 8     -0.16006       I                ***|  .                  I
 9     -0.01233       I                .  |  .                  I
10      0.15162       I                .  |***                  I
11      0.11732       I                .  |**.                  I
12      0.17589       I                .  |****                 I
13      0.08258       I                .  |**.                  I
14      0.06872       I                .  |*  .                 I
15      0.01111       I                .  |  .                  I
16      0.00702       I                .  |  .                  I
17      0.06229       I                .  |*  .                 I
18     -0.14474       I                ***|  .                  I
19      0.11326       I                .  |**.                  I
20     -0.03966       I                . *|  .                  I
21     -0.03950       I                . *|  .                  I
22     -0.03486       I                . *|  .                  I
23      0.04640       I                .  |*  .                 I
24      0.05298       I                .  |*  .                 I
```

(b) The SPAC

**FIGURE 11.19** SAS output of the RSAC and RSPAC for the model
$z_t = \phi_1 z_{t-1} + \phi_3 z_{t-3} + \phi_{1,12} z_{t-12} - \phi_1 \phi_{1,12} z_{t-13} - \phi_3 \phi_{1,12} z_{t-15} + a_t$

Autocorrelation Check of Residuals

| To Lag | Chi-Square | DF | Pr > ChiSq | ----------------------Autocorrelations---------------------- | | | | | |
|---|---|---|---|---|---|---|---|---|---|
| 6 | 6.85 | 3 | 0.0768 | -0.049 | 0.090 | 0.010 | 0.004 | -0.169 | 0.011 |
| 12 | 11.36 | 9 | 0.2521 | 0.004 | -0.083 | -0.031 | 0.086 | 0.097 | -0.011 |
| 18 | 24.83 | 15 | 0.0523 | 0.137 | 0.099 | -0.036 | -0.004 | 0.066 | -0.194 |
| 24 | 27.75 | 21 | 0.1474 | 0.056 | -0.036 | 0.025 | -0.031 | 0.087 | 0.036 |
| 30 | 33.42 | 27 | 0.1834 | 0.109 | 0.005 | 0.072 | -0.089 | -0.054 | -0.012 |

Autocorrelation Plot of Residuals

| Lag | Covariance | Correlation | -1 9 8 7 6 5 4 3 2 1 0 1 2 3 4 5 6 7 8 9 1 | Std Error |
|---|---|---|---|---|
| 0 | 0.00060764 | 1.00000 | \|                    \|********************\| | 0 |
| 1 | -0.0000300 | -.04934 | \|                 . *\| .              \| | 0.077152 |
| 2 | 0.00005477 | 0.09014 | \|                 . \|**.              \| | 0.077339 |
| 3 | 6.18103E-6 | 0.01017 | \|                 .  \| .               \| | 0.077962 |
| 4 | 2.20716E-6 | 0.00363 | \|                 .  \| .               \| | 0.077970 |
| 5 | -0.0001026 | -.16887 | \|              ***\| .               \| | 0.077971 |
| 6 | 6.40469E-6 | 0.01054 | \|                 .  \| .               \| | 0.080118 |
| 7 | 2.69106E-6 | 0.00443 | \|                 .  \| .               \| | 0.080127 |
| 8 | -0.0000507 | -.08350 | \|                .**\| .               \| | 0.080128 |
| 9 | -0.0000191 | -.03142 | \|                 . *\| .               \| | 0.080644 |
| 10 | 0.00005239 | 0.08622 | \|                 . \|**.               \| | 0.080717 |

(a) The RSAC

Partial Autocorrelations

| Lag | Correlation | -1 9 8 7 6 5 4 3 2 1 0 1 2 3 4 5 6 7 8 9 1 |
|---|---|---|
| 1 | -0.04934 | \|              . *\| .              \| |
| 2 | 0.08792 | \|              . \|**.              \| |
| 3 | 0.01876 | \|              .  \| .              \| |
| 4 | -0.00300 | \|              .  \| .              \| |
| 5 | -0.17325 | \|           ***\| .              \| |
| 6 | -0.00588 | \|              .  \| .              \| |
| 7 | 0.03734 | \|              . \|* .              \| |
| 8 | -0.07765 | \|             .**\| .              \| |
| 9 | -0.04645 | \|              . *\| .              \| |
| 10 | 0.07167 | \|              . \|* .              \| |

(b) The RSPAC

# 11.3 BOX–JENKINS ERROR TERM MODELS IN TIME SERIES REGRESSION

**Time series regression models** are employed to forecast time series that are **deterministic** in nature. That is, such models are useful when *the parameters describing a time series are not changing over time.* Chapter 6 discusses time series regression models, including polynomial trend models, dummy variable models, trigonometric models, and growth curve models. For such models each error term is assumed to be a random variable that is normally distributed with mean zero and a variance that is the same for each and every time period $t$. Moreover, the error terms are assumed to be **statistically independent.**

Often, however, when we employ a time series regression model, the RSAC, the RSPAC, and the $Q^*$ statistic indicate that the error terms are not statistically independent. In such a case we should use the three-step procedure, as described in Section 11.2, to identify a Box–Jenkins model that describes the error terms. Then, as illustrated in the following example, we forecast future values of the time series by combining the time series regression model with the Box–Jenkins model describing the error terms.

**EXAMPLE 11.6**    Consider the monthly hotel room averages given in Table 11.1. The plot of the room averages versus time given in Figure 11.1 indicates that this time series can be described by a linear trend and increasing seasonal variation. Furthermore, this plot suggests that the parameters describing this trend and seasonal variation are probably not changing very much over time. Therefore, we might consider using the dummy variable regression model

$$y_t^* = TR_t + SN_t + \varepsilon_t$$
$$= \beta_0 + \beta_1 t + \beta_2 M_1 + \beta_3 M_2 + \cdots + \beta_{12} M_{11} + \varepsilon_t$$

where $y_t^* = y_t^{.25}$ and $M_1, M_2, \ldots, M_{11}$ are dummy variables. For example,

$$M_1 = \begin{cases} 1 & \text{if period } t \text{ is January} \\ 0 & \text{otherwise} \end{cases}$$

Note that we have not defined a dummy variable for December.

The residuals from fitting this dummy variable regression model to the quartic roots of the hotel room averages form the time series that was analyzed in Example 11.5, that is, the $z_t$ values are actually the residuals. Thus, we can use the SAC in Figure 11.18 to decide whether the error terms in our regression model are independent. The spikes in the SAC for the residuals (the estimates for the error terms in our regression model) show us that the residuals are autocorrelated at several lags, including lags 1 and 12. Therefore, we believe that the error terms are autocorrelated (not statistically independent), and we should not use the regression model to forecast the quartic roots of the hotel room averages. We can, however, find a Box–Jenkins model for the error terms and combine this model with the regression model.

In Example 11.5, we tentatively identified a model for the error terms (that is, for the $z_t$ values) as

$$\varepsilon_t = \phi_1 \varepsilon_{t-1} + \phi_3 \varepsilon_{t-3} + \phi_5 \varepsilon_{t-5} + \phi_{1,12} \varepsilon_{t-12} - \phi_1 \phi_{1,12} \varepsilon_{t-13} - \phi_3 \phi_{1,12} \varepsilon_{t-15} - \phi_5 \phi_{1,12} \varepsilon_{t-17} + a_t$$

The SAS output of estimation, diagnostic checking, and forecasting that results from the *time series regression model* obtained by combining the dummy variable and error term models is given in Figures 11.20, 11.21, and 11.22. The $p$-values associated with values of $Q^*$ do not indicate that we should reject the adequacy of the model.

We complete this example by discussing exactly how the model

$$y_t^* = \beta_0 + \beta_1 t + \beta_2 M_1 + \beta_3 M_2 + \cdots + \beta_{12} M_{11} + \varepsilon_t$$

**FIGURE 11.20** SAS output of the least squares point estimates of parameters in the dummy variable regression model for hotel room occupancy, where the error terms $\varepsilon_1, \varepsilon_2, \ldots$ are described by the model
$\varepsilon_t = \phi_1 \varepsilon_{t-1} + \phi_3 \varepsilon_{t-3} + \phi_5 \varepsilon_{t-5} + \phi_{1,12} \varepsilon_{t-12} - \phi_1 \phi_{1,12} \varepsilon_{t-13} - \phi_3 \phi_{1,12} \varepsilon_{t-15} - \phi_5 \phi_{1,12} \varepsilon_{t-17} + a_t$

Conditional Least Squares Estimation

| Parameter | Estimate | Standard Error | t Value | Approx Pr > \|t\| | Lag | Variable | Shift |
|---|---|---|---|---|---|---|---|
| MU | 4.80395 | 0.01041 | 461.49 | <.0001 | 0 | QtRooty | 0 |
| AR1,1 | 0.30455 | 0.07843 | 3.88 | 0.0002 | 1 | QtRooty | 0 |
| AR1,2 | -0.21580 | 0.07824 | -2.76 | 0.0065 | 3 | QtRooty | 0 |
| AR1,3 | -0.13804 | 0.07865 | -1.76 | 0.0813 | 5 | QtRooty | 0 |
| AR2,1 | 0.28454 | 0.08449 | 3.37 | 0.0010 | 12 | QtRooty | 0 |
| NUM1 | 0.0035291 | 0.00004840 | 72.92 | <.0001 | 0 | Time | 0 |
| NUM2 | -0.04846 | 0.01140 | -4.25 | <.0001 | 0 | M1 | 0 |
| NUM3 | -0.13701 | 0.01288 | -10.63 | <.0001 | 0 | M2 | 0 |
| NUM4 | -0.10415 | 0.01433 | -7.27 | <.0001 | 0 | M3 | 0 |
| NUM5 | 0.05249 | 0.01399 | 3.75 | 0.0002 | 0 | M4 | 0 |
| NUM6 | 0.02585 | 0.01454 | 1.78 | 0.0775 | 0 | M5 | 0 |
| NUM7 | 0.19115 | 0.01417 | 13.49 | <.0001 | 0 | M6 | 0 |
| NUM0 | 0.38432 | 0.01467 | 26.20 | <.0001 | 0 | M7 | 0 |
| NUM9 | 0.41375 | 0.01411 | 29.33 | <.0001 | 0 | M8 | 0 |
| NUM10 | 0.07270 | 0.01449 | 5.02 | <.0001 | 0 | M9 | 0 |
| NUM11 | 0.04932 | 0.01286 | 3.84 | 0.0002 | 0 | M10 | 0 |
| NUM12 | -0.14248 | 0.01122 | -12.69 | <.0001 | 0 | M11 | 0 |

Constant Estimate       3.606476
Variance Estimate       0.0006
Std Error Estimate      0.024487
AIC                     -753.595
SBC                     -700.487
Number of Residuals        168
* AIC and SBC do not include log determinant.

where

$$\varepsilon_t = \phi_1 \varepsilon_{t-1} + \phi_3 \varepsilon_{t-3} + \phi_5 \varepsilon_{t-5} + \phi_{1,12} \varepsilon_{t-12} - \phi_1 \phi_{1,12} \varepsilon_{t-13} - \phi_3 \phi_{1,12} \varepsilon_{t-15} - \phi_5 \phi_{1,12} \varepsilon_{t-17} + a_t$$

has produced the point forecasts in Figure 11.22 (page 518). Note that we have observed 168 time series observations $y_1^*, y_2^*, \ldots, y_{168}^*$, and also note that

$$y_{169}^* = \beta_0 + \beta_1(169) + \beta_2(1) + \beta_3(0) + \cdots + \beta_{12}(0) + \varepsilon_{169}$$

where

$$\varepsilon_{169} = \phi_1 \varepsilon_{168} + \phi_3 \varepsilon_{166} + \phi_5 \varepsilon_{164} + \phi_{1,12} \varepsilon_{157} - \phi_1 \phi_{1,12} \varepsilon_{156} - \phi_3 \phi_{1,12} \varepsilon_{154} - \phi_5 \phi_{1,12} \varepsilon_{152} + a_{169}$$

It follows that a point forecast of $y_{169}^*$ is

$$\hat{y}_{169}^* = b_0 + b_1(169) + b_2 + \hat{\varepsilon}_{169}$$

where

$$\hat{\varepsilon}_{169} = \hat{\phi}_1 \hat{\varepsilon}_{168} + \hat{\phi}_3 \hat{\varepsilon}_{166} + \hat{\phi}_5 \hat{\varepsilon}_{164} + \hat{\phi}_{1,12} \hat{\varepsilon}_{157} - \hat{\phi}_1 \hat{\phi}_{1,12} \hat{\varepsilon}_{156} - \hat{\phi}_3 \hat{\phi}_{1,12} \hat{\varepsilon}_{154} - \hat{\phi}_5 \hat{\phi}_{1,12} \hat{\varepsilon}_{152} + \hat{a}_{169}$$

Here $b_0, b_1, b_2, \hat{\phi}_1, \hat{\phi}_3, \hat{\phi}_5,$ and $\hat{\phi}_{1,12}$ are the least squares point estimates given in Figure 11.20 and the point prediction of $a_{169}$ is $\hat{a}_{169} = 0$ (since $a_{169}$ is a future random shock). Moreover,

**FIGURE 11.21** SAS output of the RSAC and RSPAC for the dummy variable regression model for hotel room occupancy, where the error terms $\varepsilon_1, \varepsilon_2, \ldots$ are described by the model

$$\varepsilon_t = \phi_1\varepsilon_{t-1} + \phi_3\varepsilon_{t-3} + \phi_5\varepsilon_{t-5} + \phi_{1,12}\varepsilon_{t-12} - \phi_1\phi_{1,12}\varepsilon_{t-13} - \phi_3\phi_{1,12}\varepsilon_{t-15} - \phi_5\phi_{1,12}\varepsilon_{t-17} + a_t$$

```
                        Autocorrelation Check of Residuals

    To      Chi-              Pr >
    Lag    Square    DF      ChiSq    ------------------Autocorrelations------------------
     6      2.42      2      0.2986   -0.024   0.094  -0.008  -0.011  -0.037   0.054
    12      6.11      8      0.6348    0.031  -0.079  -0.033   0.051   0.097  -0.014
    18     16.91     14      0.2610    0.116   0.108  -0.025   0.008   0.061  -0.167
    24     19.15     20      0.5120    0.078  -0.017   0.025  -0.025   0.049   0.038
    30     24.01     26      0.5756    0.110   0.006   0.046  -0.078  -0.058   0.016
```

```
                        Autocorrelation Plot of Residuals

  Lag    Covariance     Correlation    -1 9 8 7 6 5 4 3 2 1 0 1 2 3 4 5 6 7 8 9 1    Std Error
   0    0.00059960       1.00000      |                    |********************|       0
   1   -0.0000142        -.02374      |                    .| .                 |    0.077152
   2    0.00005666       0.09450      |                    .|**.                |    0.077195
   3   -4.9838E-6        -.00831      |                    .| .                 |    0.077881
   4   -6.8487E-6        -.01142      |                    .| .                 |    0.077886
   5   -0.0000222        -.03697      |                   .*| .                 |    0.077896
   6    0.00003226       0.05381      |                    .|* .                |    0.078000
   7    0.00001861       0.03104      |                    .|* .                |    0.078221
   8   -0.0000471        -.07854      |                  .**| .                 |    0.078294
   9   -0.0000201        -.03348      |                   .*| .                 |    0.078762
  10    0.00003054       0.05094      |                    .|* .                |    0.078846
  11    0.00005823       0.09711      |                    .|**.                |    0.079042
  12   -8.414E-6         -.01403      |                    .| .                 |    0.079749
  13    0.00006950       0.11591      |                    .|**.                |    0.079764
  14    0.00006495       0.10832      |                    .|**.                |    0.080760
  15   -0.0000147        -.02454      |                    .| .                 |    0.081620
  16    4.61478E-6       0.00770      |                    .| .                 |    0.081664
  17    0.00003653       0.06092      |                    .|* .                |    0.081669
  18   -0.0001002        -.16719      |                 ***| .                  |    0.081939
  19    0.00004683       0.07810      |                    .|**.                |    0.083945
  20   -0.0000102        -.01698      |                    .| .                 |    0.084376
  21    0.00001472       0.02456      |                    .| .                 |    0.084396
  22   -0.0000151        -.02512      |                   .*| .                 |    0.084439
  23    0.00002967       0.04948      |                    .|* .                |    0.084483
  24    0.00002308       0.03849      |                    .|* .                |    0.084656
```

(a) The RSAC

the model

$$y_t^* = \beta_0 + \beta_1 t + \beta_2 M_1 + \beta_3 M_2 + \cdots + \beta_{12}M_{11} + \varepsilon_t$$

implies that

$$\varepsilon_t = y_t^* - (\beta_0 + \beta_1 t + \beta_2 M_1 + \beta_3 M_2 + \cdots + \beta_{12}M_{11})$$

Since we have observed $y_{168}^*, y_{166}^*, y_{164}^*, y_{157}^*, y_{156}^*, y_{154}^*$, and $y_{152}^*$, the point prediction of each of $\varepsilon_{168}, \varepsilon_{166}, \varepsilon_{164}, \varepsilon_{157}, \varepsilon_{156}, \varepsilon_{154}$, and $\varepsilon_{152}$ is given by the equation

$$\hat{\varepsilon}_t = y_t^* - (b_0 + b_1 t + b_2 M_1 + b_3 M_2 + \cdots + b_{12}M_{11})$$

For example, the past time period 166 is October and $y_{166} = 860$ (see Table 11.1). In Figure 11.20, we find that $b_0 = 4.80395$, $b_1 = .0035291$, and $b_{11} = .04932$. It follows

**FIGURE 11.21** (Continued)

Partial Autocorrelations

| Lag | Correlation | -1 9 8 7 6 5 4 3 2 1 0 1 2 3 4 5 6 7 8 9 1 |
|-----|-------------|---------------------------------------------|
| 1 | -0.02374 | |
| 2 | 0.09399 | ** |
| 3 | -0.00409 | |
| 4 | -0.02076 | |
| 5 | -0.03684 | * |
| 6 | 0.05587 | * |
| 7 | 0.04073 | * |
| 8 | -0.08959 | ** |
| 9 | -0.04583 | * |
| 10 | 0.06896 | * |
| 11 | 0.11627 | ** |
| 12 | -0.02767 | * |
| 13 | 0.08240 | ** |
| 14 | 0.13338 | *** |
| 15 | -0.01903 | |
| 16 | -0.02626 | * |
| 17 | 0.05082 | * |
| 18 | -0.15357 | *** |
| 19 | 0.08188 | ** |
| 20 | -0.00143 | |
| 21 | 0.00345 | |
| 22 | -0.00136 | |
| 23 | 0.03565 | * |
| 24 | 0.02813 | * |

(b) The RSPAC

that

$$\hat{\varepsilon}_{166} = [(860)^{.25} - (4.80395 + .0035291(166) + .04932)] = -.02377$$

If we calculate other past $\hat{\varepsilon}_t$ values similarly and plug them into the equation for the future $\hat{\varepsilon}_{169}$, we find that $\hat{\varepsilon}_{169} = .03164$. Since $b_2 = -.04846$, it follows that the point forecast of $y^*_{169}$ is

$$y^*_{169} = b_0 + b_1(169) + b_2 + \hat{\varepsilon}_{169}$$
$$= 4.80395 + .0035291(169) - .04846 + .03164 = 5.38355$$

and the point forecast for hotel room occupancy in January of year 15, $y_{169}$, is

$$\hat{y}_{169} = (5.38355)^4 = 839.99$$

Point forecasts of other future values of $y_t$ are made in a similar manner.

In Example 11.6 the time series regression model

$$y_t = TR_t + SN_t + \varepsilon_t$$

where $TR_t$ and $SN_t$ are deterministic functions of time, provided good predictions of hotel room occupancies. Using a model in which $TR_t$ and $SN_t$ are deterministic

**FIGURE 11.22** SAS output of forecasting using the dummy variable regression model for hotel room occupancy, where the error terms $\varepsilon_1, \varepsilon_2, \ldots$ are described by the model

$$\varepsilon_t = \phi_1 \varepsilon_{t-1} + \phi_3 \varepsilon_{t-3} + \phi_5 \varepsilon_{t-5} + \phi_{1,12} \varepsilon_{t-12} - \phi_1 \phi_{1,12} \varepsilon_{t-13} - \phi_3 \phi_{1,12} \varepsilon_{t-15} - \phi_5 \phi_{1,12} \varepsilon_{t-17} + a_t$$

Forecasts for variable QtRooty

| Obs | Forecast | Std Error | 95% Confidence Limits | |
|-----|----------|-----------|-----------------------|------|
| 169 | 5.3836 | 0.0245 | 5.3356 | 5.4315 |
| 170 | 5.2679 | 0.0256 | 5.2177 | 5.3180 |
| 171 | 5.2888 | 0.0257 | 5.2384 | 5.3392 |
| 172 | 5.4464 | 0.0261 | 5.3952 | 5.4976 |
| 173 | 5.4221 | 0.0263 | 5.3706 | 5.4736 |
| 174 | 5.5928 | 0.0267 | 5.5405 | 5.6452 |
| 175 | 5.8073 | 0.0268 | 5.7548 | 5.8597 |
| 176 | 5.8396 | 0.0268 | 5.7872 | 5.8921 |
| 177 | 5.4956 | 0.0268 | 5.4431 | 5.5481 |
| 178 | 5.4774 | 0.0268 | 5.4248 | 5.5300 |
| 179 | 5.2951 | 0.0269 | 5.2425 | 5.3478 |
| 180 | 5.4518 | 0.0269 | 5.3992 | 5.5044 |

(a) Forecasts of quartic roots of hotel room occupancies

| Obs | Forecasty | L95CI | U95CI |
|-----|-----------|-------|-------|
| 169 | 839.99 | 810.44 | 870.35 |
| 170 | 770.08 | 741.16 | 799.84 |
| 171 | 782.41 | 753.03 | 812.64 |
| 172 | 879.91 | 847.31 | 913.44 |
| 173 | 864.32 | 831.94 | 897.63 |
| 174 | 978.43 | 942.31 | 1015.58 |
| 175 | 1137.33 | 1096.80 | 1178.96 |
| 176 | 1162.90 | 1121.69 | 1205.23 |
| 177 | 912.15 | 877.77 | 947.53 |
| 178 | 900.10 | 866.03 | 935.16 |
| 179 | 786.15 | 755.36 | 817.87 |
| 180 | 883.39 | 849.77 | 918.00 |

(b) Forecasts of actual hotel room occupancies

functions of time implies that the trend and seasonal natures of the time series under consideration are largely **deterministic** (that is, **unchanging**) over time. Since the hotel room occupancy data exhibited a definite linear trend with well-defined seasonal variation, modeling the trend and seasonal effects by using deterministic functions of time provided good models. However, many time series exhibit trend and seasonal effects that are largely **stochastic** (that is, **changing over time**). The Box–Jenkins models of Chapters 9–12 are particularly effective when used to model such time series. This is so because the autoregressive and differencing operators in these models are designed to describe stochastic trend and seasonal effects. For example, it is best to use Box–Jenkins models to forecast the paper towel sales time series in Table 9.1 and the Wisconsin trade time series in Table 11.4 of the exercises, both of which exhibit stochastic trend and/or seasonal effects.

**TABLE 11.4 (for Exercises 11.1–11.5)  Number of Employees in Wholesale and Retail Trade in Wisconsin, 1961–1975 (Thousands of Employees)**

| Year | Jan. | Feb. | Mar. | Apr. | May | June | July | Aug. | Sept. | Oct. | Nov. | Dec. |
|------|------|------|------|------|------|------|------|------|-------|------|------|------|
| 1961 | 239.6 | 236.4 | 236.8 | 241.5 | 243.7 | 246.1 | 244.1 | 244.2 | 244.8 | 246.6 | 250.9 | 261.4 |
| 1962 | 237.6 | 235.7 | 236.1 | 242.6 | 244.5 | 246.6 | 245.7 | 247.7 | 248.9 | 251.4 | 255.9 | 263.7 |
| 1963 | 242.2 | 239.3 | 239.7 | 247.2 | 249.3 | 252.3 | 252.8 | 253.6 | 254.2 | 256.1 | 260.3 | 268.8 |
| 1964 | 250.1 | 247.9 | 249.0 | 253.8 | 258.3 | 261.3 | 261.3 | 261.9 | 263.3 | 267.3 | 270.6 | 281.5 |
| 1965 | 261.9 | 258.6 | 259.7 | 266.0 | 271.1 | 274.4 | 274.0 | 273.8 | 274.9 | 280.0 | 285.4 | 295.9 |
| 1966 | 275.4 | 273.6 | 275.9 | 281.1 | 285.2 | 289.1 | 289.2 | 288.9 | 291.1 | 295.3 | 300.2 | 310.9 |
| 1967 | 286.9 | 283.0 | 286.2 | 291.5 | 295.4 | 299.7 | 297.9 | 298.1 | 300.2 | 304.8 | 311.9 | 320.9 |
| 1968 | 298.3 | 295.5 | 297.2 | 302.7 | 306.7 | 309.1 | 308.7 | 309.9 | 310.8 | 314.7 | 321.2 | 329.0 |
| 1969 | 307.6 | 305.5 | 308.0 | 314.4 | 320.5 | 323.4 | 323.0 | 324.4 | 326.1 | 329.3 | 335.0 | 341.9 |
| 1970 | 321.8 | 317.3 | 318.6 | 323.4 | 327.1 | 327.9 | 325.3 | 325.7 | 330.0 | 333.5 | 337.1 | 341.3 |
| 1971 | 321.6 | 318.2 | 319.6 | 326.2 | 332.3 | 334.2 | 334.5 | 335.5 | 335.1 | 338.2 | 341.9 | 347.9 |
| 1972 | 329.5 | 326.4 | 329.1 | 337.2 | 344.9 | 349.6 | 351.0 | 353.8 | 354.5 | 357.4 | 362.1 | 367.5 |
| 1973 | 347.9 | 345.0 | 348.9 | 355.3 | 362.4 | 366.6 | 366.0 | 370.2 | 370.9 | 374.5 | 380.2 | 384.6 |
| 1974 | 360.6 | 354.4 | 357.4 | 367.0 | 375.7 | 381.0 | 381.2 | 383.0 | 384.3 | 387.0 | 391.7 | 396.0 |
| 1975 | 374.0 | 370.4 | 373.2 | 381.1 | 389.9 | 394.6 | 394.0 | 397.0 | 397.2 | 399.4 | | |

*Source:* State of Wisconsin Department of Industry, Labor, and Human Relations, Bureau of Research and Statistics.

# Exercises

Miller and Wichern (1977) reported 178 monthly values $y_1, y_2, \ldots, y_{178}$ of the number of people in Wisconsin employed in "trade" from 1961 to 1975 (all observations are given in units of 1000 employees). This time series is presented in Table 11.4 and is plotted in Figure 11.23 (page 520). Since the plot seems to exhibit constant seasonal variation, we will not use a predifferencing transformation. Figures 11.24 (page 520), 11.25 (page 521), and 11.26 (page 521) present the SAS output of the SAC of the values produced by each of the transformations $z_t = y_t$, $z_t = y_t - y_{t-1}$, and $z_t = y_t - y_{t-12}$. In Figure 11.27 (page 522) we present the SAS output of the SAC and SPAC of the values produced by the transformation $z_t = y_t - y_{t-1} - y_{t-12} + y_{t-13}$. **Exercises 11.1 through 11.5 are based on these outputs.**

**11.1** Should the values produced by the transformation $z_t = y_t$ be considered stationary? Explain your answer.

**11.2** Should the values produced by the transformation $z_t = y_t - y_{t-1}$ be considered stationary? Explain your answer.

**11.3** Should the values produced by the transformation $z_t = y_t - y_{t-12}$ be considered stationary? Explain your answer.

**11.4** Should the values produced by the transformation

$$z_t = y_t - y_{t-1} - y_{t-12} + y_{t-13}$$

be considered stationary? Explain your answer.

**11.5** Discuss why the model

$$z_t = a_t - \theta_1 a_{t-1} - \theta_{1,12} a_{t-12} + \theta_1 \theta_{1,12} a_{t-13}$$

where

$$z_t = y_t - y_{t-1} - y_{t-12} + y_{t-13}$$

is a reasonable tentative model describing the trade values in Table 11.4.

**FIGURE 11.23 (for Exercises 11.1–11.5)** JMP IN plot of the number of employees in wholesale and retail trade

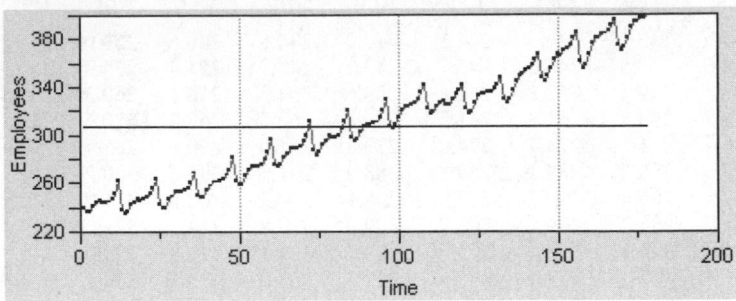

**FIGURE 11.24 (for Exercises 11.1–11.5)** SAS output of the SAC for the original trade values

Autocorrelations

| Lag | Covariance | Correlation | -1 9 8 7 6 5 4 3 2 1 0 1 2 3 4 5 6 7 8 9 1 | Std Error |
|---|---|---|---|---|
| 0 | 2174.219 | 1.00000 | \|********************\| | 0 |
| 1 | 2111.301 | 0.97106 | \|        .        ******************* \| | 0.074953 |
| 2 | 2046.143 | 0.94109 | \|       .        ******************* \| | 0.127330 |
| 3 | 1990.467 | 0.91549 | \|        .        ****************** \| | 0.161754 |
| 4 | 1953.651 | 0.89855 | \|         .        ****************** \| | 0.188630 |
| 5 | 1923.082 | 0.88449 | \|         .        ****************** \| | 0.211313 |
| 6 | 1894.387 | 0.87130 | \|          .        ***************** \| | 0.231178 |
| 7 | 1857.165 | 0.85418 | \|          .        ***************** \| | 0.248944 |
| 8 | 1822.990 | 0.83846 | \|           .        **************** \| | 0.264898 |
| 9 | 1795.368 | 0.82575 | \|           .        **************** \| | 0.279410 |
| 10 | 1781.604 | 0.81942 | \|            .        *************** \| | 0.292800 |
| 11 | 1766.588 | 0.81252 | \|            .        *************** \| | 0.305411 |
| 12 | 1754.960 | 0.80717 | \|            .        *************** \| | 0.317323 |
| 13 | 1689.253 | 0.77695 | \|            .        *************** \| | 0.328655 |
| 14 | 1622.604 | 0.74629 | \|            .        ************** \| | 0.338817 |
| 15 | 1565.605 | 0.72008 | \|            .        ************** \| | 0.347929 |
| 16 | 1526.444 | 0.70207 | \|            .        ************* \| | 0.356203 |
| 17 | 1493.548 | 0.68694 | \|            .        *************. \| | 0.363894 |
| 18 | 1462.579 | 0.67269 | \|           .        ************ . \| | 0.371108 |
| 19 | 1424.437 | 0.65515 | \|           .        ************ . \| | 0.377896 |
| 20 | 1390.875 | 0.63971 | \|           .        ************ . \| | 0.384224 |
| 21 | 1363.633 | 0.62718 | \|          .        ************ . \| | 0.390162 |
| 22 | 1347.737 | 0.61987 | \|          .        ***********  . \| | 0.395785 |
| 23 | 1328.662 | 0.61110 | \|          .        ***********  . \| | 0.401202 |
| 24 | 1312.463 | 0.60365 | \|          .        ***********  . \| | 0.406398 |

**FIGURE 11.25 (for Exercises 11.1–11.5)** SAS output of the SAC of the trade values given by the transformation $z_t = y_t - y_{t-1}$

Autocorrelations

| Lag | Covariance | Correlation | Std Error |
|---|---|---|---|
| 0 | 51.984116 | 1.00000 | 0 |
| 1 | 1.341360 | 0.02580 | 0.075165 |
| 2 | -10.104648 | -.19438 | 0.075215 |
| 3 | -16.397040 | -.31542 | 0.078001 |
| 4 | -6.537721 | -.12576 | 0.084902 |
| 5 | 0.720104 | 0.01385 | 0.085948 |
| 6 | 11.646511 | 0.22404 | 0.085961 |
| 7 | 0.382655 | 0.00736 | 0.089199 |
| 8 | -5.583873 | -.10741 | 0.089202 |
| 9 | -15.804044 | -.30402 | 0.089930 |
| 10 | -9.291756 | -.17874 | 0.095560 |
| 11 | 2.139864 | 0.04116 | 0.097431 |
| 12 | 46.868231 | 0.90159 | 0.097529 |
| 13 | 0.801322 | 0.01541 | 0.136736 |
| 14 | -9.690318 | -.18641 | 0.136746 |
| 15 | -15.285807 | -.29405 | 0.138174 |
| 16 | -6.236594 | -.11997 | 0.141665 |
| 17 | 0.881801 | 0.01696 | 0.142238 |
| 18 | 10.680823 | 0.20546 | 0.142250 |
| 19 | 0.496121 | 0.00954 | 0.143917 |
| 20 | -4.968756 | -.09558 | 0.143920 |
| 21 | -14.320935 | -.27549 | 0.144278 |
| 22 | -8.286359 | -.15940 | 0.147220 |
| 23 | 1.685671 | 0.03243 | 0.140192 |
| 24 | 42.361435 | 0.81489 | 0.148232 |

**FIGURE 11.26 (for Exercises 11.1–11.5)** SAS output of the SAC for the trade values given by the transformation $z_t = y_t - y_{t-12}$

Autocorrelations

| Lag | Covariance | Correlation | Std Error |
|---|---|---|---|
| 0 | 25.057251 | 1.00000 | 0 |
| 1 | 23.551046 | 0.93989 | 0.077615 |
| 2 | 21.700063 | 0.86803 | 0.129102 |
| 3 | 19.984942 | 0.79757 | 0.160454 |
| 4 | 18.383410 | 0.73366 | 0.182782 |
| 5 | 17.021926 | 0.67972 | 0.199736 |
| 6 | 15.647000 | 0.62448 | 0.213216 |
| 7 | 14.141135 | 0.56435 | 0.223963 |
| 8 | 12.707374 | 0.50713 | 0.232372 |
| 9 | 11.123315 | 0.44392 | 0.238946 |
| 10 | 9.421701 | 0.37601 | 0.243864 |
| 11 | 7.755107 | 0.30950 | 0.247332 |
| 12 | 6.024674 | 0.24044 | 0.249854 |
| 13 | 5.018099 | 0.20027 | 0.251045 |
| 14 | 4.119250 | 0.16439 | 0.252005 |
| 15 | 3.165849 | 0.12634 | 0.252651 |
| 16 | 2.245328 | 0.08961 | 0.253031 |
| 17 | 1.057665 | 0.04221 | 0.253222 |
| 18 | -0.103884 | -.00415 | 0.253264 |
| 19 | -0.936067 | -.03736 | 0.253265 |
| 20 | -1.623877 | -.06481 | 0.253298 |
| 21 | -2.257332 | -.09009 | 0.253398 |
| 22 | -2.941722 | -.11740 | 0.253591 |
| 23 | -3.670260 | -.14647 | 0.253918 |
| 24 | -4.472118 | -.17848 | 0.254426 |

**FIGURE 11.27 (for Exercises 11.1–11.5)** SAS output of the SAC and SPAC of the trade values given by the transformation $z_t = y_t - y_{t-1} - y_{t-12} + y_{t-13}$

Name of Variable = y

| Period(s) of Differencing | 1,12 |
|---|---|
| Mean of Working Series | 0.087273 |
| Standard Deviation | 1.438735 |
| Number of Observations | 165 |
| Observation(s) eliminated by differencing | 13 |

Autocorrelations

| Lag | Covariance | Correlation | -1 9 8 7 6 5 4 3 2 1 0 1 2 3 4 5 6 7 8 9 1 | Std Error |
|---|---|---|---|---|
| 0 | 2.069959 | 1.00000 | \|********************\| | 0 |
| 1 | 0.380397 | 0.18377 | . \|**** | 0.077850 |
| 2 | -0.056837 | -.02746 | . *\| . | 0.080436 |
| 3 | -0.021478 | -.01038 | . \| . | 0.080493 |
| 4 | -0.290834 | -.14050 | ***\| . | 0.080501 |
| 5 | -0.0045074 | -.00218 | . \| . | 0.081974 |
| 6 | 0.200142 | 0.09669 | . \|**. | 0.081974 |
| 7 | 0.041474 | 0.02004 | . \| . | 0.082662 |
| 8 | 0.187094 | 0.09039 | . \|**. | 0.082692 |
| 9 | 0.197702 | 0.09551 | . \|**. | 0.083288 |
| 10 | 0.00045630 | 0.00022 | . \| . | 0.083950 |
| 11 | -0.144889 | -.07000 | . *\| . | 0.083950 |
| 12 | -0.572732 | -.27669 | ******\| . | 0.084302 |
| 13 | -0.200208 | -.09672 | . **\| . | 0.089637 |
| 14 | 0.056730 | 0.02741 | . \|* . | 0.090268 |
| 15 | 0.0061858 | 0.00299 | . \| . | 0.090318 |
| 16 | 0.287759 | 0.13902 | . \|***. | 0.090319 |
| 17 | 0.049923 | 0.02412 | . \| . | 0.091606 |
| 18 | -0.209991 | -.10145 | . **\| . | 0.091645 |
| 19 | -0.198252 | -.09578 | . **\| . | 0.092323 |
| 20 | -0.113819 | -.05499 | . *\| . | 0.092923 |
| 21 | -0.039443 | -.01906 | . \| . | 0.093120 |
| 22 | -0.039793 | -.01922 | . \| . | 0.093144 |
| 23 | 0.106062 | 0.05124 | . \|* . | 0.093168 |
| 24 | -0.165247 | -.07983 | . **\| . | 0.093338 |

(a) The SAC

Partial Autocorrelations

| Lag | Correlation | -1 9 8 7 6 5 4 3 2 1 0 1 2 3 4 5 6 7 8 9 1 |
|---|---|---|
| 1 | 0.18377 | . \|**** |
| 2 | -0.06337 | . *\| . |
| 3 | 0.00689 | . \| . |
| 4 | -0.14706 | ***\| . |
| 5 | 0.05599 | . \|* . |
| 6 | 0.07694 | . \|**. |
| 7 | -0.00961 | . \| . |
| 8 | 0.08102 | . \|**. |
| 9 | 0.07084 | . \|* . |
| 10 | 0.00110 | . \| . |
| 11 | -0.07361 | . *\| . |
| 12 | -0.25948 | *****\| . |
| 13 | 0.01555 | . \| . |
| 14 | 0.00615 | . \| . |
| 15 | -0.03042 | . *\| . |
| 16 | 0.09184 | . \|**. |
| 17 | -0.01900 | . \| . |
| 18 | -0.04354 | . *\| . |
| 19 | -0.08056 | .**\| . |
| 20 | 0.03107 | . \|* . |
| 21 | 0.03687 | . \|* . |
| 22 | -0.06723 | . *\| . |
| 23 | 0.03476 | . \|* . |
| 24 | -0.18999 | ****\| . |

(b) The SPAC

Figure 11.28 presents the SAS output of estimation, diagnostic checking, and forecasting that is obtained when the model

$$z_t = a_t - \theta_1 a_{t-1} - \theta_{1,12} a_{t-12} + \theta_1 \theta_{1,12} a_{t-13}$$

where

$$z_t = y_t - y_{t-1} - y_{t-12} + y_{t-13}$$

is used to analyze the trade values in Table 11.4. **Exercises 11.6 through 11.9 are based on this output.**

**11.6** Identify the least squares point estimates of $\theta_1$ and $\theta_{1,12}$.

**11.7** Use the appropriate $t$-statistics to determine whether $\theta_1$ and $\theta_{1,12}$ should be retained in the model.

**11.8** Use the $p$-values associated with $Q^*$ to determine whether the model is adequate.

**11.9** Identify a point forecast of and a 95% prediction interval for $y_{179}$. Calculate a 99% prediction interval for $y_{179}$.

**FIGURE 11.28 (for Exercises 11.6–11.9)** SAS output of estimation, diagnostic checking, and forecasting for the model $z_t = a_t - \theta_1 a_{t-1} - \theta_{1,12} a_{t-12} + \theta_1 \theta_{1,12} a_{t-13}$ where $z_t = y_t - y_{t-1} - y_{t-12} + y_{t-13}$

Conditional Least Squares Estimation

| Parameter | Estimate | Standard Error | t Value | Approx Pr > \|t\| | Lag |
|---|---|---|---|---|---|
| MA1,1 | -0.18157 | 0.07727 | -2.35 | 0.0200 | 1 |
| MA2,1 | 0.38802 | 0.07342 | 5.29 | <.0001 | 12 |

| | |
|---|---|
| Variance Estimate | 1.824741 |
| Std Error Estimate | 1.35083 |
| AIC | 569.4748 |
| SBC | 575.6867 |
| Number of Residuals | 165 |

* AIC and SBC do not include log determinant.

Correlations of Parameter Estimates

| Parameter | MA1,1 | MA2,1 |
|---|---|---|
| MA1,1 | 1.000 | -0.076 |
| MA2,1 | -0.076 | 1.000 |

(a) Estimation

Autocorrelation Check of Residuals

| To Lag | Chi-Square | DF | Pr > ChiSq | Autocorrelations | | | | | |
|---|---|---|---|---|---|---|---|---|---|
| 6 | 4.27 | 4 | 0.3707 | -0.005 | -0.016 | 0.049 | -0.094 | 0.006 | 0.115 |
| 12 | 7.53 | 10 | 0.6749 | -0.049 | 0.033 | 0.108 | -0.018 | 0.019 | 0.050 |
| 18 | 12.12 | 16 | 0.7358 | -0.082 | 0.063 | -0.032 | 0.094 | 0.041 | -0.053 |
| 24 | 19.52 | 22 | 0.6133 | -0.131 | -0.040 | 0.034 | -0.023 | 0.110 | -0.077 |
| 30 | 23.50 | 28 | 0.7077 | -0.078 | 0.064 | -0.058 | -0.037 | 0.068 | -0.023 |

(b) The RSAC

**FIGURE 11.28** (Continued)

```
                          Autocorrelation Plot of Residuals

Lag    Covariance    Correlation    -1 9 8 7 6 5 4 3 2 1 0 1 2 3 4 5 6 7 8 9 1    Std Error

 0     1.824741       1.00000         |                  |********************|             0
 1    -0.0093048      -.00510         |                 .|.                   |       0.077850
 2    -0.029424       -.01613         |                 .|.                   |       0.077852
 3     0.089537       0.04907         |                 .|*.                  |       0.077872
 4    -0.171457       -.09396         |                .**|.                  |       0.078059
 5     0.011258       0.00617         |                 .|.                   |       0.078742
 6     0.209974       0.11507         |                 .|**.                 |       0.078745
 7    -0.089625       -.04912         |                 .*|.                  |       0.079757
 8     0.060443       0.03312         |                 .|*.                  |       0.079940
 9     0.197827       0.10841         |                 .|**.                 |       0.080024
10    -0.032320       -.01771         |                 .|.                   |       0.080909
11     0.034833       0.01909         |                 .|.                   |       0.080932
12     0.090915       0.04982         |                 .|*.                  |       0.080960
13    -0.150083       -.08225         |                .**|.                  |       0.081145
14     0.114404       0.06270         |                 .|*.                  |       0.081649
15    -0.057584       -.03156         |                 .*|.                  |       0.081940
16     0.170816       0.09361         |                 .|**.                 |       0.082014
17     0.075254       0.04124         |                 .|*.                  |       0.082659
18    -0.096724       -.05301         |                 .*|.                  |       0.082783
19    -0.239914       -.13148         |                ***|.                  |       0.082989
20    -0.072242       -.03959         |                 .*|.                  |       0.084242
21     0.062872       0.03446         |                 .|*.                  |       0.084355
22    -0.042878       -.02350         |                 .|.                   |       0.084440
23     0.201000       0.11015         |                 .|**.                 |       0.084479
24    -0.139882       -.07666         |                .**|.                  |       0.085345
```

(b) The RSAC (Continued)

```
                    Partial Autocorrelations

Lag    Correlation    -1 9 8 7 6 5 4 3 2 1 0 1 2 3 4 5 6 7 8 9 1

 1     -0.00510        |                .|.                   |
 2     -0.01615        |                .|.                   |
 3      0.04892        |                .|*.                  |
 4     -0.09401        |               .**|.                  |
 5      0.00743        |                .|.                   |
 6      0.11081        |                .|**.                 |
 7     -0.04078        |                .*|.                  |
 8      0.02736        |                .|*.                  |
 9      0.10097        |                .|**.                 |
10      0.00683        |                .|.                   |
11      0.00902        |                .|.                   |
12      0.03713        |                .|*.                  |
13     -0.05577        |                .*|.                  |
14      0.05326        |                .|*.                  |
15     -0.05570        |                .*|.                  |
16      0.12113        |                .|**.                 |
17      0.01247        |                .|.                   |
18     -0.05856        |                .*|.                  |
19     -0.13448        |               ***|.                  |
20     -0.04708        |                .*|.                  |
21      0.05099        |                .|*.                  |
22     -0.04347        |                .*|.                  |
23      0.09343        |                .|**.                 |
24     -0.07774        |               .**|.                  |
```

(c) The RSPAC

**FIGURE 11.28** (Continued)

Forecasts for variable y

| Obs | Forecast | Std Error | 95% Confidence Limits | |
|-----|----------|-----------|------|------|
| 179 | 404.1921 | 1.3508 | 401.5445 | 406.8397 |
| 180 | 408.7049 | 2.0910 | 404.6066 | 412.8032 |
| 181 | 386.6225 | 2.6306 | 381.4667 | 391.7783 |
| 182 | 382.4893 | 3.0769 | 376.4587 | 388.5200 |
| 183 | 385.4055 | 3.4662 | 378.6118 | 392.1992 |
| 184 | 393.5371 | 3.8161 | 386.0577 | 401.0164 |
| 185 | 402.0405 | 4.1364 | 393.9332 | 410.1477 |
| 186 | 406.7711 | 4.4337 | 398.0812 | 415.4609 |
| 187 | 406.4346 | 4.7122 | 397.1988 | 415.6703 |
| 188 | 409.2050 | 4.9752 | 399.4538 | 418.9562 |
| 189 | 409.7485 | 5.2249 | 399.5078 | 419.9892 |
| 190 | 412.2454 | 5.4633 | 401.5375 | 422.9532 |

(d) Forecasts for $y_{179}$ through $y_{190}$

**11.10** The monthly retail sales values $y_1, y_2, \ldots, y_{144}$ in U.S. sporting goods and bicycle shops from January 1987 to December 1998 are presented in Table 11.5 (page 526) and plotted in Figure 11.29(a) (page 526). Each of the 144 observations is given in millions of dollars. Figure 11.29(b) (page 526) displays the plot of the values transformed by the natural logarithm $\ln y_1$, $\ln y_2, \ldots, \ln y_{144}$. Figure 11.30 (page 527) gives the SAS output of the SAC and SPAC for the time series values produced by using the transformation $z_t = y_t^* - y_{t-12}^*$ where $y_t^* = \ln y_t$.

a. Do the values produced by the predifferencing transformation $y_t^* = \ln y_t$ appear to have a constant variance? Explain your answer.

b. Should the values produced by the transformation $z_t = y_t^* - y_{t-12}^*$ with $y_t^* = \ln y_t$ be considered stationary? Explain your answer.

c. Discuss why the models

$z_t = \delta + \phi_1 z_{t-1} + \phi_3 z_{t-3} + a_t$    at the nonseasonal level

$z_t = \delta + \phi_{1,12} z_{t-12} + a_t$    at the seasonal level

and hence,

$$z_t = \delta + \phi_1 z_{t-1} + \phi_3 z_{t-3} + \phi_{1,12} z_{t-12} - \phi_1 \phi_{1,12} z_{t-13}$$
$$- \phi_3 \phi_{1,12} z_{t-15} + a_t$$

are reasonable choices for finding the overall tentative model for the data in Table 11.5.

**11.11** Figure 11.31 (page 528) presents the SAS output of estimation, diagnostic checking, and forecasting that is obtained when the model

$$z_t = \delta + \phi_1 z_{t-1} + \phi_3 z_{t-3} + \phi_{1,12} z_{t-12}$$
$$- \phi_1 \phi_{1,12} z_{t-13} - \phi_3 \phi_{1,12} z_{t-15} + a_t$$

where

$$z_t = y_t^* - y_{t-12}^* \quad \text{and} \quad y_t^* = \ln y_t$$

is used to analyze the data in Table 11.5.

a. Identify the least squares point estimates of the parameters $\delta$, $\phi_1$, $\phi_3$, and $\phi_{1,12}$.

b. Use the appropriate $t$-statistics to determine which parameters should remain in the model.

c. Use the $p$-values associated with $Q^*$ to determine whether the model is adequate.

d. Identify a point forecast of and a 95% prediction interval for $y_{145}$.

**TABLE 11.5 (for Exercises 11.10–11.11)** Retail Sales in U.S. Sporting Goods and Bicycle Shops (× $1 million)

| Year | Jan. | Feb. | Mar. | Apr. | May | June | July | Aug. | Sept. | Oct. | Nov. | Dec. |
|------|------|------|------|------|------|------|------|------|-------|------|------|------|
| 1987 | 730 | 717 | 769 | 858 | 921 | 1018 | 980 | 1027 | 906 | 847 | 981 | 1502 |
| 1988 | 821 | 871 | 938 | 1044 | 1097 | 1155 | 1069 | 1150 | 981 | 915 | 1087 | 1698 |
| 1989 | 892 | 942 | 1095 | 1099 | 1186 | 1215 | 1125 | 1283 | 1143 | 1030 | 1233 | 1934 |
| 1990 | 1000 | 1052 | 1240 | 1182 | 1298 | 1321 | 1210 | 1340 | 1178 | 1117 | 1192 | 1857 |
| 1991 | 945 | 991 | 1151 | 1190 | 1287 | 1332 | 1299 | 1430 | 1236 | 1091 | 1205 | 1908 |
| 1992 | 998 | 1122 | 1234 | 1278 | 1300 | 1335 | 1336 | 1370 | 1198 | 1112 | 1197 | 2137 |
| 1993 | 1033 | 984 | 1217 | 1372 | 1395 | 1465 | 1467 | 1543 | 1325 | 1210 | 1390 | 2499 |
| 1994 | 1178 | 1205 | 1502 | 1566 | 1566 | 1694 | 1600 | 1755 | 1485 | 1339 | 1488 | 2640 |
| 1995 | 1239 | 1265 | 1621 | 1629 | 1668 | 1774 | 1730 | 1873 | 1593 | 1419 | 1571 | 2771 |
| 1996 | 1346 | 1327 | 1672 | 1727 | 1801 | 1925 | 1865 | 2029 | 1629 | 1488 | 1651 | 2749 |
| 1997 | 1392 | 1388 | 1683 | 1793 | 1860 | 2052 | 1924 | 2048 | 1671 | 1596 | 1738 | 2990 |
| 1998 | 1458 | 1485 | 1848 | 1919 | 2043 | 2231 | 2081 | 2143 | 1779 | 1678 | 1764 | 2979 |

*Source:* U.S. Census Bureau, Monthly Retail Trade

**FIGURE 11.29  (for Exercise 11.10)** JMP IN plot of U.S. retail sales in sporting goods and bicycle shops

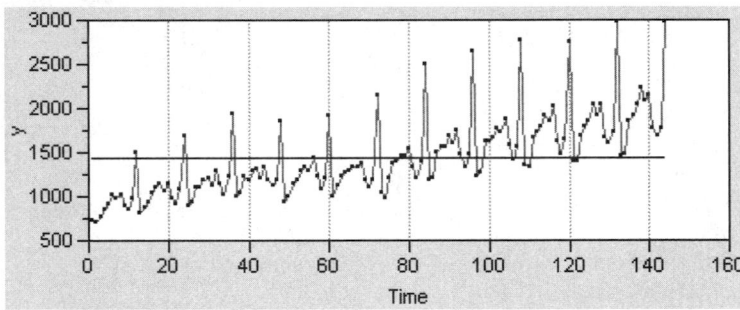

(a) Original values $y_t$

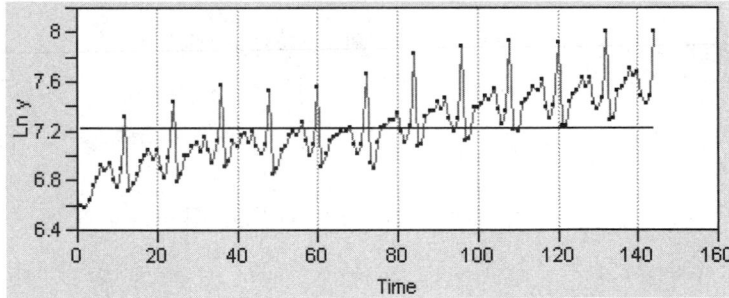

(b) Transformed values $y_t^\star = \ln y_t$

**FIGURE 11.30 (for Exercise 11.10)** SAS output of the SAC and SPAC of the values given by the transformation $z_t = y_t^* - y_{t-12}^*$ where $y_t^* = \ln y_t$ for retail sales in U.S. sporting goods and bicycle shops

```
                    Name of Variable = Lny

           Period(s) of Differencing                    12
           Mean of Working Series               0.066678
           Standard Deviation                   0.056826
           Number of Observations                    132
           Observation(s) eliminated by differencing  12
                        Autocorrelations
```

| Lag | Covariance | Correlation | -1 9 8 7 6 5 4 3 2 1 0 1 2 3 4 5 6 7 8 9 1 | Std Error |
|-----|-----------|-------------|----------------------------------------------|-----------|
| 0 | 0.0032292 | 1.00000 | \|********************\| | 0 |
| 1 | 0.0023377 | 0.72393 | \|*************\| | 0.087039 |
| 2 | 0.0018195 | 0.56345 | \|***********\| | 0.124564 |
| 3 | 0.0016512 | 0.51133 | \|**********\| | 0.142571 |
| 4 | 0.0012329 | 0.38179 | \|********\| | 0.155846 |
| 5 | 0.0010501 | 0.32519 | \|*******\| | 0.162778 |
| 6 | 0.00098565 | 0.30523 | \|******.\| | 0.167627 |
| 7 | 0.00079203 | 0.24527 | \|*****.\| | 0.171786 |
| 8 | 0.00062716 | 0.19422 | \|****.\| | 0.174419 |
| 9 | 0.00046402 | 0.14369 | \|***.\| | 0.176049 |
| 10 | 0.00026952 | 0.08346 | \|**.\| | 0.176936 |
| 11 | -7.1013E-6 | -.00220 | \|.\| | 0.177234 |
| 12 | -0.0004188 | -.12968 | ***\|.\| | 0.177234 |
| 13 | -0.0004086 | -.12654 | ***\|.\| | 0.177951 |
| 14 | -0.0003326 | -.10299 | **\|.\| | 0.178632 |
| 15 | -0.0002409 | -.07459 | *\|.\| | 0.179081 |
| 16 | -0.0000591 | -.01831 | \|.\| | 0.179316 |
| 17 | 9.87659E-7 | 0.00031 | \|.\| | 0.179330 |
| 18 | -0.0000729 | -.02259 | \|.\| | 0.179330 |
| 19 | 0.00005312 | 0.01645 | \|.\| | 0.179352 |
| 20 | 0.00018840 | 0.05834 | \|*.\| | 0.179363 |
| 21 | 0.00020766 | 0.06431 | \|*.\| | 0.179507 |
| 22 | 0.00016471 | 0.05101 | \|*.\| | 0.179681 |
| 23 | 0.00023089 | 0.07150 | \|*.\| | 0.179791 |
| 24 | 0.00002008 | 0.00622 | \|.\| | 0.180006 |

(a) The SAC

```
                Partial Autocorrelations
```

| Lag | Correlation | -1 9 8 7 6 5 4 3 2 1 0 1 2 3 4 5 6 7 8 9 1 |
|-----|-------------|----------------------------------------------|
| 1 | 0.72393 | \|**************\| |
| 2 | 0.08274 | \|**.\| |
| 3 | 0.16350 | \|***\| |
| 4 | -0.11876 | .**\|.\| |
| 5 | 0.07609 | \|**.\| |
| 6 | 0.04168 | \|*.\| |
| 7 | -0.01811 | \|.\| |
| 8 | -0.02966 | .*\|.\| |
| 9 | -0.04745 | .*\|.\| |
| 10 | -0.04284 | .*\|.\| |
| 11 | -0.12100 | .**\|.\| |
| 12 | -0.20361 | ****\|.\| |
| 13 | 0.10930 | \|**.\| |
| 14 | 0.05536 | \|*.\| |
| 15 | 0.11708 | \|**.\| |
| 16 | 0.05410 | \|*.\| |
| 17 | 0.02277 | \|.\| |
| 18 | -0.03757 | .*\|.\| |
| 19 | 0.09083 | \|**.\| |
| 20 | 0.06680 | \|*.\| |
| 21 | 0.00886 | \|.\| |
| 22 | -0.09431 | .**\|.\| |
| 23 | 0.00393 | \|.\| |
| 24 | -0.25336 | *****\|.\| |

(b) The SPAC

**FIGURE 11.31 (for Exercise 11.11)** SAS output of estimation, diagnostic checking, and forecasting for the model $z_t = \delta + \phi_1 z_{t-1} + \phi_3 z_{t-3} + \phi_{1,12} z_{t-12} - \phi_1 \phi_{1,12} z_{t-13} - \phi_3 \phi_{1,12} z_{t-15} + a_t$ where $z_t = y_t^* - y_{t-12}^*$ and $y_t^* = \ln y_t$

### Conditional Least Squares Estimation

| Parameter | Estimate | Standard Error | t Value | Approx Pr > \|t\| | Lag |
|-----------|----------|----------------|---------|-------------------|-----|
| MU    | 0.07487  | 0.01458 | 5.14  | <.0001 | 0  |
| AR1,1 | 0.62993  | 0.07249 | 8.69  | <.0001 | 1  |
| AR1,2 | 0.20816  | 0.07344 | 2.83  | 0.0053 | 3  |
| AR2,1 | -0.27124 | 0.08826 | -3.07 | 0.0026 | 12 |

| | |
|---|---|
| Constant Estimate | 0.01541 |
| Variance Estimate | 0.001409 |
| Std Error Estimate | 0.037531 |
| AIC | -488.066 |
| SBC | -476.535 |
| Number of Residuals | 132 |

\* AIC and SBC do not include log determinant.

### Correlations of Parameter Estimates

| Parameter | MU | AR1,1 | AR1,2 | AR2,1 |
|-----------|-------|--------|--------|--------|
| MU    | 1.000  | 0.057  | 0.086  | -0.019 |
| AR1,1 | 0.057  | 1.000  | -0.603 | -0.046 |
| AR1,2 | 0.086  | -0.603 | 1.000  | -0.111 |
| AR2,1 | -0.019 | -0.046 | -0.111 | 1.000  |

(a) Estimation

### Autocorrelation Check of Residuals

| To Lag | Chi-Square | DF | Pr > ChiSq | | | Autocorrelations | | | |
|--------|------------|----|-----------|--------|--------|--------|--------|--------|--------|
| 6  | 3.04  | 3  | 0.3859 | 0.025  | -0.020 | 0.038  | -0.128 | -0.019 | 0.052  |
| 12 | 5.76  | 9  | 0.7635 | 0.007  | 0.018  | 0.104  | 0.034  | 0.078  | -0.019 |
| 18 | 11.68 | 15 | 0.7029 | -0.147 | -0.078 | -0.041 | 0.024  | 0.077  | -0.058 |
| 24 | 18.75 | 21 | 0.6014 | 0.002  | 0.068  | 0.074  | -0.018 | 0.138  | -0.119 |

### Autocorrelation Plot of Residuals

| Lag | Covariance | Correlation | -1 9 8 7 6 5 4 3 2 1 0 1 2 3 4 5 6 7 8 9 1 | Std Error |
|-----|------------|-------------|---------------------------------------------|-----------|
| 0  | 0.0014086  | 1.00000  | \|********************\|  | 0        |
| 1  | 0.00003507 | 0.02490  | \|                       \|  | 0.087039 |
| 2  | -0.0000281 | -.01994  | .   \|                   \|  | 0.087093 |
| 3  | 0.00005345 | 0.03795  | .  \|*                    \|  | 0.087127 |
| 4  | -0.0001805 | -.12817  | ***\|                    \|  | 0.087252 |
| 5  | -0.0000273 | -.01938  | .   \|                   \|  | 0.088667 |
| 6  | 0.00007324 | 0.05200  | .  \|*                    \|  | 0.088700 |
| 7  | 9.68178E-6 | 0.00687  | .   \|                   \|  | 0.088930 |
| 8  | 0.00002524 | 0.01792  | .   \|                   \|  | 0.088934 |
| 9  | 0.00014693 | 0.10431  | .  \|**                   \|  | 0.088962 |
| 10 | 0.00004805 | 0.03412  | .  \|*                    \|  | 0.089883 |
| 11 | 0.00010960 | 0.07781  | .  \|**                   \|  | 0.089981 |
| 12 | -0.0000268 | -.01904  | .   \|                   \|  | 0.090490 |
| 13 | -0.0002075 | -.14730  | .***\|                   \|  | 0.090520 |
| 14 | -0.0001102 | -.07823  | . **\|                   \|  | 0.092318 |
| 15 | -0.0000577 | -.04097  | .  *\|                   \|  | 0.092819 |
| 16 | 0.00003310 | 0.02350  | .   \|                   \|  | 0.092956 |
| 17 | 0.00010871 | 0.07718  | .  \|**                   \|  | 0.093001 |
| 18 | -0.0000818 | -.05811  | .  *\|                   \|  | 0.093485 |
| 19 | 2.64752E-6 | 0.00188  | .   \|                   \|  | 0.093758 |
| 20 | 0.00009619 | 0.06829  | .  \|*                    \|  | 0.093758 |
| 21 | 0.00010385 | 0.07373  | .  \|*                    \|  | 0.094134 |
| 22 | -0.0000251 | -.01781  | .   \|                   \|  | 0.094571 |
| 23 | 0.00019460 | 0.13816  | .  \|***                  \|  | 0.094596 |
| 24 | -0.0001674 | -.11882  | . **\|                   \|  | 0.096113 |

(b) The RSAC

**FIGURE 11.31** (Continued)

Partial Autocorrelations

```
Lag    Correlation    -1 9 8 7 6 5 4 3 2 1 0 1 2 3 4 5 6 7 8 9 1
 1       0.02490      !                    .    !  .              !
 2      -0.02057      !                    .    !  .              !
 3       0.03901      !                    .   !*  .              !
 4      -0.13091      !                  ***!   .                 !
 5      -0.01054      !                    .   !  .               !
 6       0.04649      !                    .   !* .               !
 7       0.01392      !                    .   !  .               !
 8       0.00389      !                    .   !  .               !
 9       0.09829      !                    .   !**.               !
10       0.04151      !                    .   !* .               !
11       0.08554      !                    .   !**.               !
12      -0.02968      !                    . *!  .                !
13      -0.12551      !                  ***!   .                 !
14      -0.07290      !                    . *!  .                !
15      -0.03298      !                    . *!  .                !
16       0.02310      !                    .   !  .               !
17       0.04004      !                    .   !* .               !
18      -0.09093      !                    .**!  .                !
19       0.00090      !                    .   !  .               !
20       0.06712      !                    .   !* .               !
21       0.10884      !                    .   !**.               !
22      -0.01384      !                    .   !  .               !
23       0.16752      !                    .   !***               !
24      -0.08886      !                    .**!  .                !
```

(c) The RSPAC

```
Obs    Forecasty    L95CI      U95CI
145    1501.30      1394.83    1615.90
146    1529.35      1402.01    1668.26
147    1893.08      1727.19    2074.90
148    1991.05      1805.72    2195.40
149    2115.18      1909.18    2343.40
150    2324.20      2091.29    2583.06
151    2178.33      1955.15    2426.99
152    2270.59      2033.85    2534.89
153    1881.17      1682.43    2103.39
154    1784.69      1594.21    1997.93
155    1090.30      1694.07    2127.15
156    3228.17      2878.68    3620.08
```

(d) Forecasts of $y_{145}$ through $y_{156}$

**11.12** The 232 monthly values for midwestern housing starts $y_1, y_2, \ldots, y_{232}$ from January 1980 to April 1999 are plotted in Figure 11.32 (page 530). The observations are given in thousands of housing units. Figure 11.33 (page 530) is a MINITAB output of the SAC and SPAC for the time series produced by using the transformation $z_t = y_t - y_{t-12}$.

a. Should the values in Figure 11.32 be considered to have constant variance? Explain your answer.

b. Should the values produced by the transformation $z_t = y_t - y_{t-12}$ be considered stationary? Explain your answer.

c. Discuss why the model

$$z_t = \delta + \phi_1 z_{t-1} + \phi_2 z_{t-2} + \phi_3 z_{t-3} - \theta_{1,12} a_{t-12} + a_t$$

where

$$z_t = y_t - y_{t-12}$$

is a reasonable tentative model for describing the data in Figure 11.32.

**FIGURE 11.32 (for Exercise 11.12)** JMP IN plot of midwestern housing starts from January 1980 to April 1999 (1000s of housing units) *Source:* U.S. Census Bureau, Housing Starts (C-20)

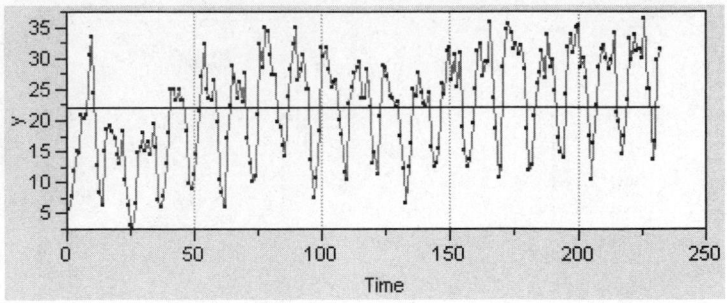

**FIGURE 11.33 (for Exercise 11.12)** MINITAB output of the SAC and SPAC of values given by the transformation $z_t = y_t - y_{t-12}$ for the midwestern housing start data

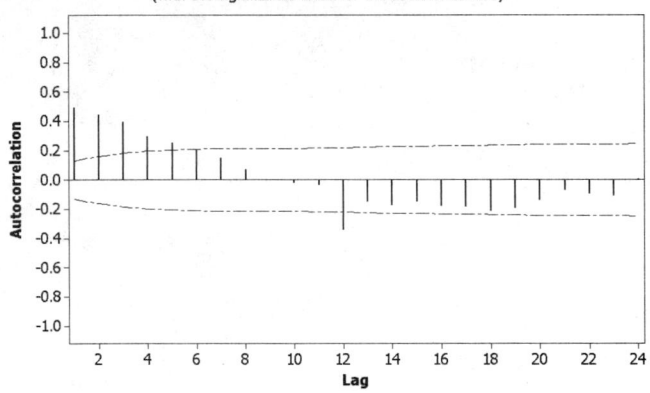

(a) The SAC

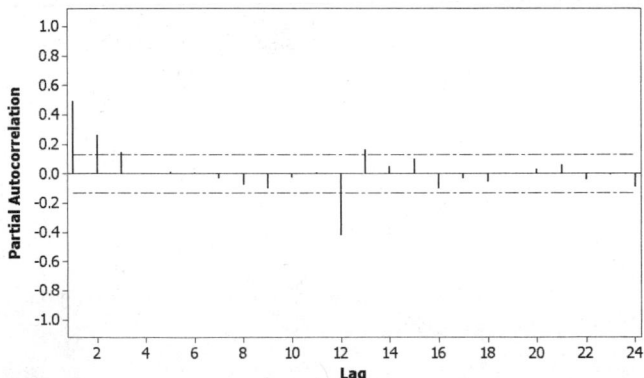

(b) The SPAC

**11.13** Figure 11.34 presents the MINITAB output of estimation, diagnostic checking, and forecasting that is obtained when the model

$$z_t = \delta + \phi_1 z_{t-1} + \phi_2 z_{t-2} + \phi_3 z_{t-3} - \theta_{1,12} a_{t-12} + a_t$$

where

$$z_t = y_t - y_{t-12}$$

is used to analyze the data in Figure 11.32.

a. Identify the least squares point estimates of the parameters $\delta$, $\phi_1$, $\phi_2$, $\phi_3$, and $\theta_{1,12}$.
b. Use the appropriate $t$-statistics to determine which parameters should remain in the model.
c. Use the $p$-values associated with the $Q^*$-statistic to determine whether the model is adequate.
d. Identify a point forecast of and a 95% prediction interval for $y_{233}$.

**FIGURE 11.34  (for Exercise 11.13)** MINITAB output of estimation, diagnostic checking, and forecasting for the model $z_t = \delta + \phi_1 z_{t-1} + \phi_2 z_{t-2} + \phi_3 z_{t-3} - \theta_{1,12} a_{t-12} + a_t$ where $z_t = y_t - y_{t-12}$

```
Final Estimates of Parameters
Type          Coef      SE Coef        T        P
AR   1      0.4214      0.0673       6.26    0.000
AR   2      0.2118      0.0698       3.03    0.003
AR   3      0.1053      0.0662       1.59    0.113
SMA 12      0.9230      0.0387      23.87    0.000
Constant   0.16171     0.02152       7.51    0.000


Differencing: 0 regular, 1 seasonal of order 12
Number of observations:  Original series 232, after differencing 220
Residuals:     SS =   1556.08   (backforecasts excluded)
               MS =      7.24  DF = 215
```

(a) Estimation

```
Modified Box-Pierce (Ljung-Box) Chi-Square statistic
Lag                  12        24        36        48
Chi-Square          8.6      15.4      28.0      38.7
DF                    7        19        31        43
P-Value           0.285     0.694     0.620     0.658
```

(b) Diagnostic checking

**FIGURE 11.34** (Continued)

```
Forecasts from period 232
                              95 Percent Limits
Period      Forecast      Lower         Upper
 233        34.1304       28.8564       39.4044
 234        35.5028       29.7796       41.2261
 235        32.6199       26.5394       38.7005
 236        32.8004       26.4324       39.1685
 237        31.5949       25.0602       38.1296
 238        34.4253       27.7749       41.0757
 239        26.6619       19.9322       33.3916
 240        21.1045       14.3213       27.8877
 241        16.5758        9.7559       23.3957
 242        17.9948       11.1497       24.8399
 243        26.4059       19.5435       33.2682
 244        32.5904       25.7162       39.4646
```

(c) Forecasting

**11.14** Consider the monthly passenger total values produced by using the transformation

$$z_t = y_t^* - y_{t-1}^* - y_{t-12}^* + y_{t-13}^*$$

where

$$y_t^* = \ln y_t$$

At the nonseasonal level the SAC of these values has spikes at lags 1 and 3 and cuts off after lag 3 and the SPAC dies down (see Figure 11.16 on page 508). This might cause us to tentatively identify the nonseasonal moving average model of order 3

$$z_t = a_t - \theta_1 a_{t-1} - \theta_2 a_{t-2} - \theta_3 a_{t-3}$$

or (since there is no spike at lag 2 in the SAC) the model

$$z_t = a_t - \theta_1 a_{t-1} - \theta_3 a_{t-3}$$

Since we use MINITAB in this example, and since MINITAB does not allow us to fit the second of these models, we will combine the first model with the

seasonal moving average model of order 1

$$z_t = a_t - \theta_{1,12} a_{t-12}$$

which was tentatively identified in Example 11.4. This gives the overall tentatively identified model

$$z_t = a_t - \theta_1 a_{t-1} - \theta_2 a_{t-2} - \theta_3 a_{t-3} - \theta_{1,12} a_{t-12}$$
$$+ \theta_1 \theta_{1,12} a_{t-13} + \theta_2 \theta_{1,12} a_{t-14} + \theta_3 \theta_{1,12} a_{t-15}$$

The MINITAB output of estimation, diagnostic checking, and forecasting for this model is given in Figure 11.35 (page 533).

a. By comparing Figure 11.35 with Figure 11.17, which is the MINITAB output of estimation, diagnostic checking, and forecasting for the model

$$z_t = a_t - \theta_1 a_{t-1} - \theta_{1,12} a_{t-12} + \theta_1 \theta_{1,12} a_{t-13}$$

discuss which of the models seems best.

b. Use SAS to analyze the monthly passenger total values by using the model

$$z_t = a_t - \theta_1 a_{t-1} - \theta_3 a_{t-3} - \theta_{1,12} a_{t-12}$$
$$+ \theta_1 \theta_{1,12} a_{t-13} + \theta_3 \theta_{1,12} a_{t-15}$$

**FIGURE 11.35 (for Exercise 11.14)** MINITAB output of estimation, diagnostic checking, and forecasting for the model $z_t = a_t - \theta_1 a_{t-1} - \theta_2 a_{t-2} - \theta_3 a_{t-3} - \theta_{1,12} a_{t-12} + \theta_1 \theta_{1,12} a_{t-13} + \theta_2 \theta_{1,12} a_{t-14} + \theta_3 \theta_{1,12} a_{t-15}$ where $z_t = y_t^* - y_{t-1}^* - y_{t-12}^* + y_{t-13}^*$ and $y_t^* = \ln y_t$

```
Final Estimates of Parameters
Type          Coef      SE Coef        T         P
MA    1      0.3596     0.0905       3.97      0.000
MA    2     -0.0894     0.0963      -0.93      0.355
MA    3      0.2185     0.0908       2.41      0.018
SMA  12      0.6600     0.0764       8.64      0.000


Differencing: 1 regular, 1 seasonal of order 12
Number of observations:  Original series 132, after differencing 119
Residuals:    SS =  0.144662  (backforecasts excluded)
              MS = 0.001258  DF = 115
```

(a) Estimation

```
Modified Box-Pierce (Ljung-Box) Chi-Square statistic
Lag                  12          24          36          48
Chi-Square          4.7        18.0        30.7        37.5
DF                    8          20          32          44
P-Value           0.791       0.585       0.530       0.744
```

(b) Diagnostic checking

| Period | Forecast | Lower95 | Upper95 |
|---|---|---|---|
| 133 | 420.018 | 391.806 | 450.261 |
| 134 | 399.576 | 367.911 | 433.967 |
| 135 | 465.670 | 422.660 | 513.057 |
| 136 | 453.626 | 409.137 | 502.953 |
| 137 | 469.492 | 420.935 | 523.650 |
| 138 | 542.982 | 484.086 | 609.044 |
| 139 | 614.892 | 545.257 | 693.421 |
| 140 | 620.603 | 547.496 | 703.472 |
| 131 | 523.481 | 459.538 | 596.322 |
| 142 | 459.205 | 401.197 | 525.599 |
| 143 | 403.530 | 350.938 | 464.005 |
| 144 | 450.137 | 389.731 | 519.905 |

(c) Forecasts for $y_{133}$ through $y_{144}$

**11.15** Consider the monthly retail sales in U.S. sporting goods and bicycle shops in Table 11.5 (page 526) that were analyzed in Exercises 11.10 and 11.11. Since a plot of these data in Figure 11.29(a) indicates a linear trend and a deterministic seasonal variation, we might consider the regression model

$$y_t^* = TR_t + SN_t + \varepsilon_t$$
$$= \beta_0 + \beta_1 t + \beta_2 M_1 + \beta_3 M_2 + \cdots + \beta_{12} M_{11} + \varepsilon_t$$

where $y_t^* = y_t^{.25}$ and $M_1, M_2, \ldots, M_{11}$ are dummy variables. For example:

$$M_1 = \begin{cases} 1 & \text{if period } t \text{ is January} \\ 0 & \text{otherwise} \end{cases}$$

Assuming independent error terms $\varepsilon_1, \varepsilon_2, \ldots$, the SAS output of estimation and diagnostic checking for the model is as given in Figure 11.36 (page 535). Since the $p$-values associated with the values of $Q^*$ are extremely small, we reject the adequacy of the model.

a.  Using Figure 11.36(b) and (c), discuss why the models

$$\varepsilon_t = \phi_1 \varepsilon_{t-1} + \phi_3 \varepsilon_{t-3} + a_t \quad \text{at the nonseasonal level}$$

$$\varepsilon_t = \phi_{1,12} \varepsilon_{t-12} + a_t \quad \text{at the seasonal level}$$

and hence,

$$\varepsilon_t = \phi_1 \varepsilon_{t-1} + \phi_3 \varepsilon_{t-3} + \phi_{1,12} \varepsilon_{t-12} - \phi_1 \phi_{1,12} \varepsilon_{t-13}$$
$$- \phi_3 \phi_{1,12} \varepsilon_{t-15} + a_t$$

for the combined model are reasonable choices for finding a tentative model for the error terms in this regression model.

b.  Figure 11.37 (page 537) presents the SAS output of estimation, diagnostic checking, and forecasting for the time series regression model which assumes that

$$\varepsilon_t = \phi_1 \varepsilon_{t-1} + \phi_3 \varepsilon_{t-3} + \phi_{1,12} \varepsilon_{t-12} - \phi_1 \phi_{1,12} \varepsilon_{t-13}$$
$$- \phi_3 \phi_{1,12} \varepsilon_{t-15} + a_t$$

Using Figure 11.37(a), (b), and (c), determine if this regression model is a reasonable model for forecasting retail sales.

c.  Compare the model of part (b) in this exercise and the model in Exercise 11.11. Which model has the smaller standard error for estimating $y_t^*$ and yields shorter prediction intervals for forecasting the retail sales $y_t$?

**11.16** Use SAS to find a time series regression model for the monthly passenger total values in Table 11.3 (page 505).

**FIGURE 11.36 (for Exercise 11.15)** SAS output of estimation and diagnostic checking for the dummy variable regression model for sporting good sales, assuming independent error terms $\varepsilon_1$, $\varepsilon_2$, ...

Conditional Least Squares Estimation

| Parameter | Estimate | Standard Error | t Value | Approx Pr > \|t\| | Lag | Variable | Shift |
|---|---|---|---|---|---|---|---|
| MU | 7.30995 | 0.01655 | 441.76 | <.0001 | 0 | Lny | 0 |
| NUM1 | 0.0052328 | 0.0001013 | 51.65 | <.0001 | 0 | Time | 0 |
| NUM2 | -0.69190 | 0.02059 | -33.60 | <.0001 | 0 | M1 | 0 |
| NUM3 | -0.67154 | 0.02059 | -32.62 | <.0001 | 0 | M2 | 0 |
| NUM4 | -0.50784 | 0.02058 | -24.68 | <.0001 | 0 | M3 | 0 |
| NUM5 | -0.46802 | 0.02058 | -22.75 | <.0001 | 0 | M4 | 0 |
| NUM6 | -0.42599 | 0.02057 | -20.71 | <.0001 | 0 | M5 | 0 |
| NUM7 | -0.37320 | 0.02057 | -18.14 | <.0001 | 0 | M6 | 0 |
| NUM8 | -0.42435 | 0.02057 | -20.63 | <.0001 | 0 | M7 | 0 |
| NUM9 | -0.35683 | 0.02056 | -17.35 | <.0001 | 0 | M8 | 0 |
| NUM10 | -0.52032 | 0.02056 | -25.30 | <.0001 | 0 | M9 | 0 |
| NUM11 | -0.60875 | 0.02056 | -29.61 | <.0001 | 0 | M10 | 0 |
| NUM12 | -0.50381 | 0.02056 | -24.50 | <.0001 | 0 | M11 | 0 |

|   |   |
|---|---|
| Constant Estimate | 7.309952 |
| Variance Estimate | 0.002536 |
| Std Error Estimate | 0.050363 |
| AIC | -439.659 |
| SBC | -401.051 |
| Number of Residuals | 144 |

\* AIC and SBC do not include log determinant.

(a) Estimation

Autocorrelation Check of Residuals

| To Lag | Chi-Square | DF | Pr > ChiSq | --------------------Autocorrelations-------------------- | | | | | |
|---|---|---|---|---|---|---|---|---|---|
| 6 | 183.15 | 6 | <.0001 | 0.643 | 0.480 | 0.500 | 0.392 | 0.317 | 0.287 |
| 12 | 228.80 | 12 | <.0001 | 0.263 | 0.244 | 0.256 | 0.156 | 0.151 | 0.226 |
| 18 | 230.74 | 18 | <.0001 | 0.031 | -0.023 | 0.019 | 0.013 | -0.045 | -0.087 |
| 24 | 244.35 | 24 | <.0001 | -0.088 | -0.084 | -0.090 | -0.139 | -0.133 | -0.137 |

Autocorrelation Plot of Residuals

| Lag | Covariance | Correlation | -1 9 8 7 6 5 4 3 2 1 0 1 2 3 4 5 6 7 8 9 1 | Std Error |
|---|---|---|---|---|
| 0 | 0.0025964 | 1.00000 | \|********************\| | 0 |
| 1 | 0.0016301 | 0.64269 | \|*************  | 0.083333 |
| 2 | 0.0012180 | 0.48020 | \|**********  | 0.112611 |
| 3 | 0.0012694 | 0.50046 | \|**********  | 0.126031 |
| 4 | 0.00099504 | 0.39230 | \|********  | 0.139149 |
| 5 | 0.00080527 | 0.31748 | \|******  | 0.146629 |
| 6 | 0.00072001 | 0.28734 | \|******  | 0.151327 |
| 7 | 0.00066712 | 0.26302 | \|*****.  | 0.155070 |
| 8 | 0.00061990 | 0.24440 | \|*****.  | 0.158138 |
| 9 | 0.00064957 | 0.25610 | \|*****.  | 0.160739 |
| 10 | 0.00039608 | 0.15616 | \|***  | 0.163548 |
| 11 | 0.00038228 | 0.15071 | \|***  | 0.164580 |
| 12 | 0.00057440 | 0.22646 | \|*****  | 0.165536 |
| 13 | 0.00007845 | 0.03093 | \|*  | 0.167674 |
| 14 | -0.0000589 | -.02321 | .  | 0.167713 |
| 15 | 0.00004933 | 0.01945 | .  | 0.167736 |
| 16 | 0.00003359 | 0.01324 | .  | 0.167751 |
| 17 | -0.0001152 | -.04541 | *\|  | 0.167759 |
| 18 | -0.0002215 | -.08734 | **\|  | 0.167844 |
| 19 | -0.0002240 | -.08831 | **\|  | 0.168159 |
| 20 | -0.0002131 | -.08401 | **\|  | 0.168481 |
| 21 | -0.0002294 | -.09044 | **\|  | 0.168772 |
| 22 | -0.0003530 | -.13918 | ***\|  | 0.169108 |
| 23 | -0.0003367 | -.13274 | ***\|  | 0.169901 |
| 24 | -0.0003485 | -.13738 | ***\|  | 0.170620 |

(b) The RSAC

**FIGURE 11.36** (Continued)

```
                          Partial Autocorrelations
   Lag    Correlation   -1 9 8 7 6 5 4 3 2 1 0 1 2 3 4 5 6 7 8 9 1
    1       0.64269     I                  .  I*************    I
    2       0.11442     I                  .  I**.             I
    3       0.26519     I                  .  I*****           I
    4      -0.05616     I                 . *I   .             I
    5       0.02568     I                  . I*  .             I
    6      -0.00348     I                  . I   .             I
    7       0.04807     I                  . I*  .             I
    8       0.03448     I                  . I*  .             I
    9       0.08133     I                  . I**.              I
   10      -0.14979     I               ***I   .              I
   11       0.06324     I                  . I*  .            I
   12       0.11118     I                  . I**.             I
   13      -0.29666     I            ******I   .              I
   14      -0.00113     I                  . I   .            I
   15      -0.01594     I                  . I   .            I
   16       0.09370     I                  . I**.             I
   17      -0.09153     I                .**I   .             I
   18      -0.07826     I                .**I   .             I
   19      -0.01884     I                  . I   .            I
   20       0.02918     I                  . I*  .            I
   21      -0.03058     I                 . *I   .            I
   22      -0.00022     I                  . I   .            I
   23      -0.03690     I                 . *I   .            I
   24      -0.09402     I                .**I   .             I
```

(c) The RSPAC

**FIGURE 11.37 (for Exercise 11.15)** SAS output of estimation, diagnostic checking, and forecasting for the dummy variable regression model for sporting good sales, assuming the error terms $\varepsilon_1, \varepsilon_2, \ldots$ are described by the model $\varepsilon_t = \phi_1\varepsilon_{t-1} + \phi_3\varepsilon_{t-3} + \phi_{1,12}\varepsilon_{t-12} - \phi_1\phi_{1,12}\varepsilon_{t-13} - \phi_3\phi_{1,12}\varepsilon_{t-15} + a_t$

Conditional Least Squares Estimation

| Parameter | Estimate | Standard Error | t Value | Approx Pr > \|t\| | Lag | Variable | Shift |
|-----------|----------|----------------|---------|-------------------|-----|----------|-------|
| MU    | 7.24013   | 0.02958   | 244.77 | <.0001 | 0  | Lny  | 0 |
| AR1,1 | 0.59377   | 0.07271   | 8.17   | <.0001 | 1  | Lny  | 0 |
| AR1,2 | 0.24789   | 0.07463   | 3.32   | 0.0012 | 3  | Lny  | 0 |
| AR2,1 | 0.40077   | 0.08727   | 4.59   | <.0001 | 12 | Lny  | 0 |
| NUM1  | 0.0057249 | 0.0004015 | 14.26  | <.0001 | 0  | Time | 0 |
| NUM2  | -0.68389  | 0.01780   | -38.43 | <.0001 | 0  | M1   | 0 |
| NUM3  | -0.66558  | 0.02085   | -31.92 | <.0001 | 0  | M2   | 0 |
| NUM4  | -0.50828  | 0.02068   | -24.57 | <.0001 | 0  | M3   | 0 |
| NUM5  | -0.46292  | 0.02176   | -21.28 | <.0001 | 0  | M4   | 0 |
| NUM6  | -0.41770  | 0.02254   | -18.53 | <.0001 | 0  | M5   | 0 |
| NUM7  | -0.36018  | 0.02267   | -15.89 | <.0001 | 0  | M6   | 0 |
| NUM8  | -0.41220  | 0.02252   | -18.30 | <.0001 | 0  | M7   | 0 |
| NUM9  | -0.34958  | 0.02151   | -16.26 | <.0001 | 0  | M8   | 0 |
| NUM10 | -0.51214  | 0.02034   | -25.17 | <.0001 | 0  | M9   | 0 |
| NUM11 | -0.59866  | 0.02065   | -28.99 | <.0001 | 0  | M10  | 0 |
| NUM12 | -0.49681  | 0.01710   | -29.06 | <.0001 | 0  | M11  | 0 |

```
            Constant Estimate      0.686953
            Variance Estimate      0.001193
            Std Error Estimate     0.034545
            AIC                    -545.57
            SBC                    -498.053
            Number of Residuals        144
    * AIC and SBC do not include log determinant.
```

(a) Estimation

Autocorrelation Check of Residuals

| To Lag | Chi-Square | DF | Pr > ChiSq | ------Autocorrelations------ | | | | | |
|--------|-----------|----|-----------|--------|--------|--------|--------|--------|--------|
| 6  | 1.20  | 3  | 0.7541 | 0.024  | -0.026 | 0.025  | -0.077 | 0.010  | 0.007  |
| 12 | 3.36  | 9  | 0.9485 | 0.025  | 0.007  | 0.106  | 0.005  | -0.043 | 0.001  |
| 18 | 10.37 | 15 | 0.7961 | -0.148 | -0.084 | -0.005 | 0.105  | 0.027  | -0.048 |
| 24 | 13.69 | 21 | 0.8824 | -0.018 | 0.016  | 0.065  | 0.021  | 0.108  | 0.049  |

Autocorrelation Plot of Residuals

| Lag | Covariance | Correlation | -1 9 8 7 6 5 4 3 2 1 0 1 2 3 4 5 6 7 8 9 1 | Std Error |
|-----|-----------|-------------|---------------------------------------------|-----------|
| 0  | 0.0011933  | 1.00000  | \|********************\| | 0 |
| 1  | 0.00002921 | 0.02447  | .  \| . | 0.083333 |
| 2  | -0.0000315 | -.02636  | . *\| . | 0.083383 |
| 3  | 0.00002995 | 0.02510  | . \|* . | 0.083441 |
| 4  | -0.0000919 | -.07699  | .**\| . | 0.083493 |
| 5  | 0.00001142 | 0.00957  | . \| . | 0.083985 |
| 6  | 7.7696E-6  | 0.00651  | . \| . | 0.083993 |
| 7  | 0.00002926 | 0.02452  | . \| . | 0.083996 |
| 8  | 7.96516E-6 | 0.00667  | . \| . | 0.084046 |
| 9  | 0.00012709 | 0.10650  | . \|** . | 0.084050 |
| 10 | 6.55841E-6 | 0.00550  | . \| . | 0.084981 |
| 11 | -0.0000511 | -.04280  | . *\| . | 0.084984 |
| 12 | 1.45169E-6 | 0.00122  | . \| . | 0.085133 |
| 13 | -0.0001772 | -.14846  | ***\| . | 0.085134 |
| 14 | -0.0000998 | -.08367  | .**\| . | 0.086913 |
| 15 | -5.801E-6  | -.00486  | . \| . | 0.087470 |
| 16 | 0.00012569 | 0.10532  | . \|** . | 0.087472 |
| 17 | 0.00003264 | 0.02735  | . \|* . | 0.088348 |
| 18 | -0.0000578 | -.04843  | . *\| . | 0.088407 |
| 19 | -0.0000211 | -.01770  | . \| . | 0.088591 |
| 20 | 0.00001921 | 0.01610  | . \| . | 0.088616 |
| 21 | 0.00007778 | 0.06518  | . \|* . | 0.088636 |
| 22 | 0.00002450 | 0.02053  | . \| . | 0.088868 |
| 23 | 0.00012866 | 0.10781  | . \|** . | 0.089001 |
| 24 | 0.00005800 | 0.04860  | . \|* . | 0.089904 |

(b) The RSAC

**FIGURE 11.37** (Continued)

```
                        Partial Autocorrelations
Lag    Correlation    -1 9 8 7 6 5 4 3 2 1 0 1 2 3 4 5 6 7 8 9 1
  1      0.02447      |                     .  *|   .               |
  2     -0.02697      |                     .  *|   .               |
  3      0.02645      |                     .   |*  .               |
  4     -0.07918      |                     .**|   .               |
  5      0.01528      |                     .   |   .               |
  6      0.00071      |                     .   |   .               |
  7      0.02948      |                     .   |*  .               |
  8     -0.00148      |                     .   |   .               |
  9      0.11073      |                     .   |**.                |
 10     -0.00186      |                     .   |   .               |
 11     -0.03274      |                     .  *|   .               |
 12     -0.00336      |                     .   |   .               |
 13     -0.13695      |                     ***|   .               |
 14     -0.08068      |                     .**|   .               |
 15     -0.01750      |                     .   |   .               |
 16      0.10917      |                     .   |**.                |
 17      0.00709      |                     .   |   .               |
 18     -0.05919      |                     .  *|   .               |
 19     -0.02038      |                     .   |   .               |
 20      0.04700      |                     .   |*  .               |
 21      0.07416      |                     .   |*  .               |
 22      0.04334      |                     .   |*  .               |
 23      0.12865      |                     .   |***                |
 24      0.04079      |                     .   |*  .               |
```

(c) The RSPAC

```
Obs    Forecasty    L95CI     U95CI
145    1520.23     1420.71   1626.73
146    1554.75     1437.02   1682.13
147    1874.64     1726.57   2035.41
148    1974.88     1808.68   2156.36
149    2096.12     1911.18   2298.97
150    2261.56     2056.33   2487.27
151    2146.10     1946.82   2365.80
152    2268.86     2054.15   2506.00
153    1921.50     1737.08   2125.50
154    1792.31     1618.37   1984.95
155    1954.32     1762.95   2166.46
156    3264.14     2942.24   3621.25
```

(d) Forecasts for $y_{145}$ through $y_{156}$

# 12

## *Advanced Box–Jenkins Modeling*

In this chapter we continue and generalize our discussion of Box–Jenkins seasonal modeling. In Section 12.1 we present a general seasonal model, which is expressed by using a mathematical device called the **backshift operator.** We also give ten guidelines for tentatively determining which special case of the general seasonal model describes a specific time series.

Section 12.2 discusses **intervention models.** These models are used when exceptional, external events affect the variable to be predicted. Examples of such events might be strikes, natural disasters (say, a hurricane or flood), and policy changes (say, a telephone company initiating a new charge for directory assistance calls). We will see that special kinds of dummy variables called **pulse functions** and **step functions** are used in building intervention models.

When employing the Box–Jenkins methodology, we use the term **transfer function model** to refer to a model that predicts future values of a time series (called the **output series**) on the basis of past values of this series and on the basis of one or more related time series (called the **input series**). Section 12.3 presents a *procedure for building a transfer function model*. We will see that this involves (1) identifying a model to describe the input series, (2) identifying a preliminary transfer function model describing the output series, and (3) using the residuals for the preliminary model to identify a model describing the error structure of the preliminary model and to form a final transfer function model.

# 12.1 THE GENERAL SEASONAL MODEL AND GUIDELINES FOR TENTATIVE IDENTIFICATION

## The General Seasonal Model

In order to discuss the general seasonal model, we need to become familiar with the symbol $B$, which is called the **backshift operator** and which shifts the subscript of a time series observation backward in time by one period. That is,

$$By_t = y_{t-1} \quad \text{for example, } By_{50} = y_{49}$$

Next the symbol $B^k$, which intuitively represents $B$ raised to a power equal to $k$, shifts the subscript of a time series observation backward in time by $k$ periods. That is,

$$B^k y_t = y_{t-k} \quad \text{for example, } B^{12} y_{50} = y_{38}$$

Although we will perform various algebraic manipulations with the backshift operator $B$, we will not discuss the theory justifying these manipulations. However, it can be shown that the manipulations are legitimate.

We will first use the backshift operator to present a **general stationarity transformation.** The transformations we previously discussed are special cases of this general transformation. We define the **nonseasonal operator** $\nabla$ to be

$$\nabla = 1 - B$$

and we define the **seasonal operator** $\nabla_L$ to be

$$\nabla_L = 1 - B^L$$

where $L$ is the number of seasons in a year ($L = 4$ for quarterly data and $L = 12$ for monthly data). Moreover, we let $y_t^*$ represent an appropriate predifferencing transformation (for example, $y_t^* = \ln y_t$ if we need to take the natural logarithms of the original time series values and $y_t^* = y_t$ if we do not need a predifferencing transformation). These are the elements in the general stationarity transformation.

---

The **general stationarity transformation** is

$$z_t = \nabla_L^D \nabla^d y_t^*$$
$$= (1 - B^L)^D (1 - B)^d y_t^*$$

where $d$ is the **degree of nonseasonal differencing** used and $D$ is the **degree of seasonal differencing** used.

---

If a time series possesses no seasonal variation, then experience with Box–Jenkins modeling indicates that setting $D = 0$ and $d = 0$, 1, or 2 will usually produce stationary time series values. Setting $D = 0$ implies that

$$z_t = \nabla_L^D \nabla^d y_t^* = \nabla_L^0 \nabla^d y_t^*$$
$$= (1 - B^L)^0 (1 - B)^d y_t^*$$
$$= (1 - B)^d y_t^*$$

which means that we are using no seasonal differencing. Setting $d = 0$ implies that

$$z_t = (1 - B)^d y_t^*$$
$$= (1 - B)^0 y_t^*$$
$$= y_t^*$$

which means that the transformed values $z_1, z_2, \ldots, z_n$ are the original predifferenced values $y_1^*, y_2^*, \ldots, y_n^*$. Setting $d = 1$ implies that

$$z_t = (1 - B)^d y_t^* = (1 - B)^1 y_t^*$$
$$= (1 - B) y_t^* = y_t^* - B y_t^*$$
$$= y_t^* - y_{t-1}^*$$

which means that the transformed values are the first regular differenced values. Setting $d = 2$ implies that

$$z_t = (1 - B)^d y_t^*$$
$$= (1 - B)^2 y_t^*$$
$$= (1 - 2B + B^2) y_t^* = y_t^* - 2B y_t^* + B^2 y_t^*$$
$$= y_t^* - 2y_{t-1}^* + y_{t-2}^*$$

which means that the transformed values are the second regular differenced values.

If a time series possesses seasonal variation, then experience with Box–Jenkins modeling indicates that setting $D = 0$ or 1 and $d = 0$ or 1 will usually produce stationary time series values. Setting $D = 1$ and $d = 0$ implies that

$$z_t = (1 - B^L)^D (1 - B)^d y_t^*$$
$$= (1 - B^L)^1 (1 - B)^0 y_t^* = (1 - B^L) y_t^*$$
$$= y_t^* - B^L y_t^*$$
$$= y_t^* - y_{t-L}^*$$

which means that the transformed values are the first seasonal differenced values. Setting $D = 1$ and $d = 1$ implies that

$$z_t = (1 - B^L)^D (1 - B)^d y_t^*$$
$$= (1 - B^L)^1 (1 - B)^1 y_t^* = (1 - B - B^L + B^{L+1}) y_t^*$$
$$= y_t^* - B y_t^* - B^L y_t^* + B^{L+1} y_t^*$$
$$= y_t^* - y_{t-1}^* - y_{t-L}^* + y_{t-L-1}^*$$

which means that the transformed values are the first regular differenced and first seasonal differenced values.

Once we have used the stationarity transformation

$$z_t = (1 - B^L)^D (1 - B)^d y_t^*$$

to transform time series values $y_1, y_2, \ldots, y_n$ possessing seasonal variation into stationary time series values $z_b, z_{b+1}, \ldots, z_n$, we use the SAC and SPAC of the values $z_b, z_{b+1}, \ldots, z_n$ to tentatively identify a Box–Jenkins model describing these values. To motivate the general seasonal model, recall that in Example 11.3 we concluded that the model

$$z_t = \delta + \phi_1 z_{t-1} + \phi_3 z_{t-3} + \phi_5 z_{t-5} - \theta_{1,12} a_{t-12} + a_t$$

where

$$z_t = y_t^* - y_{t-12}^* \quad \text{and} \quad y_t^* = y_t^{.25}$$

describes the monthly hotel room averages in Table 11.1. This model can be written as

$$z_t - \phi_1 z_{t-1} - \phi_3 z_{t-3} - \phi_5 z_{t-5} = \delta + a_t - \theta_{1,12} a_{t-12}$$

or

$$z_t - \phi_1 B z_t - \phi_3 B^3 z_t - \phi_5 B^5 z_t = \delta + a_t - \theta_{1,12} B^{12} a_t$$

or

$$(1 - \phi_1 B - \phi_3 B^3 - \phi_5 B^5) z_t = \delta + (1 - \theta_{1,12} B^{12}) a_t$$

or

$$\phi_5(B) z_t = \delta + \theta_1(B^{12}) a_t$$

Here

$$\phi_5(B) = (1 - \phi_1 B - \phi_3 B^3 - \phi_5 B^5)$$

is called a **nonseasonal autoregressive operator,** and

$$\theta_1(B^{12}) = (1 - \theta_{1,12} B^{12})$$

is called the **seasonal moving average operator of order 1.** This model for monthly room averages, and every (seasonal or nonseasonal) Box–Jenkins model, is a special case (or a slight modification) of **the general Box–Jenkins model of order $(p, P, q, Q)$.** This model is as follows.

---

**The general Box–Jenkins model of order $(p, P, q, Q)$ is**

$$\phi_p(B)\phi_P(B^L) z_t = \delta + \theta_q(B)\theta_Q(B^L) a_t$$

Here

1.   $\phi_p(B) = (1 - \phi_1 B - \phi_2 B^2 - \cdots - \phi_p B^p)$

is called the **nonseasonal autoregressive operator of order $p$.**

**2.**   $\phi_P(B^L) = (1 - \phi_{1,L}B^L - \phi_{2,L}B^{2L} - \cdots - \phi_{P,L}B^{PL})$

is called the **seasonal autoregressive operator of order** $P$.

**3.**   $\theta_q(B) = (1 - \theta_1 B - \theta_2 B^2 - \cdots - \theta_q B^q)$

is called the **nonseasonal moving average operator of order** $q$.

**4.**   $\theta_Q(B^L) = (1 - \theta_{1,L}B^L - \theta_{2,L}B^{2L} - \cdots - \theta_{Q,L}B^{QL})$

is called the **seasonal moving average operator of order** $Q$.

**5.**   $\delta = \phi_p(B)\phi_P(B^L)\mu$

is a **constant term,** where $\mu$ is the true mean of the stationary time
series being modeled, and $B\mu = \mu$.

**6.**   $\phi_1, \phi_2, \ldots, \phi_p; \phi_{1,L}, \phi_{2,L}, \ldots, \phi_{P,L}; \theta_1, \theta_2, \ldots, \theta_q; \theta_{1,L}, \theta_{2,L}, \ldots, \theta_{Q,L};$ and $\delta$
are **unknown parameters** that must be estimated from sample data.

**7.**   $a_t, a_{t-1}, \ldots$ are **random shocks** that are assumed to be statistically
independent of each other; each is assumed to have been randomly
selected from a *normal distribution* that has *mean zero* and a *variance*
that is the *same* for each and every time period $t$.

## Guidelines for Tentative Identification

Identification of the particular special form of the general Box–Jenkins model of order
$(p, P, q, Q)$ that describes a particular stationary time series $z_b, z_{b+1}, \ldots, z_n$ involves
determining the following:

**1.**   Whether the constant term $\delta$ should be included in the model

**2.**   Which of the operators $\phi_p(B)$, $\phi_P(B^L)$, $\theta_q(B)$, and $\theta_Q(B^L)$ should be included in
the model

**3.**   The order of each operator that is included in the model

Letting

$$\bar{z} = \frac{\sum_{t=b}^{n} z_t}{n - b + 1} \quad \text{and} \quad s_z = \left( \frac{\sum_{t=b}^{n} (z_t - \bar{z})^2}{(n - b + 1) - 1} \right)^{1/2}$$

denote the mean and standard deviation of the time series values $z_b, z_{b+1}, \ldots, z_n$, it follows (as in Chapter 9) that one very approximate procedure is to decide that $\bar{z}$ is statistically different from zero and thus to include the constant term

$$\delta = \phi_p(B)\phi_P(B^L)\mu$$

in the general Box–Jenkins model if the absolute value of

$$\frac{\bar{z}}{s_z/\sqrt{n-b+1}}$$

is greater than 2. Moreover, in order to determine which of the operators $\phi_p(B)$, $\phi_P(B^L)$, $\theta_q(B)$, and $\theta_Q(B^L)$ should be included in the general Box–Jenkins model, we do the following:

1.  Use the behaviors of the SAC and SPAC of the values $z_b, z_{b+1}, \ldots, z_n$ at the **nonseasonal level** to determine which (if any) of the nonseasonal operators should be utilized: the nonseasonal moving average operator of order $q$

$$\theta_q(B) = (1 - \theta_1 B - \theta_2 B^2 - \cdots - \theta_q B^q)$$

and/or the nonseasonal autoregressive operator of order $p$

$$\phi_p(B) = (1 - \phi_1 B - \phi_2 B^2 - \cdots - \phi_p B^p)$$

2.  Use the behaviors of the SAC and SPAC of the values $z_b, z_{b+1}, \ldots, z_n$ at the **seasonal level** to determine which (if any) of the seasonal operators should be utilized: the seasonal moving average operator of order $Q$

$$\theta_Q(B^L) = (1 - \theta_{1,L} B^L - \theta_{2,L} B^{2L} - \cdots - \theta_{Q,L} B^{QL})$$

and/or the seasonal autoregressive operator of order $P$

$$\phi_P(B^L) = (1 - \phi_{1,L} B^L - \phi_{2,L} B^{2L} - \cdots - \phi_{P,L} B^{PL})$$

In this regard note that Table 12.1 presents five guidelines describing nonseasonal behaviors of the SAC and SPAC and the nonseasonal operator(s) that should be used if each of these nonseasonal behaviors is observed. Table 12.2 (page 546) presents five guidelines describing seasonal behaviors of the SAC and SPAC and the seasonal operator(s) that should be used if each of these seasonal behaviors is observed. If we determine that an operator should not be used, we set this operator equal to 1.

Once we have tentatively identified an appropriate special form of the general Box–Jenkins model

$$\phi_p(B)\phi_P(B^L)z_t = \delta + \theta_q(B)\theta_Q(B^L)a_t$$

we insert the appropriate stationarity transformation

$$z_t = \nabla_L^D \nabla^d y_t^*$$

into this model to obtain the model

$$\phi_p(B)\phi_P(B^L)\nabla_L^D \nabla^d y_t^* = \delta + \theta_q(B)\theta_Q(B^L)a_t$$

## Examples

We now present three examples of using Guidelines 1–10 to help us to tentatively identify Box–Jenkins seasonal models.

**TABLE 12.1** Guidelines for Choosing Nonseasonal Operators

| Guideline | Behavior of SAC and SPAC | Nonseasonal Operator(s) to Be Used and Determination of the Form of the Operators(s) |
|---|---|---|
| 1 | SAC has spikes at lags 1, 2,..., $q$ and *cuts off* after lag $q$, and the SPAC *dies down* | $\theta_q(B) = (1 - \theta_1 B - \theta_2 B^2 - \cdots - \theta_q B^q)$<br>  = nonseasonal moving average operator of order $q$<br>Form determined by spikes in SAC. For example:<br>1. If SAC has a spike at lag 1 and cuts off after lag 1, and the SPAC dies down in a fashion dominated by damped exponential decay, use the nonseasonal moving average operator of order 1:<br>$\theta_1(B) = (1 - \theta_1 B)$<br>2. If SAC has spikes at lags 1 and 2 and cuts off after lag 2, and the SPAC dies down according to a mixture of damped exponentials and/or damped sine-waves, use the nonseasonal moving average operator of order 2:<br>$\theta_2(B) = (1 - \theta_1 B - \theta_2 B^2)$ |
| 2 | SAC *dies down,* and SPAC has spikes at lags 1, 2,..., $p$ and *cuts off* after lag $p$ | $\phi_p(B) = (1 - \phi_1 B - \phi_2 B^2 - \cdots - \phi_p B^p)$<br>  = nonseasonal autoregressive operator of order $p$<br>Form determined by spikes in SPAC. For example:<br>1. If SPAC has a spike at lag 1 and cuts off after lag 1, and the SAC dies down in a damped exponential fashion, use the nonseasonal autoregressive operator of order 1:<br>$\phi_1(B) = (1 - \phi_1 B)$<br>2. If SPAC has spikes at lags 1 and 2 and cuts off after lag 2, and the SAC dies down according to a mixture of damped exponentials and/or damped sine-waves, use the nonseasonal autoregressive operator of order 2:<br>$\phi_2(B) = (1 - \phi_1 B - \phi_2 B^2)$ |
| 3 | SAC has spikes at lags 1, 2,..., $q$ and *cuts off* after lag $q$, and the SPAC has spikes at lags 1, 2,..., $p$ and *cuts off* after lag $p$ | $\theta_q(B)$ or $\phi_p(B)$<br>If $\theta_q(B)$, form determined as discussed in Guideline 1. If $\phi_p(B)$, form determined as discussed in Guideline 2. If SAC cuts off more abruptly than SPAC, use $\theta_q(B)$. If SPAC cuts off more abruptly than SAC, use $\phi_p(B)$. If both the SAC and the SPAC appear to cut off equally abruptly,<br>1. use $\theta_q(B)$ and not $\phi_p(B)$ in a model and<br>2. use $\phi_p(B)$ and not $\theta_q(B)$ in a model.<br>Then choose the operator that yields the best model. Often $\theta_q(B)$ yields the best model. Therefore, one might first consider a model using $\theta_q(B)$. |
| 4 | SAC contains small sample autocorrelations (that is, has no spikes) at all lags and SPAC contains small sample partial autocorrelations (that is, has no spikes) at all lags. | No nonseasonal operator |
| 5 | SAC *dies down,* and SPAC *dies down* | Both $\theta_q(B)$ and $\phi_p(B)$<br>Simple forms of these operators are usually sufficient. For example, if the SAC dies down in a damped exponential fashion, and the SPAC dies down in a fashion dominated by damped exponential decay, it is appropriate to use<br>$\theta_1(B) = (1 - \theta_1 B)$ and $\phi_1(B) = (1 - \phi_1 B)$ |

**TABLE 12.2 Guidelines for Choosing Seasonal Operators**

| Guideline | Seasonal Behavior of SAC and SPAC | Seasonal Operator(s) to Be Used and Determination of the Form of the Operators(s) |
|---|---|---|
| 6 | SAC has spikes at lags $L, 2L, \ldots, QL$ and *cuts off* after lag $QL$, and the SPAC *dies down* | $\theta_Q(B^L) = (1 - \theta_{1,L}B^L - \theta_{2,L}B^{2L} - \cdots - \theta_{Q,L}B^{QL})$ <br> $=$ seasonal moving average operator of order $Q$ <br> Form determined by spikes in SAC at seasonal level. For example, if SAC has a spike at lag $L$ and cuts off after lag $L$, use the seasonal moving average operator of order 1: <br> $\theta_1(B^L) = (1 - \theta_{1,L}B^L)$ |
| 7 | SAC *dies down,* and SPAC has spikes at lags $L, 2L, \ldots, PL$ and *cuts off* after lag $PL$ | $\phi_P(B^L) = (1 - \phi_{1,L}B^L - \phi_{2,L}B^{2L} - \cdots - \phi_{p,L}B^{PL})$ <br> $=$ seasonal autoregressive operator of order $P$ <br> Form determined by spikes in SPAC at seasonal level. For example, if SPAC has a spike at lag $L$ and cuts off after lag $L$, use the seasonal autoregressive operator of order 1: <br> $\phi_1(B^L) = (1 - \phi_{1,L}B^L)$ |
| 8 | SAC has spikes at lags $L, 2L, \ldots, QL$ and *cuts off* after lag $QL$, and the SPAC has spikes at lags $L, 2L, \ldots, PL$ and *cuts off* after lag $PL$ | $\theta_Q(B^L)$ or $\phi_P(B^L)$ <br> If $\theta_Q(B^L)$, form determined as discussed in Guideline 6. If $\phi_P(B^L)$, form determined as discussed in Guideline 7. If SAC cuts off more abruptly at seasonal level than SPAC, use $\theta_Q(B^L)$. If SPAC cuts off more abruptly at seasonal level than SAC, use $\phi_P(B^L)$. If both the SAC and the SPAC appear to cut off equally abruptly at the seasonal level, <br> 1. use $\theta_Q(B^L)$ and not $\phi_P(B^L)$ in a model and <br> 2. use $\phi_P(B^L)$ and not $\theta_Q(B^L)$ in a model <br> Then choose the operator that yields the best model. Often $\theta_Q(B^L)$ yields the best model. Therefore, one might first consider a model using $\theta_Q(B^L)$. |
| 9 | SAC contains small sample autocorrelations (that is, has no spikes) at all seasonal lags and SPAC contains small sample partial autocorrelations (that is, has no spikes) at all seasonal lags | No seasonal operator |
| 10 | SAC *dies down* fairly quickly at the seasonal level, and SPAC *dies down* fairly quickly at the seasonal level | Both $\theta_Q(B^L)$ and $\phi_P(B^L)$ <br> Simple forms of these operators are usually sufficient. For example, it might be appropriate to use <br> $\theta_1(B^L) = (1 - \theta_{1,L}B^L)$ and <br> $\phi_1(B^L) = (1 - \phi_{1,L}B^L)$ |

**EXAMPLE 12.1**  We concluded in Example 11.2 that for the monthly hotel room averages in Table 11.1, the transformation

$$z_t = y_t^* - y_{t-12}^* \quad \text{where} \quad y_t^* = y_t^{.25}$$

produces stationary time series values. The SAC and SPAC of these stationary time series values are presented in Figure 11.7.

1.   At the **nonseasonal level** the SAC dies down fairly quickly, and the SPAC has spikes at lags 1, 3, and 5 and cuts off after lag 5. It follows, by Guideline 2 in Table 12.1, that we should use the nonseasonal autoregressive operator of order 5

$$\phi_5(B) = (1 - \phi_1 B - \phi_3 B^3 - \phi_5 B^5)$$

Note that we have omitted $\phi_2 B^2$ and $\phi_4 B^4$ from this operator because the SPAC has no spikes at lags 2 and 4.

2.   At the **seasonal level** the SAC has a spike at lag 12 and cuts off after lag 12, and the SPAC dies down fairly quickly. It follows, by Guideline 6 in Table 12.2, that we should use the seasonal moving average operator of order 1

$$\theta_1(B^{12}) = (1 - \theta_{1,12} B^{12})$$

By inserting these operators into the general model

$$\phi_p(B)\phi_P(B^L)z_t = \delta + \theta_q(B)\theta_Q(B^L)a_t$$

we are led to consider the tentative model

$$\phi_5(B)z_t = \delta + \theta_1(B^{12})a_t$$

or

$$(1 - \phi_1 B - \phi_3 B^3 - \phi_5 B^5)z_t = \delta + (1 - \theta_{1,12} B^{12})a_t$$

Here note that

$$\delta = \phi_p(B)\phi_P(B^{12})\mu$$
$$= (1 - \phi_1 B - \phi_3 B^3 - \phi_5 B^5)\mu$$
$$- (\mu \quad \phi_1\mu \quad \phi_3\mu \quad \phi_5\mu)$$
$$= (1 - \phi_1 - \phi_3 - \phi_5)\mu$$

We have tentatively included $\delta$ in the model because we concluded in Example 11.3 that $z$ is statistically different from zero. The model

$$(1 - \phi_1 B - \phi_3 B^3 - \phi_5 B^5)z_t = \delta + (1 - \theta_{1,12} B^{12})a_t$$

is equivalent to

$$z_t - \phi_1 B z_t - \phi_3 B^3 z_t - \phi_5 B^5 z_t = \delta + a_t - \theta_{1,12} B^{12} a_t$$

or

$$z_t - \phi_1 z_{t-1} - \phi_3 z_{t-3} - \phi_5 z_{t-5} = \delta + a_t - \theta_{1,12} a_{t-12}$$

or

$$z_t = \delta + \phi_1 z_{t-1} + \phi_3 z_{t-3} + \phi_5 z_{t-5} - \theta_{1,12} a_{t-12} + a_t$$

In Example 11.3 we concluded that this model is adequate, and we used it to forecast future monthly hotel room averages.

**EXAMPLE 12.2**   We concluded in Example 11.4 that for the monthly passenger totals in Table 11.3, the transformation

$$z_t = y_t^* - y_{t-1}^* - y_{t-12}^* + y_{t-13}^* \quad \text{where} \quad y_t^* = \ln y_t$$

produces stationary time series values. As previously discussed, the SAC and SPAC of these stationary time series values are presented in Figure 11.16.

1. At the **nonseasonal level** the SAC has a spike at lag 1 and (with the exception of a spike at lag 3) cuts off after lag 1, and the SPAC dies down fairly quickly. It follows, by Guideline 1 in Table 12.1, that we should use the nonseasonal moving average operator of order 1

$$\theta_1(B) = (1 - \theta_1 B)$$

2. At the **seasonal level** the SAC has a spike at lag 12 and cuts off after lag 12, and the SPAC has a spike at lag 12 and either cuts off after lag 12 or dies down. It follows, by either Guideline 6 or Guideline 8 in Table 12.2, that we should use the seasonal moving average operator of order 1

$$\theta_1(B^{12}) = (1 - \theta_{1,12} B^{12})$$

By inserting

$$\theta_1(B) = (1 - \theta_1 B) \quad \text{and} \quad \theta_1(B^{12}) = (1 - \theta_{1,12} B^{12})$$

into the general model

$$\phi_p(B)\phi_P(B^{12})z_t = \delta + \theta_q(B)\theta_Q(B^{12})a_t$$

we are led to try the model

$$z_t = (1 - \theta_1 B)(1 - \theta_{1,12} B^{12})a_t$$

Here we exclude $\delta$ because we concluded in Example 11.4 that $\bar{z}$ is not statistically different from zero. This model is called **multiplicative** because the operator $(1 - \theta_1 B)$ is multiplied by the operator $(1 - \theta_{1,12} B^{12})$. This model is equivalent to

$$z_t = (1 - \theta_1 B - \theta_{1,12} B^{12} + \theta_1 \theta_{1,12} B^{13})a_t$$

or

$$z_t = a_t - \theta_1 a_{t-1} - \theta_{1,12} a_{t-12} + \theta_1 \theta_{1,12} a_{t-13}$$

Note that multiplying the two operators together has yielded a model with the term $\theta_1 \theta_{1,12} a_{t-13}$. Such multiplicative terms were discussed in Chapter 11. In general, using the ten guidelines in Tables 12.1 and 12.2 will yield models with the appropriate multiplicative terms. Recall that in Example 11.4 we concluded that the above model is adequate, and we used this model to forecast future monthly passenger totals.

**EXAMPLE 12.3**   We now apply the guidelines in Tables 12.1 and 12.2 to the SAC and SPAC in Figure 11.18.

1. At the **nonseasonal level** the SPAC has spikes at lags 1 and 3 and cuts off after lag 3, and the SAC dies down. It follows, by Guideline 2 in Table 12.1, that we

should use a nonseasonal autoregressive operator of order 3 (the term $\phi_2 B^2$ is omitted because there is no spike at lag 2)

$$\phi_3(B) = (1 - \phi_1 B - \phi_3 B^3)$$

2.   At the **seasonal level** the SPAC has a spike at lag 12 and cuts off after lag 12, and the SAC dies down. It follows, by Guideline 7 in Table 12.2, that we should use the seasonal autoregressive operator of order 1

$$\phi_1(B^{12}) = (1 - \phi_{1,12} B^{12})$$

By inserting these two operators into the general model, we are led to try the model

$$(1 - \phi_1 B - \phi_3 B^3)(1 - \phi_{1,12} B^{12})z_t = a_t$$

This model is equivalent to

$$(1 - \phi_1 B - \phi_3 B^3 - \phi_{1,12} B^{12} + \phi_1 \phi_{1,12} B^{13} + \phi_3 \phi_{1,12} B^{15})z_t = a_t$$

or

$$z_t - \phi_1 z_{t-1} - \phi_3 z_{t-3} - \phi_{1,12} z_{t-12} + \phi_1 \phi_{1,12} z_{t-13} + \phi_3 \phi_{1,12} z_{t-15} = a_t$$

or

$$z_t = \phi_1 z_{t-1} + \phi_3 z_{t-3} + \phi_{1,12} z_{t-12} - \phi_1 \phi_{1,12} z_{t-13} - \phi_3 \phi_{1,12} z_{t-15} + a_t$$

Thus, we can see the rationalization for the multiplicative terms and their negative signs when this model is constructed without using the operator notation. The term $\delta$ is omitted because the data for time series $z_t$ in this case are actually the residuals from a regression model (see Example 11.6).

Note that our procedure for identifying a seasonal Box–Jenkins model involves examining the SAC and SPAC at the nonseasonal level and then examining them at the seasonal level. This procedure implicitly suggests separating the behaviors of the SAC and SPAC at the nonseasonal level from their behaviors at the seasonal level. However, it can be shown that for many seasonal Box–Jenkins models involving both nonseasonal and seasonal operators, the behaviors of the SAC and SPAC at the nonseasonal level are related to their behaviors at the seasonal level. Therefore, sometimes the behaviors of the SAC and SPAC at the nonseasonal level are related to their behaviors at the seasonal level. In spite of this, experience has shown that our procedure (and guidelines) yields tentative seasonal Box–Jenkins models that diagnostic checking procedures indicate are good final models or models that require little modification in order to form a good final model.

## Stationarity and Invertibility Conditions

The Box–Jenkins methodology requires that the model

$$\phi_p(B)\phi_P(B^L)z_t = \delta + \theta_q(B)\theta_Q(B^L)a_t$$

**TABLE 12.3** Stationarity and Invertibility Conditions on the Parameters in the First and Second Orders of $\phi_p(B)$, $\phi_P(B^L)$, $\theta_q(B)$, and $\theta_Q(B^L)$

| Operator | Stationarity Conditions | Invertibility Conditions |
|---|---|---|
| $\theta_1(B) = (1 - \theta_1 B)$ | None | $\|\theta_1\| < 1$ |
| $\theta_2(B) = (1 - \theta_1 B - \theta_2 B^2)$ | None | $\theta_1 + \theta_2 < 1$ |
| | | $\theta_2 - \theta_1 < 1$ |
| | | $\|\theta_2\| < 1$ |
| $\theta_1(B^L) = (1 - \theta_{1,L} B^L)$ | None | $\|\theta_{1,L}\| < 1$ |
| $\theta_2(B^L) = (1 - \theta_{1,L} B^L - \theta_{2,L} B^{2L})$ | None | $\theta_{1,L} + \theta_{2,L} < 1$ |
| | | $\theta_{2,L} - \theta_{1,L} < 1$ |
| | | $\|\theta_{2,L}\| < 1$ |
| $\phi_1(B) = (1 - \phi_1 B)$ | $\|\phi_1\| < 1$ | None |
| $\phi_2(B) = (1 - \phi_1 B - \phi_2 B^2)$ | $\phi_1 + \phi_2 < 1$ | None |
| | $\phi_2 - \phi_1 < 1$ | |
| | $\|\phi_2\| < 1$ | |
| $\phi_1(B^L) = (1 - \phi_{1,L} B^L)$ | $\|\phi_{1,L}\| < 1$ | None |
| $\phi_2(B^L) = (1 - \phi_{1,L} B^L - \phi_{2,L} B^{2L})$ | $\phi_{1,L} + \phi_{2,L} < 1$ | None |
| | $\phi_{2,L} - \phi_{1,L} < 1$ | |
| | $\|\phi_{2,L}\| < 1$ | |

used in describing and forecasting a time series must be both **stationary** and **invertible.** The stationarity and invertibility conditions on the parameters of the first and second orders of the operators $\phi_p(B)$, $\phi_P(B^L)$, $\theta_q(B)$, and $\theta_Q(B^L)$ are given in Table 12.3. The stationarity and invertibility conditions on the parameters of the *general* forms of the operators $\phi_p(B)$, $\phi_P(B^L)$, $\theta_q(B)$, and $\theta_Q(B^L)$ are complicated and will not be given here. However, we will say that

1.  There are stationarity conditions, but no invertibility conditions, on the parameters of any form of each of the autoregressive operators $\phi_p(B)$ and $\phi_P(B^L)$. A necessary (but not sufficient) stationarity condition on the parameters of any form of each of the operators $\phi_p(B)$ and $\phi_P(B^L)$ is that the sum of the values of the parameters in the operator is less than 1.

2.  There are invertibility conditions, but no stationarity conditions, on the parameters of any form of each of the moving average operators $\theta_q(B)$ and $\theta_Q(B^L)$. A necessary (but not sufficient) invertibility condition on the parameters of any form of each of the operators $\theta_q(B)$ and $\theta_Q(B^L)$ is that the sum of the values of the parameters in the operator is less than 1.

3.  Each of the operators $\phi_p(B)$, $\phi_P(B^L)$, $\theta_q(B)$, and $\theta_Q(B^L)$ should be checked separately.

**EXAMPLE 12.4**   We said in Example 12.1 that the model

$$(1 - \phi_1 B - \phi_3 B^3 - \phi_5 B^5)z_t = \delta + (1 - \theta_{1,12} B^{12})a_t$$

where

$$z_t = y_t^* - y_{t-12}^* \quad \text{and} \quad y_t^* = y_t^{.25}$$

adequately describes the original monthly hotel room averages in Table 11.1. A necessary (but not sufficient) stationarity condition on the parameters $\phi_1$, $\phi_3$, and $\phi_5$ in the nonseasonal autoregressive operator

$$\phi_5(B) = (1 - \phi_1 B - \phi_3 B^3 - \phi_5 B^5)$$

is

$$\phi_1 + \phi_3 + \phi_5 < 1$$

Moreover, the invertibility condition on the parameter $\theta_{1,12}$ in the seasonal moving average operator of order 1

$$\theta_1(B^{12}) = (1 - \theta_{1,12} B^{12})$$

is (from Table 12.3)

$$|\theta_{1,12}| < 1$$

Note that the preliminary point estimates $\hat{\phi}_1 = .1$, $\hat{\phi}_3 = .1$, $\hat{\phi}_5 = .1$, and $\hat{\theta}_{1,12} = .1$ satisfy these stationarity and invertibility conditions, and note that

$$\hat{\phi}_1 = .23242 \qquad \hat{\phi}_3 = -.22301 \quad \hat{\phi}_5 = -.15263 \quad \text{and} \quad \hat{\theta}_{1,12} = .47634$$

(which are the final least squares point estimates of $\phi_1$, $\phi_3$, $\phi_5$ and $\theta_{1,12}$ in Figure 11.9) also satisfy the stationarity and invertibility conditions.

# 12.2 INTERVENTION MODELS

Intervention models are used when exceptional external events, called **interventions,** affect the variable to be forecasted. Examples of interventions are strikes, natural disasters, and policy changes. As demonstrated in the following examples, we use special types of dummy variables called **step functions** and **impulse functions** to build intervention models.

**EXAMPLE 12.5**   In March 1974 the Cincinnati Bell Telephone Company initiated a policy intended to reduce the frequency of local directory assistance calls. According to this policy, each subscriber is allowed three such calls each month and then is charged 20 cents for each additional such call. Prior to March 1974 there had been no such charge. In Table 12.4 we present the monthly average number of directory assistance calls per day (Sundays excluded) made by Cincinnati Bell subscribers from January 1962 to December 1976. There are 180 observations in this table, and the number of calls in March 1974 is observation 147. In examining the plot of these data in Figure 12.1, we see that the effect of the new charge was to reduce substantially the number of calls.

To estimate the size of this reduction and to develop a model for forecasting future directory assistance calls, we use a three-step procedure.

**TABLE 12.4 Cincinnati Directory Assistance, Monthly Average Calls per Day (In Units of 100 Calls), From January 1962 to December 1976 (Read Left to Right)**

| | | | | | | | | | | | |
|---|---|---|---|---|---|---|---|---|---|---|---|
| 350 | 339 | 351 | 364 | 369 | 331 | 331 | 340 | 346 | 341 | 357 | 398 |
| 381 | 367 | 383 | 375 | 353 | 361 | 375 | 371 | 373 | 366 | 382 | 429 |
| 406 | 403 | 429 | 425 | 427 | 409 | 402 | 409 | 419 | 404 | 429 | 463 |
| 428 | 449 | 444 | 467 | 474 | 463 | 432 | 453 | 462 | 456 | 474 | 514 |
| 489 | 475 | 492 | 525 | 527 | 533 | 527 | 522 | 526 | 513 | 564 | 599 |
| 572 | 587 | 599 | 601 | 611 | 620 | 579 | 582 | 592 | 581 | 630 | 663 |
| 638 | 631 | 645 | 682 | 601 | 595 | 521 | 521 | 516 | 496 | 538 | 575 |
| 537 | 534 | 542 | 538 | 547 | 540 | 526 | 548 | 555 | 545 | 594 | 643 |
| 625 | 616 | 640 | 625 | 637 | 634 | 621 | 641 | 654 | 649 | 662 | 699 |
| 672 | 704 | 700 | 711 | 715 | 718 | 652 | 664 | 695 | 704 | 733 | 772 |
| 716 | 712 | 732 | 755 | 761 | 748 | 748 | 750 | 744 | 731 | 782 | 810 |
| 777 | 816 | 840 | 868 | 872 | 811 | 810 | 762 | 634 | 626 | 649 | 697 |
| 657 | 549 | 162 | 177 | 175 | 162 | 161 | 165 | 170 | 172 | 178 | 186 |
| 178 | 178 | 189 | 205 | 202 | 185 | 193 | 200 | 196 | 204 | 206 | 227 |
| 225 | 217 | 219 | 236 | 253 | 213 | 205 | 210 | 216 | 218 | 235 | 241 |

*Source:* Dr. A. J. McSweeny, Department of Psychology, University of West Virginia. See McSweeny (1978).

**FIGURE 12.1**
JMP IN plot of the directory assistance call data in Table 12.4

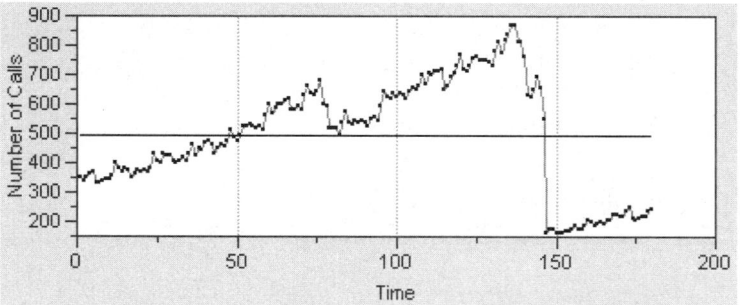

**Step 1:** Find a Box–Jenkins model describing the time series values observed before (or after) the intervention.

Consider the 146 observations before the intervention. It can be verified that taking the seasonal difference of the regular difference of the $y_t$ values produces stationary $z_t$ values and that the stationary values should be described by a seasonal moving average model. A model describing the observations before the intervention is

$$z_t = (1 - \theta_{1,12}B^{12})a_t \quad \text{where} \quad z_t = (1 - B)(1 - B^{12})y_t$$
$$= y_t - y_{t-1} - y_{t-12} + y_{t-13}$$

**Step 2:** Using appropriately defined dummy variables, find a regression model describing the intervention.

Figure 12.1 indicates that the charge (in March 1974) abruptly and permanently decreased the number of monthly average calls per day by a particular amount. The rate of increase in calls after March 1974 is similar to the rate of increase before this date and is probably due to population growth, rather than to a decay of the effect of the charge. Therefore, we hypothesize the regression model

$$y_t = CS_t + \varepsilon_t$$

The constant $C$ (which is negative) represents the decrease in the expected number of monthly average calls per day that is associated with the charge. The $S_t$ is called a step function and is defined as follows:

$$S_t = \begin{cases} 0 & \text{if } t < 147 \text{ (before March 1974)} \\ 1 & \text{if } t \geq 147 \text{ (March 1974 and after)} \end{cases}$$

**Step 3:** Modify the regression model of step 2 by (1) differencing both the $y_t$ and the dummy variables in the way that the $y_t$ values in step 1 are differenced and (2) describing the error term $\varepsilon_t$ in the regression model by using the Box–Jenkins model describing the stationary $z_t$ values of step 1.
The modified model describing the monthly average calls per day is

$$z_t = Cz_t(S) + \varepsilon_t$$

where

$$z_t = (1 - B)(1 - B^{12})y_t = y_t - y_{t-1} - y_{t-12} + y_{t-13}$$

$$z_t(S) = (1 - B)(1 - B^{12})S_t = S_t - S_{t-1} - S_{t-12} + S_{t-13}$$

and

$$\varepsilon_t - (1 - 0_{1,12}B^{12})a_t \quad \text{(from the model in step 1)}$$

Figure 12.2 presents the SAS output of estimation, diagnostic checking, and forecasting for this model. The model seems adequate, and the least squares point estimate of $C$ is −399.82270. Since the values in Table 12.4 are expressed in units of 100 calls, we estimate that the effect of the charge was to reduce the expected number of monthly average calls per day by about 40,000 calls.

**EXAMPLE 12.6**    Table 12.5 presents the number of miles flown by United Kingdom airlines from January 1963 to December 1970. Figure 12.3 is a plot of these data. Pilot strikes occurred in June and July 1968 (periods 66 and 67) and in April 1969 (period 76). In order to estimate the effects of such strikes and to develop a model for predicting future monthly airline mileages, Kendall and Ord (1990) carried out the following analysis.

**Step 1:** The first 60 observations were used to find the model

$$(1 - \phi_1 B - \phi_3 B^3)z_t = \delta + a_t \quad \text{where} \quad z_t = (1 - B^{12})y_t$$

**Step 2:** The regression model describing the interventions was

$$y_t = C_1 P_{1t} + C_2 P_{2t} + \varepsilon_t$$

**FIGURE 12.2** SAS output of estimation, diagnostic checking, and forecasting for the model
$z_t = Cz_t(S) + \varepsilon_t$   where   $z_t = (1 - B)(1 - B^{12})y_t$, $z_t(S) = (1 - B)(1 - B^{12})S_t$,   and   $\varepsilon_t = (1 - \theta_{1,12}B^{12})a_t$

Conditional Least Squares Estimation

| Parameter | Estimate | Standard Error | t Value | Approx Pr > \|t\| | Lag | Variable |
|-----------|----------|----------------|---------|------------------|-----|----------|
| MA1,1     | 0.85654  | 0.04359        | 19.65   | <.0001           | 12  | y        |
| SCALE1    | -399.82270 | 22.95216     | -17.42  | <.0001           | 0   | S        |

| To Lag | Chi-Square | DF | Pr > ChiSq |
|--------|-----------|----|-----------|
| 6      | 3.53      | 5  | 0.6183    |
| 12     | 6.83      | 11 | 0.8128    |
| 18     | 10.33     | 17 | 0.8891    |
| 24     | 15.31     | 23 | 0.8831    |
| 30     | 22.25     | 29 | 0.8098    |

Forecasts for variable y

| Obs | Forecast | Std Error | 95% Confidence Limits | |
|-----|----------|-----------|-----------------------|--------|
| 181 | 217.1092 | 23.3598   | 171.3247 | 262.8936 |
| 182 | 208.0332 | 33.0358   | 143.2842 | 272.7822 |
| 183 | 219.8708 | 40.4604   | 140.5698 | 299.1718 |
| 184 | 234.2990 | 46.7197   | 142.7301 | 325.8680 |
| 185 | 235.7922 | 52.2342   | 133.4150 | 338.1693 |
| 186 | 215.1519 | 57.2197   | 103.0033 | 327.3005 |
| 187 | 203.5945 | 61.8044   | 82.4601  | 324.7288 |
| 188 | 206.0268 | 66.0716   | 76.5288  | 335.5248 |
| 189 | 199.4998 | 70.0795   | 62.1464  | 336.8532 |
| 190 | 196.2642 | 73.8703   | 51.4810  | 341.0474 |
| 191 | 218.8361 | 77.4759   | 66.9862  | 370.6859 |
| 192 | 247.8388 | 80.9209   | 89.2368  | 406.4408 |

**TABLE 12.5** Monthly Miles Flown by United Kingdom Airlines (In Units of 1000 Miles)

|       | 1963   | 1964   | 1965   | 1966   | 1967   | 1968   | 1969   | 1970   |
|-------|--------|--------|--------|--------|--------|--------|--------|--------|
| Jan.  | 6,827  | 7,269  | 8,350  | 8,186  | 8,334  | 8,639  | 9,491  | 10,840 |
| Feb.  | 6,178  | 6,775  | 7,829  | 7,444  | 7,899  | 8,772  | 8,919  | 10,436 |
| Mar.  | 7,084  | 7,819  | 8,829  | 8,484  | 9,994  | 10,894 | 11,607 | 13,589 |
| Apr.  | 8,162  | 8,371  | 9,948  | 9,864  | 10,078 | 10,455 | 8,852  | 13,402 |
| May   | 8,462  | 9,069  | 10,638 | 10,252 | 10,801 | 11,179 | 12,537 | 13,103 |
| June  | 9,644  | 10,248 | 11,253 | 12,282 | 12,950 | 10,588 | 14,759 | 14,933 |
| July  | 10,466 | 11,030 | 11,424 | 11,637 | 12,222 | 10,794 | 13,667 | 14,147 |
| Aug.  | 10,748 | 10,882 | 11,391 | 11,577 | 12,246 | 12,770 | 13,731 | 14,057 |
| Sept. | 9,963  | 10,333 | 10,665 | 12,417 | 13,281 | 13,812 | 15,110 | 16,234 |
| Oct.  | 8,194  | 9,109  | 9,396  | 9,637  | 10,366 | 10,857 | 12,185 | 12,389 |
| Nov.  | 6,848  | 7,685  | 7,775  | 8,094  | 8,730  | 9,290  | 10,645 | 11,595 |
| Dec.  | 7,027  | 7,602  | 7,933  | 9,280  | 9,614  | 10,925 | 12,161 | 12,772 |

*Source:* Kendall and Ord (1990).

**FIGURE 12.3**

JMP IN plot of the United Kingdom airlines data in Table 12.5

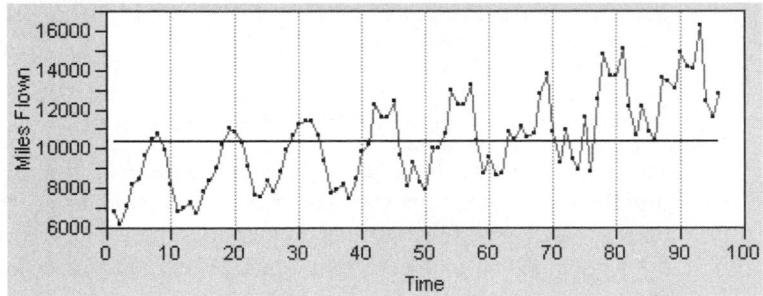

Here $P_{1t}$ and $P_{2t}$ are called pulse variables and are defined as follows:

$$P_{1t} = \begin{cases} 1 & \text{if } t = 66 \text{ or } 67 \text{ (June or July 1968)} \\ 0 & \text{otherwise} \end{cases}$$

$$P_{2t} = \begin{cases} 1 & \text{if } t = 76 \text{ (April 1969)} \\ 0 & \text{otherwise} \end{cases}$$

Therefore, $C_1$ (which is negative) represents the decrease in the expected number of United Kingdom airline miles in June 1968 (July 1968) that is associated with the pilot strike in that month. Note that the decrease in June 1968 is assumed to be the same as the decrease in July 1968. Furthermore, $C_2$ (which is negative) represents the decrease in the expected number of United Kingdom airline miles in April 1969 that is associated with the pilot strike in that month.

**Step 3:** The modified model is

$$z_t = \delta + C_1 z_t(P_1) + C_2 z_t(P_2) + \varepsilon_t$$

where

$$z_t = (1 - B^{12})y_t \qquad z_t(P_1) = (1 - B^{12})P_{1t} \qquad z_t(P_2) = (1 - B^{12})P_{2t}$$

and

$$(1 - \phi_1 B - \phi_3 B^3)\varepsilon_t = a_t$$

A constant term $\delta$ is included in the modified model because this term was included in the model of step 1. Furthermore, the autoregressive operator for $\varepsilon_t$ follows from the model of step 1. In the exercises the reader will interpret the SAS output of estimation, diagnostic checking, and forecasting for this model.

We next note that instead of starting with step 1, it can sometimes be useful to begin with step 2 and find a regression model describing the intervention. We then fit this model to the data by assuming the error terms are statistically independent and use the SAC and SPAC of the model's residuals (that is, the RSAC and the RSPAC) to find a Box–Jenkins model describing the error terms of a time series regression model. We have previously used such a procedure in Section 11.3 to find a Box–Jenkins model describing the error terms of a time series regression model.

## More General Intervention Models

The functions $CS_t$, $C_1P_{1t}$, and $C_2P_{2t}$ used in the previous examples are called **response functions** for modeling interventions. Figure 12.4 summarizes six useful response functions and the types of intervention responses that they imply. To understand these functions, suppose that an intervention occurs at time $T$. The first three response functions employ the step function

$$S_t = \begin{cases} 0 & \text{if } t < T \text{ (before the intervention)} \\ 1 & \text{if } t \geq T \text{ (at and after the intervention)} \end{cases}$$

The first function in Figure 12.4, $CS_t$, was used in Example 12.5 to model the abrupt and permanent decrease in the number of monthly average calls per day associated with the new directory assistance charge. If we thought that the decrease in the number of monthly average calls was gradual and led to a permanent change (excluding such factors as population growth), we would utilize the second function, $[C/(1 - \delta B)]S_t$. Therefore, the model would be

$$z_t = \frac{C}{(1 - \delta B)} z_t(S) + \varepsilon_t$$

**FIGURE 12.4**
Forms of intervention responses

| Type of Response | Response Function | Typical Diagram |
|---|---|---|
| Abrupt start and permanent effect | $CS_t$ | 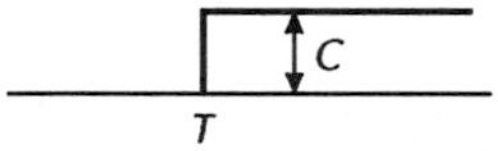 |
| Gradual start and permanent effect | $\dfrac{C}{1 - \delta B} S_t$ | 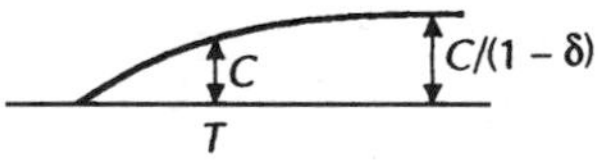 |
| Linearly changing without limit | $\dfrac{C}{1 - B} S_t$ | 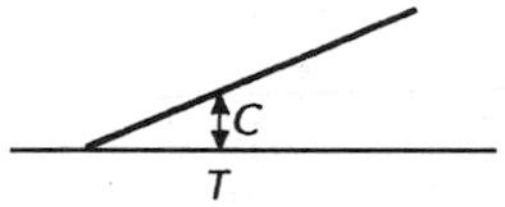 |
| Abrupt start and abrupt decay | $CP_t$ | 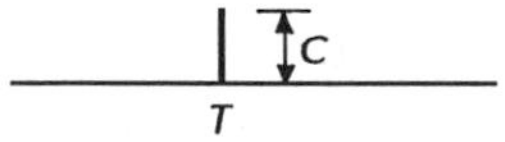 |
| Abrupt start and gradual decay | $\dfrac{C}{1 - \delta B} P_t$ |  |
| Abrupt start and gradual decay to a permanent level | $\dfrac{C_1}{1 - \delta B} P_t + \dfrac{C_2}{1 - B} P_t$ | 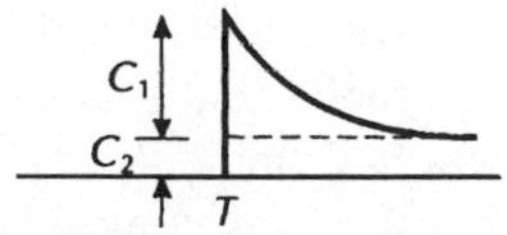 |

**FIGURE 12.5** SAS output of estimation for the model $z_t = [C/(1 - \delta B)] z_t(S) + \varepsilon_t$

<pre>
                    Conditional Least Squares Estimation

                        Standard                  Approx
Parameter    Estimate    Error      t Value    Pr > |t|    Lag    Variable
MA1,1         0.83756    0.04695     17.84      <.0001      12       y
SCALE1     -399.67998   23.08069    -17.32      <.0001       0       S
DEN1,1      -0.0068788   0.05792     -0.12      0.9056       1       S
</pre>

where $z_t$, $z_t(S)$, and $\varepsilon_t$ are the same as defined in Example 12.5. In order to give meaning to the notation $C/(1 - \delta B)$, multiply both sides of the equation for the model by $(1 - \delta B)$. Then we can see that our model is equivalent to the model

$$(1 - \delta B)z_t = Cz_t(S) + (1 - \delta B)\varepsilon_t$$

or

$$z_t - \delta z_{t-1} = Cz_t(S) + \varepsilon_t - \delta \varepsilon_{t-1}$$

or

$$z_t = Cz_t(S) + \delta z_{t-1} + \varepsilon_t - \delta \varepsilon_{t-1}$$

Figure 12.5 gives the SAS output of estimation when the model

$$z_t = \frac{C}{(1 - \delta B)} z_t(S) + \varepsilon_t$$

is used for the directory assistance data in Table 12.4. The approximate $p$-value associated with the $t$-statistic for $\delta$ is .9056 (see DEN1,1 in Figure 12.5) and indicates that $\delta$ should not be retained in the model. Therefore, our original model $z_t = Cz_t(S) + \varepsilon_t$ seems best. This result agrees with Figure 12.1, which shows the decrease in the number of monthly average calls to be abrupt rather than gradual. The third function in Figure 12.4, $[C/(1 - B)]S_t$, would be used if we thought that the charge decreased the number of calls linearly and without limit over time. This certainly is not the case. The last three response functions in Figure 12.4 employ the pulse function

$$P_t = \begin{cases} 0 & \text{if } t \neq T \\ 1 & \text{if } t = T \end{cases}$$

The fourth function, $CP_t$, was used in Example 12.6 to model the effect of the pilot strikes. This function assumes that the effect of a strike in a given month decreased the airline miles only in that month. On the other hand, the strike could cause a loss of goodwill. This could result in a decrease in mileage extending over several months, followed by a gradual (and ultimately complete) recovery in mileage. In this case we would use the fifth function, $[C/(1 - \delta B)]P_t$. If we thought that the gradual recovery of the mileage did not result in a complete recovery (some miles are permanently lost to rival carriers), we would use the sixth function

$$\frac{C_1}{1 - \delta B} P_t + \frac{C_2}{1 - B} P_t$$

# 12.3 BUILDING A TRANSFER FUNCTION MODEL

In this section we denote the $t$th values of the output series and the input series by the symbols $y_t$ and $x_t$. To illustrate the use of transfer functions, we analyze data presented by Makridakis, Wheelwright, and McGee (1983). These data consist of $n = 100$ observations of the two variables

$y_t$ = total sales (in thousands of cases) in month $t$

$x_t$ = advertising expenditure (in thousands of dollars) in month $t$

The data are presented in Table 12.6. They provide a good example of transfer function modeling.

The **general transfer function model** is

$$z_t = \mu + \frac{Cw(B)}{\delta(B)} B^b z_t^{(x)} + \varepsilon_t$$

Here

1. $z_t$ represents the stationary $y_t$ values, and $z_t^{(x)}$ represents the stationary $x_t$ values. It can be verified that *first-order regular differencing* makes both the $y_t$ values and the $x_t$ values in Table 12.6 stationary. Therefore, $z_t = y_t - y_{t-1}$ and $z_t^{(x)} = x_t - x_{t-1}$. In general, higher-order differencing may need to be applied to either the input series or the output series or both in order to achieve stationarity. In addition, the input series and the output series do not necessarily need to be differenced in the same way.

2. $\mu$ is a constant term that should be included if, when it is included in the model, the absolute $t$-value associated with its least squares point estimate is greater than 2.

3. $C$ is a scale parameter that must be estimated.

4. $b$ is the number of periods before the $x_t$ values begin to affect the $y_t$ values. To determine $b$ and tentatively identify other components of the transfer function model, we calculate the **sample cross-correlation function** between the $x_t$ and $y_t$ values. To do this, we first **prewhiten** these values. The first step in the prewhitening process is to find a Box–Jenkins model describing the $x_t$ values.

**TABLE 12.6** Monthly Total Sales (1000s of Cases) and Advertising Expenditures ($1000s)

| t | Advertising Input $x_t$ | Sales Output $y_t$ | t | Advertising Input $x_t$ | Sales Output $y_t$ | t | Advertising Input $x_t$ | Sales Output $y_t$ |
|---|---|---|---|---|---|---|---|---|
| 0 | 116.44 | 202.66 | 34 | 128.75 | 258.27 | 67 | 128.19 | 252.07 |
| 1 | 119.58 | 232.91 | 35 | 127.09 | 242.89 | 68 | 134.79 | 269.86 |
| 2 | 125.74 | 272.07 | 36 | 114.55 | 255.98 | 69 | 128.93 | 291.62 |
| 3 | 124.55 | 290.97 | 37 | 113.26 | 278.53 | 70 | 121.63 | 314.06 |
| 4 | 122.35 | 299.09 | 38 | 111.51 | 273.21 | 71 | 125.43 | 318.56 |
| 5 | 120.44 | 296.95 | 39 | 111.73 | 246.37 | 72 | 126.80 | 289.11 |
| 6 | 123.24 | 279.49 | 40 | 114.08 | 221.10 | 73 | 131.56 | 255.88 |
| 7 | 127.99 | 255.75 | 41 | 114.32 | 210.41 | 74 | 126.43 | 249.81 |
| 8 | 121.19 | 242.78 | 42 | 115.03 | 222.19 | 75 | 116.19 | 268.82 |
| 9 | 118.00 | 255.34 | 43 | 124.28 | 245.27 | 76 | 112.72 | 288.24 |
| 10 | 121.81 | 271.58 | 44 | 132.69 | 262.58 | 77 | 109.53 | 281.26 |
| 11 | 126.54 | 268.27 | 45 | 134.64 | 283.25 | 78 | 110.38 | 250.92 |
| 12 | 129.85 | 260.51 | 46 | 133.28 | 311.12 | 79 | 107.31 | 222.26 |
| 13 | 122.65 | 266.34 | 47 | 128.00 | 326.28 | 80 | 93.59 | 209.94 |
| 14 | 121.64 | 281.24 | 48 | 129.97 | 322.04 | 81 | 89.80 | 213.30 |
| 15 | 127.24 | 286.19 | 49 | 128.35 | 295.37 | 82 | 88.70 | 207.19 |
| 16 | 132.35 | 271.97 | 50 | 123.90 | 266.69 | 83 | 86.64 | 186.13 |
| 17 | 130.86 | 265.01 | 51 | 122.45 | 253.07 | 84 | 89.26 | 171.20 |
| 18 | 122.90 | 274.44 | 52 | 122.85 | 249.12 | 85 | 96.51 | 170.33 |
| 19 | 117.15 | 291.81 | 53 | 129.28 | 253.59 | 86 | 107.35 | 183.69 |
| 20 | 109.47 | 290.91 | 54 | 129.77 | 262.13 | 87 | 110.35 | 211.30 |
| 21 | 114.34 | 264.95 | 55 | 127.78 | 279.66 | 88 | 102.66 | 252.66 |
| 22 | 123.72 | 228.40 | 56 | 134.29 | 302.92 | 89 | 97.56 | 286.20 |
| 23 | 130.33 | 209.33 | 57 | 140.61 | 310.77 | 90 | 98.06 | 279.45 |
| 24 | 133.17 | 231.69 | 58 | 133.64 | 307.83 | 91 | 103.93 | 237.06 |
| 25 | 134.25 | 281.56 | 59 | 135.45 | 313.19 | 92 | 115.66 | 193.40 |
| 26 | 129.75 | 327.16 | 60 | 130.93 | 312.80 | 93 | 112.91 | 180.79 |
| 27 | 130.05 | 344.24 | 61 | 118.65 | 301.23 | 94 | 116.89 | 215.73 |
| 28 | 133.42 | 324.74 | 62 | 120.34 | 286.64 | 95 | 116.84 | 264.98 |
| 29 | 135.16 | 289.36 | 63 | 120.35 | 257.17 | 96 | 109.55 | 294.07 |
| 30 | 130.89 | 262.92 | 64 | 117.09 | 229.60 | 97 | 110.63 | 299.08 |
| 31 | 123.48 | 263.65 | 65 | 117.56 | 227.62 | 98 | 111.32 | 271.10 |
| 32 | 118.46 | 276.38 | 66 | 121.69 | 238.21 | 99 | 117.09 | 230.56 |
| 33 | 122.11 | 276.34 | | | | | | |

*Source: Forecasting: Methods and Applications* by S. Makridakis, S. C. Wheelwright, and V. E. McGee, Wiley, New York, 1983.

It can be verified that both the SAC and SPAC of the first-order regular differences of the $x_t$ values die down fairly quickly. By Guideline 5 in Table 12.1, we tentatively identify the model

$$(1 - \phi_1^{(x)}B)z_t^{(x)} = (1 - \theta_1^{(x)}B)a_t \quad \text{where} \quad z_t^{(x)} = x_t - x_{t-1}$$

This model is found to be adequate, and the least squares point estimates of $\phi_1^{(x)}$ and $\theta_1^{(x)}$ are found to be $\hat{\phi}_1^{(x)} = -.3003$ and $\hat{\theta}_1^{(x)} = -.7871$. If we solve the model for $a_t$, we obtain

$$a_t = \frac{(1 - \phi_1^{(x)}B)}{(1 - \theta_1^{(x)}B)} z_t^{(x)}$$

By substituting the least squares estimates $\hat{\phi}_1^{(x)} = -.3003$ and $\hat{\theta}_1^{(x)} = -.7871$ for $\phi_1^{(x)}$ and $\theta_1^{(x)}$, we compute the prewhitened $x_t$ values. We represent these prewhitened $x_t$ values by $\alpha_t$ and thus obtain the equation

$$\alpha_t = \frac{(1 + .3003B)}{(1 + .7871B)} z_t^{(x)}$$

To calculate prewhitened $y_t$ values, we substitute $z_t = y_t - y_{t-1}$ for $z_t^{(x)} = x_t - x_{t-1}$ in the previous equation. We represent these prewhitened $y_t$ values by $\beta_t$ and thus obtain the equation

$$\beta_t = \frac{(1 + .3003B)}{(1 + .7871)} z_t$$

The equation for $\alpha_t$, the prewhitened $x_t$ values, can be written in the equivalent form

$$(1 + .7871B)\alpha_t = (1 + .3003B)z_t^{(x)}$$

or

$$\alpha_t = -.7871\alpha_{t-1} + z_t^{(x)} + .3003z_{t-1}^{(x)}$$
$$= -.7871\alpha_{t-1} + (x_t - x_{t-1}) + .3003(x_{t-1} - x_{t-2})$$

Similarly, the equation for $\beta_t$, the prewhitened $y_t$ values, can be written in the equivalent form

$$\beta_t = -.7871\beta_{t-1} + (y_t - y_{t-1}) + .3003(y_{t-1} - y_{t-2})$$

Figure 12.6 gives the SAS output of the **sample cross-correlation function** (the **SCC**) between the $\alpha_t$ values and the $\beta_t$ values. The SCC is a listing, for $k = -10, -9, \ldots, -1, 0, 1, \ldots, 10$, of the values of

$$r_k(\alpha_t, \beta_t) = \frac{\sum\limits_{t=b}^{n-k} (\alpha_t - \bar{\alpha})(\beta_{t+k} - \bar{\beta})}{\left[\sum\limits_{t=b}^{n} (\alpha_t - \bar{\alpha})^2\right]^{1/2} \left[\sum\limits_{t=b}^{n} (\beta_t - \bar{\beta})^2\right]^{1/2}}$$

where

$$\bar{\alpha} = \frac{\sum\limits_{t-b}^{n} \alpha_t}{n - b + 1} \quad \text{and} \quad \bar{\beta} = \frac{\sum\limits_{t=b}^{n} \beta_t}{n - b + 1}$$

**FIGURE 12.6** SAS output of the SCC between the prewhitened values of advertising expenditure and the prewhitened values of sales

```
                  Correlation of y and x

       Period(s) of Differencing                    1
       Number of Observations                      99
       Observation(s) eliminated by differencing    1
       Variance of transformed series y       271.7644
       Variance of transformed series x        21.91755

            Both series have been prewhitened.


                      Crosscorrelations

Lag    Covariance    Correlation    -1 9 8 7 6 5 4 3 2 1 0 1 2 3 4 5 6 7 8 9 1

-10     1.762407        0.06171     !                   .  !*  .                !
 -9     1.901889        0.02464     !                   .  !   .                !
 -8     1.366826        0.01771     !                   .  !   .                !
 -7    -4.748175       -.06152      !                   . *!   .                !
 -6    -4.222908       -.05472      !                   . *!   .                !
 -5    -7.902604       -.10239      !                   . **!  .                !
 -4    -6.045174       -.07833      !                   . **!  .                !
 -3     4.666570        0.06047     !                   .  !*  .                !
 -2     6.975240        0.09038     !                   .  !** .                !
 -1    -3.357529       -.04350      !                   . *!   .                !
  0    -9.157557       -.11866      !                   . **!  .                !
  1    -7.390464       -.09576      !                   . **!  .                !
  2    26.271432        0.34040     !                   .  !*******             !
  3    49.041253        0.63543     !                   .  !*************       !
  4    22.236550        0.28812     !                   .  !******             !
  5   -14.682423       -.19024      !               ****!  .                    !
  6   -35.866691       -.46473      !        *********!  .                      !
  7   -31.123249       -.40327      !         ********!  .                      !
  8    -2.799674       -.03628      !                   . *!  .                 !
  9    10.285329        0.13327     !                   .  !***.                !
 10     8.423270        0.10914     !                   .  !** .                !
```

Here $r_k(\alpha_t, \beta_t)$ is called the **sample cross-correlation** between the $\alpha_t$ values and $\beta_t$ values at lag $k$ and is a measure of the linear relationship between the values of $\alpha_t$ and the values of $\beta_{t+k}$.

To interpret the SCC, we first make sure that there are no spikes at negative lags. If there were, this would mean that past $y_t$ (sales) values affect future $x_t$ (advertising) values. In this case, we could not use the transfer function methodology of this section. No such spikes exist, and thus we continue the analysis by identifying the lag where the first spike occurs in the SCC. This lag is $b$, the number of periods before the $x_t$ values begin to affect the $y_t$ values. Figure 12.6 tells us that $b = 2$, which says that it takes two months for advertising to affect sales.

5.
$$w(B) = (1 - w_1 B - w_2 B^2 - \cdots - w_s B^s)$$

is called the $z_t^{(x)}$ **operator of order s,** where $s$ represents the number of past $z_t^{(x)}$ values influencing $z_t$. Practice has shown that the first spike in the SCC will be followed (possibly after one or more lags) by a "clear dying-down pattern" that may be exponential or sinusoidal. The value $s$ is set equal to the number of lags that reside between the first spike in the SCC and the beginning of the clear dying-down pattern. In our example, if we examine Figure 12.6, the value of $s$ is not obvious. After the first spike in the SCC (at lag 2), a sinusoidal dying-down pattern appears to begin. Whether the spikes at lags 3 and 4 are part of the pattern is questionable. If both of these spikes are part of the clear dying-down pattern, then $s = 0$. However, if the spike at lag 4 is part of this pattern but the spike at lag 3 is not, then $s = 1$. If neither of these spikes is part of the pattern, then $s = 2$. Here we will (somewhat arbitrarily) set $s = 2$. This conclusion implies that we should use the operator

$$w(B) = (1 - w_1 B - w_2 B^2)$$

**6.**
$$\delta(B) = (1 - \delta_1 B - \delta_2 B^2 - \cdots - \delta_r B^r)$$

is called the $z_t$ **operator of order r,** where $r$ intuitively represents the number of its own past values to which $z_t$ is related. Practice has shown that it is reasonable to determine $r$ by examining the manner in which the sample cross-correlations die down at lags after lag $(b + s)$. Specifically, if the sample cross-correlations die down in a damped exponential fashion, it is reasonable to set $r = 1$. If the sample cross-correlations die down in a damped sine-wave fashion, it is reasonable to set $r = 2$. Since in Figure 12.6 the sample cross-correlations die down in a damped sine-wave fashion at lags after lag $(b + s) = (2 + 2) = 4$, it is reasonable to set $r = 2$. This implies that we should use the operator $\delta(B) = (1 - \delta_1 B - \delta_2 B^2)$.

**7.** $\varepsilon_t$ is an error term.

Inserting the appropriate operators into the general model

$$z_t = \mu + \frac{Cw(B)}{\delta(B)} B^b z_t^{(x)} + \varepsilon_t$$

and arbitrarily excluding $\mu$, we are led to tentatively consider the model

$$z_t = \frac{C(1 - w_1 B - w_2 B^2)}{(1 - \delta_1 B - \delta_2 B^2)} B^2 z_t^{(x)} + \varepsilon_t$$

where

$$z_t = y_t - y_{t-1} \quad \text{and} \quad z_t^{(x)} = x_t - x_{t-1}$$

Figure 12.7 is the SAS output of estimation and diagnostic checking for this model, where we assume that the error terms are statistically independent. In addition to the RSAC and the RSPAC, this output gives the **sample cross-correlation function of the residuals with the values of $x_t$** (denoted RSCC). Since Figure 12.7(b) indicates that

**FIGURE 12.7** SAS output of estimation and diagnostic checking for the model

$$z_t = \frac{C(1 - w_1 B - w_2 B^2)}{(1 - \delta_1 B - \delta_2 B^2)} B^2 z_t^{(x)} + \varepsilon_t \quad \text{where} \quad z_t = y_t - y_{t-1} \quad \text{and} \quad z_t^{(x)} = x_t - x_{t-1}$$

| Parameter | Estimate | Standard Error | t Value | Approx Pr > \|t\| | Lag | Variable |
|---|---|---|---|---|---|---|
| SCALE1 | 1.29581 | 0.04197 | 30.87 | <.0001 | 0 | x |
| NUM1,1 | -0.46439 | 0.06450 | -7.20 | <.0001 | 1 | x |
| NUM1,2 | 0.62171 | 0.06172 | 10.07 | <.0001 | 2 | x |
| DEN1,1 | 1.20637 | 0.0071342 | 169.10 | <.0001 | 1 | x |
| DEN1,2 | -0.70507 | 0.0063110 | -111.72 | <.0001 | 2 | x |

(a) Estimation

Crosscorrelation Check of Residuals with Input x

| To Lag | Chi-Square | DF | Pr > ChiSq | | | Crosscorrelations | | | |
|---|---|---|---|---|---|---|---|---|---|
| 5 | 1.84 | 1 | 0.1753 | 0.024 | -0.108 | -0.025 | 0.052 | 0.030 | -0.063 |
| 11 | 2.43 | 7 | 0.9322 | -0.015 | -0.027 | -0.045 | -0.060 | -0.006 | 0.003 |
| 17 | 4.41 | 13 | 0.9859 | -0.054 | 0.097 | 0.046 | 0.010 | 0.080 | -0.035 |
| 23 | 6.11 | 19 | 0.9977 | -0.010 | 0.006 | -0.007 | 0.007 | 0.003 | -0.136 |

(b) The RSCC

Autocorrelation Check of Residuals

| To Lag | Chi-Square | DF | Pr > ChiSq | | | Autocorrelations | | | |
|---|---|---|---|---|---|---|---|---|---|
| 6 | 27.94 | 6 | <.0001 | 0.363 | -0.154 | -0.186 | -0.230 | -0.208 | -0.051 |
| 12 | 32.49 | 12 | 0.0012 | 0.022 | -0.039 | -0.021 | 0.113 | 0.126 | 0.107 |
| 18 | 45.16 | 18 | 0.0004 | 0.005 | -0.063 | -0.235 | -0.077 | 0.179 | 0.119 |
| 24 | 48.92 | 24 | 0.0019 | 0.038 | -0.080 | -0.137 | -0.044 | -0.032 | -0.037 |

Autocorrelation Plot of Residuals

| Lag | Covariance | Correlation | -1 9 8 7 6 5 4 3 2 1 0 1 2 3 4 5 6 7 8 9 1 | Std Error |
|---|---|---|---|---|
| 0 | 3.863841 | 1.00000 | \|********************\| | 0 |
| 1 | 1.403255 | 0.36318 | \|******* | 0.104257 |
| 2 | -0.593352 | -.15357 | . ***\| | 0.117204 |
| 3 | -0.710540 | -.18597 | .****\| | 0.119371 |
| 4 | -0.889331 | -.23017 | *****\| | 0.122480 |
| 5 | -0.805354 | -.20843 | .****\| | 0.127095 |
| 6 | -0.196015 | -.05073 | . *\| | 0.130757 |
| 7 | 0.084775 | 0.02194 | \| | 0.130971 |
| 8 | -0.151466 | -.03920 | . *\| | 0.131011 |
| 9 | -0.080257 | -.02077 | \| | 0.131139 |
| 10 | 0.436151 | 0.11288 | \|** | 0.131174 |

(c) The RSAC

Partial Autocorrelations

| Lag | Correlation | -1 9 8 7 6 5 4 3 2 1 0 1 2 3 4 5 6 7 8 9 1 |
|---|---|---|
| 1 | 0.36318 | . \|******* |
| 2 | -0.32883 | *******\| . |
| 3 | 0.00978 | . \| . |
| 4 | -0.25136 | *****\| . |
| 5 | -0.08566 | . **\| . |
| 6 | -0.04182 | . *\| . |
| 7 | -0.07664 | . **\| . |
| 8 | -0.13305 | .***\| . |
| 9 | -0.03943 | . *\| . |
| 10 | 0.06876 | . \|* . |

(d) The RSPAC

the *p*-values associated with the values of $Q^*$ are large, we conclude that the prewhitened $x_t$ values are statistically independent of the error term $\varepsilon_t$. This is a necessary condition for the validity of transfer function modeling. However, since the *p*-values associated with the $Q^*$ pertaining to the RSAC are extremely small, we conclude that the error terms are statistically dependent.

To find a model describing $\varepsilon_t$, note in Figure 12.7(c) and (d) that at the nonseasonal level the RSAC dies down quickly and the RSPAC has spikes at lags 1 and 2 and cuts off after lag 2 (we ignore a spike at lag 4). By Guideline 2 in Table 12.1, a tentative model describing the error term $\varepsilon_t$ is

$$(1 - \phi_1 B - \phi_2 B^2)\varepsilon_t = a_t$$

or

$$\varepsilon_t = \phi_1 \varepsilon_{t-1} + \phi_2 \varepsilon_{t-2} + a_t$$

Figure 12.8 presents the SAS output of estimation, diagnostic checking, and forecasting for the transfer function model, assuming that this model describes $\varepsilon_t$. The RSCC and RSAC indicate that the model is adequate. Furthermore, if we add $\mu$ to the model the *t*-statistic associated with its least squares estimate indicates that it is not important. Therefore, we conclude that the transfer function model should not include $\mu$ and is a reasonable final model. In order to obtain the forecasts, we can either supply SAS with future $x_t$ values or have SAS use the model describing $x_t$ to forecast future $x_t$ values. Here we have chosen the latter option.

We consider the following example, which was adapted from Abraham and Ledolter (1983).

**EXAMPLE 12.7**   Hillmer and Tiao (1979) analyzed U.S. monthly housing starts $y_t$ and houses sold $x_t$ for the years 1965 to 1974.

**Identification of a Model Describing $x_t$ and Prewhitening of $x_t$ and $y_t$**

The model

$$z_t^{(x)} = (1 - \theta_1^{(x)}B)(1 - \theta_{1,12}^{(x)}B^{12})a_t$$

where

$$z_t^{(x)} = x_t - x_{t-1} - x_{t-12} + x_{t-13}$$

adequately describes the $x_t$ values, and we can achieve stationary $y_t$ values by using the transformation

$$z_t = y_t - y_{t-1} - y_{t-12} + y_{t-13}$$

Furthermore, since

$$a_t = \frac{1}{(1 - \theta_1^{(x)}B)(1 - \theta_{1,12}^{(x)}B^{12})} z_t^{(x)}$$

**FIGURE 12.8** SAS output of estimation, diagnostic checking, and forecasting for the model

$$z_t = \frac{C(1 - w_1B - w_2B^2)}{(1 - \delta_1B - \delta_2B^2)} B^2 z_t^{(x)} + \varepsilon_t$$

where   $\varepsilon_t = \phi_1\varepsilon_{t-1} + \phi_2\varepsilon_{t-2} + a_t$,   $z_t = y_t - y_{t-1}$,   and   $z_t^{(x)} = x_t - x_{t-1}$

Conditional Least Squares Estimation

| Parameter | Estimate | Standard Error | t Value | Approx Pr > \|t\| | Lag | Variable | Shift |
|-----------|----------|----------------|---------|-------------------|-----|----------|-------|
| AR1,1 | 0.48651 | 0.10250 | 4.75 | <.0001 | 1 | y | 0 |
| AR1,2 | -0.34014 | 0.10369 | -3.28 | 0.0015 | 2 | y | 0 |
| SCALE1 | 1.31547 | 0.03874 | 33.96 | <.0001 | 0 | x | 2 |
| NUM1,1 | -0.44079 | 0.05478 | -8.05 | <.0001 | 1 | x | 2 |
| NUM1,2 | 0.59950 | 0.05181 | 11.57 | <.0001 | 2 | x | 2 |
| DEN1,1 | 1.20697 | 0.0089842 | 134.34 | <.0001 | 1 | x | 2 |
| DEN1,2 | -0.70657 | 0.0076019 | -92.95 | <.0001 | 2 | x | 2 |

(a) Estimation

| To Lag | Chi-Square | DF | Pr > ChiSq |   | To Lag | Chi-Square | DF | Pr > ChiSq |
|--------|-----------|-----|-----------|---|--------|-----------|-----|-----------|
| 5 | 1.41 | 1 | 0.2343 |   | 6 | 7.70 | 4 | 0.1033 |
| 11 | 2.30 | 7 | 0.9417 |   | 12 | 11.54 | 10 | 0.3170 |
| 17 | 6.36 | 13 | 0.9319 |   | 18 | 23.53 | 16 | 0.1002 |
| 23 | 8.81 | 19 | 0.9765 |   | 24 | 25.99 | 22 | 0.2522 |

(b) The RSCC                                         (c) The RSAC

Forecasts for variable y

| Obs | Forecast | Std Error | 95% Confidence Limits | |
|-----|----------|-----------|------------|----------|
| 101 | 209.1095 | 1.7462 | 205.6870 | 212.5319 |
| 102 | 218.9218 | 3.1284 | 212.7903 | 225.0533 |
| 103 | 252.4898 | 7.3708 | 238.0433 | 266.9364 |
| 104 | 282.0147 | 20.9486 | 240.9563 | 323.0731 |
| 105 | 291.4291 | 34.8876 | 223.0505 | 359.8076 |
| 106 | 282.7287 | 43.8909 | 196.7042 | 368.7532 |
| 107 | 265.3541 | 48.1607 | 170.9609 | 359.7473 |
| 108 | 250.5904 | 49.7221 | 153.1369 | 348.0439 |
| 109 | 245.0200 | 50.4009 | 146.2360 | 343.8040 |
| 110 | 248.7343 | 51.1069 | 148.5666 | 348.9020 |

(d) Forecasting of $y_{101}$ through $y_{110}$ where future values of $x_t$ are forecasted by the model
$(1 - \phi_1^{(x)}B)z_t^{(x)} - (1 - \theta_1^{(x)}B)a_t$   where   $z_t^{(x)} = x_t - x_{t-1}$

and since the least squares point estimates of $\theta_1^{(x)}$ and $\theta_{1,12}^{(y)}$ are $\hat{\theta}_1^{(x)} = .20$ and $\hat{\theta}_{1,12}^{(y)} = .83$, we calculate prewhitened $x_t$ values and prewhitened $y_t$ values by the equations

$$\alpha_t = \frac{1}{(1 - .20B)(1 - .83B^{12})} z_t^{(x)}$$

and

$$\beta_t = \frac{1}{(1 - .20B)(1 - .83B^{12})} z_t$$

**FIGURE 12.9**
The SCC

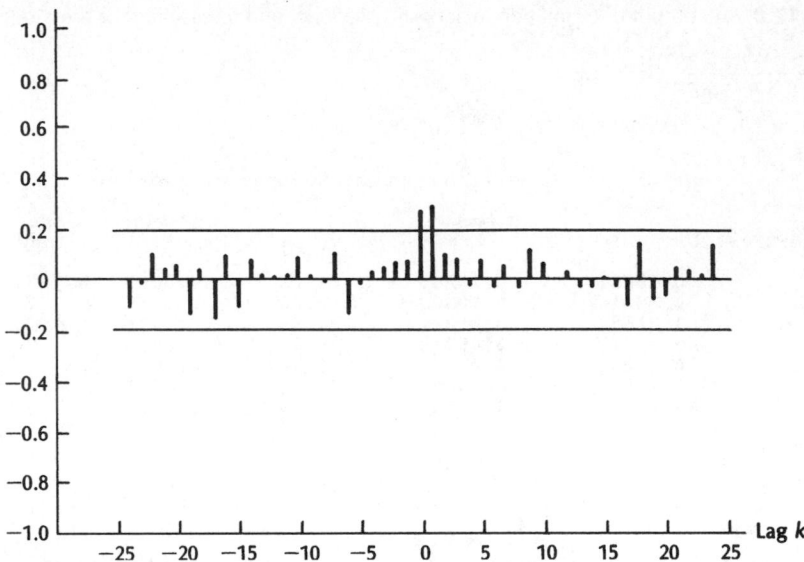

### Calculation of the SCC and Identification of a Preliminary Transfer Function Model

The SCC is presented in Figure 12.9. We note that

1. $b = 0$ is the lag at which we encounter the first spike in the SCC (which implies that the number of houses sold in a month is related to the number of housing starts in the same month).

2. The SCC appears to be dying down in a damped exponential fashion after lag 1. Since the spike at lag 1 does not appear to be part of this clear dying-down pattern, it is reasonable to set $s = 1$. Thus we should use the operator $w(B) = (1 - w_1B)$.

3. Since the sample cross-correlations die down in a damped exponential fashion at lags after lag $(b + s) = (0 + 1) = 1$, it is reasonable to set $r = 1$. This conclusion implies that we should use the operator $\delta(B) = (1 - \delta_1B)$.

Inserting the appropriate operators into the general model

$$z_t = \mu + \frac{Cw(B)}{\delta(B)} B^b z_t^{(x)} + \varepsilon_t$$

and arbitrarily excluding $\mu$, we are led to tentatively consider the model

$$z_t = \frac{C(1 - w_1B)}{(1 - \delta_1B)} B^0 z_t^{(x)} + \varepsilon_t$$

where

$$z_t = y_t - y_{t-1} - y_{t-12} + y_{t-13} \quad \text{and} \quad z_t^{(x)} = x_t - x_{t-1} - x_{t-12} + x_{t-13}$$

**FIGURE 12.10** The RSAC resulting from the model

$$z_t = \frac{C(1 - w_1 B)}{(1 - \delta_1 B)} B^0 z_t^{(x)} + \varepsilon_t$$

where   $z_t = y_t - y_{t-1} - y_{t-12} + y_{t-13}$   and   $z_t^{(x)} = x_t - x_{t-1} - x_{t-12} + x_{t-13}$

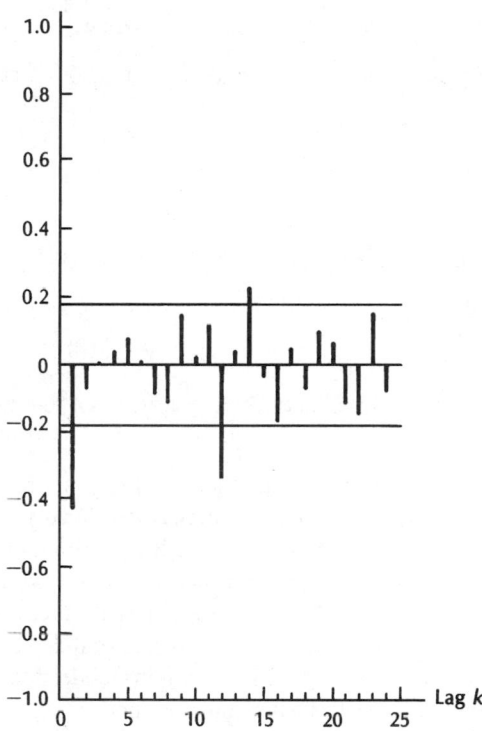

## Identification of a Model Describing $\varepsilon_t$ and of a Final Transfer Function Model

The RSAC for the tentative model is given in Figure 12.10. The p-values associated with the values of $Q^*$ pertaining to the RSAC can be calculated to be very small, indicating that the error terms $\varepsilon_1, \varepsilon_2, \ldots$ are statistically dependent. To find a model describing $\varepsilon_t$ (which represents the residuals), note that

1.   At the *nonseasonal level* the RSAC has a spike at lag 1 and cuts off after lag 1. This implies, by Guideline 1 or 3 in Table 12.1, that we should use the nonseasonal moving average operator of order 1

$$\theta_1(B) = (1 - \theta_1 B)$$

2.   At the *seasonal level* the RSAC has spikes at lags 12 and 14 and either cuts off after lag 14 or (possibly) dies down quickly. Although the behavior of the RSAC is not obvious here, it might be reasonable to conclude that the RSAC cuts off after

lag 14. If we make this assumption, by Guideline 6 or 8 in Table 12.2, we should use the seasonal moving average operator of order 1

$$\theta_1(B^{12}) = (1 - \theta_{1,12}B^{12})$$

These conclusions imply that the model

$$\varepsilon_t = (1 - \theta_1 B)(1 - \theta_{1,12}B^{12})a_t$$

describes $\varepsilon_t$, which implies that an appropriate final transfer function model would be

$$z_t = \frac{C(1 - w_1 B)}{(1 - \delta_1 B)} B^0 z_t^{(x)} + (1 - \theta_1 B)(1 - \theta_{1,12}B^{12})a_t$$

where

$$z_t = y_t - y_{t-1} - y_{t-12} + y_{t-13} \quad \text{and} \quad z_t^{(x)} = x_t - x_{t-1} - x_{t-12} + x_{t-13}$$

Here future values of $x_t$ are forecasted by the model describing $x_t$

$$z_t^{(x)} = (1 - \theta_1^{(x)}B)(1 - \theta_{1,12}^{(x)}B^{12})a_t$$

Examination of the RSAC, RSPAC, and RSCC indicates that this model is adequate.

To conclude this section, note that if there are two or more independent variables, we use the SCC to identify a transfer function of the form $Cw(B)/\delta(B)$ relating $y_t$ to each independent variable. We next add together the individual transfer functions multiplied by their respective and appropriately differenced independent variables. Then, we fit the resulting model to the appropriately differenced dependent variable, assuming that the model's error terms are statistically independent. The RSAC and RSPAC help us identify an appropriate Box–Jenkins model describing the error terms, and we thereby obtain the final transfer function model.

## Exercises

**12.1** Use the SAC and SPAC in Figure 11.27 (page 522) and the guidelines in Tables 12.1 and 12.2 to tentatively identify a model describing the trade data in Table 11.4.

**12.2** Use the SAC and SPAC in Figure 11.30 (page 527) and the guidelines in Tables 12.1 and 12.2 to tentatively identify a model describing the retail data in Table 11.5.

**12.3** Use the SAC and SPAC in Figure 11.33 (page 530) and the guidelines in Tables 12.1 and 12.2 to tentatively identify a model describing the housing starts data in Figure 11.32.

**12.4** Algebraically expand each of the following models and express $y_t$ as a function of past time series observations and of past and present random shocks.

a. $z_t = (1 - \theta_6 B^6 - \theta_{12}B^{12})a_t$   where   $z_t = y_t - y_{t-1}$

b. $z_t = (1 - \theta_6 B^6)(1 - \theta_{1,12}B^{12})a_t$   where   $z_t = y_t - y_{t-1}$

c. $z_t = (1 - \theta_1 B - \theta_2 B^2)(1 - \theta_{1,12}B^{12})a_t$   where   $z_t = y_t - y_{t-1} - y_{t-12} + y_{t-13}$

d. $(1 - \phi_1 B - \phi_2 B^2)(1 - \phi_{1,12}B^{12})y_t = \delta + a_t$

e. $(1 - \phi_{1,4}B^4)z_t = \delta + (1 - \theta_1 B - \theta_2 B^2)a_t$   where   $z_t = y_t - y_{t-4}$

f. $(1 - \phi_1 B - \phi_2 B^2)z_t = (1 - \theta_{1,12}B^{12})a_t$   where   $z_t = (1 - B^{12})(1 - B)y_t$

Table 12.7 presents the quarterly energy bills for a school system. The energy bills are the combined gas,

## TABLE 12.7 Quarterly Energy Bills for the School System

| Year | Quarter 1 | Quarter 2 | Quarter 3 | Quarter 4 |
|------|-----------|-----------|-----------|-----------|
| 1 | 344.39 ($= y_1$) | 246.63 ($= y_2$) | 131.53 ($= y_3$) | 288.87 ($= y_4$) |
| 2 | 313.45 ($= y_5$) | 189.76 ($= y_6$) | 179.10 ($= y_7$) | 221.10 ($= y_8$) |
| 3 | 246.84 | 209.00 | 51.21 | 133.89 |
| 4 | 277.01 | 197.98 | 50.68 | 218.08 |
| 5 | 365.10 | 207.51 | 54.63 | 214.09 |
| 6 | 267.00 | 230.28 | 230.32 | 426.41 |
| 7 | 467.06 | 306.03 | 253.23 | 279.46 |
| 8 | 336.56 | 196.67 | 152.15 | 319.67 |
| 9 | 440.00 | 315.04 | 216.42 | 339.78 |
| 10 | 434.66 ($= y_{37}$) | 399.66 ($= y_{38}$) | 330.80 ($= y_{39}$) | 539.78 ($= y_{40}$) |

oil, and electric bills for the school system and are expressed in units of $100. A plot of the energy bills is displayed in Figure 12.11 (page 570). **Exercises 12.5 through 12.8 are based on these energy bills.**

**12.5** Figure 12.12 (page 570) presents the SAS output of the SAC and SPAC for the seasonal differences, $z_t = y_t - y_{t-4}$, of the energy bills.
a. Explain why the seasonal differences, $z_t = y_t - y_{t-4}$, can be considered to be stationary.
b. Discuss why the model $(1 - \phi_1 B)z_t = (1 - \theta_{1,4} B^4)a_t$ where $z_t = y_t - y_{t-4}$ is a reasonable tentative model for the energy bills in Table 12.7.

**12.6** Figure 12.13 (page 571) presents the SAS output for the estimation and diagnostic checking for the model

Model 1.   $(1 - \phi_1 B)z_t = (1 - \theta_{1,4} B^4)a_t$   where
$$z_t = y_t - y_{t-4}$$

a. Is this model a reasonable model for forecasting? Explain by checking all characteristics of a good model.
b. Discuss why this model might be improved by one of the following models:

Model 2:   $(1 - \phi_1 B)z_t = (1 - \theta_{1,4} B^4)(1 - \theta_{1,5} B^5)a_t$

or

Model 3:   $(1 - \phi_1 B)z_t = (1 - \theta_{1,4} B^4 - \theta_{1,5} B^5)a_t$

**12.7** Figures 12.14 (page 572) and 12.15 (page 572) present the SAS outputs for the estimation and diagnostic checking for Models 2 and 3 in Exercise 12.6.
a. Explain why Model 2 almost fails the invertibility condition for operator $(1 - \theta_{1,4} B^4)$.

b. Explain why Model 3 fails the invertibility condition for operator $(1 - \theta_{1,4} B^4 - \theta_{1,5} B^5)$.

Note: This lack of invertibility for these two models can be shown to imply that it might be better to forecast the energy bill time series by using a time series regression model (see Exercise 12.8).

**12.8** Consider the quarterly energy bill data in Table 12.7. Since a plot of these data in Figure 12.11 indicates the existence of a quadratic trend and constant seasonal variation, we might consider the regression model

$$y_t = TR_t + SN_t + \varepsilon_t$$
$$= \beta_0 + \beta_1 t + \beta_2 t^2 + \beta_3 Q_1$$
$$+ \beta_4 Q_2 + \beta_5 Q_3 + \varepsilon_t$$

where $Q_1$, $Q_2$, and $Q_3$ are dummy variables. For example,

$$Q_1 = \begin{cases} 1 & \text{if period } t \text{ is Quarter 1} \\ 0 & \text{otherwise} \end{cases}$$

Assuming independent error terms $\varepsilon_1, \varepsilon_2, \ldots$, the SAS output of estimation and diagnostic checking for the model is given in Figure 12.16 (page 573). Since the $p$-values associated with the values of $Q^*$ are extremely small, we reject the adequacy of the model.
a. Using Figures 12.16(b) and (c), discuss why the model

$$(1 - \phi_1 B)\varepsilon_t = (1 - \theta_{1,5} B^5)a_t$$

is a reasonable tentative model for the error terms $\varepsilon_1, \varepsilon_2, \ldots$, in the time series regression model.

(Continues on page 574)

**FIGURE 12.11 (for Exercises 12.5–12.8)** JMP IN plot of quarterly
energy bills for the school system

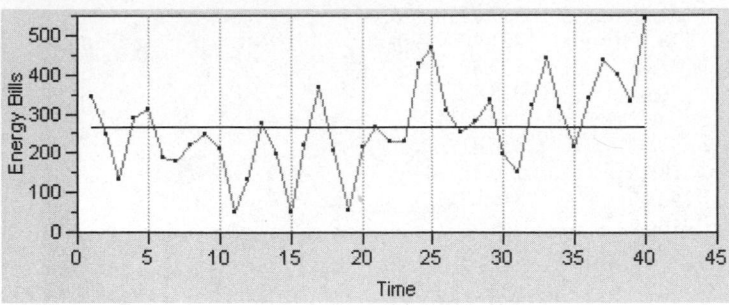

**FIGURE 12.12 (for Exercise 12.5)** SAS output of the SAC and SPAC for energy bill values given by the transformation $z_t = y_t - y_{t-4}$

```
                          Name of Variable = y

              Period(s) of Differencing                  4
              Mean of Working Series             19.26333
              Standard Deviation                 95.27317
              Number of Observations                   36
              Observation(s) eliminated by differencing  4


                              Autocorrelations

Lag    Covariance    Correlation   -1 9 8 7 6 5 4 3 2 1 0 1 2 3 4 5 6 7 8 9 1    Std Error

 0     9076.976       1.00000      |                    |********************|         0
 1     5437.664       0.59906      |             .      |***********         |   0.166667
 2     1858.937       0.20480      |             .      |****    .           |   0.218438
 3     -752.975      -.08295       |             .    **|        .           |   0.223708
 4    -3427.603      -.37762       |         .********|          .           |   0.224561
 5    -3499.087      -.38549       |         .********|          .           |   0.241556
 6    -1213.131      -.13365       |             .  ***|          .           |   0.258080
 7      451.714       0.04976      |             .      |*         .         |   0.259995
 8      803.438       0.08851      |             .      |**        .         |   0.260260
 9     1214.133       0.13376      |             .      |***       .         |   0.261095
```
(a) The SAC

```
                         The ARIMA Procedure

                       Partial Autocorrelations

Lag    Correlation    -1 9 8 7 6 5 4 3 2 1 0 1 2 3 4 5 6 7 8 9 1

 1       0.59906      |              .     |************        |
 2      -0.24032      |              . *****|        .          |
 3      -0.15090      |              .   ***|        .          |
 4      -0.34274      |              *******|        .          |
 5       0.06565      |              .      |*        .         |
 6       0.20907      |              .      |****     .         |
 7      -0.01418      |              .      |         .         |
 8      -0.20624      |              .  ****|         .         |
 9       0.03294      |              .      |*        .         |
```
(b) The SPAC

**FIGURE 12.13 (for Exercise 12.6)** SAS output of estimation and diagnostic checking for the model $(1 - \phi_1 B)z_t = (1 - \theta_{1,4}B^4)a_t$   where   $z_t = y_t - y_{t-4}$

```
                  Conditional Least Squares Estimation

                            Standard                  Approx
Parameter       Estimate      Error     t Value    Pr > |t|    Lag

MA1,1           0.95478      0.09800      9.74       <.0001      4
AR1,1           0.88047      0.11890      7.41       <.0001      1


               Variance Estimate        3602.55
               Std Error Estimate       60.02124
               AIC                      398.9242
               SBC                      402.0912
               Number of Residuals            36
         * AIC and SBC do not include log determinant.
```

(a) Estimation

```
                   Autocorrelation Check of Residuals

  To      Chi-            Pr >
  Lag    Square    DF    ChiSq    ----------------------Autocorrelations--------------------

   6      8.14      4   0.0866   -0.033   -0.040    0.113    0.035   -0.382    0.149
  12     17.98     10   0.0553    0.211   -0.043   -0.001    0.264   -0.142   -0.225
                     Autocorrelation Plot of Residuals

Lag   Covariance    Correlation   -1 9 8 7 6 5 4 3 2 1 0 1 2 3 4 5 6 7 8 9 1    Std Error

  0    3602.550      1.00000       |                    |********************|          0
  1    -118.855      -.03299       |                  . *|                    |    0.166667
  2    -144.191      -.04002       |                  . *|                    |    0.166848
  3     406.274      0.11277       |                  .  |**  .               |    0.167114
  4     127.255      0.03532       |                  .  |*   .               |    0.169215
  5   -1376.380      -.38206       |            ********|    .                |    0.169420
  6     536.159      0.14883       |                  . |***  .               |    0.191866
  7     761.490      0.21138       |                  . |****  .              |    0.195046
  8    -154.765      -.04296       |                  . *|    .               |    0.201309
  9      -4.911697   -.00136       |                  .  |    .               |    0.201563
```

(b) The RSAC

```
                   Partial Autocorrelations

Lag   Correlation   -1 9 8 7 6 5 4 3 2 1 0 1 2 3 4 5 6 7 8 9 1

  1   -0.03299      |                  . *|    .               |
  2   -0.04116      |                  . *|    .               |
  3    0.11035      |                  .  |**  .               |
  4    0.04145      |                  .  |*   .               |
  5   -0.37724      |            ********|    .                |
  6    0.14118      |                  . |***  .               |
  7    0.23067      |                  . |*****  .             |
  8    0.03595      |                  .  |*   .               |
  9   -0.02660      |                  . *|    .               |
```

(c) The RSPAC

```
                Forecasts for variable y

Obs     Forecast     Std Error      95% Confidence Limits

41      573.1082      60.0212      455.4687      690.7477
42      447.8739      79.9710      291.1336      604.6142
43      321.0303      92.5226      139.6894      502.3713
44      449.5160     101.1873      251.1926      647.8395
```

(d) Forecasting $y_{41}$ through $y_{44}$

**FIGURE 12.14  (for Exercise 12.7)**  SAS output of estimation and diagnostic checking for the model $(1 - \phi_1 B)z_t = (1 - \theta_{1,4}B^4)(1 - \theta_{1,5}B^5)a_t$   where   $z_t = y_t - y_{t-4}$

Conditional Least Squares Estimation

| Parameter | Estimate | Standard Error | t Value | Approx Pr > \|t\| | Lag |
|-----------|----------|----------------|---------|-------------------|-----|
| MA1,1 | 0.98623 | 0.09325 | 10.58 | <.0001 | 4 |
| MA2,1 | 0.34007 | 0.18833 | 1.81 | 0.0801 | 5 |
| AR1,1 | 0.95226 | 0.10474 | 9.09 | <.0001 | 1 |

```
          Variance Estimate        3213.779
          Std Error Estimate        56.6902
          AIC                      395.7385
          SBC                      400.489
          Number of Residuals          36
        * AIC and SBC do not include log determinant.
```

(a) Estimation

Autocorrelation Check of Residuals

| To Lag | Chi-Square | DF | Pr > ChiSq | --------------------Autocorrelations-------------------- | | | | | |
|--------|-----------|----|-----------|-----|-----|-----|-----|-----|-----|
| 6 | 1.16 | 3 | 0.7626 | -0.078 | -0.014 | 0.039 | -0.010 | -0.110 | 0.083 |
| 12 | 8.39 | 9 | 0.4953 | 0.113 | -0.021 | -0.042 | 0.279 | -0.127 | -0.164 |

(b) Q* statistics

**FIGURE 12.15  (for Exercise 12.7)**  SAS output of estimation and diagnostic checking for the model $(1 - \phi_1 B)z_t = (1 - \theta_{1,4}B^4 - \theta_{1,5}B^5)a_t$   where   $z_t = y_t - y_{t-4}$

Conditional Least Squares Estimation

| Parameter | Estimate | Standard Error | t Value | Approx Pr > \|t\| | Lag |
|-----------|----------|----------------|---------|-------------------|-----|
| MA1,1 | 0.83937 | 0.17581 | 4.77 | <.0001 | 4 |
| MA1,2 | 0.16063 | 0.17092 | 0.94 | 0.3542 | 5 |
| AR1,1 | 0.86570 | 0.12843 | 6.74 | <.0001 | 1 |

The ARIMA Procedure

```
          Variance Estimate        3630.941
          Std Error Estimate       60.25729
          AIC                      400.1321
          SBC                      404.8826
          Number of Residuals          36
        * AIC and SBC do not include log determinant.
```

(a) Estimation

Autocorrelation Check of Residuals

| To Lag | Chi-Square | DF | Pr > ChiSq | --------------------Autocorrelations-------------------- | | | | | |
|--------|-----------|----|-----------|-----|-----|-----|-----|-----|-----|
| 6 | 4.34 | 3 | 0.2266 | 0.008 | -0.058 | 0.154 | -0.051 | -0.252 | 0.084 |
| 12 | 15.11 | 9 | 0.0880 | 0.241 | -0.100 | 0.109 | 0.193 | -0.105 | -0.277 |

(b) Q* statistics

**FIGURE 12.16  (for Exercise 12.8)** SAS output of estimation and diagnostic checking for the energy bill dummy variable regression model, assuming independent error terms $\varepsilon_1, \varepsilon_2, \ldots$

Conditional Least Squares Estimation

| Parameter | Estimate | Standard Error | t Value | Approx Pr > \|t\| | Lag | Variable | Shift |
|-----------|----------|----------------|---------|-------------------|-----|----------|-------|
| MU | 276.63631 | 35.04850 | 7.89 | <.0001 | 0 | y | 0 |
| NUM1 | -7.45825 | 3.39603 | -2.20 | 0.0350 | 0 | Time | 0 |
| NUM2 | 0.30123 | 0.08030 | 3.75 | 0.0007 | 0 | timesq | 0 |
| NUM3 | 65.77065 | 27.15916 | 2.42 | 0.0209 | 0 | Q1 | 0 |
| NUM4 | -37.87011 | 27.09580 | -1.40 | 0.1713 | 0 | Q2 | 0 |
| NUM5 | -127.61132 | 27.05743 | -4.72 | <.0001 | 0 | Q3 | 0 |

```
                Constant Estimate        276.6363
                Variance Estimate        3656.932
                Std Error Estimate       60.47257
                AIC                      447.1895
                SBC                      457.3228
                Number of Residuals           40
        * AIC and SBC do not include log determinant.
```

(a) Estimation

Autocorrelation Check of Residuals

| To Lag | Chi-Square | DF | Pr > ChiSq | ------------------Autocorrelations------------------ | | | | | |
|--------|-----------|-----|-----------|------|-------|-------|--------|--------|--------|
| 6 | 25.10 | 6 | 0.0003 | 0.554 | 0.209 | 0.060 | -0.212 | -0.362 | -0.166 |
| 12 | 39.27 | 12 | <.0001 | -0.035 | -0.146 | -0.092 | -0.083 | -0.258 | -0.372 |

Autocorrelation Plot of Residuals

| Lag | Covariance | Correlation | -1 9 8 7 6 5 4 3 2 1 0 1 2 3 4 5 6 7 8 9 1 | Std Error |
|-----|-----------|-------------|---------------------------------------------|-----------|
| 0 | 3656.932 | 1.00000 | \|********************\| | 0 |
| 1 | 2027.405 | 0.55440 | \|*********** | 0.158114 |
| 2 | 762.648 | 0.20855 | . \|**** . | 0.200918 |
| 3 | 219.915 | 0.06014 | . \|* . | 0.206259 |
| 4 | -777.079 | -.21249 | . ****\| . | 0.206697 |
| 5 | -1325.062 | -.36234 | .******\| . | 0.212088 |
| 6 | -608.374 | -.16636 | . ***\| . | 0.227037 |
| 7 | -128.783 | -.03522 | . *\| . | 0.230064 |
| 8 | -534.503 | -.14616 | . ***\| . | 0.230199 |
| 9 | -334.855 | -.09157 | . **\| . | 0.232508 |
| 10 | -303.686 | -.08304 | . **\| . | 0.233407 |

(b) The RSAC

Partial Autocorrelations

| Lag | Correlation | -1 9 8 7 6 5 4 3 2 1 0 1 2 3 4 5 6 7 8 9 1 |
|-----|-------------|---------------------------------------------|
| 1 | 0.55440 | . \|*********** |
| 2 | -0.14266 | . ***\| . |
| 3 | 0.01048 | . \| . |
| 4 | -0.33215 | ******\| . |
| 5 | -0.12713 | . ***\| . |
| 6 | 0.20953 | . \|**** . |
| 7 | 0.01388 | . \| . |
| 8 | -0.29395 | ******\| . |
| 9 | -0.04148 | . *\| . |
| 10 | -0.10345 | . **\| . |

(c) The RSPAC

**FIGURE 12.17 (for Exercise 12.8)** SAS output of estimation, diagnostic checking, and forecasting for the energy bill dummy variable regression model, assuming the error terms $\varepsilon_1, \varepsilon_2, \ldots$ are described by the model $(1 - \phi_1 B)\varepsilon_t = (1 - \theta_{1,5}B^5)a_t$

Conditional Least Squares Estimation

| Parameter | Estimate | Standard Error | t Value | Approx Pr > \|t\| | Lag | Variable | Shift |
|-----------|----------|----------------|---------|-------------------|-----|----------|-------|
| MU | 271.66634 | 38.03439 | 7.14 | <.0001 | 0 | y | 0 |
| MA1,1 | 0.37311 | 0.17234 | 2.16 | 0.0380 | 5 | y | 0 |
| AR1,1 | 0.56211 | 0.15226 | 3.69 | 0.0008 | 1 | y | 0 |
| NUM1 | -7.44947 | 4.21594 | -1.77 | 0.0868 | 0 | Time | 0 |
| NUM2 | 0.30983 | 0.10233 | 3.03 | 0.0048 | 0 | Timesq | 0 |
| NUM3 | 68.49711 | 18.74013 | 3.66 | 0.0009 | 0 | Q1 | 0 |
| NUM4 | -34.66757 | 19.24221 | -1.80 | 0.0810 | 0 | Q2 | 0 |
| NUM5 | -128.54275 | 18.53486 | -6.94 | <.0001 | 0 | Q3 | 0 |

```
            Constant Estimate        118.9608
            Variance Estimate        2201.877
            Std Error Estimate       46.92416
            AIC                      428.472
            SBC                      441.983
            Number of Residuals        40
    * AIC and SBC do not include log determinant.
```

(a) Estimation

Autocorrelation Check of Residuals

| To Lag | Chi-Square | DF | Pr > ChiSq | | | Autocorrelations | | | |
|--------|-----------|-----|-----------|--------|--------|--------|--------|--------|--------|
| 6 | 2.49 | 4 | 0.6463 | 0.059 | -0.063 | 0.068 | -0.182 | -0.082 | -0.044 |
| 12 | 13.81 | 10 | 0.1817 | 0.039 | -0.168 | -0.061 | 0.149 | -0.162 | -0.337 |

Autocorrelation Plot of Residuals

| Lag | Covariance | Correlation | -1 9 8 7 6 5 4 3 2 1 0 1 2 3 4 5 6 7 8 9 1 | Std Error |
|-----|-----------|-------------|---------------------------------------------|-----------|
| 0 | 2201.877 | 1.00000 | \|********************\| | 0 |
| 1 | 130.819 | 0.05941 | . \|* . | 0.158114 |
| 2 | -137.791 | -.06258 | . *\| . | 0.158671 |
| 3 | 148.809 | 0.06758 | . \|* . | 0.159287 |
| 4 | -399.704 | -.18153 | . ****\| . | 0.160002 |
| 5 | -181.027 | -.08221 | . **\| . | 0.165071 |
| 6 | -96.921515 | -.04402 | . *\| . | 0.166091 |
| 7 | 85.329799 | 0.03875 | . \|* . | 0.166383 |
| 8 | -368.827 | -.16751 | . ***\| . | 0.166608 |
| 9 | -134.888 | -.06126 | . *\| . | 0.170766 |
| 10 | 328.527 | 0.14920 | . \|*** . | 0.171315 |

(b) The RSAC

**Exercise 12.8 (continued)**

b. Figure 12.17 presents the SAS output of estimation, diagnostic checking, and forecasting for the time series regression model which assumes that

$$(1 - \phi_1 B)\varepsilon_t = (1 - \theta_{1,5}B^5)a_t$$

Using Figure 12.17 and checking all the characteristics of a good model, determine if this is a reasonable model for forecasting energy bills for the school system.

c. Compare the standard error of the final time series regression model with the standard errors of the Box–Jenkins models in Exercises 12.6 and 12.7. What do you conclude based on this comparison?

**FIGURE 12.17** (Continued)

Partial Autocorrelations

```
Lag    Correlation    -1 9 8 7 6 5 4 3 2 1 0 1 2 3 4 5 6 7 8 9 1
 1       0.05941     I              .       I*    .              I
 2      -0.06634     I              .     *I     .              I
 3       0.07609     I              .      I**   .              I
 4      -0.19783     I              .  ****I     .              I
 5      -0.04637     I              .     *I     .              I
 6      -0.07170     I              .     *I     .              I
 7       0.07007     I              .      I*    .              I
 8      -0.22417     I              .  ****I     .              I
 9      -0.03901     I              .     *I     .              I
10       0.09689     I              .      I**   .              I
```

(c) The RSPAC

Forecasts for variable y

| Obs | Forecast | Std Error | 95% Confidence Limits | |
|-----|----------|-----------|-----------------------|---|
| 41 | 611.9197 | 46.9242 | 519.9500 | 703.8894 |
| 42 | 504.5760 | 53.8293 | 399.0725 | 610.0795 |
| 43 | 402.7493 | 55.8338 | 293.3171 | 512.1815 |
| 44 | 549.3194 | 56.4524 | 438.6748 | 659.9640 |

(d) Forecasts for $y_{41}$ through $y_{44}$

**12.9** Miller and Wichern (1977) analyzed 120 monthly values of average weekly total investments per month of large New York City banks. This time series is presented in Table 12.8 (page 576). Stationary time series values were produced by using the stationarity transformation

$$z_t = y_t - y_{t-1}$$

The SAC and SPAC of these stationary values are presented in Figure 12.18 (page 576).

a. Discuss why the SAC and SPAC in Figure 12.18 indicate that

$$z_t = (1 - \theta_6 B^6)(1 - \theta_{1,17} B^{12})a_t$$

or

$$z_t = (1 - \theta_6 B^6 - \theta_{12} B^{12})a_t$$

are reasonable tentative models describing the time series.

b. Figures 12.19 (page 577) and 12.20 (page 579) present the SAS outputs of estimation, diagnostic checking, and forecasting for the models in part (a). Which model seems best? Justify your answer.

**TABLE 12.8 (for Exercise 12.9)** Monthly Values of Average Weekly Total Investments at Large New York City Banks, 1965–1974 (millions of dollars)

| Year | 1965 | 1966 | 1967 | 1968 | 1969 | 1970 | 1971 | 1972 | 1973 | 1974 |
|------|------|------|------|------|------|------|------|------|------|------|
| Jan. | 5466.10 | 4565.70 | 4475.40 | 5313.20 | 5165.40 | 4550.20 | 5544.60 | 5112.20 | 4931.20 | 5435.00 |
| Feb. | 4845.90 | 4193.90 | 4785.40 | 5192.70 | 4580.80 | 4136.50 | 5342.90 | 5031.10 | 4362.80 | 5117.00 |
| Mar. | 4671.20 | 3822.40 | 4882.00 | 4807.50 | 4144.90 | 4232.10 | 5106.00 | 5551.80 | 4137.60 | 4984.00 |
| Apr. | 4528.40 | 4144.90 | 4648.70 | 4765.60 | 4509.00 | 4936.80 | 5439.20 | 5223.90 | 4316.10 | 4781.00 |
| May | 4418.10 | 3823.70 | 4656.40 | 4631.00 | 3984.80 | 4507.10 | 4863.70 | 5004.40 | 3760.80 | 3793.00 |
| June | 4461.00 | 3653.60 | 4775.30 | 4727.80 | 4030.40 | 4329.70 | 4657.20 | 4901.10 | 4247.10 | 3679.00 |
| July | 4643.70 | 3710.40 | 5017.90 | 5773.20 | 4275.20 | 4500.20 | 4988.70 | 4602.10 | 3831.90 | 3373.00 |
| Aug. | 4460.00 | 3705.80 | 4859.60 | 5298.90 | 4291.70 | 5169.40 | 4427.20 | 4746.20 | 3768.80 | 4118.00 |
| Sept. | 4260.00 | 3999.60 | 5287.40 | 5909.90 | 4324.20 | 4993.00 | 4562.60 | 5247.30 | 4154.20 | 4679.00 |
| Oct. | 4627.90 | 3694.60 | 5794.20 | 5647.80 | 4164.40 | 4879.90 | 4528.40 | 4715.10 | 4257.60 | 4144.00 |
| Nov. | 4612.40 | 3855.40 | 5832.60 | 5645.10 | 4615.90 | 5059.00 | 5330.70 | 4862.80 | 4867.90 | 4625.00 |
| Dec. | 4759.60 | 4323.90 | 5597.60 | 5965.10 | 4962.40 | 5459.80 | 5263.60 | 5039.90 | 5787.90 | 4932.00 |

*Source: Federal Reserve Bulletin,* published by the Division of Administrative Services, Board of Governors of the Federal Reserve System.

**FIGURE 12.18 (for Exercise 12.9)** SAS output of the SAC and SPAC of investment values given by the transformation $z_t = y_t - y_{t-1}$

```
                          Name of Variable = y

              Period(s) of Differencing                       1
              Mean of Working Series                    -4.48824
              Standard Deviation                        373.2907
              Number of Observations                         119
              Observation(s) eliminated by differencing        1


                              Autocorrelations

Lag    Covariance    Correlation   -1 9 8 7 6 5 4 3 2 1 0 1 2 3 4 5 6 7 8 9 1    Std Error

 0      139346        1.00000      I                   |********************|        0
 1    -8377.921       -.06012      I             .     *|      .            I     0.091670
 2    -9677.615       -.06945      I             .     *|      .            I     0.092001
 3     5797.611        0.04161     I             .      |*     .            I     0.092440
 4     1712.812        0.01229     I             .      |      .            I     0.092597
 5    -7858.935       -.05640      I             .     *|      .            I     0.092611
 6   -40647.419       -.29170      I          ******|      .            I     0.092899
 7   -22631.187       -.16241      I             .***|      .            I     0.100301
 8    -4021.092       -.02886      I             .     *|      .            I     0.102487
 9    19620.907        0.14081     I             .      |***   .            I     0.102556
10   -10503.103       -.07537      I             .    **|      .            I     0.104168
11     -356.283       -.00256      I             .      |      .            I     0.104625
12    38249.026        0.27449     I             .      |*****  .            I     0.104625
13    -5018.713       -.03602      I             .     *|      .            I     0.110511
14     6389.508        0.04585     I             .      |*     .            I     0.110610
15     7037.700        0.05051     I             .      |*     .            I     0.110770
16    -7990.619       -.05734      I             .     *|      .            I     0.110963
17    -1751.035       -.01257      I             .      |      .            I     0.111212
18   -29839.409       -.21414      I          ****|      .            I     0.111224
19     7231.594        0.05190     I             .      |*     .            I     0.114636
20   -11135.836       -.07992      I             .    **|      .            I     0.114833
21    11302.699        0.08111     I             .      |**    .            I     0.115300
22   -17005.933       -.12204      I             .    **|      .            I     0.115778
23      275.679        0.00198     I             .      |      .            I     0.116854
24    28424.609        0.20399     I             .      |****. .            I     0.116854
```

(a) The SAC

**FIGURE 12.18** (Continued)

```
                            Partial Autocorrelations

Lag      Correlation     -1 9 8 7 6 5 4 3 2 1 0 1 2 3 4 5 6 7 8 9 1
  1        -0.06012      I                  .  *I   .              I
  2        -0.07333      I                  .  *I   .              I
  3         0.03301      I                  .   I*  .              I
  4         0.01204      I                  .   I   .              I
  5        -0.05015      I                  .  *I   .              I
  6        -0.30183      I             ******I   .              I
  7        -0.23571      I              *****I   .              I
  8        -0.12707      I                .***I   .              I
  9         0.13493      I                  .   I***.              I
 10        -0.03790      I                  .  *I   .              I
 11        -0.03566      I                  .  *I   .              I
 12         0.15079      I                  .   I***.              I
 13        -0.12828      I                .***I   .              I
 14         0.00207      I                  .   I   .              I
 15         0.09751      I                  .   I** .              I
 16        -0.02160      I                  .   I   .              I
 17         0.00197      I                  .   I   .              I
 18        -0.18231      I               ****I   .              I
 19         0.08385      I                  .   I** .              I
 20        -0.07845      I                  . **I   .              I
 21         0.09631      I                  .   I** .              I
 22        -0.09483      I                  . **I   .              I
 23        -0.07664      I                  . **I   .              I
 24         0.02375      I                  .   I   .              I
```

(b) The SPAC

**FIGURE 12.19  (for Exercise 12.9)** SAS output of estimation, diagnostic checking, and forecasting for the model $z_t = (1 - \theta_6 B^6)(1 - \theta_{1,12}B^{12})a_t$   where   $z_t = y_t - y_{t-1}$

```
                    Conditional Least Squares Estimation

                              Standard                Approx
   Parameter     Estimate      Error      t Value    Pr > |t|     Lag

   MA1,1         0.24544      0.09685       2.53      0.0126        6
   MA2,1        -0.22813      0.10019      -2.28      0.0246       12

          Variance Estimate      125384.2      Correlations of Parameter
          Std Error Estimate      354.0963               Estimates
          AIC                    1736.648
          SBC                    1742.206      Parameter      MA1,1      MA2,1
          Number of Residuals        119
   * AIC and SBC do not include log determinant.  MA1,1      1.000     -0.238
                                                  MA2,1     -0.238      1.000
```

(a) Estimation

**FIGURE 12.19** (Continued)

```
                         Autocorrelation Check of Residuals

   To      Chi-            Pr >
   Lag    Square    DF    ChiSq  --------------------Autocorrelations--------------------

    6      3.32      4   0.5053   -0.120   -0.092    0.048    0.001   -0.044   -0.002
   12     13.82     10   0.1812   -0.215   -0.027    0.174   -0.052   -0.008    0.030
   18     19.17     16   0.2602   -0.042    0.052    0.090   -0.100   -0.035   -0.120
   24     29.30     22   0.1364    0.090   -0.083    0.070   -0.164    0.003    0.147
                         Autocorrelation Plot of Residuals

  Lag    Covariance    Correlation   -1 9 8 7 6 5 4 3 2 1 0 1 2 3 4 5 6 7 8 9 1    Std Error

   0         125384      1.00000     |              |********************|         0
   1     -15004.785      -.11967     |            . **|            .      |         0.091670
   2     -11581.198      -.09237     |            . **|            .      |         0.092973
   3       6002.579      0.04787     |            .   |*           .      |         0.093741
   4         99.915542   0.00080     |            .   |            .      |         0.093947
   5      -5470.189      -.04363     |            .  *|            .      |         0.093947
   6       -278.429      -.00222     |            .   |            .      |         0.094117
   7     -26948.303      -.21493     |          ****|             .      |         0.094117
   8      -3443.430      -.02746     |            .  *|            .      |         0.098155
   9      21834.574      0.17414     |            .   |***         .      |         0.098219
  10      -6548.011      -.05222     |            .  *|            .      |         0.100781
  11      -1064.297      -.00849     |            .   |            .      |         0.101008
  12       3822.607      0.03049     |            .   |*           .      |         0.101014
  13      -5299.897      -.04227     |            .  *|            .      |         0.101091
  14       6546.773      0.05221     |            .   |*           .      |         0.101239
  15      11261.131      0.08981     |            .   |**          .      |         0.101466
  16     -12476.430      -.09951     |            . **|            .      |         0.102131
  17      -4334.014      -.03457     |            .  *|            .      |         0.102943
  18     -15054.138      -.12006     |            . **|            .      |         0.103040
  19      11276.116      0.08993     |            .   |**          .      |         0.104209
  20     -10389.621      -.08286     |            . **|            .      |         0.104860
  21       8737.186      0.06968     |            .   |*           .      |         0.105408
  22     -20563.442      -.16400     |            .***|            .      |         0.105795
  23        389.133      0.00310     |            .   |            .      |         0.107910
  24      18404.622      0.14679     |            .   |***.        .      |         0.107911
```

(b) The RSAC

```
                      Partial Autocorrelations

  Lag    Correlation   -1 9 8 7 6 5 4 3 2 1 0 1 2 3 4 5 6 7 8 9 1

   1      -0.11967     |            . **|            .      |
   2      -0.10824     |            . **|            .      |
   3       0.02327     |            .   |            .      |
   4       0.00010     |            .   |            .      |
   5      -0.03731     |            .  *|            .      |
   6      -0.01403     |            .   |            .      |
   7      -0.23124     |          *****|             .      |
   8      -0.09176     |            . **|            .      |
   9       0.12471     |            .   |**          .      |
  10      -0.00991     |            .   |            .      |
  11       0.01367     |            .   |            .      |
  12      -0.00729     |            .   |            .      |
  13      -0.06224     |            .  *|            .      |
  14       0.00637     |            .   |            .      |
  15       0.08331     |            .   |**          .      |
  16      -0.00724     |            .   |            .      |
  17      -0.03777     |            .  *|            .      |
  18      -0.19674     |          ****|             .      |
  19       0.06268     |            .   |*           .      |
  20      -0.09960     |            . **|            .      |
  21       0.09737     |            .   |**          .      |
  22      -0.14267     |            .***|            .      |
  23      -0.08309     |            . **|            .      |
  24       0.06459     |            .   |*           .      |
```

(c) The RSPAC

**FIGURE 12.19** (Continued)

Forecasts for variable y

| Obs | Forecast | Std Error | 95% Confidence Limits | |
|-----|----------|-----------|-----------------------|---|
| 121 | 4937.3383 | 354.0963 | 4243.3223 | 5631.3544 |
| 122 | 4718.7522 | 500.7678 | 3737.2653 | 5700.2391 |
| 123 | 4584.7499 | 613.3128 | 3382.6789 | 5786.8210 |
| 124 | 4680.7305 | 708.1927 | 3292.6984 | 6068.7626 |
| 125 | 4444.5401 | 791.7835 | 2892.6730 | 5996.4072 |
| 126 | 4364.8010 | 867.3553 | 2664.8158 | 6064.7862 |
| 127 | 4312.2567 | 907.5759 | 2533.4406 | 6091.0728 |
| 128 | 4489.1253 | 946.0881 | 2634.8266 | 6343.4240 |
| 129 | 4602.5344 | 983.0928 | 2675.7078 | 6529.3609 |
| 130 | 4468.8182 | 1018.7543 | 2472.0965 | 6465.5399 |
| 131 | 4546.4140 | 1053.2089 | 2482.1624 | 6610.6655 |
| 132 | 4571.0661 | 1086.5716 | 2441.4249 | 6700.7072 |

(d) Forecasts of $y_{121}$ through $y_{132}$

**FIGURE 12.20 (for Exercise 12.9)** SAS output of estimation, diagnostic checking, and forecasting for the model $z_t = (1 - \theta_6 B^6 - \theta_{12} B^{12}) a_t$   where   $z_t = y_t - y_{t-1}$

Conditional Least Squares Estimation

| Parameter | Estimate | Standard Error | t Value | Approx Pr > \|t\| | Lag |
|-----------|----------|----------------|---------|-------------------|-----|
| MA1,1 | 0.22791 | 0.09544 | 2.39 | 0.0185 | 6 |
| MA1,2 | -0.20987 | 0.09746 | -2.15 | 0.0333 | 12 |

| | |
|---|---|
| Variance Estimate | 126680.7 |
| Std Error Estimate | 355.9223 |
| AIC | 1737.872 |
| SBC | 1743.43 |
| Number of Residuals | 119 |

\* AIC and SBC do not include log determinant.

Correlations of Parameter Estimates

| Parameter | MA1,1 | MA1,2 |
|-----------|-------|-------|
| MA1,1 | 1.000 | -0.195 |
| MA1,2 | -0.195 | 1.000 |

(a) Estimation

**FIGURE 12.20** (Continued)

Autocorrelation Check of Residuals

| To Lag | Chi-Square | DF | Pr > ChiSq | | | Autocorrelations | | | |
|---|---|---|---|---|---|---|---|---|---|
| 6 | 3.04 | 4 | 0.5519 | -0.118 | -0.079 | 0.041 | 0.008 | -0.046 | -0.026 |
| 12 | 12.70 | 10 | 0.2410 | -0.208 | -0.015 | 0.162 | -0.047 | -0.005 | 0.049 |
| 18 | 19.16 | 16 | 0.2603 | -0.037 | 0.050 | 0.076 | -0.094 | -0.026 | -0.163 |
| 24 | 29.11 | 22 | 0.1417 | 0.098 | -0.091 | 0.070 | -0.160 | 0.004 | 0.137 |

Autocorrelation Plot of Residuals

| Lag | Covariance | Correlation | -1 9 8 7 6 5 4 3 2 1 0 1 2 3 4 5 6 7 8 9 1 | Std Error |
|---|---|---|---|---|
| 0 | 126681 | 1.00000 | \|                  \|******************** | 0 |
| 1 | -14983.276 | -.11828 | \|              . **\|        . | 0.091670 |
| 2 | -9952.703 | -.07857 | \|              . **\|        . | 0.092943 |
| 3 | 5160.887 | 0.04074 | \|              .  \|*       . | 0.093500 |
| 4 | 1002.441 | 0.00791 | \|              .  \|        . | 0.093649 |
| 5 | -5852.092 | -.04620 | \|              .  *\|       . | 0.093654 |
| 6 | -3282.959 | -.02592 | \|              .  *\|       . | 0.093846 |
| 7 | -26331.691 | -.20786 | \|              .****\|      . | 0.093906 |
| 8 | -1941.985 | -.01533 | \|              .  \|        . | 0.097696 |
| 9 | 20565.625 | 0.16234 | \|              .  \|***      . | 0.097716 |
| 10 | -5997.211 | -.04734 | \|              .  *\|       . | 0.099957 |
| 11 | -576.811 | -.00455 | \|              .  \|        . | 0.100145 |
| 12 | 6261.104 | 0.04942 | \|              .  \|*       . | 0.100147 |
| 13 | -4665.981 | -.03683 | \|              .  *\|       . | 0.100351 |
| 14 | 6355.901 | 0.05017 | \|              .  \|*       . | 0.100465 |
| 15 | 9658.083 | 0.07624 | \|              .  \|**      . | 0.100675 |
| 16 | -11852.905 | -.09357 | \|              . **\|       . | 0.101159 |
| 17 | -3307.545 | -.02611 | \|              .  *\|       . | 0.101884 |
| 18 | -20711.765 | -.16350 | \|              .***\|       . | 0.101940 |
| 19 | 12405.541 | 0.09793 | \|              .  \|**      . | 0.104120 |
| 20 | -11485.734 | -.09067 | \|              . **\|       . | 0.104892 |
| 21 | 8818.804 | 0.06961 | \|              .  \|*       . | 0.105548 |
| 22 | -20266.993 | -.15998 | \|              .***\|       . | 0.105933 |
| 23 | 493.106 | 0.00389 | \|              .  \|        . | 0.107944 |
| 24 | 17391.873 | 0.13729 | \|              .  \|***      . | 0.107946 |

(b) The RSAC

Partial Autocorrelations

| Lag | Correlation | -1 9 8 7 6 5 4 3 2 1 0 1 2 3 4 5 6 7 8 9 1 |
|---|---|---|
| 1 | -0.11828 | \|            . **\|    . | 
| 2 | -0.09387 | \|            . **\|    . |
| 3 | 0.01992 | \|            .  \|    . |
| 4 | 0.00849 | \|            .  \|    . |
| 5 | -0.03976 | \|            .  *\|   . |
| 6 | -0.03715 | \|            .  *\|   . |
| 7 | -0.22934 | \|            .*****\|  . |
| 8 | -0.08169 | \|            . **\|   . |
| 9 | 0.12395 | \|            .  \|**  . |
| 10 | -0.00357 | \|            .  \|    . |
| 11 | 0.01343 | \|            .  \|    . |
| 12 | 0.01442 | \|            .  \|    . |
| 13 | -0.06081 | \|            .  *\|   . |
| 14 | 0.00849 | \|            .  \|    . |
| 15 | 0.08118 | \|            .  \|**  . |
| 16 | -0.00802 | \|            .  \|    . |
| 17 | -0.02899 | \|            .  *\|   . |
| 18 | -0.23204 | \|            .*****\|  . |
| 19 | 0.06647 | \|            .  \|*   . |
| 20 | -0.10646 | \|            . **\|   . |
| 21 | 0.09647 | \|            .  \|**  . |
| 22 | -0.14273 | \|            .***\|   . |
| 23 | -0.09048 | \|            . **\|   . |
| 24 | 0.05355 | \|            .  \|*   . |

(c) The RSPAC

**FIGURE 12.20** (Continued)

```
                 Forecasts for variable y

Obs       Forecast      Std Error       95% Confidence Limits

121      4920.6605      355.9223       4223.0656      5618.2555
122      4697.7522      503.3502       3711.2040      5684.3005
123      4573.2710      616.4756       3365.0010      5781.5409
124      4681.0558      711.8447       3285.8658      6076.2457
125      4474.1502      795.8666       2914.2804      6034.0200
126      4452.3151      871.8281       2743.5634      6161.0669
127      4385.3149      914.1122       2593.6878      6176.9419
128      4538.3657      954.5250       2667.5310      6409.2003
129      4644.9819      993.2949       2698.1596      6591.8042
130      4513.2343     1030.6074       2493.2808      6533.1877
131      4556.6662     1066.6155       2466.1383      6647.1941
132      4576.7063     1101.4470       2417.9100      6735.5027
```

(d) Forecasts of $y_{121}$ through $y_{132}$

**12.10** Figure 12.21 (page 582) presents the estimation, diagnostic checking, and forecasting for the tentative intervention model of the monthly miles flown by the United Kingdom airlines in Table 12.5 and Figure 12.3 of Example 12.6 (page 553). The model is

$$z_t = \delta + C_1 z_t(P_1) + C_2 z_t(P_2) + \varepsilon_t$$

where

$$z_t = (1 - B^{12})y_t$$
$$z_t(P_1) = (1 - B^{12})P_{1t}$$
$$z_t(P_2) = (1 - B^{12})P_{2t}$$
$$a_t = (1 - \phi_1 B - \phi_3 B^3)\varepsilon_t$$

a. What do the values of the $Q^*$-statistic for $K = 6$, 12, 18, and 24 (and the associated $p$-values) say about the adequacy of this tentative model?

b. Find the least squares estimates of the values $\delta$, $\phi_1$, and $\phi_3$.

c. Do the parameters $\delta$, $\phi_1$, and $\phi_3$ seem to be significantly different from zero? Justify your answer with statistical tests.

d. Find the least squares estimates of the values for $C_1$ and $C_2$.

e. Do $C_1$ and $C_2$ seem to be significantly different from zero? Justify your answer with statistical tests.

f. Interpret the numerical values for $C_1$ and $C_2$ in terms of the expected number of United Kingdom airline miles. See step 2 in Example 12.6, and use the units shown in Table 12.5.

g. Find a point forecast and a 95% prediction interval for $y_{97}$. Interpret the 95% prediction interval.

**FIGURE 12.21 (for Exercise 12.10)** SAS output of estimation, diagnostic checking, and forecasting for the model $z_t = \delta + C_1 z_t(P_1) + C_2 z_t(P_2) + \varepsilon_t$   where   $(1 - \phi_1 B - \phi_3 B^3)\varepsilon_t = a_t$

### Conditional Least Squares Estimation

| Parameter | Estimate | Standard Error | t Value | Approx Pr > \|t\| | Lag | Variable |
|---|---|---|---|---|---|---|
| MU | 665.17454 | 132.23991 | 5.03 | <.0001 | 0 | y |
| AR1,1 | 0.33039 | 0.10939 | 3.02 | 0.0034 | 1 | y |
| AR1,2 | 0.30071 | 0.10510 | 2.86 | 0.0054 | 3 | y |
| NUM1 | -2458.6 | 257.51457 | -9.55 | <.0001 | 0 | P1 |
| NUM2 | -2933.5 | 310.17635 | -9.46 | <.0001 | 0 | P2 |

(a) Estimation

| To Lag | Chi-Square | DF | Pr > ChiSq |
|---|---|---|---|
| 6 | 4.99 | 4 | 0.2884 |
| 12 | 14.73 | 10 | 0.1422 |
| 18 | 19.34 | 16 | 0.2513 |
| 24 | 20.35 | 22 | 0.5613 |

### Autocorrelation Plot of Residuals

| Lag | Covariance | Correlation | -1 9 8 7 6 5 4 3 2 1 0 1 2 3 4 5 6 7 8 9 1 | Std Erro |
|---|---|---|---|---|
| 0 | 217881 | 1.00000 | \|********************\| | |
| 1 | 5929.889 | 0.02722 | \|* . | 0.11111 |
| 2 | 1308.348 | 0.00600 | \| . | 0.11119 |
| 3 | 6242.520 | 0.02865 | \|* . | 0.11119 |
| 4 | -18539.452 | -.08509 | . **\| . | 0.11128 |
| 5 | 28921.974 | 0.13274 | \|*** . | 0.11208 |
| 6 | 37546.559 | 0.17233 | \|*** . | 0.11401 |
| 7 | -50276.472 | -.23075 | *****\| . | 0.11718 |
| 8 | -16727.546 | -.07677 | . **\| . | 0.12266 |
| 9 | 2591.755 | 0.01190 | \| . | 0.12325 |
| 10 | -6274.175 | -.02880 | . *\| . | 0.12327 |
| 11 | 4622.113 | 0.02121 | \| . | 0.12335 |
| 12 | -45382.492 | -.20829 | .****\| . | 0.12340 |

(b) The RSAC

### Partial Autocorrelations

| Lag | Correlation | -1 9 8 7 6 5 4 3 2 1 0 1 2 3 4 5 6 7 8 9 1 |
|---|---|---|
| 1 | 0.02722 | \|* . |
| 2 | 0.00527 | \|* . |
| 3 | 0.02837 | \|* . |
| 4 | -0.08680 | . **\| . |
| 5 | 0.13854 | \|***. |
| 6 | 0.16751 | \|***. |
| 7 | -0.25048 | *****\| . |
| 8 | -0.08687 | . **\| . |
| 9 | 0.05657 | \|* . |
| 10 | -0.00330 | \| . |
| 11 | -0.07719 | . **\| . |
| 12 | -0.21294 | ****\| . |

(c) The RSPAC

**FIGURE 12.21** (Continued)

```
                Forecasts for variable y

Obs       Forecast      Std Error      95% Confidence Limits

 97     11348.5979      466.7777      10433.7304      12263.4653
 98     11135.0919      491.5942      10171.5850      12098.5987
 99     14249.0899      494.2276      13280.4215      15217.7583
100     14018.4111      518.6250      13001.9248      15034.8973
101     13762.2627      527.8607      12727.6748      14796.8506
102     15594.6923      530.0207      14555.8708      16633.5139
103     14796.3606      533.7593      13750.2116      15842.5096
104     14715.1720      536.1334      13664.3700      15765.9741
105     16895.8139      537.0303      15843.2538      17948.3740
106     13048.3089      537.8243      11994.1925      14102.4252
107     12256.1309      538.3962      11200.8938      13311.3680
108     13434.8280      538.6813      12379.0320      14490.6240
```

(d) Forecasts of $y_{97}$ through $y_{108}$

**Exercises 12.11 through 12.14 deal with data analyzed by Box, Jenkins, and Reinsel (1994).** They forecast sales ($y_t$) by using a leading economic indicator ($x_t$). The historical data consist of 150 observations and are given in Table 12.9 (page 584). It can be verified that regular differencing makes both the $x_t$ and $y_t$ values stationary and that a model describing the $x_t$ values is

$$z_t^{(x)} = (1 - \theta_1^{(x)}B)a_t \quad \text{where} \quad z_t^{(x)} = x_t - x_{t-1}$$

**12.11** The SAS output of the SCC between the prewhitened values of the leading indicator and the prewhitened values of sales is given in Figure 12.22 (page 585). Use the output to rationalize the following preliminary transfer function model (where we arbitrarily include $\mu$)

$$z_t = \mu + \frac{C}{(1 - \delta_1 B)} B^3 z_t^{(x)} + \varepsilon_t$$

If we consider the general preliminary transfer function model

$$z_t = \mu + \frac{Cw(B)}{\delta(B)} B^b z_t^{(x)} + \varepsilon_t$$

carefully explain how you arrived at

a.  A tentative value of $b$.
b.  A tentative form of $w(B) = (1 - w_1 B - w_2 B^2 - \cdots - w_s B^s)$.
c.  A tentative form of $\delta(B) = (1 - \delta_1 B - \delta_2 B^2 - \cdots - \delta_r B^r)$.

**12.12** The SAS output of estimation and diagnostic checking for the preliminary transfer function model in Exercise 12.11 is given in Figure 12.23 (page 586).

a.  Find and identify the least squares point estimates of the model parameters.
b.  Do all of the model parameters seem to be significantly different from zero? Explain your answer.
c.  Consider the RSCC. What do the $p$-values associated with the $Q^*$-statistic say about whether the prewhitened input series is statistically independent of the error component? Explain your answer.
d.  Consider the RSAC. What do the values of the $Q^*$ statistic (and the associated $p$-values) say about the adequacy of the model?
e.  Should we consider the error terms $\varepsilon_1, \varepsilon_2, \ldots$ to be statistically independent or statistically dependent? Explain your answer.
f.  Describe the behavior of the RSAC.
g.  Describe the behavior of the RSPAC.
h.  Use the behavior of the RSAC and RSPAC to rationalize that the model

$$\varepsilon_t = (1 - \theta_1 B)a_t$$

is a reasonable tentative model describing $\varepsilon_t$. What guideline(s) (in Tables 12.1 and 12.2) did you use to identify this model?
i.  Use the model of part (h) describing $\varepsilon_t$ to specify an appropriate final transfer function model.

**TABLE 12.9 (for Exercises 12.11 and 12.12)** 150 Observations of Sales and a Leading Indicator

| t | Leading Indicator $x_t$ | Sales $y_t$ | t | Leading Indicator $x_t$ | Sales $y_t$ | t | Leading Indicator $x_t$ | Sales $y_t$ |
|---|---|---|---|---|---|---|---|---|
| 1 | 10.01 | 200.1 | 51 | 10.77 | 220.0 | 101 | 12.90 | 249.4 |
| 2 | 10.07 | 199.5 | 52 | 10.88 | 218.7 | 102 | 13.12 | 249.0 |
| 3 | 10.32 | 199.4 | 53 | 10.49 | 217.0 | 103 | 12.47 | 249.9 |
| 4 | 9.75 | 198.9 | 54 | 10.50 | 215.9 | 104 | 12.47 | 250.5 |
| 5 | 10.33 | 199.0 | 55 | 11.00 | 215.8 | 105 | 12.94 | 251.5 |
| 6 | 10.13 | 200.2 | 56 | 10.98 | 214.1 | 106 | 13.10 | 249.0 |
| 7 | 10.36 | 198.6 | 57 | 10.61 | 212.3 | 107 | 12.91 | 247.6 |
| 8 | 10.32 | 200.0 | 58 | 10.48 | 213.9 | 108 | 13.39 | 248.8 |
| 9 | 10.13 | 200.3 | 59 | 10.53 | 214.6 | 109 | 13.13 | 250.4 |
| 10 | 10.16 | 201.2 | 60 | 11.07 | 213.6 | 110 | 13.34 | 250.7 |
| 11 | 10.58 | 201.6 | 61 | 10.61 | 212.1 | 111 | 13.34 | 253.0 |
| 12 | 10.62 | 201.5 | 62 | 10.86 | 211.4 | 112 | 13.14 | 253.7 |
| 13 | 10.86 | 201.5 | 63 | 10.34 | 213.1 | 113 | 13.49 | 255.0 |
| 14 | 11.20 | 203.5 | 64 | 10.78 | 212.9 | 114 | 13.87 | 256.2 |
| 15 | 10.74 | 204.9 | 65 | 10.80 | 213.3 | 115 | 13.39 | 256.0 |
| 16 | 10.56 | 207.1 | 66 | 10.33 | 211.5 | 116 | 13.59 | 257.4 |
| 17 | 10.48 | 210.5 | 67 | 10.44 | 212.3 | 117 | 13.27 | 260.4 |
| 18 | 10.77 | 210.5 | 68 | 10.50 | 213.0 | 118 | 13.70 | 260.0 |
| 19 | 11.33 | 209.8 | 69 | 10.75 | 211.0 | 119 | 13.20 | 261.3 |
| 20 | 10.96 | 208.8 | 70 | 10.40 | 210.7 | 120 | 13.32 | 260.4 |
| 21 | 11.16 | 209.5 | 71 | 10.40 | 210.1 | 121 | 13.15 | 261.6 |
| 22 | 11.70 | 213.2 | 72 | 10.34 | 211.4 | 122 | 13.30 | 260.8 |
| 23 | 11.39 | 213.7 | 73 | 10.55 | 210.0 | 123 | 12.94 | 259.8 |
| 24 | 11.42 | 215.1 | 74 | 10.46 | 209.7 | 124 | 13.29 | 259.0 |
| 25 | 11.94 | 218.7 | 75 | 10.82 | 208.8 | 125 | 13.26 | 258.9 |
| 26 | 11.24 | 219.8 | 76 | 10.91 | 208.8 | 126 | 13.08 | 257.4 |
| 27 | 11.59 | 220.5 | 77 | 10.87 | 208.8 | 127 | 13.24 | 257.7 |
| 28 | 10.96 | 223.8 | 78 | 10.67 | 210.6 | 128 | 13.31 | 257.9 |
| 29 | 11.40 | 222.8 | 79 | 11.11 | 211.9 | 129 | 13.52 | 257.4 |
| 30 | 11.02 | 223.8 | 80 | 10.88 | 212.8 | 130 | 13.02 | 257.3 |
| 31 | 11.01 | 221.7 | 81 | 11.28 | 212.5 | 131 | 13.25 | 257.6 |
| 32 | 11.23 | 222.3 | 82 | 11.27 | 214.8 | 132 | 13.12 | 258.9 |
| 33 | 11.33 | 220.8 | 83 | 11.44 | 215.3 | 133 | 13.26 | 257.8 |
| 34 | 10.83 | 219.4 | 84 | 11.52 | 217.5 | 134 | 13.11 | 257.7 |
| 35 | 10.84 | 220.1 | 85 | 12.10 | 218.8 | 135 | 13.30 | 257.2 |
| 36 | 11.14 | 220.6 | 86 | 11.83 | 220.7 | 136 | 13.06 | 257.5 |
| 37 | 10.38 | 218.9 | 87 | 12.62 | 222.2 | 137 | 13.32 | 256.8 |
| 38 | 10.90 | 217.8 | 88 | 12.41 | 226.7 | 138 | 13.10 | 257.5 |
| 39 | 11.05 | 217.7 | 89 | 12.43 | 228.4 | 139 | 13.27 | 257.0 |
| 40 | 11.11 | 215.0 | 90 | 12.73 | 233.2 | 140 | 13.64 | 257.6 |
| 41 | 11.01 | 215.3 | 91 | 13.01 | 235.7 | 141 | 13.58 | 257.3 |
| 42 | 11.22 | 215.9 | 92 | 12.74 | 237.1 | 142 | 13.87 | 257.5 |
| 43 | 11.21 | 216.7 | 93 | 12.73 | 240.6 | 143 | 13.53 | 259.6 |
| 44 | 11.91 | 216.7 | 94 | 12.76 | 243.8 | 144 | 13.41 | 261.1 |
| 45 | 11.69 | 217.7 | 95 | 12.92 | 245.3 | 145 | 13.25 | 262.9 |
| 46 | 10.93 | 218.7 | 96 | 12.64 | 246.0 | 146 | 13.50 | 263.3 |
| 47 | 10.99 | 222.9 | 97 | 12.79 | 246.3 | 147 | 13.58 | 262.8 |
| 48 | 11.01 | 224.9 | 98 | 13.05 | 247.7 | 148 | 13.51 | 261.8 |
| 49 | 10.84 | 222.2 | 99 | 12.69 | 247.6 | 149 | 13.77 | 262.2 |
| 50 | 10.76 | 220.7 | 100 | 13.01 | 247.8 | 150 | 13.40 | 262.7 |

*Source: Time Series Analysis: Forecasting and Control,* 3rd ed., by G.E.P. Box, G.M. Jenkins, G.C. Reinsel, Prentice-Hall, Inc., Englewood Cliffs, 1994.

**FIGURE 12.22 (for Exercise 12.11)** SAS output of the SCC between the prewhitened values of the leading indicator and the prewhitened values of sales

```
                        Correlation of y and x

        Period(s) of Differencing                      1
        Number of Observations                       149
        Observation(s) eliminated by differencing      1
        Variance of transformed series y          3.794675
        Variance of transformed series x          0.078036

              Both series have been prewhitened.

                       Crosscorrelations

Lag   Covariance    Correlation   -1 9 8 7 6 5 4 3 2 1 0 1 2 3 4 5 6 7 8 9 1

-10   -0.028313       -.05203      |                  . *|  .                |
-9    -0.026054       -.04788      |                  . *|  .                |
-8     0.026927       0.04948      |                  . |*  .                |
-7    -0.0013061      -.00240      |                  . |   .                |
-6    -0.034684       -.06374      |                  . *|  .                |
-5     0.013016       0.02392      |                  . |   .                |
-4     0.0012583      0.00231      |                  . |   .                |
-3     0.022045       0.04051      |                  . |*  .                |
-2     0.0054125      0.00995      |                  . |   .                |
-1     0.051478       0.09460      |                  . |** .                |
 0     0.034232       0.06291      |                  . |*  .                |
 1     0.043060       0.07913      |                  . |** .                |
 2     0.010062       0.01849      |                  . |   .                |
 3     0.367442       0.67523      |                  . |*************** *    |
 4     0.246112       0.45227      |                  . |*********            |
 5     0.185447       0.34079      |                  . |*******             |
 6     0.140160       0.25757      |                  . |*****               |
 7     0.145861       0.26804      |                  . |*****               |
 8     0.107803       0.19811      |                  . |****                |
 9     0.094235       0.17317      |                  . |***                 |
10     0.053115       0.09761      |                  . |** .                |
```

**FIGURE 12.23 (for Exercise 12.12)**  SAS output of estimation and diagnostic checking for the model

$$z_t = \mu + \frac{C}{(1 - \delta_1 B)} B^3 z_t^{(x)} + \varepsilon_t \quad \text{where} \quad z_t = y_t - y_{t-1} \quad \text{and} \quad z_t^{(x)} = x_t - x_{t-1}$$

### Conditional Least Squares Estimation

| Parameter | Estimate | Standard Error | t Value | Approx Pr > \|t\| | Lag | Variable | Shift |
|-----------|----------|----------------|---------|-------------------|-----|----------|-------|
| MU | 0.02952 | 0.02414 | 1.22 | 0.2235 | 0 | y | 0 |
| SCALE1 | 4.69215 | 0.07717 | 60.80 | <.0001 | 0 | x | 3 |
| DEN1,1 | 0.72490 | 0.0074539 | 97.25 | <.0001 | 1 | x | 3 |

```
Constant Estimate       0.029517
Variance Estimate       0.06597
Std Error Estimate      0.256846
AIC                     19.9111
SBC                     28.77858
Number of Residuals       142
   * AIC and SBC do not include log determinant.
```

(a) Estimation

### Crosscorrelation Check of Residuals with Input x

| To Lag | Chi-Square | DF | Pr > ChiSq | Crosscorrelations | | | | | |
|--------|-----------|----|-----------|-------|-------|-------|-------|-------|-------|
| 5 | 12.25 | 5 | 0.0315 | 0.010 | 0.097 | -0.169 | 0.079 | -0.076 | 0.195 |
| 11 | 13.82 | 11 | 0.2433 | -0.060 | -0.017 | 0.033 | 0.034 | -0.014 | 0.070 |
| 17 | 15.28 | 17 | 0.5754 | -0.037 | -0.035 | -0.027 | -0.041 | 0.074 | 0.006 |
| 23 | 23.55 | 23 | 0.4288 | -0.158 | 0.122 | -0.018 | 0.033 | -0.081 | 0.109 |

(b) The RSCC

### Autocorrelation Check of Residuals

| To Lag | Chi-Square | DF | Pr > ChiSq | Autocorrelations | | | | | |
|--------|-----------|----|-----------|-------|-------|-------|-------|-------|-------|
| 6 | 28.11 | 6 | <.0001 | -0.400 | 0.018 | -0.042 | -0.094 | 0.142 | 0.042 |
| 12 | 35.75 | 12 | 0.0004 | -0.093 | 0.076 | -0.135 | 0.124 | -0.013 | -0.039 |
| 18 | 46.35 | 18 | 0.0003 | -0.088 | 0.055 | -0.054 | 0.141 | -0.161 | 0.075 |
| 24 | 53.59 | 24 | 0.0005 | 0.043 | -0.051 | 0.032 | -0.065 | -0.073 | 0.164 |

### Autocorrelation Plot of Residuals

| Lag | Covariance | Correlation | -1 9 8 7 6 5 4 3 2 1 0 1 2 3 4 5 6 7 8 9 1 | Std Error |
|-----|-----------|-------------|--------------------------------------------|-----------|
| 0 | 0.065970 | 1.00000 | \|********************\| | 0 |
| 1 | -0.026393 | -.40008 | ********\| . \| | 0.083918 |
| 2 | 0.0011898 | 0.01804 | . \| . \| | 0.096419 |
| 3 | -0.0027551 | -.04176 | . *\| . \| | 0.096443 |
| 4 | -0.0061943 | -.09390 | . **\| . \| | 0.096570 |
| 5 | 0.0093920 | 0.14237 | . \|***. \| | 0.097211 |
| 6 | 0.0027685 | 0.04197 | . \|* . \| | 0.098669 |
| 7 | -0.0061098 | -.09262 | . **\| . \| | 0.098794 |
| 8 | 0.0049872 | 0.07560 | . \|** . \| | 0.099404 |
| 9 | -0.0089323 | -.13540 | .***\| . \| | 0.099808 |
| 10 | 0.0081823 | 0.12403 | . \|** . \| | 0.101093 |

(c) The RSAC

**FIGURE 12.23** (Continued)

Partial Autocorrelations

| Lag | Correlation | -1 9 8 7 6 5 4 3 2 1 0 1 2 3 4 5 6 7 8 9 1 |
|-----|-------------|--------------------------------------------|
| 1 | -0.40008 |                 \|    ********\| . |
| 2 | -0.16910 |                 \|      ***\| . |
| 3 | -0.12376 |                 \|      .**\| . |
| 4 | -0.19881 |                 \|     ****\| . |
| 5 | 0.00940 |                 \|         . \| . |
| 6 | 0.11348 |                 \|        . \|**. |
| 7 | -0.02181 |                 \|        . \| . |
| 8 | 0.05657 |                 \|        . \|* . |
| 9 | -0.07268 |                 \|       . *\| . |
| 10 | 0.04532 |                 \|        . \|* . |

(d) The RSPAC

**12.13** The SAS output of estimation, diagnostic checking, and forecasting for the final model is given in Figure 12.24 (page 588).

a. Find and identify the least squares point estimates of the model parameters.

b. Do all of the model parameters seem to be significantly different from zero? Explain your answer.

c. What do the correlations of the least squares point estimates say about the adequacy of the model?

d. What do the behaviors of the RSAC and the RSPAC say about the adequacy of the model? Explain your answer.

e. What do the values of the $Q^*$-statistics for $K = 6$, 12, 18, and 24 (and the associated $p$-values) say about the adequacy of the model? Explain your answer.

f. Find a point forecast and a 95% prediction interval for $y_{151}$. Interpret the 95% prediction interval.

**12.14** Write the five SAS programs needed to carry out the transfer function analysis of the sales and leading economic indicator data. That is, write SAS programs to

a. Compute the SAC and SPAC for each of the transformations

$$z_t = x_t \quad \text{and} \quad z_t^{(x)} = x_t - x_{t-1}$$

b. Fit the tentative model describing $x_t$.

$$z_t^{(x)} = (1 - \theta_1^{(x)} B)a_t \quad \text{where} \quad z_t^{(x)} = x_t - \dot{x}_{t-1}$$

c. Compute the prewhitened $x_t$ and $y_t$ values and compute the SCC.

d. Fit the preliminary transfer function model

$$z_t = \mu + \frac{C}{(1 - \delta_1 B)} B^3 z_t^{(x)} + \varepsilon_t$$

e. Fit (and forecast with) the final transfer function model

$$z_t = \mu + \frac{C}{(1 - \delta_1 B)} B^3 z_t^{(x)} + (1 - \theta_1 B)a_t$$

**FIGURE 12.24 (for Exercise 12.13)** SAS output of estimation, diagnostic checking, and forecasting for the model

$$z_t = \mu + \frac{C}{(1 - \delta_1 B)} B^3 z_t^{(x)} + (1 - \theta_1 B)a_t \quad \text{where} \quad z_t = y_t - y_{t-1} \quad \text{and} \quad z_t^{(x)} = x_t - x_{t-1}$$

Conditional Least Squares Estimation

| Parameter | Estimate | Standard Error | t Value | Approx Pr > \|t\| | Lag | Variable | Shift |
|-----------|----------|----------------|---------|------------------|-----|----------|-------|
| MU        | 0.03040  | 0.01043        | 2.91    | 0.0042           | 0   | y        | 0     |
| MA1,1     | 0.52474  | 0.07255        | 7.23    | <.0001           | 1   | y        | 0     |
| SCALE1    | 4.70826  | 0.05792        | 81.29   | <.0001           | 0   | x        | 3     |
| DEN1,1    | 0.72428  | 0.0042986      | 168.49  | <.0001           | 1   | x        | 3     |

| | |
|---|---|
| Constant Estimate | 0.030396 |
| Variance Estimate | 0.052682 |
| Std Error Estimate | 0.229525 |
| AIC | -11.0535 |
| SBC | 0.769844 |
| Number of Residuals | 142 |

* AIC and SBC do not include log determinant.

(a) Estimation

Crosscorrelation Check of Residuals with Input x

| To Lag | Chi-Square | DF | Pr > ChiSq | ----------Crosscorrelations---------- | | | | | |
|--------|-----------|----|-----------|--------|--------|--------|--------|--------|--------|
| 5      | 10.09     | 5  | 0.0726    | 0.007  | 0.116  | -0.136 | 0.018  | -0.082 | 0.183  |
| 11     | 12.00     | 11 | 0.3640    | 0.027  | -0.004 | 0.037  | 0.060  | 0.016  | 0.088  |
| 17     | 13.77     | 17 | 0.6833    | 0.002  | -0.039 | -0.051 | -0.074 | 0.047  | 0.032  |
| 23     | 20.08     | 23 | 0.6371    | -0.167 | 0.054  | 0.005  | 0.039  | -0.074 | 0.086  |

(b) The RSCC

Autocorrelation Check of Residuals

| To Lag | Chi-Square | DF | Pr > ChiSq | ----------Autocorrelations---------- | | | | | |
|--------|-----------|----|-----------|--------|--------|--------|--------|--------|--------|
| 6      | 5.50      | 5  | 0.3582    | 0.013  | -0.000 | -0.064 | -0.056 | 0.151  | 0.081  |
| 12     | 9.89      | 11 | 0.5401    | -0.052 | 0.012  | -0.099 | 0.070  | -0.025 | -0.101 |
| 18     | 15.93     | 17 | 0.5289    | -0.128 | -0.004 | -0.016 | 0.089  | -0.100 | 0.054  |
| 24     | 21.74     | 23 | 0.5360    | 0.044  | -0.050 | -0.037 | -0.112 | -0.084 | 0.092  |

Autocorrelation Plot of Residuals

| Lag | Covariance | Correlation | -1 9 8 7 6 5 4 3 2 1 0 1 2 3 4 5 6 7 8 9 1 | Std Error |
|-----|-----------|-------------|---------------------------------------------|-----------|
| 0   | 0.052682   | 1.00000     | \|********************\|                    | 0         |
| 1   | 0.00066954 | 0.01271     | \| .                                        | 0.083918  |
| 2   | -5.3032E-7 | -.00001     | \| .                                        | 0.083932  |
| 3   | -0.0033954 | -.06445     | . *\| .                                     | 0.083932  |
| 4   | -0.0029691 | -.05636     | . *\| .                                     | 0.084280  |
| 5   | 0.0079534  | 0.15097     | . \|*** .                                   | 0.084544  |
| 6   | 0.0042760  | 0.08117     | . \|**.                                     | 0.086422  |
| 7   | -0.0027384 | -.05198     | . *\| .                                     | 0.086957  |
| 8   | 0.00063294 | 0.01201     | . \| .                                      | 0.087176  |
| 9   | -0.0052262 | -.09920     | .**\| .                                     | 0.087188  |
| 10  | 0.0036849  | 0.06995     | . \|* .                                     | 0.087979  |

(c) The RSAC

**FIGURE 12.24** (Continued)

```
                    Partial Autocorrelations

Lag    Correlation    -1 9 8 7 6 5 4 3 2 1 0 1 2 3 4 5 6 7 8 9 1

 1        0.01271     |                 .   |   .               |
 2       -0.00017     |                 .   |   .               |
 3       -0.06446     |                 .  *|   .               |
 4       -0.05496     |                 .  *|   .               |
 5        0.15335     |                 .   |***                |
 6        0.07535     |                 .   |**.                |
 7       -0.06501     |                 .  *|   .               |
 8        0.02846     |                 .   |*  .               |
 9       -0.07362     |                 .  *|   .               |
10        0.05239     |                 .   |*  .               |
```

(d) The RSPAC

```
                   Forecasts for variable y

Obs      Forecast     Std Error      95% Confidence Limits

151     262.8970       0.2295        262.4472      263.3469
152     264.2397       0.2541        263.7416      264.7378
153     263.4785       0.2766        262.9365      264.0205
154     263.4738       1.3676        260.7934      266.1542
155     263.4787       2.1861        259.1940      267.7635
156     263.4907       2.9435        257.7216      269.2599
157     263.5078       3.6530        256.3480      270.6676
158     263.5285       4.3182        255.0650      271.9921
159     263.5519       4.9421        253.8655      273.2383
160     263.5773       5.5200        252.7425      274.4120
```

(e) Forecasts of $y_{151}$ through $y_{160}$ where future values of $x_t$ are forecasted by the model $z_t^{(x)} = (1 - \theta_1^{(x)}B)a_t$   where   $z_t^{(x)} = x_t - x_{t-1}$

# Statistical Tables

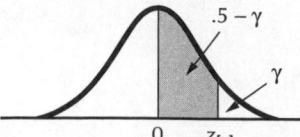

**TABLE A1** A Table of Areas under the Standard Normal Curve

| $z_{[\gamma]}$ | .00 | .01 | .02 | .03 | .04 | .05 | .06 | .07 | .08 | .09 |
|---|---|---|---|---|---|---|---|---|---|---|
| 0.0 | .0000 | .0040 | .0080 | .0120 | .0160 | .0199 | .0239 | .0279 | .0319 | .0359 |
| 0.1 | .0398 | .0438 | .0478 | .0517 | .0557 | .0596 | .0636 | .0675 | .0714 | .0753 |
| 0.2 | .0793 | .0832 | .0871 | .0910 | .0948 | .0987 | .1026 | .1064 | .1103 | .1141 |
| 0.3 | .1179 | .1217 | .1255 | .1293 | .1331 | .1368 | .1406 | .1443 | .1480 | .1517 |
| 0.4 | .1554 | .1591 | .1628 | .1664 | .1700 | .1736 | .1772 | .1808 | .1844 | .1879 |
| 0.5 | .1915 | .1950 | .1985 | .2019 | .2054 | .2088 | .2123 | .2157 | .2190 | .2224 |
| 0.6 | .2257 | .2291 | .2324 | .2357 | .2389 | .2422 | .2454 | .2486 | .2517 | .2549 |
| 0.7 | .2580 | .2611 | .2642 | .2673 | .2704 | .2734 | .2764 | .2794 | .2823 | .2852 |
| 0.8 | .2881 | .2910 | .2939 | .2967 | .2995 | .3023 | .3051 | .3078 | .3106 | .3133 |
| 0.9 | .3159 | .3186 | .3212 | .3238 | .3264 | .3289 | .3315 | .3340 | .3365 | .3389 |
| 1.0 | .3413 | .3438 | .3461 | .3485 | .3508 | .3531 | .3554 | .3577 | .3599 | .3621 |
| 1.1 | .3643 | .3665 | .3686 | .3708 | .3729 | .3749 | .3770 | .3790 | .3810 | .3830 |
| 1.2 | .3849 | .3869 | .3888 | .3907 | .3925 | .3944 | .3962 | .3980 | .3997 | .4015 |
| 1.3 | .4032 | .4049 | .4066 | .4082 | .4099 | .4115 | .4131 | .4147 | .4162 | .4177 |
| 1.4 | .4192 | .4207 | .4222 | .4236 | .4251 | .4265 | .4279 | .4292 | .4306 | .4319 |
| 1.5 | .4332 | .4345 | .4357 | .4370 | .4382 | .4394 | .4406 | .4418 | .4429 | .4441 |
| 1.6 | .4452 | .4463 | .4474 | .4484 | .4495 | .4505 | .4515 | .4525 | .4535 | .4545 |
| 1.7 | .4554 | .4564 | .4573 | .4582 | .4591 | .4599 | .4608 | .4616 | .4625 | .4633 |
| 1.8 | .4641 | .4649 | .4656 | .4664 | .4671 | .4678 | .4686 | .4693 | .4699 | .4706 |
| 1.9 | .4713 | .4719 | .4726 | .4732 | .4738 | .4744 | .4750 | .4756 | .4761 | .4767 |
| 2.0 | .4772 | .4778 | .4783 | .4788 | .4793 | .4798 | .4803 | .4808 | .4812 | .4817 |
| 2.1 | .4821 | .4826 | .4830 | .4834 | .4838 | .4842 | .4846 | .4850 | .4854 | .4857 |
| 2.2 | .4861 | .4864 | .4868 | .4871 | .4875 | .4878 | .4881 | .4884 | .4887 | .4890 |
| 2.3 | .4893 | .4896 | .4898 | .4901 | .4904 | .4906 | .4909 | .4911 | .4913 | .4916 |
| 2.4 | .4918 | .4920 | .4922 | .4925 | .4927 | .4929 | .4931 | .4932 | .4934 | .4936 |
| 2.5 | .4938 | .4940 | .4941 | .4943 | .4945 | .4946 | .4948 | .4949 | .4951 | .4952 |
| 2.6 | .4953 | .4955 | .4956 | .4957 | .4959 | .4960 | .4961 | .4962 | .4963 | .4964 |
| 2.7 | .4965 | .4966 | .4967 | .4968 | .4969 | .4970 | .4971 | .4972 | .4973 | .4974 |
| 2.8 | .4974 | .4975 | .4976 | .4977 | .4977 | .4978 | .4979 | .4979 | .4980 | .4981 |
| 2.9 | .4981 | .4982 | .4982 | .4983 | .4984 | .4984 | .4985 | .4985 | .4986 | .4986 |
| 3.0 | .4987 | .4987 | .4987 | .4988 | .4988 | .4989 | .4989 | .4989 | .4990 | .4990 |

*Source:* A. Hald, *Statistical Tables and Formulas* (New York: Wiley, 1952), abridged from Table 1. Reproduced by permission of the publisher.

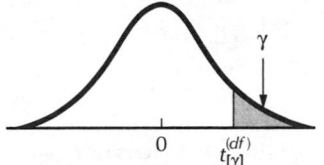

**TABLE A2** A *t*-Table: Values of $t_{[\gamma]}^{[df]}$

| $df$ | $t_{[.10]}^{(df)}$ | $t_{[.05]}^{(df)}$ | $t_{[.025]}^{(df)}$ | $t_{[.01]}^{(df)}$ | $t_{[.005]}^{(df)}$ |
|------|------|------|------|------|------|
| 1 | 3.078 | 6.314 | 12.706 | 31.821 | 63.657 |
| 2 | 1.886 | 2.920 | 4.303 | 6.965 | 9.925 |
| 3 | 1.638 | 2.353 | 3.182 | 4.541 | 5.841 |
| 4 | 1.533 | 2.132 | 2.776 | 3.747 | 4.604 |
| 5 | 1.476 | 2.015 | 2.571 | 3.365 | 4.032 |
| 6 | 1.440 | 1.943 | 2.447 | 3.143 | 3.707 |
| 7 | 1.415 | 1.895 | 2.365 | 2.998 | 3.499 |
| 8 | 1.397 | 1.860 | 2.306 | 2.896 | 3.355 |
| 9 | 1.383 | 1.833 | 2.262 | 2.821 | 3.250 |
| 10 | 1.372 | 1.812 | 2.228 | 2.764 | 3.169 |
| 11 | 1.363 | 1.796 | 2.201 | 2.718 | 3.106 |
| 12 | 1.356 | 1.782 | 2.179 | 2.681 | 3.055 |
| 13 | 1.350 | 1.771 | 2.160 | 2.650 | 3.012 |
| 14 | 1.345 | 1.761 | 2.145 | 2.624 | 2.977 |
| 15 | 1.341 | 1.753 | 2.131 | 2.602 | 2.947 |
| 16 | 1.337 | 1.746 | 2.120 | 2.583 | 2.921 |
| 17 | 1.333 | 1.740 | 2.110 | 2.567 | 2.898 |
| 18 | 1.330 | 1.734 | 2.101 | 2.552 | 2.878 |
| 19 | 1.328 | 1.729 | 2.093 | 2.539 | 2.861 |
| 20 | 1.325 | 1.725 | 2.086 | 2.528 | 2.845 |
| 21 | 1.323 | 1.721 | 2.080 | 2.518 | 2.831 |
| 22 | 1.321 | 1.717 | 2.074 | 2.508 | 2.819 |
| 23 | 1.319 | 1.714 | 2.069 | 2.500 | 2.807 |
| 24 | 1.318 | 1.711 | 2.064 | 2.492 | 2.797 |
| 25 | 1.316 | 1.708 | 2.060 | 2.485 | 2.787 |
| 26 | 1.315 | 1.706 | 2.056 | 2.479 | 2.779 |
| 27 | 1.314 | 1.703 | 2.052 | 2.473 | 2.771 |
| 28 | 1.313 | 1.701 | 2.048 | 2.467 | 2.763 |
| 29 | 1.311 | 1.699 | 2.045 | 2.462 | 2.756 |
| inf. | 1.282 | 1.645 | 1.960 | 2.326 | 2.576 |

*Source:* From "Table of Percentage Points of the *t*-Distribution," by Maxine Merrington, *Biometrika* 32 (1941), 300. Reproduced by permission of the *Biometrika* Trustees.

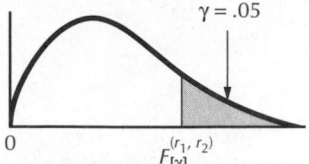

**TABLE A3** An $F$-Table: Values of $F_{[.05]}$

| Denominator Degrees of Freedom, $r_2$ | Numerator Degrees of Freedom, $r_1$ | | | | | | | | |
|---|---|---|---|---|---|---|---|---|---|
| | **1** | **2** | **3** | **4** | **5** | **6** | **7** | **8** | **9** |
| 1 | 161.4 | 199.5 | 215.7 | 224.6 | 230.2 | 234.0 | 236.8 | 238.9 | 240.5 |
| 2 | 18.51 | 19.00 | 19.16 | 19.25 | 19.30 | 19.33 | 19.35 | 19.37 | 19.38 |
| 3 | 10.13 | 9.55 | 9.28 | 9.12 | 9.01 | 8.94 | 8.89 | 8.85 | 8.81 |
| 4 | 7.71 | 6.94 | 6.59 | 6.39 | 6.26 | 6.16 | 6.09 | 6.04 | 6.00 |
| 5 | 6.61 | 5.79 | 5.41 | 5.19 | 5.05 | 4.95 | 4.88 | 4.82 | 4.77 |
| 6 | 5.99 | 5.14 | 4.76 | 4.53 | 4.39 | 4.28 | 4.21 | 4.15 | 4.10 |
| 7 | 5.59 | 4.74 | 4.35 | 4.12 | 3.97 | 3.87 | 3.79 | 3.73 | 3.68 |
| 8 | 5.32 | 4.46 | 4.07 | 3.84 | 3.69 | 3.58 | 3.50 | 3.44 | 3.39 |
| 9 | 5.12 | 4.26 | 3.86 | 3.63 | 3.48 | 3.37 | 3.29 | 3.23 | 3.18 |
| 10 | 4.96 | 4.10 | 3.71 | 3.48 | 3.33 | 3.22 | 3.14 | 3.07 | 3.02 |
| 11 | 4.84 | 3.98 | 3.59 | 3.36 | 3.20 | 3.09 | 3.01 | 2.95 | 2.90 |
| 12 | 4.75 | 3.89 | 3.49 | 3.26 | 3.11 | 3.00 | 2.91 | 2.85 | 2.80 |
| 13 | 4.67 | 3.81 | 3.41 | 3.18 | 3.03 | 2.92 | 2.83 | 2.77 | 2.71 |
| 14 | 4.60 | 3.74 | 3.34 | 3.11 | 2.96 | 2.85 | 2.76 | 2.70 | 2.65 |
| 15 | 4.54 | 3.68 | 3.29 | 3.06 | 2.90 | 2.79 | 2.71 | 2.64 | 2.59 |
| 16 | 4.49 | 3.63 | 3.24 | 3.01 | 2.85 | 2.74 | 2.66 | 2.59 | 2.54 |
| 17 | 4.45 | 3.59 | 3.20 | 2.96 | 2.81 | 2.70 | 2.61 | 2.55 | 2.49 |
| 18 | 4.41 | 3.55 | 3.16 | 2.93 | 2.77 | 2.66 | 2.58 | 2.51 | 2.46 |
| 19 | 4.38 | 3.52 | 3.13 | 2.90 | 2.74 | 2.63 | 2.54 | 2.48 | 2.42 |
| 20 | 4.35 | 3.49 | 3.10 | 2.87 | 2.71 | 2.60 | 2.51 | 2.45 | 2.39 |
| 21 | 4.32 | 3.47 | 3.07 | 2.84 | 2.68 | 2.57 | 2.49 | 2.42 | 2.37 |
| 22 | 4.30 | 3.44 | 3.05 | 2.82 | 2.66 | 2.55 | 2.46 | 2.40 | 2.34 |
| 23 | 4.28 | 3.42 | 3.03 | 2.80 | 2.64 | 2.53 | 2.44 | 2.37 | 2.32 |
| 24 | 4.26 | 3.40 | 3.01 | 2.78 | 2.62 | 2.51 | 2.42 | 2.36 | 2.30 |
| 25 | 4.24 | 3.39 | 2.99 | 2.76 | 2.60 | 2.49 | 2.40 | 2.34 | 2.28 |
| 26 | 4.23 | 3.37 | 2.98 | 2.74 | 2.59 | 2.47 | 2.39 | 2.32 | 2.27 |
| 27 | 4.21 | 3.35 | 2.96 | 2.73 | 2.57 | 2.46 | 2.37 | 2.31 | 2.25 |
| 28 | 4.20 | 3.34 | 2.95 | 2.71 | 2.56 | 2.45 | 2.36 | 2.29 | 2.24 |
| 29 | 4.18 | 3.33 | 2.93 | 2.70 | 2.55 | 2.43 | 2.35 | 2.28 | 2.22 |
| 30 | 4.17 | 3.32 | 2.92 | 2.69 | 2.53 | 2.42 | 2.33 | 2.27 | 2.21 |
| 40 | 4.08 | 3.23 | 2.84 | 2.61 | 2.45 | 2.34 | 2.25 | 2.18 | 2.12 |
| 60 | 4.00 | 3.15 | 2.76 | 2.53 | 2.37 | 2.25 | 2.17 | 2.10 | 2.04 |
| 120 | 3.92 | 3.07 | 2.68 | 2.45 | 2.29 | 2.17 | 2.09 | 2.02 | 1.96 |
| ∞ | 3.84 | 3.00 | 2.60 | 2.37 | 2.21 | 2.10 | 2.01 | 1.94 | 1.88 |

*Source:* From "Tables of Percentage Points of the Inverted Beta ($F$)-Distribution," by Maxine Merrington and Catherine M. Thompson, *Biometrika* 33 (1943), 73–88. Reproduced by permission of the *Biometrika* Trustees.

| Denominator Degrees of Freedom, $r_2$ | Numerator Degrees of Freedom, $r_1$ | | | | | | | | | |
|---|---|---|---|---|---|---|---|---|---|---|
| | 10 | 12 | 15 | 20 | 24 | 30 | 40 | 60 | 120 | ∞ |
| 1 | 241.9 | 243.9 | 245.9 | 248.0 | 249.1 | 250.1 | 251.1 | 252.2 | 253.3 | 254.3 |
| 2 | 19.40 | 19.41 | 19.43 | 19.45 | 19.45 | 19.46 | 19.47 | 19.48 | 19.49 | 19.50 |
| 3 | 8.79 | 8.74 | 8.70 | 8.66 | 8.64 | 8.62 | 8.59 | 8.57 | 8.55 | 8.53 |
| 4 | 5.96 | 5.91 | 5.86 | 5.80 | 5.77 | 5.75 | 5.72 | 5.69 | 5.66 | 5.63 |
| 5 | 4.74 | 4.68 | 4.62 | 4.56 | 4.53 | 4.50 | 4.46 | 4.43 | 4.40 | 4.36 |
| 6 | 4.06 | 4.00 | 3.94 | 3.87 | 3.84 | 3.81 | 3.77 | 3.74 | 3.70 | 3.67 |
| 7 | 3.64 | 3.57 | 3.51 | 3.44 | 3.41 | 3.38 | 3.34 | 3.30 | 3.27 | 3.23 |
| 8 | 3.35 | 3.28 | 3.22 | 3.15 | 3.12 | 3.08 | 3.04 | 3.01 | 2.97 | 2.93 |
| 9 | 3.14 | 3.07 | 3.01 | 2.94 | 2.90 | 2.86 | 2.83 | 2.79 | 2.75 | 2.71 |
| 10 | 2.98 | 2.91 | 2.85 | 2.77 | 2.74 | 2.70 | 2.66 | 2.62 | 2.58 | 2.54 |
| 11 | 2.85 | 2.79 | 2.72 | 2.65 | 2.61 | 2.57 | 2.53 | 2.49 | 2.45 | 2.40 |
| 12 | 2.75 | 2.69 | 2.62 | 2.54 | 2.51 | 2.47 | 2.43 | 2.38 | 2.34 | 2.30 |
| 13 | 2.67 | 2.60 | 2.53 | 2.46 | 2.42 | 2.38 | 2.34 | 2.30 | 2.25 | 2.21 |
| 14 | 2.60 | 2.53 | 2.46 | 2.39 | 2.35 | 2.31 | 2.27 | 2.22 | 2.18 | 2.13 |
| 15 | 2.54 | 2.48 | 2.40 | 2.33 | 2.29 | 2.25 | 2.20 | 2.16 | 2.11 | 2.07 |
| 16 | 2.49 | 2.42 | 2.35 | 2.28 | 2.24 | 2.19 | 2.15 | 2.11 | 2.06 | 2.01 |
| 17 | 2.45 | 2.38 | 2.31 | 2.23 | 2.19 | 2.15 | 2.10 | 2.06 | 2.01 | 1.96 |
| 18 | 2.41 | 2.34 | 2.27 | 2.19 | 2.15 | 2.11 | 2.06 | 2.02 | 1.97 | 1.92 |
| 19 | 2.38 | 2.31 | 2.23 | 2.16 | 2.11 | 2.07 | 2.03 | 1.98 | 1.93 | 1.88 |
| 20 | 2.35 | 2.28 | 2.20 | 2.12 | 2.08 | 2.04 | 1.99 | 1.95 | 1.90 | 1.84 |
| 21 | 2.32 | 2.25 | 2.18 | 2.10 | 2.05 | 2.01 | 1.96 | 1.92 | 1.87 | 1.81 |
| 22 | 2.30 | 2.23 | 2.15 | 2.07 | 2.03 | 1.98 | 1.94 | 1.89 | 1.84 | 1.78 |
| 23 | 2.27 | 2.20 | 2.13 | 2.05 | 2.01 | 1.96 | 1.91 | 1.86 | 1.81 | 1.76 |
| 24 | 2.25 | 2.18 | 2.11 | 2.03 | 1.98 | 1.94 | 1.89 | 1.84 | 1.79 | 1.73 |
| 25 | 2.24 | 2.16 | 2.09 | 2.01 | 1.96 | 1.92 | 1.87 | 1.82 | 1.77 | 1.71 |
| 26 | 2.22 | 2.15 | 2.07 | 1.99 | 1.95 | 1.90 | 1.85 | 1.80 | 1.75 | 1.69 |
| 27 | 2.20 | 2.13 | 2.06 | 1.97 | 1.93 | 1.88 | 1.84 | 1.79 | 1.73 | 1.67 |
| 28 | 2.19 | 2.12 | 2.04 | 1.96 | 1.91 | 1.87 | 1.82 | 1.77 | 1.71 | 1.65 |
| 29 | 2.18 | 2.10 | 2.03 | 1.94 | 1.90 | 1.85 | 1.81 | 1.75 | 1.70 | 1.64 |
| 30 | 2.16 | 2.09 | 2.01 | 1.93 | 1.89 | 1.84 | 1.79 | 1.74 | 1.68 | 1.62 |
| 40 | 2.08 | 2.00 | 1.92 | 1.84 | 1.79 | 1.74 | 1.69 | 1.64 | 1.58 | 1.51 |
| 60 | 1.99 | 1.92 | 1.84 | 1.75 | 1.70 | 1.65 | 1.59 | 1.53 | 1.47 | 1.39 |
| 120 | 1.91 | 1.83 | 1.75 | 1.66 | 1.61 | 1.55 | 1.50 | 1.43 | 1.35 | 1.25 |
| ∞ | 1.83 | 1.75 | 1.67 | 1.57 | 1.52 | 1.46 | 1.39 | 1.32 | 1.22 | 1.00 |

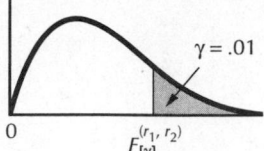

**TABLE A4** An *F*-Table: Values of $F_{[.01]}$

| Denominator Degrees of Freedom, $r_2$ | Numerator Degrees of Freedom, $r_1$ | | | | | | | | |
|---|---|---|---|---|---|---|---|---|---|
| | **1** | **2** | **3** | **4** | **5** | **6** | **7** | **8** | **9** |
| 1 | 4052 | 4999.5 | 5403 | 5625 | 5764 | 5859 | 5928 | 5982 | 6022 |
| 2 | 98.50 | 99.00 | 99.17 | 99.25 | 99.30 | 99.33 | 99.36 | 99.37 | 99.39 |
| 3 | 34.12 | 30.82 | 29.46 | 28.71 | 28.24 | 27.91 | 27.67 | 27.49 | 27.35 |
| 4 | 21.20 | 18.00 | 16.69 | 15.98 | 15.52 | 15.21 | 14.98 | 14.80 | 14.66 |
| 5 | 16.26 | 13.27 | 12.06 | 11.39 | 10.97 | 10.67 | 10.46 | 10.29 | 10.16 |
| 6 | 13.75 | 10.92 | 9.78 | 9.15 | 8.75 | 8.47 | 8.26 | 8.10 | 7.98 |
| 7 | 12.25 | 9.55 | 8.45 | 7.85 | 7.46 | 7.19 | 6.99 | 6.84 | 6.72 |
| 8 | 11.26 | 8.65 | 7.59 | 7.01 | 6.63 | 6.37 | 6.18 | 6.03 | 5.91 |
| 9 | 10.56 | 8.02 | 6.99 | 6.42 | 6.06 | 5.80 | 5.61 | 5.47 | 5.35 |
| 10 | 10.04 | 7.56 | 6.55 | 5.99 | 5.64 | 5.39 | 5.20 | 5.06 | 4.94 |
| 11 | 9.65 | 7.21 | 6.22 | 5.67 | 5.32 | 5.07 | 4.89 | 4.74 | 4.63 |
| 12 | 9.33 | 6.93 | 5.95 | 5.41 | 5.06 | 4.82 | 4.64 | 4.50 | 4.39 |
| 13 | 9.07 | 6.70 | 5.74 | 5.21 | 4.86 | 4.62 | 4.44 | 4.30 | 4.19 |
| 14 | 8.86 | 6.51 | 5.56 | 5.04 | 4.69 | 4.46 | 4.28 | 4.14 | 4.03 |
| 15 | 8.68 | 6.36 | 5.42 | 4.89 | 4.56 | 4.32 | 4.14 | 4.00 | 3.89 |
| 16 | 8.53 | 6.23 | 5.29 | 4.77 | 4.44 | 4.20 | 4.03 | 3.89 | 3.78 |
| 17 | 8.40 | 6.11 | 5.18 | 4.67 | 4.34 | 4.10 | 3.93 | 3.79 | 3.68 |
| 18 | 8.29 | 6.01 | 5.09 | 4.58 | 4.25 | 4.01 | 3.84 | 3.71 | 3.60 |
| 19 | 8.18 | 5.93 | 5.01 | 4.50 | 4.17 | 3.94 | 3.77 | 3.63 | 3.52 |
| 20 | 8.10 | 5.85 | 4.94 | 4.43 | 4.10 | 3.87 | 3.70 | 3.56 | 3.46 |
| 21 | 8.02 | 5.78 | 4.87 | 4.37 | 4.04 | 3.81 | 3.64 | 3.51 | 3.40 |
| 22 | 7.95 | 5.72 | 4.82 | 4.31 | 3.99 | 3.76 | 3.59 | 3.45 | 3.35 |
| 23 | 7.88 | 5.66 | 4.76 | 4.26 | 3.94 | 3.71 | 3.54 | 3.41 | 3.30 |
| 24 | 7.82 | 5.61 | 4.72 | 4.22 | 3.90 | 3.67 | 3.50 | 3.36 | 3.26 |
| 25 | 7.77 | 5.57 | 4.68 | 4.18 | 3.85 | 3.63 | 3.46 | 3.32 | 3.22 |
| 26 | 7.72 | 5.53 | 4.64 | 4.14 | 3.82 | 3.59 | 3.42 | 3.29 | 3.18 |
| 27 | 7.68 | 5.49 | 4.60 | 4.11 | 3.78 | 3.56 | 3.39 | 3.26 | 3.15 |
| 28 | 7.64 | 5.45 | 4.57 | 4.07 | 3.75 | 3.53 | 3.36 | 3.23 | 3.12 |
| 29 | 7.60 | 5.42 | 4.54 | 4.04 | 3.73 | 3.50 | 3.33 | 3.20 | 3.09 |
| 30 | 7.56 | 5.39 | 4.51 | 4.02 | 3.70 | 3.47 | 3.30 | 3.17 | 3.07 |
| 40 | 7.31 | 5.18 | 4.31 | 3.83 | 3.51 | 3.29 | 3.12 | 2.99 | 2.89 |
| 60 | 7.08 | 4.98 | 4.13 | 3.65 | 3.34 | 3.12 | 2.95 | 2.82 | 2.72 |
| 120 | 6.85 | 4.79 | 3.95 | 3.48 | 3.17 | 2.96 | 2.79 | 2.66 | 2.50 |
| ∞ | 6.63 | 4.61 | 3.78 | 3.32 | 3.02 | 2.80 | 2.64 | 2.51 | 2.41 |

*Source:* From "Tables of Percentage Points of the inverted Beta (*F*)-Distribution," by Maxine Merrington and Cathrine M. Thompson, *Biometrika* 33 (1943), 73–88. Reproduced by permission of the *Biometrika* Trustees.

| Denominator Degrees of Freedom, $r_2$ | Numerator Degrees of Freedom, $r_1$ | | | | | | | | | |
|---|---|---|---|---|---|---|---|---|---|---|
| | 10 | 12 | 15 | 20 | 24 | 30 | 40 | 60 | 120 | ∞ |
| 1 | 6056 | 6106 | 6157 | 6209 | 6235 | 6261 | 6287 | 6313 | 6339 | 6366 |
| 2 | 99.49 | 99.42 | 99.43 | 99.45 | 99.46 | 99.47 | 99.47 | 99.48 | 99.49 | 99.50 |
| 3 | 27.23 | 27.05 | 26.87 | 26.69 | 26.60 | 26.50 | 26.41 | 26.32 | 26.22 | 26.13 |
| 4 | 14.55 | 14.37 | 14.20 | 14.02 | 13.93 | 13.84 | 13.75 | 13.65 | 13.56 | 13.46 |
| 5 | 10.05 | 9.89 | 9.72 | 9.55 | 9.47 | 9.38 | 9.29 | 9.20 | 9.11 | 9.02 |
| 6 | 7.87 | 7.72 | 7.56 | 7.40 | 7.31 | 7.23 | 7.14 | 7.06 | 6.97 | 6.88 |
| 7 | 6.62 | 6.47 | 6.31 | 6.16 | 6.07 | 5.99 | 5.91 | 5.82 | 5.74 | 5.65 |
| 8 | 5.81 | 5.67 | 5.52 | 5.36 | 5.28 | 5.20 | 5.12 | 5.03 | 4.95 | 4.86 |
| 9 | 5.26 | 5.11 | 4.96 | 4.81 | 4.73 | 4.65 | 4.57 | 4.48 | 4.40 | 4.31 |
| 10 | 4.85 | 4.71 | 4.56 | 4.41 | 4.33 | 4.25 | 4.17 | 4.08 | 4.00 | 3.91 |
| 11 | 4.54 | 4.40 | 4.25 | 4.10 | 4.02 | 3.94 | 3.86 | 3.78 | 3.69 | 3.60 |
| 12 | 4.30 | 4.16 | 4.01 | 3.86 | 3.78 | 3.70 | 3.62 | 3.54 | 3.45 | 3.36 |
| 13 | 4.10 | 3.96 | 3.82 | 3.66 | 3.59 | 3.51 | 3.43 | 3.34 | 3.25 | 3.17 |
| 14 | 3.94 | 3.80 | 3.66 | 3.51 | 3.43 | 3.35 | 3.27 | 3.18 | 3.09 | 3.00 |
| 15 | 3.80 | 3.67 | 3.52 | 3.37 | 3.29 | 3.21 | 3.13 | 3.05 | 2.96 | 2.87 |
| 16 | 3.69 | 3.55 | 3.41 | 3.26 | 3.18 | 3.10 | 3.02 | 2.93 | 2.84 | 2.75 |
| 17 | 3.59 | 3.46 | 3.31 | 3.16 | 3.08 | 3.00 | 2.92 | 2.83 | 2.75 | 2.65 |
| 18 | 3.51 | 3.37 | 3.23 | 3.08 | 3.00 | 2.92 | 2.84 | 2.75 | 2.66 | 2.57 |
| 19 | 3.43 | 3.30 | 3.15 | 3.00 | 2.92 | 2.84 | 2.76 | 2.67 | 2.58 | 2.49 |
| 20 | 3.37 | 3.23 | 3.09 | 2.94 | 2.86 | 2.78 | 2.69 | 2.61 | 2.52 | 2.42 |
| 21 | 3.31 | 3.17 | 3.03 | 2.88 | 2.80 | 2.72 | 2.64 | 2.55 | 2.46 | 2.36 |
| 22 | 3.26 | 3.12 | 2.98 | 2.83 | 2.75 | 2.67 | 2.58 | 2.50 | 2.40 | 2.31 |
| 23 | 3.21 | 3.07 | 2.93 | 2.78 | 2.70 | 2.62 | 2.54 | 2.45 | 2.35 | 2.26 |
| 24 | 3.17 | 3.03 | 2.89 | 2.74 | 2.66 | 2.58 | 2.49 | 2.40 | 2.31 | 2.21 |
| 25 | 3.13 | 2.99 | 2.85 | 2.70 | 2.62 | 2.54 | 2.45 | 2.36 | 2.27 | 2.17 |
| 26 | 3.09 | 2.96 | 2.81 | 2.66 | 2.58 | 2.50 | 2.42 | 2.33 | 2.23 | 2.13 |
| 27 | 3.06 | 2.93 | 2.78 | 2.63 | 2.55 | 2.47 | 2.38 | 2.29 | 2.20 | 2.10 |
| 28 | 3.03 | 2.90 | 2.75 | 2.60 | 2.52 | 2.44 | 2.35 | 2.26 | 2.17 | 2.06 |
| 29 | 3.00 | 2.87 | 2.73 | 2.57 | 2.49 | 2.41 | 2.33 | 2.23 | 2.14 | 2.03 |
| 30 | 2.98 | 2.84 | 2.70 | 2.55 | 2.47 | 2.39 | 2.30 | 2.21 | 2.11 | 2.01 |
| 40 | 2.80 | 2.66 | 2.52 | 2.37 | 2.29 | 2.20 | 2.11 | 2.02 | 1.92 | 1.80 |
| 60 | 2.63 | 2.50 | 2.35 | 2.20 | 2.12 | 2.03 | 1.94 | 1.84 | 1.73 | 1.60 |
| 120 | 2.47 | 2.34 | 2.19 | 2.03 | 1.95 | 1.86 | 1.76 | 1.66 | 1.53 | 1.38 |
| ∞ | 2.32 | 2.18 | 2.04 | 1.88 | 1.79 | 1.70 | 1.59 | 1.47 | 1.32 | 1.00 |

**TABLE A5** A Durbin–Watson Table: Values of $d_{L,.05}$ and $d_{U,.05}$

| n | k = 1 | | k = 2 | | k = 3 | | k = 4 | | k = 5 | |
|---|---|---|---|---|---|---|---|---|---|---|
| | $d_{L,.05}$ | $d_{U,.05}$ | $d_{L,.05}$ | $d_{U,.05}$ | $d_{L,.05}$ | $d_{U,.05}$ | $d_{L,.05}$ | $d_{U,.05}$ | $d_{L,.05}$ | $d_{U,.05}$ |
| 15 | 1.08 | 1.36 | 0.95 | 1.54 | 0.82 | 1.75 | 0.69 | 1.97 | 0.56 | 2.21 |
| 16 | 1.10 | 1.37 | 0.98 | 1.54 | 0.86 | 1.73 | 0.74 | 1.93 | 0.62 | 2.15 |
| 17 | 1.13 | 1.38 | 1.02 | 1.54 | 0.90 | 1.71 | 0.78 | 1.90 | 0.67 | 2.10 |
| 18 | 1.16 | 1.39 | 1.05 | 1.53 | 0.93 | 1.69 | 0.82 | 1.87 | 0.71 | 2.06 |
| 19 | 1.18 | 1.40 | 1.08 | 1.53 | 0.97 | 1.68 | 0.86 | 1.85 | 0.75 | 2.02 |
| 20 | 1.20 | 1.41 | 1.10 | 1.54 | 1.00 | 1.68 | 0.90 | 1.83 | 0.79 | 1.99 |
| 21 | 1.22 | 1.42 | 1.13 | 1.54 | 1.03 | 1.67 | 0.93 | 1.81 | 0.83 | 1.96 |
| 22 | 1.24 | 1.43 | 1.15 | 1.54 | 1.05 | 1.66 | 0.96 | 1.80 | 0.86 | 1.94 |
| 23 | 1.26 | 1.44 | 1.17 | 1.54 | 1.08 | 1.66 | 0.99 | 1.79 | 0.90 | 1.92 |
| 24 | 1.27 | 1.45 | 1.19 | 1.55 | 1.10 | 1.66 | 1.01 | 1.78 | 0.93 | 1.90 |
| 25 | 1.29 | 1.45 | 1.21 | 1.55 | 1.12 | 1.66 | 1.04 | 1.77 | 0.95 | 1.89 |
| 26 | 1.30 | 1.46 | 1.22 | 1.55 | 1.14 | 1.65 | 1.06 | 1.76 | 0.98 | 1.88 |
| 27 | 1.32 | 1.47 | 1.24 | 1.56 | 1.16 | 1.65 | 1.08 | 1.76 | 1.01 | 1.86 |
| 28 | 1.33 | 1.48 | 1.26 | 1.56 | 1.18 | 1.65 | 1.10 | 1.75 | 1.03 | 1.85 |
| 29 | 1.34 | 1.48 | 1.27 | 1.56 | 1.20 | 1.65 | 1.12 | 1.74 | 1.05 | 1.84 |
| 30 | 1.35 | 1.49 | 1.28 | 1.57 | 1.21 | 1.65 | 1.14 | 1.74 | 1.07 | 1.83 |
| 31 | 1.36 | 1.50 | 1.30 | 1.57 | 1.23 | 1.65 | 1.16 | 1.74 | 1.09 | 1.83 |
| 32 | 1.37 | 1.50 | 1.31 | 1.57 | 1.24 | 1.65 | 1.18 | 1.73 | 1.11 | 1.82 |
| 33 | 1.38 | 1.51 | 1.32 | 1.58 | 1.26 | 1.65 | 1.19 | 1.73 | 1.13 | 1.81 |
| 34 | 1.39 | 1.51 | 1.33 | 1.58 | 1.27 | 1.65 | 1.21 | 1.73 | 1.15 | 1.81 |
| 35 | 1.40 | 1.52 | 1.34 | 1.58 | 1.28 | 1.65 | 1.22 | 1.73 | 1.16 | 1.80 |
| 36 | 1.41 | 1.52 | 1.35 | 1.59 | 1.29 | 1.65 | 1.24 | 1.73 | 1.18 | 1.80 |
| 37 | 1.42 | 1.53 | 1.36 | 1.59 | 1.31 | 1.66 | 1.25 | 1.72 | 1.19 | 1.80 |
| 38 | 1.43 | 1.54 | 1.37 | 1.59 | 1.32 | 1.66 | 1.26 | 1.72 | 1.21 | 1.79 |
| 39 | 1.43 | 1.54 | 1.38 | 1.60 | 1.33 | 1.66 | 1.27 | 1.72 | 1.22 | 1.79 |
| 40 | 1.44 | 1.54 | 1.39 | 1.60 | 1.34 | 1.66 | 1.29 | 1.72 | 1.23 | 1.79 |
| 45 | 1.48 | 1.57 | 1.43 | 1.62 | 1.38 | 1.67 | 1.34 | 1.72 | 1.29 | 1.78 |
| 50 | 1.50 | 1.59 | 1.46 | 1.63 | 1.42 | 1.67 | 1.38 | 1.72 | 1.34 | 1.77 |
| 55 | 1.53 | 1.60 | 1.49 | 1.64 | 1.45 | 1.68 | 1.41 | 1.72 | 1.38 | 1.77 |
| 60 | 1.55 | 1.62 | 1.51 | 1.65 | 1.48 | 1.69 | 1.44 | 1.73 | 1.41 | 1.77 |
| 65 | 1.57 | 1.63 | 1.54 | 1.66 | 1.50 | 1.70 | 1.47 | 1.73 | 1.44 | 1.77 |
| 70 | 1.58 | 1.64 | 1.55 | 1.67 | 1.52 | 1.70 | 1.49 | 1.74 | 1.46 | 1.77 |
| 75 | 1.60 | 1.65 | 1.57 | 1.68 | 1.54 | 1.71 | 1.51 | 1.74 | 1.49 | 1.77 |
| 80 | 1.61 | 1.66 | 1.59 | 1.69 | 1.56 | 1.72 | 1.53 | 1.74 | 1.51 | 1.77 |
| 85 | 1.62 | 1.67 | 1.60 | 1.70 | 1.57 | 1.72 | 1.55 | 1.75 | 1.52 | 1.77 |
| 90 | 1.63 | 1.68 | 1.61 | 1.70 | 1.59 | 1.73 | 1.57 | 1.75 | 1.54 | 1.78 |
| 95 | 1.64 | 1.69 | 1.62 | 1.71 | 1.60 | 1.73 | 1.58 | 1.75 | 1.56 | 1.78 |
| 100 | 1.65 | 1.69 | 1.63 | 1.72 | 1.61 | 1.74 | 1.59 | 1.76 | 1.57 | 1.78 |

*Source:* From J. Durbin and G. S. Watson, "Testing for Serial Correlation in Least Squares Regression, II," *Biometrika* 30 (1951), 159–178. Reproduced by permission of the *Biometrika* Trustees.

**TABLE A6** A Durbin–Watson Table: Values of $d_{L,.01}$ and $d_{U,.01}$

| n | k = 1 | | k = 2 | | k = 3 | | k = 4 | | k = 5 | |
|---|---|---|---|---|---|---|---|---|---|---|
| | $d_{L,.01}$ | $d_{U,.01}$ | $d_{L,.01}$ | $d_{U,.01}$ | $d_{L,.01}$ | $d_{U,.01}$ | $d_{L,.01}$ | $d_{U,.01}$ | $d_{L,.01}$ | $d_{U,.01}$ |
| 15 | .81 | 1.07 | .70 | 1.25 | .59 | 1.46 | .49 | 1.70 | .39 | 1.96 |
| 16 | .84 | 1.09 | .74 | 1.25 | .63 | 1.44 | .53 | 1.66 | .44 | 1.90 |
| 17 | .87 | 1.10 | .77 | 1.25 | .67 | 1.43 | .57 | 1.63 | .48 | 1.85 |
| 18 | .90 | 1.12 | .80 | 1.26 | .71 | 1.42 | .61 | 1.60 | .52 | 1.80 |
| 19 | .93 | 1.13 | .83 | 1.26 | .74 | 1.41 | .65 | 1.58 | .56 | 1.77 |
| 20 | .95 | 1.15 | .86 | 1.27 | .77 | 1.41 | .68 | 1.57 | .60 | 1.74 |
| 21 | .97 | 1.16 | .89 | 1.27 | .80 | 1.41 | .72 | 1.55 | .63 | 1.71 |
| 22 | 1.00 | 1.17 | .91 | 1.28 | .83 | 1.40 | .75 | 1.54 | .66 | 1.69 |
| 23 | 1.02 | 1.19 | .94 | 1.29 | .86 | 1.40 | .77 | 1.53 | .70 | 1.67 |
| 24 | 1.04 | 1.20 | .96 | 1.30 | .88 | 1.41 | .80 | 1.53 | .72 | 1.66 |
| 25 | 1.05 | 1.21 | .98 | 1.30 | .90 | 1.41 | .83 | 1.52 | .75 | 1.65 |
| 26 | 1.07 | 1.22 | 1.00 | 1.31 | .93 | 1.41 | .85 | 1.52 | .78 | 1.64 |
| 27 | 1.09 | 1.23 | 1.02 | 1.32 | .95 | 1.41 | .88 | 1.51 | .81 | 1.63 |
| 28 | 1.10 | 1.24 | 1.04 | 1.32 | .97 | 1.41 | .90 | 1.51 | .83 | 1.62 |
| 29 | 1.12 | 1.25 | 1.05 | 1.33 | .99 | 1.42 | .92 | 1.51 | .85 | 1.61 |
| 30 | 1.13 | 1.26 | 1.07 | 1.34 | 1.01 | 1.42 | .94 | 1.51 | .88 | 1.61 |
| 31 | 1.15 | 1.27 | 1.08 | 1.34 | 1.02 | 1.42 | .96 | 1.51 | .90 | 1.60 |
| 32 | 1.16 | 1.28 | 1.10 | 1.35 | 1.04 | 1.43 | .98 | 1.51 | .92 | 1.60 |
| 33 | 1.17 | 1.29 | 1.11 | 1.36 | 1.05 | 1.43 | 1.00 | 1.51 | .94 | 1.59 |
| 34 | 1.18 | 1.30 | 1.13 | 1.36 | 1.07 | 1.43 | 1.01 | 1.51 | .95 | 1.59 |
| 35 | 1.19 | 1.31 | 1.14 | 1.37 | 1.08 | 1.44 | 1.03 | 1.51 | .97 | 1.59 |
| 36 | 1.21 | 1.32 | 1.15 | 1.38 | 1.10 | 1.44 | 1.04 | 1.51 | .99 | 1.59 |
| 37 | 1.22 | 1.32 | 1.16 | 1.38 | 1.11 | 1.45 | 1.06 | 1.51 | 1.00 | 1.59 |
| 38 | 1.23 | 1.33 | 1.18 | 1.39 | 1.12 | 1.45 | 1.07 | 1.52 | 1.02 | 1.58 |
| 39 | 1.24 | 1.34 | 1.19 | 1.39 | 1.14 | 1.45 | 1.09 | 1.52 | 1.03 | 1.58 |
| 40 | 1.25 | 1.34 | 1.20 | 1.40 | 1.15 | 1.46 | 1.10 | 1.52 | 1.05 | 1.58 |
| 45 | 1.29 | 1.38 | 1.24 | 1.42 | 1.20 | 1.48 | 1.16 | 1.53 | 1.11 | 1.58 |
| 50 | 1.32 | 1.40 | 1.28 | 1.45 | 1.24 | 1.49 | 1.20 | 1.54 | 1.16 | 1.59 |
| 55 | 1.36 | 1.43 | 1.32 | 1.47 | 1.28 | 1.51 | 1.25 | 1.55 | 1.21 | 1.59 |
| 60 | 1.38 | 1.45 | 1.35 | 1.48 | 1.32 | 1.52 | 1.28 | 1.56 | 1.25 | 1.60 |
| 65 | 1.41 | 1.47 | 1.38 | 1.50 | 1.35 | 1.53 | 1.31 | 1.57 | 1.28 | 1.61 |
| 70 | 1.43 | 1.49 | 1.40 | 1.52 | 1.37 | 1.55 | 1.34 | 1.58 | 1.31 | 1.61 |
| 75 | 1.45 | 1.50 | 1.42 | 1.53 | 1.39 | 1.56 | 1.37 | 1.59 | 1.34 | 1.62 |
| 80 | 1.47 | 1.52 | 1.44 | 1.54 | 1.42 | 1.57 | 1.39 | 1.60 | 1.36 | 1.62 |
| 85 | 1.48 | 1.53 | 1.46 | 1.55 | 1.43 | 1.58 | 1.41 | 1.60 | 1.39 | 1.63 |
| 90 | 1.50 | 1.54 | 1.47 | 1.56 | 1.45 | 1.59 | 1.43 | 1.61 | 1.41 | 1.64 |
| 95 | 1.51 | 1.55 | 1.49 | 1.57 | 1.47 | 1.60 | 1.45 | 1.62 | 1.42 | 1.64 |
| 100 | 1.52 | 1.56 | 1.50 | 1.58 | 1.48 | 1.60 | 1.46 | 1.63 | 1.44 | 1.65 |

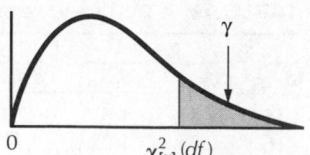

**TABLE A7** A Chi-Square Table: Values of $\chi^2_{[\gamma]}(df)$

| df | $\chi^2_{[.995]}(df)$ | $\chi^2_{[.99]}(df)$ | $\chi^2_{[.975]}(df)$ | $\chi^2_{[.95]}(df)$ | $\chi^2_{[.90]}(df)$ |
|---|---|---|---|---|---|
| 1 | .0000393 | .0001571 | .0009821 | .0039321 | .0157908 |
| 2 | .0100251 | .0201007 | .0506356 | .102587 | .210720 |
| 3 | .0717212 | .114832 | .215795 | .341846 | .584375 |
| 4 | .206990 | .297110 | .484419 | .710721 | .063623 |
| 5 | .411740 | .554300 | .831211 | 1.145476 | 1.61031 |
| 6 | .675727 | .872085 | 1.237347 | 1.63539 | 2.20413 |
| 7 | .989265 | 1.239043 | 1.68987 | 2.16735 | 2.83311 |
| 8 | 1.344419 | 1.646482 | 2.17973 | 2.73264 | 3.48954 |
| 9 | 1.734926 | 2.087912 | 2.70039 | 3.32511 | 4.16816 |
| 10 | 2.15585 | 2.55821 | 3.24697 | 3.94030 | 4.86518 |
| 11 | 2.60321 | 3.05347 | 3.81575 | 4.57481 | 5.57779 |
| 12 | 3.07382 | 3.57056 | 4.40379 | 5.22603 | 6.30380 |
| 13 | 3.56503 | 4.10691 | 5.00874 | 5.89186 | 7.04150 |
| 14 | 4.07468 | 4.66043 | 5.62872 | 6.57063 | 7.78953 |
| 15 | 4.60094 | 5.22935 | 6.26214 | 7.26094 | 8.54675 |
| 16 | 5.14224 | 5.81221 | 6.90766 | 7.96164 | 9.31223 |
| 17 | 5.69724 | 6.40776 | 7.56418 | 8.67176 | 10.0852 |
| 18 | 6.26481 | 7.01491 | 8.23075 | 9.39046 | 10.8649 |
| 19 | 6.84398 | 7.63273 | 8.90655 | 10.1170 | 11.6509 |
| 20 | 7.43386 | 8.26040 | 9.59083 | 10.8508 | 12.4426 |
| 21 | 8.03366 | 8.89720 | 10.28293 | 11.5913 | 13.2396 |
| 22 | 8.64272 | 9.54249 | 10.9823 | 12.3380 | 14.0415 |
| 23 | 9.26042 | 10.19567 | 11.6885 | 13.0905 | 14.8479 |
| 24 | 9.88623 | 10.8564 | 12.4011 | 13.8484 | 15.6587 |
| 25 | 10.5197 | 11.5240 | 13.1197 | 14.6114 | 16.4734 |
| 26 | 11.1603 | 12.1981 | 13.8439 | 15.3791 | 17.2919 |
| 27 | 11.8076 | 12.8786 | 14.5733 | 16.1513 | 18.1138 |
| 28 | 12.4613 | 13.5648 | 15.3079 | 16.9279 | 18.9392 |
| 29 | 13.1211 | 14.2565 | 16.0471 | 17.7083 | 19.7677 |
| 30 | 13.7867 | 14.9535 | 16.7908 | 18.4926 | 20.5992 |
| 40 | 20.7065 | 22.1643 | 24.4331 | 26.5093 | 29.0505 |
| 50 | 27.9907 | 29.7067 | 32.3574 | 34.7642 | 37.6886 |
| 60 | 35.5346 | 37.4848 | 40.4817 | 43.1879 | 46.4589 |
| 70 | 43.2752 | 45.4418 | 48.7576 | 51.7393 | 55.3290 |
| 80 | 51.1720 | 53.5400 | 57.1532 | 60.3915 | 64.2778 |
| 90 | 59.1963 | 61.7541 | 65.6466 | 69.1260 | 73.2912 |
| 100 | 67.3276 | 70.0648 | 74.2219 | 77.9295 | 82.3581 |

*Source:* From "Tables of the Percentage Points of the $\chi^2$-Distribution," by Catherine M. Thompson, *Biometrika* 32 (1941), 188–189. Reproduced by permission of the *Biometrika* Trustees.

| $\chi^2_{[.10]}(df)$ | $\chi^2_{[.05]}(df)$ | $\chi^2_{[.025]}(df)$ | $\chi^2_{[.01]}(df)$ | $\chi^2_{[.005]}(df)$ | df |
|---|---|---|---|---|---|
| 2.70554 | 3.84146 | 5.02389 | 6.63490 | 7.87944 | 1 |
| 4.60517 | 5.99147 | 7.37776 | 9.21034 | 10.5966 | 2 |
| 6.25139 | 7.81473 | 9.34840 | 11.3449 | 12.8381 | 3 |
| 7.77944 | 9.48773 | 11.1433 | 13.2767 | 14.8602 | 4 |
| 9.23635 | 11.0705 | 12.8325 | 15.0863 | 16.7496 | 5 |
| 10.6446 | 12.5916 | 14.4494 | 16.8119 | 18.5476 | 6 |
| 12.0170 | 14.0671 | 16.0128 | 18.4753 | 20.2777 | 7 |
| 13.3616 | 15.5073 | 17.5346 | 20.0902 | 21.9550 | 8 |
| 14.6837 | 16.9190 | 19.0228 | 21.6660 | 23.5893 | 9 |
| 15.9871 | 18.3070 | 20.4831 | 23.2093 | 25.1882 | 10 |
| 17.2750 | 19.6751 | 21.9200 | 24.7250 | 26.7569 | 11 |
| 18.5494 | 21.0261 | 23.3367 | 26.2170 | 28.2995 | 12 |
| 19.8119 | 22.3621 | 24.7356 | 27.6883 | 29.8194 | 13 |
| 21.0642 | 23.6848 | 26.1190 | 29.1413 | 31.3193 | 14 |
| 22.3072 | 24.9958 | 27.4884 | 30.5779 | 32.8013 | 15 |
| 23.5418 | 26.2962 | 28.8454 | 31.9999 | 34.2672 | 16 |
| 24.7690 | 27.5871 | 30.1910 | 33.4087 | 35.7185 | 17 |
| 25.9894 | 28.8693 | 31.5264 | 34.8053 | 37.1564 | 18 |
| 27.2036 | 30.1435 | 32.8523 | 36.1908 | 38.5822 | 19 |
| 28.4120 | 31.4104 | 34.1696 | 37.5662 | 39.9968 | 20 |
| 29.6151 | 32.6705 | 35.4789 | 38.9321 | 41.4010 | 21 |
| 30.8133 | 33.9244 | 36.7807 | 40.2894 | 42.7956 | 22 |
| 32.0069 | 35.1725 | 38.0757 | 41.6384 | 44.1813 | 23 |
| 33.1963 | 36.4151 | 39.3641 | 42.9798 | 45.5585 | 24 |
| 34.3816 | 37.6525 | 40.6465 | 44.3141 | 46.9278 | 25 |
| 35.5631 | 38.8852 | 41.9232 | 45.6417 | 48.2899 | 26 |
| 36.7412 | 40.1133 | 43.1944 | 46.9630 | 49.6449 | 27 |
| 37.9159 | 41.3372 | 44.4607 | 48.2782 | 50.9933 | 28 |
| 39.0875 | 42.5569 | 45.7222 | 49.5879 | 52.3356 | 29 |
| 40.2560 | 43.7729 | 46.9792 | 50.8922 | 53.6720 | 30 |
| 51.8050 | 55.7585 | 59.3417 | 63.6907 | 66.7659 | 40 |
| 63.1671 | 67.5048 | 71.4202 | 76.1539 | 79.4900 | 50 |
| 74.3970 | 79.0819 | 83.2976 | 88.3794 | 91.9517 | 60 |
| 85.5271 | 90.5312 | 95.0231 | 100.425 | 104.215 | 70 |
| 96.5782 | 101.879 | 106.629 | 112.329 | 116.321 | 80 |
| 107.565 | 113.145 | 118.136 | 124.116 | 128.299 | 90 |
| 118.498 | 124.342 | 129.561 | 135.807 | 140.169 | 100 |

# *Matrix Algebra for Regression Calculations*

## B.1 MATRICES AND VECTORS

A **matrix** is a rectangular array of numbers (called elements) that is composed of rows and columns. An example of a matrix is

$$\mathbf{A} = \begin{bmatrix} 1 & 5 & 3 & 10 \\ 12 & 6 & 7 & 4 \\ 9 & 2 & 11 & 8 \end{bmatrix}$$

The notation $\mathbf{A}$ is used to indicate that we are referring to a matrix rather than a number.

The **dimension** of a matrix is determined by the number of rows and columns in the matrix. Since the matrix **A** has 3 rows and 4 columns, this matrix is said to have dimension 3 by 4 (commonly written $3 \times 4$). In general, a matrix with $m$ rows and $n$ columns is said to have dimension $m \times n$. As another example, the matrix

$$
\mathbf{X} = \begin{bmatrix}
1 & 0 & 0 \\
1 & 1 & 0 \\
1 & 2 & 0 \\
1 & 0 & 1 \\
1 & 1 & 1 \\
1 & 2 & 1 \\
1 & 0 & 2 \\
1 & 1 & 2 \\
1 & 2 & 2
\end{bmatrix}
$$

has dimension $9 \times 3$, since it has 9 rows and 3 columns.

In general, a matrix with dimension $m \times n$ can be represented as

$$
\mathbf{A}_{m \times n} = \begin{bmatrix}
a_{11} & a_{12} & \cdots & a_{1j} & \cdots & a_{1n} \\
a_{21} & a_{22} & \cdots & a_{2j} & \cdots & a_{2n} \\
\vdots & \vdots & & \vdots & & \vdots \\
a_{i1} & a_{i2} & \cdots & a_{ij} & \cdots & a_{in} \\
\vdots & \vdots & & \vdots & & \vdots \\
a_{m1} & a_{m2} & \cdots & a_{mj} & \cdots & a_{mn}
\end{bmatrix}
$$

where $a_{ij}$ is the number in the matrix in row $i$ and column $j$, and the subscript $m \times n$ indicates the dimension of **A**.

A matrix that consists of one column is a **column vector,** for example,

$$
\mathbf{B}_{4 \times 1} = \begin{bmatrix} 5 \\ 3 \\ 4 \\ 1 \end{bmatrix} \quad \text{and} \quad \mathbf{C}_{3 \times 1} = \begin{bmatrix} 101 \\ 73 \\ 51 \end{bmatrix}
$$

A matrix that consists of one row is a **row vector,** for example,

$$
\mathbf{E}'_{1 \times 4} = [10 \quad 7 \quad 6 \quad 12]
$$
$$
\mathbf{F}'_{1 \times 6} = [1 \quad 2 \quad 7 \quad 11 \quad 5 \quad 8]
$$

Note that the prime mark ($'$) is used to distinguish a row vector from a column vector.

## B.2   THE TRANSPOSE OF A MATRIX

> The **transpose** of a matrix is formed by interchanging the rows and columns of the matrix.

For example, consider the matrix

$$\mathbf{A}_{2\times3} = \begin{bmatrix} 5 & 6 & 7 \\ 3 & 2 & 1 \end{bmatrix}$$

The transpose of $\mathbf{A}$, which is denoted $\mathbf{A}'$, is

$$\mathbf{A}'_{3\times2} = \begin{bmatrix} 5 & 3 \\ 6 & 2 \\ 7 & 1 \end{bmatrix}$$

Thus the first row of $\mathbf{A}$ is the first column of $\mathbf{A}'$, and the second row of $\mathbf{A}$ is the second column of $\mathbf{A}'$.

Notice that the transpose of the column vector

$$\mathbf{E}_{4\times1} = \begin{bmatrix} 10 \\ 7 \\ 6 \\ 12 \end{bmatrix}$$

is the row vector

$$\mathbf{E}'_{1\times4} = \begin{bmatrix} 10 & 7 & 6 & 12 \end{bmatrix}$$

As a last example, consider the matrix

$$\mathbf{X}_{9\times3} = \begin{bmatrix} 1 & 0 & 0 \\ 1 & 1 & 0 \\ 1 & 2 & 0 \\ 1 & 0 & 1 \\ 1 & 1 & 1 \\ 1 & 2 & 1 \\ 1 & 0 & 2 \\ 1 & 1 & 2 \\ 1 & 2 & 2 \end{bmatrix}$$

The transpose of $\mathbf{X}$ is

$$\mathbf{X}'_{3\times9} = \begin{bmatrix} 1 & 1 & 1 & 1 & 1 & 1 & 1 & 1 & 1 \\ 0 & 1 & 2 & 0 & 1 & 2 & 0 & 1 & 2 \\ 0 & 0 & 0 & 1 & 1 & 1 & 2 & 2 & 2 \end{bmatrix}$$

# B.3  SUMS AND DIFFERENCES OF MATRICES

Consider two matrices, $\mathbf{A}$ and $\mathbf{B}$, that have the same dimensions.

> The **sum** of **A** and **B** is a matrix obtained by adding the corresponding elements of **A** and **B**.

For example, for the matrices

$$\mathbf{A}_{2\times3} = \begin{bmatrix} 1 & 4 & 2 \\ 5 & 3 & 2 \end{bmatrix} \quad \text{and} \quad \mathbf{B}_{2\times3} = \begin{bmatrix} 7 & 0 & 4 \\ 3 & 1 & 5 \end{bmatrix}$$

the sum is

$$\mathbf{C}_{2\times3} = \mathbf{A}_{2\times3} + \mathbf{B}_{2\times3} = \begin{bmatrix} 1+7 & 4+0 & 2+4 \\ 5+3 & 3+1 & 2+5 \end{bmatrix} = \begin{bmatrix} 8 & 4 & 6 \\ 8 & 4 & 7 \end{bmatrix}$$

In general, if **A** and **B** have the same dimensions and $\mathbf{C} = \mathbf{A} + \mathbf{B}$,

$$c_{ij} = a_{ij} + b_{ij}$$

where

$$c_{ij} = \text{the number in } \mathbf{C} \text{ in row } i \text{ and column } j$$
$$a_{ij} = \text{the number in } \mathbf{A} \text{ in row } i \text{ and column } j$$
$$b_{ij} = \text{the number in } \mathbf{B} \text{ in row } i \text{ and column } j$$

Again consider two matrices, **A** and **B**, that have the same dimensions.

> The **difference** of **A** and **B** is a matrix obtained by subtracting the corresponding elements of **A** and **B**.

For example, for the matrices

$$\mathbf{A}_{2\times3} = \begin{bmatrix} 1 & 4 & 2 \\ 5 & 3 & 2 \end{bmatrix} \quad \text{and} \quad \mathbf{B}_{2\times3} = \begin{bmatrix} 7 & 0 & 4 \\ 3 & 1 & 5 \end{bmatrix}$$

the difference is

$$\mathbf{D}_{2\times3} = \mathbf{A}_{2\times3} - \mathbf{B}_{2\times3} = \begin{bmatrix} 1-7 & 4-0 & 2-4 \\ 5-3 & 3-1 & 2-5 \end{bmatrix} = \begin{bmatrix} -6 & 4 & -2 \\ 2 & 2 & -3 \end{bmatrix}$$

In general, if **A** and **B** have the same dimensions and $\mathbf{D} = \mathbf{A} - \mathbf{B}$,

$$d_{ij} = a_{ij} - b_{ij}$$

where

$$d_{ij} = \text{the number in } \mathbf{D} \text{ in row } i \text{ and column } j$$
$$a_{ij} = \text{the number in } \mathbf{A} \text{ in row } i \text{ and column } j$$
$$b_{ij} = \text{the number in } \mathbf{B} \text{ in row } i \text{ and column } j$$

# B.4   MATRIX MULTIPLICATION

We now consider **multiplication** *of a matrix by a number.*

> The **product of a number** $\lambda$ *and* **a matrix** $A$ is a matrix obtained by multiply-
> ing each element of **A** by the number $\lambda$.

For example, multiplying the following matrix

$$\mathbf{Z}_{2\times 3} = \begin{bmatrix} 1 & 4 & 7 \\ 3 & 2 & 3 \end{bmatrix}$$

by $\lambda = 5$, we get

$$5\mathbf{Z}_{2\times 3} = 5\begin{bmatrix} 1 & 4 & 7 \\ 3 & 2 & 3 \end{bmatrix} = \begin{bmatrix} 5(1) & 5(4) & 5(7) \\ 5(3) & 5(2) & 5(3) \end{bmatrix} = \begin{bmatrix} 5 & 20 & 35 \\ 15 & 10 & 15 \end{bmatrix}$$

In general, if $\lambda$ is a number, **A** is a matrix, and $\mathbf{E} = \lambda\mathbf{A}$,

$$e_{ij} = \lambda a_{ij}$$

where

$$e_{ij} = \text{the number in } \mathbf{E} \text{ in row } i \text{ and column } j$$
$$a_{ij} = \text{the number in } \mathbf{A} \text{ in row } i \text{ and column } j$$

We next consider **multiplication of a matrix by a matrix.**

> Consider two matrices **A** and **B** where the number of **columns** in **A** is equal to
> the number of **rows** in **B**. Then the **product of the two matrices** *A and B* is a
> matrix calculated so that the element in row $i$ and column $j$ of the product is
> obtained by multiplying the elements in row $i$ of matrix **A** by the corresponding
> elements in column $j$ of matrix **B** and adding the resulting products.

For example, consider the following matrices.

$$\mathbf{A}_{2\times 2} = \begin{bmatrix} 4 & 3 \\ 2 & 2 \end{bmatrix} \quad \text{and} \quad \mathbf{B}_{2\times 2} = \begin{bmatrix} 2 & 1 \\ 3 & 5 \end{bmatrix}$$

Suppose we wish to find the product **AB**. The number in row 1 and column 1 of the
product is obtained by multiplying the elements in row 1 of **A** by the corresponding
elements in column 1 of **B** and adding these products. We obtain

$$4(2) + 3(3) = 8 + 9 = 17$$

The number in row 1 and column 2 of the product is obtained by multiplying the elements in row 1 of **A** by the corresponding elements in column 2 of **B** and adding these products. We obtain

$$4(1) + 3(5) = 4 + 15 = 19$$

The number in row 2 and column 1 of the product is obtained by multiplying the elements in row 2 of **A** by the corresponding elements in column 1 of **B** and adding these products. We obtain

$$2(2) + 2(3) = 4 + 6 = 10$$

The number in row 2 and column 2 of the product is obtained by multiplying the elements in row 2 of **A** by the corresponding elements in column 2 of **B** and adding these products. We obtain

$$2(1) + 2(5) = 2 + 10 = 12$$

Thus the product **AB** is as follows:

$$\mathbf{A}_{2\times 2}\mathbf{B}_{2\times 2} = \begin{bmatrix} 4 & 3 \\ 2 & 2 \end{bmatrix}\begin{bmatrix} 2 & 1 \\ 3 & 5 \end{bmatrix} = \begin{bmatrix} 4(2) + 3(3) & 4(1) + 3(5) \\ 2(2) + 2(3) & 2(1) + 2(5) \end{bmatrix}$$
$$= \begin{bmatrix} 17 & 19 \\ 10 & 12 \end{bmatrix}$$

In general, we can multiply a matrix **A** with $m$ rows and $r$ columns by a matrix **B** with $r$ rows and $n$ columns and obtain a matrix **C** with $m$ rows and $n$ columns. Moreover, $c_{ij}$, the number in the product in row $i$ and column $j$, is obtained by multiplying the elements in row $i$ of **A** by the corresponding elements in column $j$ of **B** and adding the resulting products. Note that the number of columns in **A** must equal the number of rows in **B** in order for this multiplication procedure to be defined.

The multiplication procedure is illustrated in Figure B.1.

**FIGURE B.1**
An illustration of matrix multiplication

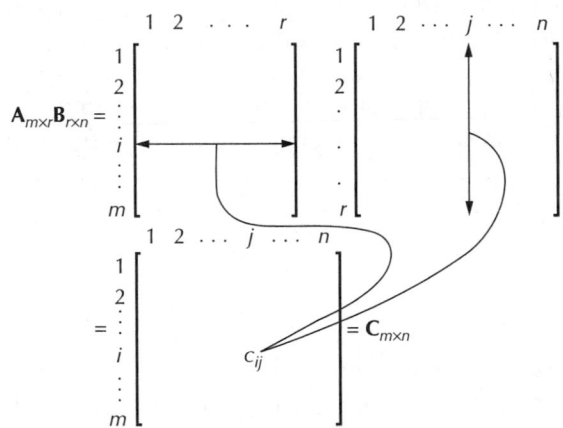

We now present several more examples. Consider the following matrices:

$$\mathbf{W}_{3\times 2} = \begin{bmatrix} 1 & 6 \\ 2 & 5 \\ 3 & 4 \end{bmatrix} \quad \mathbf{U}_{2\times 2} = \begin{bmatrix} 2 & 2 \\ 1 & 3 \end{bmatrix}$$

$$\mathbf{X}_{9\times 3} = \begin{bmatrix} 1 & 0 & 0 \\ 1 & 1 & 0 \\ 1 & 2 & 0 \\ 1 & 0 & 1 \\ 1 & 1 & 1 \\ 1 & 2 & 1 \\ 1 & 0 & 2 \\ 1 & 1 & 2 \\ 1 & 2 & 2 \end{bmatrix} \quad \mathbf{y}_{9\times 1} = \begin{bmatrix} 18 \\ 21 \\ 20 \\ 20 \\ 22 \\ 20 \\ 19 \\ 21 \\ 20 \end{bmatrix}$$

Then we find that

$$\mathbf{W}_{3\times 2}\mathbf{U}_{2\times 2} = \begin{bmatrix} 1 & 6 \\ 2 & 5 \\ 3 & 4 \end{bmatrix}\begin{bmatrix} 2 & 2 \\ 1 & 3 \end{bmatrix} = \begin{bmatrix} 8 & 20 \\ 9 & 19 \\ 10 & 18 \end{bmatrix}$$

but that

$$\mathbf{U}_{2\times 2}\mathbf{W}_{3\times 2} = \begin{bmatrix} 2 & 2 \\ 1 & 3 \end{bmatrix}\begin{bmatrix} 1 & 6 \\ 2 & 5 \\ 3 & 4 \end{bmatrix}$$

does not exist because the number of columns in $\mathbf{U}_{2\times 2}$ does not equal the number of rows in $\mathbf{W}_{3\times 2}$. Also, we find that

$$\mathbf{X}'_{3\times 9}\mathbf{X}_{9\times 3} = \begin{bmatrix} 1 & 1 & 1 & 1 & 1 & 1 & 1 & 1 & 1 \\ 0 & 1 & 2 & 0 & 1 & 2 & 0 & 1 & 2 \\ 0 & 0 & 0 & 1 & 1 & 1 & 2 & 2 & 2 \end{bmatrix}\begin{bmatrix} 1 & 0 & 0 \\ 1 & 1 & 0 \\ 1 & 2 & 0 \\ 1 & 0 & 1 \\ 1 & 1 & 1 \\ 1 & 2 & 1 \\ 1 & 0 & 2 \\ 1 & 1 & 2 \\ 1 & 2 & 2 \end{bmatrix}$$

$$= \begin{bmatrix} 9 & 9 & 9 \\ 9 & 15 & 9 \\ 9 & 9 & 15 \end{bmatrix}$$

and that

$$\mathbf{X}'_{3\times9}\mathbf{y}_{9\times1} = \begin{bmatrix} 1 & 1 & 1 & 1 & 1 & 1 & 1 & 1 & 1 \\ 0 & 1 & 2 & 0 & 1 & 2 & 0 & 1 & 2 \\ 0 & 0 & 0 & 1 & 1 & 1 & 2 & 2 & 2 \end{bmatrix} \begin{bmatrix} 18 \\ 21 \\ 20 \\ 20 \\ 22 \\ 20 \\ 19 \\ 21 \\ 20 \end{bmatrix} = \begin{bmatrix} 181 \\ 184 \\ 182 \end{bmatrix}$$

As a last example, consider the matrices

$$\mathbf{A}_{2\times2} = \begin{bmatrix} 1 & 1 \\ 2 & 2 \end{bmatrix} \quad \text{and} \quad \mathbf{B}_{2\times2} = \begin{bmatrix} 0 & 1 \\ 1 & 0 \end{bmatrix}$$

Then we find that

$$\mathbf{A}_{2\times2}\mathbf{B}_{2\times2} = \begin{bmatrix} 1 & 1 \\ 2 & 2 \end{bmatrix} \begin{bmatrix} 0 & 1 \\ 1 & 0 \end{bmatrix} = \begin{bmatrix} 1 & 1 \\ 2 & 2 \end{bmatrix}$$

In this case, **B** is said to be premultiplied by **A**, or **A** is said to be postmultiplied by **B**. Now consider

$$\mathbf{B}_{2\times2}\mathbf{A}_{2\times2} = \begin{bmatrix} 0 & 1 \\ 1 & 0 \end{bmatrix} \begin{bmatrix} 1 & 1 \\ 2 & 2 \end{bmatrix} = \begin{bmatrix} 2 & 2 \\ 1 & 1 \end{bmatrix}$$

Here **A** is said to be premultiplied by **B**, or **B** is said to be postmultiplied by **A**. Note that in this case **AB** is not equal to **BA**. In general, if **A** and **B** are matrices, then $\mathbf{AB} \neq \mathbf{BA}$.

# B.5 THE IDENTITY MATRIX

A matrix in which the number of rows is equal to the number of columns is called a **square matrix.**

For example, the following matrices are square matrices:

$$\mathbf{A}_{3\times3} = \begin{bmatrix} 3 & 4 & 1 \\ 6 & 10 & 2 \\ 3 & 1 & 5 \end{bmatrix} \qquad \mathbf{B}_{2\times2} = \begin{bmatrix} 1 & 6 \\ 2 & 3 \end{bmatrix}$$

A square matrix in which the numbers on the main diagonal (the diagonal that runs from upper left to lower right) are 1s and in which all numbers off this diagonal are zeros is called an **identity matrix** and is denoted $\mathbf{I}$.

The following are examples of identity matrices:

$$\mathbf{I}_{2\times2} = \begin{bmatrix} 1 & 0 \\ 0 & 1 \end{bmatrix} \qquad \mathbf{I}_{3\times3} = \begin{bmatrix} 1 & 0 & 0 \\ 0 & 1 & 0 \\ 0 & 0 & 1 \end{bmatrix}$$

Such a matrix is called an identity matrix because premultiplication or postmultiplication of a square $n \times n$ matrix $\mathbf{A}$ by the $n \times n$ identity matrix $\mathbf{I}$ leaves the matrix $\mathbf{A}$ unchanged. For example, if

$$\mathbf{A}_{3\times3} = \begin{bmatrix} 2 & 1 & 3 \\ 4 & 1 & 2 \\ 2 & 2 & 1 \end{bmatrix}$$

then we see that

$$\mathbf{I}_{3\times3}\mathbf{A}_{3\times3} = \begin{bmatrix} 1 & 0 & 0 \\ 0 & 1 & 0 \\ 0 & 0 & 1 \end{bmatrix}\begin{bmatrix} 2 & 1 & 3 \\ 4 & 1 & 2 \\ 2 & 2 & 1 \end{bmatrix} = \begin{bmatrix} 2 & 1 & 3 \\ 4 & 1 & 2 \\ 2 & 2 & 1 \end{bmatrix}$$

and also that

$$\mathbf{A}_{3\times3}\mathbf{I}_{3\times3} = \begin{bmatrix} 2 & 1 & 3 \\ 4 & 1 & 2 \\ 2 & 2 & 1 \end{bmatrix}\begin{bmatrix} 1 & 0 & 0 \\ 0 & 1 & 0 \\ 0 & 0 & 1 \end{bmatrix} = \begin{bmatrix} 2 & 1 & 3 \\ 4 & 1 & 2 \\ 2 & 2 & 1 \end{bmatrix}$$

In general, if $\mathbf{A}_{m\times n}$ is not a square matrix, then

$$\mathbf{A}_{m\times n}\mathbf{I}_{n\times n} = \mathbf{A}_{m\times n} \quad \text{and} \quad \mathbf{I}_{m\times m}\mathbf{A}_{m\times n} = \mathbf{A}_{m\times n}$$

# B.6 LINEAR DEPENDENCE AND LINEAR INDEPENDENCE

We now discuss two concepts known as linear independence and linear dependence. Consider the following matrix $\mathbf{A}$:

$$\mathbf{A}_{3\times3} = \begin{bmatrix} 1 & 4 & 2 \\ 3 & 2 & 6 \\ 2 & 1 & 4 \end{bmatrix}$$

Notice that the third column in this matrix is a multiple of the first column in the matrix. In particular, the third column is simply the first column multiplied by 2. That is,

$$\begin{bmatrix} 2 \\ 6 \\ 4 \end{bmatrix} = 2 \begin{bmatrix} 1 \\ 3 \\ 2 \end{bmatrix}$$

In a situation like this, when one column in a matrix $\mathbf{A}$ is a multiple of another column in matrix $\mathbf{A}$, the columns of $\mathbf{A}$ are said to be linearly dependent. More generally,

---

If one of the columns of a matrix $\mathbf{A}$ can be written as a linear combination of some of the other columns in $\mathbf{A}$, then the columns of $\mathbf{A}$ are said to be **linearly dependent.**

---

As an example, consider the matrix

$$\mathbf{A}_{3\times4} = \begin{bmatrix} 1 & 3 & 10 & 4 \\ 5 & 2 & 5 & 1 \\ 2 & 2 & 7 & 3 \end{bmatrix}$$

In this case, column 3 is the sum of column 4 plus 2 times column 2. That is,

$$\begin{bmatrix} 4 \\ 1 \\ 3 \end{bmatrix} + 2 \begin{bmatrix} 3 \\ 2 \\ 2 \end{bmatrix} = \begin{bmatrix} 4 \\ 1 \\ 3 \end{bmatrix} + \begin{bmatrix} 6 \\ 4 \\ 4 \end{bmatrix} = \begin{bmatrix} 10 \\ 5 \\ 7 \end{bmatrix}$$

Thus the columns of $\mathbf{A}$ are linearly dependent because column 3 can be expressed as a linear combination of columns 2 and 4.

---

If none of the columns in a matrix $\mathbf{A}$ can be written as a linear combination of other columns in $\mathbf{A}$, then the columns of $\mathbf{A}$ are **linearly independent.** The maximum number of linearly independent columns in a matrix $\mathbf{A}$ is called the **rank** of the matrix. When the rank of a matrix $\mathbf{A}$ is equal to the number of columns in $\mathbf{A}$, the matrix $\mathbf{A}$ is said to be of **full rank.**

---

# B.7   THE INVERSE OF A MATRIX

Now consider a square matrix $\mathbf{A}_{n\times n}$, which is of full rank.

The **inverse** of the matrix $\mathbf{A}$ is another matrix, denoted $\mathbf{A}^{-1}$, which satisfies the condition

$$\mathbf{A}\mathbf{A}^{-1} = \mathbf{A}^{-1}\mathbf{A} = \mathbf{I}_{n \times n}$$

where $\mathbf{I}_{n \times n}$ is the identity matrix with dimension $n \times n$.

It should be emphasized that $\mathbf{A}^{-1}$ exists if and only if $\mathbf{A}$ is a square matrix of full rank. As an example, consider the matrix

$$\mathbf{A}_{3\times3} = \begin{bmatrix} 9 & 9 & 9 \\ 9 & 15 & 9 \\ 9 & 9 & 15 \end{bmatrix}$$

The inverse of $\mathbf{A}$ is

$$\mathbf{A}_{3\times3}^{-1} = \begin{bmatrix} \frac{4}{9} & -\frac{1}{6} & -\frac{1}{6} \\ -\frac{1}{6} & \frac{1}{6} & 0 \\ \frac{1}{6} & 0 & \frac{1}{6} \end{bmatrix}$$

since

$$\mathbf{A}_{3\times3}\mathbf{A}_{3\times3}^{-1} = \begin{bmatrix} 9 & 9 & 9 \\ 9 & 15 & 9 \\ 9 & 9 & 15 \end{bmatrix}\begin{bmatrix} \frac{4}{9} & -\frac{1}{6} & -\frac{1}{6} \\ -\frac{1}{6} & \frac{1}{6} & 0 \\ -\frac{1}{6} & 0 & \frac{1}{6} \end{bmatrix}$$

$$= \begin{bmatrix} 1 & 0 & 0 \\ 0 & 1 & 0 \\ 0 & 0 & 1 \end{bmatrix}$$

and

$$\mathbf{A}_{3\times3}^{-1}\mathbf{A}_{3\times3} = \begin{bmatrix} \frac{4}{9} & -\frac{1}{6} & \frac{1}{6} \\ -\frac{1}{6} & \frac{1}{6} & 0 \\ -\frac{1}{6} & 0 & \frac{1}{6} \end{bmatrix}\begin{bmatrix} 9 & 9 & 9 \\ 9 & 15 & 9 \\ 9 & 9 & 15 \end{bmatrix}$$

$$= \begin{bmatrix} 1 & 0 & 0 \\ 0 & 1 & 0 \\ 0 & 0 & 1 \end{bmatrix}$$

It can be shown that $\mathbf{A}^{-1}\mathbf{A} = \mathbf{I}_{n \times n}$ if and only if $\mathbf{A}\mathbf{A}^{-1} = \mathbf{I}_{n \times n}$.

Although we will not discuss them here, general formulas exist that allow the calculation of matrix inverses. Also, computer programs are often used to calculate matrix inverses.

# B.8  THE LEAST SQUARES POINT ESTIMATES

## THE LEAST SQUARES POINT ESTIMATES

The **least squares point estimates** $b_0, b_1, b_2, \ldots, b_k$ are calculated by using the formula

$$\begin{bmatrix} b_0 \\ b_1 \\ b_2 \\ \vdots \\ b_k \end{bmatrix} = \mathbf{b} = (\mathbf{X'X})^{-1}\,\mathbf{X'y}$$

where $\mathbf{y}$ and $\mathbf{X}$ are the following column vector and matrix:

$$\mathbf{y} = \begin{bmatrix} y_1 \\ y_2 \\ \vdots \\ y_n \end{bmatrix} \quad \text{and} \quad \mathbf{X} = \begin{matrix} 0 & 1 & 2 & . & . & . & k \\ & x_1 & x_2 & . & . & . & x_k \\ \begin{bmatrix} 1 \\ 1 \\ \vdots \\ 1 \end{bmatrix} & \begin{matrix} x_{11} \\ x_{21} \\ \vdots \\ x_{n1} \end{matrix} & \begin{matrix} x_{12} \\ x_{22} \\ \vdots \\ x_{n2} \end{matrix} & \begin{matrix} . \\ . \\ \vdots \\ . \end{matrix} & \begin{matrix} . \\ . \\ \vdots \\ . \end{matrix} & \begin{matrix} . \\ . \\ \vdots \\ . \end{matrix} & \begin{matrix} x_{1k} \\ x_{2k} \\ \vdots \\ x_{nk} \end{matrix} \end{matrix}$$

Here $\mathbf{y}$ is a column vector of the $n$ observed values of the dependent variable, $y_1$, $y_2, \ldots, y_n$. To define the matrix $\mathbf{X}$, consider the regression model

$$y = \beta_0 + \beta_1 x_1 + \beta_2 x_2 + \cdots + \beta_k x_k + \varepsilon$$

Since there are $(k + 1)$ parameters in this model, the matrix $\mathbf{X}$ will consist of $(k + 1)$ columns. The columns in the matrix $\mathbf{X}$ contain the observed values of the independent variables corresponding to (that is, multiplied by) the $(k + 1)$ parameters $\beta_0, \beta_1, \beta_2, \ldots, \beta_k$. The columns of this matrix are numbered in the same manner as the parameters are numbered (see the preceding $\mathbf{X}$ matrix). In the following examples we demonstrate how to calculate the least squares point estimates.

**EXAMPLE B.1**   The least squares point estimates $b_0$, $b_1$, and $b_2$ of the parameters $\beta_0$, $\beta_1$, and $\beta_2$ in the fuel consumption model

$$y = \beta_0 + \beta_1 x_1 + \beta_2 x_2 + \varepsilon$$

are calculated by using the formula

$$\begin{bmatrix} b_0 \\ b_1 \\ b_2 \end{bmatrix} = \mathbf{b} = (\mathbf{X}'\mathbf{X})^{-1}\mathbf{X}'\mathbf{y}$$

where

$$\mathbf{y} = \begin{bmatrix} y_1 \\ y_2 \\ y_3 \\ y_4 \\ y_5 \\ y_6 \\ y_7 \\ y_8 \end{bmatrix} = \begin{bmatrix} 12.4 \\ 11.7 \\ 12.4 \\ 10.8 \\ 9.4 \\ 9.5 \\ 8.0 \\ 7.5 \end{bmatrix}$$

and

$$\mathbf{X} = \begin{bmatrix} 1 & x_{11} & x_{12} \\ 1 & x_{21} & x_{22} \\ 1 & x_{31} & x_{32} \\ 1 & x_{41} & x_{42} \\ 1 & x_{51} & x_{52} \\ 1 & x_{61} & x_{62} \\ 1 & x_{71} & x_{72} \\ 1 & x_{81} & x_{82} \end{bmatrix} = \begin{bmatrix} 1 & 28.0 & 18 \\ 1 & 28.0 & 14 \\ 1 & 32.5 & 24 \\ 1 & 39.0 & 22 \\ 1 & 45.9 & 8 \\ 1 & 57.8 & 16 \\ 1 & 58.1 & 1 \\ 1 & 62.5 & 0 \end{bmatrix}$$

with columns labeled $0, 1, 2$ and $0, 1, 2$ corresponding to $x_1, x_2$ and $x_1, x_2$.

Here, the column vector $\mathbf{y}$ is simply a vector of the observed weekly fuel consumptions, and the three columns of the $\mathbf{X}$ matrix contain the observed values of the independent variables corresponding to (that is, multiplied by) the three parameters in the model. Therefore, since the number 1 is multiplied by $\beta_0$, the column of the $\mathbf{X}$ matrix corresponding to $\beta_0$ is a column of 1s. Since the independent variable $x_1$ is multiplied by $\beta_1$, the column of the $\mathbf{X}$ matrix corresponding to $\beta_1$ is a column containing the observed average hourly temperatures (see Table 4.1). The independent variable $x_2$ is multiplied by $\beta_2$, and thus the column of the $\mathbf{X}$ matrix corresponding to $\beta_2$ is a column containing the observed chill indices (see Table 4.1).

To calculate $\mathbf{b} = (\mathbf{X}'\mathbf{X})^{-1}\mathbf{X}'\mathbf{y}$, we first find

$$\mathbf{X}'\mathbf{X} = \begin{bmatrix} 1 & 1 & 1 & 1 & 1 & 1 & 1 & 1 \\ 28.0 & 28.0 & 32.5 & 39.0 & 45.9 & 57.8 & 58.1 & 62.5 \\ 18 & 14 & 24 & 22 & 8 & 16 & 1 & 0 \end{bmatrix} \begin{bmatrix} 1 & 28.0 & 18 \\ 1 & 28.0 & 14 \\ 1 & 32.5 & 24 \\ 1 & 39.0 & 22 \\ 1 & 45.9 & 8 \\ 1 & 57.8 & 16 \\ 1 & 58.1 & 1 \\ 1 & 62.5 & 0 \end{bmatrix}$$

$$= \begin{bmatrix} 8.0 & 351.8 & 103.0 \\ 351.8 & 16874.76 & 3884.1 \\ 103.0 & 3884.1 & 1901.0 \end{bmatrix}$$

Since the columns of the matrix $\mathbf{X}'\mathbf{X}$ can be verified to be linearly independent of each other, the matrix $\mathbf{X}'\mathbf{X}$ possesses an inverse matrix $(\mathbf{X}'\mathbf{X})^{-1}$. This matrix can be computer calculated to be

$$(\mathbf{X}'\mathbf{X})^{-1} = \begin{bmatrix} 8.0 & 351.8 & 103.0 \\ 351.8 & 16874.76 & 3884.1 \\ 103.0 & 3884.1 & 1901.0 \end{bmatrix}^{-1}$$

$$= \begin{bmatrix} 5.43405 & -.085930 & -.118856 \\ -.085930 & .00147070 & .00165094 \\ -.118856 & .00165094 & .00359276 \end{bmatrix}$$

We next calculate

$$\mathbf{X}'\mathbf{y} = \begin{bmatrix} 1 & 1 & 1 & 1 & 1 & 1 & 1 & 1 \\ 28.0 & 28.0 & 32.5 & 39.0 & 45.9 & 57.8 & 58.1 & 62.5 \\ 18 & 14 & 24 & 22 & 8 & 16 & 1 & 0 \end{bmatrix} \begin{bmatrix} 12.4 \\ 11.7 \\ 12.4 \\ 10.8 \\ 9.4 \\ 9.5 \\ 8.0 \\ 7.5 \end{bmatrix}$$

$$= \begin{bmatrix} 81.7 \\ 3413.11 \\ 1157.4 \end{bmatrix}$$

Finally, we compute

$$\begin{bmatrix} b_0 \\ b_1 \\ b_2 \end{bmatrix} = \mathbf{b} = (\mathbf{X}'\mathbf{X})^{-1}\mathbf{X}'\mathbf{y}$$

$$= \begin{bmatrix} 5.43405 & -.085930 & -.118856 \\ -.085930 & .00147070 & .00165094 \\ -.118856 & .00165094 & .00359276 \end{bmatrix} \begin{bmatrix} 81.7 \\ 3413.11 \\ 1157.4 \end{bmatrix}$$

$$= \begin{bmatrix} 13.1087 \\ -.09001 \\ .08249 \end{bmatrix}$$

**EXAMPLE B.2**  Consider the sales territory performance model of Example 4.2

$$y = \beta_0 + \beta_1 x_1 + \beta_2 x_2 + \beta_3 x_3 + \beta_4 x_4 + \beta_5 x_5 + \varepsilon$$

By using the data in Table 4.2 we define the column vector $\mathbf{y}$ and matrix $\mathbf{X}$ as follows:

$$\mathbf{y} = \begin{bmatrix} y_1 \\ y_2 \\ \vdots \\ y_{25} \end{bmatrix} = \begin{bmatrix} 3669.88 \\ 3473.95 \\ \vdots \\ 2799.97 \end{bmatrix} \qquad \mathbf{X} = \begin{bmatrix} 1 & x_1 & x_2 & x_3 & x_4 & x_5 \\ 1 & 43.10 & 74065.11 & 4582.88 & 2.51 & .34 \\ 1 & 108.13 & 58117.30 & 5539.78 & 5.51 & .15 \\ \vdots & & & & & \\ 1 & 21.14 & 22809.53 & 3552.00 & 9.14 & -.74 \end{bmatrix}$$

Therefore we can calculate the least squares point estimates of $\beta_0$, $\beta_1$, $\beta_2$, $\beta_3$, $\beta_4$, and $\beta_5$ to be

$$\begin{bmatrix} b_0 \\ b_1 \\ b_2 \\ b_3 \\ b_4 \\ b_5 \end{bmatrix} = \mathbf{b} = (\mathbf{X'X})^{-1}\mathbf{X'y} = \begin{bmatrix} -1113.78788 \\ 3.61210 \\ .04209 \\ .12886 \\ 256.95554 \\ 324.53345 \end{bmatrix}$$

In concluding this section we note that the column vector $\mathbf{y}$ and the matrix $\mathbf{X}$ used to calculate the least squares point estimates $b_0$ and $b_1$ of the parameters $\beta_0$ and $\beta_1$ in the simple linear regression model are

$$\mathbf{y} = \begin{bmatrix} y_1 \\ y_2 \\ \vdots \\ y_n \end{bmatrix} \quad \text{and} \quad \mathbf{X} = \begin{bmatrix} 1 & x_1 \\ 1 & x_2 \\ \vdots & \vdots \\ 1 & x_n \end{bmatrix}$$

By using this $\mathbf{y}$ vector and $\mathbf{X}$ matrix it can be shown that

$$\begin{bmatrix} b_0 \\ b_1 \end{bmatrix} = \mathbf{b} = (\mathbf{X'X})^{-1}\mathbf{X'y} = \begin{bmatrix} \bar{y} - b_1\bar{x} \\ \dfrac{SS_{xy}}{SS_{xx}} \end{bmatrix}$$

These are the same formulas for $b_0$ and $b_1$ that we presented in Chapter 3. In fact, each general matrix algebra formula of this appendix can be shown to reduce, when considering the simple linear regression model, to the corresponding formula in Chapter 3.

# B.9 THE UNEXPLAINED VARIATION AND THE EXPLAINED VARIATION

The total variation of the dependent variable $y$ depends only on the values of $y$ and is not affected by the values of the selected independent variables. That is,

$$\text{Total variation} = SS_{yy} = \sum_{i=1}^{n}(y_i - \bar{y}_i)^2 = \sum_{i=1}^{n}y_i^2 - \frac{\left(\sum_{i=1}^{n}y_i\right)^2}{n}$$

The unexplained variation can be found by the following calculation formula:

$$\text{Unexplained variation} = \text{SSE} = \sum_{i=1}^{n}(y_i - \hat{y}_i)^2 = \sum_{i=1}^{n} y_i^2 - \mathbf{b'X'y}$$

Here, $\mathbf{b'} = [b_0 \quad b_1 \quad b_2 \quad \cdots \quad b_k]$ is a row vector (the transpose of $\mathbf{b}$) containing the least squares point estimates, and $\mathbf{X'y}$ is the column vector used in calculating the least squares point estimates $\mathbf{b} = (\mathbf{X'X})^{-1}\mathbf{X'y}$. Since

$$\text{Total variation} = \text{Unexplained variation} + \text{Explained variation}$$

we can find the explained variation by using

$$\text{Explained variation} = \text{Total variation} - \text{Unexplained variation}$$

Note that we could also find the unexplained variation directly because it follows that

$$\text{Explained variation} = \mathbf{b'X'y} - \frac{\left(\sum_{i=1}^{n} y_i\right)^2}{n}$$

**EXAMPLE B.3**   For the fuel consumption model we have computed $\mathbf{b}$ and $\mathbf{X'y}$ in Example B.1. Therefore

$$\mathbf{b'X'y} = [13.1087 \quad -.09001 \quad .08249] \begin{bmatrix} 81.7 \\ 3413.11 \\ 1157.40 \end{bmatrix}$$

$$= 13.1087(81.7) + (-.09001)(3413.11) + (.08249)(1157.40)$$

$$= 859.236$$

Furthermore, from Examples 3.3 and 3.6, we know that

$$\sum_{i=1}^{8} y_i = 81.7 \quad \text{and} \quad \sum_{i=1}^{8} y_i^2 = 859.91$$

Therefore,

$$\text{Total variation} = \text{SS}_{yy} = \sum_{i=1}^{n} y_i^2 - \frac{\left(\sum_{i=1}^{n} y_i\right)^2}{n}$$

$$= 859.91 - \frac{(81.7)^2}{2}$$

$$= 25.549$$

$$\text{Unexplained variation} = \text{SSE} = \sum y_i^2 - \mathbf{b'X'y}$$

$$= 859.91 - 859.236$$

$$= .674$$

$$s^2 = \frac{\text{SSE}}{n - (k + 1)} = \frac{.674}{8 - 3} = \frac{.674}{5} = .1348$$

$$s = \sqrt{s^2} = \sqrt{.1348} = .3671$$

$$\text{Explained variation} = \text{Total variation} - \text{Unexplained variation}$$

$$= 25.549 - .674$$

$$= 24.875$$

# B.10 THE STANDARD ERROR OF THE ESTIMATE $b_j$

It can be proven that $\sigma_{b_j}$, the standard deviation of the population of all possible values of the least squares point estimate $b_j$, is

$$\sigma_{b_j} = \sigma \sqrt{c_{jj}}$$

Here, $\sigma$ is the constant standard deviation of the different error term populations, and $c_{jj}$ is the $j$th diagonal element of $(\mathbf{X'X})^{-1}$ (we illustrate how to find $c_{jj}$ in the next example). We denote the point estimate of $\sigma_{b_j}$ by $s_{b_j}$ and refer to $s_{b_j}$ as the **standard error of the estimate $b_j$**. Since we estimate $\sigma$ by $s$, it follows that

$$s_{b_j} = s \sqrt{c_{jj}}$$

As discussed in Section 4.5, we use $s_{b_j}$ to calculate the $t$-statistic for testing $H_0: \beta_j = 0$ and to calculate a confidence interval for $\beta_j$.

---

The $t$-statistic for testing $H_0: \beta_j = 0$ versus $H_a: \beta_j \neq 0$ is

$$t = \frac{b_j}{s_{b_j}} = \frac{b_j}{s \sqrt{c_{jj}}}$$

A $100(1 - \alpha)\%$ confidence interval for $\beta_j$ is

$$\left[ b_j + t_{[\alpha/2]}^{(n-(k+1))} s_{b_j} \right] = \left[ b_j + t_{[\alpha/2]}^{(n-(k+1))} s \sqrt{c_{jj}} \right]$$

**EXAMPLE B.4**    Consider the fuel consumption model

$$y = \beta_0 + \beta_1 x_1 + \beta_2 x_2 + \varepsilon$$

In Example B.1 we have seen that

$$
(\mathbf{X'X})^{-1} = 
\begin{array}{c}
\text{row} \\
0 \\
1 \\
2
\end{array}
\begin{bmatrix}
5.43405 & -.085930 & -.118856 \\
-.085930 & .00147070 & .00165094 \\
-.118856 & .00165094 & .00359276
\end{bmatrix}
$$

$$
= 
\begin{bmatrix}
c_{00} & & \\
& c_{11} & \\
& & c_{22}
\end{bmatrix}
$$

with columns labeled 0, 1, 2.

Here, we have numbered the rows and columns of $(\mathbf{X'X})^{-1}$ as 0, 1, and 2 because the $\beta$'s in the fuel consumption model are denoted as $\beta_0$, $\beta_1$, and $\beta_2$. Thus, the diagonal element of $(\mathbf{X'X})^{-1}$ corresponding to

1.  $\beta_0$ is $c_{00} = 5.43405 \approx 5.434$
2.  $\beta_1$ is $c_{11} = .00147070 \approx .00147$
3.  $\beta_2$ is $c_{22} = .00359276 \approx .0036$

Since we have seen in Example B.3 that $s = .3671$, it follows that we calculate $s_{b_0}, s_{b_1}, s_{b_2}$, and the associated $t$-statistics for testing $H_0: \beta_0 = 0$, $H_0: \beta_1 = 0$, and $H_0: \beta_2 = 0$ as shown in Table B.1.

**TABLE B.1** Calculations of the Standard Errors of the $b_j$ Values and the $t$-Statistics for Testing $H_0: \beta_0 = 0$, $H_0: \beta_1 = 0$, and $H_0: \beta_2 = 0$ in the Fuel Consumption Model $y = \beta_0 + \beta_1 x_1 + \beta_2 x_2 + \varepsilon$

| Independent Variable | $b_j$ | $s_{b_j} = s\sqrt{c_{jj}}$ | $t = \dfrac{b_j}{s_{b_j}}$ |
|---|---|---|---|
| Intercept | $b_0 = 13.1087$ | $s_{b_0} = s\sqrt{c_{00}}$ $= .3671\sqrt{5.434}$ $= .8557$ | $t = \dfrac{13.1087}{.8557} = 15.32$ |
| $x_1$ | $b_1 = -.09001$ | $s_{b_1} = s\sqrt{c_{11}}$ $= .3671\sqrt{.00147}$ $= .01408$ | $t = \dfrac{-.09001}{.01408} = -6.39$ |
| $x_2$ | $b_2 = .08249$ | $s_{b_2} = s\sqrt{c_{22}}$ $= .3671\sqrt{.0036}$ $= .0220$ | $t = \dfrac{.08249}{.0220} = 3.75$ |

# B.11   THE DISTANCE VALUE

A $100(1 - \alpha)\%$ confidence interval for the mean value of the dependent variable when the values of the independent variables are $x_{01}, x_{02}, \ldots, x_{0k}$ is

$$\left[\hat{y} \pm t_{[\alpha/2]}^{(n-(k+1))} s \sqrt{\text{Distance value}}\right]$$

A $100(1 - \alpha)\%$ prediction interval for an individual value of the dependent variable when the values of the independent variables are $x_{01}, x_{02}, \ldots, x_{0k}$ is

$$\left[\hat{y} \pm t_{[\alpha/2]}^{(n-(k+1))} s \sqrt{1 + \text{Distance value}}\right]$$

Here

$$\hat{y} = b_0 + b_1 x_{01} + b_2 x_{02} + \cdots + b_k x_{0k}$$

and

$$\text{Distance value} = \mathbf{x}_0'(\mathbf{X}'\mathbf{X})^{-1}\mathbf{x}_0$$

where

$$\mathbf{x}_0' = [1 \quad x_{01} \quad x_{02} \quad \cdots \quad x_{0k}]$$

is a row vector containing the numbers multiplied by $b_0, b_1, b_2, \ldots, b_k$ in the equation for $\hat{y}$.

**EXAMPLE B.5**   In the fuel consumption problem, recall that a weather forecasting service has told us that the average hourly temperature in the future week will be $x_{01} = 40.0$ and the chill index in the future week will be $x_{02} = 10$. We saw in Example 4.9 that

$$\hat{y} = b_0 + b_1 x_{01} + b_2 x_{02}$$
$$= 13.1087 - .09001(40.0) + .08249(10)$$
$$= 10.333 \text{ MMcf of natural gas}$$

is the point estimate of the mean fuel consumption when $x_1$ equals 40 and $x_2$ equals 10, and is the point prediction of the individual fuel consumption in a single week when $x_1$ equals 40 and $x_2$ equals 10. To calculate the

$$\text{Distance value} = \mathbf{x}_0'(\mathbf{X}'\mathbf{X})^{-1}\mathbf{x}_0$$

note that $\mathbf{x}_0'$ is a row vector containing the numbers multiplied by the least squares point estimates $b_0$, $b_1$, and $b_2$ in the point estimate (and prediction) $\hat{y}$. Since 1 is multiplied by $b_0$, $x_{01}$ = 40.0 is multiplied by $b_1$, and $x_{02}$ = 10 is multiplied by $b_2$, it follows that

$$\mathbf{x}_0' = [1 \quad x_{01} \quad x_{02}] = [1 \quad 40 \quad 10]$$

and

$$\mathbf{x}_0 = \begin{bmatrix} 1 \\ x_{01} \\ x_{02} \end{bmatrix} = \begin{bmatrix} 1 \\ 40 \\ 10 \end{bmatrix}$$

Hence, since we have previously calculated $(\mathbf{X}'\mathbf{X})^{-1}$ (see Example B.1), it follows that

$$\text{Distance value} = \mathbf{x}_0'(\mathbf{X}'\mathbf{X})^{-1}\mathbf{x}_0$$

$$= [1 \quad 40 \quad 10] \begin{bmatrix} 5.43405 & -.085930 & -.118856 \\ -.085930 & .00147070 & .00165094 \\ -.118856 & .00165094 & .00359276 \end{bmatrix} \begin{bmatrix} 1 \\ 40 \\ 10 \end{bmatrix}$$

$$= [.80828 \quad -.0105926 \quad -.0168908] \begin{bmatrix} 1 \\ 40 \\ 10 \end{bmatrix} = .2157$$

Therefore, since we recall from Example B.3 that the standard error, $s$, is .3671, it follows that a 95% confidence interval for the mean fuel consumption is

$$\left[ \hat{y} \pm t_{[.025]}^{(8-3)} s\sqrt{\text{Distance value}} \right] = [10.333 \pm t_{[.025]}^{(5)}(.3671)\sqrt{.2157}]$$

$$= [10.333 \pm 2.571(.3671)\sqrt{.2157}]$$

$$= [10.333 \pm .438]$$

$$= [9.895, 10.771]$$

Here, $t_{[.025]}^{(5)}$ = 2.571 is based on $n - (k + 1) = 8 - 3 = 5$ degrees of freedom. Furthermore, a 95% prediction interval for the individual fuel consumption is

$$\left[ \hat{y} \pm t_{[.025]}^{(8-3)} s\sqrt{1 + \text{Distance value}} \right] = [10.333 \pm t_{[.025]}^{(5)}(.3671)\sqrt{1.2157}]$$

$$= [10.333 \pm 2.571(.3671)\sqrt{1.2157}]$$

$$= [10.333 \pm 1.04]$$

$$= [9.293, 11.374]$$

# B.12  USING SQUARED TERMS

**EXAMPLE B.6**    Consider the Fresh detergent model of Example 4.12

$$y = \beta_0 + \beta_1 x_4 + \beta_2 x_3 + \beta_3 x_3^2 + \varepsilon$$

By using the data in Table 4.6, we define the column vector

$$\mathbf{y} = \begin{bmatrix} y_1 \\ y_2 \\ \vdots \\ y_{30} \end{bmatrix} = \begin{bmatrix} 7.38 \\ 8.51 \\ \vdots \\ 9.26 \end{bmatrix}$$

and the matrix

$$\begin{array}{cccc} 1 & x_4 & x_3 & x_3^2 \end{array}$$

$$\mathbf{X} = \begin{bmatrix} 1 & -.05 & 5.50 & (5.50)^2 \\ 1 & .25 & 6.75 & (6.75)^2 \\ \vdots & \vdots & \vdots & \vdots \\ 1 & .55 & 6.80 & (6.80)^2 \end{bmatrix} = \begin{bmatrix} 1 & -.05 & 5.50 & 30.25 \\ 1 & .25 & 6.75 & 45.5625 \\ \vdots & \vdots & \vdots & \vdots \\ 1 & .55 & 6.80 & 46.24 \end{bmatrix}$$

Thus we can calculate the least squares point estimates of $\beta_0$, $\beta_1$, $\beta_2$, and $\beta_3$ to be

$$\begin{bmatrix} b_0 \\ b_1 \\ b_2 \\ b_3 \end{bmatrix} = \mathbf{b} = (\mathbf{X'X})^{-1}\mathbf{X'y} = \begin{bmatrix} 17.32437 \\ 1.30699 \\ -3.69559 \\ .34861 \end{bmatrix}$$

We have seen in Example 4.12 that

$$\hat{y} = b_0 + b_1 x_{04} + b_2 x_{03} + b_3 x_{03}^2$$
$$- 17.32437 + 1.30699(.20) - 3.69559(6.50) + .34861(6.50)^2$$
$$= 8.2933$$

is the point prediction of demand in a single sales period when the price difference is \$.20 and the advertising expenditure is \$650,000. Furthermore, since

$$\mathbf{x}_0' = [1 \quad .20 \quad 6.50 \quad (6.50)^2] = [1 \quad .20 \quad 6.50 \quad 42.25]$$

the distance value can be computed to be $\mathbf{x}_0'(\mathbf{X'X})^{-1}\mathbf{x}_0 = .06893$. Since $s = .2213$ and $n - (k + 1) = 30 - 4 = 26$, a 95% prediction interval for the demand is

$$\left[ \hat{y} \pm t_{[.025]}^{(26)} s\sqrt{1 + \text{Distance value}} \right] = [8.2933 \pm 2.056(.2213)\sqrt{1 + .06893}]$$

$$- [7.8230, 8.7636]$$

# B.13 USING INTERACTION TERMS

**EXAMPLE B.7**     Consider the Fresh detergent model of Example 4.14

$$y = \beta_0 + \beta_1 x_4 + \beta_2 x_3 + \beta_3 x_3^2 + \beta_4 x_4 x_3 + \varepsilon$$

By using the data in Table 4.6, we define the column vector

$$\mathbf{y} = \begin{bmatrix} y_1 \\ y_2 \\ y_3 \\ \vdots \\ y_{30} \end{bmatrix} = \begin{bmatrix} 7.38 \\ 8.51 \\ 9.52 \\ \vdots \\ 9.26 \end{bmatrix}$$

and the matrix

$$
\begin{array}{ccccc}
1 & x_4 & x_3 & x_3^2 & x_4 x_3
\end{array}
$$
$$
\mathbf{X} = \begin{bmatrix}
1 & -.05 & 5.50 & (5.50)^2 & (-.05)(5.50) \\
1 & .25 & 6.75 & (6.75)^2 & (.25)(6.75) \\
1 & .60 & 7.25 & (7.25)^2 & (.60)(7.25) \\
\vdots & \vdots & \vdots & \vdots & \vdots \\
1 & .55 & 6.80 & (6.80)^2 & (.55)(6.80)
\end{bmatrix}
$$

$$
\begin{array}{ccccc}
1 & x_4 & x_3 & x_3^2 & x_4 x_3
\end{array}
$$
$$
= \begin{bmatrix}
1 & -.05 & 5.50 & 30.25 & -.275 \\
1 & .25 & 6.75 & 45.5625 & 1.6875 \\
1 & .60 & 7.25 & 52.5625 & 4.35 \\
\vdots & \vdots & \vdots & \vdots & \vdots \\
1 & .55 & 6.80 & 46.24 & 3.74
\end{bmatrix}
$$

Thus we can calculate the least squares point estimates of $\beta_0$, $\beta_1$, $\beta_2$, and $\beta_3$ to be

$$
\begin{bmatrix} b_0 \\ b_1 \\ b_2 \\ b_3 \\ b_4 \end{bmatrix} = \mathbf{b} = (\mathbf{X'X})^{-1}\mathbf{X'y} = \begin{bmatrix} 29.11329 \\ 11.13423 \\ -7.60801 \\ .67125 \\ -1.47772 \end{bmatrix}
$$

We have seen in Example 4.14 that

$$\hat{y} = 29.11329 + 11.13423(.20) - 7.60801(6.50) + .67125(6.50)^2$$
$$- 1.47772(.20)(6.50)$$
$$= 8.3272$$

is the point prediction of demand in a single sales period when the price difference is \$.20 and the advertising expenditure is \$650,000. Furthermore, since

$$\mathbf{x}_0' = [1 \quad .20 \quad 6.50 \quad (6.50)^2 \quad (.20)(6.50)] = [1 \quad .20 \quad 6.50 \quad 42.25 \quad 1.3]$$

the distance value can be computed to be $\mathbf{x}_0'(\mathbf{X'X})^{-1}\mathbf{x}_0 = .07366$. Since $s = .20634$ and $n - (k + 1) = 30 - 5 = 25$, a 95% prediction interval for the demand is

$$\left[ \hat{y} \pm t_{[.025]}^{(25)} s \sqrt{1 + \text{Distance value}} \right] = [8.3272 \pm 2.060(.20634)\sqrt{1 + .07366}]$$
$$= [7.8867, 8.7678]$$

# B.14  USING DUMMY VARIABLES

**EXAMPLE B.8**   Consider the Electronics World dummy variable model of Example 4.15 (Part 3)

$$y = \beta_0 + \beta_1 x + \beta_2 D_M + \beta_3 D_D + \varepsilon$$

Using the data in Table 4.9, we define the following column vector **y** and matrix **X**

$$
\mathbf{y} = \begin{bmatrix} 157.27 \\ 93.28 \\ 136.81 \\ 123.79 \\ 153.51 \\ 241.74 \\ 201.54 \\ 206.71 \\ 229.78 \\ 135.22 \\ 224.71 \\ 195.29 \\ 242.1G \\ 115.21 \\ 197.82 \end{bmatrix} \quad \text{and} \quad \mathbf{X} = \begin{array}{c} \begin{array}{cccc} 1 & x & D_M & D_D \end{array} \\ \begin{bmatrix} 1 & 161 & 0 & 0 \\ 1 & 99 & 0 & 0 \\ 1 & 135 & 0 & 0 \\ 1 & 120 & 0 & 0 \\ 1 & 164 & 0 & 0 \\ 1 & 221 & 1 & 0 \\ 1 & 179 & 1 & 0 \\ 1 & 204 & 1 & 0 \\ 1 & 214 & 1 & 0 \\ 1 & 101 & 1 & 0 \\ 1 & 231 & 0 & 1 \\ 1 & 206 & 0 & 1 \\ 1 & 248 & 0 & 1 \\ 1 & 107 & 0 & 1 \\ 1 & 205 & 0 & 1 \end{bmatrix} \end{array}
$$

Thus we can calculate the least squares point estimates of $\beta_0$, $\beta_1$, $\beta_2$, and $\beta_3$ to be

$$
\begin{bmatrix} b_0 \\ b_1 \\ b_2 \\ b_3 \end{bmatrix} = \mathbf{b} = (\mathbf{X'X})^{-1}\mathbf{X'y} = \begin{bmatrix} 14.978 \\ .8686 \\ 28.374 \\ 6.864 \end{bmatrix}
$$

We have seen in Example 4.15 that

$$\hat{y} = b_0 + b_1(200) + b_2(1) + b_3(0)$$
$$= 14.978 + .8686(200) + 28.374(1)$$
$$= 217.07$$

is the point prediction of the sales volume in a future month for an individual store that has 200,000 households in its area and is located in a shopping mall. Furthermore, since

$$\mathbf{x}_0' = [1 \quad 200 \quad 1 \quad 0]$$

the distance value can be computed to be $\mathbf{x}_0'(\mathbf{X'X})^{-1}\mathbf{x}_0 = .21063$. Since $s = 6.34941$ and $n - (k + 1) = 15 - 4 = 11$, a 95% prediction interval for the sales volume is

$$\left[ \hat{y} \pm t_{[.025]}^{(11)} s\sqrt{1 + \text{Distance value}} \right] = [217.07 \pm 2.201(6.34941)\sqrt{1 + .21063}]$$
$$= [201.69, 232.45]$$

# B.15 THE STANDARD ERROR OF THE ESTIMATE OF A LINEAR COMBINATION OF REGRESSION PARAMETERS

Consider the Electronics World dummy variable model

$$y = \beta_0 + \beta_1 x + \beta_2 D_M + \beta_3 D_D + \varepsilon$$

In Example 4.15 we have seen that $\beta_2 - \beta_3$ is the difference between the mean monthly sales volumes in mall and downtown locations. In order to make statistical inferences about $\beta_2 - \beta_3$, we express this difference as a linear combination of the parameters $\beta_0$, $\beta_1$, $\beta_2$, and $\beta_3$ in the dummy variable model. Specifically, letting $\ell$ denote the linear combination, we write

$$\ell = \beta_2 - \beta_3 = (0)\beta_0 + (0)\beta_1 + (1)\beta_2 + (-1)\beta_3$$

In general, let

$$\ell = \lambda_0 \beta_0 + \lambda_1 \beta_1 + \lambda_2 \beta_2 + \cdots + \lambda_k \beta_k$$

be a linear combination of regression parameters. A point estimate of $\ell$ is

$$\hat{\ell} = \lambda_0 b_0 + \lambda_1 b_1 + \lambda_2 b_2 + \cdots + \lambda_k b_k$$

If the regression assumptions are satisfied, the population of all possible values of $\hat{\ell}$ is normally distributed with mean $\ell$ and standard deviation

$$\sigma_{\hat{\ell}} = \sigma \sqrt{\lambda'(\mathbf{X'X})^{-1}\lambda}$$

Here, $\lambda' = [\lambda_0, \lambda_1, \lambda_2, \ldots, \lambda_k]$ is a row vector containing the numbers multiplied by the $\beta$'s in the equation for $\ell$. Since we estimate $\sigma$ by $s$, it follows that

$$s_{\hat{\ell}} = s \sqrt{\lambda'(\mathbf{X'X})^{-1}\lambda}$$

We use $s_{\hat{\ell}}$ to calculate the $t$-statistic for testing $H_0$: $\ell = 0$ and to calculate confidence intervals for $\ell$.

---

The $t$-statistic for testing $H_0$: $\ell = 0$ versus $H_a$: $\ell \neq 0$ is

$$t = \frac{\hat{\ell}}{s_{\hat{\ell}}} = \frac{\hat{\ell}}{s\sqrt{\lambda'(\mathbf{X'X})^{-1}\lambda}}$$

A $100(1 - \alpha)\%$ confidence interval for $\ell$ is

$$\left[\hat{\ell} \pm t_{[\alpha/2]}^{(n-(k+1))} s_{\hat{\ell}}\right] = \left[\hat{\ell} \pm t_{[\alpha/2]}^{(n-(k+1))} s\sqrt{\lambda'(\mathbf{X'X})^{-1}\lambda}\right]$$

**EXAMPLE B.9**   Consider the Electronics World dummy variable model

$$y = \beta_0 + \beta_1 x + \beta_2 D_M + \beta_3 D_D + \varepsilon$$

Since we have seen in Example 4.15 that the least squares point estimates of $\beta_2$ and $\beta_3$ are $b_2 = 28.374$ and $b_3 = 6.864$, the point estimate of $\ell = \beta_2 - \beta_3$ is

$$\hat{\ell} = b_2 - b_3 = 28.374 - 6.864 = 21.51$$

Noting that

$$\ell = \beta_2 - \beta_3 = (0)\beta_0 + (0)\beta_1 + (1)\beta_2 + (-1)\beta_3$$

it follows that

$$\lambda' = [0 \quad 0 \quad 1 \quad -1]$$

and

$$\lambda = \begin{bmatrix} 0 \\ 0 \\ 1 \\ -1 \end{bmatrix}$$

Using $\lambda'$ and $\lambda$, $\lambda'(\mathbf{X'X})^{-1}\lambda$ can be computed to be .409898. Therefore, since $s = 6.34941$ and $n - (k + 1) = 15 - 4 = 11$, a 95% confidence interval for $\ell = \beta_2 - \beta_3$ is

$$\left[\hat{\ell} \pm t_{[\alpha/2]}^{(n-(k+1))} s_{\hat{\ell}}\right] = \left[\hat{\ell} \pm t_{[.025]}^{(11)} s\sqrt{\lambda'(\mathbf{X'X})^{-1}\lambda}\right]$$

$$= [21.51 \pm 2.201(6.34941)\sqrt{.409898}]$$

$$= [21.51 \pm 2.201(4.0651)]$$

$$= [12.5627, 30.4573]$$

# Exercises

**B.1** Let

$$\mathbf{A} = \begin{bmatrix} 1 & 2 \\ 3 & 1 \\ 2 & 2 \end{bmatrix}$$

a. Calculate $\mathbf{A'}$.
b. Calculate $\mathbf{A'A}$.

**B.2** Let

$$\mathbf{A} = \begin{bmatrix} 1 & 3 & 1 \\ 2 & 1 & 1 \\ 1 & 3 & 3 \end{bmatrix}$$

and $\mathbf{B} = \begin{bmatrix} 0 & .6 & -.2 \\ .5 & -.2 & -.1 \\ -.5 & 0 & .5 \end{bmatrix}$

a. Calculate $\mathbf{A} + \mathbf{B}$.
b. Calculate $\mathbf{AB}$.
c. Calculate $\mathbf{BA}$.
d. How are $\mathbf{A}$ and $\mathbf{B}$ related?

**B.3** Let

$$\mathbf{A} = \begin{bmatrix} .02 & 0 & 0 & 0 & 0 \\ 0 & .01 & 0 & 0 & 0 \\ 0 & 0 & .004 & 0 & 0 \\ 0 & 0 & 0 & .005 & 0 \\ 0 & 0 & 0 & 0 & .002 \end{bmatrix}$$

$$\mathbf{c} = \begin{bmatrix} 1000 \\ 300 \\ 500 \\ 80 \\ 250 \end{bmatrix} \quad \mathbf{x} = \begin{bmatrix} 1 \\ 2 \\ 5 \\ 4 \\ 10 \end{bmatrix}$$

a.  Calculate $\mathbf{c} + \mathbf{x}$.
b.  Calculate $\mathbf{Ac}$.
c.  Calculate $(\mathbf{Ac})'$.
d.  Calculate $(\mathbf{Ac})'\mathbf{c}$.
e.  Calculate $\mathbf{x}'$.
f.  Calculate $\mathbf{x}'\mathbf{Ax}$.

**B.4**  Suppose that $\mathbf{x}_0' = \begin{bmatrix} 1 & 2 & 5 & 25 \end{bmatrix}$ and

$$(\mathbf{X}'\mathbf{X})^{-1} = \begin{bmatrix} .05 & 0 & 0 & 0 \\ 0 & .01 & 0 & 0 \\ 0 & 0 & .10 & 0 \\ 0 & 0 & 0 & .02 \end{bmatrix}$$

a.  Calculate $\mathbf{x}_0'(\mathbf{X}'\mathbf{X})^{-1}$.
b.  Calculate $(\mathbf{X}'\mathbf{X})^{-1}\mathbf{x}_0$.
c.  Calculate $\mathbf{x}_0'(\mathbf{X}'\mathbf{X})^{-1}\mathbf{x}_c$.

**B.5**  Suppose that $\mathbf{x}_0' = \begin{bmatrix} 1 & 5 & 10 & 15 & 20 \end{bmatrix}$

$$\mathbf{X}'\mathbf{y} = \begin{bmatrix} 5000 \\ 1000 \\ 750 \\ 2000 \\ 500 \end{bmatrix}$$

$$(\mathbf{X}'\mathbf{X})^{-1} = \begin{bmatrix} .10 & 0 & 0 & 0 & 0 \\ 0 & .20 & 0 & 0 & 0 \\ 0 & 0 & .30 & 0 & 0 \\ 0 & 0 & 0 & .40 & 0 \\ 0 & 0 & 0 & 0 & .50 \end{bmatrix}$$

a.  Calculate $(\mathbf{X}'\mathbf{X})^{-1}\mathbf{X}'\mathbf{y}$.
b.  Calculate $\mathbf{x}_0'(\mathbf{X}'\mathbf{X})^{-1}$.
c.  Calculate $\mathbf{x}_0'(\mathbf{X}'\mathbf{X})^{-1}\mathbf{x}_0$.

**To work Exercises B.6 through B.9, it is useful to know** that if the matrix

$$\mathbf{A} = \begin{bmatrix} a & b \\ c & d \end{bmatrix}$$

is a $2 \times 2$ matrix, then the inverse of $\mathbf{A}$ is

$$\mathbf{A}^{-1} = \begin{bmatrix} d/D & -b/D \\ -c/D & a/D \end{bmatrix} \quad \text{where} \quad D = ad - bc$$

**B.6**  Suppose that

$$\mathbf{A} = \begin{bmatrix} 5 & 10 \\ 5 & 20 \end{bmatrix}$$

a.  Calculate $\mathbf{A}^{-1}$.
b.  Verify your result for part (a) by computing $\mathbf{A}^{-1}\mathbf{A}$ and $\mathbf{AA}^{-1}$.

**B.7**  Suppose that

$$\mathbf{A} = \begin{bmatrix} 100 & .5 \\ 200 & .10 \end{bmatrix}$$

a.  Calculate $\mathbf{A}^{-1}$.
b.  Verify your result for part (a) by computing $\mathbf{A}^{-1}\mathbf{A}$ and $\mathbf{AA}^{-1}$.

**B.8**  Suppose that

$$\mathbf{y} = \begin{bmatrix} 4 \\ 5 \\ 3 \\ 7 \\ 1 \\ 8 \\ 10 \end{bmatrix} \quad \text{and} \quad \mathbf{X} = \begin{bmatrix} 1 & 1.5 \\ 1 & 2.0 \\ 1 & 1.0 \\ 1 & 0.5 \\ 1 & 2.0 \\ 1 & 3.0 \\ 1 & 2.5 \end{bmatrix}$$

a.  Calculate $(\mathbf{X}'\mathbf{X})$.
b.  Calculate $(\mathbf{X}'\mathbf{X})^{-1}$.
c.  Calculate $\mathbf{X}'\mathbf{y}$.
d.  Calculate $(\mathbf{X}'\mathbf{X})^{-1}\mathbf{X}'\mathbf{y}$.

**B.9**  Suppose that $\mathbf{X}$ is as defined in Exercise B.8 and that

$$\mathbf{x}_0' = \begin{bmatrix} 1 & 4.0 \end{bmatrix}$$

a.  Calculate $\mathbf{x}_0'(\mathbf{X}'\mathbf{X})^{-1}$.
b.  Calculate $\mathbf{x}_0'(\mathbf{X}'\mathbf{X})^{-1}\mathbf{x}_0$.

**B.10**  Compustat, Inc., sells an electronic calculator, the CS-22. Compustat has, over the past $n = 25$ sales periods, spent different amounts of money on advertising and has had three different advertising firms handle the advertising strategy for the CS-22. The three advertising firms have different amounts of experience in the advertising field. One company has had five years of experience, while the others have had ten and fifteen years of experience, respectively. Compustat wishes to develop a regression model that relates the dependent variable

$y$ = demand for the CS-22 during a sales period (measured in units of 1000 calculators sold)

to the independent variables

$x_1$ = advertising expenditure during the sales period (measured in units of $100,000)

$x_2$ = the number of years of experience in the advertising field of the firm handling the advertising strategy for the CS-22 during the sales period

Compustat wishes to consider using the regression model

$$y = \beta_0 + \beta_1 x_1 + \beta_2 x_2 + \beta_3 x_1^2 + \varepsilon$$

Assume that a sample of $n = 25$ combinations of ($y$, $x_1$, $x_2$) values are observed and that the following calculations are made:

$$(\mathbf{X'X})^{-1} = \begin{bmatrix} .02 & 0 & 0 & 0 \\ 0 & .01 & 0 & 0 \\ 0 & 0 & .004 & 0 \\ 0 & 0 & 0 & .006 \end{bmatrix}$$

$$\mathbf{X'y} = \begin{bmatrix} 1000 \\ 300 \\ 500 \\ 100 \end{bmatrix} \quad \text{and} \quad \sum_{i=1}^{25} y_i^2 = 22,162$$

$$\text{and} \quad \sum_{i=1}^{25} y_i = 715.44$$

a. Calculate the least squares point estimates of the model parameters.
b. Calculate $\mathbf{b'X'y}$, SSE, $s^2$, and $s$.
c. Calculate the total variation, the explained variation, and $R^2$.
d. Calculate $F(\text{model})$ and use it to test the importance of the model with $\alpha = .05$.
e. Calculate for each parameter $\beta_j$ the $t$-statistic for testing $H_0$: $\beta_j = 0$ versus $H_a$: $\beta_j \neq 0$. Then, do the test by setting $\alpha = .05$ and by setting $\alpha = .01$.
f. Calculate the 95% confidence interval for each $\beta_j$.
g. Calculate a point estimate of and a 95% confidence interval for the mean demand when $200,000 is spent on advertising and the firm handling the advertising has five years of experience.
h. Calculate a point prediction of and a 95% prediction interval for the actual demand in a future sales period when $200,000 is spent on advertising and the firm handling the account has five years of experience.

i. Assume that when we use the model

$$y = \beta_0 + \beta_1 x_1 + \beta_2 x_2 + \beta_3 x_1^2 + \beta_4 x_1 x_2 + \varepsilon$$

to analyze the $n = 25$ combinations of ($y$, $x_1$, $x_2$) values, the following calculations are made:

$$(\mathbf{X'X})^{-1} = \begin{bmatrix} .02 & 0 & 0 & 0 & 0 \\ 0 & .01 & 0 & 0 & 0 \\ 0 & 0 & .004 & 0 & 0 \\ 0 & 0 & 0 & .006 & 0 \\ 0 & 0 & 0 & 0 & .002 \end{bmatrix}$$

$$\mathbf{X'y} = \begin{bmatrix} 1000 \\ 300 \\ 500 \\ 100 \\ 250 \end{bmatrix}$$

and

$$\sum_{i=1}^{25} y_i^2 = 22,162 \qquad \sum_{i=1}^{25} y_i = 715.44$$

Answer parts (a) through (h) above using this new model.

**B.11** Panasound, Inc., wishes to use the regression model

$$y = \beta_0 + \beta_1 x_1 + \beta_2 x_1^2 + \beta_3 D_B + \beta_4 D_C + \varepsilon$$

to relate the dependent variable

$y$ = sales of the Panasound Video Recorder (in thousands of units) in a sales period

to the independent variables

$x$ = advertising expenditure (in hundreds of thousands of dollars) in the sales period

and the advertising agency ($A$, $B$, or $C$) that handles the Panasound account in the sales period. To model the effect of the advertising agencies, we use dummy variables defined as follows:

$$D_B = \begin{cases} 1 & \text{if advertising agency B handles the Panasound account in the sales period} \\ 0 & \text{otherwise} \end{cases}$$

$$D_C = \begin{cases} 1 & \text{if advertising agency C handles the Panasound account in the sales period} \\ 0 & \text{otherwise} \end{cases}$$

By using data observed on these variables for $n = 25$ sales periods, the following calculations are made.

$$(\mathbf{X'X})^{-1} = \begin{bmatrix} .02 & 0 & 0 & 0 & 0 \\ 0 & .01 & 0 & 0 & 0 \\ 0 & 0 & .05 & 0 & 0 \\ 0 & 0 & 0 & .05 & 0 \\ 0 & 0 & 0 & 0 & .10 \end{bmatrix} \text{ and }$$

$$\mathbf{X'y} = \begin{bmatrix} 1000 \\ 300 \\ 50 \\ 60 \\ 50 \end{bmatrix}$$

$$\sum_{i=1}^{25} y_i^2 = 21,500 \quad \sum_{i=1}^{25} y_i = 724.57$$

a. Answer questions (a) through (f) of Exercise B.10, as these questions apply to this situation.

b. Let

$\mu_{a,A}$ = mean sales when advertising expenditure is $a$ and agency $A$ handles the Panasound account

$\mu_{a,B}$ = mean sales when advertising expenditure is $a$ and agency $B$ handles the Panasound account

$\mu_{a,C}$ = mean sales when advertising expenditure is $a$ and agency $C$ handles the Panasound account

Then, show that

$$\mu_{a,B} - \mu_{a,A} = \beta_3$$
$$\mu_{a,C} - \mu_{a,A} = \beta_4$$
$$\mu_{a,C} - \mu_{a,B} = \beta_4 - \beta_3$$
$$\mu_{a,C} - \left[ \frac{\mu_{a,B} + \mu_{a,A}}{2} \right] = \beta_4 - .5\beta_3$$

Also, find 95% confidence intervals for these differences. Interpret these intervals. Test the hypothesis that each difference is 0 by calculating the appropriate $t$-statistic and setting $\alpha = .05$. The second two differences require Section B.15.

c. Find a point estimate of and a 95% confidence interval for the mean sales when $500,000 is spent on advertising and agency $C$ handles the account.

d. Find a point prediction of and a 95% prediction interval for the actual sales in a future sales period when $500,000 is spent on advertising and agency $C$ handles the account.

**B.12** Consider Exercise 4.23.

a. Specify the row vector $\lambda'$ that would be used in part (a) of Exercise 4.23 to calculate a 95% confidence interval for

$$\mu_{[d,a,C]} - \mu_{[d,a,B]} = \beta_6 - \beta_5 + \beta_8(6.2) - \beta_7(6.2)$$

b. Specify the row vector $\mathbf{x_0'}$ that would be used to calculate the confidence and prediction intervals referred to in a part (b) of Exercise 4.23.

# *Directions and Programs to Implement Regression Analysis in SAS Version 8*

## RETRIEVING, EXAMINING, AND SAVING DATA USING THE FUEL CONSUMPTION DATA IN TABLE 4.1

### Creating a SAS Data Set Using SAS Commands

In the SAS Program Editor, write the following program. **All commands must end with a semicolon.**

| | |
|---|---|
| data fuel; | Defines WORK filename "fuel" |
|   input temp chill fuelcons; | Defines variable names for temperature, chill index, and fuel consumption |
| datalines; | |
| 28.0  18  12.4 | Values from Table 4.1 |
| 28.0  14  11.7 | |
|   ⋮    ⋮    ⋮ | |
| 62.5   0    7.5 | |
| run; | Required statement |
| proc print data = work.fuel; | Prints file work.fuel, if desired |
| run; | Required statement |

Now click on "Run" at the top of the screen and click on "Submit."

When this program is executed, it creates the SAS file called "fuel" in the WORK library.

Note: In other parts of SAS you might need to update your data by selecting "Tools" and then "Update data."

## Importing (Retrieving) a Data Set from an Excel File Using the Import Wizard

To retrieve a data set that is stored as an Excel file and import it into the WORK library in SAS System for Windows, do the following:

| | |
|---|---|
| Click | File |
| Click | Import data |
| Click | Microsoft Excel 97 or 2000 (*.xls) |
| Click | Next> |

In the box under **Where is the file located?**

| | |
|---|---|
| Type | a:\fuel.xls (assumes that file is in a: drive and that data columns have headings) or Browse to locate the file |
| Click | Next> |

In the box under **MEMBER**

| | |
|---|---|
| Type | Fuel (or any desired filename) |
| Click | Finish |

Notes: (1) An Excel file must *not be open* in Excel when being imported. (2) Alphanumeric data (data containing letters) should be imported as a Tab Delimited *.txt file. To change an Excel *.xls file to this format, open the file in Excel, save the data as a Tab Delimited *.txt file, and close the file before importing it to SAS.

## Examining, Editing, Transforming, and Graphing Data in SAS/INSIGHT

To enter SAS/INSIGHT and open a specified data set, such as work.fuel, do the following:

| | |
|---|---|
| Click | Solutions |
| Click | ASSIST |
| Click | Block Menu |
| Click | Continue |
| Click | DATA ANALYSIS |
| Click | INTERACTIVE |
| Click | Data exploration |
| Click | WORK under **Library** |
| Click | Fuel (or any desired file) under **Data set** |
| Click | Open |

Use Edit and Analyze to help edit, transform, and graph the data. The arrow in the upper left corner of the spreadsheet can be clicked to find selections for creating new variables and naming variables. Basic simple and multiple regression (no confidence or prediction intervals for future values) can be done within SAS/INSIGHT, if desired.

## Exporting (Storing) the SAS Data Set as an Excel File

To store your data file as an Excel file, do the following:

| | |
|---|---|
| Click | File |
| Click | Export data |

In the box under **LIBRARY**: select WORK.
In the box under **MEMBER**: select Fuel (or any desired file).
(Note: You will have to click on the large down arrow to find the list of data sets.)

| | |
|---|---|
| Click | Next> |
| Click | Microsoft Excel 97 or 2000 (*.xls) |
| Click | Next> |

In the box under **Where do you want to save the file?**

| | |
|---|---|
| Type | a:\fuel.xls |

(Note: Replace "a:" with any other desired drive or Browse to select a location for that file.)

| | |
|---|---|
| Click | Finish |

# SAS PROGRAMS FOR SIMPLE LINEAR REGRESSION USING THE FUEL CONSUMPTION DATA IN TABLE 4.1

## Programming Commands for Procedures to Add a Future Value, Plot Data, and Produce Regression Analysis for Simple Linear Regression

This example corresponds to the MINITAB output in Figure 3.9.

In the SAS Program Editor, write the following program. **(All commands must end with a semicolon).**

| | |
|---|---|
| data fuel; | Defines WORK filename "fuel" |
|   input temp chill fuelcons; | Defines variable names for temperature, wind chill, and fuel consumption |
| datalines; | |
|   28.0   18   12.4 | First value from Table 4.1 |
|   28.0   14   11.7 | |
|        ⋮ | |
|   62.5    0    7.5 | Last value from Table 4.1 |
|   40.0    .    . | Value of 40.0 for future temperature and periods for missing or unknown values |
| run; | Required statement |
| proc plot data = work.fuel; | Requests PROC PLOT and fuel data |
|   plot fuelcons*temp; | Plots fuel consumption on the vertical axis and temperature on the horizontal axis |
|   plot fuelcons*chill; | Plots fuelcons versus chill |
| proc reg data = work.fuel; | Requests PROC REG and fuel data |
|   model fuelcons = temp/clm cli; | Specifies the model |

$$\text{fuelcons} = \beta_0 + \beta_1 \text{temp} + \varepsilon$$

clm = 95% confidence intervals desired
cli = 95% prediction intervals desired

run;    required statement

Note: The value of 40.0 for a future temperature can be added to the data in SAS/INSIGHT.

To execute the program, click on "Run" at the top of the screen and click on "Submit."

When your program is executed, the output will appear in the Output Window, where it can be printed or saved.

There are now three windows: Program Editor (contains the program commands), Output (contains the output from the commands), and Log (contains a record of what you have done, error messages, and sometimes output). As with any Windows program, you can click on "Window" at the top of the screen to see a list of the current windows and click on a desired window or display the windows in a desired arrangement.

To recall the program to the Program Editor Window:

| | |
|---|---|
| Click | anywhere on Program Editor Window |
| Click | Run |
| Click | Recall Last Submit |

To save your program commands, follow the usual procedures for saving a file, but be sure that you click on the Program Editor Window first. The program will be saved as a *.sas file.

# SAS PROGRAMS FOR MULTIPLE LINEAR REGRESSION

## Programming Commands for Basic Multiple Linear Regression

This example uses the fuel consumption data in Table 4.1 and corresponds to the MINITAB output in Figure 4.5.

| Data fuel; | Defines WORK filename "fuel" |
|---|---|
| input temp chill fuelcons; | Defines variable names for temperature, chill index, and fuel consumption |
| datalines; | |
| 28.0    18    12.4 | First value from Table 4.1 |
| 28.0    14    11.7 | |
| . | |
| . | |
| . | |
| 62.5    0    7.5 | Last value from Table 4.1 |
| 40.0    10    . | Values of 40.0 and 10 for future temperature and chill index with period for missing or unknown value |
| run; | Required statement |

| | |
|---|---|
| proc reg data = work.fuel; | Requests PROC REG and fuel data |
| model fuelcons = temp chill/clm cli; | Specifies the model |
| | fuelcons = $\beta_0$ + $\beta_1$temp + $\beta_2$chill + $\varepsilon$ |
| | clm = 95% confidence intervals desired cli = 95% prediction intervals desired |
| run; | Required statement |

## Programming Commands for Models with Squared and Interaction Terms

This example corresponds to Figures 4.13 and 4.17.

- Create work.fresh from data in Table 4.6 and add future values

```
data fresh;
  input PriceDif AdverExp Demand;
datalines;
-.05        5.50        7.38
 .25        6.75        8.51
             .
             .
             .
 .55        6.80        6.80
 .20        6.50        .
run;
```

- Create new file work.fresh2 with two additional variables: advertising expense squared and the product of price difference and advertising expense

Note: All creation of new variables must be done within a data step. The formulas for new variables can be put between input and datalines in the original data step. A separate data step is used here in case the original file work.fresh2 is imported from a disk, CD, etc., and the future values added elsewhere, such as in SAS/INSIGHT. The new variables themselves can also be created in SAS/INSIGHT.

```
data fresh2;
  set fresh;
  AdvExpsq = AdvExp*AdvExp;
  PrAdv = PriceDif*AdvExp;
run;
```

- Regression analysis for model with squared term in Figure 4.13

$$\text{Demand} = \beta_0 + \beta_1\text{PriceDif} + \beta_2\text{AdvExp} + \beta_3\text{AdvExpsq} + \varepsilon$$

```
proc reg data = work.fresh2;
  model Demand = PriceDif AdvExp AdvExpsq/clm cli;
run;
```

- Regression analysis for model with squared and interaction terms in Figure 4.17

$$\text{Demand} = \beta_0 + \beta_1\text{PriceDif} + \beta_2\text{AdvExp} + \beta_3\text{AdvExpsq} + \beta_4\text{PrAdv} + \varepsilon$$

```
proc reg data = work.fresh2;
  model Demand = PriceDif AdvExp AdvExpsq PrAdv/
    clm cli;
run;
```

## Programming Commands for Models with Dummy Variables

This example corresponds to Figures 4.22 and 4.23.

- Create work.storeloc from data in Table 4.9 and add future values

```
data storeloc;
  input x y DM DD;
datalines;
  161      157.27      0       0
                .
                .
                .
  221      241.74      1       0
                .
                .
                .
  205      197.82      0       1
    .      200.00      1       0
run;
```

- Create new file work.storeloc2 with two new variables for the interaction of number of households and store location

```
data storeloc2;
  set storeloc;
  xDM = x*DM;
  xDD = x*DD;
run;
```

- Regression analysis for model with dummy variables in Figure 4.22

$$y = \beta_0 + \beta_1 x + \beta_2 D_M + \beta_3 D_D + \varepsilon$$

```
proc reg data = work.storeloc2;
  model y = x DM DD/clm cli;
run;
```

- Regression analysis for model with dummy variables and interaction terms in Figure 4.23

$$y = \beta_0 + \beta_1 x + \beta_2 D_M + \beta_3 D_D + \beta_4 x D_M + \beta_5 x D_D + \varepsilon$$

```
proc reg data = work.storeloc2;
  model y = x DM DD xDM xDD;
run;
```

# MODEL BUILDING USING SALES TERRITORY DATA IN TABLES 4.2 AND 5.1

## Programming Commands for the Procedure to Produce Correlations among All Variables

This example is similar to the MINITAB output in Figure 5.1.

```
proc corr data = work.salesterr;
  var Sales Time MktPoten Adver MktShare Change
    Accts WkLoad Rating;
run;
```

## Programming Commands for the Procedure to Produce Variance Inflation Factors

This example corresponds to Figure 5.2.

```
proc reg data = work.salesterr;
  model Sales = Time MktPoten Adver MktShare Change
    Accts WkLoad Rating/VIF;
run;
```

## Programming Commands for the Procedure to Use RSQUARE to Select the Two Best Submodels of Each Size

This example is similar to the MINITAB output in Figure 5.4(a).

```
proc reg data = work.salesterr;
  model Sales = Time MktPoten Adver MktShare Change
                Accts WkLoad Rating/selection =
                rsquare Best=2 adjrsq CP RMSE;
run;
```

## Programming Commands for the Procedure to Use ADJRSQ to Select the Eight Best Submodels

This example corresponds to Figure 5.4(b).

```
proc reg data = work.salesterr;
  model Sales = Time MktPoten Adver MktShare Change
                Accts WkLoad Rating/selection =
                adjrsq Best=8 CP RMSE;
run;
```

## Programming Commands for the Stepwise Procedure to Select a Model

This example is similar to the MINITAB output in Figure 5.5(a).

```
proc reg data = work.salesterr;
  model Sales = Time MktPoten Adver MktShare Change
                Accts WkLoad Rating/selection =
                stepwise SLentry = .10 SLstay = .10;
run;
```

## Programming Commands for the Backward Procedure to Select a Model

This example is similar to the MINITAB output in Figure 5.5(b).

```
proc reg data = work.salesterr;
  model Sales = Time MktPoten Adver MktShare Change
                Accts WkLoad Rating/selection =
                backward SLstay = .10;
run;
```

# RESIDUAL ANALYSIS AND DETECTING OUTLYING AND INFLUENTIAL OBSERVATIONS

## Programming Commands for Residual Analysis

Simple linear regression model for the QHIC data in Table 3.2:

$$\text{upkeep} = \beta_0 + \beta_1 \text{Value} + \varepsilon$$

- Create output file work.results that contains predicted values and residuals, and produce residual plots [corresponds to the MINITAB graphs in Figure 5.6(a) and (b)]

```
proc reg data = work.QHIC;
  model upkeep = Value;
    output out = results predicted = yhat
                  residual = resid;
proc plot data = results;
  plot resid*(Value yhat);
```

- Produce normal plot, statistical tests for normality, and stem-and-leaf plot [similar to the graphs in Figures 5.8(a) and (c)]

```
proc univariate data = work.results normal plot;
  var resid;
run;
```

## Programming Commands in Simple Linear Regression to Transform *y* for the QHIC Data in Table 3.2 to Correct for Nonconstant Variance

- Create new file work.QHIC2 with three new variables: square root, quartic root, and natural logarithm of *y*, and plot these variables versus value (corresponds to Figures 5.12, 5.13, and 5.14)

```
data QHIC2;
  set QHIC;
  SRUPKEEP = UPKEEP**.5;
  QRUPKEEP = UPKEEP**.25;
  LNUPKEEP = Log(UPKEEP);
run;
proc plot;
  plot SRUPKEEP*value;
```

```
      plot QRUPKEEP*value;
      plot LNUPKEEP*value;
   run;
```

- Regression analysis and residual analysis for the model with transformed $y$

$$\text{SRupkeep} = \beta_0 + \beta_1 \text{value} + \varepsilon$$

This is similar to the MINITAB output in Figures 5.15 and 5.16.

```
proc reg data = work.QHIC2;
  model SRUPKEEP = Value/clm cli;
  output out = results predicted = yhat
                residual = resid;
proc plot data = results;
  plot resid*(Value yhat);
proc univariate data = work.results normal plot;
  var resid;
run;
```

## Programming Commands for Residual Analysis

Multiple linear regression model for the sales territory data in Table 4.2

$$\text{sales} = \beta_0 + \beta_1 \text{Time} + \beta_2 \text{MktPoten} + \beta_3 \text{Adver} + \beta_4 \text{MktShare} + \beta_5 \text{Change} + \varepsilon$$

- Create output file work.results that contains predicted values and residuals, and produce residual plots, normal plot, tests for normality, and stem-and-leaf plot (similar to output in Figure 5.17)

```
proc reg data = work.salesterr;
  model sales = Time MktPoten Adver MktShare Change;
  output out = results predicted = yhat
                residual = resid;
Proc plot data = work.results;
  plot resid*(yhat Time MktPoten Adver MktShare
    Change);
Proc univariate data = work.results normal plot;
  var resid;
run;
```

## Programming Commands for Detecting Outlying and Influential Observations

This example uses the hospital data in Table 5.5 and the model

$$\text{hours} = \beta_0 + \beta_1 \text{xray} + \beta_2 \text{beddays} + \beta_3 \text{length} + \varepsilon$$

It is similar to the output in Figure 5.20.

```
proc reg data = work.hospital;
  model hours = xray beddays length/ r influence;
run;
```

# TIME SERIES REGRESSION

## Programming Commands for the No Trend Model of the Cod Catch Data in Table 6.1

$$y_t = \beta_0 + \varepsilon_t$$

This example is similar to the MINITAB output in Figures 6.3 and 6.10.

```
data cod;
  input y time;
datalines;
362        1
381        2
317        3
  .        .
  .        .
  .        .
365       24
  .       25
run;
data cod2;
  set cod;
  one = 1;
run;
proc plot data = work.cod2;
  plot y*time;
proc reg data = work.cod2;
  model y = one/noint clm cli;
  output out = results predicted = yhat
      residual = resid;
proc plot data = work.results;
  plot resid*time;
run;
```

## Programming Commands for the Linear Trend Model of Calculator Sales in Table 6.2

$$y_t = \beta_0 + \beta_1 t + \varepsilon_t$$

This example corresponds to Figures 6.5 and 6.11.

```
data calc;
  input y time;
datalines;
197        1
211        2
203        3

      :
      :

384       24
  .       25
  .       26
  .       27
  .       28
run;
proc plot data = work.calc;
  plot y*time;
proc reg data = work.calc;
  model y = time/clm cli dw;
  output out = results predicted = yhat
                residual = resid;
proc plot data = work.results;
  plot resid*time;
run;
```

Note: dw in the model statement produces the Durbin–Watson statistic.

## Programming Commands for Quadratic Trend Model of Loan Requests in Table 6.3

$$y_t = \beta_0 + \beta_1 t + \beta_2 t^2 + \varepsilon_t$$

This example is similar to the MINITAB output in Figures 6.7 and 6.12.

```
data loans;
  Input y time;
```

```
datalines;
297          1
249          2
340          3
              .
              .
1127        24
  .         25
  .         26
run;
data loans2;
  set loans;
  timesq = time**2;
proc plot data = work.loans2;
  plot y*time;
proc reg data = work.loans2;
  model y = time timesq/clm cli dw;
  output out = results predicted = yhat
        residual = resid;
proc plot data = work.results;
  plot resid*time;
run;
```

## Programming Commands for Plotting Transformed Monthly Hotel Data in Table 6.4

- Transforming data when a SAS data set work.hotel has already been created

```
data hotel2;
  Set hotel;
  Time=_n_;
  Lny=Log(y);
  Sqrty=y**.5;
  Qtrooty=y**.25;
run;
```

Note: Transformations must be done within a data step.

- Plot each of $y$, square root of $y$, quartic root of $y$, and natural logarithm of $y$ versus Time (similar to JMP IN output in Figures 6.15 to 6.18)

```
Proc plot data = work.hotel2;
  Plot y*Time;
  Plot Sqrty*Time;
```

```
   plot Qtrooty*Time;
   plot Lny*Time;
run;
```

## Programming Commands for Seasonal Models for the Monthly Hotel Data in Table 6.4

• Create a file work.hotel from Table 6.4 and add future values for Time

```
data hotel;
    input y;
    Lny = Log(y);
    Time = _n_;
  Datalines;
  501
  488
   .
   .
   .
  877
Run;
data future;
  input y Lny Time;
  datalines;
   .    .    169
   .    .    170
   .    .    171
   .    .    172
   .    .    173
   .    .    174
   .    .    175
   .    .    176
   .    .    177
   .    .    178
   .    .    179
   .    .    180
run;
data hotel2;
  update hotel future;
  by Time;
run;
```

Note: The future lines may be added other ways, such as adding the lines in SAS/INSIGHT.

- Create dummy variables

```
data hotel3;
  set hotel2;
  if mod(Time,12)=1 then M1=1; else M1=0;
  if mod(Time,12)=2 then M2=1; else M2=0;
  if mod(Time,12)=3 then M3=1; else M3=0;
  if mod(Time,12)=4 then M4=1; else M4=0;
  if mod(Time,12)=5 then M5=1; else M5=0;
  if mod(Time,12)=6 then M6=1; else M6=0;
  if mod(Time,12)=7 then M7=1; else M7=0;
  if mod(Time,12)=8 then M8=1; else M8=0;
  if mod(Time,12)=9 then M9=1; else M9=0;
  if mod(Time,12)=10 then M10=1; else M10=0;
  if mod(Time,12)=11 then M11=1; else M11=0
run;
```

- Regression analysis for linear trend model with dummy variables for the monthly seasonal pattern in Figure 6.19

$$\ln y = \beta_0 + \beta_1 t + \beta_2 M_1 + \beta_3 M_2 + \cdots + \beta_{12} M_{11} + \varepsilon_t$$

```
proc reg data = work.hotel3;
model Lny = time M1 M2 M3 M4 M5 M6 M7 M8 M9 M10
  M11/CLM CLI DW;
run;
```

- Regression analysis for the linear trend model with trigonometric variables for the monthly seasonal pattern in Figure 6.20

$$\ln y = \beta_0 + \beta_1 t + \beta_2 \sin\left(\frac{2\pi t}{12}\right) + \beta_3 \cos\left(\frac{2\pi t}{12}\right) + \beta_4 \sin\left(\frac{4\pi t}{12}\right) + \beta_5 \cos\left(\frac{4\pi t}{12}\right) + \varepsilon$$

```
data hotel4;
  set work.hotel2;
  pi = arcos(-1);
  two = (pi*time)/6;
  four = (pi*time)/3;
  sintwo = sin(two);
  costwo = cos(two);
  sinfour = sin(four);
  cosfour = cos(four);
proc reg data = work.hotel4;
  model Lny = time sintwo costwo sinfour cosfour/CLM
    CLI DW;
run;
```

- Regression analysis for the linear trend model with dummy variables for the monthly seasonal pattern and order 1 autocorrelation for the error term, as in Figure 6.25

$$\ln y = \beta_0 + \beta_1 t + \beta_2 M_1 + \beta_3 M_2 + \cdots + \beta_{12} M_{11} + \varepsilon_t \quad \text{where} \quad \varepsilon_t = \phi_1 \varepsilon_{t-1} + a_t$$

```
proc arima data = work.hotel3;
  identify var = Lny
  crosscor = (Time M1 M2 M3 M4 M5 M6 M7 M8 M9 M10 M11)
             noprint;
  estimate input = (Time M1 M2 M3 M4 M5 M6 M7 M8 M9
             M10 M11) printall plot;
proc arima data = work.hotel3;
  identify var = Lny
  crosscor = (Time M1 M2 M3 M4 M5 M6 M7 M8 M9 M10 M11)
             noprint;
  estimate input = (Time M1 M2 M3 M4 M5 M6 M7 M8 M9
             M10 M11)
             p=(1) printall plot;
  forecast lead = 12 out = work.fcast1;
data fcast2;
  set work.fcast1;
  Forecasty = Exp(Forecast);
  L95CI -   Exp(L95);
  U95CI =   Exp(U95);
proc print data = work.fcast2;
  var Forecasty L95CI U95CI;
run;
```

## Programming Commands for the Growth Curve Model for the Steakhouse Data in Table 6.5

This example is similar to the MINITAB output in Figures 6.22, 6.23, and 6.24.

```
data steak;
  input y Time;
datalines;
11        1
14        2
16        3
      .
      .
403       14
  .       15
run;
```

```
data steak2;
  set work.steak;
  Lny = Log(y);
run;
Proc plot data = work.steak2;
  plot y*Time;
  plot Lny*Time;
Proc reg data = work.steak2;
  model Lny = Time/clm cli dw;
run;
```

*Directions and Programs
to Implement the
Box–Jenkins
Methodology in
SAS Version 8*

# RETRIEVING, EXAMINING, AND SAVING DATA USING THE ABSORBENT PAPER TOWEL SALES IN TABLE 9.1

## Creating a SAS Data Set Using SAS Commands

In the SAS Program Editor, write the following program. **All commands must end with a semicolon.**

| | |
|---|---|
| data towel; | Defines WORK filename "towel" |
|   input y; | Difines variable name for time series |
|   time = _n_; | Creates variable for time $t$ |
|   z = dif1(y); | Creates a variable |
| | $z_t = y_t - y_{t-1}$ (first differences) |
| datalines; | |
| 15.0000 | |
| 14.4064 | |
|   . | |
|   . | |
|   . | |
| 15.6453 | |
| run; | Required statement |
| proc print data = work.towel; | Prints data set work.towel, if desired |
| run; | Required statement |

Now click on "Run" at the top of the screen and click on "Submit."

When this program is executed, it creates the SAS file called "towel" in the WORK library.

Note: In other parts of SAS you might need to update your data by selecting "Tools" and then "Update data."

## Importing (Retrieving) a Data Set from an Excel File Using the Import Wizard

To retrieve a data set that is stored as an Excel file and import it into the WORK library in SAS System for Windows, do the following:

| | |
|---|---|
| Click | File |
| Click | Import data |
| Click | Microsoft Excel 97 or 2000 (*.xls) |
| Click | Next> |

In the box under **Where is the file located?**

| | |
|---|---|
| Type | a:\towel.xls (assumes that file is in a: drive and that data columns have headings) or Browse to find the file |
| Click | Next> |

In the box under **MEMBER**

| | |
|---|---|
| Type | Towel (or any desired filename) |
| Click | Finish |

Notes: (1) An Excel file must *not be open* in Excel when being imported. (2) Alphanumeric data (data containing letters) should be imported as a Tab Delimited *.txt file. To change an Excel *.xls file to this format, open the file in Excel, save the data as a Tab Delimited *.txt file, and close the file before importing it to SAS.

## Examining, Editing, Transforming, and Graphing Data in SAS/INSIGHT

To enter SAS/INSIGHT and open a specified data set, such as work.towel, do the following:

| | |
|---|---|
| Click | Solutions |
| Click | ASSIST |
| Click | Block Menu |
| Click | Continue |
| Click | DATA ANALYSIS |
| Click | INTERACTIVE |
| Click | Data exploration |
| Click | WORK under **Library** |
| Click | TOWEL (or any desired file) under **Data set** |
| Click | Open |

Use Edit and Analyze to help edit, transform, and graph the data. Also, the arrow in the upper left corner of the spreadsheet can be clicked to find selections for creating new variables and naming variables.

## Exporting (Storing) the SAS Data Set as an Excel File

To store your data file as an Excel file, do the following:

| | |
|---|---|
| Click | File |
| Click | Export data |

In the box under **LIBRARY**: select WORK.

In the box under **MEMBER**: select Towel (or any desired file).
(Note: You will have to click on the large down arrow to find the list of data sets.)

| | |
|---|---|
| Click | Next> |
| Click | Microsoft Excel 97 or 2000 (*.xls) |
| Click | Next> |

In the box under **Where do you want to save the file?**

| | |
|---|---|
| Type | a:\towel.xls |

(Note: Replace "a:" with any other desired drive or Browse to select another location for the file.)

| | |
|---|---|
| Click | Finish |

# SAS PROGRAMS FOR NONSEASONAL DATA USING THE ABSORBENT PAPER TOWEL SALES IN TABLE 9.1

## Programming Commands for Procedures to Plot Data and Find SAC and SPAC

In the SAS Program Editor, Write the follwing program. **All commands must end with a semicolon.**

| | |
|---|---|
| proc plot data = work.towel; | Requests PROC PLOT and towel data |
| plot y*time; | Plots $y_t$ versus time. |
| plot z*time; | Plots $z_t = y_t - y_{t-1}$ versus time |
| proc arima data = work.towel; | Requests PROC ARIMA and towel data |
| identify var = y; | Generates SAC and SPAC for $y_t$ |
| identify var = y(1); | Generates SAC and SPAC for $z_t = y_t - y_{t-1}$ |
| identify var = y(1,1); | Generates SAC and SPAC for $z_t = y_t - 2y_{t-1} + y_{t-2}$ |
| run; | |

To execute the program, click on "Run" at the top of the screen and click on "Submit."

When your program is executed, the output will appear in the Output Window, where it can be printed or saved.

There are now three windows: Program Editor (contains the program commands), Output (contains the output from the commands), and Log (contains a record of what you have done, error messages, and sometimes output). As with any Windows program, you can click on "Window" at the top of the screen to see a list of the current windows and click on a desired window or display the windows in a desired arrangement.

To recall the program to the Program Editor Window:

Click        anywhere on Program Editor Window
Click        Run
Click        Recall Last Submit

To save your program commands, follow the usual procedures for saving a file, but be sure that you click on the Program Editor Window first. The program will be saved as a *.sas file.

## SAS Commands for Estimation and Forecasting with PROC ARIMA

To analyze and forecast the towel data, write the following program in the SAS Program Editor.

| | |
|---|---|
| proc arima data = work.towel; | Requests PROC ARIMA and towel data |
| identify var = y(1); | Specifies first differencing |
| estimate q = (1) noconstant printall plot; | Requests estimation and diagnostics for model $z_t = a_t - \theta_1 a_{t-1}$ |
| forecast lead = 12; | Generates forecasts for 12 periods ahead |
| run; | |

Other sample statements for PROC ARIMA:

| | |
|---|---|
| estimate q = (1,2) noconstant printall plot; | Model $z_t = a_t - \theta_1 a_{t-1} - \theta_2 a_{t-2}$ |
| estimate p = (1) noconstant printall plot; | Model $z_t = \phi_1 z_{t-1} + a_t$ |
| estimate p = (1,2) noconstant printall plot; | Model $z_t = \phi_1 z_{t-1} + \phi_2 z_{t-2} + a_t$ |
| estimate p = (1)  q = (1) printall plot; | Model $z_t = \delta + \phi_1 z_{t-1} + a_t - \theta_1 a_{t-1}$ |
| estimate p = (1,2)  q = (6) noconstant printall plot; | Model $z_t = \phi_1 z_{t-1} + \phi_2 z_{t-2} + a_t - \theta_1 a_{t-6}$ |

## Chapter 9

SAC for the Absorbent Paper Towel sales in Figure 9.3

```
proc arima data = work.towel;
  identify var = y nlag=14;
run;
```

SAC and SPAC for first differences of the Absorbent Paper Towel sales in Figures 9.7 and 9.9

```
proc arima data = work.towel;
   identify var = y(1) nlag=14;
run;
```

## Chapter 10

Estimation, diagnostics, and forecasting for the towel sales in Figures 10.1, 10.5, and 10.9.

```
proc arima data = work.towel;
   identify var = y(1) nlag=14;
   estimate q=(1) noconstant printall plot;
   forecast lead = 10;
run;
```

Estimation, diagnostics, and forecasting for viscosity readings in Figures 10.3, 10.7, and 10.10

```
proc arima data = work.viscosity;
   identify var = y nlag=14;
   estimate p=(1,2) printall plot;
   forecast lead = 10;
run;
```

# SAS PROGRAMS FOR SEASONAL DATA USING THE HOTEL DATA IN TABLE 11.1

## Predifferencing Transformations and Differencing Transformations

| | |
|---|---|
| data hotel; | Defines WORK file named "hotel" |
| input y; | Defines variable name for time series |
| time = _n_; | Creates a variable for time |
| Lny = log (y); | Performs natural log transformation of $y$ and creates variable called Lny |
| Sqrty = y**.5; | Performs square root transformation of $y$ and creates variable called Sqrty |
| QtRooty = y**.25; | Performs quartic root transformation of $y$ and creates variable called QtRooty |

| | |
|---|---|
| datalines; | |
| 501 | |
| 488 | |
| . | |
| . | |
| . | |
| 877 | |
| run; | Required statement |
| proc plot data = work.hotel; | Requests PROC PLOT and hotel data |
| plot y*time; | Plots $y$ versus time |
| plot Lny*time; | Plots natural logarithms versus time |
| plot Sqrty*time; | Plots square roots versus time |
| plot QtRooty*time; | Plots quartic roots versus time |
| proc arima data=work.hotel; | Requests PROC ARIMA and hotel data |
| identify var = QtRooty; | Generates SAC and SPAC for $y_t^* = \sqrt[4]{y_t}$ |
| identify var = QtRooty(1); | Generates SAC and SPAC for $z_t = y_t^* - y_{t-1}^*$ |
| identify var = QtRooty(12); | Generates SAC and SPAC for $z_t = y_t^* - y_{t-12}^*$ |
| identify var = QtRooty(1,12); | Generates SAC and SPAC for $z_t = y_t^* - y_{t-1}^* - y_{t-12}^* + y_{t-13}^*$ |
| run; | Required statement |

# Estimation, Diagnostics, and Forecasting

| | |
|---|---|
| proc arima data = work.hotel; | Requests PROC ARIMA and hotel data |
| identify var = QtRooty(12); | Specifies variable and first order seasonal differencing |
| estimate p = (1,3,5)   q = (12) printall plot; | Requests estimation and diagnostics for model of hotel data in Example 11.3 |
| forecast lead = 12 out = fcast1; | Generates forecasts for 12 periods ahead and stores results in a file called "fcast1" |
| data fore1; | Defines a Work file named "fore1" |
| set fcast1; | Requests WORK file called "fcast1" |
| y = Qtrooty**4; | Retransforms variable Qtrooty back to $y$ for the file "fore1" |
| Forecasty = forecast**4; | Creates variable that contains forecasts in the original units for the data set |

| | |
|---|---|
| L95CI = L95**4; | Creates variable that contains lower 95% limits in original units for the data set |
| U95CI = U95**4; | Creates variable that contains upper 95% limits in original units for the data set |
| proc print data = work.fore1; | Requests PROC PRINT and fore1 file |
| var y Forecasty L95CI U95CI; | Specifies four variables to be printed |
| run; | Required statement |

Other sample statements for PROC ARIMA:

Model of airline data in Example 11.4

```
identify var = Lny(1,12);
estimate q = (1)(12) noconstant printall plot;
```

Models of energy bill data in Exercise 12.6

```
identify var = y(4);
estimate p = (1)   q = (1)(5) noconstant printall plot;      (Model 2)
estimate p = (1)   q = (1,5) noconstant printall plot;       (Model 3)
```

# Chapter 11

Transforming data when a SAS data set work.hotel has already been created

```
data hotel2;
  set hotel;
  Time = _n_;
  Logy = Log(y);
  Sqrty = y**.5;
  Qtrooty = y**.25;
run;
```

Note: Predifferencing transformations must be done within a data step. Using this data set requires replacing hotel by hotel2 in the next two programs.

SAC and SPAC for various degrees of differencing of the hotel data as shown in Figures 11.5, 11.6, 11.7, and 11.8

```
proc arima data = work.hotel;
  identify var = QtRooty;
  identify var = QtRooty(1);
  identify var = QtRooty(12);
  identify var = QtRooty(1,12);
run;
```

Estimation, diagnostics, and forecasting for the hotel data in Figure 11.9

```
proc arima data = work.hotel;
   identify var = QtRooty(12);
   estimate p=(1,3,5) q=(12) printall plot;
   forecast lead = 12 out = work.fcast1;
data fcast2;
   set fcast1;
   Forecasty = Forecast**4;
   L95CI = L95**4;
   U95CI = U95**4;
proc print data = work.fcast2;
   var Forecasty L95CI U95CI;
run;
```

Time series regression with Box–Jenkins model for error terms in Example 11.6 and Figures 11.18, 11.20, 11.21, and 11.22

- Create work.hotel from Table 11.1 and add future values for time

```
data hotel;
   input y;
   QtRooty = y**.25;
   Time = _n_;
 Datalines;
 501
 488
   .
   .
   .
 877
Run;
data future;
   input y QtRooty Time;
   datalines;
   . . 169
   . . 170
   . . 171
   . . 172
   . . 173
   . . 174
   . . 175
   . . 176
   . . 177
   . . 178
   . . 179
   . . 180
   run;
```

```
data hotel2;
  update hotel future;
  by Time;
run;
```

Note: The future lines may be added other ways, such as adding the lines in SAS/INSIGHT.

- Create dummy variables

```
data hotel3;
  set hotel2;
  if mod(Time,12)=1 then M1=1; else M1=0;
  if mod(Time,12)=2 then M2=1; else M2=0;
  if mod(Time,12)=3 then M3=1; else M3=0;
  if mod(Time,12)=4 then M4=1; else M4=0;
  if mod(Time,12)=5 then M5=1; else M5=0;
  if mod(Time,12)=6 then M6=1; else M6=0;
  if mod(Time,12)=7 then M7=1; else M7=0;
  if mod(Time,12)=8 then M8=1; else M8=0;
  if mod(Time,12)=9 then M9=1; else M9=0;
  if mod(Time,12)=10 then M10=1; else M10=0;
  if mod(Time,12)=11 then M11=1; else M11=0;
```

- Estimation and diagnostics for time series regression with autocorrelated errors (RSAC and RSPAC correspond to SAC and SPAC in Figure 11.18)

```
proc arima data = work.hotel3;
  identify var = QtRooty
    crosscor = (Time M1 M2 M3 M4 M5 M6 M7 M8 M9 M10
                M11) noprint;
  estimate input = (Time M1 M2 M3 M4 M5 M6 M7 M8 M9
                    M10 M11)
      printall plot;
```

- Estimation, diagnostics, and forecasting for time series regression with a Box–Jenkins model for the error terms in Figures 11.20, 11.21, and 11.22

```
proc arima data = work.hotel3;
  identify var = QtRooty
    crosscor = (Time M1 M2 M3 M4 M5 M6 M7 M8 M9 M10
                M11) noprint;
  estimate input = (Time M1 M2 M3 M4 M5 M6 M7 M8 M9
                    M10 M11)
      p=(1,3,5)(12) printall plot;
  forecast lead = 12 out = work.fcast1;
data fcast2;
  set work.fcast1;
```

```
    y = QtRooty**4;
    Forecasty = Forecast**4;
    L95CI = L95**4;
    U95CI = U95**4;
  proc print data = work.fcast2;
    var y Forecasty L95CI U95CI;
  run;
```

# ADVANCED BOX–JENKINS MODELING IN CHAPTER 12

## Intervention Models for Directory Assistance Data in Figures 12.2 and 12.5 of Example 12.5

$$\text{Model 1:} \qquad z_t = C z_t(S) + \varepsilon_t$$

$$\text{Model 2:} \qquad z_t = \frac{C}{(1 - \delta B)} z_t(S) + \varepsilon_t$$

where $z_t = (1 - B)(1 - B^{12})y_t$,   $z_t(S) = (1 - B)(1 - B^{12})S_t$, and $\varepsilon_t = (1 - \theta_{1,12}B^{12})a_t$

- Create work.DirAssis with data in Table 12.4 and add future values

```
data DirectAssis;
  input y;
datalines;
    350
    339

    .
    .

    241
run;
data DirAssis2;
  set DirAssis;
  Time = _n_;
  if Time >= 147 then S=1; else S=0;
run;
data future;
  input y Time S;
```

```
datalines;
    .       181         1
    .       182         1
            .
            .
            .
    .       192         1
run;
data DirAssis3;
  update DirAssis2 Future;
  by Time S;
run;
```

Note: Future values may be added in other ways, such as through SAS/INSIGHT.

*   Plot the monthly average number of directory assisted calls per day versus time

```
proc plot data = work.DirAssis2;
  plot y*Time;
```

*   Estimation, diagnostics, and forecasting for directory assistance data in Figures 12.2 and 12.5

```
proc arima data=work.DirAssis3;
  identify var=y(1,12) crosscor=(S(1,12));
  estimate q=(12) Input=S noconstant
    printall altparm maxit=30 backlim = -3 plot;
  forecast lead=12;
  estimate q=(12) input = (0$/(1)S) noconstant
    printall altparm maxit=30 backlim = -3 plot;
  forecast lead=12;
run;
```

## Intervention Model for UK Airlines Data in Example 12.6 and Figure 12.21 of Exercise 12.10

$$z_t = \delta + C_1 z_t(P_1) + C_2 z_t(P_2) + \varepsilon_t$$

where $z_t = (1 - B^{12})y_t$, $z_t(P_1) = (1 - B^{12})P_{1t}$, $z_t(P_2) = (1 - B^{12})P_{2t}$, and $(1 - \phi_1 B - \phi_3 B^3)\varepsilon_t = a_t$

*   Create work.Ukair with data from Table 12.5 and add future values

```
Data Ukair;
  input y;
datalines;
  6827
```

```
      6178
        .
        .
        .
      12772
    run;
    data Ukair2;
      set Ukair;
      Time = _n_;
      if Time = 66 or Time = 67 then P1=1; else P1=0;
      if Time = 76 then P2=1; else P2=0;
    run;
    data Future;
      input y Time P1 P2;
    datalines;
      .     96        0          0
      .     97        0          0
            .
            .
      .    108        0          0
    run;
    data Ukair3;
      update Ukair2 Future;
      by Time P1 P2;
    run;
```

- Plot miles flown by UK airlines versus time

```
    proc plot;
      plot y*Time;
```

- Estimation, diagnostics, and forecasting in Figure 12.21 of Exercise 12.10

```
    proc arima data=work.Ukair3;
      identify var=y(12) crosscor=(P1(12) P2(12));
      estimate p=(1,3) Input=(P1 P2) printall
            maxit=30 backlim = -3 plot;
      forecast lead=12;
    run;
```

# Transfer Function Model Using Sales Data in Figures 12.6, 12.7, and 12.8

- Create work.sales from sales data in Table 12.6

```
    Data sales
      input x y;
```

```
datalines;
  116.44    202.66
  119.58    232.91
              .
              .
              .
  117.09    230.56
run;
```

- SAC and SPAC for original data and first difference of variables $x$ and $y$

```
proc arima data = work.sales;
  identify var = x;
  identify var = x(1);
  identify var = y;
  identify var = y(1);
run;
```

- Estimation and diagnostics for the tentative model

$$(1 - \phi^{(x)}B)z^{(x)} = (1 - \theta^{(x)}B)a_t$$

where $z^{(x)} = x_t - x_{t-1}$

```
proc arima data = work.sales;
  identify var = x(1);
  estimate p=(1) q=(1) noconstant printall plot;
run;
```

- Sample cross-correlation function (SCC) between the prewhitened values of advertising expenditure $x$ and prewhitened values of sales $y$ in Figure 12.6

```
proc arima data = work.sales;
  identify var = x(1) noprint;
  estimate p=(1) q=(1) noconstant;
  identify var = y(1) crosscor = (x(1)) nlag=10;
run;
```

- Estimation and diagnostics of the preliminary transfer function model in Figure 12.7

$$z_t = \frac{C(1 - w_1B - w_2B^2)}{(1 - \delta_1B - \delta_2B^2)} B^2 z_t^{(x)} + \varepsilon_t$$

where $z_t = y_t - y_{t-1}$ and $z_t^{(x)} = x_t - x_{t-1}$

```
proc arima data = work.sales;
  identify var=x(1) noprint;
  estimate p=(1) q=(1) noconstant;
  identify var=y(1) crosscor=(x(1)) nlag=10;
```

```
   estimate input = (2$(1,2)/(1,2)x) noconstant
      printall
       altparm maxit = 30 backlim = -3 plot;
 run;
```

Note: In (2$(1, 2)/(1,2) x), the 2$ corresponds to $B^b = B^2$, (1,2) corresponds to $(1 - w_1B - w_2B^2)$, and /(1,2) corresponds to $(1 - \delta_1B - \delta_2B^2)$.

- Estimation, diagnostics, and forecasting of the model in Figure 12.8

$$z_t = \frac{C(1 - w_1B - w_2B^2)}{(1 - \delta_1B - \delta_2B^2)} B^2 z_t^{(x)} + \varepsilon_t$$

where $\varepsilon_t = \phi_1\varepsilon_{t-1} + \phi_2\varepsilon_{t-2} + a_t$, $z_t = y_t - y_{t-1}$ and $z_t^{(x)} = x_t - x_{t-1}$

```
proc arima data = work.sales;
  identify var=x(1) noprint;
  estimate p=(1) q=(1) noconstant;
  identify var=y(1) crosscor=(x(1)) nlag=10;
  estimate p=(1,2) input = (2$(1,2)/(1,2)x)
          noconstant printall
             altparm maxit = 30 backlim = -3 plot;
  forecast lead = 10;
run;
```

# References

Abraham, B., and J. Ledolter. *Statistical Methods for Forecasting.* New York: Wiley, 1983.

Allmon, C. I. "Advertising and Sales Relationships for Toothpaste: Another Look." *Business Economics* (Sept. 1982): 17, 58.

Anderson, T. W. *The Statistical Analysis of Time Series.* New York: Wiley, 1971.

Anscombe, F. J., and J. W. Tukey. "The Examination and Analysis of Residuals." *Technometrics* 5 (1963): 141–160.

Armstrong, J. S., ed. *Principles of Forecasting: A Handbook for Researchers and Practitioners.* Boston: Kulwar, 2001.

Barlev, B., and H. Levy. "On the Variability of Accounting Income Numbers." *Journal of Accounting Research* (Autumn 1979): 305–315.

Bowerman, B. L., and R. T. O'Connell. *Linear Statistical Models: An Applied Approach,* 2nd ed. Boston: PWS-Kent, 1990.

Bowerman, B. L., and R. T. O'Connell. *Business Statistics in Practice,* 3rd ed. Boston: McGraw-Hill/ Irwin, 2003.

Box, G. E. P., and D. R. Cox. "An Analysis of Transformations." *Journal of Royal Statistical Society* B 26 (1964): 211–243.

Box, G. E. P., G. M. Jenkins, and G. C. Reinsel. *Time Series Analysis: Forecasting and Control,* 3rd ed. Englewood Cliffs, NJ: Prentice Hall, 1994.

Boyd, T. C., and T. C. Krehbiel. "The Effect of Promotion Timing on Major League Baseball Attendance." *Sport Marketing Quarterly* 8 (1999): 23–24.

Brocklebank, J. C., and D. A. Dickey. *SAS System for Forecasting Time Series.* Cary, NC: SAS Institute, 1986.

Brown, R. G. *Statistical Forecasting for Inventory Control.* New York: McGraw-Hill, 1959.

Brown, R. G. *Smoothing, Forecasting and Prediction of Discrete Time Series.* Englewood Cliffs, NJ: Prentice-Hall, 1962.

Brown, R. G. *Decision Rules for Inventory Management.* New York: Holt, Rinehart & Winston, 1967.

Chatfield, C. *Time-Series Forecasting.* London: Chapman & Hall/CRC, 2000.

Chatfield, C., and D. L. Prothero. "Box-Jenkins Seasonal Forecasting Problems in a Case Study" (with discussion). *Journal of the Royal Statistical Society,* A136 (1973).

Chow, W. M. "Adaptive Control of the Exponential Smoothing Constant." *Journal of Industrial Engineering,* 16, No. 5 (1965): 314–317.

Cochran, G. W., and G. M. Cox. *Experimental Designs,* 2nd ed. New York: Wiley, 1957.

Cravens, D. W., R. B. Woodruff, and J. C. Stamper. "An Analytical Approach for Evaluating Sales Territory Performance." *Journal of Marketing* 36 (1972): 31–37.

Dagum, E. B. *The X-11-ARIMA Seasonal Adjustment Method (No. 12-564E).* Ottawa: Statistics Canada, 1980.

D'Ambrosio, P., and S. Chambers. "No Checks and Balances." *Asbury Park Press,* Sept. 10, 1995.

Davis, O. L. *The Design and Analysis of Industrial Experiments.* New York: Hafner, 1956.

Dickey, D. A., W. R. Bell, and R. B. Miller. "Unit Roots in Time Series Models: Tests and Implications." *American Statistician* 49 (1986): 12–26.

Dielman, T. *Applied Regression Analysis for Business and Economics,* 3rd ed. Belmont, CA: Duxbury Press, 2001.

Draper, N., and H. Smith. *Applied Regression Analysis,* 2nd ed. New York: Wiley, 1981.

Durbin, J., and G. S. Watson. "Testing for Serial Correlation in Least Squares Regression, I." *Biometrika* 37 (1950): 409–428.

Durbin, J., and G. S. Watson. "Testing for Serial Correlation in Least Squares Regression, II." *Biometrika* 38 (1951): 159–179.

Findley, D. F., B. C. Monsell, W. R. Bell, M. C. Otto, and B. Chen. "New Capabilities and Methods of the X-12-ARIMA Seasonal-Adjustment Program." *Journal of Business and Economic Statistics* 16 (1998): 127–152.

Fuller, W. A. *Introduction to Statistical Time Series.* New York: Wiley, 1976.

Gardner, E. S. "Automatic Monitoring of Forecast Errors." *Journal of Forecasting* 2 (1983): 1–21.

Gerstenfeld, Arthur. "Technological Forecasting." *Journal of Business* 44, No. 1 (1971).

Graybill, F. A. *Theory and Application of the Linear Model.* Boston: Duxbury Press, 1976.

Harvey, Andrew C. *Forecasting, Structural Time Series Models and the Kalman Filter.* New York: Cambridge University Press, 1989.

Hillmer, S. C., and G. C. Tiao. "Likelihood Function of Stationary Multiple Autoregressive Moving Average Models." *Journal of the American Statistical Association* 74 (1979): 652–660.

Hyndman, R. J., A. B. Koehler, R. D. Snyder, and S. Grose. "A State Space Framework for Automatic Forecasting Using Exponential Smoothing Methods." *International Journal of Forecasting* 18 (2002): 439–454.

Hyndman, R. J., A. B. Koehler, J. K. Ord, and R. D. Snyder. "Prediction Intervals for Exponential Smoothing State Space Models." Working Paper Series, Department of Econometrics and Business Statistics, Monash University, Australia, 2001.

Johnson, L. A., and D. C. Montgomery. *Forecasting and Time Series Analysis.* New York: McGraw-Hill, 1976.

Kendall, M., and J. K. Ord. *Time Series,* 3rd ed. London: Edward Arnold, 1990.

Kennedy, W. J., Jr., and J. E. Gentile. *Statistical Computing.* New York: Dekker, 1980.

Kleinbaum, D., and L. Kupper. *Applied Regression Analysis and Other Multivariable Methods,* 2nd ed. Boston: Duxbury Press, 1987.

Kutner, M. H., C. J. Nachtsheim, and J. Neter. *Applied Linear Regression Models,* 4th ed. Boston: McGraw-Hill/Irwin, 2004.

Mabert, V. A. *An Introduction to Short Term Forecasting Using the Box-Jenkins Methodology.* Publication No. 2 in the American Institute of Industrial Engineers Monograph Series, 1976.

Makridakis, S., S. C. Wheelwright, and R. J. Hyndman. *Forecasting Methods and Applications,* 3rd ed. New York: Wiley, 1998.

Makridakis, S., S. C. Wheelwright, and V. E. McGee. *Forecasting Methods and Applications,* 2nd ed. New York: Wiley, 1983.

McKenzie, E. "General Exponential Smoothing and the Equivalent ARMA Process." *Journal of Forecasting* 3 (1984): 333–444.

McSweeney, A. J. "The Effects of Response Cost on the Behavior of a Million Persons: Charging for Directory Assistance in Cincinnati." *Journal of Applied Behavioral Analysis* 11 (1978): 47–51.

Mendenhall, W. *Introduction to Linear Models and the Design and Analysis of Experiments.* Belmont, CA: Wadsworth, 1968.

Mendenhall, W., and J. Reinmuth. *Statistics for Management and Economics,* 6th ed. Boston: Duxbury Press, 1989.

Miller, R. B., and D. W. Wichern. *Intermediate Business Statistics: Analysis of Variance, Regression, and Time Series.* New York: Holt, Rinehart, and Winston, 1977.

Myers, R. H. *Classical and Modern Regression with Applications,* 2nd ed. Boston: Duxbury Press, 1990.

Nelson, C. R. *Applied Time Series Analysis for Managerial Forecasting.* San Francisco: Holden-Day, 1973.

Neter, J., M. H. Kutner, C. Nachtsheim, and W. Wasserman. *Applied Linear Statistical Models,* 3rd ed. Homewood, IL: McGraw-Hill/Irwin, 1996.

Neter, J., W. Wasserman, and G. A. Whitmore. *Applied Statistics,* 3rd ed. Boston: Allyn & Bacon, 1998.

Ord, J. K., A. B. Koehler, and R. D. Snyder. "Estimation and Prediction for a Class of Dynamic Nonlinear Statistical Models." *Journal of the American Statistical Association* 92 (1997): 1621–1629.

Ott, Lyman. *An Introduction to Statistical Methods and Data Analysis,* 4th ed. Boston: Duxbury Press, 1992.

Pankratz, A. *Forecasting with Dynamic Regression Models.* New York: Wiley, 1991.

Pankratz, A. *Forecasting with Univariate Box–Jenkins Models: Concepts and Bases.* New York: Wiley, 1983.

Pena, D., G. C. Tiao, and R. S. Tsay. *A Course in Time Series Analysis.* New York: Wiley, 2001.

Rowe, G., and G. Wright. "Expert Opinions in Forecasting: The Role of the Delphi Technique." *In Principles of Forecasting: A Handbook for Researchers and Practitioners.* Boston: Kluwar, 2001.

Scheffe, H. *The Analysis of Variance.* New York: Wiley, 1959.

Searle, S. R. *Linear Models.* New York: Wiley, 1971.

Shiskin, J., A. H. Young, and J. C. Musgrave. "The X-11 Variant of the Census Method II Seasonal Adjustment Program." Technical Paper 15, Bureau of the Census, U.S. Department of Commerce, Washington, D.C., 1967.

Trigg, D. W. "Monitoring a Forecast System." *Oprational Research Quarterly* 15 (1964): 271–274.

Wheelwright, S. C., and S. Makridakis. *Forecasting Methods for Management,* 3rd ed. New York: Wiley, 1980.

Winer, B. J. *Statistical Principles in Experimental Design,* 2nd ed. New York: McGraw-Hill, 1971.

Winters, P. R. "Forecasting Sales by Exponentially Weighted Moving Averages." *Management Science* 6, No. 3 (1960): 324–342.

Wonnacott, T. H., and R. J. Wonnacott. *Introductory Statistics for Business and Economics,* 4th ed. New York: Wiley, 1990.

Wonnacott, T. H., and R. J. Wonnacott. *Regression: A Second Course in Statistics.* New York: Wiley, 1981.

# *Index*